Gale Encyclopedia of Everyday La

THIRD EDITION

Gale Encyclopedia of Everyday Law

THIRD EDITION

VOLUME I
AMERICANS WITH DISABILITIES ACT TO FIRST AMENDMENT LAW

GALE
CENGAGE Learning

Detroit • New York • San Francisco • New Haven, Conn • Waterville, Maine • London

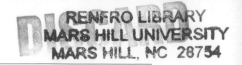
Gale Encyclopedia of Everyday Law,
Third Edition

Project Editor: Donna Batten

Editorial: Kristin Key and Brigham Narins

Product Manager: Stephen Wasserstein

Editorial Support Services: Andrea Lopeman

Indexing Services: Laurie Andriot

Rights Acquisition and Management:
Margaret Chamberlin

Composition: Evi Abou-El-Seoud

Manufacturing: Rita Wimberley

Imaging: John Watkins

Product Design: Kristine Julien

For product information and technology assistance, contact us at
Gale Customer Support, 1-800-877-4253.
For permission to use material from this text or product,
submit all requests online at **www.cengage.com/permissions.**
Further permissions questions can be emailed to
permissionrequest@cengage.com

While every effort has been made to ensure the reliability of the information presented in this publication, Gale, Cengage Learning, does not guarantee the accuracy of the data contained herein. Gale accepts no payment for listing; and inclusion in the publication of any organization, agency, institution, publication, service, or individual does not imply endorsement of the editors or publisher. Errors brought to the attention of the publisher and verified to the satisfaction of the publisher will be corrected in future editions.

LIBRARY OF CONGRESS CATALOGING-IN-PUBLICATION DATA

Gale encyclopedia of everyday law / Donna Batten, editor. -- Third edition.
p. cm. --
Summary: "The Encyclopedia, written for the layperson, is arranged alphabetically by broad subject categories and presents in-depth treatments of topics such as consumer issues, education, family, immigration, real estate, and retirement. Individual essays are organized in alphabetical order within these broad subject categories, and include information on state and local laws, as well as federal laws"-- Provided by publisher.
Includes bibliographical references and index.
ISBN 978-1-4144-9896-6 (hardback) -- ISBN 978-1-4144-9897-3 (vol. 1) -- ISBN 978-1-4144-9898-0 (vol. 2)
1. Law--United States--Popular works. I. Batten, Donna.
II. Title: Encyclopedia of everyday law.

KF387.G27 2013
349.73–dc23   2012049116

Gale, Cengage Learning
27500 Drake Rd.
Farmington Hills, MI, 48331-3535

ISBN-13: 978-1-4144-9896-6 (set)   ISBN-10: 1-4144-9896-9 (set)
ISBN-13: 978-1-4144-9897-3 (vol. 1)   ISBN-10: 1-4144-9897-7 (vol. 1)
ISBN-13: 978-1-4144-9898-0 (vol. 2)   ISBN-10: 1-4144-9898-5 (vol. 2)

This title is also available as an e-book.
ISBN-13: 978-1-4144-9899-7; ISBN-10: 1-4144-9899-3
Contact your Gale, Cengage Learning, sales representative for ordering information.

Table of Contents

Table of Contents

Contributors

In compiling this edition, we have been fortunate in being able to call upon our board of advisors and contributors who were instrumental in the compilation and the accuracy of the information in the Gale Encyclopedia of Everyday Law. We express sincere appreciation.

ADVISORY BOARD

Matthew C. Cordon

Frederick G. Grittner

Jim Heller

Matt Morrison

Anna Teller

CONTRIBUTORS

Laurie Andriot

Lauren Barrow

James Cahoy

Matthew C. Cordon

Richard Cretan

Debra DeFour

Heidi Denler

J. Alicia Elster

Mark D. Engsberg

Frederick G. Grittner

Lauri Harding

Kristy Holtfreter

David Johnstone

Sunwoo Kahng

Anne Kevlin

Frances Lynch

George A. Milite

Melodie Monahan

Joe Pascarella

Monica L. P. Robbers

Mary Hertz Scarbrough

Thomas W. Scholl III

Scott Slick

Sherrie Voss Matthews

Bridget Waldron

Eric L. Welsh

Introduction

The third edition of the *Gale Encyclopedia of Everyday Law* is a two-volume encyclopedia of practical information on laws and issues affecting people's everyday lives. Readers will turn to this work for help in answering questions such as, "What is involved in estate planning?" "Do I have any recourse to noisy neighbors?" and "What are the consequences of an expired visa?" This *Encyclopedia* aims to educate people about their rights under the law, although it is not intended as a self-help or "do-it-yourself" legal resource. It seeks to fill the niche between legal texts focusing on the theory and history behind the law and shallower guides dealing with general law.

This *Encyclopedia*, written for the layperson, is arranged alphabetically by broad subject categories and presents in-depth treatments of topics such as consumer issues, education, family, immigration, real estate, and retirement. Individual entries are organized in alphabetical order within these broad subject categories, and include background on the topic and information laws. In entries where it is not possible to include state and local information, references direct the reader to resources for further research.

The work contains 276 articles of 1,000-5,000 words each, organized within 26 broad subject categories, which are arranged alphabetically. Each article begins with a brief description of the issue's historical background, covering important statutes and cases. The body of the article is divided into subsections profiling the various U.S. federal laws and regulations concerning the topic. A third section details variations of the laws and regulations from state to state. Each article closes with a comprehensive bibliography, covering print resources and web sites, and a list of relevant national and state organizations and agencies.

HOW TO USE THIS BOOK

The *Gale Encyclopedia of Everyday Law* has been designed with ready reference in mind.

- **ENTRIES ARE ARRANGED ALPHABETICALLY WITHIN 26 BROAD CATEGORIES** and are listed in the **TABLE OF CONTENTS**

- **BOLDFACED TERMS** in the essays direct readers to a **GLOSSARY** of terms located at the end of Volume 2.

- A comprehensible **OVERVIEW OF THE AMERICAN LEGAL SYSTEM** details civil and criminal procedure, appeals, small claims court, in pro per representation, differences between local codes and state codes, and the difference between statutes and regulations.

- **STATE/FEDERAL AGENCIES AND NATIONAL ORGANIZATIONS CONTACTS** at the end of Volume 2 provide web sites for various state and federal government agencies and national organizations.

- A general **INDEX** at the back of Volume 2 covers subject terms from throughout the *Encyclopedia* and includes case and statute titles, personal names, and geographic locations.

Overview of the American Legal System

FRAMEWORK OF GOVERNMENT IN THE UNITED STATES

Basis of the American Legal System The legal system of the United States is administered and carried on by the official branches of government and many other authorities acting within their official lawmaking capacity. The original basis of the law in this country is the U.S. Constitution, which lays the framework under which each of the different branches of government operates. The Constitution also guarantees the basic civil rights of the citizens of the United States. All authority of the federal government originates from the Constitution, and the Constitution serves as the supreme law of the land. The Constitution grants to the federal government certain enumerated powers, and grants to the states any power not specifically delegated to a branch of the federal government. Under this system, states retain significant authority and autonomy. The Constitutions in each of the fifty states contain many similar provisions to those in the U.S. Constitution in terms of the basic structure of government. Under the federal and state constitutions, the U.S. legal system consists of a system of powers separated among branches of government, with a system of checks and balances among these branches.

Legislative Branches The legislative branch is the primary law-making body among the three branches, although authority emanating from the other branches also constitutes law. The legislative branch consists of Congress, and is subdivided into two lower houses, the House of Representatives and the Senate. In addition to the powers granted to Congress, the Constitution sets forth specific duties of both the House and the Senate. Each Congress meets for two sessions, with each session lasting two years. For example, the 112th Congress met in its first session in 2011 and met in its second session in 2012.

State legislatures are structured similarly, with the vast majority of these legislatures consisting of two lower houses. Many states have a house of representatives and a senate, just like Congress. Other states have different lower houses, such as a state with a house of delegates or a general assembly. Nebraska is the only state that has a unicameral legislature, meaning it only has one house.

Judicial Branches The judicial branch in the federal system consists of three levels of courts, with the Supreme Court serving as the highest court in the land. The intermediate courts in the federal system are the thirteen Courts of Appeals. The United States is divided by circuits, with each circuit consisting of a number of states. The Fifth Circuit, for example, consists of Texas, Mississippi, and Louisiana. Each court of appeals has jurisdiction to decide federal cases in its respective circuit. The trial level in the federal judicial system consists of the District Courts. Each state contains at least one district, with larger states containing as many as four districts. Congress has also established a number of lower federal courts with specialized jurisdiction, such as the bankruptcy courts and the U.S. Tax Court.

Most state court systems are similar to that of the federal system, with a three-tiered system consisting of trial courts, appellate courts, and a highest court, which is also referred to as a "court of last resort." The names of the courts are similar from state to state, such as superior court, court of appeals, and supreme court. However, some states do not follow this structure. For example, in New York, the trial level court is the Supreme Court, while the court of last resort is the Court of Appeals. Texas, as another example, has two highest courts—the Supreme Court and the Court of Criminal Appeals. In addition to the trial level courts, small claims courts or other county courts typically hear small claims, such as those seeking recovery of less than $1000.

Executive Branches The federal Constitution vests executive power in the President of the United States. The President also serves as the Commander in Chief of the Armed Forces and has the power to make treaties with other nations, with the advice and consent of the Senate. Besides those powers enumerated in Article II of the Constitution, much of the power of the executive branch stems from the executive departments, such as the Department of the Treasury and the Department of Justice. Congress has the constitutional authority to delegate power to administrative agencies, and many of these agencies fall under the executive branch and are known as executive agencies. Congress also has the authority to create agencies independent of the other branches of government, called independent agencies. Authority emanating from executive and independent agencies is law, and it is similar in many ways to legislation created by legislatures or opinions issued by courts. State executive branches and administrative agencies are similar to those of their federal counterparts.

CONSTITUTIONAL AUTHORITY

Interpretation of the Constitution At 4,543 words, the federal Constitution is not a particularly lengthy document, and does not provide many answers to specific questions of law. It has, instead, been the subject of extensive interpretation since its original ratification. In the famous 1803 case of *Marbury v. Madison*, Chief Justice John Marshall wrote an opinion of the Supreme Court, which stated that the judicial branch was the appropriate body for interpreting the Constitution and determining the constitutionality of federal or state legislation. Accordingly, determining the extent of power among the three branches of government, or determining the rights of the citizens of the United States, almost always requires an evaluation of federal cases, in addition to a reading of the actual text of the Constitution.

Powers of Congress Most of the enumerated congressional powers are contained in section 8 of Article I of the Constitution. Many courts have been asked to review congressional statutes to determine whether Congress had the constitutional authority to enact such statutes. Among these powers, the power of Congress to "regulate [c]ommerce among the several [s]tates" has been the subject of the most litigation and outside debate. A number of cases during the New Deal era under President Franklin D. Roosevelt considered the breadth of this provision, which is referred to as the Commerce Clause. After the Supreme Court determined that many of these statutes were unconstitutional, Roosevelt, after a landslide election in 1936, threatened to add additional justices to the court, in order to provide more support for his position with respect to the pieces of legislation passed during the New Deal era. The reason he gave to Congress at the time was that many of the justices were over the age of seventy, and could no longer perform their job function, but the general understanding was that he wanted justices that would approve the New Deal legislation as constitutional. The threat of this so-called "Court-packing" plan succeeded, and the Commerce Clause has been construed very broadly since then. Other powers enumerated in Article I are generally construed broadly as well.

Civil Rights Provisions in the Constitutions The main text of the Constitution does not provide rights to the citizens of the United States. These rights are generally provided in the many amendments to the Constitution. The first ten amendments, all ratified in 1791, are called the "Bill of Rights," and confer many of the cherished and fundamental rights to the citizens of the United States. Among the rights included in the Bill of Rights are the freedoms of speech and religion (First Amendment); right to keep and bear arms (Second Amendment); right to be free from unreasonable searches and seizures (Fourth Amendment); right to be free from being compelled to testify against one's self in a criminal trial (Fifth Amendment); right to due process of law (Fifth Amendment); right to a jury trial (Sixth Amendment); and right to be free from cruel and unusual punishment (Eighth Amendment).

Between 1791 and 1865, no constitutional amendments were ratified that provided civil rights to citizens. However, at the conclusion of the Civil War and during the reconstruction period following the war, three major amendments were added to the Constitution. The first was the Thirteenth Amendment, ratified in 1865, which finally abolished slavery and involuntary servitude in the United States. The Fourteenth Amendment, ratified in 1868, provided some of the most significant rights to citizens, including the guarantee of equal protection of the laws and prohibited denial of life, liberty, or property without due process of law. The Fifteenth Amendment, ratified in 1870, provided that the right to vote could not be abridged on account of race, color, or previous condition of servitude. Fifty years later, women were guaranteed the right to vote with the ratification of the Nineteenth Amendment in 1920.

Application of Constitutional Amendments Like other constitutional provisions, the judicial branch is the appropriate body to interpret the Bill of Rights and other amendments to the Constitution. The plain language of the amendments can cause some confusion, since some, by their own terms, they apply specifically to Congress, while other apply specifically to states. For example, the First Amendment begins, "Congress shall make no law respecting an establishment of religion . . ." Similarly, the Fourteenth Amendment contains a provision that states, "No State shall make or enforce any law which shall abridge the privileges and immunities of the citizens of the United States . . ." Modern courts have resolved some of these questions by ruling that the Due Process Clauses of the Fifth and Fourteenth Amendments incorporate these provisions, so many provisions apply to both the federal and state governments, despite the language in the Constitution.

State Constitutions Many state constitutions are structured similarly to the federal Constitution, except that most are more detailed than the federal Constitution. Most citizens are guaranteed basic civil rights by both the federal Constitution and their relevant state constitutions. For example, it is common for state constitutions to include provisions guaranteeing freedom of speech or equal protection, and most are phrased similarly to the provisions in the First and Fourteenth Amendments. Since the federal Constitution is the supreme law of the land, any rights provided in it are guaranteed to all citizens and cannot be lost because a state constitution's provisions conflict with the corresponding provision in the federal Constitution. A state may provide greater rights to citizens than those provided in a federal counterpart but may not remove rights guaranteed under the federal doctrine. Section 10 of Article I of the Constitution also prohibits states from making certain laws or conducting certain acts, such as passing an ex post facto law or coining money.

INTERNATIONAL TREATIES

Authority of Treaties Article VI of the Constitution provides, "This Constitution, and the Laws of the United States which shall be made in Pursuance thereof; and all Treaties made, or which shall be made, under the Authority of the United States, shall be the supreme Law of the Land." An international treaty is generally considered to be on the same footing as a piece of legislation. If a treaty and a federal statute conflict, the one enacted at a later date, or the one that more specifically governs a particular circumstance, will typically govern. State legislation may not contradict provisions contained in a treaty. Similarly, states are forbidden from entering into treaties under the provisions in Article I, Section 10.

Creation of Treaties and Other International Agreements The power to enter into treaties is vested in the President, though the executive must act with the advice and consent of the Senate, and receive the concurrence of two-thirds of the Senate before a treaty is ratified. The various Presidents have also entered into executive agreements with foreign nations when the President has not been able to receive approval from two-thirds of the Senate, or has not sought approval from the Senate. While nothing in the Constitution permits or forbids this practice, executives have entered into thousands of such agreements.

FEDERAL AND STATE LEGISLATION

Federal Legislative Process Members of Congress have the exclusive authority to introduce legislation to the floor of either the House of Representatives or Senate. Legislation is introduced to Congress in the form of bills. Most bills can originate either in the Senate or in the House, with the exception of bills to raise revenue, which must originate in the House under Article I of the Constitution. When a bill is introduced, it is designated with a bill number, and these bill numbers run sequentially through two sessions of Congress. For example, the fifty-sixth bill introduced in the House during the 108th Congress will be designated as "H.R. 56" ("H.R." is an abbreviation for House of Representatives). Likewise, the twelfth bill introduced in the Senate during the same Congress will be designated "S. 12." It is not uncommon that bills are introduced in both the House and the Senate simultaneously that address the same subject matter. These bills are referred to as "companion bills," and the actual law that is passed often contains components from both the enacted bill and its companion bill. Thousands of bills are introduced in the House and Senate each session, and a relatively small proportion is actually passed into law.

After a bill has been introduced, it is sent to one or more appropriate committees in the House or Senate. The committee or committees analyze the provisions of the bill, including the reasoning for such legislation and the expected effect of the bill if it were enacted into law. A committee conducts hearings, where it hears testimony from experts and other parties that can provide information relevant to the subject matter covered by a bill. A committee may also order the preparation of an in-depth study (called a "committee print") that provides additional background information, often in the form of statistics and statistical analysis. A number of additional documents may also be produced during the committee stage, and practically every action is documented, including the production of written transcripts of committee hearings. A committee may amend or rewrite a bill before it approves it, which generally extends the length of time that a bill remains at the committee stage. The vast majority of bills, in fact, never leave the committee stage, and these bills are commonly said to have "died in committee."

When a committee completes its consideration of a bill, it reports the bill back to the floor of the House or Senate. A committee ordinarily accompanies the bill with a report that summarizes and analyzes each bill's provisions, and provides recommendations regarding the passage of the bill. Reports, as well as other documents, are designated with unique numbers and are made available to the public. An example of a report number is "H.R. Rep. No. 112-15," which indicates that it is the fifteenth report submitted to the House of Representatives in the 112th Congress.

Members of the houses of Congress debate the bills on the floor of the relevant house. These debates are transcribed, and the text of the transcription is routinely available to the public. During this period, the relevant chamber may amend the bill. Once the debates and other activities are completed, the chamber votes to pass the bill. If the chamber approves the bill, it is sent to the other chamber, and the entire process is repeated. The version of the bill sent to the other chamber of Congress is called the "engrossed" version of the bill. The other chamber must pass this version exactly as it appears in the engrossed version, or else the bill, assuming the second chamber passes it, is sent back to the original chamber for future consideration. If the House and Senate cannot agree to a single version of a bill, a conference, or joint, committee may be convened, where members of both chambers may compromise to complete a version of a bill acceptable to both chambers. If this conference committee is successful in doing so, the bill is returned to the House and Senate for another vote.

Once a bill passes both the House and the Senate, it is sent to the President as an "enrolled" bill. The President may sign the bill and make it law. If the President does not sign the bill, and Congress is still in session, the bill becomes law automatically after ten days. If the President does not sign the bill, and Congress adjourns within ten days, the bill does not become law. The President may also reject the bill by vetoing it. Congress may override this veto with a two-thirds majority vote in both chambers.

Types of Laws Passed by Congress Laws that apply to and are binding on the general citizenry are called public laws. Each public law is designated with a public law number, and the numbering system is similar to that of reports and other documents described above. For example, Public Law Number 108-1 represents that this is the first public law passed in the 108th Congress. Congress may also pass laws that apply only to individual citizens or small classes of individuals. These laws are called private laws, and are usually passed in the context of immigration and naturalization. Private laws are numbered identically to public laws, such as, for example, Private Law Number 112-2, which is the second private law passed in the 112th Congress.

Congress also passes various types of resolutions, some of which do not constitute law and do not contain binding provisions equivalent to public laws. A single chamber of Congress may pass simple resolutions, which relate to the operations of that chamber or express the opinion of that chamber on policy issues. Both chambers may pass a concurrent resolution, which relate to the entire operation of Congress, or the express opinion of the entire Congress. Neither simple nor concurrent resolutions constitute law, and are not submitted to the President for approval. Joint resolutions, on the other hand, have the same binding effect as bills, and must be submitted to the President for final approval. Appropriations and similar measures often enter Congress as joint resolutions. Some actions, particularly the introduction of a constitutional amendment, require the use of a joint resolution, and many of these actions do not require presidential approval.

Publication of Federal Legislation Practically all documents produced by Congress during the legislative process are published by the U.S. Government Printing Office and made available to the public. Most of items produced since 1995 are now also available on the Internet in electronic formats. Legislation first appears in the form of a slip law, named as such because the Government Printing Office prints these on unbound slips of paper. At the conclusion of a session of Congress, the laws passed during that session are compiled and appear in the form of session laws, organized in chronological order. The official source for federal session laws is the U.S. Statutes at Large.

Most legislation in force in the United States is organized into a subject matter arrangement and published in the U.S. Code. A statute contained in the U.S. Code is called a codified statute. The U.S. Code consists of 50 titles, with each title representing a certain area of law. For example, Title 17 contains the copyright laws of the United States; Title 26 contains the Internal Revenue Code; and Title 29 contains most of the labor laws of the United States.

Relationship Between Federal and State Legislation Federal legislation is superior to state legislation under the provisions of Article VI of the U.S. Constitution. Thus, the courts will resolve any potential conflicts between a state statute and a federal statute by enforcing the federal statute. Federal superiority, however, does not mean that states are forbidden from enacting legislation covering the same subject matter as a federal statute; it is common for both federal and state legislation to govern similar areas of law. This is true in such areas as securities regulation, consumer protection, and labor law. Federal labor relations laws, for example, apply specifically to private employers but do not apply to public employers. Labor relations between public employers and their employees are governed generally by state labor relations laws.

If Congress wants an area of law to be governed solely by federal legislation, Congress may include a provision that such legislation preempts any state law related to the subject matter covered by the federal statute. Congress may preempt state regulation expressly through specific statutory language, or by implication based on the structure and purpose behind a federal statute. Examples of legislation that contain preemption provisions are the Employment Retirement Income Security Act of 1974, the Comprehensive Environmental Response, Compensation and Liability Act, and the Toxic Substance Control Act.

The Tenth Amendment to the federal Constitution reserves any power not delegated to the federal government to the states, or to the people. However, there have been questions among the courts and scholars regarding the extent of this amendment, and it has not generally been construed to grant any special powers to the states through its enactment. Rather, it is a clause that reserves power to the states where Congress has not acted, subject to some limitations.

Legislative Process in State Legislatures Most state legislatures follow similar processes as Congress. Each state legislature, with the exception of Nebraska, consists of two chambers. Most legislatures meet in regular session annually, though some meet biannually with special called sessions held periodically. In many states, the process of introducing a bill is streamlined, where only one chamber may introduce certain types of bills. Several states also permit citizens to initiate legislation, which is not possible in Congress. Some states allow citizens to vote directly on a proposed piece of legislation. Other states contain provisions that all citizens, once they have received a requisite number of signatures, may force the legislature to consider and vote on a particular issue.

Publication of State Legislation Most states publish enacted legislation in a similar manner as the publication of federal legislation. Laws passed during each session of a respective legislature are compiled as session laws, and laws currently in force are compiled in a subject matter arrangement. In most states, laws in force are compiled according to a numbering system similar to the U.S. Code, with title or chapter numbers representing the subject matter of the statute. Other states, most notably California and Texas, have created codes that are named to represent the subject matter of the statues contained in them. For example, the California Family Code contains the family law statutes of that state; similarly, the Texas Finance Code contains the statutes governing many of the financial operations in that state.

Bills introduced in every legislature during a current session are available on the various legislatures' Internet sites, as are the current statutes. However, very little documentation from the legislative process is published in a fashion to make it readily available to interested members of the public. Even as of the early 2010s, legal researchers interested in such information must often travel to their respective state capitol to obtain this information.

Interpretation of Legislation The language of a statute may be somewhat ambiguous regarding their application, and the courts have the responsibility to interpret or construe the language to determine the proper application of the statute. Courts have developed "canons of construction" to aid in this interpretation. The most basic form of statutory construction is consideration of the text and plain meaning of a statute. This consideration includes the process of defining the terms and phrases used in statute, including the use of a dictionary to derive the common meaning of a term. Courts will also consider the application of the statute in the context of the broader statutory scheme, which can often indicate what the purpose of the statute was when the statute was enacted.

If the plain meaning of a statute cannot be derived from the statute or statutory scheme, courts may look to the history of the legislation to determine the intent of the legislature when it enacted the statute. It is possible that Congress or a state legislature specifically addressed a concern during the legislative process, and members of the legislature may have made statements indicating how the legislature intended for the statute to apply in a particular circumstance. Locating this information requires a legal researcher to locate documentation prepared during the legislative process, in a process called "compiling" a legislative history.

Substantive vs. Procedural Laws Many of the laws passed by legislatures are considered "substantive" laws, because they create, define, and regulate legal rights and obligations. If an individual has been harmed and wants to bring litigation against the person or group that harmed him or her, substantive statutes often provide the law that governs that situation, and also include provisions regarding the appropriate damages that can be awarded to the plaintiff should the plaintiff successfully prove his or her case.

By comparison, procedural laws are those that set forth the rules used to enforce substantive laws. These laws may dictate the steps that a litigant must take to bring a suit to court, or may dictate the appropriate courts where a case may be brought. Some statutes, called statutes of limitations, also limit the amount of time in which a particular case may be brought. Procedural laws are as important as substantive laws in many respects, because a party with a valid claim may nevertheless lose a case if the proper procedures are not followed, or if the claim is not filed in the time required under a statute oflimitations.

Criminal Law vs. Civil Law Criminal laws are those designed to punish private parties for violating the provisions contained in these laws. Violations of these laws are crimes against society, and are brought as criminal actions against the alleged offenders by state or federal attorneys acting on behalf of the people. All citizens of the United States are guaranteed rights in criminal investigations and criminal trials, and law enforcement officers and prosecutors must follow certain procedures in order to protect these rights. For this reason, criminal procedure differs significantly from the procedures for bringing a civil case to court. Among the most fundamental rights is that all accused individuals are presumed innocent until the state proves them guilty beyond a reasonable doubt. This places the burden of proof in a criminal action on the state, rather than on the defendant. Title 18 of the U.S. Code contains most of the federal criminal laws, while state penal codes generally contain the state criminal laws.

The term "civil law" has different meanings in two distinct contexts. First, it refers to a system of law that differs from the common law system employed by the United States. Second, it refers to a type of law that defines rights between private parties, and, as such, differs from criminal law. Civil laws are applicable in such situations as when two parties enter into a contract with one another, or when one party causes physical injury to another party. The procedures that must be followed in a civil court case are generally less stringent than those in a criminal case. Some civil laws include provisions designed to punish wrongdoers, usually in the form of punitive, or exemplary, damages that are paid to the other party.

Municipal Ordinances and Other Local Laws Local government entities are generally created by the various states, and are typically referred to as municipalities. The powers of a municipality are limited to those granted to it by the state, usually defined in the municipal charter that created the municipality. Charters are somewhat analogous to state constitutions, and usually were created by vote of the voters in the municipality. Local governing bodies may include a city council, county commission, and/or board of supervisors, and these bodies enact ordinances that apply specifically to the locality governed by these bodies. Ordinances are similar to state legislative acts in their function. In many municipalities, ordinances are organized into a subject matter arrangement and produced as municipal codes.

Local laws often govern everyday situations more so than many state or federal laws. These laws include many provisions for public safety, raise revenue through the creation and implementation of sales and other local taxes, and govern the zoning of the municipality. Decisions regarding education are also generally made through local boards of education, though these boards are entities distinct from the municipal government. Local laws cannot contradict federal or state law, including statutory or constitutional provisions.

CASES AND CASE LAW IN THE JUDICIAL SYSTEMS OF THE UNITED STATES

Adversarial System The judicial system in the United States is premised largely on the resolution of disputes between adversaries after evidence is presented on both sides to a judge or jury during a trial. Civil cases usually involve the resolution of disputes between private parties in such areas as personal injury, breach of contract, property disputes, or resolution of domestic relations disputes. Criminal cases involve the prosecution by the state or federal government of an individual accused of violating a criminal statute. The rules and procedures that parties must follow differ between criminal and civil trials, although similarities exist between the two types of rules. Some courts, such as probate courts and juvenile courts, have been developed to hear specific types of suits in a particular jurisdiction. Other tribunals, such as small claims courts and justice of the peace courts, have also been established to resolve minor disputes or try cases involving alleged infractions of minor crimes. The systems by which parties appeal decisions are also premised on an adversarial process.

Civil Trials A party commences a civil trial by filing a petition or complaint with an appropriate court. The party bringing the suit is usually referred to as the plaintiff, though in some cases the party is referred to as the petitioner. A petition or complaint must generally name the parties involved, the cause of action, the legal theories under which recovery may be appropriate, and the relief sought from the court. Once the petition or complaint is filed with the court, the plaintiff must serve the party or parties against whom the action was brought. The party against whom the case is brought is referred to as the defendant, though in some cases this party is referred to as the respondent. A defendant generally responds to a petition or complaint by filing an answer admitting or denying liability, though the filing of a pre-answer motion or motions may precede this.

A number of events occur between the time a petition or complaint is filed with a court and the time of trial. During the pretrial stage, the parties will usually file a series of motions with the court, requesting the addition or removal of a party, limits on evidence that may be presented at trial, or the complete dismissal of the case in its entirety. Parties also collect information in a process called discovery. During discovery, parties file interrogatories, which are written questions submitted to the other party or parties; seek admissions to certain facts from the other party or parties; and take depositions, which are oral questions asked of witnesses who are under oath. The pretrial stage is very important to the eventual resolution of a dispute, and many cases are settled by the parties outside of court or dismissed before the case actually goes to trial.

When a civil case goes to trial, a judge or a jury may try it. If a judge tries a case, he or she makes findings of facts and rulings of law, and the trial is usually referred to as a bench trial. If a jury tries a case, the jury makes findings of facts, such as whether a contract existed or whether one party assaulted another party. However, the judge makes rulings of law in a jury trial. A plaintiff who wants a jury to try his or her case must usually request it as a jury demand, or else the case will proceed as a bench trial. Some types of cases, such as family law cases, are never tried with juries. If a jury is requested, the case proceeds with the selection of jurors. During this time, a specified number of jurors are selected randomly from a pool of potential jurors. Both parties are permitted to question the jurors in a process called voir dire, and may ask that a certain number of jurors be removed from the final jury.

At the beginning of a trial, both sides give opening statements, providing an overview of the evidence that will be presented during the trial. After opening statements, both sides present evidence by questioning its own witnesses (called direct examination) and introducing physical items into evidence. Each party has the right to cross-examine witnesses produced by the opposing party. All jurisdictions have developed detailed rules of evidence that must be followed by both parties. Many of these rules govern the questions that may be asked on direct or cross-examination of witnesses. If one party enters something into evidence that violates the rules of evidence, the other party must raise an objection to the entry of this evidence, and the judge may sustain or overrule this objection. Some violations of the rules of evidence may result in a mistrial, in which the entire trial process must be repeated because it would be unfair to continue with the case. Even if the rule violation is not enough to cause a mistrial, a party who may wish to appeal an adverse ruling must raise objections during trial to "preserve error" for future consideration by appellate courts. Appellate courts will generally only consider points of possible error when the party seeking the appeal raised an objection and preserved error at the trial level.

A plaintiff generally has the burden to prove a case, and always introduces evidence before the defendant. Because a plaintiff has the burden of proof, a defendant is not required to introduce evidence, though the defendant will almost always do so. After the defendant concludes his or her presentation of evidence, the plaintiff may present evidence that rebuts evidence offered by the defense. Once all evidence has been introduced, both parties make closing arguments. Closing arguments are followed by jury deliberation, in which the jury determines whether the plaintiff or plaintiffs deserve to recover, and what amount of damages is appropriate. A jury relies on jury instructions (or court charges) given to them by the court, which describe the law and procedure that the jury must use to make its decision. The percentage of jurors that must be in agreement to render a decision ranges among different jurisdictions.

Once a jury renders a verdict, the parties may file post-trial motions that may still affect the outcome of the trial. These motions may include motion for new trial, which is usually awarded if something occurred during the trial that rendered the process unfair to one of the parties; or a motion for judgment notwithstanding the verdict (commonly referred to as "JNOV"), where the court renders judgment for one party, though the jury decided in favor of the other party, because the evidence presented at trial did not support the jury's decision. A party who wishes to appeal an adverse decision may also file a notice of appeal with the trial court, indicating that it wishes to appeal the ruling to an appellate court. Filing a notice of appeal within a certain time frame (30 days is common) is required in most jurisdictions in order to appeal a case to a higher court.

Criminal Trials State and federal prosecutors initiate criminal cases, which involve charges that an individual has violated a criminal law. In all criminal cases, the state or federal government serves as the plaintiff, while the person charged is the defendant. Criminal laws, which are promulgated by the various legislatures, consist of two major types of laws: felonies and misdemeanors. Felonies consist of the more serious crimes, and carry with them the most serious punishment. Both felonies and misdemeanors can result in jail or prison time, and both will usually result in a significant fine.

Citizens are guaranteed a number of rights in the context of criminal prosecution, and exercise of these rights is often the focus of criminal trials. The Fourth Amendment of the U.S. Constitution requires that law enforcement officials obtain a search warrant, upon showing of probable cause, before conducting searches or seizures of individuals or the property of individuals. The Fifth and Sixth Amendments contain a number of guarantees to all citizens that must be provided in a criminal trial. If a citizen's constitutional rights have been violated, the state may be required to proceed without the introduction of relevant evidence obtained illegally, or may be required to terminate the criminal action altogether.

When a person is arrested for violation of a criminal law, he or she must generally be brought before a judge within twenty-four hours of the arrest. The judge must inform the individual of the charges brought against him or her, and set bail or other condition of release. After other preliminary matters, the defendant is formally charged in one of two ways. First, the prosecutors may file a "trial information," which formally states the charges against the defendant. In more serious cases, such as murder trials, a panel of citizens will be convened as a grand jury to consider the evidence against the defendant. A grand jury, unlike a trial jury, only determines whether sufficient evidence to support the criminal charge exists, and will issue an indictment if evidence is sufficient. Either the filing of a trial information, or the return of an indictment, formally begins the trial process by charging the defendant. Once the defendant has been formally charged, he or she must appear for an arraignment, where the court reads the charge and permits the defendant to enter a plea. The defendant may enter a plea of guilty or not guilty at this time. Where it is permitted or required as a prerequisite to an insanity defense, the defendant may enter a plea of not guilty by reason of insanity. In some jurisdictions, including federal courts, the defendant may plead nolo contendere, or "no contest," which means that the defendant does not contest the charges. Its primary effect is the same as a plea of guilty, and its primary significance is that a plea of nolo contendere cannot be introduced into evidence in a subsequent civil action as proof of the defendant's guilt in the criminal action. Nolo contendere pleadings may usually only be entered with the permission of the court.

The Sixth Amendment guarantees the accused in a criminal prosecution a speedy and public trial. When a defendant enters a plea of not guilty, the trial is usually scheduled within ninety days of the filing of the trial information or indictment. The Sixth Amendment also guarantees citizens accused of crimes the right to a jury trial, though a defendant may waive this right and request a bench trial. During the pre-trial stage, the defendant may file motions with the court, such as those requesting exclusion of evidence from a trial because the evidence may have been obtained illegally. A defendant may also engage in pretrial discovery, including requests to view evidence in the possession of the prosecution. The prosecution and the defendant may engage in plea bargaining, whereby the prosecution may agree to reduce charges against the defendant in exchange for a plea of guilty or nolo contendere.

When a case proceeds to a jury trial, the parties have an opportunity to question prospective jurors, similar to the selection of jurors in a civil case, except that the final number of jurors in a criminal trial is usually larger than the number used in a civil case. Both the state and the defendant have the opportunity to strike jurors from the final jury. Once the final jury is selected and the trial begins, the prosecution reads the indictment or trial information, reads the defendant's plea, and makes an opening statement. The defendant may make an opening statement immediately after the prosecution, or may wait to do so until the time the defense introduces its evidence. Introduction of evidence in a criminal case is similar to that of a civil case, and the prosecution bears the burden of proving that the defendant is guilty beyond a reasonable doubt. Until the state proves otherwise, the defendant is presumed innocent. The defendant is not required to introduce evidence since the prosecution bears the burden of proof, but if the defendant does produce evidence, the prosecution may present rebuttal evidence and cross-examine any witnesses. Once both sides have presented the evidence, each party may give a closing argument.

A jury in a criminal trial must return a unanimous verdict of "guilty" or "not guilty." If a jury fails to reach a unanimous verdict, it is referred to as a "hung" jury, and a mistrial is declared. In such a situation, a new jury must retry the entire case. If the jury returns a unanimous verdict of guilty, then the jury's duty is usually complete, since a jury in most jurisdictions is not involved in the sentencing of the defendant. A judge, when determining an appropriate sentence for a convicted defendant, considers testimony and reports from a number of different sources, such as probation officers and victims. The federal government and many state governments have established detailed sentencing guidelines that must be followed by judges in criminal cases. In addition to a sentence of imprisonment or of a fine, a court may place a convicted defendant on probation, meaning that the defendant is placed under the supervision of a local correctional program. A defendant must comply with specific terms and conditions of the probation in order to avoid time in prison or jail. Similar to probation, a judge may also give the defendant a deferred judgment, or may suspend the defendant's sentence. In either case, the defendant is given the opportunity to remove the crime from his or her criminal record by successfully completing a period of probation.

Appeals If a party in a case is not satisfied with the outcome of a trial decision, he or she may appeal the case to a higher court for review. Not all parties have the right to appeal, however, and parties must follow proper procedures for the higher court to agree to hear the appeal. During trial, parties must "preserve error" by making timely objections to violations of the rules of evidence and other procedural rules. After trial, the party seeking an appeal must file a notice of appeal with the trial court. The opposing party may file a notice of cross-appeal if that party is not satisfied with the final judgment from the lower court. The party bringing the appeal is usually referred to as the appellant (though in some cases this party is the petitioner), and the opposing party is referred to as the appellee (or respondent in some cases).

Once a party has filed a notice of appeal, both parties must comply with a series of rules of appellate procedure to continue with the appeal. The appellant usually requests that the transcript of the trial court proceeding from the trial court reporter be sent to the court of appeals. The appellant must also pay a docketing or similar fee with the court of appeals. Both parties then file briefs with the appellate court stating the facts from the case, stating the legal arguments and reasons for appeal, and requesting relief from the appellate court. Both parties have access to the other party's briefs submitted to the court. Parties also request an oral argument, where both sides are given the opportunity to make their legal arguments before the court, and answer questions from the appellate court justices. Appellate courts do not hear testimony from witnesses or consider evidence that was not introduced in the trial. Rather, a court of appeals reviews the trial court proceeding to determine whether the trial court applied substantive or procedural law to the facts of the case correctly. At the end of the appeal, the court will issue an opinion that states the conclusion of the court of appeals.

Almost all judicial systems in the United States consist of three tiers, and an intermediate appellate court hears the first level of appeals. If a party is dissatisfied with an intermediate court's opinion, the party may seek an appeal by its jurisdiction's court of last resort. In many cases, the decision of a court of last resort to hear an appeal is discretionary, and a party must petition the court to hear the appeal (intermediate appellate courts, by comparison, typically do not have this discretion). The U.S. Supreme Court is the court of last resort for all cases in the United States, including the intermediate federal courts of appeals and the highest state courts. The U.S. Supreme Court only hears cases involving the application of federal law, and in most cases, the decision to grant an appeal is completely discretionary on the part of the Supreme Court. A party seeking review from the Supreme Court must file a petition for writ of certiorari requesting that the Court review the lower court's decision, and if the Court grants the writ, the Court orders the submission of the lower court's case. The Supreme Court grants a writ of certiorari in a very small percentage of cases, usually when there is a controversial issue of federal law in question in the case.

Civil appeals and criminal appeals are similar, with two main exceptions. First, the state ordinarily may not appeal an acquittal of a criminal in a trial court case. Second, in some criminal cases, especially murder cases where the defendant has received the death penalty, the right to appeal is guaranteed and automatic.

Jurisdiction and Venue When a party bring a lawsuit in a court in the United States, the party must determine which court has appropriate jurisdiction to hear the case, and which court is the proper venue for such a suit. Jurisdiction refers to the power of a court to hear a particular case, and may be subdivided into two components: subject matter jurisdiction and personal jurisdiction. Venue refers to the appropriateness of a court to hear a case, and applies differently than jurisdiction.

A court has proper subject matter jurisdiction if it has been given the power to hear a particular type of case or controversy under constitutional or statutory provisions. For example, a county court of law may have jurisdiction to hear cases and controversies where the amount in controversy of the claim is less than $5,000. If a claimant brings a case before the county court with an amount in controversy of $7,500, the court lacks jurisdiction to hear the case and will dismiss it. Subject matter jurisdiction is often a difficult issue with respect to the jurisdiction of federal courts. Personal jurisdiction is based on the parties or property involved in the lawsuit. *In personam* jurisdiction refers to the power of a court over a particular person or persons, and usually applies when a party is a resident of a state or has established some minimum contact with that state. In rem jurisdiction, by comparison, refers to the power of a court over property located in a particular state.

Venue is often confused with jurisdiction because it applies when determining whether a particular court may hear a case. A court may have jurisdiction to hear a case, but may not be the proper venue for such a case. Statutes often provide that proper venue in a particular case is the county or location where the defendant or defendants reside. Even if a court in the county where the plaintiff resides has proper jurisdiction to hear the case, it may not be the proper venue because of a provision in a statute regarding venue.

Jurisdiction of Federal Courts Federal courts in the United States have limited jurisdiction to hear certain claims, based primarily on provisions in Article III of the U.S. Constitution. Federal courts can hear cases involving the application of the Constitution, federal statutes, or treaties. Federal courts may also hear cases where the amount in controversy is more than $75,000, and all of the parties are citizens of different states. State courts may also hear cases with federal questions or where parties reside in different states. If a party brings a case in state court and a federal court has jurisdiction to hear the case, the opposing party may remove the case to federal court. The federal court generally reviews each case to determine whether jurisdiction is appropriate. If federal jurisdiction is not appropriate, the court remands the case to state court.

Some suits may only be brought in federal court, such as those brought by or against the government of the United States. Other examples are those involving bankruptcy, patents, and admiralty.

Legal vs. Equitable Remedies Some remedies available from courts are considered "legal" remedies, while others are considered "equitable" remedies. Legal remedies are usually those involving an award of monetary damages. By comparison, a court through use of an equitable remedy may require or prohibit certain conduct from a party. The distinction between legal and equitable remedies relates to the historic distinction between "law" and "equity" courts that existed in England as far back as the fourteenth century. Law courts traditionally adhered to very rigid procedures and formalities in resolving the outcome of a legal conflict, while equity courts developed a more flexible system where judges could exercise more discretion. This system transferred to the United States, but today, most courts in the United States may hear cases in both law and equity, although the procedure and proof required to request an equitable remedy may differ from the requirements to request a legal remedy. Examples of equitable remedies are specific performance of a contract, reformation of a contract, injunctions, and restitution.

Procedural Rules of the Courts In addition to procedural laws promulgated by legislatures, judicial systems also adopt various rules of procedure that must be followed by the courts and parties to a case. Two main types of court rules exist. First, some rules have general applicability over all courts in a particular jurisdiction. Examples of such rules are rules of civil procedure, rules of appellate procedure, rules of criminal procedure, and rules of evidence. Second, some rules apply only to a particular court, and are referred to as local court rules. Many counties draft local court rules that apply to all courts in those particular counties. Local court rules are generally more specific than rules of general applicability, and both must be consulted in a given case.

Pro Se Litigants and the Right to Representation A litigant representing himself or herself, without the assistance of counsel, is called a pro se litigant. It is almost always advisable to seek counsel with respect to a legal claim, if possible. Defendants in criminal cases are entitled to legal representation, and a lawyer will be provided to a criminal if the criminal shows indigence. Such assistance in criminal cases is usually provided by a public defender's office. Claimants in civil cases, on the other hand, are not entitled to attorneys, though any of a number of legal aid societies may be willing to provide legal services free of charge. Many of these legal aid societies are subsidized by public agencies, and will accept a case only if a person meets certain criteria, usually focusing on the income of the party.

In a civil case, a court may appoint counsel after considering a number of factors, including the validity of the party's position, and the ability of the party to try the case. A party who is indigent must usually file a written motion with the court, explaining the party's indigence and need for counsel. An attorney who provides free legal assistance is said to provide a pro bono service. Attorneys are generally free to determine when they will provide pro bono services, and it is common in every jurisdiction for the number of litigants seeking the appointment of counsel to outweigh the number of attorneys willing to provide pro bono services.

If a party must continue pro se, the rules regarding sanctions of attorneys apply equally to this party. A party must verify the accuracy and reasonableness of any document submitted to the court. If any submission contains false, improper, or frivolous information, the party may be liable for monetary or other sanctions. Likewise, a pro se litigant may be held in contempt of court for failure to follow the directions of a court. Many courts provide handbooks that assist pro se litigants in following proper trial procedures.

Small Claims Courts and Other Local Tribunals Cases involving a relatively small amount in controversy may be brought before small claims court. These courts exist only at the state court level. The maximum amount in controversy for a small claims court is usually $1,000 for a money judgment sought, or $5,000 for the recovery of personal property, though these amounts vary among jurisdictions. Witnesses are sworn, as they are in any trial, but the judge in a small claims court typically conducts the trial in a more informal fashion than in a trial at the district court level. Judges may permit the admission of evidence in a small claims action that may not be admissible under relevant rules of evidence or rules of procedure. One major exception is that privileged communication is usually not admissible in a small claims action. A small claims court usually only has the power to award monetary damages. If a party is unsatisfied with the judgment of the small claims court, the party may ordinarily appeal the case to a district court or other trial court.

Alternative Dispute Resolution A variety of procedures may be available to parties, which can serve as alternatives to litigation in the court system. Alternative dispute resolution, or ADR, has become rather common, because it is typically less costly and does not involve the formal proceedings associated with a trial. Parties usually enter into one of two types of ADR: arbitration or mediation. If a case is submitted to arbitration, a neutral arbitrator renders a decision that may be binding or non-binding, depending on the agreement of the parties. An arbitrator serves a function analogous to a judge, though the presentation of each party's evidence does not need to follow the formal rules that must be followed in a judicial decision. Though parties are generally not able to appeal an arbitrator's award, parties may seek judicial relief if the arbitrator acts in an arbitrary or capricious manner, shows bias towards one of the parties, or makes an obvious mistake. Arbitration may be ordered by a court, may be required under certain laws, or may be voluntary.

Mediation is similar to arbitration because it involves the use of a neutral third party to resolve a dispute. A mediator assists the parties to identify issues in a dispute, and makes proposals for the resolution of the dispute or disputes. However, unlike arbitrators, a mediator does not have the power to make a binding decision in a case. Also unlike arbitrators, a mediator typically meets with each of the interested parties in private to hold confidential discussions. Mediation may be court-ordered, may be required under certain laws, or may be voluntary. A number of organizations, including state bar associations, offer mediation services.

A number of other forms of ADR exist. For example, parties may employ the use of a fact finder, who resolves factual disputes between two parties. In some jurisdictions, parties may be required to submit a dispute to early neutral evaluation, where a neutral evaluator provides an assessment of the strengths and weaknesses of each party's position.

Case Law in the Common Law System Cases play a very important part in the legal system of the United States, not only because courts adjudicate the claims of parties before them, but also because courts establish precedent that must be followed in future cases. The United States adopted the common law tradition of England as the basis for its legal system. Under the common law system, legal principles were handed down from previous generations, first on an unwritten basis, then through the decisions of the courts. Though legislatures possess constitutional power to make law, in a common law system there is no presumption that legislation applies to every legal problem in the area addressed by the legislation. This differs from the legal systems based on the civil law tradition derived from Roman law (the use of the term civil law also refers to noncriminal laws, as discussed below, and the two uses of the term are distinct). In a civil law system, legislatures develop codes that are presumed to apply to all situations relevant to the code, and courts are employed only to adjudicate claims. The only state in the United States that does not consider itself a "common law state" is Louisiana, which adopted the civil law tradition based on its roots in French law. Accordingly, the codes (legislation) in that state are somewhat different than those in other states.

Courts in the United States follow the doctrine of precedent, which was also adopted from the English common law system. Under this doctrine, courts not only adjudicate the claims of the parties before them, but also establish a precedent that must be followed in future cases. The ruling of a court binds not only itself for future cases, but also any courts under which the court has appellate jurisdiction. Though trial level courts make rulings of law that are binding on future cases, the doctrine of precedent is most important in the legal system at the appellate levels.

Publication of Case Law Unlike statutes, cases are usually not available in a subject matter arrangement. When a case is first published, it is issued as a "slip opinion," named as such because these are printed on unbound sheets of paper. These opinions are compiled, and eventually published in bound case reporters. Cases from the U.S. Supreme Court and from courts in many jurisdictions are contained in reporters published by government bodies, and are called official reporters. These cases and other cases are also published in the National Reporter System, originally created by West Publishing Company (now West Group) in 1879. Case reporters in this system include state cases, federal cases, and cases from specialized tribunals, such as the bankruptcy courts. Cases may be readily located by finding their citation in the National Reporter System, or in another case reporter. An example of such a citation is "*Roe v. Wade*, 93 S. Ct. 705 (1973)." "*Roe v. Wade*" refers to the names of the parties of the case; "93" refers to the volume of the reporter; "S. Ct." is an abbreviation for Supreme Court Reporter; "705" refers to the page in the reporter where the case begins; and "(1973)" refers to year the case was decided.

Cases from all three levels of the federal judicial system are published. With few exceptions, only appellate court opinions from state courts are published. Unlike appellate courts, state trial judges seldom issue formal legal opinions about their cases, although rulings of law may be available in the record of the trial court. Most legal research in case law focuses on location of appellate court decisions.

Reading a Judicial Opinion Like other types of law, reading and understanding the meaning of a judicial opinion is more of an art than a science. The opinion of the case includes the court's reasoning in deciding a case, and is binding on future courts only if a majority of the court deciding the case joins the opinion (in which case the opinion is called the majority opinion). If an opinion is written in support of the court's judgment, but is not joined by a majority of justices, then the opinion is termed a plurality. Plurality opinions are not binding on future courts, but may be highly persuasive since they support the judgment of the court. Some justices may agree with the judgment, but may not agree with the majority opinion. These justices may write concurring opinions that state their reasons in support of the judgment. These opinions have no precedential value, but may be persuasive in future cases. Similarly, justices who disagree with the judgment, the opinion, or both, write dissenting opinions that argue against the judgment or majority opinion.

Some components of a majority opinion are binding on future courts, while others are not. The actual holding or reason for deciding (traditionally referred to as the ratio decidendi) provides the rule of law that is binding precedent in future cases. By comparison, dictum is the portion of an opinion that is not essential to a court's holding, and is not binding on future courts. Dicta may include background information about the holding, or may include the judge's personal comments about the reasoning for the holding. Dicta may be highly persuasive and may alter the holdings of future cases.

ADMINISTRATIVE LAW AND PROCEDURE

Creation and Empowerment of Government Agencies Although the branches of government are primarily responsible for the development of law and resolution of disputes, much of the responsibility of the administration of government has been delegated to government agencies. While branches of government may not delegate essential government functions to agencies, agencies may administer government programs, and promulgate and enforce regulations. When a legislature creates a government agency, it does so through the passage of an enabling statute, which also describes the specific powers delegated to the agency. The Administrative Procedure Act (APA) governs agency action at the federal level, and state counterparts to the APA govern state agencies.

Types of Government Agencies Some government agencies are formed to carry out government programs, but do not promulgate regulations that carry the force of law. A number of these agencies have been established to administer such programs as highway construction, education, public housing, and similar functions. Other government agencies promulgate rules and regulations that govern a particular area of law. Examples of regulatory agencies include the Environmental Protection Agency and Nuclear Regulatory Commission, both of which promulgate regulations that are similar in function to legislation. Legislatures also create agencies that resolve dispute among parties, similar to the function of a judicial body. Agency decisions are usually referred to as agency adjudications. Examples of agencies that adjudicate claims are the National Labor Relations Board and Securities and Exchange Commission.

Agency Rulemaking Most agencies that have regulatory power promulgate regulations through a process called notice and comment rulemaking. Before a regulatory agency can promulgate a rule, it must provide notice to the public. Federal agencies provide notice in the Federal Register, a daily government publication that provides the text of proposed and final agency rules. After considering comments from the public and making additional considerations, the agency may issue a final, binding rule. The promulgation of a final rule can take months, or may take years, to complete. State agencies must follow similar procedures, including publication of proposed rules in a publication analogous to the Federal Register. Agency rules are functionally equivalent to statutes. Federal agency rules currently in force are published in a subject matter arrangement in the Code of Federal Regulations. Each state publishes its rules in force in a state administrative code.

Some agencies at the state and federal levels are required to follow more formal procedures. Agencies may not exceed the power delegated by a respective legislature, and may adopt rules without following the proper procedures provided in the enabling legislation or legislation governing administrative procedures.

Agency Adjudications Agencies with power to adjudicate claims operate similarly to a court. Such an agency considers evidence presented in a hearing, and makes a final, binding decision based on an application of the law to the facts in a case. An agency that adjudicates a claim must maintain a record of the hearing, and parties are generally able to seek judicial review of a decision, much like judicial review of a lower court decision. A court may overrule an agency decision if the agency acted in an arbitrary or capricious manner, made a decision unsupported by substantial evidence, or made a decision unsupported by the facts presented to the agency.

RELATIONSHIP AMONG VARIOUS LAWS AND OTHER AUTHORITY

Laws in the United States do not exist in a vacuum, and determining the appropriate outcome of a case may require consultation with several different types of laws. A single case may be governed by application of a statute, an administrative regulation, and cases interpreting the statute and regulation. Understanding the application of laws usually requires an understanding of the nature of legal authority.

Any authority emanating from an official government entity acting in its lawmaking capacity is referred to as primary authority, and this authority is what is binding on a particular case. Primary authority can be subdivided into two types: primary mandatory authority and primary persuasive authority. Primary mandatory authority is law that is binding in a particular jurisdiction. For example, a Fifth Circuit Court of Appeals decision is primary mandatory authority in Texas, Mississippi, and Louisiana, since the Fifth Circuit governs these states. By comparison, primary authority that is not binding in a particular jurisdiction is referred to as primary persuasive authority. It is considered persuasive because though such authority does not bind a decision-maker in a jurisdiction, the decision-maker may nevertheless be persuaded to act in a familiar fashion as the authority from outside the jurisdiction. In the example above, a Fifth Circuit decision in a court in California would be considered primary persuasive authority, and could influence the California tribunal in its decision-making.

Another type of authority—secondary authority—may also be helpful in determining the appropriate application of the law. Secondary authority includes a broad array of sources, including treatises (a term used for law book); law review articles, which are usually written by law professors, judges, or expert practitioners; legal encyclopedias, which provide an overview of the law; and several other items that provide commentary about the law. An individual who is not trained in the law (and in many cases those who are trained in the law) should ordinarily begin his or her legal research by consulting such authority to gain a basic understanding of the law that applies in a particular situation.

A final consideration that cannot be overlooked is that the law constantly changes. If a legal researcher comes across literature describing the law in a given area, he or she must always verify that the discussion in the literature reflects the current state of the law.

Legislatures and agencies constantly add new laws, and revise and amend existing laws. Similarly, courts routinely overrule previous decisions and may rule that a statute or regulation is not valid under a relevant constitutional provision. Updating legal authority involves a process of consulting supplements and other resources, and is necessary to ensure that an individual knows the current state of the law.

AMERICANS WITH DISABILITIES ACT

EDUCATIONAL ACCOMMODATIONS

Sections within this essay:

- Background
- Defining Disability
- Accommodation of Disabilities
- Reasonable Accommodation
- Testing and Examinations
- Hidden Disabilities
- Private and Religious Schools
- Postsecondary Education
- Individuals with Disabilities Education Act
- State Laws Regarding Disabled Students
- Additional Resources

BACKGROUND

Congress enacted the Americans with Disabilities Act (ADA) to prohibit **discrimination** against those with disabilities. The **statute**, first enacted in 1990, applies in the areas of employment, public accommodations, transportation, services offered by governmental entities, and other areas. The Act attempts to extend the types of rights provided under the Civil Rights Act of 1964 to those with disabilities. Included among the rights in the ADA are provisions requiring educational institutions to provide accommodations to those with disabilities.

The first success the **disability** rights movement had was with Section 504 of the Rehabilitation Act of 1973. Based on the models of previous laws that prohibited discrimination based on race or gender, Section 504 prohibits discrimination in programs or activities receiving federal financial assistance. It provides: "No otherwise qualified individual with handicaps in the United States . . . shall, solely by reason of her or his handicap, be excluded from the participation in, be denied the benefits of, or be subjected to discrimination under any program or activity receiving Federal financial assistance." This provision marks the first time the disabled were viewed as a class of people, similar to a race or gender. The disabled used Section 504 to demand and enforce equal footing as a class under the law, one that could demand facilities to accommodate their disability.

Although this language offered some protection from educational discrimination for those with disabilities, Section 504 did not go far enough. It only applied in limited situations, where the program or building used federal financial aid in the form of grants. Those with disabilities still faced discrimination in the private sector, in private schools, and in those public facilities that did not use federal grant money. The disabled still faced a great many inaccessible schools; testing situations that did not offer alternatives for the deaf, the blind, or those with other types of disability; and other, similar barriers to equal education and access.

The Americans with Disabilities Act was passed on July 26, 1990, and signed into law by President George H.W. Bush. The intention of the Americans with Disabilities Act was to fill the gaps left behind by Section 504. The ADA builds upon the legal language within

Section 504, so that applied together, both laws would cover almost any situation, public or private, that the disabled might encounter.

The ADA bars employment and educational discrimination against "qualified individuals with disabilities." Title II of the ADA applies specifically to educational institutions, requiring them to make educational opportunities, extracurricular activities, and facilities open and accessible to all students. The ADA applies equally to public and private sector institutions, although the requirements for private schools and institutions are slightly less stringent.

DEFINING DISABILITY

Section 504 of the Rehabilitation Act of 1973 defines individuals with disabilities as those who have a physical or mental impairment which substantially limits one or more major life activities; has a record of such impairment; or is regarded as having such an impairment. This category includes physiological disorders such as hearing impairment, vision impairment, or speech impairments; neurological disorders such as muscular dystrophy or multiple sclerosis; psychological disorders such as mental retardation, mental illness, or learning disabilities. The legislative definition does not spell out specific illnesses or impairments because of the difficulty of ensuring an all-inclusive list.

The deciding factor in determining whether or not a person suffers from a disability under Section 504 is whether the impairment limits one or more major life activities, such as walking, performing manual tasks, seeing, hearing, speaking, breathing, learning and/or working. The ADA defines a disability as a "physical or mental impairment that substantially limits one or more major life activity; a record of such impairment; or being regarded as having such impairment." The ADA covers obvious impairments such as difficulty in seeing, hearing, or learning, as well as less obvious impairments such as alcoholism, epilepsy, paralysis, mental retardation, and contagious and noncontagious diseases, specifically Acquired Immune Deficiency Syndrome (AIDS).

The U.S. Supreme Court, in several key decisions, narrowed the ADA's definition of disability. The Court found that people with a range of substantially limiting impairments were not people with disabilities. In 2008, Congress enacted amendments that overturned these court rulings and directed the courts in the future to construe the definition of disability in favor of broad coverage of individuals under the ADA.

The difference between the two laws, as they apply to educational institutions, is that Section 504 applies to the recipients of grant monies from the federal government, while Title II of the ADA applies only to public entities,

with some applications to private sector entities. These entities include nursery, elementary, secondary, undergraduate, or postgraduate schools, or other places of education, day care centers, and gymnasiums or other places of exercise or recreation.

ACCOMMODATION OF DISABILITIES

Section 504 of the Rehabilitation Act of 1973 and Title II of the ADA cover students in virtually any public school district, college, or university because they receive some form of federal assistance. Some private schools, colleges, and universities also receive such assistance, and students are protected under Section 504, but Title II does not apply to them. Both laws apply to all programs of a school or college, not simply academics. These include extracurricular activities such as band, clubs, or academic teams, as well as athletics and any activity that might occur off campus.

Neither law requires that all buildings be made fully accessible to students or teachers with disabilities. Those buildings constructed after the Section 504 regulation was issued in 1977 must be fully accessible. For older buildings, the law requires that the program or activity be made accessible. Often, classes or extracurricular activities are moved to another, more accessible, room to accommodate any disabled person who attends. An interpreter for the hearing-impaired or other types of assistance can be supplied.

REASONABLE ACCOMMODATION

One aim of the ADA was to make educational institutions more accessible for the disabled. This aim covers "reasonable accommodations" such as the following:

- Modification of application and testing
- Allowing students to tape-record or videotape lectures and classes
- Modification of class schedules
- Extra time allotted between classes
- Notetakers
- Interpreters
- Readers
- Specialized computer equipment
- Special education

Accommodations also includes physical changes to an educational institution's buildings, including the following:

- Installing accessible doorknobs and hardware
- Installing grab bars in bathrooms
- Increasing maneuverability in bathrooms for wheelchairs

- Installing sinks and hand dryers within reach
- Creating handicapped parking spaces
- Installing accessible water fountains
- Installing ramps
- Having curb cuts, sidewalks, and entrances that are accessible
- Installing elevators
- Widening door openings

Public accommodation is not required if a particular aid or service would result in either fundamental alteration of the services offered or the facility if the accommodation would impose an undue burden. (See *Southeastern Community College v. Davis*, 442 U.S. 397 [1979]). Under the U.S. Supreme Court's interpretation, Congress intended that undue burden and hardship must be determined on a case-by-case basis.

TESTING AND EXAMINATIONS

Section 309 of the Americans with Disabilities Act fills the gap regarding testing and examination not defined by Section 504 of the Rehabilitation Act of 1973 or Title II of the ADA. Any educational facility that receives federal money or is a public facility because it is a function of the state or local government as defined under Title II of the ADA is required to make any examination accessible to persons with disabilities. This requirement includes physical access to the testing facility, as well as any modification of the way the test is administered to assist the disabled. Modifications may include offering extended time, written instructions, or the assistance of a reader.

Many licensing and testing authorities are not covered by Section 504 or Title II. In these cases, a provision in the ADA was included to assure that persons with disabilities are not prohibited from or disallowed in any educational, professional, or other examination opportunity because a test or course is conducted in an inaccessible location or is offered without the needed modifications to assist the disabled student. Modifications may include offering an examination with the assistance of a reader, in Braille or large print format, transcribers, or the proper computer equipment to help the disabled person.

Examiners may require proof of disability, but requests for documentation of the disability must be reasonable and must be limited to support for the modification or aid requested. The student or testing applicant may be required to bear the cost of providing such documentation for examination officials. Appropriate documentation would include:

- Letter from physician or psychiatrist or other qualified individual

- Evidence of prior diagnosis
- Evidence of prior accommodation

HIDDEN DISABILITIES

Hidden disabilities are considered to be any physical or mental impairments that are not readily apparent to others. They include such conditions as learning disabilities, allergies, diabetes, and epilepsy, as well as chronic illnesses such as heart, kidney, or liver disease. There are roughly four million American students with disabilities, many with impairments that are not immediately known without medical or diagnostic testing.

PRIVATE AND RELIGIOUS SCHOOLS

The ADA defines private elementary and secondary schools as places of public accommodation that must be physically accessible to those with disabilities. However these schools are not required to provide free appropriate education or develop an individualized educational program for students with disabilities. Any private school that receives federal grant monies or any type of federal assistance would then fall under the Department of Education's regulations regarding construction and alterations to the private school's structures and buildings, where it can be conveniently and economically incorporated.

POSTSECONDARY EDUCATION

Under Section 504, colleges and universities are not required to identify students with disabilities. They are required to inform all applicants of the availability of auxiliary aids, services, and academic adjustments. It is the student's responsibility to make his or her condition known and to seek out assistance.

INDIVIDUALS WITH DISABILITIES EDUCATION ACT

In addition to the protections offered by the ADA and Section 504, another statute, the Individuals with Disabilities Education Act (IDEA), provides additional protection to those with disabilities in the context of education. The act was originally passed by Congress in 1975 but has been amended on several occasions since that time. The goals of IDEA are as follows:

- It ensures the disabled children are given a "free appropriate public education," emphasizing special education and related services that meet the specific needs of each disabled child

- It ensures the protection of the rights of disabled children and their parents

- It assists states, local governments, educational service agencies, and federal agencies to provide for the education of disabled children

- It assists states to implement a statewide system of early intervention services for disabled infants and toddlers; it ensures that educators and parents have the necessary tools to improve educational results for disabled children

- It assesses and ensures the effectiveness of efforts to educate disabled children

Unlike ADA and Section 504, which are nondiscrimination laws, IDEA is instead a grant program. It requires states that accept federal funds to provide free, appropriate public education to disabled children. Although the means by which IDEA operates differs from the ADA and Section 504, each of these statutes serve similar purposes for the most part.

STATE LAWS REGARDING DISABLED STUDENTS

Under IDEA, states that receive federal funding must conduct an approved plan for meeting guidelines in educating disabled students. Accordingly, each state has enacted a statute designed to assure compliance with guidelines. A brief summary of these statutes is as follows:

ALABAMA: The statute related to education for exceptional children is located in title 16 of the Alabama Code.

ALASKA: The statute related to education for exceptional children is located in title 14 of the Alaska Statutes.

ARIZONA: The statute related to special education for exceptional children is located in title 15 of the Arizona Revised Statutes.

ARKANSAS: The statute related to education for handicapped children is located in title 6 of the Arkansas Code.

CALIFORNIA: The statute related to special education programs is located in the California Education Code.

COLORADO: The Handicapped Children's Education Act is located in title 22 of the Colorado Revised Statutes.

CONNECTICUT: The Exceptional Children Act is located in title 10 of the Connecticut General Statutes.

DELAWARE: The statute related to education for exceptional and handicapped students is located in title 14 of the Delaware Code.

FLORIDA: The statute related to instruction of exceptional students is located in chapter 1003 of the Florida Statutes.

GEORGIA: The statute related to special education services is located in title 20 of the Georgia Code.

HAWAII: The statute related to education for exceptional children is located in chapter 301 of the Hawaii Revised Statutes.

IDAHO: The statute related to education of handicapped or others unable to attend school is located in title 33 of the Idaho Code.

ILLINOIS: The statute related to the education of disabled children is located in chapter 105 of the Illinois Compiled Statutes.

INDIANA: The statute related to special education programs is located in title 20 of the Indiana Code.

IOWA: The statute related to education of children requiring special education is contained in chapter 281 of the Iowa Code.

KANSAS: The Special Education for Exceptional Children Act is located in title 72 of the Kansas Statutes.

KENTUCKY: The statute related to special education programs is located in title 157 of the Kentucky Revised Statutes.

LOUISIANA: The statutes related to education opportunities for exceptional children is located in title 17 of the Louisiana Revised Statutes.

MAINE: The statute related to education for exceptional children is located in title 20-A of the Maine Revised Statutes.

MARYLAND: The statute related to compensatory education for disadvantaged and handicapped children is contained in the Maryland Education Code.

MASSACHUSETTS: The statute related to education of children with special needs is located in chapter 71B of the Massachusetts Laws.

MICHIGAN: The statute related to special education programs for the handicapped is located in chapter 380 of the Michigan Compiled Laws.

MINNESOTA: The statute related to special education for handicapped children is located in chapter 120 of the Minnesota Statutes.

MISSISSIPPI: The statute related to education for exceptional children is located in title 37 of the Mississippi Code.

MISSOURI: The statute related to special educational services for handicapped children is located in chapter 162 of the Missouri Revised Statutes.

MONTANA: The statute related to special education programs for handicapped children is located in title 20 of the Montana Code.

NEBRASKA: The statute related to special education is located in chapter 79 of the Nebraska Revised Statutes.

NEVADA: The statute related to education of handicapped minors is located in chapter 388 of the Nevada Revised Statutes.

NEW HAMPSHIRE: The statute related to programs of special education is located in chapter 186-C of the New Hampshire Revised Statutes.

NEW JERSEY: The statute related to classes and facilities for handicapped children is located in title 18A of the New Jersey Statutes.

NEW MEXICO: The statute related to special education for exceptional children is located in chapter 22 of the New Mexico Statutes.

NEW YORK: The statute related to children with handicapping conditions is located in sections 4401 *et seq.* of the New York Education Law.

NORTH CAROLINA: The statute related to special education programs is located in chapter 115C of the North Carolina General Statutes.

NORTH DAKOTA: The statute related to special education of exceptional children is located in title 15 of the North Dakota Century Code.

OHIO: The statute related to the education of handicapped children is located in chapter 3323 of the Ohio Revised Code.

OKLAHOMA: The statute related to special education for exceptional children is located in title 70 of the Oklahoma Statutes.

OREGON: The statute related to special education services is located in chapter 343 of the Oregon Revised Statutes.

PENNSYLVANIA: The statute related to education of exceptional children is located in title 24 of the Pennsylvania Statutes.

RHODE ISLAND: The statute related to education of handicapped children is located in title 16 of the Rhode Island General Laws.

SOUTH CAROLINA: The statute related to special education for handicapped children is located in title 59 of the South Carolina Code.

SOUTH DAKOTA: The statute related to special and prolonged educational assistance is located in title 13 of the South Dakota Codified Laws.

TENNESSEE: The statute related to special education programs is located in title 49 of the Tennessee Code.

TEXAS: The statute related to special education programs is located in the Texas Education Code.

UTAH: The statute related to the education of handicapped children is located in the Utah Code.

VERMONT: The statute related to education of handicapped children is located in title 16 of the Vermont Statutes.

VIRGINIA: The statute related to special education programs is located in title 22.1 of the Virginia Code.

WASHINGTON: The statute related to special education for handicapped children is located in title 28A of the Washington Revised Code.

WEST VIRGINIA: The statute related to education of exceptional children is located in title 18 of the West Virginia Code.

WISCONSIN: The statute related to children with exceptional needs is located in chapter 115 of the Wisconsin Statutes.

WYOMING: The statute related to programs for handicapped children is located in title 21 of the Wyoming Statutes.

ADDITIONAL RESOURCES

Americans with Disabilities Handbook. Equal Employment Opportunity Commission and U.S. Department of Justice, October 1991.

Auxiliary Aids and Services for Post-Secondary Students with Disabilities: Higher Education's Obligations Under Section 504 and Title II of the ADA. Office for Civil Rights, U.S. Department of Education. 1998.

"The Civil Rights of Students with Hidden Disabilities Under Section 504 of the Rehabilitation Act of 1973." Office for Civil Rights, U.S. Department of Education. 1995. Available at http://www2.ed.gov/about/offices/list/ocr/docs/hq5269.html (accessed November 1, 2012).

Disability.gov. Clearinghouse for information about federal government resources, pamphlets, and information regarding disabilities. Managed by the Office of Disability Employment Policy, U.S. Department of Labor. Available at http://www.disAbility.gov (accessed November 3, 2012).

Rapp, James A. *Education Law.* Newark, NJ: LexisNexis/Matthew Bender, 2005.

"Student Placement in Elementary and Secondary Schools and Section 504 of the Rehabilitation Act and Title II of the Americans with Disabilities Act." Office for Civil Rights, U.S. Department of Education, August 2010. Available at http://www2.ed.gov/about/offices/list/ocr/docs/placpub.html (accessed November 2, 2012).

ORGANIZATIONS

American Council on Rural Special Education (ACRES)

2323 Anderson Ave., Suite 226, Kansas State University
Manhattan, WA 66502
Phone: (785) 532-2737
Fax: (785) 532-7732
URL: http://acres-sped.org

American Speech Language-Hearing Association (ASHA)

1801 Rockville Pike
Rockville, MD
Phone: (301) 897-5700
Toll Free: (800) 638-8255
URL: http://www.asha.org

Children with Attention Deficit Disorders (CHADD)

8181 Professional Place, Suite 201
Landover, MD 20785
Phone: (301) 306-7070
Fax: (301) 306-7090
URL: http://www.chadd.org

Clearinghouse of Disability Information, Office of Special Education and Rehabilitative Services, U.S. Department of Education

Switzer Building Room 3132 330 C Street SW
Washington, DC 20202
Phone: (202) 205-8241
Fax: (202) 401-2608
URL: http://www2.ed.gob/about/offices/list/osers/codi.html

Dyslexia Research Institute, Inc.

5746 Centerville Road
Tallahassee, FL 32308
Phone: (850) 893-2216
Fax: (850) 893-2440
URL: http://www.dyslexia-add.org

Learning Disabilities Association of America (LDA)

4156 Library Road
Pittsburgh, PA 15234
Phone: (412) 341-1515
Fax: (412) 341-8077
URL: http://www.ldanatl.org

National Center for Learning Disabilities (NCLD)

381 Park Avenue South, Suite 1401
New York City, NY 10016
Phone: (212) 545-7510
Fax: (212) 545-9665
URL: http://www.ncld.org

AMERICANS WITH DISABILITIES ACT

PUBLIC FACILITY ACCOMMODATIONS

Sections within this essay:

- Background
- Before ADA
  - Architectural Barriers Act
  - Rehabilitation Act of 1973
  - Uniform Federal Accessibility Standards (UFAS)
- ADA and Title III
  - Physical Accommodations
  - Auxiliary Accommodations
  - Other Accommodations
- Enforcing the Law
- Additional Resources

BACKGROUND

Many people think that the Americans with Disabilities Act (ADA) primarily covers workplace accommodations. The only public accommodations they associate with ADA are handicapped parking spaces and Braille numbers on elevator buttons. In fact, the ADA's public facilities rules, as outlined in Title III of the act, are far more comprehensive than that. All sorts of buildings and businesses fall under Title III: restaurants, schools, office buildings, banks, doctors' offices, and movie theaters, to name a few. Accommodation can include anything from adjusting store shelves to constructing special ramps and entryways.

Some people mistakenly believe that ADA requires businesses to make all sorts of prohibitively expensive changes or else face stiff penalties. The truth is that ADA is designed to benefit the disabled, not to punish business owners. The key to understanding ADA is knowing what is and is not required, as well as what constitutes an acceptable accommodation.

BEFORE ADA

In years past, "disability" was not something people dealt with publicly. It was understood that those who were blind, deaf, paralyzed, or otherwise "handicapped" would not participate in ordinary life activities, such as school or work.

Attitudes changed slowly but steadily, and by the twentieth century such notable people as Helen Keller and Franklin D. Roosevelt helped break down stereotypes about disabilities. Accommodating the disabled was another matter. Only important public figures such as Roosevelt (who could not stand or walk unaided after his 1921 bout with polio) could expect that structural accommodations would be made for them, and even then those accommodations were limited in scope. There were simply some places that the disabled could not visit freely.

Architectural Barriers Act Although most people think that ADA was the first federal law regulating public facilities, in fact it was an earlier law that set the stage. The Architectural Barriers Act (ABA) was passed in 1968, and it mandated that any buildings designed, constructed, altered, or leased with federal funding had to be accessible to the disabled. This included post offices, national parks, some schools, some public housing, and mass transit systems. Because it dealt only with federally funded structures, it was (and still is) less well known than ADA, but it was an important early step.

Rehabilitation Act of 1973 As important as ABA was, it was met with a certain degree of apathy that undermined its effectiveness. Congress, eager to improve ABA compliance and equally eager for the government to create new and more comprehensive design standards, passed the Rehabilitation Act in 1973. Perhaps the most important element of this law was Section 502, which established the Architectural and Transportation Barriers Compliance Board (later called simply the Access Board). Originally created to develop as well as enforce design requirements, its role later became more focused on ensuring compliance. Beginning in 1976, the Access Board started investigating ABA non-compliance complaints against a variety of public buildings. The law covers any facility that was designed, built, altered, or leased with federal funds after 1969.

Uniform Federal Accessibility Standard (UFAS) The design requirements that are supposed to be followed under ABA are spelled out by the Uniform Federal Accessibility Standard (UFAS), which was first published in 1984. These guidelines served as a precursor of sorts to guidelines later introduced under ADA. In the early 2010s, some government agencies required compliance with both the ADA guidelines and UFAS.

ADA AND TITLE III

The Americans with Disabilities Act was signed into law on July 26, 1990. Title I of the law covers places of employment; Title II state and local governments. Title IV covers telecommunications for the deaf and hearing-impaired, and Title V covers miscellaneous items. The section of ADA that deals with public facilities is Title III.

Public accommodations include any building or outdoor space through which any person can enter, with or without a fee. Essentially, that means all buildings except for "private" clubs (any club that requires members to vote to admit an individual) and religious facilities. Among the facilities covered as listed by ADA are the following:

- Lodgings (hotels, motels, inns)
- Establishments that serve food and drink (restaurants, bars, taverns)
- Establishments that offer entertainment (theaters, stadiums)
- Places where public gatherings may be held (auditoriums, convention halls)
- Sale or rental establishments (retail stores)
- Service establishments (medical offices, law offices, funeral parlors)
- Places of public display or collection (museums, galleries, public gardens)
- Social service centers (homeless shelters, day care centers)
- Recreation/exercise establishment (golf courses, gymnasiums)

It is important to understand not only which facilities are covered under ADA, but also who is considered disabled. Under ADA guidelines, anyone who possesses a physical or mental impairment that significantly limits at least one major life function—for example, the ability to feed oneself, the ability to walk, or the ability to breathe on one's own. Alcoholics and other substance abusers are also covered if they have been shown to have a history of such abuse.

A public accommodation is expected to follow three basic guidelines under Title III of ADA. First, it cannot deny goods or services to a disabled person covered under the legislation. Second, it cannot satisfy its commitment to the legislation by offering benefits that are separate or unequal. Finally, it must offer all services in as integrated a setting as possible.

This kind of wording frightens some owners of public facilities. Retail store owners, for example, sometimes fear that Title III compliance means having to make expensive structural changes to their stores or keep people on staff to accommodate all possible disabilities. Would a small company have to install an elevator in its building? Does a restaurant have to make Braille menus and sign-language interpreters available?

In fact, ADA's Title III guidelines do offer a certain degree of leeway for facilities, but that leeway is dependent on a number of factors including cost and a facility's special needs.

Physical Accommodations Under Title III, any new building first occupied after January 26, 1993 is required to meet full ADA standards (unless the building plans had been completed before January 26, 1992). The following are among the requirements that new buildings are expected to meet:

- Doorways must be wide enough to accommodate wheelchairs; doors must be easy to open.

- Restrooms must be equipped with adequately wide stalls, grab bars, and sinks and towel dispensers easily accessible for someone in a wheelchair.

- Pay phones must be provided at more than one height, and phones with amplifiers should also be available.

- Adequate parking spaces should be set aside to accommodate disabled patrons.

- Elevators must have Braille numbers and visual as well as audible operation signals.

- Alarm systems must be audible and visible.

Existing facilities that are being remodeled (and in some cases those that are not) must make sure that alterations are ADA-compliant, as long as such changes are deemed reasonable, or, in the words of the legislation, "readily achievable." An alteration is deemed readily achievable when it can be done relatively easily and without much expense. It might not be structurally or economically feasible for a public facility with no elevator to install one, for example, but it probably is feasible to install ramps, handrails, and grab bars. Shelving in stores, telephones mounted lower on the wall, soap dispensers in bathrooms, and brighter lights are all things that can be added with little difficulty or undue expense. In cases in which alterations are difficult or impossible, alternatives can be incorporated instead. Examples include providing taped lectures of inaccessible gallery exhibits or providing a water cooler or reachable paper cups instead of installing a new accessible drinking fountain

As for new buildings, the costs of incorporating ADA-compliant accessibility features has been estimated to be less than one percent of overall construction costs. Thus, it is unlikely that the owners of a building currently under construction would be able to make a case against accessibility, nor should they want to. As more disabled people enter both the consumer market (as tourists, for example) and the workforce, it benefits building owners to make their structures ADA-compliant.

Auxiliary Accommodations A special accommodation category exists for those with visual and hearing impairments. The "auxiliary accommodations" are designed to make it easier to communicate with people who have difficulty seeing or hearing. Among the accommodations ADA can recommend are the following:

- Interpreters who speak sign language

- Special listening devices and headsets

- Texts in large print and Braille, or recorded on tape

- TDD/TTY text telephones for those with hearing impairments

As with physical alterations, auxiliary accommodations are not designed to create an undue burden on the building owner. They are also not meant to alter the nature of goods or services offered by the public facility in question. For example, a museum whose art works are too delicate to be handled may implement a "no touch" policy, even though it means that certain blind people may not be able to enjoy the exhibit fully.

Stores are not required to have signs or price tags in Braille, nor do they need to have a sign language interpreter on staff. As long as an employee can read price tags and similar information to blind shoppers, and as long as store employees can communicate with deaf customers by writing out notes, there is no requirement for businesses to incur the expense of extra assistance.

Actually, many auxiliary accommodations can be made quite inexpensively. Most ordinary computer programs can be set to display and print in large type, for example. TDD/TTY telephone units equipped with printers cost about $500, which most fair-sized businesses could afford with little difficulty.

Other Accommodations There are a number of other accommodations that in general are cost-effective to implement. For example, restaurants that need to make more room for wheelchairs may be required to move their tables around; unless they had to remove a significant number of tables and thus lose business, this should not be a burden. In fact, many restaurants add or remove tables for certain events as a matter of course. Some stores may have to relocate display racks for the same reason. Outdoor cafes that crowd sidewalks may be required to reduce the number of tables or increase the space between them. Large plants, whether indoors or outdoors, may need to be moved to make room for disabled individuals.

ENFORCING THE LAW

Since 1976 the Access Board has investigated thousands of complaints against public facilities, including post offices, military facilities, veterans hospitals, federal courthouses, and prisons. In general, the Board works with the facility to find ways to bring it into compliance. One example is the Holocaust Memorial Museum in Washington, D.C. A group of children with varying degrees of hearing impairment were touring the museum when the fire alarm went off. Because the students actually thought the alarms were part of the exhibit, and because they could not hear the evacuation notices, there was potential for serious consequences. A complaint was filed with the Access Board, which worked with the museum to install new alarms that offered a more distinct and distinguishable signal.

Another example is a homeless shelter in Phoenix, Arizona. Although rest rooms in the shelter had been renovated twice using federal funds, they were still not ADA compliant. The Access Board worked successfully with the shelter to address the issue and made the rest rooms compliant.

Those who feel that a public facility is in violation of Title III may file their complaints with the U.S. Department of Justice. In cases of repeat violations, the Department has authorization to bring lawsuits against offenders, although the more desired outcome would be correction of the problem with the help of groups such as the Access Board. The Department of Justice website that handles ADA issues is http://www.usdoj.gov/crt/ada/adahom1.htm.

ADDITIONAL RESOURCES

Disability.gov. Clearinghouse for information about federal government resources, pamphlets, and information regarding disabilities. Managed by the Office of Disability Employment Policy, U.S. Department of Labor. Available at http://www.disAbility.gov (accessed November 3, 2012).

Rhoads, Macela. *The ADA Companion Guide: Understanding the Americans with Disabilities Act Accessibility Guidelines (ADAAG) and the Architectural Barriers Act (ABA).* Hoboken, NJ: Wiley, 2010.

Young, Jonathan M. *Equality of Opportunity: The Making of ADA.* Washington, DC: National Council on Disability, 2010. Available at http://www.ncd.gov/publications/1997/equality_of_Opportunity_The_Making_of_the_Americans_with_Disabilities_Act (accessed November 1, 2012).

ORGANIZATIONS

Access Board
1331 F St. NW, Ste. 1000
Washington, DC 20004
Phone: (202) 272-0080
Fax: (202) 272-0081
URL: http://www.access-board.gov

Council for Disability Rights
205 West Randolph Street, Suite 1645
Chicago, IL 60606
Phone: (312) 444-9484
Fax: (312) 444-1977
URL: http://www.disabilityrights.org

Office of Disability Rights, Civil Rights Division, U.S. Department of Justice
950 Pennsylvania Avenue NW
Washington, DC 20530
Phone: (202) 307-2227
Fax: (202) 307-1198
URL: http://www.usdoj.gov/crt/drs/drshome.htm

U.S. Equal Employment Opportunity Commission (EEOC)
1801 L Street NW
Washington, DC 20507
Phone: (202) 663-4900
Fax: (202) 663-4494 (TTY)
URL: http://www.eeoc.gov

AMERICANS WITH DISABILITIES ACT

WORK ACCOMMODATIONS

Sections within this essay:

- Background
- Rationale
- Reasonable Accommodations
- Procedure
- Types of Reasonable Accommodations
- Additional Resources

BACKGROUND

In the United States, approximately 54 million people (19% of the population) have physical or mental disabilities or impairments that substantially limit major life activities. In an effort to avoid **discrimination** against disabled people in the workplace, Congress passed and the president signed into law in July of 1990 the Americans with Disabilities Act (ADA). One way that the ADA seeks to improve employment opportunities for disabled people is by requiring employers under certain circumstances to alter the workplace to accommodate disabilities. These alterations are known as workplace accommodations.

RATIONALE

Just like individuals of different races, colors, religions, gender, or national origin, individuals with physical or mental disabilities historically have faced discrimination. Disabled people have been excluded from mainstream society, segregated, provided with inferior or unequal services, and denied benefits that non-disabled people enjoy. What is different about the discrimination of disabled people as compared to other types of discrimination is that there is often a rational basis for treating disabled people differently from able-bodied people. Whereas there is usually no rational basis for treating, for example, a woman from South Africa differently from a woman from the United States, there may be a rational basis for treating a woman who is blind differently from a woman with good vision. The visually impaired woman may require the use of Braille, for example.

Another difference in **disability** discrimination is its intent. Many types of discrimination, such as **racial discrimination**, are rooted in hostility or hatred toward people who are different. However, discrimination against disabled individuals more often is rooted in ignorance or apathy. Some people view disabilities with pity or discomfort, leading to behavior that may patronize people with disabilities. Other people simply fail to consider or understand the needs of disabled people, leading to benign neglect or misguided efforts to assist.

The U.S. Constitution does little to protect those with mental or physical disabilities from discrimination. Courts historically have not applied the Constitution's Equal Protection Clause to discrimination of **disabled persons** with the same level of scrutiny as discrimination of such protected classes as race, religion, and gender. People with disabilities, therefore, had little or no recourse when their disabilities unfairly prevented them from getting suitable jobs. Only two-thirds of employable disabled persons in the United States were employed in the late 1980s, and many of those employed were not working to their full capacity to earn given their disabilities. By 1990, more than 8 million disabled individuals were unemployed and forced to live on welfare and other forms of government assistance. Congress began enacting federal laws in the 1960s designed to protect disabled people, but these laws did not outlaw disability discrimination by employers. Such protections did not enter the workplace until the 1990 passage of the ADA.

The ADA prohibits private and state and local government employers, as well as employment agencies and labor unions, from discriminating on the basis of disability. It does not apply to private employers with fewer than 15 employees. The ADA prohibits several specific forms of disability discrimination. One example of an ADA violation occurs when an employer fails to make reasonable accommodations to allow disabled workers to work.

REASONABLE ACCOMMODATIONS

The ADA requires employers to make reasonable accommodations to qualified persons with disabilities unless such accommodations would cause an undue hardship to the employer. A disabled person under the ADA is someone who is substantially limited in the ability to perform a major life activity or who has a record of such an impairment or who is regarded as having such an impairment. To be qualified as a disabled person under the ADA, an individual must show an ability to perform all of the essential job functions either with or without a reasonable accommodation. Courts look at mitigating measures in determining whether an individual is disabled. For example, persons who need eyeglasses may be substantially limited in the ability to read, which is a major life activity, unless they wear eyeglasses. Because eyeglasses mitigate their bad vision and allow them to read normally, they are not considered to disabled under the ADA.

The U.S. Supreme Court, in several key decisions, narrowed the ADA's definition of disability. The Court found that people with a range of substantially limiting impairments were not people with disabilities. In 2008, Congress enacted amendments that overturned these court rulings and directed the courts in the future to construe the definition of disability in favor of broad coverage of individuals under the ADA.

There are three general types of reasonable accommodations. The first type modifies the job application process to enable qualified job applicants with a disability to be considered for the job they want. The second type modifies the work environment or the manner in which the job is performed to allow disabled individuals to perform the job's essential functions. The third type modifies the workplace to allow disabled employees equal benefits and privileges as similarly situated employees without disabilities.

More specific types of reasonable accommodations may include making an office wheelchair accessible; restructuring jobs; providing part-time or modified work schedules; modifying or purchasing special furniture or equipment; changing employment policies; providing readers or interpreters; and reassigning disabled individuals to vacant positions. An employer is not required to eliminate an essential job function or fundamental duty of the job to accommodate a disabled person. An employer is not required to lower production quotas or standards that apply to all employees, although an employer is required to provide reasonable accommodations to help a disabled individual meet production quotas or standards. An employer is not required to provide disabled employees with personal use items that are necessary both on and off the job, such as hearing aids.

The ADA does not require that reasonable accommodations be made when the accommodations would cause employers an undue hardship. Undue hardship means significant difficulty or expense when compared with the employer's resources and circumstances. The employer's financial capabilities are one factor in defining undue hardship, but undue hardship also occurs when the reasonable accommodation would be unduly extensive or disruptive or would fundamentally alter the nature or operation of the business. Courts determine on a case-by-case basis whether a reasonable accommodation would be an undue hardship for the employer.

PROCEDURE

Individuals who want a reasonable accommodation must request it but need not mention the ADA or the phrase "reasonable accommodation." It is sufficient if employees simply ask for an accommodation for a medical reason. Once a request is made, employers are obligated to investigate the request and determine if the requesting employee is qualified as a disabled individual under the ADA. If that determination is positive, then the employer must begin an interactive process with that employee, determining that individual's needs and identifying the accommodation that should be made. Sometimes this is an easy process with both sides agreeing on the reasonable accommodation. Other times, the interactive process can be complicated and contentious.

Sometimes employers do not know about or understand the disability enough to determine a reasonable accommodation. In these cases, employers are entitled to obtain documentation, such as medical records or a letter from a doctor, to learn about the disability, its functional limitations, and the sort of accommodation that needs to be made. Alternatively, employers may simply ask the requesting employee about the disability and limitations. Unless the disability is obvious, that employee must provide the employer with sufficient information about the disability to help the employer determine a reasonable accommodation.

As long as the reasonable accommodation is effective in allowing the disabled individuals to perform their job functions and receive the same benefits as other, non-disabled individuals, then employers have the right to choose among reasonable accommodation options. Employers may choose options that are less expensive or easier to provide, for example. If employers offer disabled employees reasonable accommodations that employees do not want, the employers may not force the employees to accept the accommodations. If, however, the employee's refusal of the reasonable accommodation results in the individual's inability to perform the essential functions of the job, the employee may be deemed unqualified for the job. The employer may then be justified in terminating the employee.

During the hiring process, employers are not permitted to ask whether job applicants require a reasonable accommodation unless an applicant's disability is obvious, such as an applicant who uses a wheelchair, or unless the applicant voluntarily informs the employer about the disability. If the employer offers the applicant a job, it is with the condition that the applicant is able to perform the essential job functions either with or without a reasonable accommodation. Once the applicant receives the job offer, the employer may inquire about the necessity of reasonable accommodations.

The ADA also mandates that employees with disabilities be permitted to enjoy the same benefits and privileges of employment as non-disabled employees enjoy. Therefore, employers must provide reasonable accommodations to allow the disabled worker to gain access to such privileges as workplace cafeterias or lounges, gyms or health clubs, training programs, credit unions, transportation, or any other perk offered to non-disabled employees. A blind employee, for example, would not be able to read employment related notices placed on bulletin boards. In that case, the employer would have to provide a reasonable accommodation, such as sending that employee telephone messages.

TYPES OF REASONABLE ACCOMMODATIONS

An employer may restructure or modify a job as a reasonable accommodation for an employee with a disability. Job restructuring may include reallocating job functions or trading certain job functions that are difficult or impossible for the disabled worker with other job functions of a non-disabled worker. A disabled secretary who cannot climb stairs, for example, may be able to fulfill the essential functions of the job but cannot easily retrieve files from the upstairs storage

room. In this case, an appropriate accommodation would be to assign the disabled worker additional filing duties and require an able-bodied co-worker to actually retrieve the files.

A disabled worker may be entitled to a paid or unpaid leave of absence from the job as a reasonable accommodation for such reasons as the worker's need for surgery or other medical treatment, the worker's recovery from illness related to the disability, or the worker's education or training related to the disability. An employer does not have to pay the disabled worker during a disability-related leave of absence beyond the employer's own policy regarding sick pay or vacation pay. The employer is required to hold open the disabled worker's job during the leave of absence, but the employer may demonstrate that holding open the position for an extended period would constitute an undue hardship. In the event of undue hardship, the employer can fill the disabled worker's position with another employee but then must try to identify an equivalent position for the disabled worker when the leave of absence ends.

Unless doing so would cause an undue hardship to the employer, the employer must allow a disabled worker the option of a modified or part-time work schedule if required by the disability. This may be necessary for individuals who need medical treatment periodically. Another type of job modification involves workplace policies. An employer who prohibits workers from eating or drinking at their workstations may amend that policy for a worker with a disability that requires this worker to eat or drink at specific times of the day. An employer who requires employees to work at the employer's office rather than at home may alter the policy if a disabled worker can perform the essential job functions from home but cannot perform them at the office.

An employer may claim that undue hardship prevents the provision of reasonable accommodations, but undue hardship is not easy to prove. The employer must demonstrate that the specific reasonable accommodation being considered would cause significant difficulty or expense. The determination of undue hardship is made on a case-by-case basis, and courts consider such factors as the type and cost of the accommodation, the financial resources of the employer, the number of employees, and the overall impact of the accommodation on the employer's operation. An employer cannot claim undue hardship resulting from fears or prejudices about an individual's disability or fears that an accommodation would result in a morale problem with co-workers. An employer may, however, demonstrate undue hardship if an accommodation would unduly disrupt the work of other employees.

ADDITIONAL RESOURCES

Disability.gov. Clearinghouse for information about federal government resources, pamphlets, and information regarding disabilities. Managed by the Office of Disability Employment Policy, U.S. Department of Labor. Available at http://www.disAbility.gov (accessed November 3, 2012).

Gale Encyclopedia of American Law. 3rd ed. Detroit: Gale, Cengage Learning, 2011.

ORGANIZATIONS

ADA Disability and Business Technical Assistance Centers, U.S. Department of Education

Toll Free: (800) 949-4232
URL: http://wdcrobcolp01.ed.gov/Programs/EROD/org_list.cfm?category_cd=DBT

Job Accommodation Network (JAN)

PO Box 6080
Morgantown, WV 26506-6080
Toll Free: (800) 232-9675
URL: http://janweb.icdi.wvu.edu/

U.S. Equal Employment Opportunity Commission

1801 L Street, NW
Washington, DC 20507
Toll Free: (800) 669-3362
URL: http://www.eeoc.gov

ATTORNEYS

ATTORNEY-CLIENT PRIVILEGE

Sections within this essay:

- Background
- The Elements, Scope, and Application of the Attorney-Client Privilege
  - Elements of the Attorney-Client Privilege
  - Scope and Application of the Attorney-Client Privilege
- State Rules Governing Attorney-Client Privilege
- Additional Resources

BACKGROUND

The attorney-client privilege is an evidentiary rule that protects both attorneys and their clients from being compelled to disclose confidential communications between them made for the purpose of furnishing or obtaining legal advice or assistance. The privilege is designed to foster frank, open, and uninhibited discourse between attorney and client so that the client's legal needs are competently addressed by a fully prepared attorney who is cognizant of all the relevant information the client can provide. The attorney-client privilege may be raised during any type of legal proceeding, civil, criminal, or administrative, and at any time during those proceedings, pre-trial, during trial, or post-trial.

The privilege dates back to ancient Rome, where governors were forbidden from calling their advocates as witnesses out of concern that the governors would lose confidence in their own defenders. In 1577 the first evidentiary privilege recognized by the English **common law** was the attorney-client privilege. The English

common law protected the confidential nature of attorney-client communications, regardless of whether those communications took place in public or in private. The American colonies adopted this approach to the attorney-client privilege, and Delaware codified the privilege in its first constitution in 1776.

THE ELEMENTS, SCOPE, AND APPLICATION OF THE ATTORNEY-CLIENT PRIVILEGE

Elements of the Attorney-Client Privilege Because the attorney-client privilege often prevents disclosure of information that would be relevant to a legal proceeding, courts are cautious when examining objections grounded in the privilege. Most courts generally require that certain elements be demonstrated before finding that the privilege applies. Although the elements vary from **jurisdiction** to jurisdiction, a case often cited for the elements required to invoke the privileges is *United States v. United Shoe Machinery Corp.*, 89 F. Supp. 357 (D. Mass. 1950). The court in that case enumerated a five-part test: (1) the person asserting the privilege must be a client or someone attempting to establish a relationship as a client; (2) the person with whom the client communicated must be an attorney and acting in the capacity as an attorney at the time of the communication; (3) the communication must be between the attorney and client exclusively; (4) the communication must be for the purpose of securing a legal opinion, legal services, or assistance in some legal proceeding, and not for the purpose of committing a crime or **fraud**; and (5) the privilege may be claimed or waived by the client only.

Scope and Application of the Attorney-Client Privilege
The five-part test is typically the starting point in a court's analysis of a claim for privilege. Each element appears

straight-forward on its face but can be tricky to apply, especially when the client is a corporation and not a natural person. **Corporate** clients raise questions as to who may speak for the corporation and assert the attorney-client privilege on behalf of the entity as a whole. Some courts have ruled that the attorney-client privilege may only be asserted by the upper management of a corporation. A vast majority of courts, however, have ruled that the privilege may be asserted not only by a corporation's officers, directors, and board members, but also by any employee who has communicated with an attorney at the request of a corporate superior for the purpose of obtaining legal advice. *Upjohn Co. v. United States*, 449 U.S. 383, 101 S. Ct. 677, 66 L. Ed. 2d 584 (1981).

Whether the client is a person or a corporation, the attorney-client privilege belongs only to the client and not to the attorney. As a result, clients can prevent attorneys from divulging their secrets, but attorneys have no power to prevent their clients from choosing to waive the privilege and testifying in court, talking to the police, or otherwise sharing confidential attorney-client information with third parties not privy to the confidential discussions. Clients may waive attorney-client privilege expressly by their words or implicitly by their conduct, but a court will only find that the privilege has been waived if there is a clear indication that the client did not take steps to keep the communications confidential. An attorney's or a client's inadvertent disclosure of confidential information to a third party will not normally suffice to constitute **waiver**. If a client decides against waiving the privilege, the attorney may then assert the privilege on behalf of the client to shield both the client and the attorney from having to divulge confidential information shared during their relationship.

In most situations, courts can easily determine whether the person with whom a given conversation took place was in fact an attorney. However, in a few cases courts are asked to decide whether the privilege should apply to a communication with an unlicensed or disbarred attorney. In such instances, courts will frequently find that the privilege applies if the client reasonably believes that he or she was communicating with a licensed attorney. *State v. Berberich*, 978 P.2d 902 (Kan. 1999). However, courts in some jurisdictions have relaxed this standard, holding that the privilege applies to communications between clients and unlicensed lay persons who represent them in administrative proceedings. *Woods on Behalf of T.W. v. New Jersey Department of Education*, 858 F. Supp. 51 (D.N.J. 1993).

Although many courts emphasize that the attorney-client privilege should be strictly applied to communications between attorney and client, the attorney-client privilege does extend beyond the immediate attorney-client relationship to include an attorney's partners, associates, and office staff members (e.g., secretaries, file

clerks, telephone operators, messengers, law clerks) who work with the attorney in the ordinary course of their normal duties. *Gucci America, Inc. v. Guess?, Inc.*, 271 F.R.D. 58 (S.D.N.Y. 2010). However, the presence of a third party who is not a member of the attorney's firm will sometimes defeat a claim for privilege, even if that third person is a member of the client's family.

Thus, one court ruled that in the absence of any suggestion that a criminal defendant's father was a confidential agent of the **defendant** or that the father's presence was reasonably necessary to aid or protect the defendant's interests, the presence of the defendant's father at a **pretrial conference** between the defendant and his attorney invalidated the attorney-client privilege with respect to the conference. *State v. Fingers*, 564 S.W.2d 579 (Mo. App. 1978). In the corporate setting, the presence of a client's sister defeated a claim for attorney-client privilege that involved a conversation between a client-company's president and the company's attorney, since the sister was neither an officer nor director of the company and did not possess an ownership interest in the company. *Cherryvale Grain Co. v. First State Bank of Edna*, 971 P.2d 1204 (Kan. App. 1999).

Many courts have described attorney-client confidences as "inviolate." *Wesp v. Everson*, 33 P.3d 191 (Colo. 2001). However, this description is misleading. The attorney-client privilege is subject to several exceptions. Federal Rule of Evidence 501 states that "the recognition of a privilege based on a confidential relationship ... should be determined on a case-by-case basis." In examining claims for privilege against objections that an exception should be made in a particular case, courts will balance the benefits to be gained by protecting the sanctity of attorney-client confidences against the probable harms caused by denying the opposing party access to potentially valuable information.

The crime-fraud exception is one of the oldest exceptions to the attorney-client privilege. The attorney-client privilege does not extend to communications made in connection with a client seeking advice on how to commit a criminal or **fraudulent** act. In addition, client's statement of intent to commit a crime shall not be deemed privileged, even if the client was not seeking advice about how to commit it. The attorney-client privilege is ultimately designed to serve the interests of justice by insulating attorney-client communications made in furtherance of adversarial proceedings. However, the interests of justice are not served by forcing attorneys to withhold information that might help prevent criminal or fraudulent acts. Consequently, in nearly all jurisdictions attorneys can be compelled to disclose such information to a court or other investigating authorities.

A party seeking **discovery** of privileged communications based upon the crime-fraud exception must make a threshold showing that the legal advice was obtained in furtherance of the fraudulent activity and was closely related to it. The party seeking disclosure does not satisfy this burden merely by alleging that a crime or fraud has occurred and then asserting that disclosure of privileged communications might help prove the crime or fraud. There must be a specific showing that a particular document or communication was made in furtherance of the client's alleged crime or fraud.

The fact that an attorney-client relationship exists between two persons is itself not typically privileged (*United States v. Leventhal*, 961 F.2d 936 (11th Cir. 1992)). Likewise, information about the receipt of attorney's fees from a client is generally not privileged (*O'Neal v. United States*, 258 F.3d 1265, 1276 (11th Cir. 2001)). However, if disclosure of an attorney-client relationship could prove incriminating to the client, some courts will enforce the privilege (*In re Michaelson*, 511 F.2d 882 (9th Cir. 1975)). Names of clients and the amounts paid in fees to their attorneys are not normally privileged. Clients usually will not be successful in asserting the privilege against attorneys who are seeking to introduce confidential information in a lawsuit brought by a client accusing the attorney of wrongdoing. In such instances courts will not allow clients to use the attorney-client privilege as a weapon to silence the attorneys who have represented them. Courts will allow both parties to have their say in **malpractice** suits brought by clients against their former attorneys.

STATE RULES GOVERNING ATTORNEY-CLIENT PRIVILEGE

The body of law governing the attorney-client privilege comprises federal and state legislation, court rules, and **case law**. Some state court decisions decided at least in part based on their own state's court rules, case law, or legislation are:

ALABAMA: Where a defendant asserted that his guilty pleas to robbery charges were the product of his defense counsel's **coercion**, the absence of the defense counsel's **testimony** to rebut the defendant's testimony could not be excused by any assertion of the attorney-client privilege. *Walker v. State*, 827 So. 2d 863 (Ala. Crim. App., 2001).

ARIZONA: By asserting that its personnel understood the law on stacking coverage for under insured and uninsured motorist claims, the insurer affirmatively injected legal knowledge of its claims managers into the insured's **bad faith** action and thus effectively waived the attorney-client privilege as to any communications between the insurer and its **counsel** regarding the propriety of the insurer's policy of denying coverage. *State Farm Mut. Auto. Inc. Co. v. Lee*, 13 P.3d 1169 (Ariz. 2000).

ARKANSAS: Attempts by both an attorney and his secretary to communicate with the client regarding his pending criminal case were protected by the attorney-client privilege. Rules of Evid., Rule 502(b). *Byrd v. State*, 929 S.W.2d 151 (Ark. 1996).

CALIFORNIA: The attorney-client privilege is not limited to litigation-related communications, since the applicable provisions of the state Evidence Code do not use the terms "litigation" or "legal communications" in their description of privileged disclosures but instead specifically refer to "the accomplishment of the purpose" for which the lawyer was consulted. Cal. Evid. Code §§ 912, 952. *STI Outdoor v. Superior Court*, 109 Cal. Rptr. 2d 865 (Cal. App. 2001).

COLORADO: Under § 13-90-107 of the Colorado Revised Statutes, the attorney-client privilege applies to confidential matters communicated by the attorney to the client or by the client to the attorney during the course of the client obtaining counsel, advice, and direction with regard to the client's rights or obligations. *People v. Trujillo*, 144 P.3d 539 (Colo. 2006).

ILLINOIS: To prevail on an attorney-client privilege claim in a corporate context, a claimant must first show that a statement was made by someone in the corporate control group, meaning that group of employees whose advisory role to top management in a particular area is such that a decision would not normally be made without their advice or opinion and whose opinion, in fact, forms the basis of any final decision by those with actual authority. *Hayes v. Burlington Northern and Santa Fe Ry. Co.*, 752 N.E.2d 470 (Ill. App. 2001).

IOWA: A corporation's attorney-client privilege applies when a corporate employee discusses the employee's actions regarding potential liability of the corporation with corporate counsel. *Keefe v. Bernard*, 774 N.W.2d 663 (Iowa 2009).

MAINE: Counsel's inadvertent disclosure of a memorandum to opposing counsel, which summarized a telephone conference between counsel and his client, did not constitute a waiver of the attorney-client privilege, where the document was mistakenly placed in boxes of unprivileged documents that were available to opposing counsel to photocopy and the memorandum in question was labeled "confidential and legally privileged." *Corey v. Norman, Hanson & DeTroy*, 742 A.2d 933, 1999 ME 196 (Me. 1999).

MASSACHUSETTS: Hospital personnel were neither the defendant's nor his attorney's agents when they conducted a blood-alcohol test on the defendant at the attorney's request for sole purpose of gathering potentially **exculpatory** evidence, and thus the state's **grand jury subpoena** of the test results did not violate the attorney-client privilege. *Commonwealth v. Senior*, 744 N.E.2d 614 (Mass. 2001).

MICHIGAN: A Court of Appeals reviews de novo a decision regarding whether the attorney-client privilege may be asserted. *Koster v. June's Trucking, Inc.*, 625 N.W.2d 82 (Mich. App. 2000).

MINNESOTA: The presence of the defendant's wife at a joint meeting in which the defendant, his attorney, and his wife discussed financial aspects of a possible **divorce** prevented the attorney-client privilege from attaching. *State v. Rhodes*, 627 N.W.2d 74 (Minn. 2001).

NEW JERSEY: The person asserting the attorney-client privilege bears the burden to prove it applies to any given communication. *Horon Holding Corp. v. McKenzie*, 775 A.2d 111 (N.J. Super. A.D. 2001)

NEW YORK: A client's intent to commit a crime is not a protected confidence or secret for the purposes of the attorney-client privilege. N.Y. Ct. Rules, § 1200.19. *People v. DePallo*, 754 N.E.2d 751, (N.Y. 2001).

NORTH DAKOTA: A communication is confidential, for the purposes of determining the applicability of attorney-client privilege, if it is not intended to be disclosed to persons other than those to whom the disclosure is made during the course of rendering professional legal services or to those reasonably necessary for transmission of the communication during the course of rendering professional legal services. Rules of Evid., Rule 502(a)(5). *Farm Credit Bank of St. Paul v. Huether*, 454 N.W.2d 710 (N.D. 1990).

OHIO: The attorney-client privilege is not absolute, and thus the mere fact that an attorney-client relationship exists does not raise a presumption of confidentiality of all communications made between the attorney and client. *Radovanic v. Cossler*, 746 N.E.2d 1184 (Ohio App. 2000).

PENNSYLVANIA: Attorney-fee agreements and billing records are generally subject to disclosure because the privilege does not apply. *Levy v. Senate*, 34 A.3d 243 (Penn. Commonwealth Ct. 2011)

TEXAS: Physicians who were defending against a malpractice action were not entitled to discover, under fraud exception to attorney-client privilege, material relating to a **settlement** between the plaintiffs and another defendant, although the physicians alleged that disparate distribution of the settlement proceeds was a sham intended to deprive the physicians of settlement credit, since there was no evidence that the plaintiffs made or intended to make hidden distributions. Tex. R. Civ. P. Rule 192.5(a); Rules of Evid. Rule 503(d)(1). *In re Lux*, 52 S.W.3d 369 (Tex. App. 2001).

WASHINGTON: The federal constitutional foundation for the attorney-client privilege is found in the Fifth Amendment **privilege against self-incrimination**, the Sixth Amendment **right to counsel**, and the Due Process Clause of the Fourteenth Amendment, as these rights can be protected only if there is candor and free and open discussion between client and counsel. *In re Recall of Lakewood City Council Members*, 30 P.3d 474 (Wash. 2001).

ADDITIONAL RESOURCES

Attorney-Client Privilege in the United States. Eagan, MN: West, Thomson Reuters, 2011.

Walkowiak, Vincent S., Stephen M. McNabb, and Oscar Rey Rodriguez, eds. *The Attorney-Client Privilege in Civil Litigation: Protecting and Defending Confidentiality.* 5th ed. Chicago, IL: Tort Trial & Insurance Practice, American Bar Association, 2012.

ORGANIZATIONS

American Bar Association (ABA)

321 North Clark Street
Chicago, IL 60610
Phone: (312) 988-5000
Toll Free: (800) 285-2221
Fax: (312) 988-6800
URL: http://www.americanbar.org

National Lawyers Association

3000 S. Jamaica Ct., Ste. 390
Aurora, CO 80014
Toll Free: (800) 471-2994
Fax: (303) 979-6094
URL: http://www.nla.org

National Organization of Bar Counsel

515 Fifth Street, N.W.
Washington, DC 64196
Phone: (202) 638-1501
Fax: (202) 662-1777
URL: http://www.nobc.org

ATTORNEYS

ATTORNEY FEES

Sections within this essay:

- Background
  - Exceptions

- Types of Fee Arrangements
  - Hourly Fees
  - Flat or Fixed Fees
  - Contingent Fees
  - Retainer Fees
  - Statutory Fees
  - Prepaid Legal Plans
  - Pro Bono Services

- What Is Covered by Fees
  - Initial Consultation
  - Fees vs. Costs
  - Fee Sharing and Fee Splitting

- Ethical Considerations
  - IOLTA Funds
  - American Bar Association (ABA) Code and Model Rules

- Recourse and Remedies
  - Fees Owed to Attorneys Who Are Fired
  - Escrowed Funds and Retainers
  - Unreasonable Fees
  - Arbitration

- Additional Resources

BACKGROUND

The long-standing rule in the United States, derived from **common law**, is that each side to a legal controversy must pay for its own attorney. The prevailing litigant is generally not entitled to collect a reasonable attorney's fee from the loser (*Alyeska Pipeline Service Co. v. Wilderness Society*, 421 U.S. 240, 247 (1975)). This is often referred to as the American rule, as distinguished from the English rule, which permits fee-shifting and derives from court-made law.

Of course, there are numerous common-law exceptions and nearly two hundred **statutory** exceptions, with many having been enacted by Congress and state legislatures to encourage private litigants to implement **public policy**. For example, an award of attorney's fees is often statutorily designed to address the unequal bargaining and/or litigating power of big **corporations** or government against individual plaintiffs. Accordingly, provisions awarding attorneys' fees are most often found in consumer or citizen-oriented **litigation**, such as that found in **civil rights**, environmental protection, and **consumer protection** areas of law.

Under these exceptions, federal courts (and some federal agencies) may order the losing party in a lawsuit to pay the winning party's attorney's fees. In 1997, Congress enacted a **statute** that provided for the award of attorney's fees in some criminal defense cases. Additionally, the Equal Access to Justice Act (EAJA) provides for the United States to pay attorney fees in many court matters and some administrative proceedings in which the United States is a losing party and has failed to prove that its position was substantially justified.

Several states have considered proposals to limit awards of attorney's fees, especially in instances involving awards related to **medical malpractice** claims. Nevertheless, in most matters of private litigation between private parties, the American rule still applies.

Exceptions The American rule has two major common law exceptions, mostly affecting federal-court litigation: the common-benefit doctrine and the bad-faith doctrine. The common-benefit exception generally applies in cases where a particular **plaintiff** or number of plaintiffs have born the legal expenses for the benefit of a larger group of potential plaintiffs, as in shareholders' derivative suits or class actions. In these matters, district courts may equitably order that attorney fees for the plaintiffs be reimbursed from the total amount of the judgment.

The **bad faith** exception may be invoked under circumstances in which either an attorney or a party has acted in bad faith when filing or pursuing litigation, often evidenced by the frivolous nature of the particular claim. In this set of exceptions, the underlying rationale behind the award of attorney fees is not that of fee-shifting *per se,* but rather punitive in nature. [See, for example, *Hall v. Cole,* 412 U.S. 1, 5 (1973)].

TYPES OF FEE ARRANGEMENTS

Attorneys charge for their services using a variety of fee structures and arrangements. Prospective clients who retain **counsel** to represent them should know in advance what such services will cost, commit the fee agreement to a writing, and understand their recourse if they believe there has been a deviation from the agreement. This does not imply dishonesty or misrepresentation on the part of counsel, but rather, the possibility of misunderstanding or miscomprehension between counsel and client.

Attorneys consider several factors when setting their fees. These include the area of law invoked, the experience of the lawyer, the simple or complicated nature of the issue, and the amount of time it will take to legally resolve the matter. The more aggressively an attorney wages a legal battle, the more expensive it becomes. Moreover, attorneys may not be able to offer a fair quote for their fee if a prospective client has waited until the last minute to obtain legal counsel, and matters must be acted upon very quickly. In such cases, the fees will typically be higher than otherwise.

Importantly, when dealing with a law firm instead of a sole practitioner, a legal client may be surprised to find that the attorney handling much of the case is not the one who initially met with the client. If a client wishes to retain a particular attorney within the firm to handle the case, this arrangement must be expressly articulated and agreed upon.

Finally, many of the routine legal services provided by law firms are performed by paralegals, not attorneys.

When this is the case, any fee arrangement should reflect a lowered hourly rate for these services, charged separately from attorney's rates.

Hourly Fees The most common form of charging legal clients is through an hourly rate. Most attorneys charge a rate between $100 and $300 per hour. Top legal counsel, with a reputation for success in complex or highly visible cases, may charge more. Rates tend to be higher in major urban areas and in matters requiring special legal expertise (e.g., admiralty, tax, **patent** law).

The majority of attorneys charge in tenth-of-an-hour increments (every six minutes, expressed as 0.10 hours) for hourly fees. Since one-tenth of an hour (or six minutes) is the least billable amount, attorneys routinely bill for one-tenth of an hour even if only one or two minutes were physically spent on the case; for example, a quick e-mail or voice mail message; reviewing and signing correspondence; and so forth. This is neither improper nor illegal. In actuality, an attorney has dropped his or her other work to concentrate on the present case, thinking about what should be done or how it should be done; therefore, the final correspondence or voice mail does not truly reflect the actual amount of minutes spent on the matter.

Hourly charges tend to add up quickly, especially when every tenth of an hour is included. Clients may wish to discuss with their attorneys several money-saving measures, including discounted rates after a certain number of hours are worked in any month (the discounted rate applying to the excess hours). Clients may also wish to cap the total number of hours or fees charged. By the time most **discovery** is completed, both sides have a better idea of what the case is worth, and whether it is worth taking to trial. A client may request that the attorney try to settle the lawsuit once legal fees reach a certain amount. Even if the **settlement** amount is less than desired, it may be the wiser choice if additional legal fees and costs of trial would eat up the difference in dollar amount anyway.

Clients can also negotiate prior approval of major legal maneuvers, although deference to counsel's opinion should be exercised. For example, to save money, an attorney may serve written **interrogatories** upon a witness rather than take his **deposition** before a court reporter. However, if the attorney wishes to spring a question upon the witness by surprise (and to which the witness must answer immediately, without preparation), a deposition may be a smarter tactic, even though it costs more. Most conscientious attorneys discuss the pros and cons of various legal maneuvers with their clients as preparation for trial nears.

A final cost-cutting measure is to pay the top hourly rate for the best trial attorney, but ask for a less experienced attorney in the law firm, at a lower hourly rate, to handle the more routine matters. This is often the practice regardless, but either way, should be clarified in advance.

Flat or Fixed Fees Recognizing the runaway nature of hourly fees, many law firms and attorneys have established fixed or flat rates for routine legal matters, such as a simple will, a **power of attorney**, or a first DUIL (driving while under the influence of alcohol).

Typically, more complex legal matters are set up on a mixed fee basis. For example, a non-contested **divorce** may have a flat fee of $1,500, but neither party to the divorce can guarantee that it will be uncontested. An attorney's duty is to get the best advantage for his or her client. Therefore, an attorney may stipulate in a fee agreement that if some areas of the divorce settlement become contested, an hourly fee will be added to the $1,500 flat fee for the resolution of the disputed matter.

Likewise, a prospective client may be quoted a flat fee of $750 for a first-time charge of drunk driving. However, if it later turns out that the client had a previous drunk driving charge not communicated to the attorney, the fees will likely increase. Often, in matters involving a lawsuit, an attorney will charge a fixed or flat fee for all work performed up to the point of trial (or settlement), after which a separate fee will be added for each day at trial. This is because preparation for trial constitutes intense labor. Trying a case requires an entirely different set of skills and labor, resulting in additional fees (typically charged in terms of hourly or daily billing rates hour or day).

With the legal profession suffering from a recessive economy at the end of the first decade of the 2000s and early 2010s, some firms have begun to consider using alternative fee agreements, which often involve flat fees. Under these arrangements, a firm may charge a certain amount based on the value of a service rather than the time it takes the attorney to complete the task. This arrangement can often save the client money, especially when the tasks are repetitive in nature.

Contingent Fees In many litigation-oriented legal matters, the attorney representing a plaintiff will often take a percentage of the money received from either a settlement or a **jury** verdict (or judge's award) as the applicable fee. This type of fee arrangement is common in lawsuits involving money damages, such as for **personal injury**, medical **malpractice**, workers' compensation, employment **discrimination** or **wrongful** termination, and so forth. Conversely, it is common for attorneys who represent the **defendant** in such matters to charge an hourly fee.

Contingency fees are usually expressed as a percentage, and the payment of the fee is *contingent* upon success at trial or the client having prevailed in the legal matter. The fee may be based upon a percentage of the dollar amount or the value of property secured or won for the client, such as a **contract**. For this reason, attorneys carefully assess a potential lawsuit to determine the likelihood of success before they agree to represent a prospective client on a contingency fee basis.

Most contingency fee agreements quote a fee between 25 and 40 percent of the settlement, verdict or award. Importantly, this percentage may be based on the gross settlement/verdict amount, or (less commonly) the **net** amount after deductions for costs and expenses.

Many contingent-fee arrangements have a sliding-scale basis similar to the flat fee with add-on charges for complication. For example, a contingency agreement may stipulate that if the legal controversy is negotiated to a settlement prior to the filing of a lawsuit, the fee will be 25 percent of the settlement amount. If the case continues and is settled in the interim between filing and trial, the fee will be 33.33 percent (the oft-quoted one-third attorney fee). However, if the attorney must try the case, the fee will be 40 percent. Again, this sliding scale is meant to reflect the amount of work the attorney does at each stage of the litigation.

Contingency fees are not appropriate in all legal matters and may in fact violate state ethics rules. In divorce cases, for example, angry spouses may be determined to "bleed the other spouse dry" with hefty legal fees and do so by challenging each and every settlement clause in court. Contingency fees are generally not permitted in criminal defense matters and most divorce cases. Likewise, it would be inappropriate for an attorney to charge a fee contingent upon whether or not the client is awarded **custody** of children. Some states do allow contingency fees in property divisions based upon a percentage of the value of property secured for the client.

Retainer Fees For representation in a particular legal matter, a true **retainer** fee is not a separate or distinct fee, but rather an advancement of fees against what will ultimately be owed to the attorney; that is, a "down payment" or credit toward what is owed. It is a guarantee that a client has "retained" a law firm or attorney for legal representation, and that, as such, the attorney or firm will be paid for work completed in behalf of the client's case.

A variation of this type of retainer fee is actually more like a flat fee paid in advance. Sometimes an attorney will estimate the amount needed to resolve a legal matter and require the payment up front to "retain" his or her services.

In either of these retainer arrangements, a portion of the retainer fee may or may not be non-refundable. However, where the fee represents an advancement of fees for work actually done, attorneys and law firms must **itemize** the actual hours worked, or the work actually completed, to draw from the retained fee. Any excess fee will then be returned to the client.

An exception to the return of excess retainer funds involves still another classic form of retainer fee. This type of fee arrangement involves retaining a law firm or attorney to be at the service of, or on call and on demand for, (usually) a **corporate** client or wealthy individual with recurring legal problems. For a flat fee (generally on an annual basis), legal service and representation is on demand for the client, even to the extent that other clients or cases are turned down to serve the client. The retainer fee ensures that an attorney will always be available or "on call" to answer a client's legal questions, provide counsel and advice, or intervene/intercede on behalf of the client in a pending matter or dispute. This type of retainer fee is generally non-refundable, even if the client ultimately makes little use of the retained services over the subject period of retainer.

Statutory Fees For certain legal matters, the attorney fee is set by law. Whether by state law or federal statute, and as previously mentioned, the award or payment of attorney fees is generally invoked in cases involving matters of public concern (e.g., willful environmental pollution), or major violations of **constitutional rights** (e.g., civil rights violations under federal law).

At one time, the American Bar Association (ABA) favored a statutory scheme to standardize minimum fees or "recommended fee schedules" to circumvent fee-cutting competition and preserve the integrity of the legal profession. However, in 1975, the U.S. Supreme Court held that minimum fee schedules violated the Sherman Anti-Trust Act. Notwithstanding, many states and federal laws restrict maximum fees that may be charged for certain matters, as for probating a will or (with tort reform) in medical malpractice actions.

State laws awarding attorney fees, or providing for a fixed fee or percentage, or mandating court approval for a proposed fee are too varied to include herein. The following federal civil rights statutes provide for attorney fees to be paid:

- Civil Rights Act of 1964, Title II (Public Accommodations)
- Civil Rights Act of 1964, Title III (Public Facilities)
- Civil Rights Act of 1964, Title VII (Equal Employment Opportunities)
- Fair Housing Act

- Fair Labor Standards Act
- Age Discrimination in Employment Act of 1967
- Equal Credit Opportunity Act
- Voting Rights Act of 1965
- Civil Service Reform Act of 1978
- Age Discrimination Act of 1975
- Civil Rights of Institutionalized Persons Act
- Rehabilitation Act of 1973
- Individuals with Disabilities Education Act
- Americans with Disabilities Act of 1990
- Civil Rights Attorney's Fees Awards Act of 1976

Prepaid Legal Plans Usually associated with employers, unions, or **credit union** membership, prepaid legal plans operate like prepaid health organizations. Participants pay a monthly fee in exchange for access to legal advice and/or legal representation from one of the plan's member attorneys. However, most plans limit the number of services and/or number of hours of legal assistance each month. Also, types and costs for different services can vary from plan to plan. If, after consulting with legal counsel under the plan, it is determined that litigation or more intense legal work will be required, additional charges (established up front with plan membership) will apply. Additional information about prepaid legal plans can be obtained from American Prepaid Legal Services Institute (APLSI), 321 N Clark St., Chicago, IL 60601, (312) 988-5751, Website at http://www. aplsi.org. APLSI is affiliated with the American Bar Association.

Pro Bono Services The Latin term "pro bono," being shortened in common usage from "pro bono publico," literally means for the good of the public. In cases involving social injustices (e.g., **sexual harassment** by an employer, **freedom of speech** or religion, spousal abuse, discrimination in housing or employment, whistle-blowing, environmental pollution), legal fees may be waived by attorneys or nonprofit legal organizations interested in the outcome of the case, especially if it raises new and important issues of law.

Some of the organizations that may offer legal resources or **pro bono** representation include the American Civil Liberties Union (ACLU), the National Association for the Advancement of Colored People (NAACP) Legal Defense Fund, the Natural Resources Defense Council, the National Women's Law Center, and the Lambda Legal Defense and Education Fund (for gay and lesbian rights).

WHAT IS COVERED BY FEES

Initial Consultation Many attorneys do not charge for an initial private consultation. This is particularly true for plaintiff-oriented cases where the attorney will ultimately charge on a contingency fee basis. During the initial consultation, the attorney will assess the merits of success on the potential claim or lawsuit. However, if the purpose of consultation is for the rendering of a simple legal opinion, most attorneys will charge a relatively small fee; for example, less than $100.

Since everything communicated during the initial consultation is protected by **attorney-client privilege**, it is important that clients are open and honest with the attorney, providing all known information and (crucially) even the damaging facts. Even a low consultation fee is worthlessly spent if the attorney is not able to fairly assess the case because of withheld information.

During the initial consultation, the question of fees should be addressed and committed to writing. This is also an appropriate time for the client to assess the experience, skills, and effectiveness of counsel.

Fees vs. Costs Many stories abound in which seriously injured plaintiffs who win their cases nonetheless take home less money than their attorneys. In all fairness, while it is true that an attorney or law firm may receive a large share of the settlement/verdict/award, the money does not all go to the attorneys. Costs and expenses often devour the largest chunk of the proceeds. In their minds, plaintiffs are thinking they will receive two-thirds of any settlement or award, based on, for example, a 33.33 percent contingency fee. But in reality, another third of the proceeds may be spent on costs and expenses associated with the case. In the end, the injured plaintiff may go home with one third, and the law firm will keep two-thirds of the proceeds (but earn considerably less once all costs and expenses are reimbursed). This, precisely, is what contributes to the perception that the "lion's share went to the lawyers."

Such a scenario is particularly true in personal injury/medical malpractice cases that require copious amounts of medical analyses and expert-witness opinions. Trial expert witnesses charges thousands of dollars for reviewing files, rendering opinions (upon which reputations may be staked) and appearing to **testify** at trial.

But in reality, the attorneys only keep the agreed-upon fee. If they also receive monies for costs and expenses, it is merely to repay them for bills they have paid on behalf of the client. Costs are ultimately the responsibility of clients, even if initially paid by the law firm in order to move the case forward. Costs are itemized separately from the fee charged by attorneys for their legal work.

Costs include charges for all court filings (complaint, motions, discovery, etc.), process serving, investigations, mailing, photocopying, service of subpoenas for appearance of witnesses, as well as for records and document retrieval, court reporters and transcripts of depositions, motions, and other related proceedings, jury fees and mileage, expert witness fees and travel/lodging fees for both witnesses and attorneys.

Most often, costs are deducted from the gross amount of the settlement/verdict/award *after* the **deduction** of attorney fees. In other words, the attorney fee will be based on a percentage of the *gross* amount recovered, not the net amount after costs are deducted. Next will be deductions for costs and expenses paid or owing on behalf of the client. Finally, the remaining balance will represent the client's proceeds or share of the money.

Fee Sharing and Fee Splitting Generally, fee sharing or fee-splitting arrangements between attorneys do not increase the bottom-line fee paid by a client. However, there are ethical and professional rules addressing these subjects, and one recurring theme is that such arrangements must be communicated to a client in advance.

For example, ABA Model Rule 1.5(e) states that a division of fees between attorneys from different law firms may be made only if (1) the division is proportionate to the services performed by the respective attorneys, or a client agrees in writing that each attorney assumes joint responsibility for the representation; (2)the client is advised of and does not object to the participation of the additional attorneys; and (3)the total fee is reasonable.

ETHICAL CONSIDERATIONS

IOLTA Funds The Interest on Lawyers' Trust Accounts (IOLTA) program has been adopted by all state bar associations and the District of Columbia as an innovative way to do a public good; simplify accounting on clients' accounts; and prevent the temptation of misuse/abuse of earned interest on those accounts. By authority of state supreme courts or legislative acts, attorneys can deposit client funds that are too small in amount, or are deposited for too short a time to earn interest, in a state-wide IOLTA account. These accounts represent pooled, interest-bearing trust accounts.(Larger amounts from clients are placed in client bank accounts where interest inures back to the benefit of the clients.)

Since the pooled funds generate interest where none had been previously paid, IOLTA provides a public benefit without cost to taxpayers. The funds are earmarked through a local grant process to not-for-profit organizations throughout each state. They are generally used to fund civil legal services for the poor, or for law-related public education or administration of justice.

American Bar Association (ABA) Code and Model Rules
State bar associations address ethical considerations of
attorney fee-setting in their bar rules of professional
conduct or professional responsibility. All states have
similar rules, most often parallel to, or adopting *verbatim*.
the ABA Model Rules or ABA Model Code of Professional
Responsibility.

ABA Model Rule 1.5 states that a lawyer's fee must
be reasonable. The rule lists the same criteria and factors
to consider (in determining reasonableness) as those used
when lawyers first assess a legal matter and then establish
their fee arrangement with a client. These factors include
the time and labor involved, the requisite legal skills
needed, the fee customarily charged for such services, and
the experience and reputation of the lawyer.

The ABA Model Code of Professional Responsibility,
DR 2-106 prohibits clearly excessive fees. Factors to be
considered as guidelines in determining the reasonableness
or excessiveness of the fee again parallel the same
considerations recommended when first establishing fees
(see Rule 1.5, above).

More importantly, ABA Model Rule 1.5(d) prohibits
fee arrangements that (1) are contingent upon the securing
of a divorce, or the amount of **alimony** or support; or (2)
are contingent fees for legal representation in a criminal
defense matter.

RECOURSE AND REMEDIES

Attorneys cannot guarantee results. Clients must pay for
the services rendered, whether they agree with the
outcome or not. However, there are some measures that
can be taken if an attorney has done something illegal or
improper.

Fees Owed to Attorneys Who Are Fired If a client is
unhappy with an attorney's representation, and hires
another attorney, there are two caveats worthy of mention
here. First, it is a violation of an attorney's code of ethics
to work on a file or legal case while another attorney is still
officially handling it. Therefore, a client should discharge
the previous attorney in writing. Secondly, the terminated
attorney is nonetheless entitled to compensation for the
work completed thus far, and may place an attorney's **lien**
on the file/case through the court. When the client is
finally paid on the matter, the original attorney will
receive whatever compensation he or she earned. If the
original agreement was for a contingency fee, and the
second attorney completed work on the case, the
contingency fee will be split, with or without court
intervention. Many jurisdictions permit the first (discharged) attorney to be paid a reasonable hourly fee for
work completed, rather than a percentage of the

contingency. The discharged attorney will need to itemize
work done on the file prior to being discharged.

Escrowed Funds and Retainers Attorneys cannot spend
unearned retainer fees or funds advanced to the attorneys.
State bar rules require attorneys to deposit all retainer and
advance payment funds into interest-bearing accounts,
which can only be withdrawn as the legal work is
completed and billed against the account. Any interest
earned on the account is usually donated to nonprofit
legal clinics or (long-term) returned to the client.

If a client believes that an attorney has not returned
excess retainer funds, or has not accounted for the entire
amount in an itemized statement, the first step should be
in the form of registered/certified correspondence to the
attorney, requesting explanation. If such a step fails to
satisfy the client, the next contact should be to the state
bar association, which will have a forum for filing
grievances against attorneys.

Unreasonable Fees Even though attorneys have quoted
certain fees to a prospective client, they may be open to
negotiating a lower fee, based upon the client's articulated
reasons. Additionally, attorneys may allow **installment**
payments or other payment plans to help clients meet
their obligations.

However, if the fee paid is questionable, or the costs
and expenses attached to the file seem unreasonable, the
first step should be a registered/certified correspondence
to the attorney, requesting explanation. If such a step fails
to satisfy the client, the next contact should be the state
bar association, which will have a forum for filing
grievances against attorneys.

Arbitration For unresolved fee controversies between
attorney and client, **arbitration** or **mediation** may offer
an appropriate forum for resolution. This is particularly
true if the reasonableness of a fee or the costs on a file case
are questioned. The state bar association is the best place
to start, and may be able to provide either an arbitration
forum, or a list of private arbitrators and mediators skilled
in this area. Finally, it should be noted that unhappiness
with the costs or fees charged by the attorney does not
necessarily mean that the charges were unreasonable. If
the possibility of high costs was communicated to the
client in advance, along with the amount and type of fee,
the client's chance of prevailing at arbitration are slim.

Sometimes, as in personal injury cases, a client agrees
to the fee and anticipated costs (e.g., for medical expert
witnesses) and subsequently prevails at trial, but the
verdict or award is less than anticipated. A good attorney
may be willing to attempt to negotiate a reduced charge
from the expert witnesses, along with some reduction in

the attorney fee. However, the attorney is under no obligation to do either.

ADDITIONAL RESOURCES

Cohen, Henry. "Awards of Attorneys' Fees by Federal Courts and Federal Agencies." CRS Report for Congress. Updated June 20, 2008. Washington, DC: Library of Congress, Congressional Research Service. Available at http://www.fas.org/sgp/crs/misc/94-970.pdf (accessed October 1, 2012).

"Fact Sheet on Interest on Lawyers' Trust Accounts (IOLTA)." American Bar Association Commission on IOLTA. Available at http://www.nlada.org/DMS/Documents/1011300749.75 (accessed October 1, 2012).

ORGANIZATIONS

American Bar Association (ABA)

321 North Clark Street
Chicago, IL 60610

Phone: (202) 662-1000
Toll Free: (800) 285-2221
Fax: (312) 988-6800
URL: http://www.americanbar.org

National Lawyers Association

3000 S. Jamaica Ct., Ste. 390
Aurora, CO 80014
Toll Free: (800) 471-2994
Fax: (303) 979-6094
URL: http://www.nla.org

National Organization of Bar Counsel

515 Fifth Street, N.W.
Washington, DC 64196
Phone: (202) 638-1501
Fax: (202) 662-1777
URL: http://www.nobc.org

ATTORNEYS

COMMUNICATIONS BETWEEN ATTORNEY AND CLIENT

Sections within this essay:

- A Client's Relationship with an Attorney
- A Lawyer's Advertising and Solicitation
- The Interview with the Attorney
- Communicating with the Attorney
  - Fee Agreements
  - Scope of the Representation
  - Decision-Making and Status Updates
  - Confidential Information

- Problems the Attorney and Client Should Avoid
  - Conflicts of Interest
  - Other Relationships with Clients

- Terminating the Attorney-Client Relationship
- State Laws
- Additional Resources

A CLIENT'S RELATIONSHIP WITH AN ATTORNEY

A typical individual in the United States may hire an attorney in only the worst of times. The person may have been **accused** of a crime, may need to **probate** the will of a deceased loved one, may need to seek a **divorce**, or may have been injured by somebody else and needs to bring a case in a court of law to try to recover damages. In other circumstances, the person seeking legal advice may need to complete a will or sell a home and cannot do so without the assistance of an attorney.

The client may have had only limited interaction with attorneys in the past and may not fully understand what the attorney does. Moreover, the client may not know about the client's rights or the attorney's obligations under the law. A competent attorney should explain these rights and obligations to the client, and this explanation should be an important part of attorney-client communications.

In fact, the communication between the attorney and client is one of the most important aspects of the relationship. The client should know what the attorney can communicate through advertising, what communications should take place during the initial interview and in later stages of representation, and what problems may arise when the attorney represents the client. The client should also be aware that the attorney remains bound to certain obligations even after the attorney-client relationship has ended.

A LAWYER'S ADVERTISING AND SOLICITATION

Many lawyers rely heavily on advertising to attract clients. It is fairly common to see large advertisements for lawyers in the telephone book or in many different types of publications. An advertisement may include a picture of the lawyer, the lawyer's contact information, and a list of the types of cases and matters that the attorney handles. Many law firms and law offices also maintain websites that contain information about the attorneys and the cases that the attorneys have handled in the past. For instance, a website may list an attorney's educational and professional background along with a summary of verdicts from major cases the attorney has handled in the past.

Each state's rules of professional conduct strictly limit what an attorney can include in an advertisement. For instance, lawyers cannot promise certain results in a case no matter what kind of outcome the attorney has achieved in previous cases. Thus, a lawyer cannot advertise that he recovered a $1 million verdict if the advertisement suggests that the lawyer will achieve the same result in a later case. State rules generally require the attorney to include a disclaimer that the attorney cannot guarantee the same result in two different cases.

Examples of other limitations on attorney advertising include the following:

- Many states require an attorney to make certain statements about whether the attorney is certified as a specialist in a certain field.

- A number of states require an attorney to make a disclaimer or disclosure about contingent-fee arrangements.

- Most states either forbid or strictly limit endorsements and testimonials.

- Attorneys in specific practice areas may be required to issue specific disclaimers. For example, a tax attorney cannot promise that the client will be able to avoid tax penalties under the Internal Revenue Code.

Those seeking an attorney's advice should never hire an attorney based on an advertisement alone. The client should conduct interviews with a number of attorneys before deciding which attorney to hire.

THE INTERVIEW WITH THE ATTORNEY

The first direct interaction between an attorney and a client (or prospective attorney and client) will usually take place during a formal interview. This interview may take place in the attorney's office, the client's home, or some other location. The communication that takes place during this interview is important to the lawyer because of what the lawyer needs to learn and what the lawyer needs to convey during this interview.

Importantly, the lawyer needs to listen to the client's problem and understand what the client needs from the lawyer. The client may or may not know what information is relevant to a specific problem, so the lawyer will usually ask certain questions so that the lawyer has a better idea about what the client actually needs from the representation. Examples of different types of questions might include the following:

- Open questions: These types of questions are usually broad in nature and allow the client to explain

something. For example, "What happened on the night of the accident?"

- Closed questions: These questions often lead to short answers, such as simple yes or no responses. For example, "Were you drinking on the night of the accident?"

- Follow-up questions: These questions follow open or closed questions to clarify previous answers. For example, "Where did you have these drinks?"

- Leading questions: Occasionally the lawyer will ask a **leading question**, perhaps to confirm certain facts. For example, "You only had two glasses of wine before you drove, isn't that correct?"

- Summary questions: The attorney might ask a broad question at the end of the interview. For example, "Is there anything I have left out?"

By asking these questions, the lawyer will be in a better position to decide whether to offer services to a prospective client or to convey information that the client will need when deciding whether to hire the lawyer. It is possible that the attorney may refuse to take a client because of the nature of the prospective client's problem. The attorney may sometimes refer the person to another attorney, but the attorney is not required to do so. However, even if the attorney does not accept the representation, or the client decides to hire a different attorney, any communication between the attorney and the prospective client will remain confidential and privileged.

COMMUNICATING WITH THE ATTORNEY

Communications remain a vital part of the attorney-client relationship once the client has hired the attorney. The attorney is bound by a number of ethical obligations about communicating with a client, and these communications will also often be important factors in how effective an attorney's representation will be.

Fee Agreements A lawyer's fees may not be the most popular topic for either the lawyer or the client, but the lawyer is required to explain the fee arrangement in detail. Many attorneys will bill for their time by an hourly rate, often dividing an hour into fractions. For example, a lawyer may charge a client $200 per hour and divide time by 15-minute increments. The lawyer is obligated to keep close track of his or her time and to explain what the lawyer did during that time. The lawyer will then bill the client at the end of the month.

A lawyer must fulfill a **fiduciary** duty to a client, and this duty would encompass the amount of time the lawyer may spend on a certain matter or task. Thus, the lawyer cannot simply waste time or work slowly and then ethically bill the client for that entire time. On the other hand, if the attorney must have reasonably spent a certain period of time on the matter, then the attorney can bill for the time spent.

Some lawyers will offer fixed rates for certain types of services, such as the preparation of a will. Other lawyers, such as those who are involved in **personal injury litigation**, may offer a contingency fee arrangement under which the attorney will receive a fee only if the client recovers a monetary amount. As with hourly fees, the attorney must explain fix, contingency, or other fee arrangements with the client from the outset of the representation.

Scope of the Representation From the outset of the representation, the attorney and client should agree to the scope of the representation. This part of the agreement may give the lawyer the authority to act on the client's behalf without further action on the client's part. Conversely, the agreement may limit the attorney's representation. For example, an agreement might state that an attorney will handle the trial during a case but will not participate in any appeals.

Rules governing a lawyer's conduct apply to agreements affecting the scope of the representation. Many states follow the American Bar Association's Model Rules of Professional Conduct. Rule 1.2 of these Model Rules includes several provisions related to the scope of representation, including:

- A lawyer must generally abide by the client's decisions regarding the objectives of the representation, and the attorney must consult with the client about the means by which the attorney will pursue these objectives.

- A lawyer and client may agree to the scope of the representation if the limitation is reasonable under the circumstances and the client consents after being informed.

- The lawyer cannot **counsel** a client to engage in conduct that is criminal or **fraudulent**, though the attorney may discuss the consequences of a proposed course of conduct.

Decision-Making and Status Updates The attorney has the right under rules of professional conduct to control strategies and tactics used during a case. However, even with this right, an attorney must consult with a client making these decisions. Thus, a lawyer may have the right to decide whether to file a motion for **summary judgment** on a client's behalf, but the lawyer is obligated to consult with the client before doing so. As a general matter, the client retains the right to make most other major decisions, such as which claims to assert, whether to accept an offer for **settlement**, or whether to **appeal** a judgment.

In addition to consulting with a client about these major decisions, a lawyer is also under a duty to provide periodic status updates. This is true even where a lawyer may have made mistakes that could lead to a **malpractice** claim. For example, a lawyer might fail to file a complaint within the period of time established through a **statute of limitations**. The lawyer must communicate this error to the client even though the client might be able to sue the attorney later for malpractice.

Even if the failure to communicate does not give relate to malpractice, an attorney may be subject to discipline by a state **bar association** for failing to keep a client informed of a pending matter.

Confidential Information It is important for attorneys to explain to their clients that communications between them are confidential, meaning that the attorney cannot ethically divulge anything that the client says to the attorney. The reason for this rule is that the attorney needs to be completely informed about the client's case, and this often includes knowledge of private and possibly embarrassing facts. The client would be less likely to divulge this information if the attorney could tell others about what the client said. The same privilege also applies to other professionals, such as doctors.

The duty to maintain confidential information means that an attorney cannot voluntarily disclose the information. It is possible, though, that an attorney may be called to **testify** about information that a client conveyed to the attorney. In this situation, the attorney may invoke the **attorney-client privilege** and refuse to testify about the communications. The duty applies to anything the client communicated with the intent to seek legal advice, so the duty can apply to a broad range of communications. However, not all private information is privileged, nor is information that the client shared with a third party as well as the attorney.

PROBLEMS THE ATTORNEY AND CLIENT SHOULD AVOID

The attorney and client can avoid many potential problems through effective communication. These problems may include the following general categories below.

Conflicts of Interest The attorney owes a duty of loyalty to a client, meaning that the attorney represents the client's best interests and does not represent dual interests (subject to some exceptions that are usually handled through full disclosure). It is the attorney's obligation to identify possible conflicts of interest, and the client needs to disclose information that will assist the attorney in identifying possible conflicts.

A common example occurs when a lawyer has previously represented someone who is involved with the current client's case. If the former client's interests are adverse to the current client's interests, the attorney will be required to withdraw from representation unless the current client consents after full disclosure.

Other Relationships with Clients Rules of professional conduct prohibit or limit certain relationships between an attorney and client outside of the legal representation. This includes the following common situations:

- Conducting Business with the Lawyer. Before a lawyer and client can engage in business outside the attorney-client relationship, lawyer generally must receive consent from a client, must ensure that a proposed transaction is fair, and must advise the client of benefits of seeking separate counsel.

- Giving Gifts to the Lawyer. Most rules limit gifts that a client can give to a lawyer, including a gift given in a will that the lawyer drafts.

- Intimate Relationships. Rules generally forbid a lawyer from engaging in a sexual relationship with a client.

TERMINATING THE ATTORNEY-CLIENT RELATIONSHIP

Many clients do not realize that the duties and privileges that arise during representation continue even after the attorney-client relationship has ended. Thus, the attorney continues to have a duty of loyalty to the former client so that the lawyer cannot take advantage of the former client. Likewise, the attorney-client privilege continues to apply after the relationship ends.

Communication is important even if the client is unhappy with the attorney's services. In such a situation, the client should first speak to the attorney about concerns and complaints. If the attorney has behaved unethically or otherwise violated rules of professional conduct, the client may consider filing a complaint with a state disciplinary authority or seek some other remedy, such as a malpractice suit or a suit asking a court to **forfeit** an attorney's fees.

STATE LAWS

The following are examples of state laws that apply to attorney advertising.

ALABAMA: The Alabama Rules of Professional Conduct require an attorney to disclose the following: "No

representation is made that the quality of the legal services to be performed is greater than the quality of legal services performed by other lawyers."

ARIZONA: Advertisements containing information about a lawyer's fees are subject to the following: "[A]dvertisements and written solicitations indicating that the charging of a fee is the client will be liable for expenses regardless of outcome unless the repayment of such is contingent upon the outcome of the matter and . . . whether the percentage fee will be computed before expenses are deducted from the recovery"

ARKANSAS: A lawyer may not state that he or she is a specialist in a field of law unless: (1) the lawyer has been certified as a specialist by an organization that has been approved by an appropriate state authority or that has been accredited by the American Bar Association; and (2) the name of the certifying organization is clearly identified in the communication.

CALIFORNIA: Under the California Rules of Professional Conduct, an attorney may not "[s]tate that a member is a 'certified specialist' unless the member holds a current certificate as a specialist issued by the Board of Legal Specialization, or any other entity accredited by the State Bar to designate specialists pursuant to standards adopted by the Board of Governors, and states the complete name of the entity which granted certification."

COLORADO: Under the Colorado Rules of Professional Conduct, "Statements such as 'recovery, no fee' are misleading if they do not additionally mention that a client may be obligated to pay costs of the lawsuit. Any communication that states or implies the client does not have to pay a fee if there is no recovery shall also disclose that the client may be liable for costs."

NEVADA: The Nevada Rules of Professional Conduct require an attorney to disclose: "You may have to pay the opposing party's attorney fees and costs in the event of a loss."

NEW YORK: The New York Rules of Professional Conduct allow a lawyer to use testimonials or endorsements from clients, so long as the advertisement contains a disclaimer stating, "Prior results do not guarantee a similar outcome."

VERMONT: The Vermont Rules of Professional Conduct provide that "a lawyer may communicate the fact that the lawyer has been certified as a specialist in a field of law by a named organization, provided that the communication clearly states that there is no procedure in Vermont for approving certifying organizations. If, however, the named organization has been accredited by the American Bar Association to certify lawyers as specialists in a particular field of law, the communication need not contain such a statement."

VIRGINIA: The Virginia Rules of Professional Conduct provide an example of an advertising disclaimer: "Every legal matter is different. The outcome of each legal case depends upon many factors, including the facts of the case, and no attorney can guarantee a positive result in any particular case."

ADDITIONAL RESOURCES

Attorney-Client Privilege in the United States. Eagan, MN: West, Thomson Reuters, 2011.

Ewalt, Henry W., and Andrew W. Ewalt. *Through the Client's Eyes.* Chicago: American Bar Association, 2008.

Fox, Lawrence J. and Susan R. Martyn. *Your Lawyer: A User's Guide.* Charlottesville, VA.: LexisNexis, 2006.

Herman, G. Nicholas, and Jean M. Cary. *A Practical Approach to Client Interviewing, Counseling, and Decision-Making.* Charlottesville, VA: LexisNexis, 2009.

Walkowiak, Vincent S., Stephen M. McNabb, and Oscar Rey Rodriguez, eds. *The Attorney-Client Privilege in Civil Litigation: Protecting and Defending Confidentiality.* 5th ed. Chicago, IL: Tort Trial & Insurance Practice, American Bar Association, 2012.

ORGANIZATIONS

American Bar Association (ABA)
321 North Clark Street
Chicago, IL 60610
Phone: (202) 662-1000
Toll Free: (800) 285-2221
Fax: (312) 988-6800
URL: http://www.americanbar.org

National Bar Association
1225 11th Street, NW
Washington, DC 20001
Phone: (202) 842-3900
Fax: (202) 289-6170
URL: http://www.nationalbar.org

National Lawyers Association
3000 S. Jamaica Ct., Ste. 390
Aurora, CO 80014
Toll Free: (800) 471-2994
Fax: (303) 979-6094
URL: http://www.nla.org

National Organization of Bar Counsel
515 Fifth Street, N.W.
Washington, DC 64196
Phone: (202) 638-1501
Fax: (202) 662-1777
URL: http://www.nobc.org

ATTORNEYS

ENROLLING IN LAW SCHOOL

Sections within this essay:

- Introduction
- Deciding Whether to Attend Law School
- Deciding Where to Attend Law School
- Deciding Which Law School to Attend
- Applying for Law School
  – Undergraduate GPA and Course of study
  – The Law School Admission Test
  – Personal Statement and Recommendations
  – Other Criteria

- How to Stand Out as an Applicant
- Law Schools by State

INTRODUCTION

The decision to attend law school is not an easy one to make. The application process takes many months to complete, and assuming an applicant has more than one option, the applicant will need to make a critical decision about which law school to attend. Some applicants have wanted to pursue a legal career for many years, while for others the decision may have come later in life. Many have questions about exactly what it will take to make it through the law school doors.

Compared with other avenues of education, those who wish to attend law school have a relatively narrow list of options. As of 2012, the American Bar Association has accredited only 201 law schools in the entire nation. Total enrollment at these law schools was 146,288 in 2012.

There are more than twice as many programs for those seeking Masters in Business Administration (MBA) degrees. The law school numbers have grown only gradually. For instance, in 1992, the ABA accredited a total of 176 law schools, and these schools had a total enrollment 129,580.

Before engaging in the application process, a potential applicant needs to consider a few factors related to law school. The applicant should decide carefully whether to attend law school and where (geographically) the applicant may be interested in attending. The applicant should also identify schools that may be of interest, though competition for seats at various law school as well as for scholarships and other considerations can be rather fierce.

DECIDING WHETHER TO ATTEND LAW SCHOOL

There is no single "good" reason to decide to attend law school. Some pursue the degree because of their interest in civil justice. Others may envision a high salary and glamorous lifestyle, which is often portrayed in popular media. A few applicants do not even have a specific reason for attending, noting that they just thought law school would present an interesting challenge.

No matter what the reason for attending is, a prospective applicant should educate himself or herself about the realities of law school and the legal profession before deciding to pursue a career in law. It can be a very rewarding career in terms of both economics and personal satisfaction. However, law school is usually a stressful environment and one that many students find to be less satisfying than they expected. Students who may have done well in their prior educational experiences may not

Number and percentage of law students at U.S. law schools, 2009–2012

Academic year	2009–2010	2010–2011	2011–2012
Total JD enrollment	145,239	147,525	146,288
Gender			
Male	53%	53%	53%
Female	47%	47%	47%
Minority enrollment	22.40%	23.80%	24.50%

SOURCE: ABA Section of Legal Education & Admissions to the Bar. Available at: http://www.americanbar.org/groups/legal_education/resources/statistics.html

TABLE BY PREMEDIAGLOBAL. ©2013 CENGAGE LEARNING.

perform as well in what is often a highly competitive environment.

Prospective applicants should also have a realistic view of how much money they are likely to make. A person graduating from law school can make as much as $160,000 per year at large law firms. However, those jobs are difficult to obtain, and only those who attend the most highly ranked law schools or those at the very top of their classes can usually compete for those positions. The reality is that the median salary for all first-year lawyers in the private sector was about $72,000 in 2010, and a substantial number of new lawyers make between $45,000 and $60,000 per year. Thus, while a few students will enjoy large salaries when they enter into the profession, many will not make considerably more than they would if they chose another field. Too many law students incur large debt (often more than $100,000) to attend law school only to accept a position making too little money to pay back the loan.

On the other hand, a lawyer's overall satisfaction with the profession is very often not connected with the salary. Many lawyers who earn closer to the median salary report a higher satisfaction level than those who have jobs at large law firms. Thus, there are a variety of factors other than salary that a prospective applicant should consider, but the applicant should take into account the amount of debt that will be necessary to earn the law degree.

Another important point is that law students tend to have varied backgrounds. Although a law school class may have a number of students who completed pre-law programs, students in a class may have come from highly varied academic backgrounds, including the sciences and the arts.

Although backgrounds of law students tend to be high varied, a law student should have strong skills in certain areas. The American Bar Association's Section on Legal Education and **Admission to the Bar** identified

seven core skills and values that a law student should have. These are:

- Analytical and program-solving skills
- Critical reading skills
- Writing skills
- Oral communications and listening abilities
- General research skills
- Task organization and management skills
- Values of serving others and promoting justice

The ABA Section on Legal Education also noted that it will help law students to have a broad understanding of history, a fundamental understanding of political thought, basic mathematical and financial skills, a basic understanding of human behavior, and an understanding of diverse cultures.

DECIDING WHERE TO ATTEND LAW SCHOOL

Many states only have one or two law schools, so some applicants will have to make the difficult decision about the geographic location of where they want to attend law school. As a general matter, larger states with larger legal markets tend to have more law schools. California has the most, with 21 schools accredited by the American Bar Association. Florida, Illinois, New York, Ohio, and Texas each have at least nine law schools. On the other hand, 24 states have only one or two law schools within their borders.

The geographical location of a law school may affect more than where a person physically attends a school. Many schools have strong connections to certain markets, so students from those schools may have better opportunities if they remain within those markets. For instance, a student who attends a school in a large metropolitan area may find that law firms in that area tend to hire more graduates from that particular law school compared with other law schools in the state or region.

A related factor to consider is that the future law student will need to become licensed, and it may be easier to take the **bar examination** in the state where the student attended law school.

DECIDING WHICH LAW SCHOOL TO ATTEND

A prospective applicant should take several factors into account when deciding which law school to attend. Some law schools are very exclusive, and only those with the highest credentials will earn acceptance. Thus, an applicant wanting to attend Harvard, Yale, or Stanford will need to have top grades as an undergraduate with a score on the Law School Admission Test (LSAT) that ranks at or near the top in terms of percentile. Even with these high scores, there is no guarantee that a school will accept the applicant.

Other schools are relatively less selective, but that does not mean they will accept all applicants. In fact, a number of schools take pride in their selectivity, accepting only small percentages of the larger applicant pool. Many applicants will apply to numerous schools because they may face rejection by one or more of the schools they would like to attend.

Many applicants pay close attention to where various law schools rank compared with each other. The most popular ranking system is one used by *U.S. News and World Report*, which issues law school rankings in an annual issue. The magazine uses a variety of factors in its ranking system, relying heavily on statistics that each school reports to the American Bar Association. The magazine then sorts schools into "tiers." The top tier is reserved for schools in the top 50, and the remaining tiers consist of lower-ranking schools.

There is considerable debate about whether these rankings should have the influence they do, but the truth is that many applicants take these rankings seriously. A graduate of a "top tier" law school is more likely to earn a job offer from a large law firm than a graduate from a second- or third-tier school, so applicants naturally want to attend a top tier school.

Balancing these concerns is the availability of scholarship money. Some students may be able to attend a higher ranked law school, but another school may offer substantial scholarship money, including a full-tuition scholarship. The prospective applicant may be faced with a choice of attending a higher-ranked school with a tuition rate of, for instance, $40,000 or attending another law school tuition-free. The benefit of the scholarship may very well outweigh the benefit of the higher ranking, especially if the student will need to take out a loan to pay the tuition.

APPLYING FOR LAW SCHOOL

Given the highly competitive atmosphere of law school admissions, applicants will need to compile the best applications they can. Although grade point averages and LSAT scores are important, other factors can be the difference between acceptance and rejection.

Undergraduate GPA and Course of Study Most law schools will consider an applicant's undergraduate grade point average (UGPA) as part of the admissions process. Schools are required to report the UGPAs of their students to the ABA, and many schools have students with median UGPAs of 3.5 or even higher. Thus, an applicant's performance as an undergraduate is important.

Of course, not all undergraduate grades are earned in the same manner. Most schools will consider the rigors of the undergraduate program, often based on the reputation that an undergraduate program has. Thus, while no single course of study is necessary to earn admission into law school, a student who performs well in a rigorous undergraduate program may have a better chance to impress members of an admissions committee.

The Law School Admission Test The Law School Admission Test (LSAT) is a standardized test offered four times per year. It consists of five parts that take 35 minutes per part. Scores are based on a scale from 120 to 180 and are based on answers to multiple-choice questions that test a variety of reading and verbal reasoning skills.

Three of the parts on this exam include reading comprehension questions, analytical reasoning questions, and logical reasoning questions. A four section is ungraded and usually consists of test questions. A fifth section is an essay that is ungraded but is sent to law schools in which an applicant applies.

Some law schools place more emphasis on the LSAT than others, but it is an important score at any school. The top-ranked law schools typically report median LSAT scores of 165 or higher, and a student earning a score that high will stand a better chance of acceptance.

Personal Statement and Recommendations Many schools pay close attention to an applicant's personal statement. This statement needs to be well-written and well-edited, and it should stress why the applicant is distinctive compared with other applicants. Recommendations letters may likewise help the applicant to paint a more complete picture of himself or herself during the admissions process.

Other Criteria Schools may also consider a combination of many other factors. These can include any or all of those listed below.

- Graduate work
- Improvement in grades and grade distribution
- Ethnic or racial background
- Individual character and personality
- Work experience
- Motivation to study law
- State of residency
- Obstacles that have been overcome
- Past accomplishments and leadership
- Conditional admission programs

HOW TO STAND OUT AS AN APPLICANT

In 2010, *U.S. News and World Report* posed a series of questions to various law school admissions offices. One question focused on how applicants can set themselves apart from their peers. Examples of responses from three schools are:

Baylor University School of Law: "Applicants should focus on putting together a well-crafted application package that showcases their strengths and what they can contribute to the academic environment and legal profession. Some applicants make the mistake of developing answers and/or essays that are contrived or unauthentic. The key element applicants should remember is to be sincere, honest, and precise when preparing an application package."

Case Western Reserve University School of Law: "Approach the application as an opportunity to present yourself in the best perspectives. Apply early. Answer all questions, attach all addendums as applicable and make sure the application is complete in all respects. Provide timely response when we request additional information."

University of California-Berkeley School of Law (Boalt Hall): "We use a holistic review process to screen several hundreds of applications, culled from thousands we receive each year. Many of these have very similar or identical grades or LSAT scores. A well-written, substantive personal statement is often the only way an applicant can indicate the factors that set him or her apart from the rest. Other factors that could possibly distinguish applicants are a graduate degree, significant work or leadership experience, or mastery of a creative pursuit."

LAW SCHOOLS BY STATE

The law schools listed are organized by state and then alphabetically by school name. Schools are limited to those accredited by the American Bar Association. The numbers in parentheses represent each school's application fees as of 2010.

ALABAMA: Cumberland School of Law, Samford University ($50); Thomas Goode Jones School of Law, Faulkner University ($50); University of Alabama School of Law ($40).

ALASKA: Alaska does not have a law school.

ARIZONA: James E. Rogers College of Law, University of Arizona ($65); Phoenix School of Law ($50); Sandra Day O'Connor College of Law, Arizona State University ($60).

ARKANSAS: University of Arkansas School of Law ($0); William H. Bowen School of Law, University of Arkansas at Little Rock ($0).

CALIFORNIA: Boalt Hall School of Law, University of California at Berkeley ($75); California Western School of Law ($55); Chapman University School of Law ($75); Golden Gate University School of Law ($60); Loyola Law School ($65); McGeorge School of Law, University of the Pacific ($50); Pepperdine University School of Law ($60); Santa Clara University School of Law ($75); Southwestern University School of Law ($60); Stanford Law School, Stanford University ($100); Thomas Jefferson School of Law, Faulkner University ($50); University of California, Davis, School of Law ($75); UC Hastings College of the Law ($75); UCLA School of Law ($75); University of La Verne College of Law ($50); University of San Diego School of Law ($50); University of San Francisco School of Law ($60); USC Gould School of Law, University of Southern California ($75); Western State University College of Law ($60); Whittier Law School, Whittier College ($60).

COLORADO: Sturm College of Law, University of Denver ($65); University of Colorado School of Law at Boulder ($65)

CONNECTICUT: Quinnipiac University School of Law ($65); University of Connecticut School of Law ($60); Yale Law School, Yale University (n/a).

DELAWARE: Widener University School of Law ($60).

DISTRICT OF COLUMBIA: Columbus School of Law, The Catholic University of America ($65); David A. Clarke School of Law, University of the District of Columbia ($35); George Washington University Law School ($80); Georgetown University Law Center ($85); Howard University School of Law ($60); Washington College of Law, American University ($70).

FLORIDA: Dwayne O. Andreas School of Law, Barry University (n/a); Florida A&M University College of Law ($33); Florida Coastal School of Law ($0); Florida International College of Law, Florida International University ($20); Florida State University College of Law ($30); Levin College of Law, University of Florida ($30); Shepard Broad Law Center, Nova Southeastern University ($53); St. Thomas University School of Law ($60); Stetson University College of Law ($55); University of Miami School of Law ($60).

GEORGIA: Emory University School of Law ($80); Georgia State University College of Law ($50); John Marshall Law School, Atlanta ($50); Mercer University Walter F. George School of Law ($50); University of Georgia School of Law ($50).

HAWAII: William S. Richardson School of Law, University of Hawaii at Manoa ($75).

IDAHO: University of Idaho College of Law ($50).

ILLINOIS: Chicago-Kent College of Law, Illinois Institute of Technology ($0); DePaul University College of Law ($60); John Marshall Law School ($0); Loyola University Chicago School of Law ($0); Northern Illinois University College of Law ($50); Northwestern University School of Law ($100); Southern Illinois University School of Law (n/a); University of Chicago Law School ($75); University of Illinois College of Law at Urbana-Champaign ($0).

INDIANA: Indiana University School of Law, Bloomington ($50); Indiana University Robert H. McKinney School of Law, Indianapolis ($50); Notre Dame Law School, University of Notre Dame ($65); Valparaiso University School of Law ($0).

IOWA: Drake University Law School ($50); The University of Iowa College of Law ($60).

KANSAS: University of Kansas School of Law ($55); Washburn University School of Law ($40).

KENTUCKY: Louis D. Brandeis School of Law, University of Louisville ($50); Salmon P. Chase College of Law, Northern Kentucky University ($40); University of Kentucky College of Law ($50).

LOUISIANA: Loyola University New Orleans College of Law ($45); Paul M. Hebert Law Center, Louisiana State University ($50); Southern University Law Center, Southern University and A&M College ($25); Tulane University Law School ($60).

MAINE: University of Maine School of Law, University of Southern Maine ($50).

MARYLAND: University of Baltimore School of Law ($60); University of Maryland School of Law, Baltimore ($70).

MASSACHUSETTS: Boston College Law School ($75); Boston University School of Law ($75); Harvard Law School, Harvard University ($85); New England School of Law ($65); Northeastern University School of Law ($75); Suffolk University Law School ($60); Western New England College School of Law (n/a).

MICHIGAN: Michigan State University College of Law ($60); Thomas M. Cooley Law School ($0); University of Detroit Mercy School of Law ($50); University of Michigan Law School ($75); Wayne State University Law School ($50).

MINNESOTA: Hamline University School of Law ($35); University of Minnesota Law School, Twin Cities ($75); University of St. Thomas School of Law ($0); William Mitchell College of Law ($0).

MISSISSIPPI: Mississippi College School of Law ($40); University of Mississippi School of Law ($0).

MISSOURI: Saint Louis University School of Law ($55); University of Missouri School of Law, Columbia ($60); University of Missouri-Kansas City School of Law ($60); Washington University in St. Louis School of Law ($70).

MONTANA: University of Montana School of Law ($60).

NEBRASKA: Creighton University School of Law ($50); University of Nebraska-Lincoln College of Law ($50).

NEVADA: William S. Boyd School of Law, University of Nevada, Las Vegas ($50).

NEW HAMPSHIRE: Franklin Pierce Law Center, Franklin Pierce College ($55).

NEW JERSEY: Rutgers School of Law, Newark, Rutgers University-Newark ($65); Rutgers University School of Law, Camden ($65); Seton Hall University School of Law ($65).

NEW MEXICO: University of New Mexico School of Law ($50).

NEW YORK: Albany Law School, Union College ($70); Benjamin N. Cardozo School of Law, Yeshiva University ($75); Brooklyn Law School ($0); Columbia University School of Law (n/a); Cornell Law School, Cornell University ($80); CUNY School of Law, The City University of New York ($60); Fordham University School of Law ($70); Hofstra University School of Law ($0); Jacob D. Fuchsberg Law Center, Touro College ($60); New York Law School ($0); New York University School of Law ($75); Pace University School of Law ($65); St. John's University School of Law ($60); SUNY Buffalo Law School ($75); Syracuse University College of Law ($75).

NORTH CAROLINA: Charlotte School of Law (n/a); Duke University School of Law ($70); Elon University School of Law ($50); Norman Adrian Wiggins School of Law, Campbell University ($50); North Carolina Central University School of Law ($50); University of North Carolina School of Law at Chapel Hill ($75); Wake Forest University School of Law ($60).

NORTH DAKOTA: University of North Dakota School of Law ($35).

OHIO: Capital University Law School ($40); Case Western Reserve University School of Law ($40); Cleveland-Marshall College of Law, Cleveland State University ($0); Michael E. Moritz College of Law, Ohio State University ($60); Pettit College of Law, Ohio Northern University ($0); The University of Akron School of Law ($0); University of Cincinnati College of Law ($35); University of Dayton School of Law ($50); University of Toledo College of Law ($0);

OKLAHOMA: Oklahoma City University School of Law ($50); The University of Tulsa College of Law ($30); University of Oklahoma Law Center ($50).

OREGON: Lewis and Clark Law School, Lewis and Clark College ($50); University of Oregon School of Law ($50); Willamette University College of Law ($50).

PENNSYLVANIA: Beasley School of Law, Temple University ($60); Dickinson School of Law, Pennsylvania State University ($60); Duquesne University School of Law ($60); Earle Mack School of Law, Drexel University ($0); University of Pennsylvania Law School ($80); University of Pittsburgh School of Law ($55); Villanova University School of Law ($75); Widener University School of Law ($60)

RHODE ISLAND: Ralph R. Papitto School of Law, Roger Williams University ($60).

SOUTH CAROLINA: Charleston School of Law ($50); University of South Carolina School of Law ($60).

SOUTH DAKOTA: University of South Dakota School of Law ($35).

TENNESSEE: Cecil C. Humphreys School of Law, The University of Memphis ($25); University of Tennessee College of Law ($15); Vanderbilt University School of Law ($50).

TEXAS: Baylor University School of Law ($40); Dedman School of Law, Southern Methodist University ($75); South Texas College of Law ($55); St. Mary's University School of Law ($55); Texas Tech University School of Law ($50); Texas Wesleyan University School of Law ($55); The University of Texas School of Law Austin ($70); Thurgood Marshall School of Law, Texas Southern University ($55); University of Houston Law Center ($70);

UTAH: J. Reuben Clark Law School, Brigham Young University ($50); S.J. Quinney College of Law, University of Utah ($60).

VERMONT: Vermont Law School ($60).

VIRGINIA: Appalachian School of Law ($60); George Mason University School of Law ($35); Liberty University School of Law ($50); Regent University School of Law ($50); University of Richmond School of Law ($50); University of Virginia School of Law ($80); Washington and Lee University School of Law ($0); William and Mary Law School ($50);

WASHINGTON: Gonzaga University School of Law ($50); Seattle University School of Law ($60); University of Washington School of Law ($60).

WEST VIRGINIA: West Virginia University College of Law ($50).

WISCONSIN: Marquette University Law School ($50); University of Wisconsin Law School, Madison ($56).

WYOMING: University of Wyoming College of Law ($50).

ATTORNEYS

HOW TO FIND AN ATTORNEY

BACKGROUND

In 1977, the U.S. Supreme Court handed down its decision in *Bates v. State Bar of Arizona*, 433 U.S. 350, 97 S. Ct. 2691, which struck down state laws prohibiting lawyers from advertising as an unconstitutional interference with free speech. At the time, commentators widely thought that it would then be easier to find an attorney. This belief was based on the premise that since lawyers were allowed to compete in the same way as other businesses do, it would be easier to meet one's needs for legal representation and that the costs would go down.

It is true that lawyer advertising has made it easier to find an attorney. However, a challenge continues to find the right attorney to match specific needs. If the selected lawyer is inexperienced, incompetent, or lacks the willingness or ability to communicate effectively with a client, the client will not be satisfied with the lawyer's service. Furthermore, the consequences for the client could be catastrophic, such as losing a business or being unable to recover for injuries the client sustained at the hands of a liable third party. In order to find the best attorney, one needs more than a list of names, even if these are specialists in the relevant legal area. Clients are best served by asking questions before they decide on an attorney to retain.

Consumer dissatisfaction with lawyers has been a major problem. A survey taken in 1995 by Consumer's Union revealed that out of 30,000 respondents, one-third were not well satisfied with the quality of their attorneys' services. The reasons for this dissatisfaction varied, ranging from attorneys failing to keep their clients informed on the progress of their cases, failing to protect clients' interests, failing to resolve cases in a timely manner, and continually charge unreasonable fees. The reason for this widespread dissatisfaction is linked to the lack of knowledge by consumers on how to find attorneys experienced with the kinds of problems they are facing as well as knowing what questions to ask a lawyer they are considering retaining. The results of a one thousand person survey reported in the *Florida Bar Journal* revealed that the average time spent in finding a lawyer was two hours or less. Nearly one half of those surveyed said it was hard to find a good lawyer, and over a quarter of them said they did not know how to find a lawyer. It is remarkable that 80 percent of respondents said they wished there was a source for information on lawyers' credentials.

Subsequent surveys have had similar results. Moreover, with economic problems in the United States during the late 2000s and early 2010s, many clients have stressed that they want greater value in services. Finding a lawyer who provides services at an agreeable price can be an even greater challenge.

Why It Is Difficult to Find an Attorney One difficulty in finding the appropriate attorney is the ever expanding number of specialties practiced by lawyers. Specialization makes selection more complicated. Law has become more specialized because changes in technology have necessitated the development of new areas, such as Cyberlaw and Internet law. New areas of law have also been created by recently enacted laws and regulations from such federal administrative bodies as the Environmental Protection Agency. This could impact and complicate the problems of a person acquiring a business and trying to determine whether the seller or the buyer is liable for cleaning up a toxic waste site. The increasing number of laws and regulations has forced lawyers to become more specialized to keep up with new developments. Furthermore, many general areas of the law in which an attorney could become proficient, have been split up into specialties. In business law, there are specialists for mergers and acquisitions because of the complexity involved in these transactions. Even criminal law is not immune to this trend since some lawyers specialize in white collar crime.

When Do I Need A Lawyer? Potential clients should retain a lawyer for any of the following reasons:

- If they have been charged with a felony
- If they have been served with papers naming them as defendants in a lawsuit
- If their insurance coverage is less than the amount a third party is claiming due to their negligence
- If they are making a will or changing it
- If they wish to adopt a child
- If someone with whom they are involved in a business setting breaches his or her **contract** with the client

If a person is a **defendant** in a civil lawsuit and fails to appear in court, a **default judgment** will be entered by the court against the defendant, and for all practical purposes, the defendant will be unable to overturn it.

Avoiding the Dishonest or Unethical Lawyers It is relatively easy to encounter a dishonest or unethical lawyer because, with the exception of Oregon, at least some part of the disciplinary process is kept private. This means that potential clients have no way of knowing whether a complaint has been made against a lawyer if no disciplinary action has been taken. Although some complaints against lawyers are frivolous, the consumer

has no way of knowing whether the decision by the state bar not to take any action was made in **good faith**. Furthermore, the action taken may only amount to a private reprimand in the form of a letter sent to the attorney. According to a recent investigation by the *Washington Times*, lawyers guilty of serious ethical violations and felonies are at the most only suspended for a limited period of time and made to make **restitution** to the client. Even the most severe punishment, disbarment, is not permanent since in most states the attorney can apply for reinstatement in five years.

Not only are the actions taken against lawyers found guilty of ethical violations not published in many states, this information is unavailable even in publications and databases relied upon by consumers to avoid this problem. There are attorneys listed in the well-respected Martindale-Hubbell Lawyers Directory who may be under suspension, disbarred, or imprisoned. The database set up by the American Bar Association (ABA) to allow consumers to find out whether a lawyer has been sanctioned is a great deal less than helpful since no details are given as to the offense charged or the punishment given.

Out of all the complaints made against lawyers, only one-half of one per cent result in disbarment, and a total of only one and one-half percent result in any **sanction** at all, including private reprimands.

QUESTIONS TO ASK BEFORE RETAINING A LAWYER

There are four purposes to this process. First, it allows consumers to determine whether the attorney has sufficient experience not just in the specialty pertaining to their problem, but also whether the lawyer has had previously solved a similar problem for another client. Second, they can learn whether his style is suited to their goals in resolving the dispute they have with the other side. For example, if a potential client is hoping for a **settlement**, a hardball Rambo like style may backfire. Third, they will discover how well they and the attorney communicate with one another. Fourth, they can ask the attorney if they are able to devote sufficient time and resources, such as a support staff, to their case.

Consumer Reports suggests that the following questions be asked during an interview with any attorney a consumer is considering retaining:

- How many years of experience do you have in this specialty and how have you handled similar disputes in the past?
- What are the possible results from pursuing this matter?

- How long will you expect it to take to resolve this matter?

- How will you keep me informed of what is happening as the case proceeds?

- Will anyone else, such as one of your associates or paralegals, be working on my case?

- Do you charge a flat or an hourly rate and how much?

- What other expenses will there be besides your fee and how are they calculated?

- What's a reasonable approximate figure for a total bill?

- Can you give me a written estimate?

- Can some of the work be handled by members of your staff at a lower rate?

- Will unforeseen events increase the amount you charge me?

- If you charge on a contingency basis, what proportion of the amount I recover will be paid to you as your fee and can this figure be calculated after the expenses are deducted?

- How often will I be billed, and how are billing disputes resolved? If we cannot settle this, will you agree to mandatory arbitration?

- Do you need any further information from me?

- Can I do some of the work in exchange for a lower bill?

- Do you recommend that this matter be submitted to an arbitrator or mediator, and do you know anyone qualified to do this?

METHODS OF FINDING AN ATTORNEY

By Advertisement In an advertisement, consumers cannot obtain the information you need in order to make a wise decision. There is nothing upon which to judge the legal skills of the attorney, whether his style would be conducive to achieving specific goals as to how to resolve specific problem, or whether there have been any complaints against the attorney resulting in a reprimand, suspension or disbarment. It also cannot determine from an advertisement whether the attorney will be accessible enough so that they can communicate effectively with their clients and willing to take the time necessary so that they understand the possible outcomes of handling the client's case in a given manner.

By Personal Referral Friends and business acquaintances whose judgment is trusted is a good source in finding an attorney, if they have used the attorney for the same kind of problem that a consumer is facing or at least practices in a specialty pertaining to the consumer's situation. An even better source is a friend or acquaintance who actually is an active or recently retired lawyer or judge. Such persons can inform potential clients as to attorneys' reputation in the legal community.

By Published Directories

Martindale Hubbell Law Directory This annually published directory is the oldest and best known of those available today. It includes lawyers practicing in the United States as well as 159 other countries. This coverage of foreign countries will continue to become more important as laws in the United States are affected by foreign and international law.

Each individual lawyer entry will contain the date of birth, the year first admitted to a state bar, numeric codes indicating where all listed educational degrees were earned Specialized areas of law in which they practice, and a listing of representative clients, the firm where the lawyer practices, and contact information. If the entry has the bar registry designation (BR), it means that they are also listed in the Martindale Hubbell Directory for Pre-Eminent Lawyers.

Despite its enormous size, not all practicing attorneys are listed. In order for an attorney or firm to be included in this directory, they must send the appropriate information to the publisher.

Many, but not all of the attorneys and firms listed, are rated according to their degree of legal skill and whether they follow the highest ethical standards. The rating "AV" is the highest rating given. A "BV" rating is still above average in terms of legal skills and an indication the attorney subscribes to the same high ethical standards as those given the "AV" rating. The "CV" rating denotes an average rating in terms of legal skills and an indication the lawyer also follows the highest ethical standards. No attorney is given a rating without their consent. The ratings are based on confidential written evaluations by practitioners and judges in the position to know the given lawyer. There is no rating to indicate that a lawyer is below average in legal ability or that he does not follow the highest ethical standards.

Martindale Hubbell Bar Register of Pre-Eminent Lawyers Listings are restricted to those individual attorneys and firms that have earned the "AV" rating and who practice in the United States and Canada. Instead of being grouped by state and within each state by the locality in which the lawyer practices, the lawyers are first grouped according to the specialty in which they practice. Sixty specialties are included.

The primary value of these directories in your search for an attorney is that they tell you how long that lawyer has been in practice, whether he specializes in an area relevant to the problem you are facing, and whether there may be a **conflict of interest** if you retain that attorney based on the clients they represent.

The Best Lawyers in America In its 18th edition as of 2012, the information is based on the polling of thousands of lawyers who were asked which attorneys in practice for a minimum of ten years they consider to be the best in their specialty. The 2012 edition featured 43,629 lawyers in 135 practice areas.

Chambers USA This source is designed for those trying to find an attorney practicing in one of over sixty specialized areas of business and **corporate** law.

Evaluations are from leading practitioners in each specialty obtained through telephone interviews averaging thirty minutes. During these interviews, the person interviewed is asked who they consider to be the best attorney in their specialty and why they hold such a high opinion of them. This procedure, unlike the written questionnaires upon which other lawyer directories rely, allows for a more thorough investigation of the legal abilities of a given attorney. This is because an interview by telephone avoids the **bias** that is inherent in written questionnaires since the ones returned in such surveys are much more likely to be favorable. Conversely, attorneys who do not respect the abilities of another practitioner are less likely to send in their written responses.

By the Internet Several Internet sources are available to assist individuals to find lawyers. Some popular options include the following:

- Martindale Hubbell, http://www.martindale.com
- Lawyers.com, http://www.lawyers.com
- Chambers and Partners, http://www.chambersand partners.com/
- Findlaw, http://lawyers.findlaw.com/

By Lawyer Referral Services of State Bar Associations These sources are useful only to the extent they can give consumers the names of lawyers in a given locality who practice law in a given specialty and who have agreed to have their name put on the list maintained by the bar association. For a small fee, usually $25 to $30, each attorney on the list agrees to give a fifteen to thirty minute consultation. This can be helpful because consumers can get an opinion from a lawyer as to whether they have a case and whether it is worth pursuing. This can save consumers a great deal of time and effort as opposed to attempting to research the matter on their own. During the consultation, the lawyer should be able to inform the potential client whether the **statute of limitations** for filing their particular claim has expired or not. Although consumers

could do research on their own, just reading the **statute** may be insufficient to determine whether the statute of limitations has run out; they may have to read the **case law** on this matter. Regardless of what the attorney tells the consumer regarding their case, they are under no obligation to retain the lawyer's services.

The following are a short list of directory services available:

- ABA Lawyer Referral Directory – This directory lists state wide and local bar association referral services. The local referral services specify which counties they serve. Each referral service will indicate whether they give referrals for all specialties or exclude certain ones. Information is also given as to whether low fee or **pro bono** (no fee) programs are provided for low income clients.

- Law and Legal Information Directory by Steven & Jacqueline O'Brien Wasserman – This source has an alphabetical listing by state of referral services located in that **jurisdiction**. Included are entries for services provided by the state bar as well as local bar associations. Street and website addresses, regular and toll-free telephone numbers are provided. If you qualify by income, a listing of legal aid offices arranged alphabetically by state and cities within will include the same information the lawyer referral section provides.

- Web Services – If you do not have access to either of the above titles, you may obtain information on the legal referral services offered by your state bar by logging on to http://www.findlaw.com. From this site you will be led to links for each state that in turn will include links to that state's bar association and the lawyer referral service it provides.

SELECTED STATE BAR ASSOCIATION RESOURCES

Several state bar associations provide resource to assist individuals to find a lawyer. Examples include:

CALIFORNIA: The State Bar of California produces a pamphlet entitled "How Can I Find and Hire the Right Lawyer?" It is available online at http://www.calbar.ca. gov/Public/Pamphlets/HiringaLawyer.aspx.

FLORIDA: The Florida Bar produces a pamphlet entitled "How to Find a Lawyer in Florida." It is available online at the Florida bar website at http://www. floridabar.org.

ILLINOIS: The Illinois State Bar Association maintains a site entitled IllinoisLawyerFinder, which includes information about what a client should seek in a lawyer. The resource is available online at http://www.illinoislawyerfinder.com/.

NEW YORK: The New York Better Business Bureau provides a web page that describes how to find a lawyer in New York City. It also includes contact information for lawyer referral services. The site is available at http://newyork.bbb.org/how-to-find-a-lawyer-in-nyc/.

TEXAS: The State Bar of Texas provides a site that allows members of the public to search for attorneys. The site is available at http://www.texasbar.com.

ADDITIONAL RESOURCES

Lawyer Referral Directory. Annual. Standing Committee on Lawyer Referral and Information Service. Chicago, IL: American Bar Association, 2012.

Martindale Hubbell Law Directory. Annual. Summit, NJ: Martindale-Hubbell, 2012.

Profile 2000: Characteristics of Lawyer Referral and Information Service. ABA Committee on Lawyer Referral and Information Service. Chicago, American Bar Association, 1999.

ORGANIZATIONS

American Bar Association (ABA)

321 North Clark Street
Chicago, IL 60610
Phone: (202) 662-1000
Toll Free: (800) 285-2221
Fax: (312) 988-6800
URL: http://www.americanbar.org

Chicago Divorce Association

One Pierce Center
Itasca, IL 60143
Phone: (630) 860-2100

Christian Legal Society

4208 Evergreen Lane, Suite 222
Annandale, VA 22003
Phone: (703) 642-1070
URL: URL: http://clsnet.org

Help Abolish Legal Tyranny (HALT)

1612 K St. NW, Ste. 510
Washington, DC 20006
Phone: (202) 887-8255
Toll Free: (888) FOR-HALT
URL: http://www.halt.org

National Conference of Black Lawyers

116 W. 111th St., 3rd Fl.
New York, NY 10026
URL: http://www.ncbl.org

National Lawyers Association

3000 S. Jamaica Ct., Ste. 390
Aurora, CO 80014
Toll Free: (800) 471-2994
Fax: (303) 979-6094
URL: http://www.nla.org

National Lawyers Guild

126 University Place, 5th floor
New York, NY 10003-4538
URL: http://www.nlg.org/

ATTORNEYS

LICENSING OF ATTORNEYS

BACKGROUND

The terms lawyer and attorney are commonly used interchangeably with one referring to the other. In each of the 50 states and the District of Columbia, the practice of law is limited to attorneys/lawyers who have been formally registered and admitted to practice in that state or district. Being admitted to practice is generally a three-fold process: graduation from an **accredited law school**, obtaining a passing score on the multi-state and state bar examinations, and meeting all character and fitness criteria established by a state administrative board responsible for overseeing the practice of law in that state. The unlicensed practice of law, by either a layman or a trained lawyer who has failed to obtain licensure, carries serious consequences, including administrative, civil, and/or criminal sanctions.

Technically speaking, successful graduation from an accredited law school, along with passing scores on multi-state and state bar examinations, objectively determine professional **competency** of an individual to practice law. However, because **incompetency** or unprofessional conduct can result in serious harm or damage to a client, licensure is mandated to ensure the overall and continued competence of each practitioner.

As with other licensed professions, the practice of law is primarily self-policed by the state administrative body that admits each person to practice. The state maintains a continued interest in the competency of attorneys after admission to practice, and has power to suspend or **rescind** licenses to practice within the state. Most states also mandate periodic continued legal education (CLE) after law school, to ensure that lawyers stay current on changing law and procedural practice.

HISTORY

The framers of the U.S. Constitution clearly believed that the interpretation of **constitutional rights** should be entrusted to specialists. Article III provides for an independent judicial power equal in power to the executive and legislative branches that has **jurisdiction** over both states and individuals. It also created a federal judiciary with the power to determine whether Congress had exceeded its powers, and the power to review state court decisions in certain cases.

Early colonial legislation was primarily reviewed by administrative authorities in the mother countries (e.g., England, Spain, France). As colonial industry and population increased (to approximately 300,000 in 1700), review of colonial legislation came under increasing scrutiny. As for colonists, the necessity of dealing in commercial matters with English merchants, and the reliance on English law to support colonists' grievances against the crown, enhanced the desire to create a native force of legal professionals who understood the nuances of legal terms and clauses.

Apprenticeships were completed in a manner similar to England's Inns of Court. There was no formal "admission" to practice law, but, following "book" study and apprenticeship, prospective lawyers were "accepted" into practice by local and experienced members of the profession. By the time of the American Revolution, each colony had a bar of legally trained and respected professionals.

Eventually, particularly in colonial cities, the legal profession enjoyed both social status and economic success. With such status, colonial lawyers became increasingly involved in politics as well, since 25 of the 56 signatories to the Declaration of Independence were lawyers.

Formation of an Early American Legal System With newly gained American independence came a certain political antipathy toward English law, resulting in the creation of several early statutes prohibiting the citation of any English decision handed down after independence. Loyalist attorneys returned to England, and those that stayed to seize political or judicial posts under the new government found much of their talents and expertise no longer in demand. The opportunity to broaden the base of American law was considerable, with an expressed interest in Roman and French law for enlightenment and guidance. (The Code of Napoleon did not appear until the beginning of the 19th century.) However, few judges or lawyers were versed in foreign languages, and the lack of an adequate body of American **case law** to bridge the gap left the legal bar in splinters.

As a result, the quality of lawyers in the states was palpably inferior to the systemically-trained professionals of England. Early American lawyers were generally self-taught and self-read. Respected laypersons were often elected or appointed as judges to fill the gap and keep up with the newly burgeoning nation. During the early 1800s, the state of Rhode Island had a farmer serving as its **chief justice**, as well as a blacksmith serving as a member of its highest court. Early judges grappled with jurisprudential conflicts to form new law that would fit the

peculiar needs of a young growing country, particularly the needs peculiar to their own jurisdictions. Eventually, judges "rode circuits, traveling from county seat to county seat, **hearing** cases, and lawyers often traveled with them.

As the volume of new American case law grew, the uncertainty of earlier parochial court decisions gave way to more predictable and standard outcomes. Local judges increasingly strove to shape their own decisions so as to provide consistency with that of other regional (and eventually, state) jurisdictions.

By the end of the Civil War (1860s), the influence of English law on the United States was negligible, although familiar procedures, vocabulary, and conceptual approaches to legal **jurisprudence** survived and were incorporated into U.S. law. A few states originally paralleled the English system by distinguishing barristers from solicitors within the legal profession (Massachusetts, New Jersey, New York, Virginia). However, by the mid-1800s, such distinctions were dropped in favor of a single class of lawyers who dealt directly with both clients and courtrooms.

Legal Education Notwithstanding the splintered beginnings of U.S. law, the accepted preparation for becoming a lawyer remained the completion of an apprenticeship under a trained lawyer, along with self-reading of such printed sources as the American edition of William Blackstone's *Commentaries on the Laws of England,* which first appeared in the 1760s, and James Kent's *Commentaries on American Law.* Eventually, Blackstone's Commentaries sold as many copies in America as in England.

The earliest known formal legal education was at Oxford University, as early as the 1750s. William Blackstone began offering lectures on the English **common law** at that time (which became the source for his later *Commentaries*), and many smaller American universities later followed his example. In 1779, a chair of law was established at William and Mary College in Virginia. There followed a series of independent schools of law, not associated with universities or colleges, which functioned as offshoots of the apprenticeship system. The most notable of these (and credited as the first law school in the country) was the Litchfield Law School in Connecticut. Founded by Judge Tapping Reeve, the school looked much like a country schoolhouse, and operated solely on daily lectures. There were no prerequisites or entrance requirements and no final examinations. The school operated continuously from 1784 to 1833 after which, schools like Litchfield died out or merged with instruction in a university setting.

It is important to note that from the latter 1700s to the second half of the 1800s, the legal profession in the

United States was not considered academic or elite, but rather vocational and functional. The present day "law school" did not take shape until 1829, when Justice Joseph Story reorganized the separate law department at Harvard University. Prior to that time, legal studies were considered part of a broader liberal education at the universities, and non-university law schools were comparable to modern-day vocational schools.

Justice Story set up Harvard's law school curriculum as an exclusive legal education, premised on the assumption that its students had acquired a sufficient background in liberal arts prior to admission to law school. However, even the ambitious Harvard program had more intellectual pretension than substance. There were no entrance examinations, interim examinations, or final examination. The only requirement was the completion of two years at the school and the payment of fees.

By 1870, the United States had over 30 university law schools, mostly based on Story's model. In reality, however, these schools had no academic admissions requirements, and no attempt was made to ensure that students had already achieved the antecedent liberal education contemplated by Story.

LAW SCHOOL

As of 2012, there were over 200 law schools in the United States, the great majority of which had been approved by the American Bar Association (ABA) and had met somewhat stricter standards of the Association of American Law Schools. In most schools, admission is premised on scores achieved on the Law School Admission Test (LSAT), undergraduate grade point average and course of study, and other personal criteria factored in, for example, ethnic or cultural diversity or leadership or success in extra-curricular activities. Although not all law schools require a four-year undergraduate degree as a prerequisite for admission, an abundance of applicants creates a competitive edge that results in the great majority of vacancies being filled by college graduates. The formal three-year course of intensive professional training has replaced the apprenticeship form of training. Law clerkships during law school are common in both the public and private sector, and again, create a competitive edge for job placement after graduation.

THE BAR EXAMINATION

Each state prepares and administers its own written examination for applicants seeking licensure to practice law in that state. The vast majority of states incorporate the use of the Multi-state Bar Examination (MBE), a day-long multiple-choice test which challenges a candidate's basic understanding of general law and legal theories (e.g.,

torts, contracts, **criminal procedure**, constitutional rights, etc.). This is followed by another day-long written examination on a particular state law, which tests candidates' knowledge of not only state statutes, but also the state's approach to common law issues. Finally, most states add a half-day written examination on ethics and professional responsibility.

CHARACTER AND FITNESS REVIEW

State bar associations conduct character and fitness reviews of prospective candidates seeking licensure to practice law in those states. This is generally conducted through a series of multi-page applications, reference-checking, employment history verifications, reviews of letters of recommendation, and criminal background investigations.

THE ROLE OF THE ORGANIZED BAR

The Association of the Bar of the City of New York was founded in 1870 by what one lawyer referred to as the "decent part of the profession." It was a group of 75 gentlemen from this state bar that ultimately met in 1878 to form the American Bar Association (ABA). Its goal was reform: fighting corruption, drafting better laws, and raising the prestige of the profession. From this group, the Association of American Law Schools was organized for the improvement of legal education.

By 1905, the ABA began to require (of its members, not of the profession as a whole) a minimum of three years of law study prior to practicing law. In fact, the ABA had become an elitist organization, representing the upper crust of the profession, with elitist values. Early on, it promoted codes of ethics for its members in an effort to define and uphold appropriate, professional conduct. In the 2010s, the ABA Model Rules of Professional Conduct have been adopted and/or incorporated by a majority of the states.

In 1952, the Association established three years of college as a prerequisite for admission to law school. By the 21st century, a majority of law schools either required or preferred the completion of course study for a four-year bachelor's degree prior to the study of law. After completion of an additional three years of law study, a law student is awarded the degree of juris doctorate (J.D.) and becomes a candidate for **admission to the bar**.

PROCEDURE FOR LICENSE TO PRACTICE LAW

By the end of 2012, the admission to, and regulation of, the legal profession was primarily the concern of state bar associations. Each state administers its own admissions requirements and procedures, although all states generally focus on law school completion, bar examination results, and background check.

While awaiting bar examination test results, prospective candidates for admission begin filing their applications with state bar organizations and forwarding law school and undergraduate transcripts. Bar admissions committees review the total submissions for each candidate and favorably select candidates considered qualified for practice.

Most selection decisions (or declinations) are communicated by correspondence to the applicants/candidates. The successful candidate is generally admitted to practice in a formal "swearing-in" ceremony or procedure before a court. Many states require the candidates to have "sponsors" who are attorneys already admitted to practice in that state. The newly admitted attorneys receive personal identification numbers from the state bar, which are later generally added to their signatures on all court documents or **legal proceedings** handled in the practice of law.

SCOPE OF LICENSE

Few states actually issue a "license" to practice law *per se*; and generally the attorney receives a formal frame-worthy certificate evidencing admission, the display of which is required by several states.

Lawyers are only permitted to practice law in a state where they have been formally admitted. Obtaining license to practice accords each lawyer with all rights to perform all duties associated with the profession. These include counseling persons in legal matters; representing persons in a court of law, before an administrative **tribunal**, or in legal controversies; advocating persons' rights or legal positions in a legal controversy; preparing and drafting legal documents; and negotiating on behalf of other persons.

A license to practice law within a state refers to practice within the state courts. Federal trial courts generally premise their admissions on the policies of the state in which they are located. Other U.S. federal courts, particularly appellate courts, have open admissions policies, allowing attorneys to argue cases before them if they are licensed anywhere in the country.

SUSPENSION OR REVOCATION OF LICENSE

By virtue of state law, the highest court of each state generally delegates authority to state bar organizations to oversee, monitor, and discipline licensed attorneys within the state. This includes the vested authority to suspend or revoke licenses.

Generally, each state bar has an attorney grievance section that reviews and adjudicates complaints received.

Procedural due process requires that the subject attorney receive notice of the substance of the complaint received. Additionally, the attorney must be granted sufficient time to prepare a response (usually first in writing, then in a hearing). Because suspension or revocation of a license interferes with an attorney's ability to be gainfully employed, adverse decisions may be appealed in a court of law. Courts of law do not have the power to suspend or revoke an attorney's license. Their jurisdiction is limited to appellate review of a state bar's action.

However, outside of the bar association forum, an attorney may also be sued for legal **malpractice** in a court of law. If a judgment is entered against him or her, the damages are compensatory in nature (usually in the form of a monetary judgment) and payable to the complainant; the court cannot suspend or revoke the attorney's license as part of the award in the lawsuit. Nevertheless, notice of the adverse judgment may then be forwarded to the state bar for review. It is the state bar organization that will decide whether the judgment against the attorney substantively represented a breach in the model rules, **code of conduct**, or code of ethics such that a suspension or revocation of the license to practice law is warranted.

INDIVIDUAL STATE ADMISSION REQUIREMENTS

The National Conference of Bar Examiners and the American Bar Association's Section of Legal Education and Admissions to the Bar produce an annual publication entitled *Comprehensive Guide to Bar Admission Requirements*. This source contains information about character and fitness determinations; eligibility to take the various bar examinations; eligibility for initial admission to the bar; various bar exam requirements; and information about reciprocity and alternative means of admission.

RECIPROCITY

Many states open the practice of law to out-of-state applicants who have already been admitted to the bar of another state. While each state establishes its own criteria for admission, reciprocal agreements between states are common. Depending on factors such as the number of graduating law students within the state, geographic desirability (high demand for "Sunbelt" states like California, Florida, and Arizona), or average earnings compared to other states, state bars may lower or raise the threshold for admission of external candidates. Some may require prospective candidates to take the state's bar exam, while others will accept a combination of passing results on the Multi-State Bar Examination and a minimum number of years' in practice in another state. For example, as of January 2005, the states of Maine, New Hampshire, and Vermont entered into a reciprocity agreement allowing attorneys to be admitted to one another's bars without taking the bar examination for that state. The geographic proximity of the states and the frequent representation by law firms of **corporations** who operate in all three states prompted the change.

ALABAMA: The state does not offer reciprocity.

ALASKA: The state has reciprocity agreements with the following other states: CO, CT, DC, GA, IL, IN, IA, KY, MA, MI, MN, MO, NE, NH, NY, ND, OH, OK, PA, TN, TX, UT, VT, VA, WA, WV, WY.

ARIZONA: The state does not offer reciprocity.

ARKANSAS: Admission by motion went into effect in October 2004.

CALIFORNIA: The state does not offer reciprocity, but offers a shorter bar examination for attorneys licensed in other states with good standing for at least four years prior to application.

COLORADO: Other states have to reciprocate for Colorado lawyers.

CONNECTICUT: Other states have to reciprocate for Connecticut lawyers.

DELAWARE: The state does not offer reciprocity.

DISTRICT OF COLUMBIA: Lawyers who have been admitted for five years in another jurisdiction immediately preceding application for admission in DC can be admitted without examination, and other lawyers can be admitted without examination if they graduated from an ABA accredited law school and obtained certain minimum scores on the Multi-State Bar Examination and the Multi-State Professional Responsibility Examination.

FLORIDA: The state does not offer reciprocity.

GEORGIA: Georgia offers a shorter bar examination for lawyers admitted by examination and in good standing in another state for at least twelve months prior to taking its Attorneys' Examination. Admission is also offered without examination for lawyers from reciprocal states who have practiced at least five years.

HAWAII: The state does not offer reciprocity.

IDAHO: Offers reciprocity only to certain lawyers licensed in Oregon, Utah, Washington, and Wyoming. However, lawyers who have actively practiced law for at least five of the last seven years immediately preceding their applications for admission do not have to take and pass the Multi-State Bar Examination, but must take and pass the remainder of the Idaho bar examination.

ILLINOIS: Has reciprocity agreements with the following states and territories: AK, CO, CT, DC, GA, GU, IN, IA, KY, MA, MI, MN, MO, NE, NH, NMI, NY, NC, ND, OH, OK, PA, TN, TX, USVI, UT, VT, VA, WA, WV, WI, WY.

INDIANA: Has no formal reciprocity but provisionally admits lawyers who have practiced law for five years of the seven years immediately preceding their applications for admission without taking and passing the Indiana bar examination.

IOWA: Lawyers who have practiced law for five full years of the seven years immediately preceding their applications for admission to practice law in Iowa can be admitted to practice without taking and passing the Iowa bar examination.

KANSAS: Does not have reciprocity.

KENTUCKY: Kentucky has reciprocity agreements with the following states: AK, CO, CT, DC, GA, IL, IA, MA, MI, MN, MO, NE, NH, NY, NC, ND, OH, OK, PA, TN, TX, UT, WA, WV, WI, WY.

LOUISIANA: Has no express reciprocity agreements, but provisionally admits certain lawyers from other jurisdictions under special criteria.

MAINE: As of January 2005, the states of Maine, New Hampshire, and Vermont entered into a reciprocity agreement allowing attorneys to be admitted to one another's bars without taking the bar examination for that state. Shorter bar examination for lawyers in good standing in another state for at least three of the preceding five years prior to admission to practice law in Maine; shorter bar examination for lawyers in good standing in another state depending on passing score on MBE within sixty-one months of the current administration of the Maine bar examination.

MARYLAND: Has no formal reciprocity agreements, but offers shorter bar examination for lawyers in good standing in another state for at least five years of the ten years prior to application for admission in Maryland.

MASSACHUSETTS: To gain license in this state, an applicant must have been admitted to practice in another state, district or territory for at least five years prior to application for admission and be in good standing in each such state, district and territory. An applicant must be a graduate of a law school which at the time of graduation was approved by the American Bar Association or was authorized by a state **statute** to grant the degree of bachelor of laws or juris doctor.

MICHIGAN: Lawyers who have actively practiced law for three of the five years preceding their applications for admission can be admitted to practice in Michigan without taking and passing the Michigan bar examination.

MINNESOTA: Lawyers who have been, as their principal occupation, actively and lawfully engaged in the practice of law in another jurisdiction for at least five of the seven years immediately preceding application may be admitted without examination; other lawyers may be admitted based on a minimum passing score on the Multistate Bar Examination if they apply within two years of the date they passed that test in another jurisdiction

MISSISSIPPI: Mississippi has a very limited reciprocity admission rule with states who will offer similar reciprocity to Mississippi lawyers. Lawyers from other states who have practiced at least five years may be admitted after taking and passing an attorney's examination.

MISSOURI: Will admit lawyers from states that have similar reciprocity for Missouri lawyers.

MONTANA: The state does not offer reciprocity.

NEBRASKA: Lawyers who have graduated from an ABA accredited law school and who have passed a bar examination comparable to Nebraska's, including the Multi-state Professional Responsibility Examination, or who have graduated from an ABA accredited law school and who have actively and substantially practiced law for five of the last seven years prior to application for admission can be admitted to the practice of law in Nebraska without having to take and pass a written bar examination.

NEVADA: Does not have formal reciprocity agreements with any states.

NEW HAMPSHIRE: As of January 2005, the states of Maine, New Hampshire, and Vermont entered into a reciprocity agreement allowing attorneys to be admitted to one another's bars without taking the bar examination for that state. This state also has reciprocity with the following states: AK, CO, DC, GA, KY, MA, MN, MO, NB, NY, NC, ND, OK, PA, TX, UT, WA;

NEW JERSEY: The state does not offer reciprocity.

NEW MEXICO: The state does not offer reciprocity.

NEW YORK: Has reciprocity with the following states: AK, CO, DC, GA, IL, IN, IA, KY, MA, MI, MN, MO, NE, NH, NC, ND, OH, OK, PA, TN, TX, UT, VA, WA, WV, WI, WY.

NORTH CAROLINA: Has reciprocity agreements with the following states: AK, CO, CT, DC, GA, IL, IN, IA, KY, MA, MI, MN, MO, NE, NH, NY, ND, OH, OK, PA, TN, TX, UT, VT, WA, WV, WI, WY.

NORTH DAKOTA: Does not have formal reciprocity, but lawyers who have been admitted to the bar of another state or the District of Columbia for at least five years and who have been actively engaged in the practice of law for at least four of the last five years immediately preceding their applications for admission can be admitted on motion without examination. Applicants receiving particular scores on the Multi-State Bar Examination and Multi-state Professional Responsibility Examination may also be admitted on motion if their applications are received by the North Dakota Bar Board within two years of the date of the MBE examination if they were admitted in the jurisdiction in which they took that test.

OHIO: This state does not have formal reciprocity agreements with other states. However, it provisionally admits (without examination) applicants who have taken and passed a bar examination and been admitted as a lawyer in the highest court of another state or in the District of Columbia, and who have practiced law, as defined in the rule, subsequent to that admission for at least five full years of the ten years prior to filing an application. Applicants also must demonstrate that they intend to engage in the practice of law in Ohio actively on a continuing basis.

OKLAHOMA: This state has formal reciprocity agreements with the following states: AK, CO, CT, DC, GA, IL, IN, IA, KY, MA, MI, MN, MO, NE, NH, NY, NC, ND, OH, PA, TN, TX, UT, VT, VA, WA, WV, WI, WY.

OREGON: This state provisionally admits qualifying Idaho and Washington lawyers.

PENNSYLVANIA: This state has reciprocity with the following states: AK, CO, CT, DC, GA, IL, IN, IA, KY, MA, MI, MN, MO, NE, NH, NY, NC, ND, OH, OK, TN, TX, UT, VT, VA, WA, WV, WI, WY.

RHODE ISLAND: This state will provisionally admit persons admitted to the practice of law in another state, district or territory of the United States who have actively engaged in the practice law (including teaching law) there for at least five years of the last ten years immediately preceding application for admission to Rhode Island, and after taking and passing the essay portion of the Rhode Island bar examination.

SOUTH CAROLINA: Does not have formal reciprocity agreements with any states.

SOUTH DAKOTA: This state has a reciprocity agreement that went into effect in 2004. Applicants must show five years prior practice in prescribed areas.

TENNESSEE: This state will provisionally admit applicants who meet the educational requirements applicable to Tennessee bar examination applicants and have actively engaged in the practice of law in another jurisdiction for at least five years immediately preceding their applications for admission in Tennessee.

TEXAS: This state has limited admission for certain lawyers to be admitted without examination and after passage of the full student examination.

UTAH: Has reciprocity agreements with the following states: AK, CO, CT, DC, GA, ID, IL, IN, IA, KY, MA, MI, MN, MO, NE, NH, NY, NC, ND, OH, OK, PA, TN, TX, VT, VA, WA, WY.

VERMONT: As of January 2005, the states of Maine, New Hampshire, and Vermont entered into a reciprocity agreement allowing attorneys to be admitted to one another's bars without taking the bar examination for that state. Otherwise, lawyers who have been admitted to the practice of law in another jurisdiction of the United States may be admitted upon motion and without examination provided that at the time of application they have been actively engaged in the practice of law for five of the preceding ten years in one or more jurisdictions of the United States, are currently licensed to practice in at least one such jurisdiction, and are not under suspension or revocation in any jurisdiction. Any or all of the five-year admission requirement may be waived in certain circumstances. Additionally, each applicant who at the time of application has been admitted in another state and has engaged in the practice of law for less than five of the preceding ten years, and who is currently licensed to practice in at least one such jurisdiction, and is not under suspension or revocation in any jurisdiction may be admitted after examination as described in Vermont Admission Rule 6(a)-(e).

VIRGINIA: Virginia will provisionally admit lawyers from other states who reciprocate for Virginia lawyers.

WASHINGTON: This state has formal reciprocity agreements with the following states: AK, CO, CT, DC, GA, ID, IL, IN, IA, KY, MA, MI, MN, MO, NE, NH, NY, NC, ND, OH, OK, OR, PA, TN, TX, UT, VT, VA, WV, WI, WY.

WEST VIRGINIA: This state has reciprocity agreements with the following states: CO, CT, DC, IL, IN, IA, KY, MA, MI, MN, MO, NE, NY, NC, ND, OK, PA, TX, VT, VA, WA, WI.

WISCONSIN: Wisconsin will offer **provisional** admission to practicing lawyers from states that reciprocate for Wisconsin lawyers.

WYOMING: Wisconsin will offer provisional admission to practicing lawyers from states that reciprocate for Wyoming lawyers.

ADDITIONAL RESOURCES

Darrow-Kleinhaus, Suzanne. *The Bar Exam in a Nutshell.* 2d ed. Eagan, MN: West, Thomson Reuters, 2009.

Farnsworth, E. Allan. *An Introduction to the Legal System of the United States.* New York: Oceana Publications, Inc., 1999.

ORGANIZATIONS

American Bar Association (ABA)
321 North Clark Street
Chicago, IL 60610
Phone: (312) 988-5000
Toll Free: (800) 285-2221
Fax: (312) 988-6800
URL: http://www.americanbar.org

National Conference of Bar Examiners
302 South Bedford Street
Madison, WI 53703-3622
Phone: (608) 280-8550
URL: http://www.ncbex.org

ATTORNEYS

MALPRACTICE

Sections within this essay:

BACKGROUND

Malpractice is professional **negligence** or (less frequently) professional misconduct. Attorney malpractice generally implies an unreasonable lack of skill, or failure to render professional services in a manner consistent with that degree of skill, care, and learning expected of a reasonably competent and prudent member of the legal profession. Claims against attorneys (lawyers) for legal malpractice are viable in all 50 states. There is no federal law governing attorney malpractice, and state statutes typically address only the appropriate **statute of limitations** (limiting the time period) for filing claims or lawsuits against attorneys. However, state **case law** will define and set the parameters for actionable cases of malpractice within the state.

For legal malpractice to be "actionable" (having all the components necessary to constitute a viable cause of action), there must be a duty owed to someone, a breach of that duty, and resulting harm or damage that is proximately caused by that breach. The simplest way to apply the concept of proximate cause to legal malpractice is to ask whether, "but for" the alleged negligence, the harm or injury would have occurred?

ESTABLISHING THE ATTORNEY-CLIENT RELATIONSHIP

First and foremost, an attorney must owe a legal duty to a person before his or her **competency** in performing that duty can be judged. In U.S. **jurisprudence**, a lawyer has no affirmative duty to assist someone—in the absence of a special relationship with that person (such as doctor-patient, attorney-client, guardian-ward, etc.). That "special relationship" between attorney and client is generally established by mutual assent/consent. This is most often confirmed by a written "retainer" agreement in which the client expressly and exclusively retains a lawyer and his/her law firm to represent the client in a specific legal matter.

Under rare and limited circumstances, a court may infer that an attorney-client relationship existed as a matter of law, even without a **contract** or agreement between the parties, and even without the attorney's **assent**. Such a legal conclusion may be drawn from the facts presented, such as reliance on the part of the client (who believed in **good faith** that an attorney-client relationship existed) or by the fact that the attorney provided more than just informal or anecdotal opinion or answer to a question. The paying of a fee or **retainer** is not dispositive in determining whether an attorney-client relationship existed, and courts generally defer to the "client" and base their conclusions on—or at least give substantial weight to—whether the client believed such a relationship existed, confided in the attorney, and relied upon the professional relationship to his or her detriment.

In any event, once the requisite attorney-client relationship is established, the attorney owes to the client the duty to render legal service and **counsel** or advice with that degree of skill, care, and diligence as possessed by or expected of a reasonably competent attorney under the same or similar circumstances. The "circumstances" may include the area of law in which the attorney practices (although all attorneys are deemed to have basic legal skill and knowledge in the general practice of law), the customary or accepted practices of other attorneys in the area, and the particular circumstances or facts surrounding the representation. The requisite degree of skill and expertise under the circumstances is established by "expert testimony" from other practicing attorneys who share the same or similar skill, training, certification, and experience as the allegedly negligent attorney.

CONDUCT VS. PERFORMANCE

The practice of law requires state licensure. All 50 states have criteria governing admission to practice within their states. Although requirements may vary slightly, almost all states require graduation from an **accredited law school**, passing the "bar exam" (referring to the professional **bar association** of that state), and submitting to a review and investigation of one's personal background for assessment of "character and fitness" to practice law. Accordingly, all new lawyers start their profession with an acceptable level of professional competency (as determined by graduation from law school and passage of a comprehensive bar exam which gauges their professional knowledge of the law), as well as an acceptable level of character and fitness to practice law (as determined by the state bar review board).

Each state also has adopted codes of conduct, disciplinary rules, and adjudicative boards to address issues of misconduct once attorneys are admitted to practice. The American Bar Association also promulgates and promotes its Model Rules of Professional Conduct (adopted by the vast majority of states as of 2012).

Additionally, virtually all states now require periodic "updating" of technical and/or academic skills by the mandatory completion of a certain number of classroom or seminar hours each year. Attorneys may generally choose the topics in which these hours are completed, but there is usually a requirement that a minimum number of hours be completed in the area of "ethics." Attorneys who fail to complete these courses may not renew their license to practice for the upcoming year. Additional fines or penalties may apply.

That said, trained, licensed attorneys nonetheless may engage in questionable conduct, display a seeming lack of skill, or otherwise neglect or fail to properly render those duties owed to their clients, their adversaries, or to the judicial system as a whole, in their day-to-day practice of law. For those indiscretions and failures that have resulted in harm to a client, a lawsuit for legal malpractice may be an appropriate remedy.

WHAT CONSTITUTES ACTIONABLE MALPRACTICE

State laws govern the viability of causes of action for legal malpractice. The laws vary in terms of time limits to bring suit, qualifications of "expert" witnesses, cognizable theories of liability, and proper party defendants/proper party plaintiffs. Notwithstanding these differences, there are common themes for all cases, and general agreement from state to state on particular instances of nonfeasance or malfeasance of professional duties that may constitute legal malpractice.

Not all instances of malpractice involve an attorney's handling of a case for trial (although persons generally think of attorneys within the context of matters involving **litigation**). For example, an attorney may fail to file a request for variance in a county **zoning** matter involving a parcel of real property or may fail to catch an error on closing documents submitted to him/her. An attorney may erroneously advise a client about an area of law, e.g. foreign **adoption**. An attorney also may otherwise act on behalf of a client, against that client's express authority or permission. Any of these may constitute examples of actionable legal malpractice.

Omission or Failure to Do Something (Nonfeasance) At the top of the list of dreaded mistakes for any attorney is the failure to file a claim, notice, or lawsuit within the time prescribed by law. Inevitably, the client loses his or her right of action, and the entire cause is lost. Such a failure is "black and white" in the eyes of jurors, and disastrous for the client. Similarly, the failure to answer a claim, notice, or lawsuit on behalf of a client may result in **forfeiture**, loss of defense, or **default judgment** entered against a client, often **fatal** failures. A failure to appear in time to set aside a default judgment is equally serious. Unfortunately, courts do not consider that the error was made by the attorney and not the client. The client must sue the attorney for malpractice to recoup his or her loss.

Probably second to the above, in terms of occurrence and viability, is the failure to provide required notice.

Such failures may include the failure to notify potential heirs at law of a **probate** matter, failure to provide notice to creditors of a pending action, failure to post public notice regarding a real property action, failure to appear in court, or failure to notify a client of an offer to settle the case, received from the opposing party. These matters generally constitute actionable malpractice if the client has suffered harm or damage as a result of the alleged failures.

Third in line is that group of failures which are serious but not always fatal to a client's interest(s). These include such things as failure to file a certain motion in court, failure to name the right parties in a lawsuit (very serious if the time period for filing expires), failure to take or obtain certain **discovery** (documents or **evidence**), failure to object to the admission of certain evidence at trial (more serious), failure to raise certain issues or questions at depositions, public hearings, trials, arbitrations and mediations, etc.

Sometimes overlooked but nonetheless considered malpractice is the failure to communicate with a client and/or keep the client apprised of the status of the legal matter. However, such instances of malpractice are seldom "actionable" (because of impalpable damages) and are better addressed through a grievance process or letter of complaint.

The above instances of failures are not comprehensive and are intended only as representative by way of example. Not all occurrences of the above "failures" will result in actionable malpractice in all jurisdictions and under all factual scenarios.

Failure to Perform or Do Something Competently (Malfeasance) An attorney may be equally liable for malpractice if he or she performs the actions required by law but does so in an incompetent or substandard manner. For example, an attorney may timely file a cause of action in court, but the complaint may fail to contain important details or averments (allegations), resulting in **dismissal** of the suit. An attorney may take the **deposition** of a witness but ask irrelevant questions or fail to ask the necessary questions needed to elicit needed **testimony**. An attorney may prepare a last will and **testament** for a client but accidentally leave out or miswrite a very important **bequest**. An attorney may appear in time for a criminal **sentencing hearing** but be wholly unprepared or unfamiliar with the case or the issues.

All of the above examples represent situations requiring levels of skill generally attributable to or expected of any competent attorney practicing law in any state. They do not require specialized knowledge in any particular area of law and do not require advanced levels of legal experience or expertise. They are considered examples of fundamental practice of law. Breaches or failures of this type are generally preventable, avoidable, and therefore, actionable in most cases.

Within the context of litigation, it should be mentioned that in most states, a client's retention of an attorney to represent an action at trial implies that the client has delegated to the attorney all decision-making regarding the manner in which the trial should be conducted or the case should be presented. Even if the attorney loses the case, and a judgment is entered against his or her client, it does not mean that any malpractice was committed; after all, in every trial, at least one competent attorney loses and one wins. Under a broad area of attorney discretion, commonly referred to as "trial tactics," errors in judgment at trial (e.g., whether or not to present a certain witness or introduce certain evidence) which are not patently substandard for the profession, do not generally give rise to a cause of action for malpractice.

Acting Outside the Scope of Authority, Duty, or Area of Competence In addition, there are clear instances when attorneys should decline representation because they are not skilled enough—or do not possess the requisite subject matter knowledge—to provide competent representation for a client. For example, such legal matters as **wrongful death** by **medical malpractice**, complex **corporate** mergers or buy-outs, or complex financial transactions, should not be handled by new attorneys without supervision. Often, mistakes in taking on a new client are made when new attorneys want to "impress" their colleagues or superiors, or when sole practitioners need money or more cases.

An attorney retained to represent a client in one matter may unilaterally and without authority decide to represent a client, or act on the client's behalf, in another unrelated matter. The client may subsequently ratify the representation, or, if harmed, may sue for malpractice. Likewise, an attorney retained for a specific matter may unilaterally and without authority decide to accept an offer of **settlement** for a certain amount of money, without the client's authority. This is a good example of malpractice but may not be "actionable" malpractice if the client is unable to prove (by a preponderance) that he or she would have gotten more money had the matter gone to trial.

FILING A MALPRACTICE LAWSUIT

There are two important factors to remember about a cause of action for malpractice. First, a client should realize that a poor, unfair, or unexpected result does not mean that any malpractice occurred. Second, in the event that malpractice has occurred, the client must prove that he or she has suffered harm or loss due to the alleged wrongs on the part of an attorney. This is not as easy to prove as one might think. For example, if the alleged malpractice involved a matter in litigation, the client must prove that he or she would have won the case, such as in a case where the **jury** would have ruled in his or her favor, "but for" the alleged malpractice. This means that in proving a case for malpractice the client would have to actually "try" the "underlying case" before a real jury and win it in order to prove the point. Consequently, many lawsuits for malpractice are settled out of court to avoid the time, expense, and uncertainty of such a burden.

ALTERNATIVES FOR ADDRESSING MALPRACTICE

All states have attorney discipline boards or committees that accept informal or formal complaints from aggrieved clients. In matters that involve misconduct more than **incompetency**, this may be the forum of choice. Generally, disciplinary boards have authority to impose fines, order **restitution** to a client, and suspend or revoke a lawyer's license to practice law in that state. Clients also may wish to consider alternative dispute resolution, such as **arbitration** or **mediation**, to settle their claims of alleged malpractice.

It is worth noting that attorneys are generally required to advise their clients of known instances of actionable malpractice that have harmed the client or caused loss or damage. By far, the majority of attorneys are honest, competent, and committed to providing good service, and will so advise clients in the event of a known failure. However, what may appear to a layperson as "malpractice" at first blush, may in reality constitute no more than a decision or tactic employed by the attorney that conflicts with a client's expectation of likely action or outcome. Persons who believe that their attorneys may have committed malpractice are encouraged to consult with legal counsel who specialize in the area of professional malpractice.

BREACH OF FIDUCIARY DUTY

Clients who file legal malpractice claims also often file claims for breach of **fiduciary** duty. An attorney is a person in a position of trust and had a fiduciary relationship with the client. This means that the law requires the lawyer to act in the client's best interests and not engage in forms of self-dealing or situations where the attorney has a **conflict of interest**. For instance, a lawyer will often hold a client's money in trust. It would be a breach of fiduciary duty if the lawyer used these funds for the lawyers own needs, such as making a short-term investment.

Similar to facts leading to malpractice claims, facts that show a breach of fiduciary duty may lead not only to

an action for civil damages but also may be the basis for a state bar association to discipline an attorney.

SELECT STATE LAWS

The summaries listed are examples of state laws that apply to legal malpractice.

CALIFORNIA: Actions for legal malpractice must be brought within one year of discovery of a claim, with a maximum four years' limitation from the date of the alleged wrong. Proc: Section 340.6.

CONNECTICUT: Actions for legal malpractice must be brought within two years of discovery, with a maximum three years' limitation from the date of the alleged wrong. Section 52-584.

ILLINOIS: Actions for legal malpractice must be brought within a maximum of six years from discovery of the alleged wrong 735 ILCS 5/13/214/3.

KANSAS: Actions for legal malpractice must be brought within two years of discovery, with a maximum four years' limitation from the date of the alleged wrong. Section 60-513(a)(7), 60-513(c).

KENTUCKY: Actions for professional service malpractice must be brought within one year from discovery. Section 413-245.

LOUISIANA: Actions for legal malpractice must be brought within one year of the injury. This period begins when the client "knew of the existence of facts which would have enabled him to state a cause of action for legal malpractice."

MAINE: Actions for legal malpractice must be brought within two years, Section 753-A.

MISSISSIPPI: Actions for professional malpractice must be brought within two years. Section 15-1-36.

MONTANA: Actions for legal malpractice must be brought within three years from discovery, with a maximum ten years' limitation from the date of the alleged wrong. Section 27-2-206.

NEVADA: Actions for legal malpractice must be brought within four years. Section 11.207.

NEW JERSEY: New Jersey courts follow section 53 of the Restatement of the Law Governing Lawyers, which provides: "Legal-malpractice actions (for negligence ... and for fiduciary breach ...) are subject to generally applicable principles of causation and damages."

NEW YORK: New York courts have established that a **plaintiff** in a legal malpractice suit must show that but for the defendant's negligence, the plaintiff would have prevailed in the underlying action or would not have sustained any damages. However, "mere speculation about a loss resulting from an attorney's alleged omission is insufficient to sustain a **prima facie** case of legal malpractice."

PENNSYLVANIA: Under Pennsylvania law, "A cause of action for legal malpractice contains three elements: the plaintiff's employment of the attorney or other grounds for imposition of a duty; the attorney's neglect to exercise ordinary skill and knowledge; and the occurrence of damage to the plaintiff proximately caused by the attorney's misfeasance."

RHODE ISLAND: Actions for legal malpractice must be brought within three years. Section 9-1-14.1 and 9-1-14.3.

SOUTH DAKOTA: Actions for legal malpractice must be brought within three years. Section 15-2-14.2.

TENNESSEE: Actions for legal malpractice must be brought within one year Section 28-3-104.

ADDITIONAL RESOURCES

Johnson, Vincent R. *Legal Malpractice Law in a Nutshell.* Eagan, MN: West, Thomson Reuters, 2011.

———. *Legal Malpractice Law: Problems and Prevention.* Eagan, MN: West, Thomson Reuters, 2008.

Legal Malpractice: The Law Office Guide to Purchasing Legal Malpractice Insurance. Annual. Eagan, MN: West, Thomson Reuters, 2012.

ORGANIZATIONS

American Bar Association (ABA)
321 North Clark Street
Chicago, IL 60610
Phone: (202) 662-1000
Toll Free: (800) 285-2221
Fax: (312) 988-6800
URL: http://www.americanbar.org

National Bar Association
1225 11th Street, NW
Washington, DC 20001
Phone: (202) 842-3900
Fax: (202) 289-6170
URL: http://www.nationalbar.org

National Lawyers Association
3000 S. Jamaica Ct., Ste. 390
Aurora, CO 80014
Toll Free: (800) 471-2994
Fax: (303) 979-6094
URL: http://www.nla.org

National Organization of Bar Counsel
515 Fifth Street, N.W.
Washington, DC 64196
Phone: (202) 638-1501
Fax: (202) 662-1777
URL: http://www.nobc.org

BANKING

BANKING AND LENDING LAW

Sections within this essay:

- Background
- Bank Transactions
  - Checks and Other Negotiable Instruments
  - Checking Accounts
  - Funds Transfers
  - Letters of Credit
  - Secured Transactions

- Federal Reserve System
- Insurance of Deposits
- Interest Rates Charged by Banks
- Truth in Lending
- Usury Laws
- Crimes Related to Banks and Banking
- State Laws Governing Banks, Banking, and Lending
- Additional Resources

BACKGROUND

The law governing banks, bank accounts, and lending in the United States is a hybrid of federal and state **statutory** law. Consumers and businesses may establish bank accounts in banks and savings associations chartered under state or federal law. The law under which a bank is chartered regulates that particular bank. A mix of state and federal law, however, governs most operations and transactions by bank customers.

Article 3 of the **Uniform Commercial Code**, as adopted by the various states, governs transactions involving negotiable instruments, including checks. Article 4 of the Uniform Commercial Code governs bank deposits and collections, including the rights and responsibilities of **depository** banks, collecting banks, and banks responsible for the payment of a check. Other provisions of the Uniform Commercial Code are also relevant to banking and lending law, including Article 4A (related to funds transfers), Article 5 (related to letters of credit), Article 8 (related to **securities**), and Article 9 (related to secured transactions).

A number of regulations govern a check when it passes through the Federal Reserve System. These regulations govern the availability of funds available to a depositor in his or her bank account, the delay between the time a bank receives a deposit and the time the funds should be made available, and the process to follow when a check is not honored for non-payment. Federal law also provides protection to bank customers. Prompted by banking crises in the 1930s, the federal government established the Federal Deposit Insurance Corporation, which insures bank accounts of individuals and institutions in amounts up to $100,000.

A number of laws have been passed affecting banks, banking, and lending. These include:

- National Bank Act of 1864 established a national banking systems and chartering of national banks.
- Federal Reserve Act of 1913 established the Federal Reserve System. Banking Act of 1933 (**Glass-Steagall Act**) established the Federal Deposit Insurance Corporation (FDIC), originally intended to be temporary.

- Banking Act of 1935 established the FDIC as a permanent agency.
- Federal Deposit Insurance Act of 1950 revised and consolidated previous laws governing the FDIC.
- Bank **Holding Company** Act of 1956 set forth requirements for the establishment of bank holding companies.
- International Banking Act of 1978 required foreign banks to fit within the federal regulatory framework.
- Financial Institutions Regulatory and Interest Rate Control Act of 1978 created the Federal Financial Institutions Examination Council. It also established limits and reporting requirements for insider transactions involving banks and modified provisions governing transfers of electronic funds.
- Depository Institutions Deregulation and Monetary Control Act of 1980 began to eliminate ceilings on **interest rates** of savings and other accounts and raised the insurance ceiling of insured account holders to $100,000.
- Depository Institutions Act of 1982 (Gar-St. Germain Act) expanded the powers of the FDIC and further eliminated ceilings on interest rates. Competitive Equality Banking Act of 1987 established new standards for the availability of expedited funds and further expanded FDIC authority.
- Financial Institutions Reform, Recovery, and Enforcement Act of 1989 set forth a number of reforms and revisions, designed to ensure trust in the savings and loan industry.
- Crime Control Act of 1990 expanded the ability of federal regulators to combat **fraud** in financial institutions.
- Federal Deposit Insurance Corporation Act of 1991 expanded the power and authority of the FDIC considerably.
- Housing and Community Development Act of 1992 set forth provisions to combat **money laundering** and provided some regulatory relief to certain financial institutions.
- Riegle Community Development and Regulatory Improvement Act of 1994 established the Community Development Financial Institutions Fund to provide assistance to community development financial institutions.
- Riegle-Neal Interstate Banking and Branching Efficiency Act of 1994 permitted bank holding companies that were adequately capitalized and managed to acquire banks in any state.
- Economic Growth and Regulatory Paperwork Reduction Act of 1996 brought forth a number of changes, many of which related to the modification of regulation of financial institutions.
- Gramm-Leach Bliley Act of 1999 brought forth numerous changes, including the restriction of disclosure of nonpublic customer information by financial institutions. The Act provided penalties for anyone who obtains nonpublic customer information from a financial institution under false pretenses.
- Dodd-Frank Financial Reform Act of 2010 sought to curb risky practices by large U.S. banks that led to the Great Recession of 2008.

Numerous federal agencies promulgate regulations relevant to banks and banking, including the Federal Deposit Insurance Corporation, Federal Reserve Board, General Accounting Office, National Credit Union Administration, and Treasury Department.

The ability for bank customers to engage in electronic banking has had a significant effect on the laws of banking in the United States. Some laws that govern paper checks and other traditional instruments are difficult to apply to corresponding electronic transfers. As technology develops and affects the banking industry, banking law was expected to continue to change.

BANKING TRANSACTIONS

Checks and Other Negotiable Instruments Article 3 of the Uniform Commercial Code, drafted by the National Conference of Commissioners on Uniform State Laws and adopted in every state except Louisiana, governs the creation and transfer of negotiable instruments. Since checks are negotiable instruments, the provisions in Article 3 apply. Because banks are lending institutions that create notes and other instruments, Article 3 will also apply in other circumstances that do not involve checks.

A person who establishes an account at a bank may make a written order on that account in the form of a check. The account holder is called the drawer, while the person named on the check is called the payee. When the drawer orders the bank to pay the person named in the check, the bank is obligated to do so and reduce the drawer's account by the amount on the check. A bank ordinarily has no obligation to honor a check from a person other than a depositor. However, both the drawer's and payee's banks generally must honor these checks if there are sufficient funds to cover the amount of the check. The payee's bank must generally honor a check written to the order of the payee if the payee has sufficient funds to cover the amount of the check, in case the drawer of the check does not have sufficient funds. A drawer may request from the bank a **certified check**, which means the check is guaranteed. Certified checks must be honored by any bank, and, as such, are considered the same as cash.

A customer's bank has a duty to know each customer's signature. If another party forges the signature of the customer, the customer is generally not liable for the amount of the check. Banks may recover from the forger but may not generally recover from the innocent customer or a third person who in **good faith** and without notice of the **forgery** gave cash or other items of value in exchange for the check. Drawers have the right to inspect all checks charged against their accounts to ensure that no forgeries have occurred. Drawers also have rights to stop payment on checks that have been neither paid nor certified by their banks. This is done through a **stop payment order** issued by the customer to the bank. If a bank pays a check despite the stop payment order, the bank is liable to the customer for the value of the check.

Many of the rules that apply to checks apply to all negotiable instruments. Banks that serve as lending institutions routinely exchange loans for promissory notes, which are typically negotiable instruments. These instruments are considered property and may be bought and sold by other entities.

Checking Accounts Article 4 of the Uniform Commercial Code governs the operation of checking accounts, though several federal laws supplement the provisions of Article 4. The provisions of this uniform law define rights regarding bank deposits and collections. It governs such relationships as those between a depository bank and a collecting bank and those between a payor bank and its customers.

Funds Transfers Article 4A of the Uniform Commercial Code governs methods of payment whereby a person making a payment (called the "originator") transmits directly an instruction to a bank to make a payment to a third person (called the "beneficiary"). Article 4A covers the issuance and acceptance of a payment order from a customer to a bank, the **execution** of a payment order by a receiving bank and the actual payment of the payment order.

Letters of Credit Article 5 of the Uniform Commercial Code governs transactions involving the issuance of letters of credit. Such letters of credit are generally issued when a party (the "applicant") applies for credit in a transaction of some sort with a third party (the "beneficiary"). The bank will issue a letter of credit to the **beneficiary** prior to the transaction. This letter is a definite undertaking by the bank to honor the letter of credit at the time the beneficiary presents the letter. Article 5 governs issuance, amendments, cancellation, duration, transfer, and assignment of letters of credit. It also defines the rights and obligations of the parties involved in the issuance of a letter of credit.

Secured Transactions When a bank agrees to enter into a loan agreement with a bank customer, the bank will most likely acquire a security interest in property owned or purchased by the customer. This transaction, called a secured transaction, is governed by Article 9 of the Uniform Commercial Code. Article 9 was substantially revised in 2000, and the vast majority of states have now adopted the revised version. The security interest provides protection for the bank in case the customer fails to pay a debt owed to the bank, even if the customer enters **bankruptcy**. A number of steps must be followed for the bank to "perfect" the security interest, including the filing of documents with the secretary of state or other appropriate officer in the state where the customer resides.

FEDERAL RESERVE SYSTEM

The Federal Reserve Board has been delegated significant responsibility related to the implementation of laws governing banks and banking. The Board has issued more than thirty major regulations on a variety of issues affecting the banking industry. When a check passes through the Federal Reserve System, Regulation J applies. This regulation governs the collection of checks and other items by Federal Reserve Banks, as well as many funds transfers. This regulation also establishes procedures, responsibilities, and duties among Federal Reserve banks, the payors, and other senders of checks through the Federal Reserve System, and the senders of wire transmissions. Regulation J is contained in Title 12 of the **Code of Federal Regulations**, Part 210.

A second significant regulation promulgated by the Federal Reserve Board is Regulation CC, which governs the availability of funds in a bank customer's account. This regulation also governs the collection of checks. Under this regulation, cash deposits made by a customer to a bank account must be available to the customer no later than the end of the business day after the day the funds were deposited. The next-day rule also applies to several check deposits, according to the regulation, although banks are not required to make funds available for as long as five days after deposit for many other types of checks. Regulation CC also governs the payment of interest, the responsibilities of various banks regarding the return of checks. Liabilities to the bank for failure to adhere to these rules are defined by the regulation. Regulation CC is contained in Title 12 of the Code of Federal Regulations, Part 229.

Other Federal Reserve Board regulations cover a variety of transactions under a myriad of statutes. These include such provisions as those requiring equal credit opportunity; transfer of electronic funds; consumer leasing; **privacy** of consumer financial information; and truth in lending.

INSURANCE OF DEPOSITS

Congress in 1933 established the Federal Deposit Insurance Corporation, which is funded by premiums paid by member institutions. If a customer holds an account at a bank that is a member institution of the FDIC, the customer's accounts are insured for an aggregate total of $250,000. Banks that are member institutions are required to prominently display signs indicating that the bank is a member of the FDIC or a sign that states "Deposits Federally Insured to $250,000—Backed by the Full Faith and Credit of the United States Government." This applies to many banks that are chartered either federally or by state **statute**.

INTEREST RATES CHARGED BY BANKS

The federal government until the early 1980s regulated interest rates charged on bank accounts. Interest rates on savings accounts were generally limited, while interest rates on other types of accounts were generally prohibited. The Depository Institutions Deregulation Act of 1980 and Garn-St. Germain Depository Institutions Act eliminated restrictions and prohibitions on interest rates on savings, checking, money market and other types of accounts.

TRUTH IN LENDING

The Truth in Lending Act, which was part of the **Consumer Credit Protection Act**, provides protection to consumers by requiring lenders to disclose costs and terms related to a loan. Most of these disclosures are contained in a loan application. Lenders must include several of the following items:

- Terms and costs of loan plans, including annual percentage rates, fees, and points
- The total amount of principal being financed
- Payment due dates, including provisions for late payment fees
- Details of variable-interest loans
- Total amount of finance charges
- Details about whether a loan is assumable
- Application fees
- Pre-payment penalties

The Truth in Lending Act also requires lenders to make certain disclosures regarding advertisements for loan rates and terms. Specific terms of the credit must be disclosed, and if the advertisement indicates a rate, it must be stated in terms of an **annual percentage rate**, which takes into account additional costs incurred relating to the loan. Other restrictions on advertising loan rates also apply. If a bank or other lending institution fails to adhere to the provision of the Truth in Lending Act, severe penalties apply.

The Federal Reserve Board has been delegated authority to prescribe regulations to enforce the provisions of the Truth in Lending Act. These regulations are contained in Regulation Z of the Board.

USURY LAWS

Every state establishes a ceiling interest rate that can be charged by creditors. If a **creditor** charges an interest rate higher than the rate established by the state, the penalties to the creditor can be severe. Such penalties may include the **forfeiture** of the principal debt owed to the creditor by the **debtor**. Debtors that are subjected to high interest rates should consult the **usury** laws in that state to determine whether these laws may apply.

CRIMES RELATED TO BANKS AND BANKING

Congress has promulgated a number of criminal statutes applicable to crimes against banks and banking institutions. Some crimes are related to more violent acts, such as robbery, while others focus on non-violent crimes, such as money laundering. Each of the crimes listed below is contained in Title 18 of the United States Code.

- Bank **bribery** is prohibited under Title 18, sections 212 through 215.
- Theft by a bank officer or employee is prohibited under Title 18, section 656.
- False bank entry is prohibited under Title 18, section 1005.
- False statements to the FDIC are prohibited under Title 18, section 1007.
- Bank fraud is prohibited under Title 18, section 1344.
- Obstruction of an examination of a financial institution is prohibited under Title 18, section 1517.
- Money laundering is prohibited under Title 18, sections 1956 through 1960.
- Bank robbery is prohibited under Title 18, section 2113.
- Crimes involving coins and currency are prohibited under provisions in Title 18, Chapter 17.

STATE LAWS GOVERNING BANKS, BANKING, AND LENDING

All U.S. states have adopted at least a portion of the Uniform Commercial Code, including Articles 3 (1990 version), 4 (1990 version), 4A (1989 version), and 5 (1995 version). Article 9 was last revised in 2000, with the previous major revision occurring in 1972. Most state laws governing banks, banking, and lending are consistent from one state to the next. Moreover, due to federal regulation of banks and banking, states are rather limited in their ability to enact laws that differ from the majority of states.

ALABAMA: Adopted Articles 3 and 4 in 1995; Article 4A in 1992; and Article 5 in 1997. The state has adopted the Revised Article 9 (2000).

ALASKA: Adopted Articles 3 and 4 in 1993; Article 4A in 1993; and Article 5 in 1999. The state adopted the majority of the provisions in the Revised Article 9 (2000) in 2000.

ARIZONA: Adopted Articles 3 and 4 in 1993; Article 4A in 1991; and Article 5 in 1996. The state has adopted the Revised Article 9 (2000).

ARKANSAS: Adopted Articles 3 and 4 in 1991; Article 4A in 1991; and Article 5 in 1997. The state has adopted the Revised Article 9 (2000).

CALIFORNIA: Adopted Articles 3 and 4 in 1992; Article 4A in 1990; and Article 5 in 1996. The state has adopted the Revised Article 9 (2000).

COLORADO: Adopted Articles 3 and 4 in 1994; Article 4A in 1990; and Article 5 in 1996. The state has adopted the Revised Article 9 (2000).

CONNECTICUT: Adopted Articles 3 and 4 in 1991; Article 4A in 1990; and Article 5 in 1996. The state has adopted the Revised Article 9 (2000).

DELAWARE: Adopted Articles 3 and 4 in 1995; Article 4A in 1992; and Article 5 in 1998. The state adopted the majority of the provisions in the Revised Article 9 (2000) in 2000.

FLORIDA: Adopted Articles 3 and 4 in 1992; Article 4A in 1991; and Article 5 in 1999. The state has adopted the Revised Article 9 (2000).

GEORGIA: Adopted Articles 3 and 4 in 1996; Article 4A in 1993. The state has adopted the Revised Article 9 (2000).

HAWAII: Adopted Articles 3 and 4 in 1991; Article 4A in 1991; and Article 5 in 1996. The state adopted the majority of the provisions in the Revised Article 9 (2000) in 2000.

IDAHO: Adopted Articles 3 and 4 in 1993; Article 4A in 1991; and Article 5 in 1996. The state has adopted the Revised Article 9 (2000).

ILLINOIS: Adopted Articles 3 and 4 in 1991; Article 4A in 1990; and Article 5 in 1996. The state adopted the majority of the provisions in the Revised Article 9 (2000) in 2000.

INDIANA: Adopted Articles 3 and 4 in 1991; Article 4A in 1991; and Article 5 in 1996. The state adopted the majority of the provisions in the Revised Article 9 (2000) in 2000.

IOWA: Adopted Articles 3 and 4 in 1994; Article 4A in 1992; and Article 5 in 1996. The state adopted the majority of the provisions in the Revised Article 9 (2000) in 2000.

KANSAS: Adopted Articles 3 and 4 in 1991; Article 4A in 1990; and Article 5 in 1996. The state adopted the majority of the provisions in the Revised Article 9 (2000) in 2000.

KENTUCKY: Adopted Articles 3 and 4 in 1996; Article 4A in 1992; and Article 5 in 2000. The state adopted the majority of the provisions in the Revised Article 9 (2000) in 2000.

LOUISIANA: Adopted Articles 3 and 4 in 1992; Article 4A in 1990; and Article 5 in 1999. The state has adopted the Revised Article 9 (2000).

MAINE: Adopted Articles 3 and 4 in 1993; Article 4A in 1992; and Article 5 in 1997. The state adopted the majority of the provisions in the Revised Article 9 (2000) in 2000.

MARYLAND: Adopted Articles 3 and 4 in 1996; Article 4A in 1992; and Article 5 in 1997. The state has adopted the Revised Article 9 (2000).

MASSACHUSETTS: Adopted Articles 3 and 4 in 1998; Article 4A in 1992; and Article 5 in 1998. The state has adopted the Revised Article 9 (2000).

MICHIGAN: Adopted Articles 3 and 4 in 1993; Article 4A in 1992; and Article 5 in 1992. The state adopted the majority of the provisions in the Revised Article 9 (2000) in 2000.

MINNESOTA: Adopted Articles 3 and 4 in 1992; Article 4A in 1990; and Article 5 in 1997. The state adopted the majority of the provisions in the Revised Article 9 (2000) in 2000.

MISSISSIPPI: Adopted Articles 3 and 4 in 1995; Article 4A in 1992; and Article 5 in 1997. The state has adopted the Revised Article 9 (2000).

MISSOURI: Adopted Articles 3 and 4 in 1992; Article 4A in 1992; and Article 5 in 1997. The state has adopted the Revised Article 9 (2000).

MONTANA: Adopted Articles 3 and 4 in 1991; Article 4A in 1991; and Article 5 in 1997. The state has adopted the Revised Article 9 (2000).

NEBRASKA: Adopted Articles 3 and 4 in 1991; Article 4A in 1991; and Article 5 in 1996. The state has adopted the Revised Article 9 (2000).

NEVADA: Adopted Articles 3 and 4 in 1993; Article 4A in 1991; and Article 5 in 1997. The state has adopted the Revised Article 9 (2000).

NEW HAMPSHIRE: Adopted Articles 3 and 4 in 1993; Article 4A in 1993; and Article 5 in 1998. The state has adopted the Revised Article 9 (2000).

NEW JERSEY: Adopted Articles 3 and 4 in 1995; Article 4A in 1995; and Article 5 in 1998. The state has adopted the Revised Article 9 (2000).

NEW MEXICO: Adopted Articles 3 and 4 in 1992; Article 4A in 1992; and Article 5 in 1997. The state has adopted the Revised Article 9 (2000).

NEW YORK: Adopted older uniform law on negotiable instruments in 1897; Article 4A in 1990; and Article 5 in 2000. The state has adopted the Revised Article 9 (2000).

NORTH CAROLINA: Adopted Articles 3 and 4 in 1995; Article 4A in 1993; and Article 5 in 1999. The state

adopted the majority of the provisions in the Revised Article 9 (2000) in 2000.

NORTH DAKOTA: Adopted Articles 3 and 4 in 1991; Article 4A in 1991; and Article 5 in 1997. The state has adopted the Revised Article 9 (2000).

OHIO: Adopted Articles 3 and 4 in 1994; Article 4A in 1991; and Article 5 in 1997. The state has adopted the Revised Article 9 (2000).

OKLAHOMA: Adopted Articles 3 and 4 in 1991; Article 4A in 1990; and Article 5 in 1996. The state adopted the majority of the provisions in the Revised Article 9 (2000) in 2000.

OREGON: Adopted Articles 3 and 4 in 1995; Article 4A in 1992; and Article 5 in 1997. The state has adopted the Revised Article 9 (2000).

PENNSYLVANIA: Adopted Articles 3 and 4 in 1992; Article 4A in 1992; and Article 5 in 2001. The state has adopted the Revised Article 9 (2000).

RHODE ISLAND: Adopted Articles 3 and 4 in 2000; Article 4A in 1991; and Article 5 in 2000. The state adopted the majority of the provisions in the Revised Article 9 (2000) in 2000.

SOUTH CAROLINA: Adopted older uniform law on negotiable instruments in 1914; Article 4A in 1996; and Article 5 in 2001. The state has adopted the Revised Article 9 (2000).

SOUTH DAKOTA: Adopted Articles 3 and 4 in 1994; Article 4A in 1991; and Article 5 in 1998. The state adopted the majority of the provisions in the Revised Article 9 (2000) in 2000.

TENNESSEE: Adopted Articles 3 and 4 in 1994; Article 4A in 1991; and Article 5 in 1998. The state adopted the majority of the provisions in the Revised Article 9 (2000) in 2000.

TEXAS: Adopted Articles 3 and 4 in 1994; Article 4A in 1991; and Article 5 in 1998. The state has adopted the Revised Article 9 (2000).

UTAH: Adopted Articles 3 and 4 in 1993; Article 4A in 1990; and Article 5 in 1997. The state adopted the majority of the provisions in the Revised Article 9 (2000) in 2000.

VERMONT: Adopted Articles 3 and 4 in 1994; Article 4A in 1994; and Article 5 in 1998. The state adopted the majority of the provisions in the Revised Article 9 (2000) in 2000.

VIRGINIA: Adopted Articles 3 and 4 in 1992; Article 4A in 1990; and Article 5 in 1997. The state adopted the majority of the provisions in the Revised Article 9 (2000) in 2000.

WASHINGTON: Adopted Articles 3 and 4 in 1994; Article 4A in 1991; and Article 5 in 1998. The state adopted the majority of the provisions in the Revised Article 9 (2000) in 2000.

WEST VIRGINIA: Adopted Articles 3 and 4 in 1993; Article 4A in 1990; and Article 5 in 1996. The state adopted the majority of the provisions in the Revised Article 9 (2000) in 2000.

WISCONSIN: Adopted Articles 3 and 4 in 1996; and Article 4A in 1992. The state has adopted the Revised Article 9 (2000).

WYOMING: Adopted Articles 3 and 4 in 1991; Article 4A in 1991; and Article 5 in 1997. The state has adopted the Revised Article 9 (2000).

ADDITIONAL RESOURCES

Code of Federal Regulations, Title 12: Banks and Banking. U.S. Government Printing Office, 2012. Available at http://www.access.gpo.gov/nara/cfr/cfr-table-search.html (accessed November 3, 2012).

"Consumer Financial Rights." Federal Deposit Insurance Corporation, 2012. Available at http://www.fdic.gov/consumers/consumer/rights/index.html (accessed November 3, 2012).

Durkin, Thomas A., and Gregory Elliehausen. *Truth in Lending: Theory, History, and a Way Forward.* New York: Oxford University Press, 2011.

Lovett, William A. *Banking and Financial Institutions Law in a Nutshell.* 7th ed. Eagan, MN: West, Thomson Reuters, 2009.

Mannimo, Edward F., and Richard E. Kaye. *Lender Liability and Banking Litigation.* New York: Law Journal Press, 2006.

ORGANIZATIONS

Board of Governors of the Federal Reserve System, Division of Consumer and Community Affairs
20th and C Streets, NW, MS 804
Washington, DC 20551
Phone: (202) 452-3667
URL: http://www.federalreserve.gov/

Customer Assistance Group, Office of the Comptroller of the Currency
1301 McKinney, Suite 3710
Houston, TX 77010
Toll Free: (800) 613-6743
URL: http://www.occ.treas.gov/

Federal Deposit Insurance Corporation (FDIC)
550 17th Street, NW
Washington, DC 20429-9990
Toll Free: (877) ASK-FDIC
URL: http://www.fdic.gov

National Conference of Commissioners on Uniform State Laws (NCCUSL)
211 E. Ontario Street, Suite 1300
Chicago, IL 60611
Phone: (312) 915-0195
Fax: (312) 915-0187
Email: nccusl@nccusl.org
URL: http://www.nccusl.org/

BANKING

BANKS, SAVINGS & LOANS, CREDIT UNIONS

Sections within this essay:

- Background
- Types of Financial Institutions
  - Banks
  - Savings and Loan Institutions
  - Credit Unions
- Automated Teller Machines (ATMs)
- Online Banking
- Federal Laws
- Additional Resources

BACKGROUND

Banks are only one of several kinds of financial institutions that offer financial services to their patrons. The term "bank" is often used as a collective term to describe any one of the numerous forms of financial institutions. Banks, like most other bank-like financial institutions, are established by charters. A charter is official permission from a regulating authority (like a state) to accept deposits and/or to provide financial services. Charters provide the specifics of a bank's powers and obligations. State and federal governments closely regulate banks and bank accounts. Accounts for customers may be established by national and state financial institutions, all of which are regulated by the law under which they are established.

The federal government regulated and controlled **interest rates** on bank accounts for many decades. There was a cap on interest rates for savings accounts, and most interest bearing payments-on-demand deposit accounts (e.g. checking accounts) were prohibited. Banks were also prevented from offering money market accounts. However, sweeping changes in banking law in the early 1980s transformed the way banks and other financial institutions do business. For example, interest rate controls on savings accounts were eliminated by the Depository Institutions Deregulation Act of 1980 (DIDRA), and the Garn-St Germain Depository Institutions Act and the DIDRA lifted restrictions on checking and money market accounts.

One common and important service offered by banking institutions is the checking account. Federal and state laws govern the operation of checking accounts. Article 4 of the **Uniform Commercial Code**, which has been adopted at least in part by every state, enumerates the rights and obligations between financial institutions and their customers with respect to bank deposits and collections. The five principal sections of Article 4 cover:

1. general provisions and definitions

2. the actions of one bank in accepting the check of another and those of other banks that handle the check but are not responsible for its final payment

3. the actions of the bank responsible for payment of the check

4. the relationship between the bank responsible for payment of the check and its customers

5. the handling of documentary drafts, which are checks or other types of drafts that will only be honored if

---

Prudential regulators and their basic functions for banking institutions

Agency	Basic function
Office of the Comptroller of the Currency	Charters and supervises national banks and federal thrifts
Board of Governors of the Federal Reserve System	Supervises state-chartered banks that opt to be members of the Federal Reserve System, bank holding companies, thrift holding companies, and the nondepository institution subsidiaries of those institutions
Federal Deposit Insurance Corporation	Supervises Federal Deposit Insurance Corporation (FDIC)-insured state-chartered banks that are not members of the Federal Reserve System, as well as federally insured state savings banks and thrifts; insures the deposits of all banks and thrifts that are approved for federal deposit insurance; and resolves all failed insured banks and thrifts and certain nonbank financial companies
National Credit Union Administration	Charters and supervises federally chartered credit unions and insures savings in federal and most state-chartered credit unions

Note: All banking institutions that offer federal deposit insurance have a prudential regulator.

SOURCE: U.S. Government Accountability Office. *Community Banks and Credit Unions: Impact of the Dodd-Frank Act Depends Largely on Future Rule Makings*, September 2012.

TABLE BY PREMEDIAGLOBAL. ©2013 CENGAGE LEARNING.

---

certain papers are first presented to the institution responsible for payment of the draft

Checks are commercial documents called "negotiable instruments." Negotiable instruments are mainly governed by Article 3 of the Uniform Commercial Code. All states have adopted Article 3 of the Uniform Commercial Code (UCC), with some modifications, as the law governing negotiable instruments. Other types of negotiable instruments include drafts and notes. Drafts are documents ordering some type of payment to be made to a person or an institution. Checks are one kind of draft. Notes are documents promising payment will be made. A **mortgage** is a kind of note. Money, investment **securities**, and some forms of payment orders are not considered negotiable instruments under Article 3.

In the Great Depression, banks that could not meet their financial obligations to their customers or their creditors failed, going bankrupt. Because the deposits were not insured, individuals and businesses with money on deposit at the time a bank failed lost whatever was in the account immediately. The Depression and the banking crisis of the 1930s gave rise to the development of federal insurance for deposits administered by the Federal Deposit Insurance Corporation (FDIC). The program is funded from premiums paid by member institutions. Under the FDIC, individual bank accounts at insured institutions are protected up to $250,000. Multiple accounts in a single financial institution and belonging to the same customer are combined for purposes of the FDIC limits.

Banks are strictly regulated by three federal agencies. Banks are also subject to regulation by state bank regulators.

The federal agencies are given below:

- Comptroller of the Currency (for national banks)
- Federal Deposit Insurance Corporation
- Federal Reserve Board

States regulate banks through their banking commission or department of banking and finance. An official called the Commissioner or Director or Superintendent of Banks manages the state's banking commission or department of banking and finance. These state banking authorities may regulate only banks that have been chartered by the state.

The Gramm-Leach-Bliley Act of 1999 is one of the most significant pieces of banking legislation in over fifty years. This law is the result of decades of effort to restructure the U.S. financial system. The Gramm-Leach-Bliley Act is complex and far-reaching, and contains a host of banking and financial services issues. Perhaps the most important feature of the Act is that it permits formal affiliations among banks, securities firms, and insurance companies. Federal law barred such affiliations beginning in the Great Depression in the 1930s because banks speculated too much in their investments and risked depositor's funds. With the passage and implementation of 1999 Act, the entire U.S. banking industry was transformed. However, the economic recession at the end of the first decade of the 2000s revealed the same speculative fever of the 1920s by the banking industry. The largest U.S. banks were "too big to fail," so the federal government provided enormous sums of capital to bail out these institutions. As a result, Congress passed the Dodd-Frank Financial Reform Act in 2010. The act seeks to curb the excesses of the banking industry without reverting to the regulations of the 1930s.

TYPES OF FINANCIAL INSTITUTIONS

Banks In common parlance the term "bank" refers to many types of financial institutions. In addition to a bank, the term can refer to a **trust company**, a savings bank, savings and loan institution, credit union, thrift, thrift and loan, or trust company.

There is a wide variety of banking institutions. The differences among these financial institutions are the result of both history and politics. Some banks may be regulated and supervised by different federal and/or state agencies. While these institutions may appear quite similar, they actually have different rights, powers, and obligations; they may even have different tax obligations. Savings and loan associations must invest more of their assets in home mortgages than traditional banks. Trust companies manage and administer trust funds of individuals and **pension** plans but may not take deposits into checking or savings accounts. Credit unions enjoy certain tax advantages. Some banking institutions have special deposit insurance arrangements. Some financial institutions can sell other financial services or products—like insurance—and other financial institutions may not. In addition, some financial institutions must put significant cash reserves on deposit with the federal government, whereas others do not.

Banks that are chartered by the Comptroller of the Currency are called "national banks." National banks usually bear the words "national" or "national association" in their titles; sometimes they carry the letters N. A. or N. S. & T. in their titles.

Savings and Loan Institutions The primary function of savings and loan associations is the financing of long-term residential mortgages. Savings and loan associations accept deposits in savings accounts, pay interest on these accounts, and make loans to residential homebuyers. They do not make business loans of any kind, nor do they provide many of the other business services one finds in commercial banks. A privately managed home financing institution, a savings and loan accepts savings accounts from individuals and other sources. This money is then principally invested in loans for the construction, purchase, or improvement of homes.

Savings and loan associations are primarily involved in making residential loans. Consequently, they may be good sources of indirect business financing for home-owners who own substantial equity in their homes. For example, if homeowners need money for their businesses, they can refinance their homes or take out a second mortgage on the equity through a savings and loan association. The home equity loan application process at a savings and loan association is generally simpler than it is for a commercial bank because it is made on the equity of the home up to a maximum percentage of the equity, usually between 75 percent to 80 percent. The savings and loan association bears little risk if the home is located in a stable or appreciating market value area. If the

borrower defaults on the loan, the savings and loan association can foreclose the mortgage and sell the property to retire the loan, often for a profit.

Credit Unions The first credit union in the United States was formed in Manchester, New Hampshire, in 1909. As of 2012, there are over 10,000 credit unions in the United States. They control assets of nearly one trillion dollars and serve about 43% of the population. Credit unions are members–only institutions. Individuals must join a credit union to take advantage of its services but they cannot join just any credit union—they must first be eligible for membership. Most credit unions are organized to serve members of a particular community, group or groups of employees, or members of an organization or association. Large **corporations**, unions, or educational institutions are some of the groups who commonly form credit unions for their members or employees.

Federal credit unions are nonprofit, cooperative financial institutions owned and operated by their members. Credit unions are democratically controlled with members given the opportunity to vote on important issues that affect the running of the credit union. For example, the board that runs a credit union is elected by its members. Credit unions provide an alternative to banks and savings and loan associations as safe places in which to place savings and borrow at reasonable rates. Credit unions pool their members' funds to make loans to one another.

In addition to typical credit unions that serve members and provide banking and lending services, there are a few special types of credit unions that include:

- Community development credit unions: The NCUA established the Office of Community Development Credit Unions in early 1994. These credit unions serve mostly low-income members in economically distressed and/or financially deprived areas. Part of their function is to educate their members in fundamental money management concepts. At the same time, they provide an economic base in order to stimulate economic development and renewal to their communities.

- **Corporate** credit unions: These institutions do not provide services to individuals, but they serve as a sort of credit union for credit unions. Nationwide, there are over thirty federally insured corporate credit unions; they provide investment, liquidity, and payment services for their member credit unions.

AUTOMATED TELLER MACHINES (ATMs)

Most financial institutions have ATMs. Before ATMs, banks employed tellers to help their customers conduct all their banking business. Because ATMs can inexpensively perform many of the functions formerly done by tellers, ATMs have replaced many tellers in the banking institution. There are no laws requiring banks or other financial institutions to have ATMs, so having one is a business decision for each bank. ATMs offer distinct advantages over traditional teller operations in terms of their locations and hours of operation. ATMs are relatively small and can be placed where banks would not ordinarily open a branch (gas stations, hotel lobbies, airports). Furthermore, ATMs are open when banks are closed and function for twenty-four hours a day, seven days a week.

ATMs can be cost effective to operate compared to the cost of hiring and training bank tellers. Nevertheless, there are costs associated with owning and operating ATMs, including:

- buying the machine
- renting space for the ATM
- maintaining the ATM's mechanical parts
- paying personnel to load it with money and remove deposits (if any)

Banks or other financial institutions may charge patrons for using their bank's ATM as long as the bank or financial institution informs patrons of the terms and conditions of their accounts, and all applicable charges. This information is often contained in the monthly statements. On the other hand, if individuals use an ATM that does not belong to their own bank, the ATM's owner can charge them for using it. This is true even though they are gaining access to their own money kept in their own bank. Likewise, a bank can charge its patrons for using someone else's ATM machine. In this way, individuals may incur two charges for using an ATM that does not belong to the bank or financial institution at which they are customers.

ONLINE BANKING

As the Internet has grown in popularity, financial institutions have established websites that allow customers to access their accounts online, transfer funds between accounts, deposit their paychecks electronically, and pay bills automatically through recurring debits from their accounts. A 2010 Federal Reserve study found that 75% of all noncash payments are made using electronic payment methods, with checks declining to 25% Financial institutions also issue customers **debit** cards, that can be used at ATMs to withdraw cash as well as to buy goods and services form retailers. Unlike a credit card, a debit card transaction results in the purchase price being withdrawn from the consumer's account immediately. Financial institutions used to take a percentage of the

transaction price from the retailer but a 2010 federal law now limits banks to charging retailers roughly 23 cents per transaction.

There has been a process of homogenization in the banking and financial industries. Services appear to be similar in many types of institutions. Nevertheless, some important differences among institutions remain. These differences may exist among banking institutions within a single state, and among the same type of institution from state to state. For example, a Missouri state chartered bank may have authority to conduct certain forms of business that are very different from those of a Missouri savings bank. Likewise, a Missouri savings and loan may have different powers from a Missouri national bank. These various rules and powers result in a difference in services among the spectrum of financial institutions. These differences can affect factors like interest rates, issuance of credit cards, ATM services, and so forth.

FEDERAL LAWS

There are many laws that apply to financial institutions. Most of these are found in Title 12 of the United States Code. Some of the most important laws are:

- 12 U.S.C. §§ 1461-1470: Laws regulating Federal Savings and Loan Associations
- 12 U.S.C. §§ 4001-4010: The Expedited Funds Availability Act
- 12 U.S.C. § 371a: Garn-St. Germain Depository Institutions Act
- 12 USC §§ 1811-1832: Federal Deposit Insurance Corporation
- 12 U.S.C.: Banks and Banking
- 28 U.S.C. § 1348: Banking Associations as Parties to Civil Litigation

In addition to statutes, there are administrative rules that govern financial institutions. These rules have the same force and effect as actual laws passed by Congress. Title 12 of the **Code of Federal Regulations** is the site of most federal agency regulations that deal with banks and banking.

ADDITIONAL RESOURCES

"Consumer Financial Rights." Federal Deposit Insurance Corporation, 2012. Available at http://www.fdic.gov/consumers/consumer/rights/index.html (accessed November 3, 2012).

"Federal Financial Institutions Examination Council." Available at http://www.ffiec.gov/ (accessed December 18, 2012).

Lovett, William A. *Banking and Financial Institutions Law in a Nutshell.* 7th ed. Eagan, MN: West, Thomson Reuters, 2009.

ORGANIZATIONS

American Bankers Association (ABA)

1120 Connecticut Ave. NW
Washington, DC 20036
Toll Free: (800) 226-5377
Email: custserv@aba.com
URL: http://www.aba.com

Conference on State Bank Supervisors (CSBS)

1015 18th Street NW, Suite 1100
Washington, DC 20036
Phone: (202) 296-2840
Fax: (202) 296-1928
URL: http://www.csbs.org/

Federal Deposit Insurance Corporation (FDIC)

550 Seventeenth Street, NW
Washington, DC 20429
URL: http://www.fdic.gov/

National Credit Union Administration (NCUA)

1775 Duke Street
Alexandria, VA 22314
Phone: (703) 518-6300
URL: http://www.ncua.gov/

Office of the Comptroller of the Currency (OCC)

1301 McKinney Street, Suite 3710
Houston, TX 77010
URL: http://www.occ.treas.gov/

Office of Thrift Supervision (OTS)

1700 G Street, NW
Washington, DC 20552
Toll Free: (800) 842-6929
Email: consumer.complaint@ots.treas.gov
URL: http://www.ots.treas.gov

BANKING

DEBIT, CREDIT, AND GIFT CARDS

Sections within this essay:

- Background
- Debit Cards
- Credit Cards
  - The CARD Act
- Gift Cards
- Additional Resources

BACKGROUND

U.S. consumers rely on **debit**, credit, and gift cards to make their purchases. Each type of card is a payment device that allows consumers to purchase goods and services without paying cash. A host of federal laws govern these cards, the most recent being the 2009 Credit Card Accountability, Responsibility, and Disclosure Act (CARD), which expands protection to consumers by reforming the practices of credit card companies. The U.S. banking industry is heavily dependent on the use of credit and debit cards, which generate revenues through accumulating consumer debt and user fees.

Aside from the CARD Act, major federal laws that effect consumer credit include the Truth in Lending Act, the **Fair Credit Reporting Act**, and the Equal Opportunity Credit Act. The Truth in Lending Act is a federal law that sets minimum standards for the information that a **creditor** must provide in an **installment** credit **contract**. The amount being financed, the amount of the required minimum monthly payment, the total number of monthly payments, and the **annual percentage rate** (APR) must all be provided to the consumer prior to entering into a credit contract. In addition, the Truth in Lending Act regulates the advertising of credit. The Fair Credit Reporting Act (FCRA) is a federal law that regulates the activities of credit reporting bureaus. The FCRA is designed to protect the **privacy** of credit report information and to guarantee that information supplied by consumer reporting agencies (CRAs) is as accurate as possible. The Equal Credit Opportunity Act (ECOA) ensures that all consumers are given an equal chance to obtain credit. Factors such as income, expenses, debt, and credit history are always valid considerations for creditworthiness. However, there are certain areas about which it unlawful for a potential creditor to inquire. These include sex, race, national origin, or religion.

DEBIT CARDS

A debit cards is an electronic card issued by a bank which allows bank clients access to their checking account to withdraw cash or pay for goods and services. The business that accepts a debit card transaction receives payment directly from the purchaser's bank account. If the funds are not available, the debit card cannot complete the transaction. Debit cards were introduced in 1966 but they did not become popular until the 1980s and 1990s when automatic teller machines (ATMs) were available. In 1990, debit cards were used in about 300 million transactions. By 2009 this figure grew to 37.6 billion transactions. Not surprisingly, the use of checks has declined dramatically as debit cards grew in popularity and merchants declined to accept checks to combat **fraud**.

Rules for gift cards

Covered by Credit Card Act of 2009, effective on or after August 22, 2010

- Store gift cards, which can be used only at a particular store or group of stores, such as a bookstore or clothing retailer.
- Gift cards with a MasterCard, Visa, American Express, or Discover brand logo. These cards generally can be used wherever the brand is accepted.

Protections

- Limits on expiration dates. The money on a gift card is good for at least five years from the date the card is purchased. Any money added to the card at a later date must also be good for at least five years.
- Replacement cards. If the gift card has an expiration date you still may be able to use unspent money that is left on the card after the card expires. For example, the card may expire in five years but the money may not expire for seven. If your card expires and there is unspent money, you can request a replacement card at no charge. Check your card to see if expiration dates apply.
- Fees disclosed. All fees must be clearly disclosed on the gift card or its packaging.
- Limits on fees. Gift card fees typically are subtracted from the money on the card. Under the new rules, many gift card fees are limited. Generally, fees can be charged if you haven't used your card for at least one year; only one fee can be charged per month.
  - These restrictions apply to fees such as: dormancy or inactivity fees for not using your card, fees for using your card (sometimes called usage fees), fees for adding money to your card, and maintenance fees.
  - You can still be charged a fee to purchase the card and certain other fees, such as a fee to replace a lost or stolen card. Make sure you read the card disclosure carefully to know what fees your card may have.

Other prepaid cards

- These new rules apply only to gift cards, which are just one type of prepaid card. The new rules do not cover other types of prepaid cards, such as:
  - Reloadable prepaid cards that are not intended for gift-giving purposes. For example, a reloadable prepaid card with a MasterCard, Visa, American Express, or Discover brand logo that is intended to be used like a checking account substitute is not covered.
  - Cards that are given as a reward or as part of a promotion. For example, a free $15 gift card given to you by a store if you purchase merchandise or services of $100 or more may have fees or an expiration date of one year rather than five years.

SOURCE: Board of Governors, Federal Reserve System, 2012. Available at: http://www.federalreserve.gov/consumerinfo/files/wyntk_giftcard.pdf

TABLE BY PREMEDIAGLOBAL. ©2013 CENGAGE LEARNING.

When a consumer pays with a debit card, the merchant usually pays an interchange fee, popularly known as a "swipe fee," to the bank for the transaction. A Federal Reserve survey found that in 2009 the average swipe fee was 44 cents. In 2009, swipe fees generated $16.2 billion in revenue for banks. This meant that banks could take in an average of 1.3% of every consumer purchase. However, the CARD Act contained a provision proposed by Illinois Senator Dick Durbin. In what is known as the "Durbin Amendment," Congress placed limits on the amounts of swipe fees that banks could charge to merchants. Banks made billions by charging these fees. The Durbin Amendment made several rather complicated changes, including a provision that allows the Federal Reserve to cap the amount charged in debit card swipe fees. The Federal Reserve approved a limit of 21 cents per transaction, plus additional amounts depending on the size of the purchase that went into effect in 2011. The major banks, alarmed at the halving of swipe fee revenue, announced the imposition of monthly user fees, but consumer complaints led them to abandon the idea.

The Durbin Amendment also allows merchants to refuse to allow consumers to use cards for small purchases of $10 or less. Merchants may also give discounts or offer other incentives for customers using cash or debit cards. In the past, major card issuers, including Visa and MasterCard, banned the practices of setting minimums for transactions or giving discounts for use of debit cards or cash.

CREDIT CARDS

A credit card is a payment device that allows a consumer to make a purchase when the person does not have cash on hand. A bank issues a credit card with terms and conditions, including the credit limit. If the credit cardholder does not pay off the balance at the end of the billing cycle, the remaining amount is subject to interest charges.

In the early Twentieth Century, oil companies and department stores issued their own **proprietary** credit cards that could only be used at their places of business. The first bank credit card was introduced in 1951 but the Diners Club Card, introduced in 1950, was the first credit card in widespread use. Within a year, there were 20,000 Diners Club cardholders. In 1959, American Express launched a credit card, which was the first card made of plastic. Both the Diners Club and American Express cards worked in what is known as a "closed loop" system, made up of the cardholder, the merchant, and the issuer of the card. The issuer authorized and handled every aspect of the transaction. By 1959, these credit card companies introduced the maintaining of a revolving balance instead of requiring the user to pay the full bill at the end of each credit cycle. Consumers gained more flexibility in managing their finances but risked finance interest charges being added to the balance.

Bank of America in 1966 introduced the general-purpose credit card. Bank of America created the Bank-America brand, which became Visa, that it franchised to banks nationwide. That same year a national credit card system was created when a group of banks joined together to create an association that became known as MasterCard. These bankcard associations were an "open loop" system, which required interbank cooperation and funds transfers and the cards could be used at multiple, diverse stores. Visa and MasterCard remained open loop systems, and American Express, Diners Club, and Discover, which began as closed loop systems, became open loop systems. Credit cards that can be used only at the issuers' outlets remained closed loop cards.

Visa and MasterCard's organizations issue credit cards through member banks and set rules for processing credit card transactions. As credit card processing became more complicated, outside service companies began to handle work for Visa and MasterCard bank members. This cut the cost of programs and allowed smaller banks to offer credit cards.

As with debit cards, credit card companies charge merchants a swipe fee if the transaction is completed. If a cardholder has met or exceeded the credit limit on the card, the credit card company will decline the transaction. If a credit card is stolen or used fraudulently, the maximum liability under federal law for unauthorized use of a credit card is $50. If the cardholder reports the loss before the credit card is used, the card issuer cannot hold the consumer responsible for any unauthorized charges. If the loss involves a credit card number, but not the card itself, the cardholder is not liable for unauthorized use.

The credit card sector of banking is a lucrative field. Critics claimed that credit card companies encouraged consumers to have multiple credit cards and make minimum payments, which resulted in debt that would be difficult to ever pay off. Credit companies were free to raise **interest rates** at will, while the terms and conditions of their agreements were confusing to consumers. Congress finally addressed these issues with the CARD Act in 2009. The provisions of the act went into effect in 2010.

The CARD Act The CARD Act put new disclosure rules into effect. A credit card company must send cardholders a notice 45 days before they can increase the interest rate, change certain fees, such as annual fees, cash advance fees, and late fees, that apply to the account, make other significant changes to the terms of the card. If the credit card company is going to make changes to the terms of the card, it must give the cardholder the option to cancel the card before certain fee increases take effect. If the cardholders take that option, however, the credit card company may close the account and increase the monthly payment, subject to certain limitations.

The company does not have to send a 45-day advance notice if the cardholder has a variable interest rate tied to an index. If the index goes up, the company does not have to provide notice before the rate goes up. No notice is required if an introductory rate expires and reverts to the previously disclosed "go-to" rate or if the rate increases because the cardholder is in a workout agreement and has failed to make the payments as agreed.

Monthly credit card bills have begun to include information on how long it will take to pay off the balance if the cardholder only makes minimum payments. It also states how much would need to be paid each month in order to pay off the balance in three years.

The law also set new rules regarding rates, fees, and credit limits. Credit card companies can no longer increase rates for the first 12 months after the cardholder opens an account. However, there are some exceptions, such as when the card has a variable interest rate tied to an index, the rate can go up whenever the index goes up. If there is an introductory rate, it must be in place for at least six months, after which the rate can revert to the "go-to" rate the company disclosed when it issued the card. If the cardholder is more than 60 days late paying the bill, the rate can be increased. In addition, if the cardholder is in a workout agreement and does not make the payments as agreed, the rate can be increased.

The new rules state that increased rates apply only to new charges. If the credit card company does raise the interest rate after the first year, the new rate will apply only to new charges the cardholder makes. If there is a balance, the old interest rate will apply to that balance.

Restrictions on over-the-limit transactions also were included in the CARD Act. The cardholder must tell the credit card company to allow transactions that will take the cardholder over the credit limit. Otherwise, if a transaction goes over the limit, it may be turned down. If cardholder does not opt-in to over-the-limit transactions and the credit card company allows one to go through, it cannot charge an over-the-limit fee. If the cardholder opts-in to allowing transactions that exceed the credit limit, the credit card company can impose only one fee per billing cycle. In addition, the cardholder can revoke the opt-in at any time.

The law placed caps on high-fee cards. If the credit card company requires an annual fee or application fee, those fees cannot total more than 25% of the initial credit limit. For example, if the initial credit limit is $500, the fees for the first year cannot be more than $125. This limit does not apply to **penalty** fees, such as penalties for late payments.

Critics of the credit card industry raised concerns about encouraging underage consumers to have credit cards. The CARD Act mandates that persons under 21 will need to show that they are able to make payments. Otherwise, they will need a cosigner in order to open a credit card account. If a person is under age 21 and has a card with a cosigner and wants an increase in the credit limit, the cosigner must agree in writing to the increase.

The CARD Act made changes to billing and payments as well. Credit card companies must mail or deliver a credit card bill at least 21 days before a payment is due. In addition, the due date should be the same date each month. For example, the payment is always due on the 15th or always due on the last day of the month. The payment cut-off time cannot be earlier than 5 p.m. on the due date. If the payment due date is on a weekend or holiday (when the company does not process payments), the cardholder will have until the following business day to pay. For example, if the due date is Sunday the 15th, the payment will be on time if it is received by Monday the 16th before 5 p.m.

If a person makes more than the minimum payment on the credit card bill, the credit card company must apply the excess amount to the balance with the highest interest rate. There is an exception for deferred interest plans. If a purchase was made under a deferred interest plan (for example, "no interest if paid in full by March 2012"), the credit card company may let the cardholder choose to apply extra amounts to the deferred interest balance before other balances. Otherwise, for two billing cycles prior to the end of the deferred interest period, the credit card company must apply the entire payment to the deferred interest-rate balance first. Finally, credit card companies can only impose interest charges on balances in the current billing cycle.

The act also mandates reasonable penalty fees, adds additional fee protections, and requires companies to explain rate increases and to reevaluate recent rate increases. Credit card companies cannot charge a late payment fee that is greater than the minimum payment nor can they charge inactivity fees for not using the card. Credit card companies cannot charge a cardholder more than one fee for a single event or transaction that violates the cardholder agreement. For example, they cannot charge more than one fee for a single late payment.

Under the act, if a credit card company increases the APR, it must inform the cardholder why. In addition, if the APR is increased, the credit card company must reevaluate that rate increase every six months. If appropriate, it must reduce the rate within 45 days after completing the evaluation.

GIFT CARDS

Gift cards have become a substantial component of retail sales. Merchants issue a gift card that can be redeemed for merchandise or services by the holder of the cart. During the 2011 Christmas holiday shopping season, nearly $30 billion of gift cards were purchased. However, many gift card recipients never redeem their cards. One report estimated that since 2005, consumers have not used $41 billion worth of gift cards.

A complicating matter was whether merchants could set expiration dates for gift cards. Setting unreasonably short expiration dates allowed retailers to make 100 percent profit on the gift card transaction. Consumer unhappiness leads to state laws that set varying expiration times. A number of states also mandated that retailers turn over the proceeds of expired gift cards to the state treasury.

The CARD Act of 2009 addressed gift card issues as well as credit cards. Under the law, gift cards issued by stores or credit card companies, whether physical or electronic, may not expire before five years. This preempts state laws that had shorter expiration periods but continues to allow states to deal with the proceeds of expired gift card. If a gift card is reloadable, any funds added to the card must remain valid for a full five years. The law also requires that all fees must be clearly disclosed on the card or the card's packaging. Post-sale fees may be imposed only if the card has not been used for one year or more and only one post-sale fee may be charged per month. Card replacement fees are not allowed for cards that expire, but funds have not expired (typically bank issued gift cards). Lost or stolen gift card replacement fees are allowed.

The act excludes from its provisions reloadable prepaid debit cards not intended for gift giving purposes. Promotional or rewards cards given away for free by the issuer may expire in one year or have fees prior to one year.

ADDITIONAL RESOURCES

Bevans, Neal R. *Consumer Law & Protection*. Durham, NC: Carolina Academic Press, 2011.

Board of Governors of the Federal Reserve System. "What You Need to Know: New Rules for Gift Cards." Available at http://www.federalreserve.gov/consumerinfo/wyntk_giftcards.htm (accessed November 3, 2012).

ORGANIZATIONS

Federal Trade Commission (FTC)
600 Pennsylvania Avenue, N.W.
Washington, DC 20580
URL: http://www.ftc.gov

BANKING

DODD-FRANK FINANCIAL REFORM ACT

Sections within this essay:

- Background
- Enhanced Consumer Protection
- Financial Stability Oversight Council
- Ending Too Big to Fail Bailouts
- Regulating the Derivatives Market
- Mortgage Reform
- Executive Pay and Corporate Governance
- Additional Resources

BACKGROUND

The Dodd-Frank Financial Reform Act was signed into law in July 2010. The act, which makes major changes to all facets of the U.S. financial industry, came in response to the Great Recession of 2008, which lead to the loss of 8 million jobs, failed businesses, a substantial drop in housing prices, and the diminishment of personal savings. Congress placed blame for the recession at the feet of Wall Street and the largest U.S. banks. It sought to prevent the use of the questionable speculative practices that lead to meltdown of the U.S. and European economies.

The law was sponsored by Senator Christopher Dodd of Connecticut and Representative Barney Frank of Massachusetts, the Democratic chairs of the Senate and House banking committees. The bill encountered fierce opposition from Wall Street and the banking industry and barely passed the Senate. Only the votes of several Republican senators secured its passage. Though the law was signed in July 2010, as of 2012 government regulations that will implement the law remain pending. The most important provisions are described below.

ENHANCED CONSUMER PROTECTION

Dodd-Frank established a new independent watchdog, housed at the Federal Reserve, with the authority to ensure U.S. consumers get the clear, accurate information they need to shop for mortgages, credit cards, and other financial products, and protect them from hidden fees, abusive terms, and deceptive practices. An independent director appointed by the President and confirmed by the Senate leads the Consumer Financial Protection Bureau (CFPB). The bureau has a dedicated budget that is paid by the Federal Reserve system.

Congress gave the CFPB the authority to write rules for consumer protections governing all financial institutions offering consumer financial services or products. It also the authority to examine and enforce regulations for banks and credit unions with assets of over $10 billion and all mortgage-related businesses (lenders, servicers, **mortgage** brokers, and **foreclosure** scam operators), payday lenders, and student lenders as well as other non-bank financial companies that are large, such as debt collectors and consumer reporting agencies. Banks and credit unions with assets of $10 billion or less will be examined for consumer complaints by the appropriate regulator.

Congress consolidated and strengthened **consumer protection** responsibilities that had been handled by the Office of the Comptroller of the Currency, Office of Thrift Supervision, Federal Deposit Insurance Corporation, Federal Reserve, National Credit Union Administration, the Department of Housing and Urban Development, and

Federal Trade Commission. The CFPB also oversees the enforcement of federal laws intended to ensure the fair, equitable and nondiscriminatory access to credit for individuals and communities.

The Bureau includes a new Office of Financial Literacy and a national consumer complaint hotline so consumers will have, for the first time, a single toll-free number to report problems with financial products and services. It also coordinates with other regulators when examining banks to prevent undue regulatory burden. It consults with regulators before a proposal is issued and it can **appeal** regulations it believes would put the safety and soundness of the banking system or the stability of the financial system at risk.

FINANCIAL STABILITY OVERSIGHT COUNCIL

Dodd-Frank established the Financial Stability Oversight Council to recommendations to the Federal Reserve for increasingly strict rules for capital, leverage, liquidity, risk management and other requirements as companies grow in size and complexity, with significant requirements on companies that pose risks to the financial system. The council is made up of 10 federal financial regulators and an independent member and 5 nonvoting members. The Council is chaired by the Treasury Secretary and includes the Federal Reserve Board, **Securities** and Exchange Commission, Commodities and Futures Trading Commission, Office of Comptroller of the Currency, Federal Deposit Insurance Corporation, Federal Housing Finance Agency, National Credit Union Administration, Consumer Financial Protection Bureau, and an independent appointee with insurance expertise. The nonvoting members include state banking, insurance, and securities regulators.

The council is authorized to require, with a two-thirds vote and vote of the chair, that a nonbank financial company be regulated by the Federal Reserve if the council believes that there would be negative effects on the financial system if the company failed or its activities would pose a risk to the financial stability of the US. It is also authorized to approve, with a two-thirds vote and vote of the chair, a Federal Reserve decision to require a large, complex company, to divest some of its holdings if it poses a grave threat to the financial stability of the United States. However, this must be done only as a last resort.

Dodd-Frank created a new Office of Financial Research within the Treasury Department that is staffed with a highly sophisticated staff of economists, accountants, lawyers, former supervisors, and other specialists to support the council's work by collecting financial data and conducting economic analysis. Through this office and member agencies the council collects and analyzes data to identify and monitor emerging risks to the economy and make this information public in periodic reports and **testimony** to Congress every year. The law also establishes a floor for capital that cannot be lower than the standards in effect in July 2010 and authorized the Council to impose a 15-1 leverage requirement at a company if necessary to mitigate a grave threat to the financial system.

ENDING TOO BIG TO FAIL BAILOUTS

The massive infusion of capital from the U.S. government into the financial industry in 2008 and 2009 was predicated on the belief that large banks and other financial firms were "too big to fail." The financial bailouts, coupled with continued enormous executive compensation for bank officials, proved controversial and unpopular. Dodd-Frank clearly stated that taxpayers would not be responsible for saving a failing financial company or to cover the cost of its **liquidation**. The Financial Stability Oversight Council monitors systemic risk and makes recommendations to the Federal Reserve for increasingly strict rules for capital, leverage, liquidity, risk management and other requirements as companies grow in size and complexity, with significant requirements on companies that pose risks to the financial system.

The Volcker Rule (named after former Federal Reserve Chair Paul Volcker) regulators must implement regulations for banks, their affiliates and holding companies, that prohibit **proprietary** trading, investment in and sponsorship of hedge funds and private equity funds, and to limit relationships with hedge funds and private equity funds. Nonbank financial institutions supervised by the Federal Reserve also have restrictions on proprietary trading and hedge fund and private equity investments. The Council has the ability to require nonbank financial companies that pose a risk to the financial stability of the United States to submit to supervision by the Federal Reserve.

Dodd-Frank requires large, complex financial companies to periodically submit plans for their rapid and orderly shutdown should the company go under. Companies face higher capital requirements and restrictions on growth and activity, as well as divestment, if they fail to submit acceptable plans. It is hoped that the plans will help regulators understand the structure of the companies they oversee and serve as a roadmap for shutting them down if the company fails. The law also creates an orderly liquidation mechanism for the Federal Deposit Insurance Corporation (FDIC) to unwind failing systemically significant financial companies. Shareholders and unsecured creditors will bear losses and management and culpable directors will be removed. Taxpayers will bear no cost for liquidating large, interconnected financial companies. The FDIC can borrow only the amount of funds to **liquidate** a company that it expects to be repaid from the assets of the company being liquidated. The government will be first in line for repayment. Funds not repaid from the sale of the company's assets will be repaid first through the claw back of any payments to creditors that exceeded liquidation value and then assessments on large financial companies.

Dodd-Frank significantly changed the Federal Reserve's emergency lending authority to prohibit bailing out an individual company. The Secretary of the Treasury must approve any lending program, and such programs must be broad based and not aid a failing financial company. **Collateral** must be sufficient to protect taxpayers from losses. Most large financial companies that fail are expected to be resolved through the **bankruptcy** process.

REGULATING THE DERIVATIVES MARKET

A derivative is a **contract** between two parties that specifies conditions under which payments are to be made between the parties. The 2008 market crash was caused in large part by speculation in credit derivatives. Dodd-Frank sought to gain more regulatory control over derivatives. It provides the Securities and Exchange Commission and the Commodities Futures Trading Commission with authority to regulate over-the-counter derivatives so that irresponsible practices and excessive risk-taking can no longer escape regulatory oversight. The law requires central clearing and exchange trading for derivatives that can be cleared and provides a role for both regulators and clearing houses to determine which contracts should be cleared. In addition, the law requires data collection and publication through clearing houses or swap repositories to improve market transparency and provide regulators important tools for monitoring and responding to risks.

Dodd-Frank added safeguards to the system by ensuring dealers and major swap participants have adequate financial resources to meet responsibilities. Regulators have the authority to impose capital and margin requirements on swap dealers and major swap participants, not end users. The law also established a **code of conduct** for all registered swap dealers and major swap participants when advising a swap entity. When acting as counterparties to a **pension** fund, endowment fund, or state or local government, derivatives dealers are to have a reasonable basis to believe that the fund or governmental entity has an independent representative advising them.

MORTGAGE REFORM

The puncturing of the real estate bubble in late 2007 and 2008 led to a steep decline in the value of homes around the country. As of 2012, thousands of homes continued to be foreclosed and hundreds of thousands were "under water." This means that the home is valued less than the amount remaining on the mortgage loan. Many buyers bought homes beyond their means, encouraged by unscrupulous mortgage companies. Dodd-Frank established a simple federal standard for all home loans that institutions must ensure that borrowers can repay the loans they are sold. The law prohibits the financial incentives for subprime loans that encourage lenders to steer borrowers into more costly loans, including the bonuses known as "yield spread premiums" that lenders pay to brokers to inflate the cost of loans. It also prohibits pre-payment penalties that trapped many borrowers into unaffordable loans.

Dodd-Frank also established penalties for irresponsible lending. Lenders and mortgage brokers who do not comply with the new standards will be held accountable by consumers. Consumers will be entitled to up to three-years of interest payments and damages plus attorney's fees. The law also protects borrowers against foreclosure for violations of these standards.

Consumers have additional protections. For those who take out high-cost loans, the law lowers the interest rate and the points and fee triggers that define high cost loans. Lenders must disclose the maximum a consumer could pay on a variable rate mortgage, with a warning that payments will vary based on interest rate changes. Finally, the act established the Office of Housing Counseling within the Department of Housing and Urban Development to boost homeownership and rental housing counseling.

EXECUTIVE PAY AND CORPORATE GOVERNANCE

Congress was troubled by what it saw as excessive **corporate** executive compensation. The boards of directors at major **corporations** agreed to lavish compensation for top-level executives even if the executives' performance was wanting. Even more troubling were the "golden parachute" packages awarded to departing executives that were deemed exorbitant. Moreover, shareholders had virtually no chance of successfully challenging compensation packages. Dodd-Frank addressed both executive pay and corporate governance.

The act gives shareholders a say on pay with the right to a non-binding vote on executive pay and golden parachutes. This gives shareholders an opportunity to hold accountable executives of the companies they own, and a chance to disapprove where they see the kind of misguided incentive schemes that threatened individual companies and in turn the broader economy. Standards for listing on a stock exchange will require that compensation committees include only independent directors and have the authority to hire compensation consultants in order to strengthen their independence from the executives they are rewarding or punishing. The law also requires that public companies set policies to take back executive compensation if it was based on inaccurate financial statements that do not comply with accounting standards. As for the financial industry, Dodd-Frank requires federal financial regulators to issue and enforce joint compensation rules specifically applicable to financial institutions with a federal regulator.

As to corporate governance in general, the SEC was given authority to grant shareholders proxy access to nominate directors. This means that the corporation must distribute **shareholder** materials that support nominees not favored by the board of directors. These requirements may help shift management's focus from short-term profits to long-term growth and stability. The SEC also was directed to clarify disclosures relating to compensation, including requiring companies to provide charts that compare their executive compensation with stock performance over a five-year period.

ADDITIONAL RESOURCES

Code of Federal Regulations, Title 12: Banks and Banking. U.S. Government Printing Office, 2012. Available at http://www.access.gpo.gov/nara/cfr/cfr-table-search.html.

"Consumer Financial Rights." Federal Deposit Insurance Corporation, 2012. Available at http://www.fdic.gov/consumers/consumer/rights/index.html (accessed November 3, 2012).

Durkin, Thomas A., and Gregory Elliehausen. *Truth in Lending: Theory, History, and a Way Forward.* New York: Oxford University Press, 2011.

Lovett, William A. *Banking and Financial Institutions Law in a Nutshell.* 7th ed. Eagan, MN: West, Thomson Reuters, 2009.

Mannimo, Edward F., and Richard E. Kaye. *Lender Liability and Banking Litigation.* New York: Law Journal Press, 2006.

ORGANIZATIONS

Board of Governors of the Federal Reserve System, Division of Consumer and Community Affairs

20th and C Streets NW, MS 804
Washington, DC 20551
Phone: (202) 452-3667
URL: http://www.federalreserve.gov

Consumer Financial Protection Bureau

1700 G St. NW
Washington, DC 20552
Phone: (202) 435-7000
URL: http://www.consumerfinance.gov

Federal Deposit Insurance Corporation (FDIC)

550 Seventeenth Street, NW
Washington, DC 20409
Toll Free: (877) ASK-FDIC
URL: http://www.fdic.gov

BANKING

FEDERAL DEPOSIT INSURANCE CORPORATION (FDIC)

Sections within this essay:

- Background
- History
- How the FDIC Works
- Definitions
- Additional Resources

BACKGROUND

Congress created the Federal Deposit Insurance Corporation (FDIC) in 1933 to protect consumers who hold their money in banks from bank failures. Depositors—persons who hold money in savings accounts, checking accounts, certificates of deposit, money market accounts, Individual Retirement Accounts (IRAs), or Keogh accounts—have FDIC protection of up to $100,000 in the event of a bank failure. The FDIC regulates all banks that are members of the Federal Reserve System and certain banks that are not members of the Federal Reserve System. It is the FDIC's mission to monitor and regulate the banking industry, making certain that banks operate safely and legally, and to prevent bank failures while encouraging healthy competition within the industry. When a bank does fail by not having sufficient assets, the FDIC uses its money to reimburse the bank's depositors. It then sells the failed bank's assets and uses the profits to assist when other banks fail.

The FDIC employs approximately 8,000 people throughout the country. The headquarters are in Washington, D.C., but regional offices are located in Atlanta, Boston, Chicago, Dallas, Kansas City, Memphis, New York City, and San Francisco. In addition, field examiners, whose job is to conduct on-site inspections of banks, have field offices in 80 more locations throughout the country.

The FDIC has **jurisdiction** over banks in the 50 states, the District of Columbia, Guam, Puerto Rico, and the Virgin Islands. It regulates banks, enforcing rules such as the Equal Credit Opportunity Act that prohibits certain forms of **discrimination** in lending, and inspects banks to be sure they are operating profitably and legally. Banks that are insured by the FDIC pay an **assessment** four times per year to the FDIC. The amount of assessment paid by the bank depends in part on the amount of funds deposited with the bank.

HISTORY

Banking history in the United States changed forever with the Great Depression. The Great Depression began when the stock market crashed in October 1929, causing numerous banks to fail, which in turn caused bank depositors in many cases to lose most or all of their money. U.S. President Franklin Delano Roosevelt and Congress responded by creating the FDIC to guarantee the safety of bank deposits and regain the public's confidence in the banking industry. The history of the FDIC, however, may be traced back even before the Great Depression.

When the United States was formed in 1776, the thirteen original colonies each had their own banking systems, with no uniform currency and little government involvement in the banking systems. In 1791, Congress created the First Bank of the United States, a bank in

Philadelphia that closed in 1811. As the country grew, banking remained largely unregulated and inconsistent. Following the Civil War, the economy in the North prospered while the economy in the South floundered. To encourage economic stability and consistency throughout the country, the National Banking Act of 1864 created national banks as well as the Office of the **Comptroller** of the Currency (OCC), and the dollar became the national currency. Bank failures in the early twentieth century led the creation of the Federal Reserve System, a central bank that continues to oversee and regulate national banks throughout the country.

The economy grew rapidly in the 1920s until the stock market crash in 1929. Stocks quickly lost their value, and as a result, banks lost money, farm prices fell, unemployment soared, and consumers began taking their money out of banks. Many banks failed and closed, lacking sufficient funds to pay their lenders and depositors. Finally, in 1933, President Roosevelt closed all banks temporarily and enacted the Banking Act. The Banking Act of 1933 established the FDIC, giving it authority to regulate and oversee banks and to provide insurance to bank depositors.

In early 1934, the maximum amount of insurance offered by the FDIC was $2,500, but by the end of the year the maximum amount increased to $5,000. Also in 1934, Congress created an entity similar to the FDIC to protect depositors from failures of federal savings and loan institutions. This entity was known as the Federal Savings and Loan Insurance Corporation (FSLIC).

The Banking Act of 1935 made the FDIC a permanent and independent corporation. Banks continued to fail throughout the 1930s, and the FDIC honored its promise to depositors by reimbursing them up to $5,000 for money lost in bank failures. Gradually, the number of bank failures declined, and by the late 1930s banks were becoming more profitable. In 1950, the FDIC maximum amount of insurance rose from $5,000 to $10,000.

In 1960, only four banks insured by the FDIC failed. The FDIC at that time employed approximately 2,500 bank examiners, and by 1962, no banks insured by the FDIC failed. In 1966, the FDIC maximum amount of insurance rose to $15,000, and in 1969, it rose again to $20,000. In 1980, the maximum amount of insurance was $100,000. It remained at that amount as of 2002.

Inflation skyrocketed to 14 percent by 1981, and the **interest rates** for home mortgages were extremely high at 21 percent. In 1983, the FDIC continued to collect more in premiums from member banks than it paid out for bank failures, but that same year, 48 banks insured by the

FDIC failed. By 1984, the FDIC was paying more on bank failures than it collected in bank assessments, with 79 banks failing. In 1985, 125 banks failed, and in 1986, 138 banks, with assets totaling $7 billion, failed. What was worse, savings and loans were failing at an unprecedented rate, prompting Congress to act in 1989 with the Financial Institutions Reform, Recovery, and Enforcement Act (FIRREA). This act created the Resolution Trust Corporation (RTC) as a temporary agency charged with administering and cleaning up the savings and loan failures. The act also established the Savings Association Insurance Fund (SAIF), which insures deposits in savings and loan associations and charged the FDIC with administering the SAIF. The SAIF replaced the FSLIC.

In 1990, the FDIC began to increase its premium rate for the first time in its history, charging banks more to remain FDIC insured. The Federal Deposit Insurance Corporation Improvement Act of 1991 allowed the FDIC to borrow additional funds from the U.S. Treasury to rebuild its coffers. It also instructed the FDIC to set premiums for banks based upon each bank's level of risk and to close failing banks in more cost-effective ways. No longer was the FDIC permitted to repay all deposits to encourage consumer confidence. Instead Congress strictly limited the FDIC to reimburse only insured depositors and only to the maximum amount allowed by law. Congress also mandated that the Federal Reserve System not lend money to banks in financial trouble. By 1993, bank failure rates were down to their lowest number in twelve years. Congress dissolved the RTC and transferred its duties back to the FDIC that same year.

The economic recession at the end of the first decade of the 2000s severely stressed the U.S. banking system. Between 2008 and 2012, 458 banks failed. At the beginning of the banking crisis in the fall of 2007, the government temporarily increased FDIC insurance. It raised the insurance limit from $100,000 to $250,000 for each FDIC insured institution. Congress made this increase permanent in 2010.

HOW THE FDIC WORKS

Provided a financial institution is insured by the FDIC, the FDIC protects any depositor—individual or entity—regardless of whether the depositor is a U.S. citizen or resident. Federally chartered banks, as well as some state chartered banks, are protected by the FDIC. If a banking institution is FDIC-insured, it must display an official FDIC sign at each teller station. The FDIC insures deposits that are payable in the United States, while deposits that are only payable overseas do not receive FDIC protection. Investments such as stocks or mutual funds are not FDIC protected. Deposits into accounts such as savings, checking, Christmas Club, certificates of deposit (CDs) are FDIC insured, as are cashiers' checks, expense checks, loan disbursement checks, interest checks, money orders, and other negotiable instruments.

A depositor who has more than $250,000 in deposits is protected only to the extent of $250,000 per FDIC insured institution. This means that consumers who have assets exceeding $250,000 are best served by keeping no more than $250,000 in any one FDIC insured bank. A bank with more than one branch is considered to be one institution, so merely keeping funds in different branch locations may not be safe. For purposes of determining deposit insurance coverage, the FDIC will add all deposits from all branch offices of the same bank for each depositor. Deposits of more than $250,000 maintained in a single banking institution are protected so long as they are maintained in different categories of legal ownership. Examples of different categories of legal ownership include single ownership versus joint accounts, or individual retirement accounts (IRAs), Keogh accounts, or **pension** or profit-sharing accounts. Different types of accounts, however—checking, savings, certificates of deposit—are not categories of legal ownership. Money contained in separate types of accounts is added together for purposes of determining FDIC insurance coverage.

The FDIC determines legal ownership of bank deposits by examining the bank deposit account records. Assuming those records are unambiguous, the FDIC insurance goes to the individual or entity named. FDIC protection continues for up to six months following the death of a depositor as though the depositor were alive. This protection is important in cases in which the funds of the deceased are left to a survivor whose own bank deposits, combined with those of the deceased, exceed $250,000. Without this protection, the survivor would only receive $25,000 in FDIC insurance, but with this protection, the survivor may receive the insurance afforded the deceased depositor as well.

Some states have **community property** laws, meaning that the property of one spouse may legally be considered to be the property of the other spouse as well. Community property laws, however, do not affect the coverage afforded by the FDIC. Even in states that have community property laws, an account held solely in the name of one spouse will not be considered by the FDIC as also belonging to the other spouse. Accounts held in the name of both spouses will be insured by the FDIC as joint accounts. With joint accounts, the interests of each individual are added together and insured by the FDIC to the extent of $250,000. This means that if Mary and Bill have a joint savings account totaling $500,000, the FDIC would completely insure Mary's portion of $250,000 and would also completely insure Bill's portion of $250,000.

In the case of retirement funds, such as IRAs and Keogh accounts, the FDIC considers the accounts to be insured separately from other non-retirement funds held by the depositor at the same financial institution. If a depositor has both IRA and Keogh accounts at the same institution, however, those funds will be added together and insured only to the extent of $250,000. Roth IRAs are treated in the same manner as traditional IRAs.

In the case of business accounts, funds deposited in the name of a corporation or other business entity receive the same FDIC protection—up to $250,000—as do individual accounts. A business entity must not exist merely to increase the FDIC protection afforded an individual depositor; the business entity must exist to perform an "independent activity" to receive FDIC protection. When a business entity owns more than one account, even when each account is designated for different purposes, the FDIC will add the total amounts of all accounts and insure the business entity to a maximum of $250,000. This rule also applies if a corporation has separate units or divisions that are not separately incorporated. If a business entity is a **sole proprietorship**, the FDIC treats deposits of the sole proprietorship as the funds of the individual who is the sole proprietor. Those funds will be added to any other insured accounts held by the individual, and the FDIC will insure no more than $250,000.

In addition to its powers of insuring bank and savings and loan deposits, the FDIC regulates the banking industry and may, after proper notice and a **hearing**, discontinue its insurance coverage if a bank engages in overly risky banking practices. When this happens, the FDIC requires the bank to provide timely notice to its depositors of the termination of FDIC coverage.

DEFINITIONS

Bank: a financial institution, chartered by the state or federal government, that exists to keep and protect the money of depositors, disburse funds for payment on checks, issue loans to businesses and consumers, and perform other money-related functions.

Savings and loan: a financial institution, similar to a bank, whose primary purpose it to make loans to customers, most often for the purchase of homes or other real estate.

ADDITIONAL RESOURCES

"Are My Deposits Insured?" Federal Deposit Insurance Corporation, 2011. Available at http://www.fdic.gov/deposit/deposits/index.html (accessed November 3, 2012).

Gale Encyclopedia of American Law. 3rd ed. Detroit: Gale, Cengage Learning, 2011.

ORGANIZATIONS

Board of Governors of the Federal Reserve System, Division of Consumer and Community Affairs

20th and C Streets, NW MS 804
Washington, DC 20551
Phone: (202) 452-3667
URL: http://www.federalreserve.gov

Federal Deposit Insurance Corporation (FDIC)

550 Seventeenth Street, NW
Washington, DC 20409
Toll Free: (877) ASK-FDIC
URL: http://www.fdic.gov

Office of the Comptroller of the Currency

1301 McKinney Suite 3710
Houston, TX 77010
Toll Free: (800) 613-6743
URL: http://www.occ.treas.gov

Office of Thrift Supervision Consumer Program Division

1700 G Street, NW
Washington, DC 20552
Toll Free: (800) 842-6929
URL: http://www.ots.treas.gov

BANKING

INTEREST RATES

Sections within this essay:

- Background
- History
- Interest and Inflation
- State Usury Laws
- Additional Resources

BACKGROUND

In the world of banking and finance, interest is money that is paid by a borrower to a lender in exchange for the use of the credit. Money held in an account, such as a bank savings or checking account, may earn interest also because the bank has use of the money while it is held in the account and the interest constitutes payment to the account holder for the temporary use of the money.

Typically, interest is computed as a percentage of the amount borrowed, which is known as the principal. Interest may be computed on a yearly basis, which is known as simple interest. For example, if a borrower borrows $1,000 at a simple interest rate of 12 percent, with the loan due to be repaid in one year, the total interest owed on the loan is $120. Alternatively, interest may be compounded. With compounded interest, the calculation of interest occurs periodically and unpaid interest is added to the premium. For example, assuming a loan of $1,000 with a 12 percent interest rate compounded monthly, the interest that accrues during the first month of the loan is $120. That amount is added to the principal, making the total amount $1,120. The

interest accruing during the second month of the loan—12 percent of $1,120—is $134.40. With compounded interest, the interest rate stays the same but the amount of interest may increase periodically.

HISTORY

Interest on borrowed funds has existed since ancient times, but interest was not always an acceptable means of conducting business. Religious groups in the Middle Ages—Jewish, Christian, and Islamic—forbade the use of interest, considering it reprehensible. Romans in ancient times also outlawed the practice of charging interest, as did the English government until the thirteenth century. In time, and with increasing demands for credit to support the growth of **commerce** and trade, a distinction was made between moderate interest rates and excessive interest rates. Chinese and Hindu laws prohibited excessive interest rates, known as **usury**, and in 1545, England set a maximum rate of interest. Other countries followed England's practice. In the United States as of 2002, the payment of interest for loans is a widely accepted business practice, with illegal usury reserved for interest rates exceeding the maximums set by law.

INTEREST AND INFLATION

Interest rates fluctuate constantly. They are controlled by supply and demand and other economic indicators. Other factors that help determine an interest rate include the length of the loan and any **collateral** used to secure the loan in the event the borrower cannot repay the loan. Low interest rates can stimulate the economy; consumers are attracted to low interest rates on consumer goods, cars, and houses and may spend more when interest rates are low. High interest rates usually have the opposite effect.

Consumers are reluctant or unable to spend money, or spend as much money, when interest rates climb.

The Federal Reserve Board of Governors, part of the Federal Reserve System, sets a benchmark interest rate known as the prime rate. The Federal Reserve, the central bank of the United States, was founded in 1913 to help regulate the country's money supply. The goals of the Federal Reserve Board are to control inflation, maintain stable prices, and promote maximum employment and output of products for a favorable economy. This is done, in part, by raising and lowering interest rates. Low interest rates spur the economy but may lead to inflation, which harms the economy in the long term. The Federal Reserve Board looks at a range of economic indicators to help it determine what its policies should be and whether to raise, lower, or maintain the prime interest rate.

Any national bank must be a member of the Federal Reserve System and is governed by its **fiscal** policies. State banks may belong to the Federal Reserve System but are not required to; state agencies regulate state banks. Savings and loans, which are similar to banks in many ways, are regulated at the federal level by the Federal Home Loan Banks System. However, regardless of the Federal Reserve's **jurisdiction** over any financial entity, the prime interest rate is often the **arbiter** of interest rates.

Interest rates have a profound effect on the national and worldwide economies and are affected by economic changes as well. Economists like Adam Smith and David Ricardo theorized that interest rates are the key in balancing investments with savings. Marxist economists believe that interest benefits only capitalists, leaving other classes exploited, since no service is rendered to those who pay interest. Other economic theorists have deemed interest as a sort of reward for those who save, rather than spend, their money, since bank accounts and other investment vehicles typically pay interest to account holders.

Every state has its own regulations on the maximum amount of interest that can be charged for a loan. These state usury laws vary considerably as to the limits on interest that can be charged for consumer and non-consumer loans. If a company charges more than the usury limit, the legality of the loan may be questioned.

STATE USURY LAWS

ALABAMA: Legal rate of interest is 6 percent. Usury limit is 8 percent. Judgment rate is 12 percent.

ALASKA: Legal rate of interest is 10.5 percent. Usury limit is 5 percent above the Federal Reserve interest rate as of the date of the loan.

ARIZONA: Legal rate of interest is 10 percent.

ARKANSAS: Legal rate of interest is 6 percent. For consumers, the usury limit is 17 percent; for non-consumers, the usury limit is 5 percent above the Federal Reserve interest rate. Judgment rate is 10 percent per annum or the lawful agreed upon rate, whichever is higher.

CALIFORNIA: Legal rate of interest is 10 percent for consumers. Usury limit is 5 percent above the Federal Reserve Bank of San Francisco rate.

COLORADO: Legal rate of interest is 8 percent. Usury limit is 45 percent. Maximum rates to consumers is 12 percent per annum.

CONNECTICUT: Legal rate of interest is 8 percent. Usury rate is 12 percent. Interest allowed in civil suits is 10 percent.

DELAWARE: Legal rate of interest is 5 percent over the Federal Reserve Rate.

DISTRICT OF COLUMBIA: Legal rate of interest is 6 percent. General usury limit is 24 percent.

FLORIDA: Legal rate of interest is 12 percent. General usury limit is 18 percent. For loans exceeding $500,000, the maximum rate is 25 percent.

GEORGIA: Legal rate of interest is 7 percent. Usury limit for loans less than $3,000 is 16 percent, otherwise 5 percent. For loans below $250,000, interest rate must be specified in writing and in simple interest.

HAWAII: Legal rate of interest is 10 percent. Usury limit for consumers is 12 percent.

IDAHO: Legal rate of interest is 12 percent. Judgment interest is 5 percent above U.S. Treasury **Securities** rate.

ILLINOIS: Legal rate of interest is 5 percent. General usury limit is 9 percent. Judgment rate is 9 percent.

INDIANA: Legal rate of interest is 10 percent. Judgment rate is 10 percent.

IOWA: Legal rate of interest is 10 percent. Maximum rate for consumer transactions is 12 percent.

KANSAS: Legal rate of interest is 10 percent. Usury limit is 15 percent. Judgment rate is 4 percent above federal discount rate. For consumer transactions, maximum rate of interest for first $1,000 is 18 percent, otherwise 14.45 percent.

KENTUCKY: Legal rate of interest is 8 percent. Usury limit is 4 percent above Federal Reserve rate or 19 percent, whichever is less. No limit for loans exceeding $15,000. Judgment rate is 12 percent compounded annually or at a rate set by the court.

LOUISIANA: Legal rate of interest 1 percent above average prime rate, not exceeding 14 percent or less than 7 percent. Usury limit is 12 percent.

MAINE: Legal rate of interest is 6 percent. Judgment rate is 15 percent for judgments below $30,000, otherwise the 52 week average discount rate for T-Bills plus 4 percent.

MARYLAND: Legal rate of interest is 6 percent. Usury limit is 24 percent. Judgment rate is 10 percent.

MASSACHUSETTS: Legal rate of interest is 6 percent. Usury limit is 20 percent. Judgment rate is 12 percent of 18 percent if the court finds a frivolous defense.

MICHIGAN: Legal rate of interest is 5 percent. Usury limit is 7 percent. Judgment rate is 1 percent above the five year T-note rate.

MINNESOTA: Legal rate of interest is 6 percent. Usury limit is 8 percent. Judgment rate is secondary market yield for one year T-Bills.

MISSISSIPPI: Legal rate of interest is 9 percent. Usury limit is 10 percent or 5 percent above the federal reserve rate. No usury limit on commercial loans exceeding $5,000. Judgment rate is 9 percent or legally agreed upon rate.

MISSOURI: Legal rate of interest is 9 percent. Judgment rate is 9 percent.

MONTANA: Legal rate of interest is 10 percent. General usury limit is 6 percent above New York City bank's prime rate. Judgment rate is 10 percent.

NEBRASKA: Legal rate of interest is 6 percent. Usury limit is 16 percent. Judgment rate is 1 percent above bond yield equivalent to T-Bill auction price.

NEVADA: Legal rate of interest is 12 percent. No usury limit.

NEW HAMPSHIRE: Legal rate of interest is 10 percent. No general usury limit.

NEW JERSEY: Legal rate of interest is 6 percent. Usury limit generally is 30 percent for individuals and 50 percent for **corporations**.

NEW MEXICO: Legal rate of interest is 15 percent. Judgment rate is determined by the court.

NEW YORK: Legal rate of interest is 9 percent. General usury limit is 16 percent.

NORTH CAROLINA: Legal rate of interest is 8 percent. General usury limit is 8 percent.

NORTH DAKOTA: Legal rate of interest is 6 percent. General usury limit is 5.5 percent above six-month treasury bill interest rate. Judgment rate is 12 percent.

OKLAHOMA: Legal rate of interest is 6 percent. Consumer loans may not exceed 10 percent unless lender is licensed. Usury limit on non-consumer loans is 45 percent. Judgment rate is 4 percent above T-Bill rate.

OREGON: Legal rate of interest is 9 percent. Judgment rate is 9 percent or agreed upon rate, whichever is higher. Usury limit is 12 percent for loans less than $50,000.

PENNSYLVANIA: Legal rate of interest is 6 percent. General usury limit is 6 percent for loans less than $50,000. Criminal usury limit is 25 percent. Judgment rate is 6 percent.

PUERTO RICO: Legal rate of interest is 6 percent.

RHODE ISLAND: Legal rate of interest is 12 percent. Judgment rate is 12 percent. Usury limit is 21 percent or 9 percent above the interest rate charged for T-Bills.

SOUTH CAROLINA: Legal rate of interest is 8.75 percent. Judgment rate is 14 percent.

SOUTH DAKOTA: Legal rate of interest is 15 percent. Judgment rate is 12 percent.

TENNESSEE: Legal rate of interest is 10 percent. Judgment rate is 10 percent. General usury limit is 24 percent, or 4 percent above average prime rate, whichever is less.

TEXAS: Legal rate of interest is 6 percent. Judgment rate is 18 percent or contracted rate, whichever is less.

UTAH: Legal rate of interest is 10 percent. Judgment rate is 12 percent or contracted rate.

VERMONT: Legal rate of interest is 12 percent. Judgment rate is 12 percent. General usury limit is 12 percent.

VIRGINIA: Legal rate of interest is 8 percent. Judgment rate is 8 percent or contracted rate. No usury limit for corporation or business loans.

WASHINGTON: Legal rate of interest is 12 percent. General usury limit is 12 percent or 4 percent above average T-Bill rate, whichever is greater. Judgment rate is 12 percent or contracted rate, whichever is higher.

WEST VIRGINIA: Legal rate of interest is 6 percent.

WISCONSIN: Legal rate of interest is 5 percent. Judgment rate is 12 percent.

WYOMING: Legal rate of interest is 10 percent. Judgment rate is 10 percent or contracted rate, whichever is less.

ADDITIONAL RESOURCES

Gale Encyclopedia of American Law. 3rd ed. Detroit: Gale, Cengage Learning, 2011.

LoanBack. "State Usury Laws." 2011. Available at http://www. loanback.com/category/usury-laws-by-state/ (accessed November 2, 2012).

ORGANIZATIONS

American Bankers Association (ABA)

1120 Connecticut Ave. NW
Washington, DC 20036
Toll Free: (800) 226-5377
Email: custserv@aba.com
URL: http://www.aba.com

bankrate.com

11811 U.S. Highway 1
North Palm Beach, FL 33408
Phone: (561) 630-2400
URL: http://www.bankrate.com

U.S. Federal Reserve

20th Street and Constitution Avenue, NW
Washington, DC 20551
Phone: (202) 452-3819
URL: http://www.federalreserve.gov

BUSINESS LAW

ACCOUNTING REQUIREMENTS

BACKGROUND

The field of accounting embodies a set of concepts and techniques that are used to measure and report financial information about a particular economic entity (or smaller unit of an entity). An economic entity may be an individual, a for-profit or nonprofit business or organization, or a unit of government.

Accounting information is useful not only to owners of entities or their creditors, but also to business planners and forecasters, government administrators, financial analysts, and even individual employees of a company. Investors are hoping to learn as much as possible about a business enterprise before purchasing an interest, while creditors are interested in the enterprise's ability to repay obligations. Business enterprise managers need financial information to make sound business decisions. Governmental units need accurate financial profiles in order to tax and regulate. Analysts use this information to form opinions and forecast local or national economic profiles. Individual employees often have bonuses or options tied to enterprise performance.

Financial vs. Managerial Accounting Accounting practices can be divided into two broad areas of function: financial accounting and managerial accounting. Both areas are dependent upon a strong information system that can reliably capture and summarize personal and business transactional data. At the heart of all accounting practices and procedures is a basic understanding of assets and liabilities (debts). However, with the advent of computers and sophisticated software capability, tedious bookkeeping tasks largely have been relegated to the annals of history, and replaced with software programs with dynamic, proactive decision-making capability in the field of financial and managerial accounting.

Financial accounting concerns itself with external reporting of information to parties outside of the subject business or entity. To ensure consistency and structure in reporting, financial accounting is managed by many rules or standards, such as those developed by the private sector group called the Financial Accounting Standards Board (FASB). Financial reports prepared under these standards have a general-purpose orientation with which all intended user groups are familiar, thus rendering the reports ostensibly neutral and free from **bias**. Most earnings reports are based on these established measurement and reporting rules, known as generally accepted accounting principles (GAAP).

In contrast, managerial accounting benefits internal management of an entity by providing information that will assist in planning, controlling, and decision-making. In contrast to financial accounting, internal management accounting dictates its own information needs and specifies the way that data is accumulated and presented. It need not follow any particular rules or guidelines, as its intended purpose is for internal decision-making.

THE ACCOUNTING PROFESSION

Like law or medicine, the field of accounting involves specialized study and experience in a variety of disciplines. The simplest of accounting tasks is no more than detailed bookkeeping; on the other end of the spectrum is analysis of complex data and economic predictions at the global level.

Auditing services involve the examination of transactions and systems that constitute an organization's financial reports. The objective of an **audit** is to provide an independent review and report on the appropriateness and correctness of financial statements.

Tax services relate to providing help in the preparation and filing of tax returns to governmental entities, and the rendering of advice on the tax consequences of alternative filing or income-classifying actions.

Consulting services include such diverse activities as evaluating production methods or developing information systems capable of multi- data-processing tasks.

Accountants may work in areas of product costing and pricing, budgeting, or diversifying investments. They may focus on internal auditing of controls and procedures used by their employers, to safeguard company resources and develop reliable and accurate accounting information and systems. They may specialize as tax accountants, auditors, or financial managers. Their expertise is widely used in governmental agencies such as the Internal Revenue Service, General Accounting Office, or Securities and Exchange Commission.

Accountants, PAs, and CPAs Referring to oneself as an accountant *implies,* but does not require, a college education or license. It does require, at a minimum, a mastery of specialized expertise in the understanding and presentation of complex financial data. Many small business entities retain accountants/bookkeepers internally

as employees to handle the internal financial matters of the business.

Engaging in the practice of "public accounting" involves auditing, taxing, and consulting services to the general public. The term "PA" has become somewhat obsolete (or at least subsumed within the broader category of CPA) in that most, but not all, public accountants are licensed as Certified Public Accountants (CPAs) and hold themselves out as certified to engage in the practice of public accounting. CPAs have received a public accountant registration or license from an accountancy board within the **jurisdiction** in which they practice after having met all requirements for such license.

Qualification and Licensure The federal government plays no role in establishing minimum criteria for the profession, and instead defers to states. Qualification to practice accounting in each state is controlled by that state's board of accountancy.

Generally speaking, references to the term "accountant" imply a profession dictated by the fulfillment of minimum education requirements and experience. Certainly this is true for the CPA subcategory. Most colleges offer bachelors' degrees in accounting, which is almost universally a minimum requirement for employment in the field. While experience often had been substituted for education in job vacancies in the past, the technical nature of liability exposure for accounting errors has come to dictate a more comprehensive minimum educational requirement that ensures uniformity in the learning of various accounting practices and procedures.

CPA Requirements The objective of most prospective accounting professionals is the attainment of a CPA license. All CPA candidates in all 50 state jurisdictions and the District of Columba must meet minimum educational criteria, successfully pass the Uniform Certified Public Accountant (CPA) Examination, and undergo background investigation to qualify for the CPA license/certificate permitting them to practice.

All states require (New York was the last to implement, in 2009) a minimum of 150-hour education credits. This essentially equates to the completion of a standard 120-semester-hour bachelor's (baccalaureate) degree plus 30 hours of specialized course study in accounting, as in typical master's degree programs. All states have a minimum number of core semester hours in accounting that must be completed as part of the educational requirement.

The Uniform CPA Examination was adopted by all 50 states and the District of Columbia as a way to protect the **public interest** in helping to ensure that only qualified individuals become licensed as CPAs. A revised examination was implemented in 2004, and new simulations on the exam were upgraded in 2006. Subjects covered in the examination include auditing and attestation; financial accounting and reporting; regulation; and business environments and concepts.

Each state accountancy board has additional criteria that must be met in order to obtain a license to practice within that state's jurisdiction. They include minimum age, residency, and experience requirements.

PROFESSIONAL ETHICS

The Code of Professional Conduct promulgated by the American Institute of Certified Public Accountants (AICPA), the premier association of certified professionals, contains both Principles and Rules governing the profession. Accounting Principles provide the framework for the Rules, which, in turn, govern the performance of professional services by members. Compliance with the Code depends primarily on members' understanding and voluntary actions, as tempered by peer reviews and public opinion, and ultimately disciplinary proceedings when necessary.

Membership in the AICPA is limited to those practitioners who are practicing in firms enrolled in an AICPA-approved practice-monitoring program (peer review). Firms that are required to register with and be inspected by the Public Company Accounting Oversight Board (PCAOB) must have a peer review program developed and administered by the AICPA's Center for Public Company Audit Firms (Center PRP).

State boards of accountancy also regulate the type of fees that accountants may charge for their services. The majority of states do permit CPAs to accept commission-based fees, with full disclosure to clients, except in situations where CPAs perform "attest services." Generally, a CPA is prohibited from charging or accepting contingency fees for preparation of tax returns or tax refund claims, unless the CPA could reasonably expect that the claim would undergo substantive review by the taxing authority.

ACCOUNTING'S WATCHDOG

In 1997, the American Institute of Certified Public Accountants (AICPA) and the National Association of State Boards of Accountancy (NASBA) jointly approved and published significant changes to their Uniform Accountancy Act (UAA) and Uniform Accountancy Act Rules. The UAA model bill and rules were designed to provide a uniform approach to regulation of the accounting profession, which had been largely self-regulated and self-policed, as are several other professions. The changes to the UAA reflected major recommendations by a joint committee of the two organizations that studied the issue of regulation for at least one year before issuing its report. The report focused on a number of contemporary issues facing the profession, including:

- globalization of business
- demographic shifts in the profession
- expansion of services
- dynamic information and electronic technology
- legal challenges to the current regulatory system

Controlling Interstate Practice One of the most significant changes in the UAA concerns the portability of a CPA license, and mobility across state lines for CPAs engaged in interstate practice, both personally and electronically. The approach taken was to establish, under Section 23 of the UAA, a "substantial equivalency" concept. The NASBA's National Qualification Appraisal Service (NQAS) first determined which states' CPA licensure requirements were substantially equivalent to that of the UAA (Section 23). CPAs who are licensed to practice in substantially equivalent states and who plan to practice in other states that have adopted Section 23 may lawfully practice in those states by simple notification of intent. A majority of states and jurisdictions have CPA licensure requirements that were substantially equivalent to that of the UAA. As of 2012 only the U.S. Virgin Islands was found to have non-substantially equivalent requirements.

At the same time, even though the vast majority of states met the equivalency criteria, only a few were expressly serviced by NASBA to accept documentation for the reciprocal licensing and notification process. They were: Arkansas, California, Kansas, New York, North Dakota, and Oklahoma.

Regulation of Accounting Firms The UAA requires that all individuals referring to themselves as CPAs must hold a valid license obtained only after demonstrating a jurisdiction's licensing requirements [UAA Sections 3(c),5, and 14(c)]. This license must be periodically renewed by demonstrated compliance with continuing education (CPE) requirements (UAA Section 6). All licenses must comply with the accountancy law and regulations (UAA Section 10). Importantly, any individual holding a CPA license is subject to the state board of accountancy, regardless of how that individual earns his/her living or whether he or she uses the CPA title.

Under the UAA, CPAs who offer or render "attest services" (audits, reviews, and examinations of financial statements or information) for the public must do so in a CPA firm that is duly licensed by the state board of accountancy (UAA Section 7). These firms undergo peer review every three years to assure that those CPAs within the firm who supervise, sign, or authorize someone to sign "attest" engagements or reports on financial statements have met an appropriate **competency** requirement that is spelled out in professional standards.

CPAs are not required to offer general services through a CPA firm, and may offer other services through any type entity they choose as these entities are not licensed by the state board. Conversely, CPA firms using the term "CPAs" in association with the entity name are subject to regulation and discipline by the state board [UAA Section 7(a)].

Generally Accepted Accounting Principles (GAAP)
Generally Accepted Accounting Principles (GAAP) refer to a combination of authoritative standards (set by policy boards) and a common set of accounting principles, standards, and procedures that most companies use to compile their financial statements. The reason that GAAP are imposed on company reporting is to ensure that investors have an ascertained level of consistency when analyzing companies for investment purposes. Companies are expected to use GAAP when reporting their financial data via financial statements. The GAAP was not a law, but the U.S. Securities and Exchange Commission (SEC) requires that it be applied to in the financial reporting of all publicly-traded companies.

Three organizations developed or influenced the development of the GAAP in the United States: the SEC, the AICPA, and the FASB. A separate but similar set of rules and principles govern state and local government reporting, as determined by the Governmental Accounting Standards Board (GASB).

Accountants generally apply GAAP through the use of FASB pronouncements referred to as Financial Accounting Standards (FASs), which are periodically published in industry bulletins. There are more than 100 FASs that have been issued over the years. They are supplemented by formal opinions and generally accepted assumptions in a particular sub-segment of the industry. For example, there exists a general assumption that financial statements must be based on the premise that a company will continue in existence unless there is substantial **evidence** to the contrary. Accountants are guided by these formal standards, rules, and principles, but must also incorporate their own professional judgment into their practices.

In 2005, the U.S. Supreme Court overturned the **conviction** of accounting firm Arthur Andersen, previously indicted and convicted of obstructing justice for shredding documents of its work done for Enron, the energy services giant under investigation for financial wrongdoing. *U.S. v. Arthur Andersen,* No. 04-0368 (2005). The government had cited various provisions of the GAAP as evidence of wrongdoing. (However, the conviction was overturned on a technicality, involving the wording of a principal **jury** instruction that, according to the Supreme Court, was vague and failed to convey the required consciousness of wrongdoing in order to convict.)

Sarbanes-Oxley Act Following the Enron and WorldCom scandals, President George W. Bush signed into law the Sarbanes-Oxley Act of 2002 (P.L. 107-104, 116 Stat 745), which applies to publicly-traded companies and their audit firms (or CPAs actively working as auditors of, or for, publicly traded companies). There are some basic implications for accountants, including:

- The Establishment of a Public Company Accounting Oversight Board (PCAOB): Appointed and overseen by the SEC, its function is to oversee and investigate the audits and auditors of public companies, and it has sanctioning power over both firms and individuals for violations of laws, regulations, and rules.

- The Creation of Criminal Penalties and Protections for Whistleblowers: Tough penalties are available for those who destroy records, commit securities **fraud**, or fail to report fraud. The SEC established new rules covering the retention of "audit or review work papers." Other standards compel auditors to keep documentation for seven years. It is now a **felony** punishable by up to 20 years' **imprisonment** for destruction of documents in a federal or **bankruptcy** investigation.

- Other checks and balances prohibit firms from providing audit services to any public company if any of that company's top officials was employed by the firm and worked on the company's audit during the previous year. Furthermore, auditors report to and are overseen by a company's audit committee and not by its management.

Peer Review Membership in the AICPA is limited to those practitioners who are practicing in firms enrolled in an AICPA-approved practice-monitoring program (peer review). Firms that are required to register with and be inspected by the PCAOB must have a peer review program developed and administered by the AICPA's Center for Public Company Audit Firms (Center PRP).

Accounting firms that are members of the Center for Public Company Audit Firms that are not required to be registered with and inspected by the PCAOB may enroll in either the Center PRP or the AICPA PRP. Those firms that are not members of the Center for Public Company Audit Firms but want or are required to be enrolled in the Center PRP must submit an enrollment form and the Center Peer Review Committee will consider the request. All other firms have a peer review under the AICPA PRP. The AICPA's PRP was developed by and is overseen by the AICPA and administered by 41 state CPA societies across the country.

WHO'S WATCHING THE WATCHDOG?

Since the PCAOB was created in 2002, business executives and free-market groups have argued that as an accounting industry regulator the Board has wielded too much unchecked power. In early 2006, the Free Enterprise Fund joined a Nevada accounting firm in filing suit in U.S. district court in Washington challenging the constitutionality of the PCAOB. The suit alleged that the process for selecting PCAOB members violated the U.S. Constitution's separation of powers. Under Sarbanes-Oxley, which created the PCAOB, the SEC appoints them, rather than the president (confirmed by the Senate). Although the PCAOB considers its members lower-level officials not subject to Constitutional provisions, it sets its own budget and pays its members upward of $450,000 a year without Congressional oversight. Nevertheless, when Sarbanes-Oxley was being drafted, these arguments had been previously considered by constitutional scholars in Congress and several universities, and the provisions passed muster under these reviews.

Also in early 2006, the tax return-preparation giant, H&R Block Inc. revealed that it had miscalculated and understated its own state **income tax** liability for 2004 and 2005, amounting to approximately $32 million in **arrears**. The company had just settled four state class-action lawsuits related to "refund anticipation loans," where customers were advanced their tax refunds in return for a percentage of the refund being paid to H&R Block. However, the Center for Responsible Lending had alleged that the annual **interest rates** on these types of loans often turned out to be as high as 40 to 700 percent annualized. The **settlement** affected more than eight million customers.

In 2005, the General Accounting Office (GAO) performed its first audit of the SEC and released a mixed report. It found that the Commission had inadequate controls over its financial **statement** preparation process. This included a lack of sufficiently documented internal policies and procedures, raising questions of whether the balances presented in SEC's own financial statements were supported by SEC's underlying accounting records.

FINDING A GOOD ACCOUNTANT

Word-of-mouth recommendations remain the preferred method to find high-quality accountants. Checking with other business owners in the area, as well as industry trade associations, often results in recommendations of good accountants familiar with issues specific to a particular business or industry.

Users of accounting services should always check with the local Better Business Bureau and local or state professional accountancy boards to ensure that accountants' credentials are good and licenses are current.

It is possible for public accounting services to be purchased and provided over the Internet. Despite its ostensible convenience, consumers are reminded that since there is no face-to-face contact, unqualified persons may masquerade as fully-licensed accountants. Internet accountants may be physically located anywhere in the world. Therefore, any problems encountered with the purchased services may not be resolved if the provider of the service is not licensed in the consumer's state or jurisdiction. It is recommended that investigative e-mails and telephone conversations precede any commitment for services.

ACCOUNTING DISCIPLINE AND MALPRACTICE

Substantiated complaints and grievances against accountants are best addressed by state accountancy boards, most of which provide a forum and specific procedures for resolution. However, state boards are limited, for the most part, to suspensions or revocations of licenses to practice, and cannot award money damages for harm or loss.

Clients should also be sure before any work is done that a CPA provides an engagement letter outlining the work that will be performed, who will specifically perform the work, and what it will cost. In a majority of complaints received by accountancy boards that **allege** poor or incorrect services, no engagement letter had been provided that clearly described the agreement between client and CPA. In such cases, both CPA and client can only provide verbal recollections of the services, and discipline for substandard work is limited.

If substandard work performed by an accountant has caused financial loss or harm to a client, a civil lawsuit for professional **malpractice** is the most appropriate remedy (in addition to filing a complaint with the state board of accountancy). Some jurisdictions offer alternative dispute resolution (**arbitration, mediation**), which is particularly helpful if **privacy** is a consideration.

Unlike complaints filed with a state board, lawsuits carry a heavy **burden of proof** before a complaining party may recover monetary damages for substandard accounting work. As in other professional malpractice cases, expert witnesses from the same accounting discipline must **testify** that the **defendant** accountant (or accounting firm) breached its duty of care (such as those considered as GAAP) by providing services that violated GAAP or other established practices and procedures. However, and more importantly, the complaining party has the burden of showing that, but for the substandard work, the complaining party would not have suffered the financial loss or would have gained more financial benefit. By the time that costs and expenses of expert witnesses and **litigation** are taken into account, accountant malpractice suits should be considered a last resort.

Accountant malpractice lawsuits sometimes involve alleged violations of state and federal statutes relating to the sale of securities. If the attested financial statements contain errors and lead to negative market impact, investors may try to recoup damages by asserting securities claims against the accountants who prepared the statements. The statutes most commonly cited to bring such claims are the Securities Act of 1933, the Securities Act of 1934, and the Racketeer Influenced and Corrupt Organizations Act (RICO).

STATE BOARDS OF ACCOUNTANCY

ALABAMA STATE BOARD OF PUBLIC ACCOUNTANCY: Suite 226, 770 Washington Ave., P.O. Box 300375, Montgomery, AL 36130 (334) 242-5700; fax (334) 242-2711

ALASKA STATE BOARD OF PUBLIC ACCOUNTANCY: Division of Occupational Licensing, Box 110806, Juneau, AK 99811-0806 (907) 465-3811; fax (907) 465-2974

ARIZONA STATE BOARD OF ACCOUNTANCY: 100 N. 15th Ave., Suite 165, Phoenix, AZ 85007 (602) 364-0804; fax (602) 364-0903

ARKANSAS STATE BOARD OF ACCOUNTANCY: 101 East Capitol, Suite 450, Little Rock, AR 72201 (501) 682-1520; fax (501) 682-5538

CALIFORNIA BOARD OF ACCOUNTANCY: 2000 Evergreen Street, Suite. 250, Sacramento, CA 95815 (916) 263-3680; fax (916) 263-3675

COLORADO STATE BOARD OF ACCOUNTANCY: 1560 Broadway, Suite 1340, Denver, CO 80202 (303) 894-7800; fax (303) 894-7692

CONNECTICUT STATE BOARD OF ACCOUNTANCY: 30 Trinity St., Hartford, CT 06106 (860) 509-6179; fax (860) 509-6247

DELAWARE STATE BOARD OF ACCOUNTANCY: Cannon Bldg., Suite. 203, 861 Silver Lake Blvd, Dover, DE 19904 (302) 744-4511; fax (302) 739-2711

DISTRICT OF COLUMBIA BOARD OF ACCOUNTANCY: Occupational & Professional Licensing, Room 7200, 941 North Capitol St., NE, Washington, D.C. 20002 (202) 442-4461; fax (202) 442-4528

FLORIDA BOARD OF ACCOUNTANCY: 240 NW 76 Drive., Ste A, Gainesville, FL 32607 (850) 487-1395; fax: (352) 333-2508

GEORGIA STATE BOARD OF ACCOUNTANCY: 237 Coliseum Dr., Macon, GA 31217-3858 (478) 207-1300; fax (478) 207-1363

HAWAII BOARD OF ACCOUNTANCY: P.O. Box 3469, Honolulu, HI 96801 (808) 586-3000; fax (808) 586-2689

IDAHO STATE BOARD OF ACCOUNTANCY: P.O. Box 83720, Boise, ID 83720 (208) 334-2490; fax (208) 334-2615

ILLINOIS BOARD OF EXAMINERS: 100 Trade Centre Drive, Suite 403, Champaign, IL 61820 (217) 531-0950; fax (217) 531-0960

INDIANA STATE BOARD OF PUBLIC ACCOUNTANCY: Professional Licensing Agency, 302 West Washington St., Room W 072, Indianapolis, IN 46204 (317) 234-3040; fax (317) 232-2312

IOWA ACCOUNTANCY EXAMINING BOARD: 1920 SE Hulsizer Road, Ankeny, IA 50021-3941 (515) 281-5910; fax: (515) 281-7411

KANSAS BOARD OF ACCOUNTANCY: 900 S.W. Jackson St., Suite 556, Topeka, KS 66612-1239 (785) 296-2162; fax (785) 291-3501

KENTUCKY STATE BOARD OF ACCOUNTANCY: 332 West Broadway, Suite 310, Louisville, KY 40202 (502) 595-3037; fax (502) 595-4281

STATE BOARD OF CPAS OF LOUISIANA: 601 Poydras Street, Suite 1770, New Orleans, LA 70130 (504) 566-1244; fax (504) 566-1252

MAINE BOARD OF ACCOUNTANCY: #35 State House Station, Augusta, ME 04333-0035 (207) 624-8603; fax (207) 624-8637

MARYLAND STATE BOARD OF PUBLIC ACCOUNTANCY: 500 N. Calvert Street, Room 308, Baltimore, MD 21202 (410) 230-6258; fax (410) 333-6314

MASSACHUSETTS BOARD OF PUBLIC ACCOUNTANCY: 239 Causeway Street, Boston, Massachusetts 02114 (617) 727-1806; fax: (617) 727-2197

MICHIGAN BOARD OF ACCOUNTANCY: P.O. Box 30018, Lansing, MI 48909 (517) 241-9249; fax (517) 241-9280

MINNESOTA STATE BOARD OF ACCOUNTANCY: 85 E. 7th Place., Suite 125, St. Paul, MN 55101 (651) 296-7937; fax (651) 282-2644

MISSISSIPPI STATE BOARD OF PUBLIC ACCOUNTANCY: 5 Old River Place, Suite 104, Jackson, MS 39202 (601) 354-7320; fax (601) 354-7290

MISSOURI STATE BOARD OF ACCOUNTANCY: P.O. Box 1335, Jefferson City, MO 65102 (573) 526-1555; fax (573) 751-0735

MONTANA STATE BOARD OF PUBLIC ACCOUNTANCY: P.O. Box 200513, Helena, MT 59620 (406) 841-2300; fax (406) 841-2309

NEBRASKA STATE BOARD OF PUBLIC ACCOUNTANCY: P.O. Box 94725, Lincoln, NE 68509 (402) 471-3595; fax (402) 471-4484

NEVADA STATE BOARD OF ACCOUNTANCY: 1325 Airmotive Way, Suite #220, Reno, NV 89502 (775) 786-0231; fax (775) 786-0234

NEW HAMPSHIRE BOARD OF ACCOUNTANCY: 78 Regional Dr., Building 2, Concord, NH 03301 (603) 271-3286; fax (603) 271-8702

NEW JERSEY STATE BOARD OF ACCOUNTANCY: P.O. Box 45000, Newark, NJ 07101 (973) 504-6380; fax (973) 648-2855

NEW MEXICO STATE BOARD OF PUBLIC ACCOUNTANCY: 5200 Oakland NE, Suite D, Albuquerque, NM 87113 (505) 222-9850; fax (505)222-9855

NEW YORK STATE BOARD FOR PUBLIC ACCOUNTANCY: 89 Washington Ave., Albany, NY 12234 (518) 474-3817 ext. 270; fax (518) 402-5354

NORTH CAROLINA STATE BOARD OF CPA EXAMINERS: P.O. Box 12827, Raleigh, NC 27605-2827 (919) 733-4222; fax (919) 733-4209

NORTH DAKOTA BOARD OF ACCOUNTANCY: 2701 S. Columbia Rd., Grand Forks, ND 58201 (800) 532-5904; fax (701) 775-7430

ACCOUNTANCY BOARD OF OHIO: 77 S. High St., 18th Floor, Columbus, OH 43215-6128 (614) 466-4135; fax (614) 466-2628

OKLAHOMA STATE BOARD OF PUBLIC ACCOUNTANCY: 4545 N Lincoln Blvd., Suite 165, Oklahoma City, OK 73105 (405) 521-2397; fax (405) 521-3118

OREGON STATE BOARD OF ACCOUNTANCY: 3218 Pringle Rd. S.E., Suite #110, Salem, OR 97302-6307 (503) 378-4181; fax (503) 378-3575

PENNSYLVANIA BOARD OF ACCOUNTANCY: P. O. Box 2649, Harrisburg, PA 17105-2649 (717) 783-1404; fax (717) 705-5540

RHODE ISLAND BOARD OF ACCOUNTANCY: 233 Richmond St., Providence, RI 02903 (401) 222-2246; fax (401) 222-6098

SOUTH CAROLINA BOARD OF ACCOUNTANCY: Street Address: 110 Centerview Dr., Columbia, SC

Mailing Address: PO Box 11329, Columbia, S.C. 29211 (803) 896-4770; fax: (803) 896-4554

SOUTH DAKOTA BOARD OF ACCOUNTANCY: 301 E. 14th St., Suite 200, Sioux Falls, SD 57104-5022 (605) 367-5770; fax (605) 367-5773

TENNESSEE STATE BOARD OF ACCOUNTANCY: 500 James Robertson Parkway, 2nd Floor, Nashville, TN 37243-1141 (615) 741-2550; fax (615) 532-8800

TEXAS STATE BOARD OF PUBLIC ACCOUNTANCY: 333 Guadalupe Tower III, Suite 900, Austin, TX 78701-3900 (512) 305-7851; fax (512) 305-7875

UTAH BOARD OF ACCOUNTANCY: 160 East 300 South, Salt Lake City, UT 84111-2316 (801) 530-6628; fax (801) 530-65111

VERMONT BOARD OF ACCOUNTANCY: 26 Terrace St., Montpelier, VT 05609-110 (802) 828-2837; fax (802) 828-2465

VIRGINIA BOARD FOR ACCOUNTANCY: 3600 W. Broad St., Suite 378, Richmond, VA 23230 (804) 367-8505; fax (804) 367-2174

WASHINGTON STATE BOARD OF ACCOUNTANCY: P.O. Box 9131, Olympia, WA 98507-9131 (360) 753-2586; fax (360) 664-9190

WEST VIRGINIA BOARD OF ACCOUNTANCY: 122 Capitol Street, Suite 100, Charleston, WV 25301 (304) 558-3557; fax (304) 558-1325

WISCONSIN ACCOUNTING EXAMINING BOARD: 1400 East Washington Ave., P.O. Box 8935, Madison, WI 53708-8935 (608) 266-5511; fax (608) 267-3816

WYOMING BOARD OF CPAS: 2020 Carey, Cheyenne, WY 82002 (307) 777-7551; fax (307) 777-3796

ADDITIONAL RESOURCES

Borrus, Amy. "Who Watches Accounting's Watchdog?" *Business Week,* 8 February 2006. Available at http://www.businessweek .com/investor/content/feb2006/pi20060208_072238.htm (accessed December 18, 2012).

Dharan, Bala G., et al, (contributors). *Enron: Corporate Fiascos and Their Implications.* Foundation Press, 2004.

Walther, Larry, PhD., CPA, CMA. "Principles of Accounting." Online publication available at http://www.principlesof accounting.com (accessed December 18, 2012).

ORGANIZATIONS

American Institute of Certified Public Accountants
1211 Avenue of the Americas
New York, NY 10036-8775
Phone: (212) 596-6200
Fax: (212) 596-6213
URL: http://aicpa.org

Financial Accounting Standards Board

401 Merritt
Norwalk, CT 06856-5116
Phone: (203) 847-0700
Fax: (203) 849-9714
URL: http://www.fasb.org

National Association of State Boards of Accountancy

150 Fourth Avenue North, Suite 700
Nashville, TN 37219-2417
Phone: (615) 880-4200
Fax: (615) 880-4292
URL: http://www.nasba.org

BUSINESS LAW

CONFLICTS OF INTEREST

BACKGROUND

Conflicts of interest arise in several different environments. A conflict may arise when the personal interests of someone in a position of **trust** clashes with the person's professional interests. A conflict may also arise when a person has different professional responsibilities and those responsibilities collide. A person who has these types of competing interests may have difficulty in fulfilling professional obligations.

Examples of professionals that may face conflicts of interest are numerous, although such conflicts generally arise in some professions more than others. For instance, a judge may have personal interests that could be affected by the outcome of a case. Likewise, an attorney or law firm may have interests that conflict with the interests of a client. Similar problems may arise in the fields of accounting, stock analysis, education, and business, as well as federal employment. Elected officials also face conflicts of interest in fulfilling their duties and are subject to rules of ethics that regulate how the officials must handle these conflicts.

HANDLING CONFLICTS OF INTEREST

A person who faces a conflict of interest may not be able to avoid the conflict. In such an instance, the person may be required to take certain legal steps or may need to follow certain practices in order to avoid any appearance of impropriety. The following are some of the means by which conflicts of interest may be handled, either by law or as good professional practice:

- Duty of Loyalty: In **partnership** law, for example, a partner is bound by a duty of loyalty, which forbids the partner from personally engaging in a business transaction to the detriment of the partnership.

- Fairness: Some laws, such as those governing conflicts of interest within **corporations**, require that transactions involving such conflicts are fair.

- Full Disclosure: Many professionals, such as lawyers and government officials, are required by law to give full, written disclosure of any conflicts of interest.

- Recusal: Decision-makers, such as judges or members of government agencies, may choose to recuse themselves in situations where the subject of a decision involves a conflict of interest.

- Third-Party Evaluations: In some situations, such as where majority shareholders in a corporation decide to buy out minority shareholders, a neutral third party may be used to determine a fair market price for the minority shares.

FIELD OF LAW

Lawyers A lawyer's relationship with a client is based largely on trust and confidence, such that the lawyer can provide the best possible representation of the client. Because of the nature of this relationship, a lawyer may frequently encounter a conflict of interest with the client. One instance may occur when one of the lawyer's clients has an interest that clashes with an interest of another client.

The American Bar Association's (ABA) Model Rules of Professional Conduct, which have been adopted by the majority of states, forbid or restrict lawyers from representing a client if a conflict exists. Under the Model Rules, a "concurrent conflict of interest" exists when: the lawyer's representation of one client will be directly adverse to another client; or the lawyer's representation of one or more clients runs a significant risk of being materially limited by the attorney's representation of another client, a former client, or a third person.

The Model Rules allow a lawyer to represent a client notwithstanding a conflict of interest when each of the following four criteria are met: the lawyer reasonably believes that he or she can still provide competent and diligent representation in spite of the conflict; the lawyer's representation of the client is not prohibited by law; the representation does not involve an instance where a claim by one of the lawyer's clients is brought against another of the lawyer's clients in the same **litigation** or other proceeding before a **tribunal**; and each affected client provides consent in writing after being informed of the conflict.

Under the Model Rules, a lawyer may neither engage in a business practice with a client nor acquire an ownership, possessory, security, or other pecuniary interest that is adverse to the client. The exception to this rule applies when the terms of the transaction are reasonable and fair to the client and are fully disclosed in writing; the client is advised in writing that he or she should seek the advice of independent legal **counsel** regarding the transaction; and "the client gives **informed consent**, in a writing signed by the client, to the essential terms of the transaction and the lawyer's role in the transaction, including whether the lawyer is representing the client in the transaction."

Lawyers are also limited from engaging in specified conduct that would involve conflicts of interest. These types of conduct include:

- Using information relating to the representation of a client to the disadvantage of the client unless the client gives informed consent.

- Soliciting any substantial gift from a client, including a testamentary gift, unless the client is related to the lawyer.

- Negotiating an agreement that gives the lawyer literary or media right to a portrayal or accounted based on information relating to the representation.

- Providing financial assistance to a client in connection with pending or contemplated litigation, except that a lawyer may advance court costs on behalf of a client or pay the court costs and expenses of an indigent client.

- Accepting compensation for representing a client from someone other than the client, unless the client gives informed consent, the payment of compensation does not interfere with the lawyer's independence of professional judgment or with the lawyer-client relationship, and the information pertaining to the client remains confidential.

- Acquiring a **proprietary** interest in a client's cause of action or the subject matter of a client's case, except in certain situations.

- Having sexual relations with a client unless a consensual sexual relationship existed between the lawyer and client when the lawyer-client relationship began.

The Model Rules also restrict lawyers from representing a client where a conflict of interest may exist between the prospective client and another member of the firm. The Model Rules likewise limit lawyers from representing someone who has interests that are adverse to one of the lawyer's former clients.

Judges Perhaps even more than for attorneys, conflicts of interest can prevent judges from carrying out their responsibilities. The Model Code of Judicial Conduct, which was drafted by the ABA and has been adopted by the majority of states, strictly forbids a judge from taking part in a case where the judge's interest may conflict with his or her professional responsibilities. According to Canon 2 of the Model Code, "[a] judge shall avoid impropriety and the appearance of impropriety in all of the judge's activities." In a more specific provision, the Model Code states, "A judge shall not allow family, social, political or other relationships to influence the judge's judicial conduct or judgment. A judge shall not lend the prestige of judicial office to advance the private interests of the judge or others; nor shall a judge convey or permit others to convey the impression that they are in a special position to influence the judge. A judge shall not **testify** voluntarily as a character witness."

A judge who faces a conflict of interest in a case is expected to recuse himself or herself from the case. A judge who presides over a case where the judge has a conflict of interest could face **impeachment** from the bench.

ACCOUNTING

The accounting industry faced a great deal of criticism in 2001 and 2002 following a scandal involving Enron Corporation and its auditors. During the fall of 2001, Enron was the seventh-largest company in the United States. Over the period of a few months, however, the company collapsed due to accounting **fraud** and other instances of wrongdoing. In the aftermath of the scandal, Arthur Andersen, an accounting firm hired by Enron as an outside auditor, shredded hundreds of documents related to Enron. The firm was later convicted of obstruction of justice.

Prior to these scandals, accountants and accounting firms often engaged in consulting work, earning considerable fees in the process. Critics charged that accountants were reluctant to challenge clients about questionable financial activities because the accountants earned such large fees from these clients. The Enron scandal and other events that followed led to the enactment of the Sarbanes-Oxley Act of 2002, Pub. L. No. 107-204, 116 Stat. 745, which addressed these concerns.

The Sarbanes-Oxley Act restricts accounting firms from engaging in consulting work that could result in a conflict of interest. The **statute** also forbids a public accounting firm from performing an **audit** on a company where the accounting firm previously employed an officer of that company and the officer participated in an audit of the same company.

STOCK ANALYSIS

In addition to conflicts of interest in the accounting industry, critics during the early 2000s became concerned about conflicts that occurred with respect to stock analysts in **securities** firms. These concerns arose because analysts made recommendations regarding the potential value of securities in public communications. A conflict could occur in several situations, such as where a stock analyst firm had a financial relationship with a company that issued securities.

In 2002, the U.S. Securities and Exchange Commission approved rule changes that addressed conflicts of interest that may arise with respect to stock analysts. These rules include provisions relating to the following:

- Analysts are prohibited from offering or threatening to withhold a favorable rating or price target with respect to stock in order to induce companies to employ the analyst for investment banking purposes.
- Research analysts may not be supervised by a company's investment banking department. Rules also restrict communications between investment banking personnel and research analysts.
- Securities firms may not tie an analyst's compensation to a specific investment banking transaction.
- A securities firm must disclose in a research report that it received compensation for investment banking services from a company that is the subject of the report.
- A stock analyst may not personally invest in a company's securities prior to the company's initial public offering if the company is in the same business sector that the analyst covers.
- Stock analysts are required to disclose whether they own shares in companies that they recommend.

BUSINESS

Owners and managers of businesses may encounter conflicts during the course of the business. Laws governing these businesses handle conflicts by several different means. For instance, partners in a partnership are bound by a duty of loyalty that prevents the partner from competing in a business to the detriment of the partnership.

A conflict of interest is often the result of a transaction between a business, such as a corporation, and a manager of the business. The manager may take advantage of this relationship and complete a transaction that benefits himself or herself and not the corporation. In the majority of U.S. jurisdictions, the resolution of a conflict of interest for a controlling **shareholder**, director, or officer of a corporation focuses on the fairness of the transaction. The person who is involved in the transaction must prove that the transaction is the result of fair dealing and demonstrates a fair price.

MEDICAL AND SCIENTIFIC RESEARCH

Because the publication of research is so important in the medical and scientific communities, conflicts of interest may interfere with the dissemination of accurate information. For example, a pharmaceutical company that is producing a drug may fund research that is the subject of an article that is published in a reputable journal. Due to the possibility that the company's funding causes a conflict of interest with the person or entity conducting the research, most medical journals require researchers to disclose the sources of funding for their research.

FEDERAL EMPLOYMENT

Under a federal criminal statute at 18 U.S.C. § 208, federal employees are forbidden from participating "personally and substantially in his official, governmental capacity in a matter" where the employee "knew that he, his spouse, or another statutorily-listed person had a financial interest" in a particular matter. The Office of Government Ethics (OGE) has promulgated regulations that have clarified to some extent the terms of this statute.

In order to participate "personally and substantially" in an action, a federal employee must have done more than participated in a ministerial or procedural role. Prosecutors may prove that the **defendant** had requisite knowledge by proving that the defendant knew about the forbidden financial interest, even if the employee did not intend to violate the statute. Courts and the OGE have further established that the statute applies only where there is a "real possibility" of gain or loss as a result of the matter.

STATE LAW APPLYING TO ELECTED OFFICIALS

Members of state legislatures are subject to a number of rules pertaining to conflicts of interest, most of which relate to disclosure of specified types of information. According to the National Conference of State Legislatures, every state except Idaho, Michigan, and Vermont requires members of the legislative body to file personal financial disclosures. The majority of states also require disclosure of other types of information, such as the names of clients or the names of certain debtors or creditors. The following is a summary of some of these requirements.

ALABAMA: State law does not require the disclosure of the names of individual clients. Legislators must reveal any indebtedness to banks, savings and loan associations, insurance companies, **mortgage** firms, stockbrokers, bond firms, or other specified organizations.

ALASKA: State law requires disclosure of names of clients who have an interest in legislation or in other specified instances. Legislators must reveal the names and addresses of the sources of loans or loan guarantees. Certain gifts must also be disclosed.

ARIZONA: State law does not require the disclosure of the names of individual clients. Legislators must reveal the

names and addresses of certain debtors and creditors. The names of the sources of gifts of more than $500 must also be disclosed.

ARKANSAS: State law does not require the disclosure of the names of individual clients. Legislators must reveal the names and addresses of certain debtors and creditors. The sources and amount of gifts of more than $100 must be disclosed.

CALIFORNIA: State law requires disclosure of the names of certain clients. Legislators must reveal the names and addresses of certain creditors. The name of the source of any gift of more than $50 must be disclosed.

COLORADO: State law does not require the disclosure of the names of individual clients. Legislators must reveal the names and addresses of certain creditors. The name of the source of certain gifts of more than $25 must be disclosed.

CONNECTICUT: State law does not require the disclosure of the names of individual clients. Legislators must reveal the names and addresses of certain creditors.

DELAWARE: State law does not require the disclosure of the names of individual clients. Legislators must reveal the names and addresses of certain creditors. The name of the source of any gift of more than $250 must be disclosed.

FLORIDA: State law requires disclosure of the names of certain clients. Legislators must reveal every liability that is greater than the legislator's **net** worth. The name of the source of any gift of more than $100 must be disclosed.

GEORGIA: State law does not require the disclosure of the names of individual clients. The sources and actual amounts of honoraria must be disclosed.

HAWAII: State law requires disclosure of the names of certain clients. Legislators must reveal the names and addresses of certain creditors. The name of the source of certain gifts of more than $200 must be disclosed.

IDAHO: State law does not require a personal financial disclosure.

ILLINOIS: State law does not require the disclosure of the names of individual clients. The name of the source of any gift of more than $500 must be disclosed.

INDIANA: State law requires disclosure of the names of clients who the legislator has represented before a state agency for a fee. The name of the source of certain gifts of more than $100 must be disclosed.

IOWA: State law does not require the disclosure of the names of individual clients.

KANSAS: State law requires disclosure of the names of certain clients. The name of the source of any gift of more than $500 must be disclosed.

KENTUCKY: State law does not require the disclosure of the names of individual clients. Legislators must reveal the names and addresses of certain creditors. The name of the source of any gift of more than $200 must be disclosed.

LOUISIANA: State law does not require the disclosure of the names of individual clients.

MAINE: State law requires disclosure of the names of certain clients. Legislators must reveal the source of any unsecured loan of $3,000 or more. The name of the source of any gift or honoraria must be disclosed.

MARYLAND: State law does not require the disclosure of the names of individual clients. Legislators must reveal the names and addresses of certain creditors. The name of the source of certain gifts of more than $100 must be disclosed.

MASSACHUSETTS: State law does not require the disclosure of the names of individual clients. Legislators must reveal the names and addresses of certain creditors. The name of the source of certain gifts of more than $100 must be disclosed.

MICHIGAN: State law does not require a personal financial disclosure.

MINNESOTA: State law does not require the disclosure of the names of individual clients. Officials may not accept gifts from lobbyists.

MISSISSIPPI: State law does not require the disclosure of the names of individual clients.

MISSOURI: State law does not require the disclosure of the names of individual clients. The name of the source of any gift of more than $200 must be disclosed.

MONTANA: State law does not require the disclosure of the names of individual clients.

NEBRASKA: State law does not require the disclosure of the names of individual clients. Legislators must reveal the names and addresses of certain creditors. The name of the source of any gift of more than $100 must be disclosed.

NEVADA: State law does not require the disclosure of the names of individual clients. Legislators must reveal the names and addresses of certain creditors. The name of the source of any gift of more than $200 must be disclosed.

NEW HAMPSHIRE: State law does not require the disclosure of the names of individual clients. The name of the source of any gift or honorarium of more than $50 must be disclosed.

NEW JERSEY: State law does not require the disclosure of the names of individual clients. The sources of any fees, honoraria, travel expenses, or other prepaid expenses must be disclosed.

NEW MEXICO: State law does not require the disclosure of the names of individual clients.

NEW YORK: State law does not require the disclosure of the names of individual clients. The name of the source of any gift of more than $1,000 must be disclosed.

NORTH CAROLINA: State law does not require the disclosure of the names of individual clients. Legislators must reveal the names and addresses of certain creditors.

NORTH DAKOTA: State law does not require the disclosure of the names of individual clients.

OHIO: State law requires disclosure of the names of certain clients. Legislators must reveal the names and addresses of certain creditors. The name of the source of any gift of more than $75 must be disclosed.

OKLAHOMA: State law requires disclosure of the names of clients who the legislator has represented before a state agency for a fee. The name of the source of any gift of more than $200 must be disclosed.

OREGON: State law requires disclosure of the names of certain clients. Legislators must reveal the names and addresses of certain creditors. The name of the source of any gift of more than $100 must be disclosed.

PENNSYLVANIA: State law requires disclosure of the names of certain clients. Legislators must reveal the names and addresses of certain creditors. The name of the source of any gift of more than $250 must be disclosed, as well as the source of any travel reimbursement of more than $650 for a single trip.

RHODE ISLAND: State law does not require the disclosure of the names of individual clients. Legislators must reveal the names and addresses of certain creditors. The name of the source of any gift of more than $100 must be disclosed.

SOUTH CAROLINA: State law requires disclosure of the names of certain clients. Legislators must reveal the names and addresses of certain creditors. The name of the source of certain gifts of more than $200 per year must be disclosed.

SOUTH DAKOTA: State law does not require the disclosure of the names of individual clients.

TENNESSEE: State law does not require the disclosure of the names of individual clients. The name of the source of certain gifts must be disclosed.

TEXAS: State law requires, in some instances, disclosure of the names of legislator's clients who are also lobbyists. Legislators must reveal the names and addresses of certain creditors. The name of the source of any gift of more than $250 must be disclosed.

UTAH: State law does not require the disclosure of the names of individual clients.

VERMONT: State law does not require a personal financial disclosure.

VIRGINIA: State law requires disclosure of the names of certain clients, including lobbyists. The name of the source of certain gifts and travel expenses must be disclosed.

WASHINGTON: State law does not require the disclosure of the names of individual clients. Legislators must reveal the names and addresses of certain creditors. The name of the source of any gift of more than $50 must be disclosed.

WEST VIRGINIA: State law does not require the disclosure of the names of individual clients. Legislators must reveal the names and addresses of certain creditors. The name of the source of any gift of more than $100 must be disclosed.

WISCONSIN: State law requires disclosure of the names of certain clients. Legislators must reveal the names and addresses of certain creditors. The name of the source of any gift of more than $50 must be disclosed.

WYOMING: State law does not require the disclosure of the names of individual clients.

ADDITIONAL RESOURCES

Hirsch, Jerry. "Senators to Battle Over Accounting." *Los Angeles Times*, May 20, 2002.

Kerns, Peggy. "How to Deal with Conflicts of Interest." *State Legislatures*, July/August 2004, 36.

Moore, Don A., Daylian M. Cain, et al, eds. *Conflicts of Interests: Challenges and Solutions in Business Law, Medicine, and Public Policy.* New York: Cambridge University Press, 2010.

Rotunda, Ronald. "Alleged Conflicts of Interest Because of the 'Appearance of Impropriety.'" *Hofstra Law Review*, Summer 2005, 1141.

Soller, Mary Lou, and Brian A. Hill. "Financial Conflicts of Interest: The Impact on Contractors and Federal Employees." *Procurement Lawyer* (Spring 2005) 1.

ORGANIZATIONS

American Bar Association (ABA)
321 North Clark Street
Chicago, IL 60610
Phone: (202) 662-1000
Toll Free: (800) 285-2221
Fax: (312) 988-6800
URL: http://www.americanbar.org

National Conference of State Legislatures
444 North Capitol Street, N.W., Suite 515
Washington, DC 20001
Phone: (202) 624-5400
Fax: (202) 737-1069
URL: http://www.ncsl.org

BUSINESS LAW

CORPORATIONS

Sections within this essay:

- Background
- History
- Laws Governing Corporations
- Forming a Corporation
- Shareholders, Directors, and Officers
- Shares and Dividends
- State Corporation Laws
- Additional Resources

BACKGROUND

A corporation is a distinct legal entity created by **statute**. Corporations have many of the same legal rights and obligations as do individuals. They can own and sell property, they can hold profits or acquire debts, they can enter into contracts and sue or be sued, and governments can tax them. Corporations are advantageous primarily because they become legal entities that are separate and distinct from the individuals who own and control them. This separation is important because in most cases these individuals have limited or no legal liability for the corporation's wrongdoings.

HISTORY

Roman law first developed the concept of corporations, and England adopted the concept long before the founding of the United States. As the states became independent from England in 1776, they too adopted corporations as distinct legal entities and assumed **jurisdiction** over them. In the 2010s, the federal government continues to leave the control of corporations primarily to the states.

Corporations did not become commonplace in the United States until the Industrial Revolution at the turn of the nineteenth century. They then quickly developed as an efficient manner in which to conduct a large enterprise while at the same time offering a degree of protection to investors and owners from legal liability. Investors and owners increasingly were drawn to the idea of the corporation, and by the 2010s corporations had become a mainstay of domestic and international business.

There are several types of corporations. Private corporations exist to make money for their investors and owners. nonprofit corporations, such as charities, exist to help a certain group of citizens or the general public. Municipal corporations are cities. Quasi-public corporations are entities such as telephone or electric companies that exist to make a profit as well as provide a service to the general public. A public corporation exists to make a profit, but it is distinguishable because it has a large number of investors known as shareholders. Shareholders own portions, known as shares, of the public corporations and may buy, sell, or trade their shares. Closely-held corporations have shareholders also but usually a much smaller group of shareholders. Often, closely-held corporations are owned by members of a family. Shareholders in closely-held corporations usually run the business, whereas shareholders in public corporations usually do not.

Another type of corporation is the professional corporation, which may be established only by professionals such as lawyers and doctors. Professionals may establish a professional corporation to limit their personal liability for **malpractice** committed by other professionals in the corporation.

LAWS GOVERNING CORPORATIONS

Many states based their laws governing corporations on the Model Business Corporations Act, which was first approved by the American Bar Association (ABA) in 1950. This act was significantly revised by the ABA in 1969 and again in 1984. A second popular source for corporation laws is the Delaware General Corporation Law. Delaware has a history of legislation that is particularly friendly to corporations, and so many corporations historically have chosen to incorporate there (see below). Lastly, the American Law Institute has produced Principles of Corporate Governance: Analysis and Recommendations, which courts often rely upon when ruling on matters related to the conduct of a business corporation.

FORMING A CORPORATION

An individual who wishes to start a corporation is known as a promoter. The promoter must find the money to start a corporation. This financing is known as capital and can be the promoter's own money, a loan from a bank or other financial institution, or money from an investor or group of investors who lend money to the promoter typically in exchange for future corporate profits. Before legally forming the corporation, or incorporating, the promoter often locates office or building space to house the corporation, identifies the people who will run the corporation, and then prepares the documents to make the corporation a legal entity. The work accomplished by the promoter prior to incorporation often necessitates contractual arrangements such as leases and loans. Because the corporation does not officially exist yet, the promoter must be the entity that enters into contracts. Later, when the corporation is legally formed, the corporation is considered as having assented to those contracts that were formed to benefit it prior to its official birth.

Corporation laws vary from state to state, but most states have the same basic requirements for forming a corporation. Promoters must file a document called the **articles of incorporation** with the secretary of state. These articles must include the corporation's name, whether the corporation will exist for a limited period of time or perpetually, the lawful business purpose of the corporation, the number of shares that the corporation will issue to shareholders as well as the types and preferences of the shares, the corporation's registered agent and address for the purpose of accepting service of process in the event that the corporation is sued, and the names and addresses of the corporation's directors and incorporators.

A corporation must also have **bylaws**, although states generally do not require that corporations file the bylaws with the secretary of state. Bylaws are rules that dictate how the corporation is going to be run. Bylaws are fairly easy to amend. They may include rules regarding the conduct of corporate officers, directors, and shareholders and typically they designate times, locations, and voting requirements for corporate meetings.

Small corporations frequently incorporate in the state in which they operate. However, promoters can incorporate in any state they wish. Delaware is the most popular state for incorporating because the Delaware General Corporation Law has been considered to be favorable to corporate bodies. With other states recently adopting laws modeled after Delaware's, however, Delaware has lost some of its competitive edge. However, Delaware continues to lead the nation in incorporations largely because corporate attorneys throughout the country are familiar with the laws in that state since Delaware infrequently changes its corporate laws and Delaware courts specialize in legal issues regarding corporations.

SHAREHOLDERS, DIRECTORS, AND OFFICERS

Shareholders are the individuals or groups that invest in the corporations. Each portion of ownership of a corporation is known as a share of stock. An individual may own one share of stock or several shares. Shareholders have certain rights when it comes to the corporation. Perhaps the most important one is the right to vote to elect the corporation's board of directors or change the corporation's bylaws. Shareholders vote on only a very limited number of corporate issues, but they nevertheless have the right to exert some control over the corporation's dealings. **Shareholder** voting typically takes place at an annual meeting, which states usually require of corporations. Corporations or shareholders may also request special meetings when a shareholder voting issue arises. It is not always practical for shareholders, who may live in various parts of the country or the world, to attend corporate meetings. For this reason, states permit shareholders to vote by authorizing, in writing, that another person may vote on behalf of the shareholder. This manner of voting is known as proxy.

Shareholders also have the right to investigate the corporation's books. As long as the shareholder seeking to investigate the corporation's records is doing so for a proper purpose or a purpose that reasonably relates to the shareholder's financial interests, the corporation must allow the inspection. In some cases, a corporation may require that the shareholder hold a minimum number of shares or that the shares be held for a certain period of time before allowing a shareholder to inspect the corporation's books and records.

A corporation is governed by a board of individuals known as directors who are elected by the shareholders. Directors may directly manage the corporation's affairs when the corporation is small, but when the corporation is large, directors primarily oversee the corporation's affairs and delegate the management activities to corporate officers. Directors usually receive a salary for their work on the corporate board, and directors have a **fiduciary** duty to act in the best interests of the corporation. These fiduciary duties require the directors to act with care toward the corporation, to act with loyalty toward the corporation, and to act within the confines of the law. A director who breaches this fiduciary duty may be sued by the shareholders and held personally liable for damages to the corporation.

The articles of incorporation or the corporate bylaws determine how many directors will serve on the board of directors and how long the directors' terms will be. Directors hold meetings at regular intervals as defined in the corporate bylaws and, in addition, may also call special board meetings when needed. At board meetings, directors discuss issues affecting the corporation and make decisions about the corporation. Before the board can make a decision affecting the corporation, however, there must be a quorum, or certain minimum number of directors, present at the meeting. The precise number constituting a quorum may be determined by the bylaws or by statute.

The fiduciary duty held by directors requires them to act with due care, which means that the director must act reasonably to protect the corporation's best interests. Courts will find a breach of the fiduciary duty when a director engages in self-dealing or **negligence**. Self-dealing occurs when the director makes a decision on behalf of the corporation that simultaneously benefits the director's personal interests. For example, assume a director for a wholesale foods corporation also owns separately a grocery store. At a corporate board meeting, the director votes to reduce by fifty percent the cost of wholesale apples sold by the corporation to independent grocery stores. Such an act would likely benefit the director's grocery store and could hurt the corporation's profitability. A court would likely determine such an act to be a breach of the director's fiduciary duty toward the corporation.

Directors are not in breach of their fiduciary duty merely because a decision they make on behalf of the corporation results in trouble for the corporation. Directors who base their decisions on reasonable information and who act rationally in making their decisions may not be held personally liable even if those

decisions turn out to be poor ones. This legal emphasis on protecting a director's decision-making process is known as the business judgment rule.

The roles of corporate officers, typically the corporation's president, vice presidents, treasurer, and secretary, are defined by the corporate bylaws, articles of incorporation, and statutes. The president acts as the primary officer and sometimes is called the chief executive officer (CEO). The vice president is second in command and makes decisions in the president's absence. The secretary keeps track of the corporate records and takes minutes at corporate meetings. The treasurer keeps track of corporate finances. Corporate officers act as agents of the corporation and have the responsibility of negotiating contracts to which the corporation is a party. When a corporate officer signs a **contract** on behalf of the corporation, the corporation is legally bound to the terms of the contract. Officers, like directors, also have a fiduciary duty toward the corporation and may be held personally liable for acts taken on behalf of the corporation.

When a corporation engages in wrongdoing, such as **fraud**, fails to pay taxes correctly, or fails to pay debts, the people behind the corporation generally are protected from liability. This protection results from the fact that the corporation takes on a legal identity of its own and becomes liable for its acts. However, courts will in some cases ignore this separate corporate identity and render the shareholders, officers, or directors personally liable for acts they have taken on the corporation's behalf. This assignment of liability is known as piercing the corporate veil. Courts will pierce the corporate veil if a shareholder, officer, or director has engaged in fraud, illegality, or misrepresentation. Courts also will pierce the corporate veil when the corporation has not followed the **statutory** requirements for incorporation or when corporate funds are commingled with the **personal property** of an individual or when a corporation is undercapitalized or lacks sufficient funding to operate.

SHARES AND DIVIDENDS

The articles of incorporation define how many shares, or ownership portions, the corporation will issue as well as what types of stock the corporation will issue. A corporation that issues only one type of stock issues common shares, or **common stock**. Common shareholders have the right to vote and also the right to the corporation's **net** assets, also known as dividends. A corporation may designate different classes of common stock, with different voting and **dividend** rights for those shareholders. **Preferred stock** is a type of stock issued by corporations that in most cases do not grant the shareholder the right to vote. However, owners of preferred stock usually have greater rights to receive dividends than do owners of common stock.

STATE CORPORATION LAWS

The majority of states have adopted the Model Business Corporation Act (MBCA) as the basis of their own state laws, though each of these states has modified the provisions of the MBCA. The following lists the laws that govern corporations and indicates which government body provides general supervision over corporations.

ALABAMA: The state corporation statute is based on the MBCA. The Secretary of State provides general supervision over corporations.

ALASKA: The current Alaska Corporations Code was adopted in 1989.

ARIZONA: The state corporation statute is based on the MBCA. The Arizona Corporation Commission provides general supervision over corporations.

ARKANSAS: The state corporation statute is based on the MBCA. The Secretary of State provides general supervision over corporations.

CALIFORNIA: The General Corporation Law has been in effect since 1977. The Secretary of State provides general supervision over corporations.

COLORADO: The state corporation statute is based on the MBCA. The Secretary of State provides general supervision over corporations.

CONNECTICUT: The current version of the Connecticut Business Corporation Act was completed in 1997.

DELAWARE: The Delaware General Corporation Law applies to corporations. The Division of Corporations of the Secretary of State governs corporations.

DISTRICT OF COLUMBIA: The District of Columbia Business Corporation Act was adopted in 1954 and was based on the MBCA. In addition to the provision allowing for the general formation of corporations, Congress may form a corporation through the enactment of a special act.

FLORIDA: The state corporation statute is based on the MBCA. The Secretary of State provides general supervision over corporations.

GEORGIA: The state corporation statute is based on the MBCA. The Corporations Division of the Secretary of State provides general supervision over corporations.

HAWAII: The state corporation statute is based on the MBCA. The Director of the Department of Commerce and Consumer Affairs provides general supervision over corporations.

IDAHO: The state corporation statute is based on the MBCA.

ILLINOIS: The Illinois Business Corporation Act became effective on July 1984. The Secretary of State provides general supervision over corporations.

INDIANA: The state corporation statute is based on the MBCA.

IOWA: The Iowa Business Corporation Act became effective in 1989.

KANSAS: The state corporation statute is based on the Delaware General Corporation Law. The Secretary of State provides general supervision over corporations.

KENTUCKY: The state corporation statute is based on the MBCA. The Secretary of State provides general supervision over corporations.

LOUISIANA: The Business Corporations Law was enacted in 1968. No government office provides general supervision, except that documents submitted by corporations are filed with the Secretary of State.

MAINE: The state corporation statute is based on the MBCA. The Secretary of State provides general supervision over corporations.

MARYLAND: The state corporation statute is based on the MBCA. The State Department of Assessments and Taxation provides general supervision over corporations.

MASSACHUSETTS: The state corporation statute is based on the MBCA. The Corporations Division of the Secretary of the Commonwealth provides general supervision over corporations.

MICHIGAN: The Michigan Business Corporation Act became effective on January 1, 1973. The Department of

Labor and Economic Growth provides general supervision over corporations.

MINNESOTA: The Business Corporation Law became effective in 1981.

MISSISSIPPI: The state corporation statute is based on the MBCA. The Business Services Division of the Secretary of State's office provides general supervision over corporations.

MISSOURI: The Secretary of State provides general supervision over corporations.

MONTANA: The state corporation statute is based on the MBCA. The Secretary of State provides general supervision over corporations.

NEBRASKA: The state corporation statute is based on the MBCA. The Secretary of State provides general supervision over corporations.

NEVADA: The Secretary of State provides general supervision over corporations.

NEW HAMPSHIRE: The state corporation statute is based on the MBCA. The Secretary of State provides general supervision over corporations.

NEW JERSEY: The current Corporations Act was adopted to become effective in 1969. The Secretary of State provides general supervision over corporations.

NEW MEXICO: The state corporation statute is based on the MBCA. The Public Regulation Commission provides general supervision over corporations.

NEW YORK: The Secretary of State provides general supervision over corporations.

NORTH CAROLINA: The state corporation statute is based on the MBCA. The Secretary of State provides general supervision over corporations.

NORTH DAKOTA: The state corporation statute is based partially on the MBCA. The Secretary of State provides general supervision over corporations.

OHIO: The Business Services Division of the Secretary of State provides general supervision over corporations.

OKLAHOMA: The Secretary of State provides general supervision over corporations.

OREGON: The state corporation statute is based on the MBCA. The Secretary of State provides general supervision over corporations.

PENNSYLVANIA: The Business Corporation Law was enacted in 1988. The Department of State provides general supervision over corporations.

RHODE ISLAND: The state corporation statute is based on the MBCA. The Secretary of State provides general supervision over corporations.

SOUTH CAROLINA: The state corporation statute is based on the MBCA. The Secretary of State provides general supervision over corporations.

SOUTH DAKOTA: The state corporation statute is based on the MBCA. The Secretary of State provides general supervision over corporations.

TENNESSEE: The Secretary of State provides general supervision over corporations.

TEXAS: The state corporation statute is based on the MBCA. The Secretary of State provides general supervision over corporations.

UTAH: The state corporation statute is based on the MBCA. The Division of Corporations and Commercial Code of the Department of Commerce provides general supervision over corporations.

VERMONT: The Secretary of State provides general supervision over corporations.

VIRGINIA: The state corporation statute is based on the MBCA. The Secretary of State provides general supervision over corporations.

WASHINGTON: The state corporation statute is based on the MBCA. The Secretary of State provides general supervision over corporations.

WEST VIRGINIA: The Secretary of State provides general supervision over corporations.

WISCONSIN: The state corporation statute is based on the MBCA. The Department of Financial

Institutions provides general supervision over corporations.

WYOMING: The state corporation statute is based on the MBCA. The Secretary of State provides general supervision over corporations.

ADDITIONAL RESOURCES

Gevurtz, Franklin A. *Corporation Law*. 2nd ed. Eagan, MN: West, Thomson Reuters, 2010.

Macey, Jonathan R. *Macey on Corporation Laws*. New York: Aspen Publishers, 2012.

Welch, Edward P., Andrew J. Turezyn, and Robert S. Saunders. *Folk on the Delaware General Corporation Law*. 5th ed. New York: Aspen Law and Business, 2012.

ORGANIZATIONS

Association of Corporate Counsel

1025 Connecticut Avenue, NW, Suite 200
Washington, DC 20036
Phone: (202) 293-4103
URL: http://www.acc.com

Business Law Section, American Bar Association

321 North Clark Street
Chicago, Illinois 60610
Toll Free: (800) 285-2221
URL: http://www.americanbar.org/groups/business_law.html

Council of Better Business Bureaus (CBBB)

3033 Wilson Blvd, Suite 600
Arlington, VA 22201
Phone: (703) 276-0100
URL: http://www.bbb.org

Delaware Division of Corporations

401 Federal Street, Suite 4
Dover, DE 19901
Phone: (302) 739-3073
URL: http://corp.delaware.gov/

BUSINESS LAW

INDEPENDENT CONTRACTORS

Sections within this essay:

BACKGROUND

An independent contractor is a person who performs work or services for another person or company, for pay, but who is not employed by that person or company. The term itself is intended to convey the status of the individual as an *independent* worker who is a party to a *contract for specific work* (rather than a **contract** for employment), the performance of which is *not* controlled or supervised by the party requesting the service or work. As in any contract, there is no control of the physical conduct of the worker, and only the end result (i.e., the fruit of the worker's labor) is accepted or rejected. For example, persons who hold themselves out as "consultants" are often retained by companies "independent contractors" who will provide expertise and assistance without actually being employed by the company requesting their expertise.

SIGNIFICANCE

The distinction between employee and independent contractor is crucial in determining the application of several important federal and state laws, including those involving wages and withholding taxes, as well as such entitlements as eligibility for **workers' compensation**. Generally, when disputed, there is no single, dispositive test for government agencies to determine whether workers are independent contractors to a company, or employees thereof. Moreover, different criteria and legal tests are used for determining worker status, because each government agency is concerned with worker classification for a different reason. Accordingly, agencies may use their own independent worker classification criteria, without regard to what other agencies have done. By analogy, this is similar in application to that of a person who might be considered "disabled" for purposes of workers' compensation, but not for social security benefits. Also possible (but not common) is the result that a worker may be deemed an independent contractor in one state, but an employee in another.

As a general rule, someone who employs an independent contractor is not vicariously liable for damages caused by the independent contractor. However, this rule is subject to a number of exceptions. For example, if the independent contractor is engaged in an inherently dangerous activity on behalf of the contractor's employer, the employer can be liable for damages caused by the activity. State statutes in many states likewise establish vicarious liability for the acts of an independent contractor in some circumstances.

TREATMENT OF INDEPENDENT CONTRACTORS UNDER VARIOUS LAWS

Title VII Claims and the Economic Realities Test Title VII, 42 USC § 2000(e), defines an "employer" as a person or entity who employs 15 or more employees in 20 or more calendar weeks in the current or preceding calendar year. The term "employee" is only loosely defined as "an individual employed by an employer." Importantly, Title VII prohibits **discrimination** by an employer against any individual "with respect to terms, conditions, and privileges of employment." Once a company or person reaches the status of "employer" under the **statute**, there may be liability exposure for claims that independent contractors were essentially functioning as employees and therefore entitled to the same privileges and conditions as employees.

Even though Title VII protects any individual, whether an employee or independent contractor, the distinction is nevertheless important. What is meant by the **statutory** provision is that an employer cannot choose to speciously label one worker as an employee and another as an independent contractor, for the purpose of paying one less than the other or providing less benefit coverage for one than the other, or otherwise illegally discriminate between them. If two workers are substantially performing the same work, for purposes of Title VII claims of discrimination, both will be deemed employees and the employer will be required to treat them equally in "terms, conditions, and privileges of employment."

In adjudicating such claims and controversies, courts often refer to what is known as the "economic realities" of the employment relationship to make a determination of status as applied to the facts presented. In applying an "economics reality test" to the situation before it, a court will review the employment relationship of the parties to see if the worker in question is actually functioning as an employee, because the worker performs most of his work for the employer and derives most of his income from the employer. Conversely, if the worker offered his services to several companies and derived his overall income from several of them, he might be more appropriately deemed an independent contractor.

Nevertheless, other courts find the economic realities test too superficial and instead look to the **common law** for guidance. Under the common law standard, the primary emphasis is on a review of the degree of control and autonomy the worker has over his hours, methods used to complete the work, and materials used for the work. If the employer only looks to the end result, the worker is more likely an independent contractor. A milestone court decision on this matter was the case of *Viscaino v. Microsoft Corp*, (9th Cir. 1997). Microsoft had routinely brought in outside "independent contractors" to work on various software programs. Microsoft needed their expertise, but made them sign contract agreements in which they understood that they were not employees of Microsoft. Many of them worked several years in this capacity for Microsoft, and ultimately a group of them filed suit under **ERISA**, hoping to recover lost **pension** and other benefits. Microsoft defended these individuals, saying they were "independent contractors" and had accepted the work with that knowledge and understanding. The Court thought otherwise. It found that the workers had assigned desks, assigned phone numbers, and were otherwise treated essentially as Microsoft employees. In fact, the only difference was that they did not receive company-paid benefits. Microsoft lost the case.

Equal Pay Act and FLSA Likewise, claims also may be brought under the Equal Pay Act, 29 USC § 206(d), which amends the **Fair Labor Standards Act** (FLSA). Generally, for wage/hour claims, the "economic realities test" is used in determining the true status of the worker. An example of this type of claim might involve an independent contractor who is to be paid a contract amount when the work is completed, but in reality, that amount is less than the **minimum wage** or does not account for applicable overtime pay. If the worker is deemed to be actually functioning as an employee, the employer may be liable for monetary damages.

Section 1981 Claims The old **Civil Rights** law, passed during the post-Civil War era [42 USC § 1981] prohibits discrimination upon the basis of race in making and enforcing contracts. This has provided a cognizable cause of action for independent contractors involving their contractual relations with employers. (See *Danco v. Wal-Mart Stores*, 1st Cir. 1999.)

Age Discrimination in Employment Act (ADEA) Definitions found in the ADEA, 29 USC § 621, are similar to those in Title VII, except that an "employer," for purposes of the ADEA, must employ 20 or more employees for each working day in 20 or more calendar weeks in the current or preceding calendar year. Likewise, protection against **age discrimination** by employers covers both employees and independent contractors.

Veterans' Reemployment Rights Act Unlike Title VII and the ADEA, the Veterans' Reemployment Rights Act, 38 USC § 4301, defines an employer as any person or entity "that pays salary or wages for work performed or that has control over employment opportunities." Under this Act, discrimination is prohibited against applicants as well as employees, due to their absence for service-related reasons.

Family and Medical Leave Act (FMLA) Under the FMLA, an employer is defined as any person or entity that employs 50 or more employees for each working day in 20 or more calendar weeks in the current or preceding year. Eligibility for family leave is premised upon the completion of 1250 hours of service and a work status for at least 12 months. Because the FMLA incorporates FLSA definitions, the same rules would apply in determining worker status (the economic realities test).

Leased or Temporary Workers Companies ("employers") also may be liable to temporary workers who are employed through third parties (such as personnel agencies). **Case law** holds that the personnel agency is generally deemed to be a nominal employer and the end-user company is the true employer. In the alternative, some jurisdictions have found that both are joint employers of the worker.

However, where an agency is merely leasing back employees to the company and has no meaningful contact with them, only the end-user will be found to be the employer.

CONSEQUENCES FOR IMPROPER CLASSIFICATIONS

Employers are not required to withhold taxes from independent contractor earnings. Instead, they file information returns to the Internal Revenue Service and state authorities, indicating the amount paid in wages to the independent contractor. This information is also provided to the contractor on IRS Form 1099-MISC.

The Internal Revenue Code and various state laws impose substantial penalties on employers for improper classification of employees as independent contractors. Likewise, the Code imposes penalties and fines upon independent contractors who either fail to report income or who do not file self-employment quarterly returns. Additionally, the independent contractor will have to back-pay all taxes and social security deductions accrued during the misclassified period, in addition to those currently due.

Penalties to employers for failure to withhold income taxes are generally equal to 1.5 percent of the wages, plus 20 percent of the social security and **Medicare** taxes that should have been paid by the employee. There is also a liability for the unpaid portion of the *employer's* portion of the social security and Medicare taxes.

SUMMARY OF SIGNIFICANT FACTORS IN CLASSIFICATION

In summary, the following factors are key in determining whether a worker is more correctly classified as an employee:

- The worker can be terminated at will.
- A manager (or designated person) assigns, reviews, and supervises the worker's work product.
- The worker performs services that are a part of the regular operation of the business.

ADDITIONAL RESOURCES

Abraham, Kenneth S. *The Forms and Functions of Tort Law*. New York: Foundation Press, 2012.

Fishman, J.D. *Working for Yourself: Law & Taxes for Independent Contractors, Freelancers & Consultants*. 8th ed. Berkeley, CA: Nolo, 2011.

Shapo, Marshall S. *Principles of Tort Law*. 3rd ed. Eagan, MN: West, Thomson Reuters, 2010.

ORGANIZATIONS

Alabama Department of Labor Relations
649 Monroe Street
Montgomery, AL 36131
Phone: (205) 242-3460

Alaska Department of Labor and Workforce Development
PO Box 111149
Juneau, AK 99811
Phone: (907) 465-2700

Arizona Labor Division
800 W Washington St.
Phoenix, AZ 85007
Phone: (602) 542-4515

Arkansas Labor Department
10421 West Markham Street
Little Rock, AR 72205
Phone: (501) 682-4500

California Industrial Relations Department
PO Box 603
San Francisco, CA 94101
Phone: (415) 737-2600

Colorado Labor and Employment Department
600 Grant Street
Denver, CO 80203-3528
Phone: (303) 837-3801

Connecticut Labor Department
200 Folly Brook Boulevard
Wethersfield, CT 06109
Phone: (203) 566-4384

Delaware Labor Department
820 North French Street
Wilmington, DE 19801
Phone: (302) 571-2710

District of Columbia Human Rights Office
2000-14th Street NW
Washington, DC 20009
Phone: (202) 939-8740

Florida Labor and Employment Security Department
2590 Executive Circle East
Tallahassee, FL 32399
Phone: (904) 488-4398

Georgia Labor Department
148 International Boulevard
Atlanta, GA 30303
Phone: (404) 656-3011

Hawaii Labor and Industrial Relations Department
830 Punchbowl Street
Honolulu, HI 96813
Phone: (808) 548-3150

Idaho Department of Labor
317 W. Main Street
Boise, ID 83735
Phone: (208) 332-3570

Illinois Labor Department
310 South Michigan, 10th Floor
Chicago, IL 60604
Phone: (312) 793-2800

Indiana Labor Department
100 North Senate Avenue, Room 1013
Indianapolis, IN 46204
Phone: (317) 232-2378

Iowa Human Rights Department
Lucas State Office Building
Des Moines, IA 50319
Phone: (515) 281-5960

Kansas Civil Rights Commission
Landon State Office Building, No. 851, South
Topeka, KS 66612-1258
Phone: (913) 296-3206

Kentucky Labor Cabinet
127 Building, U.S. Highway 27 South
Frankfort, KY 40601
Phone: (502) 564-3070

Louisiana Labor Department
PO Box 94094
Baton Rouge, LA 70804
Phone: (225) 342-3011

Maine Labor Department
20 Union Street, PO Box 309
Augusta, ME 04333-0309
Phone: (207) 289-3788

Maryland Licensing and Regulation Department, Labor and Industry Division
501 St. Paul Place
Baltimore, MD 21202
Phone: (410) 333-4179

Massachusetts Labor Executive Office
1 Ashburton Place, Room 2112
Boston, MA 02108
Phone: (617) 727-6573

Michigan Labor Department
611 West Ottawa Street
Lansing, MI 48909
Phone: (517) 373-9600

Minnesota Labor and Industry Department
443 Lafayette Road
St. Paul, MN 55155
Phone: (651) 296-2342

Mississippi Employment Security Division
PO Box 1699
Jackson, MS 39215-1699
Phone: (601) 359-1031

Missouri Labor and Industrial Relations Department
421 Dunklin Street
Jefferson City, MO 65101
Phone: (573) 751-4091

Montana Labor and Industry Department
PO Box 1728
Helena, MT 59624
Phone: (406) 444-3555

Nebraska Labor Department
PO Box 94600
Lincoln, NE 68509
Phone: (402) 475-8451

Nevada Labor Commission
505 East King Street, Room 602
Carson City, NV 89710
Phone: (775) 885-4850

New Hampshire Labor Department
19 Pillsbury Street
Concord, NH 03301
Phone: (603) 271-3171

New Jersey Labor Department
John Fitch Plaza, CN110
Trenton, NJ 08625
Phone: (609) 292-2323

New Mexico Labor Department
1596 Pacheco Street
Santa Fe, NM 87501
Phone: (505) 827-6838

New York Labor Department
State Campus. Building 12
Albany, NY 12240
Phone: (518) 457-2741

North Carolina Labor Department
4 West Edenton Street
Raleigh, NC 27601
Phone: (919) 733-7166

North Dakota Labor Department
600 East Boulevard Avenue
Bismarck, ND 58505
Phone: (701) 224-2661

Ohio Civil Rights Commission
220 Parsons Avenue
Columbus, OH 43266-0543
Phone: (614) 466-2785

Oklahoma Labor Department
4001 Lincoln Boulevard
Oklahoma City, OK 73105
Phone: (405) 528-1500

Oregon Labor and Industries Bureau
1400 S.W. 5th Avenue, Suite 409
Portland, OR 97201
Phone: (503) 229-5737

Pennsylvania Labor and Industry Department
Labor and Industry Building
Harrisburg, PA 17120
Phone: (717) 787-3756

Rhode Island Labor Department
220 Elmwood Avenue
Providence, RI 02907
Phone: (401) 457-1800

South Carolina Labor Department
PO Box 11329
Columbia, SC 29211-1329
Phone: (803) 734-9594

South Dakota Labor Department
700 Governors Drive
Pierre, SD 57501
Phone: (605) 773-3101

Tennessee Labor Department
501 Union Building
Nashville, TN 37219
Phone: (615) 741-2582

Texas Employment Commission
101 East 15th Street
Austin, TX 78778
Phone: (512) 463-2800

Utah Commerce Department
PO Box 45802
Salt Lake City, UT 84145-0801
Phone: (801) 530-6701

Vermont Labor and Industry Department
State Office Building, 120 State Street
Montpelier, VT 05602
Phone: (802) 828-2286

Virginia Office of Economic Development
205 North 4th Street, Box 12064
Richmond, VA 23241
Phone: (804) 786-2377

Washington Labor and Industries Department
General Administration Building, HC-101
Olympia, WA 05602
Phone: (206) 753-6307

West Virginia Commerce, Labor, and Environment Department
1800 Washington Street East
Charleston, WV 25305
Phone: (304) 348-7890

Wisconsin Industry Labor and Human Relations Department
PO Box 7946
Madison, WI 53707
Phone: (608) 266-7552

Wyoming Labor and Statistics Department
122 West 25th Street, 2nd Floor East
Cheyenne, WY 82002
Phone: (307) 777-7261

BUSINESS LAW

LAWS AFFECTING SMALL BUSINESSES

Sections within this essay:

- Background
- Starting a Small Business
  - Start-Up Considerations in General
  - Obtaining Capital
  - Leasing or Buying Property
  - Insurance
  - Choosing a Business Form
  - Franchising
- Running the Business
  - Business Transactions
  - Taxes
  - Advertising
  - Intellectual Property Issues
  - Other Regulations
- Issues with Employees
- Issues with Customers
- Ending the Business
- Additional Resources

BACKGROUND

A **small business** owner may encounter numerous legal problems when starting and running a small business. Even those running small companies may have a number of legal questions, and these owners will indeed need to address legal issues as part of their management of the small business.

Although many small businesses chose to hire an attorney to help them with legal problems, it helps for owners to understand legal issues that may arise on a day-to-day basis.

A difficult problem in trying to define what these legal issues are, however, is that a small business may encounter a broad range of legal problems and issues. For instance, a person starting a small business must consider a list of legal questions and issue while starting up. The owner will then have more questions arise while running the business, including problems that rise with employees and customers. Moreover, ending a business may create even more legal problems.

This essay provides a summary of several of the major legal issues that may arise for small business owners. Another good resource to consult is the website for the U.S. Small Business Administration at www.sba.gov, which provides information about business law and regulations related to small businesses.

STARTING A SMALL BUSINESS

Start-Up Considerations in General Getting started with a business obviously involves developing an idea for the business and should involve creating a business plan. A small-business owner may need to complete a number of steps during this start-up process, and several of these steps may involve legal questions.

Although steps may vary, there are certain items that practically all small-business owners will need to complete. The website at www.bsorchecklist.org provides a list of common items, which include the following:

- Register a Business Name
- Decide on the Legal Form for the Business
- Write a Business Plan

- Create Your Own Website & Find Advertisers (Affiliates) to Link To!
- Market Research and Analysis
- Set Up a Relationship with a Counselor, if Needed
- Meet Legal/Tax Requirements for Operating a Business
- Determine the Financing You Will Need and How You Will Get It
- Plan for Risk & Health Insurance
- Set up a Financial Management & Recordkeeping System
- Hire Employees

Obtaining Capital A successful business is going to need money (capital) to become successful. The capital may come in the form of equity, which relates to ownership interest in the business. For example if a person wants to start a business has a potential investor in the business, the owner can ask for money from the investor in exchange for a percentage of ownership. Thus, although the owner does not need to repay the funds received, the owner gives up some ownership rights and may have to give up some control of the business. The other form of capital comes from debt equity, which means the owner borrows the money and must repay it with interest.

An owner can raise equity or debt capital through a variety of sources. The owner may contribute his or her own money or receive loans from friends and family, a financial institution, or a government agency. The owner may also seek investments from those who will be involved in the business and/or those who want to make a profit from their investment in the company.

If an owner borrows money to raise capital, it is important for the owner to know the details of the loan. A number of owners believe that if they take out loans by using the name of the business that the owners themselves will not be liable for the debt. However, as a practical matter, very few, if any, financial institutions will issue credit to a start-up company without a personal guarantee from the owner. Thus, if the company goes out of business—as many do—the owner will remain liable for the debt used to raise capital.

If a business raises equity capital by issuing **securities** (often in the form of shares), the business must comply with federal and state securities laws. The U.S. Securities and Exchange Commission, as well as many state securities commissions, provide information for small business owners about any regulations that may apply.

Leasing or Buying Property A small-business owners usually have to decide whether to **lease** or buy property, though few small business owners have the capital to purchase property. It is also possible to lease property and negotiate with the owner either an option to purchase the property or a right of first refusal should the owner decide to sell the property. This will give the small-business owner some options down the road if the owner has to lease property.

If the small-business owner has to lease property, the owner will need to negotiate provisions of the commercial lease. In *Legal Guide for Small Business*, the American Bar Association suggests that a small-business owner seek legal assistance when dealing with a commercial lease, given that small details are important. The ABA list several items to consider, including the following:

- Basic information, including rent and square footage
- Additional rent for excess use
- Operating expenses (which a small-business owner will want to exclude)
- Parking spaces
- A clause prohibiting competition
- A renewal option
- An expansion option
- A termination clause
- A provision regarding the security deposit
- A provision regarding use
- Provisions regarding the tenant's occupation of the property and commencement of the lease
- Provisions regarding tenant improvements
- Provisions regarding building services
- Provisions regarding compliance with the Americans with Disabilities Act
- Provisions regarding signs used to advertise and promote the business
- Provisions regarding relocation
- Provisions regarding subleasing

Insurance The ABA recommends that a small business obtain business insurance from a single source so the owner will not duplicate coverage. The ABA also suggests hiring an insurance agent that works for a number of different insurance companies so that the agent can help to find coverage from a larger number of vendors.

The agent can help the small-business owner to identify the types of insurance the owner may need. Various types of insurance may include the following:

- General liability insurance
- Product liability insurance
- Professional liability insurance
- Commercial property insurance
- Home-based business insurance

A small-business owner may also need to acquire personal insurance to protect the owner from business liabilities. The owner may also choose to form a limited liability entity, which will shield the owner from much of this financial exposure.

Choosing a Business Form There are many considerations to take into account when deciding what type of business entity to form. The business owner may run the business alone and may not want to follow all of the formalities of setting up a business. Such an owner may opt to form a **sole proprietorship**. On the other hand, an owner may want to ensure that he or she is not personally responsible for the liabilities of the business. That owner may opt to form a type of limited liability entity, such as an **S corporation** or a **limited liability company**.

In addition to liability concerns, the business form will likely affect how the business is taxed.

Franchising A popular way to operate a small business is to become part of a franchise. A franchise allows independent ownership of a small business with the benefit of the goodwill and reputation developed from the brand as a whole. For example, the owner of a McDonald's franchise owns the business and also benefits from the reputation that McDonald's has with customers. This should make it easier for the owner to develop the business than if the owner instead opened a hamburger restaurant without the brand name.

There are, however, some drawbacks to franchise agreements. The franchise fee may be very costly, and the owner may have to agree to a number of conditions for running the business. Thus, compared with a completely independent business, the franchise owner will likely have less control and will have to grow the business based largely on the business plan of the larger entity.

RUNNING THE BUSINESS

Business Transactions A small business will encounter any of a large number of possible issues on a daily basis. Many of these issues relate to contracts. Although some contracts will consist of formal documents labeled as "contracts," many other agreements also constitute contracts. For example, sales of goods involve a **contract** even if the transaction was not something written in a formal document.

The more complex a matter is, the more likely the small-business owner will need a lawyer's assistance. Thus, although the owner can write business agreements, the owner should seek legal advice when a proposed transaction is complex or otherwise has a greater chance to lead to legal problems in the future. A skilled attorney can identify potential pitfalls and draft a contract to avoid these pitfalls.

Taxes The small-business owner will need to work through a number of tax matters when starting up and running the business. The owner will need to obtain a tax identification number and will need to consider several tax-related issues. These issues include tax implications of various business forms; employment taxes for employers and self-employed individuals; filing and paying taxes; calculating business expenses and deductions; identifying and paying state and local taxes; and generally managing tax obligations.

Advertising A small business will almost always have to rely on advertising to be successful. The small-business owner will need to know how to avoid false and misleading statements in advertisements. The owner will also need to be aware of various regulations that may apply to different types of advertisements. The regulations typically apply to product labeling, advertising of specific products, telemarketing and direct marketing, environmental concerns, and online advertising.

Intellectual Property Issues Small businesses acquire interests not only real and **personal property** but also **intellectual property**. The business may create a certain trademark or service mark associated with the identity of the business. Likewise, certain businesses may obtain **patents** or own copyrights. Accordingly, small-business owners should be aware of legal issues related to the intellectual property issues as well as licensing and other concerns.

Other Regulations A myriad of other regulations may apply to a certain business. For instance, a small-business owner may need to be aware of environmental regulations that affect how the owner runs the business. As with any other aspect of running this small business, the more complex the regulation, the more likely the owner should seek legal advice about how to operate an aspect of the business properly.

ISSUES WITH EMPLOYEES

A small-business owner will usually have to address wide range of issues related to employees. Laws related to employees are usually classified under either employment law or **labor law**, with latter focusing more heavily on organized labor. The U.S. Department of Labor provides a source entitled *Employment Law Guide: Laws, Regulations, and Technical Assistance Services*, which is available at http://www.dol.gov/compliance/guide/index.htm. This source summarizes several of the main employment law issues an employer may face, including:

- Wages and hours worked;

- Safety and health standards;

- Health benefits, retirement standards, and workers' compensation;

- Other workplace standards, including lie detector tests, whistleblower protections, and layoffs;

- Work authorization for non-U.S. citizens;

- Working conditions for jobs related to federal contracts; and

- Equal employment opportunities for jobs related to federal contracts.

The Department of Labor also provides a site known as "elaws" and provides an online Employment Law Advisor to help employers better understand legal issues.

ISSUES WITH CUSTOMERS

Legal issues can obviously arise from the relationship between a small-business owner and a customer. A few issues are of particular concern. An owner must decide whether to accept credit cards and checks, or even whether to offer credit directly to customers. In the event that the owner extends credit, the owner then needs to face the possibility that the customer does not pay, meaning that the owner needs to consider collections options.

A second concern relates to **privacy** laws that could apply. Owners often come into possession of sensitive personal information about customers, such as credit card numbers, social security numbers, and so forth, and the owner needs to know the laws affecting privacy rights.

ENDING THE BUSINESS

A small-business owner will also need to consider options when ending a business, such as whether to sell the business or property owned by the business. The owner should also consider retirement issues, as well as plan for the future in the event of death.

ADDITIONAL RESOURCES

Alberty, Steven C. *Advising Small Businesses*. Deerfield, IL: Callaghan, 2012.

American Bar Association. *ABA Legal Guide for Small Business*. 2nd ed. Chicago: American Bar Association, 2010.

Batman, Jean L. *Letters for Small-Business Lawyers*. Chicago: American Bar Association, 2011.

ORGANIZATIONS

American Bar Association (ABA)

321 North Clark Street
Chicago, IL 60610
Phone: (202) 662-1000
Toll Free: (800) 285-2221
Fax: (312) 988-6800
URL: http://www.americanbar.org

NFIB: The Voice of Small Business

53 Century Blvd., Suite 250
Nashville, TN 37214
Toll Free: (800) 634-2669
URL: http://www.nfib.com

SCORE

740 15th Street, NW, American Bar Association Building
Washington, DC 20005
Phone: (202) 272-0390
URL: http://www.score.org

U.S. Chamber of Commerce

1615 H St. NW
Washington, DC 20062-2000
Phone: (202) 659-6000
URL: http://www.uschamber.com

U.S. Small Business Administration

409 3d Street, SW
Washington, DC 20416
Toll Free: (800) 827-5722
URL: http://www.sba.gov

BUSINESS LAW

LIMITED LIABILITY ENTITIES

Sections within this essay:

- Background
- Entities Without Limited Liability
- Corporations
- Limited Partnerships
- Limited Liability Partnerships
- Limited Liability Limited Partnerships
- Limited Liability Companies
- Professional Limited Liability Entities
- Issues Regarding Limited Liability Entities
  - Taxation
  - "Piercing the Veil"
  - Liability for Torts and Other Obligations
- State Laws Governing Limited Liability Entities
- Additional Resources

BACKGROUND

Since the 1990s, individuals who wish to form businesses have seen a significant increase in the types of business entities that may be formed. Laws governing these new forms of businesses limit the liability that business owners may face. In general, a person who invests in a limited liability entity is only liable for an amount equivalent to the investment made by the investor.

Some limited liability entities resemble general partnerships, except for the limitations in liability. Other entities, especially limited liability companies, are more similar to **corporations** in their structure. Although some entities are taxed in a manner similar to partnerships, other forms of limited liability entities may be taxed similar to corporations.

ENTITIES WITHOUT LIMITED LIABILITY

Owners of three types of businesses are not protected by the limited liability that other business forms offer. An owner of such a business is personally liable for the debts incurred by the business. These businesses include general partnerships, joint ventures, and sole proprietorships. General partnerships are formed when two or more agree to engage in a business for profit. A **joint venture** is similar to a general **partnership**, except that two or more people form a venture for a particular business project. A **sole proprietorship** is a business that is carried on by an individual.

The law traditionally has not treated these types of business as independent and distinct from the owners. Owners of these types of business also do not need to follow the formalities that owners of other forms of businesses, such as corporations, must follow. Moreover, these business entities generally are not governed as heavily by state and federal regulations. Thus, although limitations on liability provide considerable incentive to form a limited liability entity, other factors may lead business owners to form an entity that does not enjoy limited liability.

CORPORATIONS

The corporation is the most common form of business entity in the United States. A corporation is formed when individuals complete certain formalities, including the filing of documents known as **articles of incorporation** and the payment of fees to the proper authority. The secretary of state in most states is the official responsible for receiving the documents and filing fees from the corporations.

Traditionally, the **corporate** form of business was the preferred limited liability entity because the corporation exists separate from its owners and investors. The corporation, although an artificial entity, is treated like an individual in most respects. It may enter into contracts, it may sue or be sued, and it may own property. A corporation may also exist perpetually because it may continue to exist even when owners and investors change.

As an entity separate from its owners and investors, a corporation is liable for its own contracts. Owners and investors generally are only liable to the extent of the amount that these individuals invested in the corporation.

Many states base their laws governing corporations on the Model Business Corporation Act (MBCA), which was prepared by the Section of Business Law of the American Bar Association. However, most of these states have deviated from the MBCA with respect to some of the provisions. Other states have chosen not to follow the MBCA and have instead drafted their own statutes.

LIMITED PARTNERSHIPS

Parties form a limited partnership in a manner similar to a general partnership. The most significant difference between these two types of businesses is that some of the owners of the limited partnership, known as limited partners, do not participate in the management and control of the partnership's business. Instead, limited partners provide capital contributions to the partnership and are liable only to the extent of those capital contributions.

Like a general partnership, owners of a limited partnership enter into a partnership agreement. A limited partnership must file a certificate with an appropriate state authority, usually the secretary of state. The certificate provides the limited partnership's name and character of business, along with the names and addresses of the general and limited partners. A limited partnership's name must include "L.P.," "Ltd.," or "Limited Partnership" to identify the form of the business entity. The purpose for this requirement is to warn those who deal with the partnership that some of the partners are not personally liable for the partnership's debts.

Nearly every state adopted the Uniform Limited Partnership Act, which was approved in 1916 and again in 1976 by the National Conference of Commissioners on Uniform State Laws (NCCUSL). The NCCUSL significantly revised this uniform law in 2001. As of 2012, 18 states and the District of Columbia had adopted the revised version.

LIMITED LIABILITY PARTNERSHIPS

The limited liability partnership (LLP) emerged as a business form during the 1990s. This type of business entity is similar to a general partnership in that each partner may share in the management of the business and that each partner shares in the profits. However, unlike a general partnership, partners in an LLP do not incur personal liability for claims that are brought related to the actions of a copartner. Moreover, this form of business shields a partner from liability for the acts of the partnership's employees or agents. On the other hand, a partner in an LLP is liable for his or her own **negligence** or malfeasance and the negligence and malfeasance of anyone under the supervision and control of the partner.

Owners of an LLP register the business by filing a registration with the appropriate state authority, usually the secretary of state. Owners of an LLP may be required to prove that the entity has adequate liability insurance or assets to satisfy claims that may be brought against the business. This type of partnership must include the word "Registered Limited Liability Partnership" or the initials "LLP" in its name.

Every state allows businesses to form as LLPs. The NCCUSL in 1996 amended the Uniform Partnership Act (UPA) to include sections governing limited liability partnerships. The majority of states have adopted the revised UPA.

LIMITED LIABILITY LIMITED PARTNERSHIPS

A small minority of states recognize a form of business called the limited liability limited partnership (LLLP). An LLLP is formed when a limited partnership registers as a limited liability partnership, thus allowing partners to benefit from different limitations in liability. In other words, limited partners in an LLLP are still only liable for the partnership's debts to the extent of the limited partner's contributions, while a general partner is not personally liable for the negligence or malfeasance of another general partner.

The NCCUSL modified the Uniform Limited Partnership Act in 2001 to allow limited partnerships to register as limited liability limited partnerships. A total of 18 states and the District of Columbia had adopted the revised Act as of 2012.

LIMITED LIABILITY COMPANIES

The limited liability company (LLC) first appeared as a business form in Wyoming during the 1970s and became more prevalent during the 1990s. This type of business entity combines aspects of a partnership with aspects of a corporation. Those who form an LLC may choose to have the owners of the company (called "members") manage the company. This type of management structure is more similar to a partnership. Alternatively, an LLC may choose to have managers run the company in a structure that is more similar to a corporation. The Internal Revenue Service allows an LLC to elect whether it wants to be taxed as a partnership or as a corporation, and so this form of business offers flexibility in both management and **taxation**.

In order to form an LLC, the owners must file articles of organization with an appropriate state authority, usually the secretary of state. Articles of organization are similar to articles of incorporation, which must be filed in order to form a corporation. Owners of an LLC must also pay a filing fee at the time of registration.

Members of an LLC enjoy similar protections against liability as shareholders in a corporation, limited partners in a limited partnership, or partners in a limited liability partnership or limited liability limited partnership. These members are generally not personally liable for the debts and obligations of the LLC, except in certain circumstances.

Although every state provides for the LLC as a business entity, state laws vary. The NCCUSL completed the Uniform Limited Liability Company Act in 1996 and revised it in 2006. However, as of 2012, only five states and the District of Columbia had adopted the revised act.

PROFESSIONAL LIMITED LIABILITY ENTITIES

In many states, professionals can establish professional limited liability entities. These are usually limited to fields where the professionals must maintain licenses to practice. By forming such an entity, professionals can shield themselves individually from liability for **malpractice** committed by other shareholders or members of the entity. Common examples of such professionals include lawyers, doctors, accountants, dentists, architects, and chiropractors.

A professional limited liability entity is designated with a "P" in the abbreviation, such as "PC" for professional corporation or "PLLC" for professional limited liability company.

ISSUES REGARDING LIMITED LIABILITY ENTITIES

Taxation Corporations are taxed on one of two ways, depending on the type of corporation that has been structured. A "C Corporation," also known as a standard business corporation, is an entity that is taxed separately from its owners. Dividends that are passed on to shareholders of the corporation are also taxable, thus meaning that income received by a corporation may be

taxed twice. Another type of corporation, known as an "S Corporation" is considered to be a "pass-through" entity with respect to taxation. That is, the corporation itself is not taxed, and profits and losses are passed down as income or losses to the owners of the corporation. An **S Corporation** is taxed in a manner similar to a partnership, which is also treated as a pass-through entity.

When new forms of business entities began to emerge in the 1990s, taxation of the entity was a major consideration. Limited partnerships and limited liability partnerships were easily classified as pass-through entities. However, the Internal Revenue Service (IRS) had some difficulty in determining how an LLC should be taxed. Under regulations that existed prior to 1997, if an LLC was operated in a manner more similar to a C Corporation, then the LLC was taxed as a corporation. However, the IRS changed its regulations in 1997 to allow an LLC to select how it should be taxed. Since the passage of those regulations, LLCs have been free to operate in a manner similar to corporations, but these LLCs may elect to be taxed like partnerships.

"Piercing the Veil" Under the law governing corporations, where an owner or owners of a corporation use the corporate form of business to engage in **fraud** while hiding behind the shield of limited liability, a court may hold the owners of the corporation personally liable to a third party. This is referred to as piercing the corporate veil. Since partners in a general partnership are personally liable for the debts of the partnership, this theory of liability did not apply to entities other than corporations.

Because these new limited liability entities shield owners of businesses from personal liability, commentators have suggested that the piercing-the-veil theory can apply to LLCs and LLPs. This theory would apply only in narrow circumstances, such as where owners of an LLC or LLP fail to follow proper formalities in forming or running the business, or where the business entity is being used to perpetuate fraud.

Liability for Torts and Other Obligations Owners and managers of limited liability entities are never completely shielded from personal liability. For instance, laws that govern these types of entities do not generally shield owners or managers from liability for torts that are committed while the person is acting on behalf of the business. Whether a business owner or manager is shielded from liability with respect to his or her involvement in the business depends on the type of limited liability entity and the individual state law that governs that type of entity.

STATE LAWS GOVERNING LIMITED LIABILITY ENTITIES

ALABAMA: The state has adopted provisions of the Model Business Corporation Act. The state adopted the 1997 version of the Uniform Partnership Act, including provisions governing limited liability partnerships. The state also adopted the Uniform Limited Partnership Act and the Uniform Limited Liability Company Act.

ALASKA: The state adopted the 1997 version of the Uniform Partnership Act, including provisions governing limited liability partnerships. The state has adopted the 2001 version of the Uniform Limited Partnership Act.

ARIZONA: The state has adopted provisions of the Model Business Corporation Act. The state adopted the 1997 version of the Uniform Partnership Act, including provisions governing limited liability partnerships.

ARKANSAS: The state has adopted provisions of the Model Business Corporation Act. The state adopted the 1997 version of the Uniform Partnership Act, including provisions governing limited liability partnerships.

CALIFORNIA: The state adopted the 1997 version of the Uniform Partnership Act, including provisions governing limited liability partnerships. The state has adopted the 2001 version of the Uniform Limited Partnership Act.

COLORADO: The state has adopted provisions of the Model Business Corporation Act. The state adopted the 1997 version of the Uniform Partnership Act, including provisions governing limited liability partnerships.

CONNECTICUT: The state adopted the 1994 version of the Uniform Partnership Act.

DELAWARE: The state adopted the 1997 version of the Uniform Partnership Act, including provisions governing limited liability partnerships.

DISTRICT OF COLUMBIA: The District has adopted provisions of the Model Business Corporation Act. The District adopted the 1997 version of the Uniform Partnership Act, including provisions governing limited liability partnerships. The District has also adopted the 2001 version of the Uniform Limited Partnership Act and the 2006 version of the Uniform Limited Liability Company Act.

FLORIDA: The state has adopted provisions of the Model Business Corporation Act. The state adopted the 1997 version of the Uniform Partnership Act, including provisions governing limited liability partnerships. The state also adopted the 2001 revisions to the Uniform Limited Partnership Act.

GEORGIA: The state has adopted provisions of the Model Business Corporation Act.

HAWAII: The state has adopted provisions of the Model Business Corporation Act. The state adopted the 1997 version of the Uniform Partnership Act, including provisions governing limited liability partnerships. The state also adopted the Uniform Limited Liability Company Act and the 2001 revision to the Uniform Limited Partnership Act.

IDAHO: The state has adopted provisions of the Model Business Corporation Act. The state adopted the 1997 version of the Uniform Partnership Act, including provisions governing limited liability partnerships. The state has adopted the 2001 version of the Uniform Limited Partnership Act and the 2006 version of the Uniform Limited Liability Company Act.

ILLINOIS: The state adopted the 1997 version of the Uniform Partnership Act, including provisions governing limited liability partnerships. The state also adopted the Uniform Limited Liability Company Act and the 2001 revision to the Uniform Limited Partnership Act.

INDIANA: The state has adopted provisions of the Model Business Corporation Act.

IOWA: The state adopted the 1997 version of the Uniform Partnership Act, including provisions governing limited liability partnerships. The state also adopted the 2001 revisions to the Uniform Limited Partnership Act and the 2006 version of the Uniform Limited Liability Company Act.

KANSAS: The state adopted the 1997 version of the Uniform Partnership Act, including provisions governing limited liability partnerships.

KENTUCKY: The state has adopted provisions of the Model Business Corporation Act. The state has adopted the 2001 version of the Uniform Limited Partnership Act.

MAINE: The state has adopted provisions of the Model Business Corporation Act. The state has adopted the 2001 version of the Uniform Limited Partnership Act.

MARYLAND: The state has adopted provisions of the Model Business Corporation Act. The state adopted the 1997 version of the Uniform Partnership Act, including provisions governing limited liability partnerships.

MASSACHUSETTS: The state has adopted provisions of the Model Business Corporation Act.

MINNESOTA: The state adopted the 1997 version of the Uniform Partnership Act, including provisions governing limited liability partnerships. The state also adopted the 2001 revisions to the Uniform Limited Partnership Act.

MISSISSIPPI: The state has adopted provisions of the Model Business Corporation Act. The state adopted the 1997 version of the Uniform Partnership Act, including provisions governing limited liability partnerships.

MISSOURI: The state has adopted provisions of the Model Business Corporation Act.

MONTANA: The state has adopted provisions of the Model Business Corporation Act. The state adopted the 1997 version of the Uniform Partnership Act, including provisions governing limited liability partnerships. The state has adopted the 2001 version of the Uniform Limited Partnership Act. The state also adopted the Uniform Limited Liability Company Act.

NEBRASKA: The state has adopted provisions of the Model Business Corporation Act. The state adopted the 1997 version of the Uniform Partnership Act, including provisions governing limited liability partnerships. The state has also adopted the 2006 version of the Uniform Limited Liability Company Act.

NEVADA: The state adopted the 1997 version of the Uniform Partnership Act, including provisions governing limited liability partnerships. The state has adopted the 2001 version of the Uniform Limited Partnership Act.

NEW HAMPSHIRE: The state has adopted provisions of the Model Business Corporation Act.

NEW JERSEY: The state adopted the 1997 version of the Uniform Partnership Act, including provisions governing limited liability partnerships.

NEW MEXICO: The state has adopted provisions of the Model Business Corporation Act. The state adopted the 1997 version of the Uniform Partnership Act, including provisions governing limited liability partnerships. The state has adopted the 2001 version of the Uniform Limited Partnership Act.

NORTH CAROLINA: The state has adopted provisions of the Model Business Corporation Act.

NORTH DAKOTA: The state has adopted provisions of the Model Business Corporation Act. The state adopted the 1997 version of the Uniform Partnership Act, including provisions governing limited liability partnerships. The state also adopted the 2001 revisions to the Uniform Limited Partnership Act.

OKLAHOMA: The state adopted the 1997 version of the Uniform Partnership Act, including provisions governing limited liability partnerships. The state has adopted the 2001 version of the Uniform Limited Partnership Act.

OREGON: The state has adopted provisions of the Model Business Corporation Act. The state adopted the 1997 version of the Uniform Partnership Act, including provisions governing limited liability partnerships.

RHODE ISLAND: The state has adopted provisions of the Model Business Corporation Act.

SOUTH CAROLINA: The state has adopted provisions of the Model Business Corporation Act. The state also adopted the Uniform Limited Liability Company Act.

SOUTH DAKOTA: The state has adopted provisions of the Model Business Corporation Act. Provisions of the state's partnership **statute** are similar to 1997 version of the Uniform Partnership Act, including provisions governing limited liability partnerships. The state also adopted the Uniform Limited Liability Company Act.

TENNESSEE: The state adopted the 1997 version of the Uniform Partnership Act, including provisions governing limited liability partnerships.

TEXAS: The state has adopted provisions of the Model Business Corporation Act. The state adopted the 1997 version of the Uniform Partnership Act, including provisions governing limited liability partnerships.

UTAH: The state has adopted provisions of the Model Business Corporation Act. The state has adopted the 2001 version of the Uniform Limited Partnership Act. The state has also adopted the 2006 version of the Uniform Limited Liability Company Act.

VERMONT: The state adopted the 1997 version of the Uniform Partnership Act, including provisions governing limited liability partnerships. The state also adopted the Uniform Limited Liability Company Act.

VIRGINIA: The state has adopted provisions of the Model Business Corporation Act. The state adopted the 1997 version of the Uniform Partnership Act, including provisions governing limited liability partnerships.

WASHINGTON: The state has adopted provisions of the Model Business Corporation Act. The state adopted the 1997 version of the Uniform Partnership Act, including provisions governing limited liability partnerships.

WEST VIRGINIA: The state adopted the 1994 version of the Uniform Partnership Act. The state also adopted the Uniform Limited Liability Company Act.

WISCONSIN: The state has adopted provisions of the Model Business Corporation Act.

WYOMING: The state has adopted provisions of the Model Business Corporation Act. The state adopted the 1994 version of the Uniform Partnership Act and the 2006 version of the Uniform Limited Liability Company Act.

ADDITIONAL RESOURCES

Callison, J. William, and Maureen A. Sullivan *Limited Liability Companies: A State by State Guide to Law and Practice*. Eagan, MN: West, Thomson Reuters, 2005.

Hynes, J. Dennis, and Mark J. Loewenstein. *Agency, Partnership, and the LLC in a Nutshell*. 5th ed. Eagan, MN: West, Thomson Reuters, 2011.

Macey, Jonathan R. *Macey on Corporation Laws*. New York: Aspen Publishers, 2012.

ORGANIZATIONS

Council of Better Business Bureaus (CBBB)

4200 Wilson Blvd., Suite 800
Arlington, VA 22203-1838
Phone: (703) 525-8277
URL: http://www.bbb.org

Small Business Advancement National Center (SBANC)

UCA Box 5018, 201 Donaghey Avenue
Conway, AR 72053-0001
Phone: (501) 450-5300
Fax: (501) 450-5360
URL: http://www.sbaer.uca.edu

U.S. Chamber of Commerce

1615 H Street, NW
Washington, DC 20062-2000
Phone: (202) 659-6000
URL: http://www.uschamber.com/default

BUSINESS LAW

NONPROFIT ORGANIZATIONS

Sections within this essay:

- Background
- Purpose of a Nonprofit Organization
- Location of the Organization
- Choice of Organizational Form
  - Corporations
  - Unincorporated Associations
  - Limited Liability Companies
  - Charitable Trusts
- Meaning of Tax Exemption
- Determining Tax-Exempt Status
- Categories of Tax-Exempt Organizations
- Charitable Organizations
- Taxation of Unrelated Business Activities
- Public Charities and Private Foundations
- Reporting Requirements
- Disclosure Requirements
- Legal Protections for Officers, Directors, Employees and Volunteers
- State Laws Governing Nonprofit Corporations
- Additional Resources

BACKGROUND

Nonprofit organizations exist in the United States for a number of reasons. Many of these organizations are formed for the purpose of fulfilling needs in society by providing an organization that handles what the government would handle otherwise. Nonprofit organizations exist along with two other types of entities: for-profit businesses and government agencies. Each of these serves different purposes in society.

Many people associate nonprofit organizations and tax exemption, although not all nonprofit entities are exempt from **taxation**. Moreover, a nonprofit organization is not prohibited from earning a profit, for many of these organizations generate profits. To the contrary, the law governing nonprofit entities sets forth requirements as to what each entity must do with the profits it earns. More specifically, the law expects nonprofit organizations to devote any profits to the goal of furthering the purposes and activities of the organization.

Additionally, not all nonprofit organizations are charitable in nature. Although contributions to charitable organizations generally qualify for a charitable contribution **deduction**, some nonprofit entities that are not charitable in nature are also tax exempt.

PURPOSE OF A NONPROFIT ORGANIZATION

One of the first steps in forming a nonprofit entity is to define the purpose of the entity. This statement of purpose, which must be made in writing, will define the type of tax exemption for which that organization is qualified. The following list provides examples of the types of tax-exempt nonprofit organizations:

- Organizations formed for charitable purposes
- Organizations that advocate for social welfare
- Professional associations
- Labor organizations
- Chambers of commerce and business leagues
- Social clubs
- Homeowners associations

- Employee benefit funds
- Fraternal societies
- Political organizations

The purpose driving a for-profit business is to benefit the owners of the business. By comparison, the activities of a nonprofit entity must be conducted for the benefit of the organization and not the owners. In order to qualify for tax exempt status, the organization must benefit the public.

LOCATION OF THE ORGANIZATION

Once a person or group decides to form a nonprofit organization, one of the first issues that must be addressed is where this entity will be formed. Some states may be more attractive than others due to several factors. For instance, states such as New York and California are more intense in terms of regulating nonprofit entities than other states. Moreover, state laws may differ about the requirements the entity must satisfy to qualify for tax-exempt status.

A nonprofit organization may form under the laws in one state but operate in a different state. This option may be advantageous when the laws of one state allow those who form the nonprofit entity to fulfill the purpose of the entity better than the laws of another state. On the other hand, this option is usually more costly because both the state in which the entity is formed and the state where the entity operates will charge fees.

CHOICE OF ORGANIZATIONAL FORM

Another complicated decision that those who form nonprofit entities must make is what organization form the entity will take. In general, nonprofit entities appear in four organizational forms, including **corporations**, charitable trusts, limited liability companies, and unincorporated associations. Each of these forms has some benefits and some disadvantages that must be considered when the organization is formed.

Corporations The most common form of nonprofit organization is the corporation. A corporation is a creation of the law. Those who create a corporation must file a document known as **articles of incorporation**, which sets forth important information about the corporation itself. Once a corporation is formed, it becomes its own "person" under the law, separate from its directors, officers, or owners. The corporation itself may sue others or be sued.

A nonprofit entity benefits from forming as a corporation for two primary reasons. First, the laws governing corporations provides considerable protection to officers, directors, members, employees, and volunteers against personal liability. This means that if the corporation itself incurs liability (e.g., a third person successfully sues the corporation), those who act on the corporations

behalf usually do not incur liability. Second, the law governing corporations is generally well-settled, meaning that the rules that govern the operation of the corporation are more clearly defined.

Several states have adopted the Model Nonprofit Corporation Act, which was first drafted by the Business Law Section of the American Bar Association in 1964. It was subsequently revised in 1987 and again in 2008.

Unincorporated Associations Unlike a corporation, which must be created and structured according to the directives of state law, two or more people may form an unincorporated association without following those formalities. Those who form an unincorporated association may choose how the association should be governed, which is one of the benefits of this form of entity. Such an entity may be formed as a nonprofit entity.

However, whether those associated with the entity are liable for the entity's debts is not clear. In several states, including those that have adopted the Uniform Nonprofit Unincorporated Association Act, an unincorporated association is treated as an entity separate from its members. Where a state recognizes the association as a separate entity, then the members of the entity are probably shielded from personal liability for the association debts. On the other hand, some states may not recognize the association as separate, meaning that the members could incur personal liability.

Limited Liability Companies The **limited liability company** (LLC) is a newer form of business entity. The organizational structure of an LLC borrows from the structures of both unincorporated entities and corporations. The benefit in forming an LLC is its flexibility, since someone who creates an LLC may form the entity to appear more like a **partnership** or more like a corporation, depending on the needs and preferences of the person who is forming it. An LLC may elect to be taxed as a corporation or as a partnership.

Although the LLC form of organizational structure may provide some benefits, the use of the LLC for nonprofit entities is not well settled. Questions about the taxation of a nonprofit LLC have yet to be answered, and in some states, state law is not clear whether an LLC may be formed for nonprofit purposes. On the other hand, this form of entity provides flexibility in terms of structure and may be preferable to some nonprofit entities.

Charitable Trusts A person who wishes to set aside property for the benefit of another may form a **trust**. Unlike a corporation or LLC, a person may form a trust without filing anything with the government. Instead, the trust is formed when a person transfers property to a person or an entity, known as a **trustee**, and directs the trustee to use the transferred assets for the benefit of a third person, known as a **beneficiary**. State law dictates how a trustee must handle the property that is being used for the benefit of the beneficiary.

Some nonprofit entities are formed as charitable trusts, where the beneficiaries are not specific individuals. Instead, the trustee of a charitable trust uses the property for the benefit of a specified purpose, such as education of disadvantaged youth. The laws that apply to trusts in general also apply to charitable trusts. Because modern corporations are generally easy to form, those who wish to form a charitable nonprofit entity are more likely to form a corporation than they are to create a charitable trust.

MEANING OF TAX EXEMPTION

Although some people associate nonprofit organizations with tax-exempt organizations, certainly not all nonprofit entities are exempt from taxes. Moreover, even though a tax-exempt organization may be free from paying federal income taxes, such an organization may still be liable for other types of taxes. For instance, a tax-exempt organization may be liable for taxes on **net** investment income as well as income derived from business activities that do not relate to the organization's exempt functions (known as unrelated business activities, discussed below).

DETERMINING TAX-EXEMPT STATUS

Statutory law generally determines whether an organization is exempt from taxes. Section 501 of the Internal Revenue Code (IRC) provides the basic rules for tax-exempt status at the federal level. The Internal Revenue Service (IRS) is the federal body responsible for recognizing that an organization qualifies for tax-exempt status. An entity that wants to seek recognition for this status must file Form 1023, entitled "Application for Recognition of Exemption."

State laws regarding tax exemptions vary. Those who form nonprofit entities should consult the laws of relevant states to determine which organizations are eligible for tax-exempt status and which steps, if any, the organization must take for the state to recognize that status.

CATEGORIES OF TAX-EXEMPT ORGANIZATIONS

The IRC contains a laundry list of organizations that qualify as tax-exempt organizations. The most common of these are charitable organizations, although the IRC also includes educational, scientific, and religious organizations. Moreover, the Code includes several other types of entities, such as labor organizations, social clubs, credit unions, employee benefit trusts, and farmers' cooperatives.

CHARITABLE ORGANIZATIONS

Federal law recognizes several different forms of charitable organizations. Charitable organizations are often referred to as Section 501(c)(3) organizations, named after the section of the IRC section under which these organizations are formed. The definition of charitable has been developed through the promulgation of tax regulations and tax rulings, as well as through federal and state judicial cases. The following list includes the purposes that are generally recognized as charitable:

- Relief of poverty
- Relief of the distressed
- Advancement of religion
- Advancement of education
- Advancement of science
- Lessening the burdens of government (e.g., erecting a public building)
- Community beautification and maintenance
- Promotion of health
- Promotion of social welfare
- Promote environmental conservation
- Promotion of patriotism
- Promotion of the arts

TAXATION OF UNRELATED BUSINESS ACTIVITIES

Federal tax law distinguishes between activities that relate to the exempt functions of a nonprofit and those activities that are unrelated. Gross revenues that are gained on unrelated business activities are subject to taxation. Because most nonprofit organizations conduct some sort of business, most of these organizations must determine whether any aspect of their businesses may be characterized as an unrelated business activity.

For income of a tax-exempt organization to be taxable, the income must be produced from a trade or business that the organization carries on regularly. An organization carries on a trade or business regularly if it does so frequently and continually, as opposed to sporadically or infrequently. The income must also be unrelated to the purpose for which the organization has been formed and which forms the basis for the tax exemption. Income from activities that bear a substantial relationship to the purpose of the nonprofit entity are not subject to tax, while income from activities that do not bear a substantial relationship to the purpose of the entity are subject to taxation.

Revenue that a tax-exempt organization gains on an unrelated business activity is subject to the federal **corporate income tax** that applies to non-exempt entities. An exempt organization is entitled to certain deductions related to the business that earned this income, much like a for-profit entity may be entitled to deductions for certain activities.

PUBLIC CHARITIES AND PRIVATE FOUNDATIONS

The Internal Revenue Code distinguishes between nonprofit entities that are public charities and those that are private foundations. A public charity is one that has involvement from the public in general, earns financial support from the public in general, or has an operating relationship with a public organization. By comparison, a private foundation usually derives its financial support from one source; earns money through investment assets, rather than through contributions from the public; and makes grants to other charitable organizations instead of operating its own activities.

Private foundations are subject to certain restrictive rules and taxes for which public charities are not subject. Thus, those who form nonprofit organizations often would like to avoid the status of a private foundation. Several types of institutions are exempt from the rules governing private foundations. These institutions include certain churches, educational institutions, health care providers, and governmental units.

REPORTING REQUIREMENTS

Those organizations that are exempt from federal taxes must file what is known as an information return with the IRS. Most organizations that are entitled to tax exemptions must file a Form 990 with the IRS. This form, which is about 20 pages long, including schedules, requires an exempt entity to report on items of revenue, including a balance sheet. The form also asks the organization questions about the organization's operation, mostly relating to issues dealing with the organizations tax-exempt status. The public is entitled to inspect this form.

DISCLOSURE REQUIREMENTS

In addition to annual information returns, nonprofit organizations are required to disclose information about their operations. The reason behind these requirements is to ensure that each nonprofit organization is acting in a transparent manner. Those items that are subject to disclosure requirements include the following:

- Substantiation of charitable gifts
- Quid pro quo contributions (i.e., where a **donor** pays an amount in excess of the value of goods or services received by the nonprofit entity)
- Gifts of property
- Dispositions of contributed property
- Appraisals
- Tax shelters

LEGAL PROTECTIONS FOR OFFICERS, DIRECTORS, EMPLOYEES, AND VOLUNTEERS

State laws generally provide some protection for directors, employees, and volunteers against liability. One type of law includes volunteer protection statutes, which limit liability that may be incurred by volunteers of a nonprofit entity. Congress also enacted the Volunteer Protection Act of 1997 to provide additional protection. However, several commentators have noted that these statutes have largely failed in their purpose because the statutes generally do not prohibit lawsuits against volunteers but rather merely limit liability in some circumstances.

Other state laws limit liability for directors and officers of nonprofit organizations. These laws restrict the amount that someone can recover for damages stemming from the activities of an officer or director of a nonprofit entity. Much like volunteer protection acts, however, commentators often note that these statutes that limit liability are fairly weak.

STATE LAWS GOVERNING NONPROFIT CORPORATIONS

Several states have modeled their state laws after the Model Nonprofit Corporation Act, which was approved by the Business Law Section of the American Bar Association in 1964 and revised in 1987 and 2008. Other states have not explicitly adopted either version of the model act but may borrow provisions from the model legislation. Another source of law governing nonprofit entities appears in the form of the Uniform Unincorporated Nonprofit Association Act, which was approved by the National Conference of Commissioners on Uniform State Laws in 1996 and revised in 2008.

ALABAMA: Alabama has adopted both the Model Nonprofit Corporation Act and the Uniform Unincorporated Nonprofit Association Act. A party forms a nonprofit organization by submitting a filing to the Alabama Secretary of State.

ALASKA: A party forms a nonprofit organization by submitting a filing to the Alaska Department of Commerce, Community, and Economic Development.

ARIZONA: A party forms a nonprofit organization by submitting a filing to the Arizona Secretary of State.

ARKANSAS: Arkansas has adopted both the Model Nonprofit Corporation Act and the 2008 revision of the

Uniform Unincorporated Nonprofit Association Act. A party forms a nonprofit organization by submitting a filing to the Arkansas Secretary of State.

CALIFORNIA: A party forms a nonprofit organization by submitting a filing to the California Secretary of State.

COLORADO: Colorado has adopted the Uniform Unincorporated Nonprofit Association Act. A party forms a nonprofit organization by submitting a filing to the Colorado Secretary of State.

CONNECTICUT: A party forms a nonprofit organization by submitting a filing to the Connecticut Secretary of State.

DELAWARE: Delaware has adopted the Uniform Unincorporated Nonprofit Association Act. A party forms a nonprofit organization by submitting a filing to the Delaware Division of Corporations.

DISTRICT OF COLUMBIA: The District of Columbia has adopted the 2008 revision of the Uniform Unincorporated Nonprofit Association Act.

FLORIDA: A party forms a nonprofit organization by submitting a filing to the Florida Department of Revenue or other agency as required by state law.

GEORGIA: A party forms a nonprofit organization by submitting a filing to the Georgia Secretary of State.

HAWAII: Hawaii has adopted the Uniform Unincorporated Nonprofit Association Act. A party forms a nonprofit organization by submitting a filing to the Hawaii Department of Commerce and Consumer Affairs.

IDAHO: Idaho has adopted the Uniform Unincorporated Nonprofit Association Act. A party forms a nonprofit organization by submitting a filing to the Idaho Secretary of State

ILLINOIS: A party forms a nonprofit organization by submitting a filing to the Illinois Secretary of State

INDIANA: Indiana has adopted the Model Nonprofit Corporation Act. A party forms a nonprofit organization by submitting a filing to the Indiana Secretary of State.

IOWA: A party forms a nonprofit organization by submitting a filing to the Iowa Secretary of State.

KANSAS: A party forms a nonprofit organization by submitting a filing to the Kansas Secretary of State.

KENTUCKY: A party forms a nonprofit organization by submitting a filing to the Kentucky Secretary of State.

MAINE: A party forms a nonprofit organization by submitting a filing to the Maine Secretary of State.

MARYLAND: A party forms a nonprofit organization by submitting a filing to the Maryland State Department of Assessments and Taxation.

MASSACHUSETTS: A party forms a nonprofit organization by submitting a filing to the Massachusetts Secretary of State.

MICHIGAN: A party forms a nonprofit organization by submitting a filing to the Michigan Department of Labor and Economic Growth.

MINNESOTA: A party forms a nonprofit organization by submitting a filing to the Minnesota Secretary of State.

MISSISSIPPI: Mississippi has adopted the Model Nonprofit Corporation Act. A party forms a nonprofit organization by submitting a filing to the Mississippi Secretary of State.

MISSOURI: A party forms a nonprofit organization by submitting a filing to the Missouri Secretary of State.

MONTANA: Montana has adopted the Model Nonprofit Corporation Act. A party forms a nonprofit organization by submitting a filing to the Montana Secretary of State.

NEBRASKA: A party forms a nonprofit organization by submitting a filing to the Nebraska Secretary of State.

NEVADA: A party forms a nonprofit organization by submitting a filing to the Nevada Secretary of State.

NEW HAMPSHIRE: A party forms a nonprofit organization by submitting a filing to the New Hampshire Secretary of State.

NEW JERSEY: A party forms a nonprofit organization by submitting a filing to the New Jersey Department of the Treasury.

NEW MEXICO: A party forms a nonprofit organization by submitting a filing to the New Mexico Public Regulation Commission.

NORTH CAROLINA: North Carolina has adopted the Model Nonprofit Corporation Act. A party forms a nonprofit organization by submitting a filing to the North Carolina Secretary of State.

NORTH DAKOTA: A party forms a nonprofit organization by submitting a filing to the Business Division of the North Dakota Secretary of State.

OHIO: A party forms a nonprofit organization by submitting a filing to the Ohio Secretary of State.

OKLAHOMA: A party forms a nonprofit organization by submitting a filing to the Oklahoma Secretary of State.

OREGON: A party forms a nonprofit organization by submitting a filing to the Oregon Secretary of State.

PENNSYLVANIA: A party forms a nonprofit organization by submitting a filing to the Pennsylvania Department of State.

RHODE ISLAND: A party forms a nonprofit organization by submitting a filing to the Rhode Island Secretary of State.

SOUTH CAROLINA: South Carolina has adopted the Model Nonprofit Corporation Act. A party forms a nonprofit organization by submitting a filing to the South Carolina Secretary of State.

SOUTH DAKOTA: A party forms a nonprofit organization by submitting a filing to the South Dakota Secretary of State.

TENNESSEE: A party forms a nonprofit organization by submitting a filing to the Tennessee Department of State.

TEXAS: Texas has adopted the Uniform Unincorporated Nonprofit Association Act. A party forms a nonprofit organization by submitting a filing to the Texas Secretary of State.

UTAH: A party forms a nonprofit organization by submitting a filing to the Utah Department of Commerce.

VERMONT: A party forms a nonprofit organization by submitting a filing to the Vermont Secretary of State.

VIRGINIA: A party forms a nonprofit organization by submitting a filing to the Clerk of the State Corporation Commission.

WASHINGTON: Washington has adopted the Model Nonprofit Corporation Act. A party forms a nonprofit organization by submitting a filing to the Washington Secretary of State.

WEST VIRGINIA: West Virginia has adopted the Uniform Unincorporated Nonprofit Association Act. A party forms a nonprofit organization by submitting a filing to the West Virginia Secretary of State.

WISCONSIN: Wisconsin has adopted the Uniform Unincorporated Nonprofit Association Act. A party forms a nonprofit organization by submitting a filing to the Wisconsin Department of Financial Institutions.

WYOMING: Wyoming has adopted both the Model Nonprofit Corporation Act and the Uniform Unincorporated Nonprofit Association Act. A party forms a nonprofit organization by submitting a filing to the Wyoming Secretary of State

ADDITIONAL RESOURCES

Hopkins, Bruce R. *Starting and Managing a Nonprofit Organization: A Legal Guide.* 4th ed. Hoboken, NJ: John Wiley & Sons, Inc., 2005.

Nonprofit Governance and Management. 3rd ed. ABA Business Law Section. Chicago: American Bar Association, 2011.

Phelan, Marilyn E. *Nonprofit Organizations: Law and Taxation.* Eagan, MN: West, Thomson Reuters, 2010-2012.

Runquist, Lisa A. *The ABCs of Nonprofits.* Chicago: American Bar Association, 2005.

ORGANIZATIONS

Action Without Borders/Idealist

302 Fifth Ave., 11th Fl.
New York, NY 10001
Phone: (646) 786-6886
Fax: (212) 695-7243
URL: http://www.idealist.org/

Society for Nonprofit Organizations

PO Box 510354
Livonia, MI 48151
Phone: (734) 451-3582
URL: http://www.snpo.org/index.php

BUSINESS LAW

OFFICER AND DIRECTOR LIABILITY

Sections within this essay:

BACKGROUND

Decisions made by officers and directors of **corporations** typically have not subjected these individuals to personal liability. Even if an officer or director makes what turns out to be a bad business decision, the law does not render the person liable unless that decision violates a specific duty imposed on the officer or director.

On the other hand, the law governing corporations has expanded liability in many instances. This is especially applicable when a director or officer makes a decision that causes financial harm to a corporation, acts in their own interests in making decisions to the detriment of the corporation, or commits a wrongful act or crime.

High-profile cases involving wrongdoing by **corporate** executives in the early 2000s intensified the exposure on how decisions made by those executives can impact a large number of people. For example, Enron Corporation, an energy company based in Houston, Texas, suffered a major collapse in 2001 that led to the largest **bankruptcy** in U.S. history. Acts of **fraud** on the part of corporate officers and others caused many of the problems. Employees of the company lost most of their retirement investments as a result of the company's collapse. Other companies, such as WorldCom, Tyco International, and Global Crossing, suffered similar fates.

Both officers and directors of those corporations faced civil and criminal liability. Members of boards of directors for Enron and WorldCom agreed to pay millions of dollars out of their own pockets as part of **settlement** agreements. The U.S. Securities and Exchange Commission brought charges against top company officers, seeking to recover large fines in addition to criminal convictions. These incidents also led to major changes in federal **securities** laws regarding the potential liability for officers and directors.

OFFICERS' AND DIRECTORS' ROLES IN CORPORATE GOVERNANCE

Officer and directors share in the responsibility of governing a corporation. Shareholders in the corporation elect a board of directors to be in charge of the business. The board of directors is primarily responsible for making decisions, but not for carrying out those decisions. The task of carrying out the decisions made by the board falls on the officers, such as the chief executive officer and the chief financial officer.

State law prescribes the basic powers of officers and directors. Many states have adopted provisions of the American Bar Association's Model Business Corporation Act (MBCA) or Delaware's corporation laws. Other states have adopted their own unique laws. In general, if a state law does not provide a requirement pertaining to officers or directors, then the corporation's **articles of incorporation** and/or **bylaws** usually establish these requirements.

Officers The MBCA and the Delaware corporation **statute** allow a corporation's bylaws or board of directors to specify which officers the corporation must have. In many jurisdictions, though, state law requires each corporation to have certain officers, such as a president, secretary, and treasurer. Small corporations generally have only a few officers, such as a president who serves as the executive officer and a treasurer who serves as the financial officer. Large corporations have many more officers and subordinates.

In some instances, a state's corporation statute may dictate the functions of corporate officers. Some states allow the corporation's articles of incorporation or bylaws to dictate the officers' functions. The MBCA provides, "Each officer has the authority and shall perform the functions set forth in the bylaws or, to the extent consistent with the bylaws, the functions prescribed by the board of directors or by direction of an officer authorized by the board of directors to prescribe the functions of other officers."

The issue of the authority that is delegated to an officer usually pertains to whether the officer has bound the corporation to another party. If the officer had express authority or implied authority to enter into a transaction on behalf of a corporation, then the officer's actions could lead to liability on the part of the corporation. Typically, however, an officer of a corporation, even if the officer is the president of the corporation, has less power than the board of directors.

Directors The vast majority of states and the MBCA require corporations to have one or more directors, as specified in the corporation's articles of incorporation or bylaws. This number may be increased or decreased as needed by amending the articles or bylaws. In many states, the board of directors itself may increase or decrease its size. Most modern statutes allow corporations to compensate directors for their services. A board may take an official action if it has a quorum present at its meeting, meaning that at least half of the board members are in attendance.

A director of a corporation is well-advised to stay abreast of the activities of the board. A director has the **legal right** to have access to information that allows the director to perform his or her job. To perform properly, a director should be diligent in studying the information that is available. This may include:

- Review board meeting agendas
- Review minutes of corporation board meetings
- Inspect books and records of the corporation, as well as any other data that the director may reasonably request
- Inspect corporate facilities as appropriate

Directors may take steps to negate the possibility of becoming personally liable if the board of directors approves a questionable transaction. Under the MBCA, a board member who is present at a meeting assents to a board action unless the board member takes one of three steps. These include:

- Objecting at the beginning of a meeting to holding the meeting or transacting business at the meeting
- Dissenting or abstaining from the action and having the dissent or abstention recorded in the minutes of the meeting
- Delivering written notice of the dissent or abstention to the presiding officer of the meeting before or immediately after the adjournment of the meeting

A director who is not present at a meeting is not deemed to have assented to any action of the board in the director's absence. However, a director who votes in favor of a corporation's actions cannot later submit a dissent or abstention.

RESPONSIBILITIES OF OFFICERS AND DIRECTORS

Whereas the powers of a director or an officer usually do not give rise to liability, the responsibilities of these positions may give rise to **litigation**. Directors and officers both have certain duties to the corporation, and breach of these duties can give rise to liability.

Decision-Making Responsibilities Most duties that apply to corporate governance relate to decision-making responsibilities. Duties most clearly apply to the directors of a corporation since the directors are the decision-makers in the business. Officers have duties similar to directors, especially officers that exercise judgment or discretion. In a closely held corporation, the same individual may serve as an officer and as a director, and so the same duties would apply to the person's title in either position.

Fiduciary Duties Directors and officers have what are termed **fiduciary** duties to the corporation due to the positions of **trust** that these individuals have within the corporation. The MBCA prescribes several aspects of this type of fiduciary relationship, including:

- Act in **good faith**: this is carried out by acting honestly and dealing fairly.

- Reasonably believe that the director is acting in the corporation's best interests: reviewed objectively, the director has acted with the corporation's interests in mind, rather than his or her own.

- Exercise duties with a level of care that a person in a like position would under similar circumstances.

Duty of Care The duty of care that an officer or director must exercise relates to the diligence that the person uses to make decisions. In order to fulfill this duty, an officer or director should follow several practices, including:

- Regularly attend board and committee meetings.

- Remain informed about the business and affairs of the corporation.

- Rely on information provided by others, such as reports, financial statements, and opinions.

- Make inquiries about problems that may arise with respect to the corporation.

Duty of Loyalty The duty of loyalty requires an officer or director to act in the best interests of the corporation and not in the person's own best interest. Several instances may give rise to issues that implicate the duty of loyalty, and an officer or director should be aware of how to handle each of these instances should they arise.

- An officer's or director's **conflict of interest** may or may not cause the person to breach the duty of loyalty, but the officer or director should always disclose conflicts with other directors. The disinterested directors may elect to allow the corporation to complete a transaction where a conflict exists, but the interested director should not take part in this vote.

- If an officer or director identifies a business opportunity that could benefit the corporation, the officer or director must first allow the corporation to pursue the opportunity before pursuing the opportunity himself or herself.

- Any transaction that involves a conflict of interest or self-dealing on the part of an officer or director must be fair to the corporation.

- Any conflict of interest and subsequent actions taken by the board with respect to the conflict must be documented.

- Corporations should adopt written policies governing conflicts of interest.

- A corporation should seek independent advice regarding transactions that involve conflicts of interest.

BUSINESS JUDGMENT RULE

The business judgment rule is a doctrine developed by courts in reviewing the actions of directors. Generally, courts do not hold directors personally liable for a business decision, even when a decision turns out to be a bad one, so long as the director has not breached a duty to the corporation. A director who acts in good faith, remains informed about the corporation's business, and does not engage in self-dealing or transactions involving conflicts of interest will not be subject to personal liability.

SECURITIES REGULATIONS

The Enron and WorldCom fiascos, along with others gave rise to the Sarbanes-Oxley Act of 2002, a federal statute that placed greater controls on how publicly traded corporations must conduct business. Under this statute, officer and directors who commit fraud or other crimes face greater penalties than they did in the past. The statute also gives greater power to the Securities and Exchange Commission in investigating and prosecuting acts of wrongdoing by corporate officers and directors.

RIGHTS AND DUTIES OF SHAREHOLDERS

Shareholders in publicly-traded corporations generally are not involved in decisions made by the corporation, other than their act of electing members of the board of directors. In a closely-held corporation, however, it is common that a **shareholder** or group of shareholders control the corporation. Most courts require that the controlling shareholders uphold a duty of fairness in dealing with the non-controlling shareholders. Minority shareholders in some instances may also demand an **appraisal** of the fair value of their shares or may demand that the corporation **dissolve** due to one of several occurrences.

INSURANCE AND INDEMNIFICATION

Liability insurance and indemnification by the corporation provide protection to an officer or director of a corporation from having to pay out-of-pocket for expenses that arise due to litigation. Indemnification refers to an agreement by the corporation to pay legal fees and other expenses when an officer or director faces a civil claim or criminal prosecution. An indemnification agreement also requires the corporation to pay a settlement or judgment against an officer or director. In some instances, **public policy** may limit when a corporation may indemnify an officer or director, such as when litigation is based on intentional wrongdoing.

Liability insurance for directors and officers, also referred to as D & O insurance, is provided by third party insurers to provide protection for the corporation and the directors and officers for expenses that arise due to litigation. Most state statutes expressly permit corporations to purchase D & O insurance, although policies are very expensive, potentially costing hundreds of thousands of dollars for larger corporations.

STATE LAWS GOVERNING OFFICER AND DIRECTOR LIABILITY

Most state statutes governing corporations contain provisions that prescribe the situations in which an officer or director may be liable. Some of these state statutes are

ALABAMA: The statute imposes a duty of good faith on directors and officers. A director or an officer may not act with intent to depreciate stocks or **bonds** with the further intent to buy the depreciated stocks or bonds.

ARKANSAS: The statute does not allow a corporation to limit or eliminate liability for any of the following: breach of the duty of loyalty; acts that are not carried out in good faith or that involve intentional misconduct; unlawful distributions; transactions that involve an improper personal benefit; or any breach of duty that creates third party liability.

CALIFORNIA: The director's standard of care is to serve the corporation in good faith and in the best interests of the corporation. The director must exercise such care, including reasonable inquiry, as an ordinarily prudent person in a like position would use in similar circumstances.

CONNECTICUT: A director may be liable for the willful nonpayment of certain taxes. A director must perform duties in good faith, with care an ordinarily prudent person in a like position would exercise in a similar circumstance, and in a manner that the director reasonably believes is in the best interests of the corporation.

DELAWARE: A director may be liable for the payment of an unlawful **dividend** or from an unlawful stock purchase or redemption, unless the director's dissent or absence is noted in the corporation's minutes. Liability for breach of fiduciary duty may be limited or eliminated in some circumstances.

FLORIDA: A director who acts in good faith, in a manner that the director reasonably believes is in the best interests of the corporation, and with the degree of diligence, care, and skill that an ordinarily prudent person would exercise under similar circumstances will not be subject to personal liability.

HAWAII: A corporation may not limit or eliminate the personal liability of a director in the following instances: the director receives an a financial benefit for which the director is not entitled; the director intentionally inflicts harm on the corporation or the shareholders; or the director intentionally violates criminal law.

ILLINOIS: A director faces penalties for improperly paying dividends or distributing assets, for failing to take reasonable steps to cause notice of **dissolution** to be mailed to known creditors, or for actively carrying on a business after filing articles of dissolution. A corporate director who commits an act of commercial bride or who receives a commercial bribe is liable to the corporation for three times the aggregate amount given or received in the bribe, plus attorneys' fees.

KENTUCKY: A director is not liable for monetary damages unless the director has breached a fiduciary duty in a manner that constitutes willful misconduct or wanton or reckless disregard for the best interests of the corporation.

LOUISIANA: A director or an officer of a corporation may be liable if the corporation transacts business before capital is received or the director or officer consent to the issuance of shares in violation of the law.

MARYLAND: A corporation's charter may expand or limit the liability of a director for money damages unless: the director received an improper benefit or profit; the director is adjudicated to have been guilty of active and deliberate dishonesty that was material to the cause of action; or the director was also a director of certain banking and/or financial institutions.

NEVADA: A director may be liable for the following: breach of fiduciary duty where breach involved intentional misconduct, fraud, or knowing violation of the law;

wrongful declaration of distributions; or debts or liabilities where the director acts as the alter ego of the corporation.

NEW YORK: A director who votes for or concurs in the following actions may be liable to the corporation for the benefit of creditors and shareholders: improper declaration of a dividend; improper purchase or redemption of the corporation's shares; improper distribution of assets after dissolution; or improper loans made to the director.

TENNESSEE: A director may not participate in a transaction involving a known conflict of interest without the approval of the shareholders or other directors unless the transaction was fair; make loans to officers or directors without shareholder approval; or vote for or **assent** to distribution in violation of the law or the corporation's charter.

TEXAS: A director or an officer may demonstrate that he or she exercised ordinary care by relying on certain statements, opinions, reports, and other documents. An officer may be personally liable for tortious acts when the officer participates in the wrongdoing.

ADDITIONAL RESOURCES

Gale Encyclopedia of American Law. 3rd ed. Detroit: Gale, Cengage Learning, 2011.

Gevurtz, Franklin A. *Corporation Law.* 2nd ed. Eagan, MN: West, Thomson Reuters, 2010.

Hamilton, Robert W., and Richard D. Freer. *The Law of Corporations in a Nutshell.* 6th ed. Eagan, MN: West, Thomson Reuters, 2011.

Macey, Jonathan R. *Macey on Corporation Laws.* New York: Aspen Publishers, 2005, updated 2012.

Managing Closely Held Corporations: A Legal Guidebook. ABA Committee on Corporate Laws. Chicago: American Bar Association, 2003.

Welch, Edward P., Andrew J. Turezyn, and Robert S. Saunders. *Folk on the Delaware General Corporation Law.* 5th ed. New York: Aspen Law and Business, 2012.

ORGANIZATIONS

Association of Corporate Counsel
1025 Connecticut Avenue, NW, Suite 200
Washington, DC 20036
Phone: (202) 293-4103
URL: http://www.acc.com

Business Law Section, American Bar Association
321 North Clark Street
Chicago, Illinois 60610
Toll Free: (800) 285-2221
URL: http://www.abanet.org/buslaw/home.shtml

Council of Better Business Bureaus (CBBB)
4200 Wilson Blvd, Suite 800
Arlington, VA 22203
Phone: (703) 276-0100
URL: http://www.bbb.org

Delaware Division of Corporations
401 Federal Street, Suite 4
Dover, DE 19901
Phone: (302) 739-3073
URL: http://www.state.de.us.corp

BUSINESS LAW

PARTNERSHIPS

BACKGROUND

When two or more people carry on a business for profit, the law recognizes the existence of a general partnership. Unlike **corporations**, limited liability companies, limited partnerships, and limited liability partnerships, owners of a business do not need to follow specific formalities to form a general partnership. At the same time, however, partners are not protected from liability for the business' debts. Sole proprietorships and general partnerships are considered the "default" forms of business when an individual or more than one individual establish a business, since one form of business entity or the other is generally established if the parties do not choose an alternate form.

Partnerships are governed in the vast majority of states by one of the versions of the Uniform Partnership Act (UPA), which was originally drafted by the Uniform Law Commissioners in 1914. Prior to 1994, every state, with the exception of Louisiana, adopted the UPA. The National Conference of Commissioners on Uniform State Laws significantly revised the UPA in 1994, with subsequent modifications in 1995, 1996, and 1997. The majority of states have adopted the 1997 version of the act, which is generally referred to as the Revised Uniform Partnership Act (RUPA). The RUPA revised the UPA in several key areas, though many of the basic rules governing partnerships did not change from the older law to the new law.

The UPA and RUPA, in many ways, provide "default" rules that govern general partnerships. That is, the rules in the UPA and RUPA govern the partnership, unless the partners agree otherwise. Thus, each partner generally has a right to manage the partnership that is equal to the rights of other partners. Similarly, partners can agree how they will share profits, how they will contribute to pay for losses, how they will divide the labor, and how the partnership will **dissolve** when the partnership ends. Parties cannot, however, agree to shield personal liability from one or more of the partners. If a partner or partners want to avoid personal liability for the debts of the partnership, they will need to form one of the business entities that provide limited liability.

FORMING AND MANAGING A GENERAL PARTNERSHIP

Several of the rules related to general partnerships vary between the UPA and the RUPA. Individuals who are forming a general partnership or are concerned about management issues should consult their state statutes to determine which law is in effect in that state.

Characteristics of a General Partnership A general partnership must consist of two or more individuals or entities, including another partnership or corporation. Thus, it is possible that two very large corporations could form a partnership between the two entities, although in the modern business world, when large entities agree to form a new business entity between them, they most often form some kind of limited liability entity. In order to form a general partnership, the business must be unincorporated and intended to make a profit. The "unincorporated" requirement is obvious in that an entity that has complied with the formalities to form a corporation cannot be a partnership. Partnership law is limited to entities organized to make a profit, since partnership law is a subcategory of commercial law. Other business entities, such as corporations, do not need to be formed to seek a profit. Agreeing to share a profit creates a rebuttable presumption under the RUPA that a partnership exists.

Generally, each partner in a partnership has something to offer the business, including labor, ideas, money, and/or property. Each of the partners in a general partnership co-owns the business and has a right to manage the business with other partners. This right, however, can be modified by agreement of the partners. Similarly, partners have a general right to share profits and contribute to pay for losses, though either of these can be modified by agreement of the parties.

Many partnerships are formed when one or more partners agree to provide money, property, and other types of capital to the business ("capital partners"), while one or more of the other partners agree to provide work and other labor expertise ("labor partners"). For example, assume that two people agree to form a business to build custom furniture. One partner agrees to provide the work facility and office and also agrees to supply $100,000 to finance the business. The other partner, who is an expert in building furniture, agrees to build all of the furniture and manage the business. The first partner is the capital partner, while the latter is the labor partner. This general partnership can be beneficial to both parties if the business is successful but can cause significant problems if the business fails. Many of these problems are cause for disputes over which party should bear the burden of the losses suffered by the partnership.

Partnerships are generally categorized in three types, which are defined by the agreement of the partners. In a partnership at will, every partner has the right to end the partnership, subject to some restrictions. In a partnership for a term, the partners' agreement determines the time when a partnership will end. In a partnership for a particular undertaking, the partners' agreement indicates that completion of a particular task or goal will cause the partnership to end.

Consent and the Partnership Agreement Forming a partnership requires few specific formalities, such as a written agreement or registration with a state agency. Nevertheless, all parties that are considered partners must consent to be such. The consent may be express, such as signing a written partnership agreement or implied by the conduct of the parties. Parties do not need to agree specifically to form a "partnership;" rather, their agreement or conduct must be such that they agree to run a business for profit. Even if the parties agree that their business will not be labeled a partnership, the business may be found to be one if it meets the definition of a partnership.

If two or more individuals enter a partnership without a partnership agreement, problems are likely to arise. The **default** rules found in the UPA and the RUPA may not be sufficient for the parties based on their wants and needs when they formed the business. Similarly, the rules in the UPA and RUPA may not reflect the understanding of the parties when they entered into the business. Since all partners are liable for the debts of the partnership, if a partnership is formed inadvertently, it may cause significant problems for the partner who was not aware of the legal consequences of his or her decision. Should an individual wish to enter into a business that has not been registered as a limited liability entity, he or she should be sure to demand the drafting of a written partnership agreement so that the understanding and agreement of the parties can be reflected more clearly in a document.

Profit Sharing Agreeing to share profits is a precondition for the formation of a partnership. Sharing profits is not the same as sharing revenues. Revenues refer to all of the money received by a business, including income, receipts, or proceeds. Profits are the amount remaining of the revenue after expenses incurred by the business are subtracted. If one party agrees to share revenues with another party, but the agreement makes not stipulation for profits, then a partnership has not been formed. The focus on profits requires the partners to pay attention to the management of the entire business, not only the amount of money taken in by the business. By comparison, a person who receives revenues, but not profits, is much more likely to focus on the sales of a business but not the costs in doing business.

Partners do not need to share profits equally. Under both the UPA and the RUPA, partners can agree to the division of profits made by a business. In a situation where there is a capital partner and a labor partner, the partnership agreement will most likely include a salary for the labor partner, with the capital partner receiving the profits.

Loss Sharing An agreement to share losses in all jurisdictions is strong **evidence** that a partnership exists. Although neither the UPA nor the RUPA expressly requires an agreement to share losses to find that a partnership exists, some jurisdictions require a finding of such an agreement as a prerequisite for a finding that a partnership has been formed. Under both the UPA and the RUPA, the definition of partnership does not include sharing losses but rather requires that losses be shared in the same proportion as profits. Like many other rules in the UPA and the RUPA, the parties can agree otherwise.

Ownership and Management All partners in a general partnership are considered co-owners. By default, partners also have equal rights to manage the partnership. If an agreement contemplates joint ownership of a business for profit, as well as joint decision-making regarding the partnership's business, then the likelihood increases that a partnership exists. More difficult questions are raised when co-ownership and co-management are considered in the context of control of the partnership. For example, under the default rules in the UPA and RUPA, both a capital partner and a labor partner have equal rights to manage the partnership, even if the labor partner is much more qualified to manage the business. Similarly, all partners have the authority to bind a partnership by transacting partnership business. In almost all situations, it is beneficial to include management and control provisions in a partnership agreement to avoid conflicts.

LIABILITY AND DUTIES OF PARTNERS IN A GENERAL PARTNERSHIP

Partner as an Agent of a Partnership Under both the UPA and the RUPA, all partners serve as general agents of the partnership. Accordingly, partners may bind the partnership through their actions. They often have the actual authority to conduct partnership business, though the extent of this authority often focuses on the language included in a partnership agreement. Authority may be implied through the action or inaction of other partners in the management of the business. For example, if one partner has entered into contracts on behalf of the partnership in the past, and none of the partners has objected (assuming they have knowledge of the transaction), the partner most likely has implied authority to enter into the **contract**.

Tort Liability to Third Parties Since partners are considered agents of the partnership, a partner's wrongful act or omission can bind the partnership if the wrongdoing partner has acted within the ordinary course of the partnership's business. Such liability is referred to as vicarious liability, a term that is also used when a business is liable for the acts of an employee acting within the scope of his or her employment. Moreover, partners in a partnership generally are jointly and severally liable for torts charged against the partnership. Thus, any or all of the partners in a partnership can be sued individually for the entire amount of the injury caused by the partner. For example, if two lawyers form a general partnership, and one lawyer is liable for **malpractice**, then the person injured by the malpractice may sue the partnership, the lawyer who committed malpractice, and/or the other lawyer in the partnership. In this situation, the person who is injured could chose to sue only the lawyer who did not commit malpractice, since that lawyer is jointly and severally liable for the torts of the other partner acting in the partnership's business.

Well-planned businesses will usually avoid the seemingly harsh consequences caused by joint and several liabilities. One of the more obvious solutions is for the partnership to form a limited liability entity, such as a **limited liability partnership**. Other solutions may be provided in a partnership agreement, such as the inclusion of a provision requiring the wrongdoing partner to indemnify the other partners if the other partners are vicariously liable for the torts of the wrongdoing partner.

Contract Liability to Third Parties Under the UPA, partners are jointly liable for contractual liability of the partnership. The RUPA modifies this provision so that partners are jointly and severally liable for the contractual liability of the partnership. The difference between the two types of liability is really procedural. If partners are jointly liable, all of the partners must be sued at the same time, and omission of a partner means that the suit must be dropped. By comparison, if partners are jointly and severally liable, suits may proceed against individual partners even if some partners are omitted from the suit.

Tax Liability of Partners and Partnerships One of the most practical benefits of forming a partnership, as opposed to a corporation, is the tax treatment of partnerships by the federal government in the Internal Revenue Code. Owners of a corporation, in effect, pay double taxes. The corporation itself must pay taxes on business income. The money, which has already been taxed, is eventually distributed to pay salaries, dividends, and other forms of income to those involved in the corporation. These individuals must pay tax on the money received, even though the corporation was initially taxed. Partnerships, by comparison, are treated as so-called "pass-through" entities. The partnership itself does not pay taxes. The partnership's income "passes through" the partnership and is distributed to the partners. When the partners pay taxes on their income, this money has not yet been taxed.

Ownership of Property Since partners often contribute property for the use of the partnership, the question of ownership of this property is sometimes difficult. For example, if a partner purchases **personal property** with his own money but the property is used exclusively by the partnership, then it could be questionable whether this property is the partner's separate property or whether it is the partnership's property. The UPA creates a presumption that property acquired with partnership funds is partnership property, unless the partners intend otherwise. The RUPA extends this presumption and adds a presumption that if one or more partners purchase property in their own name and without use of partnership funds, the property is considered the separate property of the partner or partners. This is true even if the property is used for partnership purposes.

Both the partnership and individual partners can hold legal title to real property, and both the UPA and the RUPA contain provisions prescribing the conveyance of real property by partners or the partnership. Under the RUPA, partners and partnerships have the option of filing and recording a statement indicating the authority of the partners to transfer real property in the name of the partnership.

DUTIES OF THE PARTNERS

Partners in a partnership owe each other certain **fiduciary** duties. One of the more significant changes between the UPA and the RUPA was the clarification of fiduciary duties in the RUPA. Under the revised act, partners owe each other the duty of loyalty and the duty of care. The RUPA restricts the ability of partners to waive these fiduciary duties.

Duty of Loyalty The duty of loyalty refers to the duty of a partner to refrain from competing with the partnership in another endeavor or profiting individually from a transaction related to the partnership. This duty does not mean that a partner cannot further his or her own interests but that a partner may not further his or her own

interests to the detriment of the partnership. Application of this duty may arise when one of the partners owns several businesses and the potential for competition between a separate business and the partnership arises. Another situation occurs when one the partners wants to leave the partnership. It is not uncommon that the partner may take steps to set up a separate business, and establishing the new business may conflict with the interests of the partnership.

Duty of Care The duty of care does not refer to acts of mere **negligence** by a partner. For example, if a partner unintentionally makes a bad business decision, his or her negligence will not necessarily violate the duty of care. On the other hand, the duty of care proscribes **gross negligence**, recklessness, intentional misconduct, or knowing violation of the law on the part of each of the partners. Although partners cannot waive the duty of care under the RUPA, partners can hold themselves to a higher standard of care, including ordinary negligence.

DISSOCIATION AND DISSOLUTION

The RUPA made other significant changes with respect to the **dissolution** of a partnership and winding up of partnership affairs. Under the UPA, if a partner withdraws from the partnership, an event occurs that ends the partnership, the partners agree to end the partnership, or any of a number of situations occurs, the partnership dissolves. When dissolution occurs, the partnership's business generally ends, the affairs of the business wind up, and partnership property is sold. Partnership agreements, even before the enactment of the RUPA, often provide a method whereby the withdrawing partner's interests are purchased and the partnership continues. In the absence of such an agreement, the remaining partners may continue the partnership's business, but the resulting business is considered a completely new partnership.

The RUPA altered this situation, providing that when certain events occur, such as a partner's withdrawal from the partnership, the partnership is not necessarily dissolved. The RUPA introduced dissociation, whereby a partner can be dissociated from a partnership without the partnership ending. If a partner dissociates from a partnership, the partnership will not necessarily dissolve. The remaining partners can instead purchase the interests of the dissociating partner and continue partnership business.

When a partnership is dissolved, it enters a stage called winding up. Both the UPA and the RUPA provide rather detailed provisions for winding up the affairs of the partnership. One restriction is that partners who have wrongfully caused the dissolution of the partnership or have wrongfully dissociated from the partnership cannot participate in the winding up process. The most significant part of the winding up process is the **liquidation** of partnership assets and payment of partnership creditors. When the assets are liquidated, creditors who are not also partners are generally paid first. If a partner is also a **creditor** of the partnership, he or she is then reimbursed. Once each of the creditors is reimbursed, partners may recover their capital contributions. Finally, if assets remain, the partners will receive their share, in accordance with a partnership agreement or according to the provisions of the UPA or the RUPA.

STATE LAWS GOVERNING PARTNERSHIPS

The majority of states have adopted the Revised Uniform Partnership Act, though some have retained the Uniform Partnership Act. Some states have modified certain provisions of their versions of the **uniform acts**, so researchers should be sure to check their states' versions of the act to determine which provisions may differ from the uniform law. The only state that has not adopted the uniform law is Louisiana.

ALABAMA: Adopted the Revised Uniform Partnership Act in 1998. Previously adopted the Uniform Partnership Act in 1972.

ALASKA: Adopted the Uniform Partnership Act in 1917.

ARIZONA: Adopted the Revised Uniform Partnership Act in 1996. Previously adopted the Uniform Partnership Act in 1954.

CALIFORNIA: Adopted the Revised Uniform Partnership Act in 1996. Previously adopted the Uniform Partnership Act.

COLORADO: Adopted the Revised Uniform Partnership Act in 1997. Previously adopted the Uniform Partnership Act in 1931.

CONNECTICUT: Adopted the Revised Uniform Partnership Act in 1995. Previously adopted the Uniform Partnership Act in 1961.

DELAWARE: Adopted the Revised Uniform Partnership Act in 1999. Previously adopted the Uniform Partnership Act in 1947.

DISTRICT OF COLUMBIA: Adopted the Revised Uniform Partnership Act in 1997. Previously adopted the Uniform Partnership Act in 1962.

FLORIDA: Adopted the Revised Uniform Partnership Act in 1995. Previously adopted the Uniform Partnership Act in 1973.

GEORGIA: Adopted the Uniform Partnership Act.

HAWAII: Adopted the Revised Uniform Partnership Act in 1999. Previously adopted the Uniform Partnership Act in 1972.

IDAHO: Adopted the Revised Uniform Partnership Act in 1998. Previously adopted the Uniform Partnership Act in 1919.

ILLINOIS: Adopted the Uniform Partnership Act in 1917.

INDIANA: Adopted the Uniform Partnership Act in 1949.

IOWA: Adopted the Revised Uniform Partnership Act in 1998. Previously adopted the Uniform Partnership Act in 1971.

KANSAS: Adopted the Revised Uniform Partnership Act in 1998. Previously adopted the Uniform Partnership Act in 1972.

LOUISIANA: Louisiana is the only state that has adopted neither the Uniform Partnership Act nor the Revised Uniform Partnership Act. Although many of the provisions of the Louisiana law governing partnership are similar to the UPA and RUPA, individuals in Louisiana should consult the Louisiana Civil Code to determine the law of Louisiana with respect to partnerships.

MAINE: Adopted the Uniform Partnership Act in 1973.

MARYLAND: Adopted the Revised Uniform Partnership Act in 1997. Previously adopted the Uniform Partnership Act in 1916.

MASSACHUSETTS: Adopted the Uniform Partnership Act in 1922.

MICHIGAN: Adopted the Uniform Partnership Act in 1917.

MINNESOTA: Adopted the Revised Uniform Partnership Act in 1997. Previously adopted the Uniform Partnership Act in 1921.

MISSISSIPPI: Adopted the Uniform Partnership Act in 1976.

MISSOURI: Adopted the Uniform Partnership Act in 1949.

MONTANA: Adopted the Revised Uniform Partnership Act in 1997. Previously adopted the Uniform Partnership Act in 1947.

NEBRASKA: Adopted the Revised Uniform Partnership Act in 1997. Previously adopted the Uniform Partnership Act in 1943.

NEVADA: Adopted the Uniform Partnership Act in 1931.

NEW HAMPSHIRE: Adopted the Uniform Partnership Act in 1973.

NEW JERSEY: Adopted the Revised Uniform Partnership Act in 2001. Previously adopted the Uniform Partnership Act in 1919.

NEW MEXICO: Adopted the Revised Uniform Partnership Act in 1997. Previously adopted the Uniform Partnership Act in 1947.

NEW YORK: Adopted the Uniform Partnership Act in 1919.

NORTH CAROLINA: Adopted the Uniform Partnership Act in 1941.

NORTH DAKOTA: Adopted the Revised Uniform Partnership Act in 1997. Previously adopted the Uniform Partnership Act in 1959.

OHIO: Adopted the Uniform Partnership Act in 1949.

OKLAHOMA: Adopted the Revised Uniform Partnership Act in 1997. Previously adopted the Uniform Partnership Act in 1959.

OREGON: Adopted the Revised Uniform Partnership Act in 1997. Previously adopted the Uniform Partnership Act in 1939.

PENNSYLVANIA: Adopted the Uniform Partnership Act in 1915.

RHODE ISLAND: Adopted the Uniform Partnership Act in 1957.

SOUTH CAROLINA: Adopted the Uniform Partnership Act in 1950.

SOUTH DAKOTA: Adopted the Revised Uniform Partnership Act in 2001. Previously adopted the Uniform Partnership Act in 1923.

TENNESSEE: Adopted the Revised Uniform Partnership Act in 2001. Previously adopted the Uniform Partnership Act in 1917.

TEXAS: Adopted the Revised Uniform Partnership Act in 1998. Previously adopted the Uniform Partnership Act in 1961.

UTAH: Adopted the Uniform Partnership Act in 1921.

VERMONT: Adopted the Revised Uniform Partnership Act in 1998. Previously adopted the Uniform Partnership Act in 1941.

VIRGINIA: Adopted the Revised Uniform Partnership Act in 1996. Previously adopted the Uniform Partnership Act in 1918.

WASHINGTON: Adopted the Revised Uniform Partnership Act in 1998. Previously adopted the Uniform Partnership Act in 1945.

WEST VIRGINIA: Adopted the Revised Uniform Partnership Act in 1995. Previously adopted the Uniform Partnership Act in 1953.

WISCONSIN: Adopted the Uniform Partnership Act in 1915.

WYOMING: Adopted the Revised Uniform Partnership Act in 1993. Previously adopted the Uniform Partnership Act in 1917.

ADDITIONAL RESOURCES

Hynes, J. Dennis, and Mark J. Loewenstein. *Agency, Partnership, and the LLC in a Nutshell.* 5th ed. Eagan, MN: West, Thomson Reuters, 2011.

Kleinberger, Daniel S. *Agency and Partnerships: Examples and Explanations.* New York: Aspen Law and Business, 1995.

National Conference of Commissioners on Uniform State Laws. "Acts: Partnership Act." 1997. Available at http://www.

uniformlaws.org/Act.aspx?title=Partnership%20Act (accessed November 3, 2012).

"Partnership Laws of the United States: Introduction and List of Articles." USLaw.com, 1999. Available at http://www.uslaw.com/library/article/noparIntro.html (accessed October 31, 2012).

Sitarz, Daniel. *Partnerships: Laws of the United States*. New York: Nova Publishing Company, 1999.

ORGANIZATIONS

Council of Better Business Bureaus (CBBB)
4200 Wilson Blvd., Suite 800
Arlington, VA 22203-1838
Phone: (703) 276-0100
Fax: (703) 525-8277
URL: http://www.bbb.org/

National Conference of Commissioners on Uniform State Laws (NCCUSL)
211 E. Ontario Street, Suite 1300
Chicago, IL 60611
Phone: (312) 915-0195
Fax: (312) 915-0187
Email: nccusl@nccusl.org
URL: http://www.nccusl.org/

Small Business Advancement National Center (SBANC)
University of Central Arkansas
College of Business Administration
UCA Box 5018
201 Donaghey Avenue
Conway, AR 72053-0001
Phone: (501) 450-5300
Fax: (501) 450-5360
URL: http://www.saber.uca.edu/

U.S. Chamber of Commerce
1615 H Street, NW
Washington, DC 20062-2000
Phone: (202) 659-6000
Email: custsvc@uschamber.com
URL: http://www.uschamber.com

BUSINESS LAW

SHAREHOLDER RIGHTS

Sections within this essay:

BACKGROUND

Investors who purchase **corporate** stock enjoy a number of rights pertaining to their ownership. Unlike **partnership** law, where the owners of businesses are also the primary managers of the businesses, owners of a corporation generally do not run the company. Shareholders in a corporation are shielded from personal liability for the debts and obligations of the corporation. However, shareholders can lose their investments should the corporation fail.

Laws governing **corporations** in the United States are fairly standard from one state to the next. The commissioners on uniform state laws drafted the Uniform Business Corporations Act in 1928, although only three states adopted this act. The American Bar Association (ABA) in 1950 drafted the Model Business Corporation Act, which subsequently has been modified numerous times. The last major redrafting occurred in 1984, but there were substantive revisions in 2002 and 2005. Approximately 32 states have adopted the Model Act as of 2012, according to the ABA. Other states have modified their own state corporation statutes to contain sections similar to the Model Act. Delaware's corporation **statute** is also significant, since the majority of large, public corporations are incorporated in that state.

The rights of shareholders depend largely on provisions in a corporation's charter and by-laws. These are the first documents which a shareholder should consult when determining his or her rights in a corporation. Shareholders also generally enjoy the following types of rights:

- Voting rights on issues that affect the corporation as a whole
- Rights related to the assets of the corporation
- Rights related to the transfer of stock
- Rights to receive dividends as declared by the board of directors of the corporation
- Rights to inspect the records and books of the corporation

- Rights to bring suit against the corporation for wrongful acts by the directors and officers of the corporation

- Rights to share in the proceeds recovered when the corporation liquidates its assets

OWNERSHIP OF STOCK

The two broad types of financing available to a corporation include equity financing and debt financing. Equity financing involves the issuance of stock, which investors purchase and which represent a share in the ownership of the corporation. The two basic types of stock are **common stock** and **preferred stock**. Debt financing involves a loan of money from an investor to the corporation in exchange for debt **securities**, such as a bond. Holders of debt securities generally do not enjoy the same rights as shareholders in terms of voting rights, participating rights, or other rights related to the ownership of stock.

Common Stock The lowest level of stock in a corporation is common stock. The rights related to common stock depend largely on the **articles of incorporation** and by-laws of the corporation. In general, owners of common stock have voting rights in a corporation as well as rights to receive distributions of money from the corporation (dividends). In a successful corporation, common stock ownership can be very lucrative. However, if a corporation is unsuccessful, common stock owners are usually the last in line to receive a distribution of the corporation's assets when the corporation's assets are liquidated.

State statutes often vary with respect to the **default** rights of common stock owners. The corporation may also issue multiple classes of common stock, such as nonvoting common stock or common stock with special **dividend** rights.

Preferred Stock Unlike common stock, holders of preferred stock are entitled to fixed dividends and fixed rights to receive a percentage of a corporation's assets are liquidated. With respect to the dividend rights, an example of such stock would include a name such as "$20 preferred," which means the shareholder has a right to receive $20 in dividends per share before dividends are paid to common stock owners.

It is noteworthy that the board of directors in a corporation usually has the discretion to decide whether dividends are issued in a given year. If dividends are not distributed during one year, whether preferred stock owners receive dividends in a subsequent year depends on whether the preferred stock is cumulative or noncumulative. If the rights are cumulative, the corporation must be

dividends during some subsequent year. If the rights are noncumulative, the rights to receive dividends are lost if the corporation does not issue dividends in a given year.

Preferred stock owners generally do not have the same rights to vote as common stock owners. However, a corporation may grant voting rights and additional rights in its articles of incorporation or other provisions. State statutes also provide some rights to preferred stock owners by default.

Bonds and Debentures Corporations may seek to borrow money in addition to (or in lieu of) issuing stock. One method for borrowing money is to exchange the loan for a debt security that can be traded on a public market. **Bonds** are long-term debt securities that are secured by corporate assets. Debentures are unsecured debt securities. Owners of debt securities generally do not enjoy the same types of rights are owners of stock. However, a corporation may grant voting rights to the owners of debt securities. These owners may also have the right to redeem debt securities in exchange for stock.

SHAREHOLDER MEETINGS AND VOTING RIGHTS

Shareholders hold general meetings on an annual basis or at fixed times according to the by-laws of the corporation. The primary purpose of these meetings is for shareholders to elect the directors of the corporation, though shareholders may also vote on a number of additional issues. Persons with authority to do so may also call special meetings on matters that require immediate attention, though only those issues set forth in the notice of the special meeting may be the subject of the vote.

A quorum must be present at the shareholder meeting for a decision to be binding. The typical quorum consists of more than half of the outstanding shares of the corporation. This percentage may be increased or decreased in the bylaws of the corporation. Prior to each shareholder meeting, a list of shareholders eligible to vote must be prepared. Shareholders have the right to inspect the voting list at any time.

Shareholders may appoint proxies to vote their shares, which is common in publicly-held corporations. Most states prescribe few specific rules with respect to the proxy appointment, other than the issue of whether this appointment may be revoked. Proxy appointments must be in writing, and the proxy does not need to be a fellow shareholder. Since the relationship between the shareholder and the proxy is one of principal and agent, the proxy must abide by the instructions of the shareholder.

Shareholders by unanimous consent may conduct business without holding a shareholder meeting. Such actions are more common in closely held corporations, where shareholder actions are typically unanimous. In a larger, publicly held corporation, such actions are much less practical, especially because decisions of the shareholders affect a larger number of people.

Matters upon which shareholders vote, in addition to the election of the directors, depend on the issues affecting the corporation. The following are the most significant of these matters.

- Approval or disapproval of changes in the articles of incorporation

- Approval or disapproval of a merger with another corporation

- Approval or disapproval of the sale of substantially all of the corporation's assets that is not in the ordinary course of the corporation's business

- Approval or disapproval of the voluntary **dissolution** of the corporation

- Approval or disapproval of corporate transactions where some directors have a conflict of interest

- Approval or disapproval of amendments to **bylaws** or articles of incorporation

- Make nonbinding recommendations about the governance and management of the corporation to the board of directors

Concerns over inappropriate or unethical corporate decisions made by officers have led some commentators to suggest giving greater power to shareholders to affect corporate decision-making. For example, Delaware state law changed in 2009 to give shareholders greater power to nominate directors. However, a proposal in Congress that would have created a shareholder **bill of rights** failed to generate significant support, and the proposal died.

SHAREHOLDER RIGHTS, ACTIONS, AND LIABILITIES

Many of the rights afforded to shareholders are contained in each corporation's articles of incorporation or bylaws. It is also noteworthy that shareholders generally do not have the right to vote on management issues that occur in the ordinary course of the corporation's business. Many decisions of the corporation must be made by the board of directors or officers of the corporation, and in most cases, shareholders may not compel the board or officers to take or refrain from taking any action.

Shareholder Direct Litigation Shareholders can protect their ownership rights in their shares by bringing a direct action against a corporation. Such cases may involve **contract** rights related to the shares; rights granted to the shareholder in a statute; rights related to the recovery of dividends; and rights to examine the books and records of a corporation. Some cases are not appropriate for direct actions by a shareholder against a corporation, however. For example, a shareholder may not bring a direct action against a corporation by alleging that an officer has breached a **fiduciary** duty owed to the corporation. Such a case involves all shareholders and is more appropriate as a derivative action. By comparison, a shareholder may bring a direct action if he or she has been prevented from voting his or her shares in a vote.

Shareholder Derivative Litigation Shareholders may bring suit as representatives of the corporation in a derivative action. Such an action is designed to prevent wrongdoing by the officers or directors of the corporation or to seek a remedy for such wrongdoing. These suits are generally brought when the corporation itself (through its officers and directors) refuses to bring suit itself. A party bringing a derivative suit acts as a representative of an appropriate class of shareholders, and in the action the shareholders enforce claims that would be appropriate between the corporation and the officers and directors of the corporation. For example, if the officers of the corporation have breached a fiduciary duty owed to the corporation, shareholders may bring a derivative action to protect the interests of the corporation on behalf of the corporation. While these actions in many cases protect the rights of the corporation and shareholders of the corporation, these actions are often controversial. Shareholders should study the procedural and substantive provisions of state statutes to determine whether the action is appropriate and determine which formalities should be followed with respect to these actions.

Shareholder Preemptive Rights Corporations retain the right to issue new shares of stock, which could dilute the ownership of existing stockholders. Existing shareholders often hold preemptive rights, which allow the shareholders to purchase these new shares of stock before they are made available to the public. Thus, if a shareholder owns 10 percent of a corporation, and the corporation issues new stock, the shareholder would own less than 10 percent if he or she did not purchase new stock. If the shareholder exercises preemptive rights, he or she may purchase as many new shares as necessary to retain that 10 percent interest.

Shareholder Liabilities As the owners of a limited liability entity, shareholders are generally shielded from personal liability for claims against the corporation. Thus, if a corporation incurs a debt or obligation against it, creditors cannot recover the personal assets of the shareholders.

However, the average life of a corporation in the United States is only seven years, and more than half fail before seven years have elapsed. A shareholder can lose his or her entire investment if the corporation fails.

TRANSFER OF STOCK OWNERSHIP

Securities Laws Federal and state securities laws govern the distribution and exchange of stock in a corporation. Many of these laws are designed to avoid **fraud** by the corporation to the detriment of prospective or existing shareholders, so shareholders should consult relevant securities laws if they believe they have been defrauded in the sale or exchange of stock. The sale and exchange of stock through electronic media have provided new methods for defrauding investors, and new securities laws have been enacted in the past ten years to address these issues.

Conversion Rights Owners of one type of stock may want, at some point, to convert their stock to a different type of stock in the same corporation, rather than sell the stock outright. For example, an owner of preferred nonvoting stock may want to own common stock that has voting rights. If the shareholder has conversion rights, he or she may convert the preferred stock for the common stock. These rights can, and often are, limited by the corporation.

Redemption Rights Shareholders may also possess redemption rights, which permit the shareholders to redeem their stock to the corporation for a value specified in the articles of incorporation or set by the board. In other words, the shareholder can demand that the corporation repurchase the shareholder's stock. This right may be limited by the corporation.

SHARING PROCEEDS UPON LIQUIDATION OF CORPORATE ASSETS

When a corporation dissolves, one of its first actions is the **liquidation** of corporate assets. Creditors of the corporation are the first to be paid with the funds received from the liquidation. Owners of debt securities are also paid before shareholders. Once these debts are paid, the remainder is paid to the stockowners. Preferred stock is paid before common stock. Some preferred stock includes a liquidation preference that fixes a price per share of preferred stock. If preferred stock includes this preference, it must be paid before the corporation pays any amount to the common stock. Common stock owners do not have any special liquidation rights and will receive assets on dissolution only after senior claims have been paid.

STATE LAWS GOVERNING SHAREHOLDER RIGHTS

Since the majority of states have adopted the Model Business Corporation Act, shareholder rights are generally consistent from one state to the next. State statutes should be consulted to determine whether an individual state has granted any specific rights to shareholders of businesses incorporated in that state.

ALABAMA: Alabama statute is based on the Model Business Corporation Act. Shareholders are granted preemptive rights in the statute. Shareholders may bring derivative actions for fraud, dishonesty, or gross abuse on the part of the directors. Holders of 10 percent of the votes may call a special meeting.

ALASKA: A shareholder may bring a derivative action on behalf of the corporation. Each record shareholder is entitled to written notice of meetings.

ARIZONA: Arizona statute is based on the Model Business Corporation Act. Corporations must provide shareholders with a stock certificate upon request. Shareholders may petition for a special meeting.

ARKANSAS: Arkansas statute is based on the Model Business Corporation Act. Shareholders are entitled to notice of annual and special shareholder meetings. The statute grants preemptive rights to shareholders.

CALIFORNIA: The statute provides special rights to shareholders who dissent to corporate reorganization or merger.

COLORADO: Colorado statute is based on the Model Business Corporation Act. Statute provides special rules regarding entitlement to voting with respect to fractional shares. The statute provides specific rules regarding derivative actions.

CONNECTICUT: The articles of incorporation of a corporation must provide preemptive rights. The statute governs derivative suits brought by shareholders.

DELAWARE: The statute provides specific rules regarding derivative actions. The statute prescribes specific rules shareholder meetings and voting, including voting agreements and voting by proxy.

DISTRICT OF COLUMBIA: The statute is based on the Model Business Corporation Act. The statute permits derivative actions brought by shareholders, and prescribes specific rules for such actions.

FLORIDA: Florida statute is based on the Model Business Corporation Act. The statute permits derivative actions and prescribes specific rules for such actions. The statute prescribes specific rules for voting by shareholders, including voting trusts and voting agreements.

GEORGIA: Georgia statute is based on the Model Business Corporation Act. The statute does not provide preemptive rights to shareholders, except those in close corporations or in those corporations in existence prior to July 1, 1989. The statute permits derivative actions by shareholders.

HAWAII: Hawaii statute is based on the Model Business Corporation Act. The statute provides preemptive rights to shareholders. The statute permits derivative actions by shareholders and prescribes specific rules for such.

IDAHO. Idaho statute is based on the Model Business Corporation Act.

ILLINOIS: The statute permits derivative actions by shareholders. The statute requires vote of shareholders to approve mergers, acquisitions, and other significant and fundamental changes in the corporate structure.

INDIANA: Indiana statute is based on the Model Business Corporation Act. The statute restricts preemptive rights, except those provided under prior law. Shareholder derivative action is permitted, subject to some restrictions. The statute permits the creation of a disinterested committee of the corporation to consider a derivative action.

IOWA: The statute does not provide preemptive rights, which may only be granted by the articles of incorporation. The statute provides specific rules regarding shareholder meetings and shareholder voting.

KANSAS: The statute provides specific rules regarding derivative actions. The statute prescribes specific rules shareholder meetings and voting, including voting agreements and voting by proxy.

KENTUCKY: Kentucky statute is based on the Model Business Corporation Act. The statute permits derivative actions by shareholders and provides specific rules regarding representation of the corporation's rights.

LOUISIANA: The statute does not provide preemptive rights, which may only be granted in the articles of incorporation. The statute provides specific rules regarding shareholder meetings and voting, including the creation of voting trusts.

MAINE: Maine statute is based on the 1960 version of the Model Business Corporation Act. The statute grants limited preemptive rights in some circumstances. The statute permits derivative actions and prescribes specific rules regarding such actions.

MARYLAND: Maryland statute is based on the Model Business Corporation Act. The statute prescribes specific rules regarding shareholder meeting and voting, including voting by proxy.

MASSACHUSETTS: The statute does not provide preemptive rights to shareholders. The statute permits derivative suits by shareholders under appropriate circumstances.

MICHIGAN: Shareholders are permitted to bring an action to establish that the acts of directors or other managers are illegal, **fraudulent**, or willfully unfair or oppressive to the shareholders or corporation. The statute sets forth detailed rules regarding shareholder meetings and voting, including voting without a meeting and voting trusts.

MINNESOTA: The statute sets forth detailed rules regarding shareholder meetings and voting and the rights of shareholders to inspect the books and records of the corporation.

MISSISSIPPI: Mississippi statute is based on the Model Business Corporation Act.

MISSOURI: The statute permits shareholders to bring suit to enjoin ultra vires acts. The statute provides detailed rules regarding shareholder meetings and voting, including voting trusts.

MONTANA: Montana statute is based on the Model Business Corporation Act. The statute provides specific rules regarding shareholder meetings and voting, including a provision that permits shareholders to participate by telephone if the corporation consists of 50 or fewer shareholders.

NEBRASKA: Nebraska's statute is based on the Model Business Corporation Act.

NEVADA: The statute provides specific rules regarding shareholder meetings and voting, including voting trusts.

NEW HAMPSHIRE: New Hampshire statute is based on the Model Business Corporation Act.

NEW JERSEY: Statute does not provide preemptive rights for shareholders. The statute permits derivative suits subject to some restrictions, and provides specific rules regarding shareholder meetings and voting, including voting trusts and voting by proxy.

NEW MEXICO: New Mexico statute is based on the Model Business Corporation Act. The statute permits shareholder derivative suits, subject to some restrictions.

NEW YORK: In some limited circumstances, majority shareholders may incur personal liability for corporation's debts. The statute provides detailed rules regarding shareholder meetings and voting, including voting trusts.

NORTH CAROLINA: North Carolina statute is based on the Model Business Corporation Act. Shareholders under current statute do not have preemptive rights. The statute provides detailed rules regarding shareholder meetings and voting, including voting trusts and voting by proxy.

NORTH DAKOTA: Shareholder meetings are held on an annual or other periodic basis, but do not need to be held unless required by the articles of incorporation or the bylaws. A shareholder with more than 5 percent of voting power may demand a meeting.

OHIO: The statute permits derivative actions brought by shareholders. Shareholders provide detailed rules regarding shareholder meetings and voting, including voting trusts.

OKLAHOMA: The statute permits derivative actions brought by shareholders. Statute and provides detailed rules regarding shareholder meetings and voting, including voting trusts.

OREGON: Oregon statute is based on the Model Business Corporation Act. The statute provides detailed rules regarding shareholder meetings and voting, including voting trusts.

PENNSYLVANIA: The statute permits derivative actions brought by shareholder and provides detailed rules regarding these actions. The statute provides detailed

rules regarding shareholder meetings and voting, including voting trusts.

RHODE ISLAND: Rhode Island statute is based on Model Business Corporation Act. The statute permits derivative actions brought by shareholders and provides some limitation for voting trusts and shareholder agreements.

SOUTH CAROLINA: South Carolina statute is based on the Model Business Corporation Act. The statute provides detailed rules on shareholder meetings and voting, including voting trusts and voting by proxy.

SOUTH DAKOTA: South Dakota statute is based on the Model Business Corporation Act.

TENNESSEE: The statute contains special rules regarding derivative actions brought by shareholders.

TEXAS: The statute permits shareholder agreements, subject to a number of restrictions and provides detailed rules regarding shareholder meetings and voting, including voting trusts.

UTAH: Utah statute is based on the Model Business Corporation Act. The statute provides detailed rules regarding shareholder meetings and voting, including voting entitlement, voting trusts, voting agreements, and other shareholder agreements.

VERMONT: The statute does not provide preemptive rights to shareholders. The statute provides specific rules regarding voting trusts and voting by proxy and permits derivative actions brought by shareholders.

VIRGINIA: Virginia statute is based partially on the Model Business Corporations Act. The statute provides preemptive rights to shareholder by default. Statute and permits derivative actions brought by shareholders.

WASHINGTON: Washington statute is based on the Model Business Corporations Act. The statute provides preemptive rights to shareholders by default.

WEST VIRGINIA: The West Virginia statute is based primarily on the Model Business Corporation Act. The statute provides detailed rules regarding shareholder meetings and voting, including voting trusts.

WISCONSIN: The statute does not provide preemptive rights to shareholders. Statute and provides detailed rules regarding shareholder meetings and voting, including voting by proxy and voting trusts.

WYOMING: Wyoming's statute is based on the Model Business Corporations Act.

ADDITIONAL RESOURCES

Fairfax, Lisa M. *Shareholder Democracy: A Primer on Shareholder Activism and Participation.* Durham, NC: Carolina Academic Press, 2011.

Harris, Lee. *Mastering Corporations and Other Business Entities.* Durham, NC: Carolina Academic Press, 2009.

Palmiter, Alan R. *Corporations: Examples and Explanations.* New York: Wolters Kluwer Law & Business, 2012.

ORGANIZATIONS

Business Law Section, American Bar Association
740 15th Street, NW
Washington, DC 20005-1019
Phone: (312) 988-5588
URL: http://www.americanbar.org/groups/business_law.html
Email: businesslaw@americanbar.org

Center for Corporate Law, University of Cincinnati College of Law
PO Box 210040
Cincinnati, OH 45221-0040
Phone: (513) 556-6805
Fax: (513) 556-2391
URL: http://www.law.uc.edu/institutes-centers/corporate-law-center/

Council of Better Business Bureaus (CBBB)
4200 Wilson Blvd., Suite 800
Arlington, VA 22203-1838
Phone: (703) 276-0100
Fax: (703) 525-8277
URL: http://www.bbb.org/

U.S. Chamber of Commerce
1615 H Street, NW
Washington, DC 20062-2000
Phone: (202) 659-6000
Email: custsvc@uschamber.com
URL: http://www.uschamber.com

CIVIL RIGHTS

AFFIRMATIVE ACTION

Sections within this essay:

BACKGROUND

Affirmative action has been the most contentious area of **civil rights** law since the late 1950s. Despite several Supreme Court decisions, numerous **executive orders**, and laws passed by legislatures at the state and federal level, it is still considered an unsettled area of law. Because of this current lack of resolution, any article written about affirmative action may become outdated quickly with the latest law or court decision. Nevertheless, the broad outlines of what affirmative action has been and presumably will be in the future can be established.

AFFIRMATIVE ACTION DEFINED

Although the term "affirmative action" can be used in a variety of contexts, the most popular definition currently is within the arena of civil rights. There, affirmative action has been held to provide a special boost to qualified minorities, women, and disabled individuals in order to make up either for past **discrimination** or for their under representation in a specific area of the work force or academia. Although these categories of individuals have historically benefited most, affirmative action programs can also apply to other areas of discrimination, such as age, nationality, and religion.

Affirmative action can be administered in several ways. One way is through "quotas," defined as a strict requirement for a proportion or share of jobs, funding, or other placement to go to a specific group—for example, 50 percent of all new hires must be women. Another is "goals," which require agencies and institutions to exert a good-faith effort toward reaching the assigned proportion or share goal but do not require that the proportion be reached. Affirmative action can also take the form of intangible "boosts" for the respective beneficiaries of the program. For example, all men shorter than 5 feet, 8 inches will be given ten extra points on the physical fitness exam.

The reasons for affirmative action are myriad and tend to overlap, but generally two justifications have stood out. One is that the group has been discriminated against in the past, such as black Americans, and needs affirmative

153

action in order to "catch up" to the majority that has not suffered discrimination. The other is that the group is under represented in whatever area is being scrutinized, such as women in construction jobs, and needs to be helped to achieve some sort of representation in the area. Even in this situation, however, there is the tacit admission that discrimination might be the underlying cause of the under representation.

HISTORY OF AFFIRMATIVE ACTION

Affirmative action has its origins in the civil rights movement of the late 1950s and early 1960s. The movement brought a dramatic change to U.S. social life through protests, court decisions, and legislative action, culminating in the passage of the 1964 Civil Rights Act, popularly known as Title VII.

However, Title VII mentioned affirmative action in a positive sense only in the context of the American Indian. It allowed preferential treatment to be given "to individuals because they are Indians living on or near a reservation." Otherwise, Title VII outlawed discrimination in a "color blind" fashion. The relevant part of Title VII states: "Nothing contained in this [law] shall be interpreted to require any employer, employment agency, labor organization, or joint labor-management committee subject to this [law] to grant preferential treatment to any individual or to any group because of the race, color, religion, sex, or national origin of such individual or group on account of an imbalance which may exist with respect to the total number or percentage of persons of any race, color, religion, sex, or national origin employed . . . in comparison with the total number or percentage of persons of such race, color, religion, sex, or national origin in any community, State, section, or other area, or in the available work force in any community, State, section, or other area."

This part of Title VII was passed to assuage the concerns of moderate members of Congress that the Civil Rights Act would become a quota bill, requiring reverse discrimination against whites. Civil rights leaders, who for the most part felt distinctly ambivalent about affirmative action, did not object to the inclusion of this passage. Many saw affirmative action as a way of dividing working class whites from blacks and the civil rights movement from its natural allies in the labor movement.

Nevertheless, the riots of the mid- and late-1960s convinced more and more civil rights leaders that a color-blind policy of enforcing civil rights was not enough and that there had to be steps taken to ensure blacks could complete equally with whites. President Lyndon Johnson endorsed this view in a speech at Howard University in 1965 in which he stated, "You do not take a person who for years has been hobbled by chains and liberate him,

bring him to the starting line and say you are free to compete with all the others."

That same year, Johnson issued Executive Order 11246, requiring firms under **contract** with the federal government not to discriminate and to "take affirmative action to ensure that applicants are employed and that employees are treated during employment, without regard to their race, creed, color, or national origin." Although not specifying what would constitute affirmative action and not applying to any firms outside the federal government, this order is considered the first attempt at positive affirmative action by a governmental entity. The order also created the Office of Federal Contract Compliance (OFCC) to enforce this policy.

Because the term affirmative action was left intentionally vague by the executive order, however, the OFCC was unsure how to enforce it. The OFCC formulated plans in several cities, such as Cleveland and Philadelphia, to facilitate the hiring of minorities for federal government work, but for various reasons these plans were determined to be illegal or never seriously enforced. Johnson left office without any definite affirmative action plan put forth on his watch.

It was left to the Nixon administration, ironically considered an administration not particularly friendly to civil rights interests, to pick up the issue and promote the first serious affirmative action plan that required government-determined, numerically specific percentages of minorities to be hired.

In 1969, the Nixon administration picked up a plan that the Johnson administration had put forth for the construction industry in the city of Philadelphia, referred to as the Philadelphia Plan. The Johnson administration plan was faulted for not having definite minimum standards for the required affirmative action programs. The Nixon plan did issue minimum standards—specific targets for minority employees in several trades. It did not require these minimum standards be met, simply that contractors submitting bids make a "good faith" effort to achieve these targets. This allowed the administration to argue it was not setting quotas, though critics of the plan suggested the administration was in fact doing so.

The Philadelphia Plan survived several challenges, both legal and Congressional, before being accepted as legitimate. The Plan set the tone for affirmative action plans that followed. Soon, the standards put forth in the Philadelphia Plan were incorporated into Executive Order 11246 that affected all federal government contractors, who were required for the first time to provide written affirmative action plans with numerical targets.

After the implementation of the Philadelphia Plan, legislation was passed at the federal, state, and municipal level implementing affirmative action plans using the

Philadelphia Plan as a model. By the early 2010s, almost all government affirmative action plans are offshoots of the Philadelphia Plan. Its mixture of numerical targets and requirements of "good faith" effort was a milestone in the history of affirmative action.

SUPREME COURT DECISIONS ON AFFIRMATIVE ACTION

The Supreme Court has given its opinion on affirmative action on numerous occasions since the Philadelphia Plan was put into effect in 1970. By-and-large, these Supreme Court decisions were more open to the idea of affirmative action during the 1970s and early 1980s and then gradually tightened the requirements for affirmative action plans. Generally, the question before the Supreme Court regarding affirmative action plans asked what kind of scrutiny to give the plans.

Griggs v. Duke Power Co. Decided in 1971, this is generally held to have laid the foundation for affirmative action programs based on the rationale of under representation. The case involved black workers at a power plant in North Carolina who sued, arguing that the plant's requirements of a high school education or passing a standardized intelligence test in order to fill certain jobs was discriminatory. The plaintiffs argued that the requirements operated to disqualify blacks at a substantially higher rate than white applicants. The plant argued that the requirements served a legitimate business purpose.

A unanimous Supreme Court disagreed with the employer, ruling that the tests did not serve any job-related requirement. The Court pointed out that the plant had practiced discrimination in the past and that the effect of these requirements was to prevent black workers from overcoming the effects of such discrimination. "Practices, procedures, or tests neutral on their face, and even neutral in terms of intent, cannot be maintained if they operate to 'freeze' the status quo of prior discriminatory employment practices," said the court.

The effect of *Griggs v. Duke Power* was to legitimize the so-called disparate impact theory—the idea that if a qualification had a disparate impact on a specific group, an organization could justify that qualification only if it could prove a business related purpose for such a requirement. This point opened the door to forcing employers, including the government, to taking a hard look at the effect of their employment practices and their relation to race.

Regents of the University of California v. Bakke This was the first instance of the court taking a case specifically involving affirmative action. The case involved a white man, Allan Bakke, who had applied for a seat at the medical school at the University of California at Davis. Bakke was rejected, and then he sued, arguing that less qualified minorities were being allowed into the school under a quota system reserving a specific number of seats for minorities.

In a 5-4 ruling, a divided Supreme Court in 1978 ruled that the specific quota system used by the University of California at Davis was illegal but that race could be taken into consideration in determining admission slots at the school. The result was the first time the Court had held that reverse discrimination could be justified under certain circumstances.

United Steel Workers of America v. Weber and *Fullilove v. Klutznick* These two cases, decided a year apart, further legitimized the use of affirmative action as a tool for increasing minority employment. In the *Weber* case, the Supreme Court in 1979 ruled that an affirmative action plan for on-the-job training that mandated a one-for-one quota for minority workers admitted to the program was legal, since the plan was a temporary measure designed to correct an imbalance in the workforce.

In *Fullilove*, the Supreme Court upheld the "minority business enterprise" provision of Public Works Employment Act of 1977, which requires that at least 10 percent of federal funds granted for local public works projects must be used by the state or local grantee to procure services or supplies from businesses owned by minority group members.

Johnson v. Santa Clara County Transportation Agency This 1987 decision expanded the Court's protection of affirmative action programs to ones benefiting women. The Court ruled that the county agency did not violate civil rights laws by taking the female employee's sex into account and promoting her over male employee with a higher test score. By doing so, the court upheld the county's affirmative action plan directing that sex or race be considered for purpose of remedying under representation of women and minorities in traditionally segregated job categories.

City of Richmond v. J.A. Croson Beginning with this case in 1989, the Supreme Court began to cut back on the leeway it had given affirmative action programs. The Court struck down a set-aside program mandated by the city of Richmond, Virginia, which required prime contractors awarded city construction contracts to subcontract at least 30 percent of the dollar amount of each contract to one or more "Minority Business Enterprises." The Court ruled that the city failed to demonstrate compelling governmental interest justifying the plan, and the plan was not narrowly tailored to remedy effects of prior discrimination.

In handing down this ruling, the Court determined that any **judicial review** of municipal affirmative action plans would be reviewed with "strict scrutiny." Under the strict scrutiny test, defendants are required to establish they have a compelling interest in justifying the measure or that the affirmative action program advances some important governmental or societal purpose. For all practical purposes, this ruling makes it very hard to justify an affirmative action plan unless past discrimination can be shown, and the under representation of minorities is a product of that discrimination.

Adarand Constructors v. Pena In this Supreme Court case, the Court applied the standards propagated in *City of Richmond v. Croson* to the federal government, ruling that all racial classifications imposed by whatever federal, state, or local governmental actor must be analyzed by the reviewing court under strict scrutiny. The Court overturned a decision dismissing a suit brought by a contractor challenging the constitutionality of a federal program designed to provide highway contracts to minority business enterprises.

The results in *Adarand* confirmed the conservative direction in which the Supreme Court moved with respect to affirmative action plans. It seemed clear after this decision that affirmative action plans would only survive court challenges by being narrowly tailored to rectify past discrimination.

Gratz v. Bollinger and *Grutter v. Bollinger* These two cases further illustrate the complexity of the issue. Jennifer Gratz was denied admission to the University of Michigan's undergraduate program in 1995, while in 1997 Barbara Grutter was denied admission to the university's law school. Both women were white, and they claimed that the university's admissions program discriminated against white students. The university used a point system for undergraduate admissions, assigning extra points to what it considered "under-represented" racial and ethnic minorities. Since it also assigned extra points to athletes, children of alumni, and men enrolling in the nursing school, the university argued, there was nothing out of the ordinary about adding points for race as well. As for the law school, there was no point system, but race was used as a determining factor because, the university maintained, it helped promote cross-racial understanding. Civil rights organizations, academicians, political leaders, and many others took sides. Former U.S. president Gerald R. Ford

(a University of Michigan alumnus) spoke out in support of the university's system in an op-ed piece in *The New York Times* in 1999.

The court voted 6-3 to strike down the undergraduate point system, but it upheld the law school's less rigid program in a 5-4 vote. While the dual votes were not a total victory for affirmative action, they clearly showed what the courts would consider valid and what they would consider too broad a reach. More importantly, they showed that the U.S. Supreme Court, however conservative, was not ready to abolish affirmative action arbitrarily.

Developments After *Gratz* and *Grutter* The Supreme Court addressed affirmative action in the employment context when it decided *Ricci v. DeStefano* in 2009. The Court ruled in a favor of a group of white firefighters who challenged a city's decision to disregard the results of a promotional examination. The city expressed concern that the exam would have a disparate impact on minority firefighters, but the Court rejected this as a basis the disregarding the exam results.

With regard to affirmative action in higher education, many commentators and the Court itself expected the decisions in *Gratz* and *Grutter* to last for many years. However, in 2012, the Court announced that it would review an affirmative action case arising from the University of Texas. The future of affirmative action in higher education may very well depend on the result of *Fisher v. University of Texas* (**Docket** Number 11-345) during the 2012 term.

FORMS OF AFFIRMATIVE ACTION

Affirmative action can take different forms. Often affirmative actions are written into federal or state law. They can also take the form of voluntary plans or consent decrees. Occasionally, although rarely in the early 2010s, a court will impose an affirmative action plan to remedy the effects of past discrimination.

Although affirmative action has been employed in the private sector, its use has been most pronounced in the public sector, in regard to both hiring and contract requirements. Affirmative action has been broadly used across a wide spectrum of federal, state, and municipal governments.

Examples of affirmative action at the federal level are as follows:

Department of Defense: Strives to award 5 percent of Department of Defense procurement, research and development, construction, operation and maintenance contracts to minority businesses and institutions.

Federal Home Loan Banks: Provides for preservation and expansion of minority owned banks.

Department of State: Mandates at least 10 percent of amount of funds appropriated for Department of State and foreign affairs diplomatic construction projects be allocated to American minority contractors.

NASA: Requires NASA administrator to establish annual goal of at least eight percent of total value of prime contracts and subcontracts awarded to be made to small disadvantaged businesses and minority educational institutions.

Federal Communications Commission: Must ensure that minority- and women-owned businesses have opportunity to participate in providing spectrum-based services.

Department of Energy: Strives for five percent of combined total funds of Department of Energy used to carry out national security programs be allocated to minority businesses and institutions.

Department of Transportation: Requires that not less than 10 percent of funds appropriated under the Intermodal Surface Transportation Efficiency Act of 1991 be expended on small and minority businesses.

Environmental Protection Agency: Must allocate no less than 10 percent of federal funding to minority businesses for research relating to requirements of Clean Air Act Amendments of 1990.

Examples of affirmative action at the state level are:

ARKANSAS: Requires Division of Minority Business Enterprise to develop plans and participation goals for minority businesses.

CONNECTICUT: Mandates that contractors on state public works contracts make **good faith** efforts to employ minority businesses as subcontractors and suppliers, allows municipalities to set aside up to 25 percent of dollar amount of construction and supply contracts to award to minority businesses.

DISTRICT OF COLUMBIA: Requires District of Columbia agencies to allocate 35 percent of dollar amount of public construction contracts to minority businesses.

FLORIDA: Allows municipalities to set aside up to 10 percent of dollar amount of contracts for procurement of **personal property** and services to award to minority businesses.

ILLINOIS: Requires Metropolitan Pier and Exposition Authority to establish goals of awarding not less than 25 percent of dollar amount of contracts to minority contractors and not less than five percent to women contractors.

INDIANA: Requires that state agencies establish goal that five percent of all contracts awarded be given to minority businesses.

KANSAS: Allows Secretary of Transportation to designate certain state highway construction contracts, or portions of contracts, to be set aside for bidding by disadvantaged businesses only.

LOUISIANA: Requires establishment of annual participation goals for awarding contracts for goods and services and public works projects to minority- and women-owned businesses.

MARYLAND: Requires that Maryland award 14 percent of dollar amount of procurement contracts to minority businesses.

MICHIGAN: Establishes participation goals for awarding of government contracts to minority- and women-owned businesses.

NEW JERSEY: Allows municipalities to set aside certain percentage of dollar value of contracts to award to minority businesses.

NEW YORK: Allows municipalities to set aside certain percentage of dollar value of contracts to award to minority businesses.

OHIO: Provides that a prime contractor on a state contract must award subcontracts totaling no less than five percent of the total value of the contract to Minority Business Enterprises (MBE) and that the total value of both the materials purchased from MBE's and of the subcontracts awarded will equal at least seven percent of the total value of the contract.

TENNESSEE: Requires all state agencies to actively solicit bids from small businesses and minority-owned businesses whenever possible. Local education agencies and state colleges and universities may set aside up to 10 percent of their funds allocated for procurement of personal property and services for the purpose of entering into contracts with small businesses and minority-owned businesses.

Required Affirmative Action for Federal Contractors
Contractors with the federal government are required to

have affirmative action plans under various federal laws. These laws include:

Executive Order 11246: This order, signed by President Johnson and amended by President Nixon, applies to all nonexempt government contractors and subcontractors and federally assisted construction contracts and subcontracts in excess of $10,000. Under the Executive Order, contractors and subcontractors with a federal contract of $50,000 or more and 50 or more employees are required to develop a written affirmative action program that sets forth specific and result-oriented procedures to which contractors commit themselves to apply every good faith effort.

Section 503 of the Rehabilitation Act of 1973: Requires affirmative action plans in all personnel practices for qualified individuals with disabilities. It applies to all firms that have a nonexempt government contact or subcontract in excess of $10,000.

The Vietnam Era Veterans' Readjustment Assistance Act of 1974 (VEVRAA): Requires affirmative action programs in all personnel practices for special disabled veterans, Vietnam era veterans, and veterans who served on active duty during a war or in a campaign or expedition for which a campaign badge has been authorized. It applies to all firms that have a nonexempt government contract or subcontract of $25,000 or more.

What an Affirmative Action Plan Should Include The Office of Federal Contract Compliance Programs (OFCCP) suggests that non-construction contractors' written affirmative action plans include the following affirmative action as part of an action-oriented program:

- Contact with specified schools, colleges, religious organizations, and other institutions that are prepared to refer women and minorities for employment;

- Identification of community leaders as recruiting sources;

- Holding of formal briefing sessions, preferably on company premises, with representatives from recruiting sources;

- Conduct of plant tours, including presentation by minority and female employees of clear and concise explanations of current and future job openings, position descriptions, worker specifications, explanations of the company's selection process, and recruitment literature;

- Encouragement of minority and female employees to refer applicants;

- With special efforts the inclusion of minorities and women in personnel department staffs;

- The availability of minority and female employees for participation in career days, youth motivation programs, and related community activities;

- Recruitment at secondary schools, junior colleges, and colleges with predominantly minority or female enrollments;

- With special efforts the contact with minorities and women when recruiting at all schools;

- Special employment programs undertaken whenever possible, such as technical and non-technical co-op programs with predominantly black and women's colleges, summer jobs for underprivileged youth, and motivation programs for the hardcore unemployed;

- Inclusion of minority and female employees in recruiting brochures pictorially presenting work situations;

- Expansion of help-wanted advertising to regularly include the minority news media and women's interest media.

Voluntary Implementation of Affirmative Action Both private and public employers use voluntary affirmative action. However, both private and public employers must satisfy certain criteria in order to comply with Title VII. The employer must have a legitimate reason for adopting a plan. Also, the plan cannot unduly interfere with the employment opportunities of non-minority or male workers or job applicants to the extent that their interests are "unnecessarily trammeled." The EEOC has promulgated Guidelines on Affirmative Action that explain how to develop a lawful affirmative action plan under Title VII.

Often, affirmative action remedies are agreed upon to settle a discrimination case. These remedies are implemented by a consent **decree**. A court must approve provisions in consent decrees that provide for the employer's adoption of an affirmative action program. Affirmative action contained in the decree is viewed as voluntary. The action may benefit individuals who were not the victims of the discriminatory practice at issue.

ABOLISHING AFFIRMATIVE ACTION

In the 1990s, several states moved to abolish affirmative action programs. California voted in 1996 to abolish affirmative action, and Washington state voted similarly in 1998. The California ban asserts: "the state shall not discriminate against, or grant preferential treatment to, any individual or group on the basis of race, sex, color, ethnicity, or national origin in the operation of public employment, public education, or public contracting." The wording of the Washington law is identical. Both laws were passed in voter referenda.

There is no question that affirmative action remains a controversial issue in the eyes of many, and that many people would like to abolish it. Nevertheless, it seems reasonable to say that society in general is mindful that affirmative action in some form is acceptable and in fact worthwhile. Those who either favor or oppose it strongly will likely have to accept some sort of middle ground in the future.

ADDITIONAL RESOURCES

Bodensteiner, Ivan E., and Rosalie Berger Levinson. *State and Local Government Civil Rights Liability*. Eagan, MN: West, Thomson Reuters, 2011.

Killenbeck, Mark R. *Affirmative Action and Diversity: The Beginning of the End? Or the End of the Beginning?* Princeton, NJ: Policy Information Center, Educational Testing Service, 2004.

Perry, Barbara A. *The Michigan Affirmative Action Cases*. Lawrence, KS: University Press of Kansas, 2007.

Sterba, James P. *Affirmative Action for the Future*. Ithaca, NY: Cornell University Press, 2009.

ORGANIZATIONS

Office of Federal Contract Compliance Programs (OFCCP)

200 Constitution Ave., NW
Washington, DC 20210
Phone: (202) 693-0101
URL: http://www.dol.gov/ofccp/

U.S. Equal Employment Opportunity Commission (EEOC)

1801 L Street, N.W.
Washington, DC 20507
Phone: (202) 663-4900
URL: http://www.eeoc.gov/

CIVIL RIGHTS

AGE DISCRIMINATION

Sections within this essay:

- Background
  - Changing Attitudes
  - Retirement Plans

- Subtle Discrimination

- Advocacy for Older Workers

- Age Discrimination in Employment Act
  - Bona Fide Occupational Qualifications

- State Age Discrimination Laws

- Additional Resources

BACKGROUND

Age **discrimination** occurs when an older person is pressured in the workplace to leave. Under the law a person's career cannot be jeopardized solely because of age. Unfortunately, many employers resort to subtler but equally damaging tactics to thin the ranks of older workers. As of the 2010s, the term "older worker" had come to mean anyone over the age of 40. Employees who fall into this group need to understand their rights under the law so if they suspect discrimination, they can take appropriate action.

Until the early twentieth century, discrimination based on age was not a clear-cut issue in most professions. Most people worked until they reached an age at which they were no longer able to be productive. For the remainder of their lives, they would be taken care of by their families.

With the rise in industrialization and in unions, specific guidelines were set in place for how long people should stay on the job. The introduction of **pension** programs allowed workers the opportunity to stop working when they reached old age, secure in the knowledge that they would be able to take care of themselves financially. Later, government initiatives such as Social Security made it still easier for people to retire.

Beginning after World War II, dramatic changes in the workplace created a shift in policies and attitudes. Technology had made many jobs obsolete, and employees had to learn more and learn faster. As the postwar "baby boom" generation came of age, a growing emphasis on youth pervaded an increasingly crowded workplace. People who had reached old or even middle age began to face increasing pressure to leave the workforce. Sometimes they were simply forced out. Older workers who happen to be women or members of a minority group have to be particularly diligent, since they could be subject to discrimination on additional factors.

Discrimination of any kind is determined by either direct or indirect **evidence** under the law. Direct evidence can include outright statements an employer makes about a particular job candidate that shows intent to exclude. Indirect evidence can be when an employer makes job qualifications vague enough to exclude certain people even though everything looks legal and ethical. In age discrimination cases, direct evidence would be an employer telling an older worker, "You're doing that job much more slowly than the others," or "I don't think you'll be able to learn our new computer system." Indirect evidence would be when a potential employer turns down a qualified older job applicant in favor of someone younger. Of course, if the younger employee is demonstrably better qualified, it may not be a case of discrimination. Nevertheless, if a qualified older worker is passed over for a job and the employer continues to interview other candidates, the employer may be deliberately excluding the older candidate.

Changing Attitudes The "baby boom" that began at the end of World War II in 1945 and lasted until the early 1960s generated an enormous number of new employees in the 1970s and 1980s. Interestingly, many companies saw the baby boomers as detrimental to productivity. To be sure, the youthful boomers lacked the experience of mature workers, but they were also the victims of stereotypes. Companies believed that these young people, born in the heady days of the postwar economy, would be less willing to work their way up from the bottom, as their parents had done. The younger workers would probably be spoiled and arrogant, and, consequently, less productive.

At the same time, rapid advances in technology meant that workers needed to be able to adapt to new ways of doing their jobs. Many companies that had prided themselves on a policy of "lifetime employment" began to see their longtime workforce as a drain on productivity. The reasoning had less to do with any belief that older workers would be unable to master new skills than it did with the fear that the older workers had grown complacent in their jobs. Moreover, older workers commanded the highest salaries and were the most likely to incur high health care costs. As the number of baby boomers in the market increased, companies began to shift their commitment from experience to a younger, less expensive workforce that could be trained (and whose jobs were made easier by technology).

Retirement Plans While there are many older workers who want to continue in the jobs because they enjoy their work, many others continue to work because they cannot afford to retire. Thanks in large part to unions, many employees are guaranteed a good pension from their company after a set number of years, regardless of their age at retirement. Known as "30-and-Out" programs (based on a United Auto Workers deal with Chrysler in 1973), they allow workers to put in their 30 or however many years and retire with full pension benefits instead of having to wait until age 65 (when people can collect their full Social Security benefits).

Many companies offer some sort of early retirement package for employees, in part to make room for younger workers but also in part to cut down on the number of top-salaried people on the payroll. Such offers are not illegal and in fact can be beneficial to both the company and the employee. The issue takes a different turn when the employee is being pressured to accept an early retirement plan.

Setting a mandatory retirement age is illegal in most professions, although there are exceptions. Federal law recognizes ADEA exemptions in the case of such employees as air traffic controllers, federal police officers, airline pilots, and firefighters. In 1996 Congress passed legislation that allowed state and local governments to set retirement ages for these and similar employees to as young as 55. State and local judges are often required to step down at a certain age as well. In addition to mandatory retirement ages, many public safety jobs also have mandatory hiring ages, thus closing the door to potentially otherwise qualified people. The argument against mandatory retirement claims that it would be fairer to all employees to rely on periodic fitness testing, since some older workers may be just as able (or perhaps more so) to carry out their duties as younger ones.

SUBTLE DISCRIMINATION

Blatant discrimination is deplorable, but it is easy to spot and usually easy to determine accountability. More ambiguous, and thus more dangerous to older workers, is subtle discrimination. This can take many forms, and by its nature it is probably more pervasive than most people realize. Some examples are as follows:

- A longtime employee's supervisor makes comments in his or her presence about the benefits of retirement

- An employee whose company "restructures," and who subsequently ends up with a smaller office down a little-used corridor

- An employee who gets passed over for promotions, always in favor of younger staffers

- A worker who is reassigned to a job with fewer responsibilities, even if the assignment is considered a lateral move

- An employee who is no longer sent on business trips, provided membership in professional associations, or encouraged to take job-related courses

What makes subtle discrimination so much more dangerous than blatant discrimination in the minds of many experts is that it is harder to prove. Perhaps the supervisor is making comments about retirement because he or she is looking forward to being retired. Maybe the employee who was passed over for promotions has never asked to be promoted and thus is considered to be lacking in leadership initiative. Subtle forms of age discrimination may make older workers uncomfortable or unhappy enough that they will retire, even though they may not be able to pinpoint actual discrimination as their reason for leaving. The bottom line, however, is that subtle discrimination is no more acceptable in the workplace than blatant actions directed at older workers. Determining the difference between innocent remarks or coincidence and true discrimination may be difficult, but an older worker who suspects discrimination should know that taking action is a viable option.

ADVOCACY FOR OLDER WORKERS

Age discrimination has a twofold negative effect on older workers. The **tangible** effect is loss of a job or limited employment opportunities. Not only is it harder for an older worker to keep a job, but it also becomes harder for an older worker to find a new job. (Economic realities often dictate that early retirees may have to supplement their pensions before they turn 65 and collect their full Social Security benefits.) The psychological effect is that older workers become frustrated by their situation. If they are working, this could affect their productivity, which could feed the stereotypes about older workers. If they are looking for work, they may simply give up, believing that they are unemployable.

Older workers have a strong ally and resource in the form of AARP (formerly known as the American Association of Retired Persons). Founded in 1958, AARP had about 40 million members across the country as of 2012. AARP acts as an information clearinghouse for legislation and other materials, and it also serves as a powerful **lobbying** force at the federal and state level. Through its lobbying network, AARP seeks to get Congress to enact new laws, enforce existing laws, and revise flawed legislation. AARP is headquartered in Washington, D.C., but it has regional offices to serve at the local level. Its leadership works actively to combat all discrimination.

AGE DISCRIMINATION IN EMPLOYMENT ACT

Older workers have legal protection from age discrimination. The Age Discrimination in Employment Act (ADEA) was passed by Congress in 1967. The ADEA extends the law as spelled out in the Civil Rights Act of 1964, which prohibits discrimination based on race, sex, creed, color, religion, or ethnic origin. (Title VII of the Civil Rights Act is important to older workers who could suffer discrimination based on any of those factors as well.) Under the ADEA, workers age 40 and older are protected from discrimination in recruitment, hiring, training, promotions, pay and benefits, **dismissal** and layoffs, and retirement. The Older Workers Benefit Protection Act (OWBPA), passed in 1990, guarantees protection against discrimination in benefits packages. For example, OWPBA sets strict guidelines prohibiting companies from converting their pension plans in a way that would provide fewer pension dollars to older workers.

While the ADEA has been a critical factor in guarding against age discrimination, certain decisions by the U.S. Supreme Court have made it somewhat less effective. Part of the reason is that the Civil Rights Act of 1991, which amended Title VII of the 1964 Civil Rights Act, did not similarly amend the ADEA. Thus, although Title VII allows victims to recover compensatory and **punitive damages** since the 1991 **amendment**, the ADEA does not. Supreme Court decisions at the turn of the millennium suggested that using pension eligibility or high salaries as a basis for layoff decisions (a practice that generally has the greatest impact on older workers) may not be discriminatory.

In 2000, the Supreme Court ruled in *Kimel v. Florida Board of Regents* that states are protected from ADEA suits by individuals. Legislation was introduced in the U.S. Senate in 2001 that would require states agencies to waive their **immunity** from ADEA suits or else **forfeit** federal funding.

Most ADEA suits are based on charges brought before the Equal Employment Opportunity Commission (EEOC). The EEOC is responsible for investigating charges of age discrimination and seeking remedies. Rarely does it file actual lawsuits (in fact EEOC **litigation** across the board dropped through the 1990s and into the twenty-first century), but individuals are allowed to sue on their own.

In 1995 the EEOC conducted a comprehensive review of its procedures and developed new National and Local Enforcement Plans. These plans provide guidelines for dealing with discrimination issues against older workers.

The EEOC has long suffered from inadequate funding, which limits its ability to investigate charges as quickly as it would like. As a result, EEOC chooses its lawsuits carefully to ensure maximum impact.

Individuals who think they are victims of age discrimination can nevertheless turn to the local office of the EEOC for assistance. The EEOC will provide information about how to file charges at the state and federal levels. It is also useful to contact the state office of civil rights.

Bona Fide Occupational Qualifications Under the law, not all age-related job exclusions are discriminatory. In fact, both Title VII and the ADEA recognize exclusions known as bona fide occupational qualifications (BFOQs) as legitimate. For example, a kosher meat market can legitimately require that it can hire only Jewish butchers. An employer seeking a BFOQ exclusion must be able to prove that those from within an excluded group would not be able to perform the job effectively. Thus, a moving company might be able to exclude a 75-year-old as a mover because moving requires heavy lifting and driving long distances. An accounting firm would be unable to make a similar claim in trying to force a 75-year-old bookkeeper to retire solely based on age.

STATE AGE DISCRIMINATION LAWS

Several states as well as cities and counties have laws prohibiting discrimination based on age. State and local laws can be especially important because these laws may apply when the ADEA does not. For instance, these state laws often apply to employers with fewer than 20 employees.

Examples of state laws prohibiting age discrimination include:

ARIZONA: Arizona's laws that apply to age discrimination are limited to individuals who are at least 40 years of age.

CALIFORNIA: In 1997, a lower **appellate court** in California (*Marks v. Loral Corp.*) rejected a claim that an employer's use of salary to differentiate between employees was age discrimination. The California Legislature responded by rejecting the opinion and establishing **public policy** that prohibits age discrimination in employment "broadly and vigorously."

LOUISIANA: State law provides a list of practices that are prohibited because they constitute age discrimination.

OREGON: The Oregon legislature declared that "the available workforce should be utilized to the fullest extent possible." Thus, state law prohibits discrimination against an employee based on age.

TENNESSEE: State law states that it is "not unlawful" for an employer to discrimination based on age "where age is a bona fide occupational qualification reasonably necessary to the normal operation of the particular business." Other age-discrimination provisions apply to individuals who are at least 40 years of age.

TEXAS: State law prohibiting age discrimination applies to individuals who are 40 years of age or older.

WASHINGTON: State law generally prohibits discrimination in employment for employees 40 years or older, subject to some exceptions.

ADDITIONAL RESOURCES

Cotter, Anne-Marie Mooney. *Just a Number: An International Legal Analysis on Age Discrimination*. Burlington, VT: Ashgate Pub., 2008.

Friedman, Joel William. *Employment Discrimination*. New York: Aspen Publishers, 2010.

Lindemann, Barbara T., and David D. Kadue. *Age Discrimination in Employment Law*. Washington, DC: Bureau of National Affairs, 2003.

ORGANIZATIONS

AARP (American Association of Retired Persons)

601 E St. NW
Washington, DC 20049
Toll Free: (877) 434-7598
URL: http://www.aarp.org

Administration on Aging, U.S. Department of Health and Human Services

One Massachusetts Ave. NW
Washington, DC 20001
Phone: (202) 401-4634
Fax: (202) 357-3555
Email: aoainfo@aoa.hhs.gov,
URL: http://www.aoa.gov

Equal Employment Opportunity Commission (EEOC)

1801 L Street NW
Washington, DC 20507
Phone: (202) 663-4900
Fax: (202) 376-6219
URL: http://www.eeoc.gov

National Council on the Aging

1901 L Street, NW, 4th Floor
Washington, DC 20036
Phone: (202) 479-1200
URL: http://www.ncoa.org

CIVIL RIGHTS

CASTLE DOCTRINE AND STAND-YOUR-GROUND LAWS

Sections within this essay:

- Introduction
- Castle Doctrine
- Stand-Your-Ground Laws
- Controversies
- State Laws
- Additional Resources

INTRODUCTION

In 2012, much of the nation followed the story of teenager Trayvon Martin, who was shot by a neighborhood watch volunteer in a gated housing community in Florida. The incident took place outdoors, so the volunteer, George Zimmerman, likely had an opportunity to retreat if Martin had indeed attacked Zimmerman. However, under state law, Zimmerman had the right to "stand his ground," meaning that he could use force to defend himself without having to first retreat. Zimmerman based his defense on Florida's stand-your-ground law.

Florida's stand-your-ground law was an extension of the so-called castle doctrine, which allows a person to use force to protect a home through use of force. The name of the doctrine is derived from the phrase "a man's home is his castle," which had its basis in a quote from an old English case. Concerns over the right of homeowners to protect themselves, their families, and their property has led a large majority of states to adopt either the castle doctrine or a specific stand-your-ground law.

Critics have been especially critical of the stand-your-ground law, claiming that such a state law may create a modern "Wild West" atmosphere. Some statistics have suggested that the laws have increased the number of justifiable homicides. On the other hand, some studies have suggested that these laws have effectively reduced murder and violent-crime rates.

CASTLE DOCTRINE

The right to defend a home dates back to English **common law**. As a general principle, the law has placed a duty on a person to retreat from an attacker before using deadly force. An exception applies when the person is defending an attack on the person's home. Under the castle doctrine, the law imposes no duty for a person to retreat before turning on and even using deadly force against the attacker who entered the home. Deadly force is almost always allowed when such force apparently necessary to save the person from great bodily harm or death.

In the United States, the modern castle doctrine evolved from the case of *Beard v. United States*, decided by the U.S. Supreme Court in 1895. The case involved a man named Beard, who had been convicted of murder after killing a trespasser in Beard's home. The trial court had instructed the **jury** that Beard had a duty to retreat before using deadly force, but the Supreme Court disagreed, noting the long-standing principle that a person has the right to protect his home without having to retreat. Courts later expanded the principle of **self-defense** underlying the castle doctrine to apply to any circumstance where a person reasonably feared death or imminent bodily harm. Justice Oliver Wendell Holmes famously said of the doctrine, "Detached reflection cannot be demanded in the presence of an uplifted knife."

Courts have generally applied the castle doctrine to situations where a person is in an office or place of business. The rationale is that the person occupies such a place lawfully and should have the same rights as if the person were at home. The Rhode Island Supreme Court applied the rule when an attacker entered a home as a guest but then attacked after being asked to leave.

The right to use deadly force in one's home under the castle doctrine is not absolute. Generally, a person may not kill an attacker unless the person has sound reason to believe that his or her life is in danger. Likewise, courts have hesitated to apply the rule when the attacker is entitled to be on the property. In such a circumstance, the person attacked may have the duty to retreat. Some courts have also held that a person has a duty to retreat when the attacker is a co-habitant and has equal right to be in the home.

In some jurisdictions, the castle doctrine applies not only inside the home but also in the area known as the curtilage. This is the area outside the home, including the yard, the garden, a porch, or an adjacent building. However, curtilage does not extend to streets, a driveway, a parking lot, or the common areas of an apartment building.

STAND-YOUR-GROUND LAWS

Nearly every state recognizes some right of a person to use force for protection of body or home even if the person has an opportunity to retreat first. However, courts nationally have not been consistent in applying these principles, and some courts within single jurisdictions struggled to establish clear rules that should apply.

Florida was one such state. The courts there expanded the castle doctrine for years, but a series of cases in the early 2000s ended that expansion. In one case, *State v. James*, the **defendant** became engaged in a fight with his girlfriend's ex-boyfriend inside the girlfriend's apartment. The defendant shot the ex-boyfriend and later argued that he did so in self-defense. A state **appellate court** ruled against the defendant, holding that the defendant had a duty to retreat because he was only a guest in his girlfriend's home. A later case also limited the doctrine by holding that it did not apply to vehicles. The reasoning in the latter case, *Baker v. State*, was that the car gave a person an easy means of escape and was not analogous to a person who is inside a home.

These decisions in part motivated the Florida legislature to codify the common law castle doctrine as a state **statute**. Supporters of the law referred to it is the "stand your ground" law, though detractors referred to it as the "shoot first" law. The legislature amended two sections of the Florida statutes and added two more. These changes abrogated any duty to retreat before a person uses deadly force in self-defense. Instead, the law allows the person to use this force so long as the person is in a place where he or she lawfully has the right to be.

More specifically, the statute allows a person to use deadly force and does not require the person to retreat when: he or she reasonably believes that such force is necessary to prevent imminent death or great bodily harm to himself or herself or another or to prevent the imminent commission of a forcible **felony**; or that deadly force is used for home protection. The rule that applies to home protection includes dwelling, residence, or vehicle. The statute allows the person to use deadly force to protect against home invasion by establishing a presumption that a person attacked in the home has a reasonable fear of "imminent peril of death or great bodily harm to himself or herself."

The Florida statute not only grants a person who exercises self-defense **immunity** from criminal prosecution, but also grants the person immunity from **civil action** for the justifiable use of force. Moreover, if the court finds that a defendant is immune from prosecution, the court must award the defendant reasonable attorney's fees, court costs, compensation for loss of income, and expenses the defendant may have incurred in any civil action.

More than 20 states followed Florida's lead after 2005. The language in these various state statutes differs somewhat, but most establish the same basic principles. The majority of states that have not adopted a stand-your-ground law continue to follow the castle doctrine.

CONTROVERSIES

Although stand-your-ground laws have been controversial for some time, the case involving Zimmerman and Martin brought the issue to the national forefront during the spring and summer. Martin was visiting his father in Sanford, Florida, on the night of the attack. The 17-year-old visited a local convenience store on night of the shooting and was wearing a "hoodie," or hooded sweatshirt. He carried some small items, including a bag of skittles, and returned to the gated community where his father lived.

Martin encountered Zimmerman at the community. Zimmerman was a neighborhood watch volunteer, and he called 911 after he saw Martin and thought the teen looked suspicious. Zimmerman pursued Martin through the community until finally confronting the teen. Zimmerman and various witnesses disputed what happened, but Zimmerman shot Martin at close range. Martin was just several yards from the house where he was staying.

Zimmerman based his defense on the stand-your-ground law, arguing that he had a right to be in the community and that he acted in self-defense. He had a bloody nose and marks on the back of his head, suggesting that he and Martin had struggled. However, witnesses disputed Zimmerman's version of the facts, noting that the two were separated by some short distance.

The case had not been resolved as of 2012, but it brought some concerns about the stand-your-ground law to light. Without the law, Zimmerman most likely would have had an opportunity to retreat, which means he would not have been able to rely on the privilege of using deadly force. Given the victim's age in the case, as well as underlying racial tensions (Martin was black while Zimmerman is part-Hispanic), emotions ran high. A number of individuals insisted that Florida **repeal** its law.

Reports about the law's effect on have been in dispute. One report by a professor at Texas A&M reviewed crime data and determined that these stand-your-ground laws have actually led to an increase in homicides. On the other hand, author John Lott conducted his own study of both the stand-your-ground laws and the castle doctrine. He concluded that these laws have effectively reduced murder rates as well as violent crime overall. The Florida state representative who authored Florida's law has also argued that crime rates in the state fell between 2005 and 2012.

STATE LAWS

The list below summarizes whether each state has adopted the castle doctrine or a stand-your-ground law. These summaries are current as of 2012.

ALABAMA: The state has adopted a stand-your-ground law.

ALASKA: The state has adopted the castle doctrine.

ARIZONA: The state has adopted a stand-your-ground law.

ARKANSAS: The state has adopted neither the castle doctrine nor a stand-your-ground law.

CALIFORNIA: The state has adopted the castle doctrine.

COLORADO: The state has adopted a stand-your-ground law.

CONNECTICUT: The state has adopted the castle doctrine.

DELAWARE: The state has adopted the castle doctrine.

FLORIDA: The state has adopted a stand-your-ground law.

GEORGIA: The state has adopted a stand-your-ground law.

HAWAII: The state has adopted the castle doctrine.

IDAHO: The state has adopted the castle doctrine.

ILLINOIS: The state has adopted the castle doctrine.

INDIANA: The state has adopted a stand-your-ground law.

IOWA: The state has adopted neither the castle doctrine nor a stand-your-ground law.

KANSAS: The state has adopted the castle doctrine.

KENTUCKY: The state has adopted a stand-your-ground law.

LOUISIANA: The state has adopted a stand-your-ground law.

MAINE: The state has adopted the castle doctrine.

MARYLAND: The state has adopted a stand-your-ground law.

MASSACHUSETTS: The state has adopted the castle doctrine.

MICHIGAN: The state has adopted the castle doctrine.

MINNESOTA: The state has adopted the castle doctrine.

MISSISSIPPI: The state has adopted a stand-your-ground law.

MISSOURI: The state has adopted the castle doctrine.

MONTANA: The state has adopted a stand-your-ground law.

NEBRASKA: The state has adopted neither the castle doctrine nor a stand-your-ground law.

NEVADA: The state has adopted a stand-your-ground law.

NEW HAMPSHIRE: The state has adopted a stand-your-ground law.

NEW JERSEY: The state has adopted the castle doctrine.

NEW MEXICO: A state statute allows for justifiable **homicide** when defending property. However, New

Mexico courts have held that a person cannot kill another for mere **trespass**.

NEW YORK: The state has adopted the castle doctrine.

NORTH CAROLINA: The state has adopted the castle doctrine.

NORTH DAKOTA: The state has adopted the castle doctrine.

OHIO: The state has adopted the castle doctrine.

OKLAHOMA: The state has adopted a stand-your-ground law.

OREGON: The state has adopted the castle doctrine.

PENNSYLVANIA: The state has adopted a stand-your-ground law.

RHODE ISLAND: The state has adopted the castle doctrine.

SOUTH CAROLINA: The state has adopted the castle doctrine.

SOUTH DAKOTA: The state has adopted the castle doctrine.

TENNESSEE: The state has adopted a stand-your-ground law.

TEXAS: The state has adopted a stand-your-ground law.

UTAH: The state has adopted a stand-your-ground law.

VERMONT: The state has adopted neither the castle doctrine nor a stand-your-ground law.

VIRGINIA: The state has adopted neither the castle doctrine nor a stand-your-ground law.

WASHINGTON: The Supreme Court of Washington has held that a person has no duty to retreat when the person in a place where he or she may lawfully be (same effect as a stand-your-ground statute).

WEST VIRGINIA: The state has adopted the castle doctrine.

WISCONSIN: The state has adopted the castle doctrine.

WYOMING: The state has adopted the castle doctrine.

ADDITIONAL RESOURCES

Dressler, Joshua. *Understanding Criminal Law.* 6th ed. New Providence, NJ: LexisNexis, 2012.

LaFave, Wayne R. *Criminal Law.* 5th ed. Eagan, MN: West, Thomson Reuters, 2010.

Lott, John R., Jr. *More Guns, Less Crime.* 3rd ed. Chicago: University of Chicago Press, 2010.

Singer, Richard G., and John Q. La Fond. *Criminal Law: Examples and Explanations.* 5th ed. New York: Aspen, 2010.

Spitzer, Robert J. *The Politics of Gun Control.* 4th ed. Washington, DC: CQ Press, 2008.

Utter, Glenn H. *Encyclopedia of Gun Control and Gun Rights.* Phoenix, AZ: Oryx Press, 2000.

Valdez, Angela, and John E. Ferguson, Jr. *Gun Control.* 2d ed. New York: Chelsea House, 2012.

ORGANIZATIONS

Brady Center to Prevent Gun Violence

1225 Eye St. NW, Ste, 1100
Washington, DC 20005
Phone: (202) 289-7319
Fax: (202) 408-1851
URL: http://www.cphv.org

Citizens Committee for the Right to Keep and Bear Arms (CCRKBA)

Liberty Park
12500 NE 10th Pl.
Bellevue, WA 98005
Phone: (425) 454-4911
Email: AdminForWeb@ccrkba.org
URL: http://www.ccrkba.org

National Association of Criminal Defense Lawyers (NACDL)

1660 L St. NW, 12th Floor
Washington, DC 20036
Phone: (202) 872-8600
URL: http://www.nacdl.org

National Rifle Association of America (NRA)

11250 Waples Mill Rd.
Fairfax, VA 22030
Toll Free: (800) 672-3888
Email: comm@nrahq.org
URL: http://www.nra.org

CIVIL RIGHTS

CHILDREN'S RIGHTS

Sections within this essay:

- Background
- Historic Mistreatment of Children
  – The Fair Labor Standards Act (FLSA)
- Children's Rights Violations in the United States
  – Child Labor Violations
  – Benefits of Joint Custody
  – Children as Detainees
- Convention on the Rights of the Child
- State Child Labor Standards
- Additional Resources

BACKGROUND

When people in the United States think of children's rights, they usually think of children in third world countries who are victims of abusive child labor practices or insurmountable poverty. They may not realize that the rights of children are violated in the United States as well. Even though **child labor laws were passed** decades ago prohibiting employment of underage youngsters, pockets of oppressive child labor exist, literally, on U.S. soil, where child farm laborers work long hours in squalid conditions and often receive half the standard **minimum wage**. In addition, although numerous studies show that children do better when two parents are involved their upbringing, many **custody** laws make it extremely difficult for non-custodial parents to spend quality time with their children.

To be sure, the United States is still better than most countries when it comes to how children are treated. Yet the topic of children's rights is one that few people know much about. In fact, although many people know that the United Nations Convention on the Rights of the Child was formulated in 1989, they are probably unaware that the United States is one of two countries (the other is Somalia) that have not ratified the Convention. The U.S. government has given what it believes are sound reasons for not having ratified the Convention and repeatedly has affirmed its commitment to children's rights in the United States and abroad. However, there is no question that some children do fall into the cracks, and others' problems are unwisely minimized.

HISTORIC MISTREATMENT OF CHILDREN

It was not uncommon for children to be exploited before the 1930s. Children routinely worked in hazardous conditions in mills, factories, and sweatshops, and on farms. They might have begun working before they had reached their tenth birthday, and they received little in the way of wages. Labor laws did not exist to protect children or adults, but children were often subject to more exploitative conditions because they were easier to manipulate.

The plight of small children did lead to the enactment of some laws, and the federal government tried in 1918 and again in 1922, to enact national child labor laws. Both times, the effort was struck down by the U.S. Supreme Court, which ruled that it was up to the individual states to enact child labor legislation.

The Fair Labor Standards Act (FLSA) In 1938, partly in response to the Great Depression, Congress passed the **Fair Labor Standards Act** (FLSA). This law protected workers from long hours and unfair pay by establishing a 40-hour work week and a minimum wage. It also protected children from exploitation by establishing that they would have to be at least 16 to work in most non-agricultural industries. Younger children could still work certain jobs provided the hours and wages were fair. (It was still possible, in other words, for children to get a newspaper route.) FLSA was challenged in the courts soon after its passage but its constitutionality was upheld by the U.S. Supreme Court in 1941.

CHILDREN'S RIGHTS VIOLATIONS IN THE UNITED STATES

Although the United States does not have the gruesome record of children's rights violations that other countries have, it is not free of violations. Some are more subtle than others, but they do exist. **Human rights** groups monitor alleged instances of violations and work to educate the public and the government with the goal of correcting the problem.

Child Labor Violations FLSA protects, among other groups, child laborers. When it was enacted, farming was primarily a family activity, and it was understood that children would help on the family farm. Thus, the restrictions on agricultural work are much less stringent. By the end of the twentieth century, the number of family farms had dwindled, and most farming was done on large commercial establishments. But the lax restrictions remained, and farm conglomerates took advantage of this.

Under FLSA, no child under the age of 13 can work in a nonagricultural setting, and children of 14 and 15 can work but only for a set number of hours each day. For children working on a farm, the situation is quite different. Children can go to work in the fields as young as nine years old in some states, as long as they have signed parental consent.

Even with the relaxed standards for agricultural work, children are often overworked, are expected to work during what would be school hours, and are paid far less than what is legally required. A report issued in 2000 by Human Rights Watch noted that children under the age of 16 are often required to put in several hours before the school day begins; during the summer months they may work 12-hour days.

The dangers of agricultural work are surprisingly many, and for minors these dangers are even more troubling. Agricultural workers can be exposed to pesticides and other chemicals. They may be sent to work in oppressive heat but without adequate water to keep from becoming dehydrated. Often, they work with heavy or dangerous equipment—equipment that children often have little experience with. Because they work long

hours, often having to rise before dawn to begin their work, lack of sleep is a major problem. For children, this is not only more dangerous, it also curtails their ability to succeed in school. Injury is common, and children can fall or have accidents with heavy equipment or sharp objects.

It is important to remember that many adult farm workers are also exploited, forced to work long hours for little pay. Often, families are so poor and desperate that they feel compelled to give their young children permission to work on the farm, thus bringing in a small but needed amount of extra money.

Organizations such as Human Rights Watch have urged the U.S. government to revise FLSA to offer additional protection to minor children working on farms, and to ensure that farms are more careful about whom they hire and also more diligent about improving working conditions and wages.

Benefits of Joint Custody Divorce was less common before 1970 than it was by the end of the twentieth century, but children whose parents divorced were likely to be placed in the custody of one parent. The other parent might get visitation rights, but these were usually limited. For children whose parents are both loving and responsible but no longer married to each other, this can be emotionally devastating.

The concept of *joint custody* was developed in the early 1970s to **redress** this imbalance. In 1973, Indiana passed the first state joint custody **statute** in the United States. As of 2002, all states have a joint custody statute on the books. There are two types of joint custody. In *Joint legal custody* both parents share decision-making responsibility. In *Joint physical custody* children spend almost an equal amount of time with each parent. Unfortunately, joint custody is still not particularly common. In some cases, of course, there are **mitigating circumstances**. One parent may have abandoned the family or may have verbally, physically, or even sexually abused the children in question. However, for the average parent, who wants what is best for the child but is no longer able to see the child except for brief visits, the issue is one of fairness to that parent as well as the child. The majority of non-custodial parents are fathers.

According to statistics released by the U.S. Department of Health and Human Services (HHS), children who do not live with both parents are twice as likely to drop out of school, twice as likely to end up in jail, and four times as likely to need help for behavioral or emotional problems. HHS reported in 2008 that only 67 percent of children between the ages of 0 and 17 lived with both parents, down from 77 percent in 1980. Organizations such as the Children's Rights Council (CRC) raised the level of awareness on this issue to the point that joint custody, both legal and physical, became more common.

Children as Detainees Illegal aliens who try to enter the United States may be detained and deported. This is true whether the aliens are adults or children. In 2008, an estimated 7,211 children were detained by U.S. **immigration** officials. Children are detained after being picked up at U.S. borders without a parent or **guardian** and without proper documentation. The issue with these children is not that they are stopped from entering the United States illegally, but that they are held in refugee shelters run by the federal Office of Refugee Resettlement. Moreover, these children face **deportation**, often to countries where they may be persecuted. They have no right to paid legal **counsel**. Reports of mistreatment of some who are detained in jails has led human rights organizations to call for investigations.

Congress has considered various proposals that would establish an office to be in charge of ensuring that children are treated humanely while in custody and that decisions on their future would be made based on their short- and long-term needs. It would also provide for legal counsel and guardians, as necessary, to be appointed to represent the children's interests. However, these proposals have largely failed.

CONVENTION ON THE RIGHTS OF THE CHILD

In an effort to create a universally accepted set of children's rights, the United Nations General Assembly adopted the Convention on the Rights of the Child in November 1989. This document promises children the basic human rights of life and liberty, as well as access to education and health care. It also calls for protection against **discrimination** and abuse, protection from economic exploitation, and protection against torture.

While children's rights have become more visible since then, there are still many instances around the world of children's rights violations.

The United States did sign the Convention in 1995 but it was never submitted to the Senate for **ratification**. Although the government has stated that it has no intention of ratifying the Convention, it has consistently reaffirmed its commitment to children's rights.

Among the reason the United States has failed to ratify the Convention is the fact that the Convention clearly states that anyone under the age of 18 is a child. The U.S. government has reservations about how that would affect matters when a 16- or 17-year old commits a crime because in the early 2010s in certain instances that child can be tried as an adult. Also, the U.S. government says that many of the declarations included in the document are not issues for which the federal government is in charge. For example, education in the United States is controlled by the states, not the federal government.

Whether the United States eventually ratifies the Convention, it still does maintain an enviable record of honoring most children's rights. Human rights groups are convinced that the United States can and should do more, and they continue to make their points of view known in the United States and abroad.

STATE CHILD LABOR STANDARDS

Each state has established its own standards related to child labor. Every state has rules that apply to the number of days and hours children can work. These days and times are usually different during the summer months as they are during a school year.

Some state laws that apply to children under the age of 16 include (for more specific guidance, consult the state labor department in the respective state).

ALABAMA: Alabama law limits children under the age of 16 from working more than 40 hours per week and eight hours per day in non-farm employment. Children under the age of 16 cannot work past 7 p.m. or 9 p.m. during the summer months.

ALASKA: Alaska law limits children under the age of 16 from working more than six days per week in non-farm employment. Children under the age of 16 cannot work between 9 p.m. and 5 a.m.

ARIZONA: Arizona law limits children under the age of 16 from working more than 40 hours per week and eight hours per day in non-farm employment. Children under the age of 16 cannot work past 9:30 p.m.

ARKANSAS: Arkansas law limits children under the age of 16 from working more than 48 hours per week and eight hours per day in non-farm employment. Children under the age of 16 cannot work past 7 p.m.

CALIFORNIA: California law limits children under the age of 16 from working more than 40 hours per week and eight hours per day in non-farm employment. Children under the age of 16 cannot work past 7 p.m.

COLORADO: Colorado law limits children under the age of 16 from working more than 40 hours per week and eight hours per day in non-farm employment. Children under the age of 16 cannot work past 9:30 p.m.

CONNECTICUT: Connecticut law limits children under the age of 16 from working more than 40 hours per week and eight hours per day in non-farm employment. Children under the age of 16 cannot work past 7 p.m.

DELAWARE: Delaware law limits children under the age of 16 from working more than 40 hours per week and eight hours per day in non-farm employment. Children under the age of 16 cannot work past 7 p.m.

FLORIDA: Florida law limits children under the age of 16 from working more than 40 hours per week and eight hours per day in non-farm employment. Children under the age of 16 cannot work past 7 p.m.

GEORGIA: Georgia law limits children under the age of 16 from working more than 40 hours per week and eight hours per day in non-farm employment. Children under the age of 16 cannot work past 9 p.m.

HAWAII: Hawaii law limits children under the age of 16 from working more than 40 hours per week and eight hours per day in non-farm employment. Children under the age of 16 cannot work past 7 p.m.

IDAHO: Idaho law limits children under the age of 16 from working more than 54 hours per week and nine hours per day in non-farm employment. Children under the age of 16 cannot work past 9 p.m.

ILLINOIS: Illinois law limits children under the age of 16 from working more than 48 hours per week and eight hours per day in non-farm employment. Children under the age of 16 cannot work past 7 p.m.

INDIANA: Indiana law limits children under the age of 16 from working more than 40 hours per week and eight hours per day in non-farm employment. Children under the age of 16 cannot work past 7 p.m.

IOWA: Iowa law limits children under the age of 16 from working more than 40 hours per week and eight hours per day in non-farm employment. Children under the age of 16 cannot work past 7 p.m.

KANSAS: Kansas law limits children under the age of 16 from working more than 40 hours per week and eight hours per day in non-farm employment. Children under the age of 16 cannot work past 10 p.m.

KENTUCKY: Kentucky law limits children under the age of 16 from working more than 40 hours per week and eight hours per day in non-farm employment. Children under the age of 16 cannot work past 7 p.m.

MAINE: Maine law limits children under the age of 16 from working more than 40 hours per week and eight hours per day in non-farm employment. Children under the age of 16 cannot work past 7 p.m.

MARYLAND: Maryland law limits children under the age of 16 from working more than 40 hours per week and eight hours per day in non-farm employment. Children under the age of 16 cannot work past 8 p.m.

MASSACHUSETTS: Massachusetts law limits children under the age of 16 from working more than 48 hours per week and eight hours per day in non-farm employment. Children under the age of 16 cannot work past 7 p.m.

MICHIGAN: Michigan law limits children under the age of 16 from working more than 48 hours per week and 10 hours per day in non-farm employment. Children under the age of 16 cannot work past 7 p.m.

MINNESOTA: Minnesota law limits children under the age of 16 from working more than 40 hours per week and eight hours per day in non-farm employment. Children under the age of 16 cannot work past 9 p.m.

MISSISSIPPI: Mississippi law limits children under the age of 16 from working more than 40 hours per week and eight hours per day in factory, mill, cannery, or workshop employment. Children under the age of 16 cannot work past 7 p.m.

MISSOURI: Missouri law limits children under the age of 16 from working more than 40 hours per week and eight hours per day in non-farm employment. Children under the age of 16 cannot work past 7 p.m.

MONTANA: Montana law limits children under the age of 16 from working more than 40 hours per week and eight hours per day in non-farm employment. Children under the age of 16 cannot work past 7 p.m.

NEBRASKA: Nebraska law limits children under the age of 16 from working more than 48 hours per week and eight hours per day in non-farm employment. Children under the age of 16 cannot work past 7 p.m.

NEVADA: Nevada law limits children under the age of 16 from working more than 48 hours per week and eight hours per day in non-farm employment. Children under the age of 16 cannot work past 8 p.m.

NEW HAMPSHIRE: New Hampshire law limits children under the age of 16 from working more than 48 hours per week and eight hours per day in non-farm employment. Children under the age of 16 cannot work past 9 p.m.

NEW JERSEY: New Jersey law limits children under the age of 16 from working more than 40 hours per week and eight hours per day in non-farm employment. Children under the age of 16 cannot work past 7 p.m.

NEW MEXICO: New Mexico law limits children under the age of 16 from working more than 44 hours per week and eight hours per day in non-farm employment. Children under the age of 16 cannot work past 9 p.m.

NEW YORK: New York law limits children under the age of 16 from working more than 40 hours per week and eight hours per day in non-farm employment. Children under the age of 16 cannot work past 7 p.m.

NORTH CAROLINA: North Carolina law limits children under the age of 16 from working more than 40 hours per week and eight hours per day in non-farm employment. Children under the age of 16 cannot work past 7 p.m.

NORTH DAKOTA: North Dakota law limits children under the age of 16 from working more than 40 hours per week and eight hours per day in non-farm employment. Children under the age of 16 cannot work past 7 p.m.

OHIO: Ohio law limits children under the age of 16 from working more than 40 hours per week and eight hours per day in non-farm employment. Children under the age of 16 cannot work past 7 p.m.

OKLAHOMA: Oklahoma law limits children under the age of 16 from working more than 40 hours per week and eight hours per day in non-farm employment. Children under the age of 16 cannot work past 7 p.m.

OREGON: Oregon law limits children under the age of 16 from working more than 40 hours per week and eight hours per day in non-farm employment. Children under the age of 16 cannot work past 7 p.m.

PENNSYLVANIA: Pennsylvania law limits children under the age of 16 from working more than 44 hours per week and eight hours per day in non-farm employment. Children under the age of 16 cannot work past 7 p.m.

RHODE ISLAND: Rhode Island law limits children under the age of 16 from working more than 40 hours per week and eight hours per day in non-farm employment. Children under the age of 16 cannot work past 7 p.m.

SOUTH CAROLINA: South Carolina law limits children under the age of 16 from working more than 40 hours per week and eight hours per day in non-farm employment. Children under the age of 16 cannot work past 7 p.m.

SOUTH DAKOTA: South Dakota law limits children under the age of 16 from working more than 40 hours per week and eight hours per day in non-farm employment. Children under the age of 16 cannot work past 10 p.m. before a school day.

TENNESSEE: Tennessee law limits children under the age of 16 from working more than 40 hours per week and eight hours per day in non-farm employment. Children under the age of 16 cannot work past 7 p.m.

TEXAS: Texas law limits children under the age of 16 from working more than 48 hours per week and eight hours per day in non-farm employment. Children under the age of 16 cannot work past 10 p.m.

UTAH: Utah law limits children under the age of 16 from working more than 40 hours per week and eight hours per day in non-farm employment. Children under the age of 16 cannot work past 9:30 p.m.

VERMONT: Vermont law limits children under the age of 16 from working more than 40 hours per week and eight hours per day in non-farm employment. Children under the age of 16 cannot work past 7 p.m.

VIRGINIA: Virginia law limits children under the age of 16 from working more than 40 hours per week and eight hours per day in non-farm employment. Children under the age of 16 cannot work past 7 p.m.

WASHINGTON: Washington law limits children under the age of 16 from working more than 40 hours per week and eight hours per day in non-farm employment. Children under the age of 16 cannot work past 7 p.m.

WEST VIRGINIA: Under West Virginia law, no minor under the age of 16 may work during school hours under any circumstance. Children under the age of 16 cannot work past 7 p.m.

WISCONSIN: Wisconsin law limits children under the age of 16 from working more than 40 hours per week and eight hours per day in non-farm employment. Children under the age of 16 cannot work past 8 p.m.

WYOMING: Wyoming law limits children under the age of 16 from working more than 56 hours per week and eight hours per day in non-farm employment. Children under the age of 16 cannot work past 10 p.m.

ADDITIONAL RESOURCES

Davis, Samuel M. *Children's Rights Under the Law.* New York: Oxford University Press, 2011.

Freeman, Michael, ed. *Children's Health and Children's Rights* Boston: Martinus Nijhoff Publishers, 2006.

Walker, Nancy E., Catherine M. Brooks, and Lawrence S. Wrightsman. *Children's Rights in the United States: In Search of a National Policy* Thousand Oaks, CA: Sage Publications, 1999.

ORGANIZATIONS

Amnesty International USA
5 Penn Plaza
New York, NY 10001
Phone: (212) 807-8400
Fax: (212) 627-1451
URL: http://www.amnestyusa.org

Children's Rights Council
9470 Annapolis Road
Lanham, MD 20706
Phone: (301) 459-1220
URL: http://www.crckids.org

Civil Rights Division, U.S. Department of Justice
950 Pennsylvania Avenue NW
Washington, DC 20530
Phone: (202) 514-2000
Toll Free: (800) 375-5283
URL: http://www.justice.gov/crt/

Human Rights Watch
350 Fifth Avenue
New York, NY 10118
Phone: (212) 490-4700
Fax: (212) 736-1300
URL: http://www.hrw.org

CIVIL RIGHTS

CIVIL LIBERTIES

Sections within this essay:

- Overview
- The Bill of Rights
- The ACLU
- Other Organizations
- Civil Liberties Issues
  - Banning Books in Schools
  - DNA and Exoneration
  - The USA Patriot Act
  - Monitoring Domestic Phone Calls
  - Defending Targets of Discrimination
  - Safe Communities, Fair Sentences
- Additional Resources

OVERVIEW

The Declaration of Independence states that all individuals have a right to "life, liberty, and the pursuit of happiness." When the United States Constitution was signed on September 17, 1787, it further established those rights for Americans. Anyone born or living in the United States would have the right to speak or write freely on any topic, the right to choose any religion, the right to assemble peacefully for any purpose, and the right to a trial by **jury**. More than two centuries later, the Constitution still guarantees those rights.

The Constitution was hardly a perfect reflection of true civil liberties. It would be nearly a hundred years before slaves were freed and more than fifty years after that before women could vote in national elections. What has made the Constitution work is its ability to accommodate social justice and the fact that there have always been people willing to fight for civil liberties.

There have been times when people questioned whether Americans needed as many civil liberties as they have. In times of war, for example, debates over whether certain liberties must be curtailed always take place. During World War II, the federal government placed 110,000 Japanese Americans, two-thirds of whom were U.S. citizens, in internment camps. The measure was deemed necessary on account of the possible danger of **espionage** and infiltration of enemy forces. In hindsight, the government realized that this was an egregiously mistaken action (many Japanese Americans had served bravely during the war in the U.S. armed forces), and Congress issued an official apology in 1993. After the war ended, fear of Communism caused state and federal governments to pass legislation requiring certain government employees to take "loyalty oaths" assuring that they were not Communists or members of like-minded groups. The issue reached the boiling point when Senator Joe McCarthy of Wisconsin claimed that there were Communists working in the federal government. McCarthy launched a series of Senate hearings, and people who were **accused** of being Communists often lost their jobs. The Communist scare burned itself out, but not before destroying many lives.

Those who feel that civil liberties can be curtailed under special circumstances will explain that special circumstances call for special measures. Civil libertarians will remind them that there is always a danger that once the special circumstances end, there is no guarantee that the self-imposed restrictions will also end.

Many people mistakenly believe that civil libertarianism is the same as political liberalism. Civil libertarians can be liberal, conservative, or anywhere within the political spectrum. **Gun control** is a good example. Most people do not think of groups such as the National Rifle Association (NRA) as a politically liberal entity. Yet the NRA, which was founded in 1871, has long been a vocal supporter of the Second Amendment, which gives citizens the right to keep firearms. The NRA's commitment to civil liberties, as it sees them in this regard, is hardly in question even by its opponents.

THE BILL OF RIGHTS

The first ten amendments to the U.S. Constitution are commonly known as the **Bill of Rights**. They set the groundwork for what we consider our basic civil liberties. These amendments guarantee the following rights:

- Right to free speech. The First Amendment guarantees the right to **freedom of speech**, **freedom of the press**, and freedom to assemble peaceably.

- Right to bear arms. The Second Amendment guarantees each state's right to keep a **militia**, and arguably the right of individuals to keep firearms.

- No unauthorized quartering of soldiers. The Third Amendment prohibits soldiers from being quartered in private residences during peacetime without permission, nor during war time except under special circumstances.

- Freedom from **search and seizure**. The Fourth Amendment guarantees the right against search and seizure of **personal property** or private papers.

- Freedom from **self-incrimination**. The **Fifth Amendment** protects against self-incrimination and **double jeopardy**, and it guarantees due process.

- Trial by jury. Under the Sixth Amendment, individuals have a right to be tried by a jury of their peers in criminal cases. The Seventh Amendment guarantees trial by jury in civil cases involving certain set sums of money.

- Protection from excessive **bail**. The Eighth Amendment protects against excessive bail and also against cruel and unusual punishment.

- Unlisted rights and powers. The Ninth Amendment states that any rights not listed are retained by the people, and the Tenth Amendment states that powers not delegated to the federal government are retained by either the states or the people.

Other key amendments guaranteeing **civil rights** and liberties include the Thirteenth Amendment (which prohibits slavery), the Fourteenth Amendment (which granted citizenship to former slaves), the Fifteenth Amendment (which guaranteed that the right to vote could not be denied on account of race), and the Nineteenth Amendment (which granted women the right to vote). The Twenty-Fourth Amendment, ratified in 1962, prohibited the imposition of a voters' poll tax on any individual.

The Constitution was designed so that it could be amended, but the amendment process is by design not easy. Both houses of Congress must approve a proposed amendment by a two-thirds majority, and the amendment must then be ratified by three quarters of the states within a specific time frame (typically seven years). This procedure keeps the Constitution from becoming bogged down with scores of frivolous or narrow-issue amendments. This can work for or against the interests of civil libertarians. The proposed "Equal Rights Amendment" was passed by Congress in 1972 but failed to get ratified even after the **ratification** period was extended by three years. A proposed amendment in 2004 that would have imposed a constitutional prohibition on same-sex marriage did not receive enough Congressional support to be voted into existence.

Conversely, many state constitutions are amended rather frequently to adapt to new issues. A majority of states have, for instance, considered and passed constitutional amendments banning same-sex marriages during the 2000s and early 2010s.

THE ACLU

The best known civil liberties organization in the United States is the American Civil Liberties Union (ACLU). Founded in 1920, the ACLU works at the national, state, and local level through the courts, legislatures, and communities to ensure individual rights and liberties are not abridged. The ACLU has branches across the United States and maintains an active network of professionals and volunteers. The ACLU challenges legislation and any government action that it feels endanger civil rights.

The list of issues the ACLU handles is quite comprehensive and includes **discrimination**, religious freedom, **privacy**, free speech, prisoners' rights, immigrants' rights, rights of the poor, and the death penalty. The ACLU initiates lawsuits and often offers to defend those whose civil liberties have been challenged. In addition, the ACLU also issues "friend of the court" briefs for cases that go before the courts.

One of the ACLU's earliest battles was the Scopes trial in Dayton, Tennessee, in 1925. Tennessee had enacted legislation prohibiting the teaching of evolution, and the ACLU decided to seek a test case to argue for free speech. John T. Scopes volunteered to be the test case, and the ACLU agreed to provide legal **counsel**. The lead attorney was the noted defense lawyer Clarence Darrow, who argued vigorously in defense of Scopes' right to teach evolution. Although Scopes was convicted and fined $100, the case brought the issue, and the ACLU, to national prominence.

A more recent case that was a victory for the ACLU was *ACLU v. Reno*. The ACLU challenged the constitutionality of the Communications Decency Act of 1996, which prohibited "indecent" speech over the Internet. The act was too broad and sweeping, claimed the ACLU, and threatened to endanger the free exchange of ideas online. The U.S. Supreme Court agreed and voted unanimously that the act was unconstitutional.

Many people think of the ACLU as a liberal organization aimed promoting a leftist agenda. In fact, the ACLU has defended people and institutions of all political beliefs. For example, the organization has opposed the creation of "hate speech" regulations on college and university campuses. The argument is that even hateful speech is protected under the Constitution (unlike hate-based actions), and a better way to deal with hate speech is to find its root causes instead of merely banning it.

OTHER ORGANIZATIONS

Although the ACLU is the best known and most prominent civil liberties organization, other national and local groups also challenge what they see as the erosion of civil liberties. The New York Civil Liberties Union (NYCLU), for example, does much of the same legal and advocacy group that the ACLU does. (The NYCLU was actually founded in 1951 as the New York affiliate of the ACLU.) The NYCLU focuses on civil liberties issues in New York, including issues surrounding security measures put in place since the September 11, 2001, terrorist attacks against the United States. A typical example is a federal suit filed in January 2006 by the NYCLU and the New York University Civil Rights Clinic on behalf of a filmmaker who was detained in May 2005 for filming on a Manhattan street. He was warned that he needed a permit, but when he applied for one some months later his application was denied without explanation. The lawsuit filed by the NYCLU claimed that the film-permit requirement is unconstitutional.

People for the American Way, founded in 1980 by television and film producer Norman Lear, works to protect civil liberties by advocating with government agencies, providing statistics and information on civil rights activities across the country and educating the public on civil liberties issues.

The American Library Association (ALA), which has more than 64,000 members across the country, works to ensure high quality information in libraries, and public access to that information. The ALA, through its Office for Intellectual Freedom, provides information on legislation and government activity that can affect how libraries disseminate information. Its opposition to Section 215 of the **USA Patriot Act** is one example. ALA also created guidelines for librarians on how to comply with the Children's Internet Protection Act (CIPA), which requires libraries to use filters to keep minors from accessing adult material.

CIVIL LIBERTIES ISSUES

Although civil liberties groups have actively advocated on behalf of civil rights over the decades, and although they have had many successes, they are quick to point out that vigilance is the key to ensuring civil liberties are not allowed to slide. Some typical issues from the late twentieth and early twenty-first centuries include the following.

Banning Books in Schools School boards regularly attempt to ban books, with classics such as *The Adventures of Huckleberry Finn* and *Of Mice and Men* among the most frequently challenged, according to ALA. In the early years of the twenty-first century, the Harry Potter series of books, which tell the story of a young aspiring wizard and his adventures in wizard school, have become a focal point for many who oppose the focus on wizardry and magic.

School boards do not have an absolute right to remove books from school library shelves. In the case of *Board of Education v. Pico*, decided in 1982 by a 5-4 majority, the U.S. Supreme Court case ruled against the school board of Island Trees, New York, which had removed several books from the school library shelves. Included among these books were *The Fixer* by Bernard Malamud, *Slaughterhouse Five* by Kurt Vonnegut, *Best Short Stories of Negro Writers* (edited by Langston Hughes), *A Hero Ain't Nothin' But A Sandwich* by Alice Childress, and *A Reader for Writers* (edited by Jerome Archer).

The court noted that school boards do have discretion in what books to acquire for the school, and it could reject any works deemed to be "pervasively vulgar." However, Justice William Brennan wrote that "the special characteristics of the school library make that environment especially appropriate for the recognition of First Amendment rights of students."

DNA and Exoneration DNA **evidence** can be used to convict criminals, and it has successfully been used to exonerate individuals, some of whom were wrongly imprisoned for more than two decades. Often, when a person who has been convicted of a crime tries to get DNA evidence admitted as evidence, the courts are reluctant, despite the fact that such evidence could exonerate an innocent person.

Often, the person who is wrongly convicted of a serious crime such as murder or rape has a criminal record for petty crimes, which means a record already exists. Civil libertarians have argued that many of these individuals were arrested and convicted more as a matter of expediency than of true suspicion.

The Innocence Project, created in 1992 by Peter Neufeld and Barry Scheck at the Benjamin Cardozo School of Law in New York, works to exonerate people by use of post-conviction DNA, in which DNA from the crime scene is tested against the accused's DNA. Often, physical evidence from a crime is kept for many years. If the evidence includes samples of blood, hair, skin, or other evidence that can include DNA, and if that evidence has not been contaminated or corrupted, it can often be used to prove a person's innocence. Between 1992 and 2012, the Innocence Project helped exonerate 297 prisoners in a total of 36 states.

The USA Patriot Act On October 26, 2001, less than two months after the September 11 attacks, Congress passed the USA Patriot Act (Uniting and Strengthening America by Providing Appropriate Tools Required to Intercept and Obstruct Terrorism). This act gave the government greater ability to seek out and combat terrorist activity in the United States. The Patriot Act grants the Secretary of the Treasury new regulatory powers to fight **money laundering** from foreign countries in U.S. banks; secures national borders against foreign nationals who are terrorists or who support **terrorism**; eases restrictions on interception and surveillance of correspondence and communication that may link to terrorist activity; stiffens penalties against money laundering, **counterfeiting**, charity **fraud**, and similar crimes; and creates new crimes and penalties for such acts as harboring terrorists and giving terrorists material support.

Civil liberties groups complained that the Patriot Act, hastily passed in a national atmosphere of grief, anger, and fear, granted the federal government too much power over innocent people or to track private records. One of the most controversial provisions was Section 215 of the Act, which gives the FBI permission to examine business records for foreign intelligence and international terrorism investigations. Called the "library provision" because some have read it to mean that libraries will be required to turn over lists of who has checked out which books, it has been criticized as overly broad by groups such as the ACLU and the American Library Association, as well as by political leaders from both parties.

Another point of contention is the existence of National Security Letters, which give federal law enforcement agencies the authority to access an individual's personal records without first seeking a **warrant**. Opponents of this procedure said that such letters should only be issued when a reasonable connection can be made between the subject and terrorist activity. They also said that targets of these letters should have the right to challenge them in court.

Even ten years after the September 11 attacks, and even with the election of a Democrat in President Barack Obama, civil-liberties issues related to national security have remained a priority for the ACLU. The ACLU has stressed that Americans do not need to choose between safety and freedom. In September 2011, the ACLU released a report entitled *A Call to Courage: Reclaiming Our Liberties Ten Years After 9/11*, which "explores how sacrificing America's values—including justice, individual liberty, and the rule of law—ultimately undermines safety."

Monitoring Domestic Phone Calls In December 2005 *The New York Times* published a story claiming that President George W. Bush had authorized the National Security Agency to monitor domestic telephone calls without first obtaining a warrant, as required under the Federal Intelligence Surveillance Act of 1978 (FISA). The Bush Administration confirmed that the wiretaps had been authorized, but he also claimed that as president, he had the right to make such an authorization, citing a joint resolution by Congress shortly after the September 11 attacks. That resolution, President Bush said, authorized him to take whatever steps were necessary to pursue individual terrorists and terrorist groups. He insisted that his actions were legal and necessary.

Civil libertarians, however, did not see the issue the way the Bush Administration did. Groups such as the ACLU claimed that Bush had circumvented the law by failing to get the proper warrants from a special FISA court set up to serve exactly that purpose. The problem, they maintained, was not so much that the president felt compelled to conduct the wiretaps, but that he did not even inform the relevant agencies about what he was planning to do.

The rationale behind this is what makes civil liberties such a complex issue. On the one hand, the libertarians make a valid point: There was no reason for the president to bypass the FISA court, and by omitting this step he may have compromised individual freedom more than he realizes. On the other hand, the president's supporters made an equally valid observation: If just one overheard telephone conversation gave the nation a piece of valuable information (such as the location for a terrorist attack) that saves lives and destruction, the benefit is well worth the trade-off of not obtaining a warrant first.

Defending Targets of Discrimination Various forms of discrimination continue to be the focus of debates. Discrimination issues that remain at the forefront of public debate include voter suppression, treatment of immigrants, segregating schools by sex, and various gay-rights issues.

Safe Communities, Fair Sentences The ACLU has continued to stress the importance of fair treatment within the criminal justice system. Civil libertarians warn that that criminal justice system treats people of color and otherwise underprivileged unfairly compared with others. The ACLU advocates solutions that would put fewer people in prison and would reduce lengthy sentences for those who have demonstrated that they are ready to reenter society.

ADDITIONAL RESOURCES

Baker, Thomas E., and John F. Stack Jr., eds. *At War with Civil Rights and Liberties.* Lanham, MD: Rowman and Littlefield Publishers, 2006.

Darmer, M. Katherine, and Richard D. Fybel, eds. *National Security, Civil Liberties and the War on Terror.* Amherst, NY: Prometheus Books, 2011.

Foerster, Herbert N. *Banned in the USA: A Reference Guide to Book Censorship in Schools and Public Libraries.* Westport, CT: Greenwood Press, 2002.

Walker, Samuel. *Presidents and Civil Liberties from Wilson to Obama: A Story of Poor Custodians.* New York: Cambridge University Press, 2012.

ORGANIZATIONS

American Civil Liberties Union (ACLU)

125 Broad St., 18th Fl.
New York, NY 10004
Phone: (212) 549-2500
Email: info@aclu.org
URL: http://www.aclu.org/

American Library Association (ALA)

50 East Huron Street
Chicago, IL 60611
Toll Free: (800) 545-2433
URL: http://www.ala.org

People for the American Way (PFAW)

1101 15th Street NW, Suite 600
Washington, DC 20005
Phone: (202) 467-4999
URL: http://www.pfaw.org

CIVIL RIGHTS

CONCEALED CARRY LAWS

Sections within this essay:

HISTORY OF CONCEALED CARRY LAWS

The origin of concealed-carry laws dates back to the turn of the twentieth century. The Vermont Supreme Court in 1903 determined that a city **ordinance** banning concealed firearms violated the state's constitution, which guarantees the right to keep and bear arms. This case continues to control Vermont law.

By the 1920s, some states considered adopting the Uniform Revolver Act. This Act made it unlawful to carry a concealed firearm without a license. States that adopted this Act developed licensing schemes that gave authorities discretion about whether to *issue* permits. However, commentators have noted that the authorities who issued the licenses often did so unfairly. Those who received permits were often white as well as rich and connected politically.

Washington state developed a different system in the 1960s. The Washington law required licensing authorities to issue permits unless the applicant fell into a category that disqualified him or her from obtaining the permit. More than 200,000 Washington citizens obtained permits in the first 30 years after the state passed the law.

The State of Florida was the next state to have a significant influence on this area of law. The state's legislature in 1987 considered its own law requiring a licensing authority to issue permits for concealed handguns once an applicant passed a background check and completed gun-safety classes. Among the supporters of the legislation was the state's police-chief association. Although Governor Bob Graham vetoed the proposal, his successor signed bill into law in 1987. By the end of 1987, only ten states allowed their ordinary citizens to carry concealed weapons. That number grew to 49 by 2012. Jurisdictions generally require citizens to obtain permits, but in most states, a person can obtain such a permit unless the state can establish a reason why the citizen should not carry one

OBTAINING A PERMIT

Specific requirements for obtaining a permit vary from state to state. In Texas, for example, an applicant is required to show the following to obtain a concealed handgun license, or CHL:

- The applicant must be 21 years old (although members and former members of the armed forces must be 18).
- The applicant must have a clean criminal history, including military service and recent juvenile records.
- The applicant must not be under a **protective order**.
- The applicant must not be chemically dependent.
- The applicant must not be of unsound mind.

Change in states' concealed carry permit designation, 2002 and 2012

Number of states by issue designation	June 2002[1]	March 2012[2]
No-issue states that prohibit the concealed carry of handguns	7 states and the District of Columbia	1 state and the District of Columbia
Shall-issue states	29	39
May-issue states	13	10
States that do not require a permit to concealed carry	1	4

[1]The total number of states and the District of Columbia adds to 51.
[2]The total number of states and the District of Columbia adds to 55 in this analysis, because 4 states (Alaska, Arizona, Rhode Island, and Wyoming) are counted in two categories. Alaska, Arizona, and Wyoming do not require permits but are considered shall-issue; and Rhode Island provides may- and shall-issue authority. Rhode Island law provides for two mechanisms for obtaining a permit: the Rhode Island Attorney General has "may-issue" authority to issue permits under R.I. Gen. Laws § 11-47-18, and cities and towns have "shall-issue" authority, with limited discretion, to issue a permit, under R.I. Gen. Laws § 11-47-11

SOURCE: U.S. Government Accountability Office. *Gun Control States' Laws and Requirements for Concealed Carry Permits* Vary *across the Nation*, July 2012.

TABLE BY PREMEDIAGLOBAL. ©2013 CENGAGE LEARNING.

- The applicant must not be delinquent in paying fines, fees, **child support**, student loans, etc.

- The applicant must be eligible to purchase a handgun by completing the NICS check.

- The applicant must complete required training.

An applicant in Texas must also pay a licensing fee, which is set by **statute**. A first-time standard applicant must pay a filing fee of $140, while those who are renewing permits must pay a $70 fee. Others, such as a judicial officers and peace officers, pay a reduced fee.

In other states, whether a licensing authority gives a citizen a concealed weapon permit is within the authority's discretion. California law, for instance, allows a police chief or county sheriff to issue a permit, assuming the applicant can meet the following conditions:

- The applicant provides proof of good moral character.

- The applicant shows good cause for the authority to issue the license.

- The applicant is a resident of the county or city where the applicant is applying for a license.

- The applicant completed a course of training, which lasts between 16 and 24 hours.

OUT-OF-STATE PERMIT HOLDERS

A permit to carry a concealed weapon in one state does not entitle the person to carry a concealed weapon elsewhere. However, many states have made agreements with other states to recognize out-of-state permits. For example, the states of Florida, Michigan, and Missouri have agreed to recognize concealed carry permits from 37 other states. However, many of these states (including Michigan and Missouri) do not recognize permits that other states have given to nonresidents of those states.

RESTRICTIONS

Although gun owners in many states are able to obtain concealed carry licenses or permits rather easily, possession of concealed weapons is subject to a number of restrictions. For instance, federal law preempts state law and forbids a person from carrying a weapon at government facilities. This includes post offices, federal court buildings, military facilities, correctional facilities, transportation facilities (such as Amtrak), and other federal property.

States also impose a variety of restrictions, which vary from state to state. The State of Texas, for example, restricts gun possession at the following:

- Schools

- School buses

- Polling places

- Courts and court offices

- Racetracks

- Secured airport areas

- Premises were executions will be carried out

- Certain businesses where alcohol is being sold

- Locations of sporting events

Concealed guns may also be prohibited at hospitals, nursing homes, amusement parks, places of worship, government meeting locations, and some businesses.

LEGAL CHALLENGES

Parties both favoring and opposing concealed carry laws have brought legal actions to try to make changes to the law through the courts. During the early 2000s, parties in states such as New Mexico, Missouri, Minnesota, and Ohio challenged concealed carry laws in state appellate courts. However, most of these challenges failed as the courts upheld the constitutionality of these laws.

In 2008, the U.S. Supreme Court issued a ruling in *District of Columbia v. Heller*, which upheld the right of private citizens to keep and bear arms. However, Justice Antonin Scalia's majority opinion noted that restrictions on concealed weapons are generally considered constitutional. He wrote: "Like most rights, the Second Amendment right is not unlimited. It is not a right to keep and carry any weapon whatsoever in any manner whatsoever and for whatever purpose: For example, concealed weapons prohibitions have been upheld under the Amendment or state analogues . . . ."

In *McDonald v. City of Chicago*, the Court extended the decision in *Heller* to apply to states and local governments. In this case, the Court struck down a handgun ban in the City of Chicago. This decision led some to question whether other restriction on concealed weapons may also violate the Second Amendment. In fact, a U.S. District Court in Maryland in 2012, ruled that the State of Maryland violated the Second Amendment by requiring applicants to show "good and substantial reason" for a licensing authority to issue a permit. As of late 2012, an **appeal** of the decision was still pending.

CONCEALED CARRY STATISTICS

Whether concealed carry laws actually reduce crime is a matter of extensive debate. Author John R. Lott Jr. has written three editions of a book entitled *More Guns, Less Crime*, which asserts that concealed weapons laws have led to a significant decline in murder and other violent crime rates. However, other studies have contradicted Lott's findings, with one report showing that concealed carry permit holders killed a total of 117 people during a two and a half year span between 2007 and 2009.

STATE CONCEALED CARRY LAWS

In the context of concealed carry laws, states are usually divided in four categories: shall-issue, may-issue, no-issue, and unrestricted. A shall-issue state is one that does not give a licensing authority discretion about whether to issue a license. A may-issue state gives the licensing authority discretion about whether to issue the license. A no-issue state does not allow a citizen the right to carry a concealed handgun. An unrestricted state does not require a citizen to have a license to carry a concealed weapon.

ALABAMA: Alabama law suggests that it is a may-issue state. However, Alabama authorities generally give permits to all applicants, making Alabama a shall-issue state in practice.

ALASKA: Alaska is considered both a shall-issue state and an unrestricted state. State law does not require a permit, but the state will issue permits to its residents so that these residents can carry weapons in other states.

ARIZONA: Alaska is considered both a shall-issue state and an unrestricted state. State law does not require a permit, but the state will issue permits to its residents so that these residents can carry weapons in other states.

ARKANSAS: Arkansas is considered a shall-issue state.

CALIFORNIA: California is considered a may-issue state.

COLORADO: Colorado is considered a shall-issue state.

CONNECTICUT: Connecticut law suggests that it is a may-issue state. However, Connecticut authorities generally give permits to all applicants, making Connecticut a shall-issue state in practice.

DELAWARE: Delaware is considered a may-issue state.

DISTRICT OF COLUMBIA: The District of Columbia is known as a no-issue **jurisdiction**.

FLORIDA: Florida is considered a shall-issue state.

GEORGIA: Georgia is considered a shall-issue state.

HAWAII: Hawaii law give authorities discretion to issue a concealed weapon license. However, authorities do not generally issue these permits, making the state a no-issue state in practice.

IDAHO: Idaho is considered a shall-issue state.

ILLINOIS: Illinois is a no-issue state.

INDIANA: Indiana is considered a shall-issue state.

IOWA: Iowa is considered a shall-issue state.

KANSAS: Kansas is considered a shall-issue state.

KENTUCKY: Kentucky is considered a shall-issue state.

LOUISIANA: Louisiana is considered a shall-issue state.

MAINE: Maine is considered a shall-issue state.

MARYLAND: Maryland law give authorities discretion to issue a concealed weapon license. However, authorities do not generally issue these permits, making the state a no-issue state in practice.

MASSACHUSETTS: Massachusetts is considered a may-issue state.

MICHIGAN: Michigan is considered a shall-issue state.

MINNESOTA: Minnesota is considered a shall-issue state.

MISSISSIPPI: Mississippi is considered a shall-issue state.

MISSOURI: Missouri is considered a shall-issue state.

MONTANA: Montana is considered a shall-issue state.

NEBRASKA: Nebraska is considered a shall-issue state.

NEVADA: Nevada is considered a shall-issue state.

NEW HAMPSHIRE: New Hampshire is considered a shall-issue state.

NEW JERSEY: New Jersey law give authorities discretion to issue a concealed weapon license. However, authorities do not generally issue these permits, making the state a no-issue state in practice.

NEW MEXICO: New Mexico is considered a shall-issue state.

NEW YORK: New York is considered a may-issue state.

NORTH CAROLINA: North Carolina is considered a shall-issue state.

NORTH DAKOTA: North Dakota is considered a shall-issue state.

OHIO: Ohio is considered a shall-issue state.

OKLAHOMA: Oklahoma is considered a shall-issue state.

OREGON: Oregon is considered a shall-issue state.

PENNSYLVANIA: Pennsylvania is considered a shall-issue state.

RHODE ISLAND: Rhode Island is considered a shall-issue state.

SOUTH CAROLINA: South Carolina is considered a shall-issue state.

SOUTH DAKOTA: South Dakota is considered a shall-issue state.

TENNESSEE: Tennessee is considered a shall-issue state.

TEXAS: Texas is considered a shall-issue state.

UTAH: Utah is considered a shall-issue state.

VERMONT: Because of a Vermont Supreme Court decision construing the state constitution, Vermont does not have any restrictions on a person's right to carry a concealed weapon.

VIRGINIA: Virginia is considered a shall-issue state.

WASHINGTON: Washington is considered a shall-issue state.

WEST VIRGINIA: West Virginia is considered a shall-issue state.

WISCONSIN: Wisconsin is considered a shall-issue state.

WYOMING: Wyoming is considered both a shall-issue state and an unrestricted state. State law does not require a permit, but the state will issue permits to its residents so that these residents can carry weapons in other states.

ADDITIONAL RESOURCES

Lott, John R., Jr. *More Guns, Less Crime.* 3rd ed. Chicago: University of Chicago Press, 2010.

Spitzer, Robert J. *The Politics of Gun Control.* 4th ed. Washington, D.C.: CQ Press, 2008.

Utter, Glenn H. *Encyclopedia of Gun Control and Gun Rights.* Phoenix, AZ: Oryx Press, 2000.

Valdez, Angela, and John E. Ferguson, Jr. *Gun Control.* 2d ed. New York: Chelsea House, 2012.

ORGANIZATIONS

Brady Center to Prevent Gun Violence

1225 Eye St. NW, Ste, 1100
Washington, DC 20005
Phone: (202) 289-7319
Fax: (202) 408-1851
URL: http://www.cphv.org

Citizens Committee for the Right to Keep and Bear Arms (CCRKBA)

Liberty Park
12500 NE 10th Pl.
Bellevue, WA 98005
Phone: (425) 454-4911
Email: AdminForWeb@ccrkba.org
URL: http://www.ccrkba.org

National Rifle Association of America (NRA)

11250 Waples Mill Rd.
Fairfax, VA 22030
Toll Free: (800) 672-3888
Email: comm@nrahq.org
URL: http://www.nra.org

CIVIL RIGHTS

CONSTITUTIONAL RIGHTS TO PRIVACY

Sections within this essay:

- Introduction
- Personal Autonomy
  - Family and Marriage
  - Abortion Rights
  - Other Issues
- Personal Information
- Government Surveillance and Searches
  - Fourth Amendment Rights
  - USA Patriot Act and Related Legislation
- State Laws
- Additional Resources

INTRODUCTION

As modern technology continues to develop, different forms of invasion of privacy become even more prevalent. Many modern automobiles are equipped with global positioning systems that may have been considered part of science fiction just a few years earlier. A great deal of personal information is available on the Internet, and criminals are able to use this information to steal someone's identity. Moreover, even the most basic mobile phones give users the opportunity to record audio, video, and pictures.

The government, of course, is capable of using these technologies for a variety of different purposes. Protecting U.S. citizens from foreign threats, including terrorists, is a major concern for the federal government, which has taken many steps to ensure that means of transportation are safe. These means have become progressively more advanced, as new scanners can see through practically anything on a person's body. Law enforcement in general is also able to take advantage of surveillance technology to record the activities of suspects.

The U.S. Constitution protects individuals from certain government action, such as unreasonable searches and seizures and infringements on **freedom of speech**. However, many are unaware that the Constitution says nothing specifically about privacy rights. Although some Supreme Court decisions suggest that such a general right exists, the Court's decisions are not uniform in recognizing these rights. Nevertheless, several state constitutions do refer specifically to the right of privacy, and several courts have suggested that the U.S. Constitution does protect privacy in some form.

Supreme Court justice Louis D. Brandeis once famously wrote that the right to privacy means "the right to be let alone." Although many may agree that Americans should possess this right, it would be difficult to guarantee this right based on such a general principle. In nearly any circumstance involving the government's potential intrusion on privacy, the government has at least some significant interest if not a compelling interest to protect. For example, a person may want to be "left alone" and not complete a **census** questionnaire. However, the government has a sufficient interest in collecting the data as part of the census that the government's right would supersede a person's interest to be left alone.

Privacy rights in constitutional law usually arise in specific contexts. This essay addresses some of these contexts, including personal autonomy, government surveillance and searches, and personal information.

PERSONAL AUTONOMY

If the right to privacy truly were the right to be left alone, then the constitutional right to privacy would focus largely on personal autonomy. In some circumstances, specific constitutional rights would protect an individual's autonomy. For instance, the First Amendment largely protects freedom to express one's self, such as adopting styles of clothing or hair. However, neither the First Amendment nor other constitutional provisions clearly apply to some topics, and courts in the past have considered arguments that a general constitutional right to privacy may apply.

Family and Marriage One of the most commonly cited decisions regarding the right to privacy is the Supreme Court's 1965 decision in *Griswold v. Connecticut*. The case involved a Connecticut **statute** that prohibited use of contraceptives. Several individuals who assisted others to obtain contraceptives appealed fines based on the state law. These individuals argued that the ban on use of contraceptives violated their privacy rights under the Constitution.

A famous majority opinion by Justice William O. Douglas recognized that the **Bill of Rights** in the Constitution contains "penumbras, formed by emanations from those guarantees that help give them life and substance." Thus, these guarantees "create zones of privacy," in Douglas' opinion. Among those related rights include the right of association under the First Amendment; the prohibition against quartering of soldiers under the Third Amendment; protections against unreasonable searches and seizures under the Fourth Amendment; the right to avoid **self-incrimination** under the **Fifth Amendment**; and rights retained through the Ninth Amendment.

In light of his analysis, Douglas concluded that the ban on contraceptives violated privacy rights. Writing for the Court, he said: "We deal with a right of privacy older than the Bill of Rights—older than our political parties, older than our school system. Marriage is a coming together for better or for worse, hopefully enduring, and intimate to the degree of being sacred. It is an association that promotes a way of life, not causes; a harmony in living, not political faiths; a bilateral loyalty, not commercial or social projects. Yet it is an association for as noble a purpose as any involved in our prior decisions."

Later cases have seldom expanded on how the Constitution protects marital privacy. Some criticized the decision in *Griswold* by arguing that the decision did not specify what married individuals have the right to do

in private. More recent cases suggest that the Supreme Court would construe right within a marriage to focus on the liberty rights contained in the due process clauses of the Fifth and Fourteenth Amendment. Nevertheless, the Court has never overruled *Griswold*, and parties continue to cite to it to support arguments about privacy rights.

Abortion Rights Eight years after the Court's decision in *Griswold*, the Court in *Roe v. Wade* addressed whether a women had the constitutional right to an **abortion**. The **appellant** in the case argued that her right to have an abortion performed was protected by the right of privacy recognized in *Griswold*, as well as the liberty rights in the Due Process Clause of the Fourteenth Amendment and rights protected by the Ninth Amendment.

Justice William Brennan agreed that the right of privacy extended to abortion rights. He wrote: "This right of privacy, whether it be founded in the Fourteenth Amendment's concept of personal liberty and restrictions upon state action, as we feel it is, or, as the District Court determined, in the Ninth Amendment's reservation of rights to the people, is broad enough to encompass a woman's decision whether or not to terminate her pregnancy. The detriment that the State would impose upon the pregnant woman by denying this choice altogether is apparent."

Other Issues A number of later decisions, however, avoided questions of privacy rights by relying instead on other rights in the Constitution. In fact, some authors have stressed that *Roe v. Wade* was one of the last times the Court extended privacy rights in the context of personal autonomy. In *Lawrence v. Texas* (2003), the Court considered whether a state **sodomy** law was unconstitutional as applied to consensual sex between two adults of the same gender. In concluding that the state law indeed violated the Constitution, Justice Anthony Kennedy focused on liberty rights under the Fourteenth Amendment's Due Process Clause rather than the privacy rights recognized in *Griswold*.

Some parties have argued that privacy rights should extend to a person's right to die. This usually arises in the context of a person's right to refuse medical treatment or even physician-assisted suicide. However, courts have not extended the privacy rights cases to apply to the right-to-die cases.

PERSONAL INFORMATION

Several Supreme Court cases have recognized that a person has a constitutional right to privacy to avoid disclosing certain personal information. This is especially true of medical records. In *Whalen v. Roe* (1977), the

Court reviewed a New York state law requiring that the state be provided with a copy of every prescription for certain types of drugs. A group of doctors and patients challenged the law, arguing that the statute violated their privacy rights. Writing for the Court, Justice John Paul Stevens noted that one of the constitutionally protected privacy interests is an individual's interest in disclosing personal matters. Stevens, however, concluded that the New York statute did not infringe upon privacy rights because the required disclosures were no different than other private information that patients had to disclose to government authorities.

Nevertheless, some lower courts have attached significance to the Court's statement about disclosures of private personal information. For instance, the Second Circuit Court of Appeals, relying in part on *Whalen*, concluded that a person had a right to privacy under the U.S. Constitution to the person's HIV status. The court characterized the protected right as one of confidentiality as opposed to personal autonomy or independence.

GOVERNMENT SURVEILLANCE AND SEARCHES

Fourth Amendment Rights Courts have uniformly agreed that Fourth Amendment and related state constitutions protect a person from unreasonable searches and seizures where a person has a reasonable expectation of privacy. This principle largely emanates from the Supreme Court's decision in *Katz v. United States* (1967). The decision established a two-part test to determine whether the Fourth Amendment would prohibit the government from searching a person or the person's property. First, the person must have a subjective expectation of privacy in the place where the search occurred, such as a home. Second, the expectation must be one that society would accept as reasonable.

A large body of **case law** has evolved about determining when a party has a reasonable expectation of privacy. However, these cases have not expanded general privacy rights under the Constitution. In fact, in *Katz* the Court addressed the general concept of privacy, noting: "[T]he Fourth Amendment cannot be translated into a general constitutional 'right to privacy.' That Amendment protects individual privacy against certain kinds of governmental intrusion, but its protections go further, and often have nothing to do with privacy at all. Other provisions of the Constitution protect personal privacy from other forms of governmental invasion.FN5 But the protection of a person's general right to privacy—his right to be let alone by other people—is, like the protection of his property and of his very life, left largely to the law of the individual States."

USA Patriot Act and Related Legislation In response to the terrorist acts against the United States on September 11, 2001, Congress passed the **USA Patriot Act**. This Act incorporated a number of changes to existing laws, including enhanced ability to use electronic surveillance to obtain intelligence information about possible terrorists. Congress in 2008 also amended the Foreign Intelligence Surveillance Act (FISA) to increase the ability of federal investigators to intercept communications.

Several groups, including the American Civil Liberties Union, have argued that the USA Patriot Act and FISA (as amended) are unconstitutional. Among the arguments is that these Acts violate privacy rights of U.S. citizens. As of 2012, however, no court had ruled that these or similar laws violate specific privacy rights or any reasonable expectations of privacy.

STATE LAWS

A number of state constitutions contain specific provisions that guarantee privacy rights. In some instances, these rights related to government intrusions in general. In other instances, these rights relate specifically to searches and seizures.

ALASKA: Article 1, § 22 of the Alaska Constitution provides: "The right of the people to privacy is recognized and shall not be infringed. The legislature shall implement this section."

ARIZONA: Article 2, § 8 of the Arizona Constitution provides: "No person shall be disturbed in his private affairs, or his home invaded, without authority of law."

CALIFORNIA: Article I, § 1 of the California Constitution provides: "All people are by nature free and independent and have inalienable rights. Among these are enjoying and defending life and liberty, acquiring, possessing, and protecting property, and pursuing and obtaining safety, happiness, and privacy."

FLORIDA: Article I, § 23 of the Florida Constitution provides: "Every natural person has the right to be let alone and free from governmental intrusion into the person's private life except as otherwise provided herein. This section shall not be construed to limit the public's right of access to public records and meetings as provided by law."

HAWAII: Article I, § 6 of the Hawaii Constitution provides: "The right of the people to privacy is recognized and shall not be infringed without the showing of a compelling state interest. The legislature shall take affirmative steps to implement this right."

ILLINOIS: Article I, § 6 of the Illinois Constitution provides: "The people shall have the right to be secure in their persons, houses, papers and other possessions against unreasonable searches, seizures, invasions of privacy or interceptions of communications by eavesdropping devices or other means. No **warrant** shall issue without **probable cause**, supported by **affidavit** particularly describing the place to be searched and the persons or things to be seized."

LOUISIANA: Article I, § 5 of the Louisiana Constitution provides: "Every person shall be secure in his person, property, communications, houses, papers, and effects against unreasonable searches, seizures, or invasions of privacy. No warrant shall issue without probable cause supported by oath or affirmation, and particularly describing the place to be searched, the persons or things to be seized, and the lawful purpose or reason for the search. Any person adversely affected by a search or seizure conducted in violation of this Section shall have standing to raise its illegality in the appropriate court."

MONTANA: Article 2, § 10 of the Montana Constitution provides: "The right of individual privacy is essential to the well-being of a free society and shall not be infringed without the showing of a compelling state interest."

PENNSYLVANIA: Courts in Pennsylvania have recognized a general privacy right contained within the state constitution. For example, in one case, a state **appellate court** ruled that a public utility commission's authorization of a caller identification service violated privacy rights because the system provided no means of blocking the identification.

SOUTH CAROLINA: Article I, § 10 of the South Carolina Constitution provides: "The right of the people to be secure in their persons, houses, papers, and effects against unreasonable searches and seizures and unreasonable invasions of privacy shall not be violated, and no warrants shall issue but upon probable cause, supported by oath or affirmation, and particularly describing the place to be searched, the person or thing to be seized, and the information to be obtained."

ADDITIONAL RESOURCES

Alderman, Ellen, and Caroline Kennedy. *The Right to Privacy.* New York: Vintage Books, 1998.

Baker, Thomas E., and John F. Stack Jr., eds. *At War with Civil Rights and Liberties.* Lanham, MD: Rowman and Littlefield Publishers, 2006.

Darmer, M. Katherine, and Richard D. Fybel, eds. *National Security, Civil Liberties and the War on Terror.* Amherst, NY: Prometheus Books, 2011.

Glenn, Richard A. *The Right to Privacy: Rights and Liberties Under the Law.* Santa Barbara, CA.: ABC-CLIO, 2003.

Mills, Jon L. *Privacy: The Lost Right.* New York: Oxford University Press, 2008.

Moore, Adam D. *Privacy Rights: Moral and Legal Foundations.* University Park, PA: Pennsylvania State University Press, 2010.

Walker, Samuel. *Presidents and Civil Liberties from Wilson to Obama: A Story of Poor Custodians.* New York: Cambridge University Press, 2012.

ORGANIZATIONS

American Civil Liberties Union (ACLU)

125 Broad St., 18th Fl.
New York, NY 10004
Phone: (212) 549-2500
Email: info@aclu.org
URL: http://www.aclu.org/

American Library Association (ALA)

50 East Huron Street
Chicago, IL 60611
Toll Free: (800) 545-2433
URL: http://www.ala.org

Electronic Privacy Information Center

1718 Connecticut Ave. NW
Washington, DC 20009
Toll Free: (202) 483-1140
Fax: (202) 483-1248
URL: http://www.epic.org

People for the American Way (PFAW)

1101 15th Street NW, Suite 600
Washington, DC 20005
Phone: (202) 467-4999
URL: http://www.pfaw.org

Privacy Rights Clearinghouse

3108 Fifth Ave., Suite A
San Diego, CA 92103
Phone: (619) 298-3396
URL: http://www.privacyrights.org

CIVIL RIGHTS

DUE PROCESS

Sections within this essay:

BACKGROUND

Under both the Fifth and Fourteenth Amendments to the U.S. Constitution, neither the federal government nor state governments may deprive any person "of life, liberty, or property without due process of law." A similar due process provision was found in the Magna Charta, as well as early state constitutions. Chief Justice William Howard Taft explained the purpose behind the clauses in *Truax v. Corrigan* (1921) as follows: "The due process clause requires that every man shall have

the protection of his day in court, and the benefit of the general law, a law which hears before it condemns, which proceeds not arbitrarily or capriciously, but upon inquiry, and renders judgment only after trial, so that every citizen shall hold his life, liberty, property and immunities under the protection of the general rules which govern society. It, of course, tends to secure equality of law in the sense that it makes a required minimum of protection for every one's right of life, liberty, and property, which the Congress or the Legislature may not withhold."

Courts have interpreted the due process clauses as providing two distinct limitations on government. First, the clauses provide for procedural due process, which requires the government to follow certain procedures before it deprives a person of life, liberty, or property. Cases that address procedural due process usually focus on the type of notice that is required of the government or the type of **hearing** that must be held when the government takes a particular action. Second, the clauses establish substantive due process, under which courts determine whether the government has sufficient justification for its actions. Because courts use substantive due process to protect certain fundamental rights of U.S. citizens, issues related to substantive due process have been the subject of extensive debate.

PROCEDURAL DUE PROCESS

Procedural due process focuses primarily on a person's right to be heard, rather than a person's right to prevail in a dispute. Courts usually consider two broad questions in cases involving procedural due process. First, courts consider whether the government's action involves an interest in life, liberty, or property. Second, courts consider whether the procedures that the government has employed assure that a person receives fair treatment.

Deprivation of Life The term "life" in the due process clauses is not often the subject of dispute. Even where the government deprives a person of life, such as through enforcement of the death penalty, the government seldom does so without following proper procedures. Where the government has allegedly taken a life in an impermissible manner, challenges to the action are usually based on another constitutional provision. For instance, challenges to the death penalty have typically been based on the Eighth Amendment's proscription against **cruel and unusual punishment**. Similarly, arguments related to whether life begins at conception or birth, especially in **abortion** cases, focus on the liberty interests of the mother rather than the definition of "life" in the due process clauses.

Deprivation of Liberty The U.S. Supreme Court has sought on a few occasions to clarify the meaning of the term "liberty," although the term has never had a precise definition. In *Meyer v. Nebraska* (1923), the Court stated that liberty "denotes not merely freedom from bodily restraint but also the right of the individual to **contract**, to engage in any of the common occupations of life, to acquire useful knowledge, to marry, establish a home and bring up children, to worship God according to the dictates of his own conscience and generally to enjoy those privileges long recognized as essential to the orderly pursuit of happiness of free men." This statement has been cited by several subsequent Supreme Court cases.

Liberty interests are most clearly involved when the government's action results in physical restraint, especially in cases involving prisoners. In the examples, the Supreme Court determined that the government was required to provide due process because of the deprivation of liberty interests:

- Revocation of **parole** (*Morrissey v. Brewer* [1972])

- Revocation of **probation** (*Gagnon v. Scarpelli* [1973])

- Revocation of "good time credits" awarded to prisoners under state law (*Wolff v. McDonnell* [1974])

- Involuntary civil commitment to a mental institution (*Addington v. Texas* [1979])

- Transfer of a prisoner to a mental hospital (*Vitek v. Jones* [1980])

- Involuntary administration of antipsychotic medications (*Washington v. Harper* [1990])

- Transfer of inmates to a strict ("supermax") prison facility (*Wilkinson v. Austin* [2005])

By comparison, the Court has refused to recognize other forms of liberty interests related to prisoners, including the following examples:

- Remaining in a minimum security prison, as opposed to a maximum security prison (*Meachum v. Fano* [1976])

- A review of a prisoner's request to commute his life sentence (*Connecticut Board of Pardons v. Dumschat* [1981])

- Rescission of discretionary parole prior to a prisoner's release (*Jago v. Van Curen* [1981])

- Visitation, including visits from family members (*Kentucky Department of Corrections v. Thompson* [1989])

In addition to restrictions on physical freedom, liberty interests include all of the rights that are granted to the people either expressly in the Constitution, such as **freedom of speech** or freedom from unreasonable searches and seizures. Liberty also includes rights that are implied from the Constitution by the courts, such as the fundamental right for parents to raise their children.

Deprivation of Property The Constitution clearly requires that the government must provide due process before it deprives a person of real or **personal property**. The issue that is most often in dispute in this context is whether a person has a property interest in a government benefit. The Supreme Court, in *Roth v. Board of Regents* (1970), noted that, "[t]o have a property interest in a benefit, a person clearly must have more than an abstract need or desire for it. He must have more than a unilateral expectation of it. He must, instead, have a legitimate claim or entitlement to it." Hence, the key to whether a person has a property interest in a benefit is whether that person is entitled to the benefit.

To determine whether a person is entitled to a benefit, courts generally consider the terms under which the government has offered the benefit. If a government employee has a reasonable expectation that he or she will continue to receive a benefit, then the person may successfully assert that he or she has a recognized property interest in the benefit. For instance, a public employee who holds a position that is terminable at the will of either party does not generally have a property interest in that position. *Bishop v. Wood* (1976). However, where a state **statute** allows public servants to retain the positions in the absence of "misfeasance, malfeasance, or nonfeasance in office," the person could have a property interest in continued employment. *Cleveland Board of Education v. Loudermill* (1985). The Supreme Court has recognized property interests protected by the due process clauses in the following instances:

- A state statute allowing the government to aid in the collection of debts through wage garnishment without notice or a hearing violated due process rights of the person whose wages were garnished (*Sniadach v. Family Finance Corp. of Bay View* [1969])
- Welfare recipients were entitled to notice and a hearing prior to the termination of public assistance payments (*Goldberg v. Kelly* [1970])
- Suspension of a driver's license by a state department of public safety required notice and a hearing (*Bell v. Burson* [1971])
- A teacher who was employed by a junior college under a series of one-year contracts could prove entitlement to continued employment based on a provision of an employee handbook (*Perry v. Sinderman* [1972])

Procedural Requirements In some instances, the government may have deprived a person of life, liberty, or property without following any form of procedure. Other instances, where a governmental unit has followed some sort of a procedure, present more difficult questions for courts, which must consider whether the procedures were adequate for the protection of the rights involved. In this context, due process is concerned only that the governmental actor followed a fair decision-making process and not that the government reached a fair result.

Due process basically requires that a person who is deprived of a recognized right must be given some sort of notice and an opportunity for a hearing on the government's action. Where individual rights are affected by legislation, the publication of a statute is sufficient to provide notice to all individuals. On the other hand, an action by an agency or a court requires notice that will ensure that interested parties will, in fact, become aware of a proposed action.

At a minimum, a person who will be deprived of a right is entitled to a fair decision-making process by an **impartial** decision-maker. However, rather than establish a single rule that all governmental bodies must follow in terms of the specific procedures that are employed during a hearing, courts instead balance various interests when determining what procedures that a governmental entity must use. The Supreme Court in *Mathews v. Eldridge* (1976) explained these factors as follows: "First, the private interest that will be affected by the official action; second, the risk of an erroneous deprivation of such interest through the procedures used, and the probative value, if any, of additional or substitute procedural safeguards; and finally, the government's interest, including the function involved and the **fiscal** and administrative burdens that the additional or substitute procedural requirement would entail."

The Supreme Court has continued to adhere to the balancing test announced in *Mathews*, although this test does not require the government to provide a formal adversarial proceeding when it deprives a person of a right. In *Wilkinson v. Austin* (2005), the U.S. Supreme Court reviewed a case where prisoners were transferred from a state penitentiary to a so-called "supermax" facility, which was reserved for the most dangerous criminals. The state adopted an informal, nonadversarial procedure for determining which inmates would be transferred. Inmates received notice of their transfer as well as the factual basis for their transfer. Moreover, inmates had an opportunity to rebut accusations, and multiple levels of review were available for an **appeal**. After stating that the *Mathews* test still constituted good law, the Court determined that these procedures were adequate to provide due process.

SUBSTANTIVE DUE PROCESS

History The Fourteenth Amendment, ratified by the states in 1866, included among its provisions is the Privileges and Immunities Clause. This clause provides that no state "shall abridge the privileges and immunities of the citizens of the United States." Many commentators have long argued that this provision, rather than the Due Process Clause of the Fourteenth Amendment, should protect substantive rights of citizens. The Supreme Court, however, limited the application of the Privileges and Immunities Clause in the *Slaughterhouse Cases* (1872) by stating that the amendment did not create any new federal rights. The Court has rarely applied the Privileges and Immunities Clause since that time.

Although some cases during the nineteenth century suggested that due process should protect substantive rights, the Supreme Court generally avoided this question. In *Lochner v. New York* (1905), however, the Court reversed its position, ruling that a state statute limiting the number of hours that employees could work violated due process because it interfered with the workers' right to contract. After this decision, the Court engaged in a practice where it effectively substituted its own judgment for the judgment of a legislative body.

Several pieces of legislation enacted under President Franklin Roosevelt's New Deal program were challenged on due process grounds. The Court at that time continued to strike down legislation based on the due process clause under *Lochner,* and the economic beliefs of the justices conflicted with the goals of Roosevelt's legislation. In a direct clash between two of the branches of government, Roosevelt threatened to add Supreme Court justices who were more likely to uphold the statutes. Although Congress later rejected the court-packing plan, the Court nevertheless reversed its position.

By 1937, the Court no longer subjected legislation to the same type of scrutiny that it did under *Lochner*.

Modern Protection of Fundamental Rights Beginning with *United States v. Carolene Products Co.* (1938), the Court significantly revised its approach to the review of legislation. The Court presumes that legislation is constitutional and places the burden on the person challenging the law to prove that the law is not rationally related to a permissible government interest. Under this rational basis test, the Court strikes down very few pieces of legislation.

The Court's review of legislation changes when the law affects a fundamental constitutional right. A fundamental right may arise explicitly from the Constitution or may be implied from the Constitution by the courts. The application of the due process clauses in the context of the protection of fundamental rights overlaps with the application of the Equal Protection Clause. If a law classifies certain people based on their exercise of a fundamental right, then the Court applies the Equal Protection Clause to the analysis. However, if the law restricts the fundamental rights of all persons, the Court engages in a due process analysis.

Under either the Equal Protection Clause or the due process clauses, where a law infringes upon a fundamental right, the Court subjects the law to close scrutiny. Unlike laws that are reviewed under the rational basis test, the Court presumes that a law that restricts a fundamental right is unconstitutional, and the state may only prove that the law is constitutional by showing that the law is "narrowly tailored" to further a compelling governmental interest. This standard is very difficult for the government to overcome.

One of the more controversial aspects of both due process and equal protection **jurisprudence** is the recognition of the fundamental rights that the Court has determined are implied in the Constitution. Few tend to question that citizens of the United States have a fundamental right to freedom of religion, since the Constitution explicitly provides this right. However, it is less clear that citizens have a general right to **privacy** since the Constitution says nothing about these types of rights. Nevertheless, the Court has recognized a number of these implied rights, which are often identified more generally as privacy rights.

Right to Procreate The Court has long recognized that the right to procreate is a fundamental right protected by the Constitution. In *Skinner v. Oklahoma* (1942), the Court invalidated a state statute that provided for the mandatory sterilization of certain **habitual** criminals. Noting that the right to procreate was a "basic right of

man," the Court strictly limited the power of a state to impose involuntary sterilization.

Use of Contraceptives Much of the modern focus on the protection of privacy rights began with the case of *Griswold v. Connecticut* (1965), which involved a challenge of a criminal law that proscribed the use of contraceptives, even in private. According to the lead opinion written by Justice William Douglas, even though the Constitution was silent about the right to privacy, the Constitution nevertheless contained a "penumbra" of rights within the **Bill of Rights** that included the right to privacy. Since the criminal law in this case infringed upon the privacy rights of those who wished to use contraceptives, the Court ruled that it violated the Due Process Clause of the Fourteenth Amendment. Although other justices disagreed with the underlying rationale for recognizing privacy rights, the decision led to the recognition other fundamental rights in later cases.

Abortion Probably the most debated right that the Court has recognized relates to whether a woman has a right to terminate her pregnancy. In *Roe v. Wade* (1973), the Court found that a woman's right to make this decision was indeed a fundamental right protected by the Constitution. Competing with this right of the woman is the state's interest in maternal health. The Court in *Roe* established the time during which the state could not prevent a woman from having an abortion (i.e., during the first trimester of the pregnancy) and the time during which the state could place restrictions on abortions (i.e., after the first trimester).

Critics have attacked *Roe* since the decision was handed down, often on the grounds that it represents judicial activism at its worst. On the other hand, supporters have defended the decision with equal vigor on the basis that it represents one of the more important rights of women. Subsequent cases, especially *Planned Parenthood of Southeastern Pennsylvania v. Casey* (1992), have diluted *Roe* to a large extent, even though the basic holding of *Roe* has remained intact.

Sodomy Most states outlawed homosexual acts for many years through the application of **sodomy** laws. The **repeal** of these sodomy laws as they applied to homosexual acts became a focal point for gay and lesbian rights groups, much like the right to an abortion has been a focal point for women's rights groups. In the case of *Bowers v. Hardwick* (1986), however, the Court explicitly refused to recognize that the Constitution "would extend a fundamental right to homosexuals to engage in acts of consensual sodomy."

Critics argued that the Court misconstrued the basic rights at issue in *Bowers*, saying that the case was really about the right to be left alone rather than the right to engage in homosexual conduct (the case arose after police arrested a man engaged in a sex act in his own house). Seventeen years after the decision in *Bowers*, the Court reconsidered its position, and in *Lawrence v. Texas* (2003), it declared that sodomy laws were indeed unconstitutional. According to Justice Anthony Kennedy, "*Bowers* was not correct when it was decided, and it is not correct today. It ought not to remain binding precedent. *Bowers v. Hardwick* should be and now is overruled."

Marital Rights The Court in *Loving v. Virginia* (1967), recognizing a fundamental right to marriage, invalidated a state statute that forbid interracial marriage. Chief Justice Earl Warren wrote that "[t]he freedom to marry has long been recognized as one of the vital personal rights essential to the orderly pursuit of happiness by free men. Marriage is one of the 'basic **civil rights** of man,' fundamental to our very existence and survival."

Advocates for gay and lesbian rights have argued that the fundamental right to marriage should extend to same-sex couples. However, as of 2012, the Supreme Court had never accepted this argument. Should the Supreme Court agree that gay couples also enjoy marriage as a fundamental right, the ruling could effectively overrule decisions in more than 30 states.

Parental Rights In addition to marital rights, the Court has recognized several other family-related rights, including the rights of parents to raise their children as they see fit. In *Santosky v. Kramer* (1982), the Court noted that "freedom of personal choice in matters of family life is a fundamental liberty interest protected by the Fourteenth Amendment." Further, the Court recognized a "fundamental liberty interest of natural parents in the care, **custody**, and management of their child."

Custody of one's children is considered to be a fundamental right, although the Court in several cases has refused to protect the rights of unmarried fathers. Parents also have a fundamental right to keep their family together, as well as to control the upbringing of their children. This includes the rights of parents to raise their children without interference from others, including grandparents. In *Troxel v. Granville* (2000), the Court in a **plurality** opinion struck down a Washington statute that allowed any person to petition a court for visitation rights if visitation was in the best interests of the child. Under this case, even though a state statute may still allow courts to grant visitation right to grandparents (and perhaps others), such a law may not do so in a manner than infringes upon a parent's right to make decisions regarding the "care, custody, and control" of his or her children.

Other Fundamental Rights In addition to privacy rights, the Supreme Court has recognized several other fundamental rights. Among these rights are the following:

- Freedom of association
- Right to vote and participate in the electoral process
- Right to interstate travel
- Right to fairness in the criminal process

ADDITIONAL RESOURCES

Epstein, Lee, and Thomas G. Walker. *Constitutional Law for a Changing America: Institutional Powers and Constraints*. 7th ed. Washington, DC: CQ Press, 2011.

Rich, William J. *Modern Constitutional Law*. 3d ed. Eagan, Minn.: Thomson Reuters, 2011.

Rotunda, Ronald D., and John E. Nowak. *Treatise on Constitutional Law: Substance and Procedure*. 5th Ed. Eagan, MN: West, 2012.

ORGANIZATIONS

American Civil Liberties Union (ACLU)
125 Broad St., 18th Fl.
New York, NY 10004
Phone: (212) 549-2500
Email: info@aclu.org
URL: http://www.aclu.org/

Civil Rights Division, U.S. Department of Justice
950 Pennsylvania Avenue NW
Washington, DC 20530
Phone: (202) 514-2000
Toll Free: (800) 375-5283
URL: http://www.justice.gov/crt/

Human Rights Watch
350 Fifth Avenue
New York, NY 10118
Phone: (212) 490-4700
Fax: (212) 736-1300
URL: http://www.hrw.org

CIVIL RIGHTS

FIREARM LAWS

BACKGROUND

The Second Amendment of the **Constitution** provides: "A well regulated **Militia**, being necessary to the security of the free State, the right of the people to keep and bear Arms, shall not be infringed." The Supreme Court has historically defined the Second Amendment as giving states the right to maintain a militia separate from a federally controlled army. Courts have consistently held that the state and federal governments may lawfully regulate the sale, transfer, receipt, possession, and use of certain categories of firearms, as well as mandate who may and may not own a gun. As a result, there are numerous federal, state, and local laws in existence today, through which a person must navigate in order to lawfully possess a firearm.

For many years, the actual meaning of the Second Amendment's language was subject to dispute, and few Supreme Court cases ever addressed the Amendment. In *District of Columbia v. Heller* (2008), however, the Court decided that the Second Amendment guaranteed an individual right to bear arms. The decision struck down a District of Columbia law that prohibited ownership of handguns. However, the case has not had the widespread impact on **gun control** laws that some expected.

HISTORY OF GUN CONTROL LAWS

There were relatively few laws passed regarding gun control prior to the twentieth century. In fact, most legislation has been passed in the last fifty years.

- The National Firearms Act of 1934 was passed to hinder machine guns and sawed-off shotguns.

- The Firearms Act of 1938 provided for federal licensing of firearms dealers, regulated firearms transportation across state lines by dealers, outlawed the transportation of stolen guns with the manufacturer's mark eradicated or changed, and outlawed firearms from being carried by fugitives, indicted defendants or convicted felons.

- The National Firearms Act was later amended significantly by the Gun Control Act of 1968, putting more stringent control on licensed sales, buyer requirements, and the importation of sporting guns.
- Prompted by the fear of hijacking, the Undetectable Firearms Act of 1988 banned plastic and other undetectable guns.
- The Gun-Free School Zone Act of 1990 outlawed the knowing possession of firearms in school zones, and made it a crime to carry unloaded firearms within 1,000 feet of the grounds of any public or private school. The law was later held unconstitutional in 1995, in *United States vs. Lopez.*
- The 1982 assassination attempt on President Ronald Reagan resulted in the Brady Handgun Violence Prevention Act of 1993. The Brady Bill imposed a five-day waiting period before a handgun could be taken home by a buyer. Although the law also mandated that local law enforcement officers conduct background checks on prospective handgun purchasers buying from federally licensed dealers, this part of the law was struck down by the Supreme Court in 1997 in *Printz vs. United States* as unconstitutional.
- Congress passed the Federal Assault Weapons Ban as part of the Violent Crime Control and Law Enforcement Act of 1994, which prohibited manufacture of semi-automatic weapons for civilian use. The Ban expired by its own terms in 2004, and Congress had not reenacted it as of 2012.

ACQUISITION AND POSSESSION OF FIREARMS

Eligibility to Purchase or Own a Firearm In general, persons who are 21 years of age or older can purchase a firearm from a federally licensed dealer licensed to sell within the state. Purchasers of rifles or shotguns must be eighteen years or older and may purchase in any state.

However, the following classes of people are ineligible to possess, receive, ship, or transport firearms or ammunition:

- Those convicted of crimes punishable by **imprisonment** for over one year, except state misdemeanors punishable by two years or less.
- Fugitives from justice.
- Unlawful users of certain depressant, narcotic, or stimulant drugs.
- Those deemed legally incompetent and those committed to mental institutions.
- Illegal aliens.
- Citizens who have renounced their citizenship.

- Those persons dishonorably discharged from the armed services.
- Persons less than eighteen years of age for the purchase of a shotgun or rifle.
- Persons less than twenty-one years of age for the purchase of a firearm that is other than a shotgun or rifle.
- Persons subject to a court order that restrains such persons from harassing, **stalking**, or threatening an intimate partner.
- Persons convicted in any court of a **misdemeanor** crime of domestic violence.

Under limited conditions, exceptions may be granted by the U.S. Secretary of the Treasury, or through a **pardon**, restoration of rights, or setting aside of a **conviction**.

Acquiring Firearms Once a person has made the decision to purchase a gun, a federally licensed dealer will fill out a federal form 4473, which requires identifying and other information about the buyer, and record the make, model, and serial number of the firearm. The licensee initiates a background check on the buyer through the National Instant Criminal Background Check System (NCIS) to determine whether the buyer is not qualified to own a firearm. This NCIS background check may be immediate, or may take up to three business days. Prior to November 30, 1998, a five-day waiting period was required.

It is unlawful for an individual to purchase a firearm through mail-order from another state. Only licensed dealers are allowed to purchase firearms across state lines from other licensed dealers.

Provided that all other laws are complied with, a person may temporarily borrow or rent a firearm for lawful sporting purposes throughout the United States.

Antique Firearms Antique firearms and replicas are exempted from the above restrictions. Antique firearms are any firearms manufactured in or before 1898 (including any firearms with a matchlock, flintlock, percussion cap, or similar type of ignition system). Also, any replica of an antique firearm qualifies if the replica is not designed or redesigned for using rimfire or conventional centerfire ammunition; if the replica uses fixed ammunition which is no longer manufactured in the United States and which is not readily available; if the replica is of any muzzle loading rifle, shotgun, or pistol, which is designed to use black powder or a black powder substitute and which cannot use fixed ammunition. (Note: Antiques exemptions vary considerably under state laws).

Prohibited Firearms The 1994 Omnibus Crime Bill included a provision that prohibited the manufacture and sale to non-military and police, after September 13, 1994, of semi-automatic rifles equipped with detachable magazines and two or more of the following: bayonet lugs, flash suppressors, protruding pistol grips, folding stocks or threaded muzzles. There are similar guidelines on handguns and shotguns. Additionally, the manufacture and sale to non-military or police of "large-capacity" ammunition magazines (holding more than 10 rounds) were also outlawed. "Assault weapons" and "large" magazines manufactured before September 13, 1994, are exempt from the law.

Shipping Firearms Personally owned rifles and shotguns may be mailed or shipped only to dealers or manufacturers for any lawful purpose, including sale, repair, or customizing. A person may not ship a firearm to another private individual across state lines. Handguns may not be mailed but may be otherwise shipped to dealers or manufacturers for any lawful purpose. Shipping companies must be notified in writing of the contents of any shipments containing firearms or ammunition.

Transporting Firearms in Automobiles Under federal law, a person is allowed to transport a firearm across state lines from one place where it is legal to possess firearms to another place where it is legal to possess firearms. The firearm must be unloaded and in the trunk of a vehicle. If the vehicle has no trunk the firearm must be unloaded and in a locked container (not the glove compartment or console). This federal law overrides state or local laws.

Many states have laws governing the transportation of firearms. Also, many cities and localities have ordinances restricting their transportation. Travelers must be aware of these laws and comply with the legal requirements in each **jurisdiction**. There is no uniform state transportation procedure for firearms. Upon reaching one's destination, the state law—or, in some areas, municipal law—will control the ownership, possession, and transportation of the firearms.

It must be stressed that as soon as any firearm—handgun, rifle, or shotgun—is carried on or about the person, or placed in a vehicle where it is readily accessible, state and local firearms laws dealing with carrying come into play. If a person wishes to transport firearms in such a manner, it is advisable to contact the Attorney General's office in each state through which the person may travel. Reviewing an *NRA State Firearms Law Digest* is also recommended to determine whether a permit is needed and how to obtain one. While many states require a permit for this type of carrying, most will not issue such permits to non-residents, and other prohibit such carrying altogether.

Transporting Firearms on Aircraft Federal law prohibits the carrying of any firearm, concealed or unconcealed, on or about the person or in carry-on baggage while aboard an aircraft. Unloaded firearms not accessible to the passenger while aboard the aircraft are permitted when:

1. The passenger has notified the airline when checking the baggage that the firearm is in the baggage and that it is unloaded.
2. The firearm is carried in a hard-sided container.
3. The baggage in which the firearm is carried is locked and only the passenger checking the baggage retains a key. Moreover, the passenger should remain present during airport screening to provide the key, if necessary, and to lock the case afterward.
4. Ammunition must be securely packed in fiber (such as cardboard), wood or metal boxes or other packaging specifically designed for small amounts of ammunition.

Violations of transportation regulations may result in criminal prosecution and civil penalties up to $10,000 per violation. Because air carriers may impose additional requirements on the transportation of firearms and ammunition, the Transportation Security Administration advises travelers to check with specific air carriers to find out any additional transportation policies.

Transporting Firearms in Other Commercial Carriers Any passenger who owns or legally possesses a firearm being transported aboard any common or contract carrier in interstate or foreign **commerce** must deliver the unloaded firearm into the **custody** of the pilot, captain, conductor, or operator of such common or contract carrier for the duration of the trip. Check with each carrier before your trip to avoid problems.

Bus companies usually refuse to transport firearms. Trains usually allow the transportation of encased long guns if they are disassembled or the bolts removed.

Ammunition Ammunition may be bought or sold without regard for state **boundaries**. Ammunition shipments across state lines by commercial carriers are subject to strict explosives regulations. As with firearms, shipments of ammunition must be accompanied by a written notice of the shipment's contents.

It is illegal to manufacture or sell armor-piercing handgun ammunition.

Firearms in National and State Parks Generally, firearms are prohibited in national parks. Individuals in possession of an operable firearm in a national park are subject to **arrest**. Rules in state park systems vary, so inquiry should be made concerning the manner of legal firearms possession in a particular park system.

Hunters In many states, game wardens strictly enforce regulations dealing with the transportation of firearms during hunting season. Some states prohibit the carrying of uncased long guns in the passenger compartment of a vehicle after dark. For up-to-date information on these regulations, it is advisable to contact applicable fish and game authorities.

EFFECT OF *DISTRICT OF COLUMBIA V. HELLER*

In 1975, the District of Columbia approved a local law that prohibited ownership of handguns, subject to few exceptions. A group of residents challenged the law in federal court. The district court dismissed the case, but the D.C. Circuit Court of Appeals reversed, holding that the prohibition infringed on the resident's individual rights to bear arms. The Fifth Circuit had previously reached a similar conclusion, but the Ninth Circuit reached the opposite result.

The Supreme Court agreed to review the case, and in a close decision affirmed the appellate court's conclusion. Justice Antonin Scalia wrote the majority opinion, which concluded that the framers of the Constitution intended to protect each individual's right to bear arms. Two years later, the Court in *McDonald v. Chicago* ruled that the right to bear arms applied to the states as well as to the federal government.

Supporters of gun rights expected the decision to have a significant effect on gun-control laws, but that was not the case in the years immediately following the case. Justice Scalia's opinion included the statement, "Nothing in our opinion should be taken to cast doubt on longstanding prohibitions on the possession of firearms by felons and the mentally ill, or laws forbidding the carrying of firearms in sensitive places such as schools and government buildings, or laws imposing conditions on the commercial sale of arms." Lower federal courts construing the Court's decision in *Heller* have concluded that existing gun-control laws are constitutional. In fact, no federal court as of 2012 had held that a gun-control law is unconstitutional under *Heller*.

STATE AND LOCAL RESTRICTIONS ON THE POSSESSION AND TRANSPORTATION OF FIREARMS

Most states permit the carrying of a concealed weapon by a resident who has been granted a permit to do so.

Four states, Alaska, Arizona, Vermont, and Wyoming, allow residents to carry a concealed weapon without obtaining a permit. Only the State of Illinois completely prohibits the carrying of concealed weapons. Nine states are known as "may issue" states because give local law enforcement some discretion in issuing a permit. In some of these states, such as Hawaii, Maryland, and New Jersey, officials frequently decline permit applications. However, in other states, such as Alabama and Connecticut, officials almost always issue the permits. Other states are known as "shall issue" states because officials must issue a permit when an applicant meets **statutory** requirements.

Nonresident travelers should check with appropriate governmental departments before traveling to another jurisdiction with a concealed weapon; concealed weapons laws are often different for nonresidents than they are for residents.

It is important to check with local authorities a complete listing of restrictions on carrying concealed weapons in a particular state. Many states restrict carrying in bars, restaurants (where alcohol is served), establishments where packaged alcohol is sold, schools, colleges, universities, churches, parks, sporting events, correctional facilities, courthouses, federal and state government offices/buildings, banks, airport terminals, police stations, polling places, any posted private property restricting the carrying of concealed firearms, etc. In addition to state restrictions, federal law prohibits carrying on military bases, in national parks and in the sterile area of airports. National forests usually follow laws of the states in which they are located.

SPECIAL RULES GOVERNING TRAVELING WITH FIREARMS IN OTHER COUNTRIES

Most countries have special laws governing the possession and transportation of firearms by nonresidents, and in many countries individual possession of firearms is illegal. Travelers should contact the appropriate government departments to learn about the laws prior to traveling. All firearms must be declared and registered with United States Customs on form 4457. This registration must be done at a U.S. Customs and Border Protection office before leaving the U.S.

The following are summaries for Canada and Mexico.

CANADA: Visitors who wish to bring firearms into Canada must declare the firearms in writing with a "Non-Resident Firearms Declaration" form. Multiple firearms may be declared on the same form. Three copies of the unsigned declaration must be presented to a Canadian customs officer at the border. The declaration costs $50 (Canadian) and serves as a temporary license and registration certificate for up to 60 days. Visitors who plan to borrow a weapon in Canada must obtain in advance a "Temporary Firearms Borrowing license" for $30 (Canadian).

Canadian authorities recommend that visitors fill out the declaration form and make copies before arrival at the port-of-entry. Requests for photocopies at the border may be denied. The applicant is required to sign the form in front of a Customs officer at the point of entry.

Canada has three classes of firearms: non-restricted (most ordinary rifles and shotguns); restricted (mainly handguns); and prohibited (full automatics, converted automatics, handguns with a barrel length of 4 inches or less, and .25 or .32 caliber handguns among others). Prohibited firearms are not allowed in the country, but restricted firearms are allowed if an "Authorization to Transport" (ATT) has been obtained from a provincial or territorial Chief Firearms Officer before arrival at the point of entry into Canada. An ATT will not be authorized for restricted firearms intended for hunting or self-protection.

More information can be obtained from the Canadian Firearms Centre via the Internet at http://www.rcmp-grc.gc.ca/cfp-pcaf/index-eng.htm, under the heading "Visitors/Non-residents" or by calling the Canadian Firearms Centre information line.

MEXICO: According to the U.S. Department of State, Bureau of Consular Affairs, U.S. travelers to Mexico should leave their weapons at home, unless they have obtained written permission from Mexican government authorities in advance of their visit. Many U.S. residents are arrested or fined every year for firearms violations in Mexico. Many of these offenders are licensed to carry the firearms in the U.S. and only inadvertently transported a firearm to Mexico without any intention of violating the Mexican law.

ADDITIONAL RESOURCES

Spitzer, Robert J. *The Politics of Gun Control.* 4th ed. Washington, D.C.: CQ Press, 2008.

Utter, Glenn H. *Encyclopedia of Gun Control and Gun Rights.* Phoenix, AZ: Oryx Press, 2000.

Valdez, Angela, and John E. Ferguson, Jr. *Gun Control.* 2d ed. New York: Chelsea House, 2012.

ORGANIZATIONS

Brady Center to Prevent Gun Violence
1225 Eye St. NW, Ste, 1100
Washington, DC 20005
Phone: (202) 289-7319
Fax: (202) 408-1851
URL: http://www.cphv.org

Citizens Committee for the Right to Keep and Bear Arms (CCRKBA)
Liberty Park
12500 NE 10th Pl.
Bellevue, WA 98005
Phone: (425) 454-4911
Email: AdminForWeb@ccrkba.org
URL: http://www.ccrkba.org

National Rifle Association of America (NRA)
11250 Waples Mill Rd.
Fairfax, VA 22030
Toll Free: (800) 672-3888
Email: comm@nrahq.org
URL: http://www.nra.org

CIVIL RIGHTS

RACIAL DISCRIMINATION

Sections within this essay

BACKGROUND

Citizens of the United States are protected against racial **discrimination** by many laws, including Constitutional protections, **civil rights** statutes, and civil rights regulations. The Fourteenth Amendment, which provides all citizens with **equal protection** of the laws, was ratified in 1868, but the most significant changes in the law with respect to racial discrimination have occurred in the Since the 1950s. In this time, a number of landmark events have occurred and a number of landmark laws have been passed that prevent discrimination on the basis of race in many circumstances.

- In 1954, the U.S. Supreme Court ruled in *Brown v. Board of Education* that the Equal Protection Clause of the Fourteenth Amendment to the United States Constitution prohibited **segregation** in public schools on the basis of race. The Court then required public school districts to begin the process of integration "with all deliberate speed."

- The Civil Rights Act of 1964 brought about the most significant changes in civil rights protection in the history of the country. It prohibited racial and other discrimination in employment, education, and use of public accommodations and facilities.

- The **Voting Rights Act of 1965** prevented racial and other forms of discrimination with respect to access to the ballots.

- The Fair Housing Act, part of the Civil Rights Act of 1968, prohibited discrimination in the sale and renting of housing. It also extended these prohibitions to lending and other financial institutions.

- The Civil Rights Act of 1991 was designed to strengthen and improve previous civil rights legislation.

Civil rights laws do not render every form of racial discrimination unlawful. For example, laws do not proscribe general notions of racial prejudice by private individuals in most circumstances. However, when racial prejudices or preferences interfere with the rights of others, then the law is more likely to provide protection.

This distinction applies to government entities or business entities engaged in interstate **commerce**.

CONSTITUTIONAL PROTECTION AGAINST RACIAL DISCRIMINATION

Supreme Court's Involvement in Protections Against Racial Discrimination The U.S. Supreme Court has been called upon on numerous occasions to address the constitutionality of state actions that may involve racial discrimination. Prior to the enactment of the Thirteenth, Fourteenth, and Fifteenth Amendments to the U.S. Constitution, the Court rendered several decisions on the issue of slavery, many of which affected the future of the United States regarding the Civil War. The most significant of these decisions occurred in 1857, when the Court in *Scott v. Sanford* decided that slaves were not "citizens" as the term was used in the Constitution. The Court also determined Congress could not constitutionally prohibit slavery in the territories.

After the enactment of the Constitutional Amendments during the reconstruction period after the Civil War, the Court was called upon to decide a number of issues related to these amendments and civil rights legislation passed during this period. The most significant of these cases was called the **Civil Rights Cases**, in which the court restricted considerably the power of Congress to proscribe discrimination by operators of public accommodations. In 1896, the Court ruled in *Plessy v. Ferguson* that the Constitution did not prohibit states from enacting laws that distinguished people of different races. In the fifty years after *Plessy v. Ferguson*, states could constitutionally segregate members of different races under the "separate-but-equal" doctrine. The Court reversed its position in 1954 with the decision in *Brown v. Board of Education*, which also led to the enactment of the civil rights legislation by Congress.

State Action The Supreme Court has long held that the Constitution applies only to the actions of government, not to the actions of private individuals or entities. This restriction traditionally enabled private individuals to circumvent the rights provided in the Constitution. The first **casualty** was the civil rights statutes passed during Reconstruction after the Civil War. Subsequent cases involved such efforts as those by private individuals to prevent blacks from voting. Since these actions were not officially considered "state actions," the Court held that the Constitution did not apply.

The Court in more modern times has taken a more liberal view of which actions constitute state actions. In some circumstances, a state's approval of private action may constitute state action. Even if an action is not considered a state action, however, modern civil rights legislation may provide protection against private actions that is equivalent to constitutional protection.

Thirteenth Amendment Protections The United States abolished slavery in the United States when it ratified the Thirteenth Amendment in 1865. Under this amendment, slavery and involuntary servitude, except as punishment for crimes, were outlawed. The amendment also permitted Congress to enact legislation to enforce this amendment. The Supreme Court restricted Congressional power to enforce the act in the Civil Rights Cases in 1883, and relatively little **litigation** occurred over the next eighty years. However, the Court held in the 1968 case of *Jones v. Alfred H. Mayer Co.* that Congressional authority to proscribe private discrimination was granted by the Thirteenth Amendment. Since that time, the Thirteenth Amendment has served as part of the basis of authority under which Congress may enact civil rights legislation.

Fourteenth Amendment Protections One of the more controversial laws in the history of the United States is the Fourteenth Amendment to the United States. This amendment prohibits government from denying equal protection of the laws or **due process of law** to the citizens of the United States. Defining "equal protection" and "due process," however, has perplexed the U.S. Supreme Court, lower federal courts, and state courts since the **ratification** of the amendment in 1868. Although ironically the Equal Protection Clause was the basis for such historic doctrines as "separate-but-equal" in *Plessy v. Ferguson*, it has also served as the basic constitutional protection against racial discrimination by government entities in modern civil rights **jurisprudence**.

Laws designed to give preferences to whites to the detriment of members of the minority races are clearly unconstitutional. More difficult questions are raised with respect to **affirmative action** programs designed to give minorities opportunities they may lack due to a history of discrimination. Since the late 1980s, the Supreme Court has struck down several of these programs as unconstitutional. Similar problems have been raised with respect to efforts to **gerrymander** voting districts in order to ensure that minority (or nonminority) political candidates have a better chance to win seats. Unless such efforts have been designed to remedy specific instances of discrimination, they are most likely in violation of the Equal Protection Clause.

Fifteenth Amendment Protection All citizens are guaranteed the right to vote through the Fifteenth Amendment. This amendment, ratified in 1870, was designed to eradicate efforts to disenfranchise blacks during Reconstruction following the Civil War. The Supreme Court limited the application of this amendment in several cases decided between 1876 and 1903, and the Court has traditionally placed much more weight on the Fourteenth Amendment than the Fifteenth Amendment with respect to racial discrimination. This tendency applies even in cases involving allegations of **infringement** on the right to vote. The most significant exception was the case of *Smith v. Allwright* in 1944, in which the Supreme Court invalidated an election on the basis of Fifteenth Amendment protections.

State Protections Against Racial Discrimination The Thirteenth, Fourteenth, and Fifteenth Amendments, by their own terms, apply to the state governments. The Fourteenth Amendment, for example, states, "No State shall . . . deny to any person within its **jurisdiction** the equal protection of the laws." State constitutions and state laws can provide greater protection to prevent racial discrimination than federal constitution guarantees. Since the U.S. Constitution is the supreme law of the land, no state constitution or **statute** can restrict the rights granted to all citizens of the United States. In other words, the U.S. Constitution provides the minimum level of rights to citizens in this country, and states may only raise this level rather than reduce it.

Judicial Review of Constitutional Violations Supreme Court jurisprudence in the area of racial discrimination is often very confusing due to the terminology used when the Court reviews these cases. When the government classifies people differently, courts will employ various levels of scrutiny to determine whether that classification is constitutionally permissible. Many classifications are generally permissible, such as those classifications that differentiate on the basis of income for tax purposes. These classifications are presumed constitutional and will be upheld unless a party can prove that the government has no rational basis for its decision.

If a government entity makes a classification based on race, courts employ a heightened standard of review. These classifications are presumed to be unconstitutional and will be upheld only if the government can prove that the program is narrowly tailored to address a compelling government interest. Very few government programs that make racial classifications can satisfy strict scrutiny, including many affirmative action programs. The Court's position in this area can shift as new justices join the Court.

CIVIL RIGHTS ACTS AND THEIR APPLICATIONS

History of Civil Rights Acts Congress attempted to provide a number of rights to members of minority races in the Civil Rights Act of 1875. However, the Supreme Court in the Civil Rights Cases in 1883 significantly curtailed this effort by ruling that Congress did not have the authority to restrict segregation in public accommodations and public conveyances. Only state governments had the power to address racial discrimination by private actors. After the decision in *Plessy v. Ferguson,* states were able to enact legislation segregating the different races, and Congress was powerless to restrict these laws.

Beginning primarily with the Supreme Court's decision in *Brown v. Board of Education* in 1954, the Court established a more expansive view of congressional authority in the area of racial discrimination. Congress enacted a number of statutes between 1957 and 1968 that granted equal rights to all races in education, employment, voting, and many other areas relevant to interstate commerce.

Employment Employers are prohibited from discriminating on the basis of race, sex, religion, or national origin by the provisions of Title VII of the Civil Rights Act of 1964. To enforce this Act, which neither defines discrimination nor sets forth mechanisms for enforcement, Congress established the Equal Employment Opportunity Commission (EEOC). The EEOC views discrimination on a broad level, considering "discrimination" to include not only blatant acts of **bias** but also programs that have a disparate impact on minorities. The EEOC has enacted numerous regulations that give guidance to employers regarding employment discrimination.

Voting Despite the enactment of the Fifteenth Amendment, governments and private individuals used a variety of tactics to prevent blacks from exercising their right to vote. Such tactics included poll taxes, property requirements, intimidation, and other mechanisms designed to discourage blacks from voting. To address these inequities, Congress in 1965 passed the Voting Rights Act. Among other provisions, this Act prohibited requirements that voters take literacy tests or pay poll taxes prior to receiving the right to vote. Provisions in other statutes further enhanced voting rights. The Equal Protection Clause of the Fourteenth Amendment provides additional protection against discrimination in voting.

Questions focusing on the Voting Right Act typically involve efforts among state or local governments to make changes to elections, such as redistricting efforts. Governmental units in several states must "preclear" any changes to election procedures because these states have histories of racial discrimination. Preclearance means that the governmental unit must submit the changes to the Justice Department or to a three-judge panel of the U.S. District Court for the District of Columbia.

Education School segregation and desegregation were among the most controversial topics in the civil rights movement in the 1950s and 1960s. The Supreme Court's decision in *Brown v. Board of Education* outlawed segregation of blacks and whites in public schools, although studies have shown that the educational levels of white students and minority students remains unequal. The Civil Rights Act of 1964 prohibits discrimination in education on the basis of race but does not contain mechanisms to ensure that education of all students, minority or nonminority, remains entirely equal.

Initial efforts to ensure educational equality focused on forced integration of students of different races. This effort involved the process of busing students from areas with a largely black population to schools in traditionally white areas. Many of these efforts have been found to be unconstitutional. Schools in higher education sought to provide some level of equality by mandating that a certain number of minorities fill positions in entering classes. However, the Supreme Court in *Bakke v. Board of Regents* ruled that such a requirement violated the Equal Protection Clause. Although some schools continue to consider race as a factor in college admissions, the legality of such considerations are progressively becoming more questionable. For example, in 1996, the Fifth Circuit Court of Appeals ruled in the 1996 case of *Hopwood v. Texas* that the University of Texas School of Law could not consider race as a factor in the admission of law students, even though the law school traditionally did not admit many minorities. In the cases of *Gratz v. Bollinger* and *Grutter v. Bollinger*, the issue of race was considered acceptable in one scenario but not in another. Jennifer Gratz was denied admission to the University of Michigan's undergraduate program in 1995, and in 1997 Barbara Grutter was denied admission to the university's law school. Both women were white, and they claimed that the university's admissions program discriminated against white students. The university was using a point system for undergraduate admissions, assigning extra points to what it considered "underrepresented" racial and ethnic minorities. Since it also assigned extra points to athletes, children of alumni, and men enrolling in the nursing school, the university felt there was nothing problematic with assigning points for race as well. The law school did not have a point system, but it did use race used as a determining factor because, the university maintained, it helped promote cross-racial understanding. In 2003 the U.S. Supreme Court voted 6-3 to strike down the undergraduate point system, but it upheld the law school's less rigid program in a 5-4 vote. In so doing, the courts acknowledged that race could be a factor in admissions, but only one of several of equal weight.

Housing Many studies have shown a relationship between school segregation and residential segregation. If whites and minorities are segregated in the areas in which they live, the schools in these areas are more likely to be segregated as well. Some efforts to desegregate schools focused on busing students from proportionately black areas to proportionately white areas. Even these efforts, however, do not address the problem with segregation in housing. Congress passed the Fair Housing Act in 1968 to prohibit real estate sellers, landlords, and others from discriminating on the basis of race. However, this Act was not enforced or applied routinely for several years, and proving discrimination in housing can be difficult. Although the legal mechanisms to prevent discrimination are in place, societal changes are likely to be necessary to eradicate discrimination in this area.

Remedies for Civil Rights Violations The Civil Rights Act of 1991 and other federal statutes permit civil actions for a deprivation of civil rights, including violations of constitutional protections, violations of civil rights legislation, or any other antidiscrimination law. Victims of racial discrimination may recover monetary damages, including **punitive damages** and attorney's fees in appropriate circumstances. Victims may also seek an injunction or other equitable remedy.

STATE PROVISIONS REGARDING RACIAL DISCRIMINATION

Many states have established their own rights related to protection of civil rights, including racial discrimination. Several of these states have established agencies or delegated authority to existing agencies to handle civil rights claims. In some states, civil rights law preempts other ordinary tort actions and in many cases limits the amount of recovery available to litigants with complaints related to violations of civil rights.

ALABAMA: Alabama has not enacted legislation dealing specifically with civil rights.

ALASKA: Complaints for relevant civil rights violations are submitted to the Commission for **Human Rights**. Private actions are permitted, and causes of action are not preempted by administrative action. The **statute of limitations** for a civil rights action is one year.

ARIZONA: Complaints for relevant civil rights violations are submitted to the Civil Rights Advisory Board. Private actions are permitted, and causes of action are not preempted by administrative action. The statute of limitations for a civil rights action is generally two years.

ARKANSAS: Private actions are permitted, except for those related to discrimination in public employment. Causes of action are not preempted by administrative action.

CALIFORNIA: Complaints for relevant civil rights violations are submitted to the Department of Employment and Housing. Private actions are permitted, and causes of action are not preempted by administrative action. The statute of limitations for a civil rights action is three years.

COLORADO: Complaints for relevant civil rights violations are submitted to the Civil Rights Commission. Private actions are permitted for some causes of action, but causes of action are preempted by administrative action. The statute of limitations for a civil rights action is sixty days.

CONNECTICUT: Complaints for relevant civil rights violations are submitted to the Commission on Human Rights and Opportunities. Private actions are permitted, and only certain causes of action are preempted by administrative action.

DELAWARE: Complaints for relevant civil rights violations are submitted to the Human Relations Commission or Department of Labor. Some private actions are permitted, but causes of action are preempted by administrative action. The statutes of limitations vary depending on the complaint.

DISTRICT OF COLUMBIA: Complaints for relevant civil rights violations are submitted to the Commission on Human Rights. Private actions are permitted, and causes of action are not preempted by administrative action. The statute of limitations for a civil rights action is one year.

FLORIDA: Complaints for relevant civil rights violations are submitted to the Commission for Human Relations. Private actions are not permitted, and causes of action are preempted by administrative action. The statute of limitations for a civil rights action is eighty days.

GEORGIA: Some private causes of action are permitted, but none is preempted by administrative action.

HAWAII: Complaints for relevant civil rights violations are submitted to the Civil Rights Commission or Department of Commerce and Consumer Affairs. Private actions are not permitted, and causes of action are preempted by administrative action. The statute of limitations for a civil rights action is ninety days.

IDAHO: Complaints for relevant civil rights violations are submitted to the Commission on Human Rights. Private actions are permitted, and causes of action are not preempted by administrative action. The statute of limitations for a civil rights action is two years.

ILLINOIS: Complaints for relevant civil rights violations are submitted to the Human Rights Commission and Department of Human Rights. Some private actions are permitted, but causes of action are preempted by administrative action. The statute of limitations for a civil rights action is 180 days.

INDIANA: Complaints for relevant civil rights violations are submitted to the Civil Rights Commission. Private actions are permitted, and causes of action are not preempted by administrative action.

IOWA: Complaints for relevant civil rights violations are submitted to the Civil Rights Commission. Private actions are permitted, but causes of action are preempted by administrative action. The statute of limitations for a civil rights action is 180 days.

KANSAS: Complaints for relevant civil rights violations are submitted to the Commission on Human Rights. Some private actions are permitted, but causes of action are preempted by administrative action. The statutes of limitations for civil rights actions vary depending on the complaint.

KENTUCKY: Complaints for relevant civil rights violations are submitted to the Commission on Human Rights. Private actions are permitted, but causes of action are preempted by administrative action. The statute of limitations for a civil rights action is 180 days.

LOUISIANA: Louisiana civil rights statutes are limited to those regarding the handicapped.

MAINE: Complaints for relevant civil rights violations are submitted to the Human Rights Commission. Private actions are permitted, but causes of action are preempted by administrative action. The statute of limitations for a civil rights action is six months.

MARYLAND: Complaints for relevant civil rights violations are submitted to the Commission on Human Relations. Private actions are not permitted, and causes of action are preempted by administrative action. The statute of limitations for a civil rights action is six months.

MASSACHUSETTS: Complaints for relevant civil rights violations are submitted to the Commission Against Discrimination. Some private actions are permitted, and some causes of action are preempted by administrative action. The statutes of limitations vary depending on the complaint.

MICHIGAN: Complaints for relevant civil rights violations are submitted to the Civil Rights Commission. Private actions are permitted, and causes of action are not preempted by administrative action.

MINNESOTA: Complaints for relevant civil rights violations are submitted to the Department of Human Rights. Private actions are permitted, and causes of action are not preempted by administrative action. The statute of limitations for a civil rights action is one year.

MISSISSIPPI: Complaints for relevant civil rights violations are submitted to the Home Corporation Oversight Committee. Private actions are not permitted, and causes of action are preempted by administrative action.

MISSOURI: Complaints for relevant civil rights violations are submitted to the Commission on Human Rights. Some private actions are permitted, and some causes of action are preempted by administrative action. The statutes of limitations vary depending on the complaint.

MONTANA: Complaints for relevant civil rights violations are submitted to the Commission for Human Rights. Some private actions are permitted, and some causes of action are preempted by administrative action. The statutes of limitations vary depending on the complaint.

NEBRASKA: Complaints for relevant civil rights violations are submitted to the Equal Opportunity Commission. Private actions are permitted, but some causes of action are preempted by administrative action. The statute of limitations for a civil rights action is 180 days.

NEVADA: Complaints for relevant civil rights violations are submitted to the Equal Rights Commission, Labor Commission, or Banking Division. Private actions are permitted, but some causes of action are preempted by administrative action. The statutes of limitations vary depending on the complaint.

NEW HAMPSHIRE: Complaints for relevant civil rights violations are submitted to the Commission for Human Rights. Private actions are permitted, and causes of action are not preempted by administrative action. The statute of limitations for a civil rights action is 180 days.

NEW JERSEY: Complaints for relevant civil rights violations are submitted to the Division on Human Rights. Private actions are permitted, and causes of action are not preempted by administrative action. The statute of limitations for a civil rights action is 180 days.

NEW MEXICO: Complaints for relevant civil rights violations are submitted to the Human Rights Commission. Private actions are permitted, but causes of action are preempted by administrative action. The statute of limitations for a civil rights action is 180 days.

NEW YORK: Complaints for relevant civil rights violations are submitted to the Division of Human Rights, Banking Department, or State Human Rights Appeal Board. Private actions are permitted, and causes of action are not preempted by administrative action. The statute of limitations for a civil rights action is usually one year.

NORTH CAROLINA: Complaints for relevant civil rights violations are submitted to the Human Relations Commission. Private actions are not permitted, and causes of action are not preempted by administrative action.

NORTH DAKOTA: Complaints for relevant civil rights violations are submitted to the Department of Labor. Private actions are permitted, and causes of action are not preempted by administrative action. The statutes of limitations vary depending on the complaint.

OHIO: Complaints for relevant civil rights violations are submitted to the Civil Rights Commission. Some private actions are permitted, and causes of action are preempted by administrative action. The statutes of limitations vary depending on the complaint.

OKLAHOMA: Complaints for relevant civil rights violations are submitted to the Human Rights Commission. Private actions are not permitted, and causes of action are preempted by administrative action. The statute of limitations for a civil rights action is 180 days.

OREGON: Complaints for relevant civil rights violations are submitted to the Bureau of Labor and Industries. Private actions are permitted, and causes of action are not preempted by administrative action. The statute of limitations for a civil rights action is one year.

PENNSYLVANIA: Complaints for relevant civil rights violations are submitted to the Human Rights Commission. Private actions are permitted, and causes of action are not preempted by administrative action. The statute of limitations for a civil rights action is 180 days.

RHODE ISLAND: Complaints for relevant civil rights violations are submitted to the Commission for Human Rights or the Department of Labor. Some private actions are permitted, and some causes of action are preempted by administrative action. The statutes of limitations vary depending on the complaint.

SOUTH CAROLINA: Complaints for relevant civil rights violations arc submitted to the Human Affairs Commission. Private actions are permitted, and causes of action are not preempted by administrative action. The statute of limitations for a civil rights action is 180 days.

SOUTH DAKOTA: Complaints for relevant civil rights violations are submitted to the Commission of Humanities. Private actions are permitted, and causes of action arc not preempted by administrative action. The statutes of limitations vary depending on the complaint.

TENNESSEE: Complaints for relevant civil rights violations are submitted to the Human Rights Commission. Private actions are permitted, and causes of action are not preempted by administrative action. The statutes of limitations vary depending on the complaint.

TEXAS: Complaints for relevant civil rights violations are submitted to the Department of Human Resources. Private actions are permitted, and causes of action are not preempted by administrative action.

UTAH: Complaints for relevant civil rights violations are submitted to the Antidiscrimination Division. Some private actions are permitted, and some causes of action are preempted by administrative action. The statutes of limitations vary depending on the complaint.

VERMONT: Complaints for relevant civil rights violations are submitted to the Human Rights Commission. Private actions are permitted, and causes of action are not preempted by administrative action. The statutes of limitations vary depending on the complaint.

VIRGINIA: Private actions are permitted, and causes of action are not preempted by administrative action. The statutes of limitations vary depending on the complaint.

WASHINGTON: Complaints for relevant civil rights violations are submitted to the Washington State Human Rights Commission. Private actions are permitted, and causes of action are not preempted by administrative action. The statute of limitations for a civil rights action is six months

WEST VIRGINIA: Complaints for relevant civil rights violations are submitted to the Human Rights Commission. Private actions are permitted, and causes of action are not preempted by administrative action. The statute of limitations for a civil rights action is 180 days.

WISCONSIN: Complaints for relevant civil rights violations are submitted to the Department of Industry, Labor, and Human Relations. Some private actions are permitted, and some causes of action are preempted by administrative action. The statutes of limitations vary depending on the complaint.

WYOMING: Complaints for relevant civil rights violations are submitted to the Fair Employment Commission. Private actions are permitted, and causes of action are not preempted by administrative action. The statute of limitations for a civil rights action is two years.

ADDITIONAL RESOURCES

Barron, Jerome A., and C. Thomas Dienes. *Constitutional Civil Rights in a Nutshell.* 7th ed. Eagan, MN: West, Thomson Reuters, 2009.

Davis, Timothy, Kevin R. Johnson, and George A. Martinez. *A Reader on Race, Civil Rights, and American Law: A Multiracial Approach.* Durham, NC: Carolina Academic Press, 2001.

Graham, Hugh Davis. *The Civil Rights Era: Origins and Development of National Policy.* New York: Oxford University Press, 1990.

Hall, Kermit L., James W. Ely Jr., and Joel B. Grossman, eds. *Oxford Companion to the Supreme Court.* 2d ed. New York: Oxford University Press, 2005.

Higginbotham, F. Michael. *Race Law: Cases, Commentary, and Questions.* Durham, NC: Carolina Academic Press, 2001.

ORGANIZATIONS

American Civil Liberties Union (ACLU)
125 Broad St., 18th Fl.
New York, NY 10004
Phone: (212) 549-2500
Email: info@aclu.org
URL: http://www.aclu.org/

Center for Equal Opportunity (CEO)
7700 Leesburg Pike

Falls Church, VA 22043
Phone: (703) 442-0066
Email: comment@ceousa.org
URL: http://www.ceousa.org/

National Association for the Advancement of Colored People (NAACP)

4805 Mt. Hope Drive
Baltimore, MD 21215

Phone: (410) 580-5777
URL: http://www.naacp.org/

U.S. Equal Employment Opportunity Commission (EEOC)

1801 L Street, N.W.
Washington, DC 20507
Phone: (202) 663-4900
URL: http://www.eeoc.gov/

CIVIL RIGHTS

SEXUAL DISCRIMINATION

Sections within this essay:

- Background
- The Equal Pay Act
- Title VII of the Civil Rights Act
- Civil Rights Act of 1991
- Title IX
- The Pregnancy Discrimination Act and Family and Medical Leave Act
- Supreme Court Standards for Gender Discrimination
- Sexual Harassment
- State Equal Pay Laws
- Additional Resources

BACKGROUND

"Remember the ladies," Abigail Adams told her husband John in 1776 while he was helping to draft the Declaration of Independence. Unfortunately, throughout most of U.S. history, the ladies were not remembered when it came to laws, as women were treated at best as second-class citizens and at worst as the virtual property of their husbands. U.S. law has witnessed a gender revolution, starting with the passage of the Equal Pay Act in 1963. In the process, areas of the law that had never existed before, such as **sexual harassment litigation**, were articulated and applied.

Since Congress enacted the Equal Pay Act, several other laws affecting the rights of women have been enacted. They include:

- Title VII of the Civil Rights Act of 1964
- The Civil Rights Act of 1991, which expanded some of the protections granted by Title VII
- Title IX of the Education Amendments of 1972 (Title IX)
- The Pregnancy Discrimination Act of 1978
- The **Family and Medical Leave Act** of 1993

THE EQUAL PAY ACT

The Equal Pay Act, passed in 1963, was the first law to address gender inequality in the workplace and one of the first laws to benefit women explicitly since they gained the right to vote earlier in the century. The Equal Pay Act guaranteed equal pay for equal work for men and women. For the act to take effect, men and women must be employed under similar working conditions, and equal is defined as "equal skill, effort and responsibility." Overtime and travel are included among the provisions of the act.

The Equal Pay Act is part of the **Fair Labor Standards Act**, although it is unlike the other parts of the act in that there are no exceptions for executive, administrative, professional employees, or outside salespeople. However, the Equal Pay Act contains the same business exceptions as the Fair Labor Standards Act and covers only employees "engaged in commerce." In practice, this law applies to vast majority of businesses in the country.

There are four affirmative defenses to the Equal Pay Act: merit, production, seniority, and "factor other than sex." The most litigated of these defenses is the "factor other than sex" because of the ambiguous nature of the clause. For example, prior wages, profitability of the company, and evaluation of a personal interview have all been held to be a factor other than sex justifying pay discrepancies between men and women under the Equal Pay Act.

TITLE VII OF THE CIVIL RIGHTS ACT

Title VII, passed in 1964, is arguably the most important legislation protecting the equality of women in the workplace. Title VII, which was originally proposed as an anti-racial discrimination bill, included sex as a protected class largely as an afterthought. The **amendment** adding the term sex was proposed by a conservative legislator from Virginia, probably as a way of scuttling the whole bill. Despite this, Title VII passed with its protections against sexual discrimination intact.

Title VII prohibits discrimination by employers, employment agencies, and labor organizations with 15 or more full-time employees on the basis of race, color, religion, sex, or national origin. It applies to pre-interview advertising, interviewing, hiring, discharge, compensation, promotion, classification, training, apprenticeships, referrals for employment, union membership, terms, working conditions, working atmosphere, seniority, reassignment, and all other "privileges of employment."

The operative question in a Title VII sex discrimination case is whether the litigant has suffered unequal treatment because of his or her sex. Courts look at whether the disparate treatment of the employee was sex-related. If it was, it is actionable under Title VII unless the employer uses an affirmative defense; if not, it is not actionable.

Affirmative defenses under Title VII include all of the affirmative defenses under the Equal Pay Act. In addition, defenses include situations in which sex is a bona fide occupational requirement (BFOQ) for the job; when sex discrimination occurs as a result of adhering to a bona fide seniority system (unless the system perpetuates past effects of sex discrimination); or when sex discrimination is justified by "business necessity."

When employers assert a mixed motive under Title VII, that is, the action taken against the employee has both an discriminatory and non-discriminatory reason, the employer must prove by a preponderance of **evidence** that the employment decision would have been made absent the discriminatory factors.

Plaintiffs can also sue under Title VII using a theory of "disparate impact" that is, showing that while an employment decision or policy is not discriminatory on its face, it has resulted in discrimination on the basis of sex. The intent of discrimination can be inferred by the impact of the policy.

Affirmative action for women is allowed under Title VII. In the decision of *Johnson v. Transportation Agency, Santa Clara County,* the Supreme Court determined an affirmative action program that promoted a woman over a more qualified man was legal under Title VII as long as her sex was just one factor in the decision, and the affirmative action plan was carefully drafted to remedy the effects of past discrimination.

THE CIVIL RIGHTS ACT OF 1991

The Civil Rights Act of 1991 enhanced the protections granted in Title VII. It added compensatory (i.e., pain and suffering) damages and **punitive damages**, sometimes known as exemplary damages, for all victims of intentional **discrimination**. (Previously these had only been available for victims of racial discrimination.) These damages are capped from $50,000 for employers with 100 or fewer employees to $300,000 for employers with more than 500 employees. It also added a right to a **jury** trial. Previously, sex discrimination plaintiffs had to file an Equal Pay Act or **common law fraud** claim to get a jury trial.

The Act also made it easier to file disparate impact cases by reversing a 1989 Supreme Court decision and establishing that to disprove a disparate impact charge, employers must show that the practice is job related for the position in question and consistent with business necessity. In addition, the Act allows employees to file a discrimination charge at the time they are affected by the discrimination, rather than when they are first notified of the discriminatory act and the Act applies Title VII to American citizens living overseas.

TITLE IX

Title IX addresses sexual discrimination in the area of education. It applies to all federally funded educational institutions, including any college or university "any part of which is extended federal financial assistance." It provides that no person shall be excluded from participation in or be subjected to discrimination on the basis of sex in any educational activity. Title IX has wrought an enormous change on American schools and universities since its enactment in 1972. It has forced schools to equalize sports programs between men and women, resulting in a boom for women's athletics. It has caused the Supreme Court to hold single sex public colleges to be unconstitutional, most famously in the case of the Virginia Military Institute. Many hold Title IX responsible for the tremendous increase in women in postsecondary graduate schools since 1970, to the point where women now make up half of all law and medical students in the country.

THE PREGNANCY DISCRIMINATION ACT AND FAMILY AND MEDICAL LEAVE ACT

The Pregnancy Discrimination Act of 1978 protects pregnant women by stating that employers must treat pregnancy as a temporary **disability**, and they may not refuse to hire a woman or fire her because she is pregnant or compel her to take maternity leave.

The Family and Medical Leave Act of 1993 built upon the rights granted under the Pregnancy Discrimination Act. This act applies to employers of 50 or more employees, and permits up to 12 weeks of unpaid leave for the birth, **adoption**, or **foster care** placement of a child; the serious medical condition of a parent, spouse, or child; and the worker's own serious medical condition that prevents the worker from performing the essential functions of his or her job.

Except for highly paid positions, individuals must be given back their former positions or one fully equivalent. Employees are eligible for family or medical leave after working for 12 months or at least 1,250 hours. Part-time employees are eligible for such leaves as these numbers average 24 hours a week.

SUPREME COURT STANDARDS FOR GENDER DISCRIMINATION

The Supreme Court has dealt with a variety of gender discrimination cases over the years. Until 1976, it used a rational basis test to determine whether the discrimination it was reviewing was constitutional. Since 1976, beginning with the case of *Craig v. Boren,* the court has used what is referred to as "intermediate" scrutiny in regard to gender discrimination cases. This standard states that a classification based on gender must be reasonable, not arbitrary, and must serve important governmental objectives and be substantially related to the achievement of those objectives.

This scrutiny is less of standard than the court uses in **racial discrimination** cases, which are subject to strict scrutiny. A classification based on race must serve a compelling government interest and be strictly tailored to the achievement of the purpose. This standard makes courts more willing to uphold a classification based on sex than to uphold one based on racial classification.

SEXUAL HARASSMENT

Title VII prohibits acts of sexual harassment when such harassment becomes a "term or condition" of employment, when rejection of the harassment could be used as the basis for an employment decision or when such conduct creates an intimidating "hostile" work environment. The types of sexual harassment prohibited by Title VII are grouped into two categories: **quid pro quo** sexual harassment, when the harassment is directly linked to the grant or denial of an employee's economic benefits, and hostile environment harassment, when the harassment creates a difficult working environment for an employee. Because the first type of harassment is relatively straightforward, the second type has been the subject of more litigation.

The Supreme Court has ruled that a hostile working environment is created when a workplace is permeated with "discriminatory intimidation, ridicule, and insult" which is widespread enough to change the conditions of employment for the person being harassed. Hostile work environments have been held by courts to be created when female employees are subjected to pornographic pictures, to unsolicited love letters and request for dates, and sexual innuendos and crude remarks where those remarks were pervasive.

Employees can sue for sexual harassment even when they have suffered no **tangible** financial problems as a result of such harassment. They can sue even though they have not experienced concrete psychological injury because of the harassment. However, such conduct must do more than offend the employee. Moreover, the harassment does not have to be cross-gender in nature. The Supreme Court in 1998 held that same-sex harassment, such as male sexual harassment of another male, is actionable under Title VII.

Many states require employers to provide training for supervisors about sexual harassment issues. For example, in California, private employers with 50 or more employees must provide training for any supervisory employees, and this training must occur within six months of the employee assuming the supervisor position. The training must include definitions of sexual harassment under both federal and California law, and the training must focus on principles about prohibiting and preventing unlawful sexual harassment in the workplace.

STATE EQUAL PAY LAWS

Nearly every state has a state **statute** prohibiting discrimination based on gender. A majority of states have also enacted laws requiring equal pays or equal wages for members of both genders. The information below summarizes various equal pay and equal wage laws.

ALABAMA: Alabama law does not contain an equal pay or equal wage provision.

ALASKA: Alaska law prohibits discrimination in payment of wages between the sexes.

ARIZONA: Arizona law does not contain an equal pay or equal wage provision.

ARKANSAS: Arkansas law prohibits discrimination in payment of wages or compensation solely on the basis of sex.

CALIFORNIA: California law prohibits discrimination in payment of wages for equal work based on sex.

COLORADO: Colorado law prohibits discrimination in payment of wages or salary paid based solely on sex.

CONNECTICUT: Connecticut law prohibits discrimination in the amount of compensation paid based on sex.

DELAWARE: Delaware law prohibits discrimination in payment of wages for equal work based on sex.

DISTRICT OF COLUMBIA: The law of the District of Columbia does not contain an equal pay or equal wage provision.

FLORIDA: Florida law prohibits discrimination based on sex in the payment of wages for equal work.

GEORGIA: Georgia law prohibits discrimination on the basis of sex in payment of wages for equal work.

HAWAII: Hawaii law prohibits discrimination in the payment of wages for equal work based upon sex.

IDAHO: Idaho law prohibits discrimination in the payment of wages on the basis of sex for comparable work.

ILLINOIS: Illinois law prohibits discrimination between employees on the basis of sex.

INDIANA: Indiana law prohibits discrimination in wages for equal work based on sex.

IOWA: Iowa law prohibits discrimination in the payment of wages based on sex.

KANSAS: Kansas law prohibits discrimination in the payment of wages based on sex.

KENTUCKY: Kentucky law prohibits discrimination in the payment of wages based on sex.

LOUISIANA: Louisiana law does not contain an equal pay or equal wage provision.

MAINE: Maine law prohibits discrimination in payment of wages for comparable work based on sex.

MARYLAND: Maryland law prohibits wage discrimination on the basis of sex where both employees perform work of comparable character.

MASSACHUSETTS: Massachusetts prohibits discrimination in the payment of wages based on sex for work of comparable character on comparable operations.

MICHIGAN: Michigan law prohibits discrimination on the basis of sex by paying a rate less than the rate given to employees of the opposite sex for equal work.

MINNESOTA: Minnesota law prohibits discrimination in the payment of wages between employees on the basis of sex for equal work.

MISSISSIPPI: Mississippi law does not contain an equal pay or equal wage provision.

MISSOURI: Missouri law prohibits discrimination in the payment of wages as between the sexes for work of the same classification.

MONTANA: It is unlawful in Montana for an employer to pay compensation to women less than that paid to men for the same amount of work.

NEBRASKA: Nebraska law prohibits discrimination on the basis of sex for payment of wages for equal work.

NEVADA: Nevada law prohibits discrimination on the basis of sex for payment of wages for equal work.

NEW HAMPSHIRE: New Hampshire law prohibits discrimination in the payment of wages as between the sexes.

NEW JERSEY: New Jersey law prohibits discrimination in the rate or method of wage payment on the basis of an employee's sex.

NEW MEXICO: New Mexico law does not contain an equal pay or equal wage provision.

NEW YORK: New York law prohibits discrimination in the payment of wages on the basis of sex where the work is equal.

NORTH CAROLINA: North Carolina law does not contain an equal pay or equal wage provision.

NORTH DAKOTA: North Dakota prohibits discrimination in the payment of wages between employees on the basis of gender for comparable work.

OHIO: Ohio law prohibits discrimination in the payment of wages based on sex.

OKLAHOMA: Oklahoma law prohibits discrimination in the payment of wages based on sex for comparable work.

OREGON: Oregon law prohibits discrimination in the payment of wages based on sex for comparable work.

PENNSYLVANIA: Pennsylvania law prohibits discrimination in the payment of wages based on sex for equal work.

RHODE ISLAND: Rhode Island law prohibits discrimination in the payment of wages based on sex for equal work.

SOUTH CAROLINA: South Carolina law does not contain an equal pay or equal wage provision.

SOUTH DAKOTA: South Dakota law prohibits discrimination in the payment of wages based on sex for comparable work.

TENNESSEE: Tennessee law prohibits discrimination in the payment of wages based on sex for comparable work.

TEXAS: Texas law does not contain an equal pay or equal wage provision.

UTAH: Utah law does not contain an equal pay or equal wage provision.

VERMONT: Vermont law prohibits discrimination in the payment of wages based on sex for equal work.

VIRGINIA: Virginia law prohibits discrimination in the payment of wages based on sex for equal work.

WASHINGTON: Under Washington law, it is **misdemeanor** for an employer to discriminate in the payment of wages based on sex.

WEST VIRGINIA: West Virginia law prohibits discrimination based on payment of wages for comparable work.

WISCONSIN: Washington law prohibits discrimination in compensation paid for equal work on the basis of sex.

WYOMING: Wyoming law prohibits discrimination between employees on the basis of gender for payment of wages for equal work.

ADDITIONAL RESOURCES

Baumie, Amanda K. *Sexual Discrimination and Law Firm Culture on the Internet: Lawyers at the Information Age Watercooler.* New York: Palgrave Macmillan, 2009.

Farber, Daniel A. *Cases and Materials on Constitutional Law: Themes for the Constitution's Third Century.* 4th ed. Eagan, MN: West, Thomson Reuters, 2009.

Griffith, Benjamin E., ed. *Sexual Harassment in the Public Workplace.* Chicago: American Bar Association, 2011.

ORGANIZATIONS

Concerned Women for America (CWA)

1015 Fifteenth St. NW, Suite 1100
Washington, DC 20005
Phone: (202) 488-7000
Fax: (202) 488-0806
URL: http://www.cwfa.org/

MADRE

121 West 27th Street, #301
New York, NY 10001
Phone: (212) 627-0444
Fax: (212) 675-3704
URL: http://www.madre.org

National Organization For Women (NOW)

1100 H Street, NW, Third Floor
Washington, DC 20005
Phone: (202) 628-8NOW (8669)
Fax: (202) 785-8576
URL: http://www.now.org/

CIVIL RIGHTS

SEXUAL ORIENTATION

Sections within this essay:

INTRODUCTION

Certain groups of citizens, such as African Americans and women, have seen rapid progress in the expansion of their **civil rights** during the past half-century. In contrast, gay and lesbian individuals have experienced rather slow progress in their attempts for equal rights. In areas ranging from marriage and family to job **discrimination** to organizations such as the boy scouts, discrimination based on sexual orientation is still sanctioned in a variety of ways. For instance, in many areas, laws do not protect a person from being fired from a job based solely on the person's sexual orientation. One of the biggest ways sexual orientation differs from other suspect classifications such as race or sex is there is no nationwide law dealing with discrimination against gay and lesbian individuals. For example, Title VII has been consistently held not to apply to discrimination against gay and lesbian individuals. The same is true for related groups, including bisexual and transgender people.

Nevertheless, the twenty-first century has witnessed a clear movement toward gay rights in the United States. For instance, many states and municipalities have adopted sexual orientation anti-discrimination laws, and these laws generally protect people from suffering discrimination in employment and other contexts. Moreover, a number of federal policies have changed that were previously based on policies disfavoring gays and lesbians. The military, for example, had a long-standing policy of "don't ask, don't tell" implemented in 1993, which allowed a serviceman or woman to be discharged if he or she publicly admitted to being homosexual. The policy was finally reversed by President Barack Obama in 2011, allowing gays and lesbians to serve openly in the military.

THE SUPREME COURT AND GAY RIGHTS

In the absence of any national law on sexual orientation discrimination, Supreme Court decisions on these issues have assumed a great importance. The Supreme Court's record on gay rights issues has been mixed. The Court has issued four comparatively landmark decisions on gay rights since it first tackled the issue in 1985 and several other less important holdings.

Bowers v. Hardwick In this 1986 case, the Court reviewed an anti-sodomy **statute** in Georgia. The **plaintiff** was

217

arrested in his bedroom for having sex with another man. The court ruled on a 5-4 vote that the constitutional right to **privacy** did not apply to conduct between members of the same sex. In handing down this ruling, the court made a distinction between homosexual behavior and actions such as **birth control**, **abortion**, and interracial marriage. While the court had previously found that all of these were covered by the right to privacy in the due process clause of the Fourteenth Amendment, homosexual acts were not covered by this clause, according to the Court.

Romer v. Evans In contrast to *Bowers v. Hardwick*, *Romer v. Evans* was considered a significant victory for gay rights. In 1992, Colorado voters had approved Amendment 2, which prohibited or preempted any law or policy "whereby homosexual, lesbian or bisexual orientation, conduct, practices or relationships shall constitute or otherwise be the basis of or entitled any person or class of persons to have or claim any minority status, quota preference, protected status or claim of discrimination." In other words, the law banned any Colorado municipality from passing an sexual orientation anti-discrimination law.

The Supreme Court ruled in a 6-3 decision in 1996 that Amendment 2 violated homosexuals **equal protection** rights in Colorado. Applying the rational basis test, which requires that a policy or law discriminating against a specific non-protected class have a rational relationship to a legitimate **public interest**, the court determined that a "desire to harm a politically unpopular group cannot constitute a legitimate government interest." The Court noted that Amendment 2 identified homosexuals by name and denied them equal protection across the board. "[It's] shear breadth is so discontinuous with the reasons offered for it that the amendment seems inexplicable by anything but animus toward the class it affects," said the Court. The Court's decision in Evans seemed to indicate the Court would accept some equal protection rights for homosexuals, though it certainly did not offer the same protection to sexual orientation discrimination as it would to race or sex.

Boy Scouts of America v. Dale The Supreme Court did another reversal in 2000 and ruled in the case of *Boy Scouts of America v. Dale* that a private organization had a right not allow in homosexuals under the theory of freedom of association. In this case, the Boy Scouts of America had dismissed a scout leader who was openly homosexual. The court determined that a New Jersey public accommodation law, which required organizations using public facilities in the state not to discriminate on the basis of sexual orientation, violated the scouts First

Amendment rights. "Forcing a group to accept certain members may impair the ability of the group to express those views, and only those views, that it intends to express," said the Court, adding that "the presence of Dale as an assistant scoutmaster would … interfere with the Boy Scouts' choice not to propound a point of view contrary to its beliefs." This decision was differentiated from the way the court had refused to apply freedom of association rights in the past when dealing with gender and **racial discrimination**. "Until today," Justice John Paul Stevens pointed out in a dissent, "we have never once found a claimed right to associate in the selection of members to prevail in the face of a State's anti-discrimination law."

Lawrence v. Texas In 2003, the Supreme Court reconsidered its position regarding the constitutionality of **sodomy** laws as they applied to homosexual acts. In *Lawrence v. Texas,* two men were arrested and charged with sodomy when police caught them engaging in consensual sexual activity in one of the men's homes. The state courts upheld the **conviction**, relying on *Bowers v. Hardwick.* The Supreme Court, in a 6-3 decision, determined that the sodomy law violated the Due Process Clause, thus overruling *Bowers.* According to the lead opinion by Justice Anthony Kennedy, "The petitioners are entitled to respect for their private lives. The State cannot demean their existence or control their destiny by making their private sexual conduct a crime. Their right to liberty under the Due Process Clause gives them the full right to engage in their conduct without intervention of the government." Gay rights activists celebrated the decision as a major victory.

Other Supreme Court Decisions Several other Supreme Court rulings were handed down in the 1990s on the issue of gay and lesbian rights. These rulings did not have the impact of the above three, although they also yielded a mixed position on gay rights. *Onacle v. Sundowner Offshore Services* in 1998 found the Court unanimously ruling that same sex harassment was actionable under Title VII. The Court found that even though same sex harassment was not contemplated by the statute, "statutory prohibitions often go beyond the principal evil to cover reasonably comparable evil." The 1998 case of *Bragdon v. Abbott* found a divided Supreme Court allowing persons with HIV to be considered disabled under the Americans With Disabilities Act, even when the disease had not progressed to a symptomatic stage. This action was considered a major gay rights victory.

Commentators have expected the Supreme Court to address gay-rights issues in the early 2010s, but this had not happened as of 2012. The principle issue the Court may address relates to the rights of gays and lesbians to marry.

SPECIFIC ISSUES RELATED TO GAY AND LESBIAN RIGHTS

Employment A growing number of states have enacted statutes that protect individuals from employment discrimination on the basis of sexual identity. As of 2011, a total of 21 states and the District of Columbia have passed some form of non-discrimination law that protects gays and lesbians from discrimination in hiring or retention. In addition, more than 175 cities and counties have enacted non-discrimination laws. A significant number of these laws apply not only to sexual orientation but also to gender identity, so they often prevent employers from discriminating against transgender individuals.

Because the Civil Rights Act does not generally apply to sexual orientation, several groups have encouraged Congress to pass a federal non-discrimination law that would prevent discrimination in employment against gays and lesbians. As of August 2011, more than 50 businesses had endorsed this proposal, but Congress had not enacted such as statute as of 2012.

Housing In addition to non-discrimination in employment, a number of state statutes and local ordinances and laws prohibit discrimination in housing based on sexual orientation. These laws often extend to several areas of housing, including listing, buying, selling, renting, and financing. Owners and landlords in areas with non-discrimination laws cannot refuse to negotiate with a person based on sexual orientation, and many of these laws also apply to gender identity.

Marriage and Other Relationships Few issues have become as heated as the issue about whether gays and lesbians should have full marriage rights. For many years, no **jurisdiction** allowed gays and lesbians to marry legally. However, several jurisdictions began to recognize certain types of formal relationships, often labeling these relationships as civil unions.

Societal views about gay marriage have changed considerably, and by the early 2010s, a small majority of Americans have said they support gay marriage. In fact, President Barack Obama in 2012 announced that he supported gay marriage, and the Democratic Party adopted a stance supporting these marriages. By 2012, a total of six states plus the District of Columbia had laws allowing gay marriage, and the issue has come up frequently in other states as well.

Parenting Discrimination based on sexual orientation has often extended to parenting. A significant number of gays and lesbians have children through **adoption**, surrogates, **donor** insemination, or previous heterosexual relationships. Concerns arise because children of gay or lesbian couples may not be able to establish a legal relationship with both parents. For example, one parent in a same-sex union (however labeled) may be a child's biological parent, so the parent can establish a legal relationship with the child. On the other hand, the other partner in the relationship may not be able to establish this legal relationship even though both parents raise the child.

A total of 12 states as of 2012 have enacted laws allowing a second parent to jointly adopt a child, which allows both parents in the example above to establish a legal relationship with the child. In several other states, a second parent can adopt the child if the couple is married, has a civil union, or has a domestic **partnership**. On the other hand, eight states expressly prohibit joint adoption by unmarried couples.

A small number of states still effectively prohibit gays and lesbians from adopting or becoming foster parents. Some other states, though, expressly forbid discrimination in adoption or fostering children.

Gay and Lesbian Teens and Children Another area of gay and lesbian rights that has received attention relates to the rights of teens and other younger people. Groups such as the American Civil Liberties Union have advocated that gay and lesbian teens should be allowed to attend school dances with dates of the same gender. Some schools have been more active in developing policies protecting teens from discrimination, but these protections are by no means uniform.

STATE NON-DISCRIMINATION LAWS
While the Supreme Court has failed to set a consistent national policy regarding sexual orientation discrimination, many states have taken the lead in passing protections for gays and lesbians as well as bisexual and transgender individuals. A number of these laws apply in areas such as employment and public accommodations. The first of these were passed in the early 1970s, and a significant number have been passed during the past decade.

ALABAMA: The state has not passed a non-discrimination law related to sexual orientation or gender identity.

ALASKA: The state has not passed a non-discrimination law related to sexual orientation or gender identity.

ARIZONA: The state prohibits discrimination based on sexual orientation in public employment.

ARKANSAS: The state has not passed a non-discrimination law related to sexual orientation or gender identity.

CALIFORNIA: The state prohibits discrimination based on both sexual orientation and gender identity.

COLORADO: The state prohibits discrimination based on both sexual orientation and gender identity.

CONNECTICUT: The state prohibits discrimination based on both sexual orientation and gender identity.

DELAWARE: The state prohibits discrimination based on sexual orientation.

DISTRICT OF COLUMBIA: The state prohibits discrimination based on both sexual orientation and gender identity.

FLORIDA: The state has not passed a non-discrimination law related to sexual orientation or gender identity.

GEORGIA: The state has not passed a non-discrimination law related to sexual orientation or gender identity.

HAWAII: The state prohibits discrimination based on both sexual orientation and gender identity.

IDAHO: The state has not passed a non-discrimination law related to sexual orientation or gender identity.

ILLINOIS: The state prohibits discrimination based on both sexual orientation and gender identity.

INDIANA: The state prohibits discrimination based on sexual orientation or gender identity in public employment.

IOWA: The state prohibits discrimination based on both sexual orientation and gender identity.

KANSAS: The state prohibits discrimination based on sexual orientation or gender identity in public employment.

KENTUCKY: The state prohibits discrimination based on sexual orientation or gender identity in public employment.

LOUISIANA: The state has not passed a non-discrimination law related to sexual orientation or gender identity.

MAINE: The state prohibits discrimination based on both sexual orientation and gender identity.

MARYLAND: The state prohibits discrimination based on sexual orientation.

MASSACHUSETTS: The state prohibits discrimination based on both sexual orientation and gender identity.

MICHIGAN: The state prohibits discrimination based on sexual orientation or gender identity in public employment.

MINNESOTA: The state prohibits discrimination based on both sexual orientation and gender identity.

MISSISSIPPI: The state has not passed a non-discrimination law related to sexual orientation or gender identity.

MISSOURI: The state prohibits discrimination based on sexual orientation in public employment.

MONTANA: The state prohibits discrimination based on sexual orientation in public employment.

NEBRASKA: The state has not passed a non-discrimination law related to sexual orientation or gender identity.

NEVADA: The state prohibits discrimination based on both sexual orientation and gender identity.

NEW HAMPSHIRE: The state prohibits discrimination based on sexual orientation.

NEW JERSEY: The state prohibits discrimination based on sexual orientation or gender identity.

NEW MEXICO: The state prohibits discrimination based on both sexual orientation and gender identity.

NEW YORK: The state prohibits discrimination based on sexual orientation.

NORTH CAROLINA: The state has not passed a non-discrimination law related to sexual orientation or gender identity.

NORTH DAKOTA: The state has not passed a non-discrimination law related to sexual orientation or gender identity.

OHIO: The state prohibits discrimination based on sexual orientation or gender identity in public employment.

OKLAHOMA: The state has not passed a non-discrimination law related to sexual orientation or gender identity.

OREGON: The state prohibits discrimination based on both sexual orientation and gender identity.

PENNSYLVANIA: The state prohibits discrimination based on sexual orientation or gender identity in public employment.

RHODE ISLAND: The state prohibits discrimination based on both sexual orientation and gender identity.

SOUTH CAROLINA: The state has not passed a non-discrimination law related to sexual orientation or gender identity.

SOUTH DAKOTA: The state has not passed a non-discrimination law related to sexual orientation or gender identity.

TENNESSEE: The state has not passed a non-discrimination law related to sexual orientation or gender identity.

TEXAS: The state has not passed a non-discrimination law related to sexual orientation or gender identity.

UTAH: The state has not passed a non-discrimination law related to sexual orientation or gender identity.

VERMONT: The state prohibits discrimination based on both sexual orientation and gender identity.

VIRGINIA: The state prohibits discrimination based on sexual orientation in public employment.

WASHINGTON: The state prohibits discrimination based on both sexual orientation and gender identity.

WEST VIRGINIA: The state has not passed a non-discrimination law related to sexual orientation or gender identity.

WISCONSIN: The state prohibits discrimination based on sexual orientation.

WYOMING: The state has not passed a non-discrimination law related to sexual orientation or gender identity.

ADDITIONAL RESOURCES

Mohr, Richard D. *The Long Arc of Justice: Lesbian and Gay Marriage, Equality, and Rights*. New York: Columbia University Press, 2005.

Myers, David G., and Letha Dawson Scanzoni. *What God Has Joined Together? A Christian Case for Gay Marriage*. New York: Harper, 2005.

Polikoff, Nancy D. *Beyond (Straight and Gay) Marriage: Valuing All Families Under the Law*. Boston, MA: Beacon Press, 2008.

ORGANIZATIONS

American Civil Liberties Union (ACLU)

125 Broad St., 18th Fl.
New York, NY 10004
Phone: (212) 549-2500
Email: info@aclu.org
URL: http://www.aclu.org/

Human Rights Campaign

1640 Rhode Island Avenue NW
Washington, DC 20036-3278
Phone: (202) 628-4160
Toll Free: (800) 777-4723
Fax: (202) 347-5323
URL: http://www.hrc.org/

Lambda Legal Defense and Education Fund

120 Wall Street, Suite 1500
New York, NY 10005-3904
Phone: (212) 809-8585
Fax: (212) 809-0055
URL: http://www.lambdalegal.org/

CIVIL RIGHTS

USA PATRIOT ACT

BACKGROUND

In the aftermath of the terrorist attacks against the United States on September 11, 2001, President George Bush and his administration devised legislation now known as the Patriot Act (or USA Patriot Act). The Patriot Act was intended to thwart future terrorist attacks, through identification and punishment of its perpetrators. "USA Patriot Act" is an acronym for "Uniting and Strengthening America by Providing Appropriate Tools Required to Intercept and Obstruct Terrorism Act of 2001."

The proposed legislation was submitted to Congress just one week after the attacks, and quickly gained approval in both houses. It passed in the Senate without debate, and Russell Feingold (D-WI) was the lone vote against the measure. Feingold said, "Preserving our freedom is one of the main reasons that we are now engaged in this new war on terrorism. We will lose that war without firing a shot if we sacrifice the liberties of the American people." In the House of Representatives, the legislation passed 357 to 66, after receiving minor modifications. The president signed the 342-page bill into law on October 26, 2001. When he signed it, he said, "We're dealing with terrorists who operate by highly sophisticated methods and technologies, some of which were not even available when our existing laws were written. The bill before me takes account of the new realities and dangers posed by modern terrorists."

Congress declared its commitment to protecting Americans' **civil rights** and civil liberties in the "quest to identify, locate, and bring to justice the perpetrators and sponsors of the terrorist attacks," but the Patriot Act has sparked fierce debate. Proponents say the act enhances national security. Opponents, including the ACLU, contend the Patriot Act severely undercuts basic civil liberties. The ACLU has charged that the Patriot Act "vastly expand[s] the government's authority to spy on its own citizens, while simultaneously reducing checks and balances on those powers like judicial oversight, public accountability, and the ability to challenge government searches in court." Many other groups have criticized the act as well. For example, according to the National League of Cities, by mid-2005 more than 2,000 communities had passed resolutions expressing concern with civil liberties issues in the Patriot Act.

The Patriot Act's stated purpose is "to deter and punish terrorist acts in the United States and around the world, to enhance law enforcement investigatory tools, and for other purposes." The act comprises the ten categories, called titles:

- Title I: Enhancing domestic security against terrorism
- Title II: Enhancing surveillance procedures
- Title III: Abatement of international **money laundering**
- Title IV: Protecting the borders
- Title V: Removal of obstacles to investigate **terrorism**
- Title VI: Providing for victims of terrorism, public safety officers, and their families
- Title VII: Increased information sharing
- Title VIII: Strengthening criminal laws against terrorism
- Title IX: Improved intelligence
- Title X: Miscellaneous provisions

The USA Patriot Act has been scheduled to expire several times since its enactment. However, Congress and Presidents George W. Bush and Barack Obama have reauthorized and extended the Act's provisions. Obama approved an extension of several key provisions on May 26, 2011, and the extension will last until 2015.

PROVISIONS OF THE PATRIOT ACT

Title I: Enhancing Domestic Security Against Terrorism Provisions in Title I set up a Counterterrorism Fund in the U.S. Treasury, and appropriated $200 million for each **fiscal** year from 2002 through 2004. Section 106 of the title increases presidential authority to seize the property of foreign persons, organizations, or countries that the president determines "has planned, authorized, aided, or engaged in such hostilities or attacks against the United States." Title I also orders the U.S. Secret Service to develop a national network of electronic crime task forces to "purpose of preventing, detecting, and investigating various forms of electronic crimes, including potential terrorist attacks against critical infrastructure and financial payment systems."

Title II: Enhanced Surveillance Procedures This title contains the act's most controversial provisions. Title II extends the government's authority to use wiretaps under the Foreign Intelligence Survey Act of 1978 (FISA). FISA authorized the government to conduct wiretap surveillance in foreign intelligence investigations, without having to show **probable cause** to obtain a **warrant**. Typically, the Fourth Amendment requires a showing of probable cause before a warrant will be issued in a criminal case. Before the Patriot Act, the government could conduct such wiretaps only where the primary purpose was to obtain foreign intelligence. The Patriot Act expanded the Fourth Amendment exception and pursuant to section 218, FISA may be used where a "significant" purpose of the investigation is foreign intelligence gathering.

In 2001, laws did not exist regarding Internet surveillance. As the Internet grew, authorities relied on pre-Internet era wiretap laws to gather information. Essentially, whenever law enforcement personnel wanted access to Internet addresses (URLs), they sought authorization through the "pen register" and "trap and trace" laws of telephone surveillance. Pen registers capture the phone numbers of outgoing telephone calls. Trap and trace devices capture incoming phone numbers. Neither method captures the actual content of a telephone call, so investigators could obtain a **search warrant** without establishing probable cause that a crime was being committed. When faced with Internet surveillance requests, some judges applied the telephone surveillance rules, but others refused. In Section 216, the Patriot Act specifically applies pen register and trap-and-trace law to the Internet. Moreover, pen registers and trap and trace wiretaps are valid nationwide, not just in the **jurisdiction** of the court that approved it. The section does not permit examination of the content of a communication. Nevertheless, critics argue that web addresses are different than telephone numbers. According to the ACLU, "When we 'visit' a Web page what we are really doing is downloading that page from the Internet onto our computer .... That is much richer information than a single list of the people we have communicated with; it is intimate information that reveals who we are and what we are thinking about - much more like the content of a phone call than the number dialed."

Section 214 deals with **wiretapping** authority under FISA and makes it easier for authorities to obtain approval for pen register and trap and trace wiretap devices. Investigators must certify that information obtained will be relevant to an investigation, rather than the previous, stricter standard that permitted wiretaps when a line was used for communications with someone involved in terrorism.

Section 209 permits seizure of voice mail messages with a search warrant. Previously, authorities needed a wiretap order.

Title II also gives the government broad authority to share "electronic, wire, and oral interception information" gleaned from an investigation with other federal agencies. Pursuant to FISA, it also allows authorities to compel Internet service providers to disclose information about a user's e-mail activity, and to compel businesses to turn over personal information related to a criminal investigation. Moreover, section 213 provides that authorities executing a search warrant may delay notice of the search under certain circumstances. Critics **allege** this delay impinges upon a person's right to challenge the constitutionality of the search.

Pursuant to the act, the federal government may examine the library records of patrons without their knowledge. The American Library Association (ALA) has condemned this authorization, arguing that it violates user **privacy** and thereby threatens the free access to knowledge and information. The 64,000-member ALA passed the resolution in early 2003.

Section 224 is a sunset provision, intended to allay concern over the controversy in some of its sections. Accordingly, a number of the act's surveillance and intelligence- gathering provisions, if not re-approved, were set to expire on December 31, 2005. The House of Representatives voted on December 14, 2005, by a vote of 251 to 174, to extend the law for another four years. The House voted to renew sections that permit roving wiretaps. Roving wiretaps are wiretaps placed on every telephone a suspect uses. It also approved extension of provisions that permit the FBI to use secret warrants to obtain medical, business, and library records. In the Senate, however, the re-approval process was much more uncertain. Finally, the Senate and House compromised and approved a renewal of the act in March 2006.

Provisions in Title II have been successfully employed in non-terrorist cases. In an address to Congress on July 13, 2004, Attorney General John Ashcroft noted several instances where provisions in Title II were used in domestic criminal investigations. The cases cited involved sexual predators and electronic surveillance under sections 210 and 212 of the act. Ashcroft told Congress, "When it comes to saving lives and protecting freedom, we must use the Patriot Act and every legal means available to us."

Title III: Money Laundering The official name of Title III is the "International Money Laundering Abatement and Financial Anti-Terrorism Act of 2001." In passing these provisions, Congress cited International Monetary Fund figures which estimate that between two and five percent of the global gross domestic product comes from money laundering with money from illegal drug and smuggling activities. The law called these gains from money laundering the "financial fuel" of terrorist operations. According to the Justice Department, money laundering provisions have been used to:

- Freeze $136 million in assets world-wide

- Charge 113 individuals with crimes related to terrorist financing, resulting in 57 convictions or guilty pleas to date

- Establish an FBI Terrorist Financing Operations Section (TFOS)

- "Identify, investigate, **prosecute**, disrupt, and dismantle terrorist-related financial and fundraising activities" through TFOS and the Joint Terrorism Task Forces

Title IV: Border Protection Provisions in this title authorized appropriations to triple the number of U.S. Border Patrol, Customs Service, and Immigration and Naturalization Service (INS) personnel posted at the border with Canada. (In other legislation related to the September 11, 2001, attacks, in March 2003, Customs, INS, and Border Patrol became part of the newly formed Department of Homeland Security.) Provisions in this title also enhance immigration provisions. For example, the Secretary of State assumed the authority to designate domestic terrorist organizations. A domestic terrorist organization is defined as any organization that has ever used a weapon or dangerous device to cause substantial damage to property. The law also makes any non-citizen members of the group **inadmissible** to the United States. Payment of dues is a deportable offense. Moreover, aliens are inadmissible to the United States if they belong to a group "whose public endorsement of acts of terrorist activity the Secretary of State has determined undermines United States efforts to reduce or eliminate terrorist activities."

Section 416 addresses the foreign student monitoring program. It compels schools to turn over information on foreign students for analysis and investigation.

Section 412 of Title IV is another controversial section of the Patriot Act. It permits up to seven days of detention for aliens suspected of terrorism before they must be charged with a crime or removal proceedings are commenced. Moreover, an immigrant who has been charged with a violation may be held for up to six months if the immigrant's release would threaten national security.

The first Secretary of the Department of Homeland Security, Tom Ridge, stated in 2004, "We share nearly 7,500 miles of land border with Canada and Mexico, across which more than 400 million people, 130 million motor vehicles and 2.5 million rail cars pass every year. We patrol almost 95,000 miles of shoreline and navigable waters . . . . We have to get it right millions of times a week. But the terrorists only have to get it right once."

Titles V, VI, and VII These titles have not been the source of controversy. The purpose of Title V is to enhance the federal government's ability to offer rewards for information offered for terrorism investigations. Title VI is concerned with providing funds and assistance to the victims of terrorism and to public safety officers and their families, where the officers are killed or suffer catastrophic injury due to terrorism. Title VII amends the Omnibus Crime Control and Safe Streets Act of 1968 to facilitate communication among federal, state, and local authorities in the event of a terrorist attack.

Title VIII: Criminal Law Changes Title VIII's numerous sections are intended strengthen criminal laws against terrorism. This title adds offenses for terrorism against mass transportation. It also addresses domestic terrorism, defining it as involving "acts dangerous to human life that are a violation of the criminal laws of the United States or of any State" that "appear to be intended to intimidate or coerce a civilian population; to influence the policy of a government by intimidation or **coercion**; or to affect the conduct of a government by mass destruction, assassination, or **kidnapping**; and occur primarily within the territorial jurisdiction of the United States." Section 803 makes it illegal to harbor or conceal terrorists or suspected terrorists. Moreover, section 809 extends certain criminal statutes of limitations. Where the commission of certain terrorism offenses "resulted in, or created a foreseeable risk of, death or serious bodily injury to another person," the **statute of limitations** is eliminated. Section 814 is intended to deter and prevent cyber-terrorism by increasing criminal penalties for Computer **Fraud** and Abuse Act violations. It amends the **statutory** definition of "protected computers" so that computers located outside the United States are included.

Title IX: Improved Intelligence This title addresses various intelligence concerns, within the federal government, including the Central Intelligence Agency (CIA). Congress directed the CIA to set up a "National Virtual Translation Center" to provide "timely and accurate translations of foreign intelligence for all other elements of the intelligence community."

USA PATRIOT ACT SUCCESSES AND CONTROVERSIES

According to the Department of Justice's website devoted to the Patriot Act, the following successes can be attributed, wholly or in part, to the Patriot Act:

- The USA Patriot Act has allowed law enforcement to investigate terrorism using the same tools as those used to combat organized crime and drug trafficking.

- The Act has facilitated sharing of information and cooperation among government agencies, such that these agencies are able to "connect the dots" more effectively.

- The Act has updated the law to reflect new terrorist threats as well as new technologies used to combat terrorism.

- The Act has increased penalties for those who commit acts of terror.

Despite these successes and others, several groups such as the ACLU and the Electronic Privacy Information Center have continued to criticize the Act based on arguments that the Act infringes upon **constitutional rights** of U.S. citizens. Of particular concern are provisions that allow agents to intercept private communications as well as those that allow agents to conduct certain types of searches.

Despite arguments to **repeal** parts or all of the Act, however, Congress as a whole has not expressed such a desire, and the key provisions of the Act have remained intact.

ADDITIONAL RESOURCES

Abele, Robert P. *A User's Guide to the USA Patriot Act and Beyond.* Lanham, MD: University Press of America, 2005.

Gaines, Larry. *Homeland Security.* Upper Saddle River, NJ: Prentice Hall, 2011.

Posner, Steve C. *Privacy Law and the USA Patriot Act.* Newark, NJ: Matthew Bender, 2007.

Wong, Kam C. *The Impact of USA Patriot Act on American Society: An Evidence Based Assessment.* New York: Nova Science Publishers, 2007.

ORGANIZATIONS

American Civil Liberties Union (ACLU)

125 Broad St., 18th Fl.
New York, NY 10004
Phone: (212) 549-2500
Email: info@aclu.org
URL: http://www.aclu.org/

American Library Association (ALA)

50 East Huron Street
Chicago, IL 60611
Toll Free: (800) 545-2433
URL: http://www.ala.org

Department of Justice

950 Pennsylvania Ave., NW
Washington, DC 20530-0001
Phone: (202) 514-2000
URL: http://www.justice.gov/

CIVIL RIGHTS

VOTING RIGHTS

Sections within this essay:

- Background
- The Nineteenth Amendment
- Black Suffrage
- Grandfather Clauses, Literacy Tests, and the White Primary
- The Fifteenth Amendment
- The Voting Rights Act
  - Section Two and Section Five
  - Malapportioned Districts
- Minority Majority Districts
- Additional Resources

BACKGROUND

During colonial times, the right to vote (also known as being enfranchised) was severely limited. Mostly, adult white males who owned property were the only people with the right to vote. Women could not vote, though some progressive colonies allowed widows who owned property to vote. After the United States gained its independence from Great Britain, the Constitution gave the states the right to decide who could vote. Individually, the states began to abolish property requirements and, by 1830, adult white males could vote. Suffrage (the right to vote) has been gradually extended to include many people, and the U.S. Constitution has been amended several times for this purpose. A time line of major developments in

U.S. voting rights contains at least the following seventeen events:

- 1789: The first presidential election is held, electing George Washington by unanimous vote of the country's "electors," a group of mostly white male landowners.
- 1868: The Fourteenth Amendment declares that any eligible twenty-one year old male has the right to vote.
- 1870: The Fifteenth Amendment says that the right to vote cannot be denied "on account of race, color, or previous condition of servitude," thus extending the right to vote to former (male) slaves.
- 1876: Wyoming becomes a state and is the first state to give voting rights to women.
- 1884: The U.S. Supreme Court rules "grandfather clauses" unconstitutional.
- 1890: Southern states pass laws designed to limit the voting rights of African Americans. Some of the laws require voters to pay a poll tax or to prove that they can read and write.
- 1920: The U.S. Supreme Court rules that since Native Americans who live on reservations pay no state taxes, they cannot vote.
- 1920: Women gain the vote when the Nineteenth Amendment declares that the right to vote cannot be denied "on account of sex."
- 1947: A court ruling grants Native Americans the right to vote in every state.
- 1961: The Twenty-third Amendment establishes that the citizens of the District of Columbia (D.C.) have the right to vote in presidential elections. D.C. is given 3 electoral votes.

- 1964: The Twenty-fourth Amendment declares that the states cannot require citizens to pay a poll tax in order to vote in federal elections.

- 1965: Voting Rights Act bans literacy tests as a voting requirement and bars all racist voting practices in all states.

- 1971: The Twenty-Sixth Amendment lowers the voting age to 18 and gives all Americans the right to vote.

- 1975: Additions to the Voting Rights Act require translations of all election materials to be made available for non-English speaking citizens.

As this list illustrates, suffrage has been expanded to include a greater number of people belonging to diverse demographic groups based on age, sex, and race. Without a doubt, the most dramatic and controversial developments in the history of U.S. voting rights expansion involves the movement to grant suffrage to women and African Americans. For African Americans, this includes a long history of ensuring unimpeded access to the polls in order to exercise their constitutional right to vote. For women, gaining suffrage was a very long struggle as well.

THE NINETEENTH AMENDMENT

The Nineteenth Amendment to the U.S. Constitution guarantees U.S. women the right to vote. However, this right was not easily won for women. It took many decades of political agitation and protest before such a right became part of U.S. law. The struggle for women's right to vote began in the middle of the nineteenth century. A movement arose that included several generations of woman suffrage supporters, who became known as suffragettes. These women lectured, wrote articles, marched, lobbied, and engaged in acts of civil disobedience to achieve what many Americans then considered to be an enormous change in the Constitution. Few of the movement's early supporters lived to see the amendment ratified in 1920.

The amendment was first introduced in Congress in 1878, but it was not ratified until August 18, 1920. Those who supported voting rights for women used a variety of strategies to achieve their goal. Some worked to pass suffrage acts in each state, and their efforts resulted in nine western states adopting female suffrage legislation by 1912. Others used the courts to challenge male-only voting laws. Some of the more militant suffragettes organized parades, vigils, and even hunger strikes. Suffragettes frequently met resistance and even open hostility. They were heckled, jailed, and sometimes even attacked physically.

By 1916, however, almost all of the major female suffrage organizations had agreed that the best strategy was to pursue the goal of a **constitutional amendment**. The following year, New York granted suffrage to women. This was quickly followed in 1918 by President Woodrow Wilson's change in his position to support an amendment in 1918. These important events helped shift the political balance in favor of the vote for women. Then, on May 21, 1919, the U.S. House of Representatives passed the amendment, followed in two weeks by approval in the Senate. With Tennessee becoming the 36th state to ratify the amendment on August 18, 1920, the amendment had thus been ratified by three-fourths of the states. The U.S. Secretary of State, Bainbridge Colby, certified the **ratification** on August 26, 1920, and women had gained the constitutional right to vote. Women's collective experience in pursuit of this goal differed significantly from that of Black Americans, who had actually gained the right much earlier but who had to struggle against sustained efforts to curtail their exercise of this right.

BLACK SUFFRAGE

Prior to the Civil War, free blacks were denied the right to vote everywhere but in New York and several New England states. By the close of the Civil War, suffrage for African Americans had become a possibility throughout the country. The Reconstruction Act of 1867 imposed conditions on former states of the Confederacy for re-admission to the Union. Some of these conditions touched on black suffrage. For example, former Confederate states were required to call conventions to which blacks could be elected as delegates and devise new state constitutions guaranteeing voting rights to black men. By the end of registration for 1867, more than 700,000 southern black men had been added to the rolls. By 1872 there were 342 black officials elected to state legislatures and to the U.S. Congress. Despite such progressive legislation, not all black **civil rights** or suffrage measures succeeded. Constitutional amendments that would have prohibited states from imposing birth requirements, property ownership, or literacy tests, as well as giving the federal government complete control over voting rights were rejected.

Unfortunately, the progress of black voting rights can be characterized as a stumbling trajectory of success. There were gains, often followed by severe setbacks. For example, in 1870 and 1871 three Enforcement Acts were passed that strengthened the constitutional guarantee of black voting rights. Moreover, the year 1870 also witnessed the ratification of the Fifteenth Amendment. However, just a few years later, two Supreme Court decisions, *United States v. Reese* (1876) and *United States v. Cruikshank* (1876), weakened the Fourteenth and Fifteenth Amendments. By 1877, the Union was withdrawing federal troops from the South as a compromise with Democrats to allow the election of Rutherford B. Hayes as president of the United States. This move gave the largely racist Southern Democrats control over the lives of blacks including black suffrage. Accordingly, this and other like-minded groups launched a wave of repressive measures to curtail the freedoms of blacks in the South.

GRANDFATHER CLAUSES, LITERACY TESTS, AND THE WHITE PRIMARY

After the Civil War and Reconstruction, southern states employed a range of tactics to prevent blacks from exercising their right to vote. They used violence, vote **fraud**, gerrymandering, literacy tests, white primaries, among others. These tactics caused registration by blacks to drop significantly. Such measures as the poll tax, literacy tests, grandfather clauses, and the white primary proved especially effective in disfranchising blacks.

The poll tax, as it applied to primary elections leading to general elections for federal office, was abolished in the Twenty-fourth Amendment, ratified in 1964. Qualifications to vote based on some element of property ownership have a history that extends to colonial days. However, the poll tax was instituted in seven southern states following Reconstruction. The poll tax was a flat fee required before voting; it was often levied as high as $200 per person. The voting rights of poor blacks were disproportionately discriminated against in this method.

The U.S. Congress eventually came to view the financial qualification as an impediment to individuals' suffrage rights. Despite Congressional sentiment, though, a constitutional amendment was necessary to abolish poll taxes, as the poll tax had previously withstood constitutional challenges in the courts. Even with the ratification of the Twenty-fourth Amendment, some states continued to look for ways to use poll taxes as an impediment to blacks' exercising their right to vote. Finally, in the 1965 opinion in the case of *Harman v. Forssenius*, the Supreme Court struck down a Virginia law which had partially eliminated the poll tax as an absolute qualification for voting in federal elections. The Virginia law had given voters in federal elections the choice of either paying the tax or of filing a certificate of residence six months before the election. The Court found the latter requirement to be an unfair procedural requirement for voters in federal elections, particularly because the law was not imposed on those who otherwise agreed to pay the poll tax. The Court unanimously held the law to conflict with the Twenty-fourth Amendment as it penalized those who chose to exercise a right guaranteed them by the amendment.

There were many uneducated African Americans in the post-Civil War era. Literacy tests were used to help exclude them from the polls. However, whites found that literacy tests also would exclude large numbers of whites from becoming eligible voters since many whites could not read or write either. As a remedy, some jurisdictions adopted a "reasonable interpretation" clause; these laws gave voting registrars discretion to evaluate applicants' performance on literacy tests. The effect was predictable: most whites passed and most blacks did not. By the beginning of the twentieth century, almost every black had been disfranchised in the South.

Grandfather clauses, a peculiarly irksome impediment to achieving voting rights for African Americans, were enacted by seven Southern states between 1895 and 1910. These laws provided that those who had enjoyed the right to vote prior to 1866 or 1867 or their lineal descendants would be exempt from educational, property, or tax requirements for voting. Because former slaves had not been granted the right to vote until the Fifteenth Amendment was ratified in 1870, these clauses effectively excluded blacks from the vote. At the same time, grandfather clauses assured the right to vote to many impoverished, ignorant, and illiterate whites. In 1915, the U.S. Supreme Court finally declared the **grandfather clause** unconstitutional because it violated equal voting rights guaranteed by the Fifteenth Amendment.

The so-called white primary was a tactic Southern whites used in which the Democratic Party was declared a private organization that could exclude whomever it pleased. State party rules or state laws that excluded blacks from the Democratic primary virtually disenfranchised all blacks (and only blacks) by keeping them out of the election that generally determined who would hold office in a state that was dominated by the Democratic Party. In 1944, the white primary was ruled unconstitutional in the U.S. Supreme Court case of *Smith v. Allwright*.

THE FIFTEENTH AMENDMENT

The Fifteenth Amendment to the United States Constitution was ratified in 1870, just a few years after the end of the Civil War. This Amendment prohibits both federal and state governments from infringing on a citizen's right to vote "on account of race, color, or previous condition of servitude." The Fifteenth Amendment is the third of three "Reconstruction Amendments" ratified in the aftermath of the Civil War. The other two are the Thirteenth Amendment that abolished slavery, and the 14th Amendment granted citizenship to all persons, "born or naturalized in the United States."

Prior to the Fifteenth Amendment, the states were empowered to set the qualifications for the right to vote. The Fifteenth Amendment essentially transferred this power to the federal government. Its ratification, however, had little effect for nearly a century. It had practically no effect in southern states, which devised numerous ways such as poll taxes and grandfather clauses to keep blacks from voting. Over time, federal laws and Supreme Court judicial opinions eventually struck down voting restrictions for blacks. Eventually, Congress passed the Civil Rights Act of 1957 which established a commission to investigate voting **discrimination**. In addition, in 1965 the Voting Rights Act was passed to increase black voter registration by empowering the Justice Department to closely monitor voting qualifications.

THE VOTING RIGHTS ACT

The **Voting Rights Act of 1965** (VRA) is arguably the most significant piece of federal legislation aimed at enforcing and protecting the voting rights of minorities. While the Fifteenth Amendment enfranchises African Americans, it does not necessarily clear the way to the polls for them. After nearly a century of countenancing various forms of intimidation and legalistic obstructions to black voters, the federal government passed sweeping legislation that fills important gaps in African Americans' constitutional right to vote. The VRA essentially mandates access to the polls for minority groups. The VRA prevents states from enforcing a range of discriminatory practices legislated to prevent African Americans from participating in the voting process. As a result of the VRA, the federal government intervened directly in areas where African Americans had been denied the right to vote.

Section Two and Section Five Sections Two and Five of the VRA are especially important. Section 2 prohibits attempts to dilute the votes of minorities. Dilution occurs when the full effect of a block of voters is deliberately and unfairly negated. Vote dilution can occur through legislation or other situations that weaken the voting strength of minorities. Section Two prohibits cities and towns from establishing practices designed to prevent minorities a fair chance to elect candidates of their choice. Section Two is enforceable nationwide.

Section Five of the VRA requires certain designated areas of the country to obtain "pre-clearance" from the U.S. attorney general or the U.S. District Court for the District of Columbia for any changes that impact voting. These special areas are called "covered jurisdictions." Accordingly, covered jurisdictions must obtain approval before they can administer any new electoral practices. All areas in the following states are subject to Section Five pre-clearance.

- Alabama
- Alaska
- Arizona
- Georgia

- Louisiana
- Mississippi
- South Carolina
- Texas
- Virginia

Parts of the following states are also subject to pre-clearance:

- California
- Florida
- Michigan
- New Hampshire
- New York
- North Carolina
- South Dakota

Section Five was necessary because of the purpose or intent in some areas to dilute or weaken the strength of minority voters. They did this by changing electoral rules such that minorities had decreased opportunities to elect someone of their choice. Additionally, Section 5 considers the effect of a proposed change. The U.S. attorney general or the U.S. District Court for the District of Columbia considers whether the proposed change will lead to a worsening of the position of minority voters, an effect known as "retrogression."

Some have advocated for Section Five to be repealed or ruled unconstitutional because it applies only to certain states. The Supreme Court had an opportunity to review whether Section Five is constitutional in *Northwest Austin Municipal Utility District Number One v. Holder* (2009), but the Court effectively avoided the question and allowed Section Five to stand. This Section will likely remain in force unless and until Congress decides to **repeal** it.

In 1975 an important amendment was added to the VRA to include rights for language minorities. These amendments required jurisdictions to provide bilingual ballots and even translation services to those who speak any of the following languages:

- Spanish
- Chinese
- Japanese
- Korean
- Native American languages
- Eskimo languages

Malapportioned Districts The first version of the VRA was insufficient to prevent efforts to continue vote dilution. Many areas had a winner-take-all, at-large electoral system, as well as severely malapportioned districts. Malapportioning, also known as "gerrymandering," is the deliberate rearrangement of the **boundaries** of congressional districts with the intent to influence the outcome of elections. Gerrymandering either concentrates opposition votes in a few districts to gain more seats for the majority in surrounding districts (a process called packing) or diffuses minority votes across many districts (called dilution). The term came about in 1812 when Massachusetts's governor Elbridge Gerry created a district for political purposes that resembled a salamander.

The at-large electoral system where representatives are chosen area-wide dilutes minority voting strength because whites so frequently outnumber blacks. In 1973 the U.S. Supreme Court in the case of *White v. Register* ruled that at-large elections were unconstitutional if they diluted or minimized minority votes.

In terms of malapportionment, there were problems of state legislatures adhering to outmoded rural interests. For example, in the 1962 case *Baker v. Carr*, malapportionment claims from some of Tennessee's big cities were found justifiable under the Fourteenth Amendment. *Baker v. Carr* involved **apportionment** schemes whereby less populated rural counties had obtained disproportionate political strength as opposed to the densely populated cities.

Such malapportionment procedures became tinged with racism as redistricting practices maximized the political advantage or votes of one group and minimized the political advantage or votes of another. In *Gomillion v. Lightfoot*, the board of supervisors in Tuskegee, Alabama, annexed territory to increase the size of the city, but excluded all the blacks around the city. The Supreme Court found that such racial gerrymandering violated constitutional guarantees. A related case, *Reynolds v. Sims* put a stop to a gerrymandering scheme that discriminated heavily against populated urban areas in favor of rural areas and small towns. Through such cases, the U.S. Supreme Court advanced toward the goal of full and effective participation by all citizens in state government.

MINORITY MAJORITY DISTRICTS

Through the VRA, the federal government moved to guarantee access for all citizens to the ballot. Even so, the right to vote did not necessarily translate into electing representatives for voters who were in the minority. In jurisdictions, particularly in the South, voters who historically had faced **racial discrimination** (African-Americans, Latinos, Asian-Pacific Americans and Native Americans) had been unable to elect candidates of their choice unless they constituted a majority of voters in a given electoral district. In 1982, Congress amended the VRA to include requirements that certain jurisdictions provide minority voters opportunities to elect candidates of their choice.

Initially, these jurisdictions turned minority populations into a majority through re-drawing legislative districts. This created an overall racial majority from a formerly minority population in a particular district. However, this approach has serious drawbacks, especially when a minority group is not centralized, but is dispersed geographically or interspersed with other groups of voters. Consequently, these race-conscious districts encountered setbacks at the Supreme Court, which outlawed explicit "racial gerrymanders."

As a result of many legal disputes and public controversies concerning effective minority representation, courts have ordered ward-based systems (single-member districts) as remedies in vote dilution cases. This supports the concept that the best determinant of a black candidate's electoral success is the racial composition of the electoral jurisdictions. But in the 1993 Supreme Court decision of *Shaw v. Reno*, the Court declared that a North Carolina reapportionment scheme constituted racial gerrymandering under the Equal Protection Clause of the Fourteenth Amendment. This ruling allows white voters to object to what they perceive as racially motivated districting. Cases similar to *Shaw*, and cases resulting from the *Shaw* decision filled the courts. Voting rights attorneys, civil rights groups, and community activists defended majority minority voting districts and to protect them in light of the *Shaw* decision.

Many would agree that the VRA is perhaps the most significant piece of legislation designed to secure minority electoral rights. However, the VRA is vulnerable to attack on the grounds that it may overextend its original mandate. Some have argued that proponents of the VRA have confused the "right to vote" with the "right to be elected." Many people of color have won federal, state, and local elections. Their success may not have been possible without such aggressive policy measures as the VRA. Yet despite the protections of the VRA, courts continue to address controversies surrounding new methods to dilute the collective strength of black voters.

The creation of majority-black districts has been the overarching federal policy regarding minority representation after the VRA was enacted. Even so, there are many views about the need and effectiveness of majority-black districts. Likewise, the case of *Shaw v. Reno* places majority-black districting in a somewhat tenuous position as more and more groups of whites begin to assert that redistricting plans have resulted in a new kind of "political apartheid," preventing them from full and effective use of the ballot. Efforts continue to work out a solution that passes constitutional muster and it remains to be seen what that solution will be.

Voting rights issues have also arisen with regard to Latino voters. In *League of United Latin American Citizens v. Perry* (2006), the Court reviewed a challenge to the Texas state legislature's congressional redistricting plan, which modified a district that had previously consisted of a majority of Latinos of voting age. Although the plan created other districts that contained a majority of Latinos, the Court concluded that the plan nevertheless diluted the voting strength of those affected by the plan. Thus, the Court ruled that the plan violated the Voting Rights Act.

ADDITIONAL RESOURCES

Blum, Edward. *The Unintended Consequences of Section 5 of the Voting Rights Act.* Washington, DC: AEI Press, 2007.

Bullock, Charles S., and Ronald Keith Gaddie. *The Triumph of Voting Rights in the South.* Norman, OK: University of Oklahoma Press, 2009.

Dimino, Michael, Bradley Smith, and Michael Solimine. *Voting Rights and Election Law.* New Providence, NJ: LexisNexis, 2010.

Griffith, Benjamin E., ed. *America Votes! A Guide to Modern Election Law and Voting Rights.* Chicago: American Bar Association, 2008.

ORGANIZATIONS

FairVote: The Center for Voting and Democracy (CVD)

6930 Carroll Ave. Suite 610
Takoma Park, MD 20912
Phone: (301) 270-4616
Fax: (301) 270-4133
Email: info@fairvote.org
URL: http://www.fairvote.org

Federal Election Commission (FEC)

999 E Street, NW
Washington, DC 20463
Phone: (202) 424-9530
Email: Webmaster@fec.gov
URL: http://www.fec.gov/

League of Women Voters (LWV)

1730 M Street NW, Suite 1000
Washington, DC 20036-4508
Phone: (202) 429-1965
Fax: (202) 429-0854
Email: lwv@lwv.org
URL: http://www.lwv.org/

National Voting Rights Institute (NVRI)

27 School Street, Suite 500
Boston, MA 02108
Phone: (617) 624-3900
Fax: (617) 624-3911
Email: nvri@nvri.org
URL: http://www.nvri.org/

CONSUMER ISSUES

ADVERTISING

Sections within this essay:

- Background
- Bureau of Consumer Protection
  - Advertising Agency Obligations
  - Publisher Obligations
  - Franchises and Businesses
  - Telemarketing Sales
  - Environmental Marketing Practices
  - Labeling Rules

- Comparative Advertising
- FTC Litigation
- Additional Resources

BACKGROUND

The Federal Trade Commission (FTC) works to ensure that the nation's markets are efficient and free of practices which might harm consumers. To ensure the smooth operation of our free market system, the FTC enforces federal consumer protection laws that prevent **fraud**, deception, and unfair business practices. The Federal Trade Commission Act allows the FTC to act in the interest of all consumers to prevent deceptive and unfair acts or practices. In interpreting the Act, the Commission has determined that, with respect to advertising, a representation, omission, or practice is deceptive if it is likely to mislead consumers and affect consumers' behavior or decisions about the product or service. In addition, an act or practice is unfair if the injury it causes,

or is likely to cause, is substantial, not outweighed by other benefits, and not reasonably avoidable.

The FTC Act's prohibition on unfair or deceptive acts or practices broadly covers advertising claims, marketing and promotional activities, and sales practices in general. The Act is not limited to any particular medium. Accordingly, the Commission's role in protecting consumers from unfair or deceptive acts or practices encompasses advertising, marketing, and sales online, as well as the same activities in print, television, telephone and radio. For certain industries or subject areas, the Commission issues rules and guides. Rules prohibit specific acts or practices that the Commission has found to be unfair or deceptive. Guides help businesses in their efforts to comply with the law by providing examples or direction on how to avoid unfair or deceptive acts or practices. Many rules and guides address claims about products or services or advertising in general and are not limited to any particular medium used to disseminate those claims or advertising. Therefore, the plain language of many rules and guides applies to claims made on the Internet. Solicitations made in print, on the telephone, radio, TV, or online naturally fall within the Rule's scope.

BUREAU OF CONSUMER PROTECTION

The FTC's Bureau of Consumer Protection protects consumers against unfair, deceptive, or **fraudulent** practices. The Bureau enforces a variety of consumer protection laws enacted by Congress, as well as trade regulation rules issued by the Commission. Its actions include individual company and industry-wide investigations, administrative and federal court **litigation**, rule-making proceedings, and consumer and business education. In addition, the Bureau contributes to the

Commission's on-going efforts to inform Congress and other government entities of the impact that proposed actions could have on consumers. The Bureau of Consumer Protection is divided into six divisions and programs, each with its own areas of expertise. One of the divisions is the Division of Advertising Practices.

Within the Bureau of Consumer Protection is the Division of Advertising Practices and the Division of Enforcement. These entities are the nation's enforcers of federal truth-in-advertising laws. The FTC Act prohibits unfair or deceptive advertising in any medium. That is, advertising must tell the truth and not mislead consumers. A claim can be misleading if relevant information is left out or if the claim implies something that is not true. In addition, claims must be substantiated especially when they concern health, safety, or performance. The type of **evidence** may depend on the product, the claims, and what experts believe necessary. Sellers are responsible for claims they make about their products and services. Third parties such as advertising agencies or website designers and catalog marketers also may be liable for making or disseminating deceptive representations if they participate in the preparation or distribution of the advertising or know about the deceptive claims.

The Division of Advertising Practices focuses its enforcement activities on claims for foods, drugs, dietary supplements, and other products promising health benefits; health fraud on the Internet; weight-loss advertising and marketing directed to children; performance claims for computers, ISPs and other high-tech products and services; tobacco and alcohol advertising; protecting children's **privacy** online; claims about product performance made in national or regional newspapers and magazines; in radio and TV commercials, including infomercials; through direct mail to consumers; or on the Internet.

Advertising Agency Obligations Advertising agencies (and more recently, website designers) are responsible for reviewing the information used to **substantiate** ad claims. These agencies may not simply rely on an advertiser's assurance that the claims are substantiated. In determining whether an ad agency should be held liable, the FTC looks at the extent of the agency's participation in the preparation of the challenged ad and whether the agency knew or should have known that the ad included false or deceptive claims.

Publisher Obligations Like advertising agencies, catalog and magazine publishers can be held responsible for material distributed. Publications may be required to provide documentation to back up assertions made in the advertisement. Repeating what the manufacturer claims about the product is not necessarily sufficient. The

Division of Enforcement conducts a wide variety of law enforcement activities to protect consumers, including deceptive marketing practices. This division monitors compliance with Commission cease and desist orders and federal court injunctive orders, investigates violations of consumer protection laws, and enforces a number of trade laws, rules, and guides.

Franchises and Businesses The Franchise and Business Opportunity Rule requires franchise and business opportunity sellers to give consumers a detailed disclosure document at least 10 days before the consumer pays any money or legally commits to a purchase. The document must include:

- the names, addresses, and telephone numbers of other purchasers
- a fully-audited **financial statement** of the seller
- the background and experience of the business's key executives
- the cost of starting and maintaining the business
- the responsibilities of the seller and purchaser once the purchase is made

In addition, companies that make earnings representations must give consumers the written basis for their claims, including the number and percentage of owners who have done at least as well as claimed.

Multi-level marketing (MLM), sometimes known as network or matrix marketing, is a way of selling goods and services through distributors. These plans typically promise that people who sign up as distributors will get commissions two ways: On their own sales and on the sales their recruits have made.

Pyramid schemes are a form of multi-level marketing which involves paying commissions to distributors only for recruiting new distributors. Pyramid schemes are illegal in most states because the plans inevitably collapse when no new distributors can be recruited. When a plan collapses, most people except those at the top of the pyramid lose money. Lawful MLMs should pay commissions for the retail sales of goods or services, not for recruiting new distributors. MLMs that involve the sale of business opportunities or franchises, as defined by the Franchise Rule, must comply with the Rule's requirements about disclosing the number and percentage of existing franchisees who have achieved the claimed results, as well as cautionary language.

Telemarketing Sales The FTC's Telemarketing Sales Rule requires certain disclosures and prohibits misrepresentations. The Rule covers most types of telemarketing calls to consumers, including calls to pitch goods, services, sweepstakes, and prize promotion and investment opportunities. It also applies to calls consumers make in response to postcards or other materials received in the mail. Calling times are restricted to the hours between 8 a.m. and 9 p.m. Telemarketers must disclose that it is a sales call, and for which company. It is illegal for telemarketers to misrepresent any information, including facts about goods or services, earnings potential, profitability, risk or liquidity of an investment, or the nature of a prize in a prize-promotion scheme. Telemarketers must disclose the total cost of the products or services offered and all restrictions on getting or using them, or that a sale is final or non-refundable. Although most types of telemarketing calls are covered by the Rule, the Rule does not cover calls placed by consumers in response to general media advertising (except calls responding to ads for investment opportunities, credit repair services, recovery room services, or advance-fee loans). It also does not cover calls placed by consumers in response to direct mail advertising that discloses all the material information required by the Rule (except calls responding to ads for investment opportunities, prize promotions, credit repair services, recovery room services, or advance-fee loans). The Mail or Telephone Order Merchandise Rule requires companies to ship purchases when promised (or within 30 days if no time is specified) or to give consumers the option to cancel their orders for a refund.

Environmental Marketing Practices Guidelines for using environmental marketing claims have been established by the Federal Trade Commission. The guides themselves are not enforceable regulations, nor do they have the force and effect of law. These guides specifically address the application of Section 5 of the Federal Trade Commission Act that makes deceptive acts and practices in or affecting **commerce** unlawful to environmental advertising and marketing practices. Guides for the Use of Environmental Marketing Claims provide the basis for voluntary compliance with such laws by members of industry and are available from the EPA and the FTC. The guides apply to advertising, labeling, and other forms of marketing to consumers and do not preempt state or local laws or regulations. Generally, environmental claims must specify application to the product, the package, or a component of either. Environmental claims should not overstate the environmental attributes or benefit. Every express and material implied claim conveyed to consumers about an objective quality should be substantiated and other broad environmental claims should be avoided or qualified.

A product which purports to offer an environmental benefit must be backed with factual information. Green Guides govern claims that consumer products are environmentally safe, recycled, recyclable, ozone-friendly, or biodegradable. These guides apply to environmental claims included in labeling, advertising, promotional

materials, and all other forms of marketing. The guides apply to any claim about the environmental attributes of a product, package, or service in connection with the sale, offering for sale, or marketing of such product, package, or service for personal, family, or household use, or for commercial, institutional, or industrial use.

According to the guidelines, a product or package should not be marketed as recyclable unless it can be collected, separated, or otherwise recovered from the solid waste stream for reuse or in the manufacture or assembly of another package or product through an established recycling program. Products or packages that are made of both recyclable and non-recyclable components must have any recyclable claim adequately qualified to avoid consumer deception about which portions or components of the product or package are recyclable. Claims of recyclability should be qualified to the extent necessary to avoid consumer deception about any limited availability of recycling programs and collection sites. If an incidental component significantly limits the ability to recycle a product or package, a claim of recyclability would be deceptive. A product or package that is made from recyclable material, but, because of its shape, size, or some other attribute, is not accepted in recycling programs for such material, should not be marketed as recyclable.

Likewise, claims that a product or package is degradable, biodegradable, or photodegradable should be substantiated by competent and reliable scientific evidence that the entire product or package will completely break down and return to nature, such as decomposing into elements found in nature within a reasonably short time after customary disposal. Claims of degradability, biodegradability, or photodegradability should be qualified to the extent necessary to avoid consumer deception about the product or package's ability to degrade in the environment where it is customarily disposed and the rate and extent of degradation.

A recycled content claim may be made only for materials that have been recovered or otherwise diverted from the solid waste stream, either during the manufacturing process (pre-consumer) or after consumer use (post-consumer). To the extent the source of recycled content includes pre-consumer material, the manufacturer or advertiser must have substantiation for concluding that the pre-consumer material would otherwise have entered the solid waste stream. In asserting a recycled content claim, distinctions may be made between pre-consumer and post-consumer materials. Where such distinctions are asserted, any express or implied claim about the specific pre-consumer or post-consumer content of a product or package must be substantiated. For products or packages that are only partially made of recycled material, a recycled claim should be adequately qualified to avoid consumer deception about the amount, by weight, of recycled content in the finished product or package. Additionally, for products that contain used, reconditioned, or remanufactured components, a recycled claim should be adequately qualified to avoid consumer deception about the nature of such components. No such qualification would be necessary in cases where it would be clear to consumers from the context that a product's recycled content consists of used, reconditioned, or remanufactured components.

Labeling Rules The Textile, Wool, Fur, and Care Labeling Rules require proper origin and fiber content labeling of textile, wool and fur products, and care label instructions attached to clothing and fabrics.

For a product to bear the label "Made in USA," the product must be "all or virtually all" made in the United States. The term "United States," as referred to in the Enforcement Policy Statement, includes the 50 states, the District of Columbia, and the U.S. territories and possessions. "All or virtually all" means that all significant parts and processing that go into the product must be of U.S. origin. That is, the product should contain no, or negligible, foreign content. The product's final assembly or processing must take place in the United States. The Commission then considers other factors, including how much of the product's total manufacturing costs can be assigned to U.S. parts and processing and how far removed any foreign content is from the finished product. In some instances, only a small portion of the total manufacturing costs is attributable to foreign processing, but that processing represents a significant amount of the product's overall processing. Claims that a particular manufacturing or other process was performed in the United States or that a particular part was manufactured in the United States must be truthful, substantiated, and clearly refer to the specific process or part, not to the general manufacture of the product, to avoid implying more U.S. content than exists.

A product that includes foreign components may be called "Assembled in USA" without qualification when its principal assembly takes place in the United States and the assembly is substantial. For the assembly claim to be valid, the product's last substantial transformation should have occurred in the United States.

COMPARATIVE ADVERTISING

It is completely legal for a company to compare its product or service to another company's in an ad provided the comparison is truthful and accurate. However, it is illegal to mislead through an implied comparison. A statement in an ad that a product is more reliable than another because it does something that the other product may also do, can manipulatively imply a falsehood.

FTC LITIGATION

Typically, FTC investigations are non-public to protect both the investigation and the companies involved. If the FTC believes that a person or company has violated the law, the agency may attempt to obtain voluntary compliance by entering into a consent order with the company. A company that signs a consent order need not admit that it violated the law, but it must agree to stop the disputed practices outlined in an accompanying complaint. If a consent agreement cannot be reached, the FTC may issue an administrative complaint or seek injunctive relief in the federal courts. The FTC's administrative complaints initiate a formal proceeding that is much like a federal court trial but before an administrative law judge; evidence is submitted, **testimony** is heard, and witnesses are examined and cross-examined. If a law violation is found, a **cease and desist order** may be issued. Initial decisions by administrative law judges may be appealed to the full Commission. Final decisions issued by the Commission may be appealed to the U.S. Court of Appeals and, ultimately, to the U.S. Supreme Court.

In some circumstances, the FTC can go directly to court to obtain an injunction, civil penalties, or consumer **redress**. The injunction preserves the market's competitive status quo. The FTC seeks federal court injunctions in consumer protection matters typically in cases of ongoing consumer fraud.

ADDITIONAL RESOURCES

Federal Trade Commission. "FTC Issues New Rule Strengthening Consumer Protections Against Deceptive Mortgage Advertisements." Available at http://www.ftc.gov/opa/2011/07/mortgageads.shtm (accessed November 3, 2012).

Rampton, Sheldon, and John Stauber. *Trust Us, We're Experts: How Industry Manipulates Science and Gambles with Your Future.* New York: Putnam, 2000.

Wells, William, Sandra Moriarty, and John Burnett. *Advertising: Principles And Practice.* 7th ed. Upper Saddle River, NJ: Prentice Hall, 2005.

ORGANIZATIONS

Council of Better Business Bureaus (BBB)
4200 Wilson Blvd., Suite 800
Arlington, VA 22203-1838
Phone: (703) 276-0100
Fax: (703) 525-8277
URL: http://www.bbb.org

Federal Trade Commission (FTC)
600 Pennsylvania Avenue, NW
Washington, DC 20580
Toll Free: (877) FTC-HELP
URL: http://www.ftc.gov

CONSUMER ISSUES

BANKRUPTCY

Sections within this essay:

- Background
- History
- Types of Bankruptcies
- Sweeping Changes in 2005
- Jurisdiction and Procedure
- Exemptions from the Bankruptcy Estate
- Federal Bankruptcy Exemptions
- Additional Resources

BACKGROUND

Bankruptcy is a procedure, authorized under federal law, that relieves an individual or corporation of debts. With bankruptcy, debtors rarely escape completely from liability for their debts; instead, they partially or completely repay creditors under an arrangement that is court approved and authorized and in exchange, any remaining debt is forgiven.

Once considered shameful, bankruptcy still is a method of last resort for relieving financial obligations, but at the end of the twentieth century and beginning of the twenty-first century bankruptcy in the United States has become more common and more acceptable. Individuals can seek the protection of the bankruptcy courts for personal debts such as credit cards, home mortgages, and medical bills, among others. **Corporations**, farms, and even local governments also can find themselves lacking enough financial resources to pay their debts and can turn to the bankruptcy courts for help.

Bankruptcy exists to allow debtors to have a "fresh start," so that they can settle their debts and return to being productive members of society. The goal is to prevent individual debtors from becoming destitute and to prevent **corporate** debtors and other entities from becoming non-existent. At the same time, it is the goal of bankruptcy to repay creditors, at least partially. This is done by having the bankruptcy court **liquidate**, or sell, the assets of the **debtor** or restructure the debtor's finances so that creditors are paid at least part of what is owed. The bankruptcy court protects the debtor from further debt-collecting actions by the **creditor** so long as the debtor complies with the court's **liquidation** or restructuring plan. Bankruptcy thereby allows the debtor to emerge from the debt and move forward. This is why bankruptcy is sometimes referred to as "bankruptcy protection" or "bankruptcy relief." A significant deterrent to bankruptcy is the damaged credit rating that results. An individual who files for bankruptcy may have a difficult time obtaining credit for up to seven years or more.

Although federal law generally governs bankruptcies in the United States, states still govern issues and disputes over financial obligations such as rental leases, utility bills, and other contracts involving finances. Federal law concerning these issues overrides state law once a debtor files for bankruptcy protection. This is warranted by the Constitution and ensures economic stability and uniformity among the states.

HISTORY

The evolution of bankruptcy laws in the United States began in England in the sixteenth century. At that time, debtors who would not, or could not, pay their debts unhappily found themselves in debtors prison. By the

U.S. bankruptcy courts—nonbusiness[1] (consumer) cases commenced, by chapter of the bankruptcy code, during the 12-month period ending March 31, 2012

Circuit and district	Nonbusiness filings			
	Total	Chapter 7	Chapter 11	Chapter 13
Total	1,320,613	926,301	1,723	392,587
DC	918	760	4	154
1st	42,143	27,938	88	14,117
2nd	55,771	47,676	68	8,027
3rd	69,990	52,276	57	17,657
4th	90,604	58,522	111	31,971
5th	77,464	33,663	49	43,751
6th	176,331	124,455	90	51,786
7th	133,623	99,339	47	34,237
8th	75,929	56,406	11	19,512
9th	336,675	257,273	974	78,427
10th	74,764	58,098	32	16,634
11th	186,401	109,895	192	76,314

[1]Section 101 of the U.S. Bankruptcy Code defines consumer (nonbusiness) debt as that incurred by an individual primarily for a personal, family, or household purpose. If the debtor is a corporation or partnership, or if debt is related to operation of a business, the nature of the debt is business.

SOURCE: United States Courts. Available at http://www.uscourts .gov/Statistics/BankruptcyStatistics/12-month-period-ending-march.aspx

TABLE BY PREMEDIAGLOBAL. ©2013 CENGAGE LEARNING.

eighteenth century, public sentiment was shifting with the realization that imprisoning debtors was not only cruel, it also prevented creditors from ever getting paid. New laws developed that allowed debts to be reduced or forgiven in exchange for the debtor's efforts to repay them.

Before the signing of the Declaration of Independence, colonies in the United States followed the earlier, punitive English laws that imprisoned debtors. States developed their own laws regarding debtors after 1776, but these laws lacked uniformity. The U.S. Constitution in 1789 charged Congress with enacting laws concerning bankruptcy and the Bankruptcy Act of 1800 became the country's first uniform bankruptcy law.

However, three years after its enactment, Congress repealed the 1800 law over public sentiment that disfavored its emphasis on creditor rights. Congress struggled during the next century to strike the delicate balance between protecting debtors and repaying creditors. In 1841, Congress for the first time permitted debtors to choose whether to obtain bankruptcy relief rather than being forced to do so. Other bankruptcy laws came and went, but the Bankruptcy Act of 1898 and its many amendments lasted for eighty years and became the model for current bankruptcy laws in the United States. The 1898 act established special bankruptcy courts and bankruptcy trustees, charged with the duty of overseeing

bankruptcy liquidations and financial restructuring. The Bankruptcy Reform Act of 1978 replaced the 1898 act and, along with amendments passed in 1984, 1986, 1994, and 2005, this act is known as the bankruptcy code. The 2005 changes, which fall under the Bankruptcy Abuse Prevention and Consumer Protection Act (BAPCPA), introduced what many experts consider to be among the most sweeping changes to personal bankruptcy law, particularly for those who seek to liquidate their debts.

TYPES OF BANKRUPTCIES

There are generally two types of bankruptcy relief. Liquidation, governed by chapter seven of the bankruptcy code and commonly referred to as chapter seven bankruptcy, involves converting the debtor's assets into cash and using the cash to pay the creditors. The bankruptcy code defines how bankruptcy courts and trustees are to prioritize creditors. Some creditors receive only partial satisfaction, or in some cases no satisfaction, of the debt. Once the liquidation and distribution of assets to the creditors is complete, in the case of an individual debtor, the court will forgive any remaining debt. In the case of a corporation, the corporation is rendered defunct upon liquidation and distribution. There is no need to forgive remaining debts of a corporation since the corporation is no longer a legal entity for creditors to pursue.

The second type of bankruptcy relief is called rehabilitation or reorganization. This type of bankruptcy usually gives creditors a better chance of being repaid, although the duration of repayment may be extended. In a reorganization bankruptcy, the debtor may keep assets but must strictly abide by a reorganization plan that the bankruptcy court authorizes. The reorganization plan defines when and how much each creditor will be repaid, but allows the debtor to continue to function as normally as possible. While the reorganization plan is in place the court prevents creditors from pursuing additional payments from the debtor. Over time and with diligence, the debtor repays the creditors according to the reorganization plan. Once the plan is completed, remaining debts are discharged, or forgiven. If the debtor does not comply with the reorganization plan, the court may order that the debtor's assets be liquidated to pay the debts.

The most common forms of reorganization bankruptcies are chapter eleven bankruptcy, which normally applies to individuals and corporations with large and complex debts, and chapter thirteen bankruptcy, which normally applies to individual consumers. The bankruptcy code has a special chapter for family farmers, chapter twelve, but family farmers may opt to file under chapters eleven or thirteen instead. Municipalities seeking bankruptcy protection do so under chapter nine, which mandates reorganization.

SWEEPING CHANGES IN 2005

The Bankruptcy Abuse Prevention and Consumer Protection Act (BAPCPA) was signed into law in April 2005 and went into effect on October 17, 2005. This act, designed to curb instances of bankruptcy **fraud**, had a direct impact on chapter seven bankruptcies. The most significant change was a requirement for chapter seven filers to pass a means test to determine whether they might be able to file chapter thirteen and pay back their debts over a five-year period. Debtors whose income was above the state median (variable based on the number of people in the debtor's household) would be required to file chapter thirteen. Even those deemed eligible to file for chapter seven would still face stricter requirements. Mandatory debt counseling must be completed within 180 days prior to filing for bankruptcy and the debtor must provide a certificate of counseling. The debtor must also supply additional proof of assets, including the most recent year's **tax return**, **evidence** of payment from employers made 60 days before filing, and other forms and documents (including a photo ID). The amount of time before a debtor can file again for chapter seven bankruptcy has risen from six years to eight years.

Banks and credit card agencies hailed the new act as a much-needed check on an easy way out of paying legitimate debts (in 2011 there were 1.3 million filings for personal bankruptcy). Consumer advocates claimed that the new act punished those who were legitimately seeking relief and who now would have a harder time trying to get a fresh start. One development that could have an impact on this issue was a change in regulations regarding minimum monthly payments on credit card accounts. The federal government compelled banks and other credit card issuers to raise the minimum monthly payments, in some cases to double what they had been. While such a change could be a hardship on borrowers who may have trouble making higher payments, ultimately it could help lower outstanding debt by getting people to pay their credit card bills down more quickly.

In October 2005, the U.S. Department of Justice announced that it would grant temporary waivers to chapter seven filers who were affected by Hurricane Katrina, which devastated Louisiana and Mississippi. Victims of the hurricane were given additional time to get the necessary paperwork and debt counseling requirements completed before filing for bankruptcy.

In 2011, the U.S. Supreme Court issued a decision involving chapter thirteen's means test provisions. Under these provisions the debtor proposes a monthly budget that includes disposable income and living expenses. Creditors may object to the budget and payback plan if they believe the debtor has inflated monthly expenses. The Supreme Court was called on to determine whether a debtor could claim an automobile **deduction** if he did not have a loan on the vehicle. The debtor claimed the standard deduction as allowed under the law for basic necessities. However, the deduction was based on "ownership costs" for monthly loan or **lease** payments. The Supreme Court ruled that the debtor could not claim the deduction because he owned the car free and clear. He could not deduct an ownership cost he did not have. However, the debtor was entitled to claim "operating cost" deductions that include payments for insurance, maintenance, fuel, state and local registration, required inspection, parking fees, tolls, and driver's license.

JURISDICTION AND PROCEDURE

Federal **statute** requires that federal district courts maintain **jurisdiction** over bankruptcy matters. District court judges do not preside over bankruptcy cases, however. Instead, units within the district courts manage bankruptcy cases. Federal **appellate court** judges appoint bankruptcy judges to these units, and these judges, with their specialized knowledge of the bankruptcy laws and rules, preside over bankruptcy cases. Thus, the federal district courts technically have jurisdiction over bankruptcy filings but in practice refer the matters to the bankruptcy judges.

Most bankruptcy cases require that the bankruptcy court appoint a **trustee**. The bankruptcy trustee's job is to impartially administer the bankruptcy estate, which includes the assets of the debtor. Once a debtor files for bankruptcy protection, the debtor's assets, such as savings, houses, cars, jewelry, stocks, and **bonds** are examples of assets, become the bankruptcy estate, and the bankruptcy estate becomes a distinct legal entity separate from the debtor. The trustee represents the bankruptcy estate and at the direction of the bankruptcy judge may sell assets, or otherwise oversees if, when, and how the assets will be distributed to pay the debts.

In 1986, Congress permanently established a central office to oversee the work of bankruptcy trustees throughout the country. The office of the U.S. trustee has trustees, appointed by the U.S. attorney general, in each region of the United States. These appointed U.S. trustees, in turn, appoint and supervise additional trustees, ensuring that trustees do their jobs competently and honestly. U.S. trustees also have the responsibility to monitor and report fraud by debtors and abuse by creditors.

One important aspect of the bankruptcy laws is the "automatic stay." As soon as a debtor files the proper legal documents requesting bankruptcy protection, the automatic stay takes effect. This means that all efforts by creditors to collect from the debtor are, by law, frozen, and a creditor who ignores the automatic stay faces severe penalties. The automatic stay gives the debtor, the trustee, and the court time to determine the proper course of action in getting the debts repaid. A party who has a claim against the bankruptcy estate and shows good cause for not being included in the requirements of the automatic stay may ask the bankruptcy judge for "relief from the automatic stay."

When the debtor complies with the bankruptcy liquidation or reorganization plan and the plan is completed, the bankruptcy judge may discharge any remaining debt and terminate the bankruptcy case. This action also terminates the automatic stay and ends the bankruptcy court's involvement with the debtor. Typically, the debtor is left without any debts since the bankruptcy plan has repaid them or the bankruptcy court has discharged them. Also typically, the debtor is left with a poor credit rating and has difficulty borrowing money, obtaining credit cards, and financing things like homes, cars, and business ventures. Credit bureaus can report a bankruptcy for ten years after the date of filing.

Sometimes creditors offer debtors the opportunity to "reaffirm" a debt, keeping the debt and agreeing to pay it off even if it is eligible for liquidation. Debtors often do this when they feel it would be to their advantage to maintain a good relationship with certain creditors. Reaffirming a debt does not improve the debtor's credit rating, and leaves the debtor with an undischargable debt, thus defeating the purpose of bankruptcy as a form of financial relief. Many lending institutions do allow debtors to obtain credit in the form of a "secured" credit card, in which the debtor deposits money into a bank account as **collateral** against the use of the card. This can be useful for people who wish to gradually rebuild their credit ratings.

EXEMPTIONS FROM THE BANKRUPTCY ESTATE

In keeping with the goal of bankruptcy laws to rehabilitate rather than punish the debtor, the individual debtor is permitted to keep some property that otherwise would be included in the bankruptcy estate and liquidated. These are called exemptions. Exemptions ensure that the debtor is able to survive the bankruptcy process without becoming destitute and having to rely on additional government assistance once the process is complete.

Property that is commonly deemed exempt from the bankruptcy estate includes a home, a personal car, and personal items such as clothing.

The federal bankruptcy statute lists allowable exemptions that are followed in some states. However, the federal law also permits states to legislate their own list of bankruptcy exemptions (in fact, 35 states do not allow debtors to take the federal exemptions). This results in widely varying types and amounts of exemptions that depend on the debtor's state of residence. Some states allow debtors to combine state and selected federal exemption items

FEDERAL BANKRUPTCY EXEMPTIONS

In 2012, federal bankruptcy exemptions included the residence of the debtor, up to $21,625 in value; the personal vehicle, up to $3,450 in value; household furnishings, books, clothing, pets, and other personal items up to $550 per item or $11,525 in aggregate value; jewelry valued at no more than $1,450; and tools of the trade with a value of no more than $2,175. In addition, benefits such as social security, **disability**, unemployment, **alimony**, and certain pensions are exempt. A "wild card" exemption of up to $1,150, as well as up to $10,825 of unused **homestead** exemption funds, can be applied to any property.

ADDITIONAL RESOURCES

Epstein, David G. *Bankruptcy and Related Law in a Nutshell.* 8th ed. Eagan, MN: West, Thomson Reuters, 2013.

Gale Encyclopedia of American Law. 3rd ed. Detroit: Gale, Cengage Learning, 2011.

U.S. Courts. "Bankruptcy Basics." Available at http://www.uscourts.gov/FederalCourts/Bankruptcy/BankruptcyBasics.aspx (accessed November 3, 2012).

ORGANIZATIONS

American Bankruptcy Institute

44 Canal Center Plz., Ste. 404
Alexandria, VA 22314
Phone: (703) 739-0800
URL: http://www.abiworld.org

CONSUMER ISSUES

CONSUMER DEBT COLLECTION AND GARNISHMENT

Sections within this essay:

BACKGROUND

In a robust economy, such as that of the economic boom during the 1990s and early 2000s, credit comes easy and consumers often respond by overindulging in purchases and loans. Many consumers ultimately find themselves overextended in both available credit and outstanding debt. However, when credit tightens, or personal circumstances in the life of a consumer-debtor change, there can be a domino effect spreading from individual debtors all the way to the national economy.

During rough financial times, there is often nothing as difficult as picking up the telephone and informing a **creditor** that a payment will be late or not coming at all. However, this is precisely what needs to be done. Creditors often have as much at stake in a defaulting account as the **debtor**. Therefore, it is to the benefit of both parties to attempt a solution short of formal proceedings.

In order to fairly accomplish this, debtors should be acquainted with their rights and the various laws, remedies, and procedures available to both them and their creditors.

General and Secured Creditors At the outset, it is important to distinguish between two main classes of creditors, to whom debts may be in **default**. The distinction directly affects the outcome of a debt collection matter.

A secured loan is one that requires the debtor to pledge something of value as **collateral** for the loan. Home mortgages and auto loans are common examples affecting most consumers. In each of these two examples, the purchased house or the purchased automobile becomes the collateral for the loan, and the lender has a "security interest" in the collateral/property that secures the debt. When a debtor defaults in payments, the "secured creditor" can simply repossess the car or house. (A **foreclosure** on a house is a form of repossession by the lender, but federal and state laws impose additional notice requirements upon defaulting debtors. However, in the classic "land contract" sale of property at **common law**, debtors who defaulted in payments generally lost the property and all equity therein.)

On the other hand, most credit card debts, revolving credit at retail stores, student loans, etc., are unsecured

241

debts. The "general" (unsecured) creditors must file suit and win a judgment against the debtor before they can seize or sell any assets or belongings of a debtor to satisfy the debt. Once the general creditor has obtained a judgment against a defaulting debtor, the general creditor stands as a secured creditor who may then move on to levy liens or writs of **execution** against a debtor's assets and **personal property**. (See "Formal Proceedings.")

SEQUENCE OF EVENTS

Once a debtor has defaulted on making a payment as originally agreed to between the debtor and creditor, the creditor has several choices. It may contact the debtor directly, turn the matter over to an internal collections department, or turn the matter over to an external collection agency.

Internal Efforts by Original Creditor It is clearly within the best interests of both creditor and debtor to resolve the matter "internally." Depending on whether the creditor is a general or secured one, the options available are broad. Generally, however, most consumer debt (other than for houses and automobiles) is unsecured, and creditors are general creditors whose collection activities are more limited prior to obtaining an actual judgment against a debtor.

Depending upon the debtor's prior payment history with a particular creditor, no action may be taken at all, other than a friendly "reminder" letter, if a monthly payment is missed on an **installment** agreement, revolving credit account, or credit card account. Creditors are happy to charge late fees, add accrued interest to the new balance, and double the amount owed for the following month. However, after a certain number of days without payment dependent on the debtor's prior history, creditors will contact the debtor, usually by correspondence and telephone. If there is no satisfactory payment or arrangement made, most major creditors will turn the account over to an internal collections department.

Typically, letters from the internal collections department of a creditor will ask the debtor to send payment or contact the creditor immediately. The creditor will attempt to collect at least the past due payment prior to the end of the month (irrespective of the original payment due date) in order to avoid reporting the late payment to a credit reporting bureau or agency. The creditor will also attempt to secure a payment over the telephone, as well as secure staggered payments, using postdated checks, for the next three payments. At this point, it behooves the creditor to work with a debtor, because if it must turn the account over to a collection agency, it will only be paid a percentage of the amount collected from the debtor after the collection agency has been paid its share.

Collection Agencies If a creditor is unsuccessful in collecting a debt payment, it may retain an outside service, or collection agency, to continue efforts to collect on the debt. A collection agency receives a percentage of the amount recovered, usually between 10 and 50 percent, in return for its efforts. Because its chief concern is to maximize its own potential earnings on the account, a collection agency's tactics are regulated by both federal and state law.

Within five days of its first telephone call to a debtor, a collection agency must send a notice in writing that states the total amount owed, and the name of the original creditor for whom the agency is attempting to collect. The written notice must also inform the debtor that he or she has 30 days from receipt of notice to dispute the debt in writing and/or request a written verification of it.

Debtors are usually authorized at this point to make payments directly to the collections agency, which will forward the **net** balance (after deducting its percentage of the recovered amount) to the original creditor. It is imperative that, prior to making any payment, the debtor verifies that the collection agency indeed represents, and is the agent for, the principal creditor. A debtor may reasonably rely on correspondence from the collection agency, stating the name of its creditor client, as **evidence** of this.

Offers of Settlement At all stages up to this point, creditors may be open to negotiating a **settlement** in lieu of the entire amount owed. The more it will cost a creditor to pursue collection activity against a debtor, the more it may be interested in a lump sum settlement offer. However, because the creditor has incurred additional costs and expenses in pursuing collection, a proffered settlement amount may not be palpably less than the amount of the original debt. For example, a defaulted debt of $10,000 may result in the addition of late fees, accrued interest, and attorney or collection fees, such that the debtor has accumulated $14,000 in debt. If the creditor agrees to accept $10,000 in full settlement of the outstanding debt, the debtor is no further along than he was before he defaulted in the first place.

Attorneys for the Creditor If a collection agency is unable to secure payment or contact with a debtor, the next step in usually **litigation**. Once the debtor's account file has been turned over to an attorney for litigation, the debtor's chances of negotiating payment or settlement with the creditor are slim to none. Moreover, once the matter has gone this far, the debtor will most likely be responsible for the payment of all attorney fees and costs associated with collection efforts, in addition to the original debt owed. Importantly, attorneys or law firms that regularly engage in the collection of debts are subject to the provisions of the Fair Debt Collection Practices Act (FDCPA) as are collection agencies.

At this stage (even though it can legally be done at an earlier stage), the creditor, or attorney acting on its behalf, will invoke any "acceleration clause" that may be in the original loan or credit agreement. These clauses are common, but usually not acted upon until a debtor fails to pay the delinquent amounts or falls seriously behind in payments. If a debtor defaults on payments, an acceleration clause, to which the debtor has agreed in the original paperwork for the credit or loan, "accelerates" all future payments so that the entire loan balance (not just the payments in **arrears**) is immediately due and payable in full. If a debtor has not already received notice that the creditor is demanding the entire loan balance, an attorney will be certain to do this prior to filing suit against the debtor.

Of course, if the debtor was able to pay off the entire loan in question, he or she would not be in default in the first place. Even if the attorney makes one last settlement offer of a percentage of the entire balance, the likelihood of the debtor being able to pay is nil. This, then, is a very serious stage of default that will most likely result in a lawsuit being filed against the debtor.

Formal Proceedings If measures have all failed to resolve a debtor's default, creditors may file suit in local state or federal court. This makes the debt collection a matter of public record. There are very few available defenses, except those permitted by the **Uniform Commercial Code** (UCC) for defective products

Creditors' lawsuits are generally grounded in **contract**. Damages are limited to the face amount of the loan balance, accrued interest, (sometimes) attorney fees, and court costs. Creditors will sue for the entire balance owed on the account, not just the payments in arrears. They seldom ask other creditors to join them in a suit, even if those other creditors also have defaulted loans. This is because there seldom are sufficient assets to cover the entire judgment immediately, and the creditor that filed suit wants to be first in line. If a defendant-debtor fails to appear in response to the lawsuit, a **default judgment** will likely be entered against him or her.

Satisfaction of Judgment After a judgment is entered against a debtor, the prevailing creditor (now a "judgment creditor") will employ various tactics to collect on the judgment. State laws dictate the number of years a creditor may pursue collection on an outstanding judgment; typically, they are 10 to 20 years. Debtors whose attitude had been, "Go ahead and sue me, I don't have any money" are surprised to learn that any assets they acquire for the next several years can be seized or forfeited in satisfaction of an outstanding judgment.

Property Seizure and Garnishment Following successful judgment against a defaulting debtor, creditors will usually ask a court for a creditor's **hearing**, in which the debtor must make a sworn declaration of all assets and property. This may be done in writing or by oral **deposition**. Exempted property (that which cannot be seized in satisfaction of a judgment) includes a primary residence up to a certain value, vehicles not used for employment, tools used for employment, some personal effects and household goods, and life insurance/retirement proceeds. However, funds in bank accounts, extra vehicles, boats, campers, and other items of value (musical instruments, stocks and **bonds**) are subject to inclusion.

Judgment creditors generally do not go to a debtor's property and seize items. Instead, they present a copy of their court judgment, along with a "writ of execution" form, to local law enforcement officials (sheriff, marshal, constable) who will "execute" the **writ** and seize property.

A judgment creditors may also request that the court issue of writ for garnishment of the debtor's wages. If granted, the court order for garnishment is served directly upon the debtor's employer, who must comply with its terms. For ordinary garnishments (those not for **child support**, **alimony**, **bankruptcy**, or any state or federal tax), the weekly amount may not exceed the lesser of two figures: 25 percent of the employee's disposable earnings, or the amount by which an employee's disposable earnings are greater than 30 times the federal **minimum wage** (currently $7.25 an hour). The garnished amount is paid directly to the judgment creditor by the debtor's employer. Federal benefits, including Social Security, cannot be garnished.

Seized property may be sold at public auction, with proceeds returned to the judgment creditor. Most states permit "redemption" (repurchase by the debtor) of real property (real estate) sold at auction, within a specified time, such as one year. Money received at auction which is in excess of the debt owed is returned to the debtor.

FAIR DEBT COLLECTION PRACTICES ACT

The Fair Debt Collection Practices Act of 1977 (FDCPA) (15 USC 1601) protects consumers from illegal or improper practices in debt collecting. Its mandates apply only to consumer debts and not to business debts.

Furthermore, they do not apply to collection efforts made directly by the creditor to whom the debt is owed. The law is enforced by the Federal Trade Commission (FTC).

What may be perceived as improper conduct or harassment by a stressed debtor may not in fact be illegal or improper under the Act. What is prohibited of a collection agency includes the following:

- Communicating with the debtor's employer, neighbors, or anyone else for any reason except to ask where the debtor lives

- Informing any person that an attempt is being made to collect a debt from the debtor

- Sending postcards or mail that reveal the sender as a collection agency

- Contacting a debtor at a place of employment, if the debtor or the employer objects

- Telephoning a debtor before 8:00 a.m. or after 9:00 p.m.

- Using obscene, profane, or threatening language

- Make the debtor's name public as a person who fails to pay debts

- Failing to identify himself/herself as a collector; pretending to be a lawyer, law enforcement officer, or other government official

- Obtaining information from the debtor under **false pretenses**, such as taking a survey or suggesting that the debtor has committed a crime

- Contacting a debtor who has informed the collector that he or she is represented by an attorney

- Communicate in any way with a debtor who has informed the collector in writing that no more contact with the debtor is to be made

State Laws Creditors that violate the rights of debtors should be reported to the Federal Trade Commission (see Organizations at the end of this essay) or the National Consumer Law Center (see Organizations at the end of this essay), which will refer the debtor to a consumer law attorney practicing in the area. The following states permit debtors to secretly tape telephone calls from collection agencies:

- Alabama
- Alaska
- Arizona
- Arkansas
- Colorado
- District of Columbia
- Georgia
- Hawaii
- Idaho
- Indiana
- Iowa
- Kansas
- Kentucky
- Louisiana
- Maine
- Minnesota
- Mississippi
- Missouri
- Nebraska
- Nevada
- New Jersey
- New Mexico
- New York
- North Carolina
- North Dakota
- Ohio
- Oklahoma
- Rhode Island
- South Carolina
- Tennessee
- Texas
- Utah
- Virginia
- West Virginia
- Wisconsin
- Wyoming

In the remaining 15 states, a debtor must secure permission from the collector. While failure to secure permission may prevent the recording of illegal or improper collection agency tactics, it does have a chilling effect on a collector who has been asked if the conversation can be recorded. He or she will most likely not engage in improper tactics, for fear that the debtor is recording the communication, even without permission.

ADDITIONAL RESOURCES

Baird, Douglas G., et al, comp. *Commercial and Debtor-Creditor Law: Selected Statutes.* Foundation Press, 2005.

Federal Trade Commission. "Facts for Consumers: Debt Collection FAQs: A Guide for Consumers." Available at http://www.ftc.gov/bcp/edu/pubs/consumer/credit/cre18.shtm (accessed November 3, 2012).

Loonin, Deanne. *Surviving Debt.* Boston: National Consumer Law Center, 2010.

Privacy Rights Clearinghouse. "Fact Sheet 27: Debt Collection Practices: When Hardball Tactics Go Too Far." Available at https://www.privacyrights.org/fs/fs27-debtcoll.htm (accessed November 3, 2012).

ORGANIZATIONS

Consumer Response Center, Federal Trade Commission

600 Pennsylvania Avenue NW
Washington, DC 20580
Toll Free: (877) 382-4357
URL: http://www.consumer.ftc.gov

National Association of Consumer Advocates (NACA)

Phone: (202) 452-1989
URL: http://www.naca.net

National Consumer Law Center (NCLC)

Phone: (617) 542-8010
URL: http://www.consumerlaw.org

National Foundation for Credit Counseling

Toll Free: (800) 388-2227
URL: http://www.nfcc.org

CONSUMER ISSUES

CONSUMER RIGHTS AND PROTECTION

Sections within this essay:

- Background
- Warranties
  - Implied Warranties
  - Express Warranties
  - Extended Warranties

- Federal Acts
  - Food Quality Protection Act
  - Safe Drinking Water Act
  - Federal Insecticide, Fungicide, and Rodenticide Act

- Consumer Vehicle Purchases
  - Lemon Laws

- Federal Agencies
  - Consumer Product Safety Commission
  - Office of Consumer Litigation
  - Internet Fraud Complaint Center
  - U.S. Food and Drug Administration
  - Center for Biologics Evaluation and Research
  - Federal Trade Commission
  - National Highway Traffic Safety Administration

- State Laws
- Additional Resources

BACKGROUND

Consumer protection encompasses a broad range of consumer issues including, credit, utilities, services and goods. Many consumer complaints arise from simple disputes that may be resolved through communication between the consumer and the business. Others, however, may accuse a manufacturer or seller of engaging in **fraudulent** transactions. Consumers are protected under both state and federal laws. Some states have laws regarding major purchases that allow for a "cooling off" period in which the consumer can return the item or cancel the **contract** with no **penalty**. Each state Attorney General's office has some type of public protection division responsible for enforcing the rights of consumers in business and service transactions and to protect the **civil rights** of citizens. Federal standards are enforced by the Federal Trade Commission, which oversees a number of federal antitrust and consumer protection laws. The Commission seeks to ensure that the nation's markets function competitively and are vigorous, efficient, and free of undue restrictions. The Commission also works to enhance the smooth operation of the marketplace by eliminating acts or practices that are unfair or deceptive. In general, the Commission's efforts are directed toward stopping actions that threaten consumers' opportunities to exercise informed choice.

WARRANTIES

A **warranty** is the promise made by a manufacturer or seller to resolve problems the product may have. Warranties can cover the retail sale of consumer goods. Consumer goods include new products or parts which are used, bought, or leased for use primarily for personal, family, or household purposes. There are two kinds of warranties: implied warranties and express warranties.

Implied Warranties Implied warranties are unspoken, unwritten promises that are created by state law. In consumer product transactions, there are two types of implied warranties: the **implied warranty** of merchantability and the implied warranty of fitness for a particular purpose. The implied warranty of merchantability is a merchant's basic promise that the goods sold will function and have nothing significantly wrong with them. The implied warranty of fitness for a particular purpose is a promise that the seller's product can be used for some specific purpose. Implied warranties are promises about the condition of products at the time they are sold, but they do not assure that a product will last for a specific length of time. Implied warranties do not cover problems caused by misuse, ordinary wear, failure to follow directions, or improper maintenance. Generally, there is no specified duration for implied warranties under state laws. However, the state statutes of limitations for breach of either an express or an implied warranty are generally four years from date of purchase. This means that buyers have four years in which to discover and seek a remedy for problems that were present in the product at the time it was sold. It does not mean that the product must last for four years. Implied warranties apply only when the seller is a merchant who deals in such goods, not when a sale is made by a private individual.

Express Warranties Express warranties are explicit warranties. Express warranties can take a variety of forms, ranging from advertising claims to formal certificates. An express warranty can be made either orally or in writing; however, only written warranties on consumer products are covered by the **Magnuson-Moss Warranty Act**.

Extended Warranties Extended warranties are actually service contracts. Like warranties, service contracts provide repair and/or maintenance for a specific period of time; however, service contracts cost extra and are sold separately. Warranties are included in the price of the product; service contracts are not.

FEDERAL ACTS

Food Quality Protection Act The Food Quality Protection Act (FQPA) of 1996 amended the Federal Insecticide, Fungicide, and Rodenticide Act (FIFRA) and the Federal Food Drug, and Cosmetic Act (FFDCA). These amendments fundamentally changed the way EPA regulates pesticides. The requirements included a new safety standard—reasonable certainty of no harm—that must be applied to all pesticides used on food.

Safe Drinking Water Act The Safe Drinking Water Act was promulgated in 1974 to protect the quality of drinking water in the United States. This law focuses on all waters actually or potentially designed for drinking use, whether from above ground or underground sources. The

Act authorizes EPA to establish safe standards of purity and required all owners or operators of public water systems to comply with primary (health-related) standards. State governments, which assume this power from EPA, also encourage attainment of secondary standards (nuisance-related).

Federal Insecticide, Fungicide, and Rodenticide Act The primary focus of the Federal Insecticide, Fungicide, and Rodenticide Act (FIFRA), enacted in 1972, was to provide federal control of pesticide distribution, sale, and use. EPA was given authority under FIFRA not only to study the consequences of pesticide usage but also to require users (farmers, utility companies, and others) to register when purchasing pesticides. Through later amendments to the law, users were required to take exams for certification as applicators of pesticides. All pesticides used in the United States must be registered (licensed) by EPA. Registration assures that pesticides will be properly labeled and that if when used in accordance with specifications will not cause unreasonable harm to the environment.

CONSUMER VEHICLE PURCHASES

The Federal Anti-Tampering Odometer Law prohibits anyone from falsifying mileage readings in a new or used vehicle. The Federal Used Car Law requires used car dealers to post Buyers Guides on used cars. The Federal Automobile Information Disclosure Act requires new car dealerships to put a sticker on the windshield or side window of the car. This sticker must list the base price of the car and the options added and their costs, as well as the dealer's cost for transportation and the number of miles per gallon the car uses.

Dealers are not required by law to give used car buyers a three-day right to cancel. The right to return the car in a few days for a refund exists only if the dealer grants this privilege to buyers. The Federal Trade Commission's Used Car Rule requires dealers to post a Buyers Guide in every used vehicle they offer for sale. This includes light-duty vans, light-duty trucks, demonstrators, and program cars. Demonstrators are new cars that have not been owned, leased, or used as rentals, but have been driven by dealer staff. Program cars are low-mileage, current-model-year vehicles returned from short-term leases or rentals. Buyers Guides do not have to be posted on motorcycles and most recreational vehicles, nor by any seller that sells less than six vehicles a year. The Buyers Guide becomes part of the sales contract and overrides all contrary provisions. Dealers who offer a written warranty must complete the warranty section of the Buyers Guide. Dealers may offer a full or limited warranty on all or some of a vehicle's systems or components. Most used car warranties are limited and their coverage varies. A full or limited warranty is not required to cover the entire vehicle. The dealer may specify that only certain systems are covered. Some parts or systems may be covered by a full warranty; others by a limited warranty. The dealer must check the appropriate box on the Buyers Guide if a service contract is offered, except in states where service contracts are regulated by insurance laws.

Lemon Laws So-called **Lemon Laws** vary from state to state. Typically, a defect covered by the Lemon Law must be a major defect which substantially impairs the use, value, or safety of the vehicle. Lemon laws generally impose time or mileage limitations regarding when the defect must be presented to the manufacturer or dealer in order to be covered under the Lemon Law. The manufacturer must repair the defect within a reasonable number of repair attempts. If the manufacturer fails to repair the defect or defects in the vehicle within a reasonable number of repair attempts, the consumer is entitled to a repurchase or replacement of the vehicle. In some states if the defect is of such a character that there is a substantial risk of death or serious bodily injury if the vehicle is driven, the vehicle is presumed to be a lemon if the defect continues to exist after even one repair attempt. If the defect does not fall into this category, additional repair attempts are normally required. In some states, three repair attempts for a defect is enough to **warrant** a buy back or replacement. Other states require four repair attempts or more.

FEDERAL AGENCIES

While many states have enacted comprehensive products liability statutes, there is no federal products liability law. There are, however, a number of federal entities responsible for maintaining and enforcing regulation of consumer products.

Consumer Product Safety Commission The U.S. Consumer Product Safety Commission (CPSC) is an independent federal regulatory agency created to protect the public from unreasonable risks of injuries and deaths associated with some 15,000 types of consumer products. Defective product law, commonly known as products liability, refers to the liability of parties along the chain of manufacture of any product for damage caused by that product. A defective product is one that causes some injury or damage to person because of some defect in the product or its labeling or the way the product was used. Those responsible for the defect can include the manufacturers of component parts, assembling manufacturers, wholesalers, and retail stores. The CPSC uses various means to inform the public about potential risks.

These include local and national media coverage, publication of numerous booklets and product alerts, a web site, a telephone Hotline, the National Injury Information Clearinghouse, CPSC's Public Information Center and responses to **Freedom of Information Act** (FOIA) requests. For nearly 30 years the U.S. Consumer Product Safety Commission (CPSC) has operated a statistically valid injury surveillance and follow-back system known as the National Electronic Injury Surveillance System (NEISS). The primary purpose of NEISS has been to provide timely data on consumer product-related injuries occurring in the United States. NEISS injury data are gathered from the emergency departments of 100 hospitals selected as a probability sample of all U.S. hospitals with emergency departments. The system's foundation rests on emergency department surveillance data, but the system also has the flexibility to gather additional data at either the surveillance or the investigation level. Surveillance data enable CPSC analysts to make timely national estimates of the number of injuries associated with (not necessarily caused by) specific consumer products. These data also provide **evidence** of the need for further study of particular products. Subsequent follow-back studies yield important clues to the cause and likely prevention of injuries.

Office of Consumer Litigation When a client agency refers a case to the Department of Justice, the Office of Consumer **Litigation** (OCL) generally receives the referral and will either retain it or ask a United States Attorney's Office (USAO) to handle the case. Frequently, OCL and the USAO work jointly on these matters. Established in 1971, the OCL enforces and defends the consumer protection programs of the Food and Drug Administration (FDA), the Federal Trade Commission (FTC), the Consumer Product Safety Commission (CPSC), and the Department of Transportation's National Highway Traffic Safety Administration (NHTSA). OCL has responsibility for litigation under federal consumer protection laws. These include the Federal Food, Drug, and Cosmetic Act; the odometer tampering prohibitions of the Motor Vehicle Information and Cost Savings Act; the Consumer Product Safety Act; and a variety of laws administered by the Federal Trade Commission, such as the Fair Debt Collection Practices Act.

Internet Fraud Complaint Center The mission of the Internet **Fraud** Complaint Center is to combat fraud committed over the Internet. The IFCC website allows consumers nationwide to report Internet fraud; enables the development of educational programs aimed at preventing Internet fraud; offers local, state, and federal law enforcement agencies training in Internet fraud; and allows the sharing of fraud data by all law enforcement and regulatory authorities.

U.S. Food and Drug Administration The U.S. Food and Drug Administration (FDA) monitors food, cosmetics, medicines and medical devices, and ensures the safety of radiation-emitting consumer products such as microwave ovens. FDA also oversees feed and drugs for pets and farm animals. Authorized by Congress to enforce the Federal Food, Drug, and Cosmetic Act and several other public health laws, the agency monitors the manufacture, import, transport, storage, and sale of $1 trillion worth of goods annually.

Center for Biologics Evaluation and Research A biological product subject to licensure under the Public Health Service Act is any virus, therapeutic serum, toxin, antitoxin, vaccine, blood, blood component or derivative, allergenic product, or analogous product, applicable to the prevention, treatment, or cure of diseases or injuries to humans. Biological products include, but are not limited to, bacterial and viral vaccines, human blood and plasma and their derivatives, and certain products produced by biotechnology, such as interferons and erythropoietins. The Center for Biologics Evaluation and Research (CBER) is responsible for ensuring the safety and efficacy of blood and blood products, vaccines, allergenics, and biological therapeutics. CBER's regulation of biological products has expanded in recent years to include a wide variety of new products such as biotechnology products, somatic cell therapy and gene therapy, and banked human tissues.

Federal Trade Commission The Federal Trade Commission (FTC) works to ensure that the nation's markets are efficient and free of practices which might harm consumers. To ensure the smooth operation of our free market system, the FTC enforces federal consumer protection laws that prevent fraud, deception and unfair business practices. The Commission also enforces federal antitrust laws that prohibit anticompetitive mergers and other business practices that restrict competition and harm consumers.

National Highway Traffic Safety Administration The National Highway Traffic Safety Administration (NHTSA), within the U.S. Department of Transportation, was established by the Highway Safety Act of 1970, to carry out safety programs under the National Traffic and Motor Vehicle Safety Act of 1966 and the Highway Safety Act of 1966. NHTSA also carries out consumer programs established by the Motor Vehicle Information and Cost Savings Act of 1972. NHTSA has consumer information on motor vehicle safety, crash worthiness, and recalls among other areas. OCL works with NHTSA to enforce the provisions of the federal odometer tampering **statute**.

STATE LAWS

ALABAMA: State law forbids **false advertising** and automobile odometer tampering. A lawsuit may be brought by a consumer, the state attorney general, or a district attorney.

ALASKA: State law forbids false advertising and automobile odometer tampering. A lawsuit may be brought by a consumer or the state attorney general.

ARIZONA: State law forbids false advertising and automobile odometer tampering, the latter of which constitutes a **misdemeanor** offense. A lawsuit may be brought by the state attorney general.

ARKANSAS: State law forbids false advertising and automobile odometer tampering. A lawsuit may be brought by the state attorney general.

CALIFORNIA: State law forbids false advertising and automobile odometer tampering. A lawsuit may be brought by a consumer, the state attorney general, or a district or prosecuting attorney.

COLORADO: State law forbids false advertising and automobile odometer tampering. A lawsuit may be brought by a consumer, the state attorney general, or a district attorney.

CONNECTICUT: State law forbids automobile odometer tampering, which is defined as a misdemeanor offense. A lawsuit may be brought by a consumer, the state attorney general, the Commissioner of Consumer Protection.

DELAWARE: State law forbids false advertising and automobile odometer tampering. A lawsuit may be brought by a consumer or the state attorney general.

DISTRICT OF COLUMBIA: The law of the district forbids false advertising. A lawsuit may be brought by a consumer or the director of the Department of Consumer and Regulatory Affairs.

FLORIDA: State law forbids false advertising and automobile odometer tampering, the latter of which is a

felony offense. A lawsuit may be brought by a consumer or certain state officials.

GEORGIA: State law forbids false advertising and automobile odometer tampering. A lawsuit may be brought by a consumer.

HAWAII: State law forbids false advertising and automobile odometer tampering. A lawsuit may be brought by a consumer or the Consumer Protection Agency.

IDAHO: State law forbids false advertising and automobile odometer tampering. A lawsuit may be brought by a consumer or by the state.

ILLINOIS: State law forbids false advertising and automobile odometer tampering, the latter of which is a misdemeanor offense. A lawsuit may be brought by a consumer, the state attorney general, or a state attorney.

INDIANA: State law forbids false advertising and automobile odometer tampering, the latter of which is a felony offense. A lawsuit may be brought by a consumer and the state attorney general.

IOWA: State law forbids false advertising and automobile odometer tampering. A lawsuit may be brought by a consumer or the state attorney general.

KANSAS: State law forbids false advertising and automobile odometer tampering. A lawsuit may be brought by a consumer, the state attorney general, or a district attorney.

KENTUCKY: State law forbids false advertising and automobile odometer tampering. A lawsuit may be brought by a consumer or the state attorney general.

LOUISIANA: State law forbids false advertising and automobile odometer tampering, the latter of which is a misdemeanor offense. A lawsuit may be brought by a consumer or the state attorney general.

MAINE: State law forbids false advertising and automobile odometer tampering, the latter of which is class D offense. A lawsuit may be brought by a consumer or the state attorney general.

MARYLAND: State law forbids false advertising and automobile odometer tampering. A lawsuit may be

brought by a consumer, the state attorney general, or the Consumer Protection Division.

MASSACHUSETTS: State law forbids false advertising and automobile odometer tampering. A lawsuit may be brought by a consumer or the state attorney general.

MICHIGAN: State law forbids false advertising and automobile odometer tampering. A lawsuit may be brought by a consumer, the state attorney general, or a prosecuting attorney.

MINNESOTA: State law forbids false advertising and automobile odometer tampering, the latter of which is a misdemeanor offense. A lawsuit may be brought by a consumer, the state attorney general, or a county attorney.

MISSISSIPPI: State law forbids false advertising and automobile odometer tampering, the latter of which is a misdemeanor offense. A lawsuit may be brought by a consumer, the state attorney general, or a district or county attorney.

MISSOURI: State law forbids false advertising and automobile odometer tampering, the latter of which can be a criminal offense. A lawsuit may be brought by a consumer or the state attorney general.

MONTANA: State law forbids false advertising and automobile odometer tampering. A lawsuit may be brought by a consumer, the state attorney general, a county attorney, or the Department of Commerce.

NEBRASKA: State law forbids false advertising and automobile odometer tampering. A lawsuit may be brought by a consumer or the state attorney general.

NEVADA: State law forbids false advertising and automobile odometer tampering, the latter of which is a misdemeanor offense. A lawsuit may be brought by a consumer, the state attorney general, or a district attorney.

NEW HAMPSHIRE: State law forbids false advertising and automobile odometer tampering, the latter of which is a misdemeanor offense. A lawsuit may be brought by a consumer or the state attorney general.

NEW JERSEY: State law forbids false advertising and automobile odometer tampering. A lawsuit may be brought by a consumer or the state attorney general.

NEW MEXICO: State law forbids false advertising and automobile odometer tampering, the latter of which is a misdemeanor offense. A lawsuit may be brought by a consumer, the state attorney general, or a district attorney.

NEW YORK: State law forbids false advertising and automobile odometer tampering, the latter of which is a misdemeanor offense. A lawsuit may be brought by a consumer or the state attorney general.

NORTH CAROLINA: State law forbids false advertising and automobile odometer tampering. A lawsuit may be brought by a consumer or the state attorney general.

NORTH DAKOTA: State law forbids false advertising and automobile odometer tampering, the latter of which is a misdemeanor offense (or a felony offense when the **defendant** has a prior **conviction**). A lawsuit may be brought by a consumer, the state attorney general, or a state's attorney.

OHIO: State law forbids false advertising and automobile odometer tampering. A lawsuit may be brought by a consumer, the state attorney general, or a district attorney. A lawsuit may be brought by a consumer or the state attorney general.

OKLAHOMA: State law forbids false advertising and automobile odometer tampering, the latter of which is a misdemeanor offense. A lawsuit may be brought by a consumer, the state attorney general, or a district attorney.

OREGON: State law forbids false advertising and automobile odometer tampering. A lawsuit may be brought by a consumer or by the state.

PENNSYLVANIA: State law forbids false advertising and automobile odometer tampering. A lawsuit may be brought by a consumer, the state attorney general, or a district attorney.

RHODE ISLAND: State law forbids false advertising and automobile odometer tampering. A lawsuit may be brought by a consumer or the state attorney general.

SOUTH CAROLINA: State law forbids false advertising. A lawsuit may be brought by a consumer, the state attorney general, a solicitor, a county attorney, or city attorney.

SOUTH DAKOTA: State law forbids false advertising and automobile odometer tampering, the latter of which is

a misdemeanor offense (subsequent offenses are felony offenses). A lawsuit may be brought by a consumer or the state attorney general.

TENNESSEE: State law forbids false advertising and automobile odometer tampering, the latter of which is a misdemeanor offense. A lawsuit may be brought by a consumer, the state attorney general, or the Division of Consumer Affairs of the Department of Commerce and Insurance.

TEXAS: State law forbids false advertising and automobile odometer tampering. A lawsuit may be brought by a consumer, the state attorney general, a district attorney, or the state consumer protection division.

UTAH: State law forbids false advertising and automobile odometer tampering, the latter of which is a felony offense. A lawsuit may be brought by a consumer or by the state.

VERMONT: State law forbids false advertising and automobile odometer tampering. A lawsuit may be brought by a consumer, the state attorney general, or a state attorney.

VIRGINIA: State law forbids false advertising and automobile odometer tampering. A lawsuit may be brought by a consumer, the state attorney general, or a commonwealth attorney.

WASHINGTON: State law forbids false advertising and automobile odometer tampering. A lawsuit may be brought by a consumer or the state attorney general.

WEST VIRGINIA: State law forbids false advertising. A lawsuit may be brought by an injured consumer.

WISCONSIN: State law forbids false advertising and automobile odometer tampering. A lawsuit may be brought by an injured consumer.

WYOMING: State law forbids false advertising and automobile odometer tampering. A lawsuit may be brought by a consumer or the state attorney general.

ADDITIONAL RESOURCES

Bogus, Carl. *Why Lawsuits Are Good for America: Disciplined Democracy, Big Business, and the Common Law.* New York: New York University Press, 2001.

Federal Citizens Information Center, Office of Citizen Services and Innovative Technologies. *2012 Consumer Action*

Handbook. Washington, DC: U.S. General Services Administration, 2012. Available at http://www.usa.gov/topics/consumer/consumer-action-handbook.pdf (accessed November 3, 2012).

Federal Trade Commission. "Consumer Information." Available at http://www.ftc.gov/bcp/consumer.shtm (accessed November 3, 2012).

Marsh, Gene A. *Consumer Protection Law in a Nutshell*. 3rd ed. Eagan, MN: West, Thomson Reuters, 1999.

Moore, Michael J. *Product Liability Entering the 21st Century: The U.S. Perspective*. Washington, DC: Brookings Institution Press, 2001.

ORGANIZATIONS

Consumer Action (CA)

717 Market Street, Suite 310
San Francisco, CA 94103
Phone: (415) 777-9635
Fax: (415) 777-5267
URL: http://www.consumer-action.org

Federal Trade Commission (FTC)

600 Pennsylvania Avenue, NW
Washington, DC 20580
Toll Free: (877) FTC-HELP
URL: http://www.ftc.gov

National Consumers League (NCL)

1701 K Street, NW, Suite 1200
Washington, DC 20006
Phone: (202) 835-3323
Fax: (202) 835-0747
URL: http://www.nclnet.org

U.S. Consumer Product Safety Commission (CPSC)

4330 East-West Highway
Bethesda, MD 20814-4408
Phone: (301) 504-0990
Fax: (301) 504-0124
URL: http://www.cpsc.gov

CONSUMER ISSUES

CONTRACTS

Sections within this essay:

BACKGROUND

A contract is an agreement between two parties that creates an obligation to do or refrain from doing a particular thing. The purpose of a contract is to establish the terms of the agreement by which the parties have fixed their rights and duties. Courts must enforce valid contracts, unless one party has legal grounds to bar enforcement.

Consumers and commercial entities both depend on the enforceability of contracts when conducting business relations. When consumers or commercial entities enter a contract to buy goods or services at a particular price, in a particular amount, or of a particular quality, they expect the seller to deliver goods and services that conform to the contract. Manufacturers, wholesalers, and retailers similarly expect that their goods and services will be bought in accordance with the terms of the contract.

A legal action for breach of contract arises when at least one party's performance does not live up to the terms of the contract and causes the other party to suffer economic damage or other types of measurable injury. The injury may include any loss suffered by the **plaintiff** in having to buy replacement goods or services at a higher price or of a lower quality from someone else in the market. It may also include the costs and expenses incurred by the plaintiff in having to locate replacement goods or services in the first place.

Contract disputes may be governed by the **common law**, **statutory** law, or both. Each state has developed its own common law of contracts, which consists of a body of **jurisprudence** developed over time by trial and appellate courts on a case-by-case basis. Many states have been influenced by the Restatement (Second) of Contracts, which was approved by the American Law Institute (ALI) in 1979.

For contracts involving commercial transactions, all fifty states have enacted, at least partially, a body of statutory law called the **Uniform Commercial Code** (U.C.C.), which governs a variety of commercial relations involving consumers and merchants, among others. Article 2 of the U.C.C. governs the sale of goods, which are defined by the code as items that are "movable" at the time of the contract. The National Conference of Commissioners on Uniform States Laws, along with the ALI and the American Bar Association, approved a revised version of Article 2 in 2003. However, as of February 2006, no state had adopted the revised version.

State legislatures have also enacted a host of other statutes governing contracts that affect the **public interest**. For example, most states have passed legislation governing the terms of insurance contracts to guarantee that sufficient financial resources will be available for residents who are injured by accident. Congress has passed a number of laws governing contracts as well, ranging from laws that regulate the terms of **collective bargaining** agreements between labor and management to laws that regulate **false advertising** and promote fair trade.

ELEMENTS OF A CONTRACT

The requisite elements that must be established to demonstrate the formation of a legally binding contract are offer; acceptance; consideration; mutuality of obligation; **competency** and capacity; and, in certain circumstances, a written instrument.

Offer An offer is a promise to act or refrain from acting, which is made in exchange for a return promise to do the same. Some offers anticipate not another promise being returned in exchange but the performance of an act or forbearance from taking action. For example, a painter's offer to paint someone's house for $100 is probably conditioned on the homeowner's promise to pay upon completion, while a homeowner's offer to pay someone $100 to have his or her house painted is probably conditioned upon the painter's successfully performing the job. In either case, an offeree's power of acceptance is created when the offeror conveys a present intent to enter a contract in certain and definite terms that are communicated to the offeree.

Courts distinguish preliminary **negotiations** from formal legal offers in that parties to preliminary negotiations lack a present intent to form a contract. Accordingly, no contract is formed when parties to preliminary negotiations respond to each other's invitations, requests, and intimations. Advertisements and catalogues, for example, are treated as forms of preliminary negotiations. Otherwise, the seller of the goods or services would be liable for countless contracts with consumers who view the ad or read the catalogue, even though the quantity of the merchandise may be limited.

However, sellers must be careful to avoid couching their advertisements in clear and definite terms that create the power of acceptance in consumers. For example, sellers have been found liable to consumers for advertising a definite quantity of goods for sale at a certain price on a "first come, first serve" basis, after consumers showed up and offered to pay the advertised price before the goods sold out. In such situations, the seller may not withdraw the offer on grounds that market factors no longer justify selling the goods at the advertised price. Instead, courts will compel them to sell the goods as advertised.

The rejection of an offer terminates the offeree's power of acceptance and ends the offeror's liability for the offer. Rejection might come in the form of an express refusal to accept the offer or by implication when the offeree makes a **counteroffer** that is materially different from the offeror's original proposal. Most jurisdictions also recognize an offeror's right to withdraw or revoke an offer as a legitimate means of terminating the offer.

Offers that are not rejected, withdrawn, or revoked generally continue until the expiration of the time period specified by the offer, or, if there is no time limit specified, until a reasonable time has elapsed. A reasonable time is determined according to what a reasonable person would consider sufficient time to accept the offer under the circumstances. Regardless of how much time has elapsed following an offer, the death or insanity of either party before acceptance is communicated normally terminates an offer, as does the destruction of the subject matter of the proposed contract and any intervening conditions that would make acceptance illegal.

Sometimes offerees are concerned that an offer may be terminated before they have had a full opportunity to evaluate it. In this case, they may purchase an "option" to keep the offer open for a designated time. During that time the offer is deemed irrevocable, though some jurisdictions allow the offeror to revoke the offer by paying the offeree an agreed upon sum to do so.

Acceptance Acceptance of an offer is the expression of **assent** to its terms. Acceptance must generally be made in the manner specified by the offer. If no manner of acceptance is specified by the offer, then acceptance may be made in a manner that is reasonable under the circumstances. An acceptance is only valid, however, if the offeree knows of the offer, the offeree manifests an intention to accept, and the acceptance is expressed as an unequivocal and unconditional agreement to the terms of the offer.

Many offers specify the method of acceptance, whether it be oral or written, by phone or in person, by handshake or by ceremony. Other offers leave open the method of acceptance, allowing the offeree to accept in a reasonable manner. Most consumer transactions fall into this category, as when a shopper "accepts" a merchant's offer by taking possession of a particular good and paying for it at the cash register. However, what constitutes a "reasonable" acceptance will vary according to the contract.

Some offers may only be accepted by the performance or non-performance of a particular act. Once formed, these types of agreements are called unilateral contracts, and they are discussed more fully later in this essay. Other offers may only be accepted by a return promise of performance from the offeree. Once formed, these agreements are called bilateral contracts, and they are also discussed more fully later in this essay.

Problems can arise when it is not clear whether an offer anticipates the method of acceptance to come in the form of performance or a return promise. Section 32 of the Restatement (Second) of Contracts attempts to address this issue by providing that "in case of doubt an offer is interpreted as inviting the offeree to accept either by promising to perform what the offer requests or by rendering performance, as the offeree chooses." A growing number of jurisdictions are adopting this approach.

Jurisdictions are split as to the time when an airmailed acceptance becomes effective. Under the majority approach, known as "the mailbox rule," an acceptance is effective upon dispatch in a properly addressed envelope with prepaid postage, even if the acceptance is lost or destroyed in transit. Under the minority approach, acceptance is effective only upon actual receipt by the offeror, no matter what precautions the offeree took to ensure that the acceptance was properly mailed.

In certain cases acceptance can be implied from a party's conduct. Suppose a consumer orders a personal computer (PC) with exact specifications for its central processing unit (CPU), hard drive, and memory. Upon receipt, the consumer determines that the PC does not match the specs. If the consumer nonetheless pays the full amount on the invoice accompanying the PC without protest, the consumer has effectively communicated a legally binding acceptance of the non-conforming good.

Acceptance cannot generally be inferred from a party's silence or inaction. An exception to this rule occurs when two parties have a prior course of dealings in which the offeree has led the offeror to believe that the offeree will accept all goods shipped by the offeror unless the offeree sends notice to the contrary. In such instances, the offeree's silence or inaction constitutes a legally binding acceptance upon which the offeror can rely.

Consideration Each party to a contract must provide something of value that induces the other to enter the agreement. The law calls this exchange of values "consideration." The value exchanged need not consist of currency. Instead, it may consist of a promise to perform an act that one is not legally required to do or a promise to refrain from an act that one is legally entitled to do. For example, if a rich uncle promises to give his nephew a new sports car if he refrains from smoking cigarettes and drinking alcohol for five years, the law deems both the uncle's promise and the nephew's forbearance lawful consideration.

A court's analysis as to whether a contract is supported by sufficient consideration typically focuses more on the promise or performance of the offeree than the promise or performance of the offeror. Courts often say that no consideration will be found unless the offeree suffers a "legal detriment" in making the return promise or in performing the act requested by the offeror. As a general rule, legal detriment is found if the offeree relinquishes a **legal right** in fulfilling his or her contractual duties. Thus, promises to give love and affection or make a gift or donation are not sufficient consideration to support a contract because no one is under a legal duty to give or refrain from giving these things to others. Similarly a promise to perform an act that has already been completed in the past fails to offer consideration to support a new agreement.

Mutuality of Obligation Closely related to the concept of consideration is the mutuality of obligation doctrine. Under this doctrine, both parties must be bound to perform their obligations or the law will treat the agreement as if neither party is bound to perform. When an offeree and offeror exchange promises to perform, one party may not be given the absolute and unlimited right to cancel the contract. Such arrangements attempt to allow one party to perform at her leisure, while ostensibly not relieving the other party of his obligations to perform. Most courts declare these one-side arrangements null for lack of mutuality of obligation. Some courts simply invalidate such contracts for lack of consideration, reasoning that a party who is given absolute power to cancel a contract suffers no legal detriment.

To avoid having a contract subsequently invalidated by a court, the parties must be careful to limit their discretion to cancel the contract or otherwise not perform. As long as the right to avoid performance is dependent on some condition or event outside the control of the party seeking to cancel the contract, courts will find that mutuality of obligation exists. Thus, a farmer might lawfully be given the right to cancel a crop-watering service if the right to cancel were conditioned upon the amount of rain that fell during a given season, something outside the farmer's control. Nevertheless, a court would find mutuality lacking if the farmer were given the right to terminate the service short of full performance simply by giving notice of his or her intention to cancel.

Competency and Capacity A natural person who enters a contract possesses complete legal capacity to be held liable for the duties he or she agrees to undertake, unless the person is a minor, mentally incapacitated, or intoxicated. A minor is defined as a person under the age of 18 or 21, depending on the **jurisdiction**. A contract made by a minor is voidable at the minor's discretion, meaning that the contract is valid and enforceable until the minor takes some affirmative act to disavow the contract. Minors who choose to disavow their contracts entered may not be held liable for breach. The law assumes that minors are too immature, naive, or inexperienced to negotiate on equal terms with adults, and thus courts protect them from being held accountable for unwisely entering contracts of any kind.

When a party does not understand the nature and consequences of an agreement that he or she has entered, the law treats that party as lacking mental capacity to form a binding contract. However, a party will not be relieved from any contractual duties until a court has formally adjudicated the issue after taking **evidence** concerning the party's mental capacity, unless there is an existing court order declaring the party to be incompetent or insane. Like agreements with minors, agreements with mentally incapacitated persons are voidable at that person's discretion. However, a **guardian** or personal representative may ratify an agreement for an incapacitated person and thereby convert the agreement into a legally binding contract.

Contracts entered into by persons under the influence of alcohol and drugs are also voidable at that person's discretion, but only if the other party knew or had reason to know the degree of impairment. As a practical matter, courts rarely show sympathy for defendants who try to avoid contractual duties on grounds that they were intoxicated. However, if the evidence shows that the sober party was trying to take advantage of the intoxicated party, courts will typically intervene to void the contract. Persons who are intoxicated from prescription medication are treated the same as persons who are mentally incompetent or insane and are generally relieved from their contractual responsibilities more readily than are persons intoxicated from non-prescription drugs or alcohol.

Writing Requirement Not every contract need be in writing to be valid and binding on both parties. But nearly every state legislature has enacted a body of law that identifies certain types of contracts that must be in writing to be enforceable. In legal parlance this body of law is called the **statute** of frauds.

Named after a seventeenth-century English statute, the statute of frauds is designed to prevent a plaintiff from bringing an action for breach of contract based on a nonexistent agreement for which the only proof of the agreement is the plaintiff's perjured **testimony**. The statue of frauds attempts to accomplish this objective by prohibiting the enforcement of particular contracts, unless the terms of the contract are expressly reflected by written note, memorandum, or agreement that is signed by the parties or their personal representatives.

As originally conceived, the statute of frauds applied to four types of contracts: promises to pay a debt owed by another person; promises to marry; promises to perform an act that cannot possibly be performed within a year from that date of the promise; and agreements involving real estate. However, most states have since expanded the class of contracts that must be in writing to be enforceable. For example, in many jurisdictions long term leases, insurance contracts, agreements for the sale of **securities**, and contracts for the sale of goods above a specified amount are unenforceable unless the terms of the parties' agreement are memorialized in writing.

Contract Formation Under the U.C.C. The U.C.C. does not require a specific manner of expression in order for two parties to enter into an agreement. Under § 2-204, "A contract for the sale of goods may be made in any manner sufficient to show agreement, including offer and acceptance, conduct by both parties which recognizes the existence of a contract" and other means. The revised version of the U.C.C., as approved in 2003, also allows a contract to be formed through the interaction of "electronic agents," which include computer programs that may initiate a transaction without human review.

TYPES OF CONTRACTS

Contracts under Seal Early English common law required all contracts to be stamped with a seal before a party could enforce them in court. The seal memorialized the parties' intention to honor the terms of the contract. No consideration was required, since the seal symbolized a solemn promise undertaken by all parties to the contract.

With the onset of the industrial era during the eighteenth century, however, sealed contracts were increasingly seen as an impractical and inefficient impediment to fast paced commercial relations. Sealed contracts were gradually replaced by other types of agreements, including express and implied contracts. In fact, nearly all jurisdictions have eliminated the legal effect of sealed contracts. Thus, contracts under seal will not generally be enforced unless they are supported by independent consideration.

Express and Implied Contracts Express contracts consist of agreements in which the terms are stated by the parties. The terms may be stated orally or in writing. But the contract as a whole must reflect the intention of the parties. As a general rule, if an express contract between the parties is established, a contract embracing the identical subject cannot be implied in fact, as the law will not normally imply a substitute promise or contract for an express contract of the parties.

Contracts implied in fact are inferred from the facts and circumstances of the case or the conduct of the parties. However, such contracts are not formally or explicitly stated in words. The law makes no distinction between contracts created by words and those created by conduct. Thus, a contract implied in fact is just as binding as an express contracts that arises from the parties' declared intentions, with the only difference being that for contracts implied in fact courts will infer the parties' intentions from their business relations and course of dealings.

Whereas courts apply the same legal principles to express contracts and contracts implied in fact, a different body of principles is applied to contracts implied in law. Also known as quasi-contracts, contracts implied in law are agreements imposed by courts despite the absence of at least one element essential to the formation of a binding agreement. The law creates these types of fictitious agreements to prevent one party from being unjustly enriched at the expense of another.

For example, suppose that a husband and wife ask a third party to hold a sum of money in **trust** for their children, but instead of holding the money in trust, the third party absconds with it. The law will not allow the third party to keep the money simply because all the requisite elements of a formal contract have not been proven by the husband and wife. Although the law is generally wary of imposing contracts on parties who did not agree to their terms, courts will find that a contract implied in law exists when the **defendant** has been enriched at the expense of the plaintiff; the enrichment was unjust the plaintiff's own conduct has not been inequitable; and it is otherwise reasonable for the court to do so in light of the relationship between the parties and the circumstances of the case.

Bilateral and Unilateral Contracts A **bilateral contract** arises from the exchange of mutual, reciprocal promises between two persons that requires the performance or non-performance of some act by both parties. The promise made by one party constitutes sufficient consideration for the promise made by the other party. A **unilateral contract** involves a promise made by only one party in exchange for the performance or

non-performance of an act by the other party. Stated differently, acceptance of an offer to form a unilateral contract cannot be achieved by making a return promise, but only by performance or non-performance of some particular act. Accordingly, acceptance of an offer to enter a unilateral contract can be revoked until performance is complete or until the date has passed for non-performance.

It should be remembered, however, that courts are asked to interpret contracts long after they have been formed. As a result, courts will often take into account how the parties actually acted on the terms of a particular contract. Not surprisingly, courts will avoid interpreting a contract as unilateral or bilateral when such an interpretation would leave one party in the lurch or the opposite interpretation would yield a more commercially reasonable result. This is not to say that courts do not enforce one-sided agreements, but only that the evidence of the parties' understanding must be clear before a court will do so.

BREACH OF CONTRACT: DEFINITION

An unjustifiable failure to perform all or some part of a contractual duty is a breach of contract. A breach may occur when one party fails to perform in the manner specified by the contract or by the time specified in the contract. A breach may also occur if one party only partially performs his or her duties or fully performs them in a defective manner.

Courts distinguish total breaches from partial breaches. A total breach of contract is the failure to perform a material part of the contract, while a partial breach results from merely a slight deviation. In determining whether a breach is total or partial, courts typically examine the following factors: the extent to which the non-breaching party obtained the substantial benefit of the contract despite the breach; the extent to which the non-breaching party can be adequately compensated for the breach with money damages; the extent to which the breaching party has already performed or made preparations for performance; the extent to which the breaching party mitigated the hardship on both parties by not fully performing; the willful, negligent, or innocent behavior of the breaching party; and the likelihood that the breaching party will perform the remainder of the contract if allowed.

BREACH OF CONTRACT: DEFENSES

A number of defenses are available to defendants who are sued for breach of contract. For example, a defendant might assert that no breach was committed because the parties never actually formed a contract due to the lack of an offer, an acceptance, consideration, mutuality of obligation, or put in writing. Alternatively, a defendant might assert that he or she lacked capacity to enter the contract, arguing that the contract should be declared void on the grounds that the defendant was incompetent, insane or intoxicated at the time it was entered.

The law also affords defendants several other defenses in breach of contract actions. They include unconscionability; mistake; **fraud**; undue influence; and **duress**.

Unconscionability Unconscionable contracts are those that violate **public policy** by being so unjust as to offend the court's sense of fairness. Sometimes called "contracts against public policy," unconscionable contracts usually result from a gross disparity in the parties' bargaining power, as can happen when one party is a savvy business person and the other party is elderly, illiterate, or not fluent in English. However, a mere disparity in bargaining power will not suffice to overturn an otherwise valid contract, unless a court finds that the resulting contract is one that no mentally competent person would enter and that no fair and honest person would accept.

Mistake Ordinarily, to constitute a valid defense in an action for breach of contract the mistake must be a mutual one made by all of the parties to the contract. However, when the mistake is obvious from the face of the contract, knowledge of the mistake will be imputed to each party. Thus, a contract that by its terms designates a horse as the subject matter will be enforced unless both parties agree that a different subject matter was intended. On the other hand, if the same contract designates a pig as the subject matter in 99 paragraphs of the agreement, but mentions a horse in only one paragraph, a court will not force the defendant to sell his horse if it is obvious that the one paragraph contains an error.

Fraud Fraud occurs when one party intentionally deceives another party as to the nature and consequences of a contract, and the deceived party is injured as a result. In most cases, fraud requires an affirmative act, such as a willful misrepresentation or concealment of a material fact. In a few cases where a special relationship exists between the parties, such as between attorney and client, simple nondisclosure of a material fact may amount to fraud. Regardless of the underlying relationship between the parties, however, a court will not void a contract due to fraud unless the defendant demonstrates that he or she was induced to enter the contract by **fraudulent** conduct and not merely that the plaintiff made a false statement at some point in time.

Undue Influence Undue influence occurs when one party exercises such control over a second party as to overcome the independent judgment and free will of the second party. In reviewing claims of undue influence, courts look to see whether the plaintiff preyed on and exploited a known psychological or physical weakness when securing the defendant's assent to a contract. However, evidence that the plaintiff merely used aggressive and unsavory tactics in securing the defendant's asset will not suffice to overturn a contract on grounds of undue influence, unless those tactics had the effect of substituting the plaintiff's will and judgment for the defendant's.

Duress Duress consists of any wrongful act that coerces another person to enter a contract that he or she would not have entered voluntarily. **Blackmail**, physical violence, a show of force, and threats to institute **legal proceedings** in an abusive manner may all constitute sufficient duress to void a contract. However, a defendant claiming duress must demonstrate that sufficient harm was threatened or inflicted to justify finding that the defendant had no reasonable choice but to enter the contract on the terms dictated by the plaintiff.

BREACH OF CONTRACT: REMEDIES

The five basic remedies for breach of contract include money damages, **restitution**, rescission, reformation, and specific performance. A money damage award includes a sum of money that is given as compensation for financial losses caused by a breach of contract. Parties injured by a breach are entitled to the benefit of the bargain they entered, or the **net** gain that would have accrued but for the breach. The type of breach governs the extent of damages that may be recovered.

If the breach is a total breach, a plaintiff can recover damages in an amount equal to the sum or value the plaintiff would have received had the contract been fully performed by the defendant, including lost profits. If the breach is only partial, the plaintiff may normally seek damages in an amount equal to the cost of hiring someone else to complete the performance contemplated by the contract. However, if the cost of completion is prohibitive and the portion of the unperformed contract is small, many courts will only award damages in an amount equal to the difference between the diminished value of the contract as performed and the full value contemplated by the contract.

For example, if the plaintiff agreed to pay the defendant $200,000 to build a house, but the defendant only completed 90 percent of the work contemplated by the contract, a court might be inclined to award $20,000 in damages if it would cost the plaintiff twice as much to hire someone else to finish the last 10 percent. The same principles apply to damages sought for contracts that are fully performed, but in a defective manner. If the defect is significant, the plaintiff can recover the cost of repair. But if the defect is minor, the plaintiff may be limited to recovering the difference between the value of the good or service actually received and the value of the good or service contemplated by the contract.

Restitution is a remedy designed to restore the injured party to the position occupied prior to the formation of the contract. Parties seeking restitution may not request to be compensated for lost profits or other earnings caused by a breach. Instead, restitution aims at returning to the plaintiff any money or property given to the defendant under the contract. Plaintiffs typically seek restitution when contracts they have entered are voided by courts due to a defendant's incompetence or incapacity. The law allows incompetent and incapacitated persons to disavow their contractual duties but generally only if the plaintiff is not made worse off by their disavowal.

Parties that are induced to enter into contracts by mistake, fraud, undue influence, or duress may seek to have the contract set aside or have the terms of the contract rewritten to do justice in the case. Rescission is the name for the remedy that terminates the contractual duties of both parties, while reformation is the name for the remedy that allows courts to change the substance of a contract to correct inequities that were suffered. Like contracts implied in law, however, courts are reluctant to rewrite contracts to reflect the parties' actual agreement, especially when the contract as written contains a mistake that could have been rectified through pre-contract investigation. Thus, one court would not reform a contract that stipulated an incorrect amount of acreage being purchased, since the buyer could have ascertained the correct amount by obtaining a land survey before entering the contract. *Little Stillwater Holding Corp. v. Cold Brook Sand & Gravel Corp.*, 151 Misc. 2d 457, 573 N.Y.S.2d 382 (N.Y. Co. Ct. 1991).

Specific performance is an equitable remedy that compels one party to perform, as nearly as practicable, his or her duties specified by the contract. Specific performance is available only when money damages are inadequate to compensate the plaintiff for the breach. This ruling often happens when the subject matter of a contract is in dispute.

Every parcel of land by definition is unique, if for no other reason than its location. However, rare articles that are not necessarily one of a kind are still treated by the law as unique if it would be impossible for a judge or **jury** to accurately calculate the appropriate amount of damages to award the plaintiff in lieu of awarding him or her the unique article contemplated by the contract. Heirlooms and antiques are examples of such rare items for which specific performance is usually available as a remedy. However, specific performance may never be invoked to compel the performance of a personal service, since doing so would constitute slavery in violation of the Thirteenth Amendment to the U.S. Constitution.

ADDITIONAL RESOURCES

American Jurisprudence. 2d ed. Eagan, MN: Thomson/West, 2006.

Calamari, John D., and Joseph M. Perillo. *Contracts*. 4th ed. Eagan, MN: West, Thomson Reuters, 2004.

Federal Citizens Information Center, Office of Citizen Services and Innovative Technologies. *2012 Consumer Action Handbook*. Washington, DC: U.S. General Services Administration, 2012. Available at http://www.usa.gov/topics/consumer/consumer-action-handbook.pdf (accessed November 3, 2012).

Gale Encyclopedia of American Law. 3rd ed. Detroit: Gale, Cengage Learning, 2011.

Restatement (Second) of Contracts. Philadelphia: American Law Institute, 1979.

ORGANIZATIONS

Consumer Contact Services, Inc.
6125 Black Oak Blvd.
Fort Wayne, IN 46835-2654
Phone: (219) 486-2453

National Organization of Bar Counsel
515 Fifth Street, NW
Washington, DC 64196
Phone: (202) 638-1501
Fax: (202) 662-1777
URL: http://www.nobc.org

Office of Consumer Protection, Federal Trade Commission
600 Pennsylvania Ave NW
Washington, DC 20580
Toll Free: (877) 382-4357
Fax: (202) 326-3529
URL: http://www.ftc.gov/ftc/consumer.htm

CONSUMER ISSUES

CREDIT/TRUTH-IN-LENDING

Sections within this essay:

- Background
- Types of Credit
  - Same-as-Cash Credit
  - Installment Credit
  - Revolving Credit

- Interest
- Truth in Lending Act
- Credit Card Accountability, Responsibility, and Disclosure Act
- FTC Litigation
- Equal Credit Opportunity Act
- Fair Credit Reporting Act
- Credit Reports
  - Credit Report Errors
  - Accurate Negative Information

- Fair Debt Collection Practices Act
- Consumer Financial Protection Bureau
- Additional Resources

BACKGROUND

Credit is money granted by a **creditor** or lender to a **debtor** or borrower, who defers payment of the debt. In exchange for the credit, the lender gets back the money, usually paid on a monthly basis, plus finance charges or interest. Entities within the credit industry, including banks, **mortgage** lenders, and credit card companies, earn billions of dollars per year from these charges and the interest received from outstanding balances.

The government regulates the credit industry due to the potential for abuse by those who issue credit. Without government regulation, creditors could attempt to confuse debtors regarding the terms of credit or could deny credit on improper grounds, such as the race or gender of the potential debtor. **Identity theft**, which occurs when one person uses another's personal identification to commit **fraud** or other crimes, has become a major problem in the United States due to the continually increasing use of the Internet. Legislatures, including Congress, have enacted statutes in recent years that are designed to protect the credit histories of those who may be the victims of identity theft.

TYPES OF CREDIT

Same-as-Cash Credit Same-as-cash, or noninstallment, credit is the simplest form of credit. Same as cash credit is usually due after a very short term, such as 30 days. Same-as-cash credit enables consumers to take possession of property today and pay for it within a set amount of time. Many department stores offer noninstallment credit. However, many same-as-cash plans can convert to high interest credit if the customer does not pay in full on the due date.

Installment Credit With **installment**, closed-end credit, a creditor loans a particular amount of money, usually the amount of the purchase price of the goods. The full amount of the principal and interest must be paid within a pre-determined time period. Failure on the part of the debtor to pay within this time period may mean that the debtor must return the goods to the creditor.

Revolving Credit Revolving, open-end credit is found with most credit cards. Under agreement with the lender, an amount of credit is extended to the consumer. An outside limit is established, depending upon the consumer's credit history and ability to handle the debt repayment. The financial institution gives the consumer a credit card with a credit limit, and the consumer can choose how much of the available credit to use at any given time. Usually the consumer makes monthly payments. Revolving credit requires active management by the consumer. The consumer can decide to pay off the entire outstanding debt when the statement is present, pay off more than the required minimum payment, or simply make the minimum required payment.

INTEREST

Interest is the compensation paid by a debtor to a creditor for the use of the creditor's money. Over time, due to inflation, the value of money decreases. Interest on credit can be either simple or compound. Simple interest is interest charged only on the principal amount borrowed. Simple interest does not add the interest charge back to the outstanding loan during the length of the loan. Thus, simple interest charges are less than **compound interest** charges. Compound interest is interest charged not only on the principal, but on the interest accrued during the length of the loan. Compound interest is more expensive to the consumer because interest is charged on top of interest.

The amount of interest that can be charged is limited and regulated by state laws. The percentage interest rate allowed varies from state to state, depending on the type of credit being extended. A fixed interest rate does not change throughout the duration of the extension of credit. Under a variable rate loan, the **finance charge** is determined by an index, such as the "prime rate" published nationally each quarter for short-term loans charged by banks. This allows the lender to charge an interest rate that reflects current market conditions. Regardless of whether the interest rate charged is fixed or variable, the rate may not exceed the permissible rate set by state **usury** laws.

TRUTH IN LENDING ACT

The Truth in Lending Act is a federal law which sets minimum standards for the information which a creditor must provide in an installment credit **contract**. The amount being financed, the amount of the required minimum monthly payment, the total number of monthly payments, and the **annual percentage rate**

(APR) must all be provided to the consumer prior to entering into a credit contract. In addition, the Truth in Lending Act regulates the advertising of credit. The Federal Trade Commission (FTC) works to ensure that the nation's markets are efficient and free of practices that might harm consumers. To ensure the smooth operation of the free market system, the FTC enforces federal consumer protection laws that prevent fraud, deception, and unfair business practices. The Federal Trade Commission Act allows the FTC to act in the interest of all consumers to prevent deceptive and unfair acts or practices. In interpreting the Act, the Commission has determined that, with respect to advertising, a representation, omission or practice is deceptive if it is likely to mislead consumers and affect consumers' behavior or decisions about the product or service. In addition, an act or practice is unfair if the injury it causes, or is likely to cause, is substantial, not outweighed by other benefits, and not reasonably avoidable.

Following the collapse of the home real estate market in 2008, the federal government enacted new regulations under the Truth in Lending Act to protect homebuyers. Under the new regulations, lenders must give **good faith** estimates of mortgage loan costs within three business days after the consumer applies for a loan and may not collect any fees before the disclosure is provided, except for a reasonable fee for obtaining a credit report. A closing may not take place until expiration of a seven-day waiting period after the consumer receives this disclosure. The annual percentage rate (APR) must include not only the interest rate on the loan but also certain other costs related to **settlement**. In addition, the homebuyer may modify or waive both waiting periods for a documented personal financial emergency, but must receive the disclosures no later than the time of the modification or **waiver**.

CREDIT CARD ACCOUNTABILITY, RESPONSIBILITY, AND DISCLOSURE ACT

Congress passed the Credit Card Accountability, Responsibility, and Disclosure Act (CARD) in 2009. CARD sought to reform some of practices of credit card companies. The law works to curtail the practice of hiking **interest rates** on existing cardholder accounts, to reduce late fees and over-limit fees, and to require credit card companies to make credit card costs clearer to consumers.

The FTC's Bureau of Consumer Protection protects consumers against unfair, deceptive, or **fraudulent** practices. The Bureau enforces a variety of consumer protection laws enacted by Congress, as well as trade regulation rules issued by the Commission. Its actions include individual company and industry-wide investigations, administrative and federal court **litigation**, rule-making proceedings, and consumer and business education. In addition, the Bureau contributes to the Commission's on-going efforts to inform Congress and other government entities of the impact that proposed actions could have on consumers. The Bureau of Consumer Protection is divided into six divisions and programs, each with its own areas of expertise.

Within the Bureau of Consumer Protection are the Division of Advertising Practices and the Division of Enforcement. These entities are the nation's enforcers of federal truth-in-advertising laws. The FTC Act prohibits unfair or deceptive advertising in any medium. That is, advertising must tell the truth and not mislead consumers. A claim can be misleading if relevant information is left out or if the claim implies something that is not true. In addition, claims must be substantiated especially when they concern health, safety, or performance. The type of **evidence** may depend on the product, the claims, and what experts believe necessary. Sellers are responsible for claims they make about their products and services. Third parties such as advertising agencies or website designers and catalog marketers also may be liable for making or disseminating deceptive representations if they participate in the preparation or distribution of the advertising, or know about the deceptive claims.

FTC LITIGATION

Typically, FTC investigations are not revealed to the public in order to protect both the investigation and the companies involved. If the FTC believes that a person or company has violated the law, the agency may attempt to obtain voluntary compliance by entering into a consent order with the company. A company that signs a consent order need not admit that it violated the law, but it must agree to stop the disputed practices outlined in an accompanying complaint. If a consent agreement cannot be reached, the FTC may issue an administrative complaint or seek injunctive relief in the federal courts. The FTC's administrative complaints initiate a formal proceeding that is much like a federal court trial but before an administrative law judge: Evidence is submitted, **testimony** is heard, and witnesses are examined and cross-examined. If a violation of the law is found, a judge may issue a **cease and desist order**. Initial decisions by administrative law judges may be appealed to the full Commission. Final decisions issued by the Commission may be appealed *to* the U.S. Court of Appeals for the District of Columbia and, ultimately, to the U.S. Supreme Court.

In some circumstances, the FTC can go directly to court to obtain an injunction, civil penalties, or consumer **redress**. The injunction preserves the market's competitive status quo. The FTC seeks federal court injunctions

in consumer protection matters typically in cases of ongoing consumer fraud.

EQUAL CREDIT OPPORTUNITY ACT

The Equal Credit Opportunity Act (ECOA) ensures that all consumers are given an equal chance to obtain credit. Factors such as income, expenses, debt, and credit history are always valid considerations for creditworthiness. However, there are certain areas about which it unlawful for a potential creditor to inquire. These include sex, race, national origin, or religion. A creditor may ask for voluntary disclosure of this information if the loan is for real estate. This information helps federal agencies enforce anti-discrimination laws. When permitted to ask marital status, a creditor may only use the terms married, unmarried, or separated. A creditor may ask for such information in **community property** states. A creditor in any state may ask for this information if the account is joint and spouses apply together. A potential creditor many not inquire about plans a consumer may have for having or raising children, except that a creditor many inquire about court-ordered **alimony**, **child support**, or separate maintenance payments a potential debtor may to obligated to make.

As creditors decide whether to grant credit, they may not base their decision on sex, marital status, race, national origin, religion, or age (unless the applicant is a minor and without capacity to contract) or if age is used to determine the meaning of other factors important to creditworthiness. A potential creditor must consider public assistance income, part-time employment or **pension**, **annuity**, or retirement income as well as any reported alimony, child support, or separate maintenance payments.

Creditors are required to notify applicants within 30 days whether the application has been approved or denied. Creditors who reject potential consumers must provide a notice explaining either the specific reasons for rejection or the procedure for discovering the reason within 60 days.

FAIR CREDIT REPORTING ACT

The **Fair Credit Reporting Act** (FCRA) is a federal law that regulates the activities of credit reporting bureaus. The FCRA is designed to protect the **privacy** of credit report information and to guarantee that information supplied by consumer reporting agencies (CRAs) is as accurate as possible. Private credit reporting bureaus, such as TransUnion, Equifax Information Services, and Experian, maintain records of financial payment histories and public record data, along with personal identification information. The FCRA punishes unauthorized persons who obtain credit reports, as well as employees of credit reporting bureaus who furnish credit reports to unauthorized persons. The FTC also places responsibilities on those who supply the reporting bureaus with the initial information.

CREDIT REPORTS

A credit report is a type of consumer report which contains information about where a consumer lives and how that consumers pays bills. It also may show whether an individual has been sued, arrested, or has filed for **bankruptcy**. Companies called consumer reporting agencies (CRAs) or credit bureaus compile and sell consumer credit reports to businesses. Businesses use this information to evaluate applications for credit, insurance, employment, and other purposes allowed by the (FCRA).

Due to concerns about the effect of identity theft on consumer credit reports, Congress amended the FCRA in 2003 with the enactment of the Fair and Accurate Credit Transactions Act. This **statute** allows every consumer to receive a free copy of his or her credit report every twelve months. This legislation does not allow consumers to obtain a free credit report directly from a credit bureau. A consumer must instead obtain this report by phone at 1-877-322-8228; by going online at http://www.annualcreditreport.com; or by submitting a form to Annual Credit Report Request Service, PO Box 105281, Atlanta, Georgia, 30348-5281.

A person may be entitled to a free report in some other instances as well. Any consumer who is denied credit insurance or employment because of information supplied by a CRA is entitled to receive the CRA's name, address, and telephone number. If the consumer contacts the agency for a copy of the report within 60 days of receiving a denial notice, the report is free. In most other instances, however, credit bureaus may charge a fee of up to $9.95 for one of these reports.

Credit Report Errors Under the FCRA, both the CRA and the organization that provided the information to the CRA, such as a bank or credit card company, have responsibilities for correcting inaccurate or incomplete information in consumer credit reports. If a consumer disputes an item on the credit report in writing, the CRAs must reinvestigate the items in question within 30 days. After the information provider receives notice of a dispute from the CRA, it must investigate, review all relevant information provided by the CRA, and report the results to the CRA. If the information provider finds the disputed information to be inaccurate, it must notify all nationwide CRAs. Disputed information that cannot be verified must be deleted from a consumer credit report. When the reinvestigation is complete, the CRA must give the consumer written results and a free copy of the report if the dispute results in a change. If an item is changed or removed, the CRA cannot put the disputed information back into a consumer file unless the information provider verifies its accuracy and completeness, and the CRA gives the consumer a written notice that includes the name, address, and phone number of the provider. Upon a consumer request, the CRA must send a notice of a correction to anyone who received a report in the previous six months. Job applicants can have a corrected copy of their report sent to anyone who received a copy during the prior two years for employment purposes. If a reinvestigation does not resolve a dispute, consumers have a right to ask the CRA to include a statement of the dispute in the file and in future reports.

Accurate Negative Information When negative information in a consumer report is accurate, only the passage of time can assure its removal. Accurate negative information can generally stay on a consumer report for seven years. However, bankruptcy information may be reported for 10 years. Information about a lawsuit or an unpaid judgment can be reported for seven years or until the **statute of limitations** runs out, whichever is longer.

Credit counseling services can assist consumers. Some of these services contact creditors and attempt to consolidate debts, putting together repayment plans. Most of these businesses are nonprofit agencies that charge small or even no fees to provide credit counseling. Other for-profit organizations sometimes advise consumers to apply for new employee ID numbers, and then use them instead of their Social Security numbers to apply for more credit. Using an identification number in order to **defraud** creditors, however, may constitute criminal activity.

FAIR DEBT COLLECTION PRACTICES ACT

The Fair Debt Collection Practices Act is a federal law that regulates the activities of those who regularly collect debts from others. Many states have adopted similar laws regulating the practices of debt collectors. Under this law, debt collectors may contact debtors by mail, in person, by telephone, or by telegram during "convenient hours" (commonly between 8 AM and 9 PM). Debt collectors are prohibited from contacting the debtor at work if the collector knows or has reason to know that the employer forbids employees from being contacted by debt collectors at the workplace. Finally, debt collectors may not contact individuals who are represented by an attorney.

Additional provisions specify that debt collectors may not threaten violence, use obscene or profane language, repeatedly telephone to annoy or harass, make collect telephone calls, or use false or misleading information in an effort to collect the debt. Consumers who believe this law has been violated may contact the regulating body, which is the Federal Trade Commission. Consumers also have the option of filing a lawsuit against the debt collector for violation of the law.

CONSUMER FINANCIAL PROTECTION BUREAU

In the wake of the 2008 recession and the questionable practices of banks, Congress passed the Dodd-Frank Act of 2010. One provision created the Consumer Financial Protection Bureau (CFPB). The bureau is charged with giving consumers the information they need to understand the terms of their agreements with financial companies. The CFPB will issue regulations, supervise, and enforce federal consumer financial protection laws. It will restrict unfair, deceptive, or abusive acts or practices and it will take consumer complaints. It is also tasked with educating consumers about financial products and researching consumer behavior.

ADDITIONAL RESOURCES

Snyder, Stephen. *Credit after Bankruptcy: A Step-by-Step Action Plan to Quick and Lasting Recovery after Personal Bankruptcy.* Columbia, MD: Bellwether, 2000.

Weston, Liz. *Your Credit Score, Your Money & What's at Stake.* Upper Saddle River, NJ: FT Press, 2009.

ORGANIZATIONS

Council of Better Business Bureaus (CBBB)
4200 Wilson Blvd., Suite 800
Arlington, VA 22203-1838
Phone: (703) 276-0100
Fax: (703) 525-8277
URL: http://www.bbb.org

Equifax Information Services, LLC
PO Box 740241
Atlanta, GA 30374
Toll Free: (800) 685-1111
URL: http://www.equifax.com

Experian
PO Box 2002
Allen, TX 75013
Toll Free: (888) 397-3742
URL: http://www.experian.com

Federal Trade Commission (FTC)
600 Pennsylvania Avenue, N.W.
Washington, DC 20580
URL: http://www.ftc.gov

National Conference of State Legislatures
444 North Capitol Street, N.W., Suite 515
Washington, DC 20001
Phone: (202) 624-5400
Fax: (202) 737-1069
URL: http://www.ncsl.org

TransUnion
PO Box 1000
Chester, PA 19022
Toll Free: (800) 888-4213
URL: http://www.transunion.com/index.jsp

CONSUMER ISSUES

DECEPTIVE TRADE PRACTICES

BACKGROUND

Federal legislation and statutes in every state prohibit employment of unfair or deceptive trade practices and **unfair competition** in business. The Federal Trade Commission regulates federal laws designed to prohibit a series of specific practices prohibited in interstate **commerce**. Several states have established consumer protection offices as part of the state attorney general offices.

The Federal Trade Commission Act (FTCA), originally passed in 1914 and amended several times thereafter, was the original **statute** in the United States prohibiting "unfair or deceptive trade acts or practices." Development of the federal law was related to federal antitrust and trademark **infringement** legislation. Prior to the enactment in the 1960s of state statutes prohibiting deceptive trade practices, the main focus of state law in this area was "unfair competition," which refers to the tort action for practices employed by businesses to confuse consumers as to the source of a product. The tort action for a business "passing off" its goods as those of another was based largely on the **common law** tort action for trademark infringement.

Because the law governing deceptive trade practices was undefined and unclear, the National Conference of Commissioners on Uniform State Laws in 1964 drafted the Uniform Deceptive Trade Practices Act. The NCCUSL revised this uniform law in 1966. The law was originally "designed to bring state law up to date by removing undue restrictions on the common law action for deceptive trade practices." Only eleven states have adopted this act, but it has had a significant effect on other states. Most state deceptive or unfair trade practices statutes were originally enacted between the mid-1960s and mid-1970s.

APPLICABILITY OF DECEPTIVE TRADE PRACTICES STATUTES

Deceptive trade practices statutes do not govern all situations where one party has deceived another party. Most states limit the scope of these statutes to commercial transactions involving a consumer purchasing or leasing goods or services for personal, household, or family purposes. The terms used in each statute to set forth the scope of the statute are often the subject of **litigation**. The majority of states require a liberal interpretation of the terms of the deceptive trade practices statutes, including those describing the applicability of the statutes.

Trade or Commerce Several states limit the applicability of deceptive trade practices to transactions in trade or commerce. This requirement usually incorporates a broad range of profit-oriented transactions. Nevertheless, it generally excludes trade between non-merchants and similar transactions.

Consumer Transactions The appropriate **plaintiff** under most deceptive trade practices acts is a consumer, commonly defined as a person who will use a good or service for personal, family, or household purposes. The determination of whether a plaintiff is a consumer often requires use of one of two types of analysis, a subjective test and an objective test. The subjective analysis typically considers the intended use of the good or service at the time of the transaction. Thus, if a buyer of a good intends at the time of a purchase to use to good for a personal, family, or household purpose, the buyer will likely be considered a consumer under the relevant statute. The objective analysis considers whether the type of good or service involved in the transaction is ordinarily used for a personal, family, or household purpose.

Goods or Services Goods are defined under the **Uniform Commercial Code** as those items movable at the time of a purchase. Many deceptive trade practices statutes apply this definition to the requirement that goods are involved in a transaction for a deceptive trade practices statute to apply. Livestock are also usually included in the definition of a good. Statutes and courts usually define services broadly, including in the definition most activities conducted on behalf of another. Some states require that consumers seek to purchase merchandise, which incorporates goods, services, real property, commodities, and some intangibles.

Prohibited Acts and Practices Most state deceptive trade practices statutes include broad restrictions on "deceptive" or "unfair" trade practices. These states often include prohibitions against **fraudulent** practices and unconscionable practices. The Federal Trade Commission, when interpreting the FTCA, does not require that the person committing an act of deception have the intent to deceive. Moreover, the FTC does not require that actual deception occur. The FTC merely requires that a party have the capacity to deceive or commit an unfair trade practice. If a business or individual has this capacity

or tendency to deceive, the FTC under the FTCA may order the company to cease and desist the deceptive or unfair practice. State statutes similarly do not require that a company specifically intends to deceive, nor must a company always have knowledge that a statement is false to be liable for misrepresentations made to a consumer.

A consumer who has been victimized by a potential deceptive or unfair trade practice should consult the deceptive trade practice statute in that state, as well as consult **case law** applying this statute, to determine whether he or she has a cause of action. In addition to the broad prohibition against deception, most state statutes also include a list of practices that are defined as deceptive. Under the Uniform Deceptive Trade Practices Act, if a business or person engages in the following, the action constitutes a deceptive trade practice:

- Passes off goods or services as those of another
- Causes likelihood of confusion or of misunderstanding as to the source, sponsorship, approval, or certification of goods or services
- Causes likelihood of confusion or of misunderstanding as to affiliation, connection, or association with, or certification by, another
- Uses deceptive representations or designations of geographic origin in connection with goods or services
- Represents that goods or services have sponsorship, approval, characteristics, ingredients, uses, benefits, or qualities that they do not have or that a person has a sponsorship, approval, status, affiliation, or connection that he does not have
- Represents that goods are original or new if they are deteriorated, altered, reconditioned, reclaimed, used, or second-hand
- Represents that goods or services are of particular standard, quality, or grade, or that goods are of particular style or model, if they are of another
- Disparages the goods, services, or business of another by false or misleading misrepresentation of fact
- Advertises goods or services with intent not to sell them as advertised
- Advertises goods or services with intent not to supply reasonably expected public demand, unless advertisement discloses a limitation of quantity
- Makes false or misleading statements of fact concerning the reasons for, existence of, or amounts of price reductions
- Engages in any other conduct which similarly creates the likelihood of confusion or of misunderstanding

Most states include similar items in their lists of deceptive trade practices violations, even if those states

270

have not adopted the uniform act. In addition, the FTC and many states prohibit other unfair practices, including the following:

- Unfair provisions in contracts of adhesion
- Coercive or high-pressure tactics in sales and collection efforts
- Illegal conduct
- Taking advantage of bargaining power of vulnerable groups
- Taking advantage of emergency situations
- Unconscionable activities, including outrageous and offensive conduct by a business in the sale of goods or services

OTHER PRACTICES DEEMED DECEPTIVE OR UNFAIR

Debt Collection The Federal Fair Debt Collection Practices Act and state debt collection statutes govern most abuses by debt collectors in debt collection activities. Deceptive trade practices statutes may provide remedies in situations that are not covered by these debt collection statutes. For example, most debt collection statutes do not cover some forms of debt collection, such as foreclosures, repossessions, and evictions, but a deceptive trade practices statute may apply. Moreover, deceptive trade practices statutes may also permit a consumer to bring a cause of action against a **creditor** for debt collection practices of an independent agency hired by the creditor. Several cases have dealt with issues regarding misrepresentations made by debt collectors or deceptive agreements proposed by debt collectors.

Breach of Warranties Consumers have several means of enforcing a **warranty** provided in a sales or service **contract**. If a business employs deceptive practices with respect to the advertisement or negotiation of a warranty, a deceptive trade practices statute may provide a consumer a remedy in addition to a breach of warranty claim.

Insurance Most states have enacted legislation regarding deceptive practices of insurance companies, including those practices related to the sale of policies and the payment of claims. In some states, employment of a deceptive practice in insurance is also a deceptive trade practice. A deceptive trade practices statute may also provide a remedy in insurance cases where state insurance laws do not apply.

Pyramid Schemes and Similar Practices Several states prohibit certain illegal business schemes through deceptive trade practices statutes. One such scheme is a "pyramid

scheme," where investors make money by recruiting others to join and invest in a company rather than selling a product as claimed by the company. Other schemes include deceptive employment opportunity claims and misleading or deceptive game or contest promotions. Some states do not specifically include these schemes in the statute, but courts in those states may have applied provisions of the relevant deceptive trade practices statute in cases involving these schemes.

REMEDIES FOR VIOLATIONS OF DECEPTIVE TRADE PRACTICES STATUTES

A consumer who has been the victim of a deceptive trade practice has a variety of remedies. State deceptive trade practices statutes have been particularly successful due to the damages provisions included in the statutes. About half of the states provide minimum **statutory** damages to a litigant who has proven a deceptive trade practice, even if the litigant has not proven actual damages. Many states also permit courts to award treble damages, which means the actual damages to a party injured by a deceptive trade practice are tripled. Several states also permit courts to impose **punitive damages** and/or attorney's fees for these practices.

In addition to monetary damages, several other options may exist for a person injured by a deceptive trade practice. When the FTC has **jurisdiction** over a case, it may enjoin a deceptive trade practice of a company under the FTCA. Statutes in each of the states also permit government enforcement officials to seek cease and desist orders to prevent businesses from engaging in deceptive trade practices. These remedies may be available in addition to civil remedies sought by private litigants.

STATE AND LOCAL PROVISIONS PROHIBITING DECEPTIVE TRADE PRACTICES

Although many state deceptive trade practices statutes include similar provisions, application of these statutes often differs from state to state. Consumers who have been victimized by a deceptive trade practice should be sure to consult their relevant state statutes to determine the appropriate procedures to follow, the appropriate office to contact, and special requirements that must be met to bring a suit in that state. Each state has adopted some version of a deceptive trade practices statute. The following are brief summaries of these statutes.

ALABAMA: The state statute prohibits 22 specific practices, plus any other deceptive or unconscionable acts or practices. The transaction must be conducted in trade or commerce for the statute to apply. The attorney general's office or a district attorney's office may enforce the statute for violations by a business.

ALASKA: The state statute prohibits 41 specific practices, plus other unfair methods of competition and unfair or deceptive acts or practices. The transaction must be conducted in trade or commerce for the statute to apply. The attorney general's office may enforce the statute for violations by a business.

ARIZONA: The state statute prohibits deception or an omission of a material fact by one party to a transaction with the intent to deceive the other party. The transaction must involve the sale, offer for sale, or **lease** of goods, real property, services, or intangibles for the statute to apply. The attorney general's office or a county attorney's office may enforce the statute for violations by a business.

ARKANSAS: The state statute prohibits 10 specific practices, plus any other deceptive or unconscionable acts or practices. The transaction must involve the sale or advertisement of goods or services for the statute to apply.

CALIFORNIA: The state statute prohibits 23 specific practices, plus any other unfair methods of competition and unfair or deceptive practices. Parties must intend for the transaction to result in the sale or lease of goods or services to a consumer for the statute to apply.

COLORADO: The state legislature adopted the Uniform Deceptive Trade Practices Act which prohibits 43 specific practices. Transactions must be in the course of a person's business, vocation, or occupation, and involve the sale of goods, services, or real property for the statute to apply. The attorney general's office or a district attorney's office may enforce the statute for violations by a business.

CONNECTICUT: The state statute prohibits unfair methods of competition and unfair or deceptive acts or practices. The transaction must be conducted in trade or commerce for the statute to apply. The Commission of Consumer Protection or the attorney general's office may enforce the statute for violations by a business.

DELAWARE: The state legislature adopted the Uniform Deceptive Trade Practices Act which prohibits 12 specific practices, plus other conduct that creates the likelihood of a misunderstanding on the part of a consumer. The transaction must be conducted in the course of business, vocation, or occupation for the statute to apply. The attorney general's office may enforce the statute for violations by a business.

DISTRICT OF COLUMBIA: The state statute prohibits 31 specific practices, plus other unfair, deceptive, or unlawful trade practices. The transaction must involve trade practices involving consumer goods or services. The Office of Consumer Protection may enforce the statute for violations by a business.

FLORIDA: The state statute prohibits unfair methods of competition, unconscionable acts or practices, and deceptive or unfair acts or practices. A finding of a violation may be based on rules promulgated by the Federal Trade Commission. The transaction must be conducted in trade or commerce for the statute to apply. The Department of Legal Affairs or the state attorney's office may enforce the statute for violations by a business.

GEORGIA: The state legislature adopted the Uniform Deceptive Trade Practices Act which prohibits deceptive or unfair acts or practices in a consumer transaction or an office supply transaction. A number of specific examples are included in the statute. The statute applies to consumer transactions in trade or commerce. Georgia Office of Consumer Affairs may enforce the statute for violations by a business.

HAWAII: The state legislature adopted the Uniform Deceptive Trade Practices Act which prohibits 12 specific practices, plus any other conduct that creates a misunderstanding on the part of a consumer. The transaction must be conducted in the course of a business, vocation, or occupation for the statute to apply.

IDAHO: The state statute prohibits 18 specific practices, plus any misleading consumer practices or unconscionable practices. The transaction must be conducted in trade or commerce for the statute to apply. The attorney general's office may enforce the statute for violations by a business.

ILLINOIS: The state legislature adopted the Uniform Deceptive Trade Practices Act which prohibits 26 specific practices, plus other unfair methods of competition and unfair or deceptive acts or practices. Proscribed practices include concealment or omission by a business of any material fact with an intent to cause reliance by a consumer. The transaction must be conducted in trade or commerce for the statute to apply. The attorney general's office may enforce the statute for violations by a business.

INDIANA: The state statute prohibits a number of specific practices, including transactions involving contracts with unconscionable provisions. The transaction must be a consumer transaction as defined by the statute for the statute to apply. The attorney general's office may enforce the statute for violations by a business.

IOWA: The state statute prohibits four specific practices, plus any other unfair or deceptive acts, or concealment or omission of a material fact by a business with the intent to cause reliance on the part of the consumer. The transaction must involve the sale, offer of sale, or advertisement of goods, real property, or several intangible items described in the statue for the statute to apply. The attorney general's office may enforce the statute for violations by a business.

KANSAS: The state statute prohibits 11 specific practices, plus any unconscionable practices as defined by the statute. The transaction must involve the sale or lease of property or services intended for personal, family, household, business, or agricultural purposes. The attorney general's office or local prosecuting attorney's office may enforce the statute for violations by a business.

KENTUCKY: The state statute prohibits unfair or deceptive acts or practices, including unconscionable practices. The transaction must be conducted in trade or commerce for the statute to apply. The attorney general's office or county attorney's office may enforce the statute for violations by a business.

LOUISIANA: The state statute prohibits unfair methods of competition and unfair or deceptive acts or practices. The transaction must be conducted in trade or commerce for the statute to apply. The Governor's Consumer Protection Division may enforce the statute for violations by a business.

MAINE: The state legislature adopted the Uniform Deceptive Trade Practices Act. The state statute prohibits 12 specific practices, plus conduct likely to create confusion or misunderstanding to a consumer, unfair methods of competition, and unfair or deceptive acts or practices. The transaction must be conducted in trade or commerce for the statute to apply. The attorney general's office may enforce the statute for violations by a business.

MARYLAND: The state statute prohibits unfair or deceptive trade practices, including a number of practices specified in the statute. The transaction must involve the sale, offer for sale, or lease of consumer goods, real property, or services. Consumer debt collection and extension of consumer credit are also within the scope of the statute. The Division of Consumer Protection of the Attorney General's office may enforce the statute for violations by a business.

MASSACHUSETTS: The state statute prohibits unfair methods of competition and unfair or deceptive acts or practices. The transaction must be conducted in trade or commerce for the statute to apply. The attorney general's office may enforce the statute for violations by a business.

MICHIGAN: The state statute prohibits 31 specific practices, plus any other deceptive, unfair, or unconscionable acts or practices. The transaction must be conducted in trade or commerce for the statute to apply. The attorney general's office or a district attorney's office may enforce the statute for violations by a business.

MINNESOTA: The state legislature adopted the Uniform Deceptive Trade Practices Act which prohibits 13 specific practices, plus any other deceptive or unconscionable acts or practices. The transaction must be conducted in the course of business, vocation, or occupation for the statute to apply. The attorney general's office may enforce the statute for violations by a business.

MISSISSIPPI: The state statute prohibits 22 specific practices, plus any other deceptive or unconscionable acts or practices. The transaction must be conducted in trade or commerce for the statute to apply. The Attorney General's Office of Consumer Protection may enforce the statute for violations by a business.

MISSOURI: The state statute prohibits deceptive or unfair acts or concealment or omission of a material fact from a consumer. The transaction may involve the sale, offer for sale, or advertisement of any merchandise for the statute to apply. The attorney general's office may enforce the statute for violations by a business.

MONTANA: The state statute prohibits unfair methods of competition and unfair or deceptive acts or practices. The transaction must involve the sale, offer for sale, or advertisement of any real or **personal property**, services, intangibles, or anything of value. The attorney general's office may enforce the statute for violations by a business.

NEBRASKA: The state legislature adopted the Uniform Deceptive Trade Practices Act which prohibits 14 specific practices, plus unfair methods of competition, other unfair or deceptive acts or practices, and all unconscionable acts by a supplier in a consumer transaction. The transaction must be conducted in trade or commerce for the statute to apply. The attorney general's office may enforce the statute for violations by a business.

NEVADA: The state statute prohibits a number of deceptive trade practices set forth in the statute. The transaction must be conducted in the course of a business or occupation. The Commissioner of Consumer Affairs, Director of the Department of Commerce, attorney general's office, or a district attorney's office may enforce the statute for violations by a business.

NEW HAMPSHIRE: The state statute prohibits 12 specific practices, plus any unfair methods of competition or any other unfair or deceptive act or practice. The transaction must be conducted in trade or commerce for the statute to apply. The attorney general's office may enforce the statute for violations by a business.

NEW JERSEY: The state statute prohibits unconscionable commercial practices, deception, **fraud**, or the knowing concealment or omission of a material fact with the intent to cause reliance on the part of a consumer. The statute includes numerous specific prohibitions. The transaction may be conducted in conjunction with the sale or advertisement of any merchandise or real property for the statute to apply. The attorney general's office or the director of a county or municipal office of consumer affairs may enforce the statute for violations by a business.

NEW MEXICO: The state legislature adopted the Uniform Deceptive Trade Practices Act which prohibits 17 specific deceptive practices, two specific unconscionable practices, and other unfair or deceptive trade practices. The transaction must be conducted in trade or commerce for the statute to apply. The attorney general's office may enforce the statute for violations by a business.

NEW YORK: The state statute prohibits deceptive acts or practices and **false advertising**. The transaction must be conducted in business, trade, or commerce, or in the furnishing of a service in the state, for the statute to apply. The attorney general's office may enforce the statute for violations by a business.

NORTH CAROLINA: The state statute prohibits unfair methods of competition and unfair or deceptive acts or practices. The transaction must be conducted in or affect commerce, including all business activities. The attorney general's office may enforce the statute for violations by a business.

NORTH DAKOTA: The state statute prohibits deceptive acts or practices, fraud, or misrepresentation with the intent for consumer to rely on the representation. The transaction may involve a sale or advertisement of any merchandise for the statute to apply. The attorney general's office may enforce the statute for violations by a business.

OHIO: The state legislature adopted the Uniform Deceptive Trade Practices Act. The state statute prohibits 11 specific practices, plus any other deceptive or unconscionable acts or practices. The transaction must be a consumer transaction for the statute to apply. The attorney general's office may enforce the statute for violations by a business.

OKLAHOMA: The state legislature adopted the Uniform Deceptive Trade Practices Act which prohibits 11 specific deceptive trade practices. The transaction must be conducted in a course of a business, vocation, or occupation for the statute to apply. The attorney general's office or a district attorney's office may enforce the statute for violations by a business.

OREGON: The state statute prohibits 20 specific unfair or deceptive acts or practices, plus two unconscionable tactics. The transaction must be conducted in trade or commerce for the statute to apply. The attorney general's office or a district attorney's office may enforce the statute for violations by a business.

PENNSYLVANIA: The state statute prohibits 21 practices, plus other unfair methods of competition, deceptive acts or practices, or any fraudulent or deceptive conduct that is likely to create confusion to a consumer. The transaction must be conducted in trade or commerce for the statute to apply. The attorney general's office may enforce the statute for violations by a business.

RHODE ISLAND: The state statute prohibits 19 specific unfair methods of competition or unfair or deceptive practices. The transaction must be conducted in trade or commerce for the statute to apply. The attorney general's office may enforce the statute for violations by a business.

SOUTH CAROLINA: The state statute prohibits unfair methods of competition and unfair or deceptive acts or practices. The transaction must be conducted in trade or commerce for the statute to apply. The attorney general's office may enforce the statute for violations by a business.

SOUTH DAKOTA: The state statute prohibits knowing and intentional deceptive practices, plus practices involving an omission of a material fact in connection with a sale of merchandise to a consumer. The transaction must be conducted in business for the statute to apply. The attorney general's office or the state's attorney with attorney general approval may enforce the statute for violations by a business.

TENNESSEE: The state statute prohibits 30 specific practices, plus any other deceptive or unfair acts or practices. The transaction must be conducted in trade or commerce for the statute to apply. The attorney general's office may enforce the statute for violations by a business.

TEXAS: The state statute prohibits 25 specific practices, plus additional actions for breach of warranty, insurance violations, or unconscionable acts or practices. The transaction must be conducted in trade or commerce for the statute to apply. The Consumer Protection Division of the attorney general's office or a district attorney's office may enforce the statute for violations by a business.

UTAH: The state statute prohibits 15 specific unconscionable practices by a supplier in a consumer transaction, plus other deceptive acts or practices. The transaction must be a consumer transaction for the statute to apply. The Division of Consumer Protection or other state officials or agencies with authority over suppliers may enforce the statute for violations by a business.

VERMONT: The state statute prohibits unfair methods of competition and unfair or deceptive acts or practices. The transaction must be conducted in commerce for the statute to apply. The attorney general's office may enforce the statute for violations by a business.

VIRGINIA: The state statute prohibits 32 specific practices, plus any other fraudulent acts or practices. A supplier must conduct a consumer transaction for the statute to apply. The attorney general's office may enforce the statute for violations by a business.

WASHINGTON: The state statute prohibits unfair methods of competition and unfair or deceptive acts or practices. The transaction must be conducted in trade or commerce for the statute to apply. The attorney general's office may enforce the statute for violations by a business.

WEST VIRGINIA: The state statute prohibits 16 specific practices, plus other unfair methods of competition and unfair or deceptive practices. The transaction must be conducted in trade or commerce for the statute to apply. The attorney general's office may enforce the statute for violations by a business.

WISCONSIN: The state statute prohibits 14 specific practices, plus other untrue, deceptive, or misleading representations; unfair methods of competition; and unfair trade practices. The statute applies to virtually any transaction due to the broad scope of the statutory language. The Department of Agriculture, Trade, and Consumer Protection may enforce the statute for violations by a business.

WYOMING: The state statute prohibits several specific practices, plus other unfair or deceptive acts or practices. The transaction must be conducted in the scope of a business and in a consumer transaction for the statute to apply. The attorney general's office may enforce the statute for violations by a business.

ADDITIONAL RESOURCES

Carter, Carolyn L., Jonathan Sheldon, et al. *Unfair and Deceptive Acts and Practices.* 8th ed. Boston: National Consumer Law Center, 2008.

Revised Uniform Deceptive Trade Practices Act. National Conference of Commissioners on Uniform State Laws, 1966. Available at https://www.law.upenn.edu/library/archives/ulc/fnact99/1920_69/rudtpa66.txt (accessed November 2, 2012).

State Unfair Trade Practices Law: In One Volume. Riverwoods, IL: Commerce Clearing House, Inc., 2000.

U.S. Code, Title 15: Commerce and Trade, Chapter 2: Federal Trade Commission; Promotion of Export Trade and Prevention of Unfair Methods of Competition. U.S. House of Representatives, 1999. Available at http://uscode.house.gov/download/pls/15C2.txt (accessed November 2, 2012).

ORGANIZATIONS

American Council on Consumer Interests (ACCI)

240 Stanley Hall
University of Missouri
Columbia, MO 65211
Phone: (573) 882-3817
Fax: (573) 884-6571
URL: http://www.consumerinterests.org/

Call for Action (CFA)

5272 River Road, Suite 300
Bethesda, MD 20816
Phone: (301) 657-8260
Fax: (301) 657-2914
URL: http://www.callforaction.org

Consumer Action (CA)

717 Market Street, Suite 310
San Francisco, CA 94103
Phone: (415) 777-9635
Fax: (415) 777-5269
URL: http://www.consumer-action.org

Council of Better Business Bureaus (CBBB)

4200 Wilson Blvd.
Arlington, VA 22203
Phone: (703) 276-0100
Fax: (703) 525-8277
URL: http://www.bbb.org/

National Consumer Law Center (NCLC)

18 Tremont Street
Boston, MA 02108
Phone: (617) 523-8089
Fax: (617) 523-7398
URL: http://www.consumerlaw.org/

National Consumers League (NCL)

1701 K Street, NW, Suite 1201
Washington, DC 20006
Phone: (202) 835-3323
Fax: (202) 835-0747
URL: http://www.nclnet.org/

National Fraud Information Center (NFIC)

PO Box 65868
Washington, DC 20035
Toll Free: (800) 876-7060
Fax: (202) 835-0767
URL: http://www.fraud.org/

CONSUMER ISSUES

DEFECTIVE PRODUCTS

Sections within this essay:

BACKGROUND

Defective product law, commonly known as product liability, refers to the liability of parties along the chain of manufacture of any product for damage caused by that product. A defective product is one that causes some injury or damage to person as a result of some defect in the product or its labeling or the way the product was used. Those responsible for the defect can include the manufacturers of component parts, assembling manufacturers, wholesalers, and retail stores. Many states have enacted comprehensive product liability statutes. There is no federal product liability law.

THEORIES OF PRODUCT LIABILITY

Some consumer advocates believe that a products liability lawsuit is a consumer's most effective weapon against dangerous products. While the government regulates products, regulations may not require the offending company to suffer much of a **penalty**. A product liability lawsuit allows the individual citizen to **prosecute** a case against reckless, incompetent, or negligent manufacturers. Typically, product defect cases are based on **strict liability**, rather than **negligence**. It is irrelevant whether the manufacturer or supplier exercised great care. If there is a defect in the product that causes harm, that entity will be liable for it. This means that it is not necessary to prove "fault" on the part of the **defendant**. To win the case, the **plaintiff** must prove that the product was unreasonably dangerous or defective; that injury resulted from use of the defective product; and that the injury was caused by the defect in the product. A repairer, seller, or manufacturer of a defective product is liable for injuries sustained by persons using the defective product. Liability may also extend to persons who did not purchase the product but were using the product in a foreseeable manner. Also, people injured as a result of someone else using a defective product may be able to recover if their injuries were caused by the product's defect. All jurisdictions require a connection between the product defect and the injury. Many **product liability** cases turn on experts' testimony, where both plaintiff and defendant use **expert testimony** to establish or deny a link between an alleged defect and an injury. Although strict liability is most common, product liability lawsuits also include negligence theories, and breach of **warranty** theories.

Negligence A negligence theory requires the plaintiff to prove that the defendant owed a duty to the consumer. Manufacturers do, in fact, owe a duty to the users of its products and to bystanders likely to be injured. The manufacturer also has a duty in making its product to guard against injuries likely to result from reasonably foreseeable misuse of the product. The plaintiff must also show that the manufacturer breached its duty. The plaintiff should be able to prove that a reasonable manufacturer, with knowledge or constructive knowledge of the product's defect, would not have produced the product. The plaintiff also must prove injury and that the defendant's breach caused the injury.

Strict Liability Strict liability does not require that the injured plaintiff show knowledge or fault on the manufacturer's part. The plaintiff must show only that the product was sold or distributed by a defendant and that the product was unreasonably dangerous at the time it left the defendant's possession. The behavior or knowledge (or lack thereof) of a product liability defendant regarding the dangerous nature of a product is not an issue for consideration under a strict liability theory. Strict liability concerns only the condition of the product itself while a negligence theory concerns not only the product, but also the manufacturer's knowledge and conduct.

Breach of Warranty Every product comes with an **implied warranty** that it is safe for its intended use. A defective product that causes injury was not safe for its intended use and thus can constitute a breach of warranty.

TYPES OF PRODUCT DEFECTS

There are three types of product defects: design defects, manufacturing defects, and defects in marketing, sometimes known a failure to warn. Design defects exist before the product is manufactured. Manufacturing defects result from the actual construction or production of the item. Defects in marketing deal with improper instructions and failures to warn consumers of potential dangers with the product.

Design Defects In these cases injury results from a poor design, even though there may be no defect in the manufacture of the individual product. A product can be unreasonably dangerous for various reasons. The design of the product could be unreasonably dangerous, resulting in

the entire line of products being defective. Generally, in order to prove a design defect case, the plaintiff is obligated to offer a reasonable alternative design that the manufacturer could have employed, which would have prevented the injury and which would not have substantially diminished the product's effectiveness. If the **jury** finds that the plaintiff's proposed alternative is reasonable and would have eliminated the product's risk, the product is determined defective.

The manufacturer in a design defect case cannot escape liability by relying on industry standards as a defense or alleging that because the other manufacturers used the same design, the product was not defective. Theoretically, the entire industry could be producing products with design defects. However, the industry standard defense is not the same as the state of the art defense, which may be a valid defense if the defendant can show that at the time the product was built, no safer, alternative design existed. The state of the art defense protects a manufacturer from liability for a product, which was reasonably safe years earlier but by current standards might be deemed defective.

Manufacturing Defects A manufacturing defect occurs when a particular product is somehow manufactured incorrectly and in its condition is unreasonably dangerous. The plaintiff must show that the product was in its defective condition when it left the manufacturer's possession and that it was unaltered at the time it caused the injury. In short, the consumer must prove that the manufacturer caused the defect. If the defective part was a component in a larger product (for example, a defective tire on an automobile), the component producer may be liable, as well as the manufacturer of the larger product.

Marketing Defects A product can also be unreasonably dangerous absent appropriate warnings. If a product could reasonably have been designed with a higher degree of safety, a proper warning will not necessarily convert the unreasonably dangerous product into a safe, non-defective one. An appropriate warning however, can transform certain dangerous products, which would be defective without the warning, into reasonably safe ones. The warning must be thorough and conspicuous, and it must evaluate the magnitude of the risk involved in failing to abide by the manufacturer's instructions. Failure to warn, or "inadequate warning" cases refer to injuries caused as a result of a product already known to be potentially dangerous which was sold without a proper warning to the consumer. Every product has a potential to be unsafe if it is used incorrectly. Whether a warning is adequate requires weighing all the possible circumstances. Juries are typically left with the task of determining whether a given warning is adequate, appropriate, suitable, or sufficient under the specific facts of a particular case.

USED MERCHANDISE

Sellers of used merchandise may be liable depending on the factual situation. If the product was warranted or guaranteed, there may be a basis of liability. **Corporate** takeovers, purchases, and break-ups of companies may create additional potentially responsible parties who are liable for injuries caused by defective products created initially by others.

EXPORTED GOODS

A large number of products manufactured outside the United States are sold in the United States. It is estimated that 80 per cent of U.S. consumer goods are imported from China. Additionally, U.S. companies frequently outsource the production of certain components to companies in foreign countries. While it is possible to sue a foreign corporation for a defective product, the requirements of proper legal procedure are sometimes extensive.

Because the number of exports to the United States has increased significantly in the last decade, the U.S. government has entered into agreements with several countries to help ensure the safety of exported products. In 2005 the U.S. Consumer Product Safety Commission (CPSC) signed agreements with the governments of Canada and Mexico to improve the safety of products imported to and from both countries. These agreements were designed to build on the North American Security and Prosperity Partnership (SPP), signed earlier that year by the United States, Canada, and Mexico. (The SPP is a more broadly based agreement that calls for improved security to keep borders free from **terrorism** but open to trade.) In 2006, the CPSC signed a Memorandum of Understanding with the government of India to improve the safety of consumer exports to the United States. This agreement includes exchanging product safety information and providing training programs that focus on safety issues. The U.S and Chinese governments agreed in 2011 to develop means of improving the quality of Chinese-made goods. This came in the wake of a number of product recalls involving glasses, drywall, pet food, toys, and food. In 2010, the CPSC issued recalls on 220 products made in China.

COMPARATIVE FAULT

While under a products liability theory a manufacturer may be strictly liable for defects, the law recognizes that certain products are inherently dangerous and that

consumers should know that the product is dangerous when they purchase it. If a consumer uses a defective product in a manner that an ordinary consumer would and is injured as a result, then a valid case may exist. Conversely, if a consumer uses a product in a manner other than that intended by the manufacturer, the consumer may be partially at fault, despite the fact that the product may have been defective.

STATUTE OF LIMITATIONS

All states have some form of **statute of limitations**, which limits the time allowed for filing a lawsuit. The time frame in which the statute of limitations runs usually begins from the time of the injury as a result of the defect. However, most states have some form of a delayed **discovery** rule, which states that the statute does not begin to run until the injury is discovered. This may be important when the injury is not obvious, perhaps until years later. There is a related statute in some jurisdictions called a statute of repose. It essentially provides that no claim can be made based upon a defective product beyond a specified number of years after the date of manufacture.

STATE LAWS

Product liability lawsuits are usually filed in state courts. The laws governing product liability come primarily from the **common law**, where court decisions have announced legal duties, standards of liability, and defenses to claims of negligence. However, provisions of the **Uniform Commercial Code** (UCC), which has been adopted by most states, also provide product liability standards. The UCC governs the sale of goods and when they prove to be defective, the manufacturer may be held liable. Sections 2-314 and 2-315 are the most important UCC provisions, as they deal with implied and express warranties of merchantability in the sale of goods.

DAMAGES

Compensatory damages awardable in products liability cases include medical bills, reimbursement for lost wages, and property damaged as a result of the defective product. Pain and suffering experienced as a result of injury and general damages are also recoupable. In addition, if the conduct of the defendant was egregious, the plaintiff may be entitled to **punitive damages**.

CONSUMER PRODUCT SAFETY COMMISSION

The U.S. Consumer Product Safety Commission (CPSC) is an independent federal regulatory agency created to protect the public from unreasonable risks of injuries and deaths associated with some 15,000 types of consumer products. CPSC uses various means to inform the public. These include local and national media coverage, publication of numerous booklets and product alerts, a website, a telephone Hotline, the National Injury Information Clearinghouse, CPSC's Public Information Center, and responses to **Freedom of Information Act** (FOIA) requests. CPSC staff participates in voluntary standards activities for a variety of products ranging from children's products to heating units to bicycles to paper shredders.

For more than 30 years CPSC has operated a statistically valid injury surveillance and follow-back system known as the National Electronic Injury Surveillance System (NEISS). The primary purpose of NEISS has been to provide timely data on consumer product-related injuries occurring in the U.S. NEISS injury data are gathered from the emergency departments of 100 hospitals selected as a probability sample of all U.S. hospitals with emergency departments. The system's foundation rests on emergency department surveillance data, but the system also has the flexibility to gather additional data at either the surveillance or the investigation level. Surveillance data enable CPSC analysts to make timely national estimates of the number of injuries associated with (not necessarily caused by) specific consumer products. These data also provide **evidence** of the need for further study of particular products. Subsequent follow-back studies yield important clues to the cause and likely prevention of injuries.

ADDITIONAL RESOURCES

Moore, Michael J. *Product Liability Entering the 21st Century: The U.S. Perspective.* Washington, DC: Brookings Institution Press, 2001.

Owen, David G. *Product Liability in a Nutshell.* 8th ed. Eagan, MN: West, Thomson Reuters, 2008.

"Your Online Resource for Recalls." Available at http://www. recalls.gov (accessed November 2, 2012).

ORGANIZATIONS

Consumer Action (CA)
221 Main Street, Suite 480
San Francisco, CA 94105
Phone: (415) 777-9635
Fax: (415) 777-5267
URL: http://www.consumer-action.org

National Consumers League (NCL)
1701 K Street, NW, Suite 1200
Washington, DC 20006
Phone: (202) 835-3323
Fax: (202) 835-0747
URL: http://www.nclnet.org

U.S. Consumer Product Safety Commission (CPSC)
4330 East-West Highway
Bethesda, MD 20814-4408
Phone: (301) 504-7923
URL: http://www.cpsc.gov

CONSUMER ISSUES

FEDERAL TRADE COMMISSION/ REGULATION

Sections within this essay:

- Background
- Bureau of Consumer Protection
  - Division of Advertising Practices
  - Division of Enforcement
  - Division of Financial Practices
  - Division of Marketing Practices
  - Division of Planning and Information

- Bureau of Economics
- Bureau of Competition
  - Antitrust Laws
  - Mergers

- FTC Litigation
- Additional Resources

BACKGROUND

The Federal Trade Commission (FTC) works to ensure that the nation's markets are efficient and free of practices which might harm consumers. To ensure the smooth operation of our free market system, the FTC enforces federal **consumer protection** laws that prevent **fraud**, deception, and unfair business practices. The Commission also enforces federal antitrust laws that prohibit anticompetitive mergers and other business practices that restrict competition and harm consumers.

The FTC was created in 1914 to prevent unfair methods of competition in **commerce**. In 1938, Congress passed the Wheeler-Lea Amendment, which included a broad prohibition against "unfair and deceptive acts or practices." After that, the FTC was directed to administer a wide variety of other consumer protection laws, including the Telemarketing Sales Rule, the Pay-Per-Call Rule and the Equal Credit Opportunity Act. In 1975, Congress passed the Magnuson-Moss Act which gave the FTC the authority to adopt trade regulation rules which define unfair or deceptive acts in particular industries. Trade regulation rules have the force of law.

Today, the FTC is an independent agency which reports directly to Congress. The Commission is headed by five commissioners, nominated by the president and confirmed by the Senate, each serving a seven-year term. The president chooses one commissioner to act as chairman. No more than three commissioners can be of the same political party. The Commission is further divided into bureaus and divisions, which are responsible for various aspects of FTC operations.

BUREAU OF CONSUMER PROTECTION

Bureau of Consumer Protection's mandate is to protect consumers against unfair, deceptive, or **fraudulent** practices. The bureau enforces a variety of consumer protection laws enacted by Congress, as well as trade regulation rules issued by the FTC. Its actions include individual company and industry-wide investigations, administrative and federal court **litigation**, rulemaking proceedings, and consumer and business education. In addition, the Bureau contributes to the FTS's on-going efforts to inform Congress and other government entities of the impact that proposed actions could have on consumers. The Bureau of Consumer Protection is divided into six divisions and programs, each with its own areas of expertise.

Division of Advertising Practices The Division of Advertising Practices is the nation's enforcer of federal truth-in-advertising laws. Its law enforcement activities focus on claims for foods, drugs, dietary supplements, and other products promising health benefits; health fraud on the Internet; weight-loss advertising and marketing directed to children; performance claims for computers, ISPs, and other high-tech products and services; tobacco and alcohol advertising; children's **privacy** online; and claims about product performance made in national or regional newspapers and magazines; in radio and TV commercials, including infomercials; through direct mail to consumers, or on the Internet.

Division of Enforcement The Division of Enforcement conducts a wide variety of law enforcement activities to protect consumers, including ensuring compliance with administrative and federal court orders entered in consumer protection cases, conducting investigations and prosecuting civil actions to stop fraudulent, unfair or deceptive marketing and advertising practices, and enforcing consumer protection laws, rules and guidelines. This division monitors compliance with FTC cease and desist orders and federal court injunctive orders, investigates violations of consumer protection laws, and enforces a number of trade laws, rules and guides, including:

- The Mail or Telephone Order Merchandise Rule, which requires companies to ship purchases when promised (or within 30 days if no time is specified) or to give consumers the option to cancel their orders for a refund.

- The Textile, Wool, Fur and Care Labeling Rules, which require proper origin and fiber content labeling of textile, wool, and fur products, and care label instructions attached to clothing and fabrics.

- Energy Rules, which require the disclosure of energy costs of home appliances (the Appliance Labeling Rule), octane ratings of gasoline (the Fuel Rating Rule), and the efficiency rating of home insulation (the R-Value Rule).

- Green Guides, which govern claims that consumer products are environmentally safe, recycled, recyclable, ozone-friendly, or biodegradable.

Division of Financial Practices The Division of Financial Practices is responsible for developing policy and enforcing laws related to financial and lending practices affecting consumers. It also is responsible for most of the agency's consumer privacy program. Its duties include enforcement of the **Fair Credit Reporting Act** (FCRA) which ensures the accuracy and privacy of information kept by credit bureaus and other consumer reporting agencies and gives consumers the right to know what information these entities are distributing about them to creditors, insurance companies, and employers. This division also enforces the Gramm-Leach-Bliley Act (GLBA). The GLBA requires financial institutions to provide notice to consumers about their information practices and to give consumers an opportunity to direct that their personal information not be shared with non-affiliated third parties.

The Division of Financial Practices monitors the Truth in Lending Act, which requires creditors to disclose in writing certain cost information, such as the **annual percentage rate** (APR), before consumers enter into credit transactions, the Consumer Leasing Act, which requires lessors to give consumers information on **lease** costs and terms, and the Fair Debt Collection Practices Act, which prohibits debt collectors from engaging in unfair, deceptive, or abusive practices, including overcharging, harassment, and disclosing consumers' debt to third parties.

Division of Marketing Practices The Division of Marketing Practices enforces federal consumer protection laws by filing actions in federal district court on behalf of the commission to stop scams, prevent scam artists from repeating their fraudulent schemes in the future, freeze assets, and obtain compensation for scam victims. The division also is responsible for enforcement of the Telemarketing Sales Rule, which prohibits deceptive sales pitches and protects consumers from abusive, unwanted, and late-night sales calls, the 900 Number Rule, which requires sellers of pay-per-call (900 numbers) to clearly disclose the price of services, and the Funeral Rule, which requires funeral directors to disclose price and other information about their services to consumers.

Division of Planning and Information The Division of Planning and Information helps consumers get information. This Division runs the Consumer Response Center, with counselors who respond to consumer complaints and requests for information. It also supervises the Identity Theft Data Clearinghouse, with staff who educate consumers on how to protect themselves from identity theft and what to do if their identity has been stolen. Additionally, this division manages the Consumer Sentinel, a secure, online database and cyber tool available to hundreds of civil and criminal law enforcement agencies in the United States and abroad.

BUREAU OF ECONOMICS

The Bureau of Economics helps the FTC evaluate the economic impact of its actions. To do so, the Bureau provides economic analysis and support to antitrust and consumer protection investigations and rulemakings. It also analyzes the impact of government regulation on competition and consumers and provides Congress, the **Executive Branch** and the public with economic analysis of market processes as they relate to antitrust, consumer protection, and regulation.

This Bureau provides guidance and support to the agency's antitrust and consumer protection enforcement activities. In the antitrust area, the Bureau participates in the investigation of alleged anticompetitive acts or practices and provides advice on the economic merits of alternative antitrust actions. If an enforcement action is initiated, the Bureau integrates economic analysis into the proceeding (sometimes providing the expert witness at trial) and works with the Bureau of Competition to devise appropriate remedies. In the consumer protection area, this bureau provides economic support and analysis of potential commission actions in both cases and rulemakings handled by the Bureau of Consumer Protection. Bureau economists also provide analysis of appropriate **penalty** levels to deter activity that harms consumers.

The Bureau of Economics also conducts economic analyses of various markets and industries. This work focuses on the economic effects of regulation and on issues important to antitrust and consumer protection policy. Many of these analyses are published as staff reports.

BUREAU OF COMPETITION

The Bureau of Competition prevents anticompetitive mergers and other anticompetitive business practices in the marketplace. The bureau fulfills this role by reviewing proposed mergers and other business practices for possible anticompetitive effects, and, when appropriate, recommending that the FTC take formal law enforcement action to protect consumers. The Bureau also serves as a research and policy resource on competition topics and provides guidance to business on complying with the antitrust laws.

Antitrust Laws The Bureau protects competition through enforcement of the antitrust laws. These laws include: Section 5 of the Federal Trade Commission Act, which prohibits unfair methods of competition, Section 1 of the Sherman Act, which outlaws every **contract**, combination, or **conspiracy**, in restraint of trade, Section 2 of the Sherman Act, which makes it unlawful for a company to monopolize, or attempt to monopolize, trade or commerce, Section 7 of the **Clayton Act**, which prohibits mergers and acquisitions the effect of which may be substantially to lessen competition or to tend to create a **monopoly**, and Section 7A of the Clayton Act (added in 1976 by the Hart-Scott-Rodino Antitrust Improvements Act), which requires companies to notify antitrust agencies before certain planned mergers.

Mergers Most mergers actually benefit competition and consumers by allowing firms to operate more efficiently. In a competitive market, firms pass on these lower costs to consumers. However, some mergers, by reducing competition, can cost consumers many millions of dollars every year in the form of higher prices and reduced product quality, consumer choice, and innovation. The Bureau of Competition reviews mergers to determine which ones have the potential to harm consumers; thoroughly investigates those that may be troublesome; and recommends enforcement action to the FTC when necessary to protect competition and consumers. The FTC challenges only a small percentage of mergers each year. Various remedies may be suitable for transactions that pose antitrust concerns. These include **settlement**, litigation, or **abandonment** of the transaction by the parties.

FTC LITIGATION

Typically, FTC investigations are non-public to protect both the investigation and the companies involved. If the FTC believes that a person or company has violated the law or that a proposed merger may violate the law, the agency may attempt to obtain voluntary compliance by entering into a consent order with the company. A company that signs a consent order need not admit that it violated the law, but it must agree to stop the disputed practices outlined in an accompanying complaint or undertake certain obligations to resolve the anticompetitive aspects of its proposed merger. If a consent agreement cannot be reached, the FTC may issue an administrative complaint or seek injunctive relief in the federal courts. The FTC's administrative complaints initiate a formal proceeding that is much like a federal court trial but before an administrative law judge. **Evidence** is submitted, **testimony** is heard, and witnesses are examined and cross-examined. If a law violation is found, a **cease and desist order** may be issued. Initial decisions by administrative law judges may be appealed to the full commission. Final decisions issued by the commission may be appealed to the U.S. Court of Appeals and, ultimately, to the U.S. Supreme Court.

In some circumstances, the FTC can go directly to court to obtain an injunction, civil penalties, or consumer **redress**. In the merger enforcement arena, the FTC may seek a **preliminary injunction** to block a proposed merger pending a full examination of the proposed transaction in an administrative proceeding. The injunction preserves the market's competitive status quo. The FTC seeks federal court injunctions in consumer protection matters typically in cases of ongoing consumer fraud.

ADDITIONAL RESOURCES

Federal Trade Commission. "FTC Regulatory Review." Available at http://ftc.gov/ftc/regreview/index.shtml (accessed November 3, 2012).

Hyde, Henry. *Antitrust Enforcement Agencies: The Antitrust Division of the Department of Justice and the Bureau of Competition of the Federal Trade Commission: Congressional Hearing.* Darby, PA: Diane Publishing, 2000.

ORGANIZATIONS

American Antitrust Institute

2919 Ellicott Street, NW, Suite 1000
Washington, DC 20008-1022
Phone: (202) 244-9800
URL: http://www.antitrustinstitute.org

Federal Trade Commission (FTC)

600 Pennsylvania Avenue, NW
Washington, DC 20580
Toll Free: (877) FTC-HELP (382-4357)
URL: http://www.ftc.gov

CONSUMER ISSUES

IDENTITY THEFT

Sections within this essay:

BACKGROUND

The person becomes the victim of identity theft when someone else uses the person's personal information to commit **fraud** or other crimes. An individual who commits identity theft may appropriate a name, bank account number, credit card number, social security number, or other personal information. With the increase in the amount of personal information that is exchanged on the Internet, identity theft has developed into a major concern in the United States and abroad.

Both state governments and the federal government have enacted a series of statutes that are designed to deter identity theft. Many of these statutes increase penalties or expand the roles that law enforcement officials play in the investigation of identity theft. Other statutes assist victims after their identities have been stolen.

HOW IDENTITY THEFT OCCURS

The Federal Trade Commission (FTC), which serves as a clearinghouse for complaints about identity theft, has identified several means by which an identity thief may perpetrate the crime. These include the following:

- Obtaining personal information of others while on the job
- Hacking personal records
- Bribing or conning an employee who has access to personal records
- Stealing a victim's wallet or purse
- Stealing personal information through e-mail, phone, or other means, in a practice known as "phishing"
- Stealing credit or debit card numbers by capturing information in a data storage device, in a practice known as "skimming"

Consumer Sentinel Network identity theft complaints by victims' age, calendar years 2009 through 2011

Age	CY 2009		CY 2010		CY 2011	
	Complaints	Percentages[1]	Complaints	Percentages[1]	Complaints	Percentages[1]
19 and under	19,192	7	18,356	8	19,563	8
20–29	64,415	24	56,734	24	56,689	23
30–39	57,651	22	49,486	21	49,950	21
40–49	50,584	19	43,996	19	45,230	18
50–59	38,568	15	35,428	15	38,150	15
60–69	20,254	8	19,985	18	23,153	9
70 and over	13,719	5	13,011	5	15,803	6
Total reporting age	**264,383**		**236,996**		**248,538**	

[1]Percentages are based on the total number of victims reporting their age in CSN identity theft complaints for each calendar year: CY-2009 = 264,383; CY-2010 = 236,996; and CY-2011 = 248,538. 95% of the consumers who contacted the FTC reported their age in CY-2009; 94% in CY-2010; and 89% in CY-2011.

SOURCE: *Consumer Sentinel Network Data Book for January–December 2011. Federal Trade Commission, 2012.*

TABLE BY PREMEDIAGLOBAL. ©2013 CENGAGE LEARNING.

- Obtaining a person's credit report

- Rummaging through a person's trash can or the trash can of a business, in a practice known as "dumpster diving"

- Stealing personal information found in a victim's home

- Stealing mail, including bank and credit card statements, offers for new credit cards, new checks, and tax information

- Completing a change of address form so that the victim's mail is sent to another location

Once an identity thief has obtained the personal information of a victim, the **perpetrator** may engage in a number of activities. Some of these illegal activities include the following:

- Establishing a phone or wireless service in the name of the victim

- Opening new credit card accounts in the victim's name

- Calling credit card companies to change the billing address of the victim's account (so that the victim will not receive statements)

- Creating **counterfeit** checks, credit cards, or **debit** cards

- Authorizing electronic transfers in the victim's name

- Draining bank accounts

- Buying a car or taking out a automobile loan in the victim's name

- Getting a job or filing a **fraudulent tax return** in the victim's name

- Giving the victim's name to the police during an arrest

SELF-HELP MEASURES

Those who have become the victims of identity theft may take certain actions in order to protect themselves. In some situations, a person may not be aware that he has become a victim, while; in others, a person may suspect that she has been victimized, but needs to determine whether this is so. Those who believe their identity has been stolen can pursue several steps to discover if they are victims of this crime.

Determine Whether Identity Theft Has Occurred In some instances, identity theft will be obvious to the victim. A victim may receive a telephone call from a **creditor** after an identity thief has opened an account in the victim's name. In other circumstances, the victim may notice unusual charges on his or her credit card statement or unauthorized withdrawals from a checking or savings account.

Even where identity theft is not immediately obvious, a victim may experience other signs that this theft has taken place. For example, the victim may stop receiving bills or other mail, indicating that an identity thief has submitted a change of address form for the victim. Similarly, a victim may be denied credit for no apparent reason or may receive credit cards for which the victim did not apply.

Obtain a Credit Report Three nationwide consumer credit reporting companies, also referred to as credit bureaus, maintain credit reports about each consumer. These companies maintain such information as how many accounts a consumer has and whether the consumer has paid his or her bills on time. The three companies include the following: Equifax, Experian, and TransUnion. Contact information for these companies is available under "Organizations" at the conclusion of this essay.

Under amendments to the federal **Fair Credit Reporting Act**, passed in 2003, each of these credit bureaus must provide every consumer with a free copy of the consumer's credit report. The credit report cannot be obtained directly from the credit bureaus, however. Instead, these reports must be obtained from http://www.annualcreditreport.com; via phone at 877-322-8228; or by submitting a form to Annual Credit Report Request Service, PO Box 105281, Atlanta, GA 30348-5281.

In some instances under federal law, a consumer is entitled to additional free reports, such as when a company denies credit to a consumer. Moreover, some states provide free access to credit reports. Otherwise, consumers may pay up to $9.95 to order a credit report from one of the reporting services.

File a Fraud Alert Each of the three major credit bureaus maintains a fraud department. A consumer who is the victim of identity theft should contact the fraud department of one of the credit bureaus and ask that the company place a fraud alert on the consumer's account. Once a consumer has contacted one of these bureaus, this bureau is required to contact the other two.

This fraud alert indicates to a creditor that the creditor must contact the consumer before opening a new account or changing an existing account. If the consumer requests, the credit bureaus may only display the last four digits of the consumer's social security number on the credit reports.

Submit an ID Theft Affidavit When an identity thief opens a new unauthorized account, the victim may dispute the opening of the account. The Federal Trade Commission has prepared an ID Theft **Affidavit** that may be used when a consumer reports fraudulent activity and disputes an account. The ID Theft Affidavit is available at http://www.consumer.gov/idtheft/pdf/affidavit.pdf.

Report to Local Police A victim of identity theft should file a report with the victim's local police or the police in the community where the theft took place. The victim should submit a copy of the police report, or at least the number of the report, to creditors and anyone else who might require proof that the crime has occurred.

File a Complaint with the Federal Trade Commission A victim should submit a complaint with the FTC, which maintains a database of information regarding identity theft cases. Law enforcement agencies use this database during investigations. The FTC also uses this information in order to gather more data about identity theft in an effort to address the problem as a whole.

Manage Personal Information The FTC and others warn consumers that they should take active steps to protect their personal information. For credit card, bank, and phone accounts, consumers should create a password that a thief cannot guess. Similarly, a consumer should not give out personal information, via computer or otherwise, to anyone unless the consumer knows with whom he or she is dealing.

Identity Theft Insurance Some insurance companies offer policies to protect against the effects of identity theft. The cost of the coverage ranges from $20 to $100 a year and is provided as a rider on a homeowner's policy or as a standalone policy. However, the National Association of Insurance Commissioners has advised consumers that such policies will not cover direct monetary losses that are a result of identity theft. Such policies only cover expenses associated with dealing with identity theft, such as the cost of phone calls, copies, postage, and possibly legal bills. The average victim spends about $1,500 to recover from the theft, so if the policy **deductible** is high, there may be a small payout from the insurance company.

FEDERAL STATUTES

Congress has enacted a number of statutes that address identity theft. Some of these statutes focus on criminal sanctions for identity theft, while others focus more on protecting the victims of identity theft crimes.

Identity Theft and Assumption Deterrence Act The Identity Theft and Assumption Deterrence Act was passed in 1998 to establish identity theft as a federal crime. Under this law, a person who commits identity theft faces a maximum of 15 years in prison and/or a fine. The maximum term of **imprisonment** increases under some circumstances, such as when identity theft occurs in connection with drug trafficking or as a means to facilitate international **terrorism**. The **statute** also requires the FTC to receive complaints from individuals who have been victims of identity theft.

Prior to the enactment of this statute, federal law only applied to the theft of identification documents and not identifying information. The 1998 law extends its application to the theft of "means of identification," which may include any of the following:

- Name
- Social security number
- Date of birth
- Official state or government issued driver's license or identification number
- Alien registration number
- Government **passport** number

- Employer or taxpayer identification number
- Unique biometric data, including a fingerprint, a voice print, a retina or iris image, or another unique physical representation
- A unique electronic identification number, address, or routing code
- Telecommunication identifying information or access device.

Identity Theft Penalty Enhancement Act In 2004, President George W. Bush signed the Identity Theft **Penalty** Enhancement Act. The statute strengthened penalties for those who possess someone else's personal information with the intent to use the information to commit a crime. Penalties are further enhanced when the identity theft is done to commit an act of terrorism.

Fair and Accurate Credit Transactions Act Congress passed the Fair and Accurate Credit Transactions Act in 2003 in an effort to prevent identity theft, among other purposes. The statute provides that consumers may request that the credit bureaus place fraud alerts on their accounts. The act also specifies that only the last five digits of a credit card number may appear on an electronically printed receipt. This provision preempted state laws, creating a national standard. Moreover, this statute directs the FTC to prepare a model summary of the rights of consumers with respect to procedures to remedy fraud or identity theft.

Other Statutes Several other federal statutes have been enacted in an effort to combat identity theft. Some of these statutes limit the financial liability of identity theft victims. Others prohibit the release of personal information, including social security numbers.

STATE STATUTES

The various states have enacted several types of statutes that apply to identity theft cases. The following are some of the more common types of identity theft statutes.

Credit Card Skimming About half of the states have approved legislation that criminalizes the unauthorized use of encoded credit card information. In some states, such as Texas, the statute requires restaurants and bars to post signs warning employees against fraudulent use of or possession of identifying information.

Breach of Information As of 2007, 36 states had enacted statutes that require state agencies and companies to disclose security breaches that involve the potential release of personal information of consumers. In some instances,

these breaches have compromised personal information of hundreds of thousands of individuals. These statutes provide notification to those who potentially could be the victims of identity theft as a result of such a breach.

Consumer Report Security Freeze Some states allow victims of identity theft to demand that credit reporting services freeze the victims' credit reports. The provisions of these statues are similar to those found in the federal Fair and Accurate Credit Transactions Act.

Anti-Phishing California in 2005 became the first state to enact legislation to address **phishing**, which is a practice of duping Internet users into divulging personal information. As of 2012, 22 other states had enacted similar laws. Congressional attempts to enact similar legislation have failed in Congress since 2004.

STATE IDENTITY THEFT LAWS

ALABAMA: The Consumer Identity Protection Act makes identity theft either a **felony** or a **misdemeanor**, depending on whether the **defendant** has had a prior **conviction** and the amount of financial loss involved with the theft.

ALASKA: The state's statute addressing theft by deception makes identity theft either a felony or a misdemeanor, depending on the circumstances.

ARIZONA: The state has enacted legislation addressing credit card numbers on receipts and credit card skimming. The state's statute addressing theft by deception makes identity theft a felony.

ARKANSAS: The state has enacted legislation addressing credit card skimming and breach of information. The state's statute addressing financial identity fraud makes identity theft a felony.

CALIFORNIA: The state has enacted legislation addressing credit card numbers on receipts, credit card skimming and breach of information. The state's statute addressing identity theft provides for both a fine and a jail term.

COLORADO: The state has enacted legislation addressing credit card numbers on receipts.

CONNECTICUT: The state has enacted legislation addressing breach of information. The state's statute addressing identity theft makes identity theft a felony.

DELAWARE: The state has enacted legislation addressing credit card numbers on receipts, credit card skimming, and breach of information. The state's statute addressing identity theft makes identity theft a felony.

FLORIDA: The state has enacted legislation addressing credit card numbers on receipts, credit card skimming, and breach of information. The state's statute addressing criminal use of personal identification information makes identity theft either a felony or a misdemeanor, depending on the circumstances.

GEORGIA: The state has enacted legislation addressing credit card numbers on receipts and breach of information. The state's statute addressing financial identity fraud makes identity theft a crime punishable by either a fine or a term of imprisonment.

HAWAII: The state's statute addressing identity theft makes identity theft a felony.

IDAHO: The state has enacted legislation addressing credit card numbers on receipts and credit card skimming. The state's statute addressing misappropriation of personal identifying information makes identity theft a misdemeanor or a felony, depending on the circumstances.

ILLINOIS: The state has enacted legislation addressing credit card numbers on receipts, credit card skimming and breach of information. The state's statute addressing identity theft makes identity theft a misdemeanor or a felony, depending on the circumstances.

INDIANA: The state has enacted legislation addressing breach of information. The state's statute addressing identity theft makes identity theft a felony.

IOWA: The state has enacted legislation addressing credit card skimming. The state's statute addressing identity theft makes identity theft a misdemeanor or a felony, depending on the circumstances.

KANSAS: The state has enacted legislation addressing credit card numbers on receipts. The state's statute addressing identity theft makes identity theft a felony.

KENTUCKY: The state has enacted legislation addressing credit card numbers on receipts and credit card skimming. The state's statute addressing identity theft makes identity theft a crime subject to a fine or term of imprisonment.

LOUISIANA: The state has enacted legislation addressing credit card numbers on receipts, credit card skimming, and breach of information. The state's statute addressing identity theft makes identity theft a felony.

MAINE: The state has enacted legislation addressing credit card numbers on receipts, credit card skimming, and breach of information. The state's statute addressing misuse of identification makes identity theft a class D crime.

MARYLAND: The state has enacted legislation addressing credit card numbers on receipts. The state's statute addressing identity theft makes identity fraud a misdemeanor or a felony, depending on the circumstances.

MASSACHUSETTS: The state's statute addressing identity theft makes identity theft a felony.

MICHIGAN: The state has enacted legislation addressing credit card skimming. The state's statute addressing identity theft makes identity theft a felony.

MINNESOTA: The state has enacted legislation addressing breach of information. The state's statute addressing identity theft makes identity theft a crime punishable by a fine or jail term.

MISSISSIPPI: The state has enacted legislation addressing credit card skimming. The state's statute addressing fraudulent use of identity makes identity theft a crime punishable by a fine or jail term.

MISSOURI: The state has enacted legislation addressing credit card numbers on receipts and credit card skimming. The state's statute addressing identity theft makes identity theft either a felony or a misdemeanor depending on the circumstances.

MONTANA: The state has enacted legislation addressing breach of information. The state's statute addressing identity theft makes identity theft a crime punishable by a fine or a jail term.

NEBRASKA: The state has enacted legislation addressing credit card numbers on receipts. The state's statute addressing criminal impersonation makes identity theft either a misdemeanor or a felony depending on the circumstances.

NEVADA: The state has enacted legislation addressing credit card numbers on receipts, credit card skimming and breach of information. The state's statute addressing identity theft makes identity theft a felony.

NEW HAMPSHIRE: The state has enacted legislation addressing credit card skimming. The state's statute addressing identity theft makes identity theft a felony.

NEW JERSEY: The state has enacted legislation addressing credit card numbers on receipts, credit card skimming, and breach of information. The state's statute addressing identity theft makes identity theft a crime punishable by fine or jail term.

NEW MEXICO: The state has enacted legislation addressing credit card numbers on receipts. The state's statute addressing identity theft makes identity theft a misdemeanor.

NEW YORK: The state has enacted legislation addressing credit card numbers on receipts and breach of information. The state's statute addressing identity theft makes identity theft either a felony or a misdemeanor, depending on the circumstances.

NORTH CAROLINA: The state has enacted legislation addressing credit card numbers on receipts and breach of information. The state's statute addressing fraudulent identity fraud makes identity theft a felony.

NORTH DAKOTA: The state has enacted legislation addressing credit card numbers on receipts and breach of information. The state's statute addressing identity theft makes identity theft a felony.

OHIO: The state's statute addressing identity theft makes identity theft either a felony or a misdemeanor depending on the circumstances.

OKLAHOMA: The state has enacted legislation addressing credit card numbers on receipts. The state's statute addressing identity theft makes identity theft a felony.

OREGON: The state has enacted legislation addressing credit card numbers on receipts and credit card skimming. The state's statute addressing identity theft makes identity theft a felony.

PENNSYLVANIA: The state's statute addressing identity theft makes identity theft either a felony or a misdemeanor depending on the circumstances.

RHODE ISLAND: The state has enacted legislation addressing credit card numbers on receipts and breach of information. The state's Impersonation and Identity Fraud Act makes identity theft a crime punishable by fine or jail term.

SOUTH CAROLINA: The state's Personal Financial Security Act makes identity theft a felony.

SOUTH DAKOTA: The state has enacted legislation addressing credit card skimming. The state's statute addressing identity theft makes identity theft a misdemeanor.

TENNESSEE: The state has enacted legislation addressing credit card numbers on receipts and breach of information. The state's statute addressing identity theft makes identity theft either a felony or a misdemeanor depending on the circumstances.

TEXAS: The state has enacted legislation addressing credit card numbers on receipts, credit card skimming, and breach of information. The state's statute addressing identity theft makes identity theft a felony.

UTAH: The state has enacted legislation addressing credit card skimming. The state's statute addressing identity theft makes identity theft either a felony or a misdemeanor depending on the circumstances.

VERMONT: The state's statute addressing identity theft makes identity theft either a felony or a misdemeanor depending on the circumstances.

VIRGINIA: The state has enacted legislation addressing credit card numbers on receipts and credit card skimming. The state's statute addressing identity theft makes identity theft either a felony or a misdemeanor depending on the circumstances.

WASHINGTON: The state has enacted legislation addressing credit card numbers on receipts, credit card skimming, and breach of information. The state's statute addressing identity theft makes identity theft a felony.

WEST VIRGINIA: The state has enacted legislation addressing credit card skimming. The state's statute addressing identity theft makes identity theft a felony.

WISCONSIN: The state's statute addressing misappropriation of personal identifying information makes identity theft a felony.

WYOMING: The state has enacted legislation addressing credit card skimming. The state's statute addressing identity theft makes identity theft either a felony or a misdemeanor depending on the circumstances.

ADDITIONAL RESOURCES

"Fighting Back Against Identity Theft." Federal Trade Commission. Available at http://www.ftc.gov/bcp/edu/microsites/idtheft/ (accessed November 1, 2012).

Kelly, Denis G. *The Official Identity Theft Prevention Handbook Professional Edition.* New York: Sterling & Ross, 2011.

U.S. Department of Justice. "Identity Theft and Identity Fraud." Available at http://www.justice.gov/criminal/fraud/websites/idtheft.html (accessed November 2, 2012).

ORGANIZATIONS

Equifax Information Services, LLC
PO Box 740241
Atlanta, GA 30374
Toll Free: (800) 685-1111
URL: http://www.equifax.com

Experian
PO Box 2002
Allen, TX 75013
Toll Free: (888) 397-3742
URL: http://www.experian.com

Federal Trade Commission (FTC)
600 Pennsylvania Avenue, N.W.
Washington, DC 20580
URL: http://www.ftc.gov

National Conference of State Legislatures
444 North Capitol Street, N.W., Suite 515
Washington, DC 20001
Phone: (202) 624-5400
Fax: (202) 737-1069
URL: http://www.ncsl.org

TransUnion
PO Box 1000
Chester, PA 19022
Toll Free: (800) 888-4213
URL: http://www.transunion.com/index.jsp

CONSUMER ISSUES

MAIL-ORDER PURCHASES/ TELEMARKETING

Sections within this essay:

BACKGROUND

Mail order advertising has its roots in the 1800s, when Richard Sears, a railroad clerk in Minnesota, found himself with an abandoned case of pocket watches. Using his list of other railroad clerks throughout the Midwest, he marketed these watches and quickly sold them. Sears recognized immediately that an entrepreneur with a list of accurate names and addresses and a stock of quality merchandise no longer needed a store. He only needed a good message delivery vehicle and first-rate customer service. Thus began the company that would become known as Sears Roebuck. With the advent of the telephone, telemarketing followed. Along with direct mail and telemarketing came governmental regulation.

DIRECT MAIL

The U.S. Postal Inspection Service is the law enforcement branch of the U.S. Postal Service, empowered by federal laws and regulations to investigate and enforce over 200 federal statutes related to crimes against the U.S. mail, the Postal Service, and its employees. Postal inspectors investigate any crime in which the U.S. mail is used to further a scheme, whether it originated in the mail, by telephone or on the Internet. The illegal use of the U.S. mail determines a **mail fraud**. If **evidence** of a postal-related violation exists, postal inspectors may seek prosecutive or administrative action against a violator. Postal inspectors base their investigations of mail **fraud** on the number, pattern and substance of complaints received from the public.

Deceptive Mail Prevention and Enforcement Act The Deceptive Mail Prevention and Enforcement Act of 1999 requires mailings to clearly display on rules and order forms that no purchase is necessary to enter contest and state that a purchase does not improve the chance of winning. They must state the terms and conditions of the sweepstakes promotion, including rules and entry procedures; the sponsor or mailer of the promotion and principal place of business, or other contact address of sponsor or mailer; estimated odds of winning each prize; the quantity, estimated retail value, and nature of each prize; and the schedule of any payments made over time. The act imposes requirements for mail related to skill contests mailings, which must disclose the number of rounds, cost to enter each round, whether subsequent rounds will be more difficult, and the maximum cost to enter all rounds; the percentage of entrants who may solve correctly the skill contest; the identity of the judges and the method used in judging; the date the winner will be determined, as well as quantity and estimated value of each prize. The law imposed new federal standards on facsimile checks sent in any mailing. The checks must include a statement on the check itself that it is non-negotiable and has no cash value. The law prohibits mailings that imply a connection to, approval of, or endorsement by the federal government through the misleading use of a seal, insignia, reference to the postmaster general, **citation** to a federal statue, trade or brand name, or any other term or symbol, unless the mailings carry two disclaimers. The law requires companies sending sweepstakes or skill contests to establish a system and include in their mailings a telephone number or address, which consumers could use to have themselves removed from the mailing lists of such companies. The U.S. Postal Inspection Service is responsible for investigating cases of fraud when U.S. mail is used as part of the scheme.

E-mail Marketing With the growth of the Internet skyrocketing in the 1990s, marketers quickly realized that they could collect email addresses and then send marketing messages to thousands, if not millions, of consumers. Such bulk advertising flooded the in-boxes of consumers and lead to state and federal laws to curtail what has become known as "spam" emails. As of 2012, 37 states had enacted statutes regulating unsolicited electronic mail advertising. The majority of these state laws target commercial or **fraudulent** electronic mail, while a smaller number of state laws apply to unsolicited "bulk" e-mail. Most state anti-spam laws prohibit misrepresenting or falsifying the origin of or the routing information on messages; using an Internet address of a third party without permission, or including misleading information in the subject line of a message. Some states also prohibit the sale or distribution of software that is designed solely to falsify or forge the point of origin of or the routing information on email messages. Some states, such as California, require individuals who send bulk advertising messages through email to include the abbreviation "ADV" to identify a message as an advertisement. Other states have enacted statutes that call for harsher punishment for violators. The vast majority of state statutes provide for fines, rather than potential

criminal sentences, and catching a **perpetrator** who sends the spam is often difficult. Moreover, many e-mails originate from overseas, making domestic legislation much weaker.

In 2003, Congress passed a law known as the Controlling the Assault of Non-Solicited Pornography and Marketing (CAN-SPAM) Act. Under the Can-Spam Act, set up an "opt-out" system for marketers. This system permits marketers to send bulk e-mails, but requires marketers to provide a link that allows recipients to block further e-mails. Moreover, the **statute** does not permit **class action** suits against those who infringe upon the law's requirements. If a person sends a request to someone who has sent spam, and the sender continues to deliver messages to the recipient anyway, the sender can be subjected to severe penalties. the act preempts any state law that "expressly regulates the use of electronic mail to send commercial messages, except to the extent that any such statute, regulation, or rule prohibits falsity or deception in any portion of a commercial electronic mail message or information attached thereto."

900 Telephone Number Solicitations The 900 telephone numbers, in which the caller pays a fee per minute, have been used by legitimate entities. However, some mailings attempt to lure consumers into calling a 900 number claiming the consumer has won a sweepstakes or prize. Other 900 number solicitations offer products or services, such as credit repair or a travel package. People with bad credit who hope to receive a credit card by calling a 900 number might receive a list of banks to which they can apply for such a card. Those who are told to call because they're winners in a sweepstakes may receive nothing but a charge on a phone bill. Sometimes a call to a 900 number requires the consumer to listen to a long recorded sales pitch, resulting in a high phone charge.

Solicitations Disguised as Invoices Title 39, United States Code, Section 3001, makes it illegal to mail a **solicitation** in the form of an invoice, bill, or statement of account due unless it conspicuously bears a notice on its face that it is, in fact, merely a solicitation. This disclaimer must be in very large (at least 30-point) type and must be in boldface capital letters in a color that contrasts prominently with the background against which it appears. The disclaimer must not be modified, qualified, or explained, such as with the phrase "Legal notice required by law." It must be the one prescribed in the statute, or alternatively, the following notice prescribed by the U.S. Postal Service: THIS IS NOT A BILL. THIS IS A SOLICITATION. YOU ARE

UNDER NO OBLIGATION TO PAY THE AMOUNT STATED ABOVE UNLESS YOU ACCEPT THIS OFFER. Some solicitations disguise their true nature. Others identify themselves as solicitations, but only in the "fine print." A solicitation whose appearance does not conform to the requirements of Title 39, United States Code, Section 3001, constitutes **prima facie** evidence of violation of the federal False Representation Statute. Therefore, solicitations in the form of invoices, bills, or statements of account due which do not contain the large and conspicuous disclaimer required by the law will not be carried or delivered by mail if they come to the attention of the Postal Service, and will be disposed of as the Postal Service shall direct.

Sexually Oriented Mail Solicitations Consumers can have their names and the names of their minor children placed on a U.S. Postal Department list of persons who do not want to receive unsolicited sexually oriented advertisements through the mail. Form 1500, Application for Listing and/or Prohibitory Order, is available at any local post office. Thirty days after protection begins, any mailer who sends the consumer sexually oriented advertisements may be subject to civil and criminal sanctions. Names will remain on the list for five years.

TELEPHONE SOLICITATION

A telephone solicitation is a telephone call that acts as an advertisement. In some cases unlisted or non-listed numbers can be obtained from a directory assistance operator. They, along with non-published numbers, may be sold to other organizations. Some sales organizations call all numbers in numerical order for a neighborhood or area. The FCC's rules prohibit telephone solicitation calls to homes before 8 am or after 9 p.m. A person placing a telephone solicitation call must provide his or her name, the name of the person or entity on whose behalf the call is being made, and a telephone number or address at which that person or entity may be contacted. The term telephone solicitation does not include calls or messages placed with the receiver's prior consent, regarding a tax-exempt nonprofit organization, or from a person or organization with which the receiver has an established business relationship. An established business relationship exists if the consumer has made an inquiry, application, purchase, or transaction regarding products or services offered by the person or entity involved.

The Telephone Consumer Protection Act The Telephone Consumer Protection Act of 1991 (TCPA) was enacted by Congress to reduce the nuisance and invasion of **privacy** caused by telemarketing and prerecorded calls. Congress ordered the FCC to make and clarify certain regulations. The TCPA imposes restrictions on the use of automatic telephone dialing systems, of artificial or prerecorded voice messages, and of telephone facsimile machines to send unsolicited advertisements. Specifically, the TCPA prohibits autodialed and prerecorded voice message calls to emergency lines, health care facilities or similar establishments, and numbers assigned to radio common carrier services or any service for which the called party is charged for the call. The TCPA also prohibits artificial or prerecorded voice message calls to residences made without prior express consent. Telephone facsimile machines may not transmit unsolicited advertisements. Those using telephone facsimile machines or transmitting artificial or prerecorded voice messages are subject to certain identification requirements. Finally, the TCPA requires that the Commission consider several methods to accommodate telephone subscribers who do not wish to receive unsolicited advertisements, including live voice solicitations. The statute also outlines various remedies for violations of the TCPA.

Automatic Telephone Dialing Systems Automatic telephone dialing systems, also known as autodialers, generate a lot of consumer complaints. Autodialers produce, store, and dial telephone numbers using a random or sequential number generator. Autodialers are usually used to place artificial (computerized) or prerecorded voice calls. Autodialers and any artificial or prerecorded voice messages may not be used to contact numbers assigned to any emergency telephone line, the telephone line of any guest or patient room at a hospital, health care facility, cellular telephone service, or other radio common carrier service. Calls using autodialers or artificial or prerecorded voice messages may be placed to businesses, although the FCC's rules prohibit the use of autodialers in a way that ties up two or more lines of a multi-line business at the same time.

If an autodialer is used to deliver an artificial or prerecorded voice message, that message must state, at the beginning, the identity of the business, individual, or other entity initiating the call. During or after the message, the caller must give the telephone number (other than that of the autodialer or prerecorded message player that placed the call) or address of the business, other entity, or individual that made the call. It may not be a 900 number or any other number for which charges exceed local or long distance transmission charges. Autodialers that deliver a recorded message must release the called party's telephone line within 5 seconds of the time that the calling system receives notification that the called party's line has hung up.

Do Not Call Lists The FCC requires a person or entity placing live telephone solicitations to maintain a record of any consumer request not to receive future telephone solicitations from that person or entity. A record of a do-not-call request must be maintained for ten years. This request should also stop calls from affiliated entities if individuals would reasonably expect them to be included, given the identification of the caller and the product being advertised. Tax-exempt nonprofit organizations are not required to keep do-not-call lists. The Direct Marketing Association (DMA) sponsors the Telephone Preference Service (TPS) which maintains a do-no-call list. DMA members are required to use this list. Registration is free and the request remains on file for 5 years. Finally, as of 2002, many states had statewide no-call lists for residents in that state.

Some states permit consumers to file lawsuits against violators who continue to call despite the consumer being on a no-call list. Consumers can sometimes seek **punitive damages** if the caller willfully and knowingly violated do-not-call requirements. States themselves may initiate a civil suit in federal district court against any person or entity that engages in a pattern or practice of violations of the TCPA or FCC rules. While the FCC may not award monetary or other damages, it can give citations or fines to those violating the TCPA or other FCC rules regarding unsolicited telephone marketing calls. Consumers who file complaints with the FCC retain their private right of action.

THE FEDERAL TRADE COMMISSION

One of the most important enforcement agencies for direct marketers is the Federal Trade Commission (FTC), which enforces federal consumer protection laws passed by Congress and which has the authority to adopt regulations and rules interpreting and implementing those laws. There are rules on marketing to children online, on regulations for distance selling delivery requirements, for telemarketing, and many other subjects. Each of the states has similar powers and authority, usually under the office of the state's attorney general, the chief law enforcement officer of the state. The Federal Trade Commission (FTC) Telemarketing Sales Rule requires certain disclosures and prohibits misrepresentations. The Rule covers most types of telemarketing calls to consumers, including calls to pitch goods, services, sweepstakes, prize promotions, and investment opportunities. It also applies to calls consumers make in response to postcards or other materials received in the mail. Calling times are

restricted to the hours between 8 a.m. and 9 p.m. Telemarketers must disclose that it is a sales call and for which company. It is illegal for telemarketers to misrepresent any information, including facts about goods or services, earnings potential, profitability, risk or liquidity of an investment, or the nature of a prize in a prize-promotion scheme. Telemarketers must disclose the total cost of the products or services offered and all restrictions on getting or using them, and that a sale is final or non-refundable.

The FTC works to ensure that the nation's markets are efficient and free of practices which might harm consumers. To ensure the smooth operation of a free market system, the FTC enforces federal consumer protection laws that make illegal fraud, deception, and unfair business practices. The Federal Trade Commission Act allows the FTC to act in the interest of all consumers to prevent deceptive and unfair acts or practices. In interpreting the Act, the Commission has determined that, with respect to advertising, a representation, omission, or practice is deceptive if it is likely to mislead consumers and affect consumers' behavior or decisions about the product or service. In addition, an act or practice is unfair if the injury it causes, or is likely to cause, is substantial, not outweighed by other benefits, and not reasonably avoidable.

The FTC Act's prohibition on unfair or deceptive acts or practices broadly covers advertising claims, marketing and promotional activities, and sales practices in general. The Act is not limited to any particular medium. Accordingly, the Commission's role in protecting consumers from unfair or deceptive acts or practices encompasses advertising, marketing, and sales online, as well as the same activities in print, television, telephone, and radio. For certain industries or subject areas, the Commission issues rules and guides. Rules prohibit specific acts or practices that the Commission has found to be unfair or deceptive. Guides help businesses in their efforts to comply with the law by providing examples or direction on how to avoid unfair or deceptive acts or practices. Many rules and guides address claims about products or services or advertising in general and are not limited to any particular medium used to disseminate those claims or advertising. Therefore, the plain language of many rules and guides applies to claims made on the Internet. Solicitations made in print, on the telephone, radio, TV or online fall within the rule's scope.

Mail or Telephone Order Rule Shopping by phone or mail is a convenient alternative to shopping at a store. By law, a company must ship a consumer's order within the time stated in its ads. If no time is promised, the company should ship the order within 30 days after receiving it. If the company is unable to ship within the promised time, it must provide the consumer with an option notice. This notice gives the consumer the choice of agreeing to the delay or canceling the order and receiving a prompt refund. If a company does not promise a shipping time and the consumer is applying for credit, the company has 50 days to ship after receiving the order.

Bureau of Consumer Protection The FTC's Bureau of Consumer Protection protects consumers against unfair, deceptive, or fraudulent practices. The Bureau enforces a variety of consumer protection laws enacted by Congress, as well as trade regulation rules issued by the Commission. Its actions include individual company and industry-wide investigations, administrative and federal court **litigation**, rulemaking proceedings, and consumer and business education. In addition, the Bureau contributes to the Commission's on-going efforts to inform Congress and other government entities of the impact that proposed actions could have on consumers. The Bureau of Consumer Protection is divided into six divisions and programs, each with its own areas of expertise.

Within the Bureau of Consumer Protection is the Division of Advertising Practices and the Division of Enforcement. These entities are the nation's enforcers of federal truth-in-advertising laws. The FTC Act prohibits unfair or deceptive advertising in any medium. That is, advertising must tell the truth and not mislead consumers. A claim can be misleading if relevant information is left out or if the claim implies something that is not true. In addition, claims must be substantiated especially when they concern health, safety, or performance. The type of evidence may depend on the product, the claims, and what experts believe necessary. Sellers are responsible for claims they make about their products and services. Third parties such as advertising agencies or website designers and catalog marketers also may be liable for making or disseminating deceptive representations if they participate in the preparation or distribution of the advertising, or know about the deceptive claims.

Obligations of Publishers and Agencies Advertising agencies (and more recently, website designers) are responsible for reviewing the information used to **substantiate** ad claims. These agencies may not simply rely on an advertiser's assurance that the claims are substantiated. In determining whether an ad agency should be held liable, the FTC looks at the extent of the agency's participation in the preparation of the challenged ad, and whether the agency knew or should have known

that the ad included false or deceptive claims. Likewise, catalog and magazine publishers can be held responsible for material distributed. Publications may be required to provide documentation to back up assertions made in the advertisement. Repeating what the manufacturer claims about the product is not necessarily sufficient. The Division of Enforcement conducts a wide variety of law enforcement activities to protect consumers, including deceptive marketing practices. This division monitors compliance with Commission cease and desist orders and federal court injunctive orders, investigates violations of consumer protection laws, and enforces a number of trade laws, rules and guides.

FTC LITIGATION

Typically, FTC investigations are non-public to protect both the investigation and the companies involved. If the FTC believes that a person or company has violated the law, the agency may attempt to obtain voluntary compliance by entering into a consent order with the company. A company that signs a consent order need not admit that it violated the law, but it must agree to stop the disputed practices outlined in an accompanying complaint. If a consent agreement cannot be reached, the FTC may issue an administrative complaint or seek injunctive relief in the federal courts. The FTC's administrative complaints initiate a formal proceeding that is much like a federal court trial but before an administrative law judge: Evidence is submitted, **testimony** is heard, and witnesses are examined and cross-examined. If a law violation is found, a **cease and desist order** may be issued. Initial decisions by administrative law judges may be appealed to the full Commission. Final decisions issued by the Commission may be appealed to the U.S. Court of Appeals and, ultimately, to the U.S. Supreme Court. In some circumstances, the FTC can go directly to court to obtain an injunction, civil penalties or consumer **redress**. The injunction preserves the market's competitive status quo. The FTC seeks federal court injunctions in consumer protection matters typically in cases of ongoing consumer fraud.

ADDITIONAL RESOURCES

Brown, Bruce. *The Complete Guide to email Marketing* Ocala, FL: Atlantic Publishing, 2007.

Federal Citizens Information Center, Office of Citizen Services and Innovative Technologies. *2012 Consumer Action Handbook*. Washington, DC: U.S. General Services Administration, 2012. Available at http://www.usa.gov/topics/consumer/consumer-action-handbook.pdf (accessed November 3, 2012).

Fox, Vanessa. *Marketing in the Age of Google*. Hoboken, NJ: Wiley, 2012.

Rampton, Sheldon, and John Stauber. *Trust Us, We're Experts: How Industry Manipulates Science and Gambles with Your Future.* New York: Putnam, 2000.

ORGANIZATIONS

Council of Better Business Bureaus (BBB)

4200 Wilson Blvd., Suite 800
Arlington, VA 22203-1838
Phone: (703) 276-0100
Fax: (703) 525-8277
URL: http://www.bbb.org

Direct Marketing Association

PO Box 9014

Farmingdale, NY 11735
URL: http://www.the-dma.org

Federal Communications Commission (FCC)

445 12th Street SW
Washington, DC 20554
Toll Free: (888) CALL-FCC
Fax: (202) 418-0232
URL: http://www.fcc.gov

Federal Trade Commission (FTC)

600 Pennsylvania Avenue, NW
Washington, DC 20580
Toll Free: (877) FTC-HELP
URL: http://www.ftc.gov

CONSUMER ISSUES

OMBUDSMAN PROGRAMS

BACKGROUND

The term "ombudsman" is derived from the Swedish word meaning agent or representative. For as long as governments have existed, there has always been a parallel concern for the fair and equitable treatment of citizens and a guarantee that their rights are protected. The first public sector ombudsman was appointed by the Parliament of Sweden in 1809 with the express charter to protect individual citizen's rights against the excesses of government bureaucracy. The ombudsman was to receive and investigate citizen complaints against administrative acts of the government. The ombudsman concept spread across Europe and then to the United States in the 1960s. This was partly in response to the **civil rights** movement and citizen efforts for more openness in politics and government activities.

Typically, an ombudsman is a non-partisan, neutral, fact-finding person or office that takes no side in a dispute, but rather recommends solution. However, in broader usage, the term has come to mean more than just an agent or representative, but can also refer to an advocate or **trustee** who looks after the interests of a particular group or class of persons, and therefore serves as an agent of justice.

Within the United States, the term has taken on broader meaning that represents departure from the original Swedish model. While denoting an intermediary serving between citizens and the government, the term is also used to describe any machinery adopted by private organizations, such as educational institutions of higher learning, large business **corporations**, or government to investigate complaints of administrative abuses. They may be been vested with general or special **jurisdiction** over specific governmental functions, such as corrections, and may exercise advocacy in their recommendations, if granted such authority.

Throughout federal and state governments in the early 2010s public ombudsmen offices have been specially created by legislative, executive, or judicial authority to act as independent agencies monitoring the delivery of government services to certain populations, such as the elderly, disabled, juveniles, incarcerated adults, and government employees. An ombudsman is generally independent (although a government employee), **impartial**, universally accessible, and empowered only to assess and make recommendations. The American Bar Association (ABA) defines an ombudsman as "a government official who hears and investigates complaints by private citizens against government agencies."

THREE BASIC TYPES OF OMBUDS

Traditional ombuds (the gender-neutral and simpler term used for ombudspersons) operate in the public sector, and many are public employees. They typically address issues raised by members of the general public (or within their organization), usually concerning the actions or policies of a branch of government or of public officials.

Organizational ombuds are found in both public and private sectors. They typically address the concerns presented by members, employees, or contractors of a particular organization or entity concerning its policies or practices.

Advocate ombuds are also found in both public and private sectors, and also evaluate claims or complaints objectively. However, they typically are authorized or even required to advocate on behalf of individuals or groups found to be aggrieved. Importantly, and unique from other ombuds, an advocate ombud may have additional vested powers to represent an aggrieved party and litigate a problem on behalf of that party.

OMBUDSMEN PROGRAMS AS IMPETUS FOR CHANGE

One of the key roles of an ombudsman is to consider how issues and problems in individual cases may require system-wide change in order to impact organizational culture. The independence of an ombudsman's office gives it the **credibility**, respect, and ability to aggregate individual grievances and cases, and use them to promote systemic change at the top administrative levels. A systems change approach emphasizes monitoring performance, assessing outcome, and ensuring public accountability. It also promotes cross-agency collaboration and **partnership** to provide coordinated and comprehensive service throughout the system.

Typically, ombuds are intermediaries who assess problems and recommend solutions or change. Even though they have limited authority to directly act on a problem, they nonetheless hold powerful positions, because resolution and solution is the quintessential

objective of their profession. Without ombuds, an aggrieved individual must travel up the chain of command, management, or supervision to find a sympathetic ear or even an answer. However, since resolving complaints is not the primary function of management within an organization, a response to a complaint is often delegated to administrative staff, and the complaining party may get no further than a "thank you and we'll look into it and get back with you." response.

Conversely, the principal and full-time duty of an ombudsman is to provide a forum for the registering of a complaint or issue, then investigate and assess its merits, and offer recommendations or solutions to the respective parties. Advocate ombuds have additional authority to advocate the complaining party's position. Ultimately, the likelihood of more timely resolution is enhanced by the direct involvement of the ombudsman, whose duties and resources exist for the very purpose of such problem-solving.

Ombudsman programs serve a variety of functions, including educating the community; investigating allegations; monitoring programs, offices and facilities; conducting research; providing recommendations for change or improvement; and, if necessary and so authorized, bringing **litigation**.

ATTRIBUTES AND TRAITS OF OMBUDS

Probably the most important attribute of the office/position of ombudsman is that of objectivity. This implies and includes:

- the exercise of discretion and confidentiality
- the ability to provide objective leadership
- accessibility
- an absence of any conflicts of interest
- a perseverance to cut through red tape and follow through with complaints without getting stonewalled
- an ability to dissect fact from hyperbole and get to the bottom line
- an ability to mobilize political power, even if acting behind the scenes

Additionally, ombuds should have:

- sufficient **statutory** authority to carry out investigations and mandate improvement
- ready access to documents, records, witnesses, and **subpoena** power
- full independence from the agency in which the ombudsman operates

- no interference by officials or administrators of the agency or service provider that is the subject of a complaint
- assurance that the complaining party will suffer no retaliation
- good-faith **immunity** from civil liability for investigations, recommendations, and mandates
- sufficient funding and resources
- qualified staff, including legal experts to investigate and **substantiate** violations and subject matter experts.

PUBLIC SECTOR PROGRAMS

There are a few key areas involving the general welfare of the public, for which Congress has created federal ombudsman programs. They generally address the concerns of citizens whose status or condition may **warrant** extra protection or monitoring of rights. They include the elderly, those requiring long-term care in nursing facilities, juvenile offenders, and children in general. Other specialty ombudsman programs, such as for environmental protection or **small business** organizations, also have been established at the federal level.

Through special or earmarked funds and grants, federal monies assist many state ombudsman programs in several of the above areas of concern, as well as additional ones (such as **workers' compensation** or public transportation). In large jurisdictions, the monies may trickle down to local government. New York City holds the unique distinction of being the only geographic entity in the world to have an elected ombudsman.

Where there is no ombudsman office at the state level, inspectors general (including offices of an attorney general) and internal affairs programs provide much of the same function. Every state has an inspector general or attorney general, although such positions are more often concerned with systemic problems than individual grievances. However, when state inspectors general receive complaints from more than one individual, they may investigate for more systemic waste or **fraud**, or they may initiate **class action** suits on behalf of individuals with similar complaints. These organizations are parallel with ombuds in that they are intended to function independent of an agency's administration or influence.

United States Ombudsman Association (USOA) Probably the largest and most important of the public sector ombudsman organizations is the United States Ombudsman Association (USOA). Founded in 1977, it is also the oldest in North America. It serves governmental ombudsman offices across the country as well as member offices in Canada and other global sites. It publishes a legislative model of characteristic official offices, in an effort to promote and establish ombudsman offices at the international, national, state, and local levels.

SPECIAL INTERESTS

Elder Rights Under Title 42 of the United States Code (Public Health and Welfare), Congress created, among other things, several programs for older Americans. One of them was a provision for state Long-Term Care Ombudsman programs (42 USC § 3058g). Accordingly, even though federally-established and mandated, the program has been delegated to, and actually managed by, the states through block grants, special appropriations, and foundation grants, among others.

Ombuds in this sector act as advocates for residents of nursing homes, board and care facilities, and assisted living residential setups. They not only investigate complaints, but also provide information to help persons find an appropriate facility for care, and help them get quality care.

Under the federal Older Americans Act, every state is required to have an ombudsman program to address concerns within long term care (LTC) system. These ombuds not only investigate complaints, but also are authorized to advocate for improvement in the system. The best way to find a particular state's LTC ombudsman is to go to the online Web site of the National Long Term Care Ombudsman Resource Center (www.ltcombudsman.org) and click on any individual state. Another resource, MemberoftheFamily.Net (www.memberofthefamily.net), provides information for approximately 16,000 Medicare/Medicaid-certified nursing homes. It also maintains a National Watch List of homes recently cited for violations or substantiated complaints. Finally, it has an Honor Roll of facilities found to be deficiency-free.

Child Welfare As of 2005, there were more than 25 child welfare ombudsman programs in the United States. They generally address "out-of-home" situations involving minors, such as residential care facilities (public orphanages), public agencies providing health and dental care services, public **foster care** and placement agencies, and family social services agencies. Several states also extend ombudsman services to juvenile offender concerns (juvenile detention programs and juvenile corrections) under the broader umbrella of child welfare ombudsman programs.

Because children cannot legally speak for themselves, ombudsman programs involving them are generally advocacy-based, and are referred to as such like

Connecticut's Office of the Child Advocate, or Tennessee's Ombudsman for Children and Families. Ombudsman advocates for children are mostly concerned with complaints or issues involving:

- overcrowded foster homes
- abuse
- neglect
- inappropriate placements
- dangerous environment placements
- services not being provided
- state agency visitation schedules not being followed
- lack of contact with caseworkers
- death or physical injury to a child
- education and training not available or insufficient

Juvenile Corrections Starting in 1995, the Office of Juvenile Justice and Delinquency Prevention (OJJDP) within the U.S. Department of Justice began offering challenge grant money to states for use in ten specifically-earmarked activities. One of those ten priorities was the establishment of state ombudsman offices to investigate and resolve complaints relating to providers of out-of-home care to children and youths, including juvenile detention and correctional facilities. Tennessee and Maryland were the first two states to be awarded this funding specifically for ombudsman programs overseeing juvenile detention and correctional facilities.

Some key issues facing juvenile corrections ombuds include:

- expansion and accessibility of support and services for special- needs, especially mental health needs
- access to mental health services for families of juvenile offenders, to prevent youth from being placed in detention or other alternative
- preventing the juvenile justice system from becoming a safety net for at-risk youth
- expanding prevention and detention programs
- moving confined females into facilities where they can receive gender-responsive services
- intervention to prevent court involvement for at-risk youths.

Adult Corrections Likewise, a majority of adult correction facilities include some form of spokesperson representing the concerns of incarcerated persons, and this is often an ombudsman. By monitoring the relationship between inmates and prison officials, such programs have been successful at improving conditions within correctional institutions to ensure safe and humane treatment of incarcerated persons.

However, the success of an adult correctional ombudsman program has more risk and often depends on the authority of the ombudsman to pursue remedies and manage the competing interests of prisoners and officials. If inmates do not trust an ombudsman's ability to fairly address their complaints, or if prison officials feel that the ombudsman's recommendations are unreasonable, serious obstacles to harmonious relations may undermine the program. An ombudsman's statutory authority must be exercised with care to maintain balanced relationships among correctional administrators, staff, and inmates. However, when created and administered correctly, a correctional ombudsman program that remains independent of a department of corrections can palpably reduce tension within a prison facility and achieve many positive results in the overall running of the facility.

Workers' Compensation The International Association of Industrial Accident Boards and Commissions (IAIABC) (http://www.iaiabc.org/) maintains a detailed list of workers' compensation agencies, including ombuds. However, the most accessible, up-to-date, and probably the most complete of its kind is a website for the North Carolina Industrial Commission's list of U.S. workers' compensation agencies. Internet users can go to http://www.comp.state.nc.us/pages/all50.htm and have instant access to all 50 states' and DC's home pages for workers' compensation agencies, as well as contact information for state workers' compensation ombudsman offices.

Small Businesses The U.S. Small Business Administration (SBA) maintains an Office of the National Ombudsman to assist small businesses burdened with unfair or excessive federal regulatory enforcement, such as repetitive audits or investigations, excessive fines and penalties, retaliation, arbitrary or discriminatory regulatory enforcements, or other unfair actions by federal agencies. Working from a central office in Washington, DC, the SBA National Ombudsman covers only federal regulatory enforcement and compliance actions. Moreover, it can only assist small businesses, small government entities, and **nonprofit** organizations. The Environmental Protection Agency (EPA) Small Business Ombudsman Clearinghouse and Hotline serves private individuals, small communities, small business enterprises, and trade associations representing the small business sector. The office provides public mailings to update recent regulatory actions. Special attention is directed toward answering technical questions and apprising the trade associations that represent small business interests of current regulatory developments.

Students Many major colleges and universities throughout the United States and Canada have a student ombudsman on campus. The ombudsman is generally responsible for assisting students with problems involving school rules, policies, and procedures. Most often, the ombudsman is another student, preferably a graduate student who knows and understands the functions of various offices and organizations on campus. Students are able to discuss matters confidentially, knowing that a student ombudsman will consider all sides in an impartial and objective way.

Environmental Protection In 2002, the Senate Environment and Public Works Committee reauthorized an ombudsman post within the Environmental Protection Agency (EPA). Congress originally established the EPA ombudsman in 1984 to receive complaints about hazardous waste. When the authorization expired in 1988, the EPA retained the ombudsman, but transferred the office to the Office of Solid Waste and Emergency Response. The 2002 bill (S. 606) established an independent Office of the Ombudsman within the EPA. Under the Solid Waste Disposal Act, the ombudsman is authorized to render assistance, conduct investigations, make findings of fact, and forward non-binding recommendations to the EPA administrator.

Many individual states have separate offices for environmental affairs in which an ombudsman is available to investigate complaints of toxic waste or illegal hazardous material handling. However, a minority of states have independent offices dedicated for this function; most fall under the purview of other functions such as inspectors general.

Consumer Affairs To help investigate and enforce **consumer protection** laws, many states have established consumer affairs ombuds to provide the first forum for complaint and/or investigation. Arizona, California, Texas, and Virginia are examples of states maintaining such offices.

Insurance and Banking The Federal Deposit Insurance Corporation (FDIC) Office of the Ombudsman handles inquiries involving problems or complaints related to the FDIC. Although the FDIC insures almost all banks and savings associations in the United States, it may not be the primary regulator of a particular institution. Consumers should initially attempt to resolve a matter with the institution or the institution's primary regulator.

Recurring issues before the FDIC Ombudsman include those regarding bank application processes, the Bank Secrecy Act, and Regulation B and the Equal Credit Opportunity Act (ECOA), particularly relating to laws governing spousal signatures and the propriety of requesting information about an applicant's life insurance.

PRIVATE SECTOR PROGRAMS AND ORGANIZATIONS

International Ombudsman Association The International Ombudsman Association (IOA) was officially formed in 2005, following the merger of the University and College Ombuds Association (UCOA) and the Ombudsman Association (TOA). It is the largest international association of professional organizational ombuds, with over 500 members globally. The IOA offers professional training and education programs for practicing ombuds, and works to support and promote the profession through strategic partnerships with government agencies and other professional organizations.

National Credit Union Administration The Ombudsman for the National Credit Union Administration investigates complaints and recommends solutions relating to regulatory issues that cannot be resolved at a regional level. The NCUA Ombudsman assists complainants with defining options and recommending appropriate actions. This ombud does not advocate for any party, but does insure confidentiality of all interviews and records, used exclusively for internal investigation and recommendation. The NCUA Ombudsman will not handle any matter that involves a **conservatorship** or **liquidation**; that is in litigation; that involves an enforcement action where a notice of charges has been filed; or one that is within the jurisdiction of the Inspector General.

State Organizations In 1969, Hawaii became the first state to appoint an ombudsman. There are only five states in which the ombudsman office is a legislative agency:

- Alaska Office of the Ombudsman, PO Box 102636, Anchorage, AK 99510-2636, (907) 269-5290, website: http://www.ombudsman@legis.state.ak.us

- Arizona Office of the Ombudsman, 740 15th Street NW, Washington, DC 20005, (202) 992-1000, website: http://www.azleg.state.az.us/ombudsman

- Hawaii Office of the Ombudsman, 465 South King Street, 4th Fl., Honolulu, HI 96813,(808) 587-0770, website: http://complaints@ombudsman.Hawaii.gov

- Iowa Office of Citizens' Aid Ombudsman, Ola Babcock Bldg, 1112 East Grand, Des Moines, IA 50319, (888) 426-5065, website: http://www.legis.state.ia.us.ombudsman

- Nebraska Office of the Ombudsman, State Capitol, Rm. 807, PO Box 94604, Lincoln, NB 20005, (402) 471-2035, website: http://www.unicam.state.ne.us/offices/ombud.htm

ADDITIONAL RESOURCES

Administration on Aging. "Ombudsmen Program History." U.S. Department of Health and Human Services. Available at http://www.ltcombudsman.org/about-ombudsmen/program-history (accessed November 3, 2012).

"Citizen Representatives: Statewide Ombudsman." *SLGN Notes*, August 25, 2004. Available at http://www.statelocalgov.net.

Jones, Judith, and Alvin W. Cohn. "State Ombudsman Programs." *Juvenile Justice Bulletin.* U.S. Department of Justice, Office of Juvenile Justice and Prevention, February 2005.

National Long-Term Care Ombudsman Resource Center. "Locate an Ombudsman, State Agencies and Citizen Advocacy Groups." Available at http://www.ltcombudsman.org/ombudsman (accessed November 2, 2012).

ORGANIZATIONS

The American Bar Association (Commission on Legal Problems of the Elderly
740 15th St. NW
Washington, DC 20005
Phone: (202) 992-1000

Asbestos Abatement/Management Ombudsman
Washington, DC
Toll Free: (800) 368-5888
Fax: (202) 566-2848

Federal Deposit Insurance Corporation Ombudsman
E-2022, 3501 Fairfax Drive
Arlington, VA 2226
Phone: (202) 942-3040
URL: http://www.fdic.gov/regulations/resources/ombudsman/contact.html

National Credit Union Association Ombudsman
1775 Duke Street
Alexandria, VA 22314-3428
Phone: (703) 518-6510
URL: http://www.ncua.gov/about/leadership/co/pages/Ombudsman.aspx

National Long Term Care Ombudsman Resource Center
1828 L St. NW, Ste. 801
Washington, DC 20036
Phone: (202) 332-2275
URL: www.ltcombudsman.org

The Ombudsman Association
203 Towne Center Drive
Hillsborough, NJ 08844-4693
Phone: (908) 359-1184
Fax: (908) 359-7619
URL: www.ombuds-toa.org

SBA Ombudsman Hotline
Washington, DC
Toll Free: (800) 368-5888
Fax: (202) 566-0954

United States Ombudsman Association
PO Box 8096
Madison, WI 53708-8096
Phone: (608) 661-0402
URL: www.usombudsman.org

CONSUMER ISSUES

PHISHING

BACKGROUND

Phishing (analogous to fishing, and hence the term) refers to a practice where a **perpetrator** attempts to lure a victim into visiting an authentic-looking website and entering personal information. The purpose of a phishing scheme is to steal personal information from the victim in the form of account numbers, social security numbers, passwords, and so forth. Although these schemes are blatantly illegal forms of **identity theft**, those individuals who are responsible are difficult to catch and **prosecute** because they are often located overseas.

Statistics have shown that phishing has continually escalated as a problem in the United States. According to a study by RSA, an anti-phishing organization, $1 billion was lost to phishing attacks in 2011. The United States and the United Kingdom are the top two countries targeted for phishing attacks. Although legislative efforts to combat this problem have proven ineffective, consumers can take a number of steps to protect themselves from being victimized by this form of **fraud**.

PHISHING AND RELATED SCHEMES

Typical Phishing Scams A phishing scam begins with the distribution of an email that appears to be from a legitimate company, usually a bank or Internet shopping site. The email, which is typically addressed to a generic customer, such as "Dear Valued eBay Customer", often contains authentic-looking logos from a legitimate company. Messages in these emails vary, but most indicate either that the company is undergoing a process of updating its records or that the customer's account information has been compromised through fraud. The email directs the user to click on a link that takes the user to a website that also looks authentic. Once on the site, the page directs the user to enter personal information, including the user's password.

Many victims of phishing schemes are unaware of what happened to them because they have been led to believe that the email and website were authentic. The person responsible for the phishing attack creates deception by producing a URL that looks like it belongs to an actual company. A victim often sees words in the hyperlink that are associated with the company, such as "eBay" or "CitiBank," and have no idea that the URL is fake. The website that the victim visits is likewise designed to deceive the victim because it usually looks identical to a company's actual site.

Spear Phishing A more recent variation of phishing involves emails that are targeted towards employees of specific companies. Emails that are sent as part of this scheme appear to be from an employee's actual company and ask for the user to update personal information. However, like other phishing schemes, a link contained in the email message sends the user to a site that is completely unrelated to the company. This type of targeted phishing scheme has become known as "spear phishing."

Spear phishing has become prevalent. The *Wall Street Journal* reported that between January and June 2005, an estimated 35 million targeted messages were sent in the United States. This form of phishing has also proven to be effective. In one mock attack designed to study users' responses, 500 cadets from West Point received a targeted email asking for personal information. More than 80% of these cadets responded to the email and provided the requested information.

Pharming The term pharming refers to a practice where perpetrators redirect users from legitimate websites to **fraudulent** websites. This is done by exploiting weaknesses in Domain Name Service (DNS) software, which is used to resolve Internet names with the corresponding Internet Protocol (IP) address. For example, when a user enters http://www.mybank.com, DNS software resolves that name with an IP address that consists of a series of numbers, such as 201.26.156.98. When pharming has occurred with respect to that Internet name, the DNS software sends users to another IP address that does not belong to the actual business.

Evil Twins Another recent scam that is similar to phishing schemes employ the use of wireless devices. In these schemes, known as evil twin scams, attackers lure users into connecting their laptops or PDA devices into what appear to be legitimate wireless hotspots. An example of such a hotspot would be an airport lounge. Once a person has connected the wireless device, the attacker can steal information from the user.

Spyware and Keyloggers More sophisticated Internet attacks can be carried out through the use of spyware and keyloggers. Spyware that is installed unknowingly on a

victim's computer can be used to track the victim's Internet usage and steal personal information. Similarly, a keylogger that is installed on a computer can record anything that is typed on a computer, such as user names and passwords, and send that information to a perpetrator who installed the keylogger.

DIFFICULTY IN CONTROLLING PHISHING SCAMS

Several factors make it difficult for law enforcement to catch those who run phishing scams. The websites that are used in these scams are often only active for a few days, so even if law enforcement discovers a scam, the site may be removed long before it is investigated. Moreover, many of the servers that house these sites are located in foreign countries, making enforcement of domestic laws very difficult.

FEDERAL LAWS RELATED TO PHISHING ACTIVITIES

Although some members of Congress have introduced pieces of legislation focusing specifically on phishing, none of these bills have been enacted. Nevertheless, several federal laws prohibit phishing as well as other forms of fraud.

Credit Card Fraud Act Originally enacted in 1984, the Credit Card Fraud Act prohibits the purchase of goods with an "access device." Access devices include credit cards, account numbers, personal identification numbers, and similar items "that can be used, alone or in conjunction with another access device, to obtain money, goods, services, or any other thing of value, or that can be used to initiate a transfer of funds . . . ." A violation of the **statute** can result in a prison term of 15 years and a fine.

Identity Theft and Assumption Deterrence Act The Identity Theft and Assumption Deterrence Act applies to the unauthorized transfer or use of a means of identification. A means of identification includes personal information, such as a social security number or date of birth, as well as biometric data, such as a fingerprint. Although the two statutes are similar, the Identity Theft and Assumption Deterrence Act differs from the Credit Card Fraud Act in that the former defines "victim" as the person whose identity is stolen. By comparison, the Credit Card Fraud Act defines victim as the bank, credit issuer, or merchant, since one of those entities is financially responsible for any fraudulent purchases.

Fair and Accurate Credit Transaction Act Congress enacted the Fair and Accurate Credit Transaction Act in

2003 to allow consumers to check their credit reports and correct mistakes on those reports. The statute amended the **Fair Credit Reporting Act**, which is designed to protect the **privacy** of consumer information in credit reports as well as to promote accuracy in those reports.

CALIFORNIA'S ANTI-PHISHING LAW

California in 2005 became the first state to enact legislation designed specifically to deter phishing. Under the Anti-Phishing Act of 2005, it is unlawful in the state "for any person, by means of a web page, electronic mail message, or otherwise through use of the Internet, to solicit, request, or take any action to induce another person to provide identifying information by representing itself to be a business without the authority or approval of the business." Twenty-two states and Guam have also passed laws modeled on the California act seeking to curtail phishing schemes.

Unlike federal statutes, the California law provides for civil liability as opposed to criminal penalties. Some victims of phishing, including those who provide Internet access service to the public, own a web page, or own a trademark, may recover up to $500,000 for each proven violation of the statute. Other victims may recover up to $5000 for each violation of the statute. The statute also allows the state's attorney general or a district attorney in the state to bring an action to enjoin further violations.

California is also among a few states that allow consumers to place freezes on their credit reports. This option is similar to provisions in the federal Fair and Accurate Transactions Act (FACTA), although the state's option is stronger than the federal counterpart. Nevertheless, few consumers in those states take advantage of this option, primarily because it is not well advertised and it is costly.

SELF-HELP MEASURES

Without effective state or federal legislation, most experts recommend that consumers employ one of several self-help measures. These measures include increased education and awareness of the threat of phishing scams, review of credit records, placing freezes on credit reports, and using one of several different types of insurance.

Education and Awareness In 2012, the Federal Trade Commission (FTC) released a report based on a survey of identity theft victims. The report indicated that 87% of victims contacted a credit reporting agency. However, most focus group participants for the report stated that they did not have a clear understanding of their FACTA rights and did not have a clear plan for remedying their identity theft when they contacted a credit reporting

agency. Although phishing remains prevalent, many consumers have become sophisticated enough to identify fraudulent emails. Nevertheless, more advanced scams, such as spear phishing and pharming schemes, may still lure a consumer to provide personal information.

Banks, credit issuers, and other businesses have made efforts to educate their customers about the potential for phishing schemes and other fraudulent scams. Most businesses do not request personal information from their customers through email messages, and so almost all emails that request this information are illicit. Consumers who receive any suspicious correspondence requesting personal information should contact the business that apparently sent the request.

Several businesses and law enforcement agencies have joined the Anti-Phishing Working Group (APWG), which has been formed to eliminate the threat of phishing scams. Both the APWG and the FTC offer several suggestions in addition to those summarized above.

- Use anti-virus software and a firewall, and keep both up-to-date.
- Do not use email to send personal or account information.
- Review credit card and bank accounts as soon as they are received.
- Regularly log on to online accounts.
- Be cautious about opening any attachment or downloading any files from emails.
- Forward phishing emails to the appropriate authorities, including the following email addresses: spam@uce.gov (FTC); reportphishing@antiphishing.com (APWG).
- File a complaint with the FTC. More information is available online at http://www.consumer.gov/idtheft/ .

Review of Credit Records Consumers should take advantage of federal laws that allow consumers to review their credit reports. At the least, this allows consumers to identify suspicious activity that may have occurred with respect to their personal information. However, the effectiveness of this option may be limited because personal information stolen through a phishing scheme may have occurred months before the consumer checks the credit report.

Anti-Identity Theft Freeze A freeze on a credit account can prevent identity theft attackers from using a consumer's personal information for fraudulent purposes. If a phisher obtains personal information, a freeze would prevent the attacker from using the information for fraudulent purposes. On the other hand, if a consumer provides bank or credit card information to a phisher, such a freeze would not protect the consumer.

Insurance Several companies offer different types of insurance to protect consumers against instances of fraud. Some of these plans monitor a consumer's credit activity, while others reimburse victims after identity theft has occurred.

ADDITIONAL RESOURCES

ADDITIONAL RESOURCES

Federal Trade Commission Using FACTA Remedies: An FTC Staff Report on a Survey of Identity Theft Victims. Federal Trade Commission, 2012. Available at http://www.ftc.gov/os/2012/03/factareport.pdf (accessed December 14, 2012).

"Fighting Back Against Identity Theft." Federal Trade Commission. Available at http://www.ftc.gov/bcp/edu/microsites/idtheft/ (accessed November 1, 2012).

Kelly, Denis G. *The Official Identity Theft Prevention Handbook Professional Edition.* New York: Sterling & Ross, 2012.

Lynch, Jennifer. "Identity Theft in Cyberspace: Crime Control Methods and Their Effectiveness in Combating Phishing Attacks." *Berkeley Technology Law Journal*, 2005.

ORGANIZATIONS

Anti-Phishing Working Group
Email: info@apwg.org
URL: http://www.antiphishing.org

Council of Better Business Bureaus (CBBB)
4200 Wilson Blvd., Suite 800
Arlington, VA 22203-1838
Phone: (703) 276-0100
Fax: (703) 525-8277
URL: http://www.bbb.org

Federal Trade Commission (FTC)
600 Pennsylvania Avenue, N.W.
Washington, DC 20580
URL: http://www.ftc.gov

CONSUMER ISSUES

PURCHASES AND RETURNS

Sections within this essay:

- Background
- Warranties
  - Enforcing a Warranty
  - Remedies After the Warranty Expires
  - Extended Warranties
- Returning Consumer Purchases
  - Mandatory Policy Posting
- Responses to Dishonest or Unfair Merchants
- The Cooling-Off Rule
  - Exceptions to the Cooling-Off Rule
- Other Kinds of Contracts
- Additional Resources

BACKGROUND

Just about everyone has purchased something that looked like a bargain but proved to be an unfortunate mistake. Nearly all of these poor purchasing decisions do have a remedy. It is not necessary that the purchase involves a great deal of money, but there must be a genuine, serious, and material error. In these cases, the reason is clear: the parties somehow made a mistake as to what was being purchased. This general principle applies any time a merchant sells a **tangible** piece of property to an amateur consumer, even if the dealer claims the product is offered "as is."

What are the consumers' options? First, they should consider whether the merchant has any of the following policies:

- Returns:. These are policies that allow buyers to bring the product back to the merchant and get their money back for the product.
- Exchanges.: These policies allow buyers to bring back a product to the merchant and exchange it for a different product.
- Refunds.: This kind of policy allows buyers to get their money back from an unsatisfactory product; these almost always accompany return policies.

If the product itself is somehow defective, buyers should try to discover the warranties or guarantees that cover the product, if any. The product's manufacturer rather than the seller usually offer warranties, except of course in cases where the manufacturer is also the seller of the product.

However, before buyers try to return their products or make a claim under its **warranty**, there are preventive measures they can take to protect their rights as consumers.

- Particularly for more expensive items, consumers should insist on a signed, written, or printed receipt describing the product and the price that they are paying for it. The seller's business name, address, and the date of purchase should appear on the receipt. Most store cash register receipts contain this information.
- In some cases, it is reasonable to request the right to submit the product to a third party for an independent evaluation. For example, if customers are buying a car, they can ask the dealer to permit a mechanic look at it. They can ask for a refund from

the seller if the item is not as described. They can add this provision to the invoice. It will contain words similar to this: "Buyer has the right to submit this item to examination by a third party within five business days and to return to seller for a full refund if not as described."

Ultimately, it can be expensive, time-consuming, and a hassle to take a merchant to court, even **small claims court**. In many cases, a simple complaint letter may do the trick.

WARRANTIES

In most cases, any item purchased is covered by some kind of warranty. A warranty (also known as a guarantee) is a type of assurance from the manufacturer or merchant about the quality of goods or services purchased. A warranty gives consumers recourse if something they buy fails to live up to what they were promised.

Warranties take two forms: implied or expressed. A seller may also sell a product "as is," meaning that the product comes with no warrantee at all. Implied warranties are just that; they are not written or stated, but exist nonetheless. Almost everything customers buy comes with two implied warranties:

1. The **implied warranty** of merchantability: The implied warranty of merchantability warrants or guarantees that a new product will work correctly as long as customers use it for a reasonably expected purpose. For used products, the warranty of merchantability warrants or guarantees that the product will work as expected, considering its age and condition.

2. The implied warranty of fitness: The implied warranty applies when customers buy a product with a specific purpose in mind. If they explained their specific needs to the merchant, the implied warranty of fitness guarantees them that the product will meet their need.

In contrast to implied warranties, expressed warranties are usually written and included with the product. An expressed warranty may be part of an advertisement or included on a sign or display in a store, "genuine full lead crystal", or it may even be an oral description of a product's features. Most typical expressed warranties contain words to the effect that "this product is warranted against defects in materials or workmanship" for a certain time. Expressed warranties are not automatic. Most expressed warranties come directly from the product's manufacturer, although some are included in the merchant's sales **contract**.

In most states, implied warranties last indefinitely. In a few states, however, implied warranties last only as long as any expressed warranty that comes with a product. In these states, if there are no expressed warranties, the implied warranties last forever.

Enforcing a Warranty If a product is defective, the defect will show up immediately in most cases. When it does, customers can request that the seller or manufacturer fix or replace the defective merchandise. If the seller or manufacturer refuses, or if any repair work fails to fix the defect in the product, customers may have to take additional steps in order to resolve the problem.

If the product has not been completely paid for (e.g. something purchased on an **installment** plan), customers may choose to withhold payment. If they made the purchase with their credit card, they can call the credit company and instruct them to refuse payment for the purchase. Customers should use this strategy with care because not every problem or defect is serious enough to permit them to stop payment. It may be best to try to work out a compromise with the seller. If the seller refuses to cooperate, it may be helpful to seek assistance or **mediation** services through the local Better Business Bureau mediation program.

If informal means do not work, customers may have to resort to **litigation**. In most states, there is a **statute of limitations** on breach of warranty lawsuits. Typically, the **statute** ends within four years of when customers discovered the defect.

Remedies After the Warranty Expires If an item fails to perform or otherwise gives customers trouble while it is under warranty, and they have it repaired by someone authorized by the manufacturer to make repairs, the manufacturer must extend the original warranty for the time the item was in the repair shop. This rule applies in most states. In addition, customers can call the manufacturer and speak to the department that handles warranties. If the product was trouble-free during the warranty period, the manufacturer may offer to repair for a problem for free if the problem arose after the warranty expired. This may happen if the problem is a common one. Many manufacturers have fix-it lists—items with defects that do not cause a safety hazard and do not require a recall. Sometimes the manufacturer will repair these types of defects for free. Customers will not know of this remedy, though, unless they call and ask.

Extended Warranties When customers purchase a vehicle, appliance, or an electronic item the merchant may try to encourage them to buy an extended warranty (also known as "service contracts"). These are legitimate contracts. They are intended to extend the period of warranty coverage in the other manufacturer warranties that come with the product. These contracts can be a source of significant profit for stores, which get to keep up to 50% of the amount customers pay for the warranty.

Rarely will customers need to exercise their rights under an extended warranty or service contract. Quality vehicles, electronic equipment, and appliances do not usually experience problems during the first few years of their use. If they do experience problems during this time, they are usually covered by the original warranty. Besides, such merchandise often has a useful life well beyond the length of the extended warranty.

RETURNING CONSUMER PURCHASES

It is not true that consumers have a right to return almost anything they buy in a store. Although there are laws to protect consumers who buy defective products or who are led to make purchases based on misleading advertising, there is generally no rule or law that absolutely requires merchants to offer refunds, exchanges or credits on the items they sell.

There are four basic principles customers should know about returning goods they purchase in a store:

1. Merchants can set their own policies on refunds and exchanges. Generally, consumers are not entitled to either a refund or an exchange.

2. Although merchants are not required to do it, many of them will exchange non-sale items whether customers paid for them with cash, check, or credit.

3. Sale items are commonly exempt from merchants' refund and exchange policies.

4. If customers exchange a product for another one that costs less, the store can require the customers to spend the difference in cost in their store.

Because it makes their stores more attractive to customers, most retailers do offer refunds, exchanges, or credits voluntarily, although they usually impose a "reasonable time" condition for these refunds, exchanges, or credits. These kinds of policies have become so common that people have come to expect them. When retail sellers fail to post notices to the contrary, consumers often wrongly assume that the return, refund, or exchange policy exists. Therefore, before customers make a purchase at a store, try to determine the store's refund policy because these exchange privileges vary from merchant to merchant. A copy of a store's return policy should be posted near cash registers. They are also frequently printed on sales receipts.

When the item has been purchased through a mail-order catalog or an Internet website, the customer should read the return, exchange, and refund policies that are printed in the catalog or listed on the company's website. For example, Amazon.com has a "General Returns Policy" webpage that sets out in detail how a consumer can obtain a full refund, discusses items that are not returnable and states the terms for giving partial refunds

and deducting restocking fees. Under its Conditions of Use policies, any dispute or claim over products and services will be resolved by binding **arbitration** except the consumer may bring a claim in small claims court if the claim qualifies. Under these conditions both the consumer and Amazon agree to waive a **jury** trial.

Determining where to sue an Internet retailer can be difficult. If the retailer's place of business is in another state, the consumer's state court may not have personal **jurisdiction** over the **defendant** retailer. Courts have established varying "minimum contact" rules that determine if the retailer had a sufficient enough presence doing business in the consumer's state to establish personal jurisdiction. If a business regularly solicits business in the state, earns substantial revenue from goods or services sold in the state, or engages in some other regular course of conduct there, then there will usually be enough contact. To avoid a legal dispute, consumers should use a credit card for Internet purchases. If the retailer fails to refund the purchase price the consumer can notify the credit card company and dispute the purchase. The credit card company then seeks to resolve the dispute.

Before making a retail purchase, it is a good idea to find out the following:

- The store's return policy
- The store's exchange policy
- Whether the store will refund customers' money if they return a product
- Whether sales are final (this is especially important for goods that have been marked down)
- How the store's normal return policy is affected if customers have to sign a contract to buy the product,
- If customers are prevented from returning a damaged product if the product came with a separate written warranty.

Most stores that have a refund and/or exchange policy require that the item be returned within a specific time. These periods vary considerably from one merchant to the next, but most will be in the range of about seven to 90 days. The product usually must be in new condition, with the original packaging, and with the original sales receipts. There are a few retailers that will accept goods returned in any condition, at any time, and with no questions asked, but liberal return policies like these are very rare.

Mandatory Policy Posting In the past, some retailers did not post their policies reflecting imposed conditions or limits on accepting returned merchandise, and some did not accept returns at all. Naturally, this policy caused a great deal of frustration for consumers. Consequently, some states have enacted laws that require merchants or retailers to post their refund policies if they do not meet certain common expectations, such as the following:

- The store gives a full refund, an equal exchange, or some combination of these

- The customer may return the merchandise within seven days of the purchase, as long as it is returned with proof of purchase

Basically, if a merchant does not follow a typical return policy, the merchant must post the alternate return policy so that its customers are aware of the return policy.

RESPONSES TO DISHONEST OR UNFAIR MERCHANTS

If a dishonest or unfair merchant has victimized buyers, but they do not relish going to court for a remedy, they have several alternatives. If the merchant is clearly the party at fault, there are many assistants whose aid buyers can enlist. Before taking action, however, they must be sure that they are completely truthful and accurate in their claims. Here are some suggestions to alternative measures to litigation:

- Try to learn whether the offending merchant is a member of a trade organization (most belong to at least one trade group); buyers can complain to the organization.

- If customers paid for the item or service with a credit card, they can refuse to pay the bill when they get their statement from the credit card company. When they dispute a bill, their credit card company will usually give them an immediate credit for the amount in question and then reverse the credit it gave the merchant for their purchase. It will then ask for an explanation from the merchant. In some cases, a merchant will give up rather than take the time to write letters and participate in a credit dispute. If they claim they never received the merchandise for which they were charged, or that it was damaged or defective and they sent it back, the credit card company may refuse payment completely, regardless of what the merchant claims.

- Customers can contact the local Better Business Bureau or the Federal Trade Commission.

- Customers can contact their state, county, or municipal consumer affairs department. A telephone call followed by a letter to these organizations can be very effective at getting action from a recalcitrant merchant.

Most merchants just want to do business. They do not want to lose business. They want to make money on sales, not cheat customers. Likewise, most merchants will

not stand to be taken advantage of, so customers need to be sure they have their facts straight and that the disagreement is not merely a misunderstanding. However, a merchant who refuses to adjust the matter or even to be reasonable about it may have an ulterior motive.

Before customers take these steps, it is a good idea to inform the merchant about what he intends to do. Sometimes, just informing the merchant of intentions to pursue the matter is enough. However, sometimes it is not, in which case the customer should be ready to follow through on the plan of action. Before the customer sends a complaint letter to a consumer or regulatory authority, the customer might want to consider sending a copy of the letter to the merchant, in advance to advise the merchant that the letter will be sent in five business days if the matter is not resolved. Sometimes, the mere threat of action can bring about resolution.

THE COOLING-OFF RULE

If customers buy a product at a store and later change their minds, they may not be able to return the merchandise. However, federal and state laws provide certain protections for consumers who purchase items sold outside the vendor's usual place of business. For example, under the Federal Trade Commission's (FTC's) "Cooling Off Rule," consumers have until midnight of the third business day after signing a contract to cancel the contract. This rule applies when a consumer has entered the following deals:

- A door-to-door contract involving a sale over $25

- A contract for more than $25 made at a place other than the seller's regular place of business. There are similar laws in every state

The fact is the FTC's Cooling-Off Rule only applies to purchases made at a place that is not the seller's permanent place of business. For example, the law would apply to goods customers buy in their own homes, their workplaces, in a student's dormitory, or at spaces temporarily rented by the seller, like hotel or motel rooms, convention centers, fairgrounds, and community centers.

The Cooling-Off Rule guarantees the customer's right to cancel a sale and to receive a full refund. This right extends only until midnight of the third business day after the sale. If the customer notifies the seller of the intent to cancel the purchase within the **cooling-off period**, the customer is entitled to a full refund, and any contract that the customer signed must be rescinded without further obligation.

Under the FTC's Cooling-Off Rule the seller must inform customers about their cancellation rights at the time of the sale. Additionally, the seller is obligated to provide customers with two copies of a cancellation form. One the customer can keep for his records and one should be sent with the returned merchandise. The seller must also provide the customer with a copy of the contract or receipt. The contract or receipt must be in the same language that was used in the sales presentation. For example, if the presentation was made in Chinese, the contract or receipt must also be in Chinese.

The contract or receipt must contain the following information:

- date of the sale
- the seller's name and address
- an explanation of right to cancel the sale

Exceptions to the Cooling-Off Rule Some types of sales cannot be canceled even if they do occur in locations normally covered by the rule. The cooling off rule does not cover sales that have the following conditions:

- the goods or services are intended for commercial purposes
- the goods cost less than $25
- the goods are needed for an emergency
- part of the buyer's request is that the seller perform maintenance or repairs on the buyer's personal property
- the purchase results from **negotiations** whereat the site where the seller's goods are regularly sold.

Many states have similar **consumer protection** statutes that contain similar exceptions to the federal cooling-off rule.

OTHER KINDS OF CONTRACTS

In addition to the consumer protections outlined above for typical consumer products, there are also protections for other kinds of purchases. The Truth in Lending Act is a federal law that permits individuals to cancel a home improvement loan, a second **mortgage**, or other loan when the home has been pledged as security for the loan. This law does not apply to first mortgages. The law allows borrowers to cancel one of these contracts until midnight of the third business day after signing the contract. In some cases, the three-day period may be extended for up to three years. The Act requires the lender to inform borrowers about their right to cancel such contracts. Additionally, the borrower must provide a cancellation form when the borrower signs the loan documents.

Many states have enacted laws that allow consumers to cancel written contracts covering the purchase of certain goods or services within a few days of signing. These include contracts for the following:

- dance or martial arts lessons
- memberships in health clubs
- dating services
- weight loss programs
- time share properties
- hearing aids

State consumer protection agencies have a complete listing of the kinds of contracts covered in their state.

ADDITIONAL RESOURCES

American Bar Association. "Safe Shopping." 2012. Available at http://www.safeshopping.org/.

Bevans, Neal R. *Consumer Law & Protection.* Durham, NC: Carolina Academic Press, 2011.

Council of Better Business Bureaus, Inc. "Better Business Bureau Online." 2012. Available at http://www.bbbonline.org/.

USA.gov. "Consumer Protection." 2012. Available at http://www.usa.gov/topics/consumer.shtml (accessed November 1, 2013).

ORGANIZATIONS

Council of Better Business Bureaus (BBB)

4200 Wilson Blvd., Suite 800
Arlington, VA 22203-1838
Phone: (703) 276-0100
Fax: (703) 525-8277
URL: http://www.bbb.org/

Federal Trade Commission (FTC)

600 Pennsylvania Avenue, N.W.
Washington, DC 20580
Toll Free: (877) 382-4357
URL: http://www.ftc.gov/index.html

National Association of Attorneys General (NAAG)

750 First Street, NE, Suite 1100
Washington, DC 20002
Phone: (202) 326-6000
Fax: (202) 408-7014
URL: http://www.naag.org/

CONSUMER ISSUES

RECALLS BY MANUFACTURERS

Sections within this essay:

- Background
- Consumer Product Recalls
- Food, Drug, and Cosmetics Recalls
- Meat, Poultry, and Egg Safety
- Automobile Recalls
- Lemon Laws
- Additional Resources

BACKGROUND

Sometimes certain defects in a product become apparent after the product has entered the marketplace and been sold. These defects can be related to safety, such as when a certain model of automobile has problems with its braking system, where small pieces from a toy pose a choking hazard to young children, or where a medication poses a previously undiscovered, serious adverse health risk to users. Sometimes the problem is another kind of defect, as when a certain model of vacuum cleaner consistently fails to work properly. A recall may be necessary to remedy problems with a product. Recalls are procedures taken by a manufacturer to remove a product from the market. Recalls allow a manufacturer the opportunity to repair or replace the defective product. Recalls can be costly procedures for manufacturers, but are often less costly than multiple lawsuits or the loss of goodwill among consumers. Recalls may be voluntary on the part of a

manufacturer, or they may be mandated by the government.

Six agencies within the U.S. government have **jurisdiction** over recalls:

- The Consumer Product Safety Commission (CPSC) has jurisdiction over thousands of products used in homes, schools, and for sports and recreation

- The Food and Drug Administration (FDA) has oversight over food, drugs, medical devices, animal feed, cosmetics, and radiation-emitting products such as lasers, microwaves, and cell phones

- The Food Safety and Inspection Service (FSIS) of the Department of Agriculture (USDA) inspects and regulates meat, poultry products, and eggs and egg products

- The National Highway Traffic Safety Administration (NHTSA) is responsible for recalls of motor vehicles and related equipment, child safety seats, and tires

- The Coast Guard covers recreational boats and related equipment

- The Environmental Protection Agency (EPA) has recall jurisdiction over insecticides, rodenticides, fungicides, and vehicle emission testing

CONSUMER PRODUCT RECALLS

Manufacturers recall many of their own products every year when defects and/or safety risks are discovered in their products. Most recalls occur for safety-related reasons. Sometimes, a manufacturer will voluntarily recall products, and sometimes they are compelled to issue recalls.

The Consumer Product Safety Commission has jurisdiction over more than 15,000 consumer products. According to the agency, deaths, injury, and property damage from consumer product incidents costs the United States more than $700 billion a year. CPSC contends that its advocacy since 1972 has resulted in a 30 percent reduction in death and injury from consumer products. CPSC announces recalls of products that present risks to consumers because the products are either defective or violate mandatory safety standards issued by CPSC.

When a consumer discovers that a product that she owns is recalled, she should stop using it. The consumer should also follow the specific guidance in CPSC's recall announcement on that product. A product recall usually lasts indefinitely. Even if more than a year has passed since CPSC issued a recall notice, product owners should read and follow the instructions in the recall notice.

The remedies for recalled products are specific to each product, and no single remedy applies to all products. Each recall announcement is as specific as possible and details the remedy for the product. An announcement typically includes information on where the product was sold, the type and number of injuries or damage caused by the product, and contact information needed to obtain the remedy. The announcement frequently limits recalls to products manufactured during a specific time period. For example, CPSC may announce a recall on toy X, manufactured between June 17, 2005, and August 23, 2006. Owners may or may not get a refund of their recalled product.

FOOD, DRUG, AND COSMETICS RECALLS

The Food and Drug Administration is charged with overseeing the safety and effectiveness of food, drugs, and many cosmetics products. As with other consumer goods and motor vehicles, recalls may be necessary when it is determined that a consumable product may pose considerable risk of harm to individuals. In terms of food, drugs, or cosmetics, recalls may proceed under a manufacturer's own initiative, by FDA request, or by FDA order. There are three classes of recalls in descending order of urgency:

1. Class I recalls are cases in which there is a reasonable chance that the use of or exposure to a product will cause serious adverse health consequences or even death.

2. Class II recalls are cases in which exposure to a product may cause temporary or reversible adverse health consequences, or where the odds of serious adverse health consequences are not great.

3. Class III recalls are situations in which use of or exposure to a product is unlikely to cause adverse health consequences.

Examples of Class I recalls are foods found to contain botulinal toxin, foods with undeclared allergens, or mislabeling a life-saving drug. A drug that is under-strength but not used to treat life-threatening situations is one example of a Class II recall; another is where two units of blood are collected from a **donor** who has traveled to a country where malaria is endemic. Class III recalls might include container defects such as a lid that does not seal, a product that is off-taste or color, or a retail food that does not have a label in English.

Recalls may happen in three ways. First, a manufacturer or distributor may decide on its own initiative to issue a recall to remove a product from the market. Second, FDA may request a recall. Finally, two things can happen in the rare instances where a firm does not comply with FDA request. In certain circumstances the FDA has **statutory** authority to order a recall; in other cases the FDA must seek legal action under the Food, Drug, and Cosmetic Act. The FDA can prescribe a recall only when a medical device, human tissue products, or infant formula pose a risk to human health. Legal remedies available to FDA include seizure of the available product, an injunction against the manufacturer, and/or a court request for recall of the product.

A market withdrawal is a less drastic step than a recall. A market withdrawal is voluntary on the part of a manufacturer, and occurs when a product has a minor violation that would not otherwise be subject to FDA legal action. In these cases, a firm will remove its product from the market or otherwise correct the problem. For example, a product will be removed from the market if there is **evidence** that its packaging has been compromised. This can happen without any manufacturing or distribution problems.

A medical device safety alert is issued in situations involving a medical device that presents an unreasonable risk of substantial harm. These are primarily intended to inform potential users of possible hazards. In some cases, these alerts also are considered recalls.

MEAT, POULTRY, AND EGG SAFETY

The Department of Agriculture's Food Safety and Inspection Service is responsible for meat, egg products, and poultry products inspections. The Federal Meat Inspection Act provides FSIS with inspection duties for meat products sold in interstate **commerce**. FSIS also re-inspects imported meat products to ensure they meet U.S. food safety standards. The Poultry Products Inspection Act and the Egg Products Inspection Act provides similar jurisdiction over those products. For example, in an egg processing plant, an inspector would examine eggs before and after breaking, that are intended for further processing and for use as food.

FSIS works with manufacturers and distributors to uncover problems, set the parameters for recall, and monitor its implementation.

AUTOMOBILE RECALLS

The Department of Transportation's National Highway Traffic Safety Administration (NHTSA) is the federal agency authorized to issue vehicle safety standards and to require manufacturers to recall vehicles with safety-related defects (49 USC §301). Since NHTSA's inception in 1966, more than 299 million vehicles of all types, 43 million tires, and 84 million pieces of motor vehicle equipment (including child seats) have been recalled to correct safety defects. Vehicle manufacturers initiated some of these recalls. Others have come about after NHTSA investigation or through court action, instigated by the agency.

A safety defect is defined as a problem with a motor vehicle or motor vehicle equipment that poses a risk to motor vehicle safety. Moreover, it must be common to a group of vehicles of the same manufacture or design, or to items of equipment of the same type and manufacture. If a manufacturer identifies a safety defect, the manufacturer notifies NHTSA, as well as vehicle or equipment owners, dealers, and distributors. The manufacturer must then fix the problem, typically without charge to vehicle owners. NHTSA assesses the adequacy of the manufacturers' corrective action and makes sure manufacturers comply with all statutory requirements.

Vehicle owners should report possible auto safety issues to NHTSA. The combined effect of a number of similar complaints can trigger an investigation into the alleged safety defect and ultimately lead to a recall. However, there is no set number of complaints an agency must receive before launching an investigation; NHTSA reviews every report of an alleged safety issue. A report to NHTSA can be made three ways: through the agency's toll-free telephone hotline, by mail, or via the Internet. Consumers are asked to supply specific information necessary for NHTSA staff to evaluate the problem. The information is entered into NHTSA's database and a copy is forwarded to agency staff for evaluation. The agency assesses the information individually, as well as in combination with other information in its database. The information is organized according to vehicle make, model, model year, manufacturer, and the affected part, assembly or system. NHTSA staff monitor such complaints to determine whether a pattern emerges that may indicate potential safety-related problems on any specific vehicle, tires, or equipment.

The Office of Defects Investigation (ODI) within NHTSA is responsible for investigating potential safety defects. The investigative process consists of four parts:

- Screening. ODI determines whether to open an investigation. During this phase, ODI will conduct a preliminary review of consumer complaints and other information related to the alleged defect.

- Petition Analysis. ODI processes petitions for defect investigations during petition analysis.

- Investigation. ODI conducts an investigation of the alleged defect(s).

- Recall Management. Assuming the investigation leads to a recall, ODI will monitor the overall adequacy of safety recalls and the safety-relatedness of service bulletins.

In most cases, manufacturers discover safety defects through their own testing procedures, and make voluntary recalls to remedy the defects without NHTSA involvement. Federal law requires manufacturers to report the findings that safety defects exist in their product, and to take appropriate action to fix the defects. As some vehicles age, however, certain design and performance problems may occur. These problems often lead to complaints to NHTSA by vehicle owners. These consumer complaints can form the basis for a defect investigation, possibly leading to a recall.

After the NHTSA determines a safety defect or other noncompliance issue exists, manufacturers are given a reasonable time to notify, by first-class mail, all registered owners and purchasers of the affected vehicles. (State motor vehicle offices provide the names of vehicle owners.) Manufacturers must inform vehicle owners of the safety problem and provide an evaluation of its risk to the vehicle's safety. The letter must also instruct consumers on the following details:

- How to get the problem corrected
- That corrections are to be made at no charge
- When the remedy will be available
- How long the remedy will take to perform
- Who to contact if there are difficulties in obtaining the free recall work

Once NHTSA has made a defect determination, the manufacturer has three options to correct the defect: repair, replace, or refund the product. The circumstances of the defect and the overall cost of remedying the problem will determine the manufacturer's course of action. In the case of tires and equipment, the manufacturer can either repair or replace, but need not refund the tires or equipment. If a vehicle owner makes repairs before a recall is announced, manufacturers typically must still provide reimbursement to owners for costs incurred to remedy the defect.

A consumer's right to take advantage of a recall is limited by the age of the vehicle. In order to be eligible for free repairs, refund, or replacement, the vehicle must be less than 10 years old on the date the defect or noncompliance is determined. The age of the vehicle is based on the date it was sold to the first purchaser.

If a manufacturer challenges NHTSA's recall in court the manufacturer is not required to perform any repairs while the case is pending. Owners who take a vehicle in for repairs after NHTSA's decision to order a recall, but before the case is finally decided, will not be reimbursed if the court finds in favor of the manufacturer. If the court rules against the manufacturer, owners may be entitled to reimbursement upon proof that the repairs were made.

Recall remedies do not foreclose other legal remedies, but they are an additional layer of **consumer protection**. Persons who have been injured due to a safety-related defect may still bring suit against the manufacturer.

LEMON LAWS

Lemon laws, found in every state, provide another layer of protection for vehicle owners. Lemon laws entitle aggrieved consumers to a replacement vehicle, or a full refund, where the vehicle is so defective that the dealer cannot satisfactorily repair it. Before a lemon law can be invoked, the dealer must be given a reasonable opportunity to repair the defect.

Lemon laws usually apply to purchases or leases of new cars, trucks, motorcycles or motor homes. Additionally, lemon laws cover "demonstrator" or "executive" vehicles that are less than a year old and still under original warranties. Generally, the laws do not apply to purchases of mopeds or trailers.

Lemon laws vary from state to state. Basically, a mechanical defect must be one which substantially impairs the use, value, or safety of a vehicle. Lemon laws usually have time or mileage limits. A defect must be presented to the manufacturer or authorized dealer within these limits in order to be covered under the lemon law.

Once notified of a problem with a vehicle, the manufacturer must be allowed to repair the defect within a reasonable number of repair attempts. If the manufacturer cannot repair the defect in the vehicle within a reasonable number of repair attempts, the vehicle owner will be entitled to a refund or replacement. How many repair attempts constitutes a "reasonable number" varies from state-to-state, but a typical number is four repairs for the same problem within six months or a year. A lemon law may also be invoked where a vehicle with substantial defects is out of service for a certain number of days during a specified time period.

The nature of the defect also bears on the number of repair attempts permitted. If the defect could cause death or serious bodily injury, only one repair attempt will be allowed before the vehicle is presumed to be a lemon. If the defect is not so serious or potentially dangerous, then the manufacturer will be permitted additional repair attempts to correct the defect.

If an owner believes he has purchased a lemon, he should write the manufacturer and request a replacement vehicle or a refund. In some states the dealer must also be notified. Assuming the request is granted, the owner will not be allowed to keep the defective vehicle. If the defective vehicle is replaced, the manufacturer should refund repair costs and charge the owner nothing for mileage. If a refund is given instead of a replacement vehicle, the refund should include:

- The entire purchase price
- Any **sales tax** paid on the vehicle
- Finance charges
- The cost of repairs to the defective vehicle
- A **deduction** for mileage

If a manufacturer refuses to give a refund or provide a replacement of a defective vehicle, an owner may be able to get relief by submitting her complaint to an **arbitration** forum. This is often quicker and less expensive than **litigation**. In some states, if the manufacturer of the vehicle has a state certified arbitration program, the owner must use it before suing the manufacturer in court for a refund or replacement vehicle.

In some cases, a court may need to decide if a vehicle is a lemon and what remedy to provide. If an owner prevails in a lawsuit against the manufacturer, some jurisdictions allow damages worth double the vehicle's purchase price and repair costs, in addition to other costs and attorney fees.

An owner needs to provide **documentary evidence** to demonstrate that a car is a lemon. This includes all records of any repairs done, including dates of service and descriptions of the exact repairs made. This information is particularly critical when the car is repaired at some place other than the dealership where the car was purchased. In addition to repair records, an owner should retain the purchase **contract**, any written warranties, and should note on a calendar when the vehicle is at a dealership or other shop for **warranty** repairs. If a vehicle is operable, it may be driven while the appropriate authorities determine whether it is a lemon. If the vehicle is indeed a lemon, the dealership is often allowed to deduct a certain amount for mileage from the refund.

In many states consumers who purchase a used car are also covered under the lemon laws. For example, an owner who has recently purchased a used car may be entitled to cancel the purchase and receive a refund, where the vehicle fails a safety inspection. Vehicle safety inspections are mandatory in most states. Generally, the safety inspection must occur within a certain period of time after the purchase of the car, and the repairs must exceed a stated percentage of the purchase price of the car. In some states, a vehicle that has passed its inspection may still qualify as a lemon. Moreover, some jurisdictions apply lemon laws to both dealers and private sellers.

ADDITIONAL RESOURCES

Abbott, Howard, and Mark Tyler. *Safer by Design: A Guide to the Management and Law of Designing for Product Safety.* 2nd ed. Burlington, VT: Gower Publishing Co., 1997.

Howells, Geraint G. *Consumer Product Safety.* Hanover, NH: Dartmouth Publishing Co., 1999.

O'Reilly, James T. *Product Warnings, Defects, and Hazards.* 2nd ed. New York: Aspen Publishers, Inc., 1998.

"Safety Recall Compendium: A Guide for the Reporting, Notification, and Remedy of Motor Vehicle and Motor Vehicle Equipment in Accordance with Title 49 of the United States Code, Chapter 301 and Supporting Federal Regulations." Recall Management Division, Office of Defects Investigation, National Highway Traffic Safety Administration, U.S. Department of Transportation, 2001. Available at http://www-odi.nhtsa.dot.gov/recalls/documents/recompendium.pdf (accessed November 2, 2012).

"Your Online Resource for Recalls." Available at http://www.recalls.gov (accessed November 2, 2012).

ORGANIZATIONS

American Bar Association (ABA)

321 North Clark Street
Chicago, IL 60610
Phone: (312) 988-5000
Toll Free: (800) 285-2221
Fax: (312) 988-6800
URL: http://www.americanbar.org

Consumer Reports

101 Truman Avenue
Yonkers, NY 10703
URL: http://www.consumerreports.org/Recalls/

Federal Consumer Information Center (FCIC)

1800 F Street, NW, Room G-142, (XC)
Washington, DC 20405
Toll Free: (800) 326-2996
URL: http://publications.usa.gov

Food and Drug Administration (FDA), U.S. Department of Health and Human Services

5600 Fishers Lane
Rockville, MD 20857-0001
Toll Free: (888) 463-6332
URL: http://www.fda.gov
URL: http://www.recalls.gov/

National Highway Traffic Safety Administration (NHTSA)

400 Seventh Street, S.W.
Washington, DC 20590
Toll Free: (888) 327-4236
URL: http://www.nhtsa.dot.gov
URL: http://www.recalls.gov/

U.S. Consumer Product Safety Commission (CPSC)

4330 East-West Highway
Bethesda, MD 20814-4408
Phone: (301) 504-0990
Fax: (301) 504-0124
Email: info@cpsc.gov
URL: http://www.cpsc.gov/

U.S. Department of Agriculture (USDA)

1400 Independence Avenue, S.W.
Washington, DC 20250
Toll Free: (800) 535-4555
URL: http://www.fsis.usda.gov
URL: http://www.recalls.gov/

CONSUMER ISSUES

SCHEMES AND SCAMS

Sections within this essay:

- Background
- Ponzi Schemes
  – Contemporary Ponzi Schemes
- Scams
- Additional Resources

BACKGROUND

Gullible individuals regularly lose their money to criminals who promise large returns on their investments. The adage "If it sounds too good to be true, it's not" is ignored by wealthy investors as well as by the unsophisticated. The massive **fraud** committed by Bernard Madoff and Allen Stanford through their use of Ponzi schemes led to massive losses for their investors. The Federal Trade Commission (FTC) warns consumers about a multitude of scams, whether in person, over the phone, or over the Internet, yet the fraud persists. Perpetrators of fraud may be prosecuted but the money taken by them is usually gone and the prospects of repayment are slim.

PONZI SCHEMES

Ponzi schemes are **fraudulent** investment plans in which the investments of later investors are used to pay earlier investors, giving the appearance that the investments of the initial participants dramatically increased in value in a short amount of time. A Ponzi scheme promises investors exorbitant interest if they loan their money. As more

investors participate, the money contributed by later investors is paid to the initial investors, purportedly as the promised interest on their loans. A Ponzi scheme works in its initial stages but always collapses as more investors participate.

A Ponzi scheme was once was called a "bubble." It was renamed in 1920 after Charles Ponzi and his Boston-based company had collected almost $10 million from ten thousand investors by selling promissory notes that claimed to pay 50 percent profit in forty-five days. When the scheme was exposed, a Boston bank collapsed, and investors lost most of their money.

When the scheme collapses, the company files for **bankruptcy**. The U.S. Supreme Court ruled in the Ponzi case that the bankruptcy court could order all of the persons who had been paid by Ponzi during the life of the scheme to return the proceeds to the bankruptcy **trustee**, who then distributed the money on a pro rata basis to all of the other victims. This procedure has come to be known as a "clawback." The reasoning behind it is that the original investors who were paid in full did not earn interest because the money they received came from later investors.

A variant of the Ponzi scheme is an illegal pyramid sales scheme. In a pyramid sales plan, a person pays a fee to become a distributor. Once the person becomes a distributor, she receives commissions not only for the products she sells but also for products sold by individuals that she brings into the business. These new distributors are beneath the person who brought them into the pyramid scheme, so they are "under the pyramid." In illegal pyramid schemes, only the people at the top of the pyramid make substantial money because they get a commission from the products sold by everyone below them. As more people become distributors, the persons lower in the pyramid have less chance to make money.

Contemporary Ponzi Schemes The economic recession at the end of the first decade of the 2000s and the early 2010s devastated the U.S. economy and created the conditions for the collapse of numerous Ponzi schemes. By 2009, Ponzi scams in all 50 states had resulted in the loss of more than $16.5 billion. Approximately 150 Ponzi Schemes fell apart in 2009, compared to only 40 in 2008. Other statistics were illuminating as well. The FBI had assigned 650 agents to work on high-yield investment fraud cases in 2009 and the Securities and Exchange Commission (SEC) issued 82 percent more restraining orders against Ponzi schemes and securities fraud than in 2008. The Commodities Futures Trading Commission even filed 31 civil actions in 2009 against Ponzi schemes.

The most famous Ponzi scheme involved Bernard Madoff and the New York hedge fund that he owned. Hedge funds are investment monies managed by an individual or a business for the benefit of wealthy clients who place large amounts of money to the pool. They have not been subject to much federal securities regulation. Madoff promised his investors higher rates of return than normally expected. He and his firm successfully recruited more and more wealth investors, allowing the scheme to continue for years. When the stock market collapsed in 2008, the scheme came undone. Madoff was arrested in December 2008 and was later charged with securities fraud. He also faced a **civil action** brought by the SEC. Madoff admitted to investigators that the business was nothing more than a $65 billion Ponzi scheme. He pleaded guilty to 11 charges and was sentenced in June 2009 to 150 years in prison.

The bankruptcy trustee assigned to **liquidate** Madoff's investment firm wasted no time in seeking clawbacks from Madoff's wife and from investors who benefited from the scheme. He sought over $44 million in assets from Ruth Madoff, asserting that she benefited from the fraud. Multiple homes, yachts, and luxury items such as expensive watches and jewelry, were auctioned off. By the end of 2010, the trustee had filed 19 lawsuits seeking the return of $32 billion. One investor agreed to repay $7.2 billion. Other investors, including the owners of the New York Mets baseball team, fought the trustee, arguing that they had no idea that Madoff's investments were fraudulent. The owners eventually agreed to pay the trustee $162 million. By 2012 the trustee had recovered $9.1 billion of the $17.3 billion in stolen principal and was able to return billions to investors. Over 1,000 investors were paid in full.

Although the Ponzi scheme created by Allen Stanford did not draw as much attention as Madoff's, it too involved billions of dollars. Stanford's companies included Antiguan-based Stanford International Bank (SIB), Houston-based broker-dealer and investment adviser Stanford Group Company (SGC), and investment adviser Stanford Capital Management. In February 2009, the SEC filed a complaint in federal court in Dallas, alleging that acting through a network of SGC financial advisers, SIB has sold approximately $8 billion of so-called "certificates of deposit" (CDs) to investors by promising improbable and unsubstantiated high **interest rates**. These rates were supposedly earned through SIB's unique investment strategy, which purportedly allowed the bank to achieve double-digit returns on its investments for the prior 15 years.

Stanford and his associates represented to CD purchasers that their deposits were safe, claimed that the bank re-invested client funds primarily in "liquid" financial instruments (the portfolio). He also claimed that a team of over 20 analysts monitored the portfolio and it was subject to yearly audits by Antiguan regulators. After the Madoff funds collapsed, SIB tried to reassure its own investors by claiming the bank had no "direct or indirect" exposure to the Madoff scheme. The SEC alleged that none of these claims were true. By the time the fraud was revealed, Stanford had recruited 31,000 investors.

A Houston **grand jury** indicted Stanford in June 2009 on 21 counts of fraud. He was immediately jailed. The criminal **indictment** alleged that Stanford and other executives at his firm falsely claimed to have grown $1.2 billion in assets in 2001 to roughly $8.5 billion by the end of 2008. Even as Stanford announced healthy returns for his investors, the indictment alleged that he was secretly diverting more than $1.6 billion in personal loans to himself. Stanford, unlike Madoff, protested his innocence and denied he ran a Ponzi scheme. In 2012, he was convicted and sentenced to 110 years in prison.

SCAMS

The FTC has identified four popular scams have led many people to lose money. The first is known as the "Seminar Pitch." A person gets a letter or sees an infomercial promoting a seminar or conference that promises to help the person make a lot of money. The pitch suggests that the person will get valuable information about how to invest successfully or operate a profitable business. The "success stories" and testimonials seem to show that anyone who attends the seminar can make money from the investment or business program if they just follow a few steps. Some promoters even claim to have gotten rich from their own investment in the program. Consumers who invest in these "opportunities" usually find that the pay-off doesn't match the promise. In addition, they cannot recover the money they spent.

The "Nigerian Scam" is well known to most people who receive email. The sender of the email claims to be an official of a foreign government, a deposed member of royalty from a foreign country, a businessperson or the surviving spouse of a former government leader. The sender offers to transfer millions of dollars into the person's bank account in exchange for a small fee. Though the proposition defies common sense, gullible people have sent money and even bank account numbers to these con artists. Because the con artists do not live in the United States, there is little chance to recover the money.

A third common scam is the "Foreign Lottery." Scam operators convince people to buy chances in supposedly high-stakes foreign lotteries with pitches that generally follow a pattern whereby the person should send money to pay for taxes, insurance, or processing or customs fees. The amount may seem small at first, but as long as the person keeps paying, the requests for funds will keep coming for higher and higher amounts. Victims lose thousands of dollar and many scam operators either do not buy the promised lottery tickets keep the winning tickets proceeds for themselves. In addition, lottery hustlers use victims' bank account numbers to make unauthorized withdrawals or their credit card numbers to run up additional charges.

Another common means of fraud are "Check Overpayment Scams." A person may try to sell an item on an online auction, Craigslist, or through the classified section of a new newspaper. A buyer contacts the person with an offer to use a cashier's check, personal check or **corporate** check to purchase the item. At the last minute, the so-called buyer (or the buyer's "agent") comes up with a reason to write the check for more than the purchase price, and asks you to wire back the difference once you deposit the check. In **good faith** the seller deposits the check and wires the funds to the "buyer." However, the check bounces because it is **counterfeit**, leaving seller liable for the entire amount.

ADDITIONAL RESOURCES

Frankel, Tamar. *The Ponzi Scheme Puzzle: A History and Analysis of Con Artists and Victims.* New York: Oxford University Press, 2012.

Zuckoff, Michael. *Ponzi's Scheme: The True Story of a Financial Legend.* New York: Random House, 2006.

ORGANIZATIONS

Federal Trade Commission (FTC)
600 Pennsylvania Avenue, N.W.
Washington, DC 20580
Toll Free: (877) 382-4357
URL: http://www.ftc.gov/index.html

CONSUMER ISSUES

WARRANTIES

Sections within this essay:

- Background
- Types of Warranties
  - Implied Warranties
  - Express Warranties
  - Used and "As Is" Goods
  - Extended Warranties
  - Extension of Warranties to Remote Purchasers

- Magnuson-Moss Warranty Act
- Self-Help Measures
- Additional Resources

BACKGROUND

In simplest terms, a warranty (also called a guarantee) is an agreement between a seller and a buyer to ensure that a product will work properly. While the concept is simple, the actual application of a warranty can be quite complex. There is no law requiring a company to offer a written warranty on a product it manufactures or sells. The absence of a written warranty, however, does not mean that a product is not warranted to perform according to expectation. When a written warranty does exist, it binds the company under state and federal law into assuming responsibility in the event that a product malfunctions.

Warranties promise that a product will perform properly. When a product fails to perform, it will be replaced or repaired, or the consumer will be given a refund or a credit toward another product. The retail pioneer John Wanamaker, who introduced the concept of the "department store" in Philadelphia in 1876, is also credited with introducing the money-back guarantee. Wanamaker was a progressive businessman who was among the first to offer benefits such as paid vacations to his employees. He was also a deeply ethical man who believed that his customers should be satisfied with their purchases. The money-back guarantee earned the **trust** and the loyalty of Wanamaker's customers.

Trust and loyalty represent sound business practice for most companies. In fact, it is not uncommon for companies to use warranties as a selling point. By offering a better warranty than their competitors, companies are saying in effect that they believe more strongly in the quality of their products.

Warranty problems occur when the company has misstated its policy, or when the language included in the warranty is confusing. The concept of the "lifetime warranty" provides a good illustration of how this sort of confusion can develop. The Federal Trade Commission (FTC) offers the example of an automobile muffler with a so-called "lifetime" guarantee. "Lifetime" can mean the life of the automobile in which the new muffler was installed. Alternatively, it can mean the duration of the buyer's ownership of the car, or it can mean the buyer's actual lifetime. It is an unfortunate fact that some companies are unscrupulous and try to renege on their warranty agreements. But as the seemingly straightforward example of the muffler shows, sometimes the problem is misinterpretation. That said, it is the seller's responsibility to make sure that the warranty's language and intent is clear.

TYPES OF WARRANTIES

Under the law, there are two types of warranties: implied and express. Implied warranties exist under state law, as outlined in Article 2 of the **Uniform Commercial Code** (UCC). The UCC, which covers all 50 States and the District of Columbia, is a means of consolidating laws regarding **commerce** as a means of streamlining interstate legal issues. This allows each state to adopt the same definitions of, in this case, implied warranties. In 2003, a substantially revised version of Article 2 of the UCC was approved by the National Conference of Commissioners on Uniform State Laws and American Law Institute, but as of early 2006 no state had adopted the revised Article 2.

Implied Warranties Implied warranties are exactly what the term says they are: unspoken and unwritten promises made by a seller to a buyer that the product being sold works. These warranties are created through the application of the law, rather than through statements that are made by a seller. The concept that encompasses the **implied warranty** comes from **common law**, specifically, the principle of "fair value for money spent." Actually, there are two types of implied warranties, both outlined under Article 2 of the UCC.

The *implied warranty of merchantability* is simply the promise that the product sold is in good working order and will do what it is supposed to do. For instance, a vacuum cleaner is expected to pick up dirt and dust from carpets and floors. A refrigerator is expected to keep food cold. A toaster is expected to toast bread. If the consumer buys a product and the product does not work, then this constitutes a breach of the implied warranty. The seller is required to remedy the problem, whether by repairing or replacing the product. (It should be noted that the section of the UCC covering this type of implied warranty, Section 2-314, is law in every state except Louisiana.)

The *implied warranty of fitness for a particular purpose* is the promise that the seller's advice on how to use the product will be correct. For example, it a consumer asks an appliance dealer whether a particular air conditioner can cool a 600 square-foot room and the dealer says yes, that dealer has effectively created a warranty of fitness. In other words, the dealer has impliedly guaranteed that the air conditioner is fit for the purpose for which the consumer needs to use it as expressed to the seller. If the air conditioner can only cool a 400 square-foot room effectively, the dealer has breached the warranty. The idea behind this is that the dealer is expected to know which product will be best for which use.

Express Warranties An express warranty is an explicit offer made voluntarily by the seller that a product will perform according to particular expectations. The typical express warranty offers specific remedies in the event that the product is defective. Express warranties can be oral or written. Written warranties are covered under the federal Magnuson-Moss Act, which is explained in detail below. If a seller offers an express warranty, the product in question is still covered under implied warranty.

The length of a warranty may be specified, but if it is not, the general rule is that consumers have four years from the date of purchase to enforce a warranty claim. This does not mean that the product must last four years. Rather, it means that if there was a defect in the product at the time of purchase that manifests itself later, the consumer is entitled to some sort of remedy.

Used and "As Is" Goods Used goods are covered under implied warranties if the seller is a merchant who is in the business of selling similar products. A private individual who chooses to sell a toaster at a flea market is not expected to take responsibility for the product's performance.

In most states, goods can be sold "as is." These goods do not require the seller to offer even an implied warranty. What the seller is required to do for these products is make clear to consumers that the product is being sold in less than prime condition and that the consumer assumes all responsibility for any faults and flaws. Some states prohibit this practice, including Alabama, Connecticut, Kansas, Maine, Maryland, Massachusetts, Minnesota, Mississippi, New Hampshire, Vermont, Washington, West Virginia, and the District of Columbia. If a product is sold as is and it turns out to have a defect that results in **personal injury**, the seller is liable even in the absence of any warranty.

Extended Warranties Anyone who has purchased appliances, stereos, computers, or similar items knows that many stores will try to sell an "extended warranty" along with the standard one. These warranties, also known as service contracts, are often unnecessary because they duplicate current warranty coverage. The reason merchants are so eager to sell service contracts in general is that they make a handsome profit off those agreements. Service contracts are not illegal and in some cases they may be useful, but consumers are well advised to read the existing warranty before spending unnecessary money on redundant coverage.

Another important point that consumers should know is that if they do wish to purchase a service **contract**, they are allowed by law to do so up until 30 days from the regular warranty's expiration date. Stores that claim a "now or never" policy are being deceptive.

Extension of Warranties to Remote Purchasers Situations often arise where someone who purchases goods from the original buyer bring an action for breach of warranty against the original seller. The general rule under the UCC is that a buyer must have privity of contract with the original seller in order to recover for breach of either an express or an implied warranty. In other words, the person who actually purchased the goods from the buyer is the only person who can sue for breach of a warranty.

Some exceptions to this general rule may apply. For example, a third-party **beneficiary** to a seller's promise may recover from the seller even in the absence of privity of contract between the seller and the eventual buyer. The revised Article 2 of the UCC includes two new provisions that extend warranties to remote purchasers in some other circumstances, but as noted above, no state has adopted the revised Article 2.

MAGNUSON-MOSS WARRANTY ACT

In 1975, Congress passed the Magnuson-Moss Warranty Act as a means of providing comprehensive information to consumers about their rights under product warranties. It is important to note once again that companies are not required to provide written warranties on their products. If they do, however, they are subject to the regulations spelled out under Magnuson-Moss.

Oral warranties are not covered by Magnuson-Moss, nor are warranties on services or commercial products. Only written warranties on consumer goods are covered. The company issuing the warranty (the warrantor) or the seller must meet three basic requirements under the Act:

- The warranty must be designated as either full or limited.
- The warranty must be written in a single document that is clearly written and easy to understand.
- The warranty must be readily available for inspection where the product covered is being sold.

Anyone who offers a written warranty is prohibited from disclaiming or modifying implied warranties. In other words, consumers are protected under the implied warranty of merchantability no matter how broad or narrow the scope of the written warranty. The only exception is that the company can restrict the duration of an implied warranty to match that stated in a written limited warranty. If a company offers a three-year limited warranty on a product, for instance, it is permissible to limit the implied warranty to three years as well.

Magnuson-Moss prohibits companies from including tie-in sales provisions in its warranties. In other words, the company cannot state that owners of product X must use only product X accessories or have the product serviced at specific locations. However, companies can void a warranty if the consumer has it serviced or repaired inappropriately or incorrectly. Moreover, if the company can prove to the FTC that its products must be serviced or maintained through tie-in services, the FTC may waive this requirement.

No deceptive or misleading terms are permitted in a written warranty under Magnuson-Moss. A common example is a warranty covering moving parts in an item that has no moving parts. Moreover, the company cannot claim to offer services that it either cannot or will not provide.

Magnuson-Moss makes breach of warranty a violation of federal law and allows plaintiffs to recover court costs and reasonable attorney's fees. In general, most warranty-related lawsuits are brought in state courts, but **class action** suits can be brought in federal court. This is not to say that Magnuson-Moss has **litigation** as its goal. Rather, the goal is to make companies think carefully before they breach a warranty.

Under Magnuson-Moss, companies can include a provision in their warranties that requires customers to attempt to resolve warranty disputes through informal means (informal in the sense that they do not require the same rules of **evidence** and procedure as found in a courtroom). These informal means are known as dispute resolution mechanisms. For a company to be able to require this option, it has to meet certain requirements as stated in the FTC's Rule on Informal Dispute Settlement Procedures. The "rule" is actually a set of guidelines that requires the company to provide a means of resolution that is adequately funded and staffed to resolve disputes quickly, free of charge to customers, able to gather all necessary facts and make decisions independently, and audited annually to ensure compliance. This function can be performed by a third party, such as the Better Business Bureau, or by employees specifically on staff to handle warranty disputes objectively. Among the means of settling the dispute can be **conciliation**, **mediation**, and **arbitration**. If either party is still dissatisfied, the matter can still be brought to court.

While having an informal dispute procedure in place eliminates the necessity of going to court, it is clearly still enough of a burden on a company that it makes more sense to offer clear-cut warranties and honor them.

SELF-HELP MEASURES

The FTC recommends that consumers take several steps in order to minimize problems that they may have with respect to warranties. These steps include the following:

- Read the Warranty Before Buying an Item: Consumers should read a seller's full warranty and understand exactly what protection the **warrant** offers.

- Consider a Company's Reputation: Consumers who are unfamiliar with a company should consult with a local or state **consumer protection** office or Better Business Bureau.

- Save Receipts Along with the Warranty: The receipt may be necessary to document that the a consumer is the original owner.

- Perform Maintenance and Inspections That Are Required by the Warranty.

- Use the Product According to Instructions Provided by the Manufacturer: Some forms of abuse or misuse of a product could void a warranty.

- Attempt to Resolve a Problem Directly with the Seller.

- Consider Filing a Claim in **Small Claims Court**: A dispute that involves less than a relatively small amount of money, such as $750, may be resolved in small claims court. Costs in small claims court are usually low, procedures are relatively simple, and lawyers are not necessary.

The FTC provides additional information at http://www.ftc.gov/ftc/consumer.htm.

ADDITIONAL RESOURCES

Brook, James. *Sales and Leases: Examples and Explanations*. 6th ed. New York: Aspen Publishers, 2011.

Federal Trade Commission. "Facts for Consumers: Warranties." Available at http://www.ftc.gov/bcp/edu/pubs/consumer/products/pro17.shtm (accessed November 3, 2012).

Mayer, Robert N. *The Consumer Movement: Guardians of the Marketplace*. Woodbridge, CT: Twayne Publishers, 1989.

Return to Sender: Getting A Refund or Replacement for Your Lemon Car. Barron, Nancy, National Consumer Law Center, 2000.

Sheldon, Jonathan, Carolyn L. Carter, et al. *Consumer Warranty Law*. 4th ed. Boston: National Consumer Law Center, 2010.

Understanding Consumer Rights. Parisi, Nicolette, Dorling Kindersley, 2000.

ORGANIZATIONS

Consumers Union

101 Truman Avenue
Yonkers, NY 10703
Phone: (914) 378-2000
Fax: (914) 378-2928
URL: http://www.consumersunion.org

Council of Better Business Bureaus (BBB)

4200 Wilson Blvd, Suite 800
Arlington, VA 22203-1838
Phone: (703) 276-0100
Fax: (703) 525-8277
URL: http://www.bbb.org

Federal Trade Commission (FTC)

600 Pennsylvania Avenue, NW
Washington, DC 20580
Toll Free: (877) 382-4357
URL: http://www.ftc.gov

COURTS AND PROCEDURES

BURDEN OF PROOF

Sections within this essay:

- Background
  - Preponderance of the Evidence
  - Clear and Convincing Proof
  - Beyond a Reasonable Doubt

- Shifting Burden of Proof
- Appellate Courts
- Administrative Tribunals
- Additional Resources

BACKGROUND

Burden of proof refers to the responsibility each party to a controversy bears in proving its claim, defense (see below), or objection. It refers to that body of law dealing with **evidence** presented in a formal **adjudication** of a controversy which tends to prove or disprove a disputed fact. In civil cases, a general rule is that the burden of proof rests with the party advancing the matter to be proved. Courts apply three different standards in determining whether a party has met its burden of proof, discussed below.

In application, a party to a controversy must convince the adjudicative entity (court, **jury**, arbitrator, administrative law judge) to rule in its favor. It does this by presenting evidence that it believes supports its position. The party typically presents evidence to support each element of the claim or defense it proffers. How much weight and

credibility to afford each item of evidence is up to the adjudicative entity before which the evidence is presented.

Preponderance of the Evidence In most civil cases/lawsuits as well as administrative hearings, a party must prove its claim or position by a preponderance, defined as a superiority in weight, force, importance, etc. In legal terms, a preponderance of evidence means that a party has shown that its version of facts, causes, damages, or fault is *more likely than not* the correct version, as in **personal injury** and breach of **contract** suits. This standard is the easiest to meet and applies to all civil cases unless otherwise provided by law.

The concept of "preponderance of the evidence" can be visualized as a scale representing the burden of proof, with the totality of evidence presented by each side resting on the respective trays on either side of the scale. If the scale tips ever so slightly to one side or the other, the weightier side will prevail. If the scale does not tip toward the side of the party bearing the burden of proof, that party cannot prevail.

Trial lawyers will often instruct juries that their clients must prevail at trial if they have proved their positions by as little as 51 percent likelihood of probability (anything from 51 to 100 percent constitutes a preponderance of evidence). In other words, if a jury believes there is a 51-49 percent likelihood that a **defendant** (in a civil case) was negligent or liable, the plaintiff/complainant has met its burden of a preponderance of evidence, and will prevail. This is particularly helpful when juries are torn between the **testimony** of two expert witnesses presenting opposite opinions or views. Whether it is an issue of credibility or of expertise, the jury will decide which is the more likely version that warrants more evidentiary weight.

Clear and Convincing Evidence Certain civil suits require a stronger burden of proof, in terms of percentage of weight of the presented evidence. A burden to show "clear and convincing evidence" refers to more than a mere preponderance but something just short of conclusive, which would be more tantamount to the "beyond a reasonable doubt" burden used in criminal cases. However, in reality, "clear and convincing" burden of proof generally requires proof which leaves no **reasonable doubt** concerning the truth of the matters at issue.

This higher burden is generally employed when the alleged offense has special elements to establish, such as in a claim for **fraud**, for a lost will of **inheritance**, or when family members wish to withdraw life support from a loved one. In these and other cases, the stakes at risk are high and the defending party serves to lose a substantial benefit, property, or especially personal or fundamental liberty such as those protected under the First Amendment.

Beyond a Reasonable Doubt This standard of proof is used exclusively in criminal cases, and a person cannot be convicted of a crime unless a judge or jury is convinced of the defendant's guilt **beyond a reasonable doubt**. Precisely, if there is any reasonable uncertainty of guilt, based on the evidence presented, a defendant cannot be convicted.

Ostensibly, this burden requires that a trier of fact (judge, jury, **arbiter**) is fully satisfied and entirely convinced to a moral certainty that the evidence presented proves the guilt of the defendant. There is essentially no room for wavering or uncertainty as the trier of fact believes the evidence to be precise, indubitable, and leaves one with an inescapable conclusion of certainty. In contrast, in a civil trial a party may prevail with as little as 51 percent probability (a preponderance), those legal authorities who venture to assign a numerical value to "beyond a reasonable doubt" place it in the certainty range of 98 or 99 percent.

In a criminal trial, the state must prove that the defendant is guilty, and the burden of proof is always with the state for the case in chief. The defendant, carrying a presumption of innocence, has no burden of proof, and need prove nothing. A defendant may sit mute at a criminal trial, because the state has the burden of proof to show that the defendant satisfied each element of the **statutory** definition of a crime by his or her action/ participation or failure to act. Any evidence offered by the defense is generally directed toward discrediting or undermining the state's evidence, and does not contribute to any evidentiary burden.

However, if a defendant initiates to offer a defense to the jury, such as a defense of insanity, the burden technically shifts to the defendant to prove insanity and avoid a verdict of guilt. Likewise, a defendant claiming **self-defense** or **duress** carries the burden of proof to establish all elements of those defenses to either avoid or mitigate a guilty verdict.

SHIFTING BURDEN OF PROOF

In contrast to the rare circumstances where a burden of proof may shift in a criminal trial, there are several applications of such a concept in civil matters.

Generally speaking, the party that filed the action (be it a criminal complaint by the state's attorney, or a civil lawsuit by a private party), has the burden of proof to establish through evidence all the requisite elements of a prima facie case. For example, in a case for the offense of tortious battery, the complainant has the burden of proof to establish that there was a specific intent to make contact with the person of another in a harmful or offensive manner, without consent, and a harmful or offensive contact occurred.

If that burden is met, the burden of proof then shifts to the defendant in the case, who has to plead and prove any defense by a preponderance of evidence. Often, the defendant raises an affirmative defense, which will have its own elements of proof that must be met by the defendant. Of course, if the defendant raises a **counterclaim** against the **plaintiff**, the entire burden of proof shifts to the defendant on the matter of the counterclaim (or third party claim).

Another example of a shifting burden is found in employment **discrimination** cases. Once the plaintiff has met his or her burden of proof by establishing a **prima facie** case, the burden of proof shifts to the defendant to show some non-discriminatory reason for its action. If the defendant essentially meets that burden of proof by presenting legitimate reasons for the alleged action, the burden again shifts back to the plaintiff to show that the proffered "legitimate" reasons were pretextual.

A burden of proof generally attaches at the trial or adjudicatory stage. A plaintiff (in a civil case) or a petitioner (in an administrative case), or the state (in a criminal case) need only **allege** the existence of facts needed to prove each requisite element of the alleged wrong, offense, or crime. The averments or allegations contained therein are presumed to be true during this initial stage. However, at the actual trial, the party then bears the burden of proof to present evidence tending to support or prove the facts alleged in the complaint or petition. Following this presentation of the case in chief, an opposing party may then petition the court to dismiss the case (before it reaches a jury), for failure in meeting a required burden of proof.

APPELLATE COURTS

Appellate courts generally do not review the factual findings made by a trial court. Instead, appellate courts assess whether legal rulings made by the trial judge were proper, and if not, whether the errors were sufficient to reverse the trial court decision. However, in some appeals the court may reverse a trial court finding if the finding was arbitrary and capricious, clearly erroneous, or if the appeals court is empowered to review the factual record under a de novo standard. Under the arbitrary and capricious standard of review, a finding by the trial court will not be overturned unless there was no reasonable basis for making the finding. Under the clearly erroneous standard, the appeals court may overturn a finding of fact if it believes the trial court made a fundamental mistake. Certain types of cases are subject to de novo review, including **small claims court** decisions that are appealed to a higher court. In these cases the **appellate court** acts as if it was a trial court and examines the evidence as if for the first time. The lower court findings are ignored.

ADMINISTRATIVE TRIBUNALS

In matters coming before an administrative **tribunal**, such as **workers' compensation** boards, social security benefits hearings, or Internal Revenue Service audits or hearings, the burden of proof generally lies with the party claiming the benefit or beneficial treatment. The agency or board need only articulate a reasonable basis for denial of a claim or benefit. Of course, its decision can generally be appealed, but only in limited context, such as abuse of discretion. However, in cases involving the suspension, revocation, or **forfeiture** of some benefit *already being received* by a party, the burden typically rests with the agency, as it is the agency that initiates the action.

ADDITIONAL RESOURCES

Cammack, Mark. *Advanced Criminal Procedure in a Nutshell.* 2d ed. Eagan, MN: West, Thomson Reuters, 2006.

LaFave, Wayne R., Jerold H. Israel, and Nancy J. King, eds. *Criminal Procedure.* 5th ed. Eagan, MN: Thomson/West, 2009.

ORGANIZATIONS

American Bar Association (ABA)

321 North Clark Street
Chicago, IL 60610
Phone: (312) 988-5000
Toll Free: (800) 285-2221
Fax: (312) 988-6800
URL: http://www.americanbar.org

COURTS AND PROCEDURES

CAMERAS IN THE COURTROOM

Sections within this essay:

- Background
  - U.S. Supreme Court Cases

- Acceptance of Cameras in the Courtroom

- Rules Governing Media Access

- The Future of Cameras in the Courtroom

- Additional Resources

BACKGROUND

The presence of cameras in the courtroom has been debated since the 1930s. Proponents of permitting cameras contend that the public is better served by having access to court proceedings. Critics believe that the presence of cameras can turn trials into a circus and distort the behavior of witnesses, lawyers, and judges. By 2012 most states permitted cameras in the courtroom but they have different procedures governing how they may be used. The federal courts remain closed to cameras, although there is a pilot project underway in 14 U.S. District Courts to allow them.

Photographers had access to many state courts until the 1930s. The introduction of the motion picture camera dramatically changed the landscape, as movie audiences could be shown newsreels of court proceedings. In 1934, nearly 700 reporters and photographers descended on a New Jersey town where Bruno Hauptmann was on trial for **kidnapping** and murdering the baby of famous aviator Charles A. Lindbergh and author Anne Morrow

Lindbergh. The trial judge allowed still photography, but was unprepared for the barrage of flashbulbs and the presence of a newsreel camera that was smuggled inside the court. As a result, the American Bar Association in 1937 called for prohibiting photography in its Canons of Professional and Judicial Ethics. At the same time, Congress amended the Federal Rules of **Criminal Procedure** to ban cameras and any form of broadcasting from federal courts. All states except Texas and Colorado eventually adopted the ABA prohibition on cameras.

U.S. Supreme Court Cases The introduction of television in the 1950s ushered in new problems. In 1965, the U.S. Supreme Court addressed the constitutional question of whether TV cameras are injurious to a defendant's right to a fair trial. In *Estes v. Texas* the Court threw out a criminal **conviction** because the televised proceedings of the trial violated the defendant's right to due process under the Fourteenth Amendment.

The Court revisited the issue in 1981 in the case of *Chandler v. Florida.* Two men convicted of **burglary** argued that televising their trial over their objections was a denial of due process. At the time Florida was following a pilot program for televising and permitting still photography at state trials under the Florida code of judicial conduct. The defendants contended that the televising of criminal trials was inherently a denial of due process, while the state claimed that *Estes* did not establish any such constitutional rule. The Supreme Court agreed with Florida, ruling that states could provide access to the electronic media regardless of whether defendants wanted it. Moreover, the burden of showing how cameras have a prejudicial effect on a given trial would fall on the **defendant**.

ACCEPTANCE OF CAMERAS IN THE COURTROOM

The *Chandler* decision dramatically changed the legal landscape. The ABA abandoned its opposition to cameras in the courtroom and most states amended court rules to allow cameras. However, it was technology that revolutionized public access to court proceeds. In 1991 the cable television channel Court TV began televising noteworthy trials on a daily basis. The audience for these trials grew steadily, but it was the televised O.J. Simpson murder trial that drew national attention. The eleven-month trial involving Simpson, a popular sports and entertainment personality who was **accused** of murdering his former wife Nicole Brown Simpson and her friend Ronald Lyle Goldman, made celebrities out of the lawyers, judge, and some witnesses. Simpson was acquitted of the charges and some critics of cameras in the court contended that televising the trial had turned it into a circus.

Despite the criticisms of the Simpson trial, televised proceedings of high-profile cases continued to be permitting. However, some judges refused to allow cameras, fearing that they would lose control of their courtrooms.

RULES GOVERNING MEDIA ACCESS

By 2012, all 50 states allowed some level of camera presence in their courts (only the District of Columbia prohibited cameras in trial and **appellate** proceedings), but the rules governing when and where cameras are allowed vary enormously. There were 19 states with permissive rules, while the remainder gave either the judge or the parties the opportunity to reject cameras. State laws and court rules dictate how many cameras are allowed (usually, one), what they may do (remain stationary), whom they may film (never jurors and sometimes not witnesses), who may operate them (one person), what that operator may wear (appropriate dress), and when she or he may leave the courtroom (only during recess).

The federal courts have been reluctant to allow cameras. The Judicial Conference of the United States, the administrative body composed of federal judges, authorized and then killed a pilot project in the 1990s and in 1996 recommended that each circuit judicial council issue an order banning the taking of photographs and radio and television coverage of proceedings in U.S. district courts. However, in 2010 the Judicial Conference authorized a three-year pilot project to evaluate the effect of cameras in district court courtrooms, video recordings of proceedings, and publication of such video recordings. The pilot is limited to civil cases only. Proceedings may be recorded only with the approval of the presiding judge, and parties must consent to the recording of each proceeding in a case. Unless the presiding judge decides not to make the recordings publicly available, they will be posted on http://www.uscourts.gov, as well as on local participating court websites at the court's discretion.

Fourteen courts were participating in the pilot, which began in June 2011. The courts are Middle District of Alabama; Northern District of California; Southern District of Florida; District of Guam; Northern District of Illinois; Southern District of Iowa; District of Kansas; District of Massachusetts; Eastern District of Missouri; District of Nebraska; Northern District of Ohio; Southern District of Ohio; Western District of Tennessee; and Western District of Washington.

THE FUTURE OF CAMERAS IN THE COURTROOM

It is unclear whether more states will liberalize their cameras in the courtroom rules or whether the federal courts pilot project will result in permanent rules allowing cameras. It is likely that cable news channels will occasionally broadcast high-profile cases but the popularity of viewing televised trials has waned. Court TV changed its name in 2008 to TruTV. The channel now emphasizes reality programming, limiting trial coverage from morning to mid-afternoon.

ADDITIONAL RESOURCES

Cohn, Marjorie. *Cameras in the Courtroom: Television and the Pursuit of Justice.* Jefferson, NC: McFarland, 2011.

ORGANIZATIONS

American Bar Association (ABA)

321 North Clark Street
Chicago, IL 60610
Phone: (312) 988-5000
Toll Free: (800) 285-2221
Fax: (312) 988-6800
URL: http://www.americanbar.org

COURTS AND PROCEDURES

CIVIL PROCEDURE

Sections within this essay:

BACKGROUND

Civil procedure refers to that body of law—usually in the form of collective and published rules—that concerns itself with the methods, procedures, and practices used in civil proceedings. Civil proceedings are distinguished from criminal or administrative proceedings, which are governed by their own respective rules of procedure. Most, but not all, civil proceedings involve "litigation" or lawsuits between private parties or entities, such as business **corporations**) and the focus generally relates to key procedures in the **litigation** process.

Procedural law is intended to safeguard those vested rights in life, liberty, and property that are guaranteed by the U.S. Constitution. The **Fifth Amendment** to the Constitution provides that "No person shall be . . . deprived of life, liberty, or property without **due process of law**; nor shall private property be taken for public use, without just compensation." The Fourteenth Amendment to the Constitution makes those provisions applicable to the states.

In almost every civil lawsuit, there will be a prevailing party and a defeated party. Judgment against the losing party—whether it is the person who filed the claim or the person against whom the claim was made—generally means he or she will be adversely affected. The constitutional guarantee of "due process of law" ensures that persons whose rights may be adversely affected by litigation have the opportunity for their "day in court,"— to be heard and to present proof(s) in support of their claim or defense. Accordingly, before any judgment can be made for or against a party, certain procedural safeguards **warrant** that a just and **fair hearing** on the matter has been conducted and that all parties whose interests may be affected by the controversy have been notified of their right to be heard.

Civil procedure, then, helps provide the structure needed to guarantee a fair and just determination of the controversy, while also serving to move the matter through the legal system in an orderly and consistent manner. It governs such actions as the way in which service of process is made upon a **defendant**, the number of days and manner in which parties may "discover" one another's **evidence**, and the manner in which parties may present their controversies or objections to the court. Additional rules of procedure may have more simple purposes, such as uniformity or judicial economy. In any event, courts have the power and authority of law (in the absence of abuse of discretion) to dismiss lawsuits and/or deny remedies if procedural rules are not followed.

AUTHORITY

Article III of the U.S. Constitution expressly creates a federal court system, and Section 2 of that Article further declares that **jurisdiction** of the U.S. Supreme Court and courts within the federal system shall be subject to "such Regulations as the Congress shall make." Those regulations are contained in Section 1251 of Title 28 of the United States Code. Section 2072 of 28 U.S.C. 131 (The Rules Enabling Act) authorizes the Supreme Court to "prescribe general rules of practice and procedure and rules of evidence for cases in the U.S. district courts (including proceedings before magistrates thereof) and courts of appeals." Similarly, state constitutions and statutes empower the states' highest courts (usually) to regulate civil procedures in state courts.

JURISDICTION

An important and early determination to be made in each pending action is whether to file a civil lawsuit in the "forum" of a federal court or state court. A court's general authority to hear and/or "adjudicate" a legal matter is referred to as its "jurisdiction." In the United States, jurisdiction is granted to a court or court system by **statute** or by constitution. A legal decision made by a court that does not have proper jurisdiction is deemed void and non-binding upon the litigants.

Jurisdiction may be referred to as "exclusive," "original," concurrent, general, or limited. Article III, Section 2 of the U.S. Constitution limits the types of cases that federal courts may hear. Generally speaking, federal courts may hear only those cases involving federal laws, federal or sovereign parties (including states), or disputes between citizens from different states. Thus, federal courts have "limited" jurisdiction, which may be "exclusive" over a matter or party (to the exclusion of any other forum), or may be "concurrent" and shared with state courts. In matters where both federal and state courts have concurrent jurisdiction, state courts may hear federal law claims (e.g., violations of **civil rights**), and parties bringing suit may choose the forum. However, when a **plaintiff** raises both state and federal claims in a state court, the defendant may be able to "remove" the case to a federal court.

Subject Matter Jurisdiction A court is competent to hear and decide only those cases whose subject matter fits within the court's scope of authority. Courts of "limited" jurisdiction may be competent to hear only certain matters, such as those involving **probate** or juvenile cases. Even courts of broad or general jurisdiction may have certain matters removed from their jurisdiction (by statute or state constitution), such as **divorce** or **custody** matters, to be handled by other courts. If the controversy involves a parcel of real estate instead of a person, the property must be located within the territorial jurisdiction of the court.

Jurisdiction over the Parties A court must have jurisdiction not only over the subject matter of the controversy, but also the parties to the litigation. There is seldom a question of jurisdiction over the plaintiff, since by bringing the action into the court, the plaintiff consents to the court's jurisdiction over him or her. But the plaintiff must also show that the court has jurisdiction over the defendant. In general, this may be established by the defendant's consent, by the defendant's general appearance in court, or by proving a defendant's domicile within the geographic area of the court's jurisdiction (in combination with serving process upon the defendant). A fourth way of acquiring jurisdiction over a defendant relies on "long-arm statutes," which permit a court to "reach" absent defendants or defendants residing in other states by establishing their relationship with the state in which the action was filed (the "forum" state). It may be that they committed the wrongful act within the forum state or transact business within that state or own property in that state, etc.

Jurisdictional Amounts Finally, many courts limit their jurisdiction to cases in which the amount in controversy exceeds a certain minimum amount. For example, no complaint may be filed in a federal court unless the amount in controversy exceeds the sum or value of $75,000. This was the amount under the statute in 2012, and Congress will likely raise the amount in future years. Many state circuit courts have minimum "jurisdictional amounts" of between $5,000 and $25,000. Conversely, many local or district courts within state court systems have maximum jurisdictional amounts. If the amount in controversy exceeds the jurisdictional maximum, either the case must be re-filed in the next level court or the complaining party must waive his or her right to any judgment that exceeds the maximum.

VENUE

Venue refers to the geographic location of the court in which to bring an action. Most court systems (federal and state) have statutes that dictate the particular district, county or city in which a court with jurisdiction may hear a case. Usually, venue is premised on where a defendant resides or does business, where the wrongful act occurred, or alternatively, where a plaintiff resides. The general venue statute governing federal cases is 28 U.S.C.A. § 1391. Venue provisions for state courts are generally found in statutes rather than rules of civil procedure; the rules of procedure may address the way in which one motions a court for a "change of venue."

FEDERAL RULES OF CIVIL PROCEDURE (FRCP)

A major step toward establishing uniform federal procedures was undertaken in 1934, when the U.S. Supreme Court promulgated the Federal Rules of Civil Procedure (FRCP). The principal guide for practicing attorneys in civil litigation, the Rules govern all civil actions in federal courts nationwide, including federal **bankruptcy** court. The Rules are frequently amended and updated and contain Supplemental Rules sections for cases in admiralty and maritime actions, as well as "local rules" pertaining to specific courts within the federal system.

Although the Rules were intended to apply to U.S. district courts within the federal system, nearly all state courts have since replaced their own procedural rules with new rules, many of which are modeled after the FRCP. At a minimum, it can be said that the FRCP represents the dominant style of U.S. civil procedure, whether in federal or state court. Although there is not uniformity **per se**, there is general consistency of approach to matters common in most causes of action.

Parties In civil procedure, the prosecuting party (the one filing a complaint or lawsuit or petition) is referred to as a "plaintiff" or "petitioner" or "complainant" (depending on the court and the nature of the matter), while the opposing party is referred to as a "defendant" or "respondent." (For purposes of simplicity, the terms "plaintiff" and "defendant" are used exclusively herein, but imply any or all of the above, respectively.)

Any person may file a lawsuit under his or her own name, but the person must have "legal capacity" to sue (the legal **competency** to stand before the court). This requirement implies, among other factors, minimum **legal age** and mental competency. FRCP 17(c) provides that a **guardian** or conservator may sue or defend on behalf of an infant or legally incompetent person; or, if none exists, the court will appoint a "next friend" or "guardian ad litem" to represent the interest of the child or incompetent person. A deceased person may be represented in an action by the personal representative (**executor** or administrator) of the deceased's estate. FRCP 17(b) also provides that in federal court, the legal capacity of a

business corporation to sue or be sued is determined by the law under which it was organized.

Several parties may be joined in an action, as co-plaintiffs or co-defendants. Under FRCP 23 and most state rules, multiple plaintiffs who have suffered harm as a result of the actions of a common defendant may be joined together in one lawsuit called a "class action." Under such a suit, only a few plaintiffs will be named in the action, but they will represent all plaintiffs within the certified "class," and their claims must be fairly representative of the interests of all the persons within the class.

A lawsuit may become fairly complicated when the original parties (and sometimes the court) bring in third or additional parties not initially named in the suit. Parties joined on the same side are referred to as "co-parties." If co-parties raise claims against one another, such as when a defendant blames another defendant, they are "cross-parties" as to each other. However, if a "counter-claim" is raised against an opposing party, they become "counter-parties" as to the **counterclaim**. In the "caption," or heading of the original action, the parties may be referred to as co-plaintiffs, co-defendants, cross-plaintiffs, cross-defendants, counter-plaintiffs, counter-defendants, or "interested parties," depending upon the claims or defenses raised.

Commencement of an Action A lawsuit must be commenced within the limitation period provided by law (the applicable "statute of limitations"). Lawsuits not filed within the period of the applicable **statute of limitations** will be dismissed. Under the U.S. Supreme Court decision in *Erie v. Tompkins*, federal courts will apply the statute of limitations of the state in which the federal court lies. Statutes of limitations generally begin to run when the cause of action arises. Many states have exceptions that allow for "tolling" of their statutes of limitations (temporarily "stopping the clock") during periods of absence from the forum state, war, legal **incompetency**, and so forth. There are also special rules that apply if death occurs prior to the expiration of the limitations period.

Under FRCP 3 and many state jurisdictions, an action commences when a complaint is filed. However, many states do not consider the action to have commenced until service of process has been made upon the defendant. Service of process may be made by personal service of the complaint and **summons** upon the defendant (many states permit registered mail service); constructive service by notice or publication; or substituted service on a registered agent of the defendant (as for business corporations). There are strict rules that limit the use of constructive or substituted service on defendants.

Pleadings Pleadings are written formal allegations in support of either a claim or a defense, presented for the court's consideration and judgment. Under FRPC 7, pleadings are limited to a complaint and an answer, a reply (to a counterclaim), an answer to a cross-claim, a third-party complaint, and a third-party answer.

The first pleading in an action is called a "complaint." (In a minority of jurisdictions, the pleading may still be referred to as a "bill of complaint" or "declaration.") FRCP 10(a) requires that a complaint contain, at a minimum the following:

- a caption that contains the name of the court, the title of the action, the file number (provided by the court), and the names of all the parties
- a short and plain statement of facts which tend to show that the pleader is entitled to relief
- a demand for judgment for the relief to which plaintiff deems himself or herself entitled
- a signature of an attorney of record and the attorney's business address (or the party's signature and address, if not represented by an attorney)
- a short and plain statement of the grounds upon which the court's jurisdiction depends

FRCP 7 provides that the responsive pleading to a complaint is called an answer. It generally contains denials of the allegations in the complaint and/or new matters asserted as counterclaims or affirmative defenses. However, under FRCP12 and most states' rules, an interim responsive pleading may be in the form of a motion to dismiss or a motion for **summary judgment**, for such reasons as failure to state a claim, lack of jurisdiction, insufficiency of process, etc. These generally constitute "affirmative defenses" that do not speak to the specific facts alleged in the complaint but rather challenge the validity of the complaint on some other grounds.

Under FRCP 8, allegations in a pleading to which a responsive pleading is required are admitted unless they are specifically denied in the answer. Moreover, under the federal rules, the defendant is required to assert all defenses in the responsive pleading or they will be waived. As part of the responsive pleading, FRCP 13 permits the raising of a counterclaim against the plaintiff, or a cross-claim against a co-party or a third party claim against a non-party (who will be served and joined as a party). There must be a reply to a counterclaim or cross-claim. Amendments to pleadings are permitted in the furtherance of justice and on the terms deemed proper by the court (FRCP 15).

Pre-trial Procedure Following the filing of all initial pleadings, there begins a period of "discovery" which enables each party to learn of evidence held by opposing or other parties to the action. Generally speaking, the scope of allowable **discovery** is broad, with FRCP 26 providing that parties may obtain discovery on any matter, not privileged, which is relevant to the subject matter involved in the pending action. Discovery is accomplished by means of subpoenas; requests for inspection of documents, photographs, recordings, or other items of evidence; the taking of **testimony** of witnesses (usually by **deposition**); review and copying of relevant records; written **interrogatories** (questions that must be answered under oath); written requests for admissions (requiring admission or denial of the facts posed); requests for physical or mental examination of a party; and often, visitation to sites, premises, or geographic locations relevant to the case.

Also during the pre-trial period and continuing through the trial process, various "motions" may be filed with the court, requesting that the court grant an order on some matter related to the progress of the case. A motion may request immediate relief for an interim dispute. Such as a motion to compel the release of evidence, or it may request "dispositive" relief, such as a motion to dismiss the case for lack of evidence or failure to state a cause of action.

Trial At the close of discovery, parties are encouraged to review the sum total of evidence and attempt to settle the case. In many state jurisdictions, there is compulsory (but non-binding) "mediation" of the case, in which an independent panel reviews the pleadings and evidence and makes a **settlement** recommendation. If no viable settlement results, the case will move on to the trial stage. Prior to trial, attorneys for the parties will provide written requests for **jury** instructions they wish to include in the charge to the jury (FRCP 51). Attorneys will also have the opportunity to examine and rule out prospective jurors ("voir dire") for such disqualifying factors as **bias**, personal familiarity with the parties or witnesses, **felony conviction**, and legal relationship with any party or witness (such as **landlord**, employer, partner), among others (FRCP 47). These are referred to as "challenges for cause." Most jurisdictions also permit a certain number of "peremptory challenges," wherein trial attorneys may rule out prospective jurors without stating their reason for doing so. After a final jury is agreed upon and all last-minute motions have been heard, trial begins.

In general, the order of proceedings at trial are: opening statements (first plaintiff, then defendant); introduction of evidence (first plaintiff, then defendant, then rebuttal evidence); closing arguments (first plaintiff, then defendant); instructions to the jury ("jury charge") by the court; return of verdict and poll of jury; and entry of a judgment.

The normal order for the presentation of proofs (evidence) is: the plaintiff introduces all the evidence for his or her "case in chief"; the defendant then introduces his or her evidence in chief; the plaintiff then offers rebuttal evidence; and finally, the defendant may be permitted to present evidence in rebuttal of any new matter brought out in the plaintiff's rebuttal evidence (called surrebuttal). Objections to any proffered evidence must be timely made or they are waived; proper and/or permissible objections are covered in the Federal Rules of Evidence (FRE) rather than the FRCP.

Closing arguments are then made (plaintiff first, followed by defendant, then followed with plaintiff's final rebuttal), and the jury is charged and sequestered for deliberations. The jury normally renders its verdict through its foreman, and the entire jury must be present when the verdict is delivered in court. Barring any defects in form or challenges to the verdict, a judgment is declared for the prevailing party.

Prior to the delivery of a verdict, either party may motion the court for a judgment on the evidence, such as a motion for summary judgment, or for **mistrial** based upon an objection made during trial. Following delivery of a verdict, a party may move for a new trial or partial retrial (FRCP 59).

Judgment A judgment on the verdict is not the only way to prevail in a **civil action**. In fact, at the conclusion of trial, either party may motion a court for a "judgment notwithstanding the verdict," (following the party's earlier motion for a **directed verdict**), even though there has been a jury verdict for the other party.

Rather than defend a civil complaint, a party may merely consent to judgment, as in claims of debt, and such "consent judgments" are entered on the record and are as binding as a full jury verdict.

A "default judgment" may be rendered against a party if it is the result of a party's failure to take a necessary step in the action within the proper time. This generally means a failure to plead or otherwise defend within the time allowed. Since under rules of procedure, allegations not specifically denied are deemed admitted, failure to file a responsive pleading will generally result in the entry of a **default judgment** against the defendant.

Finally, under FRCP 57 and most state rules and/or statutes, courts are authorized to grant "declaratory judgments" in cases where the requested relief is in the form of a court's declaration of certain rights, status, or legal relations between parties or entities. Some examples include actions to "quiet title" to real property, actions regarding ownership, or use of **intellectual property** rights (such as copyrights or **patents**), among others. In order to invoke the court's jurisdiction in a declaratory matter, there must be an actual controversy and not a mere desire for an advisory opinion from the court.

Appeal In both federal and state courts, a party may **appeal** only final orders, decisions, or judgments. After the entry of a final order, decision, or judgment, there are strict procedural deadlines as to the number of days within which an appeal must be filed. Grounds for appeal are extremely limited. An order of a court will not be reversed unless the **appellant** can show that either the order was clearly contrary to law or that the judge abused his or her discretion.

Likewise, there is limited review of trial judgments. It is not generally sufficient to show error in the conduct of trial; the appellant must show harm or prejudice that was caused by the error, such as the introduction of evidence which the appellant argued was improper and without which the appellant most likely would have prevailed. Appellate courts disregard harmless errors or defects that do not affect the substantial rights of the parties in determining whether a particular case should be reversed. (FRCP 61)

STATE RULES OF CIVIL PROCEDURE

The first state to establish uniform rules of civil procedure was New York, which in 1848 enacted the Field Code, named after its principal author, David Dudley Field. Over the next several decades, nearly all states had either adopted the Code outright or had made other considerable changes to their procedures. As of 2012, the Code has been replaced with modified versions of the FRCP in nearly all states. Nevertheless there are procedural differences from state to state, and it is imperative that litigants are familiar with state rules before proceeding in court. Copies of state rules may often be found at public libraries, college libraries, and/or on states' official Internet websites.

ALABAMA: See Title 6 of the Alabama Code of 1975, also available at http://www.legislature.state.al.us/.

ALASKA: See Title 9 of Alaska Statutes, "Code of Civil Procedure."

ARIZONA: See Title 12 of the Arizona Revised Statutes, available at http://www.azleg.gov/.

ARKANSAS: See Title 16, Subtitle 5 of the Arkansas Code, available at http://www.arkleg.state.ar.us/assembly/2011/2012F/Pages/Home.aspx.

CALIFORNIA: See the "California Code of Civil Procedure."

COLORADO: See Title 13 of the Colorado Constitution, "Colorado Rules of Civil Procedure."

CONNECTICUT: See Title 52 of the General Statutes of Connecticut, available at http://www.cga.ct.gov/.

DELAWARE: See Title 10, Part 3 of the Delaware Code, "Courts and Judicial Procedure."

DISTRICT OF COLUMBIA: See Titles 13-17.

FLORIDA: See "Florida Rules of Civil Procedure," from the Florida Lawyers World Wide Web Resource Center at http://phonl.com/fl_law/rules/frcp//.

GEORGIA: See Title 9, Chapter 10 of the Georgia Code.

IDAHO: See Titles 1-13 of the Idaho Code.

ILLINOIS: See Code of Civil Procedure, 735 IL CS 5.

INDIANA: See Title 34 of the Indiana Code, Articles 1-57, available at http://www.state.in.us/.

IOWA: See Title X, Subtitle 3 of the Iowa Code, available at http://www.legis.state.ia.us/IACODE/.

KANSAS: See Chapters 60 and 61 of the Kansas Statutes, available at http://www.kslegislature.org/li/.

KENTUCKY: See Kentucky Rules of Court, authority found in Kentucky Constitution, Articles 109-116.

LOUISIANA: See the Louisiana Code of Civil Procedure, available at http://www.legis.state.la.us/.

MAINE: See Maine Rules of Civil Procedure, available at http://www.cleaves.org/sc-rules.htm.

MARYLAND: See "Courts and Judicial Procedures," Section 1-101, et seq., available at http://mlis.state.md.us/.

MASSACHUSETTS: See Chapters 211-262 of the General Laws of Massachusetts, "Courts, Judicial Officers and Proceedings in Civil Cases."

MICHIGAN: See "Michigan Rules of Court," available at http://www.legislature.mi.gov.

MINNESOTA: See Chapters 540-552.

MISSISSIPPI: See Title 11 of Mississippi Code of 1972, available at http://billstatus.ls.state.ms.us/.

MISSOURI: See Missouri Revised Statutes, Title XXXV, Chapters 506-517, available at http://www.moga.mo.gov/.

MONTANA: See Title 25 of state statute.

NEBRASKA: See Chapters 25 and 26 of Nebraska statutes, available at http://statutes.unicam.state.ne.us/.

NEVADA: See Titles 3-6 of the Nevada Revised Statutes.

NEW HAMPSHIRE: See Title LIII, Chapters 514-526 of the New Hampshire Revised Statutes, "Proceedings in Court."

NEW JERSEY: See Chapter 2A of the New Jersey Permanent Statutes, available at http://www.njleg.state.nj.us//.

NEW YORK: See Chapter 8 of the New York State Consolidated Laws, available at http://assembly.state.ny.us/leg/.

NORTH CAROLINA: See Chapters 1 and 1A of the North Carolina General Statutes.

NORTH DAKOTA: See Chapter 28 of the Century Code. "Judicial Procedure, Civil."

OKLAHOMA: See Title 12 of the Oklahoma Statutes.

OREGON: See Chapters 12-36 of the Oregon Revised Statutes.

PENNSYLVANIA: See Pennsylvania Constitution of 1968, Article V, Section 10C, 42 PA CS 1722.

RHODE ISLAND: See Title 9, available at http://www.rilin.state.ri.us/Pages/Default.aspx.

SOUTH CAROLINA: See Title 15 of the Code of Laws, available at http://www.scstatehouse.gov/.

SOUTH DAKOTA: See Title 15.

TENNESSEE: See Titles 19 and 20.

TEXAS: See "Civil Practice and Remedies Code," available at http://www.statutes.legis.state.tx.us/.

UTAH: See Future Title 28-"Judicial Code" of the Utah Code, available at http://www.le.state.ut.us.

VERMONT: See Title 12 of the Vermont Statutes.

VIRGINIA: See Virginia Code Section 915a, available at http://leg1.state.va.us/lis.htm.

WASHINGTON: See Title 4, "Civil Procedure," of the Revised Code of Washington, available at http://www.leg.wa.gov/pages/home.aspx.

WEST VIRGINIA: See Chapters 55-58.

WISCONSIN: See Chapters 801-847 of the Wisconsin Statutes.

WYOMING: See Title 1 of the Wyoming Statutes, available at http://legisweb.state.wy.us/LSOWEB/Default.aspx.

ADDITIONAL RESOURCES

Clermont, Kevin M. *Principles of Civil Procedure*. 3d ed. St. Paul, Minn.: West, 2012.

Hazard, Geoffrey C., John Leubsdorf, and Debra Lyn Bassett. *Civil Procedure*. 6th ed. New York: Foundation Press, 2011.

Hricik, David Charles. *Mastering Civil Procedure*. 2d ed. Durham, NC: Carolina Academic Press, 2011.

Issacharoff, Samuel. *Civil Procedure*. 3d ed. New York: Foundation Press, 2012.

ORGANIZATIONS

American Bar Association (ABA)

321 North Clark Street
Chicago, IL 60610
Phone: (312) 988-5000
Toll Free: (800) 285-2221
Fax: (312) 988-6800
URL: http://www.americanbar.org

American College of Trial Lawyers

19900 MacArthur Boulevard, Suite 530
Irvine, CA 92612
Phone: (949) 752-1801
URL: http://www.actl.com

Network of Trial Law Firms, Inc.

303 South Broadway, Suite 222
Tarrytown, NY 10591
Phone: (914) 332-4400
URL: http://www.trial.com

COURTS AND PROCEDURES

FEDERAL COURTS AND JURISDICTIONS

Sections within this essay:

- Background
- Structure and Power of the Federal Courts
  - Supreme Court of the United States
  - Federal Courts of Appeals
  - Federal District Courts
  - Specialized Federal Courts

- Jurisdiction of Federal Courts
  - Diversity Jurisdiction
  - Federal-Question Jurisdiction
  - Admiralty and Maritime Cases
  - Bankruptcy
  - Other Areas of Federal Jurisdiction

- Jurisdictions of Federal Courts in the U.S. States and Territories

- Additional Resources

BACKGROUND

Article III of the United States Constitution establishes the judicial power of the federal government. Under the Constitution, the authority of the federal judiciary extends only to certain "cases" and "controversies," which are identified by either the nature of the suit or the parties involved. The Constitution establishes the Supreme Court of the United States and permits Congress to establish "inferior" federal courts. The federal judiciary currently consists of the Supreme Court, courts of appeals in 12

regional judicial circuits, 2 intermediate appellate courts with special power to hear cases originating nationwide, a total of 94 judicial districts throughout the 50 states that contain at least 1 federal district court and 1 **bankruptcy** court, territorial courts that function as district courts in several territories, and specialized tribunals that have been established by Congress pursuant to power provided in Article I of the Constitution. The district courts serve as the trial courts in the federal system, while the courts of appeals serve as intermediate appellate courts.

The power or authority of a court to hear and decide a case or controversy is called the **jurisdiction** of the court. Jurisdiction may be divided into two broad categories: subject-matter jurisdiction and personal jurisdiction. Subject-matter jurisdiction refers to the authority of a court to hear a certain type of case, while personal jurisdiction refers to the power with which a court may bind an individual party. Most cases and controversies that can be heard by the federal judiciary consist of the following:

- Cases governed by federal law, such as the federal Constitution, federal **statutory** provisions, or federal regulations (federal question jurisdiction)
- Suits between citizens of different states (diversity jurisdiction)
- Suits between a citizen of a state and a citizen of a foreign country
- Admiralty and maritime cases
- Suits in which the United States is a party
- Suits between two states

The United States operates with a dual system of courts: the federal judiciary and the judicial systems of the states. If a party brings an action in a state court, but a federal court has jurisdiction to hear the case, the

defendant may choose to "remove" the case to the federal court, subject to several limitations set forth in Title 28 of the United States Code. The defendant is not obligated to remove such a case, and questions about whether removal is proper in a particular case are often subjects of controversy in federal courts. In a case where a federal court permits a state court case to be removed but later determines that removal was improper, the federal court will remand the case to the state court.

STRUCTURE AND POWER OF THE FEDERAL COURTS

Pursuant to its Constitutional power, Congress has established inferior courts in the federal judiciary at the intermediate appellate and trial court levels. Courts that have been established under Article III of the Constitution, including the Supreme Court of the United States, United States Courts of Appeals, and United States District Courts, are called constitutional, or Article III, courts. Congress, pursuant to powers granted in Article I, may also establish legislative, or Article I, courts. These courts are designed to carry out specific legislative directives. Examples of such courts are the United States Court of Federal Claims and the United States Tax Court.

Supreme Court of the United States The Supreme Court of the United States consists of the **chief justice** of the United States and, since 1869, eight associate justices. The number of justices varied during the first 80 years of the country's history, beginning with five justices in 1798 and growing to as many as ten in 1863. Congress retains authority under the Constitution to establish the number of associate justices. The president of the United States nominates Supreme Court justice candidates, and appointments are made "with the advice and consent of the Senate." Under Article III of the Constitution, U.S. Supreme Court justices have lifetime tenure in their positions "during time of good Behaviour." Lifetime tenure is also true of the judges in the lower constitutional courts of the federal system. The chief justice presides over the Supreme Court and also holds leadership roles on the Judicial Conference of the United States, the Administrative Office of the United States, and the Federal Judicial Center.

In the vast majority of Supreme Court decisions, the Court exercises its appellate jurisdiction. The Court may assert original jurisdiction (that is, decide a case from beginning to end) if the case involves states or a state and the federal government. These types of cases are seldom filed with the Court. In exercising its appellate jurisdiction, the Court can hear cases appealed from both lower federal courts and state supreme courts if a case involves an issue of federal law. With respect to cases originating in state court, parties must exhaust their possibilities in the state court system before the Supreme Court will consider hearing a case.

The Supreme Court is not required to hear most requests for appeals. The decision of the Supreme Court to hear an **appeal** is discretionary in almost all cases today. Unless an appeal is mandatory, which is very rare, a party who wishes for the Supreme Court to hear an appeal must file a writ of certiorari, which requests that the Court review the decision of a lower court. The Court denies writs of certiorari in the vast majority of cases. The Court today grants appeals in only about one percent of the cases filed before it each year. If the Court refuses an appeal, it permits the lower court's decision to stand but does not have any other significant meaning. For example, it is not an affirmance of the lower court's opinion.

Many of the Supreme Court's decisions involve interpretation of the Constitution. The Court established itself as the primary authority to interpret the Constitution in the famous case of *Marbury v. Madison* in 1803. As the primary interpreter, the Court may invalidate an act of Congress if the act violates a right granted under the Constitution or Congress has misused powers granted to it under the Constitution. The Court does not decide "political questions," meaning those questions that another branch of government is better suited to answer. The Court also refuses to provide advice to the other branches of government. This restriction stems from the famous refusal of Chief Justice John Jay to provide advice to President George Washington about the implications under the new Constitution of a foreign policy decision.

Federal Courts of Appeals Congress through the Judiciary Act of 1891 originally established the intermediate appellate courts in the federal judiciary to relieve the caseload on the Supreme Court justices. Prior to 1891, cases were appealed routinely to the Supreme Court, which was required in most cases to hear the appeal. The courts of appeals now have jurisdiction to hear appeals from the federal district courts in virtually all cases. Unlike the Supreme Court, courts of appeals do not have discretionary jurisdiction to decide whether to grant an appeal. Other Acts of Congress have expanded the jurisdiction of the courts of appeals to hear appeals of decisions of federal administrative agencies. Courts of appeals also have a number of additional administrative functions that have been directed by Congress.

The federal court system currently consists of 12 regional circuits, each with one court of appeals. Eleven of these circuits are numbered (for example, the Fifth Circuit governs Texas, Mississippi, and Louisiana). The twelfth circuit, the Court of Appeals of the District of Columbia, governs only Washington, D. C., but hears a number of cases involving federal agencies. Congress in 1982 created the United States Court of Appeals for the Federal Circuit, which combined the functions of the United States Court of Customs and Patent Appeals and the United States Court of Claims. The Federal Circuit's jurisdiction, unlike the regional circuits, is nationwide, although it only applies to areas of law that are dictated by Congress.

Federal District Courts The federal court system includes 94 district courts in the 50 states, Washington, DC, Puerto Rico, Guam, U.S. Virgin Islands, and Northern Marinara Islands. Most states have only one judicial district. Larger states can have between two and four districts. The district courts serve as the general trial courts of the federal system. Each district also has a bankruptcy unit, as district courts have exclusive jurisdiction over bankruptcy cases.

District courts generally have jurisdiction to hear cases involving federal law and those involving citizens of different states. If a party in a state case can prove that a federal district court has jurisdiction to hear a case, the party may remove the case to the federal court. However, the federal court may abstain from hearing a case that involves questions of both federal law and state law. A situation may also arise where a federal district court may no longer have jurisdiction to hear a case because of changes in the parties to the suit. If a case has been removed to federal district court and the federal district court lacks jurisdiction, the court on motion of one of the parties will remand the case to the appropriate state court.

Specialized Federal Courts Congress has created a number of courts in the federal system that have specialized jurisdiction. Unlike constitutional courts, judges appointed to legislative courts do not enjoy lifetime tenure, unless Congress specifically authorized a life term. Moreover, judges in legislative courts do not enjoy the Constitutional prohibition against salary reductions of judges. A summary of these courts is as follows:

- The United States Court of Appeals for the Armed Forces reviews court martial convictions from the armed forces. Only the Supreme Court of the United States can review its cases. Judges sitting on this court enjoy neither life tenure nor protection against salary reduction.

- The United States Court of Federal Claims has jurisdiction to hear a broad range of claims brought against the United States. The court was called the United States Claims Court from 1982 to 1992. Many cases brought before this tribunal are tax cases, though the court also hears cases involving litigants who were federal employees and other parties with monetary claims against the United States. Judges sitting on this court enjoy neither life tenure nor protection against salary reduction. An adverse

decision in this court is appealed to the United States Court of Appeals for the Federal Circuit.

- The United States Court of International Trade has jurisdiction to hear cases involving customs, unfair import practices, and other issues regarding international trade. This court is a constitutional court, so its judges have lifetime tenure and protection against salary reduction.

- The United States Court of Appeals for Veterans Claims reviews decisions of the Board of Veteran Appeals. Appointments of judges last 15 years. An adverse decision in this court is appealed to the United States Court of Appeals for the Federal Circuit.

- The United States Tax Court is a legislative court that resolves disputes between citizens and the Internal Revenue Service. Appointments of judges last 15 years. Adverse decisions are appealed to a court of appeals in an appropriate regional circuit.

JURISDICTION OF FEDERAL COURTS

No federal court has general jurisdiction, meaning that the court could hear any type of case brought before it in a particular location. The authority of a federal court to hear a case must be based on a federal law, whether it is the United States Constitution or a federal **statute**. Courts created by Congress with specialized jurisdiction are, of course, the most limited to hear a particular case because Congress permits these courts only to hear certain prescribed cases. The jurisdiction of constitutional courts is usually limited to one of two types of cases: cases involving a federal question and cases with parties with diversity of citizenship.

Diversity Jurisdiction Article III of the Constitution provides that a federal court may hear a controversy between citizens of different states or citizens of the United States and citizens of foreign nations. Congress in Title 28 of the United States Code limits this power by requiring that the amount in controversy exceed $75,000. The broad purpose behind diversity jurisdiction is that a state court may show **bias** towards its own citizen to the detriment of the citizen from another state. Diversity jurisdiction, to say the least, has long been a source of controversy.

One initial question in a diversity case is whether each of the parties does, in fact, reside in different states. For individuals, the question focuses on the individual's domicile rather than mere residence in a state. Thus, for example, if a party has a residence in both Texas and California, but his true domicile is Texas, then the party will be considered a citizen of Texas rather than a citizen of both states. Diversity jurisdiction requires complete diversity by all plaintiffs and all defendants in the suit, though there are limitations to this rule in the United States

Code. For example, federal courts may have diversity jurisdiction to hear a case because all parties have diverse citizenship, but the court will not have supplemental jurisdiction over parties that are joined as plaintiffs in the case or over parties that intervene as plaintiffs in the case.

More difficult questions often arise when a corporation or association is a party to the suit. The right of a corporation is, in many respects, no different than the rights of an individual, since a corporation can sue or be sued. However, a corporation does not have a "domicile" that is similar to an individual. For diversity jurisdiction purposes, Congress provides that a corporation is a citizen in the state in which it is incorporated and in the state where it has its principal place of business. For small **corporations**, this question is usually not difficult, especially if the corporation has most of its offices and business in a single state. However, large national corporations may have offices in every state, so the question is much more complex. For these types of corporations, courts look to the so-called "nerve center" of the corporation, meaning the state in which most of the corporation's business is conducted.

Federal-Question Jurisdiction The Constitution provides that federal courts have the power to hear cases that arise under the Constitution, laws, or treaties of the United States. Congress has granted this jurisdiction to federal district courts in Title 28 of the United States Code. The question of whether a case arises under a federal law is often clouded when a case involves issues with the application of both state and federal law. If a case primarily involves an issue of state law, but it also involves a remote federal issue, then the federal court is not the proper forum, and the case will be dismissed or remanded to state court. However, if a case involves important issues of both state and federal law, Congress permits a federal court, with some exceptions, to invoke supplemental jurisdiction to hear both the state claim and the federal claim in the same case.

Federal question jurisdiction must be based on the complaint of the **plaintiff**, not on the possibility of a federal defense. This limitation stems from the famous 1908 case of *Louisville & Nashville Railroad v. Mottley,* where the plaintiff anticipated a federal defense to a state law **contract** case. The Supreme Court held that the plaintiff's cause of action stated in the complaint must be based on federal law. This limitation is called the well-pleaded complaint rule. Since nothing prohibits state courts from hearing cases involving federal laws, federal courts are not required to hear all cases that involve federal laws.

Admiralty and Maritime Cases Since the development of the Constitution, federal courts have had jurisdiction to hear admiralty and maritime cases. In contract cases, the question to determine jurisdiction is whether a contract relates to maritime **commerce**, not the place where a contract was made or was to be performed. However, a contract to build or sell a ship does not give rise to admiralty jurisdiction. Admiralty jurisdiction arises in tort cases if the tort occurred in navigable waters or if a vessel has caused injuries on land.

Bankruptcy Federal courts have exclusive jurisdiction over bankruptcy cases. Each federal district court has a bankruptcy unit. Bankruptcy actions arise under Title 17 of the United States Code and generally incorporate all claims brought by a **creditor** against the **debtor** in the bankruptcy action. The federal bankruptcy laws differ from other state laws that govern the relationship between debtor and creditor, so certainly not all debtor-creditor cases are heard in federal court.

Other Areas of Federal Jurisdiction The Constitution and federal statutes provide federal jurisdiction in a number of areas in addition to those discussed above. Such areas include, for example, prize cases (those determining the rights to cargo and ships captured at sea), and **copyright**, patent, and trademark cases.

JURISDICTIONS OF FEDERAL COURTS IN THE U.S. STATES AND TERRITORIES

Each state, the District of Columbia, and Puerto Rico contain between one and four federal districts, with the number of authorized judgeships in each district varying. Other territories, including Guam, the Virgin Islands, and the Northern Mariana Island, contain district courts as well. Each state also falls within one of the twelve circuits.

ALABAMA: Located in the 11th Circuit, the state is divided into three federal districts: Northern (Birmingham), Middle (Montgomery), and Southern (Mobile).

ALASKA: Located in the 9th Circuit, the state has one federal judicial district, based in Anchorage.

ARKANSAS: Located in the 8th Circuit, the state is divided into two federal districts: Eastern (Little Rock) and Western (Fort Smith).

CALIFORNIA: Located in the 9th Circuit, the state is divided into four districts: Northern (San Francisco), Eastern (Sacramento), Central (Los Angeles), and Southern (San Diego).

COLORADO: Located in the 10th Circuit, the state has one federal judicial district, based in Denver.

CONNECTICUT: Located in the 2nd Circuit, the state has one federal judicial district, based in New Haven.

DELAWARE: Located in the 3rd Circuit, the state has one federal judicial district, based in Wilmington.

FLORIDA: Located in the 11th Circuit, the state has three federal judicial districts: Northern (Tallahassee), Middle (Jacksonville), and Southern (Miami).

GEORGIA: Located in the 11th Circuit, the state has three federal judicial districts: Northern (Atlanta), Middle (Macon), and Southern (Savannah).

GUAM: The territory contains a federal district, based in Agana.

HAWAII: Located in the 9th Circuit, the state has one federal district, based in Honolulu.

IDAHO: Located in the 9th Circuit, the state has one federal district, based in Boise.

ILLINOIS: Located in the 7th Circuit, the state has three federal districts: Northern (Chicago), Southern (East Saint Louis), and Central (Springfield).

INDIANA: Located in the 7th Circuit, the state has two federal districts: Northern (South Bend) and Southern (Indianapolis).

IOWA: Located in the 8th Circuit, the state has two federal districts: Northern (Cedar Rapids) and Southern (Des Moines).

KANSAS: Located in the 10th Circuit, the state has one federal district, based in Wichita.

KENTUCKY: Located in the 6th Circuit, the state has two federal districts: Eastern (Lexington) and Western (Louisville).

LOUISIANA: Located in the 5th Circuit, the state has three federal districts: Eastern (New Orleans), Middle (Baton Rouge), and Western (Shreveport).

MAINE: Located in the 1st Circuit, the state has one federal district, based in Portland.

MARYLAND: Located in the 4th Circuit, the state has one federal district, based in Baltimore.

MASSACHUSETTS: Located in the 1st Circuit, the state has one federal district, based in Boston.

MICHIGAN: Located in the 6th Circuit, the state has two federal districts: Eastern (Detroit) and Western (Grand Rapids).

MINNESOTA: Located in the 8th Circuit, the state has one federal district, based in St. Paul.

MISSISSIPPI: Located in the 5th Circuit, the state has two federal districts: Northern (Oxford) and Southern (Jackson).

MISSOURI: Located in the 8th Circuit, the state has two federal districts: Eastern (Saint Louis) and Western (Kansas City).

MONTANA: Located in the 9th Circuit, the state has one federal district, based in Billings.

NEBRASKA: Located in the 8th Circuit, the state has one federal district, based in Omaha.

NEVADA: Located in the 9th Circuit, the state has one federal district, based in Las Vegas.

NEW HAMPSHIRE: Located in the 1st Circuit, the state has one federal district, based in Concord.

NEW JERSEY: Located in the 3rd Circuit, the state has one federal district, based in Newark.

NEW MEXICO: Located in the 10th Circuit, the state has one federal district, based in Albuquerque.

NEW YORK: Located in the 2nd Circuit, the state has four federal districts: Northern (Syracuse), Eastern (Brooklyn), Southern (New York City), and Western (Buffalo).

NORTH CAROLINA: Located in the 4th Circuit, the state has three federal districts: Eastern (Raleigh), Middle (Greensboro), and Western (Asheville).

NORTH DAKOTA: Located in the 8th Circuit, the state has one federal district, based in Bismarck.

NORTH MARINA ISLANDS: The territory contains a federal district, based in Saipan.

OHIO: Located in the 6th Circuit, the state has two federal districts: Northern (Cleveland) and Southern (Columbus).

OKLAHOMA: Located in the 10th Circuit, the state has three federal districts: Northern (Tulsa), Eastern (Muskogee), and Western (Oklahoma City).

OREGON: Located in the 9th Circuit, the state has one federal district, based in Portland.

PENNSYLVANIA: Located in the 3rd Circuit, the state has three federal districts: Eastern (Philadelphia), Middle (Scranton), and Western (Pittsburgh).

PUERTO RICO: The territory contains a federal district, based in Hato Rey.

RHODE ISLAND: Located in the 1st Circuit, the state has one federal district, located in Providence.

SOUTH CAROLINA: Located in the 4th Circuit, the state contains one federal district, located in Columbia.

SOUTH DAKOTA: Located in the 8th Circuit, the state contains one federal district, based in Sioux Falls.

TENNESSEE: Located in the 6th Circuit, the state contains three federal districts: Eastern (Knoxville), Middle (Nashville), and Western (Memphis).

TEXAS: Located in the 5th Circuit, the state contains four federal districts: Northern (Dallas), Southern (Houston), Eastern (Tyler), and Western (San Antonio).

UTAH: Located in the 10th Circuit, the state contains one federal district, based in Salt Lake City.

VERMONT: Located in the 2nd Circuit, the state contains one federal district, based in Burlington.

VIRGIN ISLANDS: The territory contains a federal district, based in Saint Thomas.

VIRGINIA: Located in the 4th Circuit, the state contains two federal districts: Eastern (Alexandria) and Western (Roanoke).

WASHINGTON: Located in the 9th Circuit, the state contains two federal districts: Eastern (Spokane) and Western (Seattle).

WASHINGTON, D.C.: Located in the D. C. Circuit, Washington, D. C., has its own federal district.

WEST VIRGINIA: Located in the 4th Circuit, the state contains two federal districts: Northern (Elkins) and Southern (Charleston).

WISCONSIN: Located in the 7th Circuit, the state contains two federal districts: Eastern (Milwaukee) and Western (Madison).

WYOMING: Located in the 10th Circuit, the state contains one federal district, based in Cheyenne.

ADDITIONAL RESOURCES

Barnes, Patricia G. *Desk Reference on American Courts.* Washington, DC: CQ Press, 2000.

Currie, David P. *Federal Jurisdiction in a Nutshell.* 4th ed. Eagan, MN: West, Thomson Reuters, 1999.

Mulleniz, Linda, Martin Redish, and Georgene Vairo. *Understanding Federal Courts and Jurisdiction* New York: Matthew Bender, 1998.

U.S. Code, Title 28: Judiciary and Judicial Procedure. U.S. House of Representatives. Available at http://uscode.house.gov/pdf/2011/2011usc28.pdf (accessed November 4, 2012).

U.S. Courts. "Understanding Federal and State Courts." Available at http://www.uscourts.gov/EducationalResources/FederalCourtBasics/CourtStructure/UnderstandingFederalAndStateCourts.aspx (accessed November 4, 2012).

ORGANIZATIONS

Administrative Offices of the Courts

Thurgood Marshall Federal Judiciary Building, Office of Public Affairs
Washington, DC 20544
Phone: (202) 502-2600
URL: http://www.uscourts.gov/

Federal Judicial Center (FJC)

Thurgood Marshall Federal Judiciary Building
One Columbus Cir. NE
Washington, DC 20002
Phone: (202) 502-4000
URL: http://www.fjc.gov/

Supreme Court of the United States

U.S. Supreme Court Building
One First Street, N.E.
Washington, DC 20543
Phone: (202) 479-3000
URL: http://www.supremecourtus.gov/

U.S. Sentencing Commission (USSC)

Office of Public Affairs
One Columbus Circle, NE
Washington, DC 20002-8002
Phone: (202) 502-4500
URL: http://www.ussc.gov/

COURTS AND PROCEDURES

JURIES

Sections within this essay:

- Background
  - Historical Roots in England
  - Development in America from Colonial Times
  - Grand Juries as Distinct from Civil and Criminal Juries
  - Constitutional Right to a Jury Trial

- How People Are Chosen for a Jury Pool
  - Diversity and Cross Section of Community Requirement

- Selection Process at the Courthouse
  - Disqualification Grounds for Jury Service
  - Exemptions from Jury Service
  - Peremptory Challenges
  - Use of Jury Consultants

- The Function of the Jury at the Trial
  - Role as a Factfinder
  - How Juries Weigh the Evidence
  - Standards of Proof Used

- Jury Instructions and Their Purpose
  - Special Kinds of Instructions Limiting the Discretion of the Jury
  - Jury Nullification

- Issues Pertaining to the Jury's Performance of Its Duties
  - The Hung Jury and the Unanimous Requirement
  - Judge's Discretion to Set Aside Verdicts
  - Jury Sequestration

- Juror Misconduct
- Notetaking by Jurors
- Questioning of Witnesses by Jurors

- Future Prospects of the Jury System
  - Decline in the Use of Jury Trials
  - Prospects for Reform

- Additional Resources

BACKGROUND

Historical Roots in England The idea for disputes to be resolved by a jury began out of necessity. In medieval England, it had been increasingly difficult to have a peaceful society when the only way of resolving disputes was by force. The first time the idea of a right to a trial by jury was mentioned was in the Magna Carta signed by King John in 1215. However, this new right to a jury trial did not apply to everyone in England at that time. Only knights and landowners were entitled to the right not to have their lives or property taken without a **hearing** before a jury of their peers.

Development in America from Colonial Times The most famous incident in America that gave a tremendous boost to the idea of the right to have a jury trial occurred in New York in 1734. At that time New York was one of thirteen British colonies administered by a royal governor appointed by the king of England. Peter Zenger, a journalist, had written an article ridiculing this official. The British authorities in response charged Zenger with seditious libel. Zenger's lawyer, Andrew Hamilton, put on a defense stating that his client was not guilty because the statements in Zenger's article were true.

However, there were two problems with Hamilton's trial strategy. First, he was unable to bring in witnesses who could **testify** as to the truth of Zenger's article. More important, as the judge pointed out, this defense could not be used for the crime with which Zenger was charged. As an alternative, Hamilton said that the question of whether Zenger had committed seditious libel should not be decided by the judge but should be left to the jury to decide. The judge capitulated to Hamilton's request and permitted the jury to return a not guilty verdict. The jury in this case took this action based on the principle that a trial cannot be fair if the **accused** is prevented by the court from putting on a defense.

From colonial times until well into the twentieth century, not all citizens of the various states were universally allowed to serve on a jury. At first, only white men owning property were permitted to be on a jury. After the United States became a nation, states were allowed to enact their own restrictions on jury service based on race, gender, and ownership of property. Some of those denied the right to serve on a jury did not see these restrictions removed until well after they were given the right to vote.

Because in America's early history there were so few lawyers who were specifically trained in the law, juries exercised the power to decide not only factual questions concerning a case but also questions as to how the law should be interpreted in applying it to the facts of the case. Judges on their part were allowed to make comments regarding the **evidence** presented at trial. In the twenty-first century juries in all states can only decide questions of fact, such as whether a car ran a red light prior to an accident. They can no longer decide questions of law which consist of what the law is on a particular issue of the trial and how it is to be interpreted so it can be correctly applied to the facts of the case. Judges can no longer comment on the evidence because this is seen as preventing the jury from being **impartial**.

In criminal trials, it is always required that jury verdicts of guilty or innocent must be unanimous. Beginning in California in 1879, this requirement was phased out for civil trials, proceedings that do not involve criminal accusations, such as whether a driver was not careful enough in backing out of his driveway and injured a pedestrian.

Grand Juries as Distinct from Civil and Criminal Juries A **grand jury** is formed only in criminal cases. The purpose of the grand jury is not to determine whether a **defendant** is guilty or not. This group of usually 23 people meets to determine whether persons suspected by police as responsible for a crime should be indicted, allowing them to be brought to trial before a regular jury

consisting of six to twelve persons. Grand juries are required by the **Fifth Amendment** of the U.S. Constitution which says a person suspected of a crime must be indicted before he is tried. This action is considered a safeguard against prosecuting a person without any legitimate reason.

Constitutional Right to a Jury Trial Three separate provisions of the U.S. Constitution provide for the right to a trial by jury. Article III, Sec. 2 provides: "The trial of all crimes shall be by jury and such trial shall be held in the state where the said crimes have been committed." The Sixth Amendment says: "In all criminal prosecutions, the accused shall enjoy the right to a speedy and public trial by an impartial jury of the state where the said crimes shall have been committed." Finally, for civil matters, the Seventh Amendment provides: "In all suits at **common law**, where the value in controversy shall exceed twenty dollars, the right of trial by jury shall be preserved and no fact tried by a jury shall be otherwise reexamined by an court of the United States."

The first two above provisions as to criminal trials greatly overlap. The Sixth Amendment was added as part of the **Bill of Rights** that would be guaranteed by the Constitution. However, it has only been relatively recently has this right been mandatory in both federal and state courts. As to the Seventh Amendment which covers civil trials, this provision only applies to federal courts which deal only with laws passed by Congress and signed into law by the president. According to the U.S. Supreme Court in a 1999 decision, the Seventh Amendment does not apply in state courts.

HOW PEOPLE ARE CHOSEN FOR A JURY POOL

Diversity and Cross Section of Community Requirement The U.S. Supreme Court has repeatedly ruled it is necessary for a jury to be comprised of a "fair cross section of the community" in order to satisfy the trial right guaranteed by the Sixth Amendment of impartiality. The Federal Jury Selection and Service Act of 1968 was written for this same purpose. Thus, a jury pool of persons eligible to serve reflects the spectrum of society.

In order to comply with the U.S. Supreme Court rulings and the 1968 Act, all the states have had to change their laws to insure that a broad cross section will make up the jury pool. Typically names appearing on voter registration lists for each locality are drawn. Many people who are otherwise eligible are not included because they have moved to another locality or state. In order to help solve this problem, names for juror pools are drawn from the list of licensed drivers for that state. Over half the states have made this change, and some have gone even further and have drawn names from lists of customers for utilities and even welfare recipients. This initial list is referred to as a source list.

From the source list, a locality randomly draws a second list referred to as "master wheel" or "qualified wheel" depending upon the statute for that state. These lists are replenished at intervals as required by the law for that state. Questionnaires are sent to those on the "wheel" lists in order to determine whether a particular individual is qualified to serve on a jury. Because between one-quarter to one-half of these forms are not returned, some jurisdictions will send a notice requiring such persons to explain why they have not responded.

SELECTION PROCESS AT THE COURTHOUSE

Disqualification Grounds for Jury Service Each state by law lists what reasons disqualify someone from jury service. Many of these reasons are included because they may prevent explain why a person cannot listen to **testimony** and other evidence with an open mind. Prior contact with one of the parties or lawyers connected with the case as well as knowledge obtained prior to the trial is sufficient reason to excuse a person from serving on the jury for a particular case. Statements made by jurors while they are being questioned by the attorneys for both sides which indicate they are biased in favor of or against one of the parties have the same result as **discovery** that a potential juror has a prior **felony conviction**. In criminal trials it is common for an individual to be excused because of a relationship with a witness in the case.

Exemptions from Jury Service Formerly it was common for people otherwise qualified to serve on a jury to be exempt based on their occupation. Prior to a recent change in the law, New York had recognized more than a dozen such exemptions, including lawyers, doctors, clergy, dentists, pharmacists, optometrists, psychologists, podiatrists, nurses, embalmers, police officers, and firefighters. The reason given for these exemptions were that each of these groups performs functions necessary to the **public interest**. As of 2002, 26 states had eliminated occupational exemptions while an additional nine have placed strict limitations on them.

Exemptions are also granted for business or financial hardship according to the circumstances of that individual. A judge may grant a business hardship exemption if they are convinced that jury service would result in the business closing permanently. Financial exemptions are also given to employees of private businesses since in most states the employer is not required to pay them for the time spent on a jury. Other exemptions also granted on a case by case basis at the discretion of the judge or court officials include incapacitating physical or mental illnesses,

and extreme inconvenience such as having to travel a great distance to the courthouse.

Preemptory Challenges When selecting a jury, attorneys for both sides ask questions of each person sent to that courtroom to be considered for service on that case. The questions asked are designed to reveal if a particular potential juror has either a conscious or unconscious **bias** affecting their ability to be impartial. Because these questions may be intrusive and include such areas as reading habits, favorite television shows, amount of income, and feelings towards different racial, ethnic, or other groups, it is not uncommon for individuals required to answer such inquiries to be less than truthful or to give general answers that may conceal a biased attitude. A good trial lawyer senses bias without needing it stated explicitly.

States give each side a designated number of persons they can have excused without having to give reason. When a person is excused in this way, the attorney is said to have exercised a preemptory challenge. Because personal bias is often difficult to detect, the **peremptory challenge** allows lawyers to act on their instincts in order to obtain impartial juries.

Sometimes a judge will grant one side more preemptory challenges than is allowed by state law. The attorney who objects to this action and then loses his case will not be able to have the trial judge reversed by a higher court unless that lawyer has exhausted all preemptory challenges and can show to that because they were not granted the same number of preemptory challenges, one or more persons they would have found to be objectionable was able to serve on that jury.

Two decisions by the U.S. Supreme Court have placed limits on the use of preemptory challenges if the complaining side or party is able to prove that the use of preemptory challenges by the opposing lawyer were designed to exclude persons from a jury based on their race and gender. In the first of these cases, an African-American criminal defendant named Batson was convicted of **burglary**. On **appeal** to the U.S. Supreme Court, his lawyer argued the prosecution used his preemptory challenges so that no black person in the jury pool served on the jury. The Supreme Court ruled in Batson's favor for three reasons. First, excluding jurors on the basis of race denies a defendant the right to an impartial trial since it works against the cross section of the community requirement for jury membership. Second, the excluded jurors are denied the right to take part in the judicial process. Third, this use of preemptory challenges is harmful to the local community because it encourages its citizens to believe that a fair trial cannot be obtained there.

However, the Supreme Court made clear that future defendants seeking to have trial verdicts against them overturned on appeal to a higher court would have to prove certain things to that court. First, the defendant is a member of an identifiable racial group. Second, the prosecution used preemptory challenges to prevent those of the defendant's race from serving on the jury. Third, the lawyer for the defendant must show that the facts and circumstances of the case imply the prosecution did this intentionally.

Even though the defense attorney is faced with having to prove all of the above, the **prosecutor** must show the peremptory challenges were applied neutrally. Non-African American defendants have not been successful in challenging their convictions because U.S. Supreme Court decisions have declined to apply *Batson v. Kentucky* to their racial group. The principles in Batson have since been made applicable in civil as well as criminal trials.

In 1994, eight years after *Batson* was decided, the U.S. Supreme Court said preemptory challenges could not be used to exclude members of a particular gender from jury service. In *J. E. B. v. Alabama*, the state agency regulating the welfare of children filed a **paternity** action against J. E. B. for failing to pay the **child support** he owed to the mother. Alabama used its preemptory strikes to prevent nine men from serving on the jury eventually resulting in a panel consisting entirely of women. The jury found J. E. B. guilty of the charge, and he successfully argued for the application of *Batson* to his case on grounds that the use of preemptory challenges based on gender violated the constitutional principle that persons should not be discriminated against or treated unequally on the basis of sex.

However, it became questionable how useful *Batson* and *J. E. B.* will be in future cases for defendants. In 1995, in *Puckett v. Elam*, the Supreme Court said that a prosecutor's reason for excluding a juror on a preemptory challenge does not have to make any sense so long as it is applied neutrally as to the race and gender of the defendant. Justice John Paul Stevens in disagreeing with other justices on the Supreme Court, complained that the Court had made its decisions in *Batson* and *J. E. B.* meaningless.

Some state and federal courts lower than the U.S. Supreme Court have said preemptory challenges cannot be used to exclude persons of particular religious groups. Other courts on these levels have ruled in the opposite way. The U.S. Supreme Court had not resolved the difference of opinion among the courts on this issue as of late 2012.

Use of Jury Consultants There are two scenarios in which attorneys may consider using a jury consultant to assist them in selecting jurors. First, if their client is a celebrity,

there may be very strongly divided opinions among potential jurors on whether they like or dislike that client. This would be a great obstacle to finding at least an impartial jury. Second, even if their client does not provoke any strong sentiment, if he has a great deal to lose, they may still want to improve the probability of a favorable outcome. In either instance, to use a jury consultant constitutes an additional expense. The average cost is $250 per hour, and it could total anywhere from $10,000 to $250,000.

Most jury consultants have backgrounds in law, psychology, or sociology. In spite of the expertise a jury consultant may have, the profession is largely unregulated. Although jury consultants claim to be accurate in their appraising potential jurors, many scholars are skeptical. Another criticism is that using a jury consultant gives the general public the impression that a favorable verdict can be purchased if the right jury is selected. In light of this criticism, some judges have taken the initiative to have consultants appointed for indigent defendants.

The primary purpose of hiring a jury consultant is to help uncover hidden bias of potential jurors. Because preemptory challenges are limited, lawyers may be unsure about some of those questioned. The job of jury consultants is to give attorneys the criteria necessary for the ideal jury for their clients and to assist in determining what biases do not fit that criteria.

A good illustration of this principle is the trial of Daniel and Philip Berrigan in 1972, the first known use of jury consultants. The Berrigan brothers were accused of conspiring to plan violent demonstrations against the Vietnam War. The defense attorneys decided that in order to have the best jury possible they should poll those persons likely to qualify as jurors in Harrisburg, Pennsylvania, the site of the trial. The purpose of this polling was to determine which demographic groups would be most sympathetic to their clients. The results led the defense attorneys to conclude that Episcopalians, Presbyterians, and other Protestant denominations with a fundamentalist outlook would favor the prosecution, as would college graduates because of their support for the position of the U.S. government on the Vietnam conflict. Accordingly, the defense was successful in having a jury selected that consisted of entirely blue collar workers who would likely not have graduated from college and who were also of a different denomination from those listed above. This jury deadlocked at 10-2 in favor of **acquittal**. The government afterwards declined to retry the case.

There are two kinds of techniques jury consultants use. The first category is pretrial research. The easiest research in this category is attitude surveys conducted in phone or in person as was done in the *Berrigan* trial. A second technique is to form a trial simulation with a group of people representative of what the jury picked will most resemble. At the end of this mock trial, the participants are surveyed as to how persuasive each side was in general and in its use of the evidence. Also, a focus group may be formed and the facts of the case and the position of each side will be explained to it. Those in the focus group will be asked how they would decide the case and their opinion on which side had the best arguments supporting their position. A third method is personal background research made through credit checks, hand writing analysis, and an examination of property and tax records.

A second category relates to what consultants do when the trial takes place. One commonly used method is for the consultant to prepare a questionnaire for the attorney designed to uncover juror biases. Another is for the consultant to observe the facial expressions and posture of those being considered for the jury, These unconscious reactions may indicate whether the response to the questions of the lawyer are sincere or misleading. A third technique is to observe the jury during breaks for lunch. If certain persons on the jury always eat together this may indicate that alliances have formed that could impact how the juries will deliberate once the case is given to them to decide and could help determine the verdict they reach. In some cases, consultants will recruit a shadow jury resembling by various demographic factors the one actually deciding the case. This shadow jury will be interviewed during the trial for the purpose of determining how the real jury is perceiving their side.

Moreover, some jury consultants believe that people in general fall into one of two groups: those who conclude that what happens to a person is determined by the person's reaction to those events, and the rest, who believe what happens to an individual is dictated by circumstances and context.

THE FUNCTION OF THE JURY AT THE TRIAL

Role as a Factfinder In every case there are allegations made. In a civil case, they are made by the party known as the **plaintiff** while in a case involving criminal law, the party making the charges or allegations is the prosecutor who is employed by the state **jurisdiction** in which he practices. If the case involves federal law, the prosecutor is the U.S. Justice Department, a federal agency.

In order to win the case, the plaintiff, or whoever is making the allegations, must make his case by showing the allegations are true according to a given standard of proof to the satisfaction of a jury. For example, Smith alleges that Jones negligently backed his car into Smith, breaking his leg. In order to prove the allegations to be true, Smith must present evidence based on facts and testimony.

The facts that Smith is able to prove are true are then applied to see if the four elements necessary for Smith to win are proven. These elements in this **negligence** claim are the issues that the judge will submit to the jury. The issues are: did Jones owe a duty to be reasonably careful to Smith, did Jones breach or violate that duty, was this violation by Jones of his duty to Smith the cause of Smith's broken leg, and did Smith actually have his leg broken.

In its role as a fact finder, a jury decides, based on the evidence presented, what is the truth in regard to the facts of the case. The jury will decide on the four issues in the case based on the facts they have found to be true, and if their answer is yes to all four of these issues, Smith wins. In determining what their conclusion is to each of these issues, the jury is given considerable discretion even when evidence regarding the same fact conflicts to the extent that opposite inferences could be drawn. This discretion even extends to cases in which the facts are undisputed, but different inferences could still be found by a rational jury.

However, the judge still has discretion to withhold from the jury the right to decide a particular issue if he believes the evidence is insufficient for the jury to come to a reasonable conclusion. Because each of the issues that Smith must prove in his favor to the jury are essential to his case, a decision by the judge that the evidence presented is not enough to support only one of the four issues would result in Smith losing the case.

How Juries Weigh the Evidence Allowing evidence in the form of facts, such as testimony, to be admitted at trial by the judge depends on whether it is pertinent or relates to the issue the jury is asked to decide and whether it has probative value, meaning it helps to determine whether a fact is true or false. Once the evidence is actually admitted and the jury tries to reach a verdict they must evaluate this evidence as to its **credibility**. For example, if a witness saw Smith being struck by Jones's car, the jury will determine whether the facts **warrant** their accepting his testimony as being a true account of what occurred, issues such as whether the witness was close enough to see what had occurred.

Standards of Proof Used In a civil court case such as one of Smith, the plaintiff, versus Jones, the defendant, the burden is on the plaintiff to show or prove by the facts presented into evidence he has been injured by the defendant. In other kinds of civil lawsuits, such as those involving contracts between the plaintiff and defendant, the plaintiff still has the burden. The standard of proof that the plaintiff must meet is the preponderance of the evidence. This means that a fact put into evidence in supporting Smith's contention Jones was negligent is more likely to be true than false. The degree to which the jury must believe a fact is more likely to be true than not true in order to meet this standard of proof need only be by the smallest degree, and 51 percent would be sufficient.

Sometimes the rules of evidence in a given case will have a standard of proof known as clear and convincing evidence. In order to show that a fact presented into evidence is true according to this standard, the plaintiff Smith must show there is a high probability that a given fact is true or that a juror according to the evidence presented would come to firmly believe the fact alleged by Smith was true. This is a greater degree of proof than preponderance of the evidence, but it is not as high as the **beyond a reasonable doubt** standard required in criminal cases.

In a criminal trial, the plaintiff is not a person or corporation, but the state or federal government as represented by the prosecutor. The prosecutor, regardless of his title, has the responsibility of enforcing the criminal laws of his jurisdiction. The elements of the allegations a prosecutor must prove will vary with the offense charged, but in any event, it must be proven the defendant committed the offense he is accused of and that he intentionally did so willingly. Because the consequences of a criminal conviction are more severe than in a civil lawsuit, the highest standard of proof, beyond a **reasonable doubt**, is required. This **burden of proof** is always on the prosecution because a criminal defendant can remain silent if he chooses. This standard means the prosecutor must convince the jury to the point where they firmly believe the defendant is guilty as charged.

JURY INSTRUCTIONS AND THEIR PURPOSE

A jury instruction is a guideline given by the judge to the jury about the law they will have to apply to the facts they have found to be true. The purpose of the instructions is to help the jury arrive at a verdict that follows the law of that jurisdiction. In his instructions a judge may explain the legal principles pertaining to the subject matter of the case, make it clear to the jury the legal issues they must decide in order to arrive at a verdict, point out what each side must prove in order to win, and summarize the evidence he sees as relevant and explain how it relates to the issues they must decide. For example, do the facts admitted as evidence and found credible by the jury according to the preponderance of the evidence combined with the application of the legal principles of negligence law warrant a finding by the jury that Smith owed a duty to Jones to be reasonably careful in operating his car?

In giving these instructions, the judge binds the jury. The judge makes clear to the jurors that they are to apply the law to the facts as he gives it to them; they are not to substitute their own judgment as to whether a different

law should be applied or whether the law as has been explained to them is unjust. The instructions are to be given in terms a layperson can easily understand. In order to help the jury understand the instructions, the judge may give pre-instructions prior to the time immediately following the presentation of both sides of the case. However, the judge is forbidden to comment on the evidence presented in the case. It is the jury's responsibility to independently evaluate the evidence.

Special Kinds of Instructions Limiting the Discretion of the Jury The judge has a number of devices by which he can limit the discretion of the jury in applying the instructions to their deliberations. Through an additional instruction, the judge may supplement instructions he has already given. These instructions are usually given at the request of the jury to clarify some point regarding the law given in a previous instruction they do not understand. If a judge gives a mandatory instruction, this requires the jury to reach a verdict in favor of a particular party if the evidence indicates that a particular set of facts is true. Through a peremptory instruction, a jury is directed to find in favor of a particular party regardless of how credible they regard the evidence to be. The judge is taking the case away from the jury because he believes a reasonable juror could not rule in favor of the other party.

Jury Nullification Jury nullification is the right of a jury in a criminal case to disregard the evidence admitted at trial and the law as explained to them by the judge and to give a verdict of not guilty for reasons having nothing to do with the case. There may be several reasons for ignoring the evidence and the instructions of the judge. First, they may wish to use a not guilty verdict to communicate to the community their views on a social issue outside the scope of the trial. Second, having to convict a defendant may offend the jurors' sense of justice and fair play or jurors may believe the law itself is immoral.

A judge is powerless to **sanction** the jury in any way. The jury is not required to give any reason at all for its decision which cannot be appealed by the prosecution to a higher court because of the **Double Jeopardy** Clause of the Constitution that says a defendant is prohibited from being tried more than once for the same crime.

The right of jury nullification originated in what is referred to as Bushell's Case, an English court decision from 1670. William Penn, the eventual founder of Pennsylvania, was accused of holding an illegal meeting. The jury, based on inconclusive evidence, acquitted Penn and his co-defendant Bushell. The judge retaliated against the jury by fining and imprisoning them. After several weeks, Bushell asked for an appeal of the trial judge's action against the jurors. The judge for a higher court set the jury free and said that because reasonable people can look at the same evidence and come to a different conclusion, juries are free to decide as they see fit regardless of whether the judge believes they had an legally adequate reason.

Although this case is English and would not normally be binding in the United States, U.S. courts over a long period of time consistently upheld the right of juries to use the right of nullification. However, the use of this device by juries seems at least on the surface to apply only to criminal cases. Some scholars contend that it takes place in secret because the jury proceedings are confidential but have been unable to document any case that expressly endorse nullification in a civil trial.

ISSUES PERTAINING TO THE JURY'S PERFORMANCE OF ITS DUTIES

The Hung Jury and the Unanimous Requirement It is required that in order for a jury to reach a verdict, everyone must agree to the decision made. Unanimity is required in all federal court civil and criminal trials, in all state court criminal trials, and in most civil trials in those courts. Sometimes the entire jury is not able to agree on the verdict, resulting in a deadlocked or **hung jury**.

When judges are informed this situation has occurred, they tell the jury to continue the deliberations because the alternative is to have the entire case tried over again with a new jury. In order to push the jury into arriving at a verdict, judges urge those in the minority to reconsider their positions by reexamining the evidence carefully and to ask themselves whether their disagreement with the majority is still correct from their viewpoint. Although this device was popular among judges, many courts have abandoned it because it seems coercive.

Many courts now use another instruction drafted by the American Bar Association which asks jurors in the minority to reconsider their position and the evidence; jurors should change their stand only if they are convinced based on the evidence but not because they feel pressed to conform to the majority view.

Judge's Discretion to Set Aside Verdicts In a civil trial, a judge may set aside the verdict regarding how much money should be awarded by the jury to the plaintiff in **punitive damages**. These damages consist of a dollar figure the jury awards the plaintiff in order to punish the defendant. This amount is totally distinct from **compensatory damages**, which are meant to reimburse the plaintiff for lost wages as well as pain and suffering. Given the purpose of punitive damages, juries can award verdicts that in punitive damages alone amount to millions of dollars.

The Seventh Amendment to the U.S. Constitution precludes review by any court of a judgment over $20. In light of this provision, courts will not overturn an award made by a jury just because of its large size or because the judge, if he had been standing in their shoes, would have awarded a smaller sum. However, a judge may reduce the amount of the award if it is far in excess of any rational calculation. Because compensatory damages such as lost wages have formulas by which juries can arrive at an acceptable figure, the reduction of an award is usually applied to punitive damages. The specific ground judges use to justify this action is that the award was made out of "passion and prejudice."

In criminal cases, judges may disregard a jury's guilty verdict and **acquit** or grant a new trial if they believe the evidence was insufficient to support the decision made by the jurors. Judges may also set aside a verdict if they believe the verdict was reached on a basis that violates the U.S. or respective State constitution or if the legal theory on which the jury based their decision does not conform to the law.

Jury Sequestration Judges will have members of a jury sequestered or kept together in order to protect juries from outside influences This includes any communication with persons not allowed to be in contact with the jurors as well as the content of news reports concerning the case. Courts view sequestration as a great burden on the personal lives of the jurors as well as the cost involved, and it is used, therefore, only if the lawyer for the defense is able to show the judge there is prejudice in the surrounding community against the defendant, or that news reports would prevent members of the jury from being impartial. While even criminal defendants do not have the right to have the jury sequestered, it may be required under state law where a defendant could be sentenced to death.

Sequestration is more common in criminal than in civil trials and is likely to be imposed once the jury has been selected. In a civil trial, jurors are not sequestered until the jury has heard all of the evidence and has received their instructions from the judge.

Once a jury is sequestered, strict measures are imposed to insure their objectivity. For example, jurors are not allowed to use a public restroom without a court **bailiff** or marshal being present. Receiving and making telephone calls is forbidden but will not result in a trial verdict being reversed by a higher court so long as the court officer can hear the conversation and nothing pertaining to the case is mentioned. Jurors must also be transported as a group, eat together, and sleep at the same lodging.

Juror Misconduct Even if they are not sequestered, jurors are instructed not to discuss any subject pertaining to the trial prior to the time the jury begins their deliberations. This includes fellow jurors.

Each juror has a duty to report as soon as possible any incident where any person attempted to influence any member of the jury outside of the room where the jurors deliberate. Jurors must report to the court any violation they see committed by other jurors against warnings given by the judge not to discuss the case outside the jury room or against listening, reading or viewing news reports about the case. In regard to jurors' avoidance of any contact with news reports, the judge in many jurisdictions is required to explain to the jury his reason for warning them to do so.

There are a number of documented examples of juror misconduct that illustrate the above principles. The first kind of example is jurors bringing in outside information not given to them at trial. In an automobile accident case, a juror on his own visited the accident site and drew a diagram of the intersection. The next day when the jury deliberated, he showed the jury the diagram and brought into the room a copy of a book on state traffic laws, the contents of which they discussed. In a second instance communication was said to have taken place between members of the jury and a customer in a restaurant who approached their table and urged them to impose the death penalty. In these instances, what occurred was clearly prejudicial and resulted in the trial verdict being overturned.

There are some instances in which the rules about outside communication were not followed, but were not considered egregious enough to warrant the verdict being overturned. In one case, the jury did not understand what was meant by the term proximate cause. Instead of asking the judge for clarification, they brought in a dictionary to help them. Because the dictionary definition did not conflict with what the judge had told them earlier as to what that word mean, it was not considered to be prejudicial.

There have been a large number of cases where jurors have gone to the judge or other court officials after the trial is over to complain they were intimidated by other jurors into voting with the majority. Courts will not take any action at this point for these reasons. First, before deliberations have concluded, a juror can report intimidation to court officials. Second, the jury can be polled individually in **open court** to see if each person voluntarily agrees with the verdict. Third, courts are unwilling to meddle in or speculate about how the jury reached its decision; a jury's deliberations are meant to be secret in order for non-jurors not to have any influence. Outbursts of emotion, such as throwing chairs or cursing,

are looked upon by courts as consequences that should not be unexpected and will not in themselves be sufficient to have intimidated jurors into not voting according to their own evaluation of the evidence. Finally, allowing inquiries after a verdict would jeopardize the finality of a jury's decision and might result in endless additional time wasted.

Notetaking by Jurors As trials have become more complex, and the information given more difficult to remember and place in perspective, a number of states have made express permission for jurors to take notes during the trial. These states include Arizona, Arkansas, Connecticut, Missouri, New Jersey, New York, North Dakota, Ohio, Washington, Wisconsin, and Wyoming. Although only one state expressly prohibits this practice, in most jurisdictions whether members of a jury are allowed to take notes will depend upon the discretion of the judge. One survey indicated that 37 percent of the judges in state courts indicate they do not allow jurors to take notes during a trial. In federal courts, this matter is also left up to the judge.

Many judges oppose juror notetaking because in their view jurors cannot make the distinction between important and trivial evidence. As a result, the more vital evidence may not be recorded and the less important may be, making it impossible for a jury to reach a rational verdict. However, studies performed in Wisconsin and Arizona indicate that notetaking did not influenced the verdict, or distract the jurors; notes taken were accurate and did not result in the notetakers dominating non-notetakers in the jury deliberations.

Questioning of Witnesses by Jurors A small number of states have changed their laws and court rules to allow jurors to ask witnesses questions, either orally or in writing through the judge. Written questions submitted in advanced allow attorneys for both sides to make objections based either on the ground they would violate the rules governing the admission of evidence or would result in prejudice against their clients.

The states that expressly encourage judges to allow jurors to question witnesses are Arizona, Arkansas, Florida, Indiana, Iowa, Kentucky, Nevada and North Carolina. Out of these jurisdictions, Arizona, Florida, and Kentucky require that judges allow jurors to ask written questions. The respective highest state courts of Indiana and Kentucky have ruled jurors have a right to ask questions of witnesses.

Other jurisdictions give a more restricted endorsement of this practice. In Pennsylvania and Michigan, the respective state supreme courts have said it is permissible at the discretion of the trial judge. Texas does not permit jurors to question witnesses in criminal trials and Georgia law requires all questions to be written and submitted to the judge. Only Mississippi law expressly forbids jurors from questioning witnesses.

Plaintiffs of civil trials and prosecutors in criminal proceedings favor this practice because it assists them in sustaining the burden of proof required in order for them to win their case. When jurors ask questions, they are able to gain a better understanding of the facts brought into evidence, especially when it is highly technical, such as DNA analysis. Bias in members of the jury that was undetected during the selection process can be exposed through questions they ask, enabling the judge to give an instruction against this bias or removing and replacing jurors with alternates.

Defense attorneys in civil and criminal trials are against jurors questioning witnesses at least partly because it may lead to information being disclosed that could be detrimental to their case. If oral questions are permitted, it could put the defense attorney in an uncomfortable position if a truthful answer would prejudice the jury as a whole against their client. One example would be if a juror were to ask if the defendant had a prior criminal record. If the defense attorney objects to the question, the attorney runs the risk of antagonizing the jury. If the attorney chooses not to object, his client may have waived any right on appeal to a higher court that his verdict should be overturned because of the prejudicial nature of the question. Even if the questions are submitted to the judge first in writing, defense attorneys say jurors will inevitably put more weight than they should on their own questions and makes it more likely jurors will rush to judgment without taking into account all the evidence admitted at trial.

FUTURE PROSPECTS OF THE JURY SYSTEM

Decline in the Use of Jury Trials Only 2 percent of civil cases and a similar proportion of criminal cases that are not dismissed are settled by **plea bargaining** are decided by a jury.

The low percentage of criminal prosecutions being resolved by a jury trial is the result of their being settled by **plea** bargaining which helps manage the heavy caseloads in most jurisdictions. The reason for the low use of trials in civil cases is more complex. Various studies have indicated that compared to a bench trial where a case is heard only by a judge, a jury trial costs much more and lasts from twice to three times as long. The increasing complexity of what a jury has to decide in a civil trial makes such alternatives as **mediation**, negotiation, **arbitration**, and mini-trials attractive because individuals involved in the proceedings are

already knowledgeable in the subject matter of the case. The increased complexity of modern civil cases makes jurors less likely to understand the judges' instructions. Finally, the jury selection process itself tends to weed out the more well informed jurors who are able to handle complex case subject matter.

Prospects for Reform Jury reform is needed because less than half of those summoned to the courthouse bother to show up, and out of this group between 85 to 95 percent do not serve since they are either exempt, disqualified, or not chosen. Because of the increased importance placed on the ideal jury as conceived by jury consultants, less informed and qualified persons are more likely to be on a jury.

Arizona has made the following reforms: allowing jurors to take notes during a trial, allowing them to question witnesses, and permitting jurors to discuss the case among themselves prior to the time all evidence has been presented. These reforms are needed because the present laws and court rules on juries were put in place many years ago and do not reflect the advances scientists have made regarding how people retain and process new information.

In Arizona, a committee including former jurors made further recommendations such as increasing public awareness of jury service, having short opening statements prior to attorneys selecting juries, giving jurors copies of jury instructions, encouraging jurors to ask questions about these instructions, offering assistance by the judge and attorneys for both sides to a deadlocked jury, and obtaining jurors' reaction to their experience after the verdict is rendered.

ADDITIONAL RESOURCES

Abbott, Walter F. *Jury Research: A Review and Bibliography.* Philadelphia: American Law Institute, 1993.

Finkel, J., and J. Norman. *Commonsense Justice: Juror's Notions of Law.* Cambridge, MA: Harvard University Press, 1995.

Fukurai, Hiroshi, and Richard Krooth, eds. *Race in the Jury Box: Affirmative Action in Jury Section.* Albany, NY: State University of New York Press, 2003.

Hamilton, Sonya. *What Makes Juries Listen.* New York: Aspen Law, 1984.

Hans, Valerie. *The Jury System: Contemporary Scholarship.* Burlington, VT: Ashgate, 2006.

Hastie, Reid. *Inside the Jury: The Psychology of Juror Decision Making.* New York: Cambridge University Press, 1994.

Hawles, John. *Juries in Colonial America: Two Accounts, 1680-1722.* New York: Arno Press, 1972.

Lesser, Maximus. *The Historical Development of the Jury System.* New York: Gordon Press, 1976.

Moller, Erik T. *Trends in Civil Trial Verdicts Since 1985.* Santa Monica, CA: Rand Corporation, 1996.

Osborn, Albert S. *Mind of the Juror as Judge of the Facts: or the Layman's View of the Law.* Buffalo, NY: W.S. Hein, 1982.

Pabst, William R. *Jury Manual: A Guide for Prospective Jurors.* Berkeley, CA: Metro Publishing, 1985.

Stanley, Jacqueline D. *Juror's Rights.* 2nd ed. Naperville, IL: Sphinx Publishing, 1998.

Starr, V. Hale, and Mark McCormick. *Jury Section.* 4th ed. New York: Aspen Publishers, 2012.

U.S. Courts. "Jury Service." Available at http://www.uscourts. gov/FederalCourts/JuryService.aspx (accessed November 4, 2012).

Vidmar, Hans, and Valerie P. Hans. *American Juries: The Verdict.* Amherst, NY: Prometheus Books, 2007.

Worthington, George. *Inquiry into the Powers of Juries to Decide Incidentally on Questions of Law.* Buffalo, NY: W.S. Hein, 1995.

ORGANIZATIONS

American Association for Justice
777 Sixth Street, NW, Ste. 200
Washington, DC 20001
Phone: (202) 965-3500
Toll Free: (800) 424-2725
URL: http://www.justice.org

Council for Court Excellence
1717 K St., N.W.
Washington, DC 20036
Phone: (202) 785-5917
Fax: (202) 785-5922
URL: http://www.courtexcellence.org/

Fully Informed Jury Association
PO Box 59
Helena, MT 59843
Phone: (406) 793-5500
Fax: (406) 793-5500
URL: http://www.fija.org/

National Center for State Courts
300 Newport Ave.
Willamsburg, VA 23185
Phone: (757) 253-2000
Fax: (757) 220-0449
URL: http://www.ncsonline.org/

Roscoe Pound Institute
1050 31st St., NW
Washington, DC 20007
Phone: (202) 965-3500
Fax: (202) 965-0335
URL: http://www.roscoepound.org

COURTS AND PROCEDURE

PRETRIAL PROCESS AND SETTLEMENTS

Sections within this essay:

- Background
- Pretrial Conferences
- Settlement
- Additional Resources

BACKGROUND

It is a popular misconception that civil lawsuits are ultimately resolved trials. In fact, most lawsuits involving contracts, torts, domestic relations, and other civil matters end with the parties agreeing to a **settlement**. In the federal courts, 98 percent of cases settle and in state courts only about three percent of cases end with a **jury** verdict. The pretrial process that results in a trial, or more likely, a settlement is in most cases the most important phase in **litigation**.

The Federal Rules of Civil Procedure, which were created in 1938, have also served as a model for state rules of civil procedure. These federal and state rules set out how a civil lawsuit commences and how the parties and the judge will address issues involving the **discovery** process that requires the production of documents and witnesses as well as an early inquiry into the legal merits of the lawsuit. At an early stage a judge, **magistrate**, or other judicial officer will convene a pretrial status conference with the lawyers to discuss the case and to rule on any motions. The goals of the conference can be as simple as establishing a timetable for the pretrial process or as

complex as the judge conducting settlement discussions with the parties. If the parties do not settle early in the process, and discovery proceeds, the court will likely schedule an issues conference to have the parties agree on undisputed facts or points of law. If the parties do not settle before the trial date (and they often do just prior to the beginning of trial), the case will proceed to trial before a jury or just the judge.

PRETRIAL CONFERENCES

A civil lawsuit begins with the **plaintiff** filing a complaint in court that alleges an injury and requests damages or equitable relief. The **defendant**, who has been served with a copy of the complaint, has a specified amount of time to file an answer with the court. If the defendant admits liability in the answer, the plaintiff may then file a motion with the court that asks that relief be granted and judgment entered in the case. If the defendant does not file an answer, the plaintiff may then apply to the court for a **default judgment**. Most commonly, the defendant denies liability and the case moves to the next stage of the pretrial process: the **pretrial conference**.

A pretrial conference may be conducted for several purposes. These may include expediting the **disposition** of the case, helping the court establish managerial control over the case and discouraging wasteful pretrial activities. However, at the first pretrial conference the judge is likely more interested in seeing if the parties can settle the matter without the court's intervention. The judge meets with the parties' lawyers (the parties themselves are not present) in what is called a status or early conference. In 28 states, statutes or court rules mandate that certain types of disputes, such as **child custody**, must be referred to alternative dispute resolution. This typically means that the parties must work with a mediator, who is a neutral third party that renders a decision after **hearing** arguments and reviewing the **evidence**. **Arbitration** may also be an option in commercial disputes.

If referral to ADR is not mandated, the judge or magistrate will work with the lawyers on a host of issues at the status conference The judge may wish to formulate and simplify the issues in the case and eliminate frivolous claims or defenses. It is likely the judge will make schedules for the submission of pretrial briefs and motions and make rulings on motions submitted before the conference. Settlement will likely be discussed and the judge will encourage the parties to settle as quickly as possible. However, It is common to set dates for further conferences, where the possibility of settlement will again be discussed. In large, complex cases the judge and legal **counsel** will discuss the consolidation and management of the pretrial process. After the conference, the judge or magistrate will issue an order that reflect the results of the conference. This order will control the future course of the case.

In some jurisdictions the courts have split the pretrial conference into dispositional and trial management conferences. The court schedules a trial management conference to discuss administrative aspects of the case, such as scheduling. The court also schedules a dispositional conference in which the parties may discuss the possibility of a settlement. If no agreement between the parties is forthcoming at the dispositional conference, the case proceeds to trial. The parties are still free to continue negotiating, and they also may request a special pretrial hearing if an issue arises after the conference but prior to trial.

If the parties do not settle and the discovery process is concluded, the court will schedule a pretrial issues conference. The court will press the lawyers to agree to admissions of fact and documents to avoid unnecessary proof at trial and to agreed to undisputed points of law. These agreements are called stipulations. The judge will also ask the parties to identify witnesses and documents. The judge may request that the parties try to settle the case but if this fails, the case will proceed to trial.

SETTLEMENT

Most civil cases end with a settlement agreement. The parties to the lawsuit sign a **contract** that contains the terms of the bargain. For example, in a **medical malpractice** lawsuit, the plaintiff receives money damages for the alleged injury by the defendant. In return, the agreement states that the defendant does not admit to any fault or wrongdoing for the actions in question. In addition, most settlement agreements are confidential. If a party breaches confidentiality, the other party may seek **redress**.

Once the parties settle, they may file a motion asking the court to dismiss the case. This is routinely done. However, in some cases the parties want the court's oversight of the agreement. In this situation the parties file a joint stipulation asking the court to incorporate the settlement terms in a court order. If the court agrees, it gives assurance to the parties that any failure to comply with the terms may result in a request that the court intervene and compel performance.

ADDITIONAL RESOURCES

Kane, Mary Kay. *Civil Procedure in a Nutshell.* 6th ed. Eagan, MN: West, Thomson Reuters, 2007.

ORGANIZATIONS

American Bar Association (ABA)

321 North Clark Street
Chicago, IL 60610
Phone: (312) 988-5000
Toll Free: (800) 285-2221
Fax: (312) 988-6800
URL: http://www.americanbar.org

COURTS AND PROCEDURES

SELECTION OF JUDGES

Sections within this essay:

- Background and History
- Formal and Informal Requirements of Judges
- Selection of Federal Judges
  - Supreme Court, Courts of Appeals, District Courts
  - Chief Justice of the Supreme Court
  - Chief Judges
  - Bankruptcy Judges
  - Federal Magistrate Judges

- State Methods of Judicial Selection
  - Election
  - Appointment and Merit Selection
  - Reelection and Retention

- State-by-State Summary of Judicial Selection

- Additional Resources

BACKGROUND AND HISTORY

The method by which judges are selected in the United States has been the subject of debate that predates the Revolutionary War. The king of Great Britain selected colonial judges but retained considerable power over them. The colonists so resented this power that the Declaration of Independence includes the following statement in reference to injuries that the colonists endured: "He has made Judges dependent on his Will alone, for the tenure of their offices, and the amount and payment of their salaries."

The states initially adopted the appointment method for selecting judges. In the early 1800s, the states of Georgia and Indiana modified their laws so that judges of lower courts were selected by popular election. Other states, including Michigan and Mississippi, also provided for selection by popular election by the 1830s. By the time the Civil War began, 24 of the 34 states elected their judges.

Election of judges lost some of its support after the Civil War. Critics charged that political machines had become responsible for the selection of judges like any other type of politician. Judges earned the reputation of being corrupt and incompetent. To combat this perception, a few states chose to elect judges based on nonpartisan elections where judges were not associated with political parties. The idea behind this option was that the parties could not control the judges, but in reality, the electorate had difficulty making decisions without the party labels attached to the judges.

The methods of judicial selection continued to be debated into the 20th century. Some organizations and individuals began to advocate for a method of selecting judges based on merit. Plans for merit selection of judges included provisions that would ensure that candidates would not be limited to friends of politicians, and that the merit of the prospective judge would be the primary factor in determining who could be a judge. Organizations such as the American Judicature Society and the American Bar Association endorsed such plans.

The method judicial selection varies considerably now from state to state. Methods for retaining judges after their initial term has expired likewise vary among the states.

FORMAL AND INFORMAL REQUIREMENTS OF JUDGES

Formal requirements vary among the states, although many states do not have strict minimum requirements. Neither the U.S. Constitution nor any federal **statute** set forth formal qualifications for federal judges. However, other factors may determine who will earn a seat on a federal bench. Although federal law does not require a federal judge to be an attorney, the vast majority of judges have distinguished themselves professionally as lawyers. This becomes even more important at the intermediate **appellate court** and Supreme Court levels.

Moreover, though certainly not a requirement, judges generally need some record of political activity for two main reasons. First, the prospective judge's service in politics may be rewarded through an appointment to the federal bench. Second, a judge generally needs to have some level of political activity to become noticed by those who select judges in the federal system.

SELECTION OF FEDERAL JUDGES

Supreme Court, Courts of Appeals, District Courts Potential judges for positions on the benches of the U.S. Supreme Court, the courts of appeals and the district courts are nominated by the president and confirmed by the Senate. The president makes nominations after consultation with staff members in the White House and the attorney general's office. Individual members of the Senate and other political operatives may also have a say in the selection of these judges.

Once a judge is nominated, the Federal Bureau of Investigation conducts a routine security check on the nominee. The Senate Judiciary Committee is the body primarily responsible for screening judicial nominees. After conducting hearings on each candidate, the committee forwards its recommendations to the Senate as a whole. The Senate either approves or rejects a recommendation of the Senate Judiciary Committee by a simple majority vote. The decision to approve the judge is a permanent one, for under the Constitution, federal judges serve life terms.

Chief Justice of the United States The process by which the **chief justice** of the Supreme Court is selected is the same as the initial selection of a judge or justice. The president nominates a person to serve as chief justice, the Senate Judiciary Committee reviews the nomination and makes a recommendation, and the Senate as a whole votes whether to accept the recommendation of the Judiciary Committee.

Although most chief justices have previously been associate justices of the Supreme Court, this is not always the case. In 2005, President George W. Bush nominated

John Roberts to be chief justice after Roberts previously served on the D.C. Circuit Court of Appeals. Similarly, Warren Berger, a nominee of President Richard Nixon in 1969, was elevated to the position of chief justice directly from a position on the D.C. Court of Appeals.

Chief Judges Unlike the chief justice of the Supreme Court, a chief judge of a federal court assumes that position through seniority. In order to become a chief judge, a judge must satisfy the following conditions: the judge must be 64 years of age or younger; the judge must have served for at least one year on the bench; and the judge must not have served previously as a chief judge.

Bankruptcy Judges A **bankruptcy** judge serves as a judicial officer of a U.S. district court. Judges of the various courts of appeals appoint bankruptcy judges to serve in the bankruptcy courts within the various circuits. Unlike district court judges, bankruptcy judges do not serve life terms but are rather appointed to serve 14-year terms.

Federal Magistrate Judges Magistrate judges are appointed by a vote of the active judges of a particular district court. These magistrate judges fulfill duties prescribed by statute and also as directed by the district court judges. Full-time magistrate judges serve terms of eight years.

STATE METHODS OF JUDICIAL SELECTION

States vary in their methods of selecting judges, with judges elected in some states and appointed in others. Moreover, some states employ a hybrid system, where judges at one level of court are selected differently than those at another level of court. States also vary in their methods for retaining or reelecting judges.

Election More than half of the states choose judges for at least some of their judges through popular election. Nonpartisan elections are slightly more prevalent than partisan elections. The initial terms of office vary widely from state to state

Appointment and Merit Selection Many states employ nomination commissions to assist the respective governors or legislatures to select their judges. Most of these states use these commissions for initial appointments, though a few states only use them for interim appointments, such as appointments to fill vacancies. In a few states, the governor or legislature makes selections without the aid of nominating commissions.

Reelection and Retention States likewise vary in their approaches when a judge's term expires. States generally follow one of three methods. First, some judges are reelected by popular election. Second, some judges are subject to a retention election, where the judge is the only person listed on a ballot. The question posed in a retention election asks voters whether a judge should be retained. Third, some judges are reappointed to additional terms.

Since the early 2000s, some states have considered changes in how judges are selected and retained. Fears that partisan campaigns funded by special interests would undermine the integrity of the judicial system, led these states to consider ending judicial elections and moving to longer terms and retention elections instead. However, a proposal in Minnesota failed to pass the legislature in 2010 and Nevada voters defeated a **constitutional amendment** that same year that would have selected judges by a merit selection and used a modified retention plan.

STATE-BY-STATE SUMMARY OF JUDICIAL SELECTION

ALABAMA: All judges are selected by partisan elections. The initial term of office is six years. Judges are subsequently reelected to six-year terms.

ALASKA: All judges are chosen through a merit selection process involving a nominating commission. The initial term of office is three years. All judges are subject to retention elections, though subsequent terms vary depending on the level of court.

ARIZONA: Most judges are chosen through a merit selection process involving a nominating commission. The initial term of office is two years. Judges are subject to retention elections, although subsequent terms vary depending on the level of court. Judges for superior courts in counties with populations of less than 250,000 are elected by way of nonpartisan elections to four-year terms. These judges are reelected to four-year terms.

ARKANSAS: All judges are selected by nonpartisan elections. The initial term of office is eight years, except for circuit court judges, who are elected to six-year terms. Judges are subject to reelection.

CALIFORNIA: The governor appoints nominees to the supreme court and courts of appeals to 12-year terms. These judges are subject to retention elections for additional 12-year terms. Superior court judges are elected in nonpartisan elections for six-year terms and may be reelected to additional six-year terms.

COLORADO: All judges are chosen through a merit selection process involving a nominating commission. The initial term of office is two years. All judges are subject to retention elections, though subsequent terms vary depending on the level of court.

CONNECTICUT: All judges are chosen through a merit selection process involving a nominating commission. The initial term of office is eight years. After a commission reviews a judge's performance, the governor nominates the judge for retention, and the state legislature confirms.

DELAWARE: All judges are chosen through a merit selection process involving a nominating commission. The initial term of office is 12 years. An incumbent subsequently reapplies to a nominating commission and competes with other applicants to be renominated by the governor. The state senate confirms the governor's appointment.

DISTRICT OF COLUMBIA: All judges are chosen through a merit selection process involving a nominating commission. The initial term of office is 15 years. A judicial tenure commission reviews each judge's performance six months prior to the expiration of the judge's term of office.

FLORIDA: Judges for the supreme court and district courts of appeal are chosen through a merit selection involving a nominating commission. The initial term of office is one years. Judges are subject to retention elections for six-year terms. Judges for circuit courts are elected by way of nonpartisan elections to six-year terms. These judges are reelected to additional terms.

GEORGIA: All judges are selected by nonpartisan elections. The initial term of office is six years for **appellate** judges and four years for superior court judges. Judges are subsequently reelected to additional terms.

HAWAII: All judges are chosen through a merit selection process involving a nominating commission. The initial term of office is 10 years. A judicial selection commission reappoints judges to additional 10-year terms.

IDAHO: All judges are selected by nonpartisan elections. The initial term of office is six years for appellate judges and four years for district court judges. Judges are subsequently reelected to additional terms.

ILLINOIS: All judges are selected by partisan elections. The initial term of office is 10 years for appellate judges and six years for superior court judges. Judges are subject to retention elections for additional terms.

INDIANA: Appellate judges are chosen through a merit selection process involving a nominating commission for two-year terms. Appellate judges are subject to retention elections for 10-year terms. Circuit and superior court judges are generally selected through partisan election for six-year terms. Judges in some counties, however, are elected in nonpartisan elections.

IOWA: All judges are chosen through a merit selection process involving a nominating commission. The initial term of office is one year. All judges are subject to retention elections, though subsequent terms vary depending on the level of court.

KANSAS: Most judges are chosen through a merit selection process involving a nominating commission. The initial term of office is one year. These judges are subject to retention elections, though subsequent terms vary depending on the level of court. Judges in courts of 14 districts are elected in partisan elections.

KENTUCKY: All judges are elected in nonpartisan elections to eight-year terms. Judges are subsequently reelected to additional terms.

LOUISIANA: All judges are elected in partisan elections. Appellate judges are elected to 10-year terms, while district court judges are elected to six-year terms. Judges are subsequently reelected to additional terms.

MAINE: Judges are appointed by the governor for seven-year terms. Judges are reappointed by the governor, subject to confirmation by the legislature.

MARYLAND: All judges are chosen through a merit selection process involving a nominating commission to one-year terms. Appellate judges are subject to retention elections for subsequent 10-year terms. Circuit court judges are selected in nonpartisan elections.

MASSACHUSETTS: All judges are chosen through a merit selection process involving a nominating commission. Judges serve until they reach the age of 70.

MICHIGAN: Supreme court judges are elected in partisan elections to eight-year terms. Intermediate appellate court judges and circuit court judges are elected in nonpartisan elections to six-year terms. All judges are subsequently reelected to additional terms.

MINNESOTA: All judges are appointed by nonpartisan elections. The initial term of office is six years. Judges are subsequently reelected to additional terms.

MISSISSIPPI: All judges are appointed by nonpartisan elections. The initial term of office is eight years, except for chancery court and circuit court judges, who are elected to four-year terms. Judges are subject to reelection for additional terms.

MISSOURI: Appellate court judges are chosen through a merit selection process involving a nominating commission to one-year terms. These judges are subject to retention elections for 12-year terms. Circuit court judges are elected to six-year terms and are subject to reelection for additional terms.

MONTANA: Judges are elected by nonpartisan elections. Judges are subject to reelection, except that unopposed judges are subject to retention elections.

NEBRASKA: All judges are chosen through a merit selection process involving a nominating commission to three-year terms. Judges are subject to retention elections for six-year terms.

NEVADA: All judges are appointed by nonpartisan elections to six-year terms. Judges are subject to reelection for additional terms.

NEW HAMPSHIRE: All judges are appointed by the governor. Judges serve until they reach the age of 70.

NEW JERSEY: All judges are appointed by the governor to seven-year terms. Judges are reappointed by the governor with the advice and consent of the senate.

NEW MEXICO: All judges are chosen through a merit selection process involving a nominating commission.

NEW YORK: Appellate court judges are chosen through a merit selection involving a nominating commission. Judges on the Court of Appeals serve 14 years, while judges in the Appellate Division of the Supreme Court serve five-year terms. Supreme Court and county court judges are elected in partisan elections.

NORTH CAROLINA: All judges are selected in nonpartisan elections. The initial term of office is eight years, and judges are subject to reelection. Campaigns are publicly financed.

NORTH DAKOTA: All judges are selected in nonpartisan elections. The initial term of office for the supreme court is 10 years, while district court judges are elected to six-year terms. Judges are reelected to additional terms.

OHIO: All judges are selected in partisan elections for six-year terms. Judges are reelected to additional terms.

OKLAHOMA: Appellate court judges are chosen through a merit selection process involving a nominating commission to one-year terms. These judges are subject to retention elections for additional six-year terms. District court judges are selected in nonpartisan elections for four-year terms and are reelected for additional terms.

OREGON: All judges are selected in nonpartisan elections for six year terms. Judges are reelected for additional terms.

PENNSYLVANIA: All judges are selected in partisan elections for 10 year terms. Judges are subject to retention elections for additional ten-year terms.

RHODE ISLAND: All judges are chosen through a merit selection process involving a nominating commission. Judges serve life tenure.

SOUTH CAROLINA: The state employs a 10-member Judicial Merit Selection Commission to screen judicial candidates. This committee recommends candidates to the General Assembly, which appoints judges. Judges are subject to reappointment by the legislature.

SOUTH DAKOTA: Supreme court judges are chosen through a merit selection process involving a nominating commission for a three-year term. These judges are subject to retention elections for eight-year terms. Circuit court judges are selected in nonpartisan elections for eight year terms and are reelected for additional terms.

TENNESSEE: Appellate court judges are chosen through a merit selection process involving a nominating commission. These judges are subject to retention elections for additional eight-year terms. Judges in the chancery courts, criminal courts, and circuit courts are selected in partisan elections for eight-year terms and are reelected for additional terms.

TEXAS: All judges are selected in partisan elections. Appellate judges are elected to six-year terms, while district court judges are elected to four-year terms. Judges are subsequently reelected to additional terms.

UTAH: All judges are chosen through a merit selection process by a nominating committee. Judges are subject to retention elections for additional terms.

VERMONT: All judges are chosen through a merit selection process by a nominating committee for six-year terms. Judges are retained by a vote of the General Assembly for additional six-year terms.

VIRGINIA: All judges are appointed by the legislature. Supreme court justices are selected for 12 years, while lower court judges are selected for eight year terms. The legislature reappoints judges for additional terms.

WASHINGTON: All judges are selected in nonpartisan elections. Appellate court judges are elected to six-year terms, while superior court judges are elected to four-year terms. Judges are reelected for additional terms.

WEST VIRGINIA: All judges are selected through partisan election. Supreme court justices are elected for 12 years, while circuit court judges are selected for eight-year terms. Judges are reelected for additional terms. Elections are publicly financed.

WISCONSIN: All judges are selected through nonpartisan election. Supreme court justices are elected to 10-year terms, while lower court judges are elected to six-year terms. Judges are reelected for additional terms. Elections are publicly financed.

WYOMING: All judges are chosen through a merit selection process by a nominating committee for one-year terms. Judges are subject to retention elections for additional terms.

ADDITIONAL RESOURCES

Epstein, Lee, and Jeffrey A. Segal. *Advice and Consent: The Politics of Judicial Appointments*. New York: Oxford University Press, 2005.

"Judicial Selection in the States." American Judicature Society, 2012. Available at: http://www.judicialselection.us/ (accessed November 2, 2012).

Streb, Matthew J. *Running for Judge: The Rising Political, Financial, and Legal Stakes of Judicial Elections*. New York: New York University Press, 2009.

ORGANIZATIONS

Alliance for Justice

11 Dupont Circle NW, 2d Floor
Washington, DC 20036
Phone: (510) 444-6070
Fax: (510) 444-6078
URL: http://www.allianceforjustice.org

American Judicature Society

2700 University Avenue
Des Moines, IA 50311

Phone: (515) 271-2281
Fax: (515) 279-3090
URL: http://www.ajs.org

Center for Judicial Accountability

Box 69, Gedney Station
White Plains, NY 10605-0069
Phone: (914) 421-1200
Fax: (914) 428-4994
URL: http://www.judgewatch.org

COURTS AND PROCEDURES

SMALL CLAIMS COURTS

Sections within this essay:

- Background
- Anatomy of a Small Claim Action
  - Maximum Dollar Value of a Case
  - Nature of Dispute or Controversy
  - Time Limitations
  - Procedure
- Special Considerations
  - When Individuals Are Sued in Small Claims Court
  - Collecting on a Judgment
  - Small Claims for Small Business Owners
  - Small Claims in U.S. Tax Court
- State Provisions
- Additional Resources

BACKGROUND

Small claims courts are intended to resolve civil disputes involving small amounts of money, without formal rules of **evidence** and long delays. The parties involved may present their own claims or defenses or may be represented by **counsel**. However, in a handful of states, attorneys are prohibited. The cases move quickly through the court dockets, the judges often render their opinions in the same day, and the parties are generally satisfied with the quick resolution of the controversy. However, there is a downside. All small claims courts have "limited jurisdiction" (authority to hear and adjudge a matter) involving not only the dollar amount but also the subject matter of the controversy. In addition, if parties do not understand what they are doing in presenting their claim or defense, they could stand to lose, badly, and there is no going back.

ANATOMY OF A SMALL CLAIM ACTION

Resolving a dispute in small claims court is very much like conducting a mini-trial, although generally less formal. There is a claim and a defense, the presentation of evidence, and a judgment. Rules of procedure vary from state to state, but the overall process is remarkably similar.

Maximum Dollar Value of a Case The maximum dollar value of the dispute or claim varies greatly from state to state. Typically, the maximum amount plaintiffs may be awarded in a judgment ranges from $3,000 in Ohio to $10,000 in Minnesota. If the amount they are asking for in damages is more than the allowable amount in their state's small claims court system, they have two choices: either to either waive their right to any amount above and beyond the maximum allowable, or file their case in the next level of court.

Nature of Dispute or Controversy Small claims courts are mostly intended to resolve minor monetary disputes. A limited number of state small claims courts permit other forms of remedy besides money, for example, evictions or requests for the return of **personal property**. However, individuals generally cannot use small claims courts to file for **divorce**, **guardianship**, **bankruptcy**, name changes, **child custody**, or "injunctive relief" (emergency relief, usually to stop someone from doing something). In many states, they cannot sue for **defamation** (slander or libel) or **false arrest** in small claims court. Finally, they cannot sue the federal government or any of its branches, agencies, or employees in their official capacities in small claims court.

Time Limitations Each state has its own rules regarding how long individuals have to file suit, once they have been harmed or an event occurs that gives rise to a claim. The same time limits ("statutes of limitation") apply to small claims courts as to other courts. Generally, they have at least one year from the injury or event (or its **discovery**, in some cases) to file their suit.

Procedure To start the process, individuals should check with their local court clerk to find out where their small claims complaint should be filed: most states require that they file suit in a small claims court in the county wherein which the party being sued actually resides (or has business headquarters), rather than the one in which the **plaintiff** resides. Alternatively, some courts allow the suit to be filed in the district where the injury or event occurred (where "the cause of action arises").

Generally, the complaint itself may be hand-written or prepared on a special form available from the court itself, with "fill in the blanks" ease-of-completion. If individuals are composing their own complaints, they need to make sure that it contains, at a minimum, the following:

- The plaintiff's complete name and address
- The complete name and address of the party being sued
- The date of the injury or event which gives rise to the plaintiff's claim
- A brief statement of facts relating to the injury or the event, and the role that the party being sued played in it
- The type of harm that was suffered by the plaintiff as a result of it
- The amount of damages or other remedy the plaintiff seeks are asking

Individuals must also check local law to ensure that the party being sued is properly served with the complaint. In many small claims courts, a court clerk will take care of "service of process," but in many states, plaintiffs are responsible.

The court will notify plaintiffs of the date for their trials. Plaintiffs should request from the court clerk any available information that may help them with procedure unless they have retained an attorney. Generally, plaintiffs are allowed to bring witnesses to **testify** in support of their claims. Some courts may accept affidavits (sworn statements) from persons who cannot appear in person; however, since the other side has no opportunity to "cross-examine" an absent witness, most courts will give only minor consideration to affidavits. Plaintiffs' most important witnesses are themselves. Be prepared, be professional, and be brief (but to the point). They need to have extra copies of all documents, not only for the judge, but also for the opposing party. They will most likely be cross-examined not only on their **testimony**, but also and on the substance of any evidence they present.

Generally, there are no juries, and a judge or **magistrate** will decide the case. Often, the judgment is rendered immediately, and placed on the record. In other cases, individuals may receive written word of a decision and judgment within a few days. In some states, they may **appeal** a judgment, but not in all cases. The court is not responsible for collecting any judgment they have been awarded, but they can generally return to court for "post-judgment" proceedings if the other party fails to pay.

SPECIAL CONSIDERATIONS

When Individuals Are Sued in Small Claims Court If individuals have been served with a complaint, it is imperative that they respond to the court within the time indicated. Not only do they have the right to "tell their side of the story" in their defense, but they may also, in some small claims courts, be permitted to "counter-claim." The counter-claim may be related to the original complaint (tending to diminish the complaint's value or truth), or it may be wholly unrelated but still properly raised against the person who has sued them. Defendants must check local procedure for details on the permissibility of counter-claims.

Defendants may raise the defense that they were not properly "served" with court papers according to local rules. They may raise the defense that the time for filing suit against them has expired. They may raise the defense that the person suing them has not stated a viable claim or cause of action. They may raise any other defense that they believe diminishes the value or the existence of the complaint against them.

Finally, individuals being sued need to study carefully the charges against them very carefully. First and foremost, they need to develop any facts that tend to show that they are not liable. Second, they need to develop any facts that tend to diminish or reduce the amount of damages the person claims they have caused. Third, they need to develop any evidence that will support their defense (or counter-claim) and/or that will corroborate their own testimony. Finally, they should practice their presentation: they will want their side of the dispute to be logical, to-the-point, and damaging to the claims against them.

Collecting on a Judgment Before individuals sue, they should ask themselves whether it may cost them more than they may gain. Do the people they want to sue have steady employment, valuable real estate, or other **tangible** assets? In many states, judgments are collectible (with accrued interest) for ten years or more, so individuals may wish to wait, and attach assets of the judgment **debtor** down the road in the future. If individuals want to are suing a **small business** contractor, their state may permit them to file a copy of the judgment with the state licensing board. If the contractor does not post bond or pay it off, the license may be suspended or revoked. Finally, there is a danger that the judgment debtor may file for bankruptcy. Even if plaintiffs are listed as a **creditor**, they may only get pennies on every dollar of their judgment.

Small Claims for Small Business Owners If individuals own a small business, small claims court may be helpful for collecting unpaid bills because owners do not need to go through bill collectors or lawyers, which could substantially reduce their **net** profit. Often the debtor fails to appear in court, and creditors may be entitled to a **default judgment**. Nevertheless, creditors need to be wary of collecting in the future, especially if the judgment debtor is another small business that may not be around in a few years.

Small Claims in U.S. Tax Court If individuals are faced with a dispute involving the U.S. Internal Revenue Service (IRS), the federal Tax Court maintains a special division for small cases. Their case will qualify for the small case division if the disputed amount that the IRS claims they owe for any one tax year is $50,000 or less, including taxes and penalties. A case that qualifies for small claims handling is given an "S" designation. Most tax court cases are settled without a trial.

STATE PROVISIONS

ALABAMA: In Alabama, the Small Claims Division of the District Court hears claims limited to $3,000 or less.

ALASKA: In Alaska, the District Court Civil Division processes small claims that do not exceed $10,000. Each county has a District Court.

ARIZONA: In Arizona, every **Justice of the Peace** Court has a small claims division. Disputes must not exceed $2,500. All cases are heard by judges or **hearing** officers. No attorneys are allowed to represent clients in these cases. Justice Courts share **jurisdiction** with the Superior Court in cases of landlord/tenant disputes where damages are between $5,000 and $10,000. They

can hear matters regarding possession of, but not title to, real property.

ARKANSAS: In Arkansas, the Claims Court is a special civil division of the Municipal Court. Claims are limited to $5,000 or less.

CALIFORNIA: In California, individuals can file as many claims as they wish for up to $10,000 in the Small Claims Court. However, individuals may only file two (2) claims in any calendar year for up to $5,000. However, they cannot sue a guarantor for more than $4,000. A guarantor is one who promises to be responsible for the debt or **default** of another.

COLORADO: In Colorado, the County Court Civil Division processes small claims that do not exceed $7,500. Each county has a District Court. No plaintiff may file more than two claims per month or 18 claims per year in small claims courts.

CONNECTICUT: In Connecticut, the Small Claims Court is a division of the Superior Court and has a maximum jurisdictional amount of $5000. Attorneys are permitted. There are no rights of appeal. The official court form is "JD-CV-40." Individuals should call the Secretary of State at 860-509-6002 to find out if a **defendant** is a corporation and to get the address. There is a $30 filing fee.

DELAWARE: In Delaware, the Justice of the Peace Court handles both civil and criminal cases. Civil cases handled in the Justice of the Peace Court are those involving money debts, property damages, or return of personal property. The amount of damages that may be sought in the Justice of the Peace Court is limited to $15,000.

DISTRICT OF. COLUMBIA: In Washington, D.C, the Small Claims Division of the Superior Court of D.C. hears cases that are only for the recovery of money up to $5,000. The Small Claims Division of the Superior Court of D.C. hears cases that are only for the recovery of money up to $5,000.00, not including interest, attorney fees, and court costs. If both parties to an action agree, a Superior Court judge may settle a case by **arbitration**, regardless of the amount of the claim. DC Code 11-1321,1322; *McCray v. McGee*, 504 A.2d 1128 (App D.C. 1986.)

FLORIDA: In Florida, a County Court civil division handles small claims under $5,000.

GEORGIA: In Georgia, a County Magistrate Small Claims Court handles money claims under $15,000.

Individuals may file a claim in Magistrate Court with or without an attorney. They may have an attorney represent them if they choose at their own expense. The court does not appoint attorneys for civil cases.

HAWAII: In Hawaii, the Small Claims Division of the District Courts may only handle cases for the recovery of money where the amount claimed is no more than $5,000. The Small Claims Division publishes its own procedural rules.

ILLINOIS: In Illinois, the County Circuit Court processes small claims of $10,000 or less. The parties are not required to have lawyers but may choose to have one.

INDIANA: In Indiana, the Small Claims Division of the Superior Court hears claims limited to $3,000 or less ($6,000 in Marion and Allen Counties).

IOWA: In Iowa, the Small Claims Division of the Superior Court hears claims limited to $5,000 or less.

KANSAS: In Kansas, the District Court hears small claims actions. Amounts at issue are limited to $4.000.

KENTUCKY: In Kentucky, the Small Claims Division of the District Court hears cases involving small claims under $1,500.

LOUISIANA: In Louisiana, the City Court hears small claims actions. Some **eviction** cases are heard in small claims court, if the rent at issue is sufficiently small. Amounts at issue are limited to $5,000 ($2,000 for movable property).

MAINE: In Maine, the Small Claims Court is a special civil division of the District Court. Claims are limited to $6,000 or less.

MARYLAND: Maryland does not have a specific small claims court, but the District Court has exclusive jurisdiction for claims involving less than $25,000. No formal pleadings are required for claims under $5,000.

MASSACHUSETTS: In Massachusetts, small claims are heard in every District Court, in every Housing Court, and at the Boston Municipal Court. Small claim actions are limited to disputes under $7,000.

MICHIGAN: In Michigan, individuals can sue for up to $3,000 in the Small Claims Division of the District Court. Michigan does not allow attorneys in small claims court. Decisions are final and cannot be appealed. Filing fees are $17.00 for claims up to $600, and $32.00 for claims from $600 to $3,000.

MINNESOTA: In Minnesota, the Small Claims Court is part of the District Court. Claims may not exceed $10,000.

MISSISSIPPI: In Mississippi, individuals may sue in small claims court for up to $3,500.

MISSOURI: In Missouri, civil claims for $5,000 or less may be filed in Small Claims Court.

MONTANA: In Montana, the Justice Court hears small claims actions of $7,000 or less.

NEBRASKA: In Nebraska, small claims court is limited to civil (non-criminal) actions involving disputes over amounts of money owed, damage to property, or seeking the return of personal property. Judgments in small claims court may not exceed $7,500.

NEVADA: In Nevada, the Small Claims Division of the County Court hears small claims actions of $5,500 or less.

NEW HAMPSHIRE: In New Hampshire, Small Claims Courts are divisions of District Courts. A small claim action may not exceed $7,500. Attorneys are permitted.

NEW JERSEY: In New Jersey, small claim cases are heard in the Special Civil Part of the Civil Division of the Superior Court. These cases are for less than $3,000.

NEW MEXICO: In New Mexico, the County Magistrate Court is authorized to hear cases that do not exceed $10,000.

NEW YORK: In New York City, the City, District, and Justice Courts in the state have Small Claims Parts that are authorized to hear cases that do not exceed $5,000.

NORTH CAROLINA: In North Carolina, the County District Court is authorized to hear cases that do not exceed $5,000.

NORTH DAKOTA: In North Dakota, the District Court is authorized to hear small claims cases that do not exceed $10,000.

OHIO: In Ohio, civil claims for $3,000 or less may be filed in Small Claims Court.

OKLAHOMA: In Oklahoma, the District Court small claims division handles cases that do not exceed $6,000.

OREGON: In Oregon, the Small Claims Department of the Justice Court processes small claim actions involving disputes under $7,500.

PENNSYLVANIA: In Pennsylvania, District Justice Courts hear claims that do not exceed $12,000.

RHODE ISLAND: In Rhode Island, the small claims courts handle cases that do not exceed $2,500.

SOUTH CAROLINA: In South Carolina, the Magistrate Court processes small claim actions involving disputes under $7,500.

SOUTH DAKOTA: In South Dakota, the small claims court is authorized to hear cases for $12,000 or less.

TENNESSEE: In Tennessee, the Court of General Sessions hears small claims actions involving disputes under $25,000.

TEXAS: In Texas, a Justice Court handles small claims under $10,000.

UTAH: In Utah, the District Court processes small claim actions involving disputes under $10,000.

VERMONT: In Vermont, the small claims courts handle cases that do not exceed $5,000.

VIRGINIA: In Virginia, the small claims divisions of the general district courts hear disputes of $5,000 or less.

WASHINGTON: In Washington State, the District Court Civil Division processes small claims in amounts not exceeding $5,000.

WEST VIRGINIA: In West Virginia, the Magistrates Courts handle small claims with $5,000 or less in dispute.

WISCONSIN: In Wisconsin, the District Courts handle small claims of $10,000 or less.

WYOMING: In Wyoming, the Justice of the Peace Courts hear small claims of up to $6,000.

ADDITIONAL RESOURCES

Mann, Charlie. *How to Win Your Case In Small Claims Court Without a Lawyer.* Ocala, FL: Atlantic Publishing, 2009.

Warner, Ralph. *Everybody's Guide to Small Claims Court.* Berkeley, CA: Nolo Press, 2012.

COURTS AND PROCEDURES

STATE COURTS AND PROCEDURES

Sections within this essay:

- Background
- Function and Scope of State Courts
- The Concept of Jurisdiction
- General Structure of State Court Systems
- Judges and Administrative Staff
- State Provisions
- Additional Resources

BACKGROUND

The judicial powers of individual states are generally vested in various courts created by state constitution or (less frequently) state **statute**. Within the **boundaries** of each state and coexisting with state courts are numerous federal district and/or appellate courts that function independently. Also coexisting within state boundaries are various administrative tribunals that also hear and decide legal matters, such as workers' compensation boards, professional licensing boards, and state administrative tribunals. Yet, there are often local, district, and/or municipal courts within the community. At first blush, it may appear overwhelming and confusing to consider what legal matter may be decided in which forum. However, for the most part, each of the above courts has its own separate function and role in applying the laws to the controversies brought before it and administering justice to all.

FUNCTION AND SCOPE OF STATE COURTS

To understand the function and scope of state courts, it is necessary to consider them in relation to the federal court system expressly created in Article III of the U.S. Constitution. Article III also establishes the type of cases that federal courts may hear and decide (federal "jurisdiction").

Article VII of the Constitution declares that "This Constitution, and the Laws of the United States . . . and all Treaties made . . . under the Authority of the United States, shall be the supreme Law of the Land; and the Judges in every State shall be bound thereby, any Thing in the Constitution or Laws of any State to the Contrary notwithstanding." Later in the Constitution, the Tenth Amendment provides that "powers not delegated to the United States by the Constitution, nor prohibited by it to the States, are reserved to the States respectively, or to the people."

The ultimate effect these provisions have upon state courts is to reserve to them the right to hear and decide any legal matter not expressly reserved for the exclusive **jurisdiction** of federal courts (such as lawsuits between states). This matter mostly involves the "adjudication" of controversies concerning state laws, which impact the daily lives of citizens in a much greater manner than federal laws. State courts may also rule upon certain issues concerning federal law and the federal Constitution.

State legislatures are therefore free to create—and state courts are free to enforce—any law, regulation, or rule that does not conflict with or abridge the guarantees of the federal Constitution (or the state's own constitution). The wide variance, from state to state, of both structure and procedure within the court systems is precisely due to the preservation of those independent powers to the states by the U.S. Constitution.

THE CONCEPT OF JURISDICTION

A court's general authority to hear and/or "adjudicate" a legal matter is referred to as its "jurisdiction." In the United States, jurisdiction is granted to a court or court system by statute or by constitution. A court is competent to hear and decide only those cases whose subject matter fits within the court's jurisdiction. A legal decision made by a court that did not have proper jurisdiction is deemed void and non-binding upon the litigants.

Jurisdiction may be referred to as "exclusive," "original," concurrent, general, or limited. Federal court jurisdiction may be "exclusive" over certain matters or parties (to the exclusion of any other forum) or may be "concurrent" and shared with state courts. In matters where both federal and state courts have concurrent jurisdiction, state courts may hear federal law claims (e.g., violations of **civil rights**), and parties bringing suit may choose the forum. However, when a **plaintiff** raises both state and federal claims in a state court, the **defendant** may be able to "remove" the case to a federal court.

GENERAL STRUCTURE OF STATE COURT SYSTEMS

The general workhorse of a state court system is the trial court. This is the lowest level of court and is usually the forum in which a case or lawsuit originates. It may be a court of general jurisdiction, such as a circuit or superior court, or it may be a court of special or limited jurisdiction, such as a **probate**, juvenile, traffic, or family court. Some states handle "small claims" in separate courts, while others handle such claims in special divisions of the general trial courts. This is also true for probate and juvenile matters. Although someone may broadly refer to "juvenile court" or "small claims court," he or she may actually be referring to the juvenile or small claims "division" of the general circuit court.

- Probate courts primarily handle the administration of estates and the probating of **wills**. In many states, probate courts also handle such matters as **competency** hearings, applications for guardianships and adoptions, among others. In a minority of jurisdictions, probate courts may be referred to as surrogate's courts.

- Family courts hear cases involving (mostly) **custody** and **child support**, neglect and abuse cases, and, sometimes, juvenile crime or truancy. Most family courts do not handle divorces, which are generally handled by the courts of general jurisdiction.

- Traffic courts handle civil infractions and violations involving motor vehicles, petitions for reinstatement of driving privileges, and related matters. Some may handle minor (**misdemeanor**) criminal offenses related to motor vehicle-related violations. Most traffic courts do not handle automobile accident cases (as between the parties involved in an accident).

- Housing courts, or landlord-tenant courts, handle exactly that. In many jurisdictions, landlords must choose to file their cases in one of two courts, depending upon whether they seek **eviction**, injunction, etc. (landlord-tenant court), or seek money damages (**small claims court**). Other jurisdictions handle all landlord-tenant related matters in a single court.

- Small-claims courts handle all civil matters in which the dollar amount in controversy does not exceed a certain amount. If a party seeks damages in an amount greater than the jurisdictional limit of the small claims court, the party must either waive his or her right to the exceeding amount or re-file the case in a court with greater jurisdiction. The maximum jurisdictional limit of small claims courts varies greatly from state to state but mostly falls in the range of $3,000 to $7,500.

- Juvenile courts handle truancy and criminal offenses of minors. The maximum age of the minor varies from state to state but generally is either 16 or 18 years. Older juveniles who have committed serious crimes may be "bound over" to a court of general jurisdiction for determination of whether they should be tried as adults.

Importantly, states may have separate courts for criminal and civil matters. Most often, a trial court of general jurisdiction will handle both, but often on separate dockets. Many local or district courts will have limited jurisdiction for criminal matters, such as misdemeanors only. In such circumstances, a person charged with a **felony** may be arraigned in the district court and then "bound over" to the next level court (having proper jurisdiction) for criminal trial. Again, this varies greatly from state to state.

Every state has its own system to handle appeals from the trial courts. Most states have a three-tiered court system in which there are intermediate "appellate" courts that review **jury** verdicts or the opinions of trial court judges (on a limited basis and under strict criteria). These appellate courts may or may not be distinguished by separate buildings or courthouses. Often, what is referred to as a "court of appeals" is in reality a panel of justices who merely convene to hear and decide cases at the appellate level.

In a minority of states, trial court decisions receive only one appellate review at the level of the state's highest court or the court "of last resort" (generally referred to as the state's "supreme court"). Once a state's highest court has decided a matter, the only available **appeal** is to the U.S. Supreme Court. However, the Supreme Court is generally deferential to state supreme courts, and only reviews matters in very limited circumstances, such as where a state's highest court has ruled that a federal statute or treaty is invalid or unconstitutional, or where the highest courts of two or more states have ruled differently on federal issues. When a state's highest court has decided a matter that involves both federal and state issues, the U.S. Supreme Court will nonetheless refuse to review the matter if the non-federal question is decisive in the case.

JUDGES AND ADMINISTRATIVE STAFF

Whereas most federal judges are appointed to their positions, the majority of state trial court judges are elected to their positions by the general populace. Appellate (especially supreme court) justices are often appointed by state governors or legislatures but may also be elected by voters.

What does vary greatly from state to state is whether judicial elections involve partisan politics. In some states, party politics play a direct role in judgeships; in other states, a judicial candidate's party affiliation is treated as private data (such as religious affiliation) not disclosed in campaign profiles. States also vary greatly in the extent to which they permit judicial candidates to "advertise" their candidacy and/or raise campaign funds.

State courts employ a large number of support staff, who are usually public employees paid by taxpayer funds. Generally, a judge's staff may include one or more private assistants, law clerks, court reporters, bailiffs and other court officers, and court clerks. The most important administrative office of the courthouse is that of the court clerk. This is the office that stamps and dates all lawsuits filed, serves process (or verifies the parties' service of process), posts legal notices, subpoenas witnesses, **summons** and prepares juries, and sends sheriffs or other court officials out to serve writs of **execution** to collect on unpaid judgments.

STATE PROVISIONS

ALABAMA: Alabama's courts of limited jurisdiction are probate, county, justice, and recorder's courts. Its trial court of general jurisdiction is the "circuit court." Alabama has separate appellate courts for criminal and civil appeals and one supreme court.

ALASKA: Alaska has **magistrate** and district courts of limited jurisdiction. Its general trial courts are called "superior courts." Its court of last resort is its state supreme court.

ARIZONA: Courts of limited jurisdiction include "justice courts," municipal courts, and magistrate offices. The superior courts are the trial courts of general jurisdiction. Arizona has a court of appeals and a supreme court.

ARKANSAS: Arkansas operates county, municipal, common pleas, justice, and police courts of limited jurisdiction. It maintains the **common law** general jurisdiction courts of Chancery and Probate and has a single supreme court of last resort.

CALIFORNIA: California's circuit courts are the courts of general jurisdiction. It also maintains municipal and justice courts of limited jurisdiction. California has both a court of appeals and a supreme court.

COLORADO: Colorado maintains limited jurisdiction courts, including superior, juvenile, probate, county, and municipal courts. The superior court is the court of general jurisdiction. Colorado has both a court of appeals and a supreme court.

CONNECTICUT: Connecticut has juvenile, common pleas, and probate courts of limited jurisdiction. The district court is the court of general jurisdiction. Appeals go directly to the state supreme court.

DELAWARE: Delaware maintains limited jurisdictions courts for family, municipal, and justice. Its general jurisdiction court is the superior court, and appeals are made directly to the state supreme court.

FLORIDA: Florida's court of general jurisdiction is its circuit court. It also maintains county courts of limited jurisdiction. It has a district court of appeals and a state supreme court.

GEORGIA: Georgia has probate, civil justice, criminal justice, and small claims courts of limited jurisdiction. Its superior courts are the courts of general jurisdiction. The state maintains both an appeals court and a supreme court.

HAWAII: Hawaii utilizes district courts of limited jurisdiction and circuit courts of general jurisdiction. Appeals go directly to the Hawaii Supreme Court.

IDAHO: The district court is the court of general jurisdiction, but within that court is the magistrate's court of limited jurisdiction. Idaho's appeals go directly to the state supreme court.

ILLINOIS: Illinois circuit courts are the courts of general jurisdiction. The state maintains both a court of appeals and a state supreme court.

INDIANA: The Indiana Code establishes county, municipal, magistrate, probate, juvenile, and **justice of the peace** courts of limited jurisdiction. Indiana has circuit civil and criminal courts of general jurisdiction, and has both a court of appeals and a state supreme court.

IOWA: The court system includes the district court as the court of general jurisdiction, a court of appeals, and the state supreme court.

KANSAS: Kansas has probate, municipal, county, and juvenile courts of limited jurisdiction. Its district courts are courts of general jurisdiction, and appeals are made to the court of appeals and state supreme court.

KENTUCKY: Kentucky has county, justice, and police courts of limited jurisdiction. It has a claims court for claims against the state or its agencies. Kentucky's courts of general jurisdiction are its district and circuit courts, and the state maintains both a court of appeals and a state supreme court.

LOUISIANA: Louisiana has city, juvenile, mayor's justice, traffic, family, municipal, and parish courts of limited jurisdiction. It maintains both a court of appeals and a supreme court. http://www.legis.state.la.us.

MAINE: Maine has limited jurisdiction probate and district courts. Its superior courts are courts of general jurisdiction, and the court of last resort is called the "supreme judicial court."

MARYLAND: Maryland has orphans and district courts of limited jurisdiction. Its "circuit of counties" courts are the courts of general jurisdiction, and its court of appeals and court of special appeals are the courts of last resort.

MASSACHUSETTS: The state's courts of general jurisdiction are its superior courts. The state has land, probate, municipal, district, juvenile, and housing courts of limited jurisdiction. The court of last resort is the state's supreme judicial court, but the state also has a court of appeals.

MICHIGAN: Michigan's Constitution creates its courts, which include a court of appeals and a state supreme court. Michigan's courts of general jurisdiction are its circuit courts, generally at the county level. It maintains a few "recorder's courts" for criminal cases. Limited jurisdiction courts include those for common pleas, municipal, district, and probate.

MINNESOTA: Minnesota has district courts of general jurisdiction, a court of appeals and a supreme court.

MISSISSIPPI: The state maintains family, county, city police, and justice courts of limited jurisdiction, has chancery and circuit courts of general jurisdiction, and a state supreme court.

MISSOURI: The state has probate, courts of criminal correction, magistrate, and municipal courts of limited jurisdiction. Its circuit courts are courts of general jurisdiction, and the state has both a court of appeals and a state supreme court.

MONTANA: The state maintains municipal, justice, city, and workman's compensation courts of special or limited jurisdiction. The district court is the state's court of general jurisdiction, and maintains a state supreme court.

NEBRASKA: Nebraska has county, municipal, juvenile, and workers' compensation courts of limited jurisdiction. Its district court is the state's court of general jurisdiction, and it maintains a state supreme court.

NEVADA: Nevada has municipal and justice courts of limited jurisdiction. Its district court is the state's court of general jurisdiction, and it maintains a state supreme court.

NEW HAMPSHIRE: New Hampshire has probate, district, and municipal courts of limited jurisdiction. Its superior court is the state's court of general jurisdiction, and it maintains a state supreme court.

NEW JERSEY: New Jersey maintains municipal, county district, juvenile and domestic relations courts of limited jurisdiction. Its superior court is the state's court of general jurisdiction, and it maintains a state supreme court.

NEW MEXICO: New Mexico maintains probate, municipal, small claims, and magistrate courts of limited jurisdiction, as well as a court of appeals and a state supreme court.

NEW YORK: New York refers to its highest **appellate court** as its "superior court," and its courts of general jurisdiction as "supreme courts," mostly at the county level. New York City maintains several courts of limited jurisdiction for civil and criminal dockets, and the state also maintains a court of appeals.

NORTH CAROLINA: The state maintains its superior courts as courts of general jurisdiction. It has a court of appeals and a state supreme court.

NORTH DAKOTA: Its district court is the court of general jurisdiction. The county courts are courts of limited jurisdiction. North Dakota has a state supreme court.

OHIO: Ohio's Courts of Common Pleas are the courts of general jurisdiction. It also maintains municipal, county, and courts of claims are courts of limited jurisdiction. It maintains a court of appeals and the court of last resort is the state supreme court.

OKLAHOMA: See Title 20 of the Oklahoma Statutes. The district court is the court of general jurisdiction. The state maintains municipal courts of limited jurisdiction. It has separate courts of appeal for criminal and civil cases and has a supreme court of last resort.

OREGON: Oregon maintains district, county, justice, and municipal courts of limited jurisdiction. Its court of general jurisdiction is the circuit court. Oregon maintains a court of appeals and a state supreme court.

PENNSYLVANIA: Pennsylvania's Courts of Common Pleas are the courts of general jurisdiction. It also maintains municipal, traffic, and justice of the peace courts of limited jurisdiction. Its appellate courts are the superior court and the commonwealth court, and the court of last resort is the state supreme court.

RHODE ISLAND: The state maintains district, probate, family and police courts of limited jurisdiction. The court of general jurisdiction is the superior court, and the state has a supreme court.

SOUTH CAROLINA: The circuit court is the court of general jurisdiction. South Carolina maintains county, probate, magistrate, city recorders, and family courts of limited jurisdiction. The state's court of last resort is the state supreme court.

TENNESSEE: The courts of general jurisdiction include chancery court, circuit court, criminal court, and law equity court. There are limited jurisdiction courts for municipal, juvenile, domestic relations cases. Tennessee has separate courts of appeals for criminal and civil cases, and a state supreme court.

TEXAS: Texas maintains criminal district, domestic relations, juvenile, probate, and county courts of limited jurisdiction. Its court of general jurisdiction is the district court. There are separate courts of appeal for civil and criminal cases, and the state has a supreme court.

UTAH: The state has juvenile, city, and justice courts of limited jurisdiction. The district court is the court of general jurisdiction, and the state has a supreme court.

VERMONT: Vermont maintains district and probate courts of limited jurisdiction, while its superior courts are the courts of general jurisdiction. Vermont has a state supreme court.

VIRGINIA: Virginia has general district, juvenile, and domestic relations courts of limited jurisdiction. Its circuit courts are the courts of general jurisdiction, and the state supreme court is the court of last resort.

WASHINGTON: The superior court is the court of general jurisdiction. It maintains district and municipal courts of limited jurisdiction. The state has a court of appeals and a state supreme court.

WEST VIRGINIA: West Virginia has police courts of limited jurisdiction and circuit courts of general jurisdiction. The court of last resort is the supreme court of appeals.

WISCONSIN: The state maintains municipal courts of limited jurisdiction. The county circuit courts are the courts of general jurisdiction. Appeals are taken to the court of appeals and the state supreme court.

WYOMING: Wyoming maintains justice and municipal courts of limited jurisdiction. Its court of general jurisdiction is the state district court, and it has a state supreme court.

ADDITIONAL RESOURCES

Bergman, Paul, and Sara J. Berman. *Represent Yourself in Court.* Berkeley, CA: Nolo Press, 2010.

Schubert, Frank August, Mark G. Yudof, et al. *Introduction to Law and the Legal System.* 10th ed. Belmont, CA: Wadsworth Publishing, 2011.

ORGANIZATIONS

American Bar Association (ABA)

321 North Clark Street
Chicago, IL 60610
Phone: (312) 988-5000
Toll Free: (800) 285-2221
Fax: (312) 988-6800
URL: http://www.americanbar.org

CRIMINAL LAW

APPEALS

Sections within this essay:

- What Is an Appeal?
- The Basis for an Appeal
- Where Are Appeals Filed?
- The Number of Appeals
- Reversing a Conviction
- Writs
- Writs of Habeas Corpus
- The U.S. Supreme Court
- Costs
- Additional Resources

WHAT IS AN APPEAL?

An appeal is a request from a party in a lower court proceeding to a higher (appellate) court asking the **appellate court** to review and change the decision of the lower court. If a **defendant** in a criminal case is found guilty of a charge or charges, the defendant has the right to appeal that **conviction** or the punishment or **sentencing**. It is common for convicted defendants to appeal their convictions.

The defendant in a criminal trial may appeal after she or he is convicted at trial. In fact, it is very common for convicted defendants to appeal their convictions and/or sentencing. Usually only the defendant in a criminal trial may appeal. The **prosecutor** may not appeal if the defendant is acquitted (found "not guilty")

at trial. The prosecutor may not put the same defendant on trial for the same charge with the same **evidence**. This kind of retrial is known as "double jeopardy." **Double jeopardy** is expressly prohibited under the **Fifth Amendment** of the United States Constitution. However, prior to or during a criminal trial, a prosecutor may be able to appeal certain rulings, such as when a judge has ordered that some evidence be "suppressed" Appeals that take place in the midst of a trial are called interlocutory appeals. In most cases, appeals can be very complicated; the appellate court tends to enforce technical rules for proceeding with an appeal.

In criminal cases, a federal court may review a conviction after all of the usual appeals have been exhausted. A convicted defendant may request one of these reviews in a petition for a **writ** of habeas corpus—Latin for "you have the body." Only a very small percentage of these petitions are granted. In death penalty cases, these proceedings have become highly controversial. Since a judicial or prosecutor's error in a death penalty case has such extreme consequences, courts review petitions for writs of **habeas corpus** very carefully.

The procedures of appellate courts consist of the rules and practices by which appellate courts review trial court judgments. Federal appellate courts follow the Federal Rules of Appellate Procedure. State appellate courts follow their own state rules of appellate procedure. In both state and federal jurisdictions, appeals are commonly limited to "final judgments." There are exceptions to the "final judgment rule," including instances of plain or fundamental error by the trial court, questions of subject-matter **jurisdiction** of the trial court, or constitutional questions.

The issues under review in appellate court centers on written briefs prepared by the parties. These complex documents list the questions for the appellate court and enumerate the legal authorities and arguments in support of each party's position. Most appellate courts do not hear oral arguments unless there is a specific request by the parties. Few jurisdictions allow for oral argument as a matter of course. Where it is allowed, oral argument is intended to clarify legal issues presented in the briefs and lawyers are constrained to keep their oral presentations strictly to the issues on appeal. Ordinarily, oral arguments are subjected to a strictly enforced time limit. This time limit can be extended only upon the discretion of the court.

THE BASIS FOR AN APPEAL

There is an institutional preference for a trial court's rulings and findings in the U.S. judicial system. Thus, for an appellate court to hear an appeal from a lower court the aggrieved party must demonstrate to the appellate court that an error was made at the trial level. The error must have been substantial. "Harmless errors," or those unlikely to make a substantial impact on the result at trial, are not grounds for reversing the judgment of a lower court. Any error, defect, irregularity, or variance, which does not affect substantial rights, shall be disregarded.

Assuming that there was no harmless error, there are two basic grounds for appeal:

1. The lower court made a serious error of law (plain error),

2. The weight of the evidence does not support the verdict.

Plain error is an error or defect that affects the defendant's substantial rights, even though the parties did not bring this error or defect to the judge's attention during trial. Of course, some plain errors or defects affecting substantial rights may be noticed although they were not brought to the attention of the court. In any event, plain error will form a basis for an appeal of a criminal conviction.

It is much more difficult to prevail in an appeal based on the alleged insufficient **weight of evidence**. Although appellate courts review the transcripts of trials, they almost never hear actual **testimony** of witnesses, view the presentation of evidence, or hear the parties' opening and closing arguments. Consequently, they are not in the best position to assess the weight of evidence in many cases. For this reason they place much confidence in trial courts' decisions on issues of facts. In an appeal based on an alleged insufficient weight of evidence to support a verdict, the error or misjudgment of evidence must truly be egregious for a defendant to expect to prevail on appeal.

WHERE ARE APPEALS FILED?

Usually, individuals may only file an appeal with the next higher court in the same system in which the case originated. For example, if persons want to file an appeal from a decision in a state trial court, normally they may file their appeals only to the state intermediate appellate court. The party who loses on appeal may next appeal to the next higher court in the system, usually the state supreme court. The state's highest court is almost always the final word on matters of that state's law.

THE NUMBER OF APPEALS

Generally, the final judgment of a lower court can be appealed to the next higher court one time only. Thus, the total number of appeals depends on how many courts are "superior" to the court that made the contested decision, and sometimes what the next higher court decides the appeal's basis. In states with large populations, it is common to find three or even four levels of courts, while in less populous states there may be only two. There are important differences in the rules, time limits, costs, and procedures depending on whether the case is in Federal court or state court. Also, each state has different rules. Finally, even within a single state one may find that there are different rules for appeals depend on the court in which the case originated.

Filing a Notice of Appeal is the first step in the appeal process. An appellate court cannot adjudicate a case if the notice is not properly filed in a timely manner. The notice must be filed within a definite time. Time limits vary, but 30 days in civil appeals is common and up to 60 days in criminal appeals. The period within which to file usually starts on the date a final judgment in the lower court is filed.

REVERSING A CONVICTION

As noted above, appeals judges generally defer to trial court findings, particularly findings of fact (as opposed to findings of law). Appellate courts resist overruling trial court judgments and provide trial courts with wide discretion in the conduct of trials. "Prefect trials" are not guaranteed. In most cases, an appellate court will overturn a guilty verdict only if the trial court made an error of law that patently or significantly contributed to the trial's outcome. In other words, a trial judge's error will not lead to a reversal of a conviction as long as the error can reasonably be considered harmless. Most errors are deemed "harmless," and there are consequently few reversals of convictions. There are, of course, some types of errors that are so egregious that they are presumed harmful, such as the use of a coerced **confession**.

Sentencing is a different matter. When a trial court exercises its discretion in sentencing, an appellate court will rarely interfere. In some cases, however, the law specifies a particular sentence. If the judge gets it wrong, the appellate court will usually send the case back for resentencing.

WRITS

A writ is a document or an order from a higher court that directs a lower court or a government official to take some kind of action. In any given trial, a defendant may appeal a case to the next higher appellate body only once, but the defendant may file multiple writs in that same trial. Defendants may seek several types of writs from appellate judges directed at the trial court or at a lower appellate court. Most writs require advanced legal knowledge and involve detailed procedures. Defendants contemplating making an application for a writ are wise to consult **counsel**.

Courts view writs as extraordinary remedies. This means that is, courts permit them only when a criminal defendant has no other adequate remedy, such as an appeal. In other words, a defendant may seek a writ to contest an issue that the defendant could not raise in a regular appeal. This action generally applies when the alleged error or mistake is not apparent in the record of the case. Generally, courts will adjudicate writs more quickly than regular appeals. If a defendant feels wronged by actions of the trial judge, he or she may need to take a writ to obtain an early review by a higher court. Some of the most common grounds for seeking a writ include:

- the defense failed to make a timely objection at the time of the alleged error or injustice

- a final judgment has not yet been entered in the trial court, but the party seeking the writ requires immediate relief to prevent further injustice or unnecessary expense

- urgency

- the defendant has already lodged an unsuccessful appeal. Merely filing a writ that repeats the same unsuccessful grounds or arguments of an appeal is a frivolous writ and an appellate court will dismiss those writs immediately

- when an attorney has failed to investigate a possible defense

WRITS OF HABEAS CORPUS

In many countries, authorities may take citizens and incarcerate them for months or years without charging them. Those imprisoned have no legal means by which they can protest or challenge the **imprisonment**. The

framers of the U.S. Constitution wanted to prohibit this kind of occurrence in the new United States. Therefore, they included a clause in the Constitution that allows courts to issue writs of habeas corpus.

Defendants who are considering challenging the legal basis of their imprisonment—or the conditions in which they are being imprisoned—may seek relief from a court by filing an application for a "writ of habeas corpus." A writ of habeas corpus (which literally means to "produce the body") is a court order to a person or agency holding someone in **custody** to deliver the imprisoned individual to the court issuing the order. The U.S. Constitution specifically prohibits the government from suspending proceedings for writs of habeas corpus except under extraordinary circumstances, such as during times of war. However, Congress and the U.S. Supreme Court have placed many procedural hurdles in the way of inmates who seek habeas relief.

Convicted defendants have a number of options for challenging guilty verdicts and/or for seeking remedy for violations of **constitutional rights**, including motions, appeals, and writs. Note that convicted defendants must first have sought relief through the available state courts before they are permitted to seek relief in federal courts. Thus, defendants should consult lawyers to determine which remedies are available to them.

THE U.S. SUPREME COURT

The U.S. Supreme Court is the "highest" court in the land. It has authority to hear appeals in nearly all cases decided in the federal court system. It can also hear appeals that involve a "federal question," such as an issue involving a federal **statute** or an issue arising under the U.S. Constitution. The Supreme Court will generally hear cases that originate in state court only after a decision by that state's highest court. Despite the great number of criminal cases that are appealed, very few criminal cases are ever heard by the Supreme Court. Fewer than 100 cases are actually heard and decided by the Supreme Court in any given year, so the chance that a criminal case reaches the court is slim at best.

COSTS

Surprisingly, many appeals can be very inexpensive. If the appeal is focused on only one clearly defined issue of law and all sides have prepared good briefs, it may cost very little to appeal. On the other hand, appeals, such as claims that the verdict was against the weight of the evidence, typically require both the printing of the entire trial record and extensive analysis and briefing. Such appeals are relatively expensive as they can require large amounts of lawyers' time. Additionally, they often turn out to be less successful.

ADDITIONAL RESOURCES

Cammack, Mark. *Advanced Criminal Procedure in a Nutshell.* 2d ed. Eagan, MN: West, Thomson Reuters, 2006.

Federal Court of Appeals Manual: Local Rules. Eagan, MN: West, Thomson Reuters, 2012.

Israel, Jerold H., and Wayne R. LaFave. *Criminal Procedure, Constitutional Limitations in a Nutshell.* 7th ed. Eagan, MN: West, Thomson Reuters, 2006.

Wiener, Frederick Bernays. *Briefing and Arguing Federal Appeals: A New Edition of "Effective Appellate Advocacy."* Clark, NJ: Lawbook Exchange, 2001.

ORGANIZATIONS

Criminal Justice Section, American Bar Association (ABA)

740 15th Street, NW, 10th Floor
Washington, DC 20005-1009

Phone: (202) 662-1500
Fax: (202) 662-1501
URL: http://www.abanet.org/crimjust/contact.html

National Association of Criminal Defense Lawyers (NACDL)

1660 L St. NW, 12th Fl.
Washington, DC 20036
Phone: (202) 872-8600
Fax: (202) 872-8690
Email: assist@nacdl.org
URL: http://www.nacdl.org

CRIMINAL LAW

BAIL AND BAIL BOND AGENTS

Sections within this essay:

- Background
- The Bail Reform Act of 1984
  - Detention Hearing Procedures
  - Material Witnesses, Bonds on Appeal or Pending Sentencing
- Posting Bail
- Bail Bond Agents
- Additional Resources

BACKGROUND

Bail is an amount of money that a criminal **defendant** may be ordered to pay before being released from **custody** pending trial. Its purpose is to ensure a defendant's return at subsequent trial proceedings. Bail is typically determined during a defendant's first appearance in court. A judge or other court officer sets the amount and conditions of bail. At a bail **hearing**, a judge has three options:

- Release the defendant on his or her own recognizance or upon an unsecured appearance bond
- Deny bail to the accused
- Set terms of bail, including the amount of bail and any special conditions for release

In common usage, bail typically refers to criminal proceedings. However, in rare instances bail may be imposed in civil cases. Civil bail is used to directly or indirectly secure payment of a debt or to secure a performance of a civil duty. For example, bail may be employed in a civil case to **arrest** someone to prevent them from fleeing to avoid **litigation**, or it may be used to prevent an unlawful concealment or disposal of assets. The amount of bail set will be based on the probable amount of damages the **plaintiff** could collect. Sometimes the deposit may be used to pay the judgment to a plaintiff.

Bail law came to the U.S. through English tradition and laws. Even before the adoption of the U.S. Constitution and **Bill of Rights**, a judiciary act in 1789 guaranteed a right to bail in all noncapital cases. For a person charged with a capital offense (where death is a possible punishment), bail was discretionary, depending upon the seriousness of the offense. The Eighth Amendment to the U.S. Constitution provides, "excessive bail shall not be required." The U.S. Supreme Court has ruled that the Constitution permits holding a defendant without bail pending a criminal trial. No absolute right to bail exists.

Bail is not meant to act as pre-trial punishment, or as a fine. Modern bail laws reflect an intentional emphasis on non-monetary methods to ensure a defendant's appearance at trial. This is meant to avoid **discrimination** against poor defendants.

Bail may or may not be required in **misdemeanor** cases, depending upon the circumstances and seriousness of the offense. More serious misdemeanor cases and felonies often require a bail determination. Bail may come into play at three stages of a criminal proceeding:

- During the pretrial period
- Pending imposition or **execution** of sentence
- Pending **appeal** of a **conviction** or sentence

If bail is not required, a defendant may be released on his or her own recognizance. Releasing someone on personal recognizance means that the person has promised to show up for trial or other court proceedings, without posting a bond. Release on personal recognizance may be appropriate when a person has ties to the community and has lawful and steady employment. Family status is also taken into account. Before release, a defendant must sign a document promising to appear. Failure to abide by the terms of release on personal recognizance may result in revocation of the privilege, or further criminal charges, including immediate arrest. A defendant released on personal recognizance may be required to abide by certain rules. For example, the defendant may be forbidden from traveling outside of the court's **jurisdiction**, or may be forbidden from contacting the victim or the victim's family.

A court may also impose an unsecured appearance bond on a criminal defendant. A bond amount is set, but the defendant is not required to post any money. If the defendant fails to appear at subsequent proceedings, or violates any terms of the bond, he or she will be required to pay the full amount of the bond.

According to the Department of Justice's Bureau of Justice statistics, for all defendants charged with state felonies in May 2006 in the 75 most populous counties in the country:

- 58 percent were released prior to the **disposition** of their case
- 42 percent were detained, including 5 percent who were denied bail
- Of those released, 26 percent were released on their own recognizance
- 25 percent were released on a commercial surety bond
- About a third of those released failed to appear for a scheduled appearance, were rearrested for a new offense, or committed a violation that resulted in revocation of the pretrial release

THE BAIL REFORM ACT OF 1984

The Bail Reform Act of 1984, found in Title 18 of the United States Code, replaced the Bail Reform Act of 1964. The 1964 act did not allow judges in noncapital cases to consider the danger a defendant posed to the community. In some cases, this resulted in defendants who committed further violent crimes after being released on personal recognizance. The 1984 law closed this loophole, and allowed for detention where necessary for the safety of the community. In addition to the federal statutes governing bail in federal criminal cases, every state has its own bail laws.

Pursuant to federal **statute**, a detention hearing is required in cases involving violence, including any offense where the maximum sentence is life **imprisonment** or death, or for certain drug offenses where a maximum sentence of ten years or more is prescribed. Moreover, a hearing is required for certain defendants who have multiple convictions. A hearing will also be held if it appears to involve a serious risk that the defendant will flee, or where it appears that the defendant will obstruct or attempt to obstruct justice or tamper with prospective witnesses or jurors. The detention hearing must be held promptly, preferably at the time of the defendant's first appearance in court. If bail is denied, the court must issue a written order with findings of fact and a statement of the reasons for the detention.

Detention Hearing Procedures To determine what is necessary to ensure a defendant's appearance at trial, a judge or **magistrate** examines the nature and circumstances of the charges, with particular attention to whether the offense involves violence or narcotic drugs. The court may inquire into the nature and value of any property that might be offered as **collateral**. The court also examines the weight of the **evidence** against the defendant, whether the person was on **parole** or **probation** at the time of the present arrest, the nature and seriousness of danger to others in the community, and evidence of the defendant's character. When examining the history and character of a person, the court may look at:

- Physical and mental condition
- Financial resources
- Family ties
- History relating to drug and alcohol abuse
- Criminal history
- Record concerning appearance at court proceedings
- Length of residence in the community

Where a defendant poses a threat to the safety of the community, he or she may be held without bail. In other situations, federal law typically requires that a defendant in a federal criminal case be released on personal recognizance or upon execution of an unsecured appearance bond. Released defendants must not commit any crimes during the period of release. However, if a court determines that personal recognizance or an unsecured appearance bond will not reasonably assure the defendant's appearance, or determines that the safety of a person or the community is endangered, a defendant may be released upon conditions. Federal law delineates a number of conditions that may be imposed. Defendants may be required to:

- Limit travel
- Maintain or seek employment
- Undergo drug and alcohol testing

- Undergo medical, psychiatric, or psychological treatment
- Maintain or commence an educational program
- Comply with a curfew
- Refrain from excessive use of alcohol or any use of narcotic drugs
- Remain in the custody of a designated person
- Comply with periodic check-ins with authorities
- Refrain from possession of a firearm
- Refrain from contact with crime victim or others designated by the court
- Execute a bond agreement with the court or a solvent surety in an amount as is reasonably necessary to ensure the defendant's appearance
- Agree to other reasonable conditions the court may impose to ensure a defendant's appearance

Both the defendant and the government may appeal an adverse bail decision. The scope of review is limited, however. The only question for an **appellate court** is whether the trial court abused its discretion.

Material Witnesses, Bonds on Appeal or Pending Sentencing In rare instances, persons not charged with a crime may be detained, or ordered to post bond. A material witness is subject to arrest and federal release and detention laws it is shown that a **subpoena** is not sufficient to secure the person's presence in court.

A defendant who was released prior to trial on his or her own recognizance may, if convicted, be required to post a bond during the appeal process or pending **sentencing**. A court may also determine detention is required. Release is generally appropriate in cases where no sentence of imprisonment is likely, if **acquittal** or a motion for a new trial is likely, or where the court finds by clear and convincing evidence that a person is not likely to flee or pose a danger.

POSTING BAIL

Once a court has set the amount of bail, that amount, or a specified percentage, is paid to the court. Payment may be made in cash or in an approved cash substitute, such as a money order or cashier's check. A defendant may post his or her own bail, or may find another person to do so. Once bail has been posted, whether by the defendant or someone else, the court will issue a document or a court order that shows the defendant may be released.

If another person posts bond on the behalf of a defendant, the bail bond becomes a three-party **contract** between the defendant, the court, and the surety. The surety is the party who, at the request of a defendant, becomes responsible for securing the defendant's appearance in court. People who may act as a surety for a criminal bond include licensed bond agents and friends and relatives of the defendant. As part of the contract, the defendant promises to appear at future proceedings. The surety promises to **forfeit** to the court the amount of the bond if the defendant fails to appear as required.

The **penalty** for failure to appear as required after release is a fine, imprisonment, or both. Federal law provides that any term of imprisonment for failure to appear must run consecutively to any other criminal sentence. However, if uncontrollable circumstances caused the failure to appear, and if the person immediately appeared once it was possible to do so, the person will have a valid defense to the failure to appear charge.

Once a case is over and all obligations have been fulfilled, the bond money is typically returned. Sometimes administrative costs are deducted.

BAIL BOND AGENTS

Many defendants lack the financial means to post their own bail. To secure release, they may contract a commercial bond agent to act as surety for the bond. The agent posts bail after collecting a nonrefundable fee (typically 10 to 20 percent) from the defendant or family or friends. Assuming the defendant does not have money to give the agent as security, an agent will obtain other collateral, such as jewelry, **securities**, or electronics. In return, the bail bond agent agrees to pay the remaining amount to the court if the defendant fails to appear.

There are approximately 14,000 bond agents in the United States. Most states require a bond agent to be licensed. However, the license typically is not specifically for bonding purpose, but for property and **casualty** insurance. To obtain the license, the applicant must meet certain educational requirements. This allows a potential bail bond agent to be appointed by an insurance company to write bail **bonds**. The defendant pays the agent for writing the bond. In turn, the agent pays the insurance company a premium. The bail agent is responsible for bond payment in the event a defendant fails to appear and cannot be located.

To ensure a defendant's appearance in court, a bail bond agent may require a defendant to check in by telephone or in person, or may require the defendant to be monitored in some other way. In extreme cases, a bail bondsperson may place a guard on the defendant. A bail bond agent is not obligated to post bail if the agent concludes a defendant is not likely to fulfill the obligations of the bond.

Illinois, Kentucky, Oregon and Wisconsin have outlawed the practice of posting bond for profit. In those jurisdictions, a defendant may be allowed to satisfy the requirements of the bond by posting 10 percent of the bail amount with the court. Some other jurisdictions, such as Maine and Nebraska, allow commercial bail on a limited basis.

ADDITIONAL RESOURCES

"How Courts Work." Division for Public Education, American Bar Association, 2012. Available at http://www.americanbar. org/groups/public_education/resources/law_related_ education_network/how_courts_work/bail.html (accessed November 3, 2010).

ORGANIZATIONS

Professional Bail Agents of the United States
1301 Pennsylvania Ave., N.W., Suite 925
Washington, DC 20004
Phone: (202) 783-4120
URL: http://www.pbus.com/

CRIMINAL LAW

CRIMES

BACKGROUND

Criminal offenses are classified according to their seriousness. For crimes against property, the gravity of a crime is generally commensurate with the value of the property taken or damaged, thus the greater the property value, the more serious the crime. For crimes against persons, the same proportionality principle applies to bodily injury inflicted upon individuals, thus the greater the injury, the more serious the crime. However, a host of other factors can influence the seriousness of a criminal offense. These factors include whether the **defendant** had a prior criminal record; whether the defendant committed the crime with cruelty, **malice**, intent, or in reckless disregard of another person's safety; and whether the victim was a member of a protected class, such as minors, minorities, senior citizens, the handicapped, among others. Thus, a less serious crime can be made more serious by the presence of these additional factors, and a more serious crime can be made less serious by their absence.

Three categories of criminal offenses were known at **common law**, **treason**, **felony**, and **misdemeanor**, with treason being the most serious type of crime and misdemeanor being the least serious. The common law distinction between treason and felony was particularly important in England because a traitor's lands were forfeited to the Crown. Under a doctrine known as "corruption of the blood," the traitor also lost the right to **inherit** property from relatives, while the relatives lost the right to inherit from the traitor. U.S. law has never endorsed corruption of the blood as a criminal **penalty**, and so treason was dropped as a separate classification of crime in the colonies.

In the 2010s every U.S. **jurisdiction** retained the distinction between felony level criminal offenses and misdemeanor level offenses. However, most jurisdictions had added a third-tier of criminal offense, typically called an **infraction** or a petty offense. Although the definitions of all three classes differ from one jurisdiction to the next, they do share some common characteristics.

FELONIES, MISDEMEANORS, AND INFRACTIONS

The power to define a crime and classify it as a felony, misdemeanor, or infraction rests solely with the legislature at the federal level (see *U.S. v. Hudson,* 7 Cranch 32, 11 U.S. 32, 3 L.Ed. 259 [U.S. 1812]). Federal courts do not have the power to punish any act that is not forbidden by federal **statute**. Most crimes made punishable by federal law are set forth in Title 18 U.S.C. sections 1 et seq.

In the eighteenth century U.S. courts possessed the power to define crimes and establish classifications for criminal offenses. These judicially-created offenses were known as common law crimes. By the early nineteenth

---

Offense composition of the inmate population in Federal Bureau of Prison facilities, by year, from fiscal years 2006 through 2011

Offense	Fiscal year					
	2006	2007	2008	2009	2010	2011
Drugs	91,690	95,321	94,456	96,415	96,094	97,164
Weapons/explosives	27,036	28,901	30,256	31,454	32,188	33,136
Immigration	18,992	19,862	20,165	22,298	21,767	24,800
Fraud/bribery/extortion	8,426	9,268	10,229	10,493	10,930	11,462
Sex offenses	3,824	4,754	5,989	7,308	8,610	9,653
Robbery	9,428	9,099	8,965	8,712	8,493	8,289
Burglary/larceny	6,381	6,417	6,499	6,694	6,747	7,136
Homicide/aggravated assault	4,895	4,942	4,940	4,894	4,900	5,114
Court/corrections	2,174	2,209	2,192	2,180	2,183	2,200
Miscellaneous[1]	2,374	2,298	2,305	2,281	2,064	2,006
Counterfeiting/embezzlement	1,066	1,016	1,017	945	928	948
Continuing criminal enterprise[2]	430	416	412	390	374	364
National security	108	103	105	98	97	95
Total offender population	**176,824**	**184,606**	**187,530**	**194,162**	**195,375**	**202,367**

Note: Sentencing information is not available for all inmates, for example, pretrial inmates whose information has not been entered into the data system.
[1]Miscellaneous offenses include criminal civil rights violations; food and drug violations; economic espionage; destruction of an energy facility; District of Columbia offenses, such as driving while intoxicated, malicious mischief, and contributing to the delinquency of a minor; and violations of fish and game laws.
[2]Continuing criminal enterprise refers to sentencing under the Racketeer Influenced and Corrupt Organizations Act (RICO) Act (codified at 18 U.S.C. § 1961), for example, drug kingpins.

SOURCE: U.S. Government Accountability Office analysis of Bureau of Prisons data, September 2012. Available at http://www.gao.gov/assets/650/648123.pdf

---

TABLE BY PREMEDIAGLOBAL. ©2013 CENGAGE LEARNING.

---

century, federal common law crimes were under increasing attack as violating the mandate of the separation of powers established by the U.S. Constitution. Article I of the Constitution gives Congress the power to make law, while Article III gives the judiciary the power to interpret and apply it. Thus, the constitutionally limited role of federal courts precludes them from defining crimes or creating classifications for criminal offenses.

Most states have also abolished common law crimes. In these states the legislature is given the primary and often sole responsibility for defining illegal behavior (the **executive branch** in a few states plays a limited lawmaking function via **executive orders** and administrative agency rules and regulations). In the minority of states that still recognize common law crimes, judges generally are not permitted to create new common law crimes from the bench. Instead, all 50 states and the District of Columbia rely on their penal code to shape the nature and scope of their jurisdiction's criminal laws, and when a penal code designates an offense as a felony, misdemeanor, or infraction, that designation is normally deemed conclusive by the courts.

Felonies Felonies are deemed the most serious class of offense throughout the United States. Many jurisdictions separate felonies into their own distinct classes so that a repeat offender convicted of committing a felony in a

heinous fashion receives a more severe punishment than a first-time offender convicted of committing a felony in a comparatively less hateful, cruel, or injurious fashion. Depending on the circumstances surrounding the crime, felonies are generally punishable by a fine, **imprisonment** for more than a year, or both. At common law felonies were crimes that typically involved moral turpitude, or offenses that violated the moral standards of the community. In the 2010s many crimes classified as felonies were still considered offensive to the moral standards in most American communities. They included **terrorism**, treason, **arson**, murder, rape, robbery, **burglary**, and **kidnapping**, among others.

In many felonies classified under the penal code are defined not only by the length of **incarceration** but also by the place of incarceration. For example, crimes that are punishable by incarceration in a state prison are deemed felonies in a number of states, while crimes that are punishable only by incarceration in a local jail are deemed misdemeanors. For crimes that may be punishable by incarceration in either a local jail or a state prison, the crime will normally be classified according to where the defendant actually serves the sentence.

Misdemeanors A misdemeanor, a criminal offense that is less serious than a felony and more serious than an infraction, is generally punishable by a fine or incarceration in a local jail, or both. Many jurisdictions separate misdemeanors into three classes, high or gross misdemeanors, ordinary misdemeanors, and petty misdemeanors. Petty misdemeanors usually contemplate a jail sentence of less than six months and a fine of $500 or less. The punishment prescribed for gross misdemeanors is greater than that prescribed for ordinary misdemeanors and less than that prescribed for felonies, and some states even define a gross misdemeanor as "any crime that is not a felony or a misdemeanor" (see MN ST § 609.02). Legislatures sometimes use such broad definitions to provide prosecutors and judges with flexibility in charging and **sentencing** for criminal conduct that calls for a punishment combining a fine normally assessed for a misdemeanor and an incarceration period normally given for a felony.

Infractions An infraction, sometimes called a petty offense, is the violation of an administrative regulation, an **ordinance**, a municipal code, and, in some jurisdictions, a state or local traffic rule. In many states an infraction is not considered a criminal offense and thus not punishable by incarceration. Instead, such jurisdictions treat infractions as civil offenses. Even in jurisdictions that treat infractions as criminal offenses, incarceration is not usually contemplated as punishment, and when it is, confinement is limited to serving time in a local jail. Like misdemeanors, infractions are often defined in very broad language. For example, one state provides that any offense that is defined "without either designation as a felony or a misdemeanor or specification of the class or penalty is a petty offense" (see AZ ST § 13-602).

Substantive and Procedural Implications of a Crime's Classification The category under which a crime is classified can make a difference in both substantive and procedural criminal law. Substantive criminal law defines the elements of many crimes in reference to whether they were committed in furtherance of a felony. Burglary, for example, requires proof that the defendant broke into another person's dwelling with the intent to commit a felony. If a defendant convinces a **jury** that he only had the intent to steal a misdemeanor's worth of property after breaking into the victim's home, the jury cannot return a **conviction** for burglary.

The substantive consequences for being convicted of a felony are also more far reaching than the consequences for other types of crimes. One convicted of a felony is disqualified from holding public office in many jurisdictions. Felons may also lose their right to vote or serve on a jury. In several states attorneys convicted of a felony lose their right to practice law. Misdemeanants with no felony record rarely face such serious consequences.

Criminal procedure sets forth different rules that govern courts, defendants, and law enforcement agents depending on the level of offense charged. The Fourth Amendment to the U.S. Constitution allows police officers to make warrantless arrests of suspected felons in public areas so long as the arresting officer possesses **probable cause** that the suspect committed the crime. Officers may make warrantless arrests of suspected misdemeanants only if the crime is committed in the officer's presence. Police officers do not have the authority to shoot an alleged misdemeanant while attempting to make an **arrest**, unless the shots are fired in **self-defense**. Officers generally have more authority to use deadly force when effectuating the arrest of a **felon**.

Most criminal courts have limited jurisdiction over the kinds of cases they can hear. A court with jurisdiction over only misdemeanors has no power to try a defendant charged with a felony. Defendants may be charged by information, such as a formal written instrument setting forth the criminal accusations against a defendant, when they are **accused** of a misdemeanor, whereas many jurisdictions require that defendants be charged by a **grand jury** when they are accused of a felony.

Defendants charged with capital felony offenses, such as offenses for which the death penalty might be imposed as a sentence are entitled to have their cases heard by a jury of twelve persons who must unanimously agree as to the issue of guilt before returning a conviction. Defendants charged with non-capital felonies and misdemeanors may have their cases heard by as few as six jurors who, depending on the jurisdiction and the size of the jury actually impaneled, may return a conviction on a less than unanimous vote. The right to trial by jury is generally not afforded to defendants charged only with infractions or petty offenses. Defendants charged with felonies or misdemeanors that actually result in confinement to a jail or prison are entitled to the advice and representation of a court appointed **counsel** (see USCA. Const.Amend.6). Defendants charged with infractions or misdemeanors that do not result in incarceration are not entitled to court appointed counsel.

Accused felons must generally be present during their trials, while accused misdemeanants may agree to waive their right to be present. The **testimony** of defendants and witnesses may be impeached on the ground of a former felony conviction. But a misdemeanor is not considered sufficiently serious to be grounds for **impeachment** in most jurisdictions. Because of all the additional procedural safeguards afforded to defendants charged with more serious criminal offenses, defendants must usually consent to any prosecution effort to downgrade a criminal offense to a lower level at which fewer safeguards are offered.

ADDITIONAL RESOURCES

American Jurisprudence. 2d ed. Eagan, MN: Thomson/
West, 2006.

Black's Law Dictionary. 9th ed. Eagan, MN: West, Thomson
Reuters, 2009.

Gale Encyclopedia of American Law. 3rd ed. Detroit: Gale,
Cengage Learning, 2011.

Hall, Kermit L., James W. Ely Jr., and Joel B. Grossman, eds.
Oxford Companion to the Supreme Court. 2d ed. New York:
Oxford University Press, 2005.

LaFave, Wayne R., Jerold H. Israel, and Nancy J. King,
eds. *Criminal Procedure*. 5th ed. Eagan, MN: Thomson/
West, 2009.

ORGANIZATIONS

American Civil Liberties Union (ACLU)

125 Broad St., 18th Fl.
New York, NY 10004
Phone: (212) 549-2500
Email: info@aclu.org
URL: http://www.aclu.org/

Association of Federal Defense Attorneys

8530 Wilshire Blvd, Suite 404
Beverly Hills, CA 90211
Phone: (714) 836-6031
Fax: (310) 397-1001
Email: AFDA2@AOL.com
URL: http://www.afda.org

Center for Human Rights and Constitutional Law

256 S. Occidental Blvd.
Los Angeles, CA 90057
Phone: (213) 388-8693
Fax: (213) 386-9484
Email: mail@centerforhumanrights.org
URL: http://www.centerforhumanrights.org

National District Attorneys Association (NDAA)

99 Canal Center Plaza
Alexandria, VA 22314
Phone: (703) 549-9222
Fax: (703) 836-3195
URL: http://www.ndaa.org

CRIMINAL LAW

CRIMINAL PROCEDURE

Sections within this essay:

BACKGROUND

Criminal procedure is the body of state and federal constitutional provisions, statutes, court rules, and other laws governing the administration of justice in criminal cases. The term encompasses procedures that the government must follow during the entire course of a criminal case, ranging from the initial investigation of an individual suspected of criminal activity, through **arrest**, **arraignment**, **plea negotiations**, pre-trial hearings, trial, post-trial motions, pre-sentence interviews, **sentencing**, appeals, and **probation** and **parole** proceedings. The rules of criminal procedure may also apply after a **defendant** has been unconditionally released following an **acquittal**. For example, the **Double Jeopardy** Clause of the **Fifth Amendment** to the U.S. Constitution may be invoked by individuals who are facing prosecution on charges for which they have already been found not guilty.

Criminal procedures are designed to safeguard both the innocent and the guilty from indiscriminate application of substantive criminal laws, such as laws prohibiting rape, murder, **arson**, and theft, among others, and from arbitrary or abusive treatment at the hands of law enforcement, the courts, or other members of the justice system. At the federal level these safeguards are primarily set forth in three places: the Federal Rules of Criminal Procedure, Title 18 of the United States Code sections 3001 et seq., and Amendments IV, V, VI, and VIII to the U.S. Constitution. The rules and statutes reference each other, and both are designed to enforce and delineate in greater detail the rights established by the federal Constitution.

The Fourth Amendment prohibits the government from conducting unreasonable searches and seizures while investigating criminal activity and building a case against a particular suspect. The Fifth Amendment prohibits the government from compelling individuals to **incriminate** themselves, from denying individuals **due process of law**, from subjecting individuals to multiple punishments or prosecutions for a single offense, and from being prosecuted in federal court without first being indicted by a **grand jury**. The Sixth Amendment guarantees defendants the right to a speedy and public trial by an **impartial jury**, the right to be informed of all charges against them, the right to confront adverse witnesses, the right to **subpoena** favorable witnesses, and the right to an attorney. The Eighth Amendment prohibits the government from requiring excessive **bail** to be posted for pre-trial release, from imposing excessive fines, and from inflicting cruel and unusual punishments.

The freedoms safeguarded by the Fourth, Fifth, Sixth, and Eighth Amendments have two lives, one static and the other organic. Their static life exists in the original language of the amendments as they were ratified by the states in 1791, while their organic life exists in the growing body of state and federal **case law** interpreting their text, applying it, and defining its scope as different factual situations come before the courts. All of the rights protected by these four amendments, except the right to **indictment** by a grand jury, have been made applicable to state criminal proceedings via the doctrine of incorporation. Under this doctrine U.S. Supreme Court has said that no state may deny any citizen a fundamental liberty without violating the Fourteenth Amendment's Equal Protection and Due Process Clauses. The fundamental liberties guaranteed to criminal defendants by the Fourth, Fifth, Sixth, and Eighth Amendments are best understood in the context of the criminal proceeding during which they are normally triggered.

THE FOURTH AMENDMENT AND CRIMINAL PROCEDURES GOVERNING INVESTIGATION, ARREST, AND SEARCH AND SEIZURE

The Text of the Fourth Amendment The right of the people to be secure in their persons, houses, papers, and effects, against unreasonable searches and seizures, shall not be violated, and no Warrants shall issue, but upon **probable cause**, supported by Oath or affirmation, and particularly describing the place to be searched, and the persons or things to be seized.

Case Law Interpreting the Fourth Amendment Law enforcement officers are entrusted with the power to conduct investigations, make arrests, perform searches and seizures of persons and their belongings, and occasionally use lethal force in the line of duty. However, this power must be exercised within the **boundaries** of the law, and when police officers exceed those boundaries they jeopardize the admissibility of any **evidence** collected for prosecution. By and large, the Fourth Amendment and the case law interpreting it establish these boundaries.

The safeguards enumerated by the Fourth Amendment only apply against governmental action, namely action taken by a governmental official or at the direction of a governmental official. Thus, actions taken by state or federal law enforcement officials or private persons working with law enforcement officials will be subject to the strictures of the Fourth Amendment. Bugging, **wiretapping**, and other related surveillance activity performed by purely private citizens, such as private investigators, will not receive Fourth Amendment protection.

Individuals will only receive Fourth Amendment protection if they can demonstrate that they have a reasonable expectation of **privacy** in the place to be searched or the thing to be seized. The U.S. Supreme Court explained that what "a person knowingly exposes to the public, even in his own home or office, is not a subject of Fourth Amendment protection . . . . But what he seeks to preserve as private, even in an area accessible to the public, may be constitutionally protected" (see *Katz v. United States*, 389 U.S. 347, 88 S. Ct. 507, 19 L. Ed. 576 [1976]). In general the Court has said that individuals enjoy a reasonable expectation of privacy in their own bodies, **personal property**, homes, and business offices. Individuals also enjoy a qualified expectation of privacy in their automobiles.

Once it has been established that an individual possesses a reasonable expectation of privacy in a place to be searched or a thing to be seized, the Fourth Amendment's protections take hold, and the question then becomes what are the nature of those protections. Searches and seizures performed without a **warrant** (a court order approving a search, a seizure, or an arrest) based on probable cause are presumptively invalid. However, in certain situations the Supreme Court has ruled that warrantless searches may be reasonable under the circumstances and thus pass constitutional muster.

Police officers need no justification to stop someone on a public street and ask questions, and individuals are completely entitled to refuse to answer any such questions and go about their business. However, the Fourth Amendment prohibits police officers from detaining pedestrians and conducting any kind of search of their clothing without first possessing a reasonable and articulable suspicion that the pedestrians are engaged in criminal activity (see *Terry v. Ohio*, 392 U.S. 1, 88 S. Ct. 1868, 21 L. Ed. 889 [1968]). Police may not even request that a pedestrian produce identification without first meeting this standard. Similarly, police may not stop motorists without first having a reasonable and articulable suspicion that the driver has violated a traffic law. If a police officer has satisfied this standard in stopping a motorist, the officer may conduct a search of the vehicle's interior, including the glove compartment, but not the trunk unless the officer has probable cause to believe that it contains **contraband** or the instrumentalities of criminal activity. The Supreme Court has extended the power of police to **frisk** an individual in a stopped vehicle if there is reasonable suspicion to believe the individual is armed and dangerous (see *Arizona v. Johnson*, 555 U.S. 323, 129 S. Ct. 781; 172 L. Ed. 2d 694 [2009]).

The Fourth Amendment also expresses a preference for arrests to be based on a warrant. However, warrantless arrests can be made when the circumstances make it reasonable to do so. For example, no warrant is required for a **felony** arrest in a public place, even if the arresting officer had ample time to procure a warrant, so long as the officer possessed probable cause that the suspect committed the crime. Felony arrests in places not open to the public generally do require a warrant, unless the officer is in "hot pursuit" of a fleeing **felon** (see *Warden v. Hayden*, 387 U.S. 294, 87 S.Ct. 1642, 18 L.Ed.2d 782 [1967]). The Fourth Amendment also allows warrantless arrests for misdemeanors committed in an officer's presence.

The exceptions to the Fourth Amendment's warrant requirement are based on the court's reluctance to unduly impede the job of law enforcement officials. Courts attempt to strike a balance between the practical realities of daily police work and the privacy and freedom interests of the public. Requiring police officers to take the time to obtain an arrest or **search warrant** could result in the destruction of evidence, the disappearance of suspects, or both.

When an officer does seek a search or **arrest warrant**, the officer must present evidence to a neutral judge or **magistrate** sufficient to establish probable cause that a crime has been committed. The Supreme Court has said that probable cause exists when the facts within an officer's knowledge provide a reasonably trustworthy basis for a man of reasonable caution to believe that an offense has been committed or is about to be committed. Courts will deny requests when the warrant fails to describe in particularized detail the person to be arrested or the place to be searched. The evidence upon which a warrant is based need not be ultimately **admissible** at trial, but it cannot be based on knowingly or intentionally false statements or statements made in reckless disregard of the truth. Courts will usually invalidate searches, seizures, and arrests made pursuant to a defective warrant. Inaccuracies found in a warrant due to ordinary **negligence** will not typically jeopardize a warrant's validity.

THE FIFTH AMENDMENT AND CRIMINAL PROCEDURES GOVERNING POST-ARREST AND PRE-ARRAIGNMENT PROCEEDINGS

The Text of the Fifth Amendment No person shall be held to answer for a capital, or otherwise infamous crime, unless on a presentment or indictment of a Grand Jury, except in cases arising in the land or naval forces, or in the **Militia**, when in actual service in time of War or public danger; nor shall any person be subject for the same offence to be twice put in **jeopardy** of **life or limb**; nor shall be compelled in any criminal case to be a witness against himself, nor be deprived of life, liberty, or property, without due process of law; nor shall private property be taken for public use, without just compensation.

Case Law Interpreting the Fifth Amendment Once a suspect has been arrested or taken into **custody**, the rights guaranteed by the Fifth Amendment are triggered. In *Miranda v. Arizona*, 384 U.S. 436, 86 S. Ct. 1602, 16 L. Ed.2d 694 (1966), the Supreme Court held that under the Fifth Amendment's Self-Incrimination Clause, statements made to the police during custodial interrogation will later be deemed **inadmissible** at trial unless the suspect is first told that he or she has: (1) the right to remain silent; (2) the right to consult an attorney before being questioned by the police; (3) the right to have an attorney present during police questioning; (4) the right to a court appointed attorney if the defendant cannot afford to hire a private attorney; and (5) the right to be informed that any statements they do make can and will be used against them at trial.

If a suspect makes a request to consult with an attorney, the interrogation must immediately cease or any subsequent statements made without the attorney present will be ruled inadmissible. However, a suspect's request for an attorney will not prevent law enforcement from compelling the suspect to participate in a **lineup** of persons for the victim to review or from having the suspect's picture taken and shown to the victim in a photo array. In addition, a suspect may not raise the Self-Incrimination Clause as an objection to giving a writing sample, providing a voice exemplar, or taking a blood test. Applying a Fourth Amendment analysis, the Supreme Court has said that the Self-Incrimination Clause does not apply to these situations because individuals have no privacy interest in their physical characteristics.

The purpose of the right against self-incrimination is to deter the government from compelling a **confession** through force, **coercion**, or deception. Confessions produced by these methods are not only considered uncivilized by modern standards, but they are also considered unreliable, since they are often involuntary or unwitting or the result of the accused's desire to avoid further browbeating, instead of being the product of candor or a desire to confess.

The Fifth Amendment guarantees three other rights that relate to criminal procedure. First, every defendant has the right to be indicted by a grand jury before standing trial in federal court. As noted above, the Grand Jury Clause has not been made applicable to the states, and many states allow prosecutions based on information or complaint, which are written instruments prepared by the **prosecutor**. In federal criminal proceedings and in states that use the grand jury system, grand juries are normally comprised of between 16 and 23 persons from the district in which the crime occurred, and they can return an indictment against the defendant by majority vote.

Second, the Fifth Amendment prohibits the government from subjecting individuals to multiple prosecutions or multiple punishments for a single offense. This prohibition is called the right against double jeopardy. Defendants may bring motions pursuant to the Double Jeopardy Clause either before a trial to prevent a subsequent prosecution or punishment or after trial to overturn a subsequent prosecution or punishment.

Third, the Fifth Amendment guarantees every defendant the right to due process. The Due Process Clause requires that all criminal proceedings be conducted in a fair manner by an impartial judge who will allow **accused** individuals to fully present their defense, and proceedings that produce arbitrary or capricious results will be overturned as unconstitutional. The right to due process applies to every phase of criminal proceedings from pre-trial questioning to post-trial hearings and appeals, and its application to some of these proceedings will be discussed below.

THE SIXTH AMENDMENT AND CRIMINAL PROCEDURES GOVERNING POST-ARRAIGNMENT AND PRE-SENTENCING PROCEEDINGS

The Text of the Sixth Amendment In all criminal prosecutions, the accused shall enjoy the right to a speedy and public trial, by an impartial jury of the State and district wherein the crime shall have been committed, which district shall have been previously ascertained by law, and to be informed of the nature and cause of the **accusation**; to be confronted with the witnesses against him; to have compulsory process for obtaining witnesses in his favor, and to have the Assistance of **Counsel** for his defense.

Case Law Interpreting the Sixth Amendment Once a suspect has been arrested, the rights created by the Sixth Amendment take hold. The Sixth Amendment right to a speedy trial arises after a defendant has been arrested, indicted, or otherwise formally accused. Title 18 USCA sections 3161 et seq explain the nature of this right. Prior to the point of formal accusation, the government is under no constitutional or **statutory** obligation to discover or investigate criminal activity or accuse or **prosecute** suspected criminals within a particular amount of time. Nor is the Speedy Trial Clause implicated after the government has dropped criminal charges, even if the government refiles those charges at a much later date.

The Supreme Court has declined to draw a bright line separating permissible pre-trial delays from delays that are impermissibly excessive. Instead, the Court has developed a balancing test that weighs the reasons for delay against the prejudice suffered by the defendant in having to endure the delay. A delay of at least one year in bringing a defendant to trial following arrest will create a presumption that the Speedy Trial Clause has been violated. However, defendants whose own actions lengthen the pretrial phase or who fail to assert this right early in a criminal proceeding hurt their chances of prevailing on a speedy trial claim.

The point at which defendants are formally charged also triggers the Sixth Amendment right to be informed of the nature and cause of every accusation against them. Courts have interpreted this provision to have two elements. First, defendants must receive notice of any criminal accusations that the government has formally lodged against them through an indictment, information, or complaint. Second, defendants may not be tried, convicted, or sentenced for a crime that materially varies from the crime set forth in the formal charge. If either element is not satisfied and the defendant is convicted, the court will set aside the verdict and sentence.

Once a defendant has been formally charged by the prosecution in writing, the defendant will be arraigned before a court. At the arraignment the court generally reads the written charges to the defendant and attempts to determine if the defendant understands the charges or needs further explanation. Defendants are also provided with the opportunity to enter a plea of guilty or not guilty at the arraignment.

The arraignment is important for Sixth Amendment purposes because it gives rise to defendants' **right to counsel**, after which defendants are entitled to have counsel present at every "critical stage" of the proceedings. A critical stage is every stage of a criminal proceeding at which the advice of counsel is necessary to ensure defendants' right to a fair trial or every stage at which the absence of counsel might impair the preparation or presentation of a defense. Critical stages include important pre-trial hearings, such as a **hearing** upon a motion to suppress evidence, jury selection, trial, and sentencing. Noncritical stages include pre-trial procurement of defendants' **fingerprints**, blood, DNA, clothing, hair, and handwriting or voice samples. Denial of counsel to a defendant during a critical stage is considered tantamount to an unfair trial warranting the reversal of a **conviction**.

Defendants are not required to be represented by counsel but may instead choose to represent themselves throughout the course of a criminal prosecution, which is called appearing **pro se**. However, the **waiver** of the right to counsel must be done in a knowing and intelligent fashion by a defendant who is aware of the advantages to being represented by counsel. Before accepting a defendant's waiver of counsel, courts will normally explain many of these advantages to the defendant. For example, attorneys can advise their clients whether it is in their self-interest to make any statements to the police. Attorneys can also determine the propriety of bringing any pre-trial motions, including motions to dismiss the case, compel the production of **exculpatory** evidence, limit **testimony** of adverse witnesses, and suppress evidence seized in violation of the Constitution. Under case law interpreting the Fourth Amendment, not only is unconstitutionally obtained evidence rendered inadmissible at trial under the **exclusionary rule**, but any evidence derived from the constitutional violation is also subject to suppression via the "fruit of the poisonous tree" doctrine. Pro se defendants are not likely to understand these nuances of criminal procedure.

Attorneys can also influence the amount of bail that is set by a court following arrest. The Eighth Amendment prohibits courts from setting bail in an excessive amount. Criminal defense attorneys are accustomed to making arguments in favor of setting bail at a level proportionate to the severity of the crime so that gainfully employed defendants accused of less serious offenses can continue earning a living while awaiting trial. In certain instances when defendants have strong ties to a community, attorneys can convince courts to waive bail and release the defendants on their own recognizance, which means that defendants will not be incarcerated prior to trial but are obligated to appear for scheduled court appointments in a timely fashion or risk losing this privilege.

Once the trial begins, the Sixth Amendment guarantees that the defendant be tried in a court open to the public before an impartial jury. The right to a jury trial only applies to charges for which the defendant will be incarcerated upon conviction. If a defendant is tried by the court without a jury, the Sixth Amendment precludes **imprisonment** as a punishment. The right to a public trial is personal to the defendant and may not be asserted by either the media or the public in general. However, both the media and members of the public have a qualified First Amendment right to attend criminal proceedings.

The right to an impartial jury entitles the defendant to a jury pool that represents a fair cross section of the community. From the pool a panel of jurors is chosen to hear the case through a process called **voir dire**. During voir dire the presiding judge, the prosecution, and attorneys for the defense are allowed to ask members of the jury pool a variety of questions intended to reveal biases, prejudices, or other influences that might affect their impartiality.

Jurors may be excluded from service for a specific reason, called a challenge for cause, or for strategic purposes, called a peremptory strike. Attorneys for both sides may exercise an infinite number of challenges for cause, while all jurisdictions limit the number of peremptory strikes. For example, in New York state courts both the prosecution and defense receive three peremptory strikes plus one extra for each alternate juror (see NY CPLR §4109). The Equal Protection Clause of the Fourteenth Amendment also limits attorneys' use of peremptory strikes, making it unlawful to exclude jurors on account of their race (see *Batson v. Kentucky*, 476 U.S. 79, 90 L.Ed.2d 69, 106 S.Ct. 1712 [1986]). The jurors who are ultimately impaneled for trial need not represent a cross section of the community as long as they maintain their impartiality throughout the proceedings. The presence of even one biased juror impaneled to hear the case is not permitted under the Sixth Amendment.

The constitutional parameters governing the size of a jury in criminal cases are not established by the Sixth Amendment but by the Due Process Clauses of the Fifth and Fourteenth Amendments. The Supreme Court has ruled that in capital cases, such as cases in which the death penalty may be imposed a defendant's right to a fair trial requires that the jury comprises twelve members who must unanimously agree on the issue of guilt before the defendant may be convicted and sentenced to death. For non-capital cases, the Supreme Court has ruled that the Constitution permits a verdict to be rendered by a majority vote of as few as nine jurors when the panel consists of twelve. The Court has also said that the Constitution permits trial by as few as six jurors in non-capital cases but that if a six-person jury is impaneled to decide a criminal case, all six must agree on the defendant's guilt before a conviction can be returned.

After the jury has been selected, the prosecution presents its case in chief. The Sixth Amendment guarantees defendants the right to confront witnesses who **testify** against them. In all but exceptional circumstances, the type of confrontation contemplated by the Sixth Amendment is face-to-face confrontation, allowing defendants to hear evidence against them, consult with their attorneys, and participate in **cross-examination** to test the **credibility** and reliability of the victim or other prosecution witnesses.

Once the prosecution finishes presenting its case in chief, the defendant must be allowed the opportunity to put on a defense. The Sixth Amendment gives defendants the right to subpoena witnesses and compel the production of evidence favorable to their case. The Sixth Amendment guarantees this right even if an indigent defendant cannot afford to pay the expenses that accompany the use of judicial resources to subpoena evidence. Defendants are under no obligation to testify themselves, as the Fifth Amendment right to remain silent applies during trial just as fully as it does during pre-trial questioning by the police. In fact, the defense need not call any witnesses or offer any evidence at all. The prosecutor has the burden of proving the defendant's guilt **beyond a reasonable doubt**, and the defendant may decide that the prosecution's case is sufficiently weak that the jury will vote to **acquit** without hearing from the defense.

If the court hears from the defense, each side is then allowed to present rebuttal testimony after which both sides will normally rest. The Sixth Amendment right to an impartial jury prohibits jury members from deliberating before all of the evidence has been submitted, the attorneys have made their closing arguments, and the judge has read the instructions. Once deliberations begin, jurors may ask the court for clarification of the instructions and for portions of the testimony transcribed for their review. If the jurors cannot reach a verdict after discussing the evidence among themselves, the judge will try to determine if they are hopelessly deadlocked. However, the judge cannot force a jury to reach a verdict, but the judge may encourage the jurors to make every reasonable effort to resolve their differences. If the jurors remain deadlocked for a reasonable period of time after meeting with the judge, the court will declare a **mistrial** and dismiss the panel from further service.

If the jurors return a verdict of not guilty, the court will enter a judgment of acquittal, and the defendant is free to leave the courthouse without limitation or condition. If the jurors return a verdict of guilty, the case will proceed to sentencing. For lesser offenses, such as simple or petty misdemeanors, sentencing may immediately follow the verdict. For all other offenses, sentencing is usually conducted by the court in a separate hearing held several days or weeks after the verdict. Both the prosecution and defense are permitted to make arguments as to the appropriate sentence, and courts are generally given wide latitude in crafting individualized punishments within the statutory guidelines. Sometimes this discretion is curtailed by guidelines that require mandatory minimum sentences. Punishments may include any combination of community service, **forfeiture** of property, fines, probation, or **incarceration**. In 38 states and in federal court, defendants may be sentenced to death for first-degree murder, felony murder, and other similarly serious crimes.

THE EIGHTH AMENDMENT LIMITATIONS ON SENTENCING

The Text of the Eighth Amendment Excessive bail shall not be required, nor excessive fines imposed, nor **cruel and unusual punishment** inflicted.

Case Law Interpreting the Eighth Amendment A court's discretion in sentencing a defendant is also limited by the Eighth Amendment, which prohibits the imposition of excessive fines and the infliction of cruel and unusual punishment. The Excessive Fines Clause has proven to have little effect over the course of the last two centuries. Trial judges are afforded extremely wide discretion in assessing fines on criminal defendants, and they are rarely overturned on **appeal**. For a fine to be overturned there must be proof that it was arbitrary, capricious, or so grossly excessive as to amount to a deprivation of property without due process of law. As a practical matter, the cost of appealing a fine often exceeds the amount of the fine itself, thereby reducing the incentive to appeal.

On the other hand, the Cruel and Unusual Punishment Clause has been the subject of much **litigation**. This clause requires every punishment imposed by the government to be commensurate with the offense committed by the defendant. Punishments that are disproportionately harsh will be overturned on appeal. Examples of punishments that have been overturned on Eighth Amendment grounds include two Georgia statutes that prescribed the death penalty for rape and **kidnapping** (see *Coker v. Georgia*, 433 U.S. 584, 97 S. Ct. 2861, 53 L. Ed.2d 982 (1977); *Eberheart v. Georgia*, 433 U.S. 917, 97 L. Ed.2d 2994, 53 L. Ed. 2d 1104 [1977]). The Supreme Court has also ruled that criminal sentences that are inhumane, outrageous, barbarous, or shock the social consciousness also violate the Eighth Amendment. In a recent case the court ruled that it violated the Eighth Amendment to impose capital punishment for crimes committed under the age of eighteen. (see *Roper v. Simmons*, 543 U.S. 551, 125 S. Ct. 1183; 161 L. Ed. 2d 1 [2005]).

In 1972 the U.S. Supreme Court placed a moratorium on **capital punishment** throughout the United States, declaring that the statutes authorizing the death penalty were too broad and allowed for arbitrary and discriminatory application by judges and juries (see *Furman v. Georgia*, 408 U.S. 238, 92 S.Ct. 2726, 33 L.Ed.2d 346 [1972]). However, four years later the Supreme Court upheld three new state statutes that were enacted to cure those flaws (see *Gregg v. Georgia*, 428 U.S. 153, 96 S.Ct. 2909, 49 L.Ed.2d 859 [1976]). Thirty-five states and the federal government soon followed suit by revising their death penalty statutes to comply with the Eighth Amendment, and the nation's high court has since shown reluctance to closely scrutinize these statutes.

However, in 2001 the Georgia Supreme Court surprised many legal observers when it banned use of the electric chair in executing death row inmates (see *Dawson v. State*, 554 S.E.2d 137, [GA.2001]). The court said that death by electrocution violated the state constitution's prohibition against cruel and unusual punishment because it inflicted purposeless violence and needless mutilation on the prisoner, and as such made no measurable contribution to the accepted goals of punishment (see GA Const. Art. 1, § 1, par. 17). At the same time, the court stressed that it was not calling into question Georgia's entire system of capital punishment. On the contrary, the court said that death by lethal injection raised no constitutional questions because it was minimally intrusive and involved no mutilation. However, death row inmates in numerous states challenged death by lethal injection as cruel and unusual punishment. The U.S. Supreme Court upheld the constitutionality of this form of capital punishment. (see *Baze v. Rees*, 553 U.S. 35, 128 S.Ct. 1520, 171 L.Ed.2d 525 [2008]).

APPEAL AND OTHER POST-CONVICTION PROCEEDINGS

The U.S. Constitution does not guarantee the right to appeal a criminal conviction. However, every state affords defendants the right to have at least one **appellate court** review the record for trial court errors. Many of these states restrict the subject matter of what may be appealed, curtail the time in which an appeal may be taken, or permit appellate courts to issue decisions upon the record and briefs submitted by the parties without holding a hearing or entertaining oral arguments. Federal statutes grant criminal defendants in federal court the right to appeal. Only one review is granted as a matter of right, and this is to the U.S. Court of Appeals. Review of state and federal convictions by the U.S. Supreme Court is discretionary.

After incarcerated defendants have exhausted all appeals without success, they may file a **writ** of **habeas corpus**. This is a civil suit against the warden of the prison, challenging the constitutionality of the incarceration. A habeas corpus petition is not another appeal. The only basis for granting relief to a habeas corpus petitioner is the deprivation of a constitutional right. For example, an inmate might claim that he or she was denied the assistance of counsel guaranteed by the Sixth Amendment on grounds that their attorney was incompetent. Violations of the Fourth Amendment's prohibition against unreasonable searches and seizures are not grounds for granting a writ of habeas corpus.

If a defendant loses on appeal and is denied a writ of habeas corpus, most jurisdictions offer a few last-ditch remedies. If the sentence includes parole, an inmate may petition the parole board to move up the date for parole. Inmates of state prisons may ask the governor of the state in which they are imprisoned for clemency. If granted, clemency normally includes the restoration of a released inmate's **civil rights**, such as the right to vote and own a gun. A commutation of sentence is a lesser form of clemency, since it does not restore the legal rights of the inmate but only releases him or her from incarceration.

Federal inmates may ask the president of the United States for a **pardon**, which, like clemency, releases the inmate from custody and restores his or her legal rights and privileges.

ADDITIONAL RESOURCES

American Jurisprudence. 2d ed. Eagan, MN: Thomson/West, 2006.

Black's Law Dictionary. 9th ed. Eagan, MN: West, Thomson Reuters, 2009.

Gale Encyclopedia of American Law. 3rd ed. Detroit: Gale, Cengage Learning, 2011.

Hall, Kermit L., James W. Ely Jr., and Joel B. Grossman, eds. *Oxford Companion to the Supreme Court*. 2d ed. New York: Oxford University Press, 2005.

LaFave, Wayne R., Jerold H. Israel, and Nancy J. King, eds. *Criminal Procedure*. 5th ed. Eagan, MN: Thomson/West, 2009.

Samaha, Joel. *Criminal Procedure*. Belmont, CA: Wadsworth, Cengage Learning, 2011.

ORGANIZATIONS

American Civil Liberties Union (ACLU)

125 Broad St., 18th Fl.
New York, NY 10004
Phone: (212) 549-2500
Email: info@aclu.org
URL: http://www.aclu.org/

Association of Federal Defense Attorneys

8530 Wilshire Blvd, Suite 404
Beverly Hills, CA 90211
Phone: (714) 836-6031
Fax: (310) 397-1001
Email: AFDA2@AOL.com
URL: http://www.afda.org

Center for Human Rights and Constitutional Law

256 S. Occidental Blvd.
Los Angeles, CA 90057
Phone: (213) 388-8693
Fax: (213) 386-9484
Email: mail@centerforhumanrights.org
URL: http://www.centerforhumanrights.org

National District Attorneys Association (NDAA)

99 Canal Center Plaza
Alexandria, VA 22314
Phone: (703) 549-9222
Fax: (703) 836-3195
URL: http://www.ndaa.org

CRIMINAL LAW

DEATH PENALTY

Sections within this essay:

BACKGROUND

History of Death Penalty Laws The first recognized death penalty laws date back to eighteenth century B.C. and can be found in the Code of King Hammurabi of Babylon. The Hammurabi Code prescribed the death penalty for over twenty different offenses. The death penalty was also part of the Hittite Code in the fourteenth century B.C. The Draconian Code of Athens, in seventh century B.C., made death the lone punishment for all crimes. In the fifth century B.C., the Roman Law of the Twelve Tablets also contained the death penalty. Death sentences were carried out by such means as beheading, boiling in oil, burying alive, burning, crucifixion, disembowelment, drowning, flaying alive, hanging, impalement, stoning, strangling, being thrown to wild animals, and quartering (being torn apart).

In Britain, hanging became the usual method of **execution** in the tenth century A.D. In the eleventh century, William the Conqueror would not allow persons to be hanged or otherwise executed for any crime, except in times of war. However, this trend did not last long. As many as 72,000 people were executed in the sixteenth century during the reign of Henry VIII. Common execution methods used during this time included boiling, burning at the stake, hanging, beheading, and drawing and quartering. Various capital offenses included marrying a Jew, not confessing to a crime, and **treason**.

The number of capital crimes in Britain increased throughout the next two centuries. By the 1700s, over two hundred crimes were punishable by death in Britain, including stealing, cutting down a tree, and robbing a rabbit warren. However, due to the severity of the death penalty, many juries would not convict defendants if offenses were not serious. Such practices led to early reform of Britain's death penalty. From 1823 to 1837, the death sentence was eliminated for over half of the crimes previously punishable by death.

Executions and other dispositions of inmates sentenced to death, by race and Hispanic origin, 1977–2010

Race/Hispanic origin	Total under sentence of death, 1977–2010[b]	Prisoners executed		Prisoners who received other dispositions[a]	
		Number	Percent of total	Number	Percent of total
Total	7,879	1,234	15.7	3,487	44.3
White[c]	3,816	700	18.3	1,710	44.8
Black[c]	3,225	424	13.1	1,497	46.4
Hispanic	715	96	13.4	231	32.3
All other races[c, d]	123	14	11.4	49	39.8

Note: In 1972, the U.S. Supreme Court invalidated capital punishment statutes in several states (Furman v. Georgia, 408 U.S. 238 (1972)), effecting a moratorium on executions. Executions resumed in 1977 when the Supreme Court found that revisions to several state statutes had effectively addressed the issues previously held unconstitutional (Gregg v. Georgia, 428 U.S. 153 (1976) and its companion cases).
[a]Includes persons removed from a sentence of death because of statutes struck down on appeal, sentences or convictions vacated, commutations, or death by other than execution.
[b]Includes 5 persons sentenced to death prior to 1977 who were still under sentence of death on December 31, 2010; 374 persons sentenced to death prior to 1977 whose death sentence was removed between 1977 and December 31, 2010; and 7,500 persons sentenced to death between 1977 and 2010.
[c]Excludes persons of Hispanic/Latino origin.
[d]Includes American Indians, Alaska Natives, Asians, Native Hawaiians, and other Pacific Islanders.

SOURCE: *Capital Punishment, 2010—Statistical Tables*. National Prisoner Statistics Program, Bureau of Justice Statistics, U.S. Department of Justice, December 2011.

TABLE BY PREMEDIAGLOBAL. ©2013 CENGAGE LEARNING.

THE UNITED STATES AND THE DEATH PENALTY

In colonial North America, use of the death penalty was strongly influenced by European practices. When European settlers came to the new world, they brought along their practice of **capital punishment**. In the territory now recognized as the United States, the first known execution was that of Captain George Kendall in the Jamestown colony of Virginia in 1608. Kendall was executed for being a spy for Spain. In 1612, Virginia governor Sir Thomas Dale enacted the Divine, Moral, and Martial Laws, which provided the death penalty for even minor offenses such as stealing grapes, killing chickens, and trading with Indians.

Death penalty laws varied considerably from colony to colony. The Massachusetts Bay Colony held its first execution in 1630, although the Capital Laws of New England did not go into effect until many years later. The New York Colony instituted the Duke's Laws of 1665. Under these laws, offenses such as striking one's mother or father or denying the "true God" were punishable by death.

THE ABOLITIONIST MOVEMENT

The Colonial Period The abolitionist movement is rooted in the writings of European social theorists Montesquieu, Voltaire, and Bentham, and English Quakers John Bellers and John Howard. However, it was a 1767 essay, *On Crimes and Punishment,* written by Cesare Beccaria, which principally influenced thinking about punishment throughout the world. Beccaria wrote that there was no justification for the state's taking of a life. The essay gave abolitionists an authoritative voice and renewed energy, one result of which was the **abolition** of the death penalty in Austria and Tuscany. Scholars in the United States were also affected by Beccaria's work. The first known attempted reforms of the death penalty in the United States occurred when Thomas Jefferson introduced a bill to revise Virginia's capital punishment laws, recommending that the death penalty be used only in the case of murder and treason offenses. Jefferson's bill was defeated by one vote.

Other challenges to early capital punishment laws were based on the idea that the death penalty was not a true deterrent. Dr. Benjamin Rush, founder of the Pennsylvania Prison Society, believed in the brutalization effect and argued that having a death penalty actually increased criminal behavior. Benjamin Franklin and Philadelphia attorney general William Bradford supported Rush. Bradford, who would later become the U.S. attorney general, led Pennsylvania to become the first state to consider degrees of murder based on culpability. In 1794, Pennsylvania repealed the death penalty for all offenses except premeditated murder.

The Nineteenth Century In the early to mid-nineteenth century United States, the abolitionist movement gained support in the northeast. In the early part of the century, many states reduced the number of capital crimes and built state penitentiaries. In 1834, Pennsylvania became the first state to move executions away from the public by carrying them out in correctional facilities. In 1846, Michigan was the first state to abolish the death penalty for all crimes except treason. Later, Rhode Island and Wisconsin abolished the death penalty for all crimes. By the end of the century, the countries of Venezuela, Portugal, Netherlands, Costa Rica, Brazil, and Ecuador followed suit. While some states began abolishing the death penalty, most held onto it. Some states even made more crimes punishable by death, especially those committed by slaves. In 1838, in an effort to make the death penalty more acceptable to the public, some states began passing laws against mandatory death **sentencing**, instead enacting discretionary death penalty statutes. The 1838 enactment of discretionary death penalty statutes in Tennessee and later in Alabama were seen as a great reform. This introduction of sentencing discretion in the capital process was perceived as a victory for abolitionists because prior to the enactment of these statutes, all states mandated the death penalty for anyone convicted of a capital crime, regardless of circumstances. With the exception of a small number of rarely committed crimes in a few jurisdictions, all mandatory capital punishment laws were abolished by 1863.

During the Civil War, opposition to the death penalty diminished, as more attention was given to the anti-slavery movement. After the war, new developments in the means of executions emerged. In 1888, the electric chair was introduced in the state of New York. In 1890 William Kemmler became the first man executed by electrocution. Other states followed New York and used the electric chair as the primary method of execution.

The Progressive Period While some states eliminated the death penalty in the mid-nineteenth century, it was the first half of the twentieth century that marked the beginning of the Progressive Period of reform in the United States. From 1907 to 1917, six states completely outlawed the death penalty, and three limited it to the rarely committed crimes of treason and first-degree murder of a law enforcement official. These reforms did not last long. There was a frenzied atmosphere in the United States, as citizens began to panic about the threat of revolution in the wake of the Russian Revolution. In addition, the United States had recently entered World War I, and there were intense class conflicts as socialists mounted the first serious challenge to capitalism. By 1920, these circumstances led five of the six abolitionist states to return to capital punishment.

In 1924, the use of cyanide gas was introduced in the state of Nevada as a more humane way of execution. Gee Jon was the first person executed by lethal gas. The state tried to pump cyanide gas into Jon's cell while he slept,

but this proved impossible, and the gas chamber was constructed.

From the 1920s to the 1940s, there was a revival in the use of the death penalty, due, in part, to the writings of criminologists, who argued that the death penalty was a necessary social measure. In the United States, people were suffering through Prohibition and the Great Depression. There were more executions in the 1930s than in any other decade in U.S. history, an average of 167 per year.

In the 1950s, however, public sentiment began to turn against capital punishment. Many allied nations either abolished or limited the death penalty, and in the U.S., the number of executions dropped dramatically. Whereas there were 1,289 executions in the 1940s, there were 715 in the 1950s, and the number fell even further, to only 191, from 1960 to 1976. In 1966, support for capital punishment reached an all-time low. A Gallup poll showed support for the death penalty at only 42 percent.

THE UNITED STATES CONSTITUTION AND THE DEATH PENALTY

Death Penalty Challenges The 1960s brought challenges to the presumed legality of the death penalty. Before then, the Fifth, Eighth, and Fourteenth Amendments were interpreted as permitting the death penalty. However, in the early 1960s, it was suggested that the death penalty was a "cruel and unusual" punishment and therefore, unconstitutional under the Eighth Amendment. In 1958, the Supreme Court decided in *Trop v. Dulles* (356 U.S. 86) that the Eighth Amendment contained an "evolving standard of decency that marked the progress of a maturing society." Although *Trop* was not a death penalty case, abolitionists applied the Court's logic to executions and maintained that the United States had indeed progressed to a point that its "standard of decency" should no longer tolerate the death penalty. In the late 1960s, the Supreme Court began to reconsider the way the death penalty was administered. In 1968, the Court heard two cases which dealt with prosecutorial and **jury** discretion in capital cases. In *U.S. v. Jackson* (390 U.S. 570), the Supreme Court heard arguments regarding a provision of the federal **kidnapping statute** requiring that the death penalty be imposed only upon recommendation of a jury. The Court held that this practice was unconstitutional because it encouraged defendants to waive their right to a jury trial to ensure they would not receive a death sentence.

In *Witherspoon v. Illinois* (391 U.S. 510), the Supreme Court maintained that a potential juror's reservations about the death penalty were insufficient grounds to prevent that person from serving on the jury in a death penalty case. Jurors could be disqualified only if prosecutors could show that their attitudes toward capital punishment would prevent them from making an **impartial** decision about the punishment.

In 1971, the Supreme Court twice addressed the problems associated with the role of jurors and their discretion in capital cases, in *Crampton v. Ohio* and *McGautha v. California* (consolidated under 402 U.S. 183). The defendants argued it was a violation of their Fourteenth Amendment right to due process for jurors to have unrestricted discretion in deciding whether the defendants should live or die, and such discretion resulted in arbitrary and capricious sentencing. Crampton also argued that it was unconstitutional to have his guilt and sentence determined in one set of deliberations, as the jurors in his case were instructed that a first-degree murder **conviction** would result in a death sentence. The Court rejected these claims, thereby approving of unfettered jury discretion and a single proceeding to determine guilt and sentence. The Court stated that guiding capital sentencing discretion was "beyond present human ability."

Temporary Abolition of the Death Penalty The issue of the arbitrariness of the death penalty was again brought before the Supreme Court in 1972 in *Furman v. Georgia, Jackson v. Georgia,* and *Branch v. Texas* (known collectively as the landmark case *Furman v. Georgia* [408 U.S. 238]). Furman, like McGautha, argued that capital cases resulted in arbitrary and capricious sentencing. *Furman*, however, was a challenge brought under the Eighth Amendment, unlike *McGautha*, which was a Fourteenth Amendment due process claim. With the *Furman* decision the Supreme Court set the standard that a punishment would be "cruel and unusual" if it were too severe for the crime, if it were arbitrary, if it offended society's sense of justice, or if it were not more effective than a less severe penalty.

In nine separate opinions, and by a vote of 5-4, the Court held that Georgia's death penalty statute, which gave the jury full discretion in sentencing, could result in arbitrary sentencing. The Court maintained that the scheme of punishment under the statute was thus "cruel and unusual" and violated the Eighth Amendment. As a result, the Supreme Court voided forty death penalty statutes on June 29, 1972, thereby commuting the sentences of 629 death row inmates in the United States and suspending the death penalty because existing statutes were no longer valid.

Reinstatement of the Death Penalty Although the separate opinions by Justices Brennan and Marshall stated that the death penalty itself was unconstitutional, the overall conclusion in *Furman* was that the specific death penalty statutes were unconstitutional. That decision by the Court opened the door for states to revise death penalty statutes to eliminate the problems cited in *Furman*. Advocates of capital punishment began proposing new statutes that they believed would end arbitrariness of capital sentences. The states were led by Florida, which rewrote its death penalty statute only five months after *Furman*. Shortly after, 34 other states enacted new death penalty statutes. To address the unconstitutionality of unguided jury discretion, some states removed all discretion by mandating capital punishment for those convicted of capital crimes. This practice was ultimately found unconstitutional by the Supreme Court in *Woodson v. North Carolina* (428 U.S. 280 [1976]).

Other states began to limit discretion by providing sentencing guidelines for judges and juries considering death sentences. Such guidelines allowed for the introduction of aggravating and mitigating factors in sentencing. In 1976, the Supreme Court approved these discretionary guidelines in *Gregg v. Georgia* (428 U.S. 153), *Jurek v. Texas* (428 U.S. 262), and *Proffitt v. Florida* (428 U.S. 242), collectively referred to as the *Gregg* decision. This landmark decision held that the new death penalty statutes in Florida, Georgia, and Texas were constitutional, thus reinstating the death penalty in those states. Additionally, the Court maintained that the death penalty itself was constitutional under the Eighth Amendment.

In addition to sentencing guidelines, the Court approved three additional reforms in the *Gregg* decision. The first was bifurcated trials, in which there are separate deliberations for the guilt and penalty phases of the trial. Only after the jury determines that the **defendant** is guilty of capital murder does it decide in a second trial whether the defendant should be sentenced to death or given a lesser sentence of prison time. Another reform was the practice of automatic **appellate** review of convictions and sentence. The final procedural reform was proportionality review, a practice that assists states in identifying and eliminating disparities in sentencing. The state **appellate court** can use this process to compare the sentence in a case being reviewed with other cases within the state to see if it is disproportionate. Because the reforms were acknowledged by the Supreme Court, some states wishing to reinstate their death penalty sentences included them in revised statutes. However, inclusion was not required by the Court. Therefore, some of the resulting new statutes included variations on the procedural reforms found in *Gregg*.

The ten-year moratorium on executions that began with the *Jackson* and *Witherspoon* decisions ended on January 17, 1977, with the execution of Gary Gilmore by firing squad in Utah. Gilmore did not challenge his death sentence. That same year, Oklahoma became the first state to adopt lethal injection as a means of execution, though it would be five more years until Charles Brooks became the first person executed by lethal injection in Texas on December 2, 1982.

RECENT DEVELOPMENTS IN THE DEATH PENALTY

In June 2003, Governor George Ryan of Illinois stirred controversy when he commuted the death sentences of 167 inmates to life **imprisonment**. Ryan said he had concluded that the state's capital punishment system was "haunted by the demon of error." His action came three years after he ordered a moratorium on executions after **evidence** proved that 13 inmates on death row had been wrongly convicted. Ryan, a Republican, had sought office with a platform that supported capital punishment. In 2011, Illinois abolished capital punishment, the sixteenth state to do so.

In a 1989 case, the U.S. Supreme Court upheld the execution of inmates with intellectual disabilities. In the years following, however, many states enacted legislation to prohibit such executions. In 2002, in *Atkins v. Virginia*, the Supreme Court voted 6-3 that the execution of persons with intellectual disabilities is prohibited under the Eighth Amendment as **cruel and unusual punishment**.

In 2005, in another historic decision, the U.S. Supreme Court barred the execution of persons who are under the age of 18 when they commit capital crimes. The ruling in *Roper v. Simmons* followed the same reasoning used by the court in *Atkins*. In a 5-4 decision, the majority found that "evolving standards of decency" and the Eighth Amendment's prohibition of cruel and unusual punishment required the banning of juvenile executions. In its reasoning, the court gave credence to the fact that few nations in the world allow the execution of juveniles.

The use of lethal injection for capital punishment has grown in popularity. Thirty-five states, the U.S. military, and the federal government employ this method. Inmates challenged lethal injections as cruel and unusual punishment under the Eighth Amendment, filing numerous lawsuits. In 2008, the U.S. Supreme Court resolved the issue, ruling that death by lethal injection was constitutional (see *Baze v. Rees*, 553 U.S. 35, 128 S.Ct. 1520, 171 L.Ed.2d 525 [2008]).

Capital Punishment at the Federal Level In addition to the death penalty laws in many states, the federal government has also employed capital punishment for certain federal offenses, such as murder of a government official, kidnapping resulting in death, running a large-scale drug enterprise, and treason. When the Supreme Court struck down state death penalty statutes in *Furman,*

the federal death penalty statutes suffered from the same problems that the state statutes did. As a result, death sentences under the old federal death penalty statutes have not been upheld.

In 1988, a new federal death penalty statute was enacted for murder in the course of a drug kingpin **conspiracy**. The statute was modeled on the post-*Gregg* statutes that the Supreme Court had approved. Since its enactment, six people have been sentenced to death for violating this law, though none has been executed.

In 1994, President Clinton signed the Violent Crime Control and Law Enforcement Act that expanded the federal death penalty to sixty crimes, three of which do not involve murder. The exceptions are **espionage**, treason, and drug trafficking in large amounts.

Two years later, in response to the Oklahoma City bombing of a federal building, President Clinton signed the Anti-Terrorism and Effective Death Penalty Act of 1996. The Act, which affects both state and federal prisoners, restricts review in federal courts by establishing stricter filing deadlines, limiting the opportunity for evidentiary hearings, and ordinarily allowing only a single **habeas corpus** filing in federal court. Proponents of the death penalty argue that this streamlining will speed up the death penalty process and significantly reduce its cost, although others fear that quicker, more limited federal review may increase the risk of executing innocent defendants.

When he was executed on June 11, 2001, Timothy McVeigh became the first federal prisoner executed in 38 years. McVeigh was executed by lethal injection at the U. S. Penitentiary in Terre Haute, Indiana, for the April 19, 1995 Oklahoma City bombing.

WORLDWIDE ABOLITION

In the 1980s the international abolition movement gained momentum, and treaties proclaiming abolition were drafted and ratified. Protocol No. 6 to the European Convention on **Human Rights** and its successors, the Inter-American Additional Protocol to the American Convention on Human Rights to Abolish the Death Penalty, and the United Nations' Second Optional Protocol to the International Covenant on Civil and Political Rights Aiming at the Abolition of the Death Penalty, were created with the goal of making abolition of the death penalty an international norm.

Today, the Council of Europe requires new members to undertake and ratify Protocol No. 6. This requirement has, in effect, led to the abolition of the death penalty in Eastern Europe. For example, Ukraine, formerly one of the world's leaders in executions, halted the death penalty and was admitted to the Council. In addition, in June 1999, Russian president Boris Yeltsin signed a **decree** commuting the death sentence for all of the convicts on Russia's death row. In 2005, Mexico and Liberia abolished the death penalty for all crimes.

In April 1999, the United Nations Commission on Human Rights passed the Resolution Supporting World-wide Moratorium on Executions. The resolution calls on countries that have not abolished the death penalty to restrict the use of the death penalty, including not imposing it on juvenile offenders and limiting the number of offenses for which it can be imposed. Ten countries, including the United States, China, Pakistan, Rwanda, and Sudan, voted against the resolution.

Capital Punishment Today Currently, more than half of the countries in the international community have abolished the death penalty by law or by practice. However, according to Amnesty International, 58 countries retain the death penalty, including China, Iran, and the United States. In 2011 at least 680 people were executed in 21 countries, although the actual number is significantly greater, according to reports of Amnesty International. In its 2011 report it notes that China continues to execute thousands each year.

Recent Death Penalty Statistics Beginning in the 1990s the number of persons sentenced to death has declined markedly. In its 2011 report, the Bureau of Justice Statistics noted that number of new death sentences imposed in 2011 stood at 78, a decline of about 75 percent since 1996, when 315 inmates were sentenced to death. This was the lowest number of death sentences in any year since the death penalty was reinstated in 1976. Texas, which had 48 new death sentences in 1999, had only 8 in 2011. Executions also decreased in 2011. There were 43 executions in 13 states, a 56 percent decline since 1999, when there were 98. Life without **parole** has become more popular, especially in light of numerous cases where death row inmates have been found to have been innocent of their crimes.

ADDITIONAL RESOURCES

Focault, Michel. *Discipline and Punish: The Birth of the Prison.* New York: Vintage Books, 1977.

Johnson, Robert. *Death Work: A Study of the Modern Execution Process.* Belmont, CA: Wadsworth Press, 1998.

Office of Justice Programs. "Capital Punishment Statistics." Bureau of Justice Standards, U.S. Department of Justice. Available at http://bjs.ojp.usdoj.gov/index.cfm?ty=tp&tid=18 (accessed November 3, 2012).

Oshinsky, David M. *Capital Punishment on Trial.* Lawrence, KS: University Press of Kansas, 2010.

Paternoster, Robert, Robert Brame, and Sarah Bacon. *The Death Penalty: America's Experience with Capital Punishment.* New York: Oxford University Press, 2010.

Schabas, William. *The Abolition of the Death Penalty in International Law.* New York: Cambridge University Press, 1997.

ORGANIZATIONS

Death Penalty Information Center

1320 Eighteenth Street NW
Washington, DC 20036
Phone: (202) 293-6970
Fax: (202) 822-4787
URL: http://www.deathpenaltyinfo.org/

Federal Bureau of Prisons, U.S. Department of Justice

320 First Street NW
Washington, DC 20534
Phone: (202) 307-3198
URL: http://www.bop.gov/

National Institute of Corrections

1860 Industrial Circle, Suite A
Longmont, CO 80501
Toll Free: (800) 877-1461
Fax: (303) 682-0213
URL: http://www.nicic.org/

CRIMINAL LAW

DNA TESTING, FINGERPRINTS, AND POLYGRAPHS

Sections within this essay:

- Background
- Comparing the Techniques
  - Fingerprints: The First ID
  - "Lie Detectors"
  - DNA: Greater Accuracy
- DNA as an Exoneration Tool
- Additional Resources

BACKGROUND

Viewers who watch police investigation shows on television often see intrepid experts solve crimes with the aid of a fingerprint on a doorknob or a strand of DNA from a hair miles from the crime scene. While the ease with which criminals are identified is exaggerated, the general picture is correct: Both DNA and fingerprints can help identify individuals through their unique markers, which means they can be useful tools both in identifying criminals and in clearing those who have been wrongly accused.

Polygraph machines, better known as "lie detectors," are also seen on television, but are usually found on older programs. The polygraph does not actually measure whether a person has made a true or false statement; in fact, it measures changes in breathing, blood pressure, and perspiration. Polygraph proponents claim that a person who is lying will breathe more rapidly, have a faster heartbeat, and sweat more profusely than one who is telling the truth.

COMPARING THE TECHNIQUES

All three of these tools have an established place in the criminal justice system, as well as other areas of society. When determining a person's culpability in committing a crime, law enforcement experts agree that the more corroborating **evidence**, the stronger the case. Even if a person confesses and witnesses to the crime come forward, having indisputable physical evidence helps guarantee that the right person will be called to account for the crime.

Fingerprints: The First ID Fingerprints are the oldest and most accurate method of identifying individuals. No two people (not even identical twins) have the same fingerprints, and it is extremely easy for even the most accomplished criminals to leave incriminating fingerprints at the scene of a crime.

Each fingerprint has a unique set of ridges and points that can be seen and identified by trained experts. If two fingerprints are compared and one has a point not seen on the other, those fingerprints are considered different. If there are only matching points and no differences, the fingerprints can be deemed identical. There is no set number of points required, but the more points, the stronger the identification. Fingerprints can be visible or latent; latent fingerprints can often be seen with special ultraviolet lights, although on some surfaces a simple flashlight will identify the print. Experts use fingerprint powder or chemicals to set a print; they then "lift" the print using special adhesives.

The use of fingerprints for identification goes back to ancient times. In ancient Babylonia and China, thumbprints and fingerprints were used on clay tablets and seals as signatures. The idea that fingerprints might be unique to individuals dates from the fourteenth century. In 1686 the physiologist Marcello Malpighi examined fingerprints under a microscope and noted a series of ridges and loops. In 1823, another physiologist, Jan Purkinje, noted at least nine different fingerprint patterns.

The pioneer in fingerprint identification was Sir Francis Galton, an anthropologist by training, who was the first to show scientifically how fingerprints could be used to identify individuals. Beginning in the 1880s, Galton (a cousin of Charles Darwin) studied fingerprints to seek out hereditary traits. He determined through his studies not only that no two fingerprints are exactly alike, but also that fingerprints remain constant throughout an individual's lifetime. Galton published a book on his findings in 1892 in which he listed the three most common fingerprint types: loop, whorl, and arch. These classifications are still used today.

It did not take long for law enforcement officials to recognize the potential value of fingerprint evidence. Sir Edward Richard Henry, a British official stationed in India, began to develop a system of fingerprint identification for Indian criminals. (Henry created 1,024 primary fingerprint classifications.) In Argentina, Juan Vucetich, a police official, also used Galton's findings to create a fingerprint system. (He used Galton's research to make a fingerprint identification of a murderer in 1892.) By the beginning of the twentieth century, Scotland Yard had begun to compile fingerprint information using a classification system based on Henry's work, creating a Central Fingerprint Bureau. In the United States, the New York Police Department, the New York State Prison System, and the Federal Bureau of Prisons instituted a fingerprint system in 1903, and in 1905 the U.S. Army began using fingerprint identification.

The first murder case in the United States in which fingerprint evidence was used successfully was in Illinois in 1910, when Thomas Jennings was accused of murdering Clarence Hiller after his fingerprints were found at Hiller's house. Jennings appealed his **conviction**, but the Supreme Court of Illinois upheld the evidence in 1911 and Jennings was executed in February 1912. *People v. Jennings* thus established fingerprint evidence as a reliable standard.

The Federal Bureau of Investigation (FBI) established a fingerprint repository through its Identification Division beginning in 1924. This repository held fingerprint cards in a central location. Over the next 50 years the FBI processed more than 200 million fingerprint cards. To eliminate duplicate fingerprints and make it easier to store and share fingerprints among law enforcement agencies, the FBI developed the Automated Fingerprint

Identification System (AFIS) in 1991, which computerized the card system. The Integrated AFIS system (IAFIS) was introduced in 1999; a law enforcement official can request a set of criminal prints from IAFIS and get a response within two hours.

Fingerprints are kept for criminals, but civil fingerprints are also kept. People who apply for government jobs, jobs that handle confidential information, banking jobs, teaching jobs, law enforcement jobs, and any job that involves security issues can be fingerprinted. IAFIS stores civil prints as well as criminal prints.

"Lie Detectors" The word polygraph comes from the Greek for "many writings." The polygraph machine measures physiological information from the body: breathing, blood pressure, and perspiration. The faster the breathing, the higher the blood pressure, and the greater the amount of sweat, the more likely the person being tested is nervous.

Although it had been suggested in the nineteenth and early twentieth centuries that physiological changes could help determine whether a person was telling the truth, the first serious effort to apply this information came in 1920 when John Larson, a police officer in Berkeley, California, developed a device (which he called a polygraph) that could measure breathing and blood pressure. Larson believed that his invention could help determine whether a suspect was telling the truth. When the results of a polygraph test were included as evidence in a criminal case in 1923, they were challenged, and the D.C. District Circuit Court ruled in *U.S. v. Frye* that polygraph evidence needed to meet three criteria to be accepted: (1) the general scientific community must acknowledge the test's reliability, (2) the person conducting the test must be qualified to do so, and (3) it can be proven that correct procedures were followed. Known as the "Frye test," it remained the judicial standard for 70 years.

During that time, scientists worked at refining Larson's invention. Leonarde Keeler, who had worked with Larson, began developing more sensitive polygraph machines in the 1930s, even starting a polygraph school in 1948.

Through the years, polygraphs were used by law enforcement agencies, but they were not considered definitive. To begin with, the person who is hooked up to the polygraph would already be quite nervous, and to have tubes placed on the chest, a blood pressure cuff on the arm, and metal plates on the fingers would not relax most people. Moreover, there is a difference of opinion on the accuracy of polygraph tests. The American Polygraph Association has stated that *inconclusive* polygraph results are not the same as *incorrect* results. Yet typically inconclusive readings are figured in with incorrect ones when establishing a percentage of accuracy.

Polygraph experts continued to fine-tune the machines, and also developed a questioning technique that was intended to produce fewer incorrect readings (the subject is asked to respond "yes" or "no" to questions, and unrelated questions are mixed in with relevant ones; this is meant to eliminate nerves).

In 1975, federal judges were given more discretion about the admissibility of evidence under new "Federal Rules of Evidence." Thus, a judge could allow a **jury** to consider polygraph results even if they did not pass the Frye Test. In 1993, the U.S. Supreme Court issued an opinion on *Daubert v. Merrell Dow Pharmaceuticals* that definitively replaced the Frye standard. The court said that judges could admit certain scientific evidence as long as the theory behind it could have been tested, it had been subject to peer review and publication, the potential error was known, and the scientific community in general accepted the theory. In the 1998 case of *U.S. v. Scheffer,* the U.S. Supreme Court ruled that polygraph tests did not have to be admitted as evidence in military trials. (President George H.W. Bush had banned the admission of polygraph evidence from military trials in 1991, citing their unreliability.) But it did not ban polygraph evidence outright. *Daubert* grants judges the right to determine whether polygraph evidence can be used or ignored.

The polygraph has also been used to pre-screen job applicants or to test employees to measure their truthfulness about such issues as drug use or theft. In 1988 Congress passed the Employee Polygraph Protection Act (EPPA), which prohibited businesses from using polygraph evidence to pre-screen employees or to test current employees, and prohibited companies from disciplining or firing employees solely for failing a polygraph test. (Polygraphs can be used if an employer can show other evidence against an employee, but the employee still has the right to refuse.) EPPA does not apply to government workers.

DNA: Greater Accuracy The use of DNA (deoxyribonucleic acid) as a method of identification is relatively new, but it has proven an effective means of identifying criminals, and perhaps more important, eliminating people as crime suspects. A fingerprint is the only unique identification source (identical twins have the same DNA), but if a criminal leaves no prints behind, law enforcement officials must rely on minute DNA samples from blood, saliva and other bodily fluids, hair, or skin. DNA testing is also used in **paternity** disputes to determine the identity of the actual father in **custody**, **inheritance**, or **child support** suits.

DNA testing can be done by standard techniques such as restrictive fragment length polymorphisms (RFLP), polymerase chain reaction (PCR), short tandem repeat (STR), and mitochondrial analysis. In RFLP testing, a DNA sample is mixed with a chemical substance that helps examiners isolate and identify specific key fragments of the sample that can be used in comparison analysis. A drawback of RFLP is that it requires a fairly large DNA sample. With PCR, a series of chemical reactions helps generate copies of a minute DNA sample, thus amplifying a small or degraded piece of information. In STR, various DNA regions in a sample are compared with other samples for similarities. The FBI uses STR using special software that can identify thirteen of these regions in a DNA sample. Mitochondrial DNA analysis is often used for extracting samples from bones and teeth, for which the other methods are not effective.

The goal of DNA testing is to see if the sample matches an individual. Partial or familial searching of DNA databases is a new method that detect profiles that share some aspects of the crime scene DNA when no exact match is found. In states where it is allowed, a partial match may generate new leads through investigation of close relatives of the person whose profile was in the database.

Critics of DNA evidence contend that it is not as reliable as claimed. Some research scientists believe there is at times a degree of subjectivity required to make a determination as to when a match is found or when a **defendant** cannot be excluded on the basis of DNA evidence. A 2010 study found that when DNA evidence was submitted to three different labs without any accompanying facts about the case, the labs came to three different conclusions. Critics believe national standards would remedy some of these problems. In addition, they believe that analysts should only be given the DNA to analyze. Providing other case information may cause **bias** in conclusions.

The FBI keeps a computerized databank of DNA samples called CODIS (Combined DNA Index System). It has grown dramatically since states have enacted laws that mandate all persons convicted of felonies provide a DNA sample. In addition, six states collect DNA from anyone arrested, while California collects DNA from certain "suspects." There were about 1.7 million DNA profiles in 2003; by 2012 that number had grown to almost 10 million profiles. The profiles stored in CODIS can be used to convict criminals, and also to exonerate innocent people. There are numerous examples of criminals whose DNA matched a profile from an earlier crime and who were then charged with the crime; likewise, there are examples of individuals whose innocence was confirmed when DNA found at a crime scene turned out to belong to another person identified through the profiles.

DNA AS AN EXONERATION TOOL

Not only can DNA be used to convict criminals, it has successfully been used to exonerate individuals, some of whom were wrongly imprisoned for more than two decades.

Often, the person who is wrongly convicted of a serious crime such as murder or rape has a criminal record for petty crimes, which means a record already exists. These individuals are frequently convicted on eyewitness **testimony**, but without any physical evidence tying them to the crime.

The Innocence Project, created in 1992 by Peter Neufeld and Barry Scheck at the Benjamin N. Cardozo School of Law in New York, works to exonerate people by use of postconviction DNA, in which DNA from the crime scene is tested against the accused's DNA. Often, physical evidence from a crime is kept for many years. If the evidence includes samples of blood, hair, skin, or other evidence that can include DNA, it can often be used to prove that the person accused could not have committed the crime. Moreover, if it turns out that the DNA matches a profile in a database such as CODIS, the real criminal can be located and tried. From 1989 to 2010, the Innocence Project helped exonerate 297 prisoners.

Opponents of **capital punishment** have pushed for DNA testing to be used more regularly, and many of those who favor capital punishment agree that those convicted for a capital offense should be allowed to make use of all evidence. One of the fears that come with capital punishment is that the wrong person could be executed for a crime. A case involving a man who was executed in 1992 gained national attention in 2005 when Governor Mark Warner of Virginia ordered DNA testing on a 24-year-old DNA sample to determine whether Roger Keith Coleman had murdered his sister-in-law in 1981. Coleman had proclaimed his innocence, and although his DNA had been tested before his **execution**, lawyers said the **examiner** might have misinterpreted the results. Using more advanced technology, Coleman's DNA was tested in January 2006, and the results confirmed that he was in fact the killer. Although supporters of capital punishment said that claims of the death penalty's fallibility were unfounded, opponents noted that the danger of a wrongful execution still existed, and called for increased use of DNA as an identification tool.

ADDITIONAL RESOURCES

Beaven, Colin. *Fingerprints: The Origins of Crime Detection and the Murder Case That Launched Forensic Science.* New York: Hyperion, 2001.

Kerry Segrave *Lie Detectors: A Social History.* Jefferson, NC: McFarland, 2004.

Kobilinsky, Lawrence, Thomas F. Liotti, and Jamel-Oesel-Sweat. *DNA: Forensic and Legal Applications.* Hoboken, NJ: Wiley-Interscience, 2005.

Lee, Henry C., and R.E. Gaensslen, eds. *Advances in Fingerprint Technology.* Boca Raton, FL: CRC Press, 2001.

Lynch, Michael, Simon Cole, et al. *Truth Machine: The Contentious History of DNA Fingerprinting.* Chicago: University of Chicago Press, 2011.

Michaelis, Ron. *A Litigator's Guide to DNA.* Durham, NC: Academic Press, 2008.

Newton, David E. *DNA Evidence and Forensic Science.* New York: Infobase Publishing, 2008.

ORGANIZATIONS

American Polygraph Association

P. O. Box 8037
Chattanooga, TN 37414
Phone: (423) 892-3993
Fax: (423) 894-5435
URL: http://www.polygraph.org

Federal Bureau of Investigation

J. Edgar Hoover Building, 935 Pennsylvania Avenue NW
Washington, DC 20535
Phone: (202) 324-3000
URL: http://www.fbi.gov

Innocence Project

100 Fifth Avenue, Third Floor
New York, NY 10011
Phone: (212) 364-5340
Fax: (212) 364-5341
URL: http://www.innocenceproject.org

National Institute of Justice, U.S. Department of Justice

810 Seventh Street, NW
Washington, DC 20531
Phone: (202) 307-2942
URL: http://www.nij.gov

CRIMINAL LAW

DOUBLE JEOPARDY

Sections within this essay:

- Background
- Policy Considerations Underlying the Right Against Double Jeopardy
- The Common Law Development of the Right Against Double Jeopardy
  - Where Jeopardy Applies
  - When Jeopardy Attaches
  - When Jeopardy Terminates
  - What Constitutes the Same Offense
- State Court Decisions Interpreting State Constitutional Provisions Governing Double Jeopardy
- Additional Resources

BACKGROUND

The double **jeopardy** clause in the **Fifth Amendment** to the U.S. Constitution prohibits the government from prosecuting individuals more than one time for a single offense and from imposing more than one punishment for a single offense. It provides that "No person shall . . . be subject for the same offence to be twice put in jeopardy of life or limb." Most state constitutions also guarantee this right to defendants appearing in state court. Even in states that do not expressly guarantee this right in their laws, the protection against double jeopardy must still be afforded to criminal defendants because the Fifth Amendment's Double Jeopardy Clause has been made applicable to state proceedings via the doctrine of incorporation.

Under this doctrine, the Supreme Court has ruled in a series of cases that the Due Process and Equal Protection Clauses of the Fourteenth Amendment guarantee to the citizens of every state the right to exercise certain fundamental liberties. These liberties include, but are not limited to, every liberty set forth in the **Bill of Rights**, except the Second Amendment right to bear arms, the Third Amendment right against quartering soldiers, the Seventh Amendment right to trial by **jury** in civil cases, and the Fifth Amendment right to **indictment** by **grand jury**.

The concept of double jeopardy is one of the oldest in Western civilization. In 355 B.C. Athenian statesmen Demosthenes said that the "law forbids the same man to be tried twice on the same issue." The Romans codified this principle in the Digest of Justinian in 533 A.D. The principle also survived the Dark Ages (400-1066 A.D.) through the **canon law** and the teachings of early Christian writers, notwithstanding the deterioration of other Greco-Roman legal traditions.

In England the protection against double jeopardy was considered a universal maxim of the **common law** and was embraced by eminent jurists Henry de Bracton (1250), Sir Edward Coke (1628), Sir Matthew Hale (1736), and Sir William Blackstone (1769). However, the English double jeopardy doctrine was extremely narrow. It afforded protection only to defendants **accused** of capital felonies and applied only after **conviction** or **acquittal**. It did not apply to cases dismissed prior to final judgment and was not immune to flagrant abuse by the British Crown.

The American colonists were intimately familiar with the writings of Bracton, Coke, and Hale. Copies of Blackstone's Commentaries on English law were available in most of the colonies, and Blackstone's teachings were often quoted by the colonists in support of their claims that Parliament was exceeding its lawful authority.

The colonists were also familiar with how narrowly the right against double jeopardy had been defined in England. During the constitutional convention James Madison sought to enlarge the definition by making the right against double jeopardy applicable to all crimes, not just capital felonies. Yet Madison's original draft of the Double Jeopardy Clause was perceived by some as too restrictive. It provided that "No person shall be subject . . . to more than one punishment or one trial for the same offense" (*United States v. Halper*, 490 U.S. 435, 109 S. Ct. 1892, 104 L. Ed. 2d 487 [1989]). Several House members objected to this wording, arguing that it could be misconstrued to prevent defendants from seeking a second trial on **appeal** following conviction. Although the language of the Fifth Amendment was modified to address this concern, the final version ratified by the states left other questions for judicial interpretation.

POLICY CONSIDERATIONS UNDERLYING THE RIGHT AGAINST DOUBLE JEOPARDY

Five policy considerations underpin the right against double jeopardy, sometimes known as the right against former jeopardy: (1) preventing the government from employing its superior resources to wear down and erroneously convict innocent persons; (2) protecting individuals from the financial, emotional, and social consequences of successive prosecutions; (3) preserving the finality and integrity of criminal proceedings, which would be compromised were the government allowed to arbitrarily ignore unsatisfactory outcomes; (4) restricting prosecutorial discretion over the charging process; and (5) eliminating judicial discretion to impose cumulative punishments that are otherwise not clearly prohibited by law.

THE COMMON LAW DEVELOPMENT OF THE RIGHT AGAINST DOUBLE JEOPARDY

Double jeopardy **litigation** revolves around four central questions: In what type of legal proceeding does double jeopardy protection apply? When does jeopardy begin, or, in legal parlance, attach? When does jeopardy terminate? What constitutes successive prosecutions or punishments for the same offense? Although courts have answered the second and third questions with some clarity, they continue to struggle over the first and last questions.

Where Jeopardy Applies Only certain types of **legal proceedings** invoke double jeopardy protection. If a particular proceeding does not place an individual in jeopardy, then subsequent proceedings against that individual for the same conduct are not prohibited. The text of the Fifth Amendment suggests that the protection against double jeopardy extends only to proceedings threatening "life or limb." Nevertheless, the Supreme Court has established that the right against double jeopardy is not limited to capital crimes or corporeal punishment but extends to all felonies, misdemeanors, and juvenile delinquency adjudications, regardless of the punishments they prescribe.

In *Benton v. Maryland*, 39 U.S. 784, 89 S. Ct. 2056, 23 L. Ed.2d 707 (1969), the U.S. Supreme Court ruled that the Fifth Amendment's Double Jeopardy Clause is applicable to both state and federal proceedings. Prior to this ruling, an individual accused of violating state law could rely only on that particular state's protection against double jeopardy. Some states offered greater protection against double jeopardy than others, and frequently the level of protection offered was less than that offered under the federal Constitution. The Supreme Court said this was impermissible.

Relying on the doctrine of incorporation described above, the Court held that the right against double jeopardy is so important that each state must afford criminal defendants at least the same amount of protection from multiple prosecutions and punishments that is afforded by the federal government under the Fifth Amendment. Consequently, state courts cannot provide their residents with less protection against double jeopardy than is offered by federal courts, though variations in the level of protection offered can still arise when states offer their residents more protection under their state constitutional provisions than is provided under the federal Constitution.

The Supreme Court has also ruled that the right against double jeopardy precludes only subsequent criminal proceedings. It does not preclude subsequent civil proceedings or administrative proceedings (e.g., a license revocation **hearing**) against a person who has already been prosecuted for the same act or omission, even if that person is fined in the later civil or administrative proceeding. Nor is prosecution barred by double jeopardy if it is preceded by a final civil or administrative determination on the same issue.

Courts have drawn a distinction between criminal proceedings on the one hand and civil or administrative proceedings on the other, based on the different purposes served by each. Criminal proceedings are punitive in nature and serve the purposes of deterrence and retribution. Civil and administrative proceedings are more remedial in nature. Civil proceedings, for example, seek to compensate injured persons for any losses they have suffered, while administrative proceedings can serve various remedial functions (e.g., license revocation) unrelated to deterrence or retribution. Because civil, administrative, and criminal proceedings serve different objectives, a single course of conduct can give rise to multiple trials in different types of courtrooms.

The multiple legal proceedings brought against O.J. (Orenthal James) Simpson over the death of Nicole Brown Simpson and Ronald Lyle Goldman illustrate these various objectives. The state of California prosecuted Simpson for the murders of his former wife and her friend. Despite Simpson's acquittal in criminal court, the families of the two victims filed three civil suits against him. The criminal proceedings had been instituted to punish Simpson, incarcerate him, and deter others from similar behavior. The civil suits were designed in part to make the victims' families whole by compensating them with money damages for the losses they suffered.

When Jeopardy Attaches While the differences between civil, criminal, and administrative proceedings are not always perfectly clear, courts have done a much better job of explaining when jeopardy begins, or attaches. This question is crucial because any action taken by the government before jeopardy attaches, such as dismissing the indictment, will not prevent later proceedings against the same person for the same offense. Once jeopardy has attached, the full array of Fifth Amendment protections against multiple prosecutions and multiple punishments takes hold.

The U.S. Supreme Court has held that jeopardy attaches during a jury trial when the jury is sworn. In criminal cases tried by a judge without a jury, also called a bench trial, jeopardy attaches when the first witness is sworn. Jeopardy begins in juvenile delinquency adjudications when the court first hears **evidence**. If the **defendant** or juvenile enters a **plea** agreement with the prosecution, jeopardy does not attach until the plea is accepted by the court.

When Jeopardy Terminates Determining when jeopardy terminates is no less important than determining when it begins, but it is a little more complicated. Once jeopardy has terminated, the government cannot detain someone for additional court proceedings on the same matter without raising double jeopardy questions. If jeopardy does not terminate at the conclusion of one proceeding, jeopardy is said to be "continuing," and further criminal proceedings are permitted. Jeopardy can terminate in four instances: (1) after acquittal; (2) after **dismissal**; (3) after a **mistrial**; and (4) on appeal after conviction.

A jury's verdict of acquittal terminates jeopardy, and verdicts of acquittal cannot be overturned on appeal even if there is overwhelming proof of a defendant's guilt or if the trial judge committed reversible error in ruling on an

issue at some point during the proceedings. This fundamental maxim of double jeopardy **jurisprudence** entrusts the jury with the power to nullify criminal prosecutions tainted by egregious misconduct on the part of the police, the **prosecutor**, or the court, a tremendous bulwark against tyranny in a democratic society.

A jury can also implicitly **acquit** a defendant. If a jury has been instructed by the judge on the elements of a particular crime and a lesser included offense, and the jury returns a guilty verdict as to the lesser offense but is silent as to the greater offense, re-prosecution for the greater offense is barred by the Double Jeopardy Clause. For example, a jury that has been instructed as to the crimes of first- and second-degree murder will implicitly acquit the defendant of first-degree murder by returning a guilty verdict only as to murder in the second degree. A not guilty verdict as to the greater offense is inferred from the jury's silence.

Dismissals are granted by the trial court for miscellaneous procedural errors and defects that operate as an absolute barrier to prosecution. For example, the prosecution must establish that a court has **jurisdiction** over a defendant before prosecution may commence. Failure to establish jurisdiction will normally result in a dismissal upon an objection raised by the defendant. Dismissals may be entered before a jury has been impaneled, during trial, or after conviction. But jeopardy must attach before a dismissal implicates double jeopardy protection.

Once jeopardy attaches, a dismissal granted by the court for insufficient evidence terminates jeopardy and bars further prosecution with one exception. The prosecution may appeal a dismissal entered after the jury has returned a guilty verdict. If the **appellate court** reverses the dismissal, the guilty verdict can be reinstated without necessitating a second trial. A dismissal granted for lack of evidence after a case has been submitted to a jury, but before a verdict has been reached, may not be appealed by the state.

Re-prosecution is permitted and jeopardy continues against the defendant when a case is dismissed by the court at the defendant's request for reasons other than sufficiency of the evidence. For example, courts may dismiss a case when the defendant's right to a speedy trial has been denied by prosecutorial pretrial delay. The Supreme Court has held that no double jeopardy interest is triggered when defendants obtain a dismissal for reasons unrelated to their guilt or innocence (see *United States v. Scott*, 437 U.S. 82, 98 S.Ct. 2187, 57 L.Ed.2d 65 [1978]).

Mistrials are granted when it has become impracticable or impossible to finish a case. Courts typically declare mistrials when jurors fail to unanimously reach a verdict.

Like dismissals, mistrials declared at the defendant's behest will not terminate jeopardy or bar re-prosecution. Nor will a mistrial preclude re-prosecution when it is declared with the defendant's consent. Courts disagree whether a defendant's mere silence is tantamount to consent.

A different situation is presented when a mistrial is declared over the defendant's objection. Re-prosecution will be allowed only if the mistrial resulted from "manifest necessity," a standard more rigorous than "reasonably necessary" and less exacting than "absolutely necessary." A mistrial that could have been reasonably avoided will terminate jeopardy, but jeopardy will continue if the mistrial was unavoidable.

The manifest necessity standard has been satisfied where mistrials have resulted from defective indictments, disqualified or deadlocked jurors, and procedural irregularities willfully occasioned by the defendant. Manifest necessity is not present when mistrials result from prosecutorial or judicial manipulation. In each of these cases, courts balance the defendant's interests in finality against society's interest in a fair and just legal system.

Every defendant has the right to at least one appeal after conviction. If the conviction is reversed on appeal for insufficient evidence, it is treated as an acquittal, and further prosecution is not permitted. However, a defendant may be re-prosecuted when the reversal is not based on lack of evidence. The grounds for such reversals include defective search warrants, unlawful seizure of evidence, and other so-called "technicalities." Retrials in these instances are justified by society's interest in punishing the guilty. Defendants' countervailing interests are subordinated when a conviction rendered by 12 jurors is overturned for reasons unrelated to guilt or innocence.

The interests of the accused are also subordinated when courts permit prosecutors to seek a more severe sentence during the retrial of a defendant whose original conviction was thrown out on appeal. Defendants who appeal their conviction assume the risk that a harsher sentence will be imposed during re-prosecution. However, in most circumstances, courts are not permitted to impose a death sentence on a defendant during a second trial when the jury recommended life in prison during the first. The recommendation of life **imprisonment** is construed as an acquittal on the issue of **capital punishment**.

What Constitutes the Same Offense The final question courts must resolve in double jeopardy litigation is determining whether successive prosecutions or punishments are for the "same offense." Jeopardy may have already attached and terminated in a prior criminal proceeding, but the state may bring further criminal action against a person so long as it is not for the same offense. Courts have analyzed this question in several ways, depending on whether the state is attempting to re-prosecute a defendant or impose multiple punishments.

At common law a single episode of criminal behavior produced only one prosecution, no matter how many wrongful acts may have been committed during that episode. But over the last fifty years the proliferation of overlapping and related offenses has made it possible for the government to **prosecute** someone for several different crimes stemming from the same set of circumstances. For example, an individual who has stolen a car to facilitate an abduction resulting in attempted rape could be separately prosecuted and punished for auto theft, **kidnapping**, and molestation. This development has significantly enlarged prosecutors' discretion over the charging process.

The Supreme Court curbed this discretion in *Blockburger v. United States*, 284 U.S. 299, 52 S.Ct. 180, 76 L.Ed. 306 (1932). The Court said that the government may prosecute an individual for more than one offense stemming from a single course of conduct only when each offense requires proof of a fact the other does not. Blockburger requires courts to examine the elements of each offense as they are delineated by **statute**, without regard to the actual evidence that will be introduced at trial. The prosecution has the burden of demonstrating that each offense has at least one mutually exclusive element. If any one offense is completely subsumed by another, such as a lesser included offense, the two offenses are deemed the same, and punishment is allowed only for one.

Blockburger is the exclusive means by which courts determine whether cumulative punishments pass muster under the Double Jeopardy Clause. But several other methods have been used by courts to determine whether successive prosecutions are for the same offense. **Collateral estoppel**, which prevents the same parties from relitigating ultimate factual issues previously determined by a valid and final judgment, is one such method. In *Ashe v. Swenson*, 397 U.S. 436, 90 S.Ct. 1189, 25 L.Ed.2d 469 (1970), the Supreme Court collaterally estopped the government from prosecuting an individual for robbing one of six men at a poker game when a jury had already acquitted him of robbing another one of the six. Although the second prosecution would have been permitted under Blockburger because two different victims were involved, the government here was not allowed to rehearse its case and secure a conviction against a person already declared not guilty of essentially the same crime.

The "same transaction" analysis is another means by which courts determine whether successive prosecutions will survive constitutional scrutiny. It requires the prosecution to join all offenses committed during a continuous interval that share a common factual basis and display a single goal or intent. The same transaction test is used by many state courts to bar successive prosecutions for the same offense. However, no federal court has ever adopted it.

Both state and federal courts have employed the "actual evidence" test to preclude successive prosecutions for a single offense. Unlike *Blockburger*, which examines the **statutory** elements of proof, the "actual evidence" test requires courts to compare the evidence "actually" introduced during the first trial with the evidence sought to be introduced by the prosecution at the second trial. Criminal offenses are characterized as the same when the evidence necessary to support a conviction for one offense would be sufficient to support a conviction for the other.

Under the "same conduct" analysis the government is forbidden from twice prosecuting an individual for the same criminal behavior, regardless of the actual evidence introduced during trial and regardless of the statutory elements of the offense. For example, this analysis has been applied to prevent prosecuting someone for vehicular **homicide** resulting from drunk driving, when the defendant had been earlier convicted for driving while under the influence of alcohol. The second prosecution would have been permitted had the state been able to prove the driver's **negligence** without proof of his **intoxication**. The U.S. Supreme Court applied this analysis for three years before abandoning it in 1993. However, the "same conduct" analysis is still utilized by some state courts interpreting their own constitutions and statutes.

STATE COURT DECISIONS INTERPRETING STATE CONSTITUTIONAL PROVISIONS GOVERNING DOUBLE JEOPARDY

The U.S. Constitution and the Supreme Court cases interpreting it establish the minimum amount of protection that a state court must provide when it is interpreting a section of the Bill of Rights that has been made applicable to the states via the doctrine of incorporation, including instances that require a state court to interpret and apply the Double Jeopardy Clause of the Fifth Amendment. A state court interpreting the double jeopardy clause of its own constitution may provide more protection than is afforded by the U.S. Constitution but not less.

ADDITIONAL RESOURCES

American Jurisprudence. 2d ed. Eagan, MN: Thomson/West, 2006.

FindLaw. "Double Jeopardy." Available at http://supreme.lp.findlaw.com/constitution/amendment05/02.html (accessed November 1, 2012).

Gale Encyclopedia of American Law. 3rd ed. Detroit: Gale, Cengage Learning, 2011.

Hall, Kermit L., James W. Ely Jr., and Joel B. Grossman, eds. *Oxford Companion to the Supreme Court.* 2d ed. New York: Oxford University Press, 2005.

LaFave, Wayne R., Jerold H. Israel, and Nancy J. King, eds. *Criminal Procedure.* 5th ed. Eagan, MN: Thomson/West, 2009.

ORGANIZATIONS

American Civil Liberties Union (ACLU)

125 Broad St., 18th Fl.
New York, NY 10004
Phone: (212) 549-2500
Email: info@aclu.org
URL: http://www.aclu.org/

Association of Federal Defense Attorneys

8530 Wilshire Blvd., Suite 404
Beverly Hills, CA 90211
Phone: (714) 836-6031
Fax: (310) 397-1001
Email: AFDA2@AOL.com
URL: http://www.afda.org

National District Attorneys Association (NDAA)

99 Canal Center Plaza
Alexandria, VA 22314
Phone: (703) 549-9222
Fax: (703) 836-3195
URL: http://www.ndaa.org

CRIMINAL LAW

EVIDENCE

Sections within this essay:

- Background
- Admissibility
- Real Evidence
- Demonstrative Evidence
- Documentary Evidence
- Testimony
- Leading Questions
- The Lay Opinion Rule
- Character
- Hearsay
- Privileges
- Presumptions
- Judicial Notice
- Additional Resources

BACKGROUND

The law of evidence governs how parties, judges, and juries offer and then evaluate the various forms of proof at trial. In some ways, evidence is an extension of civil and **criminal procedure**. Generally, evidence law establishes a group of limitations that courts enforce against attorneys in an attempt to control the various events that the trial process presents in an adversarial setting. There are many arguments in favor of evidence law; here are five of the most common ones:

1. To ameliorate pervasive mistrust of juries

2. To further legal or social policies relating to a matter being litigated

3. To further substantive policies unrelated to the matter in suit

4. To create conditions to receive the most accurate facts in trials

5. To manage the scope and duration of trials

In the United States, the federal courts must follow the Federal Rules of Evidence (FRE); state courts generally follow their own rules, which are generally imposed by the various state legislatures upon their respective state courts. The FRE is the most influential body of American evidence law. The FRE encompasses the majority of the laws of evidence in 68 brief sections. Its language is accessible, easy to read, and mostly free of technical jargon and complicated cross-referencing. The FRE has been enormously influential in the development of U.S. evidence law. This influence in part is a result of its brevity and simplicity.

Before 1975, U.S. evidence law was mostly a creature of the **common law** tradition. The FRE was drafted and proposed by a distinguished advisory committee composed of practitioners, judges, and law professors appointed by the U.S. Supreme Court. Just 20 years after the FRE was adopted in the federal system, almost three-quarters of the states had adopted codes that closely resemble the FRE.

The FRE applies in all federal courts in both criminal and civil cases. Understanding some of the basic provisions of the FRE will enable most people to figure out what is going on at trial, even if there are deviations between the FRE and applicable state laws of evidence.

ADMISSIBILITY

Evidence comes in four basic forms:

1. Demonstrative evidence
2. **Documentary evidence**
3. **Real evidence**
4. Testimonial evidence

Some rules of evidence apply to all four types and some rules apply to one or two of them. All of these forms of evidence must be **admissible**, though, before they can be considered as probative of an issue in a trial.

If evidence is to be admitted at court, it must be relevant, material, and competent. To be considered relevant, it must have some reasonable tendency to help prove or disprove some fact. It need not make the fact certain, but at least it must tend to increase or decrease the likelihood of some fact. Once admitted as relevant evidence, the finder of fact (judge or **jury**) will determine the appropriate weight to give a particular piece of evidence. A given piece of evidence is considered material if it is offered to prove a fact that is in dispute in a case. Competent evidence is that evidence that accords with certain traditional notions of reliability. Courts are gradually diminishing the **competency** rules of evidence by making them issues related to the **weight of evidence**.

REAL EVIDENCE

Real evidence is a thing. Its existence or characteristics are considered relevant and material to an issue in a trial. It is usually an item that was directly involved in some event in the case, such as a murder weapon, the personal effects of a victim, or an artifact like a cigarette or lighter belonging to a suspect. Real evidence must be relevant, material, and competent before a judge will permit its use in a trial. The process whereby a lawyer establishes these basic prerequisites (and any additional ones that may apply) is called laying a foundation. In most cases, the relevance and materiality of real evidence are obvious. A lawyer establishes the evidence's competence by showing that it really is what it is supposed to be. Establishing that real or other evidence is what it purports to be is called **authentication**.

DEMONSTRATIVE EVIDENCE

Evidence is considered "demonstrative" if it demonstrates or illustrates the **testimony** of a witness. It is admissible when it fairly and accurately reflects the witness's testimony and is otherwise unobjectionable. Maps, diagrams of a crime scene, and charts and graphs that illustrate profits and losses are examples of demonstrative evidence.

DOCUMENTARY EVIDENCE

Evidence contained in or on documents can be a form of real evidence. For example, a **contract** offered to prove the terms it contains is both documentary and real evidence. When a party offers a document into evidence, the party must authenticate it the same way as any other real evidence, either by a witness who can identify the document or by witnesses who can establish a chain of **custody** for the document.

When people deal with documentary evidence, it is a good idea to consider these four potential pitfalls:

- Parol evidence
- Best evidence
- Authentication
- **Hearsay**

The parol evidence rule prohibits the admission of certain evidence concerning the terms of a written agreement. Parol evidence is usually considered an issue of substantive law, rather than a pure evidentiary matter.

A party can authenticate documentary evidence in much the same way as it can authenticate other real evidence. Also, some kinds of documents are essentially self-authenticating under the FRE. Some of these are:

- Acknowledged documents to prove the acknowledgment
- Certain **commercial paper** and related documents
- Certificates of the custodians of business records
- Certified copies of public records
- Newspapers
- Official documents
- Periodicals
- Trade inscriptions

The best evidence rule states that when the contents of a written document are offered in evidence, the court will not accept a copy or other proof of the document's content in place of the original document unless an adequate explanation is offered for the absence of the original. The FRE permits the use of mechanically reproduced documents unless one of the parties has raised a genuine question about the accuracy of the copy or can somehow show that its use would be unfair. Also under the FRE, summaries or compilations of lengthy documents may be received into evidence as long as the other parties have made the originals available for examination.

TESTIMONY

Evidence given in the form of testimony is perhaps the most basic type of evidence. Testimonial evidence consists of what a competent witness at the proceeding in question says in court. Generally, witnesses are competent if they meet four broad requirements:

1. The witnesses must take the oath or a substitute and understand the oath
2. The witnesses must have personal knowledge about the subject of their testimony
3. The witnesses must recall what was perceived
4. The witnesses must be able to communicate what they perceived

The courts interpret competency quite liberally, which means that testimony based on the competency of a witness is rarely excluded.

If at trial witnesses forgets their testimony, the attorney may help to refresh their memory in four ways:

1. First, the attorney can ask the judge for a recess to allow the witnesses time to calm down or otherwise collect themselves.
2. Second, the attorney can ask the witnesses a **leading question** to try to refresh their memory.
3. Third, the attorney can attempt to refresh the witness's recollection through a process known as past recollection refreshed. The witnesses must first say that they cannot remember the facts the attorney is trying to elicit from them. Then they must say that the refreshing object might help them to remember. Almost anything that they say might help them can be used to help refresh their memory such as notes, photographs, an item of clothing, a smell, or some other object.
4. Fourth, the attorney can offer a writing as a past recollection recorded. The witnesses must first claim that they cannot remember the facts the attorney is trying to elicit from them. Next, the attorney presents the writing or other recording the attorney intended to use for the witness. If the attorney can refresh the witness's memory, they will be allowed to answer the question. If the writing does not refresh their memory, they must then identify the writing as one that they made or saw when they did remember the fact in question and that they knew then that the writing was accurate.

LEADING QUESTIONS

A leading question actually suggests an answer or substitutes the words of the questioning attorney for those of the witness. Many leading questions call for answers of either "yes" or "no." But not all questions that call for an answer of "yes" or "no" are leading questions.

Judges have discretion to allow leading questions during the **direct examination** of a witness when the questions have the following traits:

- deal with simple background issues
- will help to elicit the testimony of a witness who, due to age, incapacity, or limited intelligence, is having difficulty communicating his or her evidence
- are asked of an adverse or hostile witness. Witnesses are considered adverse or hostile when their interests or sympathies may lead them to resist testifying truthfully. In most cases, an adverse party or a witness associated with an adverse party is considered hostile for the purposes of this rule

Questions that call for a narrative answer are more or less the opposite of leading questions. Questions that call for a narrative often produce long speeches that can waste the time of the court and the parties. These kinds of questions are very unpopular with courts and should be avoided.

During **cross-examination**, attorneys may only ask about subjects that were raised upon the direct examination of the witness, including **credibility**. If cross-examiners stray into a new topical area, the judge may permit them to do so in the interest of time or efficiency, but harassment of the witness is not permitted under any circumstances.

THE LAY OPINION RULE

Witnesses must answer questions in the form of statements of what they saw, heard, felt, tasted, or smelled. Usually they are not permitted to express their opinions or draw conclusions. Under the FRE, a court will permit a person who is not testifying as an expert to **testify** in the form of an opinion if the opinion is both rationally based on his perception and helps to explain the witness's testimony. Additionally, a competent layperson may provide opinions on certain subjects that are specifically permitted by rule, **statute**, or **case law**. Some of these are:

- Another person's identity
- Another person's sanity
- Demeanor, mood, or intent
- Identification of handwriting
- Intoxication or sobriety
- Ownership
- The state of health, sickness, or injury
- Speed, distance, and size
- The value of a witness's own property

Opinion testimony is not necessarily objectionable even if such testimony goes to the ultimate issue to be decided in the trial

Extrinsic evidence is evidence other than the answers of the witness whose testimony is being impeached. It may be offered to prove facts relevant to impeaching a witness. In addition to extrinsic evidence, a party may attack the credibility of another witness by attempting to show that the witness is or has:

1. Bias, prejudice, interest in the issue, or corruption
2. Criminal convictions, or other prior bad acts
3. Prior inconsistent statements
4. An untruthful character

There are some limits to questioning a witness about a prior criminal **conviction**. However, according to the FRE, a witness may generally be questioned about criminal convictions when the crime was punishable by a sentence of more than a year or involved **fraud** or a false statement such as **perjury**. Before people attempt to use such evidence in a trial, they need to understand the limits to this kind of evidence.

The FRE allows questions about prior bad acts of a witness to **impeach** that witness's credibility where, in the court's discretion, the questions will help get at the truth. Thus, an attorney may ask questions about prior inconsistent statements if the following apply:

- The questioner has a **good faith** basis for believing that the witness made an inconsistent statement
- The witness needs to be reminded of the time, place, and circumstances of the prior statement
- If the statement is written, a copy of the written statement must be provided to the opposing **counsel** upon request

Another way to impeach the testimony of a witness is to show that the witness has a character of untruthfulness. This departure from the basic rule states a party may not provide evidence of a witness's character to show that the witness acted in conformity with that character trait. The FRE permits evidence to prove a witness has a character of untruthfulness in:

- Testimony of specific instances of untruthfulness
- The opinion of another witness concerning the honesty of another witness's character
- Testimony about the target witness's reputation for truthfulness in the community.

It is important to know that a witness whose testimony is used to impeach the truthfulness of another witness may in turn be impeached.

CHARACTER

Character is a general quality usually attributed to a person. Character cannot be used to show that someone acted on a particular occasion in conformity with a particular character trait. On the other hand, habit can be used that way. A habit is a behavior; it is specific, regular, and consistently repeated. Occasionally, some character traits can be linked with a habit, so the distinction between the two can be hard to make at times.

In civil cases, evidence that a person has a character trait generally cannot be used to prove that the person acted in conformity with that character trait on a particular occasion. Evidence of character may be proved where it is an integral issue in a dispute or where a party puts character in issue. Evidence of character is used frequently in criminal trials during the **sentencing** stage to show that a convicted **defendant** merits a lesser or greater sentence or other **penalty**.

HEARSAY

The rule against hearsay is deceptively simple and full of exceptions. Hearsay is an out of court statement, made in court, to prove the truth of the matter asserted. In other words, hearsay is evidence of a statement that was made other than by a witness while testifying at the **hearing** in question and that is offered to prove the truth of the matter stated. For example, Witness A in a murder trial claimed on the stand: "Witness B (the 'declarant') told me that the defendant killed the victim." The definition of hearsay is not too difficult to understand. But the matter can become very confusing when one considers all of the many exceptions to the general rule against hearsay.

Even if a statement meets the requirements for hearsay, the statement may yet be admissible under one of the exceptions to the hearsay rule. The FRE contains nearly thirty of these exceptions. Most of them are generally available, although a few of them are limited to times when the declarant is unavailable.

There are twenty-four exceptions in the federal rules that do not require proof that the person who made the statement is unavailable. These are:

1. Business records, including those of a public agency
2. Certain public records and reports
3. Evidence of a judgment of conviction for certain purposes
4. Evidence of the absence of a business record or entry
5. Excited utterances or spontaneous statements
6. Family records concerning family history
7. Judgments of a court concerning personal history, family history, general history, or **boundaries**, where those matters were essential to the judgment
8. Learned treatises used to question an expert witness
9. Market reports, commercial publications, and the like
10. Marriage, baptismal, and similar certificates
11. Past recollections recorded

12. Recorded documents purporting to affect interests in land
13. Records of religious organizations concerning personal or family history
14. Records of vital statistics
15. Reputation concerning boundaries or general history
16. Reputation concerning family history
17. Reputation of a person's character
18. Statements about the declarant's present sense impressions
19. Statements about the declarant's then existing mental, emotional, or physical condition
20. Statements in authentic ancient documents (at least 20 years old)
21. Statements in other documents purporting to affect interests in land and relevant to the purpose of the document
22. Statements made by the declarant for the purpose of medical diagnosis or treatment
23. Statements of the absence of a public record or entry
24. The "catchall" rule

The last exception, the so-called "catchall" rule, bears some explanation. This rule does not require that the declarant be unavailable to testify. It does say that evidence of a hearsay statement not included in one of the other exceptions may nevertheless be admitted if it meets these following conditions:

- It has sound guarantees of trustworthiness
- It is offered to help prove a material fact
- It is more probative than other equivalent and reasonably obtainable evidence
- Its admission would forward the cause of justice
- The other parties have been notified that it will be offered into evidence

PRIVILEGES

In general terms, privileges are rights held by individuals that permit them to refuse to provide evidence or to prevent certain evidence from being offered against them. Privileges exist only to serve specific interests and relationships; courts give them narrow scope.

Privileges are more or less disfavored by the courts because they run contrary to the principle that all relevant evidence should be admitted in a search for truth. Accordingly, the persons or entities whose confidentiality they are meant to shield or protect can waive their privileges. Individuals who possess a privilege are known as "holders" of the privilege. Often, the nonholder who is a party to a privileged communication must assert the privilege on behalf of the holder.

Congress could not agree on how to make laws regarding privileges, so this area was left up to the courts and to state law to define. Thus, under the FRE, when a party offers evidence on a federal claim the applicable privileges are determined by the federal case law. When a party offers evidence on a state claim, the state's law of privilege applies. The federal law of privilege is still developing, and the federal courts are usually less tolerant of parties' claims to privileges than are state courts.

PRESUMPTIONS

Previously, there was a good deal of controversy among legal professionals and scholars over the effect of presumptions, but these have largely ended, at least in the federal system. Presumptions are just that: a presumption that certain evidence is what it is on its face. Sometimes, however, a presumption can be rebutted by other evidence. There are two kinds of rebuttable presumptions: those that affect the burden of producing evidence and those that affect the **burden of proof**. In most cases, courts interpret presumptions as rebuttable. A list of rebuttable presumptions includes the following:

- that a letter that has been correctly addressed and properly mailed is received by the addressee in the ordinary course of the mail
- that a person who possesses a thing is also the owner of that thing
- that a writing is dated accurately
- that a written obligation that has been surrendered to the **debtor** has been paid by the debtor (and vice versa)
- that some specific ancient documents are authentic
- that statements in the records of a process server are true
- that when a receipt for a payment on an **installment** debt is given, the debtor has paid all previous installment payments
- that the defendant was negligent when the requirements of *res ipsa loquitur* have been proven
- that money or property delivered is in fact owed to the recipient

A presumption is not considered evidence. But if an opponent to a presumption puts on no evidence to rebut the presumption, the judge or jury must assume the existence of the presumed fact. On the other hand, if an opponent to a presumption does provide evidence to rebut the presumption, the presumption has no further effect.

JUDICIAL NOTICE

Sometimes, the need for evidence on an issue in a case can be satisfied through formal admissions, stipulations, and judicial notice. Likewise, under the FRE, a judge may take judicial notice of facts that are not in issue because they are either generally known (e.g. George Washington was the first president of the United States), or they can be accurately and readily determined (e.g. the exact time of sunrise on a particular day). In addition, state and federal courts can take judicial notice of the laws of the states and of the federal system.

ADDITIONAL RESOURCES

Eszon, Jack S. *E-Z Rules for the Federal Rules of Evidence.* Chicago: CCH, Inc. 2011.

"Federal Rules of Evidence." Legal Information Institute, as amended to December 1, 2011. Available at http://www.law.cornell.edu/rules/fre/ (accessed November 4, 2012).

Graham, Michael H. *Federal Rules of Evidence in a Nutshell.* 8th ed. Eagan, MN: West, Thomson Reuters, 2011.

Ingram, J. *Criminal Evidence.* 11th ed. Cincinnati, OH: Anderson Publishing Company, 2011.

Kirkpatrick, Laird C., Christopher B. Mueller, and Charles H. Rose. *Practice Under the Rules.* 4th ed. New York: Aspen Publishers, Inc., 2012.

Leonard, David P., and Richard D. Friedman, eds. *The New Wigmore: A Treatise on Evidence: Selected Rules of Limited Admissibility: Regulation of Evidence to Promote Extrinsic Policies and Values.* New York: Aspen Law & Business, 2002.

Lilly, Graham C., Daniel J. Capra, and Stephen A. Saltzburg. *Principles of Evidence.* 6th ed. Eagan, MN: West Group, 2012.

ORGANIZATIONS

Criminal Justice Section, American Bar Association (ABA)

740 15th Street, NW, 10th Floor
Washington, DC 20005-1009
Phone: (202) 662-1500
Fax: (202) 662-1501
URL: http://www.abanet.org/crimjust/home.html

National Association of Criminal Defense Lawyers (NACDL)

1660 L St. NW, 12th Fl.
Washington, DC 20036
Phone: (202) 872-8600
Fax: (202) 872-8690
Email: assist@nacdl.org
URL: http://www.nacdl.org

National District Attorneys Association (NDAA)

99 Canal Center Plaza, Suite 510
Alexandria, VA 22314
Phone: (703) 549-9222
Fax: (703) 836-3195
URL: http://www.ndaa.org/index.html

CRIMINAL LAW

FIFTH AMENDMENT

Sections within this essay:

BACKGROUND

Having successfully won their independence from a British monarchy and Parliament that they had **accused** of being undemocratic and tyrannical, the Framers of the federal Constitution had a strong mistrust of large, centralized governments. The Framers drafted the **Bill of Rights**, consisting of the Constitution's first ten amendments, to serve as a bulwark delineating a range of individual freedoms and thus protecting them from governmental abuse. Laws enacted, implemented, or enforced by governmental officials that infringe on these freedoms are typically invalidated as unconstitutional by the judiciary.

The Fifth Amendment to the U.S. Constitution enumerates five distinct individual freedoms: (1) the right to be indicted by an **impartial grand jury** before being tried for a federal criminal offense; (2) the right to be free from multiple prosecutions or multiple punishments for a single criminal offense; (3) the right to have individual freedoms protected by **due process of law**; (4) the right to be free from government compelled **self-incrimination**; and (5) the right to receive just compensation when the government takes private property for public use.

THE TEXT OF THE FIFTH AMENDMENT

The text of the Fifth Amendment reads as follows: "No person shall be held to answer for a capital, or otherwise infamous crime, unless on a presentment or **indictment** of a Grand Jury, except in cases arising in the land or naval forces, or in the **militia**, when in actual service in time of War or public danger; nor shall any person be subject for the same offence [sic] to be twice put in **jeopardy** of **life or limb**; nor shall be compelled in any criminal case to be a witness against himself, nor be deprived of life, liberty, or property, without due process of law; nor shall private property be taken for public use, without just compensation."

Because the Framers hoped that the Constitution would be an enduring document, they generally avoided using specific language that one might find in a code or a regulation. Instead of specifying particular instances of prohibited governmental conduct in the Bill of Rights, the Framers established broad principles that government officials must take into account before encroaching on individual freedoms. In this way the Framers required future generations of citizens to determine the Constitution's meaning.

In *Marbury v. Madison*, 5 U.S. (1 Cranch) 137 (1803), the U.S. Supreme Court, per Chief Justice John Marshall, ruled that the ultimate authority for determining the Constitution's meaning lay with the judicial branch of government through the power of **judicial review**. Pursuant to this power, courts are authorized to review laws enacted by government officials and invalidate those that violate the Constitution.

APPLICABILITY OF THE FIFTH AMENDMENT TO THE STATES

As originally ratified it was unclear whether the Fifth Amendment applied only against action taken by the federal government or if it also protected freedoms from state governmental abuse. The Supreme Court in *Barron v. City of Baltimore*, 32 U.S. 243 (1833) ruled that the Fifth Amendment did not apply to the states.

This judgment settled the question until the Fourteenth Amendment was ratified in 1868. It guaranteed the citizens of every state the right to **equal protection** of the laws and the right to due process of law. Following **ratification** of the Fourteenth Amendment, the Supreme Court began making individual freedoms enumerated in the Bill of Rights applicable to the states via the doctrine of incorporation. Under this doctrine, the Court explained through a series of cases that no state may deny any citizen a fundamental liberty without violating the Fourteenth Amendment's Equal Protection and Due Process clauses. The Court has ruled that these fundamental liberties include every liberty set forth in the Bill of Rights, except the Second Amendment's right to bear arms, the Third Amendment's right against quartering soldiers, the Seventh Amendment's right to trial by jury in civil cases, and the Fifth Amendment's right to indictment by grand jury.

INTERPRETATION AND SCOPE OF THE GRAND JURY CLAUSE

The Fifth Amendment guarantees every person charged with a federal crime the right to be indicted by a grand jury. A grand jury is a group of citizens summoned to criminal court by a law enforcement official to decide whether it is appropriate to indict someone suspected of a crime. Although the right to a grand jury is mandated at the federal level by the U.S. Constitution, about one-third of the state constitutions also require indictment by grand jury for more serious violations of state laws.

Federal grand juries may consist of between 16 and 23 citizens chosen from lists of qualified state residents of **legal age**, who have not been convicted of a crime, and are not biased against the subject of the investigation. Grand jury proceedings begin with the prosecutor presenting a bill of indictment, which is a list explaining the case and possible charges. The **prosecutor** then presents **evidence** to the grand jurors in the form of exhibits, written documents, and oral **testimony** by witnesses.

Grand jurors are given wide latitude to inquire about the criminal charges and may compel the production of documents, records, and **subpoena** witnesses, including the suspect under investigation. They may also question witnesses to satisfy themselves that the evidence is credible and reliable. Unlike at trial, **hearsay** evidence is **admissible** before grand juries. But like at trial, witnesses who refuse to answer questions may be held in **contempt** and incarcerated until they provide answers, unless the question requires disclosure of information that might tend to **incriminate** the witness. The Fifth Amendment's **privilege against self-incrimination** may be successfully asserted during grand jury proceedings.

Grand juries are accusatory bodies, and prosecutors have no obligation to present **exculpatory** evidence or testimony that impeaches their witnesses. Nor do suspects enjoy an absolute right to appear before a grand jury to present their case. Suspects may appear before a grand jury with permission of the prosecutor or upon order by subpoena. Despite the prosecutor's partisan role as the government official in charge of obtaining an indictment against the accused, the prosecutor may not compromise the grand jury's function of standing between the accused and a hasty, malicious, oppressive, or corrupt prosecution (see *Wood v. Georgia*, 370 U.S. 375 [1962]). Prosecutors, for example, are prohibited from presenting false information to a grand jury, and convictions stemming from an indictment based on false information are overturned on **appeal**. Prosecutors are also prohibited from pressuring grand jurors to "rubber stamp" an indictment.

If a majority of grand jury members agree that there is sufficient reason to charge the suspect with a crime, they return an indictment carrying the words, "true bill." But if a majority of grand jurors determine that there is insufficient evidence to go forward with prosecution, they return an indictment carrying the words, "no bill."

INTERPRETATION AND SCOPE OF THE DOUBLE JEOPARDY CLAUSE

The **Double Jeopardy** Clause of the Fifth Amendment prohibits the government from prosecuting a **defendant** more than one time for a single offense or imposing more than one punishment for a single offense. Only certain types of **legal proceedings** invoke double jeopardy protection. If a particular proceeding does not place an individual in "jeopardy," then subsequent proceedings or punishments against that individual for the same conduct are not prohibited by this clause.

The text of the Fifth Amendment suggests that the protection against double jeopardy extends only to proceedings that threaten "life or limb." However, the Supreme Court has extended the right against double jeopardy beyond capital crimes and corporeal punishments to all felonies, misdemeanors, and juvenile delinquency adjudications, regardless of the punishments they prescribe. At the same time, the Supreme Court has ruled that the right against double jeopardy precludes only subsequent criminal proceedings. It does not preclude a private litigant from initiating a civil proceeding against a defendant who has already been prosecuted for a crime, which explains why O.J. Simpson could be sued in civil court by the surviving family members of Ronald Goldman and Nicole Brown Simpson after he was acquitted in criminal court of murdering them.

A crucial question in any double jeopardy analysis is when jeopardy is said to have "attached." In other words, courts must decide at what point during a criminal prosecution a defendant's right against subsequent prosecution and multiple punishments began. Actions taken by the government before jeopardy attaches, such as dismissing an indictment, will not prevent later proceedings against a person for the same offense. Conversely, once jeopardy has attached, the full panoply of protections against subsequent prosecution and multiple punishments takes hold.

The Supreme Court has ruled that jeopardy attaches during a jury trial when the jury is sworn. In criminal cases tried by a judge without a jury, jeopardy attaches when the first witness is sworn. Jeopardy attaches in juvenile proceedings when the court first hears evidence. If the defendant or juvenile enters a **plea** agreement, jeopardy does not attach until the plea is accepted.

Determining when jeopardy terminates is no less important. Once jeopardy has terminated, the government cannot hail someone into court for additional criminal proceedings without raising double jeopardy questions. If jeopardy does not terminate at the conclusion of one proceeding, it is deemed to be continuing, and further criminal proceedings are permitted. Jeopardy can terminate in four instances: (1) after an **acquittal**; (2) after a **dismissal** of a charge; (3) after a **mistrial** that was not caused by the defendant; or (4) on appeal after a **conviction**.

The final question courts must resolve in double jeopardy **litigation** is whether successive prosecutions or punishments are for the same offense. Jeopardy may have already attached and terminated in a prior criminal proceeding, but the state may bring further criminal action against a person so long as it is not for the same offense. The U.S. Supreme Court has ruled that the government is allowed to **prosecute** an individual for more than one offense stemming from a single course of conduct only when each offense requires proof of a fact that the other offenses do not (see *Blockburger v. United States*, 284 U.S. 299 [1932]). Depending on the circumstances surrounding the single course of conduct, the Court has adopted various other tests in resolving this question and has allowed lower federal and state courts to do the same.

INTERPRETATION AND SCOPE OF THE DUE PROCESS CLAUSE

The Fifth Amendment's Due Process Clause has two prongs, one procedural and one substantive. Procedural due process encompasses the process by which legal proceedings are conducted. It requires that all persons who are materially affected by a legal proceeding receive notice of its time, place, and subject matter so that they have an adequate opportunity to prepare. It also requires that legal proceedings be conducted in a fair manner by an impartial judge who will allow the interested parties to fully present their complaints, grievances, and defenses. The procedural prong of the Due Process Clause governs civil, criminal, and administrative proceedings from the pretrial stage through final appeal. Proceedings that produce arbitrary or capricious results will be overturned as unconstitutional.

Substantive due process encompasses the content or substance of particular laws applied during legal proceedings. Before World War II, the U.S. Supreme Court relied on substantive due process to overturn legislation that infringed on a variety of property interests, including the right of employers to determine the wages their employees would be paid and the number of hours they could work. Since World War II, the Supreme Court has relied on substantive due process to protect **privacy** and autonomy interests of adults, including the right to use contraception and the right to have an **abortion**.

However, the line separating procedure from substance is not always clear. For example, procedural due process guarantees criminal defendants the right to a fair trial, while substantive due process specifies that twelve jurors must return a unanimous guilty verdict before the death penalty can be imposed. The line is further blurred by judges and lawyers who simply refer to both prongs as "due process," without any express indication as to whether they mean substantive or procedural.

INTERPRETATION AND SCOPE OF THE SELF-INCRIMINATION CLAUSE

The Fifth Amendment's right against self-incrimination permits individuals to refuse to answer questions or disclose information that could be used against them in a criminal prosecution. The purpose of this right is to inhibit the government from compelling a **confession** through force, **coercion**, or deception. Confessions produced by these methods are deemed unreliable because they are often involuntary, unwitting, or the result of the accused's desire to avoid further browbeating rather than the product of candor or a desire to confess.

The Self-Incrimination Clause applies to every type of legal proceeding, whether it is civil, criminal, or administrative in nature. Traditionally, the privilege against self-incrimination was most frequently asserted during the trial phase of legal proceedings, where individuals are placed under oath and asked questions on the witness stand. However, in the twentieth century application of the privilege was extended to the pretrial stages of legal proceedings as well. In civil cases, for example, the right against self-incrimination may be asserted when potentially incriminating questions are posed in depositions and **interrogatories**.

In criminal proceedings, the U.S. Supreme Court's decision in *Miranda v. Arizona*, 384 U.S. 436 (1966) established the rules under which the Self-Incrimination Clause applies to proceedings before trial. In *Miranda*, the Court held that any statements made by a defendant while in police **custody** will be **inadmissible** during prosecution unless the police first warn the defendants that they have (1) the right to remain silent; (2) the right to consult an attorney before being questioned by the police; (3) the right to have an attorney present during police questioning; (4) the right to a court appointed attorney if the defendant cannot afford to hire a private attorney; and (5) the right to be informed that any statements they make can and will be used against them at trial.

The *Miranda* case acknowledged that these warnings were not expressly mentioned anywhere in the text of the federal Constitution. However, the Court concluded that the warnings constituted an essential part of a judicially created buffer zone that is necessary to protect rights that throughout the Bill of Rights are expressly afforded to criminal defendants. Thus, if a defendant confesses to a crime or makes an otherwise incriminating statement to the police, that statement will be generally excluded from trial unless the defendant was first read the Miranda warnings.

Because of its lack of textual support in the federal Constitution, legal observers have long predicted the demise of Miranda. Much of this speculation has been fueled by subsequent cases in which the Supreme Court carved out exceptions to Miranda. For example, the Court ruled that when a defendant makes an un-Mirandized incriminating statement followed by a later Mirandized confession, the subsequent confession should not be

excluded from trial (see *Oregon v. Elstad*, 470 U.S. 298 [1985]). However, law enforcement officials cannot completely ignore the requirement of Miranda warnings. In 2004, the Court reviewed a case in which officers interrogated a suspect for 30 to 40 minutes without Miranda warnings, eliciting a confession during the process. Once the suspect confessed, the officers gave the Miranda warnings and then led the suspect to give the same account for a second time. In this instance, the Court determined that the confession was involuntary and that this practice violated Miranda (*Missouri v. Seibert*, 542 U.S. 600 [2004]).

INTERPRETATION AND SCOPE OF THE EMINENT DOMAIN CLAUSE

When the government takes someone's property for public use, the law calls it a "taking." The Fifth Amendment permits the government to appropriate private property for public use so long as the property owner receives just compensation. The Fifth Amendment allows for governmental **appropriation** of either real estate or **personal property**, and the just compensation provision applies to both kinds of takings. In most **eminent domain** proceedings, just compensation is normally equated with the **fair market value** of the property appropriated.

The Supreme Court in 2005 sparked a national debate regarding the use of eminent domain in the decision in *Kelo v. City of New London*, 125 S. Ct. 2655 (2005). In *Kelo*, the City of New London, Connecticut condemned privately-owned properties so that the land could be used as part of a private development plan. Even though the property would be owned by private entities and used for private purposes, the development plan would increase taxes and create new jobs. These and similar reasons led the Court to decide that the city condemnation of the property constituted a "public use," thus permitting the city to take the land.

Many members of the public criticized the decision. Several state legislators responded within a few months by introducing bills that would effectively negate the decision in *Kelo*. The state proposals appeared in several different forms. Some states sought to limit the type of uses of private property that could be considered "public uses." Other states considered legislation that would prohibit the use of eminent domain for certain uses, such as private economic development projects.

STATE LAWS CONCERNING RIGHTS ENUMERATED BY THE FIFTH AMENDMENT

The U.S. Constitution and the Supreme Court cases interpreting it establish the minimum amount of protection that a state court must provide when applying a provision of the Bill of Rights to a pending controversy. The same holds true for the four clauses of the Fifth Amendment that have been made applicable to the states through the doctrine of incorporation. However, a state constitution or a state court interpreting the state constitution may provide more protection than is afforded by the U.S. Constitution but not less.

ADDITIONAL RESOURCES

American Jurisprudence. 2d ed. Eagan, MN: Thomson/West, 2006.

Gale Encyclopedia of American Law. 3rd ed. Detroit: Gale, Cengage Learning, 2011.

Hall, Kermit L., James W. Ely Jr., and Joel B. Grossman, eds. *Oxford Companion to the Supreme Court.* 2d ed. New York: Oxford University Press, 2005.

LaFave, Wayne R., Jerold H. Israel, and Nancy J. King, eds. *Criminal Procedure.* 5th ed. Eagan, MN: Thomson/West, 2009.

ORGANIZATIONS

American Civil Liberties Union (ACLU)

125 Broad St., 18th Fl.
New York, NY 10004

Phone: (212) 549-2500
Email: info@aclu.org
URL: http://www.aclu.org/

Association of Federal Defense Attorneys

8530 Wilshire Blvd., Suite 404
Beverly Hills, CA 90211
Phone: (714) 836-6031
URL: http://www.afda.org

Center for Human Rights and Constitutional Law

256 S. Occidental Blvd.
Los Angeles, CA 90057
Phone: (213) 388-8693
Fax: (213) 386-9484
URL: http://www.centerforhumanrights.org

National District Attorneys Association (NDAA)

99 Canal Center Plaza
Alexandria, VA 22314
Phone: (703) 549-9222
Fax: (703) 836 3195
URL: http://www.ndaa.org

CRIMINAL LAW

INSANITY DEFENSE

BACKGROUND

Although the insanity defense is probably the most controversial of all criminal defense strategies, it is also, somewhat ironically, one of the least used. On many occasions when it has been used, particularly in the much-publicized 1984 **acquittal** of John W. Hinckley, Jr. for the attempted assassination of President Ronald Reagan, the insanity defense has tended to provoke public debate.

The insanity defense asserts that a criminal **defendant** should not be found guilty due to the defendant's insanity. The theory behind the defense is that a person who is insane lacks the intent required to perform a criminal act because the person either does not know that the act is wrong or cannot control his or her actions even when the person understands that the act is wrong. This theory is controversial because insanity itself is difficult to define, and the circumstances in which insanity can be used to excuse criminal responsibility are difficult to characterize.

The insanity defense has existed since the twelfth century, but initially it was not considered an argument for the defendant to be found not guilty. Instead, it was a way for a defendant to receive a **pardon** or a way to mitigate a sentence. The idea that insanity could bar the **conviction** of a defendant arose in the early nineteenth century in *The Medical Jurisprudence of Insanity* by an influential scholar named Isaac Ray, as well as in the seminal decision in England called the M'Naghten case.

THE M'NAGHTEN RULE

In 1843, Daniel M'Naghten, an Englishmen who was apparently a paranoid schizophrenic under the delusion that he was being persecuted, shot and killed Edward Drummond, Secretary to British Prime minister Sir Robert Peel. M'Naghten believed that Drummond was Peel. To the surprise of the nation, M'Naghten was found not guilty on the grounds that he was insane at the time of his act. The subsequent public outrage convinced the English House of Lords to establish standards for the defense of insanity, the result subsequently referred to as the **M'Naghten Rule**.

The M'Naghten Rule provides as follows: "Every man is to be presumed to be sane, and ... that to establish a defense on the ground of insanity, it must be clearly proved that, at the time of the committing of the act, the party **accused** was laboring under such a defect of reason, from disease of mind, and not to know the nature and quality of the act he was doing; or if he did know it, that he did not know he was doing what was wrong."

The test to determine if a defendant can distinguish right from wrong is based on the idea that the defendant must know the difference in order to be convicted of a crime. Determining a defendant's ability to do so may seem straightforward enough, but dilemmas often arise in cases in which the M'Naghten standard is used. For instance, some issues focus on whether a defendant knew that his or her criminal acts were wrong or whether he or she knew that laws exist that prohibit these acts.

Criticism of the M'Naghten test often focuses on the test's concentration on a defendant's cognitive abilities. Questions also crop up about how to treat defendants who know their acts are against the law but cannot control their impulses to commit them. Similarly, the courts need to determine how to evaluate and assign responsibility for emotional factors and compulsion. Additionally, because of the rule's inflexible cognitive standard, it tends to be difficult for defendants to be found not guilty by reason of insanity. Despite these complications, M'Naghten has survived and is currently the rule in a majority of states with regard to the insanity defense (sometimes combined with the Irresistible Impulse Test, discussed below).

THE IRRESISTIBLE IMPULSE TEST

In response to criticisms of the M'Naghten Rule, some legal commentators began to suggest expanding the definition of insanity to include more than a cognitive element. Such a test would encompass not only whether defendants know right from wrong but also whether they could control their impulses to commit wrong-doing. The Irresistible Impulse Test was first adopted by the Alabama Supreme Court in the 1887 case of *Parsons v. State*. The Alabama court stated that even though the defendant could tell right from wrong, he was subject to "the **duress** of such mental disease [that] he had ... lost the power to choose between right and wrong" and that "his free agency was at the time destroyed," and thus, "the alleged crime was so connected with such mental disease, in the relation of cause and effect, as to have been the product of it solely." In so finding, the court assigned responsibility for the crime to the mental illness despite the defendant's ability to distinguish right from wrong.

The Irresistible Impulse Test gained acceptance in various states as an appendage to the M'Naghten Rule, under which right versus wrong was still considered a vital part of any definition of insanity. In some cases, the Irresistible Impulse Test was considered to be a variation on M'Naghten; in others, it was considered to be a separate test. Though the Irresistible Impulse Test was considered to be an important corrective on M'Naghten's cognitive bias, it still came under some criticism of its own. For example, it seemed to make the definition of insanity too broad, failing to take into account the impossibility of determining which acts were uncontrollable rather than merely uncontrolled, and also making it easier to fake insanity. The test was also criticized for being too narrow; like M'Naghten, the test seemed to exclude all but those totally unable to control their actions. Nevertheless, several states currently use this test along with the M'Naghten Rule to determine insanity, and the American Law Institute in its Model Penal Code definition of insanity adopted a modified version of it.

THE DURHAM RULE

The **Durham Rule**, a version of which was originally adopted in New Hampshire in 1871, was embraced by the Circuit Court of Appeals for the District of Columbia in the 1954 case of *Durham v. United States*. The Durham Rule, sometimes referred to as the "product test," provides that the defendant is not "criminally responsible if his unlawful act is the product of a mental disease or defect."

The Durham Rule was originally seen as a way of simplifying the M'Naghten Rule and the Irresistible Impulse Test by making insanity and its relation to the crime a matter of objective diagnosis. Nevertheless, such a diagnosis proved to be more difficult to prove in practice than in theory. The test was criticized because the Circuit Court has provided no real definitions of "product," "mental disease," or "defect." Because the Durham Rule proved very difficult to apply, the Circuit Court abandoned it in 1972. Currently, only the state of New Hampshire still uses the Durham Rule as a way to define insanity.

THE AMERICAN LAW INSTITUTE'S MODEL PENAL CODE TEST

In response to the criticisms of the various tests for the insanity defense, the American Law Institute (ALI) designed a new test for its Model Penal Code in 1962. Under this test, "a person is not responsible for criminal conduct if at the time of such conduct as a result of mental disease or defect he lacks substantial capacity either to appreciate the criminality of his conduct or to conform his conduct to the requirements of the law."

The Model Penal Code test is much broader than the M'Naghten Rule and the Irresistible Impulse Test. It asks whether defendants have a substantial incapacity to appreciate the criminality of their conduct or to conform their conduct to the law rather than the absolute knowledge required by M'Naghten and the absolute inability to control conduct required by the Irresistible Impulse Test.

The ALI test also requires that the mental disease or defect be a mental diagnosis. In this way, it manages to incorporate elements of all three of its predecessors: the knowledge of right and wrong required by M'Naghten, the prerequisite of lack of control in the Irresistible Impulse Test, and the diagnosis of mental disease and defect required by Durham.

Such a broad-based rule received wide acceptance, and by 1982 all federal courts and a majority of state courts had adopted the ALI test. While some states have since dropped the ALI test, and it no longer applies at the federal level, 18 states still use the ALI test in their definitions of insanity.

THE HINCKLEY TRIAL

In 1982, John W. Hinckley, who had attempted in 1981 to assassinate President Ronald Reagan, was acquitted of the crime by a District of Columbia court by reason of insanity. The enormous outrage after Hinckley's acquittal led three states to drop the insanity defense entirely (Montana, Utah, and Idaho, joined by a fourth, Kansas, in 1995). Other states reformed their insanity defense statutes, by adopting the M'Naghten standard over the Model Penal code standard, by shifting the **burden of proof** from the state to the defense, by changing their commitment and release procedures, or by adopting a "Guilty but Mentally Ill" defense. In addition, the federal courts shifted from the ALI standard to a new law eliminating the Irresistible Impulse Test for insanity defenses in federal crimes.

CURRENT APPLICATION OF THE INSANITY DEFENSE

Burden of Proof The question of who has the burden of proof with an insanity defense has been a source of controversy. Before the Hinckley verdict, a majority of states had the burden of proof rest with the state; that is, the **prosecutor** had to prove that the defendant was not insane. After the Hinckley verdict, the vast majority of states required the defense to prove that the defendant was indeed insane. In states where the burden is on the defense to prove insanity, the defense is required to show either by clear and convincing **evidence** or by a preponderance of the evidence that the defendant is insane. In states where the burden is still on prosecutors to prove sanity, they are required to prove it **beyond a reasonable doubt.**

Commitment and Release Procedures Contrary to uninformed opinion, defendants found not guilty by reason of insanity are not simply released from **custody**. They are generally committed to mental hospitals where they can be confined for longer than their prison terms would have been. In the case of *Jones v. United States*, the Supreme Court in 1983 backed this proposition, ruling that the sentence that criminal defendants would have received had they been convicted should have no bearing on how long they could be committed to a mental hospital.

After Hinckley, many states changed their commitment policies to ensure that a defendant found not guilty by reason of insanity would be required to stay in a mental hospital for a certain period of time for evaluation following acquittal. Previously, no time was specified. Also, several states changed the burden of proof for release from the state to defendants.

Distinction Between the Insanity Defense and Competency to Stand Trial All jurisdictions require that criminal defendants must be competent to stand trial, meaning that defendants understand the nature of the proceedings against them and are able to assist **counsel** in their defense. A person who is found to be mentally incompetent to stand trial is usually hospitalized for treatment until such time that the person is competent to stand trial. **Competency** does not address the guilt or innocence of a party, and so competency to stand trial should not be confused with the insanity defense.

The Federal Insanity Defense Reform Act The federal Insanity Defense Reform Act of 1984, codified at 18 U.S.C. § 17, provides: "It is an affirmative defense to a prosecution under any Federal **statute** that, at the time of the commission of the acts constituting the offense, the defendant, as a result of a severe mental disease or defect, was unable to appreciate the nature and quality of the wrongfulness of his acts. Mental disease or defect does not otherwise constitute a defense." This act, a response to the Hinckley verdict, eliminated the Irresistible Impulse Test from the insanity defense under federal law. The act also provided that "the defendant has the burden of proving the defense of insanity by clear and convincing evidence." Previously under federal law, the government had the burden of proving sanity.

Guilty but Mentally Ill Finally, the Hinckley verdict accelerated the adoption of "guilty but mentally ill" verdicts by states. The "guilty but mentally ill" verdict allows mentally ill defendants to be found criminally liable and requires them to receive psychiatric treatment while incarcerated, or, alternatively, to be placed in a mental hospital and then, when they are well enough, to be moved to a prison to serve their sentences. Laws allowing pleas and verdicts of guilty but mentally ill were first adopted in Michigan in 1975, and concurrent with or subsequent to the Hinckley trial were adopted by 12 more states.

STATUS OF THE INSANITY DEFENSE IN CRIMINAL LAW

Commentators have noted that the insanity defense is risky for criminal defendants because it virtually eliminates any possibility that prosecutors will agree to a **plea** bargain. Studies, including an eight-state investigation by the National Institute of Mental Health, have shown that the insanity defense is raised in less than one percent of all **felony** cases. This defense is successful in only a fraction of those cases.

Nevertheless, when the insanity defense is raised, it continues to spur controversy. For instance, in 2001, Andrea Yates of Texas, who allegedly suffered from a mental illness, drowned her five children in less than an hour. At her trial for capital murder, Yates' attorneys pleaded the insanity defense, arguing that she suffered post partum depression. A **jury** rejected this argument and found her guilty. She received a life sentence for the murders.

The public showed great interest in the Yates trial. Some members of the public, especially but not limited to women's groups, sympathized with Yates due to her battle with post partum depression. At her trial, four out of five psychiatrists and one psychologist testified that Yates did not know right from wrong. However, the single mental health expert called by the prosecution testified that Yates indeed knew right from wrong, and the jury eventually rejected her insanity defense. Facts later revealed that the state's expert had presented false **testimony** regarding Yates, and a Texas **appellate court** in 2005 reversed her conviction and ordered a new trial (*Yates v. State,* 171 S.W.3d 215 [Tex. App. 2005]).

The Yates case demonstrates that in some instances the insanity defense can garner some support. Nevertheless, such a defense is still difficult to prove, and states have not made significant efforts to revise their versions of the insanity defense in recent years.

THE INSANITY DEFENSE AMONG THE STATES

Kansas, Montana, Idaho, and Utah do not allow the insanity defense. In other states, the standards for proving this defense vary widely. The following provides the status of the insanity defense in each **jurisdiction**.

ALABAMA: The state uses the M'Naghten Rule. The burden of proof is on the defendant.

ALASKA: The state uses a modified version of the M'Naghten Rule. The burden of proof is on the defendant. A guilty but mentally ill verdict is allowed.

ARIZONA: The state uses a modified version of the M'Naghten Rule. The burden of proof is on the defendant. A guilty but insane verdict is allowed.

ARKANSAS: The state uses a modified version of the Model Penal Code rule. The burden of proof is on the defendant.

CALIFORNIA: The state uses the M'Naghten Rule. The burden of proof is on the defendant.

COLORADO: The state uses a modified version of the M'Naghten Rule with the Irresistible Impulse Test. The burden of proof is on the state.

CONNECTICUT: The state uses a modified version of the Model Penal Code rule. The burden of proof is on the defendant.

DELAWARE: The state uses a modified version of the Model Penal Code rule. The burden of proof is on the defendant.

DISTRICT OF COLUMBIA: The state uses the Model Penal Code rule. The burden of proof is on the defendant.

FLORIDA: The state uses the M'Naghten Rule. The burden of proof is on the state.

GEORGIA: The state uses a modified version of the M'Naghten Rule. The burden of proof is on the defendant. A guilty but mentally ill verdict is allowed.

HAWAII: The state uses the Model Penal Code rule. The burden of proof is on the defendant.

IDAHO: The state has abolished the insanity defense. The state allows a guilty but insane verdict.

ILLINOIS: The state uses a modified version of the Model Penal Code rule. The burden of proof is on the defendant.

INDIANA: The state uses a modified version of the Model Penal Code rule. The burden of proof is on the defendant.

IOWA: The state uses the M'Naghten Rule. The burden of proof is on the defendant.

KANSAS: The state has abolished the insanity defense.

KENTUCKY: The state uses the Model Penal Code rule. The burden of proof is on the defendant.

LOUISIANA: The state uses the M'Naghten Rule. The burden of proof is on the defendant.

MAINE: The state uses a modified version of the Model Penal Code rule. The burden of proof is on the defendant.

MARYLAND: The state uses the Model Penal Code rule. The burden of proof is on the defendant.

MASSACHUSETTS: The state uses the Model Penal Code rule. The burden of proof is on the state.

MICHIGAN: The state uses the Model Penal Code rule. The burden of proof is on the state.

MINNESOTA: The state uses the M'Naghten Rule. The burden of proof is on the defendant.

MISSISSIPPI: The state uses the M'Naghten Rule. The burden of proof is on the state. An acquittal by reason of insanity verdict is allowed.

MISSOURI: The state uses a modified version of the M'Naghten Rule. The burden of proof is on the defendant.

MONTANA: The state has abolished the insanity defense, although a guilty but insane verdict is allowed.

NEBRASKA: The state uses the M'Naghten Rule. The burden of proof is on the defendant.

NEVADA: The state uses the M'Naghten Rule. The burden of proof is on the defendant.

NEW HAMPSHIRE: The state uses the Durham standard. The burden of proof is on the defendant.

NEW JERSEY: The state uses the M'Naghten Rule. The burden of proof is on the state.

NEW MEXICO: The state uses the M'Naghten Rule with the Irresistible Impulse Test. The burden of proof is on the state.

NEW YORK: The state uses the Model Penal Code rule. The burden of proof is on the defendant.

NORTH CAROLINA: The state uses the M'Naghten Rule. The burden of proof is on the defendant.

NORTH DAKOTA: The state uses the Model Penal Code rule. The burden of proof is on the state.

OHIO: The state uses the M'Naghten Rule. The burden of proof is on the defendant.

OKLAHOMA: The state uses the M'Naghten Rule. The burden of proof is on the state.

OREGON: The state uses the Model Penal Code rule. The burden of proof is on the defendant.

PENNSYLVANIA: The state uses the M'Naghten Rule. The burden of proof is on the defendant.

RHODE ISLAND: The state uses the Model Penal Code rule. The burden of proof is on the defendant.

SOUTH CAROLINA: The state uses the M'Naghten Rule. The burden of proof is on the defendant.

SOUTH DAKOTA: The state uses the M'Naghten Rule. The burden of proof is on the defendant.

TENNESSEE: The state uses the Model Penal Code rule. The burden of proof is on the state.

TEXAS: The state uses the M'Naghten Rule with the Irresistible Impulse Test. The burden of proof is on the defendant.

UTAH: The state has abolished the insanity defense, but guilty but mentally ill verdicts are allowed.

VERMONT: The state uses the Model Penal Code rule. The burden of proof is on the defendant.

VIRGINIA: The state uses the M'Naghten Rule with the Irresistible Impulse Test. The burden of proof is on the defendant.

WASHINGTON: The state uses the M'Naghten Rule. The burden of proof is on the defendant.

WEST VIRGINIA: The state uses the Model Penal Code rule. The burden of proof is on the state.

WISCONSIN: The state uses the Model Penal Code rule. The burden of proof is on the defendant.

WYOMING: The state uses the Model Penal Code rule. The burden of proof is on the defendant.

ADDITIONAL RESOURCES

American Jurisprudence. 2d cd. Eagan, MN: Thomson/West, 2006.

Hermann, Donald H.J. *Mental Health and Disability Law in a Nutshell.* Eagan, MN: West, Thomson Reuters, 1997.

Reider, Laura. "Toward a New Test for the Insanity Defense: Incorporating the Discoveries of Neuroscience into Moral and Legal Theories." *UCLA Law Review*, October. 1998.

ORGANIZATIONS

American Psychological Association (APA)

750 First Street, NE
Washington, DC 20002-4242
Phone: (202) 336-5510
URL: http://www.apa.org/

Association of Federal Defense Attorneys

8530 Wilshire Blvd., Suite 404
Beverly Hills, CA 90211
Phone: (310) 397-1001
URL: http://www.afda.org

Criminal Justice Section, American Bar Association (ABA)

740 15th Street, NW, 10th Floor
Washington, DC 20005-1009
Phone: (202) 662-1500
Fax: (202) 662-1501
URL: http://www.abanet.org/crimjust/contact.html

CRIMINAL LAW

JUVENILES

BACKGROUND

In the eyes of the law, a juvenile or a minor is any person under the legal adult age. This age varies from state to state, but in most states, the District of Columbia, and in all federal districts, any person age 18 or younger is considered a juvenile. In several states, such as New York, Connecticut, and North Carolina, a juvenile is age 16 or less, and in Georgia, Illinois, Louisiana, Massachusetts, Michigan, Missouri, New Hampshire, South Carolina, Texas, and Wisconsin, a juvenile is age 17 or less. Wyoming is the only state that has established the age of juveniles to be 19 or younger (Whitehead & Lab, 1999).

As well as having upper age limits, juvenile jurisdictions also have lower age limits. Most states specify that prior to age six or seven, juveniles lack *mens rea*, or criminal intent. At this young age, juveniles also are thought to lack the ability to tell right from wrong, or *dolci incapax*. Usually, the age of the offender refers to the age of the offender at the time the offense was committed, but in some states, age refers to the offender's age at the time of apprehension. This arrangement allows for the sometimes lengthy periods it takes to clear a case.

One's status as a juvenile or as an adult is pertinent to the court's determination of the **jurisdiction** under which an offender falls—the adult or the juvenile court system. If it is decided that a juvenile will be tried in a juvenile court, most states allow the juvenile to remain under that jurisdiction until the defendant's 21st birthday.

Relying on age as a sole determinant for adulthood has been criticized by many criminologists and policy makers since individuals develop at different rates. Some youth are far more mature at 18 years of age than some adults are. Because of this discrepancy, juvenile court judges have been given broad discretion to waive juveniles to adult court for trial and **sentencing** (see later section). In rare situations, the courts also have the power to emancipate a juvenile in a civil proceeding so that he or she becomes an adult under the law and is granted certain adult privileges. For example, if a 17-year-old loses both parents and has no other living relatives, he or she could be emancipated in order to pursue **custody** of his or her younger siblings.

433

DEVELOPMENT OF THE JUVENILE JUSTICE SYSTEM

The legal concept of juvenile status, like the concept of childhood itself, is relatively new. The juvenile court system was established in the United States about two hundred years ago, with the first court appearing in Illinois in 1899. Prior to that time, children and youth were seen as miniature adults and were tried and punished as adults.

During the progressive era, which occurred between 1880 and 1920, social conditions in the United States were characterized by large waves of **immigration** and a dramatic increase in urbanization. As a direct result, hundreds of indigent children wandered the streets, and many became involved in criminal activity. Initially, children who were convicted of crimes were housed with adult criminals. Social activists, law makers, and other officials soon realized that children institutionalized with adults were learning adult criminal behaviors and were exiting those institutions ready for life careers in criminality. Because of this negative influence, separate juvenile court systems and accompanying correctional institutions were developed.

Early juvenile institutions in the United States were based on the English Bridewell institution which emphasized the teaching of life and trade skills. The idea behind teaching skills was that criminality was a result of the social environment and often was a survival mechanism. If youth were taught other skills, they were more likely to make meaningful contributions to society upon their release.

Three other types of juvenile institutions began to appear in the United States during the progressive era: houses of refuge, new reformatories, and separate institutions for juvenile females. Houses of refuge focused on the reeducation of youth and used indeterminate sentencing, religious training, and apprenticeships in various trades. The houses were organized using a military model to promote order and discipline, but the houses were often overcrowded and youth were overworked.

New reformatories, established in the mid to late 1800s, were cottages and foster homes that were often situated on farms. Family-type organization was prevalent, and hard physical labor was stressed. New reformatories suffered from the same types of problems that houses of refuge did. Separate juvenile institutions for girls appeared in the mid 1880s, and these focused on teaching domestic and child-rearing skills to girls.

The first juvenile courts operated under the philosophy of *parens patriae* first articulated in *Prince v. Massachusetts* (1944). This philosophy meant the state could act "as a parent," and gave juvenile courts the power to intervene whenever court officials felt intervention was in the best interests of the child. Any offense committed was secondary to the offender. While *parens patriae* was designed to handle youth committing criminal acts, the discretion of this philosophy became increasingly more broad and was constantly debated in court. A number of pivotal cases ensued which helped the juvenile justice system evolve.

JUVENILE CASE HISTORY

In 1838, a man by the name of Crouse took the state to court over the **incarceration** of his daughter, Mary Ann. Mary Ann Crouse was being held at a house of refuge against her father's wishes but at the behest of her mother, who felt Mary Ann had become unruly and unmanageable. Mary Ann had not committed any crime. The courts held in *Ex parte Crouse* that the house of refuge was a reformatory rather than a jail, and Mary Ann's behavior could be reformed as long as she remained there. In essence, the court ruled that the judicial system had the right to assist families with troubled youth.

Some thirty years later in *People v. Turner* (1870), Turner protested being held in a house of refuge against the wishes of both his parents. He was incarcerated because the state felt he was in danger of becoming a criminal. His parents actually won this case, and it was decided that the state should only intervene in troubled families given extreme circumstances. However, the verdict was largely ignored by the courts.

In 1905, a juvenile was given a seven-year sentence for a minor crime that would have received a far lesser sentence in an adult court. This dilemma was argued in *Commonwealth v. Fisher*. In this case, the court decided that the long sentence was necessary and in the best interests of the child, thus broadening juvenile court discretion under the *parens patriae* philosophy. It was not until *Kent v. the United States* in 1966 that the courts recognized the discretionary powers of *parens patriae* had gone too far and were perhaps encroaching on the **constitutional rights** of juveniles. In this case, 16-year-old Morris Kent had been waived to adult court without a **hearing**. Kent's attorney challenged the decision, citing a sixth Amendment violation. This case scrutinized the entire juvenile justice process, and as a result, a more formal set of procedures was established.

In 1967, another juvenile case was argued in the Supreme Court that also addressed the constitutional rights of juveniles. *In re Gault* addressed the separation of adult and juvenile courts, and Fifth and Sixth Amendment privileges for juveniles. Gerald Gault, a 15-year-old juvenile, had been sentenced to a maximum of six years in a state training school for making obscene phone calls to a woman. The case was originally heard in a very informal juvenile court proceeding. The **accused** was not represented by an attorney, and there was no transcript of the hearing. The Supreme Court ruled that the juvenile courts must protect the constitutional rights of juveniles, and rules and regulations must be imposed in the juvenile justice system.

Under our Constitution, the condition of being a boy does not constitute a kangaroo court. The traditional ideas of the juvenile court procedure, indeed, contemplated that time would be available and care would be used to establish precisely what the juvenile did and why he did it *In re Gault*, 387 U.S. 1 [1967].

The protection of juveniles' rights upheld by *In re Gault* were further reinforced by *In re Winship* (1970), in which the Supreme Court extended the reasonable standard of doubt for guilt to juveniles. However, the following year, the right to trial by a **jury** of peers for juveniles was denied by the Supreme Court in *McKeiver v. Pennsylvania*. Several reasons were presented for the denial, including the notion that the juvenile system was not meant to be an adversarial one and was instead designed to be less formal and, therefore, more protective of juveniles' **privacy**. The Supreme Court justices also felt that allowing juvenile trials by jury would be an indication that the juvenile courts had lost their usefulness.

JUVENILES AND STATUS OFFENSES

With the division of courts into adult and juvenile jurisdictions, there were a number of activities that were deemed offenses for juveniles. As a group, these are called status offenses and are such simply because of the age of the offender. Truancy, possession and consumption of alcohol, incorrigibility, curfew violations, and purchase of cigarettes are examples of status offenses. The theory behind status offenses stems from *parens patriae* in that status offenses are harmful to minors, and the courts need to protect minors from such activities.

During the late 1960s and 1970s, there was a move toward deinstitutionalizing status offenses. The movement was formalized by the 1974 Federal Juvenile Delinquency Act. Deinstitutionalization meant that juveniles who committed status offenses were diverted from the juvenile justice system to agencies outside the juvenile court's jurisdiction. The county or district attorney was given the authority to divert an offender, and this decision was made before a petition was filed (see below section on court procedure). Diversion was implemented because many legislators felt that status offenses were minor in terms of criminal nature, and juveniles were better off having their families or some other agency deal with the matter than being formally processed by the justice system. Formal processing of status offenses was thought to lead to labeling and further

delinquent acts, thus negating the whole purpose of rehabilitation. Diversion is still practiced today.

One **status offense**, incorrigibility, received a lot of attention during the 1970s. Juveniles who habitually do not obey their parents are incorrigible. With *parens patriae* still operating, many incarcerated juveniles were serving time for incorrigibility. Critics argued that almost all juveniles disobey their parents at some point, and such behavior may not always **warrant** court action. It seemed that incarceration exposed juveniles to much more severe criminality and sometimes even sexual and physical abuse. In short, juveniles came out of the system less socialized than when they entered it.

After diversion, juveniles who were adjudicated for status offenses were often classified as children in need of supervision (CHINS), persons in need of supervision (PINS), and minors in need of supervision (MINS). Today, status offenses are still illegal in all states, and many juveniles are still confined for such offenses. The Department of Justice estimated that in 1996, juvenile courts around the United States formally disposed of some 162,000 status offenses, 44,800 of which were liquor law violations (OJJDP, 2000).

EXAMPLES OF STATUS OFFENSES

Curfew Many cities, such as New Orleans, Atlanta, and Washington, D.C., require individuals under the age of 17 to be off the streets by 11 p.m. Teenagers found violating this curfew are held at a police-designated truancy center until a parent or **guardian** claims them. Parents who are determined to be aiding and abetting curfew violators are subject to fines and community service. Curfew laws have been challenged on the grounds that they violate the First Amendment by prohibiting a juvenile's right to free association. In *Qutb v. Strauss* (1993), the U.S. Court of Appeals held that curfew laws were constitutional because they are designed to protect the community.

Truancy Most local laws prohibit school-age children from taking unexcused school absences. If caught being truant, juveniles may be processed in juvenile court or processed informally. In some states, such as Virginia and Arizona, parents can also be held accountable for their children's truancy and may be fined or jailed.

JUVENILE COURT PROCEDURE

The procedure and organization of the juvenile court system is different from the adult system. After committing an offense, juveniles are detained rather than arrested. Next, a petition is drawn up which outlines the jurisdiction authority of the juvenile court over the offense and detained individuals, gives notice for the reason for the court appearance, serves as notice to the minor's family, and also is the official charging document. Once in court, the juvenile case is adjudicated, and a **disposition** is handed down. Records from juvenile courts are sealed documents, unlike adult records which are accessible by anyone under the **Freedom of Information Act**. Like diversion, this measure is designed to protect the juvenile so that one mistake does not follow the juvenile for life. Juvenile records may also be expunged upon the juvenile's eighteenth birthday provided the juvenile has met certain conditions, such as good behavior. Juvenile court procedure is also far less formal than adult court procedure.

The disposition of a juvenile case is based on the least detrimental alternative, so the legacy of *parens patriae* is still evident. However, one major controversy in juvenile dispositions is the use of indeterminate sentencing, which allows a judge to set a maximum sentence. In such cases, juveniles are monitored during their sentences and are released only when the judge is satisfied that they have been rehabilitated or when the maximum time has been served. Critics argue that this arrangement allows the judge too much discretion and is, therefore, not the least detrimental punishment.

Juvenile courts are typically organized in one of three ways: 1) as a separate entity; 2) as part of a lower court, such as a city court or district court; or 3) as part of a higher court, such as a circuit court or a superior court. The organization model varies state by state, and some states (for example, Alabama) allow each county and city jurisdiction to decide which is the best method of organization. Where the juvenile court sits has profound implications for the juvenile process.

JUVENILE WAIVER

One of the more hotly debated subjects with regard to juveniles has to do with the option to **waiver** to adult court. Currently, there are three mechanisms by which a juvenile's case may be waived to an adult court.

Judicial Waiver Offenses A judicial waiver occurs when a juvenile court judge transfers a case from juvenile to adult court in order to deny the juvenile the protections that juvenile jurisdictions provide. All states except Nebraska, New York, and New Mexico currently provide for judicial waiver and have set a variety of lower age limits (Snyder, Sickmund & Poe-Yamagata, 2000). In most states, the youngest offender who can be waived to adult court is a 17 or 18-year-old, although in some states, this age is as low as 13 or 14. Usually, the offense allegedly committed must be particularly egregious in order for the case to be

waived judicially, or there must be a long history of offenses.

Statutory Exclusion By 1997, 28 states had **statutory** exclusions, which are provisions in the law to exclude some offenses, such as first-degree murder, from juvenile court jurisdiction. This number is expected to increase.

Concurrent Jurisdiction Some states also have a legal provision which allows the **prosecutor** to file a juvenile case in both juvenile and adult court because the offense and the age of the accused meet certain criteria. Prosecutorial transfer does not have to meet the due process requirement stipulated by *Kent v. U.S.* Approximately 15 states currently have this provision, although this number is expected to increase in the next few years.

The most important case guiding juvenile waiver is *Breed v. Jones* (1975). This case designates that a juvenile cannot be adjudicated in a juvenile court and then be waived and tried in an adult court. To do so is to try the youth twice for the same crime (**double jeopardy**), which violates the **Fifth Amendment**. However, in reality, this case did not have much impact on the juvenile system since juveniles are now subject to a waiver hearing which appears to be similar to a trial except in outcome.

JUVENILES AND THE DEATH PENALTY

In a sensitive and controversial case that had repercussions well beyond the bench, a very divided (5-4) U.S. Supreme Court ruled in 2005 that executing a convicted murderer whose capital crime was committed at the age of 17 constituted "cruel and unusual punishment" under the Eighth Amendment. The decision in *Roper v. Simmons* overruled an earlier Court decision (*Stanford v. Kentucky*). Further, as applicable to the states under the Fourteenth Amendment, the decision rendered several state laws unconstitutional, causing those states (12 in all) to reverse sentences for 72 prisoners on death row who were under 18 at the time of committing capital crimes. As of 2005, at least 20 of 38 states with the death penalty had permitted its application to offenders less than 18 years old.

Prior to this decision, there had been two key court cases that had laid the foundation for juveniles to receive the death penalty.

In *Thompson v. Oklahoma* (1988), the Supreme Court overturned a death sentence for a juvenile who was 15 years old at the time he was involved in a murder. The opinion cited the failure of the state of Oklahoma to stipulate a minimum age for **execution**. This case has also set the minimum age of 16 at which a juvenile can be executed.

In *Stanford v. Kentucky* (1989), the Supreme Court ruled that it was constitutional for a state to execute a juvenile who was between the ages of 16 and 18 at the time of the offense but unconstitutional if the juvenile was under 16.

Although there have been a number of challenges to the minimum age of 16 for juvenile execution set by *Thompson v. Oklahoma,* such as *State v. Stone* (LA, 1988), *Flowers v. State* (AL, 1991), and *Allen v. State* (FL, 1994), these challenges have only gone as far as the court of appeals.

More than 360 juveniles have been executed over the years, beginning with Thomas Graunger, who was executed in 1642 in Massachusetts. The only known countries that execute juveniles are Iran, Pakistan, Yemen, and Saudi Arabia.

JUVENILES AND MANDATORY LIFE SENTENCES

In 2010, the U.S. Supreme Court ruled in *Graham v. Florida* that the reasoning employed in *Roper* should apply in mandatory life sentences for juveniles who have committed non-homicide offenses. Having ruled these life sentences **cruel and unusual punishment**, the court addressed the same issue for juveniles who were convicted of **homicide**. In 2012, the court ruled in *Miller v. Alabama* that juveniles convicted of murder may not be sentenced to life **imprisonment** without the possibility of **parole**.

ADDITIONAL RESOURCES

Hess, Karen. *Juvenile Justice.* 6th ed. Belmont, CA: Wadsworth Publishing, 2012.

Siegal, Larry J., and Brandon Welsh. *Juvenile Delinquency: Theory, Practice, and Law.* 11th ed. Belmont, CA: Wadsworth, Cengage Learning, 2011.

Taylor, Robert, and Fritsch, Eric. *Juvenile Justice.* New York: McGraw Hill, 2012.

ORGANIZATIONS

Death Penalty Information Center

1320 18th Street NW
Washington, DC 20036
Phone: (202) 293-6970
Fax: (202) 822-4787
URL: http://www.deathpenaltyinfo.org

Juvenile Justice Center, American Bar Association

740 15th Street NW
Washington, DC 20005
Phone: (202) 662-1506 .
Fax: (202) 662-1506
URL: http://www.abanet.org/crimjust/juvjust/home.htm

Juvenile Justice Clearinghouse

PO Box 6000
Rockville, MD 20849-6000
Toll Free: (800) 638-8769
Fax: (301) 519-5600
Email: tellncjrs@ncjrs.org

National Center for Juvenile Justice

710 Fifth Avenue, Suite 3000
Pittsburgh, PA 15219
Phone: (412) 227-6950
Fax: (412) 227-6955
URL: http://www.ncjj.org

Office of Juvenile Justice and Delinquency Prevention, U.S. Department of Justice

Washington, DC
URL: http://www.ojjdp.gov

CRIMINAL LAW

PLEA BARGAINING

Sections within this essay:

- Background
- Pros and Cons
- U.S. Supreme Court Cases
- The Alford Plea
- Plea Bargaining in Federal Courts
- Prohibitions and Restrictions
- State Provisions
- Additional Resources

BACKGROUND

There is no perfect or simple definition of **plea** bargaining. *Black's Law Dictionary* defines it as follows:

"[T]he process whereby the **accused** and the **prosecutor** in a criminal case work out a mutually satisfactory **disposition** of the case subject to court approval. It usually involves the defendant's pleading guilty to a lesser offense or to only one or some of the counts of a multicount **indictment** in return for a lighter sentence than that possible for the graver charge."

In practice, plea bargaining often represents not so much "mutual satisfaction" as perhaps "mutual acknowledgement" of the strengths or weaknesses of both the charges and the defenses, against a backdrop of crowded criminal courts and court case dockets. Plea bargaining usually occurs prior to trial but in some jurisdictions may occur any time before a verdict is rendered. It also is often negotiated after a trial that has resulted in a **hung jury**; the

parties may negotiate a plea rather than go through another trial.

Plea bargaining actually involves three areas of negotiation:

- Charge Bargaining: This is a common and widely known form of plea. It involves a negotiation of the specific charges (counts) or crimes that the **defendant** will face at trial. Usually, in return for a plea of "guilty" to a lesser charge, a prosecutor will dismiss the higher or other charge(s) or counts. For example, in return for dismissing charges for first-degree murder, a prosecutor may accept a "guilty" plea for **manslaughter** (subject to court approval).

- Sentence Bargaining: Sentence bargaining involves the agreement to a plea of guilty (for the stated charge rather than a reduced charge) in return for a lighter sentence. It saves the prosecution the necessity of going through trial and proving its case. It provides the defendant with an opportunity for a lighter sentence.

- Fact Bargaining: The least used negotiation involves an admission to certain facts ("stipulating" to the truth and existence of provable facts, thereby eliminating the need for the prosecutor to have to prove them) in return for an agreement not to introduce certain other facts into **evidence.**

The validity of a plea bargain is dependent upon three essential components:

- a knowing **waiver** of rights
- a voluntary waiver
- a factual basis to support the charges to which the defendant is pleading guilty

Plea bargaining generally occurs on the telephone or in the prosecutor's office at the courtroom. Judges are not involved except in very rare circumstances. Plea bargains that are accepted by the judge are then placed "on the record" in **open court**. The defendant must be present.

One important point is a prosecuting attorney has no authority to force a court to accept a plea agreement entered into by the parties. Prosecutors may only "recommend" to the court the acceptance of a plea arrangement. The court will usually take proofs to ensure that the above three components are satisfied and will then generally accept the recommendation of the prosecution.

Moreover, plea bargaining is not as simple as it may first appear. In effectively negotiating a criminal plea arrangement, the attorney must have the technical knowledge of every "element" of a crime or charge, an understanding of the actual or potential evidence that exists or could be developed, a technical knowledge of "lesser included offenses" versus separate counts or crimes, and a reasonable understanding of **sentencing** guidelines.

PROS AND CONS

Although plea bargaining is often criticized, more than 90 percent of criminal convictions come from negotiated pleas. Thus, less than ten percent of criminal cases go to trial. For judges, the key incentive for accepting a plea bargain is to alleviate the need to schedule and hold a trial on an already overcrowded **docket**. Judges are also aware of prison overcrowding and may be receptive to the "processing out" of offenders who are not likely to do much jail time anyway.

For prosecutors, a lightened caseload is equally attractive. But more importantly, plea bargaining assures a **conviction**, even if it is for a lesser charge or crime. No matter how strong the evidence may be, no case is a foregone conclusion. Prosecutors often wage long and expensive trials but lose, as in the infamous O. J. Simpson murder trial. Moreover, prosecutors may use plea bargaining to further their case against a co-defendant. They may accept a plea bargain arrangement from one defendant in return for damaging **testimony** against another. This way, they are assured of at least one conviction (albeit on a lesser charge) plus enhanced chances of winning a conviction against the second defendant. For the defendants, plea bargaining provides the opportunity for a lighter sentence on a less severe charge. If represented by private **counsel**, defendants save the cost for trial and have fewer or less serious offenses listed on their criminal records.

U.S. SUPREME COURT CASES

Article III, Section 2, Clause 3 of the U.S. Constitution provides that "The trial of all crimes, except in Cases of **Impeachment**, shall be by Jury." However, it has never been judicially determined that engaging in a plea bargaining process to avoid trial subverts the Constitution. To the contrary, there have been numerous court decisions, at the highest levels, that discuss and rule on plea bargains. The U.S. Supreme Court did not address the constitutionality of plea bargaining until well after it had become an integral part of the criminal justice system.

In *United States v. Jackson*, 390 U.S. 570 (1968), the Court questioned the validity of the plea bargaining process if it burdened a defendant's right to a **jury** trial. At issue in that case was a **statute** that imposed the death penalty only after a jury trial. Accordingly, to avoid the death penalty, defendants were waiving trials and eagerly pleading guilty to lesser charges. Justice Potter Stewart, writing for the majority, noted that the problem with the statute was not that it coerced guilty pleas but that it needlessly encouraged them.

Two years later, the Court actually defended plea bargaining in *Brady v. United States*, 397 U.S. 742 (1970), pointing out that the process actually benefited both sides of the adversary system. The Court noted that its earlier opinion in *Jackson* merely required that guilty pleas be intelligent and voluntary. The following year, in *Santobello v. New York*, 404 U.S. 260 (1971), the Court further justified the constitutionality of plea bargaining, referring to it as "an essential component of the administration of justice." The Court added that "[as long as it is] properly administered, [plea bargaining] is to be encouraged."

THE ALFORD PLEA

The most cited and familiar Supreme Court case on plea bargaining is *North Carolina v. Alford*, 400 U.S. 25 (1970). In 1970, North Carolina law provided that a penalty of life **imprisonment** would attach to a plea of guilty for a capital offense, but the death penalty would attach following a jury verdict of guilty (unless the jury recommended life imprisonment). Alford faced the death penalty for first-degree murder. Although he claimed innocence on all charges (in the face of strong evidence to the contrary), Alford pleaded guilty to second-degree murder prior to trial. The prosecutor accepted the plea, and he was sentenced to 30 years imprisonment. Alford then appealed his case, claiming that his plea was involuntary because it was principally motivated by fear of the death penalty. His conviction was reversed on **appeal**. However, the U.S. Supreme Court held that a guilty plea which represents a voluntary and intelligent choice when considering the alternatives available to a defendant is not "compelled" within the meaning of the **Fifth Amendment** just because it was entered to avoid the possibility of the death penalty. (Alford had argued that his guilty plea to a lesser charge violated the Fifth Amendment's prohibition that "No person...shall be compelled in any criminal case to be a witness against himself.") The Supreme Court reversed the court of appeals and reinstated Alford's conviction and sentence.

The term "Alford Plea" has come to apply to any case in which the defendant tenders a guilty plea but denies that he or she has in fact committed the crime. The Alford plea is expressly prohibited in some states and limitedly allowed in others. In federal courts, the plea is conservatively permitted for certain defenses and under certain circumstances only.

The U.S. Supreme Court returned to the issue of plea bargaining in 2012, deciding two important cases. In *Lafler v. Cooper*, 132 S. Ct. 1376 (2012), the Court addressed how the Sixth Amendment right to effective counsel should apply during the plea bargaining process. The Court concluded that a defendant had been denied effective assistance when the defendant would have accepted a plea bargain agreement but for the poor advice of his lawyer. In a companion case, *Missouri v. Frye*, 132 S. Ct. 1399 (2012), the Court examined a case where defense counsel failed to communicate a plea bargain offer to the client. The Court determined that this failure constituted ineffective assistance of counsel.

PLEA BARGAINING IN FEDERAL COURTS

The Federal Rules of Criminal Procedure (F.R.Crim.P), specifically Rule 11(e), recognizes and codifies the concept of plea agreements. However, because of United States Sentencing Guideline (USSG) provisions, the leeway permitted is very restrictive. Moreover, many federal offenses carry mandatory sentences, with no room for plea bargaining. Finally, statutes codifying many federal offenses expressly prohibit the application of plea arrangements. (See "Sentencing and Sentencing Guidelines.")

Federal criminal practice is governed by Title 18 of the **U.S. Code**, Part II (Criminal Procedure). Chapter 221 of Part II addresses arraignments, pleas, and trial. The U.S. Attorney's Manual (USAM) contains several provisions addressing plea agreements. For example, Chapter 9-16.300 (Plea Agreements) states that plea agreements should "honestly reflect the totality and seriousness of the defendant's conduct," and any departure must be consistent with Sentencing Guideline provisions. The Justice Department's official policy is to stipulate only to those facts that accurately represent the defendant's conduct. Plea agreements require the approval of the assistant attorney general if counts are being dismissed, if defendant companies are being promised no further prosecution, or if particular sentences are being recommended (USAM 7-5.611).

PROHIBITIONS AND RESTRICTIONS

Aside from legal considerations as to the knowing or voluntary nature of a plea, there are other restrictions or prohibitions on the opportunity to plea bargain. In federal practice, U.S. attorneys may not make plea agreements which prejudice civil or tax liability without the express agreement of all affected divisions or agencies (USAM 9-27.630). Moreover, no attorney for the government may seek, or threaten to seek, the death penalty solely for the purpose of obtaining a more desirable negotiating position for a plea arrangement (USAM 9-10.100). Attorneys are also instructed not to consent to Alford pleas except in the most unusual circumstances and only with the recommendation of assistant attorneys general in the subject matter at issue. In any case where a defendant has tendered a plea of guilty but denies that he or she committed the offense, the attorney for the government should make an offer of proof of all facts known to the government to support the conclusion that the defendant is in fact guilty (USAM 9-16.015). Similarly, U.S. attorneys are instructed to require an explicit stipulation of all facts of a defendant's **fraud** against the United States (tax fraud, Medicare/Medicaid fraud, etc.) when agreeing to plea bargain (USAM 9-16.040).

STATE PROVISIONS

Plea bargaining is not a creature of law; it is one of legal practice. Therefore, state statutes do not create the right to plea bargain, nor do they prohibit it, with one exception. In 1975, Alaska's attorney general at the time, Avrum Gross, banned plea bargaining in Alaska. Although the ban remains officially "in the books," charge bargaining has become fairly common in most of Alaska's courts. Nonetheless, Alaska has not suffered the unmanageable caseloads or backlogged trials that were predicted when the ban went into effect.

If plea bargaining appears at all in state statutes, it is generally in the context of being prohibited or restricted for certain matters or types of cases. For example, many states have prohibited plea bargaining in drunk driving cases, sex offender cases, or those involving other crimes that place the public at risk for repeat offenses or general harm. Another common provision, found in a majority of states, is a requirement that a prosecutor must inform a victim or the victim's survivors of any plea bargaining in a case. In many states, victims' views and comments regarding both plea bargaining and sentencing are factored into the ultimate decisions or determinations.

At least one state (Alabama) has expressly ruled that once a plea bargain is accepted, or there is detrimental reliance upon the agreement before the plea is entered, it becomes binding and enforceable under constitutional law (substantive due process). Ex Parte Hon. Orson Johnson, (Alabama, 1995).

ADDITIONAL RESOURCES

Attorney General. U.S. Department of Justice. "Criminal Resource Manual." Available at http://www.usdoj.gov/usao/ eousa/foia_reading_room/usam/title9/16mcrm.htm (accessed November 1, 2012).

Legal Information Institute. "Plea Bargain." Cornell University Law School. Available at http://www.law.cornell.edu/wex/ plea_bargain (accessed November 4, 2012).

Lippke, Richard. *The Ethics of Plea Bargaining.* New York: Oxford University Press, 2011.

U.S. Code, Title 18: Crimes and Criminal Procedure, Part II: Procedure, Chapter 221: Arraignment, Pleas and Trial. Available at http://www.gpo.gov/fdsys/granule/USCODE-2010-title18/ USCODE-2010-title18-partII-chap221/content-detail.html (accessed November 4, 2012).

CRIMINAL LAW

PROBATION AND PAROLE

Sections within this essay:

BACKGROUND

The use of probation and parole is governed in part by competing philosophies, classicalism and positivism. In short, classicalists believe that offenders choose their actions and, therefore, in order to prevent (or deter) future criminal acts, such individuals should be punished. Conversely, positivists believe that individuals are forced into the choice of committing crime through **no fault** of their own and, therefore, the conditions and/or behaviors that caused the action should be remedied, ultimately resulting in rehabilitation of the offender.

Legislative acts and public sentiment further dictate the application of probation and parole. Therefore, universal and consistent definitions and applications of probation and parole are not available as the methods of punishment and governing philosophies have evolved and moved toward the twenty-first century.

While these factors contribute to a lack of consistency when dealing with probation and parole, the primary obstacle to detailing specific state protocols is that the practice of granting probation and/or parole at the state level is dependent on the discretionary powers of select individuals, such as the **prosecutor**, the judicial authority, and the parole board. Information can be obtained regarding state-level agencies governing probation and parole from the American Probation and Parole Association (www.appa-net.org) and federal level parole practices from the U.S. Parole Commission (www.justice.gov/uspc/rules_procedures/2-2.pdf).

PROBATION

Definition Probation is a court-imposed **sanction** that "releases a convicted offender into the community under a conditional suspended sentence." This practice assumes that most offenders are not dangerous and will respond well to treatment. In fact, the average **probationer** is a first time and/or non-violent offender who, it is believed, will be best served by remaining in the community while serving out the sentence.

History Historically, probation does not involve **incarceration**, making it a front-end solution to address the overcrowding problem in U.S. prisons and jails. While the immediate goal of any probation program is rehabilitation, in reality, it is more a necessity than an instrument. As a result, other programs have been developed under the umbrella of community corrections that utilize elements of conditional release, resulting in the expansion of probation-type programs.

Probation developed as a result of the efforts of philanthropist John Augustus to rehabilitate convicted offenders, although references to similar practices exist as early as 437-422 B.C. It was favored because it allowed judicial authorities a great deal of discretion when imposing sentences, thereby providing the opportunity to tailor sentences to a particular offender, in theory allowing for the greatest possibility of rehabilitation. While sentences of probation vary widely across and within jurisdictions, the maximum length of time that one can be under supervision is 5 years (60 months).

The functions of probation are difficult to state definitively. It is known that at its inception, John Augustus' goal was behavioral reform. This reflects the **sentencing** goal of rehabilitation. Fundamentally, it is believed that by allowing the offender to remain in the community, the system is providing a second chance. Further, support and guidance from probation officers may achieve the aim of guiding the offender towards a law-abiding existence.

Given that probation is no longer limited to first-time, non-violent offenders who pose minimal risk to the community, the reality is significantly different. Coupled with low confidence in the effectiveness of rehabilitative success and a burgeoning offender population, actual practices tend to be dictated by conflicting goals on both an individual and administrative level. In an aggressive bid to prevent jail or prison overcrowding, several alternatives to incarceration have developed. Some such programs enable offenders traditionally incarcerated to be released into the community, thereby forcing a shift in focus from rehabilitation to control and supervision.

Intensive Supervised Probation (ISP) ISP is a form of release into the community that emphasizes close monitoring of convicted offenders and imposes rigorous conditions on that release, such as the following:

- Multiple weekly contacts with officer
- Random and unannounced drug testing
- Stringent enforcement of conditions (i.e., maintaining employment)
- Required participation in treatment, education programs, etc.

Individuals on ISP are those who most likely should NOT be in the community. The restrictions placed on them are often excessive and the level of direct, face-to-face contact required is believed to significantly deter or at least interfere with any ongoing criminal activity.

Shock Probation and Split Sentencing Shock probation/split sentencing is a sentence for a term of years, but after 30, 60, or 90 days, the offender is removed from jail or prison.

While these terms are used interchangeably, they are actually two different activities. In shock probation, the offender is originally sentenced to jail, then brought before the judge after 30, 60, or 90 days and re-sentenced to probation (Ohio scheme). In split sentencing, probation is part of the original sentence requiring no additional appearance before the judge (California scheme). Nonetheless, the terms refer to the same outcome—some jail, some community.

Revocation Since probation is a conditional release, it can be revoked, or taken away, if the conditions governing release are not met (technical violation) or if a new crime is committed during the probationary period (new offense).

Probation revocation is initiated by the probation officer's belief that a violation warranting revocation has occurred. As a result of the 1973 case *Gagnon v. Scarpelli* (411 U.S. 778), the Supreme Court decided that where "liberty interests" are involved, probationers are entitled to retain certain due process rights. Such rights include: (1) written notification of the alleged violations; (2) preliminary (or **probable cause**) **hearing** at which a judicial authority will determine whether sufficient probable cause exists to pursue the case; and (3) if warranted, a revocation hearing.

If a revocation hearing is scheduled, probationers have the right to **testify** on their own behalf, present witnesses, and have an attorney present. While the Gagnon court was vague regarding the right to court appointed **counsel** at a revocation hearing, most jurisdictions do provide the right to appointed counsel.

The standard of proof required at a revocation hearing is a "preponderance of the evidence," lower than that required at a criminal trial. Possible outcomes include return to supervision, reprimand with restoration to supervision, or revocation with **imprisonment**.

PAROLE

Definition Parole is the "conditional early release from prison or jail, under supervision, after a portion of the sentence has been served." This practice assumes that the offender successfully demonstrated conformity to the rules and regulations of the prison environment and shows an ability to conform to society's norms and laws.

History The word, parole, derives from the French "parol" meaning "word of honor" and references prisoners of war promising not to take up arms in current conflict if released. How that concept came to apply to the early release of convicted, often violent offenders is less clear. The first documented official use of early release from prison in the United States is credited to Samuel G. Howe in Boston (1847), but prior to that, other programs using pardons achieved basically the same outcome. In fact, as late as 1938, parole was simply a conditional **pardon** in many states.

Alexander Maconochie (England) ran the Norfolk Island prison. During his tenure, he instituted a system whereby inmates would be punished for the past and trained for the future. He believed that inmates could be rehabilitated so he implemented an open-ended sentencing structure where inmates had to "earn" their release by passing through three stages. Each stage increased their liberty and responsibilities. Inmates had an open time frame in which to earn the next level. Compliance advanced them; infractions resulted in a return to the previous stage, thereby lengthening the sentence. The open-ended sentences (today known as indeterminate sentencing) allowed the administration to ensure that when finally released, an offender's behavior had been successfully reformed. Eventually, Maconochie was removed from his position under criticism that his program "coddled" criminals.

At about the same time, Sir Walter Crofton was developing a similar program in Ireland using "tickets of leave." The "Irish System," as it came to be known, employed a similar practice of allowing inmates to earn credits towards early release. However, once the "ticket of leave" was achieved, release from **custody** was conditional. The releasees were supervised in the community by either law enforcement or civilian personnel who were required to secure employment and to conduct home visits. These "supervisors" represented the forerunner to today's parole officer.

In the United States, Zebulon Brockway (Superintendent) employed elements from both the Irish and Great Britain models in managing the Elmira Reformatory during the 1870s. Brockway is credited with the passage of the first indeterminate sentencing law in the United States as well as introducing the first good time system to reduce inmates' sentences. However, releasing the offenders was only part of the problem, and initially the greatest challenge was providing adequate supervision once release had been granted.

By 1913, it was clear some independent body was required to supervise inmates in the community and by 1930, Congress formally established a United States Board of Parole. It appeared, at least for awhile, that initiatives and programs were developing that could make parole a viable and useful tool of the criminal justice system. But unfortunate timing contributed ultimately to its downfall.

In 1929, the Great Depression hit the United States. An immediate result was a sharp increase in prison populations. However, the high cost of maintaining prisons as well as a lack of available personnel to staff them made new construction prohibitive and contributed to the popularity of parole. While alleviation of the overcrowding problem is often cited as a secondary (or latent) goal, the reality is that as a back-end solution, parole is vital to the maintenance of the correctional system.

With the onset of the twentieth century, philosophers began to examine the social and psychological aspects of criminal behavior. This heralded a shift from classicalist thinking towards positivism. Under positivism, actions are believed to be caused by forces beyond one's control (such forces could be psychological, biological, or sociological in origin). Therefore, parolees were now viewed as "sick" and the parole department was charged with the responsibility of "fixing" them.

Positivism is consistent with a less punitive approach to sentencing and generally involves an indeterminate sentencing structure allowing for the possibility of early release if the offender demonstrates that they have been successfully rehabilitated. As such, it fit well with the Elmira system and the timing afforded officials the opportunity to use parole as a means to relieve the overcrowded conditions that had developed during the depression.

The fact that parole involves some incarceration suggests that the average parolee has committed a more serious crime than the average probationer and, hence, poses a greater risk to the community. Therefore, primary goals of parole must include crime deterrence and offender control. Given that most offenders will eventually return to the community, a rival goal is reintegration, or the facilitation of an offender's transition from incarceration to freedom.

Unfortunately, it appeared during the 1980s that parole was failing. Street crime rates during this period skyrocketed and in many cases, the crimes were perpetrated by individuals who were released into the community prior to the official expiration of their sentence. This reality led to the development of penal philosophies espousing "tough on crime" approaches and demanding "truth in sentencing." Such philosophies warned criminals, "do the crime, do the time" and resulted in radical changes to sentencing practices across the country that indicated a return to a more punitive sentencing structure.

Revocation Since parole is a conditional release, it can be revoked or taken away if the conditions governing release are not met (technical violation) or if a new crime is committed during the probationary period (new offense). In this manner, it is similar to probation; however, it differs in that probation is governed by judicial decisions whereas parole is governed by administrative procedures. As a result of the administrative nature of parole, the revocation process is varied among the jurisdictions.

In large part, however, most minor infractions are dealt with by the parole officer and may not necessitate involvement of the parole board. Some jurisdictions empower the parole officer to immediately take a parolee into custody for 24 (New York) to 48 hours (Pennsylvania) for purposes of obtaining an **arrest warrant**. This practice is typically employed when the offender represents an immediate threat to public safety.

With respect to the legal protections afforded to parolees, the first U.S. Supreme Court case to explore this issue was *Morrissey v. Brewer* (1972). The Morrissey case explored the extension of due process rights of (1) written notice to parolee prior to general revocation proceeding; (2) identification of the violations being presented and any **evidence** being used to prove that the violation took place; (3) the right of the parolee to confront and cross-examine accusers (subject to exceptions) and (4) a written explanation for the decisions regarding the revocation of the parole and what evidence was employed in making that decision. Perhaps the greatest contribution of the Morrissey case was the creation of a two-stage process wherein probable cause that violations had occurred had to exist in order to go to the second stage, which was the actual revocation hearing.

Interestingly, the Supreme Court did not choose to create a bright line rule for the right to court-appointed counsel at a revocation hearing. For the most part, however, most jurisdictions have followed the decision in *Mempa v. Rhay* (1967). While this case specifically dealt with the rights of probationers, it has been applied recently to parolees as well. The Supreme Court wrote that "any indigent is entitled at every stage of a criminal proceeding to be represented by court-appointed counsel, where substantial rights of a criminal **accused** may be affected." In sum, the Supreme Court considered the liberty interests of the probationers and decided that a probation revocation hearing constituted a "critical stage" which dictated adherence to due process protections. This rationale has consistently been extended to include parole revocation hearings as well.

Abolishment As of 2012, 15 states (Arizona, California, Delaware, Illinois, Indiana, Kansas, Maine, Minnesota, Mississippi, Ohio, Oregon, New Mexico, North Carolina, Virginia and Washington) and the Federal government have eliminated parole programs in lieu of a determinate model of sentencing reflective of a more retributive approach to punishment.

Such an action may seem warranted given the apparent inability of the system to guarantee the protection of the citizens—but the end result is predictable. Overcrowding still represents the greatest challenge to the correctional industry. In fact, three states (Connecticut, Colorado, and Florida) reinstituted the parole boards after eliminating them due to overcrowding problems. The reality is that removal of parole ultimately leads simply to a shift in power from parole boards to prosecutors, in that the option most often exercised in states without parole is probation (see above).

ADDITIONAL RESOURCES

Abadinsky, Howard. *Probation and Parole.* 11th ed. Upper Saddle River, NJ: Prentice Hall, 2011.

Bonczar, Thomas P., and Lauren E. Glaze. *Probation and Parole in the United States.* Washington, DC: Bureau of Justice Statistics, 2011.

Champion, Dean J. *Probation, Parole, and Community Corrections.* 6th ed. Upper Saddle River, NJ: Prentice Hall, 2007.

Hoffman, Peter. "History of the Federal Parole System, Part I (1910-1972)." *Federal Probation,* September. 1997, pp. 23-31.

Hoffman, Peter. "History of the Federal Parole System, Part II (1973-1997)." *Federal Probation,* December. 1997, pp. 49-57.

ORGANIZATIONS

American Probation and Parole Association (APPA)

2760 Research Park Drive
Lexington, KY 40511-8410
Phone: (859) 244-8207
Fax: (859) 244-8001
Email: appa@csg.org
URL: http://www.appa-net.org

U.S. Parole Commission

5550 Friendship Blvd., Suite 420
Chevy Chase, MD 20815-7286
URL: http://www.justice.gov/uspc

CRIMINAL LAW

RIGHT TO COUNSEL

Sections within this essay:

- Background
- What the Sixth Amendment Guarantees
- The Miranda Case
- Invoking the Right
- Judicial Proceedings Before Trial
- Custodial Interrogation
- Lineups and Other Identification Situations
- Post-Conviction Proceedings
- Adequate Representation or Ineffective Assistance of Counsel
- Additional Resources

BACKGROUND

During the colonial period and the early years of the Republic the practice in the United States was varied with respect to providing counsel to suspects in criminal cases. The practice varied from the English method, where no counsel was provided to defendants of **felony** charges, but counsel was made available for defendants of **misdemeanor** charges. Rules in a few states allowed for the appointment of counsel where defendants could not afford to retain a lawyer. The Sixth Amendment to the U.S. Constitution states: "in all criminal prosecutions, the **accused** shall enjoy the right ... to have the assistance of counsel for his defense." At the time the Sixth Amendment was ratified, Congress enacted two laws that appeared to indicate an understanding that the Sixth Amendment guarantee was limited: counsel would not be denied to those who wished for and could afford a lawyer. Much later—in the 1930s—the Supreme Court began to expand the clause to its present scope.

Police officers ask questions of victims, witnesses, and suspects. If individuals feel that they are suspects in a criminal investigation or even that they could later be considered a suspect, they should speak with a lawyer before they speak with law enforcement officers. What they say to their lawyer is confidential and cannot be used against them. However, what they say to the police can be used against them, even if there is no recorded or written record of that conversation.

Individuals can always inform the police officer that they wish to speak with a lawyer before they answer any questions. If they are in **custody** (have been arrested or otherwise detained), the police must stop their questioning and they will be given an opportunity to speak with a lawyer. The police may return and begin to ask them questions again after a reasonable amount of time. If they have not yet spoken with a lawyer when the police return to question them, they may continue to refuse to answer any questions until they have obtained legal assistance.

WHAT THE SIXTH AMENDMENT GUARANTEES

The Sixth Amendment guarantees the right to legal counsel at all significant stages of a criminal proceeding. This right is so important that there is an associated right given to people who are unable to pay for legal assistance to have counsel appointed and paid for by the government. The federal criminal justice system and all states have procedures for appointing counsel for indigent defendants. The Sixth Amendment right to counsel has been extended to the following:

- the interrogation phase of a criminal investigation
- the trial itself
- **sentencing**
- at least an initial **appeal** of any **conviction**

If individuals are arrested in the United States they have a range of rights that give them certain protections, even if they are not a citizen of the United States. These rights include the following:

- A trial by a **jury** (in most cases)
- The jury to hear all of the witnesses and see all of the **evidence**
- Presence at the trial and while the jury is hearing the case
- The opportunity to see, hear, and confront the witnesses presenting the case against them
- The opportunity to call witnesses and to have the court issue subpoenas to compel the witnesses to appear
- The chance to **testify** themselves should they choose to do so
- The option to refuse to testify
- Access to a criminal defense lawyer. If individuals cannot afford to hire their own criminal defense lawyer, a **public defender** will represent them. This lawyer can act on their behalf before, during, and after the trial
- The right to cross-examine the witnesses giving **testimony** against them
- The right to compel the state to prove its case against them beyond a reasonable doubt

A judge will appoint an attorney for an indigent **defendant**; this attorney will be compensated at government expense if at the conclusion of the case the defendant could possibly be imprisoned for a period of more than six months. In reality, judges almost always appoint attorneys for indigents in practically every case in which a jail sentence is a possibility—regardless of how long the sentence may be. Generally, a judge will appoint the attorney for an indigent defendant at the defendant's first court appearance; for most defendants, the first court appearance is an **arraignment** or a hearing to set **bail**.

THE MIRANDA CASE

In 1966, the U.S. Supreme Court decision in *Miranda v. Arizona* ushered in a period of court-imposed restraints on the government's ability to interrogate suspects it takes into custody. This famous decision focused on **Fifth Amendment** protections against **self-incrimination**, but

it also spoke to the right to counsel. One of the most important restraints enumerated in the *Miranda* decision is the prohibition against the government's interrogation of suspects or witnesses after the suspect has invoked the right to counsel. Here's what the Miranda warnings generally say:

- You have the right to remain silent.
- Anything you say can be used against you in a court of law.
- You have the right to have an attorney present now and during any future questioning. The right to have counsel present at a custodial interrogation is necessary to protect the Fifth Amendment **privilege against self-incrimination**. A suspect detained for interrogation must be clearly informed that he has the right to consult with a lawyer and to have the lawyer with him during interrogation.
- If you cannot afford an attorney, one will be appointed to you free of charge if you wish. The Supreme Court found it necessary to mandate notice to defendants about their constitutional right to consult with an attorney. They went one step further and declared that if a defendant is poor, the government must appoint a lawyer to represent him.

The Court further instructed the police that if a suspect says he wants a lawyer, the police must cease any interrogation or questioning until an attorney is present. Further, the police must give the suspect an opportunity to confer with his attorney and to have the attorney present during any subsequent questioning.

Individuals need to remember that they can be arrested without being advised of their Miranda Rights. The Miranda rights do not protect individuals from being arrested, but they help suspects keep from unwittingly incriminating themselves during police questioning.

All the police need to **arrest** a person is **probable cause** to believe a suspect has committed a crime. Probable cause is merely an adequate reason based on the facts or events. Police are required to read or give suspects their Miranda warnings only before questioning a suspect. Failing to follow the Miranda rules may cause suspects' statements to be **inadmissible** in court; the original arrest may still be perfectly legal and valid.

Police are allowed to ask certain questions without reading the Miranda rights, including the following:

- name
- address
- date of birth
- Social Security number
- other questions necessary to establishing a person's identity

Police can also give alcohol and drug tests without Miranda warnings, but individuals being tested may refuse to answer questions.

INVOKING THE RIGHT

The Supreme Court, while not overruling *Miranda,* has moved from an outright ban on evidence obtained in violation of the rule to a more relaxed standard. In *Chavez v. Martinez,* 538 US 760, 123 S. Ct. 1994, 155 L. Ed. 2d 984 (2003), the Court held that the Self-Incrimination Clause was not violated until the government sought to introduce a defendant's self-incriminating statements. In *U.S. v. Patane,* 542 U.S. 630, 124 S.Ct. 2620, 159 L.Ed.2d 667 (2004), it ruled that the failure of police officers to properly "Mirandize" a suspect did not require the suppression of physical evidence obtained through inadmissible questioning. The Court rejected the application of the Fourth Amendment's "fruit of the poisonous tree" doctrine. This doctrine requires that when police illegally search and seize evidence, any additional evidence that is based on this tainted evidence cannot be used as well.

Law enforcement officers have tried to avoid the restrictions that *Miranda* imposes on their interrogations because reading suspects their Miranda warnings upon their arrest can discourage suspects from cooperating and confessing to their crimes. Police developed a two-stage interrogation technique in which investigators interview a suspect without advising the suspect of his Miranda rights. Once the suspect gives incriminating statements the police briefly suspend the session before "Mirandizing" the suspect and then asking him to repeat the incriminating statements. The suspect, unaware that the first statement would be inadmissible, waives these rights and repeats the incriminating statements. Courts admitted the statements made at the second stage. However, the Supreme Court in *Missouri v. Seibert,* 542 U.S. 600, 124 S.Ct. 2601, 159 L.Ed.2d 643 (2004), ruled that this two-stage method violated *Miranda.*

The right to counsel has created significant burdens on law enforcement's ability to conduct effective interrogations Several recent court decisions have begun to limit a custodial suspect's ability to invoke that right. Specifically, the Supreme Court wants to ensure that a suspect's invocation of rights is not frivolous. To do this, courts require that suspects invoke their right to counsel unequivocally, as well as in a timely manner.

If individuals are arrested or questioned, the burden is on them to invoke their right to counsel in a clear and unequivocal manner. They should receive notice that they have the right to an attorney, but law enforcement is not required to ask them whether they want an attorney, nor do they need to ask them clarifying questions if they are unclear in their request for an attorney. Not only must invoking the right to counsel be unequivocal, but courts also have begun to insist that invocations of the Miranda right to counsel be made in a timely manner. Individuals should not wait to be asked if they want a lawyer, nor should they expect the police to read them Miranda warnings before they ask for counsel.

JUDICIAL PROCEEDINGS BEFORE TRIAL

Generally, defendants are entitled to counsel from the time of their arraignment until the beginning of their trial. This is because the defendant's need for consultation, investigation, and preparation are critically important for a fair trial. The courts have gradually expanded this idea to the point that there is a legal concept of "a critical stage in a criminal proceeding" that indicates when a defendant must be represented by counsel.

CUSTODIAL INTERROGATION

Defendants who have been taken into custody and have invoked their Sixth Amendment right to counsel with respect to the offense for which they are being prosecuted may not later waive that right. However, defendants may waive their right under Miranda not to be questioned about unrelated and uncharged offenses.

What happens if the police violate the right to counsel? The remedy for violation of the Sixth Amendment rule is that any statements obtained from defendants under these circumstances will be excluded from the evidence at trial. There is one important exception to the Sixth Amendment **exclusionary rule**: evidence obtained from defendants held in custody that violates the Sixth Amendment may be used for the sole purpose of impeaching the defendants' testimony at trial.

LINEUPS AND OTHER IDENTIFICATION SITUATIONS

Lineups are considered to be "critical stage" and the prosecution may not admit into evidence in-court identification of defendants based on out-of-court lineups or show-ups if they were obtained without the presence of defendant's counsel. Courts have found that a defendant's counsel is necessary at a **lineup** because the lineup stage is filled with much potential for both intentional and unintentional errors. Without the defendant's attorney present at the lineup, these errors may not be discovered and remedied prior to trial.

This rule does not apply to other methods of obtaining identification and other evidentiary material relating to the defendant, including the following:

- blood samples
- DNA samples

- handwriting samples
- vocal samples

In these cases, there is far less chance that the absence of counsel at the time the evidence is obtained from the defendant might prevent the defendant from getting a fair trial.

The Sixth Amendment does not guarantee the presence of the defendant's counsel at a pretrial proceeding unless the physical presence of the defendant is involved. Furthermore, the defendant's presence must be required at a trial-like confrontation at which the defendant requires the advice and assistance of counsel.

POST-CONVICTION PROCEEDINGS

In a criminal trial, the law requires a lawyer for defendants to be present at the sentencing stage of the trial. If individuals are convicted of a crime and are placed on **probation**, they still have the right to counsel at a later hearing on the revocation of their probation and imposition of the deferred sentence. Due process and **equal protection** rather than Sixth Amendment rights, however, will apply in the following three post-trial hearings:

1. for granting **parole** or probation
2. for revoking parole when parole was imposed after sentencing
3. for prison disciplinary hearings

ADEQUATE REPRESENTATION OR INEFFECTIVE ASSISTANCE OF COUNSEL

Indigent defendants who are represented by appointed lawyers and defendants who can afford to hire their own attorneys are both entitled to adequate representation. But "adequate representation" does not mean perfect representation. However, an incompetent or negligent lawyer can so poorly represent a client that the court is justified in throwing out a guilty verdict based on the attorney's incompetence.

If a defendant's lawyer is ineffective at trial and on direct appeal, the defendant's Sixth Amendment right to a fair trial has been violated. In analyzing claims that a defendant's lawyer was ineffective, the principal goal is to determine whether the lawyer's conduct so undermined the functioning of the judicial process that the trial cannot be relied upon as having produced a just result. Proving this requires two steps:

1. The defendant must show that his own lawyer's job performance was deficient. The defendant must prove that his counsel made errors so serious that the lawyer did not function as the counsel guaranteed the defendant by the Sixth Amendment.

2. The defendant must show that the deficient performance unfairly prejudiced the defense. The defendant must show that his lawyer's errors were so serious as to wholly deprive the defendant of a fair trial.

Unless a defendant proves both steps, the conviction or sentence cannot be said to result from a breakdown in the judicial process such that the result is unreliable. When courts review a lawyer's advocacy of a defendant, they are deferential. Courts are bound by a strong presumption that any given lawyer's conduct falls within the range of reasonable professional assistance.

In 2012, the Supreme Court looked at the issue of ineffective counsel in the **plea bargaining** stage, deciding two important cases. In *Lafler v. Cooper*, 132 S. Ct. 1376 (2012), the Court concluded that a defendant had been denied effective assistance when the defendant would have accepted a plea bargain agreement but for the poor advice of his lawyer. In a companion case, *Missouri v. Frye*, 132 S. Ct. 1399, (2012) the Court examined a case where defense counsel failed to communicate a plea bargain offer to the client. The Court determined that this failure constituted ineffective assistance of counsel.

ADDITIONAL RESOURCES

Garcia, Alfredo. *The Sixth Amendment in Modern American Jurisprudence: A Critical Perspective (Contributions in Legal Studies)*. Greenwood Publishing Group, 1992.

Hogrogian, John G. *Miranda v. Arizona: The Rights of the Accused (Famous Trials)*. Detroit: Lucent Books, 1999.

Lewis, Anthony. *Gideon's Trumpet*. New York: Vintage Books, 1989.

National Legal Aid & Defender Association. "History of Right to Counsel." Available at http://www.nlada.org/About/About_HistoryDefender (accessed November 4, 2012).

Tomkovicz, James J. *The Right to the Assistance of Counsel: A Reference Guide to the United States*. Westport, CT: Greenwood House, 2002.

ORGANIZATIONS

Federal Defender's Association (FDA)
8530 Wilshire Blvd, Suite 404
Beverly Hills, CA 90211
Fax: (310) 397-1001
Email: defense@afda.org
URL: http://www.afda.org/

Legal Services Corporation (LSC)
750 First Street NE, Tenth Floor
Washington, DC 20002-4250
Phone: (202) 336-8800

Fax: (202) 336-8959
Email: info@lsc.gov
URL: http://www.lsc.gov/

National Association of Criminal Defense Lawyers (NACDL)

1660 L St. NW, 12th Fl.
Washington, DC 20036
Phone: (202) 872-8600
Fax: (202) 872-8690

Email: assist@nacdl.org
URL: http://www.nacdl.org

National Legal Aid & Defender Association (NLADA)

1625 K Street NW, Suite 800
Washington, DC 20006-1604
Phone: (202) 452-0620
Fax: (202) 872-103
Email: info@nlada.org
URL: http://www.nlada.org/

CRIMINAL LAW

SEARCH AND SEIZURE

Sections within this essay:

BACKGROUND

"Search and seizure" refers to the methods used by law enforcement to investigate crimes, track down **evidence**, question witnesses, and **arrest** suspects. It also refers to the legal rules governing these methods. At the federal level these rules are set forth in the Fourth Amendment to the U.S. Constitution, the Federal Rules of **Criminal Procedure**, and Title 18 of the United States Code, sections 2231 et seq. The rules and statutes refer to each other, and both are designed to provide greater detail for areas left silent by the Constitution. In addition, each state has its own set of applicable statutes, rules of procedure, and constitutional provisions. But the starting point in understanding any of these rules is the Fourth Amendment, since it sets forth the minimum amount of protection that both the state and federal government must provide against searches and seizures. Under the Due Process and Equal Protection Clauses of the Fourteenth Amendment, the U.S. Supreme Court has ruled that states may provide their citizens with more protection against searches and seizures but not less.

The American Revolution was fought in part to create a system of government that would operate within the rule of law. The rule of law is represented by the idea that the United States is a nation of laws and not of men and women. Under the rule of law, the actions of government officials are limited by the legal principles, rules, and other norms that make up the U.S. legal system and not by the arbitrary or capricious whim of an individual official. Violating these legal norms in the course of official conduct can transform a law enforcer into a law breaker.

The Framers drafted the Fourth Amendment in response to their colonial experience with British officials whose discretion in collecting revenues for the Crown often went unchecked. Local magistrates were allowed to issue general search warrants to British tax collectors upon mere suspicion that a colonist was not fully complying with the tax code. Magistrates were not authorized to question the source or strength of a tax collector's suspicion, and, once issued, general warrants permitted blanket, door-to-door searches of entire neighborhoods without regard to person, place, or time.

The **writ** of assistance was a particularly loathsome form of general **warrant**. This writ derived its name from the power of British authorities to compel local peace officers and colonial residents to "assist" in executing a

453

particular search. A writ of assistance lasted for the life of the king or queen under whom it was issued and could be enforced by any British law enforcement officer, including customs officials who often relied on them as long-term hunting licenses against suspected smugglers.

Colonial opposition to general warrants was pervasive. In Paxton's case, 1 Quincy 51 (Mass. 1761), James Otis appeared on behalf of the colonists who opposed issuance of another writ, arguing that before a warrant is valid it must be "directed to special officers and to search certain houses" for particular goods and may only be granted "upon oath made" by a government official "that he suspects such goods to be concealed in those very places he desires to search" (quoted in *Illinois v. Krull*, 480 U.S. 340 [1987]). John Adams cited Otis' argument against the writs "as the commencement of the controversy between Great Britain and America."

Ratified by the states in 1791, the Fourth Amendment put an end to writs of assistance by creating a constitutional buffer between U.S. citizens and the often intimidating power of law enforcement. It has three components: first, the Fourth Amendment establishes a **privacy** interest by recognizing the right of every citizen to be "secure in their persons, houses, papers, and effects"; second, it protects this privacy interest by prohibiting searches and seizures that are not authorized by a warrant based on "probable cause" or that are otherwise "unreasonable"; and third, for searches requiring a warrant the Fourth Amendment states that the warrant must describe with particularity "the place to be searched, and the persons or things to be seized" and be supported by "oath or affirmation" of the officer requesting its issuance.

THE TEXT OF THE FOURTH AMENDMENT AND CASE LAW INTERPRETING IT

Although **ratification** of the Fourth Amendment answered any lingering doubts about the validity of the writs of assistance in the United States, the text of the Fourth Amendment raised questions of its own about the meaning of the terms "unreasonable," "search or seizure," "warrant," "particularity," "oath or affirmation," and "probable cause," not to mention other questions about the scope of such terms as "houses, papers, and effects." The U.S. Supreme Court, lower federal courts, and state courts have spent more than 200 years grappling with these questions and continue to do so as new cases come before them.

The Text of the Fourth Amendment The Fourth Amendment reads as follows: "The right of the people to be secure in their persons, houses, papers, and effects, against unreasonable searches and seizures, shall not be

violated, and no Warrants shall issue, but upon **probable cause**, supported by Oath or affirmation, and particularly describing the place to be searched, and the persons or things to be seized."

When the Fourth Amendment Applies Like the rest of the **Bill of Rights**, the Fourth Amendment originally only applied in federal court. However, in *Wolf v. Colorado*, 338 U.S. 25 (1949), the U.S. Supreme Court ruled that the rights guaranteed by the text of the Fourth Amendment (sans the **exclusionary rule** to be discussed below) apply equally in state courts via the Fourteenth Amendment, which guarantees to the citizen of every state the right to due process and equal protection of the laws. The process by which the Supreme Court has made certain fundamental liberties protected by the Bill of Rights applicable to the states is known as the doctrine of incorporation.

Not every search and seizure that is scrutinized in state and federal court raises a Fourth Amendment issue. The Fourth Amendment only protects against searches and seizures conducted by the government or pursuant to governmental direction. Surveillance and investigatory actions taken by strictly private persons, such as private investigators, suspicious spouses, or nosey neighbors, are not governed by the Fourth Amendment. However, Fourth Amendment concerns do arise when those same actions are taken by a law enforcement official or a private person working in conjunction with law enforcement.

The Fourth Amendment does not apply even against governmental action unless defendants first establish that they had a reasonable expectation of privacy in the place to be searched or the thing to be seized. The Supreme Court has explained that what "a person knowingly exposes to the public, even in his own home or office, is not a subject of Fourth Amendment protection . . . ." But what he seeks to preserve as private, even in an area accessible to the public, may be constitutionally protected (see *Katz v. United States*, 389 U.S. 347 [1967]).

Applying this principle, the Supreme Court has ruled that individuals generally maintain a reasonable expectation of privacy in their bodies, clothing, and personal belongings. Homeowners possess a privacy interest that extends inside their homes and in the curtilage immediately surrounding the outside of their homes, but not in the "open fields" and "wooded areas" extending beyond the curtilage (see *Hester v. United States*, 265 U.S. 57 [1924]). A business owner's expectation of privacy in commercial property is less than the privacy interest afforded to a private homeowner and is particularly attenuated in commercial property used in "closely regulated" industries (i.e., airports, railroads, restaurants, and liquor establishments), where business premises may be subject to regular administrative searches by state or federal agencies for the purpose of determining compliance with health, safety, or security regulations. Automobile owners have a reasonable expectation of privacy in the cars they own and drive, though the expectation of privacy is less than a homeowner's privacy interest in his or her home.

No expectation of privacy is maintained for property and personal effects held open to the public. Things visible in "plain view" for a person of ordinary and unenhanced vision are entitled to no expectation of privacy and thus no Fourth Amendment protection. Items lying in someone's backseat, growing in someone's outdoor garden, or discarded in someone's curb-side garbage all fall within this category. However, items seen only through enhanced surveillance, such as through high-powered or telescopic lenses, may be subject to the strictures of the Fourth Amendment. Public records, published phone numbers, and other matters readily accessible to the general public enjoy no expectation of privacy. Similarly, the Supreme Court has said that individuals do not possess an expectation of privacy in their personal characteristics (see *United States v. Dionisio*, 410 U.S. 1 [1973]). Thus, the police may require individuals to give handwriting and voice exemplars, as well as hair, blood, DNA, and fingerprint samples, without complying with the Fourth Amendment's requirements.

Finally, to raise a Fourth Amendment objection to a particular search or seizure, a person must have "standing" to do so. Standing in this context means that the rights guaranteed by the Fourth Amendment are personal and may not be asserted on behalf of others. Thus, a passenger may not generally object to a police search of the owner's car and a house-guest may not generally object to a search of the homeowner's premises. These rules can become murky, however, as when a houseguest is actually living with the homeowner or owns things stored on the owner's premises.

How the Fourth Amendment Applies: The Warrant Requirement Once the Fourth Amendment applies to a particular search or seizure, the next question is under what circumstances is a warrant required. The Supreme Court has ruled that the Constitution expresses a preference for searches, seizures, and arrests conducted pursuant to a lawfully executed warrant (see *Mincey v. Arizona*, 437 U.S. 385 [1978]). A warrant is a written order signed by a court authorizing a law-enforcement officer to conduct a search, seizure, or arrest. Searches, seizures, and arrests performed without a valid warrant are deemed presumptively invalid, and any evidence seized without a warrant will be suppressed unless a court finds that the search was reasonable under the circumstances.

An application for a warrant must be supported by a sworn, detailed statement made by a law enforcement officer appearing before a neutral judge or **magistrate**. The Supreme Court has said that probable cause exists when the facts and circumstances within the police officer's knowledge provide a reasonably trustworthy basis for a person of reasonable caution to believe that a criminal offense has been committed or is about to take place (see *Carroll v. United States*, 267 U.S. 132 [1925]). Probable cause can be established by out-of-court statements made by reliable police informants, even though those statements cannot be tested by the magistrate. However, probable cause will not lie where the only evidence of criminal activity is an officer's affirmation of suspicion or belief (see *Aguilar v. Texas*, 378 U.S. 108 [1964]). On the other hand, an officer's subjective reason for making an arrest does not need to be the same criminal offense for which the facts indicate (*Devenpeck v. Alford*, 543 U.S. 146 [2004]).

Probable cause will not lie unless the facts supporting the warrant are sworn by the officer as true to the best of his or her knowledge. The officer's oath can be written or oral, but the officer must typically swear that no knowingly or intentionally false statement has been submitted in support of the warrant and that no statement has been made in reckless disregard of the truth. Inaccuracies due to an officer's **negligence** or innocent omission do not jeopardize a warrant's validity.

The Fourth Amendment requires not only that warrants be supported by probable cause offered by a sworn police officer, but it also requires that a warrant "particularly" describe the person or place to be searched or seized. Warrants must provide enough detail so that an officer with the warrant can ascertain with reasonable effort the persons and places identified in the warrant. For most residences a street address usually satisfies the particularity requirement, unless the warrant designates an apartment complex, hotel, or other multiple-unit building, in which case the warrant must describe the specific sub-unit to be searched. Warrants must describe individuals with sufficient particularity so that a person of average intelligence can distinguish them from others in the general population.

The magistrate before whom an officer applies for a warrant must be neutral and detached. This qualification means that the magistrate must be **impartial** and not a member of the "competitive enterprise" of law enforcement (see *California v. Acevedo*, 500 U.S. 565 [1991]). Thus, police officers, prosecutors, and attorneys general are disqualified from becoming a magistrate. States vary as to the requirements that candidates must possess before they will be considered qualified for the job of magistrate. Some states require that magistrates have an attorney's license, while others require only that their magistrates be literate.

How the Fourth Amendment Applies: The Reasonableness Requirement Not every search, seizure, or arrest must be made pursuant to a lawfully executed warrant. The Supreme Court has ruled that warrantless police conduct may comply with the Fourth Amendment so long as it is reasonable under the circumstances. The exceptions made to the Fourth Amendment's warrant requirement reflect the Court's reluctance to unduly impede the job of law enforcement officials. The Court has attempted to strike a balance between the practical realities of daily police work and the privacy and freedom interests of the public. Always requiring police officers to take the time to complete a warrant application and locate and appear before a judge could result in the destruction of evidence, the disappearance of suspects and witnesses, or both. The circumstances under which a warrantless search, seizure, or arrest is deemed reasonable generally fall within seven categories.

First, no warrant is required for a **felony** arrest in a public place, even if the arresting officer had ample time to procure a warrant, so long as the officer possessed probable cause that the suspect committed the crime. Felony arrests in places not open to the public generally do require a warrant, unless the officer is in "hot pursuit" of a fleeing **felon** (see *Warden v. Hayden*, 387 U.S. 294 [1967]). The Fourth Amendment also allows warrantless arrests for misdemeanors committed in an officer's presence.

Second, no warrant is required for searches incident to lawful arrest. If a police officer has made a lawful arrest, with or without a warrant, the Fourth Amendment permits the officer to conduct a search of the suspect's person, clothing, and all of the areas within the suspect's immediate reach. This kind of warrantless search is justified on grounds that it allows police officers to protect themselves from hidden weapons that might suddenly be wielded against them. Accordingly, officers are only permitted to seize items from the area in the immediate control of the arrestee.

Third, automobiles may be stopped if an officer possesses a reasonable and articulable suspicion that the motorist has violated a traffic law. Once the vehicle has pulled to the side of the road, the Fourth Amendment permits the officer to search the vehicle's interior, including the glove compartment. However, the trunk of a vehicle cannot be searched unless the officer has probable cause to believe that it contains **contraband** or the instrumentalities of criminal activity. But similar to a

search incident to arrest, once a vehicle has been lawfully impounded, its contents may be inventoried without a warrant, including the contents of the trunk.

Fourth, an officer who reasonably believes that criminal activity may be afoot in a public place is authorized to stop any person who is suspected of participating in that criminal activity and conduct a carefully limited search of the suspect's outer clothing for weapons that may be used against the officer (see *Terry v. Ohio*, 392 U.S. 1 [1968]). The officer may also ask for identification, but the suspect is under no obligation to produce it. However, a suspect's refusal to identify himself/herself together with surrounding events may create probable cause to arrest (see *People v. Loudermilk*, 241 Cal. Rptr. 208 [Cal. App. 1987]). This kind of warrantless search, called a Terry stop or a Terry **frisk**, is designed to protect officers from hidden weapons. Accordingly, items that do not feel like weapons, such as a baggie of soft, granular substance tucked inside a jacket pocket, cannot be seized during a Terry frisk, even if it turns out that the item is contraband.

Fifth, warrantless searches, seizures, and arrests may be justified by "exigent" circumstances. To determine whether exigent circumstances justified police conduct, a court must review the totality of the circumstances, including the gravity of the underlying offense and whether the suspect was fleeing or trying to escape. However, the surrounding circumstances must be tantamount to an emergency. Shots fired, screams heard, or fire emanating from inside a building have all been considered sufficiently exigent to dispense with the Fourth Amendment's warrant requirement.

Sixth, the Supreme Court has upheld brief, warrantless seizures at fixed roadside checkpoints aimed at intercepting illegal aliens (see *United States v. Martinez-Fuerte*, 428 U.S. 543 [1976]) and drunk drivers (see *Michigan v. Sitz*, 496 U.S. 444 [1990]). Both checkpoint programs passed constitutional muster because they were tailored to remedying specific problems that law enforcement could not effectively address through more traditional means, namely problems relating to policing the nation's border and ensuring roadway safety. However, when the primary purpose of a checkpoint is simply to detect ordinary criminal activity, the Supreme Court has declared it violative of the Fourth Amendment (see *Indianapolis v. Edmond*, 531 U.S. 32 [2000]).

Seventh, searches, seizures, and arrests made pursuant to a defective warrant may be justified if the officer was proceeding in "good faith." The Supreme Court has said that a search made pursuant to a warrant that is later declared invalid (i.e., it fails to meet the requirements for a valid warrant enumerated above) will still be considered reasonable under the Fourth Amendment so long as the warrant was issued by a magistrate and the defect was not the result of willful police deception (see *United States v. Leon*, 468 U.S. 897 [1984]). This exception to the warrant requirement was created so as not to punish honest police officers who have done nothing wrong while acting in accordance with an ostensibly valid warrant.

How the Fourth Amendment Applies: The Exclusionary Rule However, in 2012 the Court ruled in *United States v. Jones*, 565 U.S. ___, (2012) that when law enforcement attaches a global positioning system (GPS) device to a vehicle and uses this device to monitor the vehicle's movements, this constitutes a search under the Fourth Amendment. Law enforcement must obtain a warrant before attaching a GPS or other electronic tracking device to a vehicle.

For the more than 100 years after its ratification, the Fourth Amendment was of little value to criminal defendants because evidence seized by law enforcement in violation of the warrant or reasonableness requirements was still **admissible** during the defendant's prosecution. The Supreme Court dramatically changed Fourth Amendment **jurisprudence** when it handed down its decision in *Weeks v. United States*, 232 U.S. 383 (1914). *Weeks* involved the **appeal** of a **defendant** who had been convicted based on evidence that had been seized by a federal agent without a warrant or other constitutional justification. The Supreme Court reversed the defendant's **conviction**, thereby creating what is known as the "exclusionary rule." In *Mapp v. Ohio*, 367 U.S. 643 (1961), the Supreme Court made the exclusionary rule applicable to the states.

Designed to deter police misconduct, the exclusionary rule enables courts to exclude incriminating evidence from introduction at trial upon proof that the evidence was procured in contravention of a constitutional provision. The rule allows defendants to challenge the admissibility of evidence by bringing a pretrial motion to suppress the evidence. If the court allows the evidence to be introduced at trial and the **jury** votes to convict, the defendant can challenge the propriety of the trial court's decision denying the motion to suppress on appeal. If the defendant succeeds on appeal, however, the Supreme Court has ruled that **double jeopardy** principles do not bar retrial of the defendant because the trial court's error did not go to the question of guilt or innocence (see *Lockhart v. Nelson*, 488 U.S. 33 [1988]). Nonetheless, obtaining a conviction in the second trial would be significantly more difficult if the evidence suppressed by the exclusionary rule is important to the prosecution.

A companion to the exclusionary rule is the "fruit of the poisonous tree" doctrine. Under this doctrine, a court may exclude from trial not only evidence that itself was seized in violation of the Constitution but also any other evidence that is derived from an illegal search. For example, suppose a defendant is arrested for **kidnapping** and later confesses to the crime. If a court subsequently declares that the arrest was unconstitutional, the **confession** will also be deemed tainted and ruled **inadmissible** at any prosecution of the defendant on the kidnapping charge.

STATE COURT DECISIONS INTERPRETING CONSTITUTIONAL PROVISIONS GOVERNING SEARCH AND SEIZURE

The federal Constitution and the Supreme Court cases interpreting it establish the minimum amount of protection that a state court must provide when it is interpreting a section of the Bill of Rights that has been made applicable to the states via the doctrine of incorporation, including instances when a state court is required to interpret and apply the Fourth Amendment. A state court interpreting the search-and-seizure provisions of its own constitution may provide more protection than is afforded by the federal Constitution but not less.

ADDITIONAL RESOURCES

American Civil Liberties Union. "Search and Seizure." Available at http://www.aclu.org/criminal-law-reform/search-and-seizure (accessed November 3, 2012).

American Jurisprudence. 2d ed. Eagan, MN: Thomson/West, 2006.

Black's Law Dictionary. 9th ed. Eagan, MN: West, Thomson Reuters, 2009.

Gale Encyclopedia of American Law. 3rd ed. Detroit: Gale, Cengage Learning, 2011.

Hall, Kermit L., James W. Ely Jr., and Joel B. Grossman, eds. *Oxford Companion to the Supreme Court.* 2d ed. New York: Oxford University Press, 2005.

LaFave, Wayne R., Jerold H. Israel, and Nancy J. King, eds. *Criminal Procedure.* 5th ed. Eagan, MN: Thomson/West, 2009.

ORGANIZATIONS

American Civil Liberties Union (ACLU)
125 Broad St., 18th Fl.
New York, NY 10004
Phone: (212) 549-2500
Email: info@aclu.org
URL: http://www.aclu.org/

Association of Federal Defense Attorneys
8530 Wilshire Blvd, Suite 404
Beverly Hills, CA 90211
Phone: (714) 836-6031

Fax: (310) 397-1001
Email: AFDA2@AOL.com
URL: http://www.afda.org

Center for Human Rights and Constitutional Law
256 S. Occidental Blvd.
Los Angeles, CA 90057
Phone: (213) 388-8693
Fax: (213) 386-9484

Email: mail@centerforhumanrights.org
URL: http://www.centerforhumanrights.org

National District Attorneys Association (NDAA)
99 Canal Center Plaza
Alexandria, VA 22314
Phone: (703) 549-9222
Fax: (703) 836-3195
URL: http://www.ndaa.org

CRIMINAL LAW

SENTENCING AND SENTENCING GUIDELINES

Sections within this essay:

- Background
- Types of Sentences
- Factors Considered in Determining a Sentence
- "Three Strikes" Sentencing Laws
- Uniformity and Consistency
- Alternative Sentences
- Sentencing Commissions
- Selected State Sentencing Provisions
- Additional Resources

BACKGROUND

A sentence is a formal judgment pronouncing a specific punishment to be imposed for the **conviction** of a crime. It may involve the payment of a fine, community service, **incarceration**, or, in capital offenses, the death penalty. It also may consist of a term of **probation** or **parole** (although parole has been abolished in many states).

Sentences may be meted out directly following the entry of a verdict or at a "sentencing hearing" scheduled for a later date. In the interim, prosecutors prepare a "sentencing report" which advises the court of the defendant's prior criminal record, aggravating or **mitigating circumstances**, and other information about the **defendant** that may assist the court in deciding an appropriate punishment.

There have been concerted efforts over the years to standardize the approach toward sentencing, particularly in **felony** offenses, and to diminish judicial discretion in sentencing. These efforts reflect a vacillating but recurring perception by lawmakers and the public at large that arbitrary or discriminatory practices may interfere with fair and just sentencing in certain cases or for certain crimes. However, the U.S. Supreme Court severely limited the ability of the federal government and state governments to enact uniform sentencing guidelines when the Court ruled that these mandatory guidelines were unconstitutional.

TYPES OF SENTENCES

Listed below are the types of sentences imposed:

- A concurrent sentence is served at the same time as another sentence imposed earlier or at the same proceeding.

- A consecutive (or cumulative) sentence occurs when a defendant has been convicted of several counts, each one constituting a distinct offense or crime, or when a defendant has been convicted of several crimes at the same time. The sentences for each crime are then "tacked" on to each other, so that each sentence begins immediately upon the expiration of the previous one.

- A deferred sentence occurs when its **execution** is postponed until some later time.

- A determinate sentence is the same as a fixed sentence: it is for a fixed period of time.

- A final sentence puts an end to a criminal case. It is distinguished from an interlocutory or interim sentence.

- An indeterminate sentence, rather than stating a fixed period of time for **imprisonment**, instead declares that the period shall be "not more than" or "not less than" a certain prescribed duration of time. The authority to render indeterminate sentences is usually granted by **statute** in several states.
- A life sentence represents the **disposition** of a serious criminal case, in which the convicted person spends the remainder of his or her life in prison.
- A mandatory sentence is created by state statute and represents the rendering of a punishment for which a judge has/had no room for discretion. Generally it means that the sentence may not be suspended and that no probation may be imposed, leaving the judge with no alternative but the "mandated" sentence.
- A maximum sentence represents the outer limit of a punishment, beyond which a convicted person may not be held in custody.
- A minimum sentence represents the minimum punishment or the minimum time a convicted person must spend in prison before becoming eligible for parole or release.
- A presumptive sentence exists in many states by statute. It specifies an appropriate or "normal" sentence for each offense to be used as a baseline for a judge when meting out a punishment. The **statutory** presumptive sentence is considered along with other relevant factors (aggravating or mitigating circumstances) in determining the actual sentence. Most states have statutory "presumptive guidelines" for major or common offenses.
- A straight or flat sentence is a fixed sentence without a maximum or minimum.
- A **suspended sentence** actually has two different meanings. It may refer to a withholding or postponing of pronouncing a sentence following a conviction or it may refer to the postponing of the execution of a sentence after it has been pronounced.

FACTORS CONSIDERED IN DETERMINING A SENTENCE

Judges, not juries, determine punishments for a crime (in **capital punishment** cases, the **jury** usually decides whether to recommend death or life in prison).

The Eighth Amendment to the U.S. Constitution, made applicable to the states by the Fourteenth Amendment, provides that "Excessive **bail** shall not be required, nor excessive fines imposed, nor cruel and unusual punishments inflicted." In addition to the sentencing prohibitions contained in the Constitution, Title 18 of the United States Code, Part II (**Criminal Procedure**), Chapters 227 (Sentences), 228 (Death

Sentence), and 232 (Miscellaneous Sentencing Provisions) also govern sentencing in federal courts. Similarly, state court sentencing procedures are governed by state laws and constitutions as discussed below.

Most crimes are specifically enumerated in constitutions or statutes, and the provision that identifies the specific crime will also identify the appropriate punishment. For example, a statute may read, "Violation of this statute constitutes a **misdemeanor**, punishable by a fine not to exceed $500 or imprisonment not to exceed 30 days, or both." Given this range of potential punishment, a judge will then consider certain "aggravating" or "mitigating" circumstances to determine where along the prescribed spectrum a particular criminal's punishment should fall. Common factors considered by judges include:

- whether the offender is a "first-time" or repeat offender
- whether the offender was an **accessory** (helping the main offender) or the main offender
- whether the offender committed the crime under great personal stress or duress
- whether anyone was hurt, and whether the crime was committed in a manner that was unlikely to result in anyone being hurt
- whether the offender was particularly cruel to a victim, or particularly destructive, vindictive, etc.
- (sometimes) whether the offender is genuinely contrite or remorseful

Under Federal Rule of Criminal Procedure 32(a), before imposing a sentence, the court must afford **counsel** an opportunity to speak on behalf of the defendant. The court will address the defendant personally and ask him if he wishes to make a statement in his own behalf and to present any information in mitigation of punishment. The attorney for the government will have an equivalent opportunity to speak to the court. Similar provisions are contained in most state procedural statutes and rules. In many state courts, a victim or the survivors of a victim may also have the opportunity to address the court and recommend leniency or strictness for the sentence.

"THREE STRIKES" SENTENCING LAWS

Under the Violent Crime Control and Law Enforcement Act of 1994, the "Three Strikes" statute (18 U.S.C. § 3559[c]) provides for mandatory life imprisonment if a convicted felon:

- has been convicted in federal court of a "serious violent felony" and

- has two or more previous convictions in federal or state courts, at least one of which is a "serious violent felony." The other offense may be a serious drug offense.

The statute goes on to define a serious violent felony as including murder, **manslaughter**, **sex offenses**, **kidnapping**, robbery, and any offense punishable by 10 years or more which includes an element of the use of force or involves a significant risk of force.

The State of Washington was the first to enact a "Three Strikes" law in 1993. Since then, more than half of the states, in addition to the federal government, have enacted three strikes laws. The primary focus of these laws is the containment of recidivism (repeat offenses by a small number of criminals). California's law is considered the most far-reaching and most often used among the states.

Three strikes laws have been the subject of extensive debate over whether they are effective. Defendants sentenced to long prison terms under these laws have also sought to challenge these laws as unconstitutional. For instance, one defendant was found guilty of stealing $150 worth of video tapes from two California department stores. The defendant had prior convictions, and pursuant to California's three-strikes laws, the judge sentenced the defendant to 50 years in prison for the theft of the video tapes. The defendant challenged his conviction before the U.S. Supreme Court in *Lockyer v. Andrade* (2003), but the Court upheld the constitutionality of the law.

UNIFORMITY AND CONSISTENCY

In addition to "three strikes" laws, other state and all federal criminal statutes include mandatory sentences that require judges to impose identical sentences on all persons convicted of the same offense. Mandatory sentences are a direct result of state legislatures' or Congress' response to the public perception of judicial leniency or inconsistency in sentencing practices.

However, most crimes do not carry mandatory sentences. If sentencing is not mandatory, judges may "fit the punishment to the offender" rather than "fit the punishment to the crime." Competing theories about criminal justice help to fuel the different approaches to sentencing and punishment. These include the severity of punishment meted, and the specific objective sought by the punishment:

- Retribution: Some believe that the primary purpose of punishment should be to punish an offender for the wrong committed—society's vengeance against a criminal. The sentiment is to punish criminals and promote public safety by keeping them "off the streets."

- Rehabilitation: Others believe that the primary purpose of punishment should be to rehabilitate criminals to mend their criminal ways and to encourage the adoption of a more socially acceptable lifestyle. Most experts agree that this theory is commendable but not practical in prisons. Many criminals boast of coming out "better criminals" than they were when they entered prison.

- Deterrence: Still others argue that the perceived punishment for a crime should be so undesirable as to result in deterring someone from actually committing a crime for fear of the likely punishment. Again, the theory is commendable, but many crimes are committed on impulse or under the influence of alcohol and other drugs. Fear of punishment is usually not a deterrent under these circumstances. Moreover, repeat offenders do not fear incarceration the way that people who have been free all their lives might.

ALTERNATIVE SENTENCES

Forced to face prison overcrowding and failed attempts at deterrence or rehabilitation, many professionals in the criminal justice system have encouraged "alternative sentencing," which refers to any punishment other than incarceration. Most alternative sentences are really variations of probation, for example, a fine and community service, along with a set period of probation. Some judges have gotten more creative in their sentencing. In many jurisdictions, convicted persons have been required to do the following:

- install breathalyzer devices in their vehicles ("ignition interlocks") to prevent their operation of the vehicle without blowing into the device to determine whether their breath is free of alcohol

- carry signs which inform the community of their offense

- stay at home under "house arrest"

- complete alcohol or other drug treatment programs

- attend lectures given by crime victims

SENTENCING COMMISSIONS

The U.S. Sentencing Commission was created in 1984 as part of the Sentencing Reform Act provisions that were included in the Comprehensive Crime Control Act of 1984 (28 U.S.C. § 994). The Commission's principal purpose has been to establish uniform sentencing guidelines and practices for the federal court system. The guidelines provide 43 levels of offense seriousness that take into account not only the seriousness of the crime, but also the offender's criminal history. They apply to all federal felonies and most serious misdemeanors.

Decisions rendered by the U.S. Supreme Court in 2004 and 2005 altered the use of sentencing guidelines by state and federal courts. First, the Court in *Blakely v. Washington* (2004) ruled that the sentencing guidelines employed by the state of Washington were unconstitutional. The ruling caused many states to evaluate whether their own sentencing guidelines would survive constitutional muster. Moreover, some lower federal courts ruled that the federal sentencing guidelines were also unconstitutional. The Supreme Court resolved the question about whether mandatory provisions in the federal guidelines violated the Constitution. In two related cases, *United States v. Booker* and *United States v. Fanfan*, both decided in 2005, the Court ruled that the federal guidelines were indeed unconstitutional. According to the Court, judges may use their discretion in following the guidelines, but the guidelines may not be mandatory. Later Supreme Court cases have emphasized to federal judges that they must use the guidelines as a yardstick for a sentence but they can also employ a standard of reasonableness on a case-by-case basis.

As of 2012, twenty-two states have established sentencing commissions. The National Association of Sentencing Commissions (NASC), which includes the federal sector as a member, provides a forum, complete with national conferences, to promote the adoption of uniform or similar presumptive sentencing guidelines among jurisdictions. The legislatures in the states with guidelines have enacted laws to insure that their systems comply with *Blakely*. Though the Supreme Court removed the mandatory application of sentencing guidelines, the courts continue to rely on them in the everyday course of business.

SELECTED STATE SENTENCING PROVISIONS

ALABAMA: The Alabama Legislature formed the Alabama Sentencing Commission to study and make recommendations regarding the state's sentencing practices.

ALASKA: Alaska has judicially-created "benchmark" guidelines for felonies, with moderate **appellate** review. Parole has been abolished for most (two-thirds) felonies. There is no active sentencing commission for the state. The state legislature modified its sentencing scheme following the Supreme Court's decision in *Blakely*.

ARIZONA: Following the Supreme Court's decision in *Blakely*, state courts in Arizona have issued several rulings

regarding the constitutionality of sentencing provisions under state law.

ARKANSAS: State courts employ voluntary guidelines for felonies. There is no appellate review. Arkansas has retained its parole system. There are guidelines which incorporate intermediate sanctions, with preliminary discussions for guidelines in juvenile cases. State sentencing commission was established in 1994.

DELAWARE: Delaware utilizes voluntary guidelines for felonies and misdemeanors. Parole has been abolished in the state since 1990. There is moderate appellate review of sentencing decisions. The state's sentencing guidelines incorporate intermediate sanctions.

DISTRICT of COLUMBIA: The district in 2004 created the District of Columbia Sentencing Commission, which reports directly to the city council.

FLORIDA: In Florida, guidelines were repealed in 1997 and replaced with statutory presumptions for minimum sentences for felonies. The state sentencing commission was abolished in 1998 after the adoption of the new statutory presumptive sentences. There is moderate appellate review of sentencing determinations. Parole has been abolished in the system.

IOWA: Iowa has established a legislative commission to study sentencing reform.

KANSAS: Kansas uses presumptive guidelines for felonies, with moderate appellate review. Parole has been abolished in the state. There are no guidelines for intermediate sanctions.

MARYLAND: Maryland's legislature created the Maryland State Commission on Criminal Sentencing Policy in 1998. There are voluntary guidelines for felonies, with no appellate review. Parole has been retained.

MASSACHUSETTS: In Massachusetts, there are presumptive guidelines for felonies and misdemeanors. A proposal is pending in the legislature for appellate review of sentencing determinations. Parole has been retained.

MICHIGAN: Michigan is a member of the National Association of Sentencing Commissions. The state employs presumptive guidelines for felonies, with appellate review as authorized by statute. The state also maintains a restricted parole system.

MINNESOTA: The state has presumptive guidelines for felonies, with moderate appellate review. Parole has been abolished in the state. There are no guidelines for intermediate sanctions.

MISSOURI: Missouri uses voluntary guidelines for felonies, with no appellate review. Parole has been retained in the state.

NORTH CAROLINA: In North Carolina, there are presumptive guidelines for felonies and misdemeanors, with minimum appellate review. Since 1999, the state has incorporated a special dispositional grid for juvenile cases. Parole has been abolished in the state.

OHIO: Ohio uses presumptive narrative guidelines for felonies. There is limited appellate review. Parole has been abolished and replaced with a judicial release mechanism. The state legislature is also considering structured sentencing for juvenile offenders.

OKLAHOMA: In Oklahoma, presumptive guidelines are in place for felonies. The state has retained a limited parole system. Legislative proposals are pending for appellate review of sentencing determinations.

OREGON: Oregon has presumptive guidelines for felonies, with moderate appellate review. Parole has been abolished.

PENNSYLVANIA: Presumptive guidelines are in place for felonies and misdemeanors, with minimum appellate review. Parole has been retained.

SOUTH CAROLINA: The state employs voluntary guidelines for felonies and misdemeanors with potential sentences of one year or more.

TENNESSEE: There are presumptive guidelines for felonies, with moderate appellate review. Parole has been retained. The sentencing commission was abolished in 1995.

UTAH: The state uses voluntary guidelines for felonies and select misdemeanors (sex offenses). There is no appellate review. Parole has been retained in the state. The state also uses voluntary guidelines for its juvenile sentencing.

VIRGINIA: Virginia has voluntary guidelines for felonies, with no appellate review. Parole has been abolished. The state is studying juvenile sentencing guidelines.

WASHINGTON: The state employs presumptive guidelines for felonies, with moderate appellate review. Parole has been abolished in the state. Special guidelines for juvenile sentencing are in effect.

WISCONSIN: In Wisconsin, the state employs voluntary guidelines for felonies. Legislative proposals are pending, which do not contemplate appellate review. The proposals also contemplate the abolishment of the state's parole system, as well as the creation of a new permanent sentencing commission.

ADDITIONAL RESOURCES

Branham, Lynn S. *The Law and Policy of Sentencing and Corrections in a Nutshell.* 8th ed. Eagan, MN: West, Thomson Reuters, 2010.

Campbell, Arthur W. *Law of Sentencing.* Eagan, MN: West, Thomson Reuters, 2005.

U.S. Sentencing Commission. "2012 USSC Guidelines Manual." Available at http://www.ussc.gov/Guidelines/2012_Guidelines/index.cfm (accessed November 2, 2012).

ORGANIZATIONS

U.S. Sentencing Commission (USSC)

One Columbus Circle, N.E.
Washington, DC 20002-8002
Phone: (202) 502-4500
URL: http://www.ussc.gov/

CRIMINAL LAW

SEX OFFENDERS

Sections within this essay:

- Background
- The Impact of Jacob Wetterling
- Megan's Laws: Community Notification Laws
- Residency Restrictions for Sex Offenders
- Other Methods to Deal with Sex Offenders
  – Chemical and Surgical Castration
  – Civil Commitment
  – Amber Alerts

- Additional Resources

BACKGROUND

Society and policy makers have long struggled with finding effective ways to protect the public from sex offenders. A sex offender is a person who has been convicted of certain sex offense crimes. Examples of sex offenses include:

- Sexual conduct with a minor
- Sexual assault
- Sexual assault of spouse
- Molestation of a child
- Continuous **sexual abuse** of a child
- Infamous crimes against nature
- Lewd and lascivious acts
- Indecent exposure and public sexual indecency
- Taking a child for the purpose of prostitution

- Sexual exploitation of a minor
- Incest
- Kidnapping, aggravated **assault**, murder, unlawful **imprisonment**, and **burglary** (when the offense includes **evidence** of sexual motivation)
- Failure to register as a sex offender
- Violation of Sex Offender Registration statutes

Most offenses involving criminal sexual conduct fall within the **jurisdiction** of state law, but federal law also includes a number of sexual offenses. The offenses are found in Title 18 of the United States Code. Some of the federal offenses specifically apply to sexual offenses committed within the territorial jurisdiction of the United States or in a federal prison. Other crimes involve offenders who cross state or international borders to commit, or in the commission, of a sexual offense. For example, 18 U.S.C. section 2251 makes it illegal to knowingly print, publish, or cause to be made, "any notice or advertisement seeking or offering to receive, exchange, buy, produce, display, distribute, or reproduce any visual depiction involving the use of a minor engaging in sexually explicit conduct. This **statute** also applies when such person knows that such notice or advertisement will be, or has been, transported in interstate or foreign **commerce** by any means, including by computer."

Federal sexual offense include:

- Selling or buying of children (Section 2251A[a][b])
- Certain activities relating to material involving the sexual exploitation of minors, including both distribution and receipt of visual depictions in books, magazines, periodicals, films, and videotapes (Section 2252)

- Certain activities relating to material constituting or containing child **pornography** (Section 2252A)

- Production of sexually explicit depictions of a minor for importation into the United States (Section 2260)

- Transporting an individual in interstate or foreign commerce with the intent that the individual engage in prostitution or other illegal sexual activity (Section 2421)

- Transportation of minors in interstate or foreign commerce, with intent to engage in criminal sexual activity (Section 2423[a])

- Interstate or foreign travel with intent to engage in a sexual act with a juvenile (Section 2423[b])

- Use of interstate facilities to transmit information about an individual under the age of 16, with "the intent to entice, encourage, offer, or solicit that minor to engage in any sexual activity that can be charged as a criminal offense" (Section 2425)

THE IMPACT OF JACOB WETTERLING

On October 22, 1989, eleven-year-old Jacob Wetterling was abducted as he, his brother, and a friend rode their bikes home from a convenience store in St. Joseph, Minnesota. Law enforcement authorities arrived on the scene within minutes. No sign of Wetterling or his abductor has ever been found, despite the involvement of local authorities, the Federal Bureau of Investigation, hundreds of volunteer searchers, and more than 50,000 leads.

Jacob's disappearance spurred his family and supporters to found the Jacob Wetterling Foundation (JWF) in January 1990. The Foundation's mission is to protect children from sexual exploitation and abduction, through prevention education, victims' assistance, and legislation aimed at sex offenders. In 1991 JWF saw its first success with Minnesota's State Sex Offender Registration Act. The law provided law enforcement authorities with a comprehensive list of sex offenders in the state, something authorities lacked when Jacob was abducted.

JWF's agenda has included both state and federal legislative changes. In 1994, Congress passed the Omnibus Crime Bill. This legislation included the Jacob Wetterling Crimes Against Children and Sex Offender Registration Act. The law mandated that each state create a specific program to register sex offenders.

In 1996, the Wetterling Act was amended by Megan's Law (discussed below), and the Pam Lychner Sex Offender Tracking and Identification Act. The Lychner Act called upon the FBI to establish a national database of names and addresses of sex offenders who are released from prison. It also required lifetime registration for certain offenders. Its purpose is to make it easier for

authorities to track the movements of convicted sex offenders throughout all 50 states.

In 1997 other changes were made to the Wetterling Act. Changes included heightened registration requirements for sexually violent offenders such as members of the U.S. Armed Forces. Additional registration requirements were imposed for sex offenders who live in one state but go to school or work in another state.

In 2006, the federal Adam Walsh Child Protection and Safety Act (discussed below) replaced the Wetterling Act registration requirements with uniform standards that all states must follow.

MEGAN'S LAWS: COMMUNITY NOTIFICATION LAWS

The original impact of the Wetterling Act was to provide law enforcement authorities the means to track and locate convicted sex offenders. Community notification laws have adapted the idea to make information about sex offenders available to the public. Community notification laws, commonly referred to as sex offender registries, are most often associated with the 1994 rape and murder of seven-year-old Megan Kanka. She died just thirty yards from her own front door in Hamilton Township, New Jersey. On July 29, 1994, a neighbor lured the little girl to his house with the promise that she could see his new puppy. The neighbor was a convicted sex offender who had served time in prison for aggravated assault and attempted sexual assault against a child.

The outcry over Megan's death spurred the New Jersey Legislature to quick action. Within three months, the legislature passed the community notification law known as Megan's Law. Less than two years later, on May 17, 1996, President William Jefferson Clinton signed a federal version of the law, amending the Wetterling Act. The **amendment** required each state to provide public notification and information about sexual offenders living in the area. The law applied to all sex offenders—whether their victims were children or adults.

Sex offender registry requirements have varied by state, but share common characteristics. Convicted sexual offenders are required to register with their local law enforcement or corrections agency. This information is forwarded to a central location, such as the state police or state bureau of investigation. Information required for the registry typically includes name, address, date of birth, social security information, physical description, **fingerprints**, and photographs. **Conviction** information may also be required, as well as samples for DNA identification.

A court or registering agency informs offenders of their duty to register. Offenders typically must register within days of their release from prison or placement on supervision. Placement on the registry usually lasts ten years. Lifetime registration may be required, particularly if an offender has been denominated a "sexual predator" or where an offender has been convicted of a subsequent sexual offense.

Title I of the Adam Walsh Child Protection and Safety Act of 2006 seeks to standardize the registration process through the United States. Walsh was a child who was abducted and murdered in 1981. Title I, known as the Sex Offender Registration and Notification Act (SORNA), mandates that states change their sex offender registration laws to meet new federal guidelines. If states fail to make changes, the federal government will reduce grant money for law enforcement to the states. As of 2011, only seven states are in substantial compliance.

Under SORNA there are three tiers of offenders. Tier 1 sex offenders are required to register for 15 years, tier 2 for 25 years and tier 3 offenders must register for life. The Walsh Act also establishes a national sex offender registry and requires each state to apply identical criteria for posting offender data on the Internet. The registry is located at http://www.nsopw.gov.

According to the National Center on Missing and Exploited Children, in July 2012, approximately 747,000 convicted sex offenders were registered in the United States. Every state now collects DNA information from registrants. All though the new national sex offender registry is now available, the FBI continues to maintain a website with links to all state sex offender registry websites. The site is located at http://www.fbi.gov/hq/cid/cac/states.htm.

Law enforcement authorities may also have the obligation to disseminate information about registered sex offenders. Notification may extend to prior victims, neighbors, schools, youth organization, and other relevant individuals or groups. In some cases, community-wide notification may be required. Newspapers, television, radio, and community meetings are some of the methods used to provide community notification.

Critics of sex offender registries claim that they do little to protect most victims of sexual offenses, because most victims know the **perpetrator**. According to the U.S. Department of Justice, about seven of every ten female rape or sexual assault victims reported that the perpetrator was a relative, friend, or acquaintance.

The U.S. Supreme Court has addressed the constitutionality of sex offender registries. In *Connecticut Department of Safety v. Doe,* and in *Smith v. Doe,* both decided March 5, 2003, the court found that sex offender registries do not violate sex offenders' **constitutional rights**.

RESIDENCY RESTRICTIONS FOR SEX OFFENDERS

Residency restriction laws are a fairly new method some jurisdictions are using in an attempt to curb the actions of sex offenders. Alabama passed the first residency restriction law in 1996. The law was part of the states' Community Notification Act. It prohibited child molesters from living within 1,000 feet of a school. By 2012, 30 states had enacted residency restrictions, as well as hundreds of local governments. Though offenders have challenged these restrictions as being overly harsh and in some cases resulting in homelessness, few court challenges have been successful. However, an attempt to prevent registered sex offenders from entering Albuquerque's public libraries was ruled unconstitutional by the Tenth Circuit Court of Appeals in January 2012.

OTHER METHODS TO DEAL WITH SEX OFFENDERS

Chemical and Surgical Castration Eight states, including California and Florida, permit convicted sex offenders to be injected with Depo Provera, an FDA-approved **birth control** drug. Often called "chemical castration," Depo Provera is meant to quell the sex drive of male sex offenders by lowering their testosterone levels. The drug does not render any permanent physical change to the body. The treatment is believed to be most effective on sex offenders who possess uncontrollable biological urges that take the form of sexual fantasies that are usually only satisfied by acting on the fantasy. Both the California and Florida statutes provide for mandatory injections for repeat sex offenders, as well as discretionary injections for first-time offenders. California, Florida, and Louisiana give offenders the option to undergo surgical castration instead.

Civil Commitment Seventeen states have used civil commitment proceedings to remove **habitual** sex offenders from society for extended periods of time. The U.S. Supreme Court ruled in *Kansas v. Hendricks* (1997) that sexually violent predator (SVP) laws do not violate the Constitution's **double jeopardy** or ex post facto clauses.

Minnesota's civil commitment law for habitual sex offenders is fairly typical. Under Minnesota law, a person classified as having a "sexual psychopathic personality" or denominated a "sexually dangerous person" may be committed indefinitely in a secure treatment facility. The commitment is intended to reduce the risk of future dangerous sexual behavior. It is not meant to serve as a punishment for past crimes. Civilly committed sex offenders may be held for an indeterminate amount of time. In other words, they may be held as long as warranted to successfully treat them and to satisfy public safety concerns.

According to Minnesota's law, a person with a sexual psychopathic personality is one who:

- Has engaged in a "habitual course" of misconduct in sexual matters
- Suffers from an "utter lack of power to control" sexual impulses
- As a result of this inability to control behavior is "dangerous to other persons"

A sexually dangerous person is defined as someone who has "engaged in a course of harmful sexual conduct." This conduct creates a "substantial likelihood" of serious physical or emotional harm to another. Moreover, the person must be diagnosed with a sexual, personality or mental disorder, and found likely to engage in harmful sexual conduct in the future.

A commitment **hearing** is held to determine whether civil commitment is warranted. This hearing is usually held shortly before a sex offender is to be released from prison. Commitment proceedings could also be commenced as part of a **plea** agreement. A petition may also be filed after a person has been released from prison on a conditional or supervised release. It is not necessary that a person have committed any further sexual offenses after the release from imprisonment.

A judge makes commitment determinations in Minnesota. The judge listens to evidence on both sides, which may include evidence of past sexual misconduct that did not result in an **arrest** or conviction. The state has the burden to prove that commitment is necessary, but its **burden of proof** is not as high as in a criminal case. If the judge finds by clear and convincing evidence that the individual is a sexual psychopathic personality or a sexually dangerous person, the person will be committed to a secure treatment facility operated by the Minnesota Sex Offender Program.

Officials generally have 60 to 90 days to evaluate the inmate and report back to the court once a person has been committed. The court then holds a second hearing to determine whether an indeterminate commitment is required.

Minnesota mainly relies on group therapy to treat civilly committed sex offenders. The offender progresses through three stages: the evaluation stage, the inpatient treatment stage and the transition stage. The inpatient treatment stage consists of four parts; an offender must pass each before progressing to the next stage. The parts are accountability, insight, integration/behavior change, and preparation for the transition stage.

A review board determines when discharge, transfer, or other change in status is appropriate. Requests for such

a hearing may come from the patient, the patient's attorney, or the facility medical director. After a hearing, the review board recommends a course of action to the Commissioner of the Minnesota Department of Human Services. The Commissioner then issues an order denying or granting the petition. The Commissioner's order is subject to **appeal**, ultimately by the Minnesota Supreme Court.

By 2012, however, states had come under criticism for releasing very few sex offenders from civil commitment. Critics have argued that treatment has never been pursued by the states but that **incarceration** was the real goal. In July 2012, a Minnesota Federal District Court granted **class action** status to a group of 600 sex offenders who had been confined under the SVP. The plaintiffs argued that their treatment had been inadequate and that the application of the SVP had proved to be unconstitutional.

Amber Alerts Although not specifically targeted only at sex offenders, the **Amber Alert** system is intended to quickly and widely disseminate information about child abductions. AMBER is an acronym for "America's Missing: Broadcast Emergency Response." The system takes its name from nine-year-old Amber Hagerman, who was abducted and murdered in Arlington, Texas, in 1996. It uses various media outlets to inform the general public that a child has been abducted. Alerts go out over radio, television, email, electronic traffic-condition signs, and SMS text messages. Law enforcement typically broadcast the name and a description of the abducted child, and a description of the suspected abductor and the abductor's vehicle and license plate number, when available. The 2003 federal PROTECT Act established the federal government's role in the Amber Alert system. The law gives grant money to the states for the development or enhancement of notification for National Amber Alert Network. Every state now has an Amber Alert system. According to the U.S. Department of Justice, 584 children were recovered in 2011 due to the Amber Alert system.

ADDITIONAL RESOURCES

Cothran, Helen, ed. *Sexual Violence: Opposing Viewpoints.* Detroit: Greenhaven Press, 2003.

Office of Justice Programs. "SMART: Office of Sex Offender, Sentencing, Monitoring, Apprehending, Registering, and Tracking." U.S. Department of Justice. Available at http://www.ojp.usdoj.gov/smart/index.htm (accessed November 3, 2012).

Zilney, Laura, and Lisa Anne Zilney. *Perverts and Predators: The Making of Sexual Offending Laws.* Lanham, MD: Rowman and Littlefield, 2009.

ORGANIZATIONS

Amber Alert Program, Office of Justice Programs, U.S. Department of Justice

810 Seventh Street NW
Washington, DC 20531
URL: http://www.amberalert.gov

Jacob Wetterling Foundation (JWF)

2314 University Avenue West, Suite 14
St. Paul, MN 55114
Toll Free: (800) 325-HOPE
Fax: (651) 714-9098
URL: http://www.jwrc.org

DISPUTE RESOLUTION ALTERNATIVES

ARBITRATION

Sections within this essay:

BACKGROUND

Arbitration refers to one of several methods, collectively referred to as "alternative dispute resolution" (ADR), for resolving legal disputes other than through a formal court system. Arbitration is very similar to a trial in court, except that the claims and defenses are presented to a privately-retained neutral party ("arbitrator" or "arbiter") rather than a judge or **jury**. After listening to summary arguments and considering all the **evidence** presented in a dispute, an arbitrator renders a decision tantamount to a court decision or judgment.

Since it is intended to substitute for a trial, formal arbitration is generally as binding as a court **adjudication**.

Therefore, like it or not, a decision of an arbitrator may be appealed only under very narrow circumstances and criteria. (In fact, the arbitration agreement may designate that the decision is final and binding and cannot be appealed.) However, some forms of arbitration may be expressly designated as "non-binding." In those circumstances, one may accept or reject the arbitration decision and continue with **litigation** in the courts.

Arbitration has become a preferred alternative favored by both courts and parties for resolving disputes. All 50 states acknowledge some form of arbitration for the resolution of certain disputes. A majority of states (48 as of 2012, excepting Georgia and Mississippi) have adopted the Uniform Arbitration Act (UAA) and/or its revised version, published in 2000, or substantially similar legislation. Washington, D.C. and Puerto Rico also have adopted versions of the Act.

The use of arbitration has greatly expanded in recent years, because of the fast resolution of disputes, and the relative consistency and near-uniformity in procedural requirements (thanks to the UAA). The arbitration process also affords the parties a degree of **privacy** for sensitive or personal matters. Health care providers and insurance companies almost universally favor arbitrations because of the opportunity to avoid the publicity of court trials and jury verdicts.

CONTRACTUAL VERSUS COMPULSORY ARBITRATION

Voluntary arbitration refers to an agreement entered into by two or more parties who choose to arbitrate a matter rather than litigate the matter in court. The agreement is a binding **contract**, and if a dispute later develops, one cannot choose to ignore the arbitration agreement and file suit instead.

But arbitration is not "compulsory." It simply means that persons have voluntarily agreed in advance to arbitrate any future disputes and cannot back out of that agreement once a dispute arises. Failure to abide with "contractual arbitration" as agreed constitutes a breach of the agreement. If an individual has entered into such an agreement and later decides to file suit instead of arbitrating the dispute, the other person or party may take that individual to court to compel arbitration.

One of the most common circumstances where this situation arises is in the health care and insurance industries. When individuals enter a hospital for treatment or care, or fill out "new patient" forms for a physician, they may be asked to sign a document in which they agree to arbitrate any dispute which may arise. If they later attempt to sue the doctor or hospital for **malpractice** or a billing dispute, the agreement they signed will be presented to the court and their lawsuit will be dismissed and/or the court will order them to arbitrate the matter. The real danger in having their case dismissed is that the time limit for filing a dispute in arbitration may have expired while they were attempting to file a lawsuit in court (in some jurisdictions, a court may "stop the clock" to provide them with enough time to dismiss their court case and file it in arbitration). The lesson to learn is that they should carefully read all documents their health care provider may present to them prior to treatment or care, and they need to always be certain to retain a copy for their records.

In many states, laws prohibit health care providers from refusing to treat individuals if they will not sign a voluntary arbitration agreement. On the other hand, only in rare circumstances will a court permit them to "set aside" a signed agreement to arbitrate and allow them to file suit instead. Usually, they will have to prove to the court that they did not sign the arbitration agreement "voluntarily." For example, there is some legal precedent for allowing agreements with health care providers to be set aside (making them "voidable") when evidence shows that they were signed while under extreme **duress** or in pain, semi-conscious, etc. In even more rare circumstances, a court may find an agreement to arbitrate "unconscionable" and against **public policy** and will determine it to be null and void.

It is common practice for insurance policies (e.g., automobile, home, health, etc.) to contain language that commits an insured to the use of arbitration in the event of a dispute with the insurer. Many insureds do not realize that such language is contained in the lengthy policy language at the time they apply for insurance coverage. It often remains unknown and unrealized until a dispute arises and the insured attempts to sue his or her insurance provider. In most insurance policies, the agreement to arbitrate is not a separate document, but rather a statement contained in the policy, such as, "You agree to arbitrate any dispute relating to . . . " Individuals who sign the application for insurance coverage and have a policy issued to them have agreed to those terms.

On the other hand, "compulsory arbitration" is generally the result of express **statute** or regulation that mandates the arbitration of certain matters. The most common of these is the mandatory arbitration of labor disputes. If individuals are members of a union, the bargaining agreement for their bargaining unit will most likely contain provisions for the arbitration of all disputes. However, since the 1990s, many consumer agreements, including credit cart disputes, include compulsory arbitration. The U.S. Supreme Court has issued decisions that broaden the ability of companies to mandate arbitration in employment disputes as well as consumer disputes.

One of the most compelling reasons for mandating the arbitration of certain matters is that such matters tend to be very complex, specialized, or too time-consuming for a general jury trial. For example, a dispute over a provision in the Internal Revenue Code may be technically complicated. Instead of a jury trial, arbitration will provide the opportunity for appointment of a neutral arbitrator or panel of arbiters who may be knowledgeable and experienced in tax matters and can more readily understand the arguments presented. The "State Provisions" Section below summarizes key areas where states have mandated compulsory arbitration of certain matters.

ARBITRABILITY

If the subject matter of a particular dispute falls within the scope of subjects that the parties agreed in advance to arbitrate, then the particular dispute is "arbitrable." However, many disputes involve multiple issues, not all of which are contemplated when the arbitration agreement is executed. For example, a claim may state an arbitrable issue of **wrongful discharge** from employment. But the defense may raise an issue of untimely filing of the claim or some other procedural error or **fatal** flaw on the part of the complainant. Who decides that?

Most federal and state **appellate court** decisions have concluded that the only proper inquiry that a court should make, on a motion to compel arbitration, is (1) whether there exists a valid agreement to arbitrate between the parties, and (2) whether the agreement covers the dispute at hand. All other issues, particularly defenses such as untimeliness, **collateral estoppel**, and res judicata should properly be decided by the arbitrator.

If such an event should occur (the raising of an issue not related to the subject matter of the dispute at hand), the arbitrator may render one decision covering all or may be forced to render a separate opinion on the "arbitrability" of the separate claim or defense, without ever reaching the main issue of the dispute. Still, sometimes the arbitrability of the main issue is, in itself, the actual dispute, as often occurs in labor contracts.

WHO ARE THE ARBITRATORS?

The majority of arbitration agreements contain provisions governing the selection and appointment of an arbitrator or arbitration panel. Private arbitration contracts may designate any person or any method for choosing a person or persons as arbitrators. If an arbitration panel is elected (usually comprised of three persons), each party may nominate or appoint one arbitrator, and both sides will decide on a "neutral" third person. Or, the parties will each select one arbitrator, and the two arbitrators will then select a third "neutral." Alternatively, three "neutrals" may be selected by having each party alternately strike names on one list until only three names remain. In single-arbitrator arbitrations, an external source of available arbitrators is often consulted.

The American Arbitration Association (AAA) is the largest full-service ADR provider in the United States. It maintains a National Roster of Arbitrators and Mediators. The persons named on the roster have been nominated by leaders in their industry or profession. The AAA has strict criteria for its roster members, and those selected are generally recognized for their standing and expertise in their fields, their integrity, and their dispute resolution skills. Many are attorneys, but being one is not a requirement. Many arbitration agreements expressly designate the use of AAA as the preferred source for arbitrators.

Under the Federal Arbitration Agreement (FAA) (see below), if an arbitration agreement does not contain a provision for the naming or appointing of an arbitrator, "the court shall designate and appoint an arbitrator . . ." (9 USC Section 5).

THE ARBITRATION PROCESS

The arbitration process generally begins with the filing of a request for arbitration. This action may be performed by direct application to the forum designated in the private arbitration agreement or by court order. Parties who simply wish to arbitrate a matter should contact a local entity that offers arbitration services. Often, a local circuit or district court may have information or services

available. There are several national organizations that also offer local arbitrations or supply lists of arbitrators (see listings below).

The chosen forum will most likely furnish the parties with a copy of rules and procedures. Attorneys may or may not represent the parties. Generally, an arbitration **hearing** parallels a court trial, in that there is the taking of **testimony** from witnesses and the introduction of evidence. However, many arbitrations are conducted on the basis of "summary briefs" from each party, which outline the issues and the arguments in document form. Arbitration decisions are always in written form. A decision may or may not be appealable, depending on the forum and the agreement of the parties.

THE UNIFORM ARBITRATION ACT (UAA)

The Uniform Arbitration Act, promulgated in 1955, has been overwhelmingly adopted by state legislatures and federal district courts for alternate dispute resolution. Its popularity derives from the advantages of uniformity and thoroughness, and in 2000, the National Conference of Commissioners on Uniform State Laws approved and recommended a revised version of the UAA for enactment in all the states. The UAA provides a structured procedure to be followed in all arbitrations, and, most importantly, includes details addressing matters that are often overlooked in privately drafted arbitration agreements. The revised UAA includes provisions not addressed in the original UAA, but deemed important as a result of the increased use of arbitration. Some of the new provisions address matters such as (1) who decides the arbitrability of a dispute and by what criteria; (2) whether arbitrators have the discretion to order **discovery**, issue protective orders, decide motions for **summary judgment**, etc.; and (3) to what extent arbitrators and arbitration organizations are immune from civil lawsuits.

FEDERAL ARBITRATION

Amendment VII (1791) provides that "In all suits at **common law**, where the value in controversy shall exceed twenty dollars, the right of trial by jury shall be preserved . . ." This provision guarantees individuals their "day in court" unless they either voluntarily choose an alternative dispute resolution, or the subject matter of their dispute falls under a compulsory arbitration mandate by law. Generally, if arbitration is made compulsory, there is a right of **appeal** through the courts of an arbitration decision.

Arbitration in the federal courts may be the result of a private contractual agreement to arbitrate, a **statutory** mandate, or a court-ordered arbitration. A majority of federal courts have authorized or established at least one court-wide ADR program, which may include court-ordered **mediation**, arbitration, early neutral evaluation (ENE), etc. These measures are the result of the Civil Justice Reform Act of 1990 (CJRA) (28 USC 471 et seq.). The CJRA has changed the use of ADR from being the initiative of individual judges to being part of court-managed, district wide programs.

The Alternative Dispute Resolution Act of 1998 (ADRA) (28 USC 651 et seq.) further expands upon the CJRA by mandating that courts establish and authorize the use of ADR in all civil actions. The federal government also encourages arbitration and mediation within its own ranks. The Administrative Dispute Resolution Act of 1996 provides a mediation forum for handling disputes within agencies or between citizens and agencies (claims against the government).

Arbitration in the federal court system is governed by the Federal Arbitration Act (FAA), first enacted in 1925 and codified in 1947 under Title 9 of the United States Code. Chapter 1 of Title 9 (General Provisions) contains such directives as the method for naming or appointing an arbitrator (Section 5); for summoning witnesses to **testify** (Section 7); and for remedy and recourse for failing to arbitrate as agreed (Section 4). While the FAA is not in itself a procedural mandate, it provides an authoritative backdrop for arbitrations and commands that arbitration agreements be enforced in accordance with their terms.

Importantly, the FAA "preempts" any state law that conflicts with its pro-arbitration public policy or any state law that renders moot or limits contractual agreements to arbitrate. The rule of preemption applies in both federal and state courts (adjudicating federal claims). However, if the parties clearly express an agreement to conduct their arbitration under state law/rules (under a "choice of law" provision), the FAA will not preempt this.

STATE ARBITRATION

The following states provide for ADR (arbitration or mediation) for certain types of disputes:

ALABAMA: Alabama Code, Ch. 25-7-4 applies to labor disputes.

ALASKA: Alaska Statutes 42.40.840 and 23.40.190 address labor disputes. Family disputes are governed by 25.20.080 and 25.24.080. Disputes involving automobile warranties are governed by 45.45.355.

ARIZONA: Arizona has adopted the UAA under Sections 12-1501 to 12-1518 of the Arizona Statutes. Provisions for arbitration/mediation of family disputes is covered

under 25-381.01 to 25-381.24. Automobile warranties are covered under 44-1265.

ARKANSAS: The UAA has been adopted under Arkansas Statutes 16-108-201 to 16-108-224. Sections 11-2-201 to 11-2-206 govern labor disputes.

CALIFORNIA: California's Code contains extensive provisions for the arbitration and/or mediation of many types of disputes. Labor disputes are addressed under Sections 65, 66, and 3518. Family disputes are covered in Sections 5180 to 5183. Education matters are covered by 48260.6, 48263, 48263.5 (truancy), and 56503 (special education). There is a special provision for the arbitration of cable TV franchise disputes under 53066.1(n)(1). Environmental regulatory disputes, including issues involving pesticides, are covered under 13127(c)(1). Water rights disputes are handled under 1219. Community disputes of a business or professional nature are covered under 465 to 471.5.

COLORADO: Colorado's statutes provide ADR for labor disputes under 8-3-113. Family matters are covered by 14-10129.5. Agricultural debts are governed by 6-9-101 to 6-9-106. A special statutory provision exists for ADR of disputes involving mobile homes under 38-12-216. The UAA has been adopted under 13-22-201 to 13-22-223. Dispute resolution in general is covered by 13-22-301 to 13-22-310.

CONNECTICUT: Labor disputes are covered under Connecticut Statutes 31-91 to 31-100, 5-276 and 5-276a. Family disputes are resolved under 46b-59a. Public Act 87-316 Section 8 (1987) is covered under 42-182.

DELAWARE: Delaware's Code covers labor disputes under Title 14 Section 4002 and 4014, Title 19 Section 110 and 113, and Title 19 Section 1614. Automobile warranties are covered under Title 6 Section 5007.

FLORIDA: Florida Statutes Annotated 448.06 and 681.110(4)(9d) cover labor disputes. Family disputes are addressed under 44.101, 61.183, 39.42, 39.427 to 39.429, 39.436, 39.44, and 39.442. Automobile **warranty** disputes are provided for under 681.108 and 681.111. Mobile home disputes fall under 723.037 and 723.038. The state maintains "citizen dispute **settlement** centers" for ADR assistance under 44.201.

GEORGIA: Labor disputes are covered under Georgia Code 34-2-6(5), 25-5-1 to 25-5-14, 45-19-32, and 45-19-36. Public employee grievances and "unlawful practices" labor arbitrations are mandated under 45-19-36.

HAWAII: Hawaii Revised Statutes 371-10, 98-11(b)(1)(d), 89-12(a) and (b), 380-8, and 377-3 cover ADR for labor disputes. Automobile warranty disputes are covered under 490-2 and 313-1. Medical **conciliation** is addressed by 671-11 to 671-20. There is a special statutory provision for ADR of geothermal resources disputes under 205-5.1. International disputes are covered by 1988 Haw. Sess. Laws, Ch. 186, Sections 1-9.

IDAHO: Idaho Statutes Title 7, Special Proceedings, Chapter 9 adopts the UAA. Idaho Section 44-106 governs labor disputes.

ILLINOIS: Labor disputes are covered by Illinois Compiled Statutes, Ch. 48, paragraphs 1612, v1706, 1712, 1713(b); and Ch. 10, paragraph 26. Family disputes are covered by Ch. 40, paragraph 602.1 and 607.1. Automobile warranty disputes are covered by Ch.121.5, paragraph 1204(4). Disputes involving **public utilities** fall under Ch. 11, paragraph 702.12a. Illinois operates several nonprofit community dispute resolution centers under the auspices of Ch. 37, paragraph 851.1 to 856.

INDIANA: Labor disputes are covered under Indiana Code 5-14-1.5-6.5(2), 22-1-1-8(d), 22-6-1-7, 20-7.5-1-9 to 20-7.5-1-13. Family disputes are covered under 31-1-24-1 to 31-1-24-9 and 31-1-23-5 to 31-1-23-9. Automobile warranties are handled under 24-5-13-19. **Civil Rights** disputes are covered under 22-9-1-6. **Consumer protection** disputes are covered under 4-6-9-4(a)(4). There is a special Code provision for water rights disputes under 13-2-1-6(2).

IOWA: Labor disputes are covered under Iowa Code 20.19 to 20.20 and 679B to 679B.27. Family disputes are covered under 598.16 and 598.41(2). Agricultural debts are handled under 654a1 to 654a14. Civil Rights disputes are covered under 601A.15(3)(c). Informal dispute resolution in general is addressed under 679.1 to 679.14.

KANSAS: Kansas Statutes 5-401 to 5-422 expressly adopt the UAA. Labor disputes are covered under Kansas Statutes 44-817, 44-819(j), 44-820(c), 44-826, 44-828, 72-5413(h), 72-5427, 72-5429, 72-5430(b)(7), 72-5430(c)(7), 75-4322, 75-4323, 75-4332, and 75-4333. The ADR provisions for family disputes are covered under 23-601 to 23-607 and 23-701. Automobile warranties are handled under 50-645(e). Civil Rights disputes are covered under 44-1001 to 44-1005. There is a special

ADR provision for barbershop business disputes under 65-1824(4).

KENTUCKY: Kentucky has extensive ADR provisions in its Kentucky Revised Statutes (KRS). The UUAA has been adopted under KRS 417.045 to 417.240. Labor disputes are covered under KRS 337.425, 345.080, 336.010, 336.020, 336.140, and 336.151 to 336.156. Family disputes are covered under KRS 403.140(b) and 403.170. Automobile warranties are handled under KRS 367.860 to 367.880. Civil Rights disputes are covered under KRS 344.190 to 344.290 and 337.425. Education matters are covered under KRS 165A.350 and 360. Disputes involving the production and distribution of agricultural products are covered under KRS 260.020.030(e) and 260.020.040(l). There is a special provision for community agency funding at KRS 273.451.

LOUISIANA: Labor disputes are covered under Louisiana Statutes, Title 23, Section 6. Family disputes are covered under Title 9, Sections 351 to 356. Automobile warranties are handled under Title 23, Section 1944. Housing civil rights matters are addressed under Title 40, Section 597. Barbershop disputes are covered under Title 37, Section 381. There is a special provision for a Medical Review Panel at Title 40, Section 1299-47.

MAINE: Maine's statutes provide ADR for the following areas of dispute: Labor disputes are covered under Title 26, Section 1026, 965, 931 to 936, 979-D, 1281, 1282, and 1285. Family disputes are covered under Title 4, Section 18 (1 to 5); Title 19, Section 214 (1,4); Title 19, Section 518 (1,2, and 4); Title 19, Section 656 and 665; and Title 19, Section 752 (4). Automobile warranties are handled under Title 10, Section 1165. There is a special ADR provision for professional **negligence** claims (malpractice) under Title 24, Sections 2851 to 2859. Disputes involving the production and distribution of agricultural products are covered under Title 13, Sections 1956 to 1959.

MARYLAND: Labor disputes are covered under Maryland Code Article 6, Section 408(d) and Article 89, Sections 3, 9, and 11. Maryland also has an employment agency dispute ADR provision under Article 56, Section 169. The UAA has been adopted in its original text under gcj, Sections 3-201 to 3-235.

MASSACHUSETTS: Labor disputes are covered under Chapter 150, Sections 1 to 3 of the General Laws. There is an ADR provision for cable television disputes under Chapter 166A, Section 16. A Community Mediation provision is covered under Chapter 218, Section 43E.

MICHIGAN: ADR provisions for labor disputes are covered under MCL 432.1, 423.9 to 423.9c, 423.25, and 423.207. Family disputes are covered under MCL 552.64, 552.505, 552.513 to 552.527, and 552.531. Automobile warranties (regarding service) are handled under MCL 257.1327. A special ADR provision for general tort actions is contained under MCL 600.4951 to 600.4969. **Medical malpractice** ADR is provided for under 600.4901 to 600.4923, and more generally under 600.4951 to 600.4969. Disputes involving the production and distribution of agricultural products are covered under 290-714. A small claims conciliation statute is contained under MCL 730.147 to 730.155.

MINNESOTA: Minnesota has adopted the UAA under Statute Section 572.08 to 572.30. Labor disputes are covered under Minnesota Statutes 179.01, 179.03, 179.04, 179.06, 179.14, 179.15, and 179.02 to 179.09. Family disputes are covered under 518.167 and 518.619. Automobile warranties are handled under 325F.665. Civil Rights disputes are covered under 63.01 and 63.04 to 63.06. Conciliation Courts are provided for under 487.30. Civil Mediation is outlined under 572.31 to 572.40. Civil litigation ADR is covered separately under 484.74. There is also a statutory ADR provision for community dispute resolution programs under 494.01 to 494.04. A special provision for debtor-creditor mediation is found under 572.41, and workers' compensation disputes under 176.351(2a). Disputes involving the production and distribution of agricultural products are covered under 17.692, 17.695, and 17.697 to 17.701. Environmental issues are covered under 40.22, 40.23(3), 40.242, 40.244, 221.035F, 221.036(9), 116.072(1), and 116.072(6) to 116.072(8). Environmental waste management issues are covered separately under 115A.29(2)(a) and 115A.38(2).

MISSISSIPPI: Automobile warranty disputes are handled under Code provisions 63-17-159 and 63-17-163. Agricultural debt is addressed under 69-2-43 to 69-43-51.

MISSOURI: Labor disputes are covered under Statutes 290.400, 290.420, 290.430, 295.030 to 290.190, and 105.525. Civil Rights disputes are covered under 213.010 (1), 213.020, and 213.075.

MONTANA: Labor disputes are covered under Montana Code 39-31-307. Family disputes are covered under 26-1-81 and 40-3-111 to 40-3-127. Agricultural debt ADR is handled under 80-13-191 and 80-13-201 to 80-13-214. Civil Rights disputes are covered under 49-2-501(1), 49-2-504 to 49-2-506, and 49-2-601. Workers' compensation disputes are covered under 39-71-2401 to 39-71-2411.

There is a special Code provision for special education matters under 20-7-462(4). Medical malpractice panels are covered under 27-6-101 to 27-6-704. Disputes involving the production and distribution of agricultural products are covered under 80-1-101 and 80-11-103(9). The UAA has been adopted under MCA 27-5-111 to 27-5-324.

NEBRASKA: The UAA has been expressly adopted under Nebraska Statutes, Sections 25-2601 to 25-2622. Family disputes are covered under 42-801 to 42-823 and 42-360. Agricultural debt is covered under 2-4801 to 2-4816. Civil rights disputes are covered under 20-113.01 and 20-114(1)(2).

NEVADA: Nevada has copious provisions for ADR in its statutes. Labor disputes are covered under 288.190, 288.200, 288.205, 288.215, 288.220, 288.270, 614.010, and 614.020. Automobile warranties are handled under 598.761. Civil Rights disputes are covered under 233.020 to 233.210 and 244.161. Consumer credit disputes are covered under 598B.150. Educational dispute ADR is found under 394.11, and mobile home disputes are handled under 118B.024, 118B.025, and 118B.260.

NEW HAMPSHIRE: Labor disputes are covered by New Hampshire Statutes 273-A:1, 273-A:12, 273.215, 273.220, 273.270, 614.010 and 614.020. Automobile warranties are handled under 357.0:4.

NEW JERSEY: Labor disputes are covered under 34-13A-4 to 34-13A-16 and 34-13A-15. Civil rights disputes are covered under 52:27E-40 and 41. A general ADR provision is found at 2A:23A-1 to 2A:23A-19. Disputes involving the developmentally disabled are covered under 52:27E-40 and 41. Home warranties are covered under 46:3 B-9. Radioactive waste issues are handled under 32:31-5.

NEW MEXICO: Family disputes are covered under 40-12-1 to 40-12-6, and 40-4-9.1(B) and (J)(5). Automobile warranties are handled under 57-16A-6. Small claims are handled under 34-8A-10.

NEW YORK: Labor disputes are covered under Sections 205 and 209 for civil service, and Sections 750 to 760 for labor. Family disputes are covered under Sections 911-926. Automobile warranties are handled under Section 198-a (general business). Tax matters fall under Section 170(3a). Community Dispute Resolution Programs are governed by Sections 849-a to 849-g (judicial law).

NORTH CAROLINA: The UAA has been expressly adopted under Statutes Section 1-567.1 to 1-567.20.

Labor disputes are covered under Statutes 95-32 to 95-36. Automobile warranties are handled under 20-351.7. Civil Rights disputes are covered under 143-422.3 (unemployment) or 41A-6(6), 41A-7(a), and 41A-8 (housing).

NORTH DAKOTA: The UAA is found under Code Sections 32-29.2.01 to 39-29.2.20. Family disputes are covered under Code Sections 14-09.1-01 to 14-09.1-08, and 27-05.1-01 to 27-05.1-18. Automobile warranties are handled under 51-07-18(3). A provision for ADR of agricultural debt can be found at 6.09.10-01 to 10-09. Debtor-creditor disputes are covered under 11-26-01 to 11-26-08.

OHIO: Lengthy provisions under Ohio's Code for labor disputes are covered under 4117.02(A), (E), (H)(7), (N), 4117.14(A) and (C). Family disputes are covered under 3117.01 to 08. Automobile warranties are handled under 1345.75 and 77. Civil rights disputes (housing matters) are covered under 1901.331.

OKLAHOMA: The UAA has been adopted in its original text at Title 15, Sections 801 to 818. Automobile warranties are handled under Statute Title 15, Section 901(f). Civil Rights disputes are covered under Title 25, Sections 1505, 1704, and 1705. 22-9-1-6. General dispute resolution programs are covered under Title 12, Sections 1801 to 1813.

OREGON: Oregon's statutes covering labor disputes are found at 662.405 to 455, 662.705(4), 662.715, 662.785, and 243.650 et seq. Family disputes are covered under 107.510 to 107.615, 107.755 to 107.795, and 107.179(4).

PENNSYLVANIA: Pennsylvania Statutes, Title 42, Part VII, Chapter 73, Subchapters A, B, and C cover statutory arbitration, common law arbitration, and judicial arbitration respectively. Title 43, Section 211.31 to 39, and Title 43, Section 213.13 cover general labor disputes, as well as Title 43, Section 1101.801 and 802, and Title 43, Section 217.3. Automobile warranties are handled under Title 73, Section 1959. Civil Rights disputes are covered under Title 43, Section 957(i) (unemployment) or Title 43, Section 959(a) to (c) (employment). **Eminent domain** issues are covered under Title 52, Section 1406.15.

RHODE ISLAND: Labor disputes are covered under General Law 28-10-1, 28-9.4-10, 28-9.4-17, and 28-7-10. ADR for consumer issues is found at 42-42-5 to 42-42-7.

SOUTH CAROLINA: Codified laws in South Carolina include adoption of the UAA under Title 15, Chapter 48.

ADR provisions for labor disputes are found under 41-10-70 (wage mediation) and 41-17-10. Civil rights disputes are covered under 1-13-70 and 1-13-90 (employment). Consumer disputes are covered under 37-6-117. Employment grievances are covered under 8-17-360 and 8-17-370.

SOUTH DAKOTA: South Dakota has ADR for labor disputes under 60-10-1 to 60-10-3.

TENNESSEE: The UAA has been adopted under Statutes 29-5-301 to 29-5-320. Bank patrons may resolve their disputes under Tennessee's Code 45-1-301 to 45-1-309.

TEXAS: Labor disputes are covered under Article 5154c-1, Section 9. ADR procedures in general are covered under Article 4590f-1, Title 7, 154.001 to 154.073, Section 3.07(d).

UTAH: Family disputes are covered under 30-3-16.2 to 30-3-17.1, 30-3-4.1, and 30-3-4.3. Automobile warranties are handled under 30-20-7. Medical malpractice resolution is provided for under 78-14-1, 78-14-2, and 78-14-12 to 16.

VERMONT: Labor disputes are covered under Vermont Code Title 21, 924 and 925; Title 3, 8.25; and Title 21, 521 to 554. Special education matters are covered by Title 16, Section 2941, 2959.

VIRGINIA: The UAA is found under Code Section 8.01-581.01 to 8.01-581.016. Labor disputes are covered under Virginia's Code, 40.1-70 to 40.1-75. Family disputes are covered under 16.1-69.35 and 16.1-289.1. Automobile warranties are handled under 59.1-207.15. Civil mediation programs are found under 16.1-69.35(d). There is a special Code provision for local government dispute mediation at 15.1-945.1 et seq.

WASHINGTON: Labor disputes are covered under 49.08.010, 41.56.430, 41.56.440, 41.56.450, and 41.59.120. Family disputes are covered under 26.09.015. Automobile warranties are handled under 19.118.150. Civil Rights disputes are covered under 49.60.130. Dispute resolution centers are found at 7.75.010 to 7.75.100.

WEST VIRGINIA: West Virginia has an ADR provision for labor disputes at Code Section 21-1A-1. There is also an ADR provision for automobile warranty disputes at 46A-6A-8 and 46A-6A-9.

WISCONSIN: Wisconsin Statutes cover ADR for labor disputes under 101.24, 111.11, 111.39, 111.53-56, 111.70, and 111.77. Family disputes are covered under 753.016 (conciliation), 767.081-82, 767.001(3) and (4), 767.11, and 767.327(1) and (2). Automobile warranties are handled under 218.015(3) to (7). Civil Rights disputes are covered under 118.20 (employment), 230.85 (employment), and 1419 (governor and mediation).

WYOMING: Automobile warranties are handled under Statute 40-17-101(a) and (f). Agricultural debt is covered under 11-41-101 to 110. Environmental issues are handled under 35-11-701(a) to (c).

ADDITIONAL RESOURCES

Carbonneau, Thomas. E. *Arbitration in a Nutshell.* 2nd ed. Eagan, MN: West, Thomson Reuters, 2009.

Nolan, Dennis R. *Labor and Employment Arbitration in a Nutshell.* 2nd ed. Eagan, MN: West, Thomson Reuters, 2006.

U.S. Code, Title 9, Chapter 1, et seq: The Federal Arbitration Act. Available at http://www.law.cornell.edu/uscode/text/9 (accessed November 3, 2012).

ORGANIZATIONS

ADR Section, American Bar Association

740 15th St. NW
Washington, DC 20005
Phone: (202) 992-1000
URL: http://www.americanbar.org/groups/dispute_resolution.html

American Arbitration Association (AAA)

335 Madison Avenue, Tenth Floor
New York NY 10017-4605
Phone: (212) 716-5800
Fax: (212) 716-5905
URL: http://www.adr.org

DISPUTE RESOLUTION ALTERNATIVES

COLLABORATIVE LAW

Sections within this essay:

- Background
- State Collaborative Laws and Rules
- Uniform Collaborative Law Act
- Additional Resources

BACKGROUND

Collaborative Law is a voluntary process in which the lawyers and clients agree that the lawyers will represent the clients solely for purposes of **settlement**, and that the clients will hire new lawyers if the case does not settle. The parties and their lawyers work together to find an equitable resolution of a dispute, retaining experts as needed. No one is required to participate, and parties are free to terminate the process at any time. The process is intended to promote full and open disclosure. Information that is disclosed in a collaborative process, which is not otherwise discoverable, may not be used in any subsequent **litigation**. This form of alternative dispute resolution can be a useful and cost-effective option for amicable, non-adversarial dispute resolution. Like **mediation**, it promotes problem solving and provides solutions not possible in litigation or **arbitration**. It is used most often in **family law**, where couples are separating or divorcing.

The collaborative law movement began in the 1980s, driven by dissatisfaction with the way the legal system handles **divorce**. Lawyers and other professionals realized that many acrimonious disputes between the parties over trivial possessions and other issues were made worse by the litigation process. Emotional issues were ignored by the courts that led to costly and protracted fights that left both parties wounded by the end of the process.

Collaborative law emphasizes a team approach to resolving financial, **custody**, and other emotionally-charged issues. Mental health counselors, neutral financial advisors, accountants, parenting specialists, child specialists, vocational experts, and appraisers may be retained by both parties to work through every issued needed to settle the case. The process is similar to mediation except that lawyers for both parties replace the mediator. Though lawyers are involved, the change in rules and perspective reduces their roles as advocates for their clients. Instead, they serve as counselors and advisors. While 90 percent of all divorce cases end in a settlement, collaborative law advocates believe their process speeds up the process and leads to more amicable agreements. However, they acknowledge that both parties must agree to make the process work.

STATE COLLABORATIVE LAWS AND RULES

Collaborative law has grown in popularity since the 1990s and has been accepted as a valid dispute resolution by much of the legal community. The American Bar Association (ABA) Standing Committee on Ethics and Professional Responsibility and at least eight state bar ethics committees (Kentucky, Maryland, Minnesota, Missouri, New Jersey, North Carolina, Pennsylvania, and Washington) have expressly approved the use of collaborative law. By 2009, four states had enacted collaborative law statutes—California, North Carolina, Utah and Texas.

However, the legal community expressed its belief that collaborative law rules needed to be uniform in all 50 states. In response, the National Conference of Commissioners on Uniform State Laws set to work. This Uniform Law Commission concluded that a comprehensive **statutory** framework was necessary in order to guarantee the benefits of the collaborative process and to further enhance its use. Establishing the essential features of collaborative law in practice would eliminate confusion and ensure that ethical issues, such as the evidentiary privilege against disclosing information in future litigation, were addressed.

UNIFORM COLLABORATIVE LAW ACT

The Uniform Collaborative Law Rules/Act (UCLR/A) was promulgated by the Uniform Law Commission as an act in 2009 and was amended in 2010. The 2010 amendments created a mechanism for having the provisions of the act be adopted by court rule rather **statute**. The amended rules/act also provides states with the option to either limit application of the act to family law matters or to not impose such a limitation. Finally, the amendments give courts the discretion to approve stays of ongoing proceedings and calendaring deadlines when parties voluntarily enter into a collaborative law process.

The UCLR/A contains 23 sections (or rules if adopted in rule format). Many of these sections establish the basic framework of collaborative law. Section 3 emphasizes that a court cannot order a party to participate in the collaborative law if the party objects. Section 4 establishes minimum requirements for a collaborative law participation agreement, which the parties sign to begin the collaborative law process. The agreement must be in writing, state the parties' intention to resolve the matter through collaborative law, contain a description of the matter and identify and confirm engagement of the collaborative lawyers. The section also allows the parties to include other provisions that are not inconsistent with the act.

Section 5 states that the process begins when parties sign a participation agreement, and any party may unilaterally terminate the process at any time without specifying a reason. The process is concluded by a negotiated, signed agreement resolving the matter, or a portion of the matter and the parties' agreement that the remaining portions of the matter will not be resolved in the process. Under certain conditions the collaborative process may continue with a successor collaborative lawyer

in the event of the withdrawal or discharge of a collaborative lawyer.

Section 6 mandates an automatic application for stay of proceedings before a **tribunal** (court, arbitrator, legislative body, administrative agency, or other body acting in an adjudicative capacity) once the parties file a notice of collaborative law with the tribunal. A tribunal may require status reports while the proceeding is stayed. The scope of the information that can be requested is limited to insure confidentiality of the collaborative law process. However, Section 7 creates an exception to the stay of proceedings by authorizing a tribunal to issue emergency orders to protect the health, safety, welfare or interests of a party or family or household member. A tribunal may also waive the stay of proceedings to protect financial or other interests of a party in any critical area in any civil dispute. Section 8 authorizes a tribunal to approve an agreement resulting from a collaborative law process.

Section 9 describes a core element and the fundamental defining characteristic of the collaborative law process: Should the collaborative law process terminate without the matter being settled, the collaborative lawyer and lawyers in the law firm with which the collaborative lawyer is associated are disqualified from representing a party in a proceeding before a tribunal in the collaborative matter, except to seek emergency orders or to approve an agreement resulting from the collaborative law process. However, the disqualification requirement is further modified regarding collaborative lawyers representing low-income parties (Section 10) and governmental entities as parties (Section 11).

Section 12 details another core element of the process. Parties in the process must, upon request of a party, make timely, full, candid, and informal disclosure of information without formal **discovery**, and promptly update information that has materially changed. Parties are free to define the scope of disclosure in the collaborative process, so long as they do not violate another law.

Section 14 deals with the appropriateness of the collaborative law process. Before the parties sign a participation agreement, a collaborative lawyer is required to discuss with a prospective client factors that the lawyer reasonably believes relate to the appropriateness of the prospective client's matter for the collaborative process. The lawyer must provide sufficient information for a prospective client to make an informed decision about the material benefits and risks of the process as compared to the material benefit and risks of other reasonably available processes, such as litigation, arbitration, mediation or expert evaluation. In addition, a prospective party must be informed of the events that will terminate the process and the effect of the disqualification requirement.

Section 15 requires a collaborative lawyer to make a reasonable effort to determine if a prospective client has a history of a coercive or violent relationship with another prospective party, and if such circumstances exist, establishes criteria for beginning and continuing the process and providing safeguards.

Section 16, 17, 18, and 19 deal with the confidentiality and the future admissibility of information disclosed during the collaborative law process. Section 16 provides that oral and written communications developed in the collaborative process are confidential to the extent agreed upon by the parties or as provided by state law, other than in these sections. Section 17 is a critical provision. It creates a broad privilege prohibiting disclosure of communications developed in the process of **legal proceedings**. The provisions are similar to those in the Uniform Mediation Act and apply to party and non-party participants in the process.

Sections 18 and 19 provide for the possibility of **waiver** of this privilege by all parties, and make certain exceptions to the privilege based on important public policies such as preventing threats to commit bodily harm or a crime, abuse or neglect of a child or adult, information available under an open records act, or to prove or disprove professional misconduct or **malpractice**. Parties may agree that all or part of the process is not privileged.

Section 20 deals with the enforcement of an agreement made in a collaborative process that fails to meet the mandatory requirement for a participation agreement (Section 4), or a collaborative lawyer who has not fully complied with the disclosure requirements (Section 14). When the interests of justice so require, a tribunal has the discretion to enforce an agreement resulting from a flawed participation agreement, if the tribunal finds that the parties intended to enter into a participation agreement, and reasonably believed that they were participating in the collaborative process.

As of 2012, the UCLR/A has been adopted by the District of Columbia, Hawaii, Nevada, Texas, and Utah. Legislation was pending in Maryland, Massachusetts, and Washington.

ADDITIONAL RESOURCES

Golann, Dwight, and Jay Folberg. *Mediation: The Roles of Advocate and Neutral.* 2nd ed. New York: Aspen Publishers, 2010.

Kovach, Kimberlee. *Mediation in a Nutshell.* 2d ed. Eagan, MN: West, Thomson Reuters, 2010.

Tesler, Pauline. *Collaborative Law: Achieving Effective Resolution Without Litigation.* Chicago: American Bar Association, 2009.

ORGANIZATIONS

ADR Section, American Bar Association

740 15th St. NW
Washington, DC 20005
Phone: (202) 992-1000
URL: http://www.americanbar.org/groups/dispute_resolution.html

International Academy of Collaborative Professionals

201 N. 24th Street #240
Phoenix, AZ 85016
Phone: (480) 696-6075
Fax: (480) 2409068
URL: http://ww.collaborativepractice.com

DISPUTE RESOLUTION ALTERNATIVES

MEDIATION

Sections within this essay:

- Background
- Voluntary Versus Mandatory Mediation
- The Mediation Process
- Deciding to Mediate a Dispute
  - Finding an Appropriate Forum and Mediator(s)
  - Checklist
- Uniform Mediation Act
- Federal Mediation
- State Mediation Provisions
- Additional Resources

BACKGROUND

Mediation refers to one of several methods used to resolve legal disputes other than through formal court trial. Mediation and **arbitration** constitute methods of "alternative dispute resolution" (ADR). Arbitration is used as a substitute for trial, but mediation merely assists the parties in reaching their own resolution of a disputed matter. Instead of a judge or **jury** rendering a judgment or verdict, or an arbitrator rendering a binding decision, a "mediator" merely facilitates open discussion and tries to assist the parties in resolving their differences on their own. Mediation thus avoids the "win-lose" set-up of a trial or arbitration.

Those who go through formal mediation tend to achieve **settlement** through their own spirit of mutual compromise. For that reason, mediation may be particularly helpful or appropriate in situations where parties have an ongoing relationship (neighbors, business associates, divorcing parents of minor children, etc.) and do not want that relationship destroyed by the adversarial process of trial. In addition to being less adversarial than trial or arbitration, mediation tends to be less expensive, faster, and non-binding.

Mediation also may be used as a pretrial initiative to provide a way for litigating parties to gauge the relative strengths and weaknesses of their claims and defenses before they get to the point of trial. This does not mean that mediation is used as a practice trial; rather, it represents a joint effort in **good faith** to resolve the matter before it gets to trial. In this form of mediation, after parties consider all sides to the dispute, a recommendation for settlement is given to the parties for their consideration. If the parties are unwilling to compromise their respective positions, and no settlement of the dispute results, at least the mediation experience will have given them a better understanding of how the dispute may or may not play out in court.

VOLUNTARY VERSUS MANDATORY MEDIATION

Mediation of a dispute may occur as a result of voluntary private agreement, community program, or court order (which includes **statutory** mediation of some matters prior to trial). However, the term "mandatory mediation" may be misleading. It merely means that the parties are "forced to the table" to try to resolve their dispute prior to trial. It does not mean that they are required to settle their dispute; it merely requires that they attempt to do so in good faith. The decision to accept the outcome of the mediation and settle the matter remains voluntary. If the attempt at mediation fails to resolve the dispute, the parties may continue to litigate the matter.

A voluntary agreement to mediate a dispute may pre-exist the dispute, as in a private **contract** provision in which the parties agree to mediate any dispute that may arise in the future. Alternatively, a decision to mediate may come about after a dispute has already occurred and the parties are merely considering a way to resolve the matter without going to court.

Statutory mandatory mediation usually governs disputes concerning certain subject matters, such as labor relations, family matters (e.g., **custody** disputes), or consumer matters. Many states also have mandatory mediation provisions for civil disputes in which the dollar amount in controversy falls within a certain range. In those circumstances, mediation becomes an integral part of "pretrial procedure," promoting the resolution of the dispute at a stage before the cost of **litigation** has begun to accrue.

THE MEDIATION PROCESS

Unlike arbitration, mediation is not similar to a trial. In voluntary mediation, there is no "decision," judgment, or verdict rendered. Rather, the neutral mediator acts as a go-between and does not take sides or advocate the cause or defense of any party. The setting is more often informal than not, and the parties may or may not be represented by attorneys (usually, court-ordered mediations are handled by the attorneys representing the parties). Often, the mediation **hearing** takes place in a conference room at a local hotel, court building, or state **bar association**.

The mediation hearing itself differs substantially from a trial, in that there is generally no formal presentation of **evidence**, and generally no witness **testimony**. Rather, each party summarizes its position in written papers filed with the mediator(s) prior to the mediation. In the written summary, each party describes the evidence it intends to produce at trial, if mediation is unsuccessful. The mediation papers may include photographs, affidavits from witnesses who will appear at trial, formal opinions or reports from experts, etc. There is a summarized statement of the issues and the respective positions of the parties, as well as factual/legal arguments identifying the strengths and weaknesses of the opposing position(s). The mediator(s) will review the pre-mediation documents in order to become familiar with the issues and arguments, and thus be able to facilitate settlement. It is important that mediations are kept confidential, either by express agreement or by law, so as not to affect trial of the matter if mediation is unsuccessful.

Most often, there is a single, neutral mediator who facilitates and encourages open discussion and negotiation between the parties. However, in court ordered mediation, a panel of mediators may be selected. In many states that utilize mediation panels, the preferred number of mediators is three: one of whom is neutral in role and the other two serve as advocates for the causes of the opposing parties. In such cases, the mediators, after listening to both or all sides of the dispute, render a mediation recommendation (which sometimes is referred to as a mediation "award" or a mediation "decision," but in fact is not binding). The parties will have a set number of days to accept or reject the recommendation of the mediation panel.

In many states that have court ordered mediation, there are consequences for rejecting mediation recommendations, and/or for failure to negotiate in good faith. For example, if a party rejects a mediator's recommended "award" of a certain dollar amount to settle the case, and instead goes on to trial, that party must succeed at trial and/or improve his/her position with a substantially better verdict than that recommended in mediation. In other words, the rejection of a mediation settlement offer must be premised on a good faith belief that the party has a reasonable chance of substantially improving its position at trial. If the party fails to do better at trial, a monetary **penalty** for rejecting the recommended mediation amount may be imposed. The justification for this rule is that by rejecting mediation, the rejecting party has caused the other party to sustain the cost of trial even though the rejecting party has not ultimately obtained a better result at trial. It follows that the rejecting party should bear the cost of this.

DECIDING TO MEDIATE A DISPUTE

For individuals who have decided to attempt resolution of their disputes through private mediation, the following may prove helpful.

Finding an Appropriate Forum and Mediator(s) The local district court is a good starting source for mediation referral. Some state and local (attorney) bar associations also offer mediation programs. The nonprofit National Association for Community Mediation is comprised of member community organizations across the nation that provide local mediators and forums for the resolution of local disputes. Often, the mediators may belong to such entities as the Better Business Bureau or local chambers of **commerce**, etc. and are quite familiar with the issues presented for resolution.

If the dispute involves more national interests or parties, individuals should consult one of the more established mediation providers, such as the American Arbitration Association (AAA), which also handles mediations and supplies mediators. Most of these providers will be able to supply individuals with a list of mediators, a set of rules for the mediation, and a date and place for the mediation hearing.

If the forum individuals have chosen does not provide a mediator, but rather requests the parties to select the mediator(s), they should consider, among other factors:

- The appropriate experience
- The appropriate training
- The appropriate site (neutral)
- The fee schedule
- The "neutrality" (absence of **bias** or **conflict of interest** on the part of the mediator)

If the parties cannot agree on a mediator, the general procedure is to alternately strike names from a list (either provided by an outside source or created by the parties) until only a single name remains. Other alternatives (for panel mediation) include each party choosing any person at all (whether or not on a list) and then both parties choosing a neutral third mediator from the formal list.

Checklist Once the mediation date, time, place, and mediator(s) have been decided upon, as well as an agreed-upon procedure and/or rules, the following should assist individuals in completing the process:

- People should double check to make sure that confidentiality provisions have been included in their mediation agreement.
- They should make sure that, prior to the mediation, the subject of allocating the costs of mediation has been resolved.
- If the type of mediation allows the appearance of witnesses, individuals should double check to make sure everyone knows when and where the mediation will be held.
- They should ensure that the person who has authority to settle the matter will be present at the mediation hearing (if different from the actual parties, such as a representative from an insurance company).
- They should make sure that their mediation summary contains a concise statement of issues and positions.
- Try to identify both weaknesses and strengths of opposing positions. They should build on one and diminish the other.
- They should know in advance the least favorable offer they are willing to accept, and be prepared to consider

even less than that if surprise testimony or disclosure of previously unknown facts alters their present position.

UNIFORM MEDIATION ACT

The Uniform Mediation Act (UMA), drafted and approved for **adoption** in August 2001 by the National Conference of Commissioners on Uniform State Laws, was endorsed by the American Bar Association in early 2002. By 2011, only eleven states had adopted the UMA. The law continues to be debated in state legislatures, because of substantive changes such as those regarding confidentiality or legal privilege.

FEDERAL MEDIATION

The Alternative Dispute Resolution Act of 1998 (ADRA) (28 USC 651 et seq.) mandates that courts establish and authorize the use of ADR, including mediation and arbitration, in all civil actions. Courts maintain their individual discretion to decide at what stage in the litigation process a court offers mediation or other ADR to the parties. Local rules establish ADR procedure in the federal courts.

In the area of statutory ADR, the Federal Mediation and Conciliation Service was created by Congress in 1947 as an independent agency poised to assist and promote sound labor-management relations. It offers ADR services in a variety of formats, including dispute mediation and preventive (issue) mediation.

The U.S. Equal Employment Opportunity Commission's (EEOC) mediation program began as a pilot experiment in 1991 in four field offices. From 1999 through 2010, almost 136,000 mediations have been held and over 94,000 charges (almost 70 percent) have been successfully resolved. EEOC continues to develop and train internal mediators employed by the EEOC as well as external mediators hired on a contract basis to promote mediation as a possible resolution for some EEOC claims.

The federal government also encourages mediation and arbitration within its own ranks. Federal agencies are free to set up their own procedural ADR programs for the handling of both internal and external disputes. The Administrative Dispute Resolution Act of 1996 provides a mediation forum for handling disputes within agencies, or between citizens and agencies (claims against the government).

STATE MEDIATION PROVISIONS

The following state laws provide for ADR (mediation/arbitration) for certain types of disputes:

ALABAMA: Alabama Code, Ch. 25-7-4 applies to labor disputes.

ALASKA: Alaska Statutes 42.40.840 and 23.40.190 address labor disputes. Family disputes are governed by 25.20.080 and 25.24.080. Disputes involving automobile warranties are governed by 45.45.355.

ARIZONA: Statutory provisions for arbitration/mediation of family disputes is covered under 25-381.01 to 25-381.24. Automobile warranties are covered under 44-1265.

ARKANSAS: Arkansas Statutes 11-2-201 to 11-2-206 governs labor disputes.

CALIFORNIA: California's Code contains extensive provisions for the arbitration and/or mediation of many types of disputes. Labor disputes are addressed under Sections 65, 66, and 3518. Family disputes are covered in Sections 5180 to 5183. Education matters are covered by 48260.6, 48263, 48263.5 (truancy), and 56503 (special education). There is a special provision for the arbitration of cable TV franchise disputes under 53066.1(n)(1). Environmental regulatory disputes, including issues involving pesticides, are covered under 13127(c)(1). Water rights disputes are handled under 1219. Community disputes of a business or professional nature are covered under 465 to 471.5.

COLORADO: Colorado's statutes provide ADR for labor disputes under 8-3-113. Family matters are covered by 14-10129.5. Agricultural debts are governed by 6-9-101 to 6-9-106. A special statutory provision exists for ADR of disputes involving mobile homes under 38-12-216. Dispute resolution in general is covered by 13-22-301 to 13-22-310.

CONNECTICUT: Labor disputes are covered under Connecticut Statutes 31-91 to 31-100, 5-276 and 5-276a. Family disputes are resolved under 46b-59a. Public Act 87-316 Section 8 (1987) is covered under 42-182.

DELAWARE: Delaware's Code covers labor disputes under Title 14 Section 4002 and 4014, Title 19 Section 110 and 113, and Title 19 Section 1614. Automobile warranties are covered under Title 6 Section 5007.

FLORIDA: Florida Statutes Annotated 448.06 and 681.110(4)(9d) cover labor disputes. Family disputes are addressed under 44.101, 61.183, 39.42, 39.427 to 39.429, 39.436, 39.44, and 39.442. Automobile **warranty** disputes are provided for under 681.108 and 681.111. Mobile home disputes fall under 723.037 and 723.038. The state maintains "citizen dispute settlement centers" for ADR assistance under 44.201.

GEORGIA: Labor disputes are covered under Georgia Code 34-2-6(5), 25-5-1 to 25-5-14, 45-19-32, and 45-19-36. Public employee grievances and "unlawful practices" labor arbitrations are mandated under 45-19-36.

HAWAII: Hawaii Revised Statutes 371-10, 98-11(b)(1) (d), 89-12(a) and (b), 380-8, and 377-3 cover ADR for labor disputes. Automobile warranty disputes are covered under 490-2 and 313-1. Medical conciliation is addressed by 671-11 to 671-20. There is a special statutory provision for ADR of geothermal resources disputes under 205-5.1. International disputes are covered by 1988 Haw. Sess. Laws, Ch. 186, Sections 1-9.

IDAHO: Idaho Code Section 44-106 governs labor disputes.

ILLINOIS: Labor disputes are covered by Illinois Compiled Statutes, Ch. 48, paragraphs 1612, v1706, 1712, 1713(b); and Ch. 10, paragraph 26. Family disputes are covered by Ch. 40, paragraph 602.1 and 607.1. Automobile warranty disputes are covered by Ch.121.5, paragraph 1204(4). Disputes involving **public utilities** fall under Ch. 11, paragraph 702.12a. Illinois operates several nonprofit community dispute resolution centers under the auspices of Ch. 37, paragraph 851.1 to 856.

INDIANA: Labor disputes are covered under Indiana Code 5-14-1.5-6.5(2), 22-1-1-8(d), 22-6-1-7, 20-7.5-1-9 to 20-7.5-1-13. Family disputes are covered under 31-1-24-1 to 31-1-24-9 and 31-1-23-5 to 31-1-23-9. Automobile warranties are handled under 24-5-13-19. **Civil Rights** disputes are covered under 22-9-1-6. **Consumer protection** disputes are covered under 4-6-9-4(a)(4). There is a special Code provision for water rights disputes under 13-2-1-6(2).

IOWA: Labor disputes are covered under Iowa Code 20.19 to 20.20 and 679B to 679B.27. Family disputes are covered under 598.16 and 598.41(2). Agricultural debts are handled under 654a1 to 654a14. Civil Rights disputes are covered under 601A.15(3)(c). Informal dispute resolution in general is addressed under 679.1 to 679.14.

KANSAS: Labor disputes are covered under Kansas Statutes 44-817, 44-819(j), 44-820(c), 44-826, 44-828, 72-5413(h), 72-5427, 72-5429, 72-5430(b)(7), 72-5430 (c)(7), 75-4322, 75-4323, 75-4332, and 75-4333. The ADR provisions for family disputes are covered under 23-601 to 23-607 and 23-701. Automobile warranties are handled under 50 645(e). Civil Rights disputes are covered under 44-1001 to 44-1005. There is a special ADR provision for barbershop business disputes under 65-1824(4).

KENTUCKY: Kentucky has extensive ADR provisions in its Kentucky Revised Statutes (KRS). Labor disputes are covered under KRS 337.425, 345.080, 336.010, 336.020, 336.140, and 336.151 to 336.156. Family disputes are covered under KRS 403.140(b) and 403.170. Automobile warranties are handled under KRS 367.860 to 367.880. Civil Rights disputes are covered under KRS 344.190 to 344.290 and 337.425. Education matters are covered under KRS 165A.350 and 360. Disputes involving the production and distribution of agricultural products are covered under KRS 260.020.030(e) and 260.020.040(l). There is a special provision for community agency funding at KRS 273.451.

LOUISIANA: Labor disputes are covered under Louisiana Statutes, Title 23, Section 6. Family disputes are covered under Title 9, Sections 351 to 356. Automobile warranties are handled under Title 23, Section 1944. Housing civil rights matters are addressed under Title 40, Section 597. Barbershop disputes are covered under Title 37, Section 381. There is a special provision for a Medical Review Panel at Title 40, Section 1299-47.

MAINE: Maine's statutes provide ADR for the following areas of dispute: Labor disputes are covered under Title 26, Section 1026, 965, 931 to 936, 979-D, 1281, 1282, and 1285. Family disputes are covered under Title 4, Section 18 (1 to 5); Title 19, Section 214 (1,4); Title 19, Section 518 (1,2, and 4),; Title 19, Section 656 and 665; and Title 19, Section 752(4). Automobile warranties are handled under Title 10, Section 1165. There is a special ADR provision for professional **negligence** claims (**malpractice**) under Title 24, Sections 2851 to 2859. Disputes involving the production and distribution of agricultural products are covered under Title 13, Sections 1956 to 1959.

MARYLAND: Labor disputes are covered under Maryland Code Article 6, Section 408(d) and Article 89, Sections 3, 9, and 11. Maryland also has an employment agency dispute ADR provision under Article 56, Section 169.

MASSACHUSETTS: Labor disputes are covered under Chapter 150, Sections 1 to 3 of the General Laws. There is an ADR provision for cable television disputes under Chapter 166A, Section 16. A Community Mediation provision is at Chapter 218, Section 43E.

MICHIGAN: MCR 2.403 (Michigan Court Rules) covers court-ordered mediations of civil actions involving money damages or division of property. Domestic relations mediation is governed by MCR 3.211. Mediation of health care matters is covered under Michigan statutes MCL 600.4901 to 600.4923. ADR provisions for labor disputes are covered under MCL 432.1, 423.9 to 423.9c, 423.25, and 423.207. Disputes involving the production and distribution of agricultural products are covered under 290-714. A small claims conciliation **statute** is contained under MCL 730.147 to 730.155.

MINNESOTA: Labor disputes are covered under Minnesota Statutes 179.01, 179.03, 179.04, 179.06, 179.14, 179.15, and 179.02 to 179.09. Family disputes are covered under 518.167 and 518.619. Automobile warranties are handled under 325F.665. Civil Rights disputes are covered under 63.01 and 63.04 to 63.06. Conciliation Courts are provided for under 487.30. Civil Mediation is outlined under 572.31 to 572.40. Civil litigation ADR is covered separately under 484.74. There is also a statutory ADR provision for community dispute resolution programs under 494.01 to 494.04. A special provision for debtor-creditor mediation is found under 572.41, and workers' compensation disputes under 176.351(2a). Disputes involving the production and distribution of agricultural products are covered under 17.692, 17.695 and 17.697 to 17.701. Environmental issues are covered under 40.22, 40.23(3), 40.242, 40.244, 221.035F, 221.036(9), 116.072(1), and 116.072(6) to 116.072(8). Environmental waste management issues are covered separately under 115A.29(2)(a) and 115A.38(2).

MISSISSIPPI: Automobile warranty disputes are handled under Code provisions 63-17-159 and 63-17-163. Agricultural debt is addressed under 69-2-43 to 69-43-51.

MISSOURI: Labor disputes are covered under Statutes 105.525, 290.400, 290.420, 290.430, and 295.030 to 290.190. Civil Rights disputes are covered under 213.010 (1), 213.020, and 213.075.

MONTANA: Labor disputes are covered under Montana Code 39-31-307. Family disputes are covered under 26-1-81 and 40-3-111 to 40-3-127. Agricultural debt ADR is handled under 80-13-191 and 80-13-201 to 80-13-214. Civil Rights disputes are covered under 49-2-501(1), 49-2-504 to 49-2-506, and 49-2-601. Workers' compensation disputes are covered under 39-71-2401 to 39-71-2411. There is a special Code provision for special education matters under 20-7-462(4). **Medical malpractice** panels are covered under 27-6-101 to 27-6-704. Disputes involving the production and distribution of agricultural products are covered under 80-1-101 and 80-11-103(9).

NEBRASKA: Family disputes are covered under 42-801 to 42-823 and 42-360. Agricultural debt is covered under 2-4801 to 2-4816. Civil rights disputes are covered under 20-113.01 and 20-114(1)(2).

NEVADA: Nevada has copious provisions for ADR in its statutes. Labor disputes are covered under 288.190, 288.200, 288.205, 288.215, 288.220, 288.270, 614.010, and 614.020. Automobile warranties are handled under 598.761. Civil Rights disputes are covered under 233.020 to 233.210 and 244.161. Consumer credit disputes are covered under 598B.150. Educational dispute ADR is found under 394.11, and mobile home disputes are handled under 118B.024, 118B.025, and 118B.260.

NEW HAMPSHIRE: Labor disputes are covered by New Hampshire Statutes 273-A:1, 273-A:12, 273.215, 273.220, 273.270, 614.010 and 614.020. Automobile warranties are handled under 357.0:4.

NEW JERSEY: Labor disputes are covered under 34-13A-4 to 34-13A-16 and 34-13A-15. Civil rights disputes are covered under 52:27E-40 and 41. A general ADR provision is found at 2A:23A-1 to 2A:23A-19. Disputes involving the developmentally disabled are covered under 52:27E-40 and 41. Home warranties are covered under 46:3 B-9. Radioactive waste issues are handled under 32:31-5.

NEW MEXICO: Family disputes are covered under 40-12-1 to 40-12-6, and 40-4-9.1(B) and (J)(5). Automobile warranties are handled under 57-16A-6. Small claims are handled under 34-8A-10.

NEW YORK: Labor disputes are covered under Sections 205 and 209 for civil service, and Sections 750 to 760 for labor. Family disputes are covered under Sections 911-926. Automobile warranties are handled under Section 198-a (general business). Tax matters fall under Section 170(3a). Community Dispute Resolution Programs are governed by Sections 849-a to 849-g (judicial law).

NORTH CAROLINA: Labor disputes are covered under Statutes 95-32 to 95-36. Automobile warranties are handled under 20-351.7. Civil Rights disputes are covered under 143-422.3 (unemployment) or 41A-6(6), 41A-7 (a), and 41A-8 (housing).

NORTH DAKOTA: Family disputes are covered under Code Sections 14-09.1-01 to 14-09.1-08, and 27-05.1-01 to 27-05.1-18. Automobile warranties are handled under 51-07-18(3). A provision for ADR of agricultural debt can be found at 6.09.10-01 to 10-09. Debtor-creditor disputes are covered under 11-26-01 to 11-26-08.

OHIO: Lengthy provisions under Ohio's Code for labor disputes are covered under 4117.02(A), (E), (H)(7), (N); 4117.14(A) and (C). Family disputes are covered under 3117.01 to 08. Automobile warranties are handled under 1345.75 and 77. Civil rights disputes (housing matters) are covered under 1901.331.

OKLAHOMA: Automobile warranties are handled under Statute Title 15, Section 901(f). Civil Rights disputes are covered under Title 25, Sections 1505, 1704, and 1705. General dispute resolution programs are covered under Title 12, Sections 1801 to 1813.

OREGON: Oregon's statutes covering labor disputes are found at 662.405 to 455, 662.705(4), 662.715, 662.785, and 243.650 et seq. Family disputes are covered under 107.510 to 107.615, 107.755 to 107.795, and 107.179(4).

PENNSYLVANIA: Pennsylvania Statutes, Title 43, Section 211.31 to 39, and Title 43, Section 213.13 cover general labor disputes, as well as Title 43, Section 1101.801 and 802, and Title 43, Section 217.3. Automobile warranties are handled under Title 73, Section 1959. Civil Rights disputes are covered under Title 43, Section 957(i) (unemployment) or Title 43, Section 959(a) to (c) (employment). **Eminent domain** issues are covered under Title 52, Section 1406.15.

RHODE ISLAND: Labor disputes are covered under General Law 28-10-1, 28-9.4-10, 28-9.4-17, and 28-7-10. ADR for consumer issues is found at 42-42-5 to 42-42-7.

SOUTH CAROLINA: Codified laws in South Carolina include ADR provisions for labor disputes under 41-10-70 (wage mediation) and 41-17-10. Civil rights disputes are covered under 1-13-70 and 1-13-90 (employment). Consumer disputes are covered under 37-6-117. Employment grievances are covered under 8-17-360 and 8-17-370.

SOUTH DAKOTA: South Dakota has ADR for labor disputes under 60-10-1 to 60-10-3.

TENNESSEE: Bank patrons may resolve their disputes under Tennessee's Code 45-1-301 to 45-1-309.

TEXAS: Labor disputes are covered under Article 5154c-1, Section 9. ADR procedures in general are covered under Article 4590f-1, Ttitle 7, 154.001 to 154.073, Section 3.07(d).

UTAH: Family disputes are covered under 30-3-16.2 to 30-3-17.1, 30-3-4.1, and 30-3-4.3. Automobile warranties are handled under 30-20-7. Medical malpractice resolution is provided for under 78-14-1, 78-14-2, and 78-14-12 to 16.

VERMONT: Labor disputes are covered under Vermont Code Title 21, 924 and 925; Title 3, 8.25; and Title 21, 521 to 554. Special education matters are covered by Title 16, Section 2941, 2959.

VIRGINIA: Labor disputes are covered under Virginia's Code, 40.1-70 to 40.1-75. Family disputes are covered under 16.1-69.35 and 16.1-289.1. Automobile warranties are handled under 59.1-207.15. Civil mediation programs are found under 16.1-69.35(d). There is a special Code provision for local government dispute mediation at 15.1-945.1 et seq.

WASHINGTON: Labor disputes are covered under 49.08.010, 41.56.430, 41.56.440, 41.56.450, and 41.59.120. Family disputes are covered under 26.09.015. Automobile warranties are handled under 19.118.150. Civil Rights disputes are covered under 49.60.130. Dispute resolution centers are found at 7.75.010 to 7.75.100.

WEST VIRGINIA: West Virginia has an ADR provision for labor disputes at Code Section 21-1A-1. There is also an ADR provision for automobile warranty disputes at 46A-6A-8 and 46A-6A-9.

WISCONSIN: Wisconsin Statutes cover ADR for labor disputes under 101.24, 111.11, 111.39, 111.53-56, 111.70, and 111.77. Family disputes are covered under 753.016 (conciliation), 767.081-82, 767.001(3) and (4), 767.11, and 767.327(1) and (2). Automobile warranties

are handled under 218.015(3) to (7). Civil Rights disputes are covered under 118.20 (employment), 230.85 (employment), and 1419 (governor and mediation).

WYOMING: Automobile warranties are handled under Statute 40-17-101(a) and (f). Agricultural debt is covered under 11-41-101 to 110. Environmental issues are handled under 35-11-701(a) to (c).

ADDITIONAL RESOURCES

"About the American Arbitration Association." Available at http://www.adr.org/ (accessed November 2, 2012).

Golann, Dwight, and Jay Folberg. *Mediation: The Roles of Advocate and Neutral.* 2nd ed. New York: Aspen Publishers, 2010.

Kovach, Kimberlee. *Mediation in a Nutshell.* 2d ed. Eagan, MN: West, Thomson Reuters, 2010.

ORGANIZATIONS

ADR Section, American Bar Association
740 15th St. NW
Washington, DC 20005
Phone: (202) 992-1000
URL: http://www.americanbar.org/groups/dispute_resolution.html

American Arbitration Association (AAA)
335 Madison Avenue, Tenth Floor
New York, NY 10017-4605
Phone: (212) 716-5800
Fax: (212) 716-5905
URL: http://www.adr.org

National Association for Community Mediation
1527 New Hampshire Avenue NW
Washington, DC 20036-1206
Phone: (202) 667-9700
URL: http://www.nafcm.org

National Institute for Dispute Resolution
1726 M Street NW, Ste. 500
Washington, DC 20036
Phone: (202) 466-4764

DISPUTE RESOLUTION ALTERNATIVES

MINI-TRIALS

Sections within this essay:

- Background
- Mini-trials Distinguished From Other Forms of ADR
- Mini-trials in Federal Courts
- State Provisions
- Additional Resources
- Organizations

BACKGROUND

A mini-trial is an alternative method for resolving a legal dispute from a formal court trial. Mini-trials, like mediations and arbitrations, constitute unique forms of "alternative dispute resolution" (ADR) favored by courts and litigants alike. There has been a general increase in all forms of ADR in recent years because of the advantages offered: reduced cost, fast resolution, **privacy**, and less adversity in effect.

A mini-trial is really not a trial at all. Rather, it is a **settlement** process in which the parties present highly summarized versions of their respective cases to a panel of officials who represent each party (plus a "neutral" official) and have authority to settle the dispute. The presentation generally takes place outside of the courtroom, in a private forum. After the parties have presented their best case, the panel convenes and tries to settle the matter.

MINI-TRIALS DISTINGUISHED FROM OTHER FORMS OF ADR

A mini-trial most resembles a **mediation hearing**, in that there is a presentation by each party of a summarized version of his or her case to a panel of persons for the purpose of resolving or settling the dispute. Also like mediation, the parties are generally not bound to an outcome, and may end the process at an impasse.

However, there is one important difference between a mediation and a mini-trial. In mediation, the mediator is a neutral third party who does not take the side of either party, but instead tries to facilitate open communication between the parties themselves in order to achieve compromise and settlement. Even in court-ordered mediations conducted by a panel of mediators, the focus is still on the parties; the mediators merely issue a recommendation to the parties for settlement consideration.

Conversely, in a mini-trial, the mediators themselves are agents and advocates for the parties, and they, rather than the parties, work out a settlement after hearing opposing sides to the controversy (each goes into the mini-trial with advance authorization to settle the matter for a certain dollar amount or under other conditions or criteria). The parties present their cases (usually through their attorneys) but do not take active roles in the settlement **negotiations** nor generally do their attorneys. The decision-makers in a mini-trial are the actual members of the panel (excepting any neutral member, who may play the role of expert, advisor on substantive law, etc.).

One might ask why the parties themselves do not facilitate the settlement directly in a mini-trial. The answer is two-fold. First, parties involved in a controversy tend to approach and/or perceive the matter subjectively rather than objectively. Parties also tend to inject emotion or **bias** into their negotiations and will seldom compromise unless they have been introduced to damaging information that tends to diminish their claim or defense. Therefore, officials who are one step removed from the controversy, even if they serve as advocates for their respective parties, tend to approach the dispute more objectively. Secondly, the officials at a mini-trial tend to be well-seasoned and experienced in similar matters. For example, they may be representatives of the insurance carrier for the party, top-level management of a business that is party to a dispute, or privately-retained consultants with technical expertise in the subject matter. For these reasons, they may be better equipped to dissect and sort out opposing **evidence** and arguments.

Mini-trials also differ from another ADR technique, the "summary trial" or "summary **jury** trial." Both mini-trials and summary jury trials involve the presentation of each side's case, usually without live **testimony**, but with opening and closing statements and an outline of evidence they intend to produce at trial. However, summary trials are actually presented before mock juries, who issue advisory "verdicts." Following a jury determination, the parties and their attorneys will attempt settlement.

Finally, a mini-trial differs from other forms of ADR in that it is usually conducted after formal **litigation** has already been undertaken. Parties to a lawsuit generally stipulate to "stay" pending litigation (put a hold on further advancement of the litigation) until the mini-trial is concluded. Thus, mini-trial does not, in and of itself, represent an alternative forum for the resolution of a dispute (such as **arbitration**), but rather it represents a pre-trial alternate attempt to settle the matter before lengthy trial begins. The outcome of the mini-trial is generally confidential and advisory only, and the parties may proceed to trial if settlement negotiations fail.

MINI-TRIALS IN FEDERAL COURTS

The Alternative Dispute Resolution Act of 1998 (ADRA) (28 USC 651 et seq.) mandates that courts authorize, establish, and promote the use of ADR, including mediation, arbitration, mini-trial and summary jury trial in all civil actions. Federal district courts maintain their individual discretion to decide at what stage in the litigation process a court may offer ADR to the parties. Local rules establish ADR procedure in the federal courts.

The federal government also encourages the use of ADR in general within its own ranks. The Administrative

Dispute Resolution Act of 1996 provides a forum for handling disputes within agencies or between citizens and agencies (claims against the government). Federal agencies are free to set up their own procedural ADR programs for the handling of both internal and external disputes. For example, the U.S. **Code of Federal Regulations** (CFR) contains several ADR program provisions for federal agencies that contemplate mini-trials (as one of several alternatives); examples include the Federal Aviation Administration (FAA) (14 CFR 17.45), the Department of Energy (10 CFR 1023.8), and the Department of Housing and Urban Development (24 CFR 7.2).

STATE PROVISIONS

Generally speaking, state provisions for mini-trials are contained in comprehensive statutes or rules addressing ADR programs in their entirety. It is fair to say that if a court system has a formal ADR program, it will be receptive to the request for a mini-trial. The following state laws provide for ADR of certain types of disputes. Within those provisions, or at the request of the parties, mini-trials may be substituted for other forms of ADR (with the exception of **statutory** mandatory arbitration).

ALABAMA: Alabama Code, Title 6, Chapter 6 covers ADR, including mini-trials.

ALASKA: Family disputes are governed by Alaska Statutes 25.20.080 and 25.24.080. Disputes involving automobile warranties are governed by 45.45.355.

ARIZONA: Statutory provisions for arbitration/mediation of family disputes are covered under 25-381.01 to 25-381.24. Automobile warranties are covered under 44-1265.

ARKANSAS: Title 16, Subtitle 1-17 of the Arkansas Statutes covers ADR, including mini-trials.

CALIFORNIA: California's Code contains extensive provisions for ADR of many types of disputes. Title 2, Division 3, Part 1, Chapter 4.5, Article 5 addresses ADR in general. Family disputes are covered in statutory Sections 5180 to 5183. Education matters are covered by 48260.6, 48263, 48263.5 (truancy), and 56503 (special education). There is a special provision for the arbitration of cable TV franchise disputes under 53066.1(n)(1). Environmental regulatory disputes, including issues involving pesticides, are covered under 13127(c)(1). Water rights disputes are handled under 1219. Community disputes of a business or professional nature are covered under 465 to 471.5.

COLORADO: Colorado's statutes provide ADR for family matters under 14-10129.5. Agricultural debts are governed by 6-9-101 to 6-9-106. A special statutory provision exists for ADR of disputes involving mobile homes under 38-12-216. Dispute resolution in general is covered by 13-22-301 to 13-22-310.

CONNECTICUT: Chapter 909 of the Connecticut Statutes cover ADR in general. Family disputes are resolved under 46b-59a. Public Act 87-316 Section 8 (1987) is codified under 42-182.

DELAWARE: Delaware's Code, Title 10, Chapter 57 addresses ADR in general. Automobile warranties are covered under Title 6 Section 5007.

FLORIDA: Florida Statutes Annotated cover ADR of family disputes under 44.101, 61.183, 39.42, 39.427 to 39.429, 39.436, 39.44, and 39.442. Automobile **warranty** disputes are provided for under 681.108 and 681.111. Mobile home disputes fall under 723.037 and 723.038. The state maintains "citizen dispute settlement centers" for ADR assistance under 44.201.

GEORGIA: Title 15, Chapter 23 under the Georgia Code addresses ADR.

HAWAII: Division 4, Title 32, Chapter 613 covers ADR in general. Automobile warranty disputes are covered under Hawaii Revised Statutes 490-2 and 313-1. Medical **conciliation** is addressed by 671-11 to 671-20. There is a special statutory provision for ADR of geothermal resources disputes under 205-5.1. International disputes are covered by 1988 Haw. Sess. Laws, Ch. 186, Sections 1-9.

IDAHO: Idaho Code Section 44-106 governs labor disputes.

ILLINOIS: Illinois Compiled Statutes address ADR of family disputes in Ch. 40, paragraph 602.1 and 607.1. Automobile warranty disputes are covered by Ch.121.5, paragraph 1204(4). Disputes involving **public utilities** fall under Ch. 11, paragraph 702.12a. Illinois operates several nonprofit community dispute resolution centers under the auspices of Ch. 37, paragraph 851.1 to 856.

INDIANA: Family disputes are covered under Indiana Code 31-1-24-1 to 31-1-24-9 and 31-1-23-5 to 31-1-23-9. Automobile warranties are handled under 24-5-13-19. **Civil Rights** disputes are covered under 22-9-1-6. **Consumer protection** disputes are covered under

4-6-9-4(a)(4). There is a special Code provision for water rights disputes under 13-2-1-6(2).

IOWA: Subtitle 5, Chapter 679 to 679.14 addresses ADR. Family disputes are covered under Iowa Code 598.16 and 598.41(2). Agricultural debts are handled under 654a1 to 654a14. Civil Rights disputes are covered under 601A.15(3)(c).

KANSAS: Kansas Statutes Chapter 60, Article 2 addresses ADR in general. The ADR provisions for family disputes are covered under 23-601 to 23-607 and 23-701. Automobile warranties are handled under 50-645(e). Civil Rights disputes are covered under 44-1001 to 44-1005. There is a special ADR provision for barbershop business disputes under 65-1824(4).

KENTUCKY: Kentucky has extensive ADR provisions in its Kentucky Revised Statutes (KRS). Family disputes are covered under KRS 403.140(b) and 403.170. Automobile warranties are handled under KRS 367.860 to 367.880. Civil Rights disputes are covered under KRS 344.190 to 344.290 and 337.425. Education matters are covered under KRS 165A.350 and 360. Disputes involving the production and distribution of agricultural products are covered under KRS 260.020.030(e) and 260.020.040(l). There is a special provision for community agency funding at KRS 273.451.

LOUISIANA: Family disputes are covered under Louisiana Statutes Title 9, Sections 351 to 356. Automobile warranties are handled under Title 23, Section 1944. Housing civil rights matters are addressed under Title 40, Section 597. Barbershop disputes are covered under Title 37, Section 381. There is a special provision for a Medical Review Panel at Title 40, Section 1299-47.

MAINE: Maine's statutes provide ADR for the following areas of dispute: family disputes are covered under Title 4, Section 18 (1 to 5); Title 19, Section 214 (1,4); Title 19, Section 518 (1,2, and 4); Title 19, Section 656 and 665; and Title 19, Section 752(4). Automobile warranties are handled under Title 10, Section 1165. There is a special ADR provision for professional **negligence** claims (**malpractice**) under Title 24, Sections 2851 to 2859. Disputes involving the production and distribution of agricultural products are covered under Title 13, Sections 1956 to 1959.

MARYLAND: Maryland has an employment agency dispute ADR provision under Article 56, Section 169.

MASSACHUSETTS: There is an ADR provision for cable television disputes under Chapter 166A, Section 16. A Community Mediation provision is at Chapter 218, Section 43E.

MICHIGAN: MCR 2.403 (Michigan Court Rules) covers court-ordered ADR (mediations) of civil actions involving money damages or division of property. Domestic relations ADR is governed by MCR 3.211. ADR of health care matters is covered under Michigan statutes MCL 600.4901 to 600.4923. Disputes involving the production and distribution of agricultural products are covered under 290-714. A small claims conciliation **statute** is contained under MCL 730.147 to 730.155.

MINNESOTA: Chapter 486.76 of the Minnesota Statutes addresses ADR. Family disputes are covered under 518.167 and 518.619. Automobile warranties are handled under 325F.665. Civil Rights disputes are covered under 63.01 and 63.04 to 63.06. Conciliation Courts are provided for under 487.30. Civil Mediation is outlined under 572.31 to 572.40. Civil litigation ADR is covered separately under 484.74. There is also a statutory ADR provision for community dispute resolution programs under 494.01 to 494.04. A special provision for debtor-creditor mediation is found under 572.41, and workers' compensation disputes under 176.351(2a). Disputes involving the production and distribution of agricultural products are covered under 17.692, 17.695 and 17.697 to 17.701. Environmental issues are covered under 40.22, 40.23(3), 40.242, 40.244, 221.035F, 221.036(9), 116.072(1), and 116.072(6) to 116.072(8). Environmental waste management issues are covered separately under 115A.29(2)(a) and 115A.38(2).

MISSISSIPPI: Title 11, Chapter 15 of the Mississippi Code addresses ADR in general. Automobile warranty disputes are handled under Code provision 63-17-159 and 63-17-163. Agricultural debt is addressed under 69-2-43 to 69-43-51.

MISSOURI: ADR of civil rights disputes is covered under Statutes 213.010(1), 213.020, and 213.075.

MONTANA: Title 25, Chapter 21, Part 5 of the Montana Code addresses ADR generally. Family disputes are covered under 26-1-81 and 40-3-111 to 40-3-127. Agricultural debt ADR is handled under 80-13-191 and 80-13-201 to 80-13-214. Civil Rights disputes are covered under 49-2-501(1), 49-2-504 to 49-2-506, and 49-2-601. Workers' compensation disputes are covered under 39-71-2401 to 39-71-2411. There is a special Code provision for special education matters under 20-7-462

(4). **Medical malpractice** panels are covered under 27-6-101 to 27-6-704. Disputes involving the production and distribution of agricultural products are covered under 80-1-101 and 80-11-103(9).

NEBRASKA: Family disputes are covered under 42-801 to 42-823 and 42-360. Agricultural debt is covered under 2-4801 to 2-4816. Civil rights disputes are covered under 20-113.01 and 20-114(1)(2).

NEVADA: Chapter 232.548 covers general ADR provisions in its statutes. Automobile warranties are handled under 598.761. Civil Rights disputes are covered under 233.020 to 233.210 and 244.161. Consumer credit disputes are covered under 598B.150. Educational dispute ADR is found under 394.11, and mobile home disputes are handled under 118B.024, 118B.025, and 118B.260.

NEW HAMPSHIRE: New Hampshire Statutes cover ADR of automobile warranties under 357.0:4.

NEW JERSEY: Title 2A, Chapter 23A provides for ADR in general. Civil rights disputes are covered under 52:27E-40 and 41. A general ADR provision is found at 2A:23A-1 to 2A:23A-19. Disputes involving the developmentally disabled are covered under 52:27E-40 and 41. Home warranties are covered under 46:3 B-9. Radioactive waste issues are handled under 32:31-5.

NEW MEXICO: Chapter 34, Article 6-44 addresses ADR in general. Family disputes are covered under 40-12-1 to 40-12-, and 40-4-9.1(B) and (J)(5). Automobile warranties are handled under 57-16A-6. Small claims are handled under 34-8A-10.

NEW YORK: Article 75 of the Civil Practice and Law Rules address ADR. Additionally, family disputes are covered under Sections 911-926. Automobile warranties are handled under Section 198-a (general business). Tax matters fall under Section 170(3a). Community Dispute Resolution Programs are governed by Sections 849-a to 849-g (judicial law).

NORTH CAROLINA: Chapter 1, Article 45A covers ADR. Automobile warranties are handled under Statutes 20-351.7. Civil Rights disputes are covered under 143-422.3 (unemployment) or 41A-6(6), 41A-7(a), and 41A-8 (housing).

NORTH DAKOTA: Title 32, Chapter 32-42 covers ADR generally. Family disputes are covered under Code Sections 14-09.1-01 to 14-09.1-08 and 27-05.1-01 to

27-05.1-18. Automobile warranties are handled under 51-07-18(3). A provision for ADR of agricultural debt can be found at 6.09.10-01 to 10-09. Debtor-creditor disputes are covered under 11-26-01 to 11-26-08.

OHIO: Article 2711 of the Ohio Code addresses ADR generally. Family disputes are covered under 3117.01 to 08. Automobile warranties are handled under 1345.75 and 77. Civil rights disputes (housing matters) are covered under 1901.331.

OKLAHOMA: Title 12, Chapter 37, 1809 provides generally for ADR. Automobile warranties are handled under Statute Title 15, Section 901(f). Civil Rights disputes are covered under Title 25, Sections 1505, 1704, and 1705. General dispute resolution programs are covered under Title 12, Sections 1801 to 1813.

OREGON: Most ADR provisions are generally discussed in Oregon's statutes, Chapter 36. Family disputes are covered under 107.510 to 107.615, 107.755 to 107.795, and 107.179(4).

PENNSYLVANIA: Pennsylvania Statutes address ADR of disputes involving automobile warranties under Title 73, Section 1959. Civil Rights disputes are covered under Title 43, Section 957(i) (unemployment) or Title 43, Section 959(a) to (c) (employment). **Eminent domain** issues are covered under Title 52, Section 1406.15.

RHODE ISLAND: ADR for consumer issues is found at 42-42-5 to 42-42-7.

SOUTH CAROLINA: Codified laws in South Carolina include ADR provisions for civil rights disputes under 1-13-70 and 1-13-90 (employment). Consumer disputes are covered under 37-6-117. Employment grievances are covered under 8-17-360 and 8-17-370.

SOUTH DAKOTA: South Dakota has statutory ADR for labor disputes under 60-10-1 to 60-10-3.

TENNESSEE: Title 29, Chapter 5 of the Tennessee Code addresses ADR. Bank patrons may resolve their disputes under Tennessee's Code 45-1-301 to 45-1-309.

TEXAS: Government Code, Title 10, Subtitle A, 2008 provides for ADR in general. ADR procedures are also addressed in Texas Code Article 4590f-1, Title 7, 154.001 to 154.073, Section 3.07(d).

UTAH: Family disputes are covered under 30-3-16.2 to 30-3-17.1, 30-3-4.1, and 30-3-4.3. Automobile warranties are handled under 30-20-7. Medical malpractice resolution is provided for under 78-14-1, 78-14-2, and 78-14-12 to 16.

VERMONT: Chapter 192 of the Vermont Code generally addresses ADR. Special education matters are covered by Title 16, Section 2941 and 2959.

VIRGINIA: Title 11-71.1 of the Virginia Code addresses ADR in general. Family disputes are covered under 16.1-69.35 and 16.1-289.1. Automobile warranties are handled under 59.1-207.15. Civil mediation programs are found under 16.1-69.35(d). There is a special Code provision for local government dispute mediation at 15.1-945.1 et seq.

WASHINGTON: Titles 7.04 and 7.75 address ADR. Family disputes are covered under 26.09.015. Automobile warranties are handled under 19.118.150. Civil Rights disputes are covered under 49.60.130. Dispute resolution centers are found at 7.75.010 to 7.75.100.

WEST VIRGINIA: Chapter 55, Article 15 of the West Virginia Code addresses ADR generally. There is also an ADR provision for automobile warranty disputes at 46A-6A-8 and 46A-6A-9.

WISCONSIN: Wisconsin Statutes, Chapter 802-12 covers ADR generally. Family disputes are covered under 753.016 (conciliation), 767.081-82, 767.001(3) and (4), 767.11, and 767.327(1) and (2). Automobile warranties are handled under 218.015(3) to (7). Civil Rights disputes are covered under 118.20 (employment), 230.85 (employment), and (esoterically) 1419.

WYOMING: Automobile warranties are handled under Statute 40-17-101(a) and (f). Agricultural debt is covered under 11-41-101 to 110. Environmental issues are handled under 35-11-701(a) to (c).

ADDITIONAL RESOURCES

"About the American Arbitration Association." Available at http://www.adr.org/ (accessed November 2, 2012).

American Bar Association. "What You Need to Know about Dispute Resolution: The Guide to Dispute Resolution Processes." Available at http://www.americanbar.org/content/dam/aba/migrated/2011_build/dispute_resolution/draftbrochure.authcheckdam.pdf (accessed November 4, 2012).

Schachner, Robert W. *How and When to Be Your Own Lawyer.* New York: Avery Publishing Group, Inc., 1995.

Ventura, John. *Law for Dummies*. 2nd ed. New York: Wiley, John & Sons, Inc., 2005.

ORGANIZATIONS

ADR Section, American Bar Association

740 15th St. NW
Washington, DC 20005
Phone: (202) 992-1000

URL: http://www.americanbar.org/groups/dispute_reso lution.html

American Arbitration Association (AAA)

335 Madison Avenue, Tenth Floor
New York, NY 10017-4605
Phone: (212) 716-5800
Fax: (212) 716-5905
URL: http://www.adr.org

DISPUTE RESOLUTION ALTERNATIVES

NEGOTIATION

Sections within this essay:

- Background
- The Role of Negotiations in ADR
  - Arbitration
  - Mediation
  - Minitrials
  - Summary Jury Trials
  - Early Neutral Evaluation
  - Conclusion: Negotiation, ADR, and Civil Litigation

- Additional Resources

BACKGROUND

Negotiations consist of written and oral communications undertaken for the purpose of reaching agreement. When undertaken in **good faith**, negotiations include a process of give-and-take, whereby each party to the negotiations presents its position, critiques opposing positions, explores points of common ground, highlights divisive issues, proposes compromises and resolutions, and determines whether a mutually acceptable arrangement can be agreed upon to resolve the matters in dispute. When undertaken in **bad faith**, negotiations often are reduced to rancorous posturing aimed at assigning blame rather than reaching an amicable **settlement**.

Lawyers are constantly negotiating in civil **litigation**. Yet negotiation is not always used often enough, or extensively enough, to avoid litigation. Legal observers have suggested that a factor contributing to the high cost of litigation is the fear that the first side to propose settlement weakens its negotiating position. Since appearing eager to settle is taken as demonstrating a lack of confidence in one's case, both sides concentrate on **discovery** and preparing for trial so as to strengthen their hands for future negotiation while legal fees continue to mount.

The same fear does not ordinarily impede alternative dispute resolution proceedings, where a negotiated settlement is typically the goal for both parties. Alternative dispute resolution refers to an array of practices, procedures, and techniques that are used to resolve legal disputes by means other than formal civil litigation. Known more commonly as ADR, alternative dispute resolution is usually less costly and more time-efficient than civil litigation. ADR can also be more confidential than civil litigation. Court proceedings, records, and transcripts are generally open to public scrutiny and inspection in most civil litigation and cannot be sealed from the public absent an extraordinary justification. By contrast, parties to ADR proceedings can agree to insulate their dispute and its resolution from the public.

Early Puritan, Quaker, and Dutch settlers were among the first in North America to employ alternative means in resolving legal disputes. These tightly knit communities of settlers preferred even-tempered negotiations to adversarial litigation and treated litigation as a last resort to try only when procedures such as **mediation** and **arbitration** (discussed in detail below) failed to produce an acceptable and effective settlement. However, the term "alternative dispute resolution" was not coined in the United States until sometime during the 1970s, when it drew diverse support from influential members of society, including Chief Justice Warren Berger and consumer rights advocate Ralph Nader. Both Berger and Nader emphasized the perspective of the average citizen, who they said has neither the time nor the money to spend getting bogged down in drawn out court battles. Instead, Berger and Nader argued that average citizens find out-of-court negotiation alternatives to be a more palatable course, at least when done evenhandedly.

Congress helped fuel the ADR movement in the 1980s and 1990s by passing a series of legislative acts. In 1980 it passed the Dispute Resolution Act, which provides financial incentives for state governments and private entities to explore innovative approaches to negotiation and dispute resolution (28 U.S.C. app. section 1 et seq; Pub. L. No. 96-190, 94 Stat. 17 [1980]). In 1990 Congress passed the Administrative Dispute Resolution Act, which encourages federal agencies to use mediation and arbitration for prompt and informal resolution of disputes (5 U.S.C.A. sections 571 et seq; Pub.L. 101-552, Nov. 15, 1990, 104 Stat. 2738, and renumbered and amended Pub.L. 102-354, Aug. 26, 1992, 106 Stat. 944, 946). Eight years later Congress passed the Alternative Dispute Resolution Act of 1998, which requires all federal district courts to establish an ADR program, making at least one form of ADR available to all federal civil litigants (28 U.S.C.A. sections 651 et seq; Pub.L. 100-702, Title IX, Nov. 19, 1988, 102 Stat. 4659). By 2001 approximately ninety to ninety-five percent of all legal disputes were being resolved outside of trial by using negotiation through some form of ADR.

THE ROLE OF NEGOTIATIONS IN ADR

A wide variety of processes, practices, and techniques fall within the definition of "alternative dispute resolution." Arbitration and mediation are the best known and most frequently used types of ADR, but not the only ones. Minitrials, early neutral evaluations, and summary **jury** trials are less well-known forms of ADR. Many of these ADR techniques have little in common except that negotiation plays a prominent role in each. Parties to ADR procedures generally agree that a negotiated settlement is worth pursuing before investing time and money in full-blown civil litigation.

Arbitration Arbitration is the process of referring a dispute to an **impartial** intermediary chosen by the parties who agree in advance to abide by the arbitrator's award that is issued after a **hearing** at which all parties have the opportunity to be heard. Arbitration resembles traditional civil litigation in that a neutral intermediary hears the disputants' arguments and imposes a final and binding decision that is enforceable by the courts. One difference

is that in arbitration the disputants elect to settle any future disputes by arbitration before a dispute actually arises, whereas with civil litigation the judicial system is generally chosen by a disgruntled party after a dispute has materialized. Another difference is that the disputants to an arbitration select the intermediary who will serve as arbitrator, whereas parties to civil litigation have little to no control over who will preside as the judge in judicial proceedings.

Arbitration also resembles litigation in that many parties use arbitration as a springboard to negotiation. Parties who know that their dispute will wind up in arbitration often fail to commence serious negotiations until shortly before or shortly after the arbitration proceedings have begun. Frequently, negotiations will continue simultaneously with the arbitration proceedings, meaning the parties' representatives will discuss settlement outside the hearing room while the hearing itself is underway inside. Arbitration can even expedite negotiations, since the parties know that once the arbitrator has issued a decision, the decision is typically final and rarely appealable.

There are two different forms of arbitration: private and judicial arbitration. Private arbitration is the most common form of ADR. Sometimes referred to as contractual arbitration, private arbitration is the product of an agreement to arbitrate drafted by the parties who enter a relationship anticipating that disputes will arise, but who mutually desire to keep any such disputes out of the courts. Private arbitration agreements typically identify the person who will serve as arbitrator. The arbitrator need not be a judge or government official. Instead, the arbitrator can be a private person whom the parties feel will have sufficient knowledge, experience, and equanimity to resolve a dispute in a reasonable manner. In some states, legislation prescribes the qualifications one must satisfy to be eligible for appointment as an arbitrator.

A private arbitrator's power is derived completely from the arbitration agreement, which may also limit the issues the arbitrator has authority to resolve. Private arbitration agreements are supported in many states by statutes that provide for judicial enforcement of agreements to arbitrate and arbitrator-rendered awards. However, statutes governing private arbitration often set forth criteria that must be followed before an arbitration agreement will be binding on both parties and enforced by a court. If those criteria are satisfied, a court will normally deem the arbitrator's decision final and enforceable. The losing party may only **appeal** the decision upon a showing of **fraud**, misrepresentation, arbitrariness, or capriciousness by the arbitrator.

Private arbitration is the primary method of settling labor disputes between unions and employers. For example, unions and employers almost always include an arbitration clause in their formal negotiations, known as **collective bargaining** agreements. By doing so, they agree to arbitrate future employee grievances over wages, hours, working conditions, and job security. Many real estate and insurance contracts also make arbitration the exclusive method of negotiating and resolving certain disputes that can arise between the parties entering those types of relationships.

Judicial arbitration, sometimes called court-annexed arbitration, is a non-binding form of arbitration, which means that any party dissatisfied with the arbitrator's decision may choose to go to trial rather than accept the decision. However, most jurisdictions prescribe a specific time period within which the parties to a judicial arbitration may elect to reject the arbitrator's decision and go to trial. If this time period expires before either party has rejected the arbitrator's decision, the decision becomes final, binding, and just as enforceable as a private arbitrator's decision.

Judicial arbitration is usually mandated by **statute**, court rule, or regulation. Many of these statutes were enacted to govern disputes for amounts that exceed the **jurisdiction** of **small claims court** but fall short of the amount required for trial in civil court. For example, in New York State claims for over $3,000 and for less than $10,000 must be submitted to non-binding judicial arbitration (NY CPLR Rule section 3405). Ten federal district courts also have mandatory programs for non-binding judicial arbitration that are funded by Congress. For example, rule 30 of the Local Rules of Court for the U.S. District Court for the Western District of Missouri provides that cases designated for compulsory, non-binding arbitration are those in which the damage award could not reasonably be expected to exceed $100,000.

Because judicial arbitration is mandatory but non-binding, it often serves as a means of facilitating negotiation between the parties to a dispute. Civil court calendars are frequently backlogged with hundreds of lawsuits. States hope that by mandating non-binding arbitration for certain disputes the parties will see the value of a negotiated settlement where both parties compromise their positions, since their positions would likely be compromised were their dispute to be resolved in civil court. Seldom do litigants receive everything they ask for in their petitions, complaints, and answers.

Private and judicial arbitration are generally less costly and more time efficient than formal civil litigation. It has been estimated that the average arbitration takes 4 to 5 months while litigation may take several years. The cost of arbitration is minimal compared to civil trials as well, since the American Arbitration Association (AAA) charges only a nominal filing fee and the arbitrator may even work without a fee to broaden his or her professional experience.

Mediation Mediation is a rapidly growing ADR technique. It consists of assisted negotiations in which the disputants agree to enlist the help of a neutral intermediary, whose job it is to facilitate a voluntary, mutually acceptable settlement. A mediator's primary function is to identify issues, explore possible bases for agreement, discuss the consequences of reaching impasse, and encourage each party to accommodate the interests of other parties through negotiation. However, unlike arbitrators, mediators lack the power to impose a decision on the parties if they fail to reach an agreement on their own.

Mediation is sometimes referred to as **conciliation**, or conciliated negotiation. However, the terms are not necessarily interchangeable. Conciliation focuses more on the early stages of negotiation, such as opening the channels of communication, bringing the disputants together, and identifying points of mutual agreement. Mediation focuses more on the later stages of negotiation, exploring weaknesses in each party's position, investigating areas where the parties disagree but might be inclined to compromise, and suggesting possible mutually agreeable outcomes. Conciliation and mediation typically work well when the disputants are involved in a long-term relationship, such as husband and wife, wholesaler and retailer, and manufacturer and distributor, to name a few. Mediation and conciliation also work well for "polycentric" problems that are not easily solved by all-or-nothing solutions, as with certain antitrust suits involving a myriad of complex issues.

Although some jurisdictions have enacted statutes that govern mediation, most mediation proceedings are voluntary for both parties. Accordingly, a mediator's influence is limited by the autonomy of the parties and their willingness to negotiate in good faith. Thus, a mediator can go no further than the parties themselves are willing to go. Since agreements reached by mediation bear the parties' own imprint, however, many observers feel that they are more likely to be adhered to than decisions imposed by an arbitrator or court. Disputants who participate in mediation without representation of legal **counsel** are also more likely to adhere to settlements when the alternative is to pursue civil litigation, where attorneys fees consume a significant portion of any monetary award granted to the parties.

Minitrials A minitrial is a process by which the attorneys for the parties present a brief version of the case to a panel, often comprised of the clients themselves and a neutral intermediary who chairs the process. Expert witnesses (and less frequently, lay witnesses) may be used in presenting the case. After the presentation, the clients, normally top management representatives who by now are more aware of the strengths and weaknesses of their positions, attempt to negotiate a settlement of the dispute. If a negotiated settlement is not reached, the parties may allow the intermediary to mediate the dispute or render a non-binding advisory opinion regarding the likely outcome of the case were it to be tried in civil court.

Minitrials are increasingly used by businesses to resolve large-scale disputes involving **product liability** questions, antitrust issues, billion dollar construction contracts, and mass tort or disaster litigation. The federal government also makes use of minitrials for disputes involving telecommunications. The **Code of Federal regulations** establishes procedures whereby individuals and entities under investigation by the FCC can request a minitrial prior to commencement of more formal administrative proceedings (47 CFR section 1.730).

Minitrials are often effective because they usually result in bringing top management officials together to negotiate the legal issues underlying a dispute. Early in the negotiation process, upper management is sometimes pre-occupied by the business side of a dispute. Minitrials tend to shift management's focus to the outstanding legal issues. Minitrials also allow businesses to share information with each other and with their attorneys, providing a forum for initial face-to-face negotiations. Management also generally prefers the time-saving, abbreviated nature of minitrials over the more time-consuming and costly civil-litigation alternative. Minitrials expedite negotiations as well, by making them more realistic. Once the parties have seen their case play out in court, even in truncated fashion, the parties are less likely to posture over less relevant or meaningless issues.

Summary Jury Trials Summary jury trials are an ADR technique used primarily in federal courts, where parties are provided with the opportunity to "try" their cases before an advisory panel of jurors, without having to face the final and possibly adverse decision of a regular jury in civil court. The purpose of the summary jury trial is to facilitate pretrial termination of cases in which a significant impediment to negotiation is disagreement between the attorneys or parties regarding a civil jury's likely findings on liability or damages in the case. Like minitrials, summary jury trials give the parties a chance to reach a preliminary assessment of the strengths and weaknesses of their positions and proceed with negotiations from a common starting point, namely the advisory jury's findings. Both summary jury trials and minitrials can ordinarily be scheduled and completed before formal civil cases would normally reach a court's **docket**.

Summary jury trials are presided over by a judge or **magistrate** in federal district court. A ten-member jury venire is presented to counsel for consideration. Counsel are provided with a short character profile of each juror and then given two challenges to arrive at a final six-member jury for the proceeding. Each attorney is given one hour to describe his or her client's case to the jury. After counsel's presentations, the presiding judge or magistrate delivers to the jury a brief statement of the applicable law, and the jury retires to deliberate. Juries are encouraged to return a consensus verdict, but they may return a special report that anonymously lists the view of each juror as to liability and damages. After the verdict or special report has been returned, counsel meet with the presiding judge or magistrate to discuss the verdict and to establish a timetable for settlement negotiations. Evidentiary and procedural rules are few and flexible.

Early Neutral Evaluation Early neutral evaluation is an informal process by which a neutral intermediary is appointed to hear the facts and arguments of counsel and the parties. After the hearing, the intermediary provides an evaluation of the strengths and weaknesses of the parties' positions and the parties' potential exposure to liability for money damages. The parties, counsel, and intermediary then engage in discussions designed to assist the parties in identifying the agreed upon facts, isolating the issues in dispute, locating areas in which further investigation would be useful, and devising a plan to streamline the investigative process. Settlement negotiations and mediation may follow, but only if the parties desire. In some jurisdictions, early neutral evaluation is a court-ordered ADR technique. However, even in these jurisdictions the parties are given the option of hiring their own neutral intermediary or having the court appoint one.

The objective of early neutral evaluation is to obtain an early assessment of the parties' dispute by a credible outsider who has no interest in the outcome of the dispute but who has sufficient knowledge and experience to sift through the facts and issues and find the ground shared by the parties and the ground separating them. Much like in the other forms of ADR, the success of early neutral evaluation depends largely on the disputants' faith in the neutral intermediary. It also depends in large part on the disputants' willingness to compromise and settle the dispute. Successful early neutral evaluations can lead directly to meaningful negotiations.

Conclusion: Negotiation, ADR, and Civil Litigation The procedures and techniques discussed above are the most commonly employed methods of ADR. Negotiation plays an important role in each method, either primarily or secondarily. However, there are countless other ADR methods, many of which modify or combine the above methods. For example, it is not uncommon for disputants to begin negotiations with early neutral evaluation and then move to non-binding mediation. If mediation fails, the parties may proceed with binding arbitration. The goal with each type of ADR is for the parties to find the most effective way of resolving their dispute without resorting to litigation. The process has been criticized as a waste of time by some legal observers who believe that the same time could be spent pursuing the claims in civil court, where negotiation also plays a prominent role and litigants are protected by a panoply of formal rights, procedures, and rules. But many participants in unsuccessful ADR proceedings believe it is useful to determine that their disputes are not amenable to a negotiated settlement before commencing a lawsuit.

Despite its success over the past three decades, ADR is not the appropriate choice for all disputants or all legal disputes. Many individuals and entities still resist ADR because it lacks the substantive, procedural, and evidentiary protections available in formal civil litigation. For example, parties to ADR typically waive their rights to object to **evidence** that might be deemed **inadmissible** under the rules of court. **Hearsay** evidence is a common example of evidence that is considered by the parties and intermediaries in ADR forums but that is generally excluded from civil trials. If a disputant believes that he or she would be sacrificing too many rights and protections by waiving the formalities of civil litigation, ADR will not be the appropriate method of dispute resolution.

ADDITIONAL RESOURCES

American Jurisprudence. 2d ed. Eagan, MN: Thomson/West, 2006.

Ezzell, Bill. "Inside the Minds of America's Family Law Courts: The Psychology of Mediation Versus Litigation in Domestic Disputes." *Law and Psychology Review* 25, rev. 119, Spring, 2001.

Gale Encyclopedia of American Law. 3rd ed. Detroit: Gale, Cengage Learning, 2011.

HG.org. Global Legal Resources. "Alternative Dispute Resolution (ADR)." Available at http://hg.org/adr.html (accessed November 1, 2012).

ORGANIZATIONS

Academy of Experts

2 South Square
London, UK WC1R 5HT
URL: http://www.academy-experts.org

Coast to Coast Mediation Center

715 Hygeia Ave
Encinitas, CA 92023
Toll Free: (800) 748-6462
Fax: (760) 634-2628
URL: http://www.ctcmediation.com

National Association For Community Mediation

1527 New Hampshire Avenue
Washington, DC 20036-1206
Phone: (202) 667-9700
Fax: (650) 329-9342
URL: http://www.nafcm.org

EDUCATION

ADMINISTERING MEDICINE

Sections within this essay:

- Background
- General Policy Overview
- Authority
- Common Provisions
- State Laws
- Additional Resources

BACKGROUND

Administering medicine to children and adolescents while on the premises of local schools is an inescapable reality for contemporary educators. The increasing incidence of students needing to take medicine during the course of a school day has forced school systems and all but a handful of state legislatures to enact and implement regulations and policies addressing the matter.

The most reported medications administered within school settings are, in descending order, ADHD medications (for Attention Deficit Hyperactivity Disorders), nonprescription medications, asthma medications, analgesics, and anti-seizure medications. Also common are antibiotics and vitamins.

Seriously ill and/or heavily medicated students are rarely allowed to attend classes, so the issues do not center on them. But for those children who are only marginally ill or disabled, the issue pits educational systems against society at large. Schools must consider safeguarding other children and staff from contagious disease, the prevention of disruption in the classroom by students exhibiting symptoms of illness, the control of cross-medicating (the sharing or selling of medication between classmates), and the potential for self-medication abuse while on school premises. On the other side of the issue, the social realities of the increasing number of households with two working parents (or single working parent households), coupled with employment that does not allow for "sick day" benefits to attend to children's illnesses, often results in sick children being sent to school, with or without medication to take.

Faced with the growing problem of exposure to liability in conjunction with the administration of medicine (and in many circumstances, the administration of controlled substances), schools have mobilized over the years and demanded both guidance and protection from liability by state legislatures. Not all states have addressed the issue at the state level, and persons needing information are best advised to start with their local school districts.

GENERAL POLICY OVERVIEW

- The only federal law that deals with school administration of medication is Section 504 of the Americans with Disabilities Act. Under this section, schools are required to provide for the health needs of children with chronic health problems. The school has to provide whatever health assistance is needed to meet the needs of a disabled child, including the dispensing of medications.

- Guidelines may be found at either state or local levels. School boards, superintendents, individuals, and other school personnel, in collaboration with local physician or medical advisory committees, develop most local policies. When individuals are searching for applicable policies or regulations, they should always start at the local level and work up.

- Many states have **sovereign immunity** laws that shield public employees, including school personnel and nurses, etc., from liability for **negligence**. Local procedures and policies generally require parents' signatures to release school districts and employees from liability.

- Many state and local policies permit "delegation" of medication administration (usually restricted to licensed nurses) to trained but unlicensed assistive personnel (UAPs) within school settings. They may be school principals, teachers, secretaries, or administrative assistants within the health services office. Certain duties cannot be delegated, such as secured storage of controlled substances.

- Self-administration policies vary greatly from state to state and within school districts. Many require student assessment for age and maturity; others simply require authorizations from prescribers and parents. Almost all include signed releases of liability.

- States may require compulsory medication, in the form of immunizations/vaccinations of school children, as prerequisites to school attendance. All states require immunization for hepatitis B vaccinations. Many have additional requirements for measles, varicella, tetanus, and diphtheria. Schools may offer free or low-cost immunizations to students in conjunction with these requirements.

AUTHORITY

Federal law mandates that children with health needs receive school health services (e.g., the Education of All Handicapped Children Act of 1975 [P.L. 94-142]; Section 504 of the Rehabilitation Act of 1973 [P.L. 93-112]). But federal law does not specifically address the administering of medicine at the individual school level. Administering medicine entails physically providing it to the ultimate user, the patient.

Federal laws and regulations that do not expressly address, but nonetheless impact, the administration of medication within schools deal mostly with controlled substances. They include:

- The Controlled Substances Act, 21 U.S.C. 801

- The Uniform Controlled Substances Act of 1994, 21 U.S.C. 802

- Title 21 (Food and Drugs) of the **Code of Federal Regulations**, Chapter II (Drug Enforcement Administration, Section 1300 [21 CFR 1300.01 et seq.])

The above federal references identify and define those substances included as "controlled substances" (any drug as defined in the five categories of the Acts). They include all opiates and their derivatives, hallucinogenic substances, anabolic steroids, and several psychotropic substances. Within school settings, most drugs used to treat ADHD are controlled substances, as is Ritalin. Controlled substances generally fall under the purview of local drug enforcement agencies, which derive their ultimate authority from the Federal Drug Enforcement Administration.

Students who need medications administered to them during the school day already have legal possession (or their parents do) of any controlled substances. The school's role is therefore limited to ensuring safe **custody**, storage, and administering of the medication, once a valid authorization is received from parents/a physician.

Most states have enacted statutes that delegate to school systems and school boards the authority to implement local policies addressing the administration of medicine on school premises. But those regulations and policies must comply and coordinate with state laws concerning the "unauthorized practice of medicine" or "unauthorized practice of nursing."

COMMON PROVISIONS

Typical state or local policies contain certain key provisions; the two most basic requirements are parental consent and a medication order from the prescribing physician (dentist, physician assistant, nurse practitioner, etc.). Most regulations or policies require that a medication plan be completed by the school nurse or health service employee and that it contains minimum required information such as emergency contacts and telephone numbers, allergies and known side effects, the quantity of the medication delivered to the school, plans for administering medication on school field trips or planned events, and information on self-administration. An individual student log, documenting dates and times of administered medicine, is usually part of the plan on file and ultimately becomes part of the school health record.

Requirements for self-administration of medications evoke more controversy. Students who suffer from asthma and similar respiratory illnesses may suffer undue panic or anxiety attacks when separated from their inhalers. On the other hand, a few asthmatic (and other) students nationwide have been known to sell off their medications to fellow students looking for a "high" or quick thrill. In schools where students are permitted to keep asthma medication close at hand, there are generally strict instructions as to where the medication may be stored (e.g., locker or backpack) and (sometimes) reserved rights on the part of the school to monitor self-administration. (If schools retain an "overseeing" role in self-medication, they may expose themselves to more liability if they are not protected with **immunity**).

Policies generally should require that all medication brought to school, whether prescriptive or over-the-counter (OTC), remain in original labeled containers. Of key concern is the access to life-sustaining medications administered by injection, such as insulin and epinephrine (to treat emergency allergic reactions). All parenteral medications and drugs controlled by the Drug Enforcement Agency must be appropriately secured by the schools (and many of them require refrigeration, as well). In such circumstances, even those students approved for self-administration must report to a school representative to receive the required medication and any dosage paraphernalia (such as a syringe) if needed. Medication dosages/pills should be counted upon arrival and recounted when tendered to school employees.

STATE LAWS

ALABAMA: The state has published "recommended guidelines" prepared by an advisory task force comprised of members from Alabama's State Department of Education and the Alabama Department of Public Health. The policy differs from others in that it expressly notes that school nurses may not delegate the administration of medications to unlicensed personnel, pursuant to Alabama's Nurse Practice Act (Title 34-21-1) and the 1993 state guidelines for Delegation of Nursing Functions to Assistive Personnel. The guidelines "are not meant to be regulatory" for local education agencies (LEAs), but intend to offer "best practice" recommendations. The guidelines allow for self-administration of prescription medication by students if permitted by local school board policy. The guidelines are available at http://www.schoolhealth.org/adminmed.html.

ALASKA: No applicable provisions.

ARIZONA: Title 15 of the Arizona Revised Statutes, Chapter 15-344, provides for the administration of prescription, **patent**, or **proprietary** medications by school employees. The law delegates authority to establish policies and procedures to local school district governing boards.

ARKANSAS: No applicable provisions.

CALIFORNIA: The California Education Code 49423, 49423.6 requires the state board of education to adopt regulations regarding the administration of prescription medication in public schools. There is no express delegation of authority.

COLORADO: Colorado Dept. of Reg. Agencies, Chapter XIII, Section 7, and Colorado Board of Health Regulations, Chapter 9, Section 105, address school administration of medications. There is no express delegation of authority.

CONNECTICUT: Connecticut General Statute 10-212a, as well as Connecticut State Agencies Regulation 10-212a-2, 5, and 6 authorize school boards of education to adopt written policies. A new Connecticut law passed in 2001 (the first of its kind in the nation) expressly prohibits teachers, counselors, and other school personnel from recommending psychiatric drugs for schoolchildren. The state requires schools to document any skipped dose and the reasons for it.

DELAWARE: The Code of Delaware Regulations 72-000-008, Section 800-9, is applicable to school nurses; there is no express delegation of authority.

DISTRICT OF COLUMBIA: D.C. Code 31-2432 to 2434 requires the D.C. Board of Education and Department of Human Services to issue joint rules and regulations. D.C. schools must obtain authorization from the student's parent or **guardian**, as well as orders/instructions from the licensed physician before administering medication.

FLORIDA: Florida Statutes Annotated 232.46 requires district school boards to adopt local policies and procedures.

GEORGIA: State Board of Education Rule 160-4-8-.01 (2000) requires each school system to develop a Student Services Plan that provides guidelines for its various components including school health services. The state's School Health Nurse Resource Manual (2001) provides suggested models for each school system to implement the rule. Each model includes administration of medication as a school nurse function.

HAWAII: Hawaii Revised Statute 321-242 establishes a statewide school health services program, including statewide requirements for medication administration. Hawaii Administrative Code 11-146-4 is also applicable.

IDAHO: No applicable provisions.

ILLINOIS: 105 Illinois Compiled Statutes Annotated 5/10-20.14b requires school boards to develop local policies for school administration of medication.

INDIANA: Indiana's 511 Indiana Administrative Code 7-21-8 establishes written medication administration policies for public schools operating special education programs only.

IOWA: Iowa Administrative Code 41.12(11) requires local education agencies offering special education programs to establish medication administration policies.

KANSAS: KAR 60-15-101 (2009) states that only a licensed registered professional nurse (or a physician provider) has the authority to delegate the administration of medication or other nursing procedures in schools to unlicensed assistive personnel (UAP) and only with appropriate and adequate training, supervision and performance evaluation of the UAP. KAR 60-15-102 (2009) requires that nursing procedures (including medication administration) in the schools can only be delegated by a licensed registered professional nurse.

KENTUCKY: KRS 156.502 (2002) requires health services to be provided in a school setting by a licensed physician, registered nurse or a delegated school employee who has been trained by a physician or nurse. Health services are defined in the statute as providing direct health care, including the administration of medication.

LOUISIANA: Louisiana Revised Statute 17:436.1 prescribes policies for delegating of administration of medications in schools to unlicensed personnel. Louisiana Administrative Code 28:1.929 requires school boards to establish guidelines consistent with state policy.

MAINE: 20-A Maine Revised Statutes Annotated, Section 254, Subsection 5, requires schools to adopt local written policies and procedures.

MARYLAND: The Annotated Code of Maryland, Education 7-401, in conjunction with Administrative Regulation 13A.05.05.08 and .10, requires county boards of education to adopt policies for administration and storage of medication within school systems.

MASSACHUSETTS: Massachusetts was one of the earliest to have a statute in place, dating from the early 1970s. New regulations were promulgated in 1993, and old ones were updated. Four statutes in the Massachusetts General Laws are pertinent. Chapter 71, Section 53, requires registered nurses in all public school districts; Chapter 94C, the Controlled Substance Act, gives the Commissioner of Public Health authority to make certain exceptions for delegation of duties to unlicensed personnel; Chapter 112 (The Nurse Practice Act) has been amended to include regulations governing the delegation of nursing tasks; and Chapter 71, Section 54B contains registration requirements for students receiving medications. 105 Code of Massachusetts Reg. 210.003 to 210.009 requires schools to adopt local policies consistent with the above laws and regulations.

MICHIGAN: MCL 380.1178 (Revised School Code, Act 451 of 1976) was amended in March 2000, to provide immunity from criminal or civil actions for school personnel who administer medication to pupils pursuant to parent/physician authorizations and instructions. The law does not protect **gross negligence** or willful and wanton misconduct. There is no express delegation of authority.

MINNESOTA: Minnesota Statutes Annotated 121A.22 requires local school boards to develop prescription medication administration procedures in conjunction with health care professionals.

MISSISSIPPI: Code 41-79-1 (1988) states that a school nurse can provide preventive health services to students to facilitate optimal development and prevent serious health problems. Code 41-79-3 (2000) authorizes each school district to employ a school nurse, known as the Health Service Coordinator, in compliance with the school nurse intervention program established by the State Department of Health.

MISSOURI: Chapter 167 of the Missouri Revised Statutes, "Pupils and Special Services," Section 167.627 (August 2001) addresses state requirements of self-administered medications for asthma "or other potentially life-threatening respiratory illnesses." Section 167.181 discusses compulsory immunizations. Section 167.191 expressly prohibits children with contagious diseases from attending school, with penalties of "not less than five nor more than one hundred dollars" for violations.

MONTANA: No applicable provisions.

NEBRASKA: Nebraska Revised Statutes 71-6718 to 6742, in conjunction with Nebraska Administrative Code, Chapters 59 and 95, regulate the administration of medication in schools by unlicensed personnel through **competency** assessments and procedural requirements.

NEVADA: Nevada Administrative Code 632.226 requires school nurses (rather than local school boards) to develop procedures.

NEW JERSEY: Concerning self-administration of medication by school pupils for asthma, **Public Law** 2001, c.061 (S1372 2R) amends Public Law 1993, c.308, and supplements Chapter 40 of Title 18A of the New Jersey Statutes. In addition, New Jersey Administrative Code 6A:16-2.3 requires district boards of education to adopt written policies.

NEW MEXICO: New Mexico, through its 6 N.M. Administrative Code 4.2.3.1.11.3.2(d), requires the supervisory school nurse to develop and implement written policies and procedures for clinical services, including the administration of medication.

NEW YORK: No applicable provisions.

NORTH CAROLINA: North Carolina General Statute 115C-307(c) authorizes school boards of education to permit school personnel to administer prescriptive medications with parents' written authorizations.

NORTH DAKOTA: No applicable provisions.

OHIO: Ohio Revised Code 3313.713 requires local school boards of education to adopt policies permitting school employees to administer medication. In February 2000, Ohio became the 50th state to allow advanced-practice nurses to prescribe medication (under physician supervision). In school settings, they have no independent authority to prescribe.

OKLAHOMA: Under 70 Oklahoma Statutes Annotated 1-116.2, school nurses and other school personnel must administer medications according to **statutory** requirements, which contain no express delegation of authority.

OREGON: Oregon Revised Statutes 339.869 and 339.870, in conjunction with Oregon Administrative Rule 581-021-0037, require local school district boards to adopt policies.

PENNSYLVANIA: Pennsylvania has no statutory authority, but it has a regulation, 22 Pa. Code 7.13, that requires school districts to develop medication administration policies that are consistent with state department of health guidelines. Title 24 (Education) of the Pennsylvania Consolidated Statutes Annotated, PSA 24-13, Article XIV, School Health Services, Sections 13-1413 and 13-1414 address supplemental duties of school physicians and care and treatment of pupils.

RHODE ISLAND: Title 16 (Education), Chapter 16-21 (Health and Safety of Pupils), Section 16-21-22 provides for self-medication by students who have provided schools with medical documentation. The law also provides for

immunity from civil damages for those negligently administering epinephrine or prescription inhalers; it does not protect gross negligence or willful/wanton conduct from liability. The Code of R.I. Rules 14-000-011, Section 18 requires schools to develop procedures that include specified minimum requirements.

SOUTH CAROLINA: No applicable provisions, but the Charleston County School District has policies comparable to most states.

SOUTH DAKOTA: Article 46:13 addresses medication administration, including self-administration, through delegation of tasks generally within the purview of licensed registered nurses. There is no express mention of application to schools.

TENNESSEE: Tennessee Code Annotated 49-5-415 requires licensed health care professionals to administer medications, but school boards may authorize unlicensed personnel to assist students with self-administration.

TEXAS: House Bill 1688, signed into law by Governor Perry in June 2001, amends Texas Chapter 38, Education Code, to add provisions regarding self-administration of prescription asthma medicine by public school students while on school property or at school-related events or activities. School-based Health Centers and their services are generally discussed in Chapter 38.011. Texas Education Code 22.052 provides for immunity from civil liability conditioned upon the adoption of compliant school district policies.

UTAH: Utah Code Annotated 53A-11-601 authorizes schools to develop policies.

VERMONT: Vermont has no statutory guidance, but Code of Vermont Rule 22-000-006, Section 4220, requires schools to incorporate specified procedures into their local administration regulations.

VIRGINIA: The Code of Virginia, as amended, Section 22.1-274.2 and Section 22.1-78, address self-administration by students of asthma medication; permissions are granted for each school year and renewed annually. The Code delegates to local school superintendents the authority to establish additional regulations for administration of medicines to students. The Code of Virginia 54.1-3408 authorizes school boards to train employees to administer drugs.

WASHINGTON: The Revised Code of Washington, RCW 28A.210.260, addresses administration of oral medication in public and private schools. It delegates policy-making to public school districts and private schools. RCW 28A.210.270 expressly provides for immunity from liability for school employees.

WEST VIRGINIA: West Virginia Code of State Rules 126-25-1 and 126-27-1 establish standards for administration of oral, topical, and emergency medication in West Virginia public schools by persons not licensed as health care providers. Code 18-5-22a requires school boards of education to develop policies.

WISCONSIN: Wisconsin Statute 118.29 requires school boards to develop policies, including authorizing school employees to administer medications.

WYOMING: The Wyoming Administrative Code, Education, Chapter 6, Section 17(a)(i)(F) requires school districts to establish local programs for handling, storage, and administration of medications.

ADDITIONAL RESOURCES

Lewis, Keeta de Stefano, and Bonnie J. Bear. *Manual of School Health: A Handbook for School Nurses, Educators, and Health Professionals.* 3d ed. St. Louis, MO: Saunders, Elsevier, 2008.

Loschiavo, Janice. *Fast Facts for the School Nurse: School Nursing in a Nutshell.* New York: Springer Publishing, 2011.

EDUCATION

ATHLETICS

Sections within this essay:

- Background
- Amateur vs. Professional Athletics
- High School Athletic Associations
- Collegiate Athletic Associations
- Professional Sports Associations
- Relationship Between Professional Sports Leagues and College Athletics
- Other Legal Issues Affecting Amateur and Professional Athletes
- Title IX and Sex Discrimination in Amateur Athletics
  – Background
  – Parties Subject to Liability
  – Standards for Liability
  – Student-Athletes' Title IX Claims
  – Coaches' Title IX Claims
  – Remedies
  – Criticisms of Title IX
- Additional Resources

BACKGROUND

The law governing amateur athletes is an amalgam of statutes, regulations, rules, procedures, and judicial decisions that apply to individual athletes, the academic institutions for which they compete, and most persons employed by those academic institutions. This body of law spans several areas of American **jurisprudence**, including **tort law**, tax law, **antitrust law**, and

civil **rights** law, among others. Thus, the law governing amateur athletics is not a single body of law unto itself.

AMATEUR VS. PROFESSIONAL ATHLETES

The most basic difference between amateur and professional athletes lies in the rewards that each group receives for athletic performances. Generally speaking, amateur athletes are not paid for their athletic performances, though the U.S. Gymnastics Association and the U.S. Figure Skating Association now allow member athletes to sponsor commercial products so long as the money earned is placed into **trust**. Professional athletes, by contrast, are typically paid annual salaries plus incentives tied to individual and team performance.

Athletic scholarships are the biggest reward offered to amateur athletes. Athletic scholarships pay for some or all of a student-athlete's tuition, including room and board, as long as the student-athlete remains enrolled at the school, continues to participate in the athletic program for which the scholarship was awarded, and maintains academic eligibility. Amateur athletes who are compensated for their performance in any way beyond their athletic scholarships can be stripped of their amateur status by National Collegiate Athletic Association (NCAA) or other college athletic organizations.

HIGH SCHOOL ATHLETIC ASSOCIATIONS

Each state has established an athletic association that establishes rules and guidelines under which most schools in that state must adhere. These rules and guidelines cover topics such as the general eligibility of student athletes, including age restrictions; residency requirements; restrictions on supervised practices when a sport is not in session; policies related to broadcasting and sponsorship;

and codes of conduct. These associations also set forth rules for individual sports.

COLLEGIATE ATHLETIC ASSOCIATIONS

Headquartered in Shawnee, Kansas, the NCAA is the governing body that regulates athletic competitions among many colleges and universities. Colleges and universities must elect to join the NCAA, and once they do they relinquish ultimate **jurisdiction** over their athletic programs, student-athletes, and coaches. To remain a member of the association, colleges and universities have to abide by NCAA rules, regulations, and policies.

Pursuant to its governing authority, the NCAA has established criteria that college athletes must satisfy to stay eligible for NCAA sanctioned athletic competitions. One of these criteria is that student-athletes be in good academic standing and maintain a certain minimum grade-point average. Schools and coaches are subject to NCAA restrictions regulating how high school students may be recruited, while both coaches and athletes are subject to discipline for violating NCAA rules relating to use of illegal or banned substances, gambling, point-shaving, and **bribery**.

The NCAA conducts its own investigations of alleged rule violations and assesses penalties based on the severity of the violation, after giving the suspected offender an opportunity to be heard during a public proceeding in which most fundamental legal rights may be invoked. Penalties may be assessed against an offending school, coach, or athlete and entail loss of scholarships and post-season awards, fines, **probation**, suspensions, **forfeiture** of games, and forfeiture of tournament and playoff opportunities.

Schools with repeat offenses may receive particularly harsh punishment. For instance, the NCAA cancelled the entire 1987 football season for Southern Methodist University (SMU) after investigators found numerous rule violations related to the football team, including payments to players that amounted to more than $600,000. The so-called "death penalty" that the NCAA administered in the SMU case is the harshest punishment that the NCAA has ever administered, but it is indicative of the level of power that the NCAA holds over athletic programs. In 2012, the NCAA issued harsh sanctions against Pennsylvania State University for the failure of school administrators and coaches to deal with **child abuse** committed by a former assistant football coach, Jerry Sandusky, over a long period of time on the Penn State campus.

Some schools, particularly smaller colleges, choose not to be members of the NCAA. More than 280 colleges belong to the National Association of Intercollegiate Athletics (NAIA), which is based in Olathe, Kansas. The NAIA sanctions more than a dozen sports for men and women. Two-year colleges, on the other hand, belong to the National Junior College Athletic Association (NJCAA), based in Colorado Springs, Colorado. Member schools of the NAIA and NJCAA are subject to similar rules as schools that are members of the NCAA.

Most colleges and universities also belong to athletic conferences. These conferences establish additional rules under which their members must operate. Athletic conferences also coordinate efforts to market their sports teams and provide for plans by which revenues from athletics are shared by member schools.

PROFESSIONAL SPORTS ASSOCIATIONS

Professional sports teams in the National Football League (NFL), Major League Baseball (MLB), the National Hockey League (NHL), and the National Basketball Association (NBA) are also governed by voluntary associations, but their associations are comprised of individual owners who purchase professional sports franchises and agree to abide by the rules, policies, and procedures established by the league. Also known as the constitution and by-laws, these rules, policies and procedures generally govern the circumstances under which franchises may move their team from one city to another; players may be drafted, sign contracts, become free agents, and receive retirement pensions; and owners, coaches, and players may be fined, suspended, banned, or otherwise punished. The league's constitution and by-laws may also be influenced by the terms of any **collective bargaining agreement** entered into between franchise owners and labor representatives for the players' union and by any applicable antitrust laws (i.e., federal laws that protect trade and **commerce** from restraints, monopolies, **price-fixing**, and price **discrimination**).

RELATIONSHIP BETWEEN PROFESSIONAL SPORTS LEAGUES AND COLLEGE ATHLETICS

Professional sports leagues generally do not have an official relationship with college athletic associations. In some sports, especially baseball and hockey, the best high school players often develop their skills in minor professional leagues rather than colleges. On the other hand, most highly talented football and basketball players traditionally have played in college as amateurs before moving on to play professionally.

Beginning primarily in the 1990s, top high school basketball stars began skipping the college ranks altogether and joining professional teams. With the success and popularity of such individuals as Kevin Garnett, Kobe

Bryant, and LeBron James, each of whom were drafted directly out of high school, more NBA teams began selecting high school players in the NBA draft. In the 2006 **collective bargaining** agreement between the NBA and the players, drafting athletes out of high school was prohibited. The NFL forbids players from entering the NFL draft until a minimum of three years has elapsed since the players have graduated from high school.

OTHER LEGAL ISSUES CONFRONTING AMATEUR AND PROFESSIONAL ATHLETES

Amateur and professional athletes must comply with state and federal laws that exist independent of the rules established by the athletic association in which they are members. Nonetheless, many professional and amateur athletes are surprised to learn of the extent to which they must understand the intricacies of civil and criminal law if they want to stay out of court. For example, professional athletes are required to pay **income tax** to every state in which they appear to play a game, and not just to the state in which their teams play home games. Amateur athletes may be taxed on the funds they receive for athletic scholarships when those funds exceed the cost of tuition, room, board, and necessary supplies.

Many amateur and professional athletes are also surprised to learn that they can be held civilly and criminally liable for injuries they inflict on other athletes during competition, even in contact sports such as hockey and football. Contact-sport athletes consent to some contact as part of the game and assume the risk for injuries that are sustained during the normal and ordinary course of an athletic contest. But under the **common law**, no athlete assumes the risk for injuries that result from the reckless or intentional misconduct of another athlete. Depending on the laws of the state in which an injury is inflicted, the blameworthiness of the misconduct, and the severity of the injury, athletes who recklessly or intentionally injure competitors during an athletic contest may be prosecuted in criminal court or sued in civil court for battery, **assault**, or other such related unlawful acts. A minority of jurisdictions allow athletes to recover for injuries sustained from the negligent conduct of competitors.

In some cases academic institutions may be held liable for injuries suffered by athletes. As a general rule, coaches, trainers, and referees must exercise reasonable care to prevent foreseeable injuries to athletes, and under no circumstances may a school employee encourage athletes to injure opponents or competitors. If a school employee fails to exercise the degree of care that is reasonable under the circumstances, the school itself may be held vicariously liable under the doctrine of respondent superior, which makes principals liable for the wrongful

acts of their agents, when those acts are committed in the ordinary course and scope of the agent's authority.

Because the relationship between the law and amateur and professional athletes can be complicated, many colleges, universities, and pro sports franchises require athletes to attend classes that introduce them to a variety of legal issues. Some of these classes are geared solely toward male athletes. Given the number of highly publicized cases in which male athletes have been **accused** of sexual assault and violence, these classes are intended to help male athletes avoid situations where they can get themselves into trouble.

TITLE IX AND SEX DISCRIMINATION IN AMATEUR ATHLETICS

Sex discrimination is a hotly debated and litigated issue in amateur athletics. Title IX of the Education Amendments Act of 1972 provides that "[n]o person in the United States shall, upon the basis of sex, be excluded from participation in, be denied the benefits of, or be subjected to discrimination under any education program or activity receiving federal financial assistance" (20 U.S.C.A. §§ 1681 *et seq.*). The phrase "education program or activity" has been broadly interpreted to include athletic programs. Title IX may be enforced by the federal government in an administrative proceeding or by a private individual in civil court. The law guarantees **equal protection** at all federally funded academic institutions for both male and female student-athletes and male and female persons employed by school athletic programs.

Background Congress enacted Title IX to serve as a catalyst against sex discrimination at federally funded academic institutions, to encourage the development of athletic programs for female student athletes, and to stimulate female participation in school sports. Within eleven years of Title IX's enactment, statistics revealed that progress was being made toward these goals. In 1983, more than 150,000 women were participating in college sports, compared with 32,000 in 1972, while the number of colleges and universities offering athletic scholarships to women increased from 60 in 1974 to 500 in 1981. By 2010, about 242,000 women engaged in athletics in the NCAA. In 2011, girls made up 41 percent of high school athletes, up 5 percent from 1991.

The U.S. Department of Education (DOE), acting through the Office of Civil Rights (OCR), is primarily responsible for implementing Title IX. The OCR promulgates regulations to enforce Title IX, initiating administrative proceedings against alleged violators and terminating federal funding for proven violators. Although neither Title IX nor any of its amendments expressly authorizes an individual to bring a lawsuit against a violator independent of an action brought by the DOE or OCR, the U.S. Supreme Court has ruled that Title IX implies a private cause of action pursuant to which aggrieved individuals may seek **redress** for sex discrimination in federal court without first having exhausted their administrative remedies (*Cannon v. University of Chicago* [1979]).

Parties Subject to Liability Title IX conditions the offer of federal funding on each funding recipient's promise not to discriminate on the basis of sex, in what amounts to a **contract** between the government and the funding recipient. Elementary schools, junior high schools, high schools, and both undergraduate and graduate colleges and universities must comply with Title IX if they receive federal funding and wish to continue receiving it. However, federally funded recipients may be exempted from liability under Title IX if they have had a continuous policy and tradition of admitting students of only one gender (20 U.S.C.A. § 1681[a][5]). Federally funded recipients are also exempt from Title IX suits that arise from employment discrimination claims over jobs in which sex is a bona fide occupational qualification, as might be the case for persons hired to clean or monitor locker rooms and toilet facilities.

As noted above, athletic departments and athletic programs infrequently receive federal funding directly from the federal government. The same holds true for directors, coaches, trainers, and other individuals employed by school athletic programs. Instead, school boards, school districts, colleges, and universities are the most common recipients of federal funding, and thus they are also the most common targets of Title IX **litigation**. Since Title IX has been interpreted as abrogating the states' Eleventh Amendment **immunity** in this area of law, state governments themselves may also be sued in federal court for discrimination that occurs at one of their federally-funded, state-sponsored academic institutions.

Standards for Liability Title IX bars sex discrimination in any interscholastic, intercollegiate, intramural, or club athletic program offered by a federally-funded academic institution. This prohibition has two prongs. The first prong prohibits sex discrimination against students participating in or seeking to participate in a school-sponsored sport. The second prong prohibits sex discrimination against persons employed or seeking employment with a school sponsored athletic program, including persons employed or seeking employment as athletic directors, athletic coordinators, coaches, physical therapists, trainers, or any other job within a school's athletic program.

Under both prongs, the law requires federally funded academic institutions to guarantee equal opportunity for student-athletes and employees without regard to gender. Ten specific factors may be considered in determining whether this obligation has been met: (1) the particular sports and levels of competition selected by an institution to accommodate members of both sexes; (2) the quality and quantity of equipment and supplies that are provided to teams of each gender; (3) the scheduling of games and practice time; (4) travel and per diem allowances; (5) the opportunities to receive coaching and academic tutoring; (6) the compensation of coaches and tutors; (7) the provision of locker rooms, as well as practice and competitive facilities; (8) the provision of medical and training facilities and services; (9) the provision of housing and dining facilities and services; and (10) the publicity afforded to each gender's athletic programs (34 C.F.R. § 106.41).

The circumstances of each case determine how much weight is allotted to a given factor in resolving Title IX disputes. Nonetheless, a significant portion of litigation has focused on the first factor, and courts will normally ask three questions when evaluating whether an academic institution has taken steps to effectively accommodate athletes of both sexes: (1) Does the number of athletic opportunities provided for males and females proportionately represent their respective overall enrollments to a substantial degree? (2) Does the academic institution have a history of expanding programs to accommodate female interests and abilities in sports? and, of so, (3) Has that institution fully and effectively accommodated those interests and abilities? If a preponderance of the **evidence** offered during a Title IX proceeding answers these questions in the affirmative, the **defendant** will normally prevail. Plaintiffs are more likely to prevail when the defendant has a poor or inconsistent record on these issues.

Student-Athletes' Title IX Claims A court's analysis will also depend on whether the **plaintiff** is a disgruntled student-athlete or a disgruntled employee. For disgruntled student-athletes, Title IX does not compel federally funded educational institutions to sponsor one program for each gender in every sport the institution sponsors. However, if a school sponsors only one program for a sport, then that school must allow members of both sexes to try out for the team, unless the sport is a contact sport, in which case the school may limit participation to one gender. Conversely, if a school sponsors only one program for a contact sport and then allows members of both sexes to compete for the team, the school may not exclude an athlete from the team on account of his or her gender. "Contact" sports include boxing, wrestling, rugby, ice hockey, football, and basketball (45 C.F.R. § 86.41).

Disgruntled students may also **allege** that they have been victims of **sexual harassment** in violation of Title IX. Sexual harassment typically consists of receiving unwanted sexually oriented comments, receiving unwanted sexually oriented physical contact, or working in a sexually charged environment. The threshold of liability is higher for sexual harassment than it is for sex discrimination. To prevail on a Title IX sexual harassment claim, a plaintiff must show that the institution was aware of the harassment, exercised control over both the harassed and the environment in which the harassment occurred, and that harassment was serious enough to have the systemic effect of denying the victim equal access to participate in an athletic program. Mere name-calling or teasing will not give rise to a Title IX harassment claim, even when the offensive comments single out differences in gender.

Courts are more inclined to find that offensive comments give rise to Title IX liability when they are made by a coach or a person acting in an official capacity for the academic institution. Plaintiffs are less likely to prevail when the offensive behavior takes the form of student-on-student or athlete-on-athlete harassment. In such instances, the plaintiff must not only prove that the academic institution was aware of the harassment and had authority to stop the harassment, but also that the harassment was so severe, pervasive, and objectively offensive that it amounted to deliberate indifference by the institution in failing to stop it. Thus, sexual harassment by fans, athletes, or coaches from opposing schools is generally not actionable.

Coaches' Title IX Claims The **statutory** proscription against sex discrimination in education programs and activities encompasses employment discrimination, which means that any person working for an athletic program at a federally funded academic institution is entitled to protection from Title IX. The law protects employees in all aspects of their employment, ranging from hiring and compensation to promotion, demotion, suspension, and termination, regardless of the position held by the employee and regardless of whether the federally funded academic institution is a tiny elementary school or an enormous Division I university.

Since 1990, a large number of Title IX employment discrimination complaints have been filed by college coaches. Frequently, these claims allege that the head coach of a women's college team is being discriminated against because she is being paid less than the head coach of the men's team for the same sport and from the same school. Courts will consider several factors in evaluating these claims, including the following: (1) the differing rates of compensation; (2) the duration of the contracts; (3) provisions relating to contract renewal; (4) the relative training and experience of the two coaches; (5) the nature of the coaching duties performed by each; (6) working conditions; (7) professional standing; (8) other terms and conditions of employment; and (9) other professional qualifications.

Remedies A plaintiff instituting a private action to enforce Title IX may not ordinarily recover **compensatory damages**, unless the plaintiff offers evidence that the discrimination was willful, deliberate, or intentional. Injunctive relief is the remedy most regularly sought in Title IX actions. Injunctions may take the form of an order compelling an academic institution to cease an offending practice or an order compelling the institution to take specific action to level the playing field for the victims of discrimination. Prevailing Title IX plaintiffs may also recover attorney's fees and expert witness fees pursuant to 42 U.S.C.A. § 1988. Additionally, when the Title IX defendant is a state government, plaintiffs may pursue remedies available under the Civil Rights Act, which prohibits discrimination by state actors (42 U.S.C.A. § 1983). Both compensatory and **punitive damages** are recoverable in section 1983 actions.

Litigants who are unhappy with a federal agency's decision made pursuant to Title IX may generally **appeal** that decision to a federal district court as provided in 20 U.S.C.A. § 1683. However, if the agency's decision involves terminating or refusing to grant or to continue financial assistance upon a finding of failure to comply with Title IX requirements, then **judicial review** may only be pursued as provided in 5 U.S.C.A. § 701 et seq. Title IX does not contain a **statute of limitations**, so both administrative agencies and judicial bodies rely on the most analogous **statute** of limitations provided by the law of the state from which the discrimination complaint originated.

Criticisms of Title IX Title IX is not without its critics. This is particularly true of those who are involved with low-profile men's sports, such as wrestling or diving. According to some critics, schools have eliminated some smaller men's sports in order to finance women's sports. Supporters of Title IX have countered that the smaller sports have been sacrificed because schools refuse to divert money from men's sports that produce the most revenue, particularly football and basketball.

Because Title IX only applies to schools accepting federal funding, about a third of the states have enacted similar laws that ban discrimination. These states include Alaska, California, Florida, Georgia, Hawaii, Illinois, Iowa, Maine, Minnesota, Nebraska, New Jersey, New Mexico, New York, Rhode Island, South Dakota, Washington, and Wisconsin.

ADDITIONAL RESOURCES

Brake, Deborah. *Getting in the Game: Title IX and the Women's Sports Revolution.* New York: New York University Press, 2010.

Gale Encyclopedia of American Law. 3rd ed. Detroit: Gale, Cengage Learning, 2011.

Managing Legal Issues in College Athletics: Proactive Strategies for Administrators. Horsham, PA: LRP Publications, 2004.

ORGANIZATIONS

National Education Association (NEA)

1201 16th Street, NW
Washington, DC 20036
Phone: (202) 833-4000
Fax: (202) 822-7170
URL: http://www.nea.org

EDUCATION

BILINGUALISM

Sections within this essay:

- Background
  - Types of Bilingual Education
  - Conflicting Philosophies

- Historical Perspective
- Landmark Legislation
  - Setting the Stage
  - Civil Rights Act (1964)
  - Bilingual Education Act (1968)
  - English Language Acquisition Act (2001)
  - *Lau v. Nichols* (1974)

- State and Local Initiatives
- Programs
- Additional Resources

BACKGROUND

As of 2009, there were 5.3 million children in the United States who were classified as Limited English Proficient (LEP). For much of the twentieth century these students would have been placed in so-called "immersion programs," in which they would be taught solely in English until they understood it as well or better than their native tongue. Beginning in the 1960s there was a gradual shift toward bilingual education, in which students can master English while retaining their native-language skills.

Types of Bilingual Education There is a difference between bilingual programs and English as a Second Language (ESL) programs, although bilingual programs include an ESL component. Bilingual programs are designed to introduce students to English gradually by working with them in both English and their native tongue. The students are able to master English without losing proficiency in the native language. In bilingual or dual language immersion, the class typically includes English speaking students and LEP students who share the same native language. Instruction is given in both English and the native language. In developmental or late-exit programs, all students share the same language; instruction begins in that language but gradually shifts to English as the students become more proficient.

Transitional or early-exit programs are similar to developmental programs, except that the goal is mastery of English rather than bilingualism. Students who become proficient in English are transferred to English-only classes.

Bilingualism is not generally a goal in ESL programs. In *sheltered English or structured immersion programs*, LEP students are taught in English (supplemented by gestures and other visual aids). The goal is acquisition of English. *Pull-out ESL programs* include English-only instruction, but LEP participants are "pulled out" of the classroom for part of the day for lessons in their native tongue.

Conflicting Philosophies Bilingual education in the United States is a complex cultural issue because of two conflicting philosophies. On the one hand is the idea that the United States welcomes people from all societies and all walks of life. Immigrants have long seen the States as the "Land of Opportunity," in which individuals can rise to the top through hard work and determination. They can build new identities for themselves, but they can also hold on to their past culture without fear of reprisal. At the same time, the United States is also the great "melting pot" in which immigrants are expected to assimilate if they wish to avail themselves of the many opportunities for freedom and success. Everyone who comes to the States, so they are told, should want to *become* American.

Thus there are people who believe strongly that erasing an immigrant's native tongue is erasing a key cultural element. People are entitled to speak and use their native languages as they please; anything less goes against the freedom for which the United States stands. Besides, having proficiency or fluency in more than one language is a decided advantage in a world that has become more interdependent.

There are other people who believe, equally strongly, that everyone who lives and works in the United States should speak, read, and write in English. Those who oppose bilingual programs for LEP students believe that allowing children to learn in their native tongue puts them at a disadvantage in a country in which English is the common language. A student whose instruction is in another language, they say, may never master English. This closes doors to opportunities including higher education and choice of career.

There is no uniform opinion even among immigrant parents of LEP children. Some parents want their children to be taught in their native tongue as a means of preserving their culture. Others, wishing their children to have the same opportunities as native speakers of English, want their children to be taught in English from the outset.

The one point on which everyone seems to agree is that LEP children deserve the best educational opportunities available, and any language program must be structured enough to give them a good foundation, while remaining flexible enough to meet their varied needs.

HISTORICAL PERSPECTIVE

Although we tend to think of bilingualism in the United States as a modern issue, in fact it has always been a part of our history. In the early days of exploration and colonization, French, Spanish, Dutch, and German were as common as English. By 1664, the year that the British took control of New York from the Dutch, there were some 18 languages (not including the native American tongues) spoken in lower Manhattan alone. No doubt many of the inhabitants of the colony were conversant in more than two languages.

German and French remained common in colonial North America. Many Germans educated their children in German-language schools. Although many colonial leaders (among them Benjamin Franklin) complained

about bilingualism, it was generally accepted. In fact, during and after the American Revolution, such documents as the **Articles of Confederation** were published in both English and German.

During the nineteenth century millions of immigrants came to the United States and brought their languages with them. German remained popular, as did other European tongues. Spanish was introduced when the United States took possession of Texas, Florida, and California from Spain.

The enormous wave of **immigration** that began in the 1880s and lasted until the early 1920s brought a change in sentiment toward bilingual education. The goals of voluntary assimilation were gradually replaced by strident calls for "Americanization." In Puerto Rico, Hawaii, and the Philippines (which the United States had acquired after the Spanish-American War in 1898), English was to be the language of instruction even though most of these new Americans spoke no English at all. In 1906, Congress passed a law, the first language law ever passed, requiring naturalized citizens to be able to speak English. Anti-bilingual sentiment got stronger as more immigrants poured into the United States. Anti-German sentiment, which reached its peak when the United States entered World War I in 1917, caused some communities to ban the use of German in public.

By the end of the war, bilingualism had fallen out of favor even in areas where it had thrived. In 1924 strict immigration quotas sharply reduced the number of new foreigners coming into the United States. For almost the next 40 years, bilingual education in U.S. schools was almost exclusively based on variations of immersion; students were taught in English no matter what their native tongue was, and those who did not master English were required to stay back in the same grade until they became proficient.

LANDMARK LEGISLATION

Setting the Stage Bilingual education in the United States was pushed back into the spotlight as a direct result of the 1959 revolution in Cuba. After Fidel Castro overthrew the dictatorship and established a Communist government, many middle- and upper-class Cubans fled to the United States. A large number of these refugees settled in Florida. Well-educated but with little in the way of resources, they were assisted quite generously by the federal and state governments.

Among this assistance was ESL instruction, provided by the Dade County (Florida) Public Schools. In addition, the school district launched a "Spanish for Spanish Speakers" program. In 1963, a bilingual education program was introduced at the Coral Way

Elementary School in Miami. Directed by both U.S. and Cuban educators, the program began in the first through third grades. U.S. and Cuban students received a half day of English and a half day of Spanish instruction; at lunch time and recess and during music and art classes the groups were mixed together. Within three years the district was able to report benefits for both groups of students, who were now not only bilingual but also bicultural. This was no accident: the goal of the Coral Way initiative was to promote exactly this level of fluency.

The Civil Rights Act (1964) The Civil Rights Act of 1964 did not address bilingual education directly, but it opened an important door. Title VI of the Act specifically prohibits **discrimination** on the basis of race, color, or national origin in any programs or activities that receive federal financial assistance. What this means, among other aspects, is that school districts that receive federal aid are required to ensure that minority students are getting the same access to programs as non-minorities. This minority group includes language minority (LM) students, defined as students who live in a home in which a language other than English is spoken. (Although some LM students are fluent in English, many are classified as LEP.) Title VI's critical role in bilingualism would be made clear a decade later in the *Lau v. Nichols* case.

Bilingual Education Act (1968) The Elementary and Secondary Education Act of 1968 was another important step for bilingual education. In particular, Title VII of that act, known as the Bilingual Education Act (BEA), established federal policy for bilingual education. Citing its recognition of "the special educational needs of the large numbers children of limited English-speaking ability in the United States," the Act stipulated that the federal government would provide financial assistance for innovative bilingual programs. Funding would be provided for the development of such programs and for implementation, staffing and staff training, and long-term program maintenance.

English Language Acquisition Act (2001) However, Title VII was repealed as part of the **No Child Left Behind Act of 2001**. The law replaced BEA with the English Language Acquisition Act, or Title III. Title III ended federal funding for bilingual education and stated that it was up to each state to determine the best way to teach children English. The law holds "state educational agencies, local educational agencies, and schools accountable for increases in English proficiency and core academic content knowledge of limited English proficient children" by requiring "demonstrated improvements in English

proficiency" each year, and yearly progress reports on "limited English proficient children, including immigrant children and youth." Title III emphasized teaching English to LEP students without supplementing it with native-language instruction for those who may need it.

Lau v. Nichols Probably the most important legal event for bilingual education was the *Lau v. Nichols* case, which was brought against the San Francisco Unified School District by the parents of nearly 1,800 Chinese students. It began as a discrimination case in 1970 when a poverty lawyer decided to represent a Chinese student who was failing in school because he could not understand the lessons and was given no special assistance. The school district countered that its policies were not discriminatory because it offered the same instruction to all students regardless of national origin. The lack of English proficiency was not the district's fault.

Lower courts ruled in favor of the San Francisco schools, but in 1974 the U.S. Supreme Court ruled unanimously in favor of the plaintiffs. Justice William O. Douglas stated simply that "there is no equality of treatment merely by providing students with the same facilities, textbooks, teachers, and curriculum; for students who do not understand English are effectively foreclosed from any meaningful education." The Court cited Title VI of the Civil Rights Act, noting that the students in question fall into the protected category established therein.

What *Lau v. Nichols* did not do was establish a specific bilingual policy. Individual school districts were responsible for taking "affirmative steps" toward reaching the goal of providing equal educational opportunities for all students.

STATE AND LOCAL INITIATIVES

In the 1960s there were no state bilingual programs; many states actually had English-only instruction laws on their books. After the Civil Rights Act and the Bilingual Education Act, states began to take more initiative. In 1971, Massachusetts became the first state to establish a bilingual mandate. Under this mandate, any school that had 20 or more students of the same language background was required to implement some sort of bilingual program.

A decade later, 11 more states had passed bilingual education laws, and an additional 19 offered some sort of legislative efforts in that direction. Today, bilingual or ESL education is offered in some form by every state. Not surprisingly, those states with the highest concentration of immigrants (New York, California, Texas, and Florida) tend to have the most comprehensive programs. In fact, according to the most recent data from the National

Clearinghouse for English Language Acquisition (NCELA), 18 of the 20 urban school districts with the highest LEP enrollment are in one of these four states. Some states fund all bilingual education programs; others fund only bilingual or only ESL programs.

It should be noted that bilingual needs can differ widely from state to state or district to district. According to the U.S. Department of Education, Spanish-speaking students make up nearly three-quarters of all LEP students in the United States. But in a district in which the predominant foreign language is Chinese, Vietnamese, or Hindi, the needs would of course be geared toward those languages. Local schools can create effective bilingual programs based on their specific needs. At the William Barton Rogers School in Boston, for example, a transitional program for middle-school LEP students who speak Vietnamese has met with success; likewise, a program for elementary school students in the Madawaska School District in Maine has been successful with French-speaking students.

Because each state's needs are different, and because those needs are subject to change, the best way to get comprehensive and up-to-date information on each state's initiatives is to contact individual state education departments (see below).

PROGRAMS

Obtaining information about bilingual grants, programs, and other initiatives is much easier today than it was in the past thanks to the Internet. Federal, state, and local government agencies offer a surprising variety of information on their websites. Those who do not own a computer can access these sites at any local public library. Following is a sampling of what is available.

The U.S. Department of Education's Office of English Language Acquisition establishes and implements policy and national dissemination efforts of the bilingual education programs that serve limited English proficient (LEP) children and adults. It administers a state grant system. The funds are distributed to states based on a formula that takes into account the number of immigrant and LEP students in each state. States must develop annual measurable achievement objectives for LEP students that measure their success in achieving English language proficiency and meeting challenging state academic content and achievement standards. Schools use the funds to implement language instruction programs designed to help LEP students achieve these standards. In 2011 the office awarded 56 grants, with the average grant $12 million.

A good beginning resource for anyone who wishes to find out about programs, grants, and other information on bilingual education and bilingual initiatives is the National Clearinghouse for English Language Acquisition. Funded by the Office of English Language Acquisition, this organization collects and analyzes information and also provides links to other organizations. The NCBE website (http://www.ncbe.gwu.edu) is a comprehensive starting point.

Each state's department of education provides information on its statewide and local bilingual initiatives; the easiest way to find this information is to visit individual state education department websites. Also, large cities such as New York, Miami, Houston, Los Angeles, and San Francisco provide information on their websites about their comprehensive bilingual programs.

ADDITIONAL RESOURCES

Baker, Colin. *Foundations of Bilingual Education and Bilingualism.* 5th ed. Bristol, UK: Multilingual Matters, 2011.

Crawford, James. *Bilingual Education: History, Politics, Theory, and Practice.* 3rd ed. Los Angeles: Bilingual Educational Services, Inc., 1995.

Garcia, Olfelia, and Jo Anne Kliefgen. *Educating Emergent Bilinguals.* New York: Teachers College Press, 2010.

ORGANIZATIONS

Center for Applied Linguistics
4646 40th Street, NW
Washington, DC 20016
Phone: (202) 362-0700
Fax: (202) 362-3740
URL: http://www.cal.org

National Association for Bilingual Education (NABE)
1220 L Street, NW, Suite 605
Washington, DC 20005
Phone: (202) 898-1829
Fax: (202) 789-2866
URL: http://www.nabe.org

National Clearinghouse for English Language Acquisition (NCELA)
The George Washington University
Center for the Study of Language and Education
2011 I St. NW, Ste. 300
Washington, DC 20006
Phone: (202) 467-0867
Fax: (800) 531-9347
URL: http://www.ncela.gwu.edu

National Education Association (NEA)
1201 16th Street, NW
Washington, DC 20036
Phone: (202) 833-4000

Fax: (202) 822-7170
URL: http://www.nea.org

National Multicultural Institute (NMCI)
3000 Connecticut Avenue, NW, Suite 438
Washington, DC 20008
Phone: (202) 483-0700
Fax: (202) 483-5233
URL: http://www.nmci.org

Office of English Language Acquisition. U.S. Department of Education
400 Maryland Avenue, SW

Washington, DC 20202
Phone: (202) 401-4300
Fax: (202) 205-1229
URL: http://www2.ed.gov/about/offices/list/oela

Teachers of English to Speakers of Other Languages (TESOL)
700 South Washington Street, Suite 200
Alexandria, VA 22314
Phone: (703) 836-0774
Fax: (703) 836-7864
URL: http://www.tesol.org

EDUCATION

CODES OF CONDUCT

Sections within this essay:

- Background
- Basic Conduct Issues
- More Serious Violations
- Violence and Other Extreme Behavior
  – Identifying Troubled Students
- Conduct and Technology
  – Acceptable Use Policies
  – Cell Phones and Smart Phones
- Getting Information
- Additional Resources

BACKGROUND

Among the many ingredients for successful schools is a student body that is not only eager to learn but also well behaved. Children are taught the difference between good and poor behavior from an early age, and ideally that training goes with them into the classroom. Teachers and school administrators are expected to serve as role models, and they also have an obligation to ensure that students meet certain conduct expectations.

Codes of conduct are designed to serve both the classroom and the individual. They outline students' rights, ensuring that no student will be penalized or singled out based on anything but a violation of established rules. They also outline students' responsibilities, thus letting individual students know that they need

to meet certain standards for their own sake and that of the entire class.

"Conduct" covers such a wide variety of behaviors that establishing a formal code within a school system is a complicated matter. A violation of conduct rules can be anything from passing notes in class to carrying a concealed weapon into the building. It is up to the school administration, often working in conjunction with parents and students, to set rules and to enforce them.

A typical school code of conduct begins with an outline of rights and responsibilities for both the students and the faculty. It then lists different infractions (often categorized at different levels of severity) and prescribes appropriate disciplinary measures. It should also explain the student's right to **appeal** any disciplinary action.

It is important to remember that both the students and the faculty have rights and responsibilities. Students have the right to be informed of the school district's policies and regulations. They also have the right to know the academic requirements of each course and to be advised of their progress. Students have **privacy** rights as well; their personal possessions are generally off limits. If the school has reason to believe that a student is carrying something illegal, such as a knife, that becomes a different matter. Desks and lockers are school property, and schools can inspect them without student permission.

Teachers, likewise, have the right to be able to do their job without distractions. They also have the right to discipline students in an appropriate manner when necessary. Most codes of conduct are written with enough flexibility to allow teachers some leeway when choosing disciplinary action.

If a student is **accused** of committing a serious offense that results in suspension or expulsion, he or she has the right to appeal the decision under due process rules of law. No student can be singled out for punishment on the basis of race, sex, color, religion, **disability**, or national origin. Moreover, in most cases, school **jurisdiction** applies to the actual school grounds, but codes of conduct are valid when students are attending school-related functions off the actual school property.

BASIC CONDUCT ISSUES

The classroom is designed to provide students with a structured environment in which they can learn. In most cases the classroom model works quite well, but it fails to take simple human nature into consideration. Children, even those who are normally well behaved, will try to test the rules for two simple reasons. First, they are away from their parents, which makes them feel independent even though a teacher may be watching them. For this reason, some students habitually come to class late or skip class altogether. Second, as children learn to socialize they seek ways to generate attention, even negative attention for being disruptive, for example, by always talking out of turn or playing the class clown.

In years past, schools offered courses in what was known as "civics." Civics courses often included instruction on the importance of integrity, honesty, and respect for others. Civics courses have fallen out of favor for the most part, although many schools do offer some sort of course work focusing on understanding values. Nonetheless, there are always students who will break the rules.

The point teachers and administrators stress is that even minor infractions can represent more serious behavior problems, and failure to offer discipline and guidance can lead some students to more disruptive or harmful violations.

Among the more innocuous types of behavior that constitute conduct violations are the following:

- Repeatedly coming to class without appropriate supplies (books, gym clothes, etc.)
- Leaving school property without permission
- Defacing school property (vandalizing books, for example)
- Wearing inappropriate clothing
- Bringing radios or CD players to class
- Truancy

Clearly each of these infractions warrants different punishment. Probably the most common punishment is having the student stay after school. Faculty and administrators have a variety of other options, however. They can give a warning or reprimand, have a student conference, have a parent conference, change the student's

class schedule, or impose a suspension. The student who brings a radio to class might benefit most from a reprimand (and from having the radio confiscated for the day). The student who cuts class regularly may require more direct involvement with teachers and parents. Students who drive to school could have their parking privileges revoked if they leave school grounds without permission.

MORE SERIOUS VIOLATIONS

When students commit more serious violations, a good code of conduct should be able to address the problematic behavior and prescribe appropriate punishment. Among those more serious violations are the following:

- Cheating or plagiarizing
- Using profane, obscene, or ethnically offensive language
- Possessing pornographic material
- Theft (from another student or from the school)
- Gambling on school grounds
- Threatening the safety of another student
- Fighting with another student

Students who commit these more serious offenses will face stronger punishment. But no school district wants merely to punish a student and let an incident drop, particularly in light of the heightened sensitivity to school violence. Intervention programs often begin with conferences between the student and his or her parents or guardians and teachers and school administrators. Discipline can be rehabilitative in form. Instead of being suspended from class, for example, a student might be assigned to do a community service project. Someone who vandalizes a school building may have to repair that damage instead of merely paying for it.

VIOLENCE AND OTHER EXTREME BEHAVIOR

For many years school violence was thought to exist only in poor inner-city schools, with most of that violence directed against specific students (gangs, for example). During the 1990s, a series of highly publicized sniper attacks, many in affluent suburban schools, changed the public's perception of school violence. The National Center for Education Statistics (NCES) noted that during the 2009–10 school year, 85 percent of public schools reported that one or more of these incidents of violence, theft, or other crimes had taken place, amounting to an estimated 1.9 million crimes.

It is simplistic to say that a code of conduct would have kept some of the most deadly sniper attacks from taking place. That said, a code of conduct does send a clear message to students that certain behavior will not be tolerated, including teasing and bullying. Some of the students who killed their fellow students were said to have been bullied and taunted by their classmates over a period of years. NCES reported that in 2009, about 28 percent of students ages 12–18 reported being bullied at school during the school year.

Identifying Troubled Students Truly troubled students who might have tendencies to resort to extreme violence against their peers and teachers cannot be stopped simply by a code of conduct. What a code of conduct can do, however, is help identify behavior patterns in children early on. A youngster who is constantly disrupting class and breaking rules is clearly having trouble adjusting, and the school can work with the youngster and the parents to identify the problem. The class bully needs to be disciplined, but without some sort of additional action (such as counseling) the discipline becomes merely punitive. Not every troubled student will react violently, of course, but that does not mean the school has no obligation to reach out and help when help seems appropriate. Regarding serious crime, students who commit **felony** offenses are removed automatically from most schools; if under age these individuals may be placed in a juvenile detention facility where they can continue their education; if over 16 they can be tried as an adult for their crimes and imprisoned if convicted.

CONDUCT AND TECHNOLOGY

The Internet has vastly expanded educational resources and opportunities for students and teachers. Students use the Internet both as a research tool and a means of communicating. The question responsible administrators and teachers need to ask is precisely what sort of research and communication the students are doing. There is a big difference between using the Internet to find biographical material of a local author, for example, and logging onto websites to find out the latest gossip about a favorite pop music star. More dangerous still, some students may use a school email account to join a chat group. Teenagers in particular may feel that they possess enough maturity to make informed choices about what they are doing, but they may inadvertently lead themselves into harm's way. The not uncommon reports of adults being arrested for trying to meet up with minors they met in chat rooms are a red flag for most school districts.

Many districts avoid the issue by not providing students with their own email accounts. They argue, quite convincingly, that student email is difficult to monitor and ties up too many resources that could be used for other activities. A number of educators, however, believe that email has become so essential that students should be trusted with the responsibility until they do something to violate that **trust**. Software programs that filter email and Internet sites are only a partial solution; a student who wants to view a particular site may be resourceful enough to be able to get past such barriers. Beyond those students who might willfully engage in irresponsible activity online, there are also students who may unwittingly create trouble for themselves or others. A student who is not computer savvy might inadvertently disclose personal information over the Internet, for example.

With the rise of text messaging and **social media** such as Facebook and Twitter, students have even more avenues to communicate with each other. While such technologies are for the most part used responsibly, school administrators have had to deal with abuses. These include the creation of fake Facebook pages that target other students, teachers, and administrators. The growth in cyber-bullying has also raised serious concerns. In some cases students who have been bullied and humiliated online have attempted or committed suicide. Bullied students have also responded with violent attacks in schools. NCES reported that in 2009, approximately 6 percent of students ages 12–18 reported being cyber-bullied during the school year. States have responded by passing bullying laws. As of 2010, 44 states had laws regarding bullying, and 30 of those included some mention of electronic forms of harassment. In 2012, New York enacted a law that requires schools to take action when students experience cyber-bullying or other forms of harassment. It ensures that school districts take immediate steps to end harmful behavior, prevent recurrences, and ensure the safety of the targeted students. The legislation also establishes improved training to help teachers and administrators better prevent and respond to bullying and other harmful acts. With laws such as New York's in effect, school administrators have responded by putting in place cyber-bullying rules in their codes of conduct.

Acceptable Use Policies Districts that do offer email accounts to students have found that establishing an "acceptable-use" policy is essential to maintaining good "netiquette" among students. An acceptable-use policy begins by setting ground rules for when and how students can use the Internet and email. Typically, students are expected to use appropriate language, to avoid off-limit sites and chat rooms, and to refrain from misuse of email, such as spamming (sending unsolicited mass postings to hundreds of email addresses). Students are also prohibited from using Internet information inappropriately (for example, downloading term papers or plagiarizing from websites). Students are advised that the school has the right to review all electronic correspondence to ensure compliance with the established rules, and anyone violating those rules can be disciplined. For serious or repeat offenses, a student's Internet privileges can be revoked. Both students and parents are usually required to sign the acceptable-use policy.

Cell Phones and Smart Phones Most schools now allow students to bring cell phones and smart phones to school, but require that they be turned off during class. Schools that ban phones find it difficult to enforce the policy. A 2010 Pew Internet & American Life Project study found that 65 percent of cell-owning teens at schools that completely ban phones bring their phones to school everyday anyway. The study also found that over 40 percent of cell and smart phone users sent text messages in at least one class a day. Smart phones typically have a camera installed, which has led to inappropriate photos of students and the sharing of them via email and text messaging.

GETTING INFORMATION

Although codes of conduct follow the same basic pattern, they vary not only from district to district but from school to school. The easiest way to find out about a particular school's code of conduct is to contact the school administration directly. Most likely, the school will have some sort of handbook listing the code, along with guidelines for punishing violations. Individual schools and school districts with websites may also post their conduct rules online.

ADDITIONAL RESOURCES

Kafka, Judith. *The History of "Zero Tolerance" in American Public Schooling*. New York: Palgrave Macmillan, 2011.

Thomas. R. Murray. *Violence in America's Schools: Understanding, Prevention, and Responses*. Lanham, MD: R&L Pub., 2009.

Twemlow, Stuart, and Frank Sacco. *Preventing Bullying and School Violence*. Arlington, VA: American Psychiatric Association, 2011.

ORGANIZATIONS

National Center for Education Statistics (NCES)

1990 K Street, NW, Room 9103
Washington, DC 20006
Phone: (202) 502-7350
Fax: (202) 502-7475
URL: http://www.nces.ed.gov

National Education Association (NEA)

1201 16th Street, NW
Washington, DC 20036
Phone: (202) 833-4000
Fax: (202) 822-7170
URL: http://www.nea.org

National Governors Association (NGA)

401 North Capitol Street
Washington, DC 20001
Phone: (202) 624-5300
Fax: (202) 624-5313
URL: http://www.nga.org

National School Boards Association (NSBA)

1680 Duke Street
Alexandria, VA 22314
Phone: (703) 838-67220
Fax: (703) 683-7590
URL: http://www.nsba.org

EDUCATION

COMPETENCY TESTING

Sections within this essay:

BACKGROUND

Testing students for academic achievement or competency is not new. As early as the 1970s, some states were making adequate performance on "exit examinations" a prerequisite for high school graduation. This was done in an effort to enhance teacher quality as well as student achievement during an era when many questions were raised by parents, educators, and the public at large about the seeming lack of basic skills in high school graduates.

While varying and inconsistent approaches have been taken to measure student performance at the elementary school level, there is more unison in setting certain minimum criteria for graduation from high school. The vast majority of states require an overall accumulation of "Carnegie units" (reflecting the number of classroom hours spent learning) in addition to passing grades in certain core subjects. By 2010, 26 states required "exit exams" in addition to accumulated credit hours in order for students to receive diplomas evidencing high school graduation. These exams affect two-thirds of the nation's high school students.

"EXIT EXAMINATIONS" FOR HIGH SCHOOL GRADUATES

Following years of complaints from both employers and academic institutions of higher learning that many high school graduates lacked basic educational skills in reading, writing, and math, both legislators and educators agreed to work toward raising educational standards nationwide. This has resulted in renewed focus on learning rather than remediation and more accountability for teachers and school systems.

Educational standards (and correlative exams) for gauging performance have been criticized in the past for being local or parochial in substance, making grades and class standing a "relative" achievement based only upon how well others in the same school system or state performed. The Education Reform Act helped standardize student performance on a national level, but new questions were raised as to whether teachers were actually enhancing learning skills or merely "teaching to the test," (i.e., merely teaching those things they knew students would be tested on, in order to make the school and/or the teacher appear favorably on assessment reviews).

However, questions remain as to which system is the best to assess the academic competency of graduating students. By far the most often used tool of assessment is the multiple-choice examination, in many cases combined with a writing sample. This, in combination with passing grades in key subjects and a minimum number of credit units, seems to be the growing method of choice for ensuring minimum competency levels of high school graduates in the United States. Because graduation from high school may be dependent upon passing an "exit exam," the process has been dubbed "high stakes testing."

LEGAL AUTHORITY FOR SETTING EDUCATIONAL STANDARDS

Most education reform since the 1980s has focused on "performance-based standards" which ostensibly indicate a minimum level of academic achievement that all graduating students should have mastered. Some important laws concerning standards-based school reform include the following:

- The No Child Left Behind Act, signed into law in January 2002, refines and makes major **amendment** to Title I (see below). Among other factors (like substantial flexibility for states in the use of federal funds), the new law requires states to assess reading and math skills in students from grades three to eight on an annual basis.

- The Educate America Act (20 USC 5801 et seq.) is only binding upon states that accept its grant funding (nearly all) but sets as its primary goal the development of strategies for setting statewide student performance standards and for assessing achievement of those standards.

- Title I of the Improving America's Schools Act of 1994 (20 USC 6301 et seq.) contains an explicit set of requirements for states to submit plans for challenging content and performance standards and assessing student mastery of the requirements in order to receive Title I funds (the largest federal school aid program).

- The Individuals with Disabilities Education Act (IDEA) (20 USC 1400 et seq.) was substantially amended in 1997. The Act requires that states that receive grant funds under its auspices must develop IEPs (individual education plans) for students with disabilities or who are deemed in need of special services. The 1997 amendments required states to develop policies and procedures to allow students with disabilities to participate in state and district-wide testing programs, with necessary accommodations.

LEGAL CHALLENGES TO EDUCATIONAL TESTING

Courts have had numerous opportunities over the decades to pass on the validity of education testing in conjunction with high school graduation and promotion (e.g., to the next grade level). Most legal challenges have been grounded in the Due Process Clause and the **Equal Protection** Clause of the Fourteenth Amendment to the U.S. Constitution. Challenges to testing of special education students have invoked IDEA and Section 504 of the Rehabilitation Act of 1973.

Due Process Claims The Due Process Clause of the Fourteenth Amendment prohibits a state from depriving "any person of life, liberty or property without due process of law." Over the years, it has been held by several courts that the receipt of a high school diploma was a "property interest" which a state could not deprive an individual of without **due process of law**. Additionally, some courts have found that students have a constitutionally protected "liberty" interest in avoiding the stigma or impaired career advancement that accompanies the failure to achieve high school graduation. (See, e.g., the *Goss* case, 419 U.S. at 574.)

The key to "due process" is the requirement of substantial notice to a person of the manner in which he or she may be denied or deprived of such an interest (graduation from high school) or, alternatively stated, substantial notice of what will be required of the student in order to graduate. With respect to testing, some courts have held that two years' advance notice that graduation was conditioned upon the passing of an exit exam in addition to credit hour completion was adequate; other courts have demanded more time.

Still other courts have held that students had no protected property interest in the expectation that a former, lower standard would continue to be accepted as the threshold for academic promotion to the next grade or graduation. (See, e.g., *Bester v. Tuscaloosa*, 722 F.2d 1514, 11th Circuit).

In determining whether denial of a high school diploma based on a failure to pass a minimum competency exit exam is unconstitutional, courts balance "the private interests of the [students], the risk of an improper deprivation of such interest and the governmental interest involved" (*Mathews v. Eldridge*, 424 U.S. 319). Almost all cases presented on these issues have turned on whether the school system had provided prospective graduates with adequate notice of new diploma requirements.

Equal Protection Claims Similarly, the Equal Protection Clause of the Fourteenth Amendment guarantees that no person will be denied the equal protection of the laws in the enjoyment and/or exercise of personal rights as that enjoyed by other persons in like circumstances. In order to ensure equal protection for students, school systems must uniformly apply educational standards and testing procedures across the board (with legal accommodations factored in for learning disabled or special needs students).

Generally, courts are more likely to uphold a testing program if there is a presence of additional factors such as opportunities for retesting, remedial or tutorial programs, and the availability of alternative ways to obtain a diploma.

HIGH SCHOOL GRADUATION EXIT OPTIONS

While no standardized national test has been implemented for use as a criterion in the granting of a high school diploma, states have developed several ways in which students may meet graduation requirements.

Standard Diploma Each state offers a standard diploma to students who have met the regular requirements for graduation. These are commonly the completion of a minimum number of Carnegie Units or credits (with passing grades), an attendance requirement, and (in an increasing number of states) a passing score on an exit exam. "Honors" diplomas are variations of standard diplomas in which student achievers may choose elective courses or independent studies in addition to their core studies. Such diplomas may also indicate accelerated or advanced coursework.

Individual Education Plan (IEP) Diploma Students with special needs may be offered an alternative way to earn a high school diploma through completion of individual education plans constructed specifically to the needs of the student. Some states allow modified coursework to count as standard coursework and, therefore, award a standard diploma; others offer "certificates of attainment" or "special certificate of completion" to indicate the student's fulfillment of special criteria for graduation.

Occupational Diploma Several states offer work/study diplomas, the most effective of which are those offered in conjunction with exit exams, to ensure that elective coursework directed toward occupational interests does not compromise minimum skill levels in core subject areas.

STATE LAWS

ALABAMA: Alabama high school graduates must meet minimum credit hour criteria plus pass an exit examination. The state offers exit options of standard diplomas, IEP diplomas, certificates of attendance only, honors diplomas, and occupational diplomas.

ALASKA: Alaska requires exit exams for high school graduation. The state does offer standard diplomas, IEP diplomas, and certificates of attendance as exit options.

ARIZONA: Graduation from an Arizona high school requires both credit hour completion and an exit exam. Only standard diplomas are granted.

ARKANSAS: Arkansas high school students must meet the credit hour criteria for graduation and pass an exit exam. The state offers exit options of standard diplomas, IEP diplomas, and certificates of attendance only.

CALIFORNIA: California has state-mandated credit hour requirements that must be met for graduation as well as an exit exam. The state generally offers standard and honors program diplomas.

COLORADO: There are no state-level requirements for high school graduation. Local education associations may establish their own credit hour requirements as well as exit examination criteria. In addition to the standard diploma, a work/study diploma may be granted, as well as IEP diplomas.

CONNECTICUT: Connecticut high school students must meet the credit hour criteria for graduation. The state offers exit options of standard diplomas, IEP diplomas, certificates of attendance only, honors diplomas, and GED diplomas.

DELAWARE: Delaware high school students must meet the credit hour criteria for graduation. The state offers exit options of standard diplomas and certificates of attendance only.

DISTRICT OF COLUMBIA: High school students must meet the credit hour criteria only. The state offers exit options of standard diplomas, IEP diplomas, or certificates of attendance only.

FLORIDA: Florida high school students must meet the credit hour criteria plus pass an exit examination. The state offers exit options of standard diplomas, IEP diplomas, certificates of attendance, and honors diplomas.

GEORGIA: In Georgia, high school students must meet the credit hour criteria plus pass an exit examination. The state offers exit options of standard diplomas, IEP diplomas, and certificates of attendance.

HAWAII: Hawaii students must meet the credit hour criteria. The state offers exit options of standard diplomas, IEP diplomas, certificates of attendance only, or honors diplomas.

IDAHO: High school students must meet the credit hour criteria and pass an exit exam. The state offers standard diplomas only.

ILLINOIS: High school students in Illinois must meet the credit hour criteria for graduation. The state offers exit options of standard diplomas or certificates of attendance only.

INDIANA: Indiana high school students must meet the credit hour criteria plus pass an exit examination. The state offers exit options of standard diplomas, honors diplomas, or GED diplomas. It awards a certificate of achievement for special education students for whom a diploma track is not appropriate.

IOWA: Iowa high school students must meet the credit hour criteria only. However, in addition to state minimum credit requirements, local education boards may establish additional requirements for graduation. The state offers exit options of standard diplomas or IEP diplomas only.

KANSAS: In Kansas, high school students must meet the credit hour criteria to be granted a standard diploma. Kansas law also authorizes local school boards to grant diplomas under separate or special criteria.

KENTUCKY: Kentucky high school students need only meet the credit hour criteria for graduation, but as of 2002, the state was implementing assessment examinations. The state offers exit options of standard diplomas, IEP diplomas, and honors diplomas.

LOUISIANA: High school students in Louisiana must meet the credit hour criteria plus pass an exit examination. The state offers exit options of standard diplomas and certificates of attendance only.

MAINE: Maine high school students must meet the credit hour criteria. The state offers exit options of standard diplomas or IEP diplomas.

MARYLAND: In Maryland, high school students must meet the credit hour criteria plus pass an exit examination. The state offers exit options of standard diplomas, IEP diplomas, certificates of attendance only, or GED diplomas.

MASSACHUSETTS: Massachusetts high school students must meet the credit hour criteria and pass an exit exam. The state offers standard diplomas only, but IEP diplomas may be authorized by local school boards. In addition, part of the credit requirements for standard diplomas and the distribution of credits are left to the discretion of local authorities.

MICHIGAN: Michigan high school students must meet locally established criteria for graduation. They receive local high school diplomas with or without state endorsements. If local criteria require exit exams, depending on the performance level on an exit exam, state endorsements will appear on the transcripts. Generally, Michigan schools also offer IEP diplomas and certificates of attendance.

MINNESOTA: In Minnesota, high school students must pass an exit examination and demonstrate mastery of 24 standards. In return, they are granted a state endorsed standard diploma.

MISSISSIPPI: Mississippi high school students must meet the credit hour criteria plus pass an exit examination. The state offers exit options of standard diplomas or certificates of attendance only.

MISSOURI: Missouri requires that high school students meet the credit hour criteria for receiving a diploma. The state offers exit options of standard diplomas, IEP diplomas, certificates of attendance only, or honors diplomas.

MONTANA: In Montana, high school students must meet the credit hour criteria. The state offers exit options of standard diplomas or IEP diplomas.

NEBRASKA: Nebraska high school students must meet the credit hour criteria, but part of the credit requirements and/or the distribution of credits are left to the discretion of local education authorities. The state offers exit options of standard diplomas, certificates of attendance only, or a locally-determined modified diploma for special needs.

NEVADA: High school students in Nevada must meet the credit hour criteria plus pass an exit examination. The state offers exit options of standard diplomas, certificates of attendance only, or adult diplomas.

NEW HAMPSHIRE: In New Hampshire, high school students must meet the credit hour criteria. The state offers exit options of standard diplomas, IEP diplomas, and certificates of attendance only.

NEW JERSEY: New Jersey high school students must meet the credit hour criteria plus pass an exit examination. The state offers standard diplomas only.

NEW MEXICO: New Mexico high school students must meet the credit hour criteria plus pass an exit examination. The state offers exit options of standard diplomas, IEP diplomas, certificates of attendance only, or "career readiness" diplomas.

NEW YORK: In New York, high school students must meet the credit hour criteria plus pass an exit examination. The state offers exit options of standard diplomas, IEP diplomas, certificates of attendance only, honors diplomas, or an annotated local diploma.

NORTH CAROLINA: North Carolina high school students must meet the credit hour criteria plus pass an exit examination. The state offers exit options of standard diplomas, IEP diplomas, certificates of attendance only, and honors diplomas.

NORTH DAKOTA: In North Dakota, high school students must meet the credit hour criteria. The state offers exit options of standard diplomas, IEP diplomas, or certificates of attendance only.

OHIO: Ohio high school students must meet the credit hour criteria plus pass an exit examination. The state offers exit options of standard diplomas, honors diplomas, or a diploma of adult education.

OKLAHOMA: Oklahoma high school students must meet the credit hour criteria. The state offers standard diplomas only.

OREGON: In Oregon, high school students must meet the credit hour criteria. The state offers exit options of standard diplomas or certificates of attendance only.

PENNSYLVANIA: Pennsylvania high school students must meet locally established criteria for graduation and pass an exit examination. The state offers standard diplomas or GED diplomas only.

RHODE ISLAND: In Rhode Island, high school students must meet the credit hour criteria. The state offers standard diplomas only.

SOUTH CAROLINA: South Carolina high school students must meet the credit hour criteria plus pass an exit examination. The state offers exit options of standard diplomas or certificates of attendance only.

SOUTH DAKOTA: South Dakota high school students must meet the credit hour criteria. The state offers standard diplomas only.

TENNESSEE: In Tennessee, high school students must meet the credit hour criteria plus pass an exit examination. The state offers exit options of standard diplomas, IEP diplomas, certificates of attendance only, or honors diplomas.

TEXAS: Texas high school students must meet the credit hour criteria plus pass an exit examination. The state offers exit options of standard diplomas or certificates of attendance only.

UTAH: Utah high school students must meet the credit hour criteria. The state offers exit options of standard diplomas or certificates of attendance only.

VERMONT: In Vermont high school students must meet the credit hour criteria. The state offers exit options of standard diplomas or certificates of attendance only.

VIRGINIA: Virginia high school students must meet the credit hour criteria plus pass an exit examination. The state offers exit options of standard diplomas, IEP diplomas, certificates of attendance only, honors diplomas, GED diplomas, and special diplomas.

WASHINGTON: In Washington, high school students must meet the credit hour criteria and pass an exit exam. The state offers standard diplomas only.

WEST VIRGINIA: West Virginia high school students must meet the credit hour criteria. The state offers exit options of standard diplomas or IEP diplomas only.

WISCONSIN: In Wisconsin, high school students must meet the credit hour criteria. The state offers exit options of standard diplomas or certificates of attendance only.

WYOMING: Wyoming high school students must meet the credit hour criteria. The state offers exit options of standard diplomas or certificates of attendance only.

ADDITIONAL RESOURCES

Conan, Neal. "Analysis: How Standardized Testing Changes Teaching and Learning." *Talk of the Nation (NPR)*, March 21, 2002.

Demerath, Peter. *Producing Success: The Culture of Personal Advancement in an American High School.* Chicago: University of Chicago Press, 2009.

Nichols, Sharon, and Berliner, David. *Collateral Damage: How High-Stakes Testing Corrupts America's Schools.* Cambridge, MA: Harvard Education Press, 2007.

Ravitch, Diane. *The Death and Life of the Great American School System: How Testing and Choice Are Undermining Education.* New York: Basic Books, 2011.

ORGANIZATIONS

Institute of Education Sciences

555 New Jersey Ave. NW
Washington, DC 20208
Phone: (202) 219-1385
URL: http://ies.ed.gov

EDUCATION

COMPULSORY EDUCATION

———————————■———————————

———————————■———————————

BACKGROUND

What Are Compulsory Attendance Laws? Compulsory attendance laws are statutes put into force by state governments that require parents to have their children attend a public or state accredited private or parochial school for a designated period. Each state by law determines when this period starts and ends. Almost all states require a child to begin attending school at an age ranging from five to seven years. The age when a child may stop going to school varies from sixteen to eighteen.

To learn about the age requirements for your state, look in the telephone directory under the listing for state government agencies for either the department or board of education or the office or department of public instruction.

History and Development of Compulsory Attendance Laws Modern compulsory attendance laws were first

531

enacted in Massachusetts in 1853, followed by New York in 1854. By 1918, all states had compulsory attendance laws. One reason for the acceptance by the states of these laws was the belief that the public school was the best means to improve the literacy rate of the poor and to help assimilate an immigrant population that grew at a high rate between the mid-nineteenth to the early twentieth centuries. Another explanation is that as children were required to attend school for a number of years, factory owners found it more difficult to exploit the cheap and plentiful child labor. This argument is substantiated by Alabama's decision for a period of time to **repeal** its compulsory attendance law due to pressure put upon state authorities by a company opening a large textile mill in that state. This industry was notorious for its use of child labor.

Penalties for Non-Compliance Failure to comply is a **misdemeanor** in almost every state. The penalties include fines for the first offense ranging from $20 to $100 and increasing thereafter for subsequent offenses from $250 to $1000 depending upon the **jurisdiction**. Most states also have the option of **sentencing** parents for as long as 30 days in jail. Some states provide for alternatives such as community service or counseling. In the case of home schooling, although the prosecution is not required to show the parent intended to break the law, it must still prove in some jurisdictions that home education does not provide an adequate alternative.

STATUTORY EXEMPTIONS FROM COMPULSORY ATTENDANCE LAWS

Child's Circumstances Most states will not enforce these laws against parents whose children are physically or mentally disabled, are employed, or have received a designated education level, typically a high school diploma or its equivalent.

Equivalent Education Equivalent education may be obtained in a state accredited private school or a parochial school. According to a ruling by the U.S. Supreme Court in *Pierce v. Society of Sisters*, states must recognize these schools as providing an education equivalent to that of the public schools so long as they follow state laws and regulations that bear a reasonable relationship to the interest the state has in educating its citizens and do not burden the religious practices of the parochial schools. These conditions placed upon non-public schools, including home schools, are permitted under the United States Constitution because the public schools must follow these regulations as well.

All non-public schools must qualify under the laws of that state as schools in order to be considered capable of providing an equivalent education. The criteria used include such factors as whether the school is established, the quality of the teaching, the soundness of the curriculum, how many hours per day are spent for instruction, how many days of the year the school is engaged in teaching, and whether the teachers are certified. Private, parochial, and home schools may have to comply with any combination of the above factors.

COURT CASE EXEMPTIONS FROM COMPULSORY ATTENDANCE LAWS

Exemptions Accepted by Some Courts

- A threat to the health, safety, or welfare of a student if the parents can show the threat is imminent.
- The child has reached the age of majority.
- The child becomes mentally or physically disabled. However, this ground is now used less frequently because of special services for the disabled mandated by federal law.
- The parent objects to classes because the content violates their religious beliefs or practices.
- Either hazardous conditions are present between the child's home and his designated public school or the distance between the student's home and the school exceeds a distance provided by **statute**.

Exemptions Rejected by Some Courts

- A parent's belief a given teacher is incompetent or otherwise not qualified to teach.
- A parent's belief the school is doing a poor job of educating his or her children.
- Objections to racial integration by the parents on religious grounds.

EARLY U.S. SUPREME COURT CHALLENGES

Meyer v. Nebraska (1923) This decision struck down a state law prohibiting any instructor, either in a public or a private school, from teaching in a language other than English. The Court took this action because of the arbitrary interference from state officials in the right of parents to provide education for their children as they saw fit. The statute was arbitrary because it bore no relationship to a legitimate state purpose and violated the part of the Due Process clause of the 14th Amendment to the Constitution that says no person may be deprived of liberty without **due process of law**. In this case, the right of the parents to employ a teacher to instruct their children in their native language fell under the right to determine how they were to be educated.

Pierce v. Society of Sisters (1925) In this case, the Court said an Oregon law that made it mandatory for parents to send their children to public school was unconstitutional. As in *Meyer,* this law was unrelated to the legitimate state goal of educating children because it interfered with the fundamental right of parents to exercise control over how their children were to be taught. Forcing parents to have the educational options for their children limited to public schools infringed upon the above right and was an abuse of the state's police power to insure the health, safety, and morality of all localities in that jurisdiction. This standardization went against the sentiment of the Court often quoted in the part of their opinion that declares a child is not the creature of the state and that the responsibility for educating children should rest with the parents.

This decision is also important because it made clear that state governments had to permit private schools to operate. No challenge has since been made on this point.

Farrington v. Tokushige (1927) The Hawaii legislature had passed a law strictly regulating hours, textbooks, and curriculum of schools that taught in the native language of the students. In striking down this law, the Court was indicating that this amount of regulation of private schools was unreasonable and that parents had the right to exercise control over how their children were educated without restrictions that were unrelated to any rational state goal.

HOME SCHOOLING AS AN ALTERNATIVE TO PUBLIC SCHOOL EDUCATION

Why Parents Home School and Its Acceptance by State Governments Home schooling is permitted in all 50 states. Studies show that most parents home school out of the religious **conviction** that the authority and power to instruct their children should remain with them and not be given to outside authority. Another reason cited is the declining academic standards of public schools as indicated by decreasing scores on standardized tests beginning in the 1960s. Some parents object to what is being taught on religious, moral, or philosophical grounds.

Legal Requirements for Home Schools Parents choosing to home school face many of the same hurdles encountered by parochial and private schools. In addition, the question may arise as to whether home instruction in a given state will come under the exemption routinely given to private schools because a home school is not established in the same way as are other non-public schools. In states in which laws remain unclear about what qualifies home instruction to be considered a school, the courts have

given the term "school" a broad meaning as a place where instruction of children takes place. This definition eliminates the requirement that a school have its own facilities. So long as the home school meets the standards applied to schools established in the normal sense, the home school comes under the private school exemption.

Once a home school is considered by state statute or **case law** to be a school, it must comply with regulations to insure that students taught at home have an equivalent education. First, many states require parents to notify appropriate authorities, often the local school superintendent, of their intention to instruct their children at home. At this point, some states also make it mandatory for parents to obtain approval from designated local officials of the content of their curriculum and other aspects of how they will teach before they begin instructing their children. Some home school parents have gone to court claiming these officials are not objective in assessing home school programs because public school funding is often determined by the number of students enrolled. The courts have rejected these claims because of the difficulty in proving school officials' **bias** caused their negative decisions and the deference courts give to decisions of administrative officials.

The second requirement home schools face is that they must meet time or durational requirements as well as teach a list of designated subjects at a minimum for their curriculum. They must do so according to the standards applied to public schools or those required of home schools.

Third, a number of states require the parent to be certified as a teacher. When parents home school for religious reasons and challenge such laws in court as interfering with their religious practices, the courts have decided to uphold such laws. The courts side with the state officials because they believe the interest of the state in education outweighs the burden on religious practices. The courts contend that if parents do not meet the certification requirements public school teachers are subject to, they are unable to meet the **burden of proof** of showing they are able to provide an equivalent education as required by state law and regulation.

Fourth, state regulations often require the progress of the students instructed at home to be measured by standardized tests that are widely recognized as valid indicators. The tests must be taken at designated times in the student's studies. In some jurisdictions, the parents must maintain a portfolio of their children's work that is evaluated by state certified teachers.

In addition to these requirements, home schools are subject in some states to visits by state officials to assess the quality of the instruction. This practice is considered permissible by the courts so long as the visits do not hinder parents' efforts to instruct and that these appearances do not occur often. If parents do not wish to consent to these visits, they are given in some jurisdictions the option of going to court to convince a judge an equivalent education is being given.

HOME SCHOOLING CONSTITUTIONAL DEFENSES

Due Process Fundamental Rights In *Meyer v. Pierce* and *Farrington v. Tokushige,* U.S. Supreme Court cases of the 1920s, the fundamental right of parents to direct the education of their children was established. These decisions are still heavily cited today by those claiming the right to home school in federal and state courts. They contend that because these decisions have given parents this right, its denial violates the right of due process. If a right is deemed to be fundamental, it is based on the premise that it is provided for in the U.S. Constitution.

Due Process Vagueness Under the Due Process clause, parents of home schooled children have contended the compulsory attendance statutes of their state were so vague and ambiguous, they were unconstitutional because a reasonably intelligent person would not be able to determine when he was violating the law and the person deciding whether such violation had occurred had no clear standards to go by in making his ruling.

Frequently, the **litigation** in this area revolves around the meaning of such terms as "equivalent education" or "private school." The meaning of these terms is important in these cases because it is upon these and other similarly worded phrases that states have granted exemptions from their compulsory attendance laws and their penalties.

Due Process Arbitrariness The Due Process clause has also been used to challenge these laws by claims that officials have too much leeway in performing their duty to apply the law. Although court cases involving this issue have not been decided in favor of the parents, the U.S. Supreme Court in a context other than home instruction has said that any decision involving a fundamental right must be made by an **impartial** party. In spite of subsequent U.S. Supreme Court cases which affirmed this principle in home schooling cases, the parents were unsuccessful.

Free Exercise By definition, a claim for exemption based on free exercise can only be used, if at all, by those who have home instruction for religious reasons. The only U.S. Supreme Court case that has ever decided any case involving home teaching is *Wisconsin v. Yoder.* Decided in 1972, it involved an Amish group who challenged the compulsory attendance laws of their state. For three centuries, the members of this religious sect taught their children at home in accordance with their religious belief that education in a public school would violate the tenets of their faith. The Amish pointed out this home education gave their children the skills to function effectively in a society that was isolated from the general public.

Unlike the decisions in *Meyer v. Pierce* and *Farrington v. Tokshige,* the Amish in *Yoder* did not rely upon due process grounds, but on the belief that compulsory attendance laws of Wisconsin violated the Free Exercise clause of the U.S. Constitution prohibiting interference by the government with practices found to be religious and not just personal preferences. The Court balanced the interest of the state in educating children against the right of the Amish to practice their religious beliefs and concluded the state of Wisconsin had failed to show the state interest of educating its citizens outweighed the interest of the Amish in not having governmental interference with their religious practices.

In weighing and balancing the interests of these opposing parties, the Court sharply limited the use of *Yoder* to persons engaged in home schooling for future cases. The Court noted the three-century tradition of home education and that its content did enable Amish children to be able to function as adults in their separate society. Therefore, the state interest present in this case was rendered irrelevant by the Amish isolation from general society. Through the use of this balancing test and its limited application of the Free Exercise clause to an unusual religious group, the court could affirm the interest of the state in educating its citizens, allowing the compulsory attendance laws to stand. In fact, lower federal court cases subsequent to *Yoder* have decided against other religious groups that instruct their children at home because they lacked the isolation of the Amish from modern life.

With this decision, a principle was established giving in theory greater protection to those who gave home instruction for religious reasons. However, the requirement that the belief of the party claiming Free Exercise protection was religious, and not one of personal preference or philosophy, and that the compulsory attendance law would severely impact such a belief would in practice be difficult to satisfy. The weight of cases subsequent to *Yoder* indicates it is far easier for the state to show the regulation fulfills a compelling or merely legitimate interest.

Only two state supreme court cases decided after *Yoder* involving home schooling parents using the Free Exercise clause resulted in a successful conclusion for the parents. Those states are Michigan in *Michigan v. DeJonge,* decided in 1993, and North Carolina in *Delconte v. State of North Carolina,* rendered in 1985.

Free Speech There have been few successful cases on such claims, but a notable example is *In re Falk,* a New York Family Court case decided in 1981. So far there have been no state or U.S. Supreme Court cases upholding the use of the right of free speech under the 1st Amendment as a defense by parents against these laws.

Right to Privacy The few cases that have used this defense for prosecution under compulsory attendance laws have not found courts to be receptive to it. The one case decided in favor of the parents was a trial court decision in Massachusetts that is not binding outside the state or to any great extent within that jurisdiction.

Ninth Amendment The Ninth Amendment says that the rights of the citizens of each state are not limited by those listed in the Constitution. The contention by parents that a right to home school is implied by this provision has only been agreed with by *Perchemlides v. Frizzle,* the case mentioned under the right of **privacy**.

ACCESS OF HOME SCHOOLING STUDENTS TO PUBLIC SCHOOL FACILITIES AND ACTIVITIES

Home School Parents' View Parents who choose to home school cope with a number of disadvantages. These include isolation, the lack of opportunity to participate in scholastic sports and other extra-curricular activities, and the lack of resources available in public schools, such as a library or instruction in specialized courses. In surveys, a majority of home school parents expressed the desire to have their children enroll in a public school on a part-time basis in order to take special courses that are beyond the parents' ability to teach or to participate in extra-curricular activities including athletics. Most of the litigation on part-time enrollment involves whether these children should be allowed to play on the athletic teams of public schools.

Oppositions' View Opposition to access of public schools by those students not enrolled full-time is strong at the local, state, and national levels. Town and city boards of education, state athletic associations, and national trade groups, such as the National School Boards Association, have been against access by outside students because of fairness and administrative reasons. They argue that accessibility by non-enrolled students, including those home schooled, is unfair because since these students have chosen not to enroll, they should not be entitled to benefit from the limited resources of public schools. From an administrative point of view, the public schools would be faced with additional burdens such as providing supervision to a greater number of students participating in a class or activity and having perhaps to transport some students at times different from those of full-time enrolled students.

Furthermore, they argue that the U.S. Constitution does not provide a right for someone not enrolled in a public school to participate in any of its classes or other activities, including athletics. Home school parents have challenged these policies in the courts by using the Free Exercise clause of the First Amendment and the Due Process and Equal Protection provisions of the 14th Amendment.

Constitutional Arguments Raised in Court Judges have, with few exceptions, been unreceptive to the claims of home school parents. Their unwillingness to grant the parents and their children what they want is based on the general principle cited by school administrators and others that there is no constitutional right to participate in any public school program, including athletics. Instead, whether a student is allowed to join a club or athletic team of a public school is a privilege local school officials can choose to grant or deny at their discretion. Courts agree with them that sports and other extra-curricular activities are an integral part of a student's education in a public school, and this legitimate objective would be frustrated if students not enrolled full time were allowed to participate.

In regard to the specific constitutional arguments put forth by home school parents, courts have said that because there is no burden placed on the religious faith and practices of those in home schools, there is no violation of the Free Exercise clause. Fourteenth Amendment claims based on Equal Protection and Due Process have also generally failed. The interest of the public school officials in efficiently carrying out their administrative responsibilities outweighs any concern of the home school students' not being treated equally. Due Process claims also are usually unsuccessful because denial of access to public schools and their programs does not amount to a denial of a fundamental right under the U.S. Constitution. The liberty the parents are entitled to under the U.S. Constitution is inapplicable here because, since participation by home school children in public school activities and programs is a privilege that may be granted or denied, parents only have an expectation their offspring will be allowed to participate. Therefore, no constitutional claim under Due Process is viable.

In addition, courts view the parents' decision to educate their children at home as an exercise of their

constitutional rights, and it is inconsistent for the parents to benefit from the public education they have chosen to reject.

Legislative Action In recent years, a number of states have chosen to address this problem through their legislatures. Oregon, Idaho, and Florida have enacted laws allowing children educated at home to take part in what is offered by the public schools. Each of these states places conditions on these **statutory** provisions which may require submission to a greater degree of oversight and monitoring than home school students and parents would experience otherwise. For example, a student may have to submit additional documentation to prove to the satisfaction of local school officials that the state home school regulations are being followed. They may also have to obtain a designated minimum score on a standardized test considered credible by that state as well as satisfy all the district eligibility and other requirements governing the behavior and performance expected of students enrolled full-time in public schools.

What is unique about the Florida statute is that it openly recognizes a state interest in the participation in public school programs and activities of students educated at home. This is significant because the outcome of many court cases involving children educated at home turns on the view of the courts as to whether the rights of these children are outweighed by the interests of the state in public education. Because these statutes have been passed only recently, it is difficult to assess their impact. However, making participation an interest of the state may result in less opposition to the presence of students who are not enrolled full-time.

Other jurisdictions, such as Maine, provide for access to the public school by children educated at home by obtaining approval from the local school superintendent. The decision to allow a home school student to participate will continue to be made on a case-by-case basis. However, the Maine statute and others similar to it require the superintendent not to make these decisions arbitrarily.

KEEPING CURRENT ON NEW DEVELOPMENTS IN YOUR STATE

Compulsory education laws and their impact on home schooling are subject to frequent changes in any jurisdiction. New laws passed by the legislature, administrative regulations handed down by those state agencies given the responsibility over educational matters, and new court decisions can all affect parents who educate their children at home. Organizations, especially the Home

School Legal Defense Association, monitor closely new developments at the state and federal level. In addition, every state now has a website where you can access recent court decisions as well as the code of laws for that jurisdiction. Many states have also made their code of administrative regulations available to the public. These materials are generally searchable by key words in court decisions, administrative regulations, and the code of laws.

ADDITIONAL RESOURCES

Aquila, Frank. *School Law for K-12 Educators*. Thousand Oaks, CA: Sage Publications, 2007.

Bauer, Susan Wise, and Jessie Wise. *The Well-Trained Mind: A Guide to Classical Education at Home*. 3d ed. New York: Norton, 2009.

Gathercole, Rachel. *The Well-Adjusted Child: The Social Benefits of Homeschooling*. Toronto: Mapletree Pub. Co., 2007.

Ray, Brian D. *Home Schooling on the Threshold: A Survey of Research at the Dawn of the New Millennium*. Salem, OR: National Home Education Institute, 1999.

ORGANIZATIONS

Education Law Association (ELA)
300 College Park
Dayton, OH 45469-2280
Phone: (937) 229-3589

Home School Legal Defense Association
PO Box 3000
Purcellville, VA 20139-9000
Phone: (540) 338-5600
URL: http://www.hslda.org/

National Association for Legal Support of Alternative Schools
PO Box 2823
Santa Fe, NM 87504
Phone: (505) 471-6928
URL: http://nalsas.org

National Home Education Research Institute
PO Box 13939
Salem, OR 97309
Phone: (503) 364-1490
URL: http://nheri.org

Parents Rights Organization
12571 Northwinds Drive
St. Louis, MO 63146-4503
Phone: (314) 434-4171

EDUCATION

CURRICULUM

Sections within this essay:

BACKGROUND

According to *Black's Law Dictionary*, "curriculum" refers to the "set of studies or courses for a particular period, designated by a school or branch of a school." But curriculum also refers to the complete range of activities designed by an educational institution to foster education. Fundamentally, curriculum outlines what students are supposed to learn and how they are to do it. Because there is much room for divergence of personal viewpoints in these issues, a school's curriculum fosters some of the most emotional and contentious debates in education law.

From a legal perspective, curriculum issues focus on two areas:

* The range of courses or instructional programs available to students

* The aggregate of activities, materials, procedures, and instructional aids used in the instructional program

Local school boards and officials typically make the decisions regarding curriculum and instructional materials for their schools, although some state authorities may limit their discretion to some extent.

The subject of curricula touches on federal, state, and local government authority, every course taught in school, and every level of school. The standards and objectives of every state differ with respect to curricula in their schools. All of this makes for a very extensive topic. A focus on the curricula in public schools from kindergarten through grade twelve (primary through secondary grades) touches on the key elements of the topic while reducing the scope of the topic to manageable proportions.

The curricula for primary and secondary schools are designed to integrate across the various grade levels. They are also intended to provide a coherent and comprehensive educational experience for each student who undertakes and completes all grade levels. Curricula are also meant to accommodate the many differences in learning styles and abilities and to account for different interests and aptitudes. Thus, a thoughtful school curriculum offers a broad range of options and tracks. Students either elect or are placed in these options or tracks based on diagnostic counseling, academic performance, and consultation with parents and students. Each state sets curricular policy that applies to schools within its **jurisdiction**, but local and individual variations occur according to the degrees of freedom allowed by the basic policy.

AUTHORITY OVER EDUCATIONAL CURRICULA

Some may be surprised to learn that the federal government does not determine what students should know and be able to do in any subject at any level of schooling. Instead, implementing standards for students' performance is left to state and local authorities and to some extent with parents. There are some 16,000 school districts in the United States. Each one is administered and financed by a local community and by one of 50 state departments of education. This extensive local control, one of the defining characteristics of American education, has caused school standards to correlate with the socioeconomic status of the communities in which they are located.

Federal Authority As stated above, the federal government has historically played a minor role in education. In fact, the Constitution relegates most of the responsibility for education to the states. Thus, until the 1960s, the federal government largely stayed away from education. While the trend for the federal government to become involved in education issues has continued, even today, the total spending by the federal government accounts for less than 10 percent of the total spent for K-12 education. But because of heavy federal regulation, these federal dollars wield a disproportionate amount of influence.

Federal programs and regulations increased dramatically after 1965. As of 2012, the Department of Education spent over $68 billion per year on K-12 and higher education expenses, and hundreds of education programs are scattered throughout many other federal agencies. Most are designed to help disadvantaged children, though their records of success vary.

Perhaps the most prominent role of the federal government in terms of curricula has been to enforce and enhance rights to educational opportunities and educational equality. This function has involved the enforcement of **constitutional rights** to education and an adequate curriculum. These federal efforts have generally focused on guaranteeing equality of access to educational content rather than the content or purpose of the instruction itself. Other than these affirmative efforts, the federal government has hesitated to establish or control a school's curriculum. Rather, the government's role has been more to encourage schools to modify and improve curriculum, and currently, these suggestions are being backed up with funding and do not merely rely on persuasion.

State Authority The states are the entities primarily responsible for the maintenance and operation of public schools. The states are also heavily involved in the establishment, selection, and regulation of curriculum, teaching methods, and instructional materials in their schools.

Each state's constitution requires it to provide a school system where children may receive an education. Many state constitutions also contain express provisions for creating educational curricula. Some state constitutions even empower state authorities to select textbooks and educational materials. Besides constitutional authority, state governments also have authority to legislate in this area, or they can authorize officials to establish, select, and regulate curriculum.

State legislatures have frequently exercised their authority to mandate specific courses to be taught in public schools. They have also set mandatory requirements for students to graduate. In cases where state rules and regulations for courses do exist, they must be followed. Local school districts may, however, offer courses and activities in the instructional program beyond those required by state **statute**. Other states delegate more of their authority. They usually prescribe a model curriculum framework, allowing local authorities to develop their own curricula based on the general state goals.

In many jurisdictions, state authorities adopt textbooks and instructional materials. Local boards and educators then may select from among the pre-approved materials. Generally, local authorities have the authority to declare state-adopted instructional materials unacceptable. States may mandate the use of uniform, adopted textbooks within a school's instructional program, but such exercise of power is rare. Instead, local boards are usually allowed to select materials to supplement the state-selected materials.

Local Authority It is well established that local school boards or districts hold a great deal of authority over the curricula in their schools. Their authority is paramount except when there are overriding federal and state concerns. Otherwise, the local school board has complete discretion to determine what courses to offer, continue, or discontinue. Federal and state governments may impose minimum standards with which local boards must conform, but local boards of education are generally permitted to supplement or expand courses or activities and materials.

The history of **litigation** with respect to curricula shows that courts rarely interfere with a local board's authority to select and regulate the curriculum within its jurisdiction. By comparison, there are limits on the relative authority of teachers, students, parents, and the rest of the community. Local school boards have discretion over issues relating to the curriculum that it deems most suitable for students. This extends to the teaching methods that are to be employed and include the books and other educational tools to be used.

Parental Authority Parents are free to direct the education of their children, including the choice of a private school. However, states have the power to regulate private schools, with the exception of religious institutions.

Parents are particularly active in issues relating to special education which is available for children with disabilities. A child's **disability** must adversely affect the child's educational performance in order for the child to receive special education assistance. The Individuals with Disabilities Education Act (20 U.S.C. §§ 1400 et seq.) is a federal law that contains a process for evaluating a child's special needs and for prescribing an individualized education program for children with special needs. Most states have enacted their own laws that parallel the Act.

Homeschooling—legal in all fifty states—is an increasingly popular option for some families. It is perhaps the greatest expression of parental control over the curriculum issues that affect their children. Home-schooling requires a large time commitment on the part of the family. There may be additional requirements as well. For example, in some states parents need to register their intent to homeschool with the state's department of education or the parent's local district school board. Furthermore, many states require annual **evidence** of home-schooled children's progress.

IDEOLOGICAL CONTENT

Schools may decide upon curricula based upon local community views and values as to educational content and methodology. Even so, school boards are limited in their ability to remove materials from the curriculum, especially when a removal is based exclusively on "ideological content." Decisions about the curriculum cannot be used to dictate views on politics, nationalism, religion, or other matters of opinion.

When trying to insure the school board's discretion is being exercised in a constitutionally permissible manner, the intent of the board members should be examined. Courts are not limited to examining the objective motivation of the board but may consider individual motives and even the mental processes of individual board members.

CURRICULUM AND FREE SPEECH

Activities in the classroom are supervised by faculty and are designed to teach or convey particular knowledge or skills to students. Consequently, school boards and educators must have broad control over the approval of the materials used. In view of school board responsibilities in this respect, state laws have almost uniformly required subordinate employees, including the classroom teacher, to follow the board's curriculum choices and related mandates. Teachers certainly enjoy a degree of academic freedom and First Amendment rights; these rights do not give teachers the authority to disregard the curriculum directives of the board. In sum, the courts have declared that individual teachers may not simply teach what they please.

A school board authority almost always extends to classroom expression. Thus, public schools may limit classroom speech to promote certain educational goals. This also touches on the use of public school facilities by groups that promote a certain agenda or otherwise exercise their right to free speech. Although a school may occasionally open a classroom for other purposes, there is no doubt that during instructional periods the classrooms are reserved for the teaching of a particular course for credit. In such periods, classroom speech and expression may be reasonably restricted.

As we have seen, a school's curriculum includes actual instruction as well as classroom materials. For example, textbooks, lab equipment, and other routine instructional materials are used to support a school's curriculum. These are subject to the school board's control. Additionally, displays in or around the classroom or the school may be curricular in nature. These materials are therefore subject to broad control by school authorities.

MAKING CURRICULUM DECISIONS

Decisions about a school's curriculum must be based upon legitimate pedagogical concerns. On occasion, these concerns have included teaching material, classroom expression, or other matters criticized on the grounds of the following issues:

- Advocacy of political or similar matters
- Bias or prejudice
- Conformity or nonconformity to shared or community values
- Distraction from an educational atmosphere
- Inability to teach prescribed curriculum because of disagreements with course content
- Lack of neutrality on religious matters
- Quality or professionalism
- Sexually harassing speech
- Suitability or unsuitability for intended students

- Vulgarity, **profanity**, nudity, sexuality, drug use, violence or other inappropriate themes

The definition of "legitimate pedagogical concerns" may be outlined in state statutes or regulations. State Education Board policies also may be relevant.

An important consideration is the age, maturity, and sophistication of the students to whom educational material is to be provided. A school's oversight or authority over curriculum matters is greater where younger students are involved.

Schools need to identify pedagogical concerns before making decisions about a curriculum. Curricular decisions should not be made after a parent or someone else makes a complaint about ideological issues, and when there has been no pedagogical review. Such decisions are as suspect as the self-serving comments that attempt to justify those decisions made after the fact and not based on the previous record.

NO CHILD LEFT BEHIND ACT

The passage of the federal No Child Left Behind Act of 2001 (NCLB) marked a major change in the way the federal government dealt with public education. To receive federal education funds, states must implement statewide accountability systems covering all public schools and students. These systems must be based on challenging state standards in reading and mathematics, annual testing for all students in grades 3-8, and annual statewide progress objectives ensuring that all groups of students reach proficiency within 12 years. School districts and schools that fail to make adequate yearly progress (AYP) toward statewide proficiency goals will, over time, be subject to improvement, corrective action, and restructuring measures aimed at getting them back on course to meet state standards. Schools that meet or exceed AYP objectives or close achievement gaps will be eligible for State Academic Achievement Awards. The act also requires states to set "one high, challenging standard" for its students. Each state is given the authority to define what counts as "one high, challenging standard," but the curriculum standards must be applied to all students, rather than having different standards for students in different cities or other parts of the state.

Because the act relies on standardized testing to measure how well all U.S. students are performing, curriculum standards have shifted to emphasize teaching a narrower subset of skills that school administrators believe will enhance test performance. Critics call this practice of "teaching to the test" as undermining the broader curriculum that students should receive. NCLB's emphasis on reading, writing, and mathematics has reshaped curriculum standards in every state.

NATIONAL STANDARDS

In terms of national trends, the consensus has been moving toward establishing a set of national standards for education. So far, there are voluntary national standards for math, science, and history. There are standards being developed for other subjects as well.

Many factors go into decisions about the development and implementation of curriculum in U.S. schools. Some of these are:

- whether the state and/or district has curriculum guidelines
- whether state and local guidelines conflict with each other
- whether there are a large number of students requiring bilingual education
- whether the state or district requires schools to follow their guidelines or allows them to develop their own curricula
- for schools that retain local autonomy over curricular decisions, whether they may choose to adopt or ignore state or district guidelines

For the latter, the school's choice is likely to be influenced by the school's history of achievement, community standards, financial resources, and how it understands the relationship between these factors and the curriculum guidelines being provided by the state or district.

The issue of standards for learning and teaching has developed in the United States in recent years as policymakers, legislators, educators, parents, and community leaders have all shown an increasing concern with students' achievement levels. The word "standards" has been used in many ways during public discussions. Sometimes the term has been used to represent established levels of achievement; in other cases it refers to commonly shared sets of academic subject content, such as those embodied in state curriculum guidelines.

Curricular guidelines have been used to set standards in many states and have been linked to state-administered achievement tests. Standards in the United States also include more informal means by which schools maintain and promote the desired levels of achievement for their students. These achievement levels for schools and for students have usually been extrapolated from community expectations, and local communities continue to greatly influence curriculum and instructional decisions made at the school level. In the end, standards are partly a result of local decisions, such as those governing the selection of textbooks and those affecting a school's policy on the promotion or retention of students. The guides to standards have developed significantly, and school districts are feeling their influence.

By 2009, the National Governors Association, the National Association of Secondary School Principals, the Council of Great City Schools, and the American Federation of Teachers (AFT) all publicly supported national standards.

ADDITIONAL RESOURCES

Nichols, Sharon, and Berliner, David. *Collateral Damage: How High-Stakes Testing Corrupts America's Schools.* Cambridge, MA: Harvard Education Press, 2007.

Ravitch, Diane. *The Death and Life of the Great American School System: How Testing and Choice Are Undermining Education.* New York: Basic Books, 2011.

Yudof, Mark G., David L. Kirp, Betsy Levin, and Rachel F. Moran. *Educational Policy and the Law.* 5th ed. Belmont, CA: Wadsworth Group, 2011.

ORGANIZATIONS

Alliance for Parental Involvement in Education (ALLPIE)
PO Box 59
East Chatham, NY 12060
Phone: (518) 392-6900
Email: allpie@taconic.net
URL: http://www.croton.com/allpie/

American Association of School Administrators (AASA)
1615 Duke St.
Alexandria, VA 22314
Phone: (703) 528-0700
Fax: (703) 841-1543
Email: Info@aasa.org
URL: http://www.aasa.org/

Education Law Association (ELA)
300 College Park 0528
Dayton, Ohio 45469
Phone: (937) 229-3589
Fax: (937) 229-3845
Email: ela@udayton.edu
URL: http://www.educationlaw.org/

Institute of Education Sciences
555 New Jersey Ave. NW
Washington, DC 20208
Phone: (202) 219-1385
URL: http://ies.ed.gov

National School Boards Foundation (NSBF)
1680 Duke Street
Alexandria, VA 22314-3493
Phone: (703) 838-6722
Fax: (703) 548-5516
Email: info@nsba.org
URL: http://www.nsba.org/index.htm

U.S. Department of Education
400 Maryland Avenue, SW
Washington, DC 20202
Toll Free: (800) USA-LEARN
Fax: (202) 401-0689
Email: customerservice@inet.ed.gov
URL: http://www.ed.gov

EDUCATION

DESEGREGATION/BUSING

Sections within this essay:

- Background
- Before Desegregation
  - The Fourteenth Amendment
    Plessy v. Ferguson
  - *Brown v. Board of Education*
- Desegregation in Theory and Practice
  - Busing and "White Flight"
  - The Needs of the Children
- Innovative Approaches
  - Magnet Schools
- Resegregation of Public Schools
- Additional Resources

BACKGROUND

One of the most important rights Americans have is the right to a free public education. No child in the United States, whether native- or foreign-born, can be denied access to a public school for elementary and secondary education. While in theory this means that everyone is entitled to the *same* educational experience, in fact that is not necessarily the case. Public schools can vary dramatically from community to community simply because some districts have more money to spend on education than others.

For years, **segregation** of black and white students was quite common. In some places, it was common because local and state laws mandated segregation in one form or another. In other places it was common because neighborhoods were segregated (often by choice) and students went to the closest schools. From the late nineteenth century to the mid-twentieth century, segregated schools were protected by the concept of "separate but equal," upheld by the U.S. Supreme Court in 1896. **Separate but equal** was overturned in 1954 in the famous *Brown v. Board of Education* decision, but segregation in the schools continued. In the 1960s and 1970s, efforts were made to desegregate schools across the country. Many of these efforts succeeded, but many failed. A number of desegregation efforts, begun with the best of intentions, turned out to be more divisive than inclusive.

Desegregation is one of the most complex issues educators and parents face. In the 1950s, desegregation was about blacks and whites. When people used the word "minority," they meant blacks. As of 2012, the entire concept of minorities and diversity has shifted. Minorities can include blacks, Central and South Americans, Southeast Asians (Vietnamese, Cambodian, Laotian), Arabs, and a host of others. These multiple ethnicities existed in large cities for decades, but in the 21st century people are more mobile and even small communities can have a dozen or more ethnic minorities. Consequently, communities cannot merely take a "one size fits all" approach. Finding the right approach to desegregation, or rather, to encouraging diversity in the schools, is an ongoing challenge to school districts across the country.

BEFORE DESEGREGATION

Education was not always the universally accepted right that it is today in the United States. Although some communities did make education a priority, the United States was primarily an agricultural society until the twentieth century.

Children might learn to work the land or be apprenticed to a tradesman after having only a few years of formal schooling. Many children had no formal education. Slave children had only as much education as their masters allowed or tolerated; most slave owners did not encourage their slaves even to learn to learn to read or write.

The Fourteenth Amendment The Thirteenth Amendment to the U.S. Constitution, ratified shortly after the end of the Civil War, prohibited slavery and involuntary servitude. But it did not specifically grant citizenship to freed slaves, and Southern states took advantage of this omission. Congress redressed the balance with the Fourteenth Amendment, which was ratified in 1868. The amendment stated that all citizens, whether by birth or by **naturalization**, were guaranteed **equal protection** under the law, and called for Federal intervention if states failed to comply. Former Confederate states that wished to rejoin the United States were required to sign the Fourteenth Amendment before being readmitted.

What the Fourteenth Amendment did not do was guarantee equal rights. Southern states used the "separate but equal" argument, which allowed them to keep blacks and whites separate as long as they did not deprive them of basic legal rights. Eventually, this arrangement led to a series of discouraging developments that relegated blacks in the South to inferior status.

Plessy v. Ferguson One of the factors affected by Southern unwillingness to recognize blacks as equals was public transportation. In 1890, the General Assembly of Louisiana passed a law requiring railroads to provide separate cars for whites and blacks, with the stipulation that the separate cars be of equal quality and comfort. The law was immediately attacked by **civil rights** groups, and to force the question of whether it was constitutional, a black man, Adolph Plessy, deliberately broke it by taking a seat in a whites-only car. The law was found constitutional by regional and state courts and went to the U.S. Supreme Court in 1896. The Court ruled seven to one against Plessy and thus established as constitutional the concept of "separate but equal." This concept was a springboard for what was called the "Jim Crow" system. Named for a character in a black minstrel show, the Jim Crow laws made segregation not merely acceptable but mandatory. Over the next several decades, "separate but equal" became pervasive, particularly in the South. Although there were some civil rights gains for blacks in the ensuing years, a definitive victory against Jim Crow did not come until 1954.

Brown v. Board of Education "Separate but equal" may have seemed unconscionable to many, but it was the law in many states. In the 1950s, 17 states and the District of Columbia had laws prohibiting **school desegregation**. It was clear to most educators, parents, and children that there could be no such thing as a separate but equal education. Several cases appeared before the U.S. Supreme Court to challenge the constitutionality of segregated schools, and the Court's unanimous ruling on *Oliver Brown et al. v. Board of Education of Topeka, Kansas* on May 17, 1954, turned the doctrine of school segregation on its head. "Separate educational facilities," said the Court, "are inherently unequal."

Although the Brown decision marked the beginning of the end for sanctioned segregation in the schools, segregation's end did not come immediately. In fact, in the late 1950s and early 1960s, several Southern governors, notably Orval Faubus of Arkansas, Ross Barnett of Mississippi, and George Wallace of Alabama, vigorously defended segregation. Not until President Lyndon B. Johnson signed the Civil Rights Act of 1964 was desegregation dealt a definitive blow throughout the United States.

DESEGREGATION IN THEORY AND PRACTICE

Throughout the 1960s it became evident that desegregation was not a clear-cut issue by any means. As communities struggled with finding the best ways to desegregate, the racial divide seemed to grow rather than diminish.

Southern states, which had borne the brunt of the negative publicity about segregation, began to point out that the Northern states were equally culpable, albeit in a different way. For years the South had *de jure* segregation—in other words, segregation mandated by law. In the North, while there were no segregation laws on the books, most blacks and whites lived in separate enclaves; often the groups did not mix, and their children attended local schools. Thus, in the North there was *de facto* segregation in the schools because neighborhoods were segregated.

Busing and "White Flight" Among the methods communities tried to desegregate the schools was the busing of black students to predominantly white schools. Since the black schools tended to be in poorer neighborhoods and had fewer resources, it seemed to make sense to bus black students to white schools until a balance of black and white students was attained. The case in the U.S. Supreme Court that set the ground rules for all future busing decisions in the courts was *Swann v. Charlotte-Mecklenburg Board of Education,* which was decided in 1970. Two years earlier, the Court had ruled in *Green v. County School Board* that the school board had the responsibility to integrate the schools and to do so promptly. The Charlotte-Mecklenburg (Virginia) school board was found to be out of compliance and was assigned a plan known as the Finger Plan (named for the man who devised it). Under the Finger Plan, schools throughout the district were to work to attain more racial balance in the schools by busing children into the schools.

Busing is one illustration of how difficult it is to achieve true desegregation. In the decades after *Swann*, other communities implemented busing. Invariably, busing is not well-received by blacks or whites. Legislating action is one thing, but legislating attitude is quite another. In many large urban cities, whites who could afford to move to the suburbs, where the population (and consequently the schools) were predominantly white, left inner-city schools with dwindling white student populations. In Denver, the school district was found to be practicing "subtle racism" by the U.S. Supreme Court in *Keyes v. School District No. 1*. A busing program was implemented, but the way the system was initially set up many elementary school students spent half a day in a de facto segregated school and half a day in an integrated school.

The 1974 case of *Milliken v. Bradley* addressed the issue of "white flight" to the suburbs by suggesting that one remedy would be to bus suburban children into the inner city schools in which whites were the minority. The U.S. Supreme Court ruled that suburban students could not be used to desegregate inner city schools. White flight continued. Because most of the people left behind were poor or working-class, cities lost a tax base. As cities became poorer, less money was spent on education. Blacks and other minorities who could afford to move did so, and the inner city populations became statistically poorer. Over time, many of the largest cities in the United States had public schools that were racially imbalanced and sadly in need of funding for maintenance, basic supplies, and more teachers.

The Needs of the Children Lost in many of these contentious proceedings was the simple question of what was best for the child. Children are not born with a predisposition to racial prejudice, but they are forced to live with the decisions of adults. In the inner cities, public education has not improved, and in affluent communities, de facto segregation is still common. While some see desegregation efforts such as busing as a positive move, others argue that the money spent on busing programs would be better spent in revitalizing poor neighborhoods and schools so that children can get a good education in their own neighborhood. But that brings back the question of segregated neighborhoods.

Many people from all ethnic and racial backgrounds look at desegregation with a mix of cynicism and resignation.

INNOVATIVE APPROACHES
Educators, government officials, and parents have all sought approaches to desegregation that are not merely superficial. Thinking up these approaches and implementing them is a challenge, but the fact that people are willing to seek alternatives to court-order remedies that may have inherent weaknesses is a start.

Magnet Schools Many communities have created "magnet schools" which students from across a community attend. These schools often emphasize particular courses of study—science or the arts, for example. Magnet schools, properly funded, can provide educational and social opportunities for children across a wide spectrum of racial and ethnic lines. Magnet schools do not keep people from moving out of the cities, however. In some places school districts have attempted to lure suburban students into inner city magnet schools. In Connecticut, cities such as Hartford and New Haven have created magnet schools that have been well received. One of the goals of these schools is to draw students from the predominantly white suburbs. As part of the state's desegregation efforts, suburban students can take part in a program called Open Choice that allows them to transfer to the inner city schools at no additional cost. Under normal circumstances, a student who goes to a district other than his or her own would have to pay tuition and transportation costs. In Connecticut, those costs are underwritten by the state.

Magnet schools are seen by many as a better way to achieve integration than charter schools, which are often created specifically to serve the needs of local neighborhoods and may not have racial or ethnic diversity as their prevailing goal (although as public entities they are subject to anti-discrimination laws).

RESEGREGATION OF SCHOOLS
The ability of school districts to promote desegregation of their schools was severely restricted by the U.S. Supreme Court in *Parents Involved in Community Schools v. Seattle School District No. 1*, 551 U.S. 701 (2007). The Court struck down the guidelines used by the Seattle, Washington and Louisville, Kentucky school districts, finding that such plans violated the Equal Protection Clause of the Fourteenth Amendment. Though four justices voted to end the use of race in public education to promote diversity, Justice Anthony

Kennedy issued a separate opinion that said that race could still be taken into account if the programs were more narrowly tailored.

In 1998, the Seattle school district established guidelines on high school assignments. Because some schools were more popular than others, a series of "tiebreakers" were used to determine who was given open slots. The first tiebreaker gave preference to students who had a sibling enrolled in the high school. The next tiebreaker was based on the racial composition of the school and the race of the individual student. The racial composition of the Seattle schools was 41 percent white and 59 percent nonwhite. If the school was not within 10 percent of the district's overall racial balance, then the school would admit students whose race would help bring the school into balance. The district employed these tiebreakers because most white students live in the northern section of Seattle, while nonwhites mostly live in southern areas of the city. By 2000 many white students were not admitted to one of the four high schools in northern Seattle, leading to the formation of Parents Involved in Community Schools. This organization filed a federal lawsuit, arguing that the tiebreaker system violated the Equal Protection Clause of the Fourteenth Amendment.

In the second case, the Jefferson County Schools located in the greater Louisville, Kentucky area established in 2001 a voluntary school assignment plan. The racial composition of the schools was 34 percent black and 66 percent white. The Louisville plan denied admission to grade schools if the student's race would contribute to the school's racial imbalance. A white mother filed a federal lawsuit challenging the plan after her son was denied the right to transfer to a grade school that was close to their home because the transfer would have an adverse effect on school desegregation.

The Supreme Court, in a 5–4 decision, struck down both plans, finding that the plans did not survive strict constitutional scrutiny. Chief Justice John Roberts found that the plans were "directed only to racial balance, pure and simple," which violated the Equal Protection Clause. He concluded that the "way to stop **discrimination** on the basis of race is to stop discriminating on the basis of race." Roberts noted that in *Brown v. Board of Education*, the Court ruled that schoolchildren could not be told where they could go to school based "on the color of their skin." The school districts had failed to demonstrate that they should be allowed to do this once again even for very different reasons. In his view it made no difference if the school districts had worthy goals in mind if they were "free to discriminate on the basis of race to achieve it."

Justice Anthony Kennedy supplied the fifth vote to strike down the two plans but he was not prepared to remove race as a consideration in ensuring diversity. Kennedy disagreed with Roberts' conclusion that race could not be taken into account, stating that "The **plurality** opinion is too dismissive of the legitimate interest government has in ensuring all people have equal opportunity regardless of race." He suggested that schools could take into account race if they did not single out individual students. The drawing of school attendance zones, "strategic site selection of new schools," and directing resources at special programs such as magnet schools were possible ways of avoiding "the status quo of racial isolation in schools." Kennedy's concurring opinion emerged as the basis for any future plaintiffs to challenge other school diversity plans, which are currently in use by over 1,000 school districts throughout the United States. Dissenting Justice Stephen Breyer concluded that without the use of such assignment plans he believed that the resegregation by race of the public schools was inevitable.

ADDITIONAL RESOURCES

Baugh, Joyce. *The Detroit School Busing Case: Milliken v. Bradley and the Controversy over Desegregation.* Lawrence, KS: University Press of Kansas, 2011.

Baum, Howell. *Brown in Baltimore: School Desegregation and the Limits of Liberalism.* Ithaca, NY: Cornell University Press, 2010.

Clotfelter, Charles. *After "Brown": The Rise and Retreat of School Desegregation.* Princeton, NJ: Princeton University Press, 2006.

Schwartz, Bernard. *Swann's Way: The School Busing Case and the Supreme Court.* New York: Oxford University Press, 1986.

Shujaa, Mwalimu J., ed. *Beyond Desegregation: The Politics of Quality in African-American Schooling.* Thousand Oaks, CA: Corwin Press, 1996.

ORGANIZATIONS

Center for Education Reform

1001 Connecticut Avenue NW, Suite 204
Washington, DC 20036
Phone: (202) 822-9000
Fax: (202) 822-5077
URL: http://www.edreform.com

Educational Opportunities Section, Civil Rights Division, U.S. Department of Justice

950 Pennsylvania Avenue NW, PHB
Washington, DC 20530
Phone: (202) 514-4092
Fax: (202) 514-8337
URL: http://www.usdoj.gov

National Association for the Advancement of Colored People (NAACP)
4805 Mt. Hope Drive
Baltimore, MD 21215
Toll Free: (877) 622-2728
URL: http://www.naacp.org

National Center for Education Statistics (NCES)
1990 K Street NW
Washington, DC 20006
Phone: (202) 502-7300
URL: http://www.nces.ed.gov

National Education Association (NEA)
1201 16th Street NW
Washington, DC 20036
Phone: (202) 833-4000
URL: http://www.nea.org

U.S. Department of Education
400 Maryland Avenue SW
Washington, DC 20202
Toll Free: (800) 872-5327
URL: http://www.ed.gov

EDUCATION

DISCIPLINE AND PUNISHMENT

BACKGROUND

Current Issues In the 1990s and 2000s, educators, law enforcement agencies, governments, courts, parents, and the general citizenry in the United States considered new and troubling questions pertaining to student conduct. The late 1990s witnessed a number of spectacular on-campus crimes by juveniles, including acts of murder, suicide, **assault**, and massive property damage. The seriousness of these events brought attention to the problems public schools face in managing students who act out in life-threatening criminal ways. Clampdown reaction to enhanced security and student protection competed with legal concerns about student **constitutional rights**, particularly the right to due process. Other widespread crimes in schools, such as physical conflicts between students, student drug use, weapon possession, and theft, disrupted the academic setting and all too often frustrated the true goals of education: teaching and learning.

Definition The word discipline is akin to the word disciple. Discipline in one sense means learning, just as the word disciple refers to one who learns. Additional meanings of discipline suggest the complexity of the subject as it pertains to individuals (in this case specifically minors) and the U.S. public school system. Discipline refers to training and experience that corrects, molds, and strengthens individuals' mental faculties and moral character. It also refers to punishment that intends to correct and that is enforced by those in authority or may be self-imposed.

Discipline likewise refers to the control gained by enforcing obedience, and it pertains to the systematic orderly behavior defined by codes or rules set forth by institutions for their members. Moreover, discipline refers to self-control and to the development of skills that help individuals resist temptation, act positively, and function both independently and cooperatively in ways that enhance personal development and community life. All of these definitions have been central to educators' efforts to find the most effective and useful way to support child development and learning.

Origin of Corporal Punishment In the colonial era, the Puritan belief that humankind is innately tainted by the Original Sin of Adam and Eve led adults to see children as contaminated by an evil element that needed to be driven out by force. Puritans believed that all disobedience and academic error was the work of Satan, and children's innate proclivity for evil had to be destroyed through pain and humiliation. The idea that suffering can correct unwanted behavior became fundamental to institutional design, whether that design was the stocks in which prisoners were displayed for public abuse or the raised stools and dunce caps intended to correct student misbehavior or ignorance through humiliation. "To spare the rod," it was believed, led inevitably to spoiling the child, so slapping, spanking, and whipping were generally understood as beneficial educational tools. These beliefs persisted. Indeed, as late as 1977, in *Ingraham v. Wright*, the U.S. Supreme Court ruled that spanking did not violate students' rights, noting the widespread use of corporal punishment to maintain discipline in educational settings. Corporal punishment remained legal thereafter in more than 20 states.

HISTORY

The U.S. Constitution does not address the subject of public education. Apparently the founding fathers thought the implementation of schools ought to be the sole responsibility of the states. Initially, education was for the wealthy, and a belief persisted through the eighteenth century that poor individuals were not educable or were not worthy of being educated. In 1852, however, then secretary of state of Massachusetts Horace Mann urged that states be obliged to offer public education to all children. The revolutionary idea behind this **plea** was that all individuals could and should be educated irrespective of economic class.

During the middle of the nineteenth century, some U.S. educators studied European models, such as the theories of Philipp Emanuel von Fellenberg (1771-1844), who urged that corporal punishment not be used for academic errors and suggested that learning occurred best with encouragement and kindness. Francis Parker introduced European ideas into the public school system in Quincy, Illinois. What came to be known as the progressive Quincy Movement attached kindergarten to elementary education and extended into the early grades the idea of learning through play. These pedagogical developments examined connections between education and discipline and considered teachers' roles in creating environments conducive to learning.

By 1910 attendance at public school was mandatory; children were thus absent on a daily basis from parental direction and placed under the authority of educators. This transfer extended teachers' roles to parental disciplinarians; teachers functioned *in loco parentis*, meaning in the place of parents. During the first decades

of the 1900s, as teachers were stepping further into these parental roles, state legal systems were beginning to evolve ways to handle juvenile offenders which intended to distinguish them from adult perpetrators. One value attached to this development asserted that while adults should be punished for their crimes, children should be rehabilitated for theirs, thus formalizing a beginning to the separation between juvenile misconduct and suffering as its remedy.

At the beginning of the twentieth century, good discipline was evinced by students sitting quietly while they learned by rote. The conventional wisdom saw education as a process of controlling student behavior while information was transferred from teacher to student. This model continues to shape concepts about classroom activities and goals. Challenging this model, however, were the increasingly popular post-World War II theories of Benjamin Spock (1903-1998), who disapproved of rigid child-rearing techniques and urged adults, parents and teachers alike, to be more affectionate and flexible. Some critics of Spock's theories asserted that they contributed to a growing attitude of permissiveness and relativity that blurred children's understanding of right and wrong and encouraged self-defeating traits like selfishness, indolence, or noncompliance.

In the second half of the twentieth century, health-care professionals and educators became more informed about how student misbehavior may be connected to physiological or psychological problems, like attention deficit disorder, hyperactivity, or emotional disturbance. Changes in the family unit, increase in the Hollywood celebration of violence, and effects of illegal drug use also affected students' ability and willingness to learn in school. Moreover, in the 1990s and 2000s, juveniles committed serious felonies on school property, some of which converted schools temporarily to war zones. Reactions to these events caused many people to advocate for a return to more stringent controls of students, which in some circles acquired the label zero tolerance.

CODES OF CONDUCT

In taking charge of students and teaching them, twentieth-century educators repeatedly faced the challenge of designing codes of conduct. Doing so required attention to multiple and sometimes seemingly conflicting issues: school organizational needs, the goals of education, and the nebulous area of personal rights both for those in charge and for those being controlled. Educators had to identify features conducive for learning and then set forth rules and consequences for misconduct that would allow problem children to be handled constructively while the behaving majority of students continued to learn without disruption. In short, educators had to define ways to support classroom productivity, encourage student academic progress, and bring misbehaving individuals back to positive conduct so that they could resume learning. In this task, educators, administrators, and staff became increasingly conscious of legal issues connected to students' rights, juvenile legal status, and the handling of student crime. All of these issues were addressed independently by different school boards across the nation and handled differently by school boards and courts over time.

Creating Codes of Conduct The issues involved in the process of developing these codes of conduct constitute an important part of pedagogical debate and ongoing courtroom deliberation. For example, some judicial decisions have attempted to define those school requirements and regulations that a court would deem "reasonable." Under these decisions, a properly written document must meet four criteria in order to carry a legal presumption of validity:

- The rules had to be in writing: Regulations students had to obey without a specific verbal command must be in writing.

- The rules had to be specific: Policies had to be clearly stated to students, and without referring to an outside source or document the rules had to explain what was expected and what was prohibited.

- The writing had to be authorized: The writer of the rules had to have the authority to define them.

- The written rules had to be published: The **code of conduct** had to be printed and distributed, for example in student handbooks, in letters home to parents, in public announcements during class time and assemblies, and in postings on bulletin boards.

Richard Curwin, a professor of Education at San Francisco State University, devised criteria for making codes of conduct more effective. His suggestions were:

- To use positive rather than negative statements
- To be definite about proper and prohibited behavior
- To be brief
- To spell out consequences

Thus, the courts began the process of educating the educators on how to arrange the business of school so that when it responded to misbehavior its rulings would be deemed valid in the legal setting.

Content of Codes In light of their wisdom, experience, and training, educators have devised codes of conduct to meet their schools' particular goals and challenges. Some school codes employ step programs that

distinguish first-time offenders from repeat offenders. These codes hand down mild penalties for first-offense students but then graduate the penalties for the misconduct of repeat offenders. In these cases, students face consequences determined by their records of behavior. Thus, for a repeat offender, a minor **infraction** might carry the serious **penalty** of suspension while the same infraction might elicit only a verbal reminder for the first-time offender. Some schools set aside special classrooms for extra training in matters of self-control, conflict resolution, and cooperation. Schools elicit parents' participation and support in encouraging their children back to positive behavior and academic progress.

Discipline policies state clearly that rules benefit everyone in the educational community and are in effect inside school buildings, on school property, inside school-owned vehicles, and at school-sponsored activities on or off campus. Codes include rules about attendance, absence, and tardiness. They outline steps for parents to take in excusing their children from class and instruct teachers how to keep records of student attendance. Patterns of unexcused absence or tardiness are quantified and carry penalties or repercussions that relate to the extent of the patterns of absence. Misbehaving students might be detained in the classroom after other students are free to go on to non-classroom activities, or they might be required to attend a Saturday detention period. During these times, students might be given extra academic work or be required to perform maintenance chores on school property. Repeat offenders are subject to a number of potential penalties, including the following: removal from school; removal from class to a study room; placement in an on-sight suspension area; suspension for a specified time; and expulsion. Although individuals who act out are arguably the ones most in need of education and support, they tend to be separated from others.

When students break the law on school property, police officers must take over for educators. Students who use alcohol or other drugs, who have in their possession or deliver to others controlled substances, who carry weapons, or who assault others are all subject to the same laws they would face elsewhere in the community. Therefore, these forms of misconduct are not within the school's **jurisdiction** solely. Students can be charged for crimes committed on school property; they can go to court and face court decisions that place them in juvenile detention centers. Clearly, school codes must address a vast range of conduct and take into consideration innumerable factors that lie in or beyond the education setting. The codes must respond legally, in line with community, state, and federal laws on issues connected to **discrimination**, harassment, gender, and **disability**. Academic codes of conduct aim to support educational goals and be in line with criminal and civil laws. Often times the courts have had the task of deciding if the codes achieve this end.

STUDENTS' CONSTITUTIONAL RIGHTS AND SELECTED CASES

Educators have to negotiate the complicated terrain of competing entities, managing difficult students yet remaining mindful of their constitutional rights, such as rights to **privacy**, **just cause**, and due process. When criminal acts in schools involve law enforcement, certain subjects, conflicts, and events may come before the courts. Courts elucidate legal issues but not once and for all; these judgments can be subsequently redefined, upheld, or found unconstitutional. Questions recur pertaining to the application of Fourteenth Amendment protections to students as these individuals are subjected to school regulations.

Issues pertaining to a student's right to privacy, to reasonable cause for **search and seizure**, and to technicalities about *Miranda* rights all were examined in *New Jersey v. T.L.O.* (1985), a case involving a juvenile (known only by her initials) who was suspected of smoking and whose purse was found to contain cigarettes, rolling paper, a bag of hashish, and some file cards containing what appeared to be a list of amounts received for drug sales. The Supreme Court had to evaluate the relative rights of the student's right to privacy against the school's need to enforce an orderly environment. One of its conclusions was that education requires a disciplined environment and that means the authority to educate entails the authority to discipline.

In the 1986 case of *In re William G.*, a California court decided that students as a group have the right to be protected by school officials from dangerous items or substances and to have enforced an environment conducive for learning. In many cases, the courts have to balance competing entities or claims to rights by opposite parties. In *Bethel v. Fraser* (1986) and again in *Vernonia v. Acton* (1995), the U.S. Supreme Court decided that students' rights are secondary to students' safety. These and many other cases produce the body of court decisions which evolve social understanding of the law as it applies in ever-changing circumstances.

COLUMBINE AND ITS AFTERMATH: ZERO TOLERANCE

On April 20, 1999 at Columbine High School in Littleton, Colorado, two heavily armed students killed twelve students and one teacher and seriously wounded nearly two dozen others before killing themselves. The

following month in Conyers, Georgia, a 15-year-old student wounded six other students. In December, an Oklahoma middle-school student took a semiautomatic handgun to school and wounded five students. Although these incidents were covered heavily in the media, they were by no means unique occurrences. From July 1, 2009 to June 30, 2010, 33 students died in school-related acts of violence.

These and other murders perpetrated by children against classmates and teachers have caused a furor of reactive security measures, precaution taking, and a new commitment to stringent control. Zero tolerance, which initially referred to students carrying weapons to school, fueled and increased provisions for suspension and expulsion. In Chicago, in the wake of commitment to zero tolerance, suspensions and expulsions jumped to an average of 90 per week, mostly Latinos and African Americans. Proponents of more stringent codes pointed to the staggering fact that everyday in the United States 12 children are killed by gunshot. The fact that one day they were gathered together in their deaths at Columbine brought national consciousness to a new level. Many schools nation-wide, particularly in urban settings, instigated entry-area body and bag searches, stricter dress codes, and random **drug testing**. Yet critics of this stringent disciplinary action urged educators to return to a positive vision of students and search for punishments that teach rather than using those that increase the dropout rate.

STATE LAWS REGARDING CORPORAL PUNISHMENT

As of 2012, 28 states outlawed corporal punishment in schools. In the remaining states, more than 200,000 students nationally are subjected to some form of corporal punishment. This number is significantly lower than in previous generations of students.

The following list indicates those states that have banned corporal punishment.

ALASKA: The state banned corporal punishment in 1989.

CALIFORNIA: The state banned corporal punishment in 1986.

CONNECTICUT: The state banned corporal punishment in 1989.

DELAWARE: The state banned corporal punishment in 2003.

HAWAII: The state banned corporal punishment in 1973.

ILLINOIS: The state banned corporal punishment in 1993.

IOWA: The state banned corporal punishment in 1989.

MAINE: The state banned corporal punishment in 1975.

MARYLAND: The state banned corporal punishment in 1993.

MASSACHUSETTS: The state banned corporal punishment in 1971.

MICHIGAN: The state banned corporal punishment in 1989.

MINNESOTA: The state banned corporal punishment in 1989.

MONTANA: The state banned corporal punishment in 1991.

NEBRASKA: The state banned corporal punishment in 1988.

NEVADA: The state banned corporal punishment in 1993.

NEW HAMPSHIRE: The state banned corporal punishment in 1983.

NEW JERSEY: The state banned corporal punishment in 1867.

NEW YORK: The state banned corporal punishment in 1985.

NORTH DAKOTA: The state banned corporal punishment in 1989.

OREGON: The state banned corporal punishment in 1989.

PENNSYLVANIA: The state banned corporal punishment in 2005.

RHODE ISLAND: The state banned corporal punishment in 1977.

SOUTH DAKOTA: The state banned corporal punishment in 1990.

VERMONT: The state banned corporal punishment in 1985.

VIRGINIA: The state banned corporal punishment in 1989.

WASHINGTON: The state banned corporal punishment in 1993.

WEST VIRGINIA: The state banned corporal punishment in 1994.

WISCONSIN: The state banned corporal punishment in 1988.

EMERGING DISCIPLINARY THEORIES

Many theories about discipline shift attention from external punishment and reward systems to internalization of socialization skills and moral sense. For example, in *Schools Without Failure*, William Glasser explains the short-term value of external punishment and the limitations of trying to control others through fear tactics. Theorists like Abraham Maslow, in *Motivation and Personality*, and W. Edwards Deming, in *Out of the Crisis*, suggest a return to humane education principles and affirmation of human goodness. Many thinkers want educational institutions to find their path into a new way of being that creates the learning moment, sees misbehavior as an opportunity, and instills faith in human nature as it pursues learning and instructs through misconduct. Marvin Marshall, in *Discipline Without Stress, Punishment, or Rewards*, urges people to remember that so long as they are manipulated by outward threats of punishment or hopes of reward, they may be neglecting intrinsic values which in the end are the ones that satisfy, induce self-control, and energize toward self-improvement. These affirmations have to be balanced with the seriousness of turn-of-the-millennium juvenile crimes and the awesome responsibility of educators to keep children safe while they engage in learning.

ADDITIONAL RESOURCES

Avery, Gary. *Safety, Order, and Discipline in American Schools: Defining the Authority of Educators and Law Enforcement Personnel.* Los Angeles: Law Advisory Group, Inc., 2001.

Bear, George. *School Discipline and Self-Discipline: A Practical Guide to Promoting Prosocial Student Behavior.* New York: Guilford Press, 2010.

Glasser, William. *Schools Without Failure.* New York: Harper & Row, 1969.

Kafka, Judith. *The History of "Zero Tolerance" in American Public Schooling.* New York: Palgrave Macmillan, 2011.

Marshall, Marvin. *Discipline without Stress, Punishments, or Rewards: How Teachers and Parents Promote Responsibility and Learning.* Cypress, CA: Piper Press, 2001.

Thomas. R. Murray. *Violence in America's Schools: Understanding, Prevention, and Responses.* Lanham, MD: R&L Pub., 2009.

Unger, Harlow G. *Encyclopedia of American Education.* 3rd ed. New York: Facts on File, 2007.

ORGANIZATIONS

Center for Effective Discipline
155 W. Main Street, Suite 1603
Columbus, OH 43215
Phone: (614) 221-8829
URL: http://www.stophitting.com

National Association of Elementary School Principals (NAESP)
1615 Duke St.
Alexandria, VA 22314
Toll Free: (800) 386-2377
URL: http://naesp.org

National Education Association (NEA)
1201 16th St., NW
Washington, DC 20036
Phone: (202) 833-4000

EDUCATION

DRUG TESTING

Sections within this essay:

- Background
- State Court Decisions
- Additional Resources

BACKGROUND

Mandatory drug testing in public schools is a relatively new issue for the law. Introduced during the late 1980s and expanding over the next decade, the practice of analyzing student urine for illegal drugs is carried out in a small but growing percentage of schools nationwide. Hundreds out of the nation's 60,000 school districts require some form of testing. Thus students in thousands of individual schools are affected, and more districts have indicated their interest in adopting testing, too. Currently, the practice has been ruled constitutional in one form by the U.S. Supreme Court.

School drug-testing grew out of the so-called war on drugs. Prior to the 1980s, citizens were rarely tested for drugs except by law enforcement officers and primarily when there were grounds for suspicion. Exceptions existed in a few areas, notably in the routine testing of college and pro athletes and prison inmates. But along with other sweeping social changes, the drug war introduced the idea of so-called mandatory suspicionless testing in the workplace. After spreading from the public to the private sector, the trend reached public high schools in with the testing of student athletes in the late 1980s.

Legally, mandatory suspicionless drug testing has proved controversial both in the workplace and school. The practice raises questions about how to balance a perceived social need for health and safety with **privacy** concerns. Not surprisingly, in light of its rulings favorable to workplace testing, the U.S. Supreme Court upheld suspicionless student drug testing in 1995. The Court already viewed the privacy rights of public school students as being lower than those generally enjoyed by adult citizens. Now, the majority saw an important social need for schools to combat drug usage, viewing the loss of student privacy as inconsequential.

Following the 1995 decision, school districts began to require drug tests for students who wanted to participate in extracurricular activities such as band and choir. This led to lawsuits challenging the testing requirement but the U.S. Supreme Court upheld the tests in 2002.

Important legal milestones include the following:

- The Supreme Court defined students' reduced Fourth Amendment rights in *New Jersey v. T.L.O.* (1985), where it ruled that schools do not have to follow the customary requirements of having **probable cause** or a **warrant** in order to carry out searches. Instead, school authorities must follow only a simple standard based on "the dictates of reason and common sense."

- In its first landmark drug-testing ruling, the Supreme Court upheld the suspicionless drug-testing of railroad employees who are involved in accidents in *Skinner v. Railway Labor Executives' Ass'n* (1989). The court held that the government has a compelling interest in public safety that overrides Fourth Amendment rights of the employees.

- In a second critical ruling on drug-testing, the Court upheld the suspicionless drug testing of U.S. Customs Service employees in sensitive positions that involve extraordinary safety and national security hazards in *National Treasury Employees Union v. Von Raab* (1989).

- The Supreme Court upheld the constitutionality of mandatory suspicionless drug-testing of student athletes in *Vernonia v. Acton* (1995). Applying its rulings in *Skinner* and *Von Raab*, the Court found that the students' Fourth Amendment rights were outweighed by the government's interest in drug-free schools when it approved a school's policy of random suspicionless testing of student athletes. In the wake of its landmark ruling, hundreds of school districts nationwide adopted similar policies.

- The U.S. Supreme Court in *Board of Education v. Earls* (2002) upheld a school's right to require random drug-testing as a condition for participation in extracurricular activities besides sports.

STATE COURT DECISIONS

As a policy matter, student drug testing in public schools is widely determined by school districts. State legislatures have thus far not intruded, leaving these determinations to the discretion of local school boards. As such, policies vary widely nationwide, and even from district to district within given states. Most schools still have no testing policy, but those that have adopted policies tend to fall into two categories: mandatory suspicionless testing is required of students who wish to play intramural athletics, or, more broadly, it is required not only of athletes but also of students wishing to participate in extracurricular clubs and organizations.

Legal direction on school policies has come from the courts. The highest-profile challenges to the policies have been brought in federal court on Fourth Amendment grounds, but some cases have been brought on state constitutional grounds, too. State constitutions often have broader privacy protections than are found under the federal constitution, thus providing powerful legal grounds for plaintiffs who want to challenge overly aggressive school policies.

The first state constitutional challenge against mandatory testing of student athletes came in *Wilson v. Ridgefield Park Board of Education* (1997). The American Civil Liberties Union brought the case against Ridgefield Park, New Jersey school board, arguing that the policy violated state constitutional privacy rights. A state superior court judge agreed, additionally finding that the school had no **evidence** of a severe drug problem among athletes, and temporarily blocked enforcement of the policy pending trial. But before the case could be heard, the school board dropped the policy in a 1998 **settlement**.

State courts in Indiana, Oregon, and Pennsylvania have also found constitutional problems with school policies. Some state courts have addressed policies resulting from the expansion of student testing to other extracurricular activities. In rejecting one such policy, the Colorado state supreme court applied the U.S. Supreme Court's 1995 standard from *Vernonia v. Acton* when it held that high school marching band members have a higher expectation of privacy than student athletes who undress in locker rooms in *Trinidad School District No. 1 v. Lopez* (1998). In other state **litigation**, school districts in Maryland and Washington discontinued policies following lawsuits.

ADDITIONAL RESOURCES

Gale Encyclopedia of American Law. 3rd ed. Detroit: Gale, Cengage Learning, 2011.

Kafka, Judith. *The History of "Zero Tolerance" in American Public Schooling.* New York: Palgrave Macmillan, 2011.

Office of National Drug Control Policy. "What You Need to Know about Drug Testing in Schools." Available at https://www.ncjrs.gov/ondcppubs/publications/pdf/drug_testing.pdf (accessed November 2, 2012).

Palmer, Kris E., ed. *Constitutional Amendments: 1789 to the Present.* Detroit: Gale, Cengage Learning, 2000.

ORGANIZATIONS

American Civil Liberties Union (ACLU)

125 Broad St., 18th Fl.
New York, NY 10004
Phone: (212) 549-2500
Email: info@aclu.org
URL: http://www.aclu.org/

Drug-Free Schools Coalition

203 Main St., PMB 327
Flemington, NJ 08822
Phone: (908) 284-5080

National School Boards Association (NSBA)

1680 Duke Street
Alexandria, VA 22314
Phone: (703) 684-7590
URL: http://www.nsba.org

EDUCATION

FINANCE/FUNDING

Sections within this essay:

- Background
- What is Funded?
- Sources of Funding
  - Federal Revenues
  - State Funding
  - Local Funding

- Sources of Information
- Additional Resources

BACKGROUND

More than half a century ago Adlai Stevenson said, "The most American thing about America is the free common school system." The public school system in the United States is free only in the sense that all students have a right to attend. According to the National Center for Education Statistics (NCES), it cost an average of just over $10,000 per student to keep public elementary and high schools (known in the education community as "el-hi") operating in academic year 2007-2008. Overall the revenues raised for that school year totaled over $596 billion.

These revenues came from the federal government, state governments, and local government. (Local government includes individual towns as well as larger municipalities and county governments.) Over 91 percent of these revenues came from the states. The federal government contributed only 9 percent of the revenues. That may seem low, but in fact the federal government has historically contributed only a small portion of public education funds.

Funding for education has always been a contentious issue. Some people believe that education funding should be much higher than it is to ensure that students get the best education they can with the best resources and the most motivated teachers. Others believe that educational expenses should be kept in check so that schools will focus on teaching students instead of adding educational "bells and whistles" that do little to provide real educational value. What constitutes bells and whistles, of course, makes the debate more challenging. In the early and mid 1980s many education experts argued that computers in the classroom were a waste of tax dollars. By the mid 1990s it was clear that computers were in the classroom to stay, a necessary and essential element in the education process. By 2012, issuing tablet computers such as the iPad to students was becoming popular.

Still, there are many other issues for people to debate. For example, does increased funding increase student achievement? How long should school equipment last before it is replaced? Do school districts need to fund extracurricular activities, such as athletic teams? The issue of school vouchers (discussed in detail in a separate entry) has raised enormous questions in some communities. The idea of allowing parents to earmark some of their tax dollars for private schooling has generated much controversy. Clearly, taking money away from the public schools puts them at a greater financial disadvantage than they already are. Yet it does children little good to know that the public school they attend is in the first year of a turnaround that may last several more years. Regardless of the many controversies surrounding public education funding, it remains vitally important and guarantees that all children in the United States have access to school.

WHAT IS FUNDED?

Educational funding covers a wide variety of expenditures, all of which are necessary to keep school systems running. The U.S. Department of Education defines *current expenditures* as those that take care of a schools' day-to-day operations. Current expenditures include instruction (for example, teacher salaries, textbooks and other equipment), non-instruction (such as cafeteria services and in-school bookstores), and support services (including nurses, libraries, administration, and maintenance). Other expenditures include *facilities equipment and construction*, which covers new school construction including renovation and expansion of older buildings. It also includes the purchase of land on which to build new school structures. *Replacement equipment* includes expenditures for items that are purchased for the long term (furniture, for example). School districts also spend money on programs such as adult education, community colleges, and various other programs that are not actually a part of public el-hi education. School districts often have to borrow money to meet major expenses (such as new school construction) even after they receive government funding. Along with the other expenditures, schools also have to figure in interest expenses as they pay back long-term debt.

SOURCES OF FUNDING

Before reading about federal, state, and local funding, it is important to remember that each state has a different breakdown of funds, based on such factors as how much federal funding it gets. Some states get more in federal funding, while others get significantly less. Likewise, state contributions can vary significantly. In Vermont, three-quarters of school funding comes from the state, while in New Hampshire less than 10 percent comes from state funding.

Much of these rates are based on the types of programs that exist within each state or the internal tax structure. A state that has more federal education programs for children may end up with a higher percentage of federal funds overall. In general, the breakdowns tend to work. That said, whenever one source cuts back, it has an effect on the other sources. If, for example, the federal government were to decrease its educational contribution across the board by two percent, that would mean states and local communities would have to make up the shortfall. If either of those sources made cutbacks, the remaining source would feel more pressure to contribute more. If the necessary funding was simply not there, the result would either be higher taxes or reduced services.

Federal Revenues The federal government contributes money to schools directly and indirectly. Part of this funding comes from the U.S. Department of Education, but other agencies contribute as well. The U.S. Department of Health and Human Services, for example, contributes to education through its Head Start program, while the U.S. Department of Agriculture funds the School Lunch program for students who cannot afford to pay for their own lunches. Even with these added contributions, the federal government accounts for less than 10 percent of school revenues. Using its own words, the Department of Education has long seen its role as "a kind of emergency response system" that fills gaps when state and local sources are inadequate to meet key needs. (For example, the 1944 **GI Bill**, a post-secondary program rather than el-hi program, helps fund college educations for nearly eight million World War II veterans.)

The Education Department's measures are not always merely stop-gap. During and after World War II, Congress passed the **Lanham Act** (1941) and the Impact Aid laws (1950) to compensate school districts that housed military and other nontaxable federal installations. Today, the federal government continues to compensate communities that house such institutions. Moreover, Title I of the Elementary and Secondary Education Act of 1965 guaranteed aid to disadvantaged children in poor urban and rural communities. The Higher Education Act, passed the same year, provided financial aid programs to help qualifying students meet college expenses. The **No Child Left Behind Act of 2001** required states to establish accountability standards as a condition for receiving federal funds.

State Funding The states provide most of the funding that keeps public el-hi schools running in the U.S. The states raise this money through a variety of means including various taxes. Some states raise money for education through state-sponsored lottery games. Doing so is somewhat controversial because, while the schools may benefit from the added revenue, some see the lottery as nothing more than state-sponsored gambling, a potentially addictive activity that particularly affects poorer individuals.

Each state has an Education Department that oversees state programs (such as state university systems) as well as individual school districts. In some states a governing body, such as the Board of Regents in New York, plays a significant role. The New York Board of Regents provides a series of examinations for students to establish proficiency in various subjects based on established state standards. Many students in New York receive a Regents diploma as well as their regular school diploma when they graduate high school.

State funding for education can cause huge disagreements with the state among communities. The question state governments face constantly is how to distribute the revenues evenly to ensure that each school district gets its fair share. New York and Pennsylvania offer two examples of how state funds can be fought over. New York City holds nearly half the population of the state, yet it receives proportionally less per student from the state government than other districts in New York. Residents of upstate New York have little desire to see their state tax dollars sent to New York City schools, which they see as too bureaucratic and wasteful. Residents of central Pennsylvania feel the same about education expenditures in Philadelphia and Pittsburgh.

Urban and rural areas have separate needs and challenges. A large city may have an established infrastructure that allows its school officials to approach private companies for assistance. A local computer company may donate computer equipment to the city schools, for example. Yet city schools are often decrepit (many school buildings in New York City are heated by coal furnaces), classes are crowded, and teacher turnover is high. In rural areas, classes are unlikely to be overcrowded, and teachers may stay longer in one place. But having fewer students can also mean having access to fewer resources, and there may not be enough students in a given district to justify the expense of, for example, a special education program for developmentally disabled children.

Local Funding Local sources make up nearly as much revenue as state sources. Local sources include intermediate revenues from county or township governments, but the bulk of local funding comes from individual community school districts. Some of the local revenues come from sources such as revenues from student activities and food services. Most of the money comes from property taxes, which are raised to cover all community services as well as education. All homeowners pay taxes based on a local **assessment** of their houses. Local school budgets are mapped out by elected officials, including mayors and council members, as well as the local board of education. Residents are able to vote on local school budgets in regularly scheduled elections.

Funding schools with local dollars has benefits and drawbacks. The primary benefit of local funding is accountability. Taxpayers can see exactly how their money is being spent. They can see the new cafeteria at the high school, the new science lab equipment, the new textbooks. The local elected officials who submit school budgets to the voters know that if they fail to keep the promises they make, those same voters will remove them from office in the next election.

Members of the community also have more say in how local dollars are spent. Those who have children in the school system will be particularly interested in how tax dollars are spent. Some of them may become quite active in school affairs by participating in the Parent Teacher Association (PTA) or on the local board of education.

This arrangement can be a drawback to local funding as well as a benefit. Because members of the community know they have a say in the school budgetary process, they may be more likely to examine each expenditure carefully. This scrutiny is not the problem. What creates difficulties is when local residents perceive expenses as unnecessary. Those who no longer have children in the school system may be reluctant to see their property taxes increase for programs that will bring them little if any benefit. Senior citizens likewise may be reluctant to support tax increases (even though in many communities they get a **property tax** break). People who feel that teacher salaries are already too high or that the old gym is perfectly fine for the students or that new instruments for the marching band are an extravagance may vote down any school budget increases.

Local elected officials need to be able to show community residents the positive side of spending more money on the schools. Better-equipped schools attract better teachers. Better teachers prepare students better, and more students achieve success. This improvement in turn means more young families, since for young families the quality of the schools is the most important factor when they choose a place to live. As the community becomes more attractive to outsiders, property values will go up; often the rise in value more than offsets the extra cost incurred by taxes. Of course, higher property values may also mean higher tax assessments, so for the homeowner who has no children and no plans to move, the process of increased values may feel like a personal financial burden rather than tax dollars at work. For these and other reasons local funding is more complex than it would appear to be.

SOURCES OF INFORMATION

The federal government offers a number of sources of revenue information through the U.S. Department of Education (which oversees NCES), and other sources. Each state has its own education department, which can provide information about state education funding. Because education is such a critical issue to so many people, elected officials are a good source of statistical information on school revenues. Local government sources and boards of education are useful resources for information about local funding. Most public libraries compile information about local school revenue issues as well.

ADDITIONAL RESOURCES

Hanushek, Eric, and Alfred Lindseth. *Schoolhouses, Courthouses, and Statehouses: Solving the Funding-Achievement Puzzle in America's Public Schools*. Princeton, NJ: Princeton University. Press, 2009.

ORGANIZATIONS

National Center for Education Statistics (NCES)

1990 K Street, NW, Room 9103
Washington, DC 20006
Phone: (202) 502-7350
Fax: (202) 502-7475
URL: http://www.nces.ed.gov

National Education Association (NEA)

1201 16th Street, NW
Washington, DC 20036
Phone: (202) 833-4000
Fax: (202) 822-7170
URL: http://www.nea.org

National School Boards Association (NSBA)

1680 Duke Street
Alexandria, VA 22314
Phone: (703) 838-67220
Fax: (703) 683-7590
URL: http://www.nsba.org

EDUCATION

FOR-PROFIT HIGHER EDUCATION

Sections within this essay:

- Background
- Accreditation
- Structure of For-Profit Education
- Recruiting Students
- Costs
- Outcomes
- Additional Resources

BACKGROUND

Most students seek post-secondary education at public or nonprofit institutions. However, a growing number of Americans attend for-profit schools. Approximately 1.1 million students enrolled for the 2008-2009 school year at for-profit schools. These schools attract non-traditional students, which include those who delayed college, who work part-time or full-time while attending school, are independent of their parents, or have dependents other than a spouse. The growth of for-profit schools has increased dramatically since the early 1990s, when Congress enacted a law that allows up to 90 percent of a for-profit school's revenue to come from federal student loans and federal Pell grants.

For-profit schools have existed for decades. Local business colleges, schools of cosmetology, and vocational schools issue certificates to students who successfully complete the course of study. In the 1990s, two-thirds of

for-profit schools enrolled students in training programs lasting less than one year. While certificate and diploma offerings have continued to grow, growth in degree programs has been more significant.

For-profit schools have established programs that grant associate, bachelor's, and graduate degrees. Between 2004 and 2010, the number of associate degrees awarded by for-profit schools increased 77 percent, while bachelor's degrees increased 136 percent. In addition, these new schools marketed themselves regionally and nationally. By the late 1990s investors recognized the low risk potential for profit and began purchasing and investing in for-profit colleges. In 2009, 76 percent of the students attending for-profit schools were enrolling in a school that was either owned by a company traded on a major stock exchange or a private equity firm. By 2012 there was also mounting criticism over for-profit recruiting tactics, low student retention rates, inadequate student support and career placement services, and the federal funding of these institutions.

ACCREDITATION

There are two types of accreditation for institutions of higher learning. Institutional accreditation indicates that a membership organization approved by the U.S. Department of Education has conducted a peer review of the institution and certified that the college or university meets specified school-wide standards of quality. Institutional accreditation is essential for all colleges and universities and is required for any school to receive federal financial aid funds from the Department of Education. There are regional and national accreditation organizations. The American Commission of Career Schools and Colleges (ACCSC) is a nonprofit organization created for the purpose of nationally accrediting for-profit schools. Many for-profit schools have national accreditation, while most academically oriented, nonprofit and public schools have regional accreditation. For-profit schools with national accreditation offer vocational, career, or technical programs. Most importantly, many regionally accredited schools will not accept transfer credits earned at a nationally accredited school. However, a number of the larger for-profit schools have obtained regional accreditation.

There is also programmatic accreditation. Instead of certifying an entire institution, programmatic accreditation certifies that a specific degree or certificate program meets standards expected within a particular field or profession. Different professions and different states place a different emphasis on programmatic accreditation. For example, most states will only license recent law school graduates to practice law if they graduated from a program accredited by the American Bar Association. On the other hand, no state laws mandate that diagnostic sonographers graduate from programs accredited by the Commission on Accreditation of Allied Health Education Programs. However, most employers seek to hire only registered sonographers and registration is not open to recent graduates of non-accredited degree programs. While state law does not create an absolute barrier to practicing for students from unaccredited programs, the practical effect can be the same for many students.

A 2012 U.S. Senate Committee report on for-profit schools criticized for-profits for being inconsistent in how they disclose this lack of programmatic accreditation. Some note this fact in an obscure part of their website or in the fine print of the enrollment agreement. In addition, students have been recruited into non-accredited programs under the mistaken belief that their time and money would lead to a valuable credential and access to a job field.

STRUCTURE OF FOR-PROFIT EDUCATION

Unlike nonprofit schools, for-profit schools rely on part-time and adjunct instructors. They are frequently hired on a short-term basis to help minimize educational costs. In 2012, most instructors worked part-time. Many students attend for-profit schools by going to a classroom, but the growth of online colleges since the early 2000s has made this option very popular. The course structure for online colleges consists of self-directed reading from books and website, online discussion threads, online tests, individual written assignments or power-point presentations, and a few courses that include group assignments. Interaction with the teacher is primarily through text-based chat rooms, discussion posts, and direct emails. Some courses feature video or audio lecture components. Curriculum is highly-structured, with students having fewer electives and choices than they would have in a nonprofit school.

RECRUITING STUDENTS

Unlike nonprofit schools, for-profit schools spend a large part of their budgets recruiting students. In 2009 the education companies that the Senate Committee studied spent $4.2 billion, or nearly 23 percent of their revenue, on marketing, advertising, recruiting, and admissions staffing, compared with $3.2 billion, or more than 17 percent of revenue, on instruction. Those same schools employed over 35,000 recruiters, or about one recruiter for every 53 students attending a for-profit college in 2010.

Critics have charged that this intensive recruiting forced recruiters to mislead prospective students with regard to the cost of the program, the availability of federal aid, the time to complete the program, the completion rates of other students, the job placement rate of other students, the transferability of credits, or the reputation and accreditation of the school. A 2011 Government Accountability Office (GAO) undercover recording project, along with internal documents, confirmed these practices were being used. Before a ban on incentive compensation was put in place in 2011, recruiters' salaries at many for-profit schools were directly tied to enrolling a certain number of new students.

For-profit schools gather contact information of prospective students by paying third-party companies known as "lead generators" that specialize in gathering and selling information. Lead generators advertise themselves as a free and reliable way to get information about college, but lead generator websites generally direct students only to schools that pay them. Some of these lead generators have a history of engaging in online marketing using aggressive and misleading methods. Many for-profit schools and lead generators have targeted servicemembers, veterans, spouses and family members because of their eligibility for military benefits.

COSTS

Most for-profit colleges charge higher tuition than comparable programs at community colleges and state public universities. For-profit bachelor's degree programs average 20 percent more than the cost of a similar program at public universities. Associate degrees average more than four times the cost of degree programs at comparable community colleges, while certificate programs average four and a half times the cost at community colleges. For-profit schools rarely set tuition below available federal student aid.

Most students use federal direct loans and Pell grants to finance their for-profit school education. Under a federal law, for-profit schools may receive 90 percent of their revenue from federal education aid. In the 2009 academic year for-profit schools received $32 billion, 25 percent of the total federal student aid program funds. Pell grants increased at twice the rate of the program as a whole. The 2012 Senate Committee report estimated that in 2009, when all sources of federal funds, including military and veterans' benefits, were included, the 15 publicly traded for-profit education companies received 86 percent of their revenues from federal funds.

OUTCOMES

Community colleges and two-year for-profit programs both have low student retention rates. Half their students drop out within a year. However, nearly all students attending a for-profit college take out loans to attend, compared with just 13 percent of community-college students. Critics of for-profit schools contend the schools must spend more on instruction and support services to increase the success rate.

For those students who complete programs to be security guards, medical assistants and law enforcement officers, the income they earn may not be enough to pay off their student loans. Federal law places an important check on for-profit schools by setting a percentage of students who may **default** on federal student loans before the school loses eligibility for federal student aid. In 2012, the Department of Education issued new regulations that

raise the percentage of defaults at 35 percent for students in security guard, medical assistant, and law enforcement programs. Under the new regulation, which does not go into effect until 2015, programs will remain eligible for federal aid if they meet at least one of three tests in a given year: at least 35 percent of former students are repaying their loan balance; yearly educational-debt payments of typical graduates account for a maximum of 12 percent of their total income; and those payments account for no more than 30 percent of their discretionary income. Programs would have to fail all three tests in the same year for three out of four years before losing aid eligibility. More than 190 programs at 93 colleges failed all three measures in 2012.

ADDITIONAL RESOURCES

Christensen, Clayton, and Henry Eyring. *The Innovative University: Changing the DNA of Higher Education from the Inside Out.* San Francisco: Jossey-Bass, 2011.

Hentschket, Guilbert, et al, eds. *For-Profit Colleges and Universities: Their Markets, Regulation, Performance, and Place in Higher Education.* Sterling, VA: Stylus Publishing, 2010.

ORGANIZATIONS

U.S. Department of Education

400 Maryland Ave., SW
Washington, DC 20202
Toll Free: (800) 872-5327
URL: http://www.ed.gov

EDUCATION

HOMESCHOOLING

Sections within this essay:

- Background
- Homeschooling Laws by State
- Additional Resources

BACKGROUND

According to U.S. Department of Education estimates, more than 1.5 million students were homeschooled in the United States in 2007. These students comprised 2.9 percent of the school-age population in Kindergarten through grade 12, compared to approximately 1.1 million students (2.2 percent of the school-age population) in 2003. The Home School Legal Defense Association believes the number of students homeschooled is significantly higher; the organization estimates that in 2011-12, about 2 million students were homeschooled.

In 2007, the most common reason parents gave for homeschooling was a desire to provide religious or moral instruction (36 percent of students). This reason was followed by a concern about the school environment (such as safety, drugs, or negative peer pressure) (21 percent), dissatisfaction with academic instruction (17 percent), and "other reasons" including family time, finances, travel, and distance (14 percent). Parents of about 7 percent of homeschooled students cited the desire to provide their child with a nontraditional approach to education as the most important reason for homeschooling, and the parents of another 6 percent of students cited a child's health problems or special needs.

Prior to 1980, states generally either expressly prohibited homeschooling, or they did not address the issue. By 2012, all states permit homeschooling. Some states specifically permit homeschool students to enroll in public school classes or extracurricular activities. In other states without such statutes, when challenged by homeschooling parents, courts have found that a student does not have a right to participate. Oftentimes, state rules concerning sports or other competitive interscholastic activities preclude participation by students who are not full time.

States vary on how they approach enforcing the **statutory** restrictions on homeschooling. In some jurisdictions, home instructors bear the burden to show they are complying with the law. In other states, the state bears the burden to show that a homeschool does not meet legal requirements. Some states have not addressed the issue.

The **No Child Left Behind Act of 2001** does not apply to homeschooled students. However, according to the Individuals with Disabilities Education Act, children with disabilities are entitled to a "free, appropriate public education." This entitlement applies to homeschooled children as well, and means that a homeschooled child with a **disability** is entitled to special education and related services at public expense with public supervision and direction. The services must be provided in conformity with a child's individual education plan.

Homeschool statutes and regulations typically fall into four categories:

- Instructor qualification requirements: A handful of states require home instructors to possess a teaching certification or a bachelor's degree. Some other states have a general requirement that parents be qualified to teach.

- Pupil assessment requirements: More than half the states require homeschooled pupils to be tested or assessed for academic progress.

- Visitation requirements: Some jurisdictions require that homeschools allow visits and observation by state education officials.

- Instruction requirements: Depending upon the **jurisdiction**, homeschools may be required to provide instruction that is "substantially equivalent" or "comparable" to public school programming. Certain subjects may be required.

HOMESCHOOLING LAWS BY STATE

ALABAMA: Alabama does not have any laws that specifically address homeschooling. Parents may opt to enroll children under the church school option, which does not require teacher certification. Church schools have little regulation, other than some requirements to report attendance. Under the private tutor option, teachers must be certified. The tutor must teach for at least three hours a day for 140 days each calendar year, and must file with the proper authorities a report describing subjects taught and periods of instruction.

ALASKA: Alaska exempts children from compulsory attendance when they are educated in their home by a parent or legal **guardian**. There are no prescribed teacher qualifications, nor any requirements to assess or file any information. The state has the burden to show that the child is not receiving proper instruction.

ARIZONA: Within 30 days after homeschooling begins, the parent or guardian is required to file an **affidavit** of intent to homeschool. The affidavit is filed with the county school superintendent. The state does not prescribe any teacher certification requirements for homeschool instructors, nor are there any requirements for assessment or standardized testing. Required subjects are reading, grammar, math, social studies and science.

ARKANSAS: Parents are required to notify the local public school superintendent of the intent to homeschool, and provide information on the curriculum, the schedule, and the qualification of the parent/teacher. There are no subjects specifically required for instruction. Most students are required to take achievement tests selected by the state board of education. Refusing to participate in testing may result in a prosecution for truancy.

CALIFORNIA: The state does not have a specific homeschooling **statute**. Several options are available. First, the homeschool may qualify as a private school if, among other requirements, the teacher is "capable of teaching" and instruction is in English. As a variation, students may enroll in a private school satellite program and receive independent study from that school. Another option is instruction provided by a certified private tutor. Finally, students may enroll in an independent study program at home, through a public school.

COLORADO: Statute provides that homeschooling programs "shall be subject only to minimum state controls." Instruction must be by a parent, guardian, or adult relative designated by the parents, but teacher certification is not required. Parents must give notice that they are homeschooling, keep certain records, and submit students for testing or evaluation per state requirements.

CONNECTICUT: Although no statutes address homeschooling, Connecticut State Department of Education regulations permit it when the instruction is "equivalent" to public school instruction. Teacher certification and testing are not required, although a portfolio review with school authorities is used to determine whether instruction in required courses has been provided. Required courses are reading, writing, spelling, English, grammar, geography, arithmetic, United States history, and citizenship. Parents must file a notice of intent to homeschool.

DELAWARE: There are three options provided by statute: single-family homeschool, multiple family homeschool, and single-family homeschool coordinated with the local school district. Attendance and enrollment must be reported. There are no requirements for teacher qualifications or testing.

DISTRICT OF COLUMBIA: Homeschooling falls under laws regarding "private instruction." There are no requirements for teacher certification or student testing. No specific subjects must be taught.

FLORIDA: Florida has a notification requirement in its homeschool law. The state also requires that instructors maintain a portfolio containing specified information. The portfolio must be preserved for two years and be available for inspection, although there is no requirement that authorities actually inspect it. Parents are not required to be certified. However, where the private tutor law is used, instructors must be certified. There is also a statutory provision describing how multiple homeschools may operate as a private school. Students must be tested or evaluated annually only where the homeschool is operated by the parent or guardian.

GEORGIA: Parents must file a declaration of intent. Instruction must include, but may not be limited to, reading, language arts, math, social studies, and science. The school day is four and one-half hours. Parents must write an annual progress report, and retain it for three years. The parent must have at least a high school diploma or GED equivalency, and students must submit to a national standardized achievement test every three years, beginning in third grade.

HAWAII: Parents must provide a notice of intent to homeschool and keep a record of planned curriculum. There are no certification requirements. Students must take a standardized achievement test of the parent's choice in grades 3, 5, 8, and 10. Parents must submit an annual progress report.

IDAHO: Students are exempt from compulsory attendance if they are "comparably" instructed to those in public schools. There are no teacher certification requirements, nor are assessment tests mandated.

ILLINOIS: A homeschool is considered to be a private school. A statute provides that children in a private school are in compliance with the compulsory attendance law where they are instructed in English and where the instruction corresponds to that given to children of a corresponding age and grade in public school. Teacher qualifications and standardized testing are not prescribed.

INDIANA: Children may attend an alternative form of "equivalent" instruction when it is conducted in English. Teachers need not be certified; testing is not required. Parents must maintain attendance records.

IOWA: Parents must submit an annual private instruction report. For students age eight and older, instruction must be by or under the supervision of a certified teacher, or alternatively, instruction must be provided which results in "adequate progress" for the student. For students not under the auspices of a certified teacher, yearly assessments are required. Several options are available to satisfy the assessment requirement.

KANSAS: Homeschools may register as a non-accredited private school, for which there are no required subjects of instruction. The teacher must be "competent"; there is no testing requirement.

KENTUCKY: Although there is no specific statute on homeschooling, students may be homeschooled by following laws for private, parochial, or church regular day schools. Standardized testing is not required. Teacher certification is not required. Enrollment reports must be made to the local school board.

LOUISIANA: Homeschool students are exempt from compulsory attendance requirements if a parent applies and receives approval for a program that offers a "sustained curriculum of quality at least equal to that offered by public schools." The state also provides for home-based private schools. Standardized tests are required under the first option, but there are no requirements regarding teacher certification.

MAINE: The state has a homeschool statute, and has an option for non-approved private schools. Under the first option, there are no specified teacher requirements, but students must submit to an annual assessment. Under the private school option, teacher competence is subject to approval, but students do not need to submit to assessment.

MARYLAND: Three options are available to exempt a student from compulsory attendance laws. The "church umbrella option" provides instruction under the supervision of a bona-fide church organization. Students may also be homeschooled under a state approved "non-public school umbrella." The "portfolio option" requires supervision by a public school superintendent. None of the options requires teacher certification or testing.

MASSACHUSETTS: Students are excused from compulsory attendance laws if they are being instructed in a manner that has been approved in advance by the superintendent or the school committee. Required subjects are reading, writing, English language and grammar, geography, arithmetic, drawing, music, history and constitution of United States, citizenship, health, physical education, and good behavior. There are no teacher certification requirements. Students must take standardized tests or submit to an approved, alternative form of assessment.

MICHIGAN: A child may be educated at home by a parent or legal guardian in reading, spelling, mathematics, science, history, civics, literature, writing, and English grammar. Parents are not required to notify the state, and the burden is on the state to show that a child is not receiving an adequate education. The teacher certification requirement was held to be unconstitutional by the Michigan Supreme Court.

The state also has a nonpublic school option, which does require certified instructors.

MINNESOTA: Parents may qualify to teach their children in one of six ways, including certification, working under the direct supervision of a qualified instructor, or by holding a baccalaureate degree. Students must take achievement tests, but the results do not need to be submitted to the school district. Required topics are reading, writing, literature, fine arts, math, science, history, geography, government, health, and physical education. Parents must either submit to an on-site visit or provide documentation to show compliance with education laws.

MISSISSIPPI: Parents must file a certificate of enrollment. The child must be enrolled in a "legitimate home instruction program." There are no teacher certification requirements and no provision for mandatory testing or assessment.

MISSOURI: Homeschools must maintain specific records, although there is no requirement to submit them. There are no mandatory testing or teacher certification requirements. Students must have 1,000 hours of instruction, including a minimum 600 hours in reading, math, social studies, language arts, and science. At least 400 hours must be in the homeschool location.

MONTANA: 720 hours of instruction are required for grades 1-3, and 1,080 for grades 4-12. Homeschools must provide the same basic instructional program as public schools. Parents must notify authorities of the intent to homeschool. There are no mandatory testing or teacher certification requirements.

NORTH CAROLINA: Annual standardized testing is required for English, grammar, reading, spelling, and math. The school must operate for a nine-month period of instruction. Parents must possess a high school diploma or GED. Parents must keep certain records and must provide a notice of intent to homeschool.

NORTH DAKOTA: A certified teacher must administer standardized tests to students in grades 4, 6, 8, and 10. Parents who are not certified teachers may fulfill teacher requirements in other ways, including possession of a baccalaureate degree, and supervision by a certified teacher for those who possess a high school diploma or GED. Parents must file an annual notice of intent to homeschool and must maintain annual reports.

NEBRASKA: Homeschools operate under private school laws. Parents must affirm under oath that instruction in language arts, mathematics, science, social studies, and health are being provided to the child. There are no mandatory testing or teacher certification requirements. Elementary students must have 1,032 hours of instruction; high school students must have 1,080 hours.

NEVADA: English, science, math, and social studies are required subjects. Parents must provide **evidence** that they are providing "equivalent instruction of the kind and amount" as public schools. Parents must provide annual notification of homeschooling status. There are no mandatory testing or teacher certification requirements.

NEW HAMPSHIRE: Parents must provide notification of homeschooling. They must also maintain a portfolio of records and materials used. There are no teacher certification requirements. A number of choices exist to satisfy testing and assessment requirements.

NEW JERSEY: There are no specific statutes addressing homeschooling. Students may be homeschooled under a law that provides for instruction for "equivalent" education elsewhere than a public school. There are no mandatory testing or teacher certification requirements.

NEW MEXICO: The law contains a notification requirement, and parents must possess a high school diploma or a GED. There is no requirement of mandatory testing. Instruction must include reading, language arts, mathematics, social studies, and science.

NEW YORK: The law specifies numerous required subjects that vary depending upon grade level. Instruction must be "at least substantially equivalent" to public school instruction. Parents must provide notice of homeschooling, file individualized instruction plans, and file other required reports in a timely manner. Teachers must be "competent." Most students are required to take one of five approved standardized tests at specified intervals. The student must achieve a composite score above the thirty-third percentile.

OHIO: The homeschool law requires instruction in language arts, geography, U.S. and Ohio history, government, math, health, physical education, fine arts, first aid, and science. Parents must provide annual notification of homeschooling, which includes an outline of the intended curriculum. Teacher requirement can be satisfied several ways, including working under the direction of someone with a baccalaureate degree. Parents have three options to satisfy standardized testing requirements. Ohio law also provides for non-chartered schools for parents who object to government-controlled education because of "truly held religious beliefs." Different requirements apply to these schools, including a **waiver** of the testing requirement.

OKLAHOMA: The state has a constitutional provision which appears to guarantee the right to homeschool, but no specific statutes on the subject. There are no mandatory testing or teacher certification requirements.

OREGON: The parent or legal guardian must provide initial notification to the school district, but need not file annually. Teacher qualifications are not prescribed. Students must be assessed in grades 3, 5, 8, and 10; more testing or oversight over the homeschool may be required when students perform below specified limits. Children with disabilities will be assessed according to the individualized education plan (IEP).

PENNSYLVANIA: Parents must provide an affidavit initially and annually thereafter; the affidavit must include information on the courses taught, assurances that instruction will be in English, and certification that none of the adults in the home have been convicted of certain criminal offenses within the last five years. Parents must annually provide a portfolio for review, which includes an annual review by qualified personnel who will determine whether the child's education is appropriate. The program for a special needs child must meet special approval requirements. Parents must have a high school diploma or equivalent, and standardized testing must be done and reported for students in grades 3, 5, and 8. Other statutes provide alternatives, including instruction by a private tutor (who must be certified to teach in the state), and teaching in the home as an extension of a religious day school. The state has mandated an extensive list of required subjects, which vary with grade level.

RHODE ISLAND: Rhode Island requires attendance that is "substantially equal" to public schools. Required subjects include reading, writing, geography, math, U.S. and Rhode Island history and principles of government, English, and physical education. Instruction must be "thorough and efficient." Teacher qualifications are unspecified. There is no statutory requirement of standardized testing.

SOUTH CAROLINA: Statutes in this state delineate three different homeschooling options. First, parents may teach at home with an approved program of instruction. School must run for four and one-half hours per day for 180 days. Parents must have at least a high school diploma

or GED, and students must be assessed annually. Second, parents may become members of the South Carolina Association of Independent Home Schools and comply with the association's standards. Finally, parents may join an association of homeschools with no fewer than 50 members. Students in the latter two categories are not required to undergo annual testing.

SOUTH DAKOTA: Children are permitted to be homeschooled if the program provides for instruction for an equivalent period of time as the public schools. Required subjects are language arts and mathematics. Parents must apply for permission to homeschool, and students in grades 2, 4, 8, and 11 must take standardized tests. No teacher requirements are prescribed. No person may teach more than 22 students.

TENNESSEE: Three options exist. Parents or legal guardians may homeschool after they notify the local school district. Instruction must be four hours per day. Other options are to associate with a church-related school, or to operate as a satellite of one. Teacher qualifications and testing requirements vary depending upon the option selected.

TEXAS: The state does not have a specific homeschooling statute, but court decisions have established the right for homeschools to operate under private school rules. Required subjects are reading, spelling, grammar, math and good citizenship. There is no requirement of standardized testing. State law specifically prohibits Texas colleges from discriminating against homeschooled applicants.

UTAH: Parents must file an annual affidavit with the local school district. Required subjects are language arts, math, science, social studies, arts, health, and computer literacy. The law does not prescribe teacher qualifications or standardized testing. Parents are responsible for evaluation of instruction.

VERMONT: The law requires instruction in reading, writing, math, citizenship, history, United States and Vermont government, physical education, health, English, American and other literature, science and fine arts. Annual notice is required; notice must include a detailed description of the program of study. Teacher requirements are not specified, but students must be evaluated annually. Several options exist to satisfy the evaluation requirement.

VIRGINIA: This state has four statutory options for homeschoolers. First is the typical homeschool statute, which requires notice to the district. Parents must set forth the program of instruction and teach language arts and math. Parents may qualify as teachers in one of four ways. The second option is for students and parents who are conscientiously opposed to attendance at school due to a bona fide religious belief. These students are exempt from the requirements in the homeschool statute. Third, the state has a certified tutor statute. Fourth, groups of homeschooling families may band together to become a private school. These schools are not regulated. Only students under the first option must submit to an annual standardized test or assessment.

WASHINGTON: Students may obtain their education either under the homeschool statute or operate as an extension of a private school. Under the first option, parents must provide equivalent hours of instruction as public schools. Planned and supervised instruction must include occupational education, science, math, language, social studies, history, health, reading, writing, spelling, and art and music appreciation. Teacher qualification requirements can be satisfied in a number of ways. Standardized tests on an annual basis are required, but need not be submitted to the school district. Under the second option, parents must be supervised by a certified teacher who evaluates the student's progress.

WEST VIRGINIA: This state provides for homeschooling either under an "approval" or "notice" method. The approval method must be approved by the board and is for a term equal to that of the school district. Under the notice option, parents submit evidence that they possess a high school diploma or its equivalent, and provide an outline of the program of instruction. No testing is required under the first option; testing and evaluation under the latter option may be fulfilled in several ways.

WISCONSIN: A homeschool program must include at least 875 hours of instruction. Instruction must provide a "sequentially progressive curriculum of fundamental instruction" in reading, language arts, math, social studies, science, and health. Parents must provide

information annually to show compliance. Standardized tests are not required, and no teacher qualifications are specified.

WYOMING: Parents must annually submit a curriculum plan to the school board. This program must provide a "sequentially progressive curriculum" in reading, writing, math, civics, history, literature, and science. The law does not delineate teacher requirements or call for standardized testing.

ADDITIONAL RESOURCES

Aquila, Frank. *School Law for K-12 Educators.* Thousand Oaks, CA: Sage Publications, 2007.

Gathercole, Rachel. *The Well-Adjusted Child: The Social Benefits of Homeschooling.* Toronto: Mapletree Pub. Co., 2007.

National Center for Education Statistics. "Fast Facts: Homeschooling." U.S. Department of Education. Available at http://nces.ed.gov/fastfacts/display.asp?id=91 (accessed November 2, 2012).

Ray, Brian D. *Home Schooling on the Threshold: A Survey of Research at the Dawn of the New Millennium.* Salem, OR: National Home Education Institute, 1999.

ORGANIZATIONS

Home School Legal Defense Association
Purcellville, VA 20134
Phone: (540) 338-5600
URL: http://www.hslda.org/

National Home Education Network
PO Box 1652
Hobe Sound, FL 33475-1652
Fax: (413) 581-1463
URL: http://www.nhen.org/

U.S. Department of Education
400 Maryland Ave. SW
Washington, DC 20202
Toll Free: (800) 872-5327
URL: http://www.ed.gov/

EDUCATION

NO CHILD LEFT BEHIND ACT OF 2001

Sections within this essay:

- Background
- Provisions of No Child Left Behind
  - Title I
  - Adequate Yearly Progress
  - Failure to Meet AYP Goals
  - Title II: Teacher Accountability
  - Sex Education and School Prayer
  - School Safety and Drug Use

- Criticism of No Child Left Behind
  - Education as Domain of the States; NCLBA as an Unfunded Federal Mandate
  - Emphasis on Standardized Testing

- The Future of NCLBA
- Additional Resources

BACKGROUND

On January 8, 2002, President George W. Bush signed into law the No Child Left Behind Act of 2001 (NCLBA). This legislation reauthorized, and provided major reform, to the Elementary and Secondary Education Act of 1965 (ESEA).

The Cold War and the Soviet Union's successful launch of the Sputnik spacecraft in October 1957 brought calls for improvements to the nation's educational system. In the early 1960s, President John F. Kennedy developed proposals to ensure that American students were competitive with students around the world. His proposals were intended to guarantee that students of every race, religion, and social standing would receive a good education. After Kennedy's assassination, President Lyndon B. Johnson revised Kennedy's proposals, and oversaw their introduction in Congress. Part of Johnson's "War on Poverty," ESEA was the most expansive federal education legislation ever passed. The bill passed with little debate and in only three months' time.

ESEA provided federal funding for 90 percent of the nation's public and parochial schools. Title 1, the law's most important provision, provides guidelines for the education of "educationally disadvantaged" students. It also provides funds: more than 80 percent of the original **appropriation** under ESEA went to ESEA. In 2012, over $14 billion was appropriated for Title 1. According to the Department of Education, 13 million students in public and private schools are served through Title I.

Part of ESEA's legacy has been controversy. Prior to ESEA, educational policy decisions had been almost exclusively in the hands of state and local governments. Critics have charged that the federal government has become too involved in regulating educational matters better left to local school districts. The federal government now provides approximately seven percent of the total funding for elementary and secondary schools.

Critics of ESEA also charged that Title 1 had done little to raise student performance, because it did not mandate accountability for academic results. No Child Left Behind was crafted to address that issue. According to Congress, the two goals of NCLBA are accountability for schools and teachers, and closing the achievement gap for students of lower socioeconomic backgrounds, "so that no child is left behind." No Child Left Behind's lofty and worthy goals brought it broad bipartisan support in Congress, but its implementation has engendered considerable controversy.

PROVISIONS OF NO CHILD LEFT BEHIND

No Child Left Behind is comprised of hundreds of pages of text. The law is divided into ten sections, called titles. The titles are:

- Title I: Improving Academic Achievement of the Disadvantaged
- Title II: Preparing, Training, and Recruiting High-Quality Teachers and Principals
- Title III: Language Instruction for Limited English Proficient and Immigrant Students
- Title IV: Twenty-first Century Schools
- Title V: Promoting Parental Choice and Innovative Programs
- Title VI: Flexibility and Accountability
- Title VII: Indian, Native Hawaiian, and Alaska Native Education
- Title VIII: Impact Aid Program
- Title IX: General Provisions
- Title X: Repeals, Redesignations, and Amendments to Other Statutes

Title I Title 1 of NCLBA amends and expands Title I of ESEA and has as its purpose "to ensure that all children have a fair, equal, and significant opportunity to obtain a high-quality education and reach, at a minimum, proficiency on challenging State academic achievement standards and state academic assessments." More specifically, Title I encompasses the following goals and methods:

- Using high-quality academic assessments and other methods to measure progress against common expectations for student academic achievement
- Closing the achievement gap between high- and low-performing children, especially the gaps between minority and nonminority students, and between disadvantaged children and their more advantaged peers
- Meeting the needs of children in need of reading assistance, including minority students, English-language learner students, students with disabilities, and poor students
- Careful distribution and targeting of resources
- Holding schools, local educational agencies, and states accountable for improving the academic achievement of all students
- Improving and strengthening accountability, teaching, and learning by using state assessment systems

Adequate Yearly Progress No Child Left Behind requires that schools demonstrate that each student is on grade level, in key areas such as math and reading, by 2014. Schools that cannot demonstrate this proficiency stand to lose federal funding. States must set goals that will demonstrate schools are making "adequate yearly progress" (AYP) in math and reading on the way to the 2014 deadline. Initially only math and reading/language arts were required to be assessed. However, by the school year 2007-2008, science assessments had to be administered at least once during grades 3-5, grades 6-9, and grades 10-12.

States set their own minimum levels of improvement, which must be measurable in terms of student performance. School districts and schools must achieve these minimum levels within NCLBA time frames. States select a "starting point" based on the performance of its lowest-achieving demographic group or of the lowest-achieving schools in the state (the higher of the two). The state then sets a level that schools must reach after two years to show adequate yearly progress. After that, subsequent thresholds are set for at least every three years. As states raise their target goals over time, increasing numbers of students are expected to meet them. After 12 years, all students in the state are expected to attain the proficient level on state reading and math assessments.

School districts are required to make an annual report to the public. This NCLBA report card describes academic achievement for the district at large, for each individual school, and by grade level. The report cards classify student performance as basic, proficient, or advanced. Moreover, the report cards disaggregate the data by student subgroups according to race, ethnicity, gender, English language proficiency, migrant status, **disability** status and low-income status. All students must be evaluated, and each subgroup must meet the AYP goals or the school as a whole fails. A district's report card also tells which schools have been identified as needing improvement, corrective action, or restructuring.

NCLBA requires states to provide academic achievement awards to recognize schools that close achievement gaps between groups of students or that exceed academic achievement goals. States may also use Title I money for financial rewards for teachers. Schools that have made the greatest gains in closing the achievement gap or in exceeding achievement goals receive the designation of "distinguished schools."

Failure to Meet AYP Goals The consequences of failure to meet AYP, as defined by a state, depend upon how long the school has failed to do so. A Title I school that has not met state goals for two years is called a "School in Need of Improvement" (SINI). SINI designation means that the school will receive extra help to improve its standing. The school must develop a two-year improvement plan, and local education agencies must provide assistance in development and implementation. Students from low-income families are particularly targeted for assistance when a school is designated as needing improvement. These students may receive free tutoring and other homework help. Students from low-income families are also allowed to transfer to other non-SINI public schools in the district. The district must provide transportation for the student. A school that has failed to make adequate yearly progress for three years, in addition to the consequences above, must offer students from low-income families supplemental educational services from a state-approved provider. Supplemental educational services include tutoring and remedial classes.

Drastic changes await schools that do not attain adequate yearly progress in the fourth or fifth years. In the fourth year, in addition to previous remedial actions, a district must implement certain corrective actions to improve the school. Corrective actions include replacing staff and fully implementing a new curriculum. In the fifth year, a school district must implement plans to restructure the school. Options for restructuring include:

- Reopening the school as a charter school

- Replacing all or most of school staff

- Turning over the school operations to the state or to a private company with a demonstrated record of effectiveness

Concerns grew year-by-year as more schools were failing to make adequate yearly progress. By 2010, 38 percent of the schools were failing, up from 29 percent in 2006. In 2011, several states had a failure rate of over 50 percent. The law allowed states to set their own annual benchmarks, provided they reached 100 percent proficiency by 2012-13. Some states refused to raise their benchmarks any further or asked the Department of Education for waivers. In 2012, with the encouragement of the department, 32 states and the District of Columbia were granted waivers from the provisions of NCLB.

Title II: Teacher Accountability Teachers are held to an increased accountability standard under NCLBA. The act prohibits teaching with a temporary, **provisional**, or emergency teaching certificate. However, under the law, states are encouraged to find ways of alternative certification to allow talented individuals to teach subjects they know.

Teachers in core academic subjects must be "highly qualified." Core subjects are English, reading or language arts, mathematics, science, foreign languages, civics and government, economics, arts, history and geography. Highly qualified means teachers must have full certification, a bachelor's degree and demonstrated competence in subject

knowledge and teaching. Title II includes grants intended to strengthen teacher quality, and funding for other teacher quality-related programs. Under Title II, states and individual schools are required to document that they are complying with the highly qualified teacher requirements.

Sex Education and School Prayer Under NCLBA, schools must emphasize abstinence, and may not use federal funds for programs to distribute condoms or other contraceptives in the school. School districts must certify each year that their policies do not prevent or deny participation in constitutionally protected prayer in elementary and secondary schools.

School Safety and Drug Use NCLBA provides funds to states to award to school districts for drug- and violence-prevention programs. These programs must address specific local needs and involve parents. Under Title IV, states are required to establish a uniform management and reporting system to collect information on school safety and drug use. Reporting must include anonymous student and teacher surveys and incident reports prepared by school officials. Students have the option to change schools under certain circumstances when school safety is an issue. Students are eligible for school choice when they attend a "persistently dangerous school," as defined by state law. Any child who has been the victim of a violent crime on the grounds of his or her school is also eligible for school choice.

CRITICISM OF NO CHILD LEFT BEHIND

Numerous groups oppose No Child Left Behind. Criticism of NCLBA typically falls into three different categories. First, as with ESEA, critics charge that NCLBA causes the federal government to intrude too much into what has traditionally been the domain of the states. Second, opponents contend that NCLBA has resulted in unfunded federal mandates, which essentially pass financial problems from the federal government to state and local governments. Finally, detractors **allege** that the law places too much emphasis on standardized testing and stringent teacher qualifications.

Speaking on behalf of its 2.7 million members, the National Education Association (NEA) is an outspoken opponent of the law. The NEA argues that NCLBA requires stringent accountability, but does not provide adequate funding necessary for schools to meet those requirements. The NEA also claims that NCLBA punishes schools rather than providing assistance, and that it promotes privatization of education.

Education as Domain of the States; NCLBA as an Unfunded Federal Mandate The United States Constitution strikes a balance between powers reserved for the federal government, and those given to the states. The Tenth Amendment provides, "The powers not delegated to the United States by the Constitution, nor prohibited by it to the States, are reserved to the States respectively, or to the people." The Supreme Court has established in rulings that the Constitution does not implicitly or explicitly delegate education matters to the federal government. In fact, in the landmark *Brown v. Board of Education* case from 1954, the Supreme Court recognized, "Education is perhaps the most important function of state and local governments." Nevertheless, the federal government has often involved itself in education policies without running afoul of the Constitution.

Congress is able to enact legislation over education because of another constitutional provision, the spending clause in Art. I, sec. 8, clause 1: "The Congress shall have Power To lay and collect Taxes, Duties, Imposts and Excises, to pay the Debts and provide for the common Defence and general Welfare of the United States." Under the spending clause, if federal funds are merely an inducement to meet certain conditions, the federal government may intrude on an area normally reserved to the states.

The Supreme Court has held that Congress must meet certain requirements where it relies on the spending clause to enact legislation over which it has no specific authority. Such legislation must:

- Not be prohibited by other constitutional provisions
- Be in pursuit of the "general welfare"
- Be related to the federal interest in particular national projects or programs
- Be unambiguous in describing the conditions for the states' receipt of federal funds, to enable states to knowingly decide to participate or not

Critics of NCLBA charge that the law is unclear in describing what states must do to receive federal funds. Critics support this contention by referring to the Department of Education's massive efforts to clarify the act, as evidenced by regulations, guidance documents, and letters and other communication to various state and local officials.

Often related to the criticism that the federal government is interfering with the traditional domain of the states, some critics contend that No Child Left Behind has resulted in billions of dollars of unfunded mandates. Supporters of the law argue that NCLBA does not present an unfunded mandate, because states are not required to adopt the federal program.

Emphasis on Standardized Testing One recurring criticism of No Child Left Behind is that it forces teachers to "teach to the test" in order to get students to pass standardized tests. These critics say that a consequence of

teaching to the test is that teacher creativity and student learning are stifled. Moreover, critics charge that it is unrealistic to expect learning disabled students and non-English speaking students to pass the test. Another criticism related to testing is that the law often leads to anomalous results. For example, in 2009, Georgia and neighboring South Carolina had nearly identical scores on a national reading test for fourth graders (around 26 percent proficiency). However, the results were dramatically different on their state tests. South Carolina's fourth-graders had a 36 percent proficiency rating in reading, while Georgia's was 87 percent.

THE FUTURE OF NCLBA

The law has been up for reauthorization since 2007. In 2010, President Barack Obama proposed major changes to NCLBA. The changes included calls for college- and career-ready standards, more great teachers and principals, robust use of data, and a more flexible and targeted accountability system based on measuring annual student growth. However, the evaluation of teachers' performance would be measured in part by student test scores. As of mid-2012, Congress was still debating how to update the law.

ADDITIONAL RESOURCES

Ravitch, Diane. *The Death and Life of the Great American School System: How Testing and Choice Are Undermining Education.* New York: Basic Books, 2011.

Yudof, Mark G., David L. Kirp, Betsy Levin, and Rachel F. Moran. *Educational Policy and the Law.* 5th ed. Belmont, CA: Wadsworth Group, 2011.

ORGANIZATIONS

National Education Association (NEA)
1201 16th Street, NW
Washington, DC 20036-3290
Phone: (202) 833-4000
Fax: (202) 822-7974
URL: http://www.nea.org

National School Boards Association (NSBA)
1680 Duke Street
Alexandria, VA 22314
Phone: (703) 838-6722
Fax: (703) 683-7590
Email: goacinfo@nsba.org

U.S. Department of Education
400 Maryland Ave., SW
Washington, DC 20202
Toll Free: (800) 872-5327
URL: http://www.ed.gov

EDUCATION

SCHOOL PRAYER/PLEDGE OF ALLEGIANCE

Sections within this essay:

- Background
- School Prayer
  - Constitutional Basis for Ban
  - Types of Prayer Banned
  - Permissible Private Prayer and Secular Study of Religion
  - Permissible "Minute of Silence"
  - Congressional Action
- Limits on Pledge of Allegiance
- State and Local Laws
- Additional Resources

BACKGROUND

Prayer and the Pledge of Allegiance in public schools remain controversial legal issues. Since the mid-twentieth century, the federal courts have placed limits upon state power to require or even permit these popular cultural practices. Two landmark Supreme Court decisions in the 1960s banned prayer in public school, and subsequent decisions have mostly strengthened the ban. By comparison, the courts generally have held since the 1940s that the Pledge of Allegiance is permissible, provided that it is voluntary. Nonetheless, some individuals have brought lawsuits in the 2000s, arguing that the Pledge violates the Establishment Clause of the First Amendment to the U.S.

Constitution because the Pledge contains the phrase "under God."

Prayer was a common practice in colonial American schools, which were often merely offshoots of a local Protestant church. Along with Bible study, this tradition continued after U.S. independence and flourished well into the nineteenth century. But historical forces changed education. As **immigration** multiplied the ethnic and religious identities of Americans, modernization efforts led by education reformers like Horace Mann gradually minimized religious influences in schools. Although this secular reform swept cities, where diverse populations often disagreed on what religious practice to follow in schools, much of the United States retained school prayer.

As the twentieth century brought legal conflicts, the stage was set for even more far-reaching changes. From 1910 onward, lawsuits challenged mandatory Bible reading in public schools on the ground that students should not be forced to practice a faith other than their own. By the mid-century, social and religious tensions had pushed **litigation** through the federal courts. Subsequently, the Supreme Court ruled repeatedly that school prayer, Bible reading, and related religious practices are violations of the First Amendment. The decisions stand as critical modern mileposts in the contest between federalism and states' rights:

- The Supreme Court first ruled against public school prayer in the 1962 case of *Engle v. Vitale*. The decision struck down a New York State law that required public schools to begin the school day either with Bible reading or recitation of a specially-written, non-denominational prayer.

- One year later, in *District of Abington Township vs. Schempp* (1963), the Supreme Court struck down voluntary Bible readings and recitation of the Lord's Prayer in public schools.

- In 1980, in *Stone v. Graham*, the Supreme Court ruled against a Kentucky law that required the posting of the Ten Commandments in all public school classrooms.

- In 1981, the Supreme Court ruled in *Widmar v. Vincent* that a state university could not prohibit a religious group from using facilities that were made open for use by organizations of all other kinds. Congress responded three years later with the Equal Access Act, guaranteeing religious student groups the same rights of access to school facilities as other student groups.

- In the 1980s and 1990s, some states enacted so-called "moment of silence" or "minute of silence" laws with the intent of allowing students to conduct private prayer or spiritual reflection in the classroom. Although the Supreme Court found an early Alabama law unconstitutional in *Wallace v. Jaffree* (1985), subsequent laws have generally survived legal challenges.

- In 1992, in *Lee v. Weisman*, the Supreme Court ruled that school officials violated the First Amendment by inviting clergy to give an invocation and a benediction at a public high school graduation.

- In *Santa Fe Independent School District v. Doe* (2000), the Supreme Court ruled against a Texas school district policy of facilitating prayers over the public address system at football games and holding popular elections to choose the student selected to deliver the prayer.

The Pledge of Allegiance is one of the nation's most honored secular symbols, viewed by many in the same light as the National Anthem. Written in 1892 by the socialist Francis Bellamy, the Pledge of Allegiance first appeared in a national family magazine, Youths' Companion, and later was modified by Congress and President Dwight D. Eisenhower in 1954 to include a reference to God. Many public schools featured the pledge as part of the school day throughout the mid-twentieth century.

Legal controversy in public schools grew out of a dispute over religious freedom. In the 1930s, West Virginia mandated compulsory saluting of the flag and recitation of the Pledge. After members of Jehovah's Witnesses objected on religious grounds, students were expelled from school. The Supreme Court first upheld the state law but reversed itself three years later in *West Virginia State Board of Education v. Barnette* (1943). The Court held that schools may not coerce or force students into reciting the Pledge, observing the existence of an individual right of conscience to sit silently while others

recited. Most schools responded by making the pledge voluntary.

Contemporary legal challenges to the Pledge have been sporadic, yet they are still passionate and often draw considerable interest from the press. High-profile cases in the late 1990s and 2000s involved lawsuits against schools that instituted mandatory requirements and punished students who did not comply. Interest in the issue intensified again in 2001 following terrorist attacks upon the United States, which prompted states and school districts to revive long-dormant laws requiring students to recite the pledge. The U.S. Supreme Court in 2004 agreed to review a case involving the question of whether the Pledge violates the Constitution, but the Court decided the case on procedural grounds and did not rule on the constitutionality of the Pledge.

SCHOOL PRAYER

Constitutional Basis for Ban Since 1962, the Supreme Court's rejection of school prayer has rested upon its interpretation of the First Amendment. That interpretation has hardly varied, even in the face of public outrage, political opposition, and scholarly criticism. The court's decisions have remained largely consistent across several cases for four decades.

As one of the constitution's most powerful and sweeping guarantees of freedom, the First Amendment is generally thought to contain two contrasting principles with respect to religion. These are announced in the opening words of the amendment, which contains two clauses: "Congress shall make no law respecting an establishment of religion, or prohibiting the free exercise thereof." In constitutional law, the first clause is referred to as the Establishment Clause, and the second as the Free Exercise Clause.

Broadly general in their language, the two clauses say nothing about how to apply them. Thus their practical meaning is chiefly known through the ways courts interpret them in individual cases. Under the Establishment Clause, courts have generally held that government is forbidden to enact laws aiding any religion or creating an official religion. Under the Free Exercise Clause, courts have usually held that government is also forbidden to interfere with an individual's free exercise of religion, including the areas of belief, practice, and propagation.

Both principles require a position of government neutrality toward religion but of a different and seemingly contradictory kind. In practice, the two principles easily overlap. Advocates of school prayer have long argued that banning the practice is a violation of religious freedom guaranteed by the Free Exercise Clause. Opponents have argued that the rights to free exercise are outweighed by the prohibition laid out in the Establishment Clause.

How the tension between these principles is resolved lies at the heart of the school prayer ban.

In school prayer cases, the Supreme Court has repeatedly given the Establishment Clause precedence. From the earliest case, *Engel v. Vitale*, the Court has held that public school prayer is "wholly inconsistent" with the Establishment Clause. The majority opinion went out of its way to stress that the Court did not oppose religion itself. Instead, the opinion stated that "each separate government in this country should stay out of the business of writing or sanctioning official prayers and leave that purely religious function to the people themselves and to those the people choose to look to for religious guidance."

Types of Prayer Banned To date, the Supreme Court has never sanctioned any form of prayer spoken aloud in classrooms under the direction of officials in public schools. In a variety of decisions, it has repeatedly held or affirmed lower court rulings that several types of prayer are unconstitutional:

- Voluntary
- Mandatory
- Sectarian, as in the Lord's Prayer
- Non-sectarian or non-denominational, as in the state-authored prayer at issue in *Engel v. Vitale*
- Teacher or student-led classroom prayer
- Invocations or benedictions

From the start, these decisions have shown no tolerance for attempts to tailor prayers to make them more acceptable to a majority of citizens. In fact, the very first prayer case arose after the State of New York commissioned the writing of an original 22 word prayer that it determined would cover a broad spectrum of religious belief; the prayer was approved by Protestant, Catholic, and Jewish leaders who stated their goal was to avoid causing sectarian disputes. Yet the Supreme Court ruled that the prayer's non-denominational nature gave it no constitutional protection.

On Establishment Clause grounds similar to the prayer ban, the Supreme Court has also struck down related activities and practices involving religious worship in schools:

- Religious invocations at graduation ceremonies
- Prayers read by religious representatives
- Student-led prayers at assemblies and sporting events
- Posting of the Ten Commandments in schools

Permissible Private Prayer and Secular Study of Religion Although the prayer ban has proven largely comprehensive, the Supreme Court has not banned religion from schools. Instead, it has held that context is critical in determining what is permissible and impermissible.

The Supreme Court has never banned students from praying voluntarily and privately on their own, provided there is no state intervention. Students simply must do so without the guidance or **coercion** of school authorities. Religious student groups may meet after school like other student clubs, as guaranteed by the federal Equal Access Act, and pray on their own.

Study of religion is also constitutionally permitted. Even in its earliest prayer cases, the Supreme Court noted that schools were free to discuss religion within the context of a secular course of instruction, such as, for instance, a history course.

Between 1971 and 1990 the Supreme Court used a three-part test to determine whether state programs involving religion were permitted under the Establishment Clause. Following the standard first announced in *Lemon v. Kurtzman* (1971), the Court upheld a challenged religious program if it met all three conditions:

- It has a secular purpose
- It has a primary effect that neither advances nor inhibits religion
- It does not excessively entangle government with religion

This test began losing validity in the 1990s as the Supreme Court refused to apply it. Shifts in the court's analytical approach did not signal a reversal on doctrine, however; in fact, in 1992, the majority upheld its original school prayer ruling of 30 years earlier, and subsequent decisions extended the ban to prayers at public school events. By 2001, the test for compliance with the Establishment Clause generally required that a school policy demonstrate a secular purpose that neither advances nor inhibits religion in its principal effect. Courts continued to carefully scrutinize such policies to see that they did not endorse, show favoritism toward, or promote religious ideas.

Permissible "Minute of Silence" During the 1980s, school prayer advocates were in search of new approaches that might prove constitutional. The so-called moment of silence has proven the most successful strategy, despite an early setback in which Alabama's requirement that school children be required to observe a moment of silence each day was held unconstitutional by the Supreme Court in *Wallace v. Jaffree* (1985).

However, states subsequently crafted laws that did survive constitutional review. One example is Virginia's minute of silence law, which requires children to begin the school day with a minute to "meditate, pray or engage in silent activity." In July 2001, a panel of the 4th U.S.

Circuit Court of Appeals upheld the constitutionality of the law, noting that it "introduced at most a minor and nonintrusive accommodation of religion" and, because it allowed any type of silent reflection, served both religious and secular interests. The U.S. Supreme Court declined to hear an **appeal** in the case, thus upholding Virginia's law. Legal observers predicted the law's success would lead to more such legislation in other states; as many as 18 states already permit moments of silence under law. In 2009 and 2010, federal appeals courts held "minute of silence" laws constitutional in Texas and Illinois.

Congressional Action Responding to public demand for school prayer, federal lawmakers have occasionally sought a remedy of their own. Few advocates of school prayer believe legislation can survive **judicial review**. Thus, the chief proposal to enjoy perennial favor is the idea of a **constitutional amendment**.

Following the first 1962 prayer ruling, lawmakers flooded Congress with such proposals but never passed any. Attempts were revived over the decades, with the most serious coming in the late 1990s. But constitutional amendments face difficult legal hurdles. Even before a proposed amendment can be sent for a state-by-state vote on **ratification**, it must pass by a two-thirds majority in the House of Representatives. Historically, lawmakers are reluctant to tamper with the Constitution. Thus in June 1998, House members voted 224 to 203 in favor of a school prayer amendment, but that simple majority fell far short of the two-thirds majority needed for approval.

Another Congressional effort has borne some success for school prayer advocates. In 1984, with strong backing from conservative religious groups, Congress passed and President Ronald Reagan signed the Equal Access Act. The law requires any federally-funded public secondary school to allow all school clubs, including religious organizations, equal access to facilities. As representatives of the state, teachers and officials are instructed not to encourage or solicit participation in these activities.

LIMITS ON PLEDGE OF ALLEGIANCE

In *West Virginia State Board of Education v. Barnette* (1943), the Supreme Court ruled that requiring the Pledge of Allegiance in public schools violated the First and Fourteenth Amendments. The case grew out of West Virginia's passage of legislation requiring the pledge and flag-saluting. Lawmakers had intended them to be part of instruction on civics, history, and the Constitution, and they defined non-compliance as insubordination that was punishable by expulsion from school. Parents of expelled students were also subject to fines. After Jehovah's Witnesses students were expelled, their parents brought suit contending that the law infringed upon their religious beliefs, which they said required them not to engage in these secular practices.

The Supreme Court found two constitutional violations. The state law violated the Fourteenth Amendment's requirement of due process and the First Amendment's requirements of religious freedom and free speech upon the state. At heart, said the Court, were the principles of freedom of thought and government by consent. Critically, the majority observed a right of individuals to be free from official pressure to state a particular opinion, including that they honor their government. The opinion declared that "no official, high or petty, can prescribe what shall be orthodox in politics, nationalism, religion, or other matters of opinion or force citizens to confess by word or act their faith therein."

In the 1990s, the American Civil Liberties Union (ACLU) repeatedly defended students in school districts who suffered reprisals for failing to participate in the Pledge of Allegiance. In 1998, for instance, the ACLU filed a federal lawsuit against the Fallbrook Union High School District of San Diego, California, after school officials required a dissenting student to stand silently during the pledge, leave the classroom, or face detention; settling the case out of court, the school district agreed to change its policy.

A decision by a three-judge panel of the Ninth Circuit Court of Appeals in 2002 stirred the debate over whether the Pledge violates the Constitution. Michael A. Newdow, an avowed atheist, challenged a policy of the Elk Grove (California) Unified School District that required students to recite the Pledge. According to Newdow, because the Pledge includes the phrase "under God," the school's required recitation amounted to an unconstitutional endorsement of religion. The panel of the Ninth Circuit agreed with Newdow and held that the school district had violated the Constitution. The full panel of the Ninth Circuit allowed the decision to stand, but the school district appealed to the U.S. Supreme Court. In *Elk Grove Unified School District v. Newdow* (2004), the Court reversed the Ninth Circuit, but only because the Court determined that Newdow did not have standing to bring the case. Accordingly, the Court did not rule on the question of whether the Pledge violates the Establishment Clause.

In 2005, Newdow again challenged the constitutionality of the Pledge by bringing suit in a federal district court in California. The court followed the previous decision of the Ninth Circuit and determined that the Pledge indeed violated the Constitution. However, in 2010, the Ninth Circuit Court of Appeals overturned the district court ruling and its own precedent, finding that the Pledge of Allegiance did not violate the Establishment Clause because Congress' "ostensible and predominant purpose was to inspire patriotism and that the context of the Pledge [...] demonstrate[s] that it is a predominantly patriotic exercise." For these reasons, the phrase "one Nation under God" did not turn this patriotic exercise into a religious activity. Later in 2010, the First Circuit Court of Appeals upheld a New Hampshire law that required schools to schedule voluntary recitation of the Pledge of Allegiance.

STATE AND LOCAL LAWS

Despite many Supreme Court rulings against public school prayer, the legal picture in states is far from uniform. In some states and cities, politicians and school officials have simply ignored the Court's prayer decisions. Some school districts continue to allow classroom prayer in the absence of any direct legal challenge. Still others invite litigation, seeing in each lawsuit an opportunity to press the judiciary to reconsider the four-decade-old ban. Thus while federal judicial decisions may say one thing, the practical reality is widely acknowledged to be another; ongoing has been the norm for years, with school prayer lawsuits frequently seeing national legal organizations representing both sides in what originate as local disputes.

The situation for the Pledge of Allegiance in public schools is also mixed. Most states, in fact, still have decades-old laws relating to the pledge. The majority of states mention some form of school participation in their laws, while about 20 states require students to recite it.

ADDITIONAL RESOURCES

Dierenfield, Bruce. *The Battle over School Prayer: How Engel V. Vitale Changed America.* Lawrence, KS: University Press of Kansas, 2007.

Gale Encyclopedia of American Law. 3rd ed. Detroit: Gale, Cengage Learning, 2011.

Greenawalt, Kent. *Does God Belong in Public Schools?* Princeton, NJ: Princeton University Press, 2005.

Long, Emma. *The Church-State Debate: Religion, Education and the Establishment Clause in Post War America.* New York: Continuum, 2012.

Palmer, Kris E., ed. *Constitutional Amendments: 1789 to the Present.* Detroit: Gale, Cengage Learning, 2000.

ORGANIZATIONS

American Civil Liberties Union (ACLU)

125 Broad St., 18th Fl.
New York, NY 10004
Phone: (212) 549-2500
Email: info@aclu.org
URL: http://www.aclu.org/

American Family Association

PO Box 2440
Tupelo, MS 38803
Phone: (662) 844-5036
Fax: (662) 842-7798
URL: http://www.afa.net

Americans United for Separation of Church and State

1301 K St. NW, Ste. 850E
Washington, DC 20005
Phone: (202) 466-3234
Fax: (202) 466-2587
URL: http://www.au.org

EDUCATION

SPECIAL EDUCATION/ DISABILITY ACCESS

Sections within this essay:

- Background
- Individuals with Disabilities Education Act
  - Free and Appropriate Public Education
  - State Educational Agencies
  - Local Educational Agencies
  - Individualized Education Programs
  - Parental Involvement
- Additional Legislation Protecting Children with Disabilities
  - Section 504 of the Rehabilitation Act of 1973
  - Americans with Disabilities Act
- Definition of Disability and Eligibility for Special Education Services
- Placement of Children with Disabilities
- Procedures for Alleging Violations of Statutes Protecting Disabled Children
- State Provisions Regarding Special Education and Disability Access
- Additional Resources

BACKGROUND

Students with mental and physical disabilities in the United States were historically segregated from other students in most educational systems. While special programs were modified to provide different types of training for disabled children, these children were ordinarily separated from the mainstream students, not only to protect the children in special education but also to avoid disruption among other students without disabilities. The majority of disabled children did not attend school at all.

The move toward the recognition of rights for disabled students began with the famous 1954 case, *Brown v. Board of Education*, which established that "separate but equal" accommodations in education were not, in fact, equal. As other **civil rights** movements gained momentum throughout the 1960s, proponents for rights of disabled individuals also began to assert the rights of these individuals. Two landmark federal district court decisions in 1971 and 1972, *PARC v. Pennsylvania* and *Mills v. Board of Education*, established that denying education to children with disabilities and denying the proper procedures in such cases violated protections under the Fourteenth Amendment to the United States Constitution. A number of other cases since then have further established rights of disabled children.

A number of federal statutes have formed the basis for guaranteeing rights of disabled children since the mid-1970s. The following is a summary of these statutes:

- Rehabilitation Act of 1973: This act established that those who receive federal financial assistance cannot discriminate on the basis of a **disability**.
- Education for All Handicapped Children Act (EAHCA): Passed in 1975, this act provided support to state special education programs to provide free appropriate public education to disabled children.
- Perkins Act: Passed in 1984, this act required that ten percent of federal funding for vocational education must support the education of disabled students.

- Handicapped Children's Protection Act of 1986: This act amended the EAHCA to provide attorney's fees and costs to be awarded to parents who prevailed in an EAHCA case.

- Education to the Handicapped Act Amendments of 1986: These acts added early intervention services for three- to five-year-olds, with incentive programs for younger children with disabilities.

- Individuals with Disabilities Education Act (IDEA): Passed in 1990, this act amended the EAHCA by modifying a number of the provisions in the original **statute**. Congress added several amendments to IDEA in 2004.

- Americans with Disabilities Act (ADA): Passed in 1990, this major piece of legislation set forth broad prohibitions against **discrimination** of disabled individuals by most employers, public agencies, and those who provide public accommodations. Two titles in the Act apply specifically to schools. Congress approved several amendments to the ADA in 2008.

INDIVIDUALS WITH DISABILITIES EDUCATION ACT

The Individuals with Disabilities Education Act (IDEA) is primarily a funding statute. It requires that each state educational authority develop a policy that ensures free appropriate public education is being provided to all children with disabilities by local agencies. The amount of funding is determined on a state-by-state basis by the number of disabled children between the ages of 3 and 21 who are receiving special education and/or other related services. At the center of IDEA is a requirement that a local educational agency develop on at least an annual basis an individualized education program for each disabled child. This plan states the current educational status of the child and sets forth goals and objectives for the child to meet. Room for parental consent or involvement is provided at each step in the child's education.

In 2004, Congress amended IDEA by enacting the Individuals with Disabilities Education Improvement Act of 2004. The 2004 Act was designed to bring IDEA into line with the No Child Left Behind Act. These amendments establish financial incentives for states to improve their special education systems. These laws effectively require states to employ qualified teachers and to establish goals for special education students. Moreover, states must establish assessment levels for students with special needs. A state that fails to comply with these requirements can lose federal funding, and parents of students in failing schools have the option to move their children to different schools.

Although the No Child Left Behind Act has been the subject of criticism, it remained the law as of 2012.

Free and Appropriate Public Education IDEA defines free appropriate public education as special education and related services that are provided at public expense, under public supervision and direction. Free appropriate public education must also meet standards set forth by state educational agencies; must include appropriate education at the preschool, elementary, and secondary levels; and must be provided in conformity with individualized education programs required under IDEA.

State Educational Agencies IDEA shifts responsibility for ensuring that educational programs are in compliance with the provisions of IDEA to state education agencies. These agencies are required to promulgate a complaint procedure that provides the following services:

- Receive and resolve complaints against state or local education agencies

- Review appeals from decisions regarding a local education agency complaint

- Conduct independent on-site investigations

- Set forth a 60-day time limit to investigate and resolve complaints

- Allow time extensions only in exceptional circumstances

- Review relevant information and issue written decisions

- Provide an enforcement mechanism

Local Educational Agencies As the primary entity required to develop individualized educational programs for each disabled child in a particular locality, local educational agencies are at the center of the provision of IDEA. Residency of each child is the primary consideration for determining which local educational agency has responsibility for developing these educational programs. In some cases, determining the appropriate local agency can become difficult, particularly if the child's parents live in different districts. Many states have included provisions providing that the child's residency is that of the parent.

Individualized Education Programs Local educational agencies must include a number of components in each individualized education program for each disabled child in its district. Among these components are the following:

- Descriptions of each child's current educational status, which describes the disabled child's cognitive skills, linguistic ability, emotional behavior, social skills and behavior, and physical ability

- Details of "measurable annual goals, including benchmarks or short-term objectives" related to the specific needs of each child, according to the provisions in IDEA

- Description of the instructional setting or placement of each disabled child

- Details of developmental, corrective, and other services designed to facilitate placement in a regular class or designed to allow disabled children to benefit from special education

- Additional specific statements required by IDEA, which relate to each child's progress, needs, advancement, and goal.

Parental Involvement Parents are involved in each stage of the development of a child's individualized education program. Such participation in this process includes the following:

- Parents must approve each stage of the implementation of the individualized education program

- Parents participate in initial meetings and annual meetings reviewing the programs established for their children

- Parents and school districts must sign an individualized education program before each school year begins

- School districts must redevelop a new program for a disabled child at the request of a parent

- Parents are entitled to request a meeting at any time regarding the individualized education program

ADDITIONAL LEGISLATION PROTECTING CHILDREN WITH DISABILITIES

Section 504 of the Rehabilitation Act of 1973 Prior to the enactment of the Americans with Disabilities Act, the statute that provided the most comprehensive rights to disabled children other than IDEA was the Rehabilitation Act of 1973. This act forbids any entity that receives federal financial funding from discriminating on the basis of disability. The act protects all individuals with physical or mental impairments that substantially limit their major life activities. Major life activities under this description include an individual's ability to care for himself or herself, performance of manual tasks, walking, seeing, hearing, speaking, breathing, learning and working. If an entity, such as a school, violates the provisions of the Rehabilitation Act, the Department of Education will investigate. The most likely remedy for these violations is termination of federal financial assistance to the entity.

Americans with Disabilities Act The Americans with Disabilities Act (ADA), passed by Congress in 1990, provides many of the same protections for disabled children as the Rehabilitation Act of 1973. However, unlike the Rehabilitation Act, the prohibitions under the ADA are not limited to those that receive federal financial assistance. The ADA is applicable in other areas as well where the provisions of the Rehabilitation Act may not provide protection. This is particularly true with respect to architectural barriers to a building. Part II of the ADA, which is applicable to public schools, requires accessibility for the entire program. Part III, applicable to private schools, contains similar provisions.

Congress amended the ADA in 2008 primarily to ensure that courts apply its provisions broadly.

DEFINITION OF DISABILITY AND ELIGIBILITY FOR SPECIAL EDUCATION SERVICES

All school districts in the United States are required by law to identify, locate, and evaluate children with disabilities. Once this has occurred, school districts have a duty to evaluate whether the children are eligible for special education and then begin to develop individualized education programs for them. IDEA and the corresponding regulations define "children with disabilities" as those suffering from at least one of the following conditions:

- Mental retardation
- Hearing impairment
- Speech or language impairment
- Visual impairment
- Serious emotional disturbance
- Orthopedic impairment
- Autism
- Traumatic brain injury
- Specific learning disability
- Other health impairments

These disabilities must have adverse effects on disabled children for the children to be eligible for special education and services. The definition of disability and the application of this definition is broader under other statutes. The Americans with Disabilities Act, for example, employs a three-part definition of "disability." For the ADA to apply to an individual, the individual's physical or mental impairment must substantially limit the individual's major life activities. This individual must also have a record of such an impairment and be generally regarded as having such an impairment. Physical impairment can include any physiological disorder or condition, cosmetic disfigurement, or anatomical loss affecting one or more of several major body systems, as defined by the statute. Mental impairment may include any mental or psychological disorder, such as mental retardation, organic brain syndrome, emotional or mental illness, and specific learning disabilities. Since the definition is broader under the ADA, a child with a disability may request accommodation under the ADA, but the same child may not be eligible for special education under the provisions of IDEA.

Like the ADA, the provisions of the Rehabilitation Act of 1973 regarding the definition of disability are broader than those of IDEA. For example, a child with Acquired Immune Deficiency Syndrome may not be eligible for special education under IDEA. However, the same child may not be discriminated against on the basis of his or her disease, since AIDS and other diseases are considered disabilities under the Rehabilitation Act.

PLACEMENT OF CHILDREN WITH DISABILITIES

Placement of children with disabilities under IDEA occurs after the development of an individualized education program, described above. Local agencies must take into account a variety of factors, many of which are described in relevant regulations concerning the implementation of IDEA. Such considerations include the child's performance on aptitude and achievement tests; parental input; recommendations from teachers; the physical condition of the child; the social and cultural background of the child; and the adaptive behavior of the child. If the local agency fails to provide appropriate placement, the child's parent(s) may place the child unilaterally and seek reimbursement from the agency.

Several requirements under IDEA apply to the placement of a child. Although placement should be as close to the child's home as possible, there is no absolute requirement that the school selected is the closest to the child's home. If the closest school would not provide what would be considered free appropriate public education, the agency may select a more suitable school, even if it is farther away. The placement must be in the least restrictive environment, which generally restricts the ability of a school to segregate children with special education needs. Only in cases where the disability is so severe that regular classroom attendance would not be appropriate can complete **segregation** occur. This provision is often referred to as a mainstreaming requirement.

The placement of a child must be reviewed annually. If placement is changed, an existing individualized education program must support it, since placement itself is based on the IEP. Parents must be notified under IDEA requirements, and several states require that parental consent must be obtained before a local agency can make a change in placement for a disabled child.

PROCEDURES FOR ALLEGING VIOLATIONS OF STATUTES PROTECTING DISABLED CHILDREN

Since IDEA is a funding statute, if a local agency fails to provide free appropriate public education to a disabled child, the remedy is that the agency loses its federal funding. Many parents of disabled children, however, seek judicial and other remedies when they feel the education being provided to their child is not sufficient. The initial body required under IDEA and other statutes to hear a complaint is the state education authority, which must hold an **impartial** hearing. Specific procedures that must be followed are set forth in IDEA regulations. Once the state education authority makes its decision, a parent may **appeal** to another state-level agency. Parents should consult their own state's laws to determine which is the appropriate agency for such an appeal.

Judicial bodies, including either a federal or a state court, may review administrative proceedings. Judicial action may not take place until the parties have exhausted each of their administrative remedies. The most typical remedy sought by parents in cases involving special education is injunctive or declaratory relief, although in some cases, monetary damages may be appropriate.

Complaints for **infringement** of the ADA in schools should be filed with the Department of Education. Once administrative remedies have been exhausted, parties may seek **judicial review**. Like the remedies under IDEA, most parents seek injunctive or declaratory relief, such as a court order requiring that a school provide the requested access.

STATE PROVISIONS REGARDING SPECIAL EDUCATION AND DISABILITY ACCESS

Special education and disability access have become controlled primarily by federal **statutory** schemes. This is true even though most educational regulation is governed by state statute. Under IDEA, if a state or local agency fails to provide the minimum provisions required by the statute, the state or local entity may lose federal funding. States may, however, provide greater protection than is afforded by the federal statutes.

Parents with disabled children should consult with the state educational agencies, as well as applicable state laws, to determine what rights their children may have in their particular state. The following is a listing of the appropriate agencies in each state.

ALABAMA: The primary state educational agency is the Special Education Services division of the Alabama State Department of Education.

ALASKA: The primary state educational agency is the Special Education Office of the State Department of Education and Early Development.

ARIZONA: The primary state educational agency is Exceptional Student Services of the Arizona State Department of Education.

ARKANSAS: The primary state educational agency is the Special Education Unit of the Arkansas Department of Education.

CALIFORNIA: The primary state educational agency is the Special Education Division of the California Department of Education.

COLORADO: The primary state educational agency is the Exceptional Student Leadership Unit of the Colorado Department of Education.

CONNECTICUT: The primary state educational agency is the Bureau of Special Education and Pupil Services of the Connecticut Department of Education.

DELAWARE: The primary state educational agency is the Exceptional Children Department of the Delaware Department of Education.

DISTRICT OF COLUMBIA: The primary state educational agency is the Office of Special Education for District of Columbia Public Schools.

FLORIDA: The primary state educational agency is the Education for Exceptional Students Department of the Florida Department of Education.

GEORGIA: The primary state educational agency is the Division of Exceptional Students of the Georgia Department of Education.

HAWAII: The primary state educational agency is the Quality Student Support Branch of the Department of Education.

IDAHO: The primary state educational agency is the Special Education Team within the Idaho State Department of Education.

ILLINOIS: The primary state educational agency is the Special Education Office of the Illinois State Board of Education.

INDIANA: The primary state educational agency is the Division of Exceptional Learners of the Department of Education.

IOWA: The primary state education agency is the Bureau of Student and Family Support Services of the Department of Education.

KANSAS: The primary state educational agency is Special Education Services within the Kansas State Department of Education.

KENTUCKY: The primary state educational agency is the Division of Exceptional Children Services of the Kentucky Department of Education.

LOUISIANA: The primary state educational agency is the Division of Educational Improvement and Assistance of the Louisiana Department of Education.

MAINE: The primary state educational agency is the Office of Special Services of the Maine Department of Education.

MARYLAND: The primary state educational agency is the Division of Special Education of the Maryland State Department of Education.

MASSACHUSETTS: The primary state educational agency is the Special Education Programs division of the Massachusetts State Department of Education.

MICHIGAN: The primary state educational agency is the Office of Special Education and Early Intervention Services.

MINNESOTA: The primary state educational agency is the Office of Special Education of the Minnesota Department of Children, Families, and Learning.

MISSISSIPPI: The primary state educational agency is the Office of Special Education of the Mississippi State Department of Education.

MISSOURI: The primary state educational agency is the Division of Special Education of the Missouri State Department of Education.

MONTANA: The primary state educational agency is the Special Education Division of the Montana Office of Public Instruction.

NEBRASKA: The primary state educational agency is the Office of Special Education of the Nebraska Department of Education.

NEVADA: The primary state educational agency is the Division of Special Education of the Nevada Department of Education.

NEW HAMPSHIRE: The primary state educational agency is the Bureau of Special Education of the New Hampshire Department of Education.

NEW JERSEY: The primary state educational agency is the Office of Specialized Populations of the New Jersey State Department of Education.

NEW MEXICO: The primary state educational agency is the Special Education Bureau of the State of New Mexico Department of Education.

NEW YORK: The primary state educational agency is the Vocational and Educational Services for Individuals with Disabilities of the New York State Education Department.

NORTH CAROLINA: The primary state educational agency is the Exceptional Children Division of the North Carolina Department of Public Instruction.

NORTH DAKOTA: The primary state educational agency is the Office of Special Education of the North Dakota Department of Public Instruction.

OHIO: The primary state educational agency is the Office for Exceptional Children within the Ohio Department of Education.

OKLAHOMA: The primary state educational agency is the Special Education Services Division of the Oklahoma State Department of Education.

OREGON: The primary state educational agency is the Office of Special Education of the Oregon Department of Education.

PENNSYLVANIA: The primary state educational agency is the Bureau of Special Education of the Pennsylvania Department of Education.

RHODE ISLAND: The primary state educational agency is the Office of Diverse Learners of the Rhode Island Department of Education.

SOUTH CAROLINA: The primary state educational agency is the Office of Exceptional Children of the South Carolina Department of Education.

SOUTH DAKOTA: The primary state educational agency is the Office of Special Education of the Division of Education Resources and Services.

TENNESSEE: The primary state educational agency is the Division of Special Education of the Tennessee Department of Education.

TEXAS: The primary state educational agency is the Division of IDEA Coordination of the Texas Education Agency.

UTAH: The primary state educational agency is the Special Education Services division of the Utah State Office of Education.

VERMONT: The primary state educational agency is the Vermont Student Support Services Team.

VIRGINIA: The primary state educational agency is the Division of Special Education and Student Services of the Virginia Department of Education.

WASHINGTON: The primary state educational agency is the Special Education Section of the Office of Superintendent of Public Instruction.

WEST VIRGINIA: The primary state educational agency is the Office of Special Programs of the West Virginia Department of Education.

WISCONSIN: The primary state educational agency is the Special Education Team within the Department of Public Instruction.

WYOMING: The primary state educational agency is the Special Programs Unit of the Wyoming Department of Education.

ADDITIONAL RESOURCES

Dodd, Victoria J. *Practical Education Law for the 21st Century.* Durham, NC: Carolina Academic Press, 2010.

Imber, Michael, and Tyll van Geel. *A Teacher's Guide to Education Law.* 4th ed. New York: Routledge, 2010.

Latham, Peter S. *Special Education Law.* Boston: Pearson/Allyn and Bacon, 2008.

Rothstein, Laura, and Scott F. Johnson. *Special Education Law.* 4th ed. Thousand Oaks, CA: Sage Publications, 2010.

ORGANIZATIONS

Council for Exceptional Children (CEC)

2900 Crystal Drive, Suite 1000
Arlington, VA 22202-3557
Toll Free: (888) 232-7733
URL: http://www.cec.sped.org

National Association of Special Education Teachers

1250 Connecticut Ave, NW, Suite 200
Washington, DC 20036
Toll Free: (800) 754-4421
URL: http://www.naset.org

National Education Association (NEA)

1201 16th St., NW
Washington, DC 20036
Phone: (202) 833-4000
URL: http://www.nea.org

U.S. Department of Education

Department of Education Building
400 Maryland Ave., SW
Washington, DC 20202
Toll Free: (800) 872-5327
URL: http://www.ed.gov

EDUCATION

STUDENT LOANS

Sections within this essay:

- Background
- Federal Direct Loan Program
- Additional Resources

BACKGROUND

The financing of U.S. postsecondary education relies on student loans. In 2010, $100 billion of student loans were taken out and the total amount of outstanding student loans reached $1 trillion. The federal government and private lenders offer student loans, but most students take out federal loans. Federal loans do not cost taxpayers any money, as the **interest rates** generate a profit and student loans are not dischargeable in **bankruptcy**.

The federal government first became involved in 1965, when it began guaranteeing student loans provided by banks and nonprofit lenders. The Federal Family Education Loan (FFEL) program was the only federal student loan program until 1992, when Congress enacted a direct loan program. Under the direct loan program, the federal government loans money to students, eliminating private lenders. It was believed direct lending would be less costly to taxpayers. Congress originally mandated that 60 percent of loans nationwide had to be direct loans, but in 1994 it passed a law that barred the Department of Education from encouraging or requiring colleges to switch to the direct loan program, in the belief that this maximized choice. However, the private lending industry used their substantial resources to recruit or retain colleges and universities for the guaranteed loan program. As a result, direct loan participation declined dramatically.

By 2007, the direct loan program had reached the lowest share of total federal student loans since it began in the 1990s. However, the Great Recession of 2008 reversed this trend as the private credit market tightened up and lenders abandoned the guaranteed loan program. By 2010, direct loans were rising and political leaders debated whether FFEL should continue. Opponents of FFEL believed the subsidies paid to private lenders could be better used to fund direct loans. In 2010, President Barack Obama signed a law that eliminated the FFEL program for all new loans made as of July 1, 2010. All future federal loans will be made under the Direct Loan program. The Congressional Budget Office estimated that ending the FFEL program would generate $68.7 billion in savings over the ten years and help increase funding for federal grants-in-aid to students.

FEDERAL DIRECT LOAN PROGRAM

The federal Direct Loan Program offers low-interest loans for students and parents to help pay for the cost of a student's education after high school. The lender is the U.S. Department of Education, though the loan servicer can be a private business. There are several repayment options under the program. Students and parents apply by filling out the Free Application for Federal Student Aid (FAFSA), an application that collects financial information.

The Direct Loan Program offers four types of loans. Subsidized loans are for students with demonstrated financial need, as determined by federal regulations. No

Average federal loan amount per Full-Time Equivalent (FTE) student in constant 2010 dollars, 1973–74 to 2010–11

Year	Average federal loan amount per FTE
1973–74	$985
1974–75	$925
1975–76	$766
1976–77	$811
1977–78	$925
1978–79	$1,094
1979–80	$1,451
1980–81	$1,849
1981–82	$1,850
1982–83	$1,640
1983–84	$1,807
1984–85	$1,997
1985–86	$1,992
1986–87	$1,988
1987–88	$2,297
1988–89	$2,272
1989–90	$2,130
1990–91	$2,093
1991–92	$2,114
1992–93	$2,165
1993–94	$2,867
1994–95	$3,367
1995–96	$3,682
1996–97	$3,746
1997–98	$3,813
1998–99	$3,850
1999–00	$3,853
2000–01	$3,803
2001–02	$3,863
2002–03	$4,153
2003–04	$4,570
2004–05	$4,776
2005–06	$4,825
2006–07	$4,829
2007–08	$5,156
2008–09	$5,872
2009–10	$6,431
2010–11	$6,368

Note: The figures reported here reflect total student loan amounts divided across all students, including nonrecipients. Loan numbers do not include private nonfederal loans, which provide funding for students but do not involve subsidies.

SOURCE: Trends in Student Aid, 2011. CollegeBoard Advocacy & Policy Center. Available at http://trends.collegeboard.org/student_aid

TABLE BY PREMEDIAGLOBAL. ©2013 CENGAGE LEARNING.

interest is charged while a student is in school at least half time, during the **grace period**, and during deferment periods. Unsubsidized loans are not based on financial need. Interest is charged during all periods, even during the time a student is in school and during grace and deferment periods. PLUS loans are unsubsidized loans for the parents of dependent students and for graduate and professional students. PLUS loans help pay for education expenses up to the cost of attendance minus all other financial assistance. Interest is charged during all periods.

Consolidation loans allow eligible federal student loans to be combined into one direct consolidation loan.

Subsidized direct loans are the most popular program. Dependent undergraduates may borrow up to $31,000 over four years and independent undergraduates may borrow up to $57,500. Post-graduate and professional students may borrow up to $138,500 over the course of their studies. In most cases a school will disburse loan money by crediting it to the student's school account to pay tuition and fees, room and board, and other authorized charges. If the loan disbursement amount exceeds the school's charges, the school will pay the student the remaining balance of the disbursement directly by check or other means.

When a student graduates, drops below half time, or withdraws from an academic program, the student will receive a six month grace period for Direct Subsidized and Unsubsidized Loans. The grace period begins the day after the student stops attending school on at least a half-time basis. Once the grace period ends, the student must begin repaying all student loans. There is no grace period for a Direct PLUS Loan. The repayment period for a PLUS Loan begins on the day after the final loan disbursement is made.

A borrower will have 10 to 25 years to repay student loans, depending on the repayment plan the borrower selected. With the standard plan, the borrower pays a fixed amount each month until the loans are paid in full. Monthly payments will be at least $50, and the loan must be repaid in up to 10 years. The standard plan is a good one if the borrower can handle higher monthly payments because the loan will be repaid more quickly.

Under the extended repayment plan, a borrower must have more than $30,000 in Direct Loan debt and must not have an outstanding balance on a Direct Loan as of October 7, 1998. Under the extended plan the borrower has 25 years for repayment and two payment options: fixed or graduated. Fixed payments are the same amount each month, as with the standard plan, while graduated payments start low and increase every two years. This is a good plan if the borrower needs to make smaller monthly payments, but the borrower will pay more interest.

With the graduated repayment plan, payments start out low and increase every two years. The length of the repayment period will be up to ten years. If the borrower expects income to increase steadily over time, this plan may be a good choice. The monthly payment will never be less than the amount of interest that accrues between payments. Although monthly payments will gradually increase, no single payment under this plan will be more than three times greater than any other payment.

The income contingent plan gives the borrower flexibility to meet Direct Loan obligations without causing undue financial hardship. However, it does not apply to parent PLUS loans. Each year, monthly payments are calculated on the basis of **adjusted gross income** (AGI, plus spouse's income), family size, and the total amount of the Direct Loans. Under this plan the borrower pays each month the lesser of two options: the amount the borrower would pay if the borrower repaid the loan in 12 years multiplied by an income percentage factor that varies with the borrower's annual income, or 20 percent of monthly discretionary income. If the payments are not large enough to cover the interest that has accumulated on the loans, the unpaid amount will be capitalized once each year. However, capitalization will not exceed 10 percent of the original amount owed when the borrower entered repayment. Interest will continue to accumulate but will no longer be capitalized. The maximum repayment period is 25 years. If the loan is not fully repaid after 25 years under this plan, the unpaid portion will be discharged. The borrower may, however, have to pay taxes on the amount that is discharged.

Under the income-based repayment plan, which was introduced in 2007, the required monthly payment will be based on the borrower's income during any period when the borrower has a partial financial hardship. The monthly payment may be adjusted annually. The maximum repayment period under this plan may exceed 10 years. If the borrower meets certain requirements over a specified period of time, the borrower may qualify for cancellation of any outstanding balance of loans. In 2010, Congress enacted an **amendment** that starting in 2014, will forgive student loan debt after 20 years under this plan.

ADDITIONAL RESOURCES

Gobel, Reyna. *Graduation Debt: How to Manage Student Loans and Live Your Life*. Indianapolis, IN: Cliff's Notes, 2010.

ORGANIZATIONS

U.S. Department of Education

400 Maryland Ave., SW
Washington, DC 20202
Toll Free: (800) 872-5327
URL: http://www.ed.gov

EDUCATION

STUDENT RIGHTS/FREE SPEECH

Sections within this essay:

- Background
- Free Speech Rights in Public Schools
  - *West Virginia State Board of Education v. Barnette*
  - *Tinker v. Des Moines Independent Community School District*
  - *Bethel School District No. 403 v. Fraser*
  - *Hazelwood School District v. Kuhlmeier*
  - Elementary and Secondary Student Rights Since *Hazelwood*

- Higher Education Free Speech Issues
  - Recognizing Student Groups
  - Mandatory Student Fees
  - Hate Speech Codes

- Additional Resources

BACKGROUND

When the U.S. Supreme Court decided its first free speech case involving students and the public schools, the idea that students had any right to free speech would have been considered laughable at best, dangerous at worst. At that time, school was considered a privilege to attend, and rules or regulations the school sought to enforce were untouchable. This generalization was collectively true at the elementary, secondary and college levels of education.

Student rights to free speech did not really become an issue until the Vietnam War, when more and more students found themselves at opposite ends of the political spectrum from their teachers and school administrators. The Supreme Court's 1969 decision in *Tinker v. Des Moines Independent Community School District* opened the floodgates to school free speech **litigation**, and while court decisions have certainly gone back and forth between the right to free speech and the need to impose discipline and respect the feelings of all students, there has never been any attempt to go back to the strict free speech restrictions of the pre-Vietnam War era.

Public school free speech rights for students can be divided into those applying to elementary and secondary students and those dealing with college issues. Since college students are adults, the First Amendment situations dealt with are substantially different. Analyzing student free speech rights in this way can give a cohesive picture of those rights for students today.

FREE SPEECH RIGHTS IN PUBLIC SCHOOLS

Free speech rights in public elementary and secondary schools have undergone a remarkable transformation in the past 40 years, from nonexistence to a perpetual tension between those rights and the need for schools to control student behavior in order to preserve the sanctity of the learning environment. Today, it would be most accurate to say that public school students have some First Amendment rights in schools, but certainly not as many as adults do. Although *Tinker* was the landmark case that set forth the standards by which current student free speech cases are judged, the first case that suggested students had some First Amendment rights was decided much earlier—during World War II, to be exact.

West Virginia State Board of Education v. Barnette

This 1943 case marked the first time the Supreme Court ever conceded students had First Amendment rights. During World War II, the West Virginia State Board of Education passed a law requiring all students to salute the flag and recite the Pledge of Allegiance. Several students and their parents who were members of the Jehovah's Witnesses challenged the policy, arguing their religion prevented them from swearing allegiance to anyone but God, and so they could not recite the Pledge of Allegiance. The Supreme Court decided the students were in the right, and on First Amendment grounds struck down the West Virginia **ordinance** as violating the right of free expression.

"Educating the young for citizenship is reason for scrupulous protection of constitutional freedoms of the individual," said the Court, "if we are not to strangle the free mind at its source and teach youth to discount important principles of our government as mere platitudes." The Court determined that students had the right not to be coerced by school administrators into doing something that disagreed with their religious beliefs. Free speech in this case meant the right not to say something, in this case, the Pledge of Allegiance.

Tinker v. Des Moines Independent Community School District

After Barnette, the student First Amendment rights front was quiet in the courts, until the case of *Tinker v. Des Moines Independent Community School District* in 1969 shattered the peace and made sure there would be controversy for a long time to come. The Vietnam War was raging full force when the students at a Des Moines, Iowa high school decided to wear black armbands to school one day to protest what they saw as an unjust struggle. The school administrators learned of their plan and passed a rule banning black armbands from the school and suspending any student caught wearing one. The students wore the armbands anyway, and as a result were suspended. They sued the school district.

In writing in favor of the students for the majority, Justice Abe Fortas wrote these iconic words: "It can hardly be argued that either students or teachers shed their **constitutional rights** to **freedom of speech** or expression at the schoolhouse gate … School officials do not possess absolute authority over their students. Students in school as well as out of school are 'persons' under our Constitution. They are possessed of fundamental rights that the State must respect … In the absence of specific showing of constitutionally valid reasons to regulate their speech, students are entitled to freedom of expression of their views."

But Fortas added an important **caveat**: conduct that "materially disrupts classwork or involves substantial

disorder or invasion of the rights of others is, of course, not immunized by the constitutional guarantee of freedom of speech." In other words, not all student conduct is First Amendment protected, only that which does not disturb the classroom environment or invade the rights of others. This standard, also known as the "material and substantial disruption test," has basically remained the standard by which the school's right to prescribe free speech is examined at the secondary level as well as at public colleges and universities.

After *Tinker,* a host of cases were brought at the lower court level litigating public school free speech issues. Many of these came down on the side of freedom of expression for students. Many lower courts found themselves asking, after *Tinker*, what student speech can in fact be regulated.

Bethel School District No. 403 v. Fraser

The Supreme Court finally attempted to set some limits on student First Amendment rights in the 1986 case of *Bethel School District No. 403 v. Fraser.* Matthew Fraser made a speech at an assembly full of obscenities and innuendoes. When school officials attempted to discipline him for his speech, he sued. The Supreme Court sided with the school.

The Court found that Fraser had failed the "substantial disorder" part of the *Tinker* test. Chief Justice Warren Burger, writing for the majority, said that schools have a responsibility to instill students with "habits and manners of civility as values." The effect of Fraser's speech, suggested Berger, was to undermine this responsibility; therefore, he did not receive First Amendment protection for it. Bethel served notice that the Supreme Court saw limitations on student free speech rights. The next big school First Amendment case decided by the court served to emphasize that point.

Hazelwood School District v. Kuhlmeier

The school newspaper at Hazelwood East High School in Missouri was courting controversy when it decided to publish an article on pregnancy among students naming names, as well as an article on students of divorced parents. The principal of the school censored both articles from the school paper. The student editors of the newspaper sued.

In 1988, the Supreme Court handed down its decision: a complete defeat for the students. The majority of the court claimed *Tinker* did not apply to this case, since the school newspaper was a school-sponsored activity. According to the Court, when an activity is school sponsored, school officials may censor speech as long as such **censorship** is reasonably related to legitimate educational concerns. The Court went on to define these concerns broadly, stating that school officials would have the right to censor material that is "ungrammatical, poorly written, inadequately researched, biased or prejudiced, vulgar or profane, or unsuitable for immature audiences, or inconsistent with shared values of a civilized social order."

Hazelwood did distinguish between school-sponsored publications and other activities, and publications and activities that were not school sponsored, which the Court suggested would be given greater free-speech leeway. Nevertheless, the *Hazelwood* decision was clearly a defeat for student free speech rights. School officials were now allowed to censor school newspapers, as well as other school sponsored activities such as theatrical productions, in "any reasonable manner."

Elementary and Secondary Student Rights Since *Hazelwood* In *Santa Fe Independent School District v. Doe* (2000), the Supreme Court ruled that students may not use a school's loudspeaker system to offer student-led, student-initiated prayer. Before football games, members of the student body of a Texas high school elected one of their classmates to address the players and spectators. These addresses were conducted over the school's loudspeakers and usually involved a prayer. Attendance at these events was voluntary. Three students sued the school arguing that the prayers violated the Establishment Clause of the First Amendment. A majority of the Court rejected the school's argument that since the prayer was student initiated and student led, as opposed to officially sponsored by the school, it did not violate the First Amendment. The Court held that this action did constitute school-sponsored prayer because the loudspeakers that the students used for their invocations were owned by the school.

In *Morse v. Frederick* (2007), the Supreme Court ruled the First Amendment does not prevent school administrators from suppressing student speech at a school-supervised event that is reasonably viewed as promoting illegal drug use. The principal suspended a student after he displayed a banner reading "BONG HITS 4 JESUS" across the street from the school during the 2002 Olympic torch relay event. The Court upheld the principal, concluding that he displayed the sign at a school event, the sign promoted the use of illegal drugs, and that the principal had a compelling interest in deterring drug use by her students.

HIGHER EDUCATION FREE SPEECH ISSUES

Institutions of higher education have generally been held to have less control over student free speech rights than elementary and high school teachers and administrators. In part, this position reflects the fact that college students are adults. However, there have still been areas of controversy in post-secondary student free speech rights,

generally having to do with funding issues. The latest area of controversy has been with so-called "hate codes," which ban certain types of speech considered offensive from college campuses.

Recognizing Student Groups One way in which colleges and universities have traditionally imposed free speech restrictions on students is by determining which student groups they will recognize. Such recognition traditionally allows these groups to share in mandatory fees, receive space for offices, and to hold meetings on college campuses. Generally speaking, colleges are held to have made available a "limited public forum" to such groups, and as such are limited in the restrictions they can impose.

In the 1973 case of *Healy v. James,* the Supreme Court established that a college or university could not refuse to recognize an organization simply because university officials had an unproven fear of school disruption. *Healy* applied the material and substantial disruption test of *Tinker* to the college environment and found that unless the school had a compelling reason to believe that a group, in this case, Students for a Democratic Society, would seriously interfere with learning on the campus environment, it could not deny recognition.

In 1981, the Court went further in the case of *Widmar v. Vincent.* Involving the decision by the University of Missouri to refuse to recognize and grant access to university property to a religious group, the Court ruled that the University's decision to do so, while allowing access to several secular based groups, violated the First Amendment. The Court's decision in *Widmar* effectively meant that any decision by a college to deny recognition to a particular group was going to be analyzed with strict scrutiny and most likely struck down.

While none of these cases has reached the Supreme Court, one of the most litigated issues of the past thirty years involving recognition of student groups has involved recognition of homosexual groups. Generally speaking, nearly all attempts by colleges to refuse to recognize gay groups have been held to violate these groups, First Amendment rights.

Mandatory Student Fees Mandatory student fees constitute another area in which colleges and universities have faced free speech issues. These fees are generally collected by colleges as part of student tuition, and then distributed to a wide variety of groups.

Colleges usually do not impose restrictions in terms of ideology on which groups receive these fees, but they have in the past denied funding to groups promoting a religious viewpoint. However, in 1995 in *Rosenberger v. Rector of the University of Virginia,* the Supreme Court struck down these restrictions at the University of Virginia and ruled the University could not silence the expression of selected viewpoints by denying the groups student fee money. The *Rosenberger* decision stated colleges have to be rigidly neutral in distributing student fee money and cannot discriminate on the basis of content or viewpoint without violating the First Amendment.

A related issue concerning mandatory student fees has been whether it violates a student's First Amendment rights to be forced to pay fees that fund groups with which the student disagrees. In 2000, in the case of *Board of Regents v. Southworth*, the Supreme Court determined that it does not, as long as the money is distributed in a neutral fashion, and does not favor one viewpoint over another.

Hate Speech Codes Hate speech codes have been passed by colleges that seek to restrict speech considered offensive to other groups on campus, particularly speech that is believed to be racist or sexist. While a case involving these hate speech codes has not yet reached the Supreme Court, lower courts have been divided over their constitutionality.

ADDITIONAL RESOURCES

Alexander, Kern, and M. David Alexander. *The Law of Schools, Students and Teachers.* 4th ed. Eagan, MN: West, Thomson Reuters, 2009.

Barron, Jerome A., and C. Thomas Dienes. *First Amendment Law in a Nutshell.* 4th ed. Eagan, MN: West, Thomson Reuters, 2009.

Farber, Daniel. *The First Amendment: Concepts and Insights.* New York: Foundation Press, 2002.

Lloyd, Heather K. "Injustice in Our Schools: Students' Free Speech Rights Are Not Being Vigilantly Protected." *Northern Illinois University Law Review*, Spring, 2001.

ORGANIZATIONS

Coalition For Student & Academic Rights (COSTAR)

Post Office Box 491
Solebury, PA 18963
Phone: (215) 862-9096
Fax: (215) 862-9097
URL: http://www.co-star.org/index.html

Freedom Forum First Amendment Center

1207 18th Ave. South
Nashville, TN 37212
Phone: (615) 727-1600
Fax: (615) 727-1319
Email: info@fac.org
URL: http://www.freedomforum.org/first/default.asp

Student Press Law Center (SPLC)

1815 N Fort Myer Drive, Suite 900
Arlington, VA 22209-1817
Phone: (703) 807-1904
URL: http://splc.org/

EDUCATION

TEACHERS' RIGHTS

Sections within this essay:

BACKGROUND

Teachers in the United States enjoy a number of rights pertaining to their employment, including recognition of certain freedoms, prohibition against certain forms of **discrimination**, and significant protections against **dismissal** from their position. These rights are derived from state and federal constitutional provisions, state and federal statutes, and state and federal regulations.

Constitutional provisions provide protection to teachers at public schools that are generally not available to teachers at private schools. Since public schools are state entities, constitutional restrictions on state action limit some actions that public schools may take with respect to teachers or other employees. Rights that are constitutional in nature include the following:

- Substantive and procedural due process rights, including the right of a teacher to receive notice of termination and a right to a **hearing** in certain circumstances
- Freedom of expression and association provided by the First Amendment of the **Bill of Rights**
- Academic freedom, a limited concept recognized by courts based on principles of the First Amendment
- Protection against unreasonable searches and seizures by school officials of a teacher's **personal property** provided by the Fourth Amendment

Though private school teachers do not generally enjoy as much of the constitutional protection as public school teachers, statutes may provide protection against discrimination. The Civil Rights Act of 1964, for example, protects teachers at both public and private schools from racial, sexual, or religious discrimination. Private school teachers may also enjoy rights in their contracts that are similar to due process rights, including the inability of a private school to dismiss the teacher without cause, notice, or a hearing.

TEACHER CERTIFICATION

Certification Requirements Every state requires that teachers complete certain requirements to earn a teacher's certificate in order to teach in that state. Most states extend this requirement to private schools, though some jurisdictions may waive this for certain sectarian or denominational schools. The requirements that must be satisfied and the procedures that must be followed to earn certification vary from state to state. Requirements generally include completion of a certified education program, completion of a student teaching program, acceptable performance on a standardized test or tests, and submission of background information to the appropriate state agency in charge of accreditation. Some states require more extensive physical and mental testing of teachers and a more extensive background check. Some states also require **drug testing** of applicants prior to certification. An increasing number of states now require teachers to complete a satisfactory number of continuing education credits to maintain certification.

Denial or Revocation of Teaching Certificate Courts have held consistently that teaching certificates are not contracts. Thus, requirements to attain or maintain a certificate may be changed and applied to all teachers and prospective teachers. The certification process is administered by state certifying agencies in each state, and most of these agencies have been delegated significant authority with respect to the administration of these rules. Despite this broad delegation, however, the state agencies may not act arbitrarily, nor may these agencies deny or revoke certification on an arbitrary basis. Some state statutes provide that a certificate may be revoked for "just cause." Other common **statutory** grounds include the following:

- Immoral conduct or indecent behavior
- **Incompetency**
- Violations of ethical standards
- Unprofessional conduct
- Misrepresentation or **fraud**
- Willful neglect of duty

TENURE AND DISMISSAL OF TEACHERS

Tenure Most states protect teachers in public schools from arbitrary dismissal through tenure statutes. Under these tenure statutes, once a teacher has attained tenure, his or her **contract** renews automatically each year. School districts may dismiss tenured teachers only by a showing

of cause, after following such procedural requirements as providing notice to the teacher, specifying the charges against the teacher, and providing the teacher with a meaningful hearing. Most tenure statutes require teachers to remain employed during a probationary period for a certain number of years. Once this probationary period has ended, teachers in some states will earn tenure automatically. In other states, the local school board must take some action to grant tenure to the teacher, often at the conclusion of a review of the teacher's performance. Tenure also provides some protection for teachers against demotion, salary reductions, and other discipline. However, tenure does not guarantee that a teacher may retain a particular position, such as a coaching position, nor does it provide indefinite employment.

Prior to attaining tenure, a probationary teacher may be dismissed at the discretion of the school district, subject to contractual and constitutional restrictions. Laws other than those governing tenure will apply to determine whether a discharge of a teacher is wrongful. If a probationary teacher's dismissal does not involve discrimination or does not violate terms of the teacher's contract, the school district most likely does not need to provide notice, summary of charges, or a hearing to the teacher.

In the absence of a state tenure **statute**, a teacher may still attain de facto tenure rights if the customs or circumstances of employment demonstrate that a teacher has a "legitimate claim of entitlement for job tenure." The U.S. Supreme Court recognized this right in the case of *Perry v. Sindermann*, which also held that where a teacher has attained de facto tenure, the teacher is entitled to due process prior to dismissal by the school district.

State laws do not govern the tenure process at private schools. However, a contract between a private school district and a teacher may provide tenure rights, though enforcement of these rights is related to the contract rights rather than rights granted through the state tenure statute.

Dismissal for Cause A school must show cause in order to dismiss a teacher who has attained tenure status. Some state statutes provide a list of circumstances where a school may dismiss a teacher. These circumstances are similar to those in which a state agency may revoke a teacher's certification. Some causes for dismissal include the following:

- Immoral conduct
- Incompetence
- Neglect of duty
- Substantial noncompliance with school laws

- **Conviction** of a crime
- Insubordination
- Fraud or misrepresentation

Due Process Rights of Teachers The Due Process Clause of the Fourteenth Amendment, like its counterpart in the **Fifth Amendment**, provides that no state may "deprive any person of life, liberty, or property, without due process of law." This clause applies to public school districts and provides the minimum procedural requirements that each public school district must satisfy when dismissing a teacher who has attained tenure. Note that in this context, due process does not prescribe the reasons why a teacher may be dismissed, but rather it prescribes the procedures a school must follow to dismiss a teacher. Note also that many state statutory provisions for dismissing a teacher actually exceed the minimum requirements under the Due Process Clause.

The U.S. Supreme Court case of *Cleveland Board of Education v. Loudermill* is the leading case involving the question of what process is due under the Constitution. This case provides that a tenured teacher must be given oral or written notice of the dismissal and the charges against him or her, an explanation of the **evidence** obtained by the employer, and an opportunity for a fair and meaningful hearing.

TEACHER CONTRACTS

The law of contracts applies to contracts between teachers and school districts. This law includes the concepts of offer, acceptance, mutual **assent**, and consideration. For a teacher to determine whether a contract exists, he or she should consult authority on the general law of contracts. This section focuses on contract laws specific to teaching and education.

Ratification of Contracts by School Districts Even if a school official offers a teacher a job and the teacher accepts this offer, many state laws require that the school board ratify the contract before it becomes binding. Thus, even if a principal of a school district informs a prospective teacher that the teacher has been hired, the contract is not final until the school district accepts or ratifies the contract. The same is true if a school district fails to follow proper procedures when determining whether to ratify a contract.

Teacher's Handbook as a Contract Some teachers have argued successfully that provisions in a teacher's handbook grant the teacher certain contractual rights. However, this is not common, as many employee handbooks include clauses stating that the handbook is not a contract. For a provision in a handbook to be legally binding, the teacher must demonstrate that the actions of the teacher and the school district were such that the elements for creating a contract were met.

Breach of Teacher Contract Either a teacher or a school district can breach a contract. Whether a breach has occurred depends on the facts of the case and the terms of the contract. Breach of contract cases between teachers and school districts arise because a school district has terminated the employment of a teacher, even though the teacher has not violated any of the terms of the employment agreement. In several of these cases, a teacher has taken a leave of absence, which did not violate the employment agreement, and the school district terminated the teacher due to the leave of absence. Similarly, a teacher may breach a contract by resigning from the district before the end of the contract term (usually the end of the school year).

Remedies for Breach of Contract The usual remedy for breach of contract between a school district and a teacher is monetary damages. If a school district has breached a contract, the teacher will usually receive the amount the teacher would have received under the contract, less the amount the teacher receives (or could receive) by attaining alternative employment. Other damages, such as the cost to the teacher in finding other employment, may also be available. Non-monetary remedies, such as a court requiring a school district to rehire a teacher or to comply with contract terms, are available in some circumstances, though courts are usually hesitant to order such remedies. If a teacher breaches a contract, damages may be the cost to the school district for finding a replacement. Many contracts contain provisions prescribing the amount of damages a teacher must pay if he or she terminates employment before the end of the contract.

Collective Bargaining by Teachers Teachers' contractual rights often arise through **collective bargaining** through teachers' unions. For more information regarding collective bargaining by teachers, see Education: Teacher's Unions/Collective Bargaining.

TEACHER FREEDOMS AND RIGHTS

Freedom from Discrimination The Equal Protection Clause of the Fourteenth Amendment of the Constitution protects teachers at public schools from discrimination based on race, sex, and national origin. These forms of discrimination are also barred through the enactment of Title VII of the Civil Rights Act of 1964, which was amended in 1972 to include educational institutions. This law provides that it is an unlawful employment practice for any employer to discriminate against an individual based on the race, color, religion, sex, or national origin of the individual. Title IX of the Education Amendments of 1972 provides protection against discrimination based on sex at educational institutions that receive federal financial assistance. Title VII and IX also prohibit **sexual harassment** in the workplace.

A teacher who has been subjected to discrimination has several causes of action, though proof in some of these cases may be difficult. A teacher may bring a cause of action under section 1983 of Title 42 of the United States Code for deprivation of rights under the Equal Protection Clause (or other constitutional provision). However, to succeed under this cause of action, the teacher would need to prove that the school had the deliberate intent to discriminate. Similarly, a teacher bringing a claim under Title VII must demonstrate that the reasons given by a school for an employment decision were false and that the actual reason for the decision was discrimination.

Academic Freedom Teachers in public schools have limited freedoms in the classroom to teach without undue restrictions on the content or subjects for discussion. These freedoms are based on rights to freedom of expression under the First Amendment of the Bill of Rights. However, the concept of academic freedom is limited. The content taught by a teacher must be relevant to and consistent with the teacher's responsibilities, and a teacher cannot promote a personal or political agenda in the classroom. Factors such as the age, experience, and grade level of students affect the latitude in which a court will recognize the academic freedom of a teacher.

Freedom of Expression A leading case in First Amendment **jurisprudence** regarding protected forms of expression is *Pickering v. Board of Education*. This case involved a teacher whose job was terminated when he wrote to a local newspaper an editorial critical of the teacher's employer. The Supreme Court held that the school had unconstitutionally restricted the First Amendment rights of the teacher to speak on issues of public importance. Based on *Pickering* and similar cases, teachers generally enjoy rights to freedom of expression, though there are some restrictions. Teachers may not materially disrupt the educational interest of the school district, nor may teachers undermine authority or adversely affect working relationships at the school.

Freedom of Association Similar to rights to freedom of expression, public school teachers enjoy rights to freedom of association, based on the First Amendment's provision that grants citizens the right to peaceful assembly. These rights generally permit public school teachers to join professional, labor, or similar organizations; run for public office; and similar forms of association. However, teachers may be required to ensure that participation in these activities is completely independent from their responsibilities to the school.

Freedom of Religion The First Amendment and Title VII of the Civil Rights Act of 1964 provide protection against religious discrimination by school districts against teachers. Teachers may exercise their religious rights, though there are certain restrictions to such rights. This existence of restrictions is particularly relevant to the public schools, since public schools are restricted from teaching religion through the Establishment Clause of the First Amendment. Thus, for example, a teacher is free to be a practicing Christian, yet the teacher cannot preach Christianity in the classroom.

Privacy Rights Teachers enjoy limited rights to personal **privacy**, though courts will often support disciplinary action taken by a school district when a teacher's private life affects the integrity of the school district or the effectiveness by which a teacher can teach. Thus, for example, a teacher may be terminated from his or her position for such acts as **adultery** or other sexual conduct outside marriage, and courts will be hesitant to overrule the decisions of the school board.

Age The Age Discrimination in Employment Act of 1967, with its subsequent amendments, provides protection for teachers over the age of 40 against **age discrimination**. Under this act, age may not be the sole factor when a school district terminates the employment of a teacher. If a teacher charges a school district with age discrimination, the school district has the burden to show that some factor other than age influenced its decision.

Pregnancy The Pregnancy Discrimination Act of 1978 provides protection for teachers who are pregnant. Under this act, a school district may not dismiss or demote a pregnant teacher on the basis of her pregnancy, nor may a district deny a job or deny a promotion to a pregnant teacher on the basis of her pregnancy.

Regulating a Teacher's Private Life Schools, of course, have the authority to regulate activities of teachers while they are teaching. However, schools often implement policies that affect a teacher's life outside of the classroom. For instance, teachers are generally forbidden from entering into sexual relationships with their students, even if the student has reached the **age of consent**. This type of policy ensures that a teacher does not take advantage of a younger student who may look up to the teacher as a role model. The potential for harm to the student is quite obvious.

In other areas, a school's authority to regulate teacher behavior is less clear. The rise of **social media** in the late 2000s gave individuals the ability to share personal information even more freely than they could in the past. Millions of people became members of websites such as Facebook. However, schools quickly became concerned about teachers becoming "friends" with their students on Facebook or otherwise sharing private information that students can see. Accordingly, many schools ban teachers from having active Facebook accounts.

Some teachers have challenged restrictive policies in court, but the schools often win. For instance, a teacher in Connecticut was fired because his MySpace page contained inappropriate material that students could access. The teacher sued the school, but a federal district court dismissed the suit after concluding that the school could find the teacher's conduct to be disruptive to school activities.

STATE AND LOCAL LAWS REGARDING TEACHERS' RIGHTS

Each state provides laws governing education agencies, hiring and termination of teachers, tenure of teachers, and similar laws. Teachers should consult with statutes and education regulations in their respective states, as well as the education agencies that enforce these rules, for additional information regarding teachers' rights. Moreover, teachers should review their contracts, **collective bargaining agreement**, and/or employee handbook for specific provisions that may have been included in an agreement.

The following information summarizes the grounds on which a state may revoke or suspend a teaching certificate or on which a district may dismiss or suspend a teacher.

ALABAMA: Teacher's certificate may be revoked for immoral conduct, or unbecoming or indecent behavior. Teachers may be dismissed or suspended on similar grounds, except that tenured teachers may not be suspended or terminated on political grounds.

ALASKA: Teacher's certificate may be revoked or suspended for incompetency, immorality, substantial noncompliance with school laws or regulations, violations of ethical or professional standards, or violations of contractual obligations. Teachers may be dismissed or suspended by local school boards on similar grounds.

ARIZONA: Teacher's certificate may be revoked or suspended for immoral or unprofessional conduct,

evidence of unfitness to teach, failure to comply with various statutory requirements, failure to comply with student disciplinary procedures, teaching sectarian books or doctrine, or conducting religious exercises. Teachers may be dismissed or suspended on similar grounds. Probationary employees may be dismissed when they are unsuited or not qualified. Permanent employees may be discharged only for cause, and are entitled to due process.

ARKANSAS: Teacher's certificate may be revoked for cause. Teachers may be dismissed for any cause that is not arbitrary, capricious, or discriminatory.

CALIFORNIA: Permanent teachers may be dismissed for immoral or unprofessional conduct, dishonesty, incompetency, evident unfitness for service, a physical or mental condition unfitting for a teacher to instruct or associate with children, persistent violation of school laws or regulations, conviction of a **felony** or crime involving moral turpitude, or alcoholism or drug abuse rendering teacher unfit for service. Teacher's certificate may be revoked or suspended on the same grounds as those for dismissal or suspension.

COLORADO: Teacher's certificate may be annulled, revoked, or suspended if certificate has been obtained through fraud or misrepresentation; teacher is mentally incompetent; teacher violates statutes or regulations regarding unlawful sexual behavior, use of controlled substances, or other violations. Teachers may be dismissed on similar grounds.

CONNECTICUT: Teacher's certificate may be revoked if certificate has been obtained through fraud or misrepresentation; teacher has neglected duties or been convicted of a crime involving moral turpitude; teacher has been neglectful of duties; or other due and sufficient cause exists. Teachers may be dismissed on similar grounds.

DELAWARE: Teacher's certificate may be revoked for immorality, misconduct in office, incompetency, willful neglect of duty, or disloyalty. Teachers may be dismissed or suspended on similar grounds.

FLORIDA: Teacher's certificate may be revoked or suspended for obtaining certificate by fraud, incompetence, gross immorality or an act involving moral turpitude, revocation of a teaching certificate in another state, conviction of a crime other than a minor traffic violation, breach of teaching contract, or delinquency in **child support** obligations. Teachers may be dismissed or suspended on similar grounds.

GEORGIA: Teachers may be dismissed for incompetency, insubordination, willful neglect of duties, immorality, encouraging students to violate the law, failure to secure and maintain necessary educational training, and any other good and sufficient cause.

HAWAII: Teacher's certificate may be revoked for conviction of crime other than traffic offense or if the employer finds that teacher poses a risk to the health, safety, or well being of children. Teacher may be dismissed for inefficiency, immorality, willful violations of policies and regulations, or other good and **just cause**.

IDAHO: Teacher's certificate may be revoked for gross neglect of duty, incompetence, breach of contract, making a false statement on application for certificate, conviction of a crime involving moral turpitude or drugs or a felony offense involving children. Grounds for revocation of a teacher's certificate are also grounds for dismissal.

ILLINOIS: Teacher's certificate may be revoked or suspended for immorality, health condition detrimental to students, incompetence, unprofessional conduct, neglect of duty, willful failure to report **child abuse**, conviction of certain sex or narcotics offenses, or other just cause. Teachers may be dismissed on similar grounds.

INDIANA: Teacher's certificate may be revoked for immorality, misconduct in office, incompetency, willful neglect of duty, or improper cancellation of a contract. Permanent and semi-permanent teachers may be dismissed on similar grounds.

IOWA: Teacher's certificate may be revoked for any cause that would have permitted refusal to grant the certificate. Teachers may be dismissed for just cause.

KANSAS: Teacher's certificate may be revoked for immorality, gross neglect of duty, annulling a written contract, or any other cause that would have justified refusal to grant the certificate.

KENTUCKY: Teacher's certificate may be revoked for immorality, misconduct in office, incompetency, willful neglect of duty, or submission of false information. Teachers may be dismissed or suspended on similar grounds.

LOUISIANA: Permanent teachers may be dismissed for incompetence, dishonesty, willful neglect of duty, or membership or contribution to an unlawful organization.

MAINE: Teacher's certificate may be revoked for evidence of child abuse, gross incompetence, or fraud. Teachers may be dismissed on similar grounds.

MARYLAND: Teachers may be dismissed or suspended for immorality, misconduct in office, insubordination, incompetency, or willful neglect of duty.

MASSACHUSETTS: Teacher's certificate may be revoked for cause. Teachers may be dismissed for inefficiency, incapacity, conduct unbecoming of a teacher, insubordination, failure to satisfy teacher performance standards, or other just cause.

MICHIGAN: Teacher's certificate may be revoked or suspended for conviction of **sex offenses** and crimes involving children. Teachers may be dismissed for reasonable and just causes or failure to comply with school law.

MINNESOTA: Teacher's certificate may be revoked or suspended for immoral character or conduct, failure to perform the terms of a contract without just cause, gross inefficiency, willful neglect of duty, failure to meet requirements for licensing, or fraud or misrepresentation in obtaining a license. Teachers may be dismissed on similar grounds.

MISSISSIPPI: Teachers may be dismissed or suspended for incompetency, neglect of duty, immoral conduct, intemperance, brutal treatment of a pupil, or other good cause.

MISSOURI: Teacher's certificate may be revoked or suspended for incompetency, cruelty, immorality, **drunkenness**, neglect of duty, annulling a written contract without consent from the local board, or conviction of a crime involving moral turpitude. Teachers may be dismissed on similar grounds.

MONTANA: Teacher's certificate may be revoked or suspended for false statements on an application for the certificate, any reason that would have disqualified the person from receiving a certificate, incompetency, gross neglect of duty, conviction of a crime involving moral turpitude, or nonperformance of an employment contract. Teachers may be dismissed on similar grounds.

NEBRASKA: Teacher's certificate may be revoked for just cause, including incompetence, immorality, intemperance, cruelty, certain crimes, neglect of duty, unprofessional conduct, physical or mental incapacity, or breach of contract. Teachers may be dismissed for just cause, as defined by statute.

NEVADA: Teacher's certificate may be revoked for immoral or unprofessional conduct, unfitness for service, physical or mental incapacity, conviction of a crime involving moral turpitude or sex offenses, advocacy of the overthrow of the government, persistent refusal to obey rules, or breach of a teaching contract. Teachers may be dismissed or suspended on similar grounds.

NEW HAMPSHIRE: Teachers may be dismissed for immorality, incompetence, failure to conform to regulations, or conviction of certain crimes.

NEW JERSEY: Teacher's certificate may be revoked if teacher is a noncitizen; certificate may be suspended if teacher breaches contract. Teachers may be dismissed on similar grounds.

NEW MEXICO: Teacher's certificate may be revoked or suspended for incompetency, immorality, or any other good and just cause. Teachers may be dismissed for good cause.

NEW YORK: Teacher's certificate may be revoked if teacher is unfit to teach due to moral character or if teacher fails to complete a school term without good cause. Teachers may be dismissed on similar grounds.

NORTH CAROLINA: Teachers may be dismissed for inadequate performance, immorality, insubordination, neglect of duty, physical or mental incapacity, **habitual** or excessive use of alcohol or other controlled substances, or conviction of a crime involving moral turpitude.

NORTH DAKOTA: Teacher's certificate may be revoked or suspended for any cause that would permit refusal to issue the certificate, incompetency, immorality, intemperance, cruelty, commission of a crime, refusal to perform duties, violation of professional codes, breach of teacher contract, or wearing religious garb. Teachers may be dismissed on similar grounds.

OHIO: Teacher's certificate may be revoked for intemperance, immorality, incompetence, **negligence**, or other conduct unbecoming of the position. Teachers may be dismissed on similar grounds, including assisting a student to cheat on an achievement, ability, or proficiency test.

OKLAHOMA: Teachers may be dismissed for immorality, willful neglect of duty, cruelty, incompetency, teaching

disloyalty to the U.S. government, moral turpitude, or criminal sexual activity.

OREGON: Teacher's certificate may be revoked or suspended for conviction of certain crimes (including sale or possession of a controlled substance), gross neglect of duty, gross unfitness, or wearing religious dress at school. Teachers may be dismissed or suspended on similar grounds.

PENNSYLVANIA: Teacher's certificate may be revoked for incompetency, cruelty, negligence, immorality, or intemperance. Teachers may be dismissed on similar grounds.

RHODE ISLAND: Teacher's certificate may be revoked, or teacher may be dismissed, for good and just cause.

SOUTH CAROLINA: Teacher's certificate may be revoked for just cause, including incompetence, willful neglect of duty, willful violation of state board rules, unprofessional conduct, drunkenness, cruelty, crime, immorality, conduct involving moral turpitude, dishonesty, evident unfitness, or sale or possession of narcotics. Teachers may be dismissed on similar grounds.

SOUTH DAKOTA: Teacher's certificate may be revoked or suspended for any cause that would have permitted refusal of the certificate, violation of teacher's contract, gross immorality, incompetency, flagrant neglect of duty, or conviction of a crime involving moral turpitude. Teachers may be dismissed on similar grounds.

TENNESSEE: Teacher's certificate may be revoked if teacher is guilty of immoral conduct. Teachers may be dismissed or suspended on similar grounds, including incompetence, inefficiency, neglect of duty, unprofessional conduct, and insubordination.

TEXAS: Teacher's certificate may be revoked or suspended if teacher's activities are in violation of the law, the teacher is unworthy to instruct the youth of the state, the teacher abandons his or her contract, or the teacher is convicted of a crime. Teachers may be dismissed or suspended on similar grounds.

UTAH: Teacher's certificate may be revoked or suspended for immoral or incompetent conduct, or evidence of unfitness for teaching. Teachers may be dismissed for cause.

VERMONT: Teacher's certificate may be revoked for cause. Teachers may be dismissed for just and sufficient cause. Teachers may be suspended for incompetence, conduct unbecoming of a teacher, failure to attend to duties, or failure to carry out reasonable orders and directions of superintendent or board.

VIRGINIA: Teachers may be dismissed for incompetency, immorality, noncompliance with school laws or rules, certain **disability**, and convictions of certain crimes. Teachers may be suspended for good and just cause when the safety or welfare of children is threatened.

WASHINGTON: Teacher's certificate may be revoked for immorality, violation of a written contract, intemperance, a crime involving child neglect or abuse, or unprofessional conduct. Teachers may be dismissed for sufficient cause.

WEST VIRGINIA: Teacher's certificate may be revoked for drunkenness; untruthfulness; immorality; unfitness due to physical, mental or moral defect; neglect of duty; using **fraudulent**, unapproved, or insufficient credit; or other cause. Teachers may be dismissed or suspended on similar grounds.

WISCONSIN: Teacher's certificate may be revoked for incompetency, immoral conduct, or conviction of certain felonies. Tenured teachers may be dismissed on similar grounds.

WYOMING: Teacher's certificate may be revoked or suspended for incompetency, immorality, other reprehensible conduct, or gross neglect of duty. Teachers may be dismissed on similar grounds.

ADDITIONAL RESOURCES

Dodd, Victoria J. *Practical Education Law for the 21st Century.* Durham, NC: Carolina Academic Press, 2010.

Imber, Michael, and Tyll van Geel. *A Teacher's Guide to Education Law.* 4th ed. New York: Routledge, 2010.

McCarthy, Martha M., Nelda H. Cambron-McCabe, and Stephen B. Thomas. *Legal Rights of Teachers and Students.* Boston: Pearson/Allyn and Bacon, 2004.

Osborne, Allan G., and Charles J. Russo. *The Legal Rights and Responsibilities of Teachers: Issues of Employment and Instruction.* Thousand Oaks, CA: Corwin, 2011.

Underwood, Julie, and L. Dean Webb. *School Law for Teachers: Concepts and Applications.* Upper Saddle River, NJ: Pearson/Merrill Prentice Hall, 2006.

ORGANIZATIONS

American Association of School Administrators (AASA)

1615 Duke St.
Alexandria, VA 22314
Phone: (703) 528-0700
Fax: (703) 841-1543
Email: Info@aasa.org
URL: http://www.aasa.org/

American Federation of Teachers (AFT)

555 New Jersey Avenue, NW
Washington, DC 20001
Phone: (202) 879-4400
URL: http://www.aft.org/

Education Law Association (ELA)

300 College Park
Dayton, OH 45469
Phone: (937) 229-3589
Fax: (937) 229-3845
URL: http://www.educationlaw.org/

Education Policy Institute (EPI)

6900 Wisconsin Ave., Suite 606
Bethesda, MD 20815
Phone: (202) 657-5207
Fax: (202) 244-7584
URL: http://www.educationalpolicy.org/

National Education Association (NEA)

1201 16th Street, NW
Washington, DC 20036
Phone: (202) 833-4000
URL: http://www.nea.org/

EDUCATION

TEACHER'S UNIONS/ COLLECTIVE BARGAINING

Sections within this essay:

BACKGROUND

In 1935 Congress passed the National Labor Relations Act (Wagner Act), which guarantees the right of private employees to form and join unions to bargain collectively. The vast majority of states have extended this right to public employees, including teachers at public school districts. Many states require school districts to bargain collectively with teachers who have formed a union. Other states require districts to meet with teachers' representatives. Some states expressly prohibit collective bargaining by public school teachers or other public employees.

A wide range of provisions may be negotiated in collective bargaining between teachers' unions and school districts. Some subjects are mandatory, while others are merely permitted or even prohibited. State law governs the appropriateness of subjects to be bargained. The following are some of the matters that are often the subject of this bargaining:

- Academic freedom
- Curriculum
- Wages and salaries
- Training
- Hours, workload, and teaching responsibilities
- Tenure and probationary period
- Promotion
- Reappointment
- Reclassification and reduction
- Evaluation procedures
- Grievance procedures
- Personnel files
- Student discipline
- Retirement benefits
- Sick leave
- Leaves and sabbaticals

CONSTITUTIONAL CONSIDERATIONS REGARDING UNIONS

The First Amendment of the **Bill of Rights** provides: "Congress shall make no law . . . prohibiting . . . the right of people peaceably to assemble." This right, as applied to the states through the Fourteenth Amendment of the Constitution, has been interpreted to give teachers and other employees the right to free association, including the right to join a union, such as the National Education Association or the American Federation of Teachers. However, the Constitution does not grant teachers the right to bargain collectively with employers. This right is based on applicable provisions in state constitutions, federal statutes, or state statutes. Similarly, teachers do not have a constitutional right to strike, though other federal law or state law may permit teachers to strike.

FORMING AND JOINING A UNION TO BARGAIN COLLECTIVELY

Laws governing the representation process are often quite complex. This process prefaces the collective bargaining process and involves numerous considerations, including types of employees that will constitute a "bargaining unit," as well as the selection of an appropriate union to represent teachers. In the public school sector, state law affects both of these determinations. Some states exclude certain employees from a bargaining unit, including supervisors and individuals in management positions.

Bargaining Units Teachers seeking to join for collective bargaining must define an appropriate bargaining unit. Under most labor relations statutes, only those individuals who share a "community of interests" may comprise an appropriate bargaining unit. Community of interests generally means that the teachers have substantial mutual interests, including the following:

- Wages or compensation
- Hours of work
- Employment benefits
- Supervision
- Qualifications
- Training and skills
- Job functions
- Contact with other employees
- Integration of work functions with other employees
- History of collective bargaining

Many state statutes prescribe certain requirements or considerations with respect to bargaining units in the public sector. For example, some statutes require labor boards to avoid over-proliferation of bargaining units. Moreover, some statutes also set forth specific bargaining units, such as those for faculty, staff, maintenance, and similar distinctions.

Representation Procedures The National Labor Relations Act and most state statutes provide formal processes for designation and recognition of bargaining units. If a

dispute arises with respect to union representation, many states direct parties to resolve these dispute with the public employment relations board in that state. After the bargaining units are organized, members may file a petition with the appropriate labor board. The labor board will generally determine that **jurisdiction** over the bargaining unit is appropriate, that the proposed bargaining unit is appropriate, and that a majority of employees approve the bargaining unit through an election. Several procedures are usually in place in the **statute** and rules of the labor board to ensure that the vote is uncoerced and otherwise fair. After this election, the labor board will certify the union as the exclusive representative of the bargaining unit. Once a union is certified, usually for a one-year period, neither employees nor another union may petition for a new election.

OBLIGATIONS AND RESOLUTION OF CONFLICTS IN COLLECTIVE BARGAINING

Exclusivity and Good Faith in Bargaining Agreement Once a union has been elected, both public and private school boards are bound to deal exclusively with that union. The elected union must bargain for the collective interests of the members of the bargaining unit. Both the school district and the union representing teachers must bargain in **good faith**. The duty of parties to bargain in good faith is important in the collective bargaining process, since **negotiations** between school districts and unions can become intense and heated.

Interpretations of the term "good faith" under the National Labor Relations Act typically focus on openness, fairness, mutuality of conduct, and cooperation between parties. Many state statutes define "good faith" similarly, though some states provide more specific guidance regarding what constitutes good faith bargaining. Some states also provide a list of examples that are deemed instances of bargaining in **bad faith**. Refusal to negotiate in good faith constitutes an **unfair labor practice** under the National Labor Relations Act and many state statutes.

Terms of the Collective Bargaining Agreement Most state statutes do not require schools to bargain on issues involving the educational policy of the school board. Many states require school boards and unions to bargain on "wages, hours, and terms and conditions of employment." Some states limit bargaining to such mandatory issues as benefits, insurance, or sick leave. When a state statute includes mandatory subjects, these subjects must be bargained over at the request of either the school board or the teachers' union. If either party refuses to negotiate over a mandatory subject, state statutes generally deem this a refusal to negotiate in good faith and, thus, an unfair labor practice.

In the absence of **statutory** language specifying the scope of collective bargaining, teacher unions and school boards must consult relevant **case law** in that state to determine if the courts have set forth parameters. Other limitations to collective bargaining may also be present. A **collective bargaining agreement**, for example, cannot violate or contradict existing statutory law or constitutional provisions. Similarly, the collective bargaining agreement should recognize **contract** rights that may already exist through other agreements.

Impasse Negotiations may fail to lead to a completed agreement between a teachers' union and a school board. When good faith efforts fail to resolve the dispute or disputes between the parties, a legal impasse occurs. At the time impasse occurs, active bargaining between the parties is usually suspended.

Parties usually go through a series of options once an impasse has occurred, though public and private school teachers' options may differ. The first step after an impasse is declared is usually **mediation**. When parties employ a mediator, the mediator acts as a neutral third party to assist the two sides in reaching a compromise. Mediators lack power to make binding decisions, and they are employed only as advisors. Many state statutes require use of mediators in the public sector upon declaration of an impasse. Private sector unions and schools may employ a federal mediator, though federal labor laws do not prescribe further options regarding dispute resolution.

If mediation fails, many state statutes require the parties to employ a fact-finder, who analyzes the facts of the bargaining process and seeks to recognize a potential compromise. The parties are not bound by the recommendations of the fact-finder, though it may influence public opinion regarding the appropriate resolution of the dispute. The recommendations are particularly influential in the public sector, where the school board is a government body consisting of elected officials, and teachers and other staff are public employees. However, this step in the process may not bring resolution to the dispute. In some states, fact-finding is the final stage of impasse resolution, leaving the parties to bargain among themselves.

A third option is **arbitration**, though this is generally only employed in the public education sector. An arbitrator is a third party who performs functions similar to a fact-finder, yet the arbitrator's decision is binding on both parties. In several states, arbitration is permissive, meaning parties may submit their dispute to an arbitrator after fact-finding if they so desire. Some states mandate use of binding arbitration, often as an alternative to the right to strike.

Strikes If efforts for impasse resolution fail between a teachers' union and a school district, teachers may choose to strike to persuade or coerce the board to meet the demands of the union. A lockout by an employer is the counterpart to a strike. The right to strike in the private sector is guaranteed under the National Labor Relations Act. However, only about half of the states have extended this right to teachers in the public sector. These states usually limit this right under the respective labor laws. Where teachers do not have the right to strike, state statutes often impose monetary or similar penalties on those who strike illegally.

In states where strikes are permitted in the public sector, teachers often must meet several conditions prior to the strike. For example, a state may require that a bargaining unit has been certified properly, that methods for impasse resolution have been exhausted, that any existing collective bargaining agreement has expired, and that the union has provided sufficient notice to the school board. The purpose of such conditions is to give the parties an opportunity to avoid a strike, which is usually unpopular with both employers and employees.

COLLECTIVE BARGAINING IN HIGHER EDUCATION

Collective bargaining in higher education differs somewhat from bargaining by primary and secondary school teachers. The National Labor Relations Act applies to many private institutions of higher education, which usually have much higher revenues and many more employees than private schools at the primary or secondary level. In many states, the same statutes that govern bargaining at the primary or secondary level govern collective bargaining in higher education. In other states, however, the statutes prescribe different rules with respect to state universities than they do with school districts. Governance of a public university is often much more complex than governance at a primary or secondary school, and the interests of the employees is often much more diverse among university faculty members and other employees than the interests of high school, middle school, or elementary school teachers and employees. Whereas a primary or secondary school may require only a minimal number of bargaining units, a large university may require several bargaining units to represent the various interests of the employees of the university.

STATE AND LOCAL PROVISIONS GOVERNING COLLECTIVE BARGAINING

The National Labor Relations Act (NLRA) governs labor relations in private schools, subject to some limitations. A teachers' union of a private school should determine whether the NLRA applies to its school. State labor statutes generally govern labor relations between public school districts and teachers' unions. These provisions are summarized below. Collective bargaining statutes differ considerably from state to state, with some states providing much more guidance and specific rules than others.

ALABAMA: Teachers have a general right to join or refuse to join a labor organization.

ALASKA: Certified employees and school boards must follow specific procedures set forth in the statute. Under the state's Public Employment Relations Act, student representatives must be permitted to attend meetings and have access to documents in negotiations between a postsecondary education institution and a bargaining representative. The statute also permits a strike, with some limitations, by public school employees after mediation if a majority of employees vote by secret ballot to do so.

ARIZONA: Arizona has not enacted a collective bargaining statute governing public schools. Teachers in this state should consult relevant case law to determine when collective bargaining is permitted.

ARKANSAS: Teachers have a general right to organize and bargain collectively.

CALIFORNIA: An extensive statutory scheme is provided for governing collective bargaining between public schools and bargaining representatives, under the Public School Employee Relations Act. The statute limits the scope of representation to matters related to wages, employment hours, and other terms and conditions of employment. Employer and employee representatives are required to "meet and negotiate." If impasse is declared, mediation and, if necessary, fact-finding are required. Arbitration is permitted, but it is not required by statute.

COLORADO: Collective bargaining is permitted by statute. Teachers have a limited right to strike.

CONNECTICUT: A statute permits collective bargaining by members of the teaching profession. However, the state prohibits professional employees from striking and allows courts to enforce this prohibition.

DELAWARE: Public school employees are permitted to bargain collectively. Majority vote is required for union representation from all eligible members of the bargaining unit. The state prohibits strikes by teachers.

FLORIDA: The state constitution guarantees the right to collective bargaining but prohibits strikes by public employees. State statute defines "good faith bargaining," requiring parties to meet at reasonable times and places with the intent to reach a common accord.

HAWAII: Statute permits bargaining by all public employees. Statute defines certain bargaining units, including some supervisory employees. Mediation, fact-finding, and arbitration are provided in the statute. Strikes are permitted, but only in certain narrow circumstances.

IDAHO: Statute prescribes procedures for bargaining between a school board and certificated school employees.

ILLINOIS: Educational employees at all levels permitted to bargain under the Illinois Educational Labor Relations Act. However, several types of employees, including supervisors, managers, confidential employees, short-term employees, and students, are excluded from bargaining by statute. Impasse procedures include mediation and fact-finding. Arbitration is permitted. Strikes are permitted after several conditions set forth in the statute are met.

INDIANA: Certificated educational employees permitted to bargain by statute. Statute prescribes certain subjects that may be bargained and certain subjects that may be discussed. Strikes are prohibited.

IOWA: All public employees permitted to bargain collectively. Mediation and fact-finding required for impasse resolution. The state labor board at the request of the school board or union may order binding arbitration. Strikes are prohibited.

KANSAS: Statute permits bargaining by all public employees. Employer retains a number of rights, including right to direct work of employees. Strikes are prohibited.

LOUISIANA: No collective bargaining statute governs public schools. Teachers in this state should consult relevant case law to determine when collective bargaining is permitted.

MAINE: Statute permits collective bargaining by all public employees. Strikes by all state employees are prohibited.

MARYLAND: Statute permits bargaining by all certified and noncertified public school employees.

MASSACHUSETTS: Statute permits bargaining by all public employees. Strikes by public employees are prohibited.

MICHIGAN: Statute permits bargaining by public employees. Negotiations by teachers limited under some circumstances. Strikes by public employees are prohibited.

MINNESOTA: Statute permits bargaining by all public employees. State permits strikes only under certain circumstances, including completion of impasse resolution.

MISSISSIPPI: Strikes by teachers are illegal by statute.

MISSOURI: Teachers at public schools have the right to bargain collectively. Statute does not grant a right to strike.

MONTANA: Statute permits bargaining by all public employees. Courts have construed state statute to permit the right to strike.

NEBRASKA: Statute permits bargaining by all public employees. State restricts supervisors from joining a bargaining unit but permits some administrators, subject to restrictions, to join such a bargaining unit with teachers. Strikes by teachers are prohibited.

NEVADA: Statute permits bargaining by all public employees. Strikes by public employees are illegal by statute.

NEW HAMPSHIRE: Statute permits bargaining by all public employees. Impasse resolution procedures must be implemented within the time period specified by the statute. Strikes by public employees are illegal by statute.

NEW JERSEY: Statute permits bargaining by all public employees but excludes standards of criteria for employee performance from the scope of negotiation.

NEW YORK: Statute permits bargaining by all public employees. The statute limits the scope of negotiations to matters related to wages, employment hours, and other terms and conditions of employment. Arbitration is required by statute when an impasse is declared. Strikes by public employees are prohibited.

NORTH CAROLINA: Statute prohibits collective bargaining by all public employees. Statute also prohibits strikes by public employees.

NORTH DAKOTA: Statute permits bargaining by certificated school employees. Strikes by school employees are prohibited.

OHIO: Statute permits bargaining by public employees. Strikes by public employees are prohibited.

OKLAHOMA: Statute permits bargaining by all public school employees. Strikes by teachers are prohibited.

OREGON: Statute permits bargaining by all public employees. Impasse resolution procedures include mediation and fact-finding. Strikes are permitted after impasse resolution procedures have been implemented.

PENNSYLVANIA: Statute permits bargaining by all public employees under the Public Employee Relations Act. Statute limits which employees may be included in a single bargaining unit. Public school districts are not required to bargain over the "inherent management policy" of the district. Strikes by public employees are permitted after conditions set forth in the statute are met.

RHODE ISLAND: Statute permits bargaining by all certified public school employees. Strikes by public school employees are prohibited.

SOUTH DAKOTA: Statute permits bargaining by all public employees. Strikes by public employees are prohibited.

TENNESSEE: Negotiations by professional educators governed by the Education Professional Negotiations Act. Strikes by education professionals are prohibited.

TEXAS: Statute prohibits public employees from entering into a collective bargaining agreement. Statute also prohibits strikes by public employees.

UTAH: Statute permits union membership by public employees.

VERMONT: Statute permits bargaining by public school teachers, with representation election administered by the American Arbitration Association. Strikes by state employees are prohibited by statute.

VIRGINIA: Strikes by public employees are prohibited by statute.

WASHINGTON: Statute permits bargaining by public employees, including certified educational employees. Strikes by public employees are prohibited by statute.

WEST VIRGINIA: No collective bargaining statute governs public schools. Teachers in this state should consult relevant case law to determine when collective bargaining is permitted.

WISCONSIN: A 2011 statute mandates that all public employee unions, except those covering police officers, firefighters, or state troopers, can only collectively bargain on wage issues. However, wage increases would be limited to the rate of inflation or less. Unions will no longer be able to bargain with state and local governments over health care costs, pensions, and working conditions.

WYOMING: Statute permits right to bargain as a matter of **public policy**.

ADDITIONAL RESOURCES

Carrell, Michael, and Christina Heavrin. *Labor Relations and Collective Bargaining: Private and Public Sectors.* 10th ed. Upper Saddle River, NJ: Prentice Hall, 2012.

Kearney, Richard. *Labor Relations in the Public Sector.* 4th ed. Boca Raton, FL: CRC Press, 2008.

Yudof, Mark G., David L. Kirp, Betsy Levin, and Rachel F. Moran. *Educational Policy and the Law.* 5th ed. Belmont, CA: Wadsworth Group, 2011.

ORGANIZATIONS

American Arbitration Association (AAA)
335 Madison Avenue, Floor 10
New York, NY 10017
Phone: (212) 716-5800
Fax: (212) 716-5905
URL: http://www.adr.org/

American Association of School Administrators (AASA)
1615 Duke St.
Alexandria, VA 22314
Phone: (703) 528-0700
Fax: (703) 841-1543
Email: Info@aasa.org
URL: http://www.aasa.org/

American Federation of Teachers (AFT)
555 New Jersey Avenue, NW
Washington, DC 20001
Phone: (202) 879-4400
URL: http://www.aft.org/

Education Law Association (ELA)
300 College Park
Dayton, OH 45469
Phone: (937) 229-3589
Fax: (937) 229-3845
URL: http://www.educationlaw.org/

Education Policy Institute (EPI)
4401-A Connecticut Ave., NW
Washington, DC 20008
Phone: (202) 244-7535
Fax: (202) 244-7584
URL: http://www.educationalpolicy.org/

National Education Association (NEA)
1201 16th Street, NW
Washington, DC 20036
Phone: (202) 833-4000
URL: http://www.nea.org/

EDUCATION

TRUANCY

BACKGROUND

Truancy, also called skipping school, is defined by all states as unexcused absences from school without the knowledge of a parent or **guardian**. It has been romanticized through literature and films by characters such as Tom Sawyer and Ferris Bueller as the harmless mischief juveniles do on sunny days. But the fact is juveniles who are school-aged are required by all states to attend school, whether that school be public, private, parochial, or some other educational forum. Truancy is, therefore, a **status offense** as it only applies to people of a certain age. The school age of a juvenile varies from state to state, with most states requiring attendance either from age six to age 17 or from age five to 18. There are a number of exceptions, such as Pennsylvania, which denotes school age as between eight and 17 and Illinois which denotes school age as between seven and 16.

The number of days required in order for a juvenile to be labeled "truant" varies by school, school district, and state. State legislation tends to provide some guidelines for school districts by setting a maximum number of absences allowed. School districts then tighten these guidelines. For example, in Pennsylvania, a truant is a school-aged juvenile who is absent from school more than three times after a notice of truancy has been sent to the juvenile's home. In Louisiana, a juvenile is deemed truant after the fifth unexcused absence from school, provided the absences occur in a single month. Many school districts define truancy as any unexcused absence, where unexcused means the student has left school property without parental or school permission.

THE RATIONAL FOR TRUANCY LAWS

Compulsory education was strongly influenced by labor unions who were trying to keep children from working. The participation of children in the labor force kept adult wages low. Compulsory attendance in schools also lifted some authority of parents over their children to the state, as parents could no longer force their children to work. The state's authority in school attendance was underscored in *Prince v. Massachusetts* (1944). In this case, the Supreme Court decided that the state had the right to uphold **child labor laws** and parents' authority could not preempt that of the state. Therefore, children had to attend school whether their parents supported education or not.

In research conducted by the Office for Juvenile Justice and Delinquency Prevention, links between truancy and other, more serious forms of delinquency have been delineated. For example, the links between truancy and substance abuse, **vandalism**, auto theft, and

611

gang behavior have all been established in criminology literature. The link between truancy and later, violent offenses has been established in studies that examine male criminality. In turn, adults who were truants as juveniles tend to exhibit poorer social skills, have lower paying jobs, are more likely to rely on welfare support, and have an increased likelihood of **incarceration**.

Residents have also put pressure on schools and lawmakers to tighten truancy laws as groups of young people loitering in public during school hours often appear threatening. In Tacoma, Washington, an increase in truancy was associated with an increase in juvenile perpetrated property crimes, such as **burglary** and vandalism. This increase in juvenile daytime crime led to a program targeting the enforcement of truancy laws in this state.

Those school districts with the highest truancy rates also have the lowest academic achievement rates. This link is usually established through truancy policies that deem automatic failure in courses where students are regularly absent. Therefore, students who do not attend school on a regular basis are unlikely to graduate from high school. Between 2000 and 2010 there have been approximately three million young adults each year aged between 16 and 24 who have either failed to complete high school or not enrolled in high school (National Center for Education Statistics, 2012). This number represents about 7.5 percent of young adults in the United States. Within this group, there are a disproportionate number of minority students; for example, 15 percent of Hispanics are not completing high school (NCES, 2012).

Failure in high school not only affects the individual, but it also affects society. Affected students cannot attend college, and are more likely to have low paying jobs and feel political apathy; they then can constitute a loss in tax revenue, may experience health problems, and place a strain on social services. Moreover, they experience problems finding a full time job and are more likely to be unemployed than adults with a college degree.

EXTENT OF THE TRUANCY PROBLEM

Although there are currently no national statistics available on the extent of truancy, many states and cities do keep their own statistics which are often used to influence policy. For example, in the 2008-2009 school year, California reported that 24 percent of its 6.2 million public school children, some 1.5 million students, were truant. In that same school year, Wisconsin reported that over 15 percent of its school children were truant. Of that number 62 percent were African American students. Research suggests that the number of truants is highest in inner city, public schools, where there are large numbers of students and where a large percentage of the student population participates in the free lunch program.

CORRELATES OF TRUANCY

The following factors have been found to have associations with truancy in that the likelihood of truancy is increased given the presence of these variables. First are family factors, such as lack of supervision, physical and psychological abuse, and failure to encourage educational achievement. Second are school factors which can range from inconsistent enforcement of rules to student boredom with curriculum. Economic factors are a third correlate, and these could be factors such as high family mobility or parents with multiple jobs. Last are student characteristics such as drug and alcohol abuse, ignorance of school rules, and lack of interest in education.

ENFORCING TRUANCY LAWS

In all states, the first body responsible for enforcing truancy laws is usually the school. School officials, such as school truancy officers, teachers, and school principals, refer truancy cases to juvenile court **jurisdiction**. However, if truant individuals are found in a public area, they may be detained by police or taken to a detention facility.

Arizona was the first state in the United States to implement and enforce a get-tough approach to truancy laws. Research on truancy in Arizona began in the early 1990s. Pima County had the highest truancy rate in the state during this time period; in fact, truants from this county made up half of all truants in the state. Because of the extent of the problem, Pima County began a program called ACT Now (Abolish Chronic Truancy) which aimed to strictly enforce state and district truancy laws and offer a diversion program to address the root causes of truancy. The program also sought to provide serious sanctions for both juveniles and their parents if truancy persisted or if conditions specified by the diversion program were not met. School districts, school administrators, law enforcement personnel, and community agencies are involved in this program.

Once a student has one unexcused absence from school, a letter is sent home to the student's parents explaining the consequences of truancy. After a third unexcused absence, the juvenile is referred to the Center for Juvenile Alternatives (CJA) which makes a recommendation to the juvenile court. A letter is sent to the juvenile's parents explaining the diversion program or the alternative court imposed sanctions, and the parents decide which course of action they would prefer.

The diversion program consists of counseling, parenting classes, support groups, etc. Very often parents have no idea that their child is missing school, or they do not seem to care. Support groups and classes teach parents about the value of education and also help parents communicate more effectively with their teenagers. In their report, the CJA will identify which type of intervention is best for the family, and the juvenile and his or her parents will be referred accordingly. Both parents and the juvenile must sign an agreement promising to abide by the conditions of the diversion program. Successful completion of the program results in the truancy case being dismissed.

The ACT Now program has been formally evaluated by the American Prosecutors Research Institute (APRI), and each school district involved in the program has shown a steady decrease in the number of truancies each year. In the district with the highest percentage of truancies, ACT Now helped reduce truancies by 64 percent within two years. This program and versions of it are financially supported by the Department of Justice and have been implemented in many other states.

GETTING TOUGH ON PARENTS

Many states also hold parents accountable for their children's truancy, and Arizona was the first state to implement such laws. The rationale behind this movement was to coerce parents into taking an active role in their children's education and for all parties to take truancy laws and school attendance seriously. In Virginia, parents can be fined and jailed for failure to adequately supervise school-aged children, which includes making sure they are attending school. In Pennsylvania, parents can also be fined and jailed if they have not taken reasonable steps to ensure their child is attending school. In Texas and many other states, similar laws have recently been passed.

EXAMPLES OF TRUANCY LAWS

Although states vary in their responses to truancy, their laws in defining truancy are fairly similar. Below are some examples for various states.

CALIFORNIA: Any school-aged child who is absent from school without valid excuse three full days in one school year or tardy or absent for more than any 30-minute period during one school day on three occasions during the school year or any combination thereof is considered truant and should be reported to the supervisor of the school district.

CONNECTICUT: A truant is a child between the ages of five and 18 who is enrolled in any public or private school and has four unexcused absences in a month or 10 in any school year. A **habitual** truant is a child of the same age who has 20 unexcused absences from school during a school year.

ILLINOIS: A truant is defined as any child subject to compulsory schooling who is absent from school unexcused. Absences that are excused are determined by the school

board. A chronic or habitual truant is a school-age child who is absent without valid cause for 10 percent of 180 consecutive days. The truant officer in Illinois is responsible for informing parents of truancy and referring the case to juvenile court.

LOUISIANA: Any student between the ages of seven and seventeen is required to attend school. A student is considered truant when the child has been absent from school for five school days in schools operating on a semester system and for ten days in schools not operating on a semester basis. A student may be referred to juvenile court for habitual absence when all reasonable efforts by school administrators have failed and there have been five unexcused absences in one month. The school principal or truancy officer shall file a report indicating dates of absences, contacts with parents, and other information.

VIRGINIA: Any student between the ages of five and 18 is subject to compulsory school attendance. After a pupil has been absent for five days during the school year without a valid excuse, a notice is sent to parents outlining the consequences of truancy. A conference with school officials and parents is arranged within fifteen school days of the sixth absence. Once a truant has accumulated more than seven absences during the school year, the case will be referred to juvenile and domestic relations court.

ADDITIONAL RESOURCES

Bye, Lynn. *Truancy Prevention and Intervention.* New York: Oxford University Press, 2010

ORGANIZATIONS

National Center for Juvenile Justice
710 Fifth Avenue, Suite 3000
Pittsburgh, PA 15219
Phone: (412) 227-6950
Fax: (412) 227-6955
URL: http://www.ncjj.org

OERI At Risk, U.S. Department of Education
555 New Jersey Avenue NW, Room 610
Washington, DC 20005
Phone: (202) 208-5521

Office of Juvenile Justice and Delinquency Prevention, U.S. Department of Justice
Washington, DC
URL: http://www.ojjdp.gov

EDUCATION

TYPES OF SCHOOLS

Sections within this essay:

- Background
- Public Schools
- Private and Parochial Schools
- Charter Schools
  – Privatization
- Homeschooling
- Vocational Education
- Distance Learning
- Additional Resources

BACKGROUND

For parents and students alike, the type of education available within their community is critically important. Many people, in fact, choose the communities in which they live on the basis of the quality of the local schools. Some parents choose to send their children to public school, believing that public education provides a more well-rounded experience for children. Others feel that private education offers students a more varied and creative course of study. Those who wish to instill within their children a sense of their religion may choose religious (often called parochial) schools; these schools provide religious instruction along with the general academic program. In recent years, a growing number of parents have turned to homeschooling, which they feel allows them more control over what and how their children learn.

Each system has its advantages and drawbacks; choosing the best system is determined by a number of considerations. For example, a child who lives in an affluent community with a well-respected public school system will likely want to take advantage of this free education. A child in a poorer community, or one who needs more individualized attention, may fare better in a private school, where classes are smaller and teachers can focus more fully on specific issues. Children in small rural communities, who may have to travel dozens of miles to go to school, may profit more by being homeschooled, or they may be able to hook up to schools via technology (a concept known as distance learning). How a child is educated depends on his or her abilities and needs, the expectations of parents, and the available choices. For parents and children to make informed choices, they need to understand what each type of school offers.

PUBLIC SCHOOLS

In an address to educators in 1948, the statesman Adlai Stevenson said, "The most American thing about America is the free common school system." The concept of providing free public education to all children was born in Boston in 1635 with the establishment of a public institution that still exists today as the Boston Latin School. By the time of the American Revolution, free public schools were quite common in the northern colonies; in the South, schooling was done primarily at home until after the Civil War. By the end of the nineteenth century, public education was available to children across the country. Then, as now, the quality of education varied, sometimes dramatically, from region to region. Today, public school curricula are regulated by state and local governments.

According to the National Center for Educational Statistics, there were 13,809 public school districts in the United States in academic year 2008-2009. There are approximately 99,000 public schools in the United States; 67,000 of those schools are elementary (kindergarten through sixth grade). The rest are mostly secondary (middle and high schools), although a small number of schools go from kindergarten to 12th grade (K-12). These schools employ some 3 million teachers and serve more than 77 million students.

Public schools are funded primarily by state and local sources; the federal government historically has provided less than 10 percent of public education funding. Each school district has a board of education or similar administrative group to oversee the schools' performance; each state has an education department that sets academic standards for the school districts to follow.

The public school experience varies widely from district to district. A large city such as New York or Los Angeles has to address the education of hundreds of thousands of students with extraordinarily diverse needs. A small rural school district may have only a few hundred students who all come from a similar background. Affluent suburban communities with more local funding may pay higher salaries to attract the best teachers; this makes for strong suburban school districts but leaves poorer areas underserved. State governments do try to **redress** this imbalance (by giving more funds to poorer districts, for example) but often they meet with limited success.

PRIVATE AND PAROCHIAL SCHOOLS

Unlike public schools, private schools do not rely on government funding. They are supported by tuition, by grants from charitable organizations, and in the case of religious schools, by religious institutions. As of the 2008-2009 school year, there were approximately 33,000 private schools in the United States, with some 437,000 teachers serving about 6 million students. Private schools include nonsectarian schools and religious schools covering many denominations (the term *parochial* usually denotes Catholic schools but can mean other Christian or Jewish institutions).

Tuition costs for private schools vary. By 2011, however, the average cost of a private school education had reached over $21,000 per year. Nonsectarian private schools were the most expensive and Catholic schools were the least. Why would parents send their children to private schools when they have the option of sending them to public school for free?

For some, private school represents a stronger curriculum than public education can offer and a more personalized one as well. Public schools are generally much larger than private schools, and class size is also larger. Fewer students per teacher means that the teacher can spend more time one-on-one with each student.

The atmosphere in private and parochial schools is also different, sometimes vastly so, from that of public schools. A private school can focus its attention on a student's particular talents, such as music or science. As for parochial schools, they can provide religious instruction that no public school would be allowed to offer. This religious instruction is included in a curriculum that is generally strong academically.

Not merely the educational experience but also the social experience weighs in the minds of many parents. Schools that are unsafe (which could include anything from a building with antiquated electrical and heating systems to a school with a high rate of juvenile crime) make for a difficult atmosphere in which to learn. In general, these problems are more likely to develop in a public school than in a private one.

Teacher salaries tend to be lower in private schools, although some private schools offer teachers perks such as free meals and even free housing on campus. This gives private institutions more of a competitive edge against public systems that can pay quite well. Parents often perceive this as a sign that private school teachers are more committed to teaching than some of their public school counterparts.

CHARTER SCHOOLS

Charter schools are most simply described as a cross between public and private schools. These schools are often created by teacher and parent groups who are dissatisfied with the bureaucracy that surrounds public education. The rules and regulations that shape a public school district, charter proponents argue, can cripple innovation in the schools. The result may be an uninspired and uninspiring educational program that fails to challenge students or meet their true needs.

The first charter school in the United States opened in St. Paul, Minnesota in 1993. As of the beginning of the school year 2009, there were some 5,000 charter schools operating in 40 states and the District of Columbia, serving 1.6 million students. In the following states, a charter school law has not been passed: Alabama, Kentucky, Maine, Montana, Nebraska, North Dakota, South Dakota, Vermont, Washington, and West Virginia.

Typically, a charter school will be proposed by a group consisting of teachers, parents, and community leaders. Local and state organizations provide funding for charter schools, approve their programs, and monitor their quality. Charter schools are "public" in this sense, but unlike traditional public schools they are freed from traditional regulation. In general, the number of students per charter school is lower than in a traditional school, and there are also more teachers per pupil.

Proponents of charter schools claim that the structure not only enhances autonomy from oppressive bureaucracy but also increases accountability. Because they are monitored carefully, they have little room to do poorly. If they fail to accomplish their goal, they are closed. Moreover, because parents actively choose to send their children to charter schools, the school administrators know that if they fail to provide what they promise, parents and students will go elsewhere.

Opponents of charter schools say that they are merely private schools cloaked in a public-school mantle, allowing like-minded individuals to opt out of the public school system at the expense of those schools. This makes it even harder, they maintain, for public schools to excel. Proponents counter that charter schools create a healthy competition that forces school districts to offer more and better services to students in their traditional schools.

Privatization One of the more controversial ideas in the public school arena is whether to privatize public school districts. This issue gained national attention in 2001 when the state of Pennsylvania initiated plans to take over the Philadelphia city school district and **contract** with a private firm to administer the city's schools. The move met with widespread opposition despite the fact that Philadelphia public schools had been in decline for some time. The main problem with allowing a private firm to take control of a public school district, say opponents, is that the emphasis will be on cutting costs rather than enhancing education. For-profit firms claim that they improve schools by streamlining and cutting unnecessary costs. School privatization has been tried in some districts, but the long-term benefits or drawbacks remain to be seen.

HOMESCHOOLING

A growing number of parents are choosing to turn away from public and private schools and instead educate their children in their own homes. In 2007, some 1.5 million students between the ages of 5 and 17 were being schooled at home. Approximately 84 percent of these children are schooled completely in their homes; the remaining students are schooled primarily in their homes but also go part-time to a traditional school.

In general, the makeup of a homeschooling family is fairly traditional. Most of these families (80 percent) are two-parent families, and most of them have three or more children. Typically, one parent works while the other assumes the primary role of teacher, although the other parent may also be involved in the education process as well.

The most common reason parents give for homeschooling (a reason voiced by nearly all of them) is that they feel they can provide a better education for their children at home than the schools can. They may feel that the local school's curriculum is inadequate, or that it focuses on the wrong areas. Some parents feel that traditional schools fail to teach values to children; they school their children at home to provide a strong moral education. Or they may school their children at home for religious reasons; they may feel that the public school system is too secular for their tastes. A small number of parents turn to homeschooling because they cannot afford to send their children to a private school.

In some cases, parents who homeschool their children seek and receive a degree of public school support in the form of supplies, curricular assistance, and allowing homeschoolers to participate in the school's extracurricular programs. Frequently, the parents of homeschoolers do not avail themselves of these resources, preferring to keep the education centered around the home classroom. Homeschooled children are of course required to demonstrate that they are learning at the proper educational level, and parents are expected to provide structured classes, homework, tests, and projects.

VOCATIONAL EDUCATION

Before the twentieth century, education for many young people consisted of learning a trade, which usually meant serving as an apprentice to an experienced tradesman. Apprentices learned to be blacksmiths or cabinetmakers or carpenters. In some smaller towns, children were apprenticed to professions such as law. Since the early twentieth century public high schools have offered a version of these apprenticeships in the form of vocational education (also called occupational education). This includes shop and home economics courses, as well as courses geared toward specific occupations such as electrician or automobile mechanic or cosmetologist.

DISTANCE LEARNING

In 2009–10, some 53 percent of public school districts had high school students enrolled in distance education courses. Distance education courses are defined as courses that are credit-granting, technology-delivered, have either the instructor in a different location than the students and/or have the course content developed in, or delivered from, a different location than that of the students. By comparison, in 2002–03, approximately 30 percent of public school districts had high school students enrolled in distance education courses. There were over 1.3 million high school student enrollments in distance education courses in 2009–10, an increase of over 1 million enrollments from 2004–05, when there were just over 300,000 enrollments.

The benefits of distance learning are clear: access to lessons not otherwise available. This arrangement is useful for students living in remote rural areas, but it also proves effective in urban locations. While a distance learning experience is not the same as a person-to-person lesson, it opens up avenues for new experiences. Moreover, many distance learning programs are interactive and thus engage children in a way designed to hold their attention. As technology becomes more efficient and less expensive, it is likely that distance learning will make up a growing element of elementary and secondary education.

ADDITIONAL RESOURCES

Lubienski, Christopher, and Peter Weitzel. *The Charter School Experiment: Expectations, Evidence, and Implications.* Cambridge, MA: Harvard Education Press, 2010.

Ravitch, Diane. *The Death and Life of the Great American School System: How Testing and Choice Are Undermining Education.* New York: Basic Books, 2011.

Yudof, Mark G., David L. Kirp, Betsy Levin, and Rachel F. Moran. *Educational Policy and the Law.* 5th ed. Belmont, CA: Wadsworth Group, 2011.

ORGANIZATIONS

Center for Education Reform
1001 Connecticut Avenue NW, Suite 204
Washington, DC 20036
Phone: (202) 822-9000
Fax: (202) 822-5077
URL: http://www.edreform.com

National Association of Elementary School Principals (NAESP)
1615 Duke Street
Alexandria, VA 22314
Phone: (703) 684-3345
URL: http://www.naesp.org

National Association of Secondary School Principals (NASSP)
1904 Association Drive
Reston, VA 20191
Phone: (703) 860-0200
URL: http://www.nassp.org

National Center for Education Statistics (NCES)
1990 K Street NW
Washington, DC 20006
Phone: (202) 502-7300
URL: http://www.nces.ed.gov

National Education Association (NEA)
1201 16th Street NW
Washington, DC 20036
Phone: (202) 833-4000
URL: http://www.nea.org

U.S. Department of Education
400 Maryland Avenue SW
Washington, DC 20202
Toll Free: (800) 872-5327
URL: http://www.ed.gov

EDUCATION

VIOLENCE AND WEAPONS

Sections within this essay:

BACKGROUND

Two major issues are central to the school safety debate—Fourth Amendment rights in **search and seizure** and the extent of a school's authority in controlling the school environment and its occupants. Although all states impose minimal guidelines, each school and school district is responsible for its own governing policies. Setting the standard for all states is the 1994 Improving America's Schools Act which amended the Elementary and Secondary Education Act of 1965. Title IV of the Improving Schools Act, called Safe and Drug-Free Schools and Communities, outlines legislation and initiatives to make schools safe.

Violence in school has received much public attention during the past two decades because incidents of school violence in which students and/or teachers have died of gunshot wounds have occurred across the United States. According to the National Center for Educational Statistics (NCES), from July 1, 2009, through June 30, 2010, there were 33 school-associated violent deaths in elementary and secondary schools in the United States. Of the 33 student, staff, and nonstudent school-associated violent deaths occurring between July 1, 2009, and June 30, 2010, 25 were homicides, 5 were suicides, and 3 were legal interventions.

The school setting is unique in that it forces large groups of people together for extended periods of time in small areas. Many state legislatures have recognized that certain acts committed under these circumstances have potentially greater harmful effects to the health and safety of people and have implemented legislation accordingly.

WEAPONS AT SCHOOL

Violence at school often involves the use of weapons. Traditionally, weapons prohibited on school grounds referred to firearms and explosives, but recently, many states have widened these guidelines. For example, in Kansas, weapons include firearms, explosive devices, bludgeons, metal knuckles, throwing stars, electronic stun guns, specific types of knives (such as switchblades and butterfly knives), and any weapon that "expels a projectile by the action of an explosive" (e.g., gunpowder). Other states have gone much further than these specifications. Georgia defines weapons in its school laws as items complying with these descriptions:

> any pistol, revolver, or any weapon designed or intended to propel a missile of any kind, or any

dirk, bowie knife, switchblade knife, ballistic knife, any other knife having a blade of three or more inches, straight-edge razor, razor blade, spring stick, metal knuckles, blackjack, any bat, club, or other bludgeon-type weapon, or any flailing instrument consisting of two or more rigid parts connected in such a manner as to allow them to swing freely, which may be known as a nun chahka, nun chuck, nunchaku, shuriken, or fighting chain, or any disc, of whatever configuration, having at least two points or pointed blades which is designed to be thrown or propelled and which may be known as a throwing star or oriental dart, or any weapon of like kind, and any stun gun or taser (Code 1-33).

Ramifications of Possessing Weapons on School Grounds In nearly all states, possession of a firearm on school property is a class C or class D **felony**. In addition to having the right to file criminal charges, all school districts have an automatic expulsion policy for students caught with any type of weapon on school property, an action which can be appealed on a case-by-case basis. Such policies are mandated by the Gun-Free Schools Act of 1994. Special education students are protected from automatic expulsion under the Individuals with Disabilities Education Act (IDEA). A special education student who is found to be possessing a weapon on school grounds is subject to removal from the school to an interim setting for a period of up to 45 days. During this time, the incident is studied, and if the possession of the weapon was not due to the student's **disability**, that student can be punished in the same way as a non-special education student.

Some states, for example, Kansas and Florida, have also adopted laws that allow for the revocation of students' driver's licenses if they are found guilty of possessing a firearm or drugs on school property. Kansas goes so far to say that the state can revoke a student's driver's license for any behavior engaged in by a student that was likely to result in serious bodily injury to others at school.

Holding Parents Accountable In nearly all states, parents can be held accountable for damages resulting from their child's criminal actions on school property, provided that child is living with the parents. This law means that parents of any student who vandalizes school property or attacks other students or teachers can be held liable. In addition, parents who allow minors access to firearms can be prosecuted on criminal charges, such as contributing to the delinquency of a minor.

Holding Teachers Accountable Many states have adopted laws that require teachers to report a crime that they know

or have reason to believe was committed on school property or at a school activity. Failure to do so may result in criminal prosecution for a **misdemeanor**. Lacking uniformity on this issue, school districts vary greatly with regard to making criminal charges.

LIMITATIONS ON SCHOOL AUTHORITY

Another area that has been debated by the courts is the extent of school authority. Under the Gun Free School Zones Act of 1995, a firearm could not be brought within 1,000 feet of a school. The Supreme Court, in a rare decision that overturned this Congressional Act, decided in *United States v. Lopez* (1995) that it was unconstitutional to declare schools gun-free zones in this manner. Further, the court held that claims of increased school violence could not override Second Amendment **constitutional rights**.

There have been other challenges to school authority under the Fourteenth Amendment which allows for due process. Students must be given notification of charges against them, in addition to an opportunity to defend themselves and to be represented when being expelled or suspended. A written school policy on the appeals process is recommended.

CONSTITUTIONAL RIGHTS OF STUDENTS

With the advent of increased availability of drugs and weapons for juveniles during the last twenty years, search and seizure laws have been challenged by many students who felt their constitutional rights were violated by unreasonable searches at school. Fourth Amendment protection against search and seizure was argued in the courts for years and was finally resolved in *New Jersey v. T.L.O.* (1985). In this case, a teacher had searched a student's possessions after the student was found smoking a cigarette. Subsequently, the teacher found marijuana and drug paraphernalia. There were two major questions raised by this case. First was whether students who are searched on school property have Fourth Amendment privileges and, second, what determines **probable cause** for a search. In other instances, a **warrant** is required before a search can be conducted.

The courts held that Fourth Amendment privileges do extend to students, but school authorities can search without a warrant provided the search is reasonable in inception and reasonable in scope. However, in order for law enforcement personnel to conduct a search, a warrant must be procured. This point becomes important in light of the number of schools which have their own police officers. Thus, in order for a search to take place, there must be the following conditions:

There are reasonable grounds for suspecting that the search will turn up **evidence** that the student has violated or is violating either the law or the rules of the school. Such a search will be permissible in its scope when the measures adopted are reasonable and related to the objectives of the search and are not excessively intrusive in light of the age and sex of the student and the nature of the **infraction** (*New Jersey v. T.L.O.* 1985, p. 733).

Whether a search is reasonable in inception has been interpreted as a search based on reasonable suspicion, which is very similar to probable cause. The extent of reasonable suspicion must be much higher for more intrusive searches. For example, a search of a student's locker requires a low level of reasonable suspicion, but in order for a student to be strip searched, there must be a much higher degree of reasonable suspicion. Law enforcement personnel can only conduct a body cavity search after a warrant has been procured. Further, in order for the search to comply with the law, the search must be in proportion to the suspicion. A student should not be strip searched to find ten dollars that has been stolen.

Locker searches are also affected by individual school policies. Some schools maintain that lockers are school property and, therefore, school administrators can conduct random searches of lockers. The courts have held this is permissible provided that students are notified of this policy in writing.

Metal Detectors in Schools Metal detectors have been installed in schools around the country as a means of decreasing the number of weapons being brought to school. A metal detector is a type of mass search that has been challenged as a violation of Fourth Amendment privileges. The courts in several states, such as Florida, Louisiana and Tennessee, have held that metal detectors are not violating Fourth Amendment rights and are held to the same legal standards as metal detectors in other facilities, such as airports. Metal detectors are, therefore, considered administrative searches and may provide reasonable suspicion for further individualized searches. Some states have also noted that there is a need to violate **privacy** to some degree in order for the safety of the greater group. California has stipulated that a written policy detailing policies and the use of metal detectors be given to students and should be based on information about the dangers of students' weapons at school.

Drug Testing The U.S. Supreme Court has approved the use of mandatory, random drug tests to students who are student athletes or who wish to participate in other extracurricular activities. The Court ruled in *Vernonia School District 47J v. Action* (1995) that urine testing of student athletes was reasonable on the grounds that school order and discipline outweigh individual students' privacy. Further, student athletes should have a reduced expectation of privacy given that their grades and medical history are subject to scrutiny, and they are often placed in a communal setting for dressing and showering. In *Board of Education v. Earls* (2002), the Court upheld a school's right to require random drug-testing as a condition for participation in extracurricular activities besides sports.

Vehicle Searches Searches of students' vehicles that are parked on school grounds are subject to the *T.L.O.* guidelines. However, like locker searches, it is prudent for school districts to have a written policy regarding vehicle searches and even some type of parking permit system that clearly outlines the school's policy on vehicle searches.

ADDITIONAL RESOURCES

Kafka, Judith. *The History of "Zero Tolerance" in American Public Schooling.* New York: Palgrave Macmillan, 2011.

Simpson, Sally, et al, eds. "Strain Theory and School Crime," in *Of Crime and Criminality.* Thousand Oaks, CA: Pine Forge Press, 2000.

ORGANIZATIONS

Florida Department of Education
Turlington Building, 325 West Gaines Street
Tallahassee, FL 32399-0400
URL: http://www.firn.edu/doe/

National Center for Juvenile Justice
710 Fifth Avenue, Suite 3000
Pittsburgh, PA 15219
Phone: (412) 227-6950
Fax: (412) 227-6955
URL: http://www.ncjj.org

National Drug Strategy Network, Criminal Justice Policy Foundation
1225 I Street NW, Suite 500
Washington, DC 20005-3914
Phone: (202) 312-2015
Fax: (202) 842-2620
URL: http://www.ndsn.org

National Resource Center for Safe Schools
101 SW Main Street, Suite 500
Portland, OR 97204
Phone: (503) 275-0131
Fax: (503) 275-0444

Office of Juvenile Justice and Delinquency Prevention, U.S. Department of Justice
Washington, DC
URL: http://www.ojjdp.gov

Safe Learning
160 E. Virginia Street #290
San Jose, CA 95112
Phone: (408) 286-8505
Fax: (408) 287-8748
URL: http://www.safe-learning.com

U.S. Department of Education
400 Maryland Ave., SW
Washington, DC 20202-0498
Toll Free: (800) 872-5327
URL: http://www.ed.gov

Violence Policy Center
1140 19th Street, NW, Suite 600
Washington, DC 20036
URL: http://www.vpc.org

ESTATE PLANNING

ESTATE AND GIFT TAX

Sections within this essay:

- Background
- Gift Tax
  - Gift Splitting
  - Gift Tax Return
  - Unified Credit
- Estate Tax
  - Taxable Estate
- Recipients
- Economic Growth and Tax Relief Reconciliation Act of 2001
- Generation-Skipping Transfer Tax
- Farmers and Small Business Owners
- State Taxes
- Additional Resources

BACKGROUND

Estate and gift taxes are a **statutory** method of **taxation** that are imposed on large transfers of money and/or property during an individual's lifetime or at death. Gift taxes are imposed on transfers made during an individual's lifetime. Estate taxes are imposed on transfers made as a result of death. Most gifts are not subject to the gift tax and most estates are not subject to the estate tax. According to the Internal Revenue Service, in 2011 only about 3 percent of all estates were subject to estate taxes. Estate and gift taxes are

methods the government uses to limit dynastic or familial wealth. Estate taxes are sometimes called death taxes.

An alternative form of death tax is an **inheritance** tax, which is a tax levied on individuals receiving property from the estate. Federal law does not provide for an inheritance tax, although some states have enacted such laws. A number of individual states also have enacted estate tax laws.

Although the taxation of gifts and estates may seem complex, the calculation of estate and gift taxes is similar to the calculation of personal income taxes. As with the **income tax**, there are exemptions and credits that are applied before the progressive rate schedule is applied. Estate taxes are different in that they are calculated over a lifetime, rather than year by year.

GIFT TAX

According to the Internal Revenue Code, a person gives a gift when he gives property (including money), to another without the expectation of receiving something of approximately equal value in return. A gift may also be the use of or income from property. Selling something at less than its full value, or making an interest-free or reduced interest loan, may also constitute a gift.

Although any gift has the potential to be taxable, there are a number of exceptions. For 2012, the first $13,000 given to any one person during the calendar year is not subject to the gift tax. Moreover, gifts to a spouse, a political organization, or charities are generally also exempt.

Gift Splitting If a married couple makes a gift to a third party, the gift can be considered as made one-half by each person. This is known as gift splitting. Both spouses must agree to split the gift. Gift splitting allows a married couple in 2012 to give up to $26,000 to a person annually without making a taxable gift. If a gift is split, the couple should file a gift **tax return** proving the agreement to split the gift existed. This is true even where half of the split gift is less than $13,000.

Gift Tax Return A gift tax return is filed with annual income taxes on Form 709. This form is required for gifts of over $13,000 to someone other than a spouse, or where a married couple is splitting a gift. If the gift is something the recipient cannot actually possess, enjoy, or receive income from until sometime in the future, Form 709 must be filed. It must also be filed where a person gives his or her spouse an interest in property that will be ended by some future event.

A gift tax return is not required for gifts to political organizations and gifts made for payment of tuition or medical expenses. A gift tax return is not required for certain charitable gifts, including those made to a qualified conservation **easement**. Under certain circumstances, a charitable gift also need not be reported if the gift is for an entire interest in property.

Unified Credit Most gifts above the annual exemption are still not subject to tax because each taxpayer is allowed a lifetime credit against taxable gifts and estate. This credit reduces or eliminates the amount of taxes owed. A unified credit applies to both the gift tax and the estate tax. The unified credit is subtracted from any gift tax owed by the taxpayer. Unified credit used against a gift tax in one year reduces the amount of credit that can be applied against a gift tax in later years. The total amount used against a gift tax reduces the credit available to use against estate tax. In other words, any unified credit not used against gift tax during the taxpayer's lifetime is available to reduce or eliminate an estate tax.

Previously, the law provided the same unified credit amount for both the estate tax and the gift tax. Under current law, however, the unified credit against taxable gifts is $1,772,800. The unified credit for estate purposes is the same amount for 2012.

ESTATE TAX

A person's taxable estate is defined as the gross estate less allowable deductions. Gross estate means the value of all property in which the decedent had an interest at the time of death. The gross estate includes life insurance proceeds payable to the estate or the heirs, the value of certain annuities payable to the estate or heirs, and the value of certain property transferred three years or less prior to death. Estate taxes are due to the

IRS nine months from the date of death. The estate tax return is Form 706.

Taxable Estate The taxable estate includes the value of all property and assets owned at the time of death plus any gifts made in the three years prior to death. Allowable deductions from a decedent's taxable estate include funeral expenses, debts the decedent owed at the time of death, costs of administering and settling the estate, and the marital **deduction**. The marital deduction encompasses the value of property that passes from an estate to a surviving spouse.

Any unified credit not used to eliminate gift tax can be used to eliminate or reduce estate tax. The maximum tax rate for the estate of a person who died in 2012 is 35 percent.

RECIPIENTS

The recipient of a gift or an estate is not liable for the gift or estate tax. An estate's **executor** is responsible for payment of any estate tax that is due; the **donor** is responsible for payment of a gift tax, if one is due. Moreover, gifts and inheritances are not subject to income tax.

ECONOMIC GROWTH AND TAX RELIEF RECONCILIATION ACT OF 2001

The federal estate tax law was enacted in 1916; 1997 amendments to the estate and gift tax laws raised the amount of unified credit over a nine-year period. In 2001 Congress further amended estate and gift tax laws.

The 2001 legislation increased the amount that is exempt from estate tax, while reducing the maximum tax rates on taxable property. The 2001 law provided that the federal estate tax would be completely eliminated in 2010. However, after estate tax expired, Congress passed a law that retroactively reinstated it. The new law set rates for 2011 and 2012. This law is set to expire on December 31, 2012, which means that in 2013 the estate tax laws will revert back to the laws that were in effect in 2001/2002 if Congress does nothing.

GENERATION-SKIPPING TRANSFER TAX

Generation-skipping **transfer tax** (GST) applies when a person omits their own children as beneficiaries and instead leaves the inheritance directly to their grandchildren. The GST exemptions match the estate tax exemptions, and the top tax rate is now 35 percent.

FARMERS AND SMALL BUSINESS OWNERS

A driving force behind the 1997 and 2001 changes to estate and gift tax laws was to provide some relief to farmers of family-owned farms and other **small business** owners. Because these two groups often possess a significant amount of business assets, they are more likely than other taxpayers to be subject to estate taxes. Congress responded by enacting provisions for special-use valuation of farmland, a family-business deduction, and **installment** payment of estate taxes.

A special formula to reduce the value of real estate is employed where heirs continue to use the property as a family farm or business. Moreover, they may not sell it to a non-relative for at least 10 years. This special use valuation serves to reduce the **market value** of the real estate of most farms by anywhere from 40 to 70 percent.

For estates where farm and business assets amount to more than 35 percent of the gross estate, the estate tax may be paid in installments over a 14-year period. The law provides reduced **interest rates**, and only interest payments are required for the first five years.

STATE TAXES

Federal law previously included a credit for state death taxes, but the 2001 law changes phased out the state tax credit and replaced it with a deduction for state estate taxes paid. This change in the federal law spurred some states to reduce or eliminate their state death taxes.

ADDITIONAL RESOURCES

Internal Revenue Service. "Publication 950: Introduction to Estate and Gift Taxes." October 2011. Available at http://www.irs.gov/publications/p950/index.html (accessed November 2, 2012).

McNulty, John, and Garyson, M.P. *Federal Estate and Gift Taxation in a Nutshell.* Eagan, MN: West, Thomson Reuters, 2011.

ORGANIZATIONS

American College of Trust and Estate Counsel

3415 South Sepulveda Boulevard., Suite 330
Los Angeles, CA 90034
Phone: (310) 398-1888
Fax: (310) 572-7280

National Academy of Elder Law Attorneys, Inc.

1604 North Country Club Road
Tucson, AZ 85716
Phone: (520) 881-4005
Fax: (520) 325-7925
URL: http://www.naela.com/

ESTATE PLANNING

GUARDIANSHIPS AND CONSERVATORSHIPS

BACKGROUND

If an individual becomes unable to handle his or her own affairs there are two major areas of concern. These are the individual's physical welfare decisions and the management of the individual's finances. A guardianship is the appointment of an individual to provide care and to make personal decisions for a minor or incapacitated person.

A **guardian** may be nominated by a will, by a **trust** document, or by any person via a petition with the court. The person for whom a guardian is appointed is called a ward. Generally, the ward cannot provide food, clothing, or shelter for him or herself without assistance. A conservatorship is the appointment of an individual or a corporation with **trustee** powers, to manage the financial affairs of a minor or other person who cannot manage his or her own financial matters. A conservator is not authorized to make decisions regarding the personal care as a guardian does. The person for whom a conservator is appointed is called a protected person. The court may appoint a conservator for a single transaction or indefinitely. A person may need a guardian or a conservator or both and the same person can be appointed in both capacities.

GUARDIANSHIP

Guardianship is established by a court order. The court grants the guardian authority and responsibility to act on behalf of another person. The relationship is **fiduciary**, which means that the guardian is obliged to act in the best interests of the ward. The court supervises the guardian to assure proper actions on behalf of the ward. An individual may serve as guardian of a minor or of an incapacitated person. For a minor, the court considers which individual's appointment will be in the best interest of the minor. In some states, a minor ward over fourteen can nominate his or her own choice for guardian. Any competent person may be appointed guardian for an incapacitated person. The appointee might be the spouse, an adult child or parent of the ward, or any responsible adult with whom the ward is residing.

To establish a guardianship, a petition is typically filed in state court where the ward lives. This petition usually names the potential guardian and provides information about the parties' relationship (if any) and any pertinent information about the heirs or estate of the ward. If the ward is a minor, information about the minor's parents and whether and where they are living is generally necessary. In the case of an adult ward, if mental incapacity is the reason for the petition, medical documentation should accompany the filing. Notice of the time and place of the **hearing** is given to the potential ward and other persons specified by **statute**.

The documents are served on the interested parties at which point the proposed ward or his or her relatives can object to the guardianship request. A hearing is held. If the court finds sufficient **evidence** to order the guardianship, it may issue subsequent orders, which govern the relationship and the guardian's actions. The court may appoint a guardian if it finds the person is incapacitated and the appointment is necessary to provide continuing care and supervision of the person. Incapacity can result from any number of conditions, including, but not limited to mental illness, mental deficiency, mental disorder, physical illness or **disability**, or chronic use of alcohol or other drugs. Essentially, the court must be convinced that the individual lacks sufficient understanding or capacity to make or communicate responsible decisions. The court may terminate a guardianship if a subsequent hearing proves that the need for a guardian no longer exists, or in the case of a minor, when the child reaches the **age of majority**.

A guardianship restricts the individual's right to **contract**, marry, spend money, make decisions about their own care, or create a new will. The guardian may make personal decisions for the ward such as living arrangements, education, social activities, and authorization or withholding of medical or other professional care, treatment, or advice. A guardian must submit written reports to the court according to the court's orders and the law of the **jurisdiction** in which the guardianship takes place. Generally, a guardian is not charged with managing the income or property of the incapacitated person; however, the guardian may receive funds payable for the support of the ward such as social security as a representative payee.

If a guardianship is contested, the court may appoint a disinterested third party to investigate and make recommendations. Usually called a **guardian ad litem**, this person evaluates both the necessity for a guardianship, and the appropriateness of the proposed guardian. The ward may also hire separate legal **counsel**. If the proposed ward is indigent, the court sometimes appoints counsel.

GUARDIANSHIP OF MINORS

Guardianship of a minor is typically appropriate when a child is permanently living with someone other than a parent. This might occur if both parents died, or if one parent died and the other is incarcerated or otherwise absent. Guardianships of minors are often established when neither parent is able to provide a safe, secure home for the child because of drug abuse, alcoholism, and other serious personal problems.

The difference between guardianship and **adoption** is that guardianship does not sever the biological parents' rights and responsibilities. Guardianship of a child means that a caregiver is responsible for the care and **custody** of the child. This arrangement allows the guardian to access services on behalf of the child. Unlike adoption, a birth parent can return to court at any time and ask for the guardianship to be terminated.

When a guardian is appointed for a minor child, the court may impose conditions. One common condition is a requirement that the guardian attend parenting classes. Courts sometimes require that grandparent guardians attend grandparent caregiver support groups. Not only are judges aware that parenting techniques have changed in recent years, but if the child's parents are drug addicts, alcoholics, or abusive toward children, it may be appropriate to question why the grandparents will do a better job raising the grandchildren than they did raising their own children. Grandparents seeking guardianship should be prepared to address these issues.

Guardianship of the Estate Even if a minor child lives with one or both parents, in some states a guardianship is required if the child inherits property worth more than $20,000. After the court appoints a guardian, an inventory and **appraisal** must be filed, and annual or bi-annual accountings must also be filed with the court until the child reaches age eighteen.

De Facto Custodian De Facto Custodian laws give caregivers the same standing as parents in custody cases if they satisfy the definition of de facto custodian. They must be the primary caregiver and must be providing financial support of a child who has lived with the de facto custodian for a certain period of time.

Standby Guardianship These laws were originally designed in response to the AIDS crisis and allow a terminally ill parent to designate a standby guardian to take over the day to day care of a child in the event of parental incapacity. There is a Sense of Congress in the Adoption and Safe Families Act (ASFA) that States should pass these laws.

Permanent Guardianship Permanent guardianships are for children in state custody. In some states permanent guardianship status may be granted by the juvenile court after it is proven that it is in the best interest of the child that the birth parent should never have physical custody of the child. A birth parent is prohibited from petitioning the court to terminate this permanent guardianship once it is granted.

Subsidized Guardianship Some states have programs that provide a monthly subsidy payment to grandparents and other relatives who obtain guardianship of the children they are raising. Subsidized guardianships are designed for those children who have been in state custody, with a relative or non-relative providing the care, for at least six months and in some states up to two years. The subsidy is sometimes less than the **foster care** payment in that state but usually more than the Temporary Assistance for Needy Families (TANF) child-only grants. Continued eligibility for the subsidy is typically re-determined annually. The subsidy payments usually end when the guardianship terminates or when the child turns 18, although several states continue the subsidy until the child reaches age 21 or 22 provided he or she is attending school. States have some similar programs that do not require the child to be in state custody.

CONSERVATORSHIP

Unlike a guardian, a conservator has no power or responsibility over the individual. Only the money and property falls within the conservator's jurisdiction. A conservator has power to invest funds of the estate and to distribute sums reasonably necessary for the support, care, education or benefit of the protected person and any legal dependents of the protected person. Either an individual or a corporation with general power to serve as a trustee may be appointed conservator for a protected person. Typically, state laws provide a preferred order of priority for those who may be considered by the court for appointment. A conservator has the powers and responsibilities of a fiduciary and is held to the standard of care applicable to a trustee. The conservator files an inventory of the estate of the protected person with the court and accountings of the administration of the estate.

Conservatorship is established by petitioning the court. The petition can be filed by the person to be protected, or by any person interested in the estate, affairs, or welfare of the protected person. This appointee could be a parent or guardian, or any individual or entity adversely affected by improper management of the property and affairs of the protected person. In most states, the person to be protected must be represented by an attorney. The court also typically requires an

independent physician's report. The court may appoint a conservator if it finds that an individual is unable to manage property and financial affairs effectively for reasons including, but not limited to, mental illness, mental deficiency, mental disorder, physical illness or disability, chronic use of drugs, chronic **intoxication**, confinement, detention by a foreign power, or disappearance.

A conservatorship terminates upon the death of the protected person or upon a court determination that the disability of the protected person has ceased. The protected person, the personal representative of the protected person, the conservator, or any other interested person or entity may petition the court to terminate the conservatorship. Upon termination, title of the assets passes to the former protected person, or if deceased, as provided by the protected person's will.

INVOLUNTARY COMMITMENT

A person who is a danger to self or others can, under certain conditions, be court ordered to a mental hospital. Most states allow commitment to public and private mental hospitals, either as a voluntary patient accepted by the institution or under a court order of involuntary commitment. Legal standards surround the process by which those who are mentally ill can be forced to receive treatment. State laws and rules regarding involuntary commitment are subject to the due process clause of the Fourteenth Amendment, which guarantees the right to be free from governmental restraint and the right not to be confined unnecessarily.

If a guardian or person is not agreeable to a voluntary commitment, state law provisions typically provide a procedure for emergency involuntary hospitalization. In the event of a voluntary hospitalization, a person, or that person's court-ordered guardian, requests admission to the hospital. The hospital can retain the patient indefinitely or discharge the patient provided the staff determines discharge is in the best interest of the patient and the community. In many states, a patient on a voluntary admission who wishes to leave must give the institution three days notice. This gives the hospital the opportunity to apply for involuntary commitment of the patient, if the staff determines that is appropriate. The facility will then typically retain the patient until the court hearing.

PUBLIC FIDUCIARY

A public fiduciary is a governmental official appointed to serve as guardian, conservator, or personal representative for those individuals or estates with no one else willing or capable of serving. The public fiduciary may file a petition with the court to be named guardian/conservator if the public fiduciary believes such a request is warranted. The court appoints the public fiduciary if the court finds sufficient evidence that a person or estate is in need of the services of the public fiduciary.

REPRESENTATIVE PAYEE

Sometimes involuntary commitment or even a guardianship or conservatorship is not the best solution. If an elderly person is no longer able to remember to write out checks but can still remember how to eat regularly and take medication appropriately, a representative payeeship may often be an option. A representative payeeship is an arrangement whereby a person's Social Security and/or Supplemental Security Income (SSI) checks, or even his or her private **pension** checks, are issued to another person who is the representative payee. This person can be a family member, friend, social worker, attorney, or accountant. Additionally, many utility companies, if requested, will contact a representative third party prior to the termination of services to an elderly person. Sometimes this is sufficient to assure that an elderly person does not have essential services disconnected.

POWER OF ATTORNEY

A **power of attorney** is an authorization for one person to transact business on behalf of another. It can be specific as to one instance, or it can include any conceivable business transaction. Power of attorney documents were once considered void if the maker became mentally incompetent. Most states have now adopted the Uniform Durable Power of Attorney Act which provides that a power of attorney will survive even though its maker has become mentally incompetent.

While a power of attorney is a simple document to draft, it has inherent pitfalls. Power of attorney can be a useful safeguard against potential unknown future incapacity, but it empowers someone else to handle the financial affairs of an incapacitated person. As a result, it may give rise to family disputes and even emergency court filings in a time of family crisis. And, unlike a court appointed guardian or conservator, there is no one charged with overseeing the action of the individual with the power of attorney.

JOINT OWNERSHIP

Most common in married couples' financial situations is joint ownership. Individual access to bank accounts can be had by either joint owner, even if the other joint owner is incapacitated. For this reason, elderly people sometimes place an adult child's name on their accounts. This is a simple and effective way of insuring that the child can continue to pay the parent's bills if the parent is unable to do so. It does, however, give the child the legal ability to

withdraw everything from the entire account. Placing an adult child's name jointly on an asset can also present problems to the parent if the child incurs debts, is sued, or gets divorced. Since joint ownership means just that, the result can be that the asset which was once solely the parent's can become subject to the adult child's creditors or soon to be ex-spouse.

While joint **tenancy** can transfer assets at death without any type of **probate** proceedings, the legal implications of joint tenancy are governed by state law and will vary from state to state. In some states with **community property** law, property owned by spouses in joint tenancy will not receive the same tax treatment when one spouse dies. The joint tenancy property can lose important benefits otherwise available to the survivor. Finally, because jointly-owned assets transfer directly to the survivor, such property passes outside of a will. A parent can unintentionally leave his or her property to the child who is the joint owner, rather than having the property divided equally among several children.

STATE LAW PROVISIONS

ALABAMA: See Alabama Uniform Guardianship and Protective Proceedings Act, Alabama Code §26-2A-1 et seq. for conservatorship and guardianship laws.

ALASKA: See Alaska Statutes, Title 13: Decedents' Estates, Guardianships, Transfers, and Trusts, Chapter 13: Protection of Persons Under Disability and Their Property, §13.26.090 et seq. for guardianship and conservatorship laws.

ARIZONA: See Arizona Revised Statutes, Title 14: Decedents' Estates, Guardianships, Protective Proceedings and Trusts, Chapter 5: Protection of Persons Under Disability and Their Property, §14-5101 et seq. for guardianship and conservatorship codes.

ARKANSAS: See Arkansas Code, Title 28: **Wills**, Estates, and Fiduciary Relationships, Subtitle 5: Fiduciary Relationships, Chapter 65: Guardians Generally, §28-65-101 et seq. for guardianship laws.

CALIFORNIA: See California Probate Code, Division 4: Guardianship, Conservatorship, and Other Protective Proceedings, Part 3: Conservatorship, §1800 et seq. for conservatorship laws.

COLORADO: See Colorado Revised Statutes, Volume 5, Title 15: Probate, Trusts, and Fiduciaries, Article 14: Persons Under Disability—Protection, §15-14-101 et seq. for guardianship and conservatorship laws.

CONNECTICUT: See General Statutes of Connecticut, Volume 12, Title 45a: Probate Courts and procedure, Chapter 802h: Protected Persons and Their Property, §45a-644 et seq. for conservatorship laws.

DELAWARE: See Delaware Code, Title 12, Chapter 39: Guardianship, §3901 et seq. for guardianship laws.

DISTRICT OF COLUMBIA: See District of Columbia Code, Chapter 20: Guardianship, Protective Proceedings, and Durable Power of Attorney, §21-2001 et seq. for guardianship and conservatorship laws.

FLORIDA: See Florida Statutes Annotated, Title 43 (XLIII): Domestic Relations, Chapter 744: Guardianship, §744.1012 et seq. for guardianship laws.

GEORGIA: See Georgia Code §29-5-1 et seq. for guardianship laws.

HAWAII: See Hawaii Uniform Probate Code, Article V: Protection of Persons Under Disability and Their Property, §560:5-301 et seq. for laws on guardianships and protective proceedings.

IDAHO: See Idaho Statutes, Title 15: Uniform Probate Code, Chapter 5: Protection of Persons Under Disability and Their Property, §15-5-101 et seq. for guardianship and conservatorship laws.

ILLINOIS: See Illinois Compiled Statutes, Chapter 755: Estates, Probate Act of 1975, 755 ILCS 5/, Article XIa, Guardians for Disabled Adults, 755 ILCS 5/11a-2 et seq. for guardianship laws.

INDIANA: See Indiana Code, Title 29: Probate, Article 3: Guardianships and Protective Proceedings, IC 29-3-1 et seq. for guardianship laws.

IOWA: See Iowa Code, Title XV: Judicial Branch and Judicial Procedures, Subtitle 4: Probate–Fiduciaries, 633: Probate Code, §633.551 et seq. for guardianship and conservatorship laws.

KANSAS: See Kansas Statutes, Chapter 59: Probate Code, Article 30: Guardians or Conservators, §59-3001 et seq. for guardianship/conservatorship laws.

KENTUCKY: See Kentucky Revised Statutes, Title XXXIII, Chapter 387, §387.500 et seq. for guardianship and conservatorship laws.

LOUISIANA: See Louisiana Statutes Annotated, Civil Code, Art. 389 et seq. for laws on interdiction proceedings.

MAINE: See Maine Revised Statutes, Title 18-A: Probate Codes, Article V: Protection of Persons under Disability and Their Property, §5-101 et seq. for guardianship and conservatorship laws.

MARYLAND: See Maryland Statutes, Article: Estates and Trusts, §13-101 et seq. for guardianship laws.

MASSACHUSETTS: See General Laws of Massachusetts, Chapter 201, Guardians and Conservators, §1 et seq. for guardianship and conservatorship laws.

MICHIGAN: See Michigan Compiled Laws, Act 386 of 1998, Article V, Protection of an Individual Under Disability and His or Her Property: Part I, §700.5101 et seq. (for general provisions); Part 3, §700.5301 et seq. (for guardianship codes); and Part 4, §700.5401 et seq. (for conservatorship codes).

MINNESOTA: See Minnesota Statutes, Chapter 525: Probate Proceedings, §525.539 et seq. for guardianship and conservatorship laws.

MISSISSIPPI: See Mississippi Code, Title 93: Domestic Relations, Chapter 13: Guardians and Conservators, §93-13-5 et seq. for guardianship laws, and §93-13-251 for conservatorship laws.

MISSOURI: See Missouri Revised Statutes, Chapter 475: Probate Code–Guardianship, Section 475.010 et seq. for guardianship and conservatorship laws.

MONTANA: See Montana Code Annotated, Title 72: Estates, Trusts, and Fiduciary Relationships, Chapters 1-5: Uniform Probate Code, Part 3 (Chapter 5): Guardians of Incapacitated Persons, §72-5-101 et seq. for guardianship/conservatorship laws.

NEBRASKA: See Nebraska Uniform Probate Code, Revised Statutes, Chapter 30, §30-2619 et seq. for guardianship and conservatorship laws.

NEVADA: See Nevada Revised Statutes, Chapter 159: Guardianships, §159.013 et seq. for guardianship laws.

NEW HAMPSHIRE: See New Hampshire Revised Statutes, Title 44, Guardians and Conservators, Chapter

464-A, §464-A1 et seq. for guardianship and conservatorship laws.

NEW JERSEY: See New Jersey Permanent Statutes, Title 3B, Administration of Estates—Decedents and Others, §3B:12-1, §3B:12-25 et seq. for guardianship laws.

NEW MEXICO: See New Mexico Statutes Annotated, Chapter 45: Uniform Probate Code, §45-5-101 et seq. for guardianship and conservatorship laws.

NEW YORK: See New York State Consolidated Laws, Mental Hygiene, Title EA81, Article 81: Proceedings for Appointment of a Guardian for Personal Needs or Property Management, §81.01 et seq. for guardianship laws.

NORTH CAROLINA: See North Carolina General Statutes, Chapter 35A: **Incompetency** and Guardianship, Subchapter 1: Proceedings to Determine Incompetence, Article 1: Determination of Incompetence, §35A-1101 et seq. for guardianship laws.

NORTH DAKOTA: See North Dakota Century Code, Article V: Protection of Persons Under Disability and Their Property, Chapter 30.1-26 et seq. for guardianship and conservatorship laws.

OHIO: See Ohio Revised Code, Title 21, Chapter 11, §2111.01 et seq. for guardianship laws.

OKLAHOMA: See Oklahoma State Statutes, Title 30: Oklahoma Guardianship Act, §30-1-101 et seq. for guardianship laws.

OREGON: See Oregon Revised Statutes, Chapter 125: Protective Proceedings, §125.005 et seq. for guardianship and conservatorship laws.

PENNSYLVANIA: See Pennsylvania Consolidated Statutes, Title 20: Decedents, Estates and Fiduciaries, Chapter 55: Incapacitated Persons, §5501 et seq. for guardianship laws.

RHODE ISLAND: See Rhode Island General Laws, Title 33: Probate Practice and Procedure, Chapter 33-15: Limited Guardianship and Guardianship of Adults, §33-15-1 et seq. for guardianship and conservatorship laws.

SOUTH CAROLINA: See South Carolina Code Annotated, Article 5: Protection of Persons Under Disability and Their Property, §62-5-101 et seq. for guardianship and conservatorship laws.

SOUTH DAKOTA: See South Dakota Codified Laws, Chapter 29A-5: South Dakota Guardianship and Conservatorship Act, §29A-5-101 et seq. for guardianship and conservatorship laws.

TENNESSEE: See Tennessee Code, Title 34: Guardianship–Estates of Incompetents, Chapter 11: Guardianships and Conservatorships Generally, §34-11-101 et seq. for conservatorship laws.

TEXAS: See Texas Probate Code, Chapter XIII: Guardianship, Part 1, Subpart A, §601 et seq. for guardianship laws.

UTAH: See Utah Uniform Probate Code, Title 75, Chapter 05: Protection of Persons under Disability and Their Property, §75-5-301 et seq. for guardianship and conservatorship laws.

VERMONT: See Relations, Part IV: Fiduciary Relations, Chapter III: Guardian and Ward, Subchapter XII: Total and Limited Guardianship for Mentally Disabled Adults, §3060 et seq. for guardianship laws.

VIRGINIA: See Virginia Code, Title 37.1: Institutions for the Mentally Ill; Mental Health Generally, Chapter 4, Article 1.1: Guardianship and Conservatorship, §37.1-134.6 et seq. for guardianship laws.

WASHINGTON: See Revised Code of Washington (RCW), Title 11—Probate and Trust Law, Chapters 11.88 and 11.92, §11.88.005 et seq. and §11.92.010 et seq. for guardianship laws.

WEST VIRGINIA: See West Virginia Code, Chapter 44A, West Virginia Guardianship and Conservatorship Act, §44A-1-1 et seq. for guardianship laws.

WISCONSIN: See Wisconsin Statutes, Chapter 880: Guardians and Wards, Subchapter 1: General Provisions, §880.01 et seq. for guardianship laws.

WYOMING: See Wyoming Statutes, Title 3: Guardians and Ward, §3-1-101 et seq. for guardianship/conservatorship laws.

ADDITIONAL RESOURCES

Teaster, Pamela. *Public Guardianship*. Westport, CT: Praeger, 2010.

ORGANIZATIONS

Elder Law Project Legal Services for Cape Cod and Islands, Inc.

460 West Main Street
Hyannis, MA 02601
Phone: (508) 775-7020

National Academy of Elder Law Attorneys, Inc.

1604 North Country Club Road
Tucson, AZ 85716

Phone: (520) 881-4005
Fax: (520) 325-7925
URL: http://www.naela.com/

National Alliance for the Mentally Ill

2107 Wilson Blvd., Suite 300
Arlington, VA 22201
Phone: (703) 524-7600
URL: http://www.nami.org/

ESTATE PLANNING

INTESTACY

Sections within this essay:

BACKGROUND

When a person dies (the decedent), a major concern for those surviving the decedent is how to distribute the decedent's property, or the estate. An age-old problem, this issue has mattered greatly in the past, and it still does. Accordingly, the law has developed to govern not only how the decedent's personal property and real property is distributed to heirs but also how important privileges as well as debts and other responsibilities are passed down to later generations.

Because this issue reaches into ancient times and the consequences of **inheritance** can be so important, there is an enormous body of **statutory** and **case law** relating to "who gets what" when someone dies. There are several key components to these laws. For example, there are laws about **wills**, trusts, and other methods of leaving property in addition to wills, jurisdiction of **probate** courts, qualifications and duties of executors of wills, and estate and inheritance taxes. Tax consequences for the estate and heirs are important considerations when individuals plan their estates. Whether individuals die with a will or intestate, there are tax consequences for estates and potentially for those who would **inherit** property according to the laws of intestacy. The negative tax consequences and other potentially unintended consequences that can flow from dying intestate are major reasons that prompt people to create wills.

INTESTACY

When a decedent does not leave a legally binding will, this state is called dying intestate. The estate of a decedent (an estate is the sum of the decedent's property) who dies intestate is distributed according to the intestacy laws where the decedent was domiciled and/or where the decedent owned real property. Federal law leaves the creation of intestacy laws largely up to the states. Consequently, intestacy laws and judicial decisions vary from state to state. Intestacy statutes basically "create" a will for the decedent if the individual died intestate.

The most common way for individuals to influence how their property gets distributed when they die is to create a will. Wills are legal documents that help heirs and courts; local, state and federal governments; and the decedent's creditors know how to distribute that person's property upon death.

Partial Intestacy If someone dies and has made a will, all state laws strongly favor the decedent's intentions as expressed in his will. However, even if the individual has made a will, it is possible for the person to die partially intestate. This situation occurs when a gift in the will is invalid for some reason, or if the terms of the will simply do not cover all of the property. For example, if the will only disposes of personal property (like jewelry, art, automobiles, and antiques), the **personal property** will be distributed to those named in the will according to the terms of the will. However, if the individual had purchased a parcel of land after the will was made and failed to later include that land in the will, then the real estate may pass to the heirs under the laws of intestacy. In some states, if an otherwise valid will is not properly filed with the probate court within a specific time, the entire estate will be distributed according to the state intestacy scheme. Needless to say, these situations may not at all be what the decedent wanted to happen.

Determining Who Will Receive a Share of an Intestate Estate If individuals die intestate, their state's intestacy laws will make assumptions about how they would want to leave their property. Some of these assumptions may be correct, and others may result in the distribution of property in a manner far different from their wishes. The law will determine who will inherit the property (heirs) and how the property will be divided among the heirs, but it cannot determine who will receive specific items of property. For example, the law may state that the two children, a daughter and a son, will each take one half of the estate, but it may not say that the daughter should receive the decedent's mother's wedding ring and the decedent's son should receive the decedent's antique desk. Leaving such issues for a judge or other official to determine can cause squabbles among heirs, expense to the estate, and long delays in disposing of the property.

For the most part, states assume that the closer individuals are related to someone, the more likely the decedent would want the property to go to those persons when the decedent dies. In this way, intestate laws generally favor blood relations over other types of relationships. It is also common for state laws to require that heirs survive the decedent by a certain amount of time. This time can be expressed in hours, days, or months, depending on the state. These rules become important when there is an event in which several members of a family are killed at or about the same time. They generally apply whether or not the decedent had a will.

Intestacy Laws and Surviving Spouses Of course, there are also many laws that pertain to surviving spouses of decedents who die intestate. Like other aspects of intestacy, these laws vary considerably from state to state. While it seems safe to assume that the spouse will inherit the entire estate if the decedent dies without a will, this is not necessarily the case. It is true that spouses usually inherit the greatest portion of the decedent's estate; however, intestacy laws almost always divide the estate between the decedent's spouse, children, and sometimes even the decedent's parents. If there are no spouse or children, and if the decedent's parents are dead, then the estate usually is distributed among the decedent's siblings or other relatives according to specific rules delineated in the statutes.

It is crucial to keep in mind that state intestacy laws can differ significantly from one state to the next. For example, most states set aside an allowance for a surviving spouse and/or children. This can be true whether or not there is a will. This amount is usually modest, but it is free from any other claims against the estate or debts of the decedent. In these cases, the spouse and/or children take a specific dollar amount of the estate. Their doing so occurs before the creditors, heirs, and other beneficiaries receive their shares of what remains. There are great differences in these allowances among the states. For example, this amount is set at $50,000 in California, but only $2,000 in Delaware. If there is no will, many states also give the surviving spouse a definite financial interest in any real estate owned by the decedent, such as "one-half," or a "life estate."

Intestacy and Marital Property The portion of an estate that is distributed to the spouse of a decedent who dies intestate depends to some extent on other laws governing marital property in the decedent's state. For example, in states which employ a **community property** scheme, spouses generally own equal rights to all marital property, regardless of whose name is on the title of the property. But this general rule has some important exceptions. There are currently nine community property states: Arizona, California, Idaho, Louisiana, Nevada, New Mexico, Texas, Washington, and Wisconsin.

In a typical situation involving community property for a decedent who dies intestate, the decedent's share of the community property owned at the time of death will pass automatically to the surviving spouse. Property that the decedent owned individually (e.g. certain property owned prior to the marriage) is usually divided between the surviving spouse and any children. The spouse usually takes one quarter of this individual property and surviving children take the remaining three-quarters of the property. For individuals living in a community property state, the complexity of the intestacy and other probate laws make it especially important to contact competent legal advice when planning their estates.

TYPICAL INTESTACY DISTRIBUTION METHODS

What happens to their property if individuals die without a will? The answer to this question depends on many factors. Because of the variability of the response, it is perhaps best to explain through illustrations. Here are four examples of some of the most common distribution methods under typical intestacy laws.

If the Intestate Decedent Is Married but Has No Children

- If the intestate decedent is married but has no children, most people would probably think that the decedent's surviving spouse would take everything in the estate. However, most states distribute between one-third to one-half of the estate to the surviving spouse. Anything remaining generally goes to the decedent's surviving parent or parents. If both of the decedent's parents are dead, many state intestate statutes **decree** that the remaining portion be distributed among the decedent's surviving brothers and sisters.

If the Intestate Decedent Is Married and Has Children

- If the intestate decedent is married and has children, it seems reasonable to assume that the surviving spouse/parent would take all of the deceased spouse's property, especially if the children are minors at the time of the decedent's death. Yet, most intestacy statutes distribute just one-third to one-half of the decedent's property to the surviving spouse. The remainder is divided among the decedent's surviving children, regardless of their ages.

If the Intestate Decedent Is a Single Person with Children

- If the intestate decedent is a single person with children, state intestacy laws uniformly decree that the entire estate will be distributed equally among the children, regardless of their ages or circumstances. For example, an adult child will receive the same amount as a minor child, and a wealthy child will take the same

share as a child in more modest circumstances. The only determining factor is the blood relation to the decedent. Most states also make no distinction between siblings of whole blood and siblings of half blood. Thus, in a case where a decedent has children from two marriages, each child from both marriages will take an equal share of the decedent's estate. Likewise, intestacy laws in all states treat legally adopted children the same as full-blooded relations of the decedent. The laws may differ significantly with respect to the decedent's stepchildren and illegitimate children.

If the Intestate Decedent Is a Single Person with No Children

- If the intestate decedent is a single person with no children, most state intestacy laws favor the decedent's parent(s) in the distribution of his/her property. If both parents predecease the decedent, many states divide the property among the decedent's surviving brothers and sisters.

Intestacy laws that distribute property to surviving children and other relatives use various formulas to divide the property. In a state that employs a "per capita" method, the heirs receive equal shares. For example, if there are eleven heirs of a decedent who dies intestate, each will receive one-eleventh of the decedent's estate. Other states have more complicated schemes that determine the amount of an heir's share according to the degree of relationship to the decedent. For example, let us say that a decedent has two adult children. One of these children is dead, but has two surviving children (the decedent's grandchildren). So in the present case, the decedent's surviving adult child would take one half of the estate and the decedent's two grandchildren would share their deceased parent's half share, each taking one-quarter of the estate. These examples show that the methods of distributing property under intestacy law can range from fairly simple to quite complex.

Escheat If the intestate decedent has no living spouse, children, parents, or siblings, intestacy laws provide mechanisms to determine other blood relatives qualified to take the estate. Overall, there is a strong statutory preference to distribute the decedent's property to heirs, regardless of how remote they may be to the decedent. Sometimes, the search for heirs can be time-consuming and expensive. The estate bears the expense of a search for heirs. However, in those rare cases where no living **heir** can be located, then the decedent's estate will escheat to the state, that is, the state takes ownership of the decedent's property. Escheat is rare and almost never what the decedent wanted or expected to happen with the estate.

ESTATE AND INHERITANCE TAX CONSIDERATIONS

When a person dies the federal and state governments may impose taxes on the transfer of the property. This is true whether the person dies with a will or intestate. These taxes are calculated according to the rules of estate tax law. In some cases, the property received by heirs may also be taxed according to inheritance tax laws. The inheritance tax is usually determined by the amount of property received by the **beneficiary**, as well as by the beneficiary's relationship to the decedent. Basically, it is a tax on the right to receive the property. Every state except Nevada imposes either an estate tax or an inheritance tax; some states employ both. Inheritance taxes are not levied in addition to federal estate taxes because the federal law allows an offset for the payment of state death taxes. The maximum taxes in states with inheritance taxes are:

- Delaware 16%
- Kansas 15%
- Kentucky 16%
- Indiana 15%
- Iowa 15%
- Maryland 10%
- Massachusetts 16%
- Michigan 17%
- Mississippi 16%
- Montana 32%
- Nebraska 18%
- New Hampshire 15%
- New Jersey 16%
- North Carolina 17%
- Ohio 7%
- Oklahoma 15%
- Pennsylvania 15%
- South Dakota 30%
- Tennessee 13%

Currently, the estate of a decedent is liable for a tax if the estate exceeds $650,000. The United States has recently enacted new laws that will increase this amount in certain increments over the next several years. In calculating the value of an estate for tax purposes one starts with the premise that all property owned by the decedent at the time of death is potentially subject to tax. This amount can be modified by several factors:

- The decedent's debts
- Certain transfers to charity
- Certain transfers to the decedent's spouse
- Some **casualty** and theft losses

An intestate estate is the most exposed to estate and inheritance tax liability. The greater the value of the estate, the greater the tax burden on the estate—and potentially on the beneficiaries of the estate. This fact is a powerful inducement for many people to seek estate-planning advice. There are several methods to shield the value of an estate from estate and inheritance tax laws. Along with the creation of a will, some of these methods may include the creation of a **trust**, purchasing life insurance policies, and making transfers of property prior to one's death, known as inter vivos gifts. Attorneys and accountants provide for more specific information about estate and inheritance tax rules.

Individuals who do have wills and believe they would distribute their property differently than their state's intestacy distribution plan should consult their attorneys for advice on estate planning and wills. Likewise, if they believe they are the beneficiaries of an intestate decedent's estate, they should check with their own attorneys for information about the specific laws governing their particular situation and advice about how to proceed to claim their share of the estate. Intestacy laws differ in very significant ways from state to state; understanding their applicability to you may require the advice from an attorney.

ADDITIONAL RESOURCES

The American Bar Association Guide to Wills & Estates. American Bar Association, Times Books, 1995.

Mennell, Robert L. *Wills and Trusts in a Nutshell*. Eagan, MN: West, Thomson Reuters, 2007.

Palermo, Michael T. "Crash Course in Wills and Trusts." Available at http://www.caregiver.com/articles/general/trust_and_wills.htm (accessed October 31, 2012).

ORGANIZATIONS

American Academy of Estate Planning Attorneys

9360 Towne Centre Drive, Suite 300
San Diego, CA 92121
Toll Free: (800) 846-1555
Fax: (858) 453-1147
Email: information@aaepa.com
URL: http://www.aaepa.com

American College of Trust and Estate Counsel

3415 South Sepulveda Boulevard, Suite 330
Los Angeles, CA 90034
Phone: (310) 398-1888
Fax: (310) 572-7280
Email: info@actec.org
URL: http://www.actec.org

Americans for Tax Reform (ATR)

1920 L Street NW, Suite 200
Washington, DC 20036
Phone: (202) 785-0266
Fax: (202) 785-0261
URL: http://www.atr.org

**National Academy of Elder Law
Attorneys, Inc.**

1604 North Country Club Road
Tucson, AZ 85716
Phone: (520) 881-4005
Fax: (520) 325-7925
URL: http://www.naela.com

National Network of Estate Planning Attorneys, Inc.

One Valmont Plaza, Fourth Floor
Omaha, NE 68154-5203
Toll Free: (800) 638-8681
Email: webmaster@netplanning.com
URL: http://www.netplanning.com

Taxation Section, American Bar Association

740 15th Street NW, 10th Floor
Washington, DC 20005-1009
Phone: (202) 662-8670
Fax: (202) 662-8682
Email: taxweb@staff.abanet.org
URL: http://www.abanet.org/tax/home.html

ESTATE PLANNING

LIFE INSURANCE

Sections within this essay:

BACKGROUND

A life insurance policy is simply a **contract** between an insurance company and the person who buys the policy, the policyholder. In exchange for payment of a specified sum of money, known as a premium, the life insurance company pays a named **beneficiary** a certain amount of money if specific events occur while the policy is in force.

In life insurance policies the most common event is the death of the person who is insured, in which case the payment is made to the beneficiary, which may be a person, a **trust** or other legal entity, or the estate of the owner. Some policies also allow the owner to surrender the policy for its cash value or to take advance payments on the insurance in the event of diagnosis of a terminal condition. The sale of life insurance in the United States has historically been a highly competitive commission sales business with a number of products which combine life insurance and investments.

TYPES OF LIFE INSURANCE

Despite their various names, all life insurance policies fall into either individual or group insurance policies. The difference between Individual and Group Life has become less distinct. Many associations sponsor life insurance plans that are called Group Life coverage but which actually require the same underwriting criteria as for Individual Life.

Individual Life Insurance Individual Life insurance generally is underwritten taking into account the actuarial risk of death of the one individual being insured. Life insurance companies' underwriters typically use a combination of factors that statistics indicate equate with the risk of death. These include, but are not limited to applicant's age, applicant's gender (except in states which have unisex rate requirements), height and weight, family and applicant health history, marital status, number of children, hazardous occupations, tobacco use, alcohol use, dangerous hobbies, and foreign travel.

Group Life Insurance Group Life insurance policies cover the lives of multiple persons within a group. Group Life insurance historically was based on the risk characteristics of the group as a whole. The group might consist of employees of a business, members of a professional organization, members of a **credit union**, or perhaps members of a **labor union**. There are many other possibilities for these groups. The owner of the master group policy is the group itself, such as the employer, the union, the association, or whatever the group may be.

Second-To-Die and First-To-Die Insurance Most so-called Second-to-Die policies which pay upon the death of the second of two insured people are still regarded as Individual Life insurance. Similarly the so-called First-to-Die life insurance, where the lives of a small number of people are covered and the life insurance is payable on the first death, is also Individual Life insurance. First-to-Die is often used to cover partners in a business. The proceeds can be used to buy out the share of the partner who dies first.

Term Life Insurance Either Group or Individual polices can be Term Life Insurance. Term Life Insurance is basic insurance in the event of death. The policy owner pays a premium to the insurance company; it can typically be paid monthly, quarterly, or annually. If the insured dies during the time period that the payments are being made, the insurance company pays the face amount of the life insurance to the beneficiary. As the risk of death increases as people get older, the premium generally also increases. At advanced ages, term insurance costs are extremely expensive.

Cash Value Life Insurance Cash Value Life Insurance has the same benefits of Term Life Insurance with a savings or investment account. There are several types of Cash Value Life policies.

Traditional Whole Life and Universal Life In Traditional Whole Life and Universal Life Insurance policies, money that does not go to pay insurance costs or the sales representative's commission is invested by the insurance company in fixed dollar type investments. Whole-life policies combine life coverage with an investment fund. Cash value builds tax-free each year, and policyholders can usually borrow against the cash accumulation fund without being taxed. Universal life is a whole-life policy that combines term insurance with a money-market-type investment that pays a market rate of return. To get a higher return, these policies generally do not guarantee a certain rate. However, sales of universal policies tend to be higher than those of plain whole life, due to the higher potential yield.

Variable Life and Variable Universal Life In Variable Life and Variable Universal Life policies, money that does not go to pay insurance costs or the sales representative's commission is invested by the insurance company in **securities mutual fund** accounts selected by the owner from among the insurer's available choices. Returns are not guaranteed. Variable products are regulated as securities under the Federal Securities Laws and must be sold with a prospectus.

INSURABLE INTEREST

A basic requirement for all types of insurance is the person who buys a policy must have an insurable interest in the subject of the insurance. With respect to life insurance, an insurable interest means a substantial interest engendered by love and affection in the case of persons related by blood and a lawful and substantial economic interest in the continued life of the insured in other business related cases. Everyone has an insurable interest in their own lives and in the lives of their spouses and dependents. Business partners may have an insurable interest in each other, and a corporation may have an insurable interest in its employees' lives. The insurable interest requirement is designed to prevent people from taking out a life insurance policy on some randomly selected persons and then killing them to get the insurance proceeds. The rule also prevents life insurance from becoming a gambling device and prevents someone from taking out insurance policies simply because people are known smokers or known to drink and drive. However, it is not necessary for the beneficiary to have an insurable interest in the life of the insured.

EXAMINATIONS

On larger policies, most life insurance companies require the applicant to undergo a physical examination by a medical professional. Samples of the applicant's blood and urine typically are taken by a paramedical person contracted by the insurance carrier to conduct such tests. The insurer will typically also request the applicant's medical records from his or her physicians and have them reviewed by the underwriters. The insurer usually will also check the applicant's health history with the Medical Information Bureau (MIB).

MIB is a not-for-profit incorporated association of U.S. and Canadian life insurance companies. It is a provider of information and database management services to the financial services industry. Organized in 1902, MIB now consists of over 600 member insurance companies who agree to share information in the form of medical and avocation codes. There are approximately 230 codes, which MIB uses to signify different medical conditions. Some of the codes indicate risks involving hazardous avocations or adverse driving records. While the MIB does not report actual details about the person's medical condition or problem, the codes alert insurance companies to the fact that there was information obtained and reported by a member insurance company on this particular impairment or avocation risk. Individuals can request their own MIB record and can request that the company correct any errors. There is a small processing fee to obtain a report, which is waived if the request is within 60 days of an adverse underwriting decision. All MIB codes are supposed to be purged seven years from the report date.

CLAIMS

Every life insurance policy specifies certain actions that must take place after a loss has occurred. Typically the beneficiary provides the life insurance company with a **certified copy** of the death certificate. After proof of the death is submitted to the insurance company, the life insurance company should promptly pay the benefits, assuming that the premiums were paid, making the policy in force. Even if premiums on the policy were not currently being paid, the policy may still have been in a paid status, or the company may have failed to send the necessary notices of cancellation, in which case it may be possible to recover on the policy. Usually, once the policy is at least two years old it is beyond the incontestable period and must be paid, except in extraordinary circumstances.

Denial of Claims The most common reason life insurance companies use to deny claims is that there was a material misrepresentation in connection with the insurance purchase. The claim regarding material misrepresentation may arise out of the original application for the insurance or from an **amendment** to the application or in an application for reinstatement. A material misrepresentation sufficient to deny a claim cannot be just any incorrect statement. A material misstatement is almost always one that if it had been disclosed would have meant refusal by the insurer to issue the policy. The most commonly alleged misrepresentations involve an applicant's medical history. Delays in processing claims can sometimes result from legal questions regarding whether the policy was currently in force as of the date of death, or, if the death was a result of foul play, any possibility that the beneficiary may have played a role in the death.

Exclusions An exclusion is a part of an insurance policy which describes a condition or type of loss that is not covered by the policy. In life insurance, a common exclusion is an exception for accidental deaths caused by acts of war or while in active military service. Certain activities may also fall under the exclusion category. Some policies have an exclusion for deaths that occur while the insured was involved in the commission of a **felony**, or deaths resulting from suicide.

INSURANCE REGULATION

Because insurance companies handle large amounts of money on behalf of individuals and businesses, the level of **public interest** is sufficient to **warrant** governmental regulation. Historically, the purpose of insurance regulation has been to maintain the insurers' financial **solvency** and soundness and to guarantee the fair treatment of current and prospective policyholders and beneficiaries. There is no central Federal regulatory agency to specifically oversee insurance companies, and as a result, insurance companies in the United States are regulated by the individual states. These regulations include rules about matters such as forms, rates, sales agents, and general insurance business practices.

State laws regulating insurance business also include rules about unfair trade practices and unfair claims practices. It is illegal to refuse to sell insurance to someone because of the person's race, color, sex, religion, national origin, or ancestry. In some states the list of prohibited classifications includes marital status, age, occupation, language, **sexual orientation**, physical or mental impairment, or the geographic location where a person lives. Insurance underwriting decisions generally must be based on reasons that are related in some way to risk. A person has the right to be informed of any reason for refusal to issue an insurance policy.

RATES

Insurance companies have a range of payment or premium levels which can be charged for insurance. These are based on such factors as the applicant's age and health condition. Rating factors must be reasonably related to the risk being insured. The rates and rating factors for insurance must be filed with the insurance regulatory agency for each state where the insurance is to be sold. While a policyholder may elect to cancel an insurance policy at any time by giving notice to the insurance company, once a policy is issued, the insurance company cannot simply revoke it at will. The insurance company can only cancel the policy for reasons specifically outlined in the policy. State laws typically put limits on what an insurance company can include in the cancellation section of its policies. Generally, policies will be subject to cancellation only for some type of serious misrepresentation by the policyholder or for failure to pay the required premium on time. State law often requires insurers to allow a **grace period** of as much as 30 days after a payment is late before any insurance coverage can be terminated. Once the grace period expires, however, reinstatement is the sole option of the insurance company.

MINORS AS BENEFICIARIES

While children can lawfully be named as beneficiaries on a life insurance policy, the insurance company will not be permitted to pay benefits to a minor. The funds would likely be dispersed to the legal **guardian** of the minor child. Many divorced parents are shocked to discover that naming their minor children as beneficiaries makes their ex-spouse the direct recipient of any insurance proceeds. This situation can be avoided by creating a trust which can hold the funds until the children are of **legal age**.

ADDITIONAL RESOURCES

Briys, Eric. *Insurance: From Underwriting to Derivatives: Asset Liability Management in Insurance Companies*. New York: Wiley, John & Sons, Inc., 2001.

Silverman, Rachel Emma. *The Wall Street Journal Complete Estate Planning Guidebook*. New York: Crown Publishing Group, 2011.

Walsh, James. *True Odds: How Risks Affects Your Life*. Aberdeen, WA: Silver Lake Publishing, 1998.

ORGANIZATIONS

American Council of Life Insurers

1001 Pennsylvania Avenue, N.W.
Washington, DC 20004
Phone: (202) 624-2416
Fax: (202) 624-2319
URL: http://acli.com

National Alliance of Life Companies

10600 West Higgins Road, Suite 607
Rosemont, IL 60018
Phone: (847) 699-7008
Fax: (847) 699-7119
URL: http://www.nalc.net

National Association of Independent Life Brokerage Agencies (NAILBA)

8201 Greensboro Drive, Suite 300
McLean, VA 22102
Phone: (703) 610-9020
Fax: (703) 610-9005
URL: http://www.nailba.com

ESTATE PLANNING

LONG-TERM CARE PLANNING

Sections within this essay:

- Background
- Planning For Long-Term Care
  - Long-Term Care Insurance
  - Combined Life and Long-Term Care Insurance
  - Reversible Mortgages
  - Annuities
  - Trusts
- Additional Resources

BACKGROUND

Long-term care is a range of services and support that elderly and disabled individuals need to meet their health or personal needs over a long period of time. Most long-term care is not medical care, but rather assistance with the basic personal tasks of everyday life, sometimes called "Activities of Daily Living." These activities may include bathing, dressing, using the toilet, transferring to and from a bed or chair, caring for incontinence, and eating. Other common long-term care services and support are assistance to complete what is called Instrumental Activities of Daily Living. These are household and other tasks that an individual may do everyday, such as housework, preparing and cleaning up after meals, taking medication, shopping for groceries or clothes, using the telephone or other communication devices, managing money, caring for pets, and responding to emergency alerts such as fire alarms.

The U.S. Department of Health and Human Services estimates that in 2009 about 80 percent of care at home was done by unpaid caregivers and that one in four Americans in that year (almost 66 million people) were unpaid caregivers to an adult or child. The remaining 20 percent of paid caregiving in the home is provided by home health care or personal care agencies. Those who require care outside the home purchase services to live in an assisted living or nursing facilities. The cost for long-term care can be very expensive and can drain the savings of elderly persons. The need for long-term care planning has risen with the aging of the post-World War II "Baby Boomer" generation. In 2010, one year of care at home, consisting of a total of 18 hours per week from a home health aide, cost an average of $19,656. The average cost for one year of care in a nursing home was over $74,825 for a semi-private room (typically a room for two people).

Consumer surveys reveal common misunderstandings about which public programs pay for long-term care services. Many people believe they can rely on **Medicare** to pay for their long-term care services. However, Medicare only pays for long-term care if a person requires skilled services or rehabilitative care for a short period of time. Medicare does not pay for non-skilled assistance with Activities of Daily Living, which makes up the majority of long-term care services. Individuals have to pay for long-term care services that are not covered by a public or private insurance program. **Medicaid** is a joint federal and state program that pays for the largest share of long-term care services. However, Medicaid only covers persons whose income is below a certain level and there are minimum state eligibility requirements. Such requirements are based on the amount of assistance a person needs with Activities of Daily Living. Other federal programs such as the Older Americans Act and the

Department of Veterans Affairs pay for long-term care services, but only for specific populations and in certain circumstances.

Most employer-sponsored or private health insurance, including health insurance plans, cover only the same kinds of limited services as Medicare. If they do cover long-term care, it is typically only for skilled, short-term, medically necessary care. There is an increasing number of private payment options that can help pay for long-term care services. These include long-term care insurance, reverse mortgages, life insurance options, and annuities. Therefore, long-term care planning is essential.

PLANNING FOR LONG-TERM CARE

In 2008, 21 million people required long-term care services. About 70 percent of people over age 65 require some type of long-term care services during their lifetime, with 40 percent of these people requiring nursing home care. People often put off planning for long-term care because they do not want to think about a time when they might need it. Most people first learn about long-term care when they or a loved one needs care. However, if people wait until they need services to start planning, their options may be limited. They may not be able to find the information they need to make decisions or they may not have the money needed to pay for the services they want. They may also have to rely on their family or others to make these decisions.

In terms of estate planning, long-term care planning is essentially a way to protect as much of a person's assets as possible if they need to use long-term care. There are a number of financial products that promise to relieve the burden of long-term care. These include long-term care insurance, combined life and long-term care insurance policies, reverse mortgages, trusts, and annuities.

Long-Term Care Insurance Long-term care insurance policies provide flexibility and allow for a great deal of choice. Persons can select a range of care options and benefits that allow them to get the services they need, where they need them. The cost of a long-term care policy is based on the type and amount of services that are covered, how old the person is when buying the policy, and any optional benefits choosen, such as benefits that increase with inflation. If a person is in poor health or already receiving long-term care services, the company may refuse to insure that person. In some cases, a person may be able to buy a limited amount of coverage, or coverage at a higher "non-standard" rate.

Many long-term care insurance policies have limits on how long or how much they will pay. Some policies will pay the costs of your long-term care for two to five years. Some insurance companies offer policies that will pay long-term care costs for as long as the person lives, no matter how much it costs. But there are very few companies today that offer such unlimited or lifetime policies. However, some companies do have a "high coverage option" which might offer a $1 million lifetime limit. Most policies sold today are "comprehensive" policies. They typically cover care and services in a variety of long-term care settings including a person's home, adult day service centers, hospice care, respite care, assisted living facilities, Alzheimer's special care facilities, and nursing homes. In the home setting, comprehensive polices generally cover skilled nursing care; occupational, speech, physical, and rehabilitation therapy; and help with personal care, such as bathing and dressing. Many policies also cover some homemaker services, such as meal preparation or housekeeping as long as it is in conjunction with the personal care services you receive.

When a policyholder starts receiving benefits is based on the policy's "benefit trigger," which is the length of the elimination period the person selects. Benefit triggers are the criteria insurance policies use to determine when long-term care begins. Usually, the benefit triggers are defined in terms of Activities of Daily Living or cognitive impairments. For example, most policies pay benefits when a person needs help with two or more of six Activities of Daily Living or when they have a cognitive impairment.

The "elimination period" is the amount of time that must pass after a benefit trigger occurs but before the person starts receiving payment for services. An elimination period is like the **deductible** on car insurance, except it is measured in time rather than by dollar amount. Most policies allow the policyholder to choose an elimination period of 30, 60, or 90 days. During the elimination period, the person must cover the cost of any services. Some policies specify that in order to satisfy an elimination period, the person must receive paid care or pay for services during that time.

Once benefits begin, most policies pay the costs up to a pre-set limit. Other policies pay a pre-set cash amount for each day that the person meets the benefit trigger whether the person receives paid long-term care services on those days or not. These "cash disability" policies offer more flexibility but are much more expensive.

Most people buy long-term care insurance directly from an insurance agent, financial planner, or broker. States regulate which companies can sell long-term care insurance and the products that they can sell. There are more than 100 companies offering long-term care insurance nationally, but 15 to 20 insurers sell most policies. However, since 2010, major insurance companies including MetLife, Prudential, and John Hancock have stopped selling policies because they proved to be unprofitable.

Many private and public employers, including the federal government and a growing number of state governments, offer group long-term care programs as a voluntary benefit. Employers do not typically contribute to the premium cost (as they do with health insurance), but they often negotiate a favorable group rate. If a person is currently employed, it may be easier to qualify for long-term care insurance through the employer than it is to purchase a policy from a private insurance company.

The cost of a long-term care policy varies greatly based on the age of the person at the time of purchase, the policy type, and the coverage selected. In 2007, the average annual premium cost for individual buyers across all ages and policy types was about $2,207. Excluding the 20 percent of people who elected lifetime coverage, the average policy from 2007 covered 4.8 years worth of benefits with a daily benefit amount of $160. Most people selected a comprehensive policy that covers both facility and at-home care, and they also purchased some form of automatic inflation protection.

Combined Life and Long-Term Care Insurance The cost of long-term care insurance has risen steadily. A 2012 report by Limra, an industry-funded research group, found that the number of policy buyers had declined 38 percent since 2004. However, some insurance companies have found success with alternatives to traditional insurance. Sales of hybrid products that combine some type of life insurance with a long-term-care benefit have been rising as traditional policies have faded. Limra found that sales of such "life combination" products jumped 56 percent in 2011, the third consecutive year of double-digit gains. For example, New York Life's Asset Preserver is a universal-life policy that allows money paid into the policy as a single upfront premium to be tapped for long-term care. If the insured doesn't use the benefit in his lifetime, it is payable to his beneficiaries.

Traditional life insurance policies may be used to fund long-term care. An Accelerated Death Benefit is a feature included in some life insurance policies that allows the policyholder to receive a tax-free advance on the life insurance death benefit while the person is still alive. Sometimes the person must pay an extra premium to add this feature to the life insurance policy, while some insurance companies include it in the policy for little or no cost.

There are different types of Accelerated Death Benefits, each of which serves a different purpose. Depending on the type of policy, a person may be able to receive a cash advance on their life insurance policy's death benefit if they are terminally ill, have a life-threatening diagnosis, need long-term care services for an extended amount of time, or are permanently confined to a nursing home and incapable of performing Activities of Daily Living, such as bathing or dressing.

The amount of money received from these types of policies varies, but typically the accelerated benefit payment amount is capped at 50 percent of the death benefit. Some policies, however, allow the policyholder to use the full amount of the death benefit. For Accelerated Death Benefit policies that cover long-term care services, the monthly benefit that can be used for nursing home care is typically equal to two percent of the life insurance policy's face value. The amount available for home care (if it is included in the policy) is typically half that amount.

Life settlements allow policyholders to sell their life insurance policy for its present value to raise cash for any reason. This option is usually only available to women age 74 and older and to men age 70 and older. The proceeds may be used to pay for long-term care services.

Viatical settlements allow policyholders to sell their life insurance policy to a third party and use the money to pay for care. A viatical **settlement** is like a life settlement, but it is only possible if the person is terminally ill. During the settlement process, a viatical company pays the person a percentage of the death benefit on the life insurance policy that is based on life expectancy. The viatical company then owns the policy and is its **beneficiary**. The viatical company also takes over payment of premiums on the policy. As a result, the person gets money to pay for care, and the viatical company receives the full death benefit after the person dies. Unlike the life settlement, money received from a viatical settlement is tax-free if the person has a life expectancy of two years or less or is chronically ill, and the viatical company is licensed in the states in which it does business.

Reversible Mortgages The use of reversible mortgages to pay the cost of long-term care has also become popular. A reverse **mortgage** is a special type of home equity loan that allows people to receive cash against the value of their home without selling it. The homeowner can choose to receive a lump-sum payment, a monthly payment, or a **line of credit**. The homeowner must use the funds to pay off any existing mortgages or other debt against the home and to make required home repairs. There are no restrictions on how the homeowner uses the remainder of the money. As long as the homeowner spends the payments in the month they are received, the money is not taxable and does not count towards income or affect Social Security or Medicare benefits. It also does not count as income for Medicaid eligibility. Reverse mortgages are available to homeowners age 62 and older.

Unlike traditional mortgages, loan applicants do not have to provide an income or credit history to get the loan.

Annuities Another option is for a person to enter into an **annuity contract** with an insurance company to help pay for long-term care services. In exchange for a single payment or a series of payments, the insurance company will send the person an annuity, which is a series of regular payments over a specified period of time. There are two types of annuities: immediate long-term care and deferred long-term care.

With an immediate long-term care annuity, the insurance company sends a specified monthly income in return for a single premium payment. This option is available regardless of a person's current health status, so if the person does not qualify for long-term care insurance because of age or poor health or is already receiving long-term care, the person can still purchase an annuity. The insurance company converts the single premium payment into a guaranteed monthly income stream for a specified period of time or until the person dies. How much a person receives in income each month depends on the amount of the initial premium, the person's age, and gender. Since women tend to live longer than men, women generally receive a smaller monthly payment over a longer period of time than do men of the same age.

Deferred long-term care annuities are available to people up to age 85. Similar to other annuities, in exchange for a single premium payment, the person receives a stream of monthly income for a specified period of time. The annuity creates two funds: one for long-term care expenses and another separate fund that the person can use however they desire. The person can access the long-term care fund immediately, but must wait until a specified day in the future to access the separate cash portion. The rules of the annuity define how much can be accessed on a monthly basis from the long-term care fund and how much can be accessed on an annual basis from the cash fund. To qualify for a deferred long-term care annuity, the applicant must satisfy some health criteria.

Trusts A **trust** is a legal entity that allows a person (the trustor) to transfer assets to another person (the **trustee**). Once the trustor establishes the trust, the trustee manages and controls the assets for the trustor or for another beneficiary. A trust can provide flexible control of assets for the benefit of minor children. Another common use of a trust is to provide flexible control of assets for an older adult or a person with a **disability**, which could include a person or the person's spouse. Two types of trusts can help pay for long-term care services: charitable remainder and Medicaid Disability.

A charitable remainder trust allows a person to use their own assets to pay for long-term care services while contributing to a charity of their choice and reducing their tax burden at the same time. The trust can be designed so that the person receives payments from the trust to use for long-term care services while alive. When the person dies, the balance of the funds in the trust goes to the selected charity. Because this is a charitable donation, the person receives tax deductions for the **fair market value** of the assets that go to the charity.

Medicaid disability trusts are limited to persons with disabilities who are younger than age 65 and qualify for public benefits. Parents, grandparents, or legal guardians often set up these trusts to benefit persons with disabilities, and a nonprofit organization manages the assets. This is the only kind of trust that is exempt from rules regarding trusts and Medicaid eligibility.

ADDITIONAL RESOURCES

Loverde, Joy. *The Complete Eldercare Planner*. New York: Three Rivers Press, 2009.

Matthew, Joseph. *Long-Term Care: How to Plan and Pay for It*. 8th ed. Berkeley, CA: Nolo Press, 2010.

ORGANIZATIONS

Department of Health and Human Services

200 Independence Avenue, S.W
Washington, DC 20201
Toll Free: (877) 696-6775
URL: http://www.hhs.gov

National Care Planning Council

PO Box 1118
Centerville, UT 84014
Phone: (801) 298-8676
Toll Free: (800) 989-8137
Fax: (801) 295-3776
URL: http://www.longtermcarelink.net

ESTATE PLANNING

POWER OF ATTORNEY

Sections within this essay:

- Background
- Agent
- Creating a Power of Attorney
- Types of Powers of Attorney
  – General Power of Attorney
  – Special or Limited Power of Attorney
  – Springing Power of Attorney
  – Durable Power of Attorney
- Revoking a Power of Attorney
- Additional Resources

BACKGROUND

A power of attorney is a legal instrument that individuals create and sign; it gives someone else the authority to make certain decisions and act for the signer. The person who has these powers is called an "agent" or "attorney-in-fact." The signer is the "principal." Merely because the word "attorney" is used does not mean that the agent must be a lawyer.

Even if principals have delegated authority to an agent through a power of attorney, they can still make important decisions for themselves. But their agents may act for them as well. Their agents must follow directions as long as the principal is capable of making decisions for themselves. A power of attorney is simply one way to share authority with someone else.

As a principal, if the principal's decisions conflict with those of the agent, the principal's decision will govern, assuming that the agent confers with the principal prior to taking an action. Be aware that if the agent has acted on the principal's behalf and acted within the scope of authority granted by the power of attorney, then the principal may be obligated by the terms and conditions of his actions. If the agent does not respect the principal's wishes, the principal should revoke the power of attorney.

Principals can revoke their agent's authority at any time if they become dissatisfied with the agent's performance. If they do not revoke a power of attorney themselves, it will automatically expire upon their death. The power of attorney is not a substitute for a will. Upon the principal's death, either the will or the state's law of **intestacy** will govern the distribution of the estate.

AGENT

The person designated to be the agent assumes certain responsibilities. First and foremost, the agent is obligated to act in the principal's best interest. The agent must always follow the principal's directions. Agents are "fiduciaries," which means that the agent must act with the highest degree of **good faith** in behalf of their principals.

Although an agent is supposed to make decisions in the principal's best interest and to use the principal's money and other assets only for the principal's benefit, the agent nevertheless has great freedom to act as he or she pleases. Thus, it is crucial that trustworthy individuals are chosen to execute a power of attorney. Before selecting an agent, principals should ask themselves the following questions:

- Do I trust the candidate for agent?
- Will the agent understand my feelings and my point of view?

- Will the agent follow my wishes if I am ever incapacitated?
- Will the agent do the necessary work and spend the time to properly handle my affairs?
- Will the agent be able to visit me or to keep in contact by phone?
- Is this person informed about finances?
- Will the agent need to seek the help of experts?

An agent's relationship with the principal is governed by several basic rules. The agent must:

- keep his money separate from the principal's
- keep detailed records concerning all transactions he engages in on the principal's behalf
- not stand to profit by any transaction where the agent represents the principal's interests
- not make a gift or otherwise transfer any of the principal's money, **personal property**, or real estate to himself unless the power of attorney explicitly states he can do so

Principals usually grant their agents fairly broad powers to manage their finances and to conduct financial transactions in their behalf. Even so, principals can grant their agents as much or as little authority as they think reasonable. Typical powers include the authority to do the following:

- act for the principal with respect to inheritances or claim property to which the principal is otherwise entitled
- collect the principal's Social Security, **Medicare** or other governmental benefits
- conduct real estate transactions (purchase, sell, **mortgage**, etc.)
- conduct transactions with banks and other financial institutions
- file and pay the principal's state, federal, and local taxes
- hire a lawyer to represent the principal in court
- make investment decisions for the principal (purchase and sell stocks, **bonds**, mutual funds, etc.)
- manage the principal's retirement funds
- purchase or sell insurance policies and annuities for the principal
- run the principal's business
- use the principal's money to pay the principal's living expenses

Whatever powers the principal gives the agent, the agent must act for the principal's best interests, maintain accurate records, keep the principal's property separate from his or hers and avoid conflicts of interest.

Agents are sometimes paid for their work on the principal's behalf. This depends on the nature of the relationship between the agent and the principal, as well as the nature of the agent's duties. In most situations where the agent's duties are fairly simple, there is no payment for the performance of those duties. If, however, the agent is burdened with substantial responsibilities (such as running a business or managing a complex transaction), payment for the agent's services may be appropriate. If the principal wishes to or expects to pay the agent, the principal should clearly say so and outline the details of payment in the power of attorney. Because of the importance of the agent's duties and the potential for mistake, misunderstanding, or even outright over-reaching, the agent will usually be required to maintain separate and accurate records and make them available to the principal or to persons the principal designates.

CREATING A POWER OF ATTORNEY

When individuals create a power of attorney they are stating what they want their agent to be able to do for them. For the power of attorney to be effective the principal must be competent to give this authority. In other words, the principal must know and understand what types of decisions need to be made. If the principal is mentally competent, but physically unable to sign his name, any mark the principal makes with the full intention that others regard the mark as the principal's signature will be acceptable.

In most cases when individuals create a power of attorney, their signature on the form should be witnessed by a **notary public**. If the power of attorney grants the power to sell, **lease**, or otherwise dispose of the principal's real estate, the principal should also have the power of attorney recorded with the Registry of Deeds. The Registry of Deeds usually will be located in the county courthouse wherein which the property is located. The principal should give the agent the original power of attorney document to show to any person, business, or organization involved in the transactions. The principal should keep a copy for his records. If the principal intends to delay the agent's ability to conduct business for the principal, he may choose to keep the original document himself until such time as he wants the power of attorney to be used.

In order to create a legally effective power of attorney, the principal must be mentally competent. The principal needs to know and understand what he is doing. A person who is mentally incapacitated cannot meet these requirements. The law does not require the principal to hire a lawyer to draft the power of attorney. However, if the principal intends to grant important powers to the agent, it is a good idea to seek legal advice before the principal signs the document. The principal should make sure that he understands the details built into the power of attorney as well as the potential for legal or financial difficulties it may present.

In most instances, all the principal needs to do to create a legally valid power of attorney is properly complete and sign (before a notary public) a fill-in-the-blanks form that is a few pages long. Besides the nearly universal requirement for a power of attorney to be witnessed by a notary republic, there are few formalities to executing a power of attorney. Some states require a certain number of competent witnesses to watch the principal sign the document before the notary, and some states recommend certain forms, but none of them are mandatory to create a valid power of attorney. But some powers can be delegated to an agent only if they are specifically mentioned in the power of attorney document. Those requiring explicit language include the power to do the following:

- make gifts of the principal's money or other assets
- amend the principal's will or **community property** agreement
- name beneficiaries of the principal's insurance policies

If the principal is married and is concerned about what would happen if the principal's spouse became ill and needed nursing home care or other long-term care, the principal may want to add some additional specifically authorized powers. It may be helpful for **Medicaid** eligibility to include the power to revoke a community property agreement and to transfer property from the disabled spouse to the principal. It is a good idea to consult with a lawyer about these more complicated issues.

When individuals create a power of attorney, they can name two or more people to serve as agents at the same time. They can also name an alternate agent to assume powers under the power of attorney under certain circumstances, such as the death or incapacity of the first agent. Before principals give authority under their power of attorney to more than one person at the same time, they should consider whether confusion or some other conflict may result. It is wise to discuss the potential advantages and disadvantages with a lawyer before giving powers of attorney to more than one person.

TYPES OF POWERS OF ATTORNEY

General Power of Attorney A general power of attorney is one that permits the agent to conduct practically every kind of business or financial transaction—with the principal's assets—without any restraints. Because of the great harm to the principal's financial well-being that an incompetent or untrustworthy agent can cause with a general power of attorney, the principal should be extremely careful in choosing an agent. Additionally, the principal should maintain vigilance over the agent's transactions in the principal's behalf.

Special or Limited Power of Attorney A special power of attorney, also known as a limited power of attorney, is created to empower an agent to perform a specific act or acts. For example, if the principal is unable to do it himself, he can prepare a special power of attorney so that the agent can complete the purchase or sale of real estate. Most powers of attorney carefully define and enumerate the scope of the agent's authority. Thus, most powers of attorney are limited powers of attorney.

Springing Power of Attorney Any power of attorney can be written so that it becomes effective as soon as the principal signs it. But, the principal can also specify that the power of attorney goes into effect only upon the occurrence of some triggering event. In other words, it "springs" into effect at a later date, if ever. The triggering event can be something as simple as the principal's reaching a certain age or when a certain calendar date occurs. It can also be much more specific, such as if and when a doctor certifies that the principal has become incapacitated. These kinds of springing powers of attorney enable individuals to keep control over their affairs unless and until they become incapacitated, when it springs into effect. They are also known as durable powers of attorney.

Durable Power of Attorney Unless a power of attorney specifically says otherwise, an agent's authority ends if the principal becomes mentally incapacitated. On the other hand, a power of attorney may state explicitly that it is to remain in effect and not be limited by any future mental incapacity of the principal. A power of attorney with this sort of clause is called a durable power of attorney. The word "durable" means that the principal's agent can continue to conduct business for the principal if the principal becomes incapacitated.

Because of their potential utility to individuals who lack capacity after executing them, durable powers of attorney are arguably the most important form of these versatile legal documents. Durable powers of attorney are intended to address cases wherein which the following applies:

- The principal intends the agent to have authority only if the principal becomes incapacitated.
- The principal intends for the power of attorney to take effect immediately and to REMAIN in effect regardless of the principal's future disability.

The principal must list the specific powers under the durable power of attorney that are given to the agent and when those powers are to take effect. The agent must still act in the principal's best interest, making decisions and using the principal's assets only for the principal's benefit. In North Carolina and South Carolina, a principal must record the power of attorney with the appropriate county authorities for it to be durable.

The alternatives to creating a durable power of attorney may not be what the principal intends. If the principal has not executed a durable power of attorney and subsequently the principal becomes mentally incapacitated, a court may appoint a **guardian** or conservator for the principal. A **guardianship** or **conservatorship** must be established by a **probate** court. It is usually easier and much less expensive to manage one's affairs with a power of attorney.

Like all powers of attorney, a durable power of attorney ends or ceases to carry authority upon the death of the principal. It is fruitless to attempt to give the agent authority to handle matters for the principal after the principal's death. Actions such as attempting to pay the principal's debts, making funeral or burial arrangements, or transferring the principal's property to the people who **inherit** it cannot be legally accomplished through a power of attorney executed by a decedent. If the principal wants the agent to have authority to conclude affairs after the principal's death, a will must be prepared that names the agent as the principal's **executor**.

In addition to the principal's death, a durable power of attorney will end if any of the following applies:

- The principal revokes it. As long as the principal is mentally competent, he or she can revoke a durable power of attorney any time.

- A court invalidates the power of attorney. This does not happen very often; however, a court will declare a power of attorney invalid if the court finds that the principal lacked mental **competency** when the power of attorney was executed, or that the principal was the victim of **fraud** or undue influence.

- The principal gets a **divorce**. In Alabama, California, Colorado, Illinois, Indiana, Minnesota, Missouri, Pennsylvania, Texas and Wisconsin, if the principal's spouse is also the agent and the two get a divorce, the authority of the principal's former spouse-agent is automatically terminated by **statute**. In any state, however, it is wise to revoke a durable power of attorney after a divorce and make a new one.

- No agent is available to serve. A durable power of attorney will terminate if no one is available to serve as agent. To avoid this dilemma, a principal can name an alternate agent in the power of attorney.

There are two general types of durable powers of attorney: a durable power of attorney for finances, and a durable power of attorney for health care. Depending on the terms of the document, the durable power of attorney for finances allows the agent to serve the interests of the principal in financial matters before, during, or after the agent becomes incapacitated. The durable power of attorney for health care authorizes the agent to make medical decisions for the principal if the principal cannot otherwise make those decisions. An agent's authority over the principal's financial and health-care decisions can be included in the same power of attorney; however, some durable powers of attorney for finances do not give the agent the legal authority to make medical decisions for the principal. Sometimes financial and health-care powers are combined in one document to create a durable power of attorney.

A durable power of attorney for health care differs from a **living will**. The durable power of attorney for health care grants a third party—the agent—the authority to make decisions for the principal about the principal's health care. In most states, though, a living will (also called a Health-care Directive or Directive to Physicians), is a document wherein which the principal informs his doctors of his preferences about certain kinds of medical treatment and life-sustaining procedures in the event the principal cannot communicate his wishes. The living will does not mediate the principal's desires through an agent or other third party. If a living will is prepared properly, a physician is legally bound to respect the wishes in the living will. If for some reason a doctor finds he cannot honor the living will, he is obligated to transfer the principal's care to another doctor who will. Living **wills** are fairly simple documents, with most states now providing fill-in-the-blanks living will forms.

REVOKING A POWER OF ATTORNEY

All powers of attorney automatically expire upon the principal's death. Some powers of attorney expire on a particular date set by the principal. It is important to know that all powers of attorney are revocable if the right conditions are met. There are many reasons to revoke a power of attorney, an important one being loss of confidence in the agent; however, the principal does not need a reason to revoke the power of attorney.

Power of attorney can be revoked at any time, as long as the principal is of sound mind. To revoke a power of attorney, the principal must do so in writing. Typically, the principal merely needs to prepare a simple statement containing the following:

- The principal's name and date.
- The principal's claim to be of sound mind.
- The principal's explicit desire to revoke the durable power of attorney.

- The date the original durable power of attorney was executed.
- The name of the principal's agent or agents.
- The principal's signature.

It is important to distribute copies of this revocation statement to the agent and to any institutions and agencies, such as banks and hospitals, that may have had notice of the principal's power of attorney. If the power of attorney is on file with a county records department, the statement revoking the power of attorney should be filed in the same place. After the durable power of attorney is revoked, the principal can 1) execute a new power of attorney naming someone else as agent to handle the principal's affairs; or 2) handle the affairs independently.

ADDITIONAL RESOURCES

EagleLink. "Power of Attorney." 2002. Available at http://www.eaglelink.com/law-review/poa.htm (accessed November 1, 2012).

Irving, Shae. *The Financial Power of Attorney Workbook*. Berkeley, CA: Nolo Press, 1997.

USLegalForms.com. "Power of Attorney Forms." Available at http://www.uslegalforms.com/powerofattorney/ (accessed November 1, 2012).

ORGANIZATIONS

American Academy of Estate Planning Attorneys
9360 Towne Centre Drive, Suite 300
San Diego, CA 92121
Toll Free: (800) 846-1555

Fax: (858) 453-1147
Email: information@aaepa.com
URL: http://www.aaepa.com

American College of Trust and Estate Counsel
3415 South Sepulveda Boulevard, Suite 330
Los Angeles, CA 90034
Phone: (310) 398-1888
Fax: (310) 572-7280
Email: info@actec.org
URL: http://www.actec.org

National Academy of Elder Law Attorneys, Inc.
1604 North Country Club Road
Tucson, AZ 85716
Phone: (520) 881-4005
Fax: (520) 325-7925
URL: http://www.naela.com

National Network of Estate Planning Attorneys, Inc.
One Valmont Plaza, Fourth Floor
Omaha, NE 68154-5203
Toll Free: (800) 638-8681
Email: webmaster@netplanning.com
URL: http://www.netplanning.com

ESTATE PLANNING

PROBATE AND EXECUTORS

BACKGROUND

Probate is a legal proceeding by which a deceased person's property is distributed to the rightful heirs and/or beneficiaries. Probate proceedings are governed by the law of the state where the deceased person resided at the time of death and by the probate laws of any other state where the property was owned. The main purpose of probate is transferring title of the decedent's property to the heirs and/or beneficiaries. If the decedent had no assets, there is typically no need for probate. Probate also allows for collection of taxes due and payment of outstanding debts. The term "probate" refers to a "proving" of the existence of a valid Will or determining and "proving" who one's legal heirs are if there is no Will.

All property of a decedent may not be subject to the probate process. Life insurance, retirement accounts, real estate held as joint tenants with right of survivorship and other joint **tenancy** property can pass directly to the appropriate **beneficiary** automatically. The involvement of the court to transfer such property is not required. Property held in the **trust** is not subject to probate. A bank account or motor vehicle title may also specify a death beneficiary and thus be exempt from the probate process.

An Executor or Personal Representative (sometimes referred to as "The PR") is the person or institution named in a will and appointed by a court to carry out the will's instructions and to handle all of the matters of probate. Duties of the Personal Representative include making an inventory and **appraisal** of all property and appropriately distributing the estate.

PERSONAL REPRESENTATIVE

The Personal Representative (also called the "executor" or "executrix" if there is a Will or the "administrator" or "administratix" if there is no Will) is appointed as part of the probate proceeding. The Personal Representative can either be an entity, one individual, or two or more individuals (although this arrangement can become extremely complicated).

Duties The Personal Representative has the responsibility for managing the estate in accordance with established probate rules and procedures of the **jurisdiction** where the probate takes place. Responsibilities of a Personal Representative include:

- Locating, inventorying, and obtaining an appraisal of the assets of the decedent
- Receiving payments owed to the estate, including unpaid salary, vacation pay, or other benefits due the decedent
- Opening a checking account for the estate
- Determining how property is distributed
- Noticing potential creditors
- Investigating the validity of claims against the estate
- Paying bills, debts, valid claims and expenses of administrating the estate
- Discontinuing utilities and credit cards, closing accounts and notifying appropriate private and governmental agencies of the death
- Filing and paying income and estate taxes
- Closing the probate

Compensation Personal Representatives are generally compensated about 2% of the probate estate for their work. This varies moderately from state to state and generally decreases as a percentage as the size of the estate increases. All fees and reimbursed expenses are subject to court approval. Additional fees may be allowed if permitted by the court in certain circumstances. However, if a Personal Representative is incompetent or does not perform as required, the court may deny compensation, and the Personal Representative may be held personally responsible for any damages caused. Liability may arise from improperly managing the assets of the estate, failing to collect claims and moneys due the estate, overpaying claimants, selling an asset without authority or at an inappropriate price, neglecting to file tax returns promptly, or distributing property incorrectly to beneficiaries.

PROBATE COURT

Probate usually occurs in the local court where the deceased permanently resided at the time of death. If the deceased did not have a Will, each state will have its own pattern for distributing the deceased's real property. Generally it is necessary to go through probate or, in the case of smaller estates, a less formal procedure that is still under the general supervision of the probate court, before the deceased's property can be legally distributed. If a person dies with a Will (which is known as dying "testate"), a court must provide an opportunity to allow others to object to the Will. A number of objections might invalidate a Will, for example, an **allegation** that there is a later Will or that the Will was made at a time the deceased was mentally incompetent. Additional challenges to a Will can include

forgery, improper **execution** (signature), or a claim that the decedent was subject to undue influence. Dying without a Will is known as dying **intestate**; however, such estates remain subject to the law and rules of the probate code of the decedent's domiciled jurisdiction.

The Personal Representative typically must file a probate petition and notify all those who would have legally been entitled to receive property from the deceased if the deceased died without a Will, plus all those named in the Will, and give anyone who chooses a chance to file a formal objection to the Will.

A **hearing** on the probate petition is typically scheduled several weeks to months after the matter is filed. If no objections are filed the court generally approves the petition and formally appoints the Personal Representative. While it is not required that there be representation by an attorney in probate court, probate is a rather formalistic procedure. The death of a family member is typically a stressful time even when the death is expected, such as with a person of quite advanced age or with someone who is terminally ill. Employing an attorney may be the less expensive alternative in the long run.

Ancillary Probate The probate court or division has jurisdiction over all **personal property** the deceased owned, plus all the real property the deceased owned which is located in that same state. If the decedent owned out of state real property, the laws of that jurisdiction will apply, unless there is a Will. If there is no Will, probate is usually required in each state where the real property is situated, in addition to the home state. Even if there is a Will, after it is admitted to probate in the home state, it usually must be submitted to probate in each other jurisdiction in which the deceased owned real property. A separate probate action for such circumstances is known as **ancillary** probate. Some states require the appointment of a Personal Representative who is a local resident to administer the in-state property.

Will Contests A Will Contest take place where a second, different Will of the decedent is produced or in the event there is an objection to the Will. An individual or entity must have proper standing to contest a Will. This means they must have a claim for some type of interest in the estate based on either another Will or a lawful relationship to the decedent. If the Will is held invalid, the probate court may invalidate all provisions or only the challenged portion. If the entire Will is held invalid, generally the proceeds are distributed under the laws of **intestacy** of the probating state. The fact that the decedent even attempted to create a new Will may invalidate the older one, even if the new Will is found not to be valid. Hiring an attorney is usually necessary to determine whether contesting a Will is even worth the expense.

Lawsuits In addition to a Will Contest, estates can be involved in other lawsuits. Estates are legal entities, which can file suit, and be sued. Typically, such suits involve prior acts of the decedent which gave rise to some claim. There are time limits involving such claims if the estate is to be sued. Potential claimants would be considered potential creditors.

CREDITORS

Rules regarding notification of creditors are different for each state. However, in every state, creditors must make a claim for any amounts owed within a fixed period of time. This claim can be made directly to the Personal Representative in some jurisdictions, but in other jurisdictions, it must be made with the court. The PR can pay the claim out of the estate, but if the PR disputes its validity, the **creditor** must seek a court order to receive payment. If there is not enough money to pay all the debts of the estate, state law dictates which creditors are paid first. It is not possible to "inherit" a debt. Beneficiaries and Personal Representatives are not personally liable for the debts of the estate, although the court may order estate property sold to pay certain creditor claims.

AVOIDING PROBATE

In many estate plans, the Trust is the central tool that is used to control and manage property. A Trust continues despite the incapacity or death of the grantor. It determines how a **Trustee** is to act with respect to the Trust estate. It determines how property is to be distributed after the death of the grantor. A properly drawn Trust is a separate entity that does not die when the creator dies. The successor Trustee can take over management of the Trust estate and pay bills and taxes and promptly distribute the Trust assets to the beneficiaries, without court supervision, if the Trust agreement gives the Trustee that power. Trusts, unlike **Wills**, are generally private documents. The public would be able to see how much the descendent owned and who the beneficiaries were under a Will, but typically not with a Trust. Like a Will, however, a Trust can be used to provide for minor children, children from a prior marriage, and a second spouse in the same trust; transfer a family-operated or closely-held business; provide for pets; provide for charities; and remove life insurance benefits from a taxable estate, while still controlling the designation of insurance beneficiaries.

TAXES

One of the duties of the PR is to pay all taxes due the federal government and the state government, including estate tax, real **property tax**, and prior to death **income tax.**

Individual Income Tax In the United States, even death does not relieve the liability for income tax. Even if the taxpayer is dead on December 31, an income **tax return** has to be filed for the year of death. As always, the income tax return is due by April 15th of the following year. Only the income received and any deductions paid through the date of death will be reported on the return. Income such as dividends and interest received after the date of death will not be reported on the individual income tax return but on the estate income tax return. Any medical deductions on the decedent's part paid within one year of the date of death may be deducted on the final return. All other deductions must have been paid before death to be allowable.

Estate Income Tax Income which comes in after the date of death should not be reported on the decedent's personal income tax return. Interest, dividends, or other income paid to the estate must be reported on the estate income tax return. A separate tax identification number is obtained for the estate. This separate tax return lists the **taxable income** such as dividends, interest, **capital gains**, and rents, and allows for deductions such as legal and executor's fees. If the estate has been distributed and closed during the tax year, each beneficiary must list his or her proportionate share of the taxable income on his or her personal tax return. If the estate is open, the taxes are paid from the estate.

STATE LAW

Trusts are often created as an alternative to or in conjunction with a Will. Trusts are today usually considered an estate planning tool. The Uniform Probate Code (UPC) includes provisions dealing with affairs and estates of the deceased and laws dealing with nontestamentary transfers such as trusts. The theory behind the Code is that wills and trusts are in close relationship and thus in need of unification. Since its creation, 18 states have adopted the UPC in its entirety and other states have adopted some provisions of the Code.

ARIZONA: Without a Will, all property passes to the surviving spouse unless there are children of the decedent. If there are children only the separate property and the one-half of **community property** that belongs to the decedent passes to the surviving spouse. The remaining goes to the children unless the children are not also children of the surviving spouse, in which case one-half of the intestate separate property and all of the community property that belonged to the decedent passes to the children. Creditors have four months to notice the estate regarding claims.

CALIFORNIA: In California Probate **statutory** attorneys and Personal Representatives' fees are usually calculated based on the gross value of the estate. California has a simplified legal process known as a spousal confirmation proceeding in which, if no one objects, the court approves the transfer of all assets to the spouse. This procedure can only be used for married couples.

FLORIDA: Florida **public policy** protects the spouse and, in some circumstances, children from total disinheritance. Absent a premarital agreement, a surviving spouse may have **homestead** rights, elective share rights, family allowance rights, and exempt property rights. In addition, certain surviving children of the decedent may also have homestead rights, pretermitted child rights, family allowance rights, and exempt property rights.

SOUTH CAROLINA: Without a Will, all assets go to the surviving spouse unless there are children in which case one-half goes to the children. Protective provisions of the South Carolina Probate Code grant a spouse who is left out of a Will an election to take a one-third share of the estate. A similar provision grants a share to a child who is left out of a parent's will written before the child's birth.

SOUTH DAKOTA: South Dakota has adopted the Uniform Probate Code.

TEXAS: Texas changed its probate code to void most no-contest provisions as long as **probable cause** exists for bringing the contest, and the contest was brought and maintained in **good faith**.

UTAH: Utah has adopted the Uniform Probate Code.

WEST VIRGINIA: Without a Will, all assets go to the surviving spouse unless there are children, in which case one-half goes to the children. If there is a Will, the surviving spouse can also renounce the Will and take the elective share instead. The elective share depends on the length of the marriage. Renouncing the Will requires that papers be filed with a court within certain time frames.

ADDITIONAL RESOURCES

Averill, Lawrence, Jr., and Mary Radford. *Uniform Probate Code and Uniform Trust Code in a Nutshell.* 6th ed. Eagan, MN: West, Thomson Reuters, 2010.

McNulty, John, and Garyson, M.P. *Federal Estate and Gift Taxation in a Nutshell.* Eagan, MN: West, Thomson Reuters, 2011.

ORGANIZATIONS

Elder Law Project Legal Services for Cape Cod and Islands, Inc.

460 West Main Street
Hyannis, MA 02601
Phone: (508) 775-7020

National Academy of Elder Law Attorneys, Inc.

1604 North Country Club Road
Tucson, AZ 85716
Phone: (520) 881-4005
Fax: (520) 325-7925
URL: http://www.naela.com/

ESTATE PLANNING

TRUSTS

Sections within this essay:

BACKGROUND

A trust is a legal entity created for the purpose of holding, managing, and distributing property for the benefit of one or more persons. A trust can hold cash, **personal property**, or real property, or it can be the **beneficiary** of life insurance proceeds. In the most basic sense, a trust is just another form of a **contract**. Centuries ago, English landowners, in order to insure the continued wealth of the family, put their estates in trust to be controlled and managed under the terms of the trust agreement for an indefinite period of time. Once the land was placed in trust, the landowners controlled but technically no longer owned the land. As wealth was primarily measured at that time in history by the amount of land owned, the trust arrangement allowed the landowners **immunity** from creditors and may have absolved them of certain feudal obligations. While feudal concerns no longer exist and wealth is held today in many forms other than land, the concept of placing property in third party hands for the benefit of another while avoiding creditors has survived. A trust remains in many circumstance an effective tool to insure that the trust creator's wishes regarding the trust assets are complied with for many years, even during periods of the creator's mental **incompetency** or after death.

TYPES OF TRUSTS

A trust can be created during a person's lifetime and survive the person's death. A trust can also be created by a Will and formed after death. Once assets are put into the trust they belong to the trust itself, not the **trustee**, and remain subject to the rules and instructions of the trust contract. Most basically, a trust is a right in property, which is held in a **fiduciary** relationship by one party for the benefit of another. The trustee is the one who holds title to the trust property, and the beneficiary is the person who receives the benefits of the trust. While there are a number of different types of trusts, the basic types are revocable and irrevocable.

Revocable Trusts Revocable Trusts are created during the lifetime of the trustmaker and can be altered, changed, modified or revoked entirely. Often called a **Living Trust**, these are Trusts in which the trustmaker transfers the title of a property to a Trust, serves as the initial Trustee, and has the ability to remove the property from the Trust during his or her lifetime. Revocable Trusts are extremely helpful in avoiding **probate**. If ownership of assets is transferred to a revocable trust during the lifetime of the trustmaker so that it is owned by the trust at the time of the trustmaker's death, the assets will not be subject to probate.

Although useful to avoid probate, a revocable trust is not an asset protection technique as assets transferred to the trust during the trustmaker's lifetime will remain available to the trustmaker's creditors. It does make it somewhat more difficult for creditors to access these assets since the **creditor** must petition a court for an order to enable the creditor to get to the assets held in the trust. Typically, a revocable trust evolves into an irrevocable trust upon the death of the trustmaker.

Irrevocable Trust An Irrevocable Trust is one which cannot be altered, changed, modified or revoked after its creation. Once a property is transferred to an Irrevocable Trust, no one, including the trustmaker, can take the property out of the Trust. It is possible to purchase Survivorship Life Insurance, the benefits of which can be held by an Irrevocable Trust. This type of survivorship life insurance can be used for estate tax planning purposes in large estates, however, survivorship life insurance held in an Irrevocable Trust can have serious negative consequences.

Asset Protection Trust An Asset Protection Trust is a type of Trust that is designed to protect a person's assets from claims of future creditors. These types of Trusts are often set up in countries outside of the United States, although the assets do not always need to be transferred to the foreign **jurisdiction**. The purpose of an Asset Protection Trust is to insulate assets from creditor attack. These trusts are normally structured so that they are irrevocable for a term of years and so that the trustmaker is not a current beneficiary. An asset protection trust is normally structured so that the undistributed assets of the trust are returned to the trustmaker upon termination of the trust provided there is no current risk of creditor attack, thus permitting the trustmaker to regain complete control over the formerly protected assets.

Charitable Trust Charitable Trusts are trusts which benefit a particular charity or the public in general. Typically Charitable Trusts are established as part of an estate plan to lower or avoid imposition of estate and gift tax. A charitable remainder trust (CRT) funded during the grantor's lifetime can be a financial planning tool, providing the trustmaker with valuable lifetime benefits. In addition to the financial benefits, there is the intangible benefit of rewarding the trustmaker's altruism as charities usually immediately honor the donors who have named the charity as the beneficiary of a CRT.

Constructive Trust A Constructive Trust is an implied trust. An Implied Trust is established by a court and is determined from certain facts and circumstances. The court may decide that, even though there was never a formal declaration of a Trust, there was an intention on the part of the property owner that the property be used for a particular purpose or go to a particular person. While a person may take legal title to property, equitable considerations sometimes require that the equitable title of such property really belongs to someone else.

Special Needs Trust A Special Needs Trust is one which is set up for a person who receives government benefits so as not to disqualify the beneficiary from such government benefits. This is completely legal and permitted under Social Security rules provided that the disabled beneficiary cannot control the amount or the frequency of trust distributions and cannot revoke the trust. Ordinarily when a person is receiving government benefits, an **inheritance** or receipt of a gift could reduce or eliminate the person's eligibility for such benefits. By establishing a Trust, which provides for luxuries or other benefits which otherwise could not be obtained by the beneficiary, the beneficiary can obtain the benefits from the Trust without defeating his or her eligibility for government benefits. Usually, a Special Needs Trust has a provision which terminates the Trust in the event that it could be used to make the beneficiary ineligible for government benefits.

Special needs has a specific legal definition and is defined as the requisites for maintaining the comfort and happiness of a disabled person, when such requisites are not being provided by any public or private agency. Special needs can include medical and dental expenses, equipment, education, treatment, rehabilitation, eye glasses, transportation (including vehicle purchase), maintenance, insurance (including payment of premiums of insurance on the life of the beneficiary), essential dietary needs, spending money, electronic and computer equipment, vacations, athletic contests, movies, trips, money with which to purchase gifts, payments for a companion, and other items to enhance self-esteem. The list is quite extensive. Parents of a disabled child can establish a Special Needs Trust as part of their general estate plan and not worry that their child will be prevented from receiving benefits when they are not there to care for the child. **Disabled persons** who expect an inheritance or other large sum of money may establish a Special Needs Trust themselves, provided that another person or entity is named as Trustee.

Spendthrift Trust A Spendthrift Trust is a Trust that is established for a beneficiary which does not allow the beneficiary to sell or pledge away interests in the Trust. A Spendthrift Trust is protected from the beneficiaries' creditors, until such time as the Trust property is distributed out of the Trust and given to the beneficiaries.

Tax By-Pass Trust A Tax By-Pass Trust is a type of Trust that is created to allow one spouse to leave money to the other, while limiting the amount of Federal Estate tax that would be payable on the death of the second spouse. While assets can pass to a spouse tax-free, when the surviving spouse dies, the remaining assets over and above the exempt limit would be taxable to the children of the couple, potentially at a rate of 55%. A Tax By-Pass Trust avoids this situation and saves the children perhaps hundreds of thousands of dollars in Federal taxes, depending upon the value of the estate.

Totten Trust A Totten Trust is one that is created during the lifetime of the grantor by depositing money into an account at a financial institution in his or her name as the Trustee for another. This is a type of revocable Trust in which the gift is not completed until the grantor's death or an unequivocal act reflecting the gift during the grantor's lifetime. An individual or an entity can be named as the beneficiary. Upon death, Totten Trust assets avoid probate. A Totten Trust is used primarily with accounts and **securities** in financial institutions such as savings accounts, bank accounts, and certificates of deposit. A Totten trust cannot be used with real property. A Totten Trust provides a safer method to pass assets on to family than using joint ownership. To create a Totten Trust, the title on the account should include identifying language, such as "In Trust For," "Payable on Death To," "As Trustee For," or the identifying initials for each, "IFF," "POD," "ATF." If this language is not included, the beneficiary may not be identifiable. A Totten Trust has been called a "poor man's" trust because a written trust document is typically not involved and it often costs the trustmaker nothing to establish.

PARTIES TO A TRUST

There are typically three main parties to a Trust. The Trust Maker, sometimes called the Grantor or Maker, is the person who creates the Trust. The Trustee is the person or entity named to hold the legal title to the Trust

estate. There may be one or several Trustees. The Beneficiaries are the persons who the Trust Creator intended to benefit from the Trust estate. The rights of the beneficiaries depend on the terms of the Trust. Beneficiaries have the equitable title to the property held in the Trust. During the lifetime of the Trustmaker, the Trustmaker, Trustee and Beneficiary can all be the same individual. This is most often the case in Revocable Trusts.

Trustmaker The Trust Creator, sometimes called the Grantor or Trustmaker, is the person who started out as owner of the property that is to be transferred to and held by the Trust. The trustmaker makes an agreement with the trustee agreeing to convey his or her property into the name of the trustee for the benefit of the beneficiaries.

Trustee A Trustee is a person or institution selected to follow the instructions provided by the **declaration of Trust**. A Trustee has a very high "fiduciary duty" to act with the utmost **good faith** in dealing with the Trust estate. Many grantors and their respective spouses act as the initial Trustees of a revocable living Trust. In this way they remain in control until they are incapacitated or die. Then pre-selected successor Trustees are appointed in accordance with the terms of the declaration of Trust. Usually spouses, family members or trusted friends are selected as successor Trustees. Trustees should be knowledgeable about financial matters, be trustworthy, know how to manage and invest the Trust estate, care about the beneficiaries of the Trust, and have the financial capacity to reimburse the Trust in the event that they make serious mistakes. If a bank or **Trust company** is selected to serve as a Trustee of a Trust, it will usually charge a fee for this service, which is paid from the Trust estate.

Because the beneficiary, trustmaker, and the trustee can be the same person, the trustmaker and trustee can agree that the trust creator keep complete control over the trust by retaining the right to remove and replace the trustee, sell or transfer the original trust property, **dissolve** or revoke the trust, and change the trust beneficiaries.

Beneficiaries The Beneficiaries are the persons whom the Trust Creator intended to benefit from the Trust estate. Beneficiaries are said to have the "equitable title" to the property held in the Trust. The rights of the beneficiaries depend on the terms of the Trust. The trust agreement can provide that the beneficiaries have almost complete control over the manner in which trust assets are held and managed, as well as control over the timing and dollar amounts of distributions, or the beneficiaries could be given absolutely no control. The decision as to how trust powers are apportioned depends on the trustmaker's objectives, their trust and confidence in the trustee, and the tax consequences.

Once the trustmaker of a revocable trust dies and the trust becomes irrevocable, an anti-alienation clause usually protects the assets held in the trust from being used as **collateral** by the beneficiaries. Thus, creditors cannot force a trustee to make a distribution to the trust beneficiaries and the assets held in a trust can remain outside the reach of the beneficiaries' creditors.

REASONS FOR TRUST CREATION

Asset Control A trust can be used to maintain control over the trust assets for a designated period of time which may survive death.

Tax Savings Tax and asset protection aspects of trusts depend on the financial situation of the creator and the type of trust used. In certain circumstances, a trust can achieve substantial tax savings yet not achieve asset protection from creditors of the trustmaker. Everyone gets a lifetime credit against Federal Estate Taxes that permits a transfer of up to $675,000 free from Estate Tax. Individuals and married couples with a total estate value less than $675,000 in 2000 (the amount gradually increased to the year 2006) did not need a trust to save on Federal Estate or Gift Tax. For those who are married, there is an unlimited marital **deduction**. All estate taxes can be avoided upon the death of the first spouse to die. However, the surviving spouse would have to remarry and give the entire estate to the new spouse in order to get another unlimited marital deduction. Many people would rather their own children benefit from their estate, rather than having a surviving spouse pass it on to a new spouse. A trust can accomplish this. The trustmaker can establish a tax by-pass Trust to hold property for children, while still allowing the trust funds to provide for the surviving spouse. This arrangement enables the trustmaker to place up to $675,000 in a Trust for the benefit of the surviving spouse and children which will not be subject to estate tax upon the death of the surviving spouse. Coupled with the surviving spouse's estate and gift tax credit, the children could then **inherit** up to $1,350,000 free from Federal Estate and Gift Tax. At current Federal Estate Tax rates, this could amount to a significant savings of hundreds of thousands of dollars.

Asset Protection Assets may be put in trust because the trust creator has confidence in the prospective trustee's knowledge, experience, or ability to properly manage the type of assets to be transferred into the trusts. The utilization of a trustee in such circumstances may have the additional advantage of relieving the beneficiaries of what may otherwise be a burden.

Avoiding a Conservatorship If property is held in a Trust, a successor Trustee can step in and take over management, without the delay and expense of going to court to appoint a conservator to manage the property, if the Trust Creator becomes disabled. This may be particularly important if the trustmaker is self-employed or owns a portion of a business or **partnership**.

Avoiding Probate In many estate plans, the Trust is the central tool that is used to control and manage property. A Trust continues despite the incapacity or death of the grantor. It determines how a Trustee is to act with respect to the Trust estate. It determines how property is to be distributed after the death of the grantor. A properly drawn Trust is a separate entity that does not die when the creator dies. The successor Trustee can take over management of the Trust estate and pay bills and taxes, and promptly distribute the Trust assets to the beneficiaries, without court supervision, if the Trust agreement gives the Trustee that power. Trusts, unlike **Wills**, are generally private documents. The public would be able to see how much the descendent owned and who the beneficiaries were under a Will, but typically not with a Trust. Like a Will, however, a Trust can be used to provide for minor children, children from a prior marriage and a second spouse in the same trust; transfer a family-operated or closely-held business; provide for pets; provide for charities; and can remove life insurance benefits from a taxable estate, while still controlling the designation of insurance beneficiaries.

STATE LAW

Trusts are often created as an alternative to or in conjunction with a Will. Trusts are today usually considered an estate planning tool. The Uniform Probate Code includes provisions dealing with affairs and estates of the deceased and laws dealing with nontestamentary transfers such as trusts. The theory behind the Code is that wills and trusts are in close relationship and thus in need of unification. Since its creation, over thirty percent of states have adopted most provisions of the Code.

ADDITIONAL RESOURCES

Condon, Gerald. *Beyond the Grave: The Right Way and the Wrong Way of Leaving Money to Your Children (and Others)*. New York: HarperCollins, 2001.

McKinley, Kevin. *Make Your Kid a Millionaire: Eleven Easy Ways Anyone Can Secure a Child's Financial Future*. New York: Simon & Schuster, 2002.

Palermo, Michael T. "Crash Course in Wills and Trusts." Available at http://www.caregiver.com/articles/general/trust_and_wills.htm (accessed October 31, 2012).

ORGANIZATIONS

Elder Law Project Legal Services for Cape Cod and Islands, Inc.

460 West Main Street
Hyannis, MA 02601
Phone: (508) 775-7020

National Academy of Elder Law Attorneys, Inc.

1604 North Country Club Road
Tucson, AZ 85716
Phone: (520) 881-4005
Fax: (520) 325-7925
URL: http://www.naela.com

ESTATE PLANNING

WILLS

Sections within this essay:

BACKGROUND

A will, sometimes known as a "last will and testament," is a legal document that provides written instructions for the distribution of a decedent's property. Generally, people should consider making a will if they care how their property will be distributed when they die, they want to name the person who will handle financial and legal matters they may leave behind, or they want to name a **guardian** for their minor children.

WHAT IS IN A TYPICAL WILL?

A will most likely will include the following provisions:

- Your name (the **testator**)
- The name of your spouse and the date of your marriage, if any
- The name of your children (and how you wish any foster and stepchildren to be treated), if any
- A statement revoking any wills you may have previously made
- Your nomination of a personal representative to administer the estate and usually at least one alternate
- A list of powers that you want your personal representative to have (these are often enumerated in your state's statutes)
- A list of any special gifts
- Instructions for distributing the remainder of your estate after your debts, taxes, and expenses incurred in administering your estate have been paid
- A **waiver** of any surety bond requirements

Your will may not cover everything that you consider "your property." The following types of property are examples of assets that may pass directly to a **beneficiary** you have named in a separate document:

- **pension** plan assets
- 401(k) plan assets
- life insurance
- annuities
- property held through a "trust"

These assets would usually pass to beneficiaries you have previously named in documents under the supervision of the manager of the pension plan, the company sponsoring the 401(k), life insurance companies, annuities, and in a **trust** instrument. However, if you name "my estate" the beneficiary of any of these kinds of assets, then your will would control who receives the property and benefits. Be aware that by doing this your eventual beneficiaries may experience some significant delays and/or some important tax disadvantages.

Your will should be prepared and properly executed (signed by you and a certain number of competent witnesses) while you still have legal capacity. Thus, if you want a will, you should have one prepared and sign it according to the applicable state law while you have full control over your mental functions. If you wait until you suffer an accident or an illness, it could be too late.

THE PERSONAL REPRESENTATIVE

When you die, your personal representative (also known as an administrator or **executor**) will gather and inventory all of your property at the time of your death. Most states require the personal representative to post a surety bond covering his/her actions, although you can explicitly waive this requirement in your will. The personal representative will also determine your outstanding debts, pay your legitimate debts, and distribute the remaining property according to the instructions in your will. Your personal representative will be appointed in a **probate** proceeding. The personal representative must usher your property through the probate process, subject to your state's probate rules and procedures. In many states, the court maintains tight control over the activities of the personal representative. For example, the personal representative must obtain the court's permission to sell, distribute, or otherwise take action with respect to property in your estate.

It is important to choose someone who you think will be competent and trustworthy to serve as your personal representative. The personal representative will have access to all of your property and the authority to conduct certain business on your behalf. To the extent that you can, it is a good idea to choose a person with some business experience, intelligence, and high integrity. Your will should name the person you wish to nominate as your

personal representative. You will probably also name one or more alternates to serve in the event that your first choice for personal representative is unwilling or unable to serve. Because you cannot speak in your own behalf, your will acts as your voice to inform the probate court about who you think will be best suited to this job.

CHANGING A WILL

The most common reasons to change your will after it has been executed include the following:

- You get married or divorced
- Your family increases through the birth or **adoption** of child
- There is a death of a family member or of a beneficiary
- There arc changes in the Federal Estate Tax laws or State Tax laws that may affect your estate
- There is a substantial change in the value of your estate
- You change the nature of your property holdings, which impacts your distribution plans
- A potential guardian, executor, or **Trustee** moves away, dies, or refuses to serve in that capacity
- Your children reach the **age of majority**, or are old enough to manage financial matters on their own
- You move to a different state
- You need or want to eliminate gifts to certain people

To change your will, there are two basic choices, and professional assistance is in order for both. First, you can prepare and properly execute an entirely new will that revokes the previous will. Second, you can prepare and properly execute a **codicil** to the will. A codicil is a separate document that adds to and/or replaces one or more provisions in an existing will. What makes the most sense for you will depend on the facts and circumstances. For example, if there is a new tax provision that favors provisions in existing wills, but not new wills, or there may be a question subsequently raised about your mental competence, a codicil would generally be the best choice.

Codicils were used frequently in the past, but lawyers now use computer technologies that can quickly integrate any changes you want to make—even minor ones—into an entirely new will that is up to date. Because of the ease of making the changes, the fees charged to make these modifications are usually modest. Your lawyer may even suggest revisions to your will that take account of new laws, tax rules, and changes in your circumstances that you may have overlooked in your previous will. Regardless of the ease of making these changes, never try to make changes in your will on your own. If you write in the margins, add material, cross out words, lines, or sections of the original will you could possibly create some confusion or ambiguity and thereby invite unpleasant and protracted will contests.

COMPETENCY

Someone trying to have your will accepted for probate generally must establish that you were of sound mind and memory at the time you executed your will. Even if one becomes old, frail, and forgetful, it is difficult to get a court to regard a will as invalid. Generally, those who witnessed the will being signed will almost always say that the deceased was of sound mind; was aware of his surroundings, the day or date, and who his family members were; and knew that he was signing a will. The burden then shifts to the person challenging the will to prove it should not be accepted for probate.

Courts maintain a strong presumption that a will is valid. Thus, it can be costly and difficult to prove that someone was mentally incompetent, made a mistake, or was subject to **fraud**, **coercion**, **duress**, or undue influence when making and/or executing the will. If the testator suffers weakened mentality after the will was made has no bearing. The validity of the will is only called into question should an incompetent testator want to change the will at a later date.

CONTESTING OR CHALLENGING A WILL

Will contests challenge the admissibility of wills in probate courts. It is a kind of **litigation** that questions whether a will should be properly admitted by the court as **evidence** of a decedent's wishes regarding the distribution of his estate, appointment of guardians for minor children, or other issues dealing with the decedent's estate. One may not contest the validity of a will merely because that person does not like the will's provisions. A will's validity is not determined by one's sense of "fairness" of the will's contents. Nor is a will's validity determined by how reasonable the will's provisions appear nor on the timing of disbursements.

Despite the feelings of a decedent's family or friends, a will is most likely to be challenged by someone claiming one of the following:

- the will was not properly written, signed or witnessed, or did not meet the state's formal requirements
- the decedent lacked mental capacity at the time the will was executed
- the decedent was a victim of fraud, force, or undue influence
- the will is a forgery

If a will contest is successful, the entire document may be thrown out. Alternatively, the probate court may reject only the part of the will that was challenged. If the entire will is disallowed, the court will distribute the decedent's property as if the person died without a will. If possible, the court may use a previous will, but such action will depend on state law and the facts and circumstances of the case.

If someone files an objection to your will or produces another will, a "will contest" has begun. Will contests are not uncommon, but few people actually win one. They can be very expensive and create lengthy delays in the distribution of an estate's assets. Not just anyone can contest a will. A person must have legal "standing" to object to a will. What constitutes standing is determined by state law, but generally it means someone who either is a party mentioned in a will or perhaps should have been a party to the will based on a legal relationship to the decedent. For example, if a decedent revises his will and the later will is less favorable to someone than an earlier will, that person has standing. Someone may initiate a will contest to have a different person, bank, or **trust company** serve as the personal representative for an estate or as a trustee of trusts created by the will. Some of the most common challenges to wills come from potential heirs or beneficiaries who received less than they had anticipated.

DISINHERITING

Can you disinherit your child? The answer is generally yes. To do so, you must explicitly state that you intend to disinherit that child in your will. If your child is a minor, the state laws typically provide some sort of allowance out of the assets of your estate to support your child until he or she reaches the age of majority.

Can you disinherit your spouse? The answer is generally no. But if you and your spouse waived the right to be included in each other's estate in a prenuptial or postnuptial agreement, you may then entirely omit your spouse from taking anything under your will. In the absence of such an agreement, you can limit the amount your spouse will receive to a statutorily defined minimum. All states have laws that shield a surviving spouse from being completely cut off.

Typically, your surviving spouse could choose between the property you left to him or her in your will or a **statutory** share set by state law. Depending on the state law where you reside, this spousal share is usually one-third or one-half of your estate. The rules for calculating the amount of the share differ remarkably from state to state. Additionally, in **community property** states, the surviving spouse already owns half of the community property at the death of the other spouse.

The threat of will contest and the expense and delay they occasion prompts competent lawyers to encourage their clients to avoid completely cutting someone out. Instead, it may be advisable to leave the person a relatively small amount and put in an "in terrorum" clause. These clauses state that if the person contests the will, he or she will **forfeit** that small amount. The consequences of will contests are another important reason most people should avoid a do-it-yourself will. Lawyers are trained and experienced to prepare wills and will make sure the wording and **execution** is done according to the law. If it seems possible that someone may later claim that the testator lacked competence, the lawyer can produce qualified medical and other witnesses at the execution ceremony to ameliorate those claims.

DIVORCE

The effect of a **divorce** on the legality or sufficiency of a will depends on your state's law. In some states, a divorce **decree** will automatically revoke your entire will. In other states, a divorce will only revoke the provisions that would distribute assets to your former spouse, not the will itself. In either case, should you experience a divorce, you should review the property arrangements in your will. This is also true of other important documents, such as life insurance policies and bank accounts. This is such a fundamental principle that divorce courts frequently require litigants to address these issues as part of divorce decrees.

DYING WITHOUT A WILL

If you die without having made a will (also known as dying "intestate"), the probate court will appoint a personal representative for your estate. This representative is frequently known as an "administrator." The administrator will receive creditors' claims against your estate, pay debts, and distribute your remaining property according to the laws of your state. There are many differences between dying **testate** and dying **intestate**. The main difference, however, is that an intestate estate is distributed to beneficiaries according to the distribution plan established by state law; a testate estate is distributed according to the decedent's instructions provided in the decedent's will.

GUARDIANS

A major impetus for making a will is to provide for the care of minor children. If you have a minor child or children you may want to choose a guardian to serve in your place should you die before your children reach the age of majority. There are two basic types of legal guardians: a guardian of the person and a guardian of the estate of minor children. These functions can be performed by one person. The guardian of the person is responsible for decisions about the health, education, and welfare of the minor child. The guardian of the estate is responsible for the child's property and for managing finances for the minor child.

When one natural parent dies, generally the other natural parent is appointed as the guardian for minor children, whether or not the parents were married at the time. If someone besides a surviving natural parent of a minor child is named as guardian in a will, the surviving natural parent can contest that nomination. The court will then determine whether the appointment of the other parent as the guardian would be detrimental to the best interests of the minor child. Courts strongly prefer that children be placed in the **guardianship** of their natural parents whenever possible. It is very difficult from a legal standpoint to overcome this presumption. However, if both natural parents are deceased, it is important to name a guardian for minor children, to ensure the children (and their financial assets) will be cared for by someone the parents trust.

LIFE INSURANCE

It is not a good idea to name a beneficiary for your insurance in your will. This adds an unnecessary level of administration and expense as insurance proceeds become caught up in the probate process. Because life insurance proceeds generally pass to your beneficiaries free of the claims of your creditors, passing insurance proceeds through your will may unnecessarily subject your life insurance proceeds to your estate's debts. Currently, you may contact your insurance company to ask for a beneficiary form on which you name your life insurance beneficiaries. If your life insurance is part of your employer's benefit plan, your employer may provide you with insurance beneficiary forms. With the forms from your insurance company or employer, you may name the beneficiaries of your choice and file the new beneficiary designation with the insurance company or with your employer. Do not forget to ask for written confirmation that the form was received and properly filed. In the event of your death, the insurance company would pay the insurance proceeds directly to the beneficiaries you have named without having your beneficiaries go through the delay, expense, and trouble of probate.

LOST WILLS

Sometimes, a family knows that a deceased relative made a will, but the will cannot be found. Missing wills raise many legal issues. The outcomes of these situations depend on the specific facts and circumstances, as well as on the law of the state in which the deceased resided. If the will is missing because the deceased attempted to revoke it, depending on state law, an earlier will or the state's rules on interstate **succession** would determine how to distribute the deceased's estate. If the will is missing because it was destroyed in an explosion or fire, the probate court may accept a photocopy of the will. The court may also accept the lawyer's draft or computer file. In either of these cases, the court will require evidence that the deceased executed the original will according to state law.

MOVING FROM STATE TO STATE

The laws of all states differ with respect to wills. If you move to a different state after you make and execute your will, it may be a good idea to have your will reviewed by a lawyer in your new state. A will properly drafted and executed in your former state—and that would be valid in your former state—will typically be regarded as valid under the law of your new state.

Do not forget that the laws in your new state may be more favorable than the laws of your previous state. For example, your new state may have different processes to "prove" the will or may permit some probate matters to be handled on a less formal and less expensive basis. Sometimes this can be accomplished simply by adding language that refers to certain statutory provisions in your new state's laws.

Sometimes complications will occur because different states maintain different statutory classifications of property. The differences between states without community property schemes and those that have them can create important complications. If your will was executed in a state that does not have a community property scheme and you subsequently move to a community property state (or vice versa), you may want to confer with a lawyer in your new state to determine whether to create a new will to achieve your intended result.

REVOKING A WILL

As mentioned above, a change in your marital status may revoke all of your will, or it may revoke the part of your will relating to your former spouse. If you are mentally competent at the time you do it, you can revoke your will by burning it, tearing it up, or otherwise destroying it. Be aware that revoking your will must be properly witnessed and recorded. If not, someone may later claim that your will was simply "lost" and not revoked. Thus, copies of the will you thought you had revoked can be produced and duly probated. Alternatively, someone may claim that

you lacked mental competence at the time you "attempted" to revoke your will.

PROBATE

Probate is the process by which legal title of your property will be transferred from your estate to your beneficiaries. If you die with a will ("testate"), the probate court determines if your will is valid, hears any objections to your will, orders that your creditors be paid, and supervises the process to assure that property remaining is distributed in accordance with the terms and conditions of your will. The cost of probating your estate is determined either by state law or by practice and custom in your community. The usual cost to probate an estate varies between 3% and 7% of the value of the estate.

TAXES

As part of his or her duties, your personal representative will file tax returns for your estate to report the assets of your estate. The personal representative will also file an estate **income tax** return to report any income generated by your estate. For probates filed in 2012, the first $5 million was excluded from estate taxes. For amounts over $5 million, the tax rate was 35 percent. Merely making and executing a will does not reduce federal estate tax. However, through competent legal advice on estate planning, including the careful crafting of your will, you can minimize or avoid these taxes. Such tax benefits would not be available to you and your family if you died without a will.

TYPES OF WILLS

Do-It-Yourself Wills So-called do-it-yourself wills are wills that individuals create themselves, usually with the aid of self-help legal literature. There are numerous guides, form books, websites, and fill-in-the-blank literature in the marketplace geared for non-lawyers. This material purports to help you create a valid will and avoid the costs of hiring an attorney to prepare a will for you. While this may be true in some cases, there is much to be cautious about. Mainly, the consequences of preparing a do-it-yourself will can be potentially devastating. If you die and your will is declared to be invalid, you will not be around to explain what you had intended to accomplish in your will. Instead, a probate court will either interpret your will or distribute your property according to the state intestacy scheme. Keep in mind that your will is an important legal document. If it is not prepared and executed according to state law, your entire will can be set aside by a probate court. Additionally, just about anyone who envisions an alternative distribution of your estate can contest a do-it-yourself will. If it does not meet some very stringent tests mandated by state law, the court can disregard your do-it-yourself will.

Oral Wills Oral wills are those whose contents and terms are merely spoken to a witness or witnesses, but not written down. There is great potential for fraud or even simple misunderstanding in oral wills. In most cases an "oral will" is only recognized by a probate court when made by members of the armed services or merchant marine in active service in time of conflict. Oral wills are not uncommon in situations in which a person feels he or she does not have time to prepare a written will and have it properly executed.

Death-Bed Wills Deathbed wills are those created and executed when the testator is facing imminent death. These wills may be perfectly valid and binding, but the closer to the testator's death the will is prepared the more likely it is to be challenged. The contest is usually based on a premise that the testator lacked sufficient mental capacity or was subject to undue influence. As previously stated, challenges can lead to costly and protracted will contests.

A deathbed will can potentially lead to errors. Its hasty preparation can be such that the will may not distribute the property in the manner that the testator intended. Hasty preparation can also fail to take advantage of some features that can reduce or eliminate the Federal Estate Tax. It is also more likely that the will would be found invalid because it does not conform to some legal requirement. These are some of the reasons many lawyers urge their clients or potential clients to create and execute their wills while they are still of sound mind and body.

Holographic Wills A holographic will is one that you have written yourself. They are generally handwritten, although some states may allow for a holographic will to be created on a typewriter or with word processing software. These kinds of wills are not allowed in some states, but other states permit this kind of informal will. In states that permit them, the laws relating to holographic wills can be very specific or restrictive. For example, California requires that you write all material provisions entirely by hand and that you must sign your holographic will. On occasion, a holographic will is better than no will at all. In cases where the holographic will creates an ambiguity or an unintended result, it may have been better to have no will at all.

Self-Probating Wills You can help simplify the probate process by adding to your will the affidavits (sworn statements) of the witnesses who saw you signing your will. When these affidavits are included with a will, it is sometimes called a "self-probating will." In the affidavits, the witnesses state that they saw you execute or sign the will, that you asked them to be witnesses to the will, that you appeared mentally competent at the time, and you acted voluntarily. Without these affidavits, the process is more complicated and lengthy. In those cases, the executor would usually need to contact the original witnesses and have them appear in probate court (if they can). Before the personal representative or executor can even file your will in probate court, the witnesses would usually appear in court (or sometimes provide an **affidavit**) to state the circumstances surrounding the execution of the will. This **testimony** helps to "prove" that the will is genuine.

Probate courts usually permit your will to be filed along with the affidavits, without the need to summon witnesses or obtain new affidavits. The court then gives notice to other heirs at law who are given a specific amount of time to file any objections to the will being admitted to probate. If any of these choose to challenge your will, the probate court is more likely to require your witnesses to come into court (if they are still available) to **testify** about the circumstances in which your will was signed. In some states, self-authenticating affidavits are not accepted in situations where the testator dies shortly after the will is signed, or the will was not executed with the assistance of a licensed attorney.

Living Wills A **Living will** is something of a misnomer. It does not direct how your property is to be disposed of after you die. Rather, it is a document that specifies the general kinds of medical care you would want—or not want—in the event you became unable to communicate with your health care providers. Living wills are sometimes known as "medical directives" or "medical declarations."

ADDITIONAL RESOURCES

Averill, Lawrence, Jr., and Mary Radford. *Uniform Probate Code and Uniform Trust Code in a Nutshell.* 6th ed. Eagan, MN: West, Thomson Reuters, 2010.

McNulty, John, and Garyson, M.P. *Federal Estate and Gift Taxation in a Nutshell.* Eagan, MN: West, Thomson Reuters, 2011.

Mennell, Robert L. *Wills and Trusts in a Nutshell.* Eagan, MN: West, Thomson Reuters, 2007.

Palermo, Michael T. "Crash Course in Wills and Trusts." Available at http://www.caregiver.com/articles/general/trust_and_wills.htm (accessed October 31, 2012).

ORGANIZATIONS

American Academy of Estate Planning Attorneys
9360 Towne Centre Drive, Suite 300
San Diego, CA 92121
Toll Free: (800) 846-1555
Fax: (858) 453-1147
Email: information@aaepa.com
URL: http://www.aaepa.com

American College of Trust and Estate Counsel
3415 South Sepulveda Blvd., Suite 330
Los Angeles, CA 90034
Phone: (310) 398-1888
Fax: (310) 572-7280
Email: info@actec.org
URL: http://www.actec.org

National Academy of Elder Law Attorneys, Inc.
1604 North Country Club Road
Tucson, AZ 85716
Phone: (520) 881-4005
Fax: (520) 325-7925
URL: http://www.naela.com

National Network of Estate Planning Attorneys, Inc.
One Valmont Plaza, Fourth Floor
Omaha, NE 68154-5203
Toll Free: (800) 638-8681
Email: webmaster@netplanning.com
URL: http://www.netplanning.com/

FAMILY LAW

ADOPTION

BACKGROUND

The decision to adopt a child can be one of the most rewarding that an individual or couple can make. As with any rewarding decision, it can be extraordinarily complex. Those who wish to adopt a child must be willing not merely to welcome a new life into their hearts; they must also be willing to deal with legal and bureaucratic issues that can easily take as long as a typical pregnancy. The key to adopting successfully is to do one's homework: finding reputable attorneys and agencies, knowing the pros and cons of different types of adoptions, and understanding the need to be actively involved at every step without allowing impatience or frustration to take control.

People adopt for a variety of reasons. Many adoptive parents cannot have children. Others want to provide a loving environment for children in need of a home; many parents who adopt have already given birth to children. Some people choose to adopt "special needs" children (children with disabilities, for example). The reasons for adoption notwithstanding, the most important requirement for adoptive parents is that they accept adoption as being as irreversible as the birth process.

Beginning in the last decades of the twentieth century, overseas adoptions became increasingly common. More prospective parents turned to Russia, China, and South and Central America for adoption. This trend was spurred on by several factors, the two most important being easier availability and less fear of legal challenges. Domestic adoptions are not subject to widespread legal challenges, but it is not impossible for birth parents or birth relatives to initiate proceedings to revoke an adoption. For these reasons, it is critically important to work with people who are experienced in the adoption process and who understand what makes for a successful adoption.

TYPES OF ADOPTION

When people talk about adoption they usually mean "unrelated adoption," the adoption of a child who has no blood or marriage ties to the adoptive parent. Often a grandparent or aunt or uncle will adopt a child whose parents have died or who cannot serve in their role as parents. Step-parents often adopt their step-children as a means of creating a stronger emotional and legal bond within the family. These adoptions are generally much easier and less complicated than a typical unrelated adoption.

When individuals or couples choose to adopt, they have several options.

Domestic Adoptions People who wish to adopt a child who is as close to them culturally and physically as possible will often opt for domestic adoptions. A white couple may want to adopt a white baby, a black couple a black baby, and so on. Because there are more minority children available for adoption, prospective parents almost always have a longer wait if they wish to adopt a white child.

Multiethnic Adoptions Often a prospective parent is unconcerned about the race or ethnicity of the child. Or the parent may actively seek a child of a different race or ethnic group. Multiethnic adoptions (also called trans-ethnic or transracial adoptions) are generally easier when the parents seek a minority child, again, because there are more minority children available for adoption.

International Adoptions Because there are many more children overseas who are waiting to be adopted (in particular, many more who are under one year old), it is often easier for parents to adopt from another country. This action involves extra steps, of course, including dealing with both the U.S. government and the adoptee's government as well. A number of adoption agencies specialize in overseas adoptions.

The costs associated with adoption depend on the type of adoption and the age of the child, among other factors. An agency or other intermediary should be able to give you a detailed breakdown of how much you should expect to pay for the adoption. Agencies are also be able to provide information on sources for funding and possible tax breaks for adoptive parents.

THE ADOPTION PROCESS

Adoption is a complex process, but it follows a fairly predictable sequence of events. The first step for those who are serious about adopting is to contact someone who can provide assistance. Some people try to handle the adoption process themselves. Because the laws are so complex, doing so is illegal in a number of jurisdictions, and the sheer volume of regulations is often more than the average untrained person can handle.

Most people turn to adoption agencies when they decide to adopt a child. Agencies can be public or state-licensed private groups. Some agencies specialize in specific types of adoption, as mentioned above. Agencies place children whose birth parents have voluntarily surrendered their rights to their offspring or whose birth parents have had their parental rights terminated. Because agencies have considerable experience with adoptions, they can often make the process run more smoothly. A number of people, however, turn to "private placement," in which the biological parent or parents place the child directly with the adoptive parents. Often this action involves a third party (typically a lawyer, doctor, or a member of the clergy) who brings the biological and adoptive parents together and who then acts as an intermediary. Private placement is illegal in Connecticut, Delaware, and Massachusetts, and it is strictly regulated in several other states.

The next step after choosing a third party in the adoption is to arrange for a "home study." This is an evaluation of the prospective parent's fitness to raise a child. Not surprisingly, the process is detailed. A prospective parent is interviewed, often by several people. The parent's home is visited, and letters of reference and recommendation are asked for. The prospective parent needs to provide information about his or her physical and emotional health, financial status, employment history, marital history, and so on. The process is by necessity extremely thorough.

If the child has not yet been born, the prospective parent or the intermediary (whether an agency or an individual) selects a pregnant woman who has decided to give up her baby for adoption. If the child has been born, the prospective parent is offered a chance to meet him or her (for domestic adoptions). Obviously, a prospective parent may not be able to meet a child from overseas right away, but pictures and often videotapes of the child are made available. Some agencies do require that the prospective parent visits the country of the child's birth to meet with the child before the process is finalized. Meeting the child is an important turning point in the adoption process because it is the first chance for the parent and child to bond, if only for a brief time.

At this point the goal is to make sure all the legal requirements have been met. Many forms need to be filled out and filed with different courts and government agencies. For domestic adoptions, the child may be placed with the adoptive family for supervision to ensure that the adjustment is smooth before the adoption is finalized. This step depends on the state laws and the courts. Overseas adoptions by necessity cannot require a supervised adjustment period, so usually when the parent makes a second trip it is to take **custody** of the child. Before this action can be accomplished, however, the child must be granted U.S. citizenship. This step involves more paperwork but usually does not take long. However, adoptive parents should be prepared to wait just in case, since two government bureaucracies are at work instead of one.

Each state has its own regulations regarding the adoption process, so it is important to learn the laws governing your particular state and also to know that the intermediary you choose has a thorough knowledge of your state's laws and requirements.

OBSTACLES TO THE ADOPTION PROCESS

The adoption process is not thorough simply because bureaucrats like to make people fill out dozens of forms. Adoption is a permanent decision, and each adoption needs to be made ironclad to avoid difficulties later on.

Probably the greatest fear adoptive parents have is that the birth parents will change their minds and petition to get their children back. Although the laws are thorough, sometimes a birth parent will challenge an adoption for any one of a number of reasons. Most states allow birth mothers to revoke or withdraw their consent to give up their children for adoption; in some states this can be done at any time before the adoption has been finalized. By law, birth mothers actually cannot give consent to an adoption until after their babies have been born; Alabama, Hawaii, Washington, and Wisconsin allow prebirth consent in certain circumstances. But there are strict rules regarding consent. A birth parent who has been proved to have deserted the child, for example, has no **legal right** to give or revoke consent.

Putative Fathers Many adoptees are the children of single women who may not even know the fathers' identity. Sometimes, birth fathers may wish to exercise their rights to claim their children. Unwed, or "putative" fathers can establish certain rights thanks to changes in state laws since the 1970s. That said, a putative father needs to prove that he has actually earned these rights. Putative fathers have to prove their commitment to their children by having signed the birth certificate, provided support for the child, and communicated with him or her, and by having obtained a court order establishing **paternity**. They should also have submitted their names to a registry of putative fathers in their states. Moreover, in most cases all of these steps need to have been taken *before* a birth mother has made a petition to the court to give up her child for adoption. Court cases involving putative fathers who tried to revoke adoptions after claiming they knew nothing of their children's births have resulted in many states clarifying their laws. Putative fathers may have the law on their side, but again, only if they can prove they are truly concerned for their children's welfare.

Single Parent Adoptions Some find it surprising that no state prohibits adoption by a single adult. In fact, this has

been true since the early adoption laws were passed during the nineteenth century. However, a single parent usually has to prove that the adoption is in the child's best interest, and it is possible that a judge may rule that it is not in the child's best interest to allow adoption by the single adult.

Multiethnic Issues Within pockets of the adoption community the question of whether to allow children of one race or color to be adopted by parents of another race or color is a source of heated controversy. Some people believe that mixed-race adoptions are a good practice because they break down racial, ethnic, and cultural barriers. Others see mixed-race adoptions as a means of diluting the cultural and ethnic heritage of adopted children.

Multiethnic adoption presents a compelling problem for two reasons. One is that, as noted above, there are many more minority children available for adoption (including mixed-race children). The other is that there are many more whites than minorities who are willing to adopt. Insisting on matching race to race can leave many children without available parents to adopt them. For children of mixed ancestry, matching race to race is hardly possible.

Federal law protects parents and children from this dilemma. The Multi-Ethnic Protection Act (MEPA) of 1994 states that no adoption agencies that receive federal funds can deny or delay a placement based on race or ethnicity. Occasionally there are still some court cases that raise the issue, but parents who work with a reputable agency and knowledgeable attorneys should not have to worry.

MEPA does not cover children of American Indian (Native American) ancestry. The Indian Child Welfare Act of 1978 was passed to protect American Indian children from being taken away from their families for adoption without parental or tribal consent. This action was apparently not uncommon in years past, and the protection is thus important. Unfortunately, some have read the law to mean that no child with Indian ancestry can be legally adopted, even with the birth parent's consent, without tribal approval. Complicating the matter is the unclear definition of Indian ancestry; some tribes may consider a person with one drop of Indian blood to be Indian. Clearly there are many layers to this issue, and it requires careful evaluation by the prospective parent with the help of knowledgeable intermediaries.

Gay and Lesbian Adoptions A rather contentious issue is whether gay and lesbian couples and individuals can adopt a child. As of 2012, only two states—Mississippi and Utah—explicitly prohibited a same-sex couple from adopting a child. Similar laws in Arkansas and Florida were struck down as unconstitutional in separate cases in 2010. Same-sex couples have full adoption rights in the states of California, Connecticut, Florida, Illinois, Indiana, Maine, Massachusetts, New Jersey, New York, Oregon, and Vermont, as well as the District of Columbia and the territory of Guam.

Same-sex couples nevertheless continue to run into legal hurdles, even when one of the partners is the biological parent of the child. Thirty states as of 2012 did not have laws that explicitly allow both partners to be recognized as parents. Six states restricted or prohibited same-sex couples from adopting a child. In such a situation, the nonbiological parent may not have legal rights to the children as a true parent. Advocates have sought legislative and judicial remedies for these issues, and adoption in this context has remained an evolving area of law.

Open Adoption Open adoption allows the birth family to have visitation rights with the child and the adoptive family. The idea is that maintaining contact with the birth family is beneficial for the child. In some cases it may be, but it can also create uncomfortable situations in which the child ends up being forced to make a choice most children should never have to make. An open adoption can take place only if both the adoptive and birth parents sign an agreement and only if that agreement meets the approval of the court. Different states have different rules about open adoption procedures and also different approaches for addressing whether open adoptions are legally enforceable.

Again, this issue requires careful consideration by prospective parents. In some cases agencies encourage open adoption, but if you wish to adopt a child and open adoption makes you uncomfortable, you should make your concerns known early on.

Searching for Birth Parents Whether an adopted child may want to know his or her birth parents does not come up at the time of adoption but the question is worth thinking about early on. State laws vary widely on whether adopted children can have access to the names of their biological parents. Often those parents do not want contact with the child. Even if they do, the situation can be problematic for all parties. The issue is not really within the scope of this discussion, but adoption agencies and intermediaries should be able to answer questions about it. Bear in mind that, according to figures from the National Council on Adoption, no

more than two percent of adopted adults search for their biological parents.

GETTING INFORMATION

Probably the best first step is to conduct some research, either through materials available at the public library or over the Internet. There are a number of adoption-related websites, but keep in mind that not all of them offer the same quality of information. The National Adoption Information Clearinghouse, which is run by the U.S. Department of Health and Human Services' Administration on Children and Families, may be a good starting point. Its web address is http://www.acf.hhs.gov/.

Because each state's laws vary so widely, it is critically important to check with state government agencies that regulate adoption to determine your specific rights and responsibilities.

There are numerous adoption agencies, and it makes sense to get information from several before making a decision on which one would be the best option. Once you choose an agency, you will be working with that group for the next several months, so make sure you are comfortable with your choice.

ADDITIONAL RESOURCES

Fairfax, Jennifer. *The Adoption Law Handbook: Practice, Resources, and Forms for Family Law Professionals.* ABA Section on Family Law. Chicago: American Bar Association, 2011.

Mabry, Cynthia R., and Lisa Kelly. *Adoption Law: Theory, Policy, and Practice.* 2d ed. Buffalo, NY: William S. Hein & Co., 2010.

Reiniger, Douglas H. *Adoption Law Institute.* New York: Practising Law Institute, 2008.

ORGANIZATIONS

Administration for Children and Families, U.S. Department of Health and Human Services

370 L'Enfant Promenade SW
Washington, DC 20447
Phone: (202) 401-2337
URL: http://www.acf.gov

National Council for Adoption (NCFA)

225 N. Washington St.
Alexandria, VA 22314-2561
Phone: (703) 299-6633
Fax: (703) 299-6004
URL: https://www.adoptioncouncil.org

FAMILY LAW

CHILD ABUSE/CHILD SAFETY/ DISCIPLINE

Sections within this essay:

- Background
- History
- Defining Child Abuse
- Preventing Child Abuse
- Mandatory Reporting Laws
- State Laws
- Additional Resources

BACKGROUND

Child abuse occurs when a parent or caretaker physically, emotionally, or sexually mistreats or neglects a child resulting in the physical, emotional, or sexual harm or exploitation; imminent risk of harm or exploitation; or in extreme cases, the death of a child. Laws regarding child abuse seek to protect children while at the same time allowing parents the right to raise and discipline their children as they see fit. Controversies over child abuse laws arise when parents or guardians feel that the government is interfering in their private family lives.

HISTORY

Child abuse has a lengthy history. Children have always been subject to abuse by their parents or other adults, and for many centuries laws failed to protect them. Children under English **common law** were considered the property of their fathers until the late 1800s; American colonists in the seventeenth and eighteenth centuries carried this tradition to the early years of the United States.

In the early 1870s, child abuse captured the nation's attention with news that an eight-year-old orphan named Mary Ellen Wilson was suffering daily whippings and beatings at her foster home. With no organization in existence to protect abused children, the orphan's plight fell to attorneys for the American Society for the Prevention of Cruelty to Animals (ASPCA). These attorneys argued that laws protecting animals from abuse should not be greater than laws protecting children. Mary Ellen Wilson's case went before a judge, who convicted the foster mother of **assault and battery** and gave her a one year sentence. More significantly, the orphan's case generated enough outrage over child abuse that in 1874, citizens formed the New York Society for the Prevention of Cruelty to Children.

Child abuse captured the country's attention again in 1962, when an article appearing in the Journal of the American Medical Association described symptoms of child abuse and deemed child abuse to be medically diagnosable. Within ten years, every state had statutes known as mandatory reporting laws. Mandatory reporting laws require certain professionals—doctors and teachers, for example—to report to police suspected child abuse situations. A 1974 federal law further bolstered efforts to eliminate child abuse by funding programs to help individuals identify and report child abuse and to provide shelter and other protective services to victims.

DEFINING CHILD ABUSE

Child abuse may involve physical abuse that causes injury. The most obvious types of physical child abuse include children who are beaten, burned, or shaken. Child abuse may involve **sexual abuse**, although sexual abuse need not result in physical injury to the child for it to be illegal. Sexual abuse may include inappropriate touching, fondling, or even sexual intercourse. Finally, child abuse may involve neglect that places a child at risk, such as when a child who is left alone without adult supervision, or a child who is left enclosed and unattended in a car.

PREVENTING CHILD ABUSE

In addition to state laws criminalizing child abuse, states have agencies, known as child protective services, that investigate suspected child abuse cases involving the child's parent or **guardian**. When a suspected case of child abuse involves an adult other than the child's parent or guardian, law enforcement agencies such as police departments typically conduct the investigation. An investigation may include a law officer or case worker visiting and interviewing the child. Parents, guardians, and other possible witnesses such as doctors or teachers also may be questioned during an investigation.

Once an investigation is completed, the child protective service or law enforcement agency determines whether the **evidence** substantiates child abuse. If it does, then the agency will intervene. There is a spectrum of intervention modalities. In less severe cases of child abuse—for example, when a parent unwittingly leaves a child in a car while making a quick stop in a grocery store—intervention may be nothing more than requiring the parent to meet with a social worker to learn about the dangers of leaving a child unattended. If it appears to the investigating agency that an abused child is in imminent danger, the agency may take the child from the parents and place the child temporarily in a foster home until the parents demonstrate their willingness to stop the abuse. In extreme cases of child abuse, the investigating agency may seek assistance from a court to terminate the parental rights. When this happens, the child may be placed for permanent **adoption**.

Child protective services, in addition to investigating allegations of child abuse, maintain records regarding child abuse. These records are kept in a central registry, and in some states, parties such as **child care** providers or adoption agencies have access to the central registry. The goal of the central registry is to help child protective services, and sometimes other parties, know whether an individual has a history of abusing children. Although this information can be invaluable in preventing future child abuse, central registries may contain false or unsubstantiated accounts of child abuse, implicating innocent individuals. For this reason, some groups oppose central registries and argue that child protective services have too much power. One such group, Victims of Child Abuse Laws (VOCAL), seeks a reform in child abuse laws to better protect the rights of parents, who may be falsely **accused** of child abuse or neglect.

VOCAL, and groups like it, maintain that it is too easy for false accusations about child abuse to lead to the removal of children from their parents and their homes. False reports of child abuse can come from children seeking attention or attempting to avoid reasonable forms of discipline. False reports of child abuse also may result from animosity between parents, such as when parents are in the midst of **divorce** and **custody** battles over their children. The evidence of child abuse is sometimes nothing more than a young child's **testimony**. Proponents of child abuse law reform maintain that police and other officials can easily manipulate a young child to support allegations of child abuse. The ramifications of a false report of child abuse can be serious: officials may remove children from their homes and place them in **foster care** or permanent new adoptive homes, emotionally scarring both children and parents.

Another difficult issue in the arena of child abuse concerns discipline. There are many different views regarding what constitutes discipline and where the line should be drawn between reasonable parental discipline and child abuse. For example, some parents feel that spanking or hitting a child is abusive behavior; other parents rely on spanking, or the threat of a spanking, to teach children to obey and behave. Using physical measures to discipline children is known as corporal punishment. In trying to prevent child abuse, legal and governmental agencies attempt to balance the parents' right to raise their children in the manner they feel is appropriate with the child's right to be safe and unharmed.

Some forms of child abuse are caused not by a parent's willful abuse, but rather, by a parent's **negligence**. One common, and oftentimes tragic, form of neglect occurs when a parent accidentally leaves a sleeping baby in a car on a warm day. In the sun, the interior of a car can heat within minutes to more than 100 degrees, temperatures that a baby cannot survive. Whether to charge parents in these situations with child abuse is a divisive issue. Some people maintain that careless parents should be prosecuted; other people believe that a parent who loses a child due to the parent's mistake suffers enough without being prosecuted.

MANDATORY REPORTING LAWS

The vast majority of states, including several American territories, have enacted laws that require certain individuals to report instances of child abuse. These individuals are usually those with frequent contact with children and include social workers, teachers, physicians, mental health professionals, child-care providers, medical examiners, law enforcement officers, and lawyers. In most jurisdictions, these individuals must issue a report when the individual suspects or has reason to believe that child abuse has occurred.

In several states, professionals must report child abuse even if means divulging confidential and privileged information. For instance, communication with a doctor is ordinarily privileged, meaning that the doctor cannot divulge the communication with the patient. However, if the patient informs the doctor of an act of child abuse, the doctor may have a duty to report the abuse notwithstanding the privilege.

STATE LAWS

ALABAMA: Statute defines child abuse as harm or threatened harm of physical abuse, neglect, sexual abuse, sexual exploitation, or emotional/mental injury against a child under the age of 18. Statute contains an exemption for religious reasons for a parent's failure to obtain medical help for the child.

ALASKA: Statute defines child abuse as harm or threatened harm of physical abuse, neglect, sexual abuse, sexual exploitation, or emotional/mental injury of a child under the age of 18. Statute contains an exemption for religious reasons for a parent's failure to obtain medical help for the child.

ARIZONA: Statute defines child abuse as inflicting or allowing physical abuse, neglect, sexual abuse, sexual exploitation, emotional/mental injury, or **abandonment** of a child under the age of 18. Statute contains an exemption for Christian Scientists or unavailability of reasonable resources for a parent's failure to obtain medical help for the child.

ARKANSAS: Statute defines child abuse as intentionally, knowingly, or negligently without cause inflicting physical abuse, neglect, sexual abuse, sexual exploitation, abandonment or emotional/mental injury of a child under the age of 18. Statute contains exemptions for poverty or corporal punishment.

CALIFORNIA: Statute defines child abuse as inflicting by non-accidental means physical abuse, neglect, sexual abuse, or sexual exploitation of a child under the age of 18. Statute contains exemptions for religion, reasonable force, and informed medical decision.

COLORADO: Statute prohibits threats to a child's health and welfare due to physical abuse, neglect, sexual abuse, sexual exploitation, emotional/mental injury, or abandonment. Statute contains exemptions for corporal punishment, reasonable force, religious practices, and cultural practices.

CONNECTICUT: Statute prohibits injuries inflicted by non-accidental means involving physical abuse, neglect, sexual abuse, sexual exploitation, emotional/mental injury, or abandonment. Statute contains exemption for Christian Scientists.

DELAWARE: Statute prohibits injuries inflicted by non-accidental means involving physical abuse, neglect, sexual abuse, sexual exploitation, emotional/mental injury, or abandonment. Statute contains exemption for religion.

DISTRICT OF COLUMBIA: Statute prohibits persons from inflicting and requires people to take reasonable care not to inflict injuries involving physical abuse, neglect, sexual abuse, sexual exploitation, or emotional/mental injury. Statute contains exemption for poverty and religion.

FLORIDA: Statute prohibits any willful or threatened act that harms or is likely to cause harm of physical abuse, neglect, sexual abuse, sexual exploitation, abandonment, or emotional/mental injury. Statute contains exemptions for religion, poverty, or corporal punishment.

GEORGIA: Statute prohibits injuries inflicted by non-accidental means involving physical abuse, neglect, sexual abuse, or sexual exploitation. Statute contains exemption for religion and corporal punishment.

HAWAII: Statute prohibits acts or omissions resulting in the child being harmed or subject to any reasonably foreseeable, substantial risk of being harmed with physical abuse, neglect, sexual abuse, sexual exploitation, or emotional/mental injury. Statute contains no exemptions.

IDAHO: Statute prohibits conduct or omission resulting in physical abuse, neglect, sexual abuse, sexual exploitation, abandonment, or emotional/mental injury. Statute contains exemption for religion.

ILLINOIS: Statute prohibits persons from inflicting, causing to be inflicted, allowing to be inflicted, creating a substantial risk of, or committing or allowing to be committed physical abuse, neglect, sexual abuse, sexual exploitation, or emotional/mental injury. Statute contains exemptions for religion, school attendance, and plan of care.

INDIANA: Statute prohibits any act or omission resulting in physical abuse, neglect, sexual abuse, sexual exploitation, abandonment, or emotional/mental injury. Statute contains exemptions for religion, prescription drugs, or corporal punishment.

KENTUCKY: Statute prohibits harm or threat of harm, or infliction or allowance of infliction of physical abuse, neglect, sexual abuse, sexual exploitation, abandonment, or emotional/mental injury. Statute contains exemptions for religion.

MARYLAND: Statute prohibits harm or substantial risk of harm resulting in physical abuse, neglect, sexual abuse, sexual exploitation, or emotional/mental injury. Statute contains no exemptions.

MICHIGAN: Statute prohibits harm or threatened harm of physical abuse, neglect, sexual abuse, sexual exploitation, or emotional/mental injury. Statute contains exemptions for religion.

MISSISSIPPI: Statute prohibits persons from causing or allowing to be caused physical abuse, neglect, sexual abuse, sexual exploitation, or emotional/mental injury. Statute contains exemption for religion and corporal punishment.

NEBRASKA: Statute prohibits knowingly, intentionally, or negligently causing or permitting physical abuse, neglect, sexual abuse, sexual exploitation, or emotional/mental injury. Statute contains no exemptions.

NEW MEXICO: Statute prohibits knowingly, intentionally, or negligently causing or permitting physical abuse, neglect, sexual abuse, sexual exploitation, abandonment, or emotional/mental injury. Statute contains exemption for religion.

NORTH DAKOTA: Statute prohibits serious harm caused by non-accidental means resulting in physical abuse, neglect, sexual abuse, sexual exploitation, abandonment, or emotional/mental injury. Statute contains no exemptions.

OKLAHOMA: Statute prohibits harm or threat of harm resulting in physical abuse, neglect, sexual abuse, sexual exploitation, abandonment, or emotional/mental injury. Statute contains exemptions for religion or corporal punishment.

PENNSYLVANIA: Statute prohibits recent act or failure to act resulting in physical abuse, neglect, sexual abuse, sexual exploitation, or emotional/mental injury. Statute contains exemptions for religion or poverty.

SOUTH DAKOTA: Statute prohibits threat with substantial harm resulting in physical abuse, neglect, sexual abuse, sexual exploitation, abandonment, or emotional/mental injury. Statute contains no exemptions.

TENNESSEE: Statute prohibits persons from committing or allowing to be committed physical abuse, neglect, sexual abuse, sexual exploitation, or emotional/mental injury. Statute contains no exemptions.

UTAH: Statute prohibits harm or threat of harm resulting in physical abuse, neglect, sexual abuse, sexual exploitation, or emotional/mental injury. Statute contains no exemptions.

WASHINGTON: Statute prohibits harm of health, welfare, or safety resulting from physical abuse, neglect, sexual abuse, or sexual exploitation. Statute contains exemptions for Christian Scientists, corporal punishment, or physical **disability**.

ADDITIONAL RESOURCES

Child Welfare Information Gateway. *Child Abuse and Neglect.* Washington, DC: U.S. Department of Health and Human Services, Administration for Children and Families, 2011.

Katz, Sanford N. *Family Law in America.* New York: Oxford University Press, 2011.

Oliphant, Robert E., and Nancy Ver Steegh. *Family Law: Examples and Explanations.* 3d ed. New York: Aspen Publishers, 2010.

ORGANIZATIONS

Administration for Children and Families, U.S. Department of Health and Human Services

370 L'Enfant Promenade SW
Washington, DC 20447
Phone: (202) 401-2337
URL: http://www.acf.gov

American Professional Society on the Abuse of Children

350 Poplar Avenue
Elmhurst, IL 60126
Toll Free: (877) 402-7722
URL: http://www.apsac.org

Prevent Child Abuse America

228 South Wabash Avenue
Chicago, IL 60604
Phone: (312) 663-3520
URL: http://www.preventchildabuse.org

FAMILY LAW

CHILD SUPPORT/CUSTODY

Sections within this essay:

- Background
- Child Custody
  – Joint Custody
  – Split Custody
  – Custody Disputes

- Child Support
- Mediation
- State Laws
- Additional Resources

BACKGROUND

In more ancient times, fathers had sole rights to **custody** of children. Since custody was connected to **inheritance** and property laws, mothers had no such rights. Beginning in the late nineteenth century, courts began to award custody of young boys and of girls of all ages solely to mothers on the presumption that mothers are inherently better caretakers of young children. Most states followed this maternal preference and mothers almost always received custody. Eventually, many state courts found this preference to be unconstitutional, and gender-neutral custody statutes replaced maternal preference standards in 45 states by 1990. As of the early 2010s, the custody arrangement is typically part of the **divorce decree**. The decree provides specifics as to where the child will live, how visitation will be handled, and who will provide financial support.

Courts consider custody and child support issues as subject to change until the child involved reaches the **age of majority**. In many divorces physical custody is awarded to the parent with whom the child will live most of the time. Often, the custodial parent shares joint legal custody with the noncustodial parent, meaning that the custodial parent must inform and consult with the noncustodial parent about the child's education, health care, and other concerns. In this situation, courts may order visitation, sometimes called temporary custody, between the child and the noncustodial parent. A clear schedule with dates and times is often incorporated into the decree. Child support is usually paid by the noncustodial parent to the custodial parent. States have formulas to assist judges in determining the appropriate amount of child support.

CHILD CUSTODY

Joint Custody Some states have a presumption that joint custody is in the best interest of the child, while other states have no provision for it. Advocates of joint custody claim it lessens the feeling of losing a parent that children may experience after a divorce and that it is fair to both parents. However, because of the high degree of cooperation joint custody requires, courts resist ordering it if either of the parents does not want it or if there is **evidence** of past **domestic violence**. Later problems regarding medical or education decisions concerning the child may develop necessitating long and lengthy court proceedings.

Split Custody Split custody is an arrangement in which the parents divide custody of their children, with each parent being awarded physical custody of one or more children. In general, courts try to avoid split custody because it separates siblings, which is usually not considered to be in the best interest of the child.

Custody Disputes Many states have adopted a standard that places primary emphasis on the best interests of the child when custody is disputed. Today, courts exercise their discretion in awarding custody, considering all relevant factors, including marital misconduct, to determine the children's best interests. The court may consider such matters as the wishes of the child's parents; the wishes of the child; the relationship between each parent and the child, and any other person who interacts with the child (including step-parents); the child's adjustment to home, school, community; the mental and physical health of all individuals involved; which parent will foster a positive parent-child relationship between the child and the other parent; who was the primary caretaker; the nature and extent of **coercion**, if any, by a parent in obtaining an agreement regarding custody; and whether either parent has complied with an order to attend domestic relations education if the state requires it. Domestic violence is considered not to be in the best interest of a child and in many states a parent's **conviction** for any domestic violence can weigh heavily against that parent's bid for custody.

CHILD SUPPORT

In determining child support obligations, courts generally hold that each parent should contribute in accordance with his or her means. Child support is a mutual duty, although the primary caretaker of preschool children may not be required to obtain employment. All states have enacted some form of the Uniform Reciprocal Enforcement of Support Act (URESA). URESA is a uniform law designed to facilitate the interstate enforcement of support obligations. URESA allows an individual who is due **alimony** or child support from someone who lives in a different state to bring action for receipt of the payments in the home state. This measure circumvents such problems as expense and inconvenience inherent in traveling from one state to another in pursuit of support.

The National Conference of Commissioners on Uniform State Laws (NCCUSL) approved the Uniform Interstate Family Support Act (UIFSA) in 1992. The goal was to replace URESA, though several states retained parts or all of URESA even when enacting the UIFSA. The NCCUSL amended the UIFSA in 2008, and as of 2012, a total of 10 states had adopted the amended version.

In response to federal legislation, state laws regarding child support payments have become more severe. State laws can require employers to withhold child support from the paychecks of parents who are delinquent for one month. Employers are to be held responsible if they do not comply fully. State laws must provide for the imposition of liens against the property of those who owe support. Unpaid support must be deducted from federal and state **income tax** refunds. Expedited hearings are required in support cases.

MEDIATION

Mediation is a centered resolution process assisted by an **impartial** trained third party to assist the parties in reaching an informed and consensual agreement. Many parents find the process useful in figuring out which custody and visitation arrangement can work best for them and their child. Mediation typically provides a non-adversarial setting in which to resolve the conflicts that arise over financial, parenting, and other issues. It allows the parents to control many aspects of the court process, rather than deferring to a judge. Additionally, parties who are able to reach an agreement in mediation can save significant court costs and attorneys' fees.

STATE LAWS

State law varies considerably with respect to divorce. States have differing residency requirements, property rules, and spousal support provisions.

ALABAMA: Both parents have an equal right to the custody of their children. Alabama law creates a presumption in favor of joint custody, whereby the parental rights of both parties remain intact, with one parent as the primary custodian of the children and the other as the secondary custodian. Under this arrangement, both parents remain involved in the decision making responsibilities regarding the children, with each parent having "tie breaking" authority regarding certain issues, such as education, health and dental care, religion, civic and cultural activities, and athletic involvement. Child support is determined under the Alabama Child Support Guidelines, unless the Court finds grounds to deviate from the guidelines. In Alabama, the Department of Human Resources is responsible for enforcing child support obligations. The court retains **jurisdiction** to modify child support, up or down, until the children reach the age of 19.

ALASKA: The court determines custody in accordance with the best interests of the child and may consider all relevant factors. Domestic violence may be considered contrary to the best interest of the child. There is no presumption in favor of sole custody or joint custody. Joint custody may be ordered if both parents agree and submit a written parenting plan and such joint custody is in the child's best interest. Child support is based on Flat

Percentage of Income model. Support terminates at age 18, or 19 if child is enrolled in high school or the equivalent and is residing with custodial parent. Court may not require either parent to pay for post-majority college tuition.

ARIZONA: There is no presumption in favor of joint custody. Joint custody may be granted if both parents agree, the parents submit a parenting plan, and the order is in the child's best interests. Evidence of domestic violence must be considered contrary to the best interests of the child. In determining the best interests of the child, the court can consider: the wishes of the child's parents; the wishes of the child; the interaction among the child and relatives; the child's adjustment to school, home, and community; the mental and physical health of the parties; which parent is more likely to involve the child in the life of the other parent; if either parent has been the primary care giver; the nature and extent of coercion used by a parent in obtaining a written agreement regarding custody; whether either parent has complied with an order to attend domestic relations education. The non-custodial parent is entitled to reasonable visitation, which shall not be restricted unless the court finds serious endangerment to the child. Child support guidelines are based on Income Shares Model, and award is calculated on **gross income**. Support terminates at age 18, or when the child graduates from high school. The court may not order the parents to pay for the college education costs of the child.

ARKANSAS: The court shall determine custody in accordance with the best interests of the child. Child Support guidelines adopt Varying Percentage of Income Model, basing noncustodial parent's obligation on a percentage of **net** income, which percentage decreases as income increases. Support terminates at age 18 or when child graduates from high school. Parents cannot be compelled to pay for the college education of their children.

CALIFORNIA: There is no presumption in favor of joint or sole custody; custody shall be awarded to both parents jointly or to either parent as is in the best interests of the child. However, where the parties agree to joint custody, then joint custody shall be presumed to be in the best interests of the child. In awarding custody, the court shall consider which parent is more likely to foster a positive relationship between the child and the other parent. An explicit link between custody and child support is made by the provision that a court may order financial compensation to one parent for those periods of time the other parent fails to assume caretaking responsibility.

There may be additional financial compensation awarded to a parent who has been repeatedly thwarted by the other parent in attempts to exercise custody/visitation. State-wide Uniform Guidelines are an Income Shares model, explicitly taking into consideration the time each parent has custody of the child.

COLORADO: Joint custody, with one parent designated residential custodian, may be awarded when the parties submit a parenting plan. If no plan is submitted, the court shall determine custody in accordance with the best interests of the child. Child Support Guidelines are based on Income Shares model, based on gross income of both parents. Support terminates at age 18 or when child graduates from high school. Parents cannot be compelled to pay for the college education of their children.

CONNECTICUT: If the parents agree to joint custody, then it is presumed that joint custody is in the best interests of the child, and the court must state its reasons for denial of joint custody. The court may award joint legal custody with primary physical custody to one parent. Visitation may be granted to grandparents or any person if it is in the child's best interests. Child Support guidelines are based on the Income Shared Model, taking into consideration the net income of both parents. Child support terminates when the child reaches 18 years of age.

DELAWARE: State law does not presume that joint custody is in a child's best interests, but Delaware courts prefer to award joint custody. A court may order joint or sole custody for six months to give parents an opportunity to show that they will cooperate with the order. After that, the court can make the order permanent.

DISTRICT OF COLUMBIA: There is no presumption as to the form of legal custody. The court may order frequent and continuing contact between each party and the child. The court's order shall be based on the best interests of the child. The court can consider the wishes of the parents, the wishes of the child, the interaction and interrelationship among all family members, the mental and physical health of all parties, the capacity of the parties to communicate, the demands of parental employment, the age and number of children, the parents' financial ability to support the custody arrangement and the impact of governmental assistance. Child support guidelines are a hybrid model, sharing aspects of both the income shares and percentage of income model. The award is based on parties' gross incomes, with a self-support reserve for each parent. By **statute**, a child is entitled to support until age 21.

FLORIDA: The court must order that parental responsibility for a minor child be shared by both parents, unless it is detrimental to the child. The court may grant to one party the ultimate responsibility over specific aspects of the child's welfare. The court shall order sole parental responsibility with or without visitation to the other parent when it is in the best interests of the child. The court may order rotating custody. Child Support Guidelines are the Income Shares Model of support, figured on net income. Health insurance, childcare, and education expenses are added to the basic award. Support terminates at age 18, or 19 if the child will graduate from high school by that time.

GEORGIA: The court may award joint custody and may consider agreements of the parties, if they are in the best interests of the child. The court shall award custody according to the best interests of the child. If a child is 14 years old or older, the child shall have the right to select the parent with whom he desires to live, and such selection shall be controlling unless the parent is not fit. The court may consider family violence in making a decision. Visitation shall be ordered unless there is a history of family violence. Child support is **statutory**. It is the flat percentage of income model, calculated on gross income, with most extra expenses being a deviation factor.

HAWAII: Custody is determined according to the best interests of the child. If a child is of sufficient age and capacity to reason, so as to form an intelligent preference, the child's wishes can be considered. Joint custody may be awarded at the discretion of the court. Visitation may be awarded to grandparents or any person interested in the welfare of the child. Guidelines set out in court rule follow the Melson Formula. Support is calculated on net income, with allowances for household members.

IDAHO: Idaho law establishes a presumption favoring joint custody, either in the form of joint physical custody or joint legal custody. An Idaho court will consider the best interests of the child when making a custody decision.

ILLINOIS: There is no presumption for or against joint custody. Custody is determined based on the best interests of the child, considering the parents' and the child's wishes. Child support guidelines are statutory, based on a flat percentage of income model based on net income.

INDIANA: Joint custody may be awarded if it is in the child's best interests. The relevant factors for determining custody are the parents' and child's wishes, the interaction and relationship of the child with any person who may significantly affect his or her best interests, the mental and physical health of all individuals involved, and a pattern of domestic violence. Child support guidelines are set out in the Indiana Rules of Court. The guidelines are based on the income shares model, based on gross income. Support may include sums necessary for a child's education, including post-majority education.

IOWA: If either party requests joint custody, there is a presumption of joint custody. If the court does not grant joint custody, it must clearly state its reasons why joint custody is not in the best interests of the child. Joint custody does not necessarily require joint physical care. Physical care shall be awarded as is in the best interests of the child. Child support guidelines are enacted by the supreme court of Iowa by court rule. The guidelines are based on the income shares model, based on gross income.

KANSAS: Kansas law does not establish a presumption favoring joint custody. A court will consider the best interests of the child when making a custody determination. A court in Kansas may also order mediation if the parties cannot agree on an important issue in the case.

KENTUCKY: The court may grant joint custody to the child's parents if it is in the child's best interests. The court may not consider conduct of a custodian that does not affect his or her relationship to the child, nor may it consider **abandonment** of the family residence if it was to avoid physical harm. Child support guidelines are set out by statute. The guidelines are based on the income shares model, based on gross income. Support may include sums necessary for a child's education, including post-majority education.

LOUISIANA: The court shall award custody in accordance with the parents' agreement, unless the best interests of the child require otherwise. If there is no agreement or if the agreement is not in the best interests of the child, the court shall award joint custody, unless custody by one parent is shown by clear and convincing evidence to serve the child's best interests. Factors for determining the child's best interests include a stable environment and the primary caretaker preference. The parent not awarded custody is entitled to reasonable visitation. Child support guidelines are statutory. They are based on the Income Shares Model and the gross income of the parents.

MAINE: State law does not establish a presumption favoring joint custody. When the parties have agreed to shared parental rights and responsibilities, the court shall make such an award absent substantial evidence that it should not be ordered. In making an award of parental rights and responsibilities, the court applies the best interests of the child standard. The court may not apply a preference for one parent over the other on account of either parent's gender or the child's age and gender. The court may order grandparent or third party visitation. Child support guidelines are statutory. They are based on the Income Shares Model, based on gross income.

MARYLAND: The court may award joint custody or sole custody. The court shall deny custody to a party if the court has reasonable grounds to believe that the party abused or neglected the child and that there is a likelihood of further abuse or neglect. Child support guidelines set out by statute. The guidelines are based on the income shares model, based on gross income.

MASSACHUSETTS: Each parent must submit to the court a shared custody implementation plan. The court may modify or grant the plan. The court may reject the plan and award sole custody to one parent. Child Support Guidelines are provided in the Massachusetts Court Rules, promulgated by the Supreme Judicial Court. The Massachusetts guidelines are a hybrid form of the Percentage of Income model and Income Shares Model. Support is calculated on the gross income of the non-custodial parent, but then offset by a percentage of income of the custodial parent over a certain floor. Support for education of the child is through age 21.

MICHIGAN: Custody is awarded based on the best interests of the child, based on the following factors: moral character and prudence of the parents; physical, emotional, mental, religious and social needs of the child; capability and desire of each parent to meet the child's emotional, educational, and other needs; preference of the child, if the child is of sufficient age and maturity; the love and affection and other emotional ties existing between the child and each parent; the length of time the child has lived in a stable, satisfactory environment and the desirability of maintaining continuity; the desire and ability of each parent to allow an open and loving relationship between the child and other parent; the child's adjustment to his/her home, school, and community; the mental and physical health of all parties; permanence of the family unit of the proposed custodial home; any evidence of domestic violence; and other factors. There is a joint custody presumption if the parties agree to joint custody. The court may also award joint custody if one party requests joint custody and the court finds it to be in the best interests of the child. In deciding whether to grant joint custody, the court shall consider all of the above factors plus whether the parents will be able

to cooperate and whether the parents have agreed to joint custody. Child support payments are made through the Michigan **Friend of the Court** Bureau. Child support guidelines are contained in the Michigan Friend of the Court Child Support Manual. The guidelines are based on the Income Shares Model, calculated on each parent's net income.

MINNESOTA: If both parents request joint custody, there is a presumption that such an arrangement is in the best interests of the child, unless there has been spousal abuse. Sole custody can be awarded based on the best interests of the child. Additional visitation may be ordered for wrongful denial of or interference with visitation orders. Child support guidelines are based on the Varying Percentage of Income formula, calculated on net income.

MISSISSIPPI: Custody is determined based on the best interests of the child. Joint custody may be awarded if both parents request joint custody, and if they so request joint custody, there is a presumption that joint custody is in the best interests of the child. The court may order any of the following: joint physical custody to one or both parents, with legal custody to one or both parents; physical custody to both parents, with legal custody to one parent; physical custody to one parent, with legal custody to both parents; custody to a third party if the parents have abandoned the child or are unfit. Child support guidelines are based on the Flat Percentage of Income model, calculated on net income.

MISSOURI: The court determines custody based on the best interests of the child. Custody can be joint legal, joint physical, sole legal, sole physical, or any combination. An award of joint custody is encouraged. Child support guidelines are based on the Income Shares Formula, calculated on gross income.

MONTANA: Each parent is required to submit, either jointly or separately, a proposed "parenting plan." Sole or joint parenting is awarded based on the best interests of the child. Child support guidelines are set out in the Montana Administrative Rules. The support guidelines are based on the Melson Formula, calculated on net income.

NEBRASKA: The court makes a custody determination based on the best interests of the child, which include the relationship of the child to each parent; the desires and wishes of the child; the general health, welfare, and social behavior of the child; and credible evidence of any abuse in the household. Joint custody may be awarded when both parents agree to such an arrangement. Child support guidelines were established by court rule and are contained in the Rules of the Supreme Court. The guidelines are based on the Income Shares Formula and are calculated on net income.

NEVADA: Best interests of the child is the standard. The court awards custody in the following order of preference unless in a particular case the best interest of the child requires otherwise: to both parents jointly or to either parent; to a person or persons in whose home the child has been living and where the child has had a wholesome and stable environment; to any person related within the third degree of consanguinity; to any other person or persons whom the court finds suitable and able to provide proper care. In determining the best interests of the child, the court considers: the wishes of the child if the child is of sufficient age and maturity; any nomination by a parent for a **guardian**; whether either parent has engaged in domestic violence. A finding of domestic violence creates a rebuttable presumption that custody would not be appropriate by the **perpetrator**. Child support guidelines are based on the varying percentage of income model. Support is figured by applying a percentage to the obligor's gross income, which percentage gradually decreases as the income rises.

NEW HAMPSHIRE: Joint legal custody is presumed to be in the best interests of the child, unless the child has been abused by one of the parents. Custody is awarded based on preference of the child, education of the child, findings and recommendations of a neutral mediator, and other factors. Child support amounts are set out by statute. The guidelines are based on the Income shares model figured on net income.

NEW JERSEY: Sole or joint custody may be awarded based on the needs of the child. There is no preference for either parent and no preference for joint custody. Child support guidelines are contained in New Jersey Court Rules. The guidelines are based on the Income Shares model figured on net income.

NEW MEXICO: Joint custody is presumed to be in the best interests of the child. The court may award joint or sole custody according to the best interests of the child, upon consideration of five enumerated factors. Child support guidelines are based on the Income Shares Model, calculated on gross income.

NEW YORK: Joint or sole custody is determined according to the best interests of the child. Neither parent is entitled to a preference. Child support guidelines are based on the Income Shares Model, calculated on net income.

NORTH CAROLINA: Joint or sole child custody is determined according to the interests and welfare of the child. There is no presumption that either parent is better suited to have custody. The court considers all relevant factors, including acts of domestic violence and the safety of the child. Child support guidelines are based on the Income Shares Model and calculated on gross income.

NORTH DAKOTA: State law does not establish a presumption favoring joint custody. A family court will consider the child's best interests when making a custody decision. A custody order will generally remain in effect for at least two years unless the court determines that grounds exist to modify the order.

OHIO: If at least one parent requests shared parenting and files a plan that is in the child's best interests and approved by the court, the court may allocate parental rights and responsibilities of the child to both parents and issue a shared parenting order. Otherwise, the court, consistent with the child's best interests, allocates parental rights and responsibilities primarily to one parent. Child support guidelines are based on the Income Shares Model and are calculated on net income. Termination of child support is at age 18 or graduation from high school, whichever occurs later.

OKLAHOMA: State law does not establish a presumption favoring joint custody, and a court may award custody to one or both parents. The court will consider the child's best interests when making the custody determination.

OREGON: The court may order joint custody if the parents agree, but if one parent objects, the court cannot order joint custody. An order for joint custody may specify one home as the primary residence of the child and designate one parent to have sole power to make decisions regarding specific matters while both parents retain equal rights and responsibilities for other matters. When ordering sole custody, the court can consider the conduct, marital status, income, social environment or lifestyle of either party only if it is shown that these factors are causing or may cause damage to the child. Any person who has established emotional ties creating a parent/child relationship with a child may petition for custody, placement, or visitation. The child support guidelines formula is based on the Income Shares Formula, calculated on gross income.

PENNSYLVANIA: State law does not establish a presumption favoring joint custody. Before awarding custody, the court may require the parents to undergo counseling.

RHODE ISLAND: State law does not establish a presumption favoring joint custody, and no state statute lists factors for the court to consider. A court will grant custody based on the best interests of the child, taking into account the child's wishes, the parents' wishes, the mental and physical health of the parents, the stability of the child's home, and the ability of each parent to encourage and foster a relationship with the child's other parent.

SOUTH CAROLINA: State law does not establish a presumption favoring joint custody, and no state statute lists factors for the court to consider. The court will consider the child's preference when the child is age 12 or older.

SOUTH DAKOTA: State law does not establish a presumption favoring joint custody, and no state statute lists factors for the court to consider. The court will take into account the child's preferences, and the child's moral and mental well-being.

TENNESSEE: State law establishes a presumption in favor of joint custody, labeled as "shared parenting." The court will consider several statutory elements to determine the best interests of the child.

TEXAS: Joint or sole custody is determined according to the best interests of the child. The court considers the best interests of the children when deciding upon the terms and conditions of the rights of the parent with visitation. Child support guidelines, by statute, are based on a percentage of income of the noncustodial parent's net income. Support terminates at age 18 or graduation from high school, whichever is later. No statute or **case law** requires support for college.

UTAH: The court considers the best interests of the child along with the past conduct and demonstrated moral standards of the parties. There is a presumption that a spouse who has been abandoned is entitled to custody. State law contains advisory guidelines for visitation schedules, broken down by age of the child. Child support guidelines are based on the income shares model, calculated on gross income. Support terminates at age 18 or when the child graduates from high school. In a divorce action, the court may order support to the age of 21.

VERMONT: State law does not establish a presumption favoring joint custody, but a court will award joint custody if it is in the child's best interests.

VIRGINIA: State law does not establish a presumption favoring joint custody. The court will consider several statutory elements when deciding the child's best interests.

WASHINGTON: State law does not establish a presumption favoring joint custody. The court will consider several statutory elements when deciding the child's best interests.

WEST VIRGINIA: There is a presumption in favor of the parent who has been the primary caretaker of the child. There is no provision for joint custody. Child support guidelines are based on the income shares model, calculated on **adjusted gross income**. Support terminates at age 20, or up to age 20 if the child is still enrolled in secondary school. The court may award support for college tuition.

WISCONSIN: State law establishes a presumption favoring joint custody, and a court will award joint custody when parents show they can cooperate when performing their responsibilities toward their child. The court will consider several statutory elements when deciding the child's best interests.

WYOMING: State law does not establish a presumption favoring joint custody. The court will consider several statutory elements when deciding the child's best interests.

ADDITIONAL RESOURCES

De Witt, John Gregory, Peter N. Swisher, and Sheryl L. Wolf. *Understanding Family Law*. 3d ed. Newark, NJ: LexisNexis, 2005.

Galatzer-Levy, Robert M., Louis Kraus, and Jeanne Galatzer-Levy, eds. *The Scientific Basis of Child Custody Decisions*. 2d ed. Hoboken, NJ: Wiley, 2009.

Katz, Sanford N. *Family Law in America*. New York: Oxford University Press, 2011.

Oliphant, Robert E., and Nancy Ver Steegh. *Family Law: Examples and Explanations*. 3d ed. New York: Aspen Publishers, 2010.

ORGANIZATIONS

Administration for Children and Families, U.S. Department of Health and Human Services
370 L'Enfant Promenade SW
Washington, DC 20447

Phone: (202) 401-2337
URL: http://www.acf.gov

Fax: (312) 988-6800
URL: http://www.americanbar.org

American Bar Association (ABA)
321 North Clark Street
Chicago, IL 60610
Phone: (312) 988-5000
Toll Free: (800) 285-2221

Children's Rights Council
9470 Annapolis Road, Suite 310
Lanham, MD 20706
Phone: (301) 459-1220
URL: http://www.crckids.org

FAMILY LAW

COHABITATION

Sections within this essay:

- Background
- Unmarried Cohabitation Compared with Marriage
  - Criminal Statutes
  - Legal Status and Discrimination
  - Acquisition of Property
  - Children
  - Adoption
  - Eligibility for Benefits
- Recognition of Domestic Partners
- Common Law Marriage
- Agreements Between Unmarried Cohabitants
  - Validity
  - Provisions of Written Cohabitation Agreements
  - Wills and Durable Power of Attorney for Health Care
- State and Local Provisions Regarding Cohabitation
- Additional Resources

BACKGROUND

The law has not traditionally looked favorably upon individuals living together outside marriage. However, the law in this area has changed considerably in the past 50 years, and cohabitation has increased dramatically. In 1960, about 450,000 couples reportedly lived together outside marriage. This number increased to 1.6 million in 1980, 2.9 million in 1990, 4.2 million in 1998, and 5.5 million in 2000. By 2012, the number had increased to more than 7.5 million.

In some respects, unmarried cohabitation can be beneficial from a legal standpoint. Unmarried partners may define the terms of their relationship without being bound by marriage laws that can restrict the marriage relationship. When a relationship ends, unmarried cohabitants need not follow strict procedures to **dissolve** the living arrangement. Moreover, unmarried couples can avoid the so-called "marriage tax" in the Internal Revenue Code that provides a greater tax rate for married couples than it does for two unmarried individuals (notwithstanding efforts to eliminate this **penalty**).

On the other hand, unmarried cohabitants do not enjoy the same rights as married individuals, particularly with respect to property acquired during a relationship. Marital property laws do not apply to unmarried couples, even in long-term relationships. Moreover, laws regarding distribution of property of one spouse to another at death do not apply to unmarried couples. Children of unmarried couples have traditionally not been afforded the same rights as children of married couples, though most of these laws have now been revised to avoid unfairness towards offspring.

A fairly recent trend among both heterosexual and homosexual couples who live together is to enter into contracts that provide rights to both parties that are similar to rights enjoyed by married couples. In fact, many **family law** experts now recommend that unmarried cohabitants enter into such arrangements. Further changes in the laws may also afford greater rights to unmarried partners who live together. However, such arrangements may be invalid in some states, particularly where the **contract** is based on the sexual relationship of the parties.

UNMARRIED COHABITATION COMPARED WITH MARRIAGE

Family laws related to marriage simply do not apply to unmarried couples. More specifically, marriage creates a legal status between two individuals that gives rise to certain rights to both parties and to the union generally. Unmarried cohabitants do not enjoy this status and do not enjoy many of the rights afforded to married couples. Thus, if a couple is married for two years, and a spouse dies, the other spouse is most likely entitled to receive property, insurance benefits, death benefits, etc. from the other spouse's estate. Even if an unmarried couple lives together for 20 years, when one partner dies, the other is not guaranteed any property or benefits.

Though many groups support legal reforms providing protection to unmarried cohabitants that would be analogous to laws governing marriage, very few such laws exist today. Unmarried cohabitants need to know what laws do exist in their state and cities and know what their options are regarding contractual agreements that may provide rights that are analogous to marital rights.

Criminal Statutes Laws prohibiting cohabitation and sexual relations outside marriage were very common until about the 1970s. Though most of these laws have been repealed or are no longer enforced, they still exist in some state statutes. Five states still have laws prohibiting cohabitation, which is usually defined as two individuals living together as husband and wife without being legally married. Several states prohibit fornication, which is usually defined as consensual sexual intercourse outside marriage. However, many of these laws have been struck down as unconstitutional.

While most of these criminal laws are clearly antiquated, they are sometimes enforced. In the U. S. Supreme Court case of *Bowers v. Hardwick* in 1986, the court upheld the enforcement of a criminal **statute** prohibiting **sodomy** between two homosexual men. Criminal statutes proscribing private sexual activity do not violate the federal constitution under *Bowers*, though some state courts have held that similar statutes are unconstitutional under the relevant state constitutions.

Legal Status and Discrimination A person living as an unmarried cohabitant with another might face some form of **discrimination**. For example, an employer may expressly forbid employees from living together outside marriage and may terminate the employment of an employee who does cohabit with someone else outside marriage. Such discrimination in employment is not generally forbidden, either under federal law or under the laws of most states. Some state cases have, however, upheld the rights of individuals cohabiting outside wedlock.

Acquisition of Property Marital and **community property** laws govern the ownership of property acquired during a marriage. The characterization of property acquired by unmarried cohabitants is less clear. Some property acquired by unmarried couples may be owned jointly, but it may be difficult to divide such property when the relationship ends. Similarly, if one partner has debt problems, a **creditor** may seek to attach property owned jointly by both partners as if the partner owing the debt solely owned the property. Problems such as these are even more complicated if one partner dies without a will, since the surviving partner has no right to the other partner's property unless the property is devised to the surviving partner.

Children Children born out of wedlock have not traditionally enjoyed the same legal protections as children born in wedlock. Such children were historically referred to as "bastards" in a legal context. Though many restrictions on illegitimate children have been repealed, legitimate (or legitimated) children still enjoy some rights that frustrate illegitimate children. This discrepancy is particularly clear with respect to **inheritance**. In most states, a child born in wedlock does not need to establish **paternity** to recover from the father. However, a child born out of wedlock generally must establish paternity before he or she can recover from the father.

Adoption State laws have traditionally prevented unmarried couples from adopting children. Though some states have begun permitting unmarried couples to adopt, these couples still face difficulties. Married couples, on the other hand, are permitted to adopt and are usually preferred over unmarried individuals.

Eligibility for Benefits Recent changes of policy by insurance companies permit unmarried couples to purchase life insurance policies on the life of the other partner or jointly purchase homeowners' insurance on a house owned by both partners. However, an unmarried couple will often have more trouble jointly obtaining automobile insurance covering an automobile owned by both partners. Similarly, unmarried couples continue to face serious problems with respect to family health insurance coverage paid or co-paid by an employer. A recent trend among some states, municipalities, and private employers is to extend benefits to registered "domestic partners."

RECOGNITION OF DOMESTIC PARTNERS

Several states and municipalities have adopted a system whereby unmarried cohabitants (heterosexual or homosexual) may register as "domestic partners." Other states and municipalities permit domestic partners to recover benefits. These classifications provide some rights that are analogous to marital rights, though these rights are certainly limited. The greatest benefit in registering as domestic partners is that each partner enjoys insurance coverage, family leave, and retirement benefits similar to married couples, though these rights are considerably more restricted than rights afforded to married couples. However, these rights are not generally recognized outside the **jurisdiction** that permits registration of domestic partners.

COMMON LAW MARRIAGES

A minority of states continue to recognize **common law**, or informal, marriages. Such a marriage requires more than mere cohabitation between a man and a woman. The couple generally must agree to enter into a martial arrangement, must cohabit with one another, and must hold themselves out as husband and wife to others. Parties that enter into such marriages enjoy the same rights as couples married in a formal ceremony, including rights related to insurance and other benefits, property distribution on **dissolution** of the marriage, and distribution of property upon the death of one spouse.

Proof that the marriage exists is often the most difficult aspect of a common law marriage, and this issue often arises after the relationship has ended either in death or **divorce**. For example, the question of whether a common law marriage exists may arise after one of the partners in a relationship dies and the other seeks to prove that the partners were informally married to receive property through the other partner's estate. Similarly, when a relationship ends, a partner may seek to prove that an informal marriage exists to seek property distribution under marital or community property laws.

Though a minority of states recognize common law marriages, all states will recognize the validity of a common law marriage if it is recognized in the state where the parties reside, agreed to be married, and hold themselves out as husband and wife. Common law marriages apply only to partners who are members of the opposite sex.

AGREEMENTS BETWEEN UNMARRIED COHABITANTS

Validity Unmarried cohabitants can provide rights to one another that are analogous to rights granted to married couples by entering into a contract or contracts with one another. The validity of such agreements was the subject of the well-publicized case of *Marvin v. Marvin* in the California Supreme Court. In this case, the court held that an express or implied agreement between a couple living together outside wedlock to share income in consideration of companionship could be legally enforceable. The majority of states now recognize these agreements, though many require that the agreement be in writing. Only a small number of recent cases have held that contracts between unmarried cohabitants are unenforceable.

When an agreement expressly includes consideration of sexual services provided by one of the parties, a court is more likely to find the contract unenforceable. For example, if one partner agrees to share his or her income in return for the other partner's love and companionship, a court may find that the contract implicates meretricious sexual activity and refuse to enforce the contract. Proving an oral agreement or an implied contract between unmarried cohabitants is also difficult, and several courts have refused to recognize such an agreement due to lack of proof.

Provisions of Written Cohabitation Agreements Written cohabitation agreements usually involve financial and property arrangements. Parties can provide arrangements analogous to community or marital property laws or can provide other arrangements that are more favorable to the couple. Parties should consult with a lawyer prior to entering into such an agreement to ensure that the provisions are enforceable.

Wills and Durable Power of Attorney for Health Care Nothing prevents unmarried cohabitants from leaving estate property to the other partner upon death in a will. Alternatively, **intestate succession** laws may not provide that any of the property will pass from one cohabitant to another, since **intestacy** laws are limited to marital and other family relationships. A fellow cohabitant might be able to get a share of the intestate's estate by arguing that the parties entered into a financial or property-sharing arrangement, though such claims are often difficult to prove. A will is generally the best method to ensure that a partner's property is given to the person he or she designates.

Another complicated situation can arise if one cohabitant is disabled and requires a **guardian**. To ensure that one partner is named guardian or is otherwise able to make decisions for the other partner, the parties can prepare a document providing durable **power of attorney** to the other partner. Under this arrangement, the person granted durable power of attorney could make health-care decisions for the disabled person. Similarly, a party can draft a **living will** (also called a health-care directive) that dictates the wishes of the party regarding life-prolonging treatments.

STATE AND LOCAL PROVISIONS REGARDING COHABITATION

Sixteen states recognize common law marriages, though several of these states have repealed their laws and only recognize these marriages entered into prior to a certain date. Several states and municipalities now recognize domestic relations rights, providing a registry, extension of benefits, or both. Unmarried cohabitants should check with the state and local laws in their jurisdictions to determine what rights may be available to them.

ALABAMA: The state recognizes common law marriages.

ALASKA: The state does not recognize common law marriages.

ARIZONA: The state does not recognize common law marriages.

ARKANSAS: The state does not recognize common law marriages.

CALIFORNIA: The state does not recognize common law marriages. Domestic partnerships are granted throughout the state.

COLORADO: The state recognizes common law marriages. Designated **beneficiary** agreements are granted throughout the state.

CONNECTICUT: The state does not recognize common law marriages. The state extends benefits to domestic partners.

DELAWARE: The state does not recognize common law marriages. The state recognizes civil unions.

DISTRICT OF COLUMBIA: The District recognizes domestic partnerships.

FLORIDA: The state does not recognize common law marriages.

GEORGIA: The state recognizes common law marriages entered into before January 1, 1997.

HAWAII: The state does not recognize common law marriages. The state extends benefits to domestic partners and provides a domestic partner registry.

IDAHO: The state recognizes common law marriages enter into before January 1, 1996.

ILLINOIS: The state does not recognize common law marriages.

INDIANA: The state does not recognize common law marriages.

IOWA: The state recognizes common law marriages.

KANSAS: The state recognizes common law marriages.

KENTUCKY: The state does not recognize common law marriages.

LOUISIANA: The state does not recognize common law marriages.

MAINE: The state does not recognize common law marriages. The state recognizes domestic partnerships.

MARYLAND: The state does not recognize common law marriages. The state recognizes limited domestic **partnership** rights.

MASSACHUSETTS: The state does not recognize common law marriages.

MICHIGAN: The state does not recognize common law marriages.

MINNESOTA: The state does not recognize common law marriages.

MISSISSIPPI: The state does not recognize common law marriages.

MISSOURI: The state does not recognize common law marriages.

MONTANA: The state recognizes common law marriages.

NEBRASKA: The state does not recognize common law marriages.

NEVADA: The state does not recognize common law marriages. The state created a domestic partnership registry.

NEW HAMPSHIRE: The state recognizes common law marriages but only for inheritance purposes.

NEW JERSEY: The state does not recognize common law marriages. The state recognizes domestic partnerships.

NEW MEXICO: The state does not recognize common law marriages.

NEW YORK: The state does not recognize common law marriages.

NORTH CAROLINA: The state does not recognize common law marriages.

NORTH DAKOTA: The state does not recognize common law marriages.

OHIO: The state recognizes common law marriages entered into prior to October 10, 1991.

OKLAHOMA: The state recognizes common law marriages.

OREGON: The state does not recognize common law marriages. The state extends benefits to domestic partners.

PENNSYLVANIA: The state recognizes common law marriages.

RHODE ISLAND: The state recognizes common law marriages.

SOUTH CAROLINA: The state recognizes common law marriages.

TENNESSEE: The state does not recognize common law marriages.

TEXAS: The state recognizes common law marriages. Travis County extends benefits to domestic partners.

UTAH: The state recognizes common law marriages. Neither the state nor any municipality in the state provides specific rights to domestic partners.

VERMONT: The state was the first to recognize "civil unions," which extend rights to homosexual partners that are similar to rights granted to married couples. The state also extends benefits to domestic partners. The state does not recognize common law marriages.

VIRGINIA: The state does not recognize common law marriages.

WASHINGTON: The state does not recognize common law marriages. The state extends benefits to domestic partners.

WEST VIRGINIA: The state does not recognize common law marriages. Neither the state nor any municipality in the state provides specific rights to domestic partners.

WISCONSIN: The state does not recognize common law marriages. The state recognizes domestic partnerships.

WYOMING: The state does not recognize common law marriages.

ADDITIONAL RESOURCES

De Witt, John Gregory, Peter N. Swisher, and Sheryl L. Wolf. *Understanding Family Law.* 3d ed. Newark, NJ: LexisNexis, 2005.

Katz, Sanford N. *Family Law in America.* New York: Oxford University Press, 2011.

Lind, Goran. *Common Law Marriage: A Legal Institution for Cohabitation.* New York: Oxford University Press, 2008.

Oliphant, Robert E., and Nancy Ver Steegh. *Family Law: Examples and Explanations.* 3d ed. New York: Aspen Publishers, 2010.

ORGANIZATIONS

Alternatives to Marriage Project

PMB 136, 10002 Aurora Ave. N. #36
Seattle, WA 98133
Phone: (347) 987-1068
URL: http://www.unmarried.org/

Focus on the Family

Colorado Springs, CO 80995
Toll Free: (800) 232-6459
URL: http://www.focusonthefamily.com/

Lambda Legal Defense and Education Fund

120 Wall Street, Suite 1500
New York, NY 10005-3904
Phone: (212) 809-8585
Fax: (212) 809-0055
URL: http://www.lambdalegal.org

FAMILY LAW

DIVORCE/SEPARATION/ANNULMENT

BACKGROUND

In primitive civilizations, marriage and marriage **dissolution** were considered private matters which did not require involvement of any authority above the individuals in the relationship. The Romans first placed marriage and divorce under state regulation during the reign of Augustus. When Christianity spread about 300 A.D., governments came under religious control.

The Catholic Church did not permit divorce unless one of the parties had not been converted to Christianity prior to marriage, which then made the marriage null and void.

During the early 1500s, the Protestant Reformation began a slow movement in Europe to separate the laws governing marriage from the precinct of the Roman Catholic Church. Henry VIII wanted the Catholic Church to grant him a divorce from Catherine of Aragon because all the male offspring she bore died shortly after birth, and Henry believed he could secure a male **heir** by marrying another woman. When Pope Clement VII refused, Henry took control of Church properties in England and made himself head of the Anglican Church. This separation from the Vatican made divorce possible in England by an act of Parliament. Still, divorce remained rare; when it occurred it was a costly legislative process and could only be initiated by husbands. The resistance toward and rarity of divorce continued well into the nineteenth century.

Divorce law in the American colonies was somewhat influenced by the British, but more so by the colonists themselves. England did not want its American colonies to enact any type of law that conflicted with English law. Thus, a colonial divorce was not considered final until the English monarch had approved it. Nevertheless, several colonies adopted their own laws permitting divorce, often under odd circumstances. Under one late seventeenth century Pennsylvania law, if a married man committed **sodomy** or bestiality, his punishment was castration, after which the wife was permitted to divorce him. In Connecticut, divorce was allowed on the grounds of **adultery**, desertion, and the husband's failure in his **conjugal** duties. In Massachusetts, divorce was permitted if one of the parties committed adultery.

The U.S. Constitution left divorce regulation to the states. State legislatures passed laws that granted divorce based on a showing of fault. If a divorce was contested, the divorcing spouse was required to establish, before a court, specific grounds for the action. If the court felt that the divorcing spouse had not sufficiently proven the grounds alleged, the petition for divorce could be denied and the case dismissed.

The most common traditional grounds for divorce were cruelty, desertion, and adultery. Other grounds included nonsupport or neglect, alcoholism or other drug addiction, insanity, criminal **conviction**, and voluntary separation. In 1933, New Mexico became the first state to allow divorce on the ground of incompatibility. In 1969, California completely revised its divorce laws, providing that a filing party merely show **irreconcilable differences** resulting in an irremediable breakdown of the marriage. California's was the first comprehensive "no-fault" divorce law, and it inspired nationwide divorce law reform. In 1970, the National Conference of Commissioners on Uniform State Laws prepared a Model Marriage and Divorce Act, which provides for no-fault divorce if a court finds that the marriage is "irretrievably broken." As of 2012, six states had enacted this model law. Moreover, nearly every state legislature has enacted laws allowing no-fault divorces or divorces after a specified period of separation. Some states replaced all traditional grounds with a single no-fault provision. Other states added the ground of irreconcilable differences to existing statutes. In those states a divorce petitioner remains free to file for divorce under traditional grounds.

As of 2012, about half of all marriages ended in divorce. According to statistics compiled by the U.S. Census Bureau, 9.2 out of every 1,000 men divorced in 2009, while 9.7 out of every 1,000 women divorced.

NO-FAULT DIVORCE

By 1987, all 50 states had adopted no-fault divorce laws, exclusively or as an option to traditional fault-grounded divorce. Despite the obvious advantages, no-fault divorce laws sometimes leave parties with no real remedy for harmful acts of a spouse. Most states have laws that prevent one spouse from suing the other. Fault has survived in some aspects of divorce proceedings. Under current theories, marital misconduct is irrelevant to the divorce itself, but it may be relevant to related matters such as **child custody**, **child support**, and child visitation rights; spousal maintenance; and property distribution.

LEGAL SEPARATION

Legal separation is similar to a divorce in that papers are filed and there is often a **custody** or **property settlement** ordered by the court, but the parties remain married.

There may be benefits to this type of arrangement, but they are few. In most states, it is difficult to convert a legal separation into a divorce, and it requires beginning the process over with the filing of a divorce petition.

ANNULMENT

Annulment is a legal process in which a court essentially determines the parties were never legally married to begin with and the marriage is null and void. Annulments are not often granted, but grounds for doing so include if one party is incapable of consent, due to mental state or **intoxication**; **fraud** about some aspect of the marriage; or a failure to **consummate** the marriage. Annulments are regulated by state law.

PROPERTY DISTRIBUTION

Property distribution includes issues of real estate, **personal property**, cash savings, stocks, **bonds**, savings plans, and retirement benefits. The statutes that govern property division vary by state, but they can generally be grouped into two types: equitable distribution and **community property**.

Equitable Distribution Most states follow the equitable distribution method. Generally, this method provides that courts divide assets in a fair and equitable manner. Some equitable distribution states look to the conduct of the parties and permit findings of marital fault to affect property distribution. In others only fault relating to economic welfare is relevant in property distribution. Yet other states entirely exclude marital misconduct from consideration in **disposition** property. Equitable distribution rules give the court considerable discretion in dividing property between the parties. The courts consider the joint assets held by the parties and separate assets that the parties either brought with them into the marriage or inherited or received as gifts during the marriage. Generally, if the separate property is kept separate during the marriage and not commingled with joint assets, then the court will recognize that it belongs separately to the individual spouse and will not divide it along with the marital assets.

Equitable distribution states consider contributions (often including homemaker contributions) by each spouse made to the marriage. If one party made a greater contribution, the court may grant that person more of the joint assets. Some states do not consider a professional degree earned by one spouse during the marriage to be a joint asset but do acknowledge any financial support contributed by the other spouse and let that be reflected in the property distribution. Other states do consider a professional degree or license to be a joint marital asset and have devised various ways to distribute it or its benefits.

Community Property States that follow community property laws provide that nearly all the property acquired during the marriage belongs to the marital "community," such that the husband and wife each have a one-half interest in it upon death or divorce. It is presumed that all property acquired during the marriage by either spouse, including **earned income**, belongs to the community. Property obtained by gift or through **inheritance** is considered separate, unless it is commingled with community property. Upon divorce each party gets all separate property, as well as one-half of the community property.

Military Pay In 1982, Congress passed a law, the Uniformed Services Former Parties' Protection Act, that permits state courts to treat military retired pay as property. In community property states and many other states, a formula is used when the member has already retired. But for an active duty member, there may be no state law that specifies how the award is to be calculated.

SPOUSAL SUPPORT

Alimony, or spousal maintenance, is the financial support that one spouse provides to the other after divorce. It is separate from, and in addition to, the division of marital property. It can be either temporary or permanent. Factors relevant to an order of maintenance include the age and marketable skills of the intended recipient, the length of the marriage, and the income of both parties. Maintenance is most often used to provide support to a spouse who was financially dependent on the other during the marriage. Many states allow courts to consider marital fault in determining whether, and how much, maintenance should be granted.

TEMPORARY ORDERS

Between the time a dissolution action is filed and the time a judgment of dissolution becomes effective, the court may use temporary orders to resolve any issue in the case, including temporary support and temporary allocation of assets. Temporary orders address the immediate concerns of the parties, but also frequently form the basis for the permanent orders in the final **decree**.

COURT PROCESS

Jurisdiction over a divorce case is usually determined by residency. That is, a divorcing spouse is required to bring the divorce action in the state where she or he maintains a permanent home. States are obligated to acknowledge a divorce obtained in another state. This rule is from the Full Faith and Credit Clause of the U.S. Constitution, which requires states to recognize the valid laws and court orders of other states. Under the Due Process Clause of the Fourteenth Amendment to the U.S. Constitution, a state must make divorce available to everyone. If a party seeking divorce cannot afford the court expenses, filing fees, and costs attached to the serving or publication of legal papers, the party may file for divorce free of charge. Typically, in a divorce proceeding or dissolution action the parties are referred to as the "petitioner," and the "respondent." The petitioner is the spouse who initiates the dissolution proceeding. The other spouse is the respondent. A dissolution action begins with one spouse filing a document known as a petition or complaint. The other spouse must then be served with these papers and has a specific time frame in which to respond. The ultimate goal of any dissolution action is to obtain a decree or judgment. The decree will resolve every issue in the case, including child support and visitation, division of assets and debts, and spousal support.

There are basically three methods for securing a divorce decree. If the respondent is properly served, but never files a response, the petitioner can request that the court order the divorce by **default**. Also, the couple may agree on all the issues in the case and obtain a decree by **settlement**, stipulation, or agreement. If the parties cannot agree, the case can be decided by a judge after a trial.

INSURANCE

Insurance is considered a form of property in a divorce. The owner of the insurance policy controls the policy and has the right to name the beneficiaries. Although some laws prohibit the changing of insurance policies while a divorce is pending, once a divorce is final, insurance can become an important issue. Divorce is a qualifying event for benefits under Consolidated Omnibus Budget Reconciliation Act of 1985 (COBRA). Under this act, any person who would lose employer-based coverage because of divorce can choose to purchase continued coverage for up to 36 months. The Act applies to employers with 20 or more employees, but the coverage is not automatic. The spouse seeking coverage must contact the employer within 60 days of the qualifying event and complete the necessary paperwork. Some decrees include a provision for life insurance on the provider, to protect the support order.

DIVORCE FROM PARENTS (EMANCIPATION)

One method children can use to "divorce" their parents is to become emancipated. The word "emancipation" means to become free from the control or restraint of another. In the context of emancipated minors, **emancipation** is a legal procedure whereby children become legally responsible for themselves and their parents are no longer responsible. Emancipated children are freed from parental custody and control and are adults for most legal purposes. Parents of a child have not only responsibility for the child but also legal control over any money the child may earn. Many famous child performers and athletes have sued their parents, often claiming that money earned by the child star was mismanaged, and seeking to have the courts declare the child an adult. In fact, it is possible for a child or a teenager to seek legal emancipation and be declared an adult before age 18, although the process can be difficult. In order to become emancipated, a minor must convince a judge he or she has a place to live and sufficient money and income to be self-supporting. Since minors are not permitted to sign legally binding contracts such as rental agreements, proving such self-sufficiency can be difficult. Emancipation does not require any proof of abuse or neglect by the parents. It can be granted for educational purposes, if a teenager is starting college early and wants to rent an apartment. Many young actors and musicians who are not fighting with their parents over money seek emancipation to avoid strict **child labor laws**. Emancipation laws vary from state to state. Some states have no age restrictions, while others set the age from 14 to 17. Some states also require parental consent or **acquiescence**, which may be demonstrated by **circumstantial evidence**. Emancipation is typically automatic when a teenager marries or joins the military; however, emancipation does not override age restrictions for getting married. Some states require the emancipated teen to undergo counseling with an appointed advisor.

An emancipated minor is entitled to make almost all medical, dental, and psychiatric care decisions, enter into a **contract**, sue and be sued, make a will, buy or sell property, and apply for a work permit without parental consent. The emancipated minor is obligated to self-support but must also follow state laws regarding such requirements as compulsory school attendance. Federal age rules relating to actions such as selective service registration and voting rights do not change simply because a minor is emancipated.

STATE LAWS

State law varies considerably with respect to divorce. States have various residency requirements, property rules, and spousal support provisions. In the United States, each state regulates its own domestic relations. Most courts ignore marital fault in determining whether to grant a divorce, but many still consider fault in setting future obligations between the parties. To determine the rights and obligations of the parties in a dissolution proceeding, one must consult the divorce laws for the state in which the divorce was filed.

ALABAMA: The party filing for divorce must have resided in the State for at least six months before filing for divorce. At a minimum, Alabama law has a 30-day waiting period before a divorce can be granted.

ALASKA: No period of residence is required. After filing of complaint, however, 30 days must elapse before divorce action may be heard. A divorce may be granted on any of the following grounds: failure to consummate the marriage at the time of the marriage and continuing at the commencement of the action; adultery; conviction of a **felony**; willful desertion for a period of one year; cruel and inhuman treatment calculated to impair health or endanger life; personal indignities rendering life burdensome; incompatibility of temperament; **habitual** gross **drunkenness** contracted since marriage and continuing for one year prior to the commencement of the action; incurable mental illness when the spouse has been confined to an institution for a period of at least 18 months immediately preceding the commencement of the action; addiction of either party, subsequent to the marriage, to the habitual use of opium, morphine, cocaine, or a similar drug. Parties may jointly petition for dissolution of marriage on ground of incompatibility of temperament causing an irremediable breakdown of the marriage, so long as they have agreed to property distribution, support, custody, and visitation. Alaska's equitable distribution **statute** establishes a three-tier version of the dual classification model. Property acquired during the marriage, except for gifts and inheritance, is classified as marital property, and is divided equitably upon divorce. Property acquired before the marriage is not marital property but can be divided upon divorce if "the balancing of the equities between the parties requires it." The court may allow an amount of money for spousal support, for either a limited time or an indefinite time, in gross or in installments, without regard to fault.

ARIZONA: One party must be domiciled in the state for 90 days prior to the filing of the action. Arizona requires only that the filing party **allege** irretrievable breakdown of the marriage. Arizona is a community property state. Property held in common must be divided equitably without regard to marital conduct. The court may consider excessive or abnormal expenditures, destruction, concealment, or **fraudulent** disposition of community, joint **tenancy**, and other property held in common in dividing the property. Spousal support may be granted to either spouse if the spouse seeking such support is unable, through appropriate employment, to provide self-support or is the custodian of a child at home. Support can also be awarded if a spouse contributed to the educational opportunities of the other spouse or had a long marriage and is of an age that may preclude employment. If spousal support is awarded it is without regard to marital fault. Factors the court will consider include: the couple's standard of living during marriage; the duration of the marriage; the age, employment history, earning ability, and physical and emotional condition of the recipient spouse; financial resources and earning abilities of parties; any reduced income or career opportunities; and excessive or abnormal expenditures, destruction, concealment or fraudulent disposition of community assets.

ARKANSAS: Presence is required in the state by one party for 60 days before commencement of the action, plus another 30 days before the final decree may be entered. Grounds for divorce in Arkansas include voluntary separation without **cohabitation** for 18 months; impotency; felony conviction; habitual drunkenness for one year; cruel and barbarous treatment; indignities to the person; adultery; three year separation by reason of confinement for incurable insanity; and willful nonsupport. Marital property is divided equally between the parties unless the court finds that equal division is inequitable. The only unusual aspect of Arkansas equitable distribution law is its treatment of property held as tenants by the entireties, which is divided by legal title. Spousal support may be awarded to either party in fixed installments for a specific period of time.

CALIFORNIA: Either party must be a resident of the state for six months, and a resident of the county for three months. A filing party need only allege irreconcilable differences or incurable insanity. California is a community property state. Community property is property acquired by either party during the marriage in any type of joint form. Unless the parties otherwise agree, the court divides the community property estate equally. The court may award spousal support in an amount and for a period of time that the court determines is just and reasonable, based upon the standard of living established during the marriage. In awarding spousal support, there is a goal that the supported spouse be self-supporting within a reasonable period of time. The court retains jurisdiction to modify spousal support in all cases of marriages over ten years unless the parties otherwise agree. There is a presumption for spousal support decreases on the recipient's cohabitation.

COLORADO: Either party must be domiciled in the state for 90 days before commencement of the

proceeding. A filing party need only allege irretrievable breakdown of the marriage. Colorado adopts the traditional dual classification of property under Uniform Marriage and Divorce Act. Separate property, defined as property owned before the marriage and property acquired by gift or inheritance, is retained by the owning party. Marital property includes property that is not separate property, property acquired during the marriage, including the increase in value of separate property. The court divides the marital property as it deems just, without regard to marital fault, considering the contributions of each spouse to the acquisition of the marital property, the value of each party's separate property, the economic circumstances of the parties, and the depletion of separate property for marital purposes. The court may order spousal support if a spouse lacks sufficient property to provide for his/her reasonable needs, is unable to support him/herself through appropriate employment, or is the custodian of a child whose age or condition makes it inappropriate for the spouse to seek employment outside the home.

CONNECTICUT: There is no residence requirement for filing; however, the Decree of Divorce can only be entered after one party has been a resident for a year. The party filing may allege irretrievable breakdown of the marriage or that the parties have lived apart for 18 months due to incompatibility, with no reasonable prospect of reconciliation. Adultery, fraudulent contract, desertion for one year, seven years' absence, habitual intemperance, intolerable cruelty, **sentencing** to **imprisonment** for life, or the commission of any infamous crime involving a violation of conjugal duty and punishable by imprisonment for over one year are also valid grounds. The court values and distributes all property and awards spousal support by considering the causes of the dissolution; the length of the marriage; the age, health, station, occupation, amount and sources of income, vocational skills, employability, estate, liabilities, and needs of each party; opportunity for future acquisition of capital assets and income; contribution of each party to the marital and separate estates.

DELAWARE: The state recognizes no-fault grounds as well as the traditional grounds for divorce. A court in Delaware will issue a divorce decree upon a finding that the marriage is irretrievably broken and that reconciliation is improbable. The court will conclude that a marriage is irretrievably broken when one of the following occurs: (1) voluntary separation; (2) separation caused by respondent's misconduct; (3) separation caused by respondent's mental illness; or (4) separation caused by incompatibility.

DISTRICT OF COLUMBIA: The party filing must live in the jurisdiction for six months. The parties must have mutually and voluntarily lived separate and apart without cohabitation for a period of six months, or the parties must have lived separate and apart for one year. Factors for equitable division of property include length of the marriage, and the age, health, and occupation of parties. The court takes into consideration the value of homemaker services. The court may grant spousal support and may decree that a party retains dower rights in the other's estate.

FLORIDA: One party must live in the state for six months prior to the commencement of the action. The filing party need only allege irretrievable breakdown of the marriage or spousal mental incapacity for three years. If there are minor children, or if a claim of irretrievable breakdown is denied, the court may order counseling, continue the proceedings for three months, or take such other action as may be in the best interests of the parties and children of the marriage. Florida follows an equitable distribution of property policy, based on dual classification of property into separate and marital estates. In distributing the marital estate, the court presumes a 50/50 division, but that may be altered by factors including the contribution to the marriage by each spouse, including homemaker services; the economic circumstances of the parties' the duration of the marriage; any interruption in career or educational opportunities; the contribution of each spouse to the acquisition, enhancement, and production of income or marital assets; and any action during the pending divorce proceedings which depletes marital assets. The court may grant spousal support to either party, which may be permanent or rehabilitative in nature. The court may order periodic payments or payments in lump sum, or both. The court may consider the adultery of each spouse. The court considers the standard of living established during the marriage, the duration of the marriage, the age and health of the parties, the financial resources of the parties, the time necessary to become fully employed, and the contribution of the parties to the marriage.

GEORGIA: One spouse must have resided in Georgia for six months prior to filing. Grounds include irretrievable breakdown; mental incapacity or impotency at the time of the marriage; fraud in obtaining the marriage; adultery; desertion for one year; conviction of an offense involving moral turpitude and imprisonment for two or more years; habitual intoxication or other drug addiction; cruel treatment; and incurable mental illness. A dual classification system was adopted, with separate property comprising property acquired before marriage, property acquired by gift, and property acquired by inheritance. Temporary or permanent spousal support may be granted, except in cases of adultery and desertion. The court may consider the conduct of the parties toward one another, in addition to needs and ability to pay, in deciding whether to award spousal support. If spousal support is to be awarded, the court considers, in deciding the amount, the standard of living established during the marriage, duration of marriage, age and physical and emotional condition of the parties, contributions to the marriage, and financial condition of the parties.

HAWAII: The filing party must have lived in Hawaii for six months prior to filing. The filing party need only allege irretrievable breakdown of the marriage or that the parties have lived separate and apart for more than two years. Hawaii law provides for equitable distribution of all property, whether community, joint, or separate. The court considers the condition in which each party will be left by the divorce, the burdens imposed upon either party for the benefit of the children of the parties, and all other circumstances of the case. The court may award indefinite or rehabilitative periodic spousal support. The court considers the respective merits of the parties, the usual occupation of the parties during the marriage, and the vocational skills and employability of the party seeking spousal support.

IDAHO: The state recognizes no-fault grounds as well as the traditional grounds for divorce. Traditional grounds include adultery, extreme cruelty, willful desertion, willful neglect, habitual intemperance, conviction of a felony, or permanent insanity.

ILLINOIS: The filing party must have lived in the state for 90 days prior to filing. The filing party need only allege irreconcilable differences causing the irretrievable breakdown of the marriage. Fault grounds are impotency, **bigamy**, adultery, desertion for one year, habitual drunkenness or other drug addiction for two years, an attempt to take the life of the other, physical or mental cruelty, conviction of a felony or other infamous crime, or infecting the other with a sexually transmitted disease. Illinois law provides for equitable distribution of marital property upon divorce, without regard to marital misconduct, based on dual classification of property. Marital property is all property acquired during the marriage, except property acquired by gift, **bequest**, devise, or descent, and property acquired before the marriage. The court may award rehabilitative, periodic, or permanent spousal support, without regard to marital misconduct. Spousal support terminates on cohabitation.

INDIANA: The party filing must live in the state for six months and for three months in the county where the petition is filed. The party filing need only allege irretrievable breakdown of the marriage. Fault grounds include conviction of a felony, impotency existing at the time of the marriage, and incurable insanity for three years. Division of property carries a presumption that equal division is just and reasonable. The presumption may be overcome by sufficient proof. Rehabilitative spousal support may be granted for a maximum of three years. The court may order permanent periodic spousal support if a spouse is physically or mentally incapacitated or where a spouse lacks sufficient property and is the custodial parent of a child whose incapacity requires the **guardian** to forego employment.

IOWA: The complainant must live in the jurisdiction one year. Divorce may be granted upon breakdown of the marriage relationship to the extent that the legitimate objects of matrimony have been destroyed and there remains no reasonable likelihood that the marriage can be saved. Marital property is property acquired during the marriage except that acquired by gift or bequest. The court may grant limited or indefinite spousal support.

KANSAS: The state recognizes no-fault grounds as well as the traditional grounds for divorce. Traditional grounds include (1) failure to perform a material marital duty or obligation; or (2) incompatibility by reason of mental illness or mental incapacity of one or both spouses.

KENTUCKY: The filing party must reside in the state for 180 days prior to filing. The filing party need only allege irretrievable breakdown of marriage. The decree cannot be entered until the parties have lived separate and apart for at least 60 days. Kentucky follows an equitable division of property theory, based on dual classification of property found in the Uniform Marriage and Divorce Act. Property is divided without regard to marital misconduct. Spousal support may be rehabilitative, periodic, or lump sum. The court may order spousal support only if it finds that the spouse seeking spousal support lacks sufficient property, is unable to be self supporting, or is the custodian or a child whose age or condition makes it appropriate that the custodian not seek employment outside the home.

LOUISIANA: Six months residence is required of the filing party. Except in the case of a covenant marriage, divorce shall be granted upon motion of either spouse upon proof of 180 days' lapse since service or petition and separation of 180 days before filing of motion. Louisiana is a community property state. Community assets and liabilities are divided so that each spouse receives property of equal value. The court may award final periodic support, up to 1/3 of the obligor's **net** income, to a party free from fault based on the needs of that party and the ability of the other to pay.

MAINE: The state recognizes no-fault grounds as well as the traditional grounds for divorce. Traditional grounds include (1) adultery; (2) impotence; (3) extreme cruelty; (4) utter desertion continued for 3 consecutive years prior to the commencement of the action; (5) gross and confirmed habits of intoxication from the use of liquor or drugs; (6) nonsupport, when one spouse has sufficient ability to provide for the other spouse and grossly, wantonly or cruelly refuses or neglects to provide suitable maintenance for the complaining spouse; (7) cruel and abusive treatment; (8) mental illness requiring confinement in a mental institution for at least seven consecutive years prior to the commencement of the action.

MARYLAND: Maryland requires residence or one year residence if the cause of action for divorce occurred outside the state. Marital property is defined as property acquired during the marriage. This includes pensions and profit sharing plans. In dividing the marital property, the court considers: contributions, monetary and non-monetary, of each party to the well-being of the family; the value of the property interest of each party; the economic circumstances of the parties at the time the award is made; the circumstances that contributed to the estrangement of the parties; the duration of the marriage; the age of each party; the physical and mental condition of each party; how and when specific marital property or interest in a **pension**, retirement, profit sharing, or deferred compensation plan was acquired; contribution of non-marital property to entireties property; any spousal support award; any other factor deemed necessary. The court may award rehabilitative or indefinite spousal support, periodic or lump sum. Indefinite spousal support, however, is awardable only if the requesting spouse cannot reasonably be expected to make substantial progress toward becoming self-sufficient or the parties' respective standards of living would be unconscionably disparate.

MASSACHUSETTS: Either party can be a resident if the cause of action occurred within the state. Otherwise, there is a one-year residency requirement. Fault grounds include: adultery; impotency; desertion for one year; confirmed habits of intoxication caused by the use of alcohol or other drugs; cruel and abusive treatment; and refusal to provide suitable spousal support. The parties also have the option of filing affidavits that the marriage is irretrievably broken, and can then, within 90 days, file a separation agreement. Parties may also file a complaint alleging irretrievable breakdown without a separation agreement, and the court may order the divorce after six months have elapsed. The court may assign to either the husband or the wife part of the estate of the other. The court may award periodic or lump sum spousal support. Factors in awarding spousal support include: homemaker's contributions; the employability of each party; the needs of each party; the opportunity for the future acquisition of capital assets and income.

MICHIGAN: Immediately prior to filing for divorce, one of the parties must have been a resident for 180 days and a resident of the county where the divorce is filed for 10 days. The filing party need only allege breakdown of the marriage relationship to the extent that the objects of matrimony have been destroyed and there remains no reasonable likelihood that the marriage can be preserved. The court can award one spouse any property owned by the other party if it appears from the **evidence** in the case that the party contributed to the acquisition, improvement, or accumulation of the property. Either spouse may be ordered to pay spousal support "in gross" or otherwise. Factors to be considered include the ability of either spouse to pay and the respective circumstances of the parties.

MINNESOTA: One of the parties must have been a resident for 180 days immediately before the petition for divorce is filed. The petition may be filed in a county where either spouse resides. The filing party need allege irrevocable breakdown of the marriage relationship demonstrated by living separate and apart for 180 days or serious marital discord adversely affecting the attitude of one or both parties. In dividing marital property, the court considers the contribution of each spouse to the acquisition of the property, including homemaker contributions; the economic circumstances of the parties; the length of the marriage; the age and health of the parties; the occupation of the parties; the amount and sources of income of the parties; the vocational skills of the parties; the employability of each spouse; the liabilities and needs of the parties, and the opportunity for further acquisition of capital assets; any prior marriage of each spouse; any other factor necessary to achieve equity and justice between the parties. The court may order temporary or permanent spousal support, without regard to marital fault, after the consideration of eleven factors, including need, the ability to become employed, the standard of living during the marriage, the duration of the marriage, loss of earnings, and the age and condition of both parties.

MISSISSIPPI: One of the parties must have been a resident for at least six months prior to filing and not have secured residency solely for the purpose of procuring a divorce. There are special venue provisions based on whether the divorce is no-fault or fault-based. Irreconcilable differences are sufficient for divorce. Other grounds include: impotence; adultery; imprisonment; alcoholism and/or other drug addiction; confinement for incurable insanity for at least three years before the divorce is filed; the wife was pregnant by another man at the time of the marriage without husband's knowledge; willful desertion for at least one year; cruel and inhumane treatment; spouse lacked mental capacity at time of marriage; **incest**; bigamous marriage. Mississippi is an equitable distribution dual classification state. Either spouse may be awarded spousal support if it is equitable.

MISSOURI: One of the parties must be a resident of Missouri for 90 days before filing. The dissolution petition must be filed in the county where the **plaintiff** resides. There is a 30-day waiting period after filing before the dissolution will be granted. Irretrievable breakdown of marriage is sufficient for divorce. Missouri adopted the Uniform Marriage and Divorce Act. The court may award rehabilitative, periodic, or lump sum spousal support. The spousal support shall be in such amounts and for such periods of time as the court deems just.

MONTANA: One of the parties must be a resident of Montana for 90 days immediately prior to filing. The dissolution of marriage petition must be filed in the county where the petitioner has been a resident for the previous 90 days. The party must allege irretrievable breakdown of marriage, supported by evidence that the parties have lived separate and apart for 180 days. Montana adopted the all-property provisions of the Uniform Marriage and Divorce Act. The court may divide, without regard to marital misconduct, the property of the parties and assets belonging to either or both. Either spouse may be awarded spousal support. The award is made without regard to marital fault.

NEBRASKA: One of the parties must have been a resident for at least one year, or the marriage must have been performed in Nebraska and one of the parties lived in Nebraska for the entire marriage. The dissolution may be filed in a county where either spouse lives. There is a 30-day waiting period after service of the petition before the court can decide the case. Irretrievable breakdown of marriage or lack of mental capacity at time of marriage is sufficient to obtain a divorce. The parties keep any separate property acquired before the marriage. All marital property, which includes gifts and inheritances acquired during the marriage, may be divided. Either spouse may be ordered to pay reasonable spousal support, without regard to marital fault.

NEVADA: One of the parties must have lived in Nevada for at least six weeks prior to filing to divorce. The filing party need only allege. Nevada is a community property state. The court can make an unequal disposition of community property if the court finds a compelling reason to do so. The court may award such spousal support to the husband or the wife in a specified principal sum or a specified period of payments.

NEW HAMPSHIRE: Both parties must be residents of the state when the divorce is filed, or the spouse filing for divorce must have been a resident of New Hampshire for one year immediately prior to the filing of the divorce and the other spouse was personally served with process in New Hampshire, or the cause of divorce must have arisen in New Hampshire and one of the parties must be living in New Hampshire when the divorce is filed for. Irreconcilable differences, which have caused irremediable breakdown of the marriage, are sufficient grounds for divorce. The court may award spousal support to either party in need, either temporary or permanent, for a definite or indefinite period of time.

NEW JERSEY: One party must be a resident of New Jersey for at least one year prior to the filing for divorce, unless the cause of divorce is adultery and took place in New Jersey, in which case one of the spouses must be a resident at the time of filing. Living separate and apart for 18 months and no reasonable prospect of reconciliation is sufficient to obtain a no-fault divorce in New Jersey. Marital property is property legally and beneficially acquired during the marriage, except for property acquired by gift, devise, interstate **succession**, except that gifts between spouses are considered marital property. Either party may be awarded spousal support without regard to marital fault. Spousal support may be permanent or rehabilitative.

NEW MEXICO: One of the parties must have been a resident of New Mexico for at least six months immediately preceding the filing and have a home in New Mexico. Incompatibility because of discord and conflicts of personalities such that the legitimate ends of the marriage relationship have been destroyed, preventing any reasonable expectation of reconciliation, is **just cause**. New Mexico is a community property state. Each spouse retains his/her separate property acquired before the marriage. Separate property comprises property designated as such by written agreement, gifts, or inheritances. Community property shall be divided equally between the parties. "Quasi-community property," defined as property acquired outside New Mexico, which would be community property if acquired in New Mexico, is also divided equally. Either spouse may be awarded a just and proper amount of spousal support, without regard to marital fault. Factors considered include: duration of the marriage, parties' current and future earning capacities, **good faith** efforts to maintain employment or become self-supporting, needs and obligations of each spouse, age and health of each spouse, amount of property each spouse owns, standard of living during the marriage, medical and life insurance maintained during the marriage, assets of the parties, each spouse's liabilities, and any marital settlement agreements.

NEW YORK: If both spouses resided in New York at the time of the filing of the divorce and the grounds for divorce arose in New York, there is no residency requirement. No-fault divorce is obtainable by living separate and apart. Fault grounds include: adultery; **abandonment** for one year; imprisonment for three or more consecutive years; and cruel and inhuman treatment. Separate property comprises property acquired before the marriage, gifts, inheritances, increase in value of separate property, and property acquired in exchange for separate property. Marital property is property acquired during the marriage and not separate property. Marital property is divided based on factors including custodial provisions; dissipation; and contributions as spouse, parent, wage earner, and homemaker. Either spouse may be awarded maintenance without regard to marital fault.

NORTH CAROLINA: Either spouse must have been a resident of North Carolina for at least six months prior to filing for divorce. Living separate and apart without cohabitation for one year is sufficient grounds to obtain a no-fault divorce. Separate property comprises any property acquired before the marriage, gifts and inheritances, property acquired in exchange for separate property, increase in value of separate property, expectation of a non-vested pension, retirement, or other deferred compensation rights. Marital property is property acquired during the marriage. Either spouse may be awarded spousal support. The amount, duration, and manner of payment is in the court's discretion; however, an award of spousal support is barred by "illicit sexual behavior."

NORTH DAKOTA: The state recognizes no-fault grounds as well as the traditional grounds for divorce. Traditional grounds for divorce include adultery, extreme cruelty, willful desertion, willful neglect, abuse of alcohol or controlled substances, and conviction of felony.

OHIO: The spouse filing the divorce must have been a resident of Ohio for at least six months and a resident of the county for at least 90 days immediately prior to filing.

Incompatibility is sufficient to obtain a divorce. Divorce may be obtained by filing a separation agreement, according to specific procedures. Each party retains separate property, defined as gifts, inheritances, property acquired prior to the marriage, income or **appreciation** of separate property, and individual proceeds from **personal injury** awards. Marital fault and spousal support are not to be considered in the division of property. Either spouse may be awarded reasonable spousal support, in real property or personal property or both, or by decreeing a sum of money, payable either in gross or by installments, from future income or otherwise. Marital fault is not a consideration.

OKLAHOMA: Either party must have been a resident of Oklahoma for six months immediately prior to filing for divorce. Incompatibility is sufficient to obtain a divorce. Each spouse keeps separate property, defined as property owned prior to the marriage, gifts, and inheritances. All property held or acquired jointly during the marriage is divided between the spouses in a just and equitable manner. Marital fault is not a factor. Spousal support may be awarded to either spouse, in money or property, in lump sum or installments, having regard for the value of the property at the time of the award. Marital fault is not a consideration.

OREGON: If the marriage was not performed in Oregon, one spouse must have been a resident for six months immediately prior to filing. If the marriage was performed in Oregon and either spouse is a resident of Oregon, there is no residency requirement. Irreconcilable differences between the spouses that have caused the irretrievable breakdown of the marriage is the only grounds on which to obtain a divorce. Fault is abolished completely. Regardless of whether the property is held jointly or individually, there is a presumption that the spouses contributed equally to the acquisition of the property, unless proven otherwise. Either spouse may be required to make allowances for support of the other for his or her life or for a shorter period, having regard to the circumstances of the parties respectively.

PENNSYLVANIA: Either spouse must have been a resident for at least six months before filing. Pennsylvania's no-fault provisions require **allegation** of an irretrievable breakdown of the marriage with the spouses living separate and apart without cohabitation for two years. The couple can also file alleging irretrievable breakdown of the marriage with affidavits from both spouses that they consent to the divorce. The divorce can then be granted after 90 days. Separate and apart is defined as no cohabitation but is not precluded by living in the same residence. The parties retain their separate property, defined as property acquired before marriage, acquired in exchange for separate property, gifts and inheritances, and property designated separate by valid agreement. All other property is marital and is divided by the court equitably between the parties. A court may allow alimony to either party only if it finds that alimony is necessary. Pennsylvania has statewide spousal support guidelines that are presumed to be correct unless there is a showing that the amount would be unjust or inappropriate under the circumstances of the case.

RHODE ISLAND: Either spouse must have been a resident for one year prior to filing. Irreconcilable differences, which have caused the irremediable breakdown of the marriage, are sufficient grounds to obtain a divorce. Each spouse shall keep separate property, defined as property owned prior to the marriage, gifts, and inheritances. All property held or acquired jointly during the marriage is to be divided in an equitable manner. Marital fault is not a factor. Spousal support may be awarded to either spouse, in money or property, in lump sum or installments. Marital fault is not an issue.

SOUTH CAROLINA: If both spouses are residents, the spouse filing for divorce must have been a resident for three months. If one of the spouses is not a resident, then the other spouse must have been a resident for one year. No-fault grounds are sufficiently established by the couple living separate and apart without cohabitation for one year. Fault grounds include: adultery; alcoholism or other drug addiction; physical abuse or reasonable apprehension of physical abuse; and willful desertion. During the marriage, a spouse acquires a vested special equity and ownership right in marital property. Each party retains separate property, defined as property acquired before the marriage, by gift or inheritance, in exchange for separate property, or from an increase in value of separate property. All other property is marital, subject to division on divorce. Fault is a factor. Either spouse may be awarded spousal support; however, no alimony may be awarded to a spouse who commits adultery.

SOUTH DAKOTA: The spouse filing the divorce must be a resident of South Dakota or a member of the Armed Forces stationed in South Dakota at the time of filing and must remain a resident until the divorce is final. Irreconcilable differences, which have caused the irretrievable breakdown of the marriage, are sufficient to obtain a divorce. Marital fault is not to be considered in apportioning the property. Either spouse may be awarded permanent or time-limited maintenance, based on the needs of the spouses.

TENNESSEE: No residency requirement if the party filing was a resident of Tennessee when the grounds for divorce arose. If the cause for divorce arose outside of Tennessee, then either spouse must have been a resident of Tennessee for six months. Irreconcilable differences are sufficient to obtain a divorce if there is no denial of this ground or if the spouses submit an executed marital dissolution agreement. Fault grounds include: impotence; adultery; conviction of a felony and imprisonment; alcoholism and/or other drug addiction; wife is pregnant by another man at the time of the marriage without husband's knowledge; and refusing the move to Tennessee with a spouse and willfully absenting oneself from a new residence for two years. Each spouse keeps separate property, defined as property owned prior to the marriage, gifts and inheritances, property acquired in exchange for separate property, and income and appreciation of separate property. All property held or acquired jointly during the marriage shall be divided between the couple. Marital fault is not a factor. Spousal support may be lump sum, periodic, or rehabilitative, based on sixteen factors. Rehabilitative support is favored.

TEXAS: One of the parties must have resided in Texas for six months and must have resided for 90 days in the county prior to the filing of the petition There is a 60-day waiting period between filing for and granting of divorce. That the marriage has become unsupportable because of discord or conflict that has destroyed the legitimate ends of marriage is sufficient grounds to obtain a no-fault divorce. Texas is a community property state. Property acquired by either spouse during the marriage is presumed to be community property, and such property shall be divided equally. The court may also divide property acquired by either party during the marriage while residing outside the state of Texas which would have been community property had the parties been residing in Texas. The court may award maintenance for a spouse in limited circumstances. Spousal support may be ordered if the spouse from whom maintenance is sought has been convicted of **domestic violence** within 2 years before the suit for dissolution. Spousal support may also be ordered if the duration of the marriage is over 10 years and the spouse seeking maintenance lacks sufficient property to provide for his/her reasonable minimum needs, is unable to support him/herself through employment because of an incapacitating physical or mental **disability**, is the custodial of a child who requires substantial care and supervision on account of a physical or mental disability, or clearly lacks earning ability in the labor market to provide for minimum reasonable needs. A maintenance award may not last longer than three years unless there is a compelling impediment to the recipient spouse obtaining gainful employment.

UTAH: Either spouse must have been a resident of Utah or a member of the armed forces stationed in Utah and a resident of the county where the divorce is filed for more than three months immediately prior to the filing. There is a 90-day waiting period after filing before a divorce may be granted. Irreconcilable differences are sufficient grounds for a divorce to be granted. All of the couple's property, including gifts, inheritances, and any property acquired prior to or during the marriage is divided by the court. Either spouse may be ordered to pay an equitable amount of spousal support, based on fault and the equity of equalizing the parties' incomes. Typically the court will not order spousal support for a period longer than the marriage existed.

VIRGINIA: One of the spouses must have been a resident of Virginia for at least six months prior to filing for divorce. Living separate and apart without cohabitation is sufficient grounds for a no-fault divorce. Marital property comprises property acquired during the marriage, excluding gifts from third parties and inheritances. Separate property is property acquired before the marriage, gifts from third parties and inheritances, any increase in value of separate property, and property acquired in exchange for separate property. The court cannot order the conveyance of separate or marital property not titled in the names of both parties, but it can award a monetary payment. Either spouse may be awarded maintenance, to be paid either in a lump sum, periodic payments, or both.

WASHINGTON: The spouse filing for dissolution must be a resident of Washington or a member of the armed forces stationed in Washington. The court will not act on the petition for divorce until 90 days after the filing of the complaint and service of the **summons**. Irretrievable breakdown of marriage is sufficient grounds for the court to order a divorce. Washington is a community property state. The court divides community property in a just and equitable manner, without regard to marital conduct. Property acquired in another state is "quasi-community property" and is divided as community property. The court may award rehabilitative, periodic, or lump-sum alimony to either spouse without regard to marital fault.

WEST VIRGINIA: One party must have been a resident for one year immediately prior to the filing. If the marriage was performed in West Virginia and one spouse is a resident at the time of filing, there is no residency requirement. Irreconcilable differences are sufficient grounds for a no-fault divorce. The court divides the marital property equally. Marital property is property acquired during the marriage and the increases in value of separate property that is the result of the use of marital funds or work performed by either party during the marriage. Either spouse may be ordered to provide the other spouse with spousal support; however, spousal support will not be ordered for a party who committed adultery, was convicted of a felony during the marriage, or deserted or abandoned the other spouse for six months.

WISCONSIN: One of the spouses must have been a resident of Wisconsin for six months and a resident of the county where the divorce is filed for thirty days immediately prior to filing. Irretrievable breakdown of marriage is sufficient grounds for divorce. Wisconsin is a community property state. The court may also divide any spouse's separate property in order to prevent a hardship for a spouse or for the children of the marriage. The court may award rehabilitative, limited, or indefinite maintenance, without regard to marital misconduct. Additionally, the court may combine spousal and child support payments into a single family support payment.

WYOMING: The spouse filing for divorce must have been a resident of Wyoming for 60 days immediately prior to filing, or if the marriage was performed in Wyoming, then the spouse filing must have resided in Wyoming from the time of the marriage until the time of the filing. Irreconcilable differences are sufficient to obtain a divorce. The state follows a plan of equitable distribution of all property of both spouses, including gifts and inheritances. Either spouse may be awarded spousal support.

ADDITIONAL RESOURCES

De Witt, John Gregory, Peter N. Swisher, and Sheryl L. Wolf. *Understanding Family Law.* 3d ed. Newark, NJ: LexisNexis, 2005.

Katz, Sanford N. *Family Law in America.* New York: Oxford University Press, 2011.

Oliphant, Robert E., and Nancy Ver Steegh. *Family Law: Examples and Explanations.* 3d ed. New York: Aspen Publishers, 2010.

Rice, Larry, and Nick Rice. *The Complete Guide to Divorce Practice: Forms and Procedures for the Lawyer.* 4th ed. Chicago: American Bar Association, 2012.

ORGANIZATIONS

Administration for Children and Families, U.S. Department of Health and Human Services

370 L'Enfant Promenade SW
Washington, DC 20447
Phone: (202) 401-2337
URL: http://www.acf.gov

American Academy of Matrimonial Lawyers

150 N. Michigan Ave, Suite, 1420
Chicago, IL 60601
Phone: (312) 263-6477
URL: http://www.aaml.org

American Bar Association (ABA)

321 North Clark Street
Chicago, IL 60610
Phone: (312) 988-5000
Toll Free: (800) 285-2221
Fax: (312) 988-6800
URL: http://www.americanbar.org

Association of Certified Family Law Specialists

1500 W. El Camino Ave., Suite 158
Sacramento, CA 95833
Phone: (916) 217-4076
URL: http://www.acfls.org/

FAMILY LAW

DOMESTIC VIOLENCE

Sections within this essay:

- Background
- History of Police Responses to Domestic Violence
- Federal Legislation
- State Legislation
- Civil and Other Proceedings
- Domestic Violence and the Workplace
- Domestic Violence and Firearms
- Stalking
- Battered Women's Syndrome
- Identifying Signs of Domestic Violence
- Additional Resources

BACKGROUND

Domestic violence consists of acts committed in the context of an adult intimate relationship. It is a continuance of aggressive and controlling behaviors, including physical, sexual, and psychological attacks, that one adult intimate does to another. Domestic violence is purposeful and instrumental behavior directed at achieving compliance from, or control over, the abused party. It is one of the most under-reported crimes in the United States. According to a report issued by the National Center for Injury Prevention and Control and other agencies in 2010, more than 35 percent of women and more than 28 percent of men have experienced rape, physical violence, or **stalking** by an intimate partner during their lifetime.

Legal definitions of domestic violence are usually delineated by the relationship between the parties and by the nature of the perpetrator's abusive behaviors. For example, the relationship may be a current spouse, a former spouse, a family member, a child, parents of a child in common, unmarried persons of different genders living as spouses, intimate partners of the same gender, dating relationships, and persons offering refuge. Such definitions recognize that victims may not be exclusively women, and domestic assaults may not just occur between heterosexual couples. The types of behavior frequently encountered in domestic violence are physical attacks, sexual attacks, psychological abuse, and the destruction of property or pets.

HISTORY OF POLICE RESPONSES TO DOMESTIC VIOLENCE

Police responses to domestic violence have historically been clouded by notions, for example, the idea that a wife is the "property" of a husband and he has the right to carry out whatever behavior is necessary to "keep her in line." This idea and others like it reflect attitudes held by the greater society. Further aggravating the situation was the perception that domestic violence is not "real police work," and such disputes are private matters that should be kept within the household. Prior to 1980, when domestic situations were brought to the attention of police, calls were often diverted by dispatchers, given a lower priority, or officers responded to the scene and departed again as quickly as possible without achieving any type of meaningful intervention. Laws such as the "rule of thumb" (whereby it was legal for a husband to beat his wife with a stick not wider than his thumb) were still on the books until very recently.

Prior to the 1980s, the practice of police agencies was to use **mediation** in domestic incidents. But ironically, much of this so-called mediation was done only when one spouse was present. Several prominent court cases helped change legislation. In 1972, Ruth Bunnell was killed as a result of police non-intervention. The case of **wrongful death** against the City of San Jose was dismissed in the California Court of Appeals but received much publicity. In 1985, a **jury** verdict awarded $2.3 million in favor of **plaintiff** Tracy Thurman who sued the Torrington, CT police department after they repeatedly failed to **arrest** her abusive husband (*Thurman v. City of Torrington,* 1985). Her husband eventually caused her serious bodily injury.

Beginning in the late 1980s, there were many attempts to change the way police departments intervened in domestic violence situations. Inspired by Sherman's Minneapolis experiment, many police agencies adopted preferred or mandatory arrest policies. Arrest both acknowledges that society views domestic violence as a criminal offense and also provides immediate safety for the victim. Accompanying these new arrest policies were civil proceedings.

FEDERAL LEGISLATION

The 1994 Violence Against Women Act (VAWA), with additions passed in 1996, outlined grant programs to prevent violence against women and established a national domestic violence hotline. In addition, new protections were given to victims of domestic abuse, such as confidentiality of new address and changes to **immigration** laws that allow a battered spouse to apply for permanent residency.

According to the VAWA Act, a domestic violence **misdemeanor** is one in which someone is convicted for a crime "committed by an intimate partner, parent, or **guardian** of the victim that required the use or attempted use of physical force or the threatened use of a deadly weapon" (Section 922 [g][9]). Under these guidelines, an intimate partner is a spouse, a former spouse, a person who shares a child in common with the victim, or a person who cohabits or has cohabited with the victim.

Another area this act addresses is interstate traveling for the purposes of committing an act of domestic violence or violating an order of protection. A convicted abuser may not follow the victim into another state, nor may a convicted abuser force a victim to move to another state. Previously, orders of protection issued in one **jurisdiction** were not always recognized in another jurisdiction. The VAWA specifies full faith and credit to all orders of protection issued in any civil or criminal proceeding, or by any American Indian tribe, meaning that those orders can be fully enforced in another jurisdiction. Forty-seven states have now passed legislation that recognizes orders of protection issued in other jurisdictions. Three states, Alaska, Montana, and Pennsylvania, require that an out of state order be filed with an in state jurisdiction before the order can be enforced.

There are several landmark cases that have been decided under these interstate provisions. For example, in *United States v. Gluzman* (NY), the **defendant** traveled from New Jersey to New York with the intention of killing her estranged husband. The weapons she took with her were used in the murder. Gluzman was convicted for this crime. In *United States v. Sterkel* (1997), the defendant was convicted of interstate stalking after traveling from Utah to Arizona to threaten his former boss.

The VAWA also allows victims of domestic abuse to sue for damages in civil court. However, this part of the VAWA was overturned by the U.S. Supreme Court in *Brzonkala v. Morrison* (2000) in which the court held that Congress did not have the authority to implement such a law.

Another goal of the VAWA was to influence state legislators, particularly in regard to arrest policy for domestic situations. In order to receive Federal funding, states must adopt certain responses. The Act reads: VAWA 1994: (1) To implement mandatory arrest or pro-arrest programs and policies in police departments, including mandatory arrest programs and policies for protection order violations (Part U, § 2101). This act has had a profound effect on state laws governing domestic abuse.

STATE LEGISLATION

By 2012, every state had enacted legislation defining domestic or intimate-partner violence, though these definitions vary widely. In a minority of jurisdictions, domestic violence between unmarried couples is limited to those who either lived together or shared a child. The vast majority of states recognize domestic violence within same-sex relationships.

Until the 1990s, many states still had laws that required an officer to witness an **assault** before making an arrest. Today, officers in all states can arrest someone they suspect has committed a domestic assault without having witnessed the event. The majority of states have adopted preferred arrest policies which require police to either arrest one or both parties at the scene, or write a report justifying why an arrest is not made. Arrest policies do differ by jurisdiction even in the same state. Some states, such as New York, Wisconsin, and Minnesota, have adopted mandatory arrest policies which dictate that an officer must make an arrest at a domestic situation. Such policies were adopted after it was realized how serious domestic situations could be for the victims and their children. An arrest is usually made after the following conditions have been satisfied:

- There is **probable cause** of a crime;

- The suspect and the victim fit the definition of having a domestic relationship;

- The suspect's alleged act fits the definitions of domestic assault;

- There is reason to believe that the domestic abuse will continue if the suspect is not arrested and/or there is **evidence** of injury;

- The incident was reported within 28 days of occurrence.

Usually, if any of these conditions is not satisfied, the officer may use his or her discretion in deciding whether to make an arrest. Although different states have variations on definitions of domestic violence, most are similar to the following example.

MINNESOTA: Domestic abuse means (1) physical harm, bodily injury, or assault; (2) the infliction of fear of imminent physical harm, bodily injury, or assault; or (3) terrorist threats or criminal sexual conduct (518B.01).

CIVIL AND OTHER PROCEEDINGS

There are several available civil options that can provide for the safety of victims of domestic assaults and their families, such as an order of protection or a judicial ex parte order. All 51 states have allowances for orders of protection. An order of protection can prohibit the abuser from contacting, attacking, striking, telephoning, or disturbing the peace of the victim; force the abuser to move from a residence shared with the victim; order the abuser to stay at least 100 yards away from the victim, his or her place of residence, and place of employment; order the abuser to attend counseling; and prohibit the abuser from purchasing a firearm. Orders of protection may also include a provision for the safety of children and others living in the home.

An ex parte order requires the abusive cohabitant to temporarily vacate the premises. Issued only after the battered spouse seeks it, this order is sometimes referred to as a temporary restraining order. In most states, a cohabitant refers to a person who has a sexual relationship with the victim and has lived with the victim for at least 90 days during the year prior to the order being filed. A victim who is threatened with imminent harm, has already been harmed by the abuser, and/or already has an order of protection against the abuser has no other legal remedy than to seek a restraining order. In most states, an attorney is needed to get a restraining order.

Violation of an order of protection is the equivalent of **contempt** of a court order. In many states, police policy is to arrest violators automatically. A violator can also be fined and jailed and may be charged with a misdemeanor or a **felony**.

DOMESTIC VIOLENCE AND THE WORKPLACE

Domestic violence can reach beyond the home and into the workplace. Although a victim may leave the home and go to a shelter or change her or his address, the abuser usually knows where the victim works. Not only do abusers harass their partners at work, domestic violence can lead to missed days of work because of injuries or court appearances. Federal and state legislation has recently been amended so that victims of domestic violence are not penalized by employers for missed work.

At the Federal level, **Labor Law** Section 593 (1) states that when a victim of domestic violence voluntarily terminates his or her job, he or she is eligible for unemployment benefits. The Penal Law, Section 215.14, passed in 1996, makes it a crime to penalize an employee who has been a victim of or a witness to a criminal offense and who must attend court. Further, both state and federal guidelines mandate that employers maintain a safe work environment.

DOMESTIC VIOLENCE AND FIREARMS

Under the 1994 VAWA Act, it is illegal for individuals who have been convicted of a domestic-violence related incident or who have an order of protection against them to possess a firearm. Specifically, federal law prohibits the shipping, transporting, possessing, or receiving firearms or ammunition. Military and law enforcement personnel are not exempt from this law, even if they carry weapons when they are on duty. Questions about this policy should be directed to local branches of the Alcohol, Tobacco and Firearms (ATF) Office.

It is illegal for a person to possess a firearm while subject to a court order restraining such a person from harassing, stalking or threatening an intimate partner or the child of an intimate partner (18 U.S.C. § 922[g][8]). It is also illegal to transfer a firearm to a person subject to a court order that restrains such a person from harassing, stalking, or threatening an intimate partner or the child of an intimate partner (18 U.S.C. § 922[d][8]).

It is illegal to possess a firearm after **conviction** of a misdemeanor crime of domestic violence. This prohibition applies to persons convicted of such misdemeanors at any time, even if the conviction occurred prior to the new law's effective date (18 U.S.C. § 922[g][9]).

Further, the **Gun Control** Act, which was amended in 1996, also makes it illegal to possess a firearm and/or ammunition if the individual is subject to an order of protection or if the individual has been convicted of a misdemeanor domestic assault.

STALKING

Domestic situations may also involve stalking of the victim by the estranged partner. Stalking usually involves repeated threatening or harassing behaviors, such as phone calls, following or shadowing a person, appearing at a person's home or place of employment, vandalizing property, and any other activity that makes a person fear for his or her safety. Stalking laws vary greatly from state to state, with some requiring a minimum of two acts or other proof that the event was not an isolated occurrence, and others specifying that the threat of harm must be imminent. Some states also include activities such as lying-in-wait, surveillance, and non-consensual communication.

In its 1998 research on state codes and stalking, the National Institute of Justice defined stalking as "a course of conduct directed at a specific person that involves repeated visual or physical proximity; non-consensual communication; or verbal, written, or implied threats, or a combination thereof, that would cause a reasonable person fear," with repeated meaning on two or more occasions. There are three types of stalking: erotomania, which is often committed by a female and is a delusional obsession with a **public figure** or someone out of the stalker's reach; love obsessional, which involves individuals' stalking someone with whom they think they are in love; and simple obsessional, which is stalking by someone the victim knows. Domestic violence stalking fits into this last category and is usually perpetrated by an ex-spouse or lover, employer or co-worker.

As of 2012, a minority of states included stalking among items in crime reporting related to domestic violence. However, many incidents of stalking are not reported, so data about stalking is difficult to measure.

The following examples of state legislation on stalking illustrate differences in definitions of and punishment for stalking.

DISTRICT OF COLUMBIA: Stalking refers to more than one incident of willfully, maliciously, and repeatedly following or harassing; or without a legal purpose, willfully, maliciously, and repeatedly following or harassing another person with the intent of causing emotional distress or creating reasonable fear of death or bodily injury. Harassment refers to engaging in a course of conduct either in person, by telephone, or in writing, directed at a specific person, which seriously alarms, annoys, frightens, or torments the victim; or engaging in a course of conduct either in person, by telephone, or in writing, which would cause a reasonable person to be seriously alarmed, annoyed, frightened, or tormented. Such an offense can be punishable by a fine of not more than $500 or **imprisonment** of up to 12 months or both (Title 22, Section 504). A second offense occurring within two years can result in a fine of up to $750 and/or imprisonment for up to one and a half years. A third offense is punishable by a fine of not more than $1500 and/or imprisonment for up to three years.

TENNESSEE: (a)(1) A person commits the offense of stalking who intentionally and repeatedly follows or harasses another person in such a manner as would cause that person to be in reasonable fear of being assaulted or suffering bodily injury or death.

(A) "Follows" means maintaining a visual or physical proximity over a period of time to a specific person in such a manner as would cause a reasonable person to have a fear of an assault, bodily injury, or death;

(B) "Harasses" means a course of conduct directed at a specific person, which would cause a reasonable person to fear a sexual offense, bodily injury, or death, including, but not limited to, verbal threats, written threats, **vandalism**, or physical contact that was non-consensual;

(C) "Repeatedly" means on two (2) or more occasions.

(b)(1) Stalking is a Class A misdemeanor.

In Tennessee, if there is a subsequent violation of this law within a seven-year period, the offense becomes a class E felony. A subsequent violation denotes a class C felony.

BATTERED WOMEN'S SYNDROME

A phenomenon which has received much attention in the realm of domestic violence and particularly with women who kill is battered women's syndrome (BWS), which is a subcategory of post-traumatic stress disorder (PTSD). According to Walker, battered women's syndrome is:

> A group of usually transient psychological symptoms that are frequently observed in a particular recognizable pattern in women who report having been physically, sexually, and/or seriously psychologically abused by their male domestic partners.

BWS develops as a battering relationship unfolds. This is typically a three-stage process that includes: (1) small incidents of verbal and minor physical abuse that begin infrequently but increase in frequency; (2) actual acute battering that often causes serious injury needing medical attention; and (3) a cycle where the abuser is contrite to the abused and ultimately teaches the abused to be submissive and passive toward further abuse.

A woman displaying symptoms of BWS may be apathetic toward subjects or activities for which she used to be enthusiastic, she may become involved in drug or alcohol abuse, and she may also experience completely different attitudes and emotions toward her spouse than she did before the abuse began. The importance in knowing about BWS lies in recognizing predictable, psychological effects caused by domestic violence. BWS is now recognized in legislation by many states and is considered when defending battered wives who kill their spouses. BWS is not used as a defense but more as an indication of the defendant's state of mind or as a mitigating circumstance. A reasonable fear of imminent danger (especially used in **self-defense**) can be proven using BWS.

IDENTIFYING SIGNS OF DOMESTIC VIOLENCE

Montgomery County (MD) Sheriff's Department suggests that the following behaviors may indicate domestic violence to a police officer or dispatcher:

- The victim is very fearful of the partner
- The victim states that the partner is extremely jealous
- The victim describes the relationship as full of conflict
- The victim makes references to being forced to have sexual relations with the partner
- The victim states police have often been called to the home
- The victim states that the partner controls everything the victim does

Police and attorneys should recommend the victim apply for an order of protection if the victim has been abused or threatened, and if either of the following is present:

- The victim fears further abuse
- The victim needs the abuser out of the home in order to protect herself and/or her family
- The abuser has threatened to take the children
- The victim cannot or does not wish to file criminal charges
- The victim wants the abuser to attend a counseling program
- The victim wants a period of separation from the abuser but is unsure whether to file for **divorce** or **custody** yet

- Criminal charges are pending and the victim fears for her safety
- The victim's children have been abused

ADDITIONAL RESOURCES

Domestic Violence Practice and Procedure. Eagan, MN: West, Thomson Reuters, 2011.

Goldscheid, Julie, and Robin Runge. *Employment Law and Domestic Violence: A Practitioner's Guide*. ABA Commission on Domestic Violence. Chicago: American Bar Association, 2009.

Hamilton, Melissa. *Expert Testimony on Domestic Violence: A Discourse Analysis*. El Paso, TX: LFB Scholarly Pub., 2009.

Kiesel, Diane. *Domestic Violence: Law, Policy, and Practice*. Newark, NJ: LexisNexis, 2007.

Lemon, Nancy K.D. *Domestic Violence Law*. 3d ed. Eagan, MN: West, Thomson Reuters, 2009.

ORGANIZATIONS

Commission on Domestic and Sexual Violence, American Bar Association
740 15th Street NW
Washington, DC 20005-1022
URL: http://www.americanbar.org/groups/domestic_violence.html

Futures Without Violence
100 Montgomery Street, The Presidio
San Francisco, CA 94129
Phone: (415) 678-5500
Fax: (415) 529-2930
URL: http://www.futureswithoutviolence.org

National Coalition Against Domestic Violence
One Broadway, Suite B210
Denver, CO 80203
Phone: (303) 839-1852
Fax: (303) 831-9251
URL: http://www.ncadv.org/

National Council of Juvenile and Family Court Judges
PO Box 89507
Reno, NV 89507
Toll Free: (800) 527-3223
URL: http://www.ncjfcj.org

National Domestic Violence Hotline
PO Box 161810
Austin, TX 78716
Toll Free: (800) 787-3224
URL: http://www.thehotline.org/

FAMILY LAW

EMANCIPATION

Sections within this essay:

- Background
- Age
- Automatic Emancipation
- Petition to Courts
- Criteria for Emancipation
- Rights, Privileges, and Duties Inherent in Emancipation
- Examination of Certain State Provisions on Emancipation
- Additional Resources

BACKGROUND

Historically, parents are responsible for their children. They are also required to feed, clothe, educate, and act in their children's best interest until they reach the "age of majority" or the age in which, for most purposes, the children are considered to be adults. State law can allow a minor to ask a state court to determine that the minor is able to assume adult responsibilities before reaching the **age of majority**. The term emancipation refers to the point at which a minor becomes self-supporting, assumes adult responsibility for his or her welfare, and is no longer under the care of his or her parents. Upon achieving emancipation, the minor thereby assumes the rights, privileges, and duties of adulthood before actually reaching the "age of majority" (adulthood). At that point, the minor's parents are no longer responsible for that child

and, also, have no claim to the minor's earnings. During the court proceedings and before granting emancipation, the court considers, primarily, the best interests and level of maturity of the minor and confirms that the minor is able to financially support him or herself.

However, even when minors achieve emancipation, they cannot take part in any activity such as purchasing and/or drinking alcohol, voting, or getting married which, by **statute**, may require that the participant have attained an older age.

Close to half of the states, including New York and Pennsylvania, provide no separate **statutory** provisions for emancipation. Instead, these states rely on the fact that emancipation is automatically achieved upon a minor getting married, joining the armed forces, or reaching the age of majority which is now lower (usually eighteen years of age) than what was once commonly mandated as 21 years of age.

AGE

Generally, the statutory age in which a minor can petition a court for emancipation is at least 16 years or older but below the age of majority (which among the vast majority of states is eighteen years of age). California allows a minor of the age of 14 to petition its courts for emancipation.

AUTOMATIC EMANCIPATION

Even though minors may be under the age of majority, certain actions on their part will cause them to be emancipated from their parents' care and control even without seeking a court order. These actions are usually limited to the following:

- Joining the armed forces
- Getting married

- Reaching the actual age of majority (which is 18 years of age in most states)

The state of Michigan also allows for a temporary automatic emancipation when minors are in police **custody** and emergency medical care is required. The minors are considered emancipated and allowed to consent to such care. This emancipation ends when the medical care or treatment is completed.

PETITION TO COURTS

Minors petitioning their state courts for emancipation from their parents' care and control are normally required to prove their age and that they are residents of the state where the petition is being filed. They must tell the court why they seek emancipation. Parents must be given notice of the proceeding. Also, the minors must show the court that they are of sufficient maturity to care for themselves. This means that they are able to support themselves financially, provide for their own shelter, and make decisions on their own behalf. Some states require that the minors already support themselves and live totally or partially on their own. Most statutes exclude state financial support or "general assistance" when determining minors' ability to support themselves.

The court then looks at all the **evidence** in order to determine whether emancipation is in the minor's best interest. Also, since an order for emancipation must be in the minor's best interest, if the minor's situation changes, such an order may be rescinded by the court and the minor declared to be returned to the parents' care and control. The state of Illinois allows for court decrees of "partial" emancipation, where the court clearly states the limits of emancipation, if such an order is in the best interests of the minor.

States with no statutory provision or procedures for minors to apply for emancipation may still determine or confirm that minors have been emancipated. Minors file a petition with the court and provide the information necessary (such as proof of financial independence, adequate housing arrangements, and sufficient maturity) for the court to determine that such a confirmation of emancipation from parental care and control is in the best interests of the minor.

CRITERIA FOR EMANCIPATION

Criteria for determining whether a **decree** declaring emancipation is in the minor's best interest vary among the states. However, certain criteria can commonly be found:

- The minors' ability to support themselves financially, either currently or in the future

- The minors are currently living apart from their parents or have made adequate arrangements for future housing
- The minors can adequately make decisions for themselves
- The minors are attending school or have already received a diploma
- The minors exhibit sufficient maturity to function as adults

RIGHTS, PRIVILEGES, AND DUTIES INHERENT IN EMANCIPATION

Once declared to be emancipated, minors have the same rights, privileges, and duties in society as adults. Although the specific aspects vary among the states, generally, emancipated minors can do the following:

- Enter into contracts and leases
- Be a party to a lawsuit, either as a **plaintiff** or a **defendant**, in their own name
- Buy or sell real estate or other property
- Write a valid will
- Inherit property
- Enroll in school
- Get married
- Agree to various types of medical treatments

Emancipated minors can also vote and obtain a driver's license but only if they are of sufficient age to do so.

EXAMINATION OF CERTAIN STATE PROVISIONS ON EMANCIPATION

Of the states with specific emancipation provisions, some of the more significant state requirements include the following:

ALABAMA: In Alabama, the age of majority is 19. The Alabama code describing the emancipation procedure is designed to expand the rights of minors over the age of 18 but under the age of majority. Parents can file an emancipation petition with the court or the minor seeking emancipation can file the petition if that minor has no parents or if a living parent is insane or has abandoned the minor. The court will then decide if a decree of emancipation is in the "interest of such minor."

CALIFORNIA: In California, the age of majority is 18. Minors are considered emancipated without court intervention if they are married, are a member of the armed forces, or have previously been declared emancipated by a California court. Otherwise, in order to seek court mandated emancipation, the minors must be no younger than fourteen years old, be already living apart from their parents, be able to demonstrate the ability to take adequate care of themselves financially, and not receive any income from illegal or criminal activity.

If the court grants the order of emancipation, the minor then has the privilege and right to: sign contracts; approve medical care; buy, **lease**, and sell real property; be the plaintiff or defendant in a lawsuit; write a will; live in their own home; go to school; and get a work permit. If the minor's situation changes, the court has the ability to end the emancipation and advise the minor's parents that they are once again responsible for the minor.

FLORIDA: The age of majority in Florida is 18. In order to seek a court mandated emancipation, minors must submit a statement of "character, habits, income, and mental capacity for business, and an explanation of how the needs of the minor with respect to food, shelter, clothing, medical care, and other necessities will be met." In addition, minors must state whether they are party to any court action taking place in Florida or another state. Minors must also submit a statement explaining why they seek an order of emancipation. Parents must be notified of any such proceeding.

The court then asks for any additional evidence to determine if the decree of emancipation is in the minors' best interest. If the order of emancipation is granted, the minor will have all of the rights, responsibilities, and privileges of anyone who has reached the age of majority (18 years of age).

ILLINOIS: The age of majority in Illinois is 18. The Illinois statute allows the court to give an order of emancipation to a "mature minor who has demonstrated the ability and capacity to manage his (or her) own affairs and to live wholly or partially independent of his (or her) parents." The Illinois statute also seeks to tailor the content of the emancipation order to fit the needs of the minor seeking the order.

The statute states that for an order of emancipation from the court to be valid, neither the parents nor the minor can offer any objections. Also, the court will examine the situation and determine whether a full or partial order of emancipation will be given. Also, once the emancipation order is entered, the court will determine what adult privileges and rights, in addition to the right to enter into contracts, will be given the minor. Only those rights listed in the order will be in effect for that minor.

In order to seek a court mandated emancipation order, the minor must be at least 16 years old but under 18 years old. The minor must confirm that he or she lives in Illinois, explain why he or she wants a complete or partial order of emancipation, demonstrate that he or she is a "mature minor," and show that he or she has lived on their own.

MASSACHUSETTS: The age of majority in Massachusetts is 18. There is no formal means for a minor to become emancipated from parents, and most judges will not grant requests. In some rare instances, however, a judge will grant a request when emancipation is in a child's best interests.

In 2009, a state **appellate** judge ruled that a child does not become emancipated simply by having a child. The court noted that other states have issued similar rulings.

MICHIGAN: The age of majority in Michigan is 18. The Michigan statute defines emancipation as the "termination of the rights of the parents to the custody, control, services and earnings of a minor." Absent an order of emancipation, the statute confirms that parents are responsible for supporting their minor children. In fact, one or both parents can object to the emancipation proceedings. In that case, the court may decide to dismiss the proceedings.

The Michigan statute states the four ways that a minor can be emancipated without a court order as being marriage, reaching the age of majority (18 years of age), joining the armed forces, and temporarily while in police custody in order to consent to needed medical treatment.

The statute requires the petition to the court to be brought by the minor. The minors must submit information showing that they can take care of themselves financially, without seeking assistance from the state of Michigan. Minors must also show the court that they can take care of their other personal needs as well. The petition to the court must include a statement from an adult sufficiently familiar with the minor that the individual can offer information that explains to the court why emancipation is "in the best interest of the minor."

At this point, the court may seek additional information and may ask someone from the court staff to investigate the situation further and report back to the court. The court then determines if an order of emancipation is in the minor's best interests.

If the minor is emancipated, the adult rights and responsibilities applicable to the minor do not include those limited by age and by law such as using and purchasing alcohol and voting. However, they do include signing contracts, being a plaintiff or defendant to a lawsuit, keeping whatever money the minor earns, living away from the parents, approving health care and medical procedures, getting married, writing a will, and enrolling in school.

If the minor's circumstances change, the emancipation order can be rescinded by the court. If that happens, the parents "are not liable for any debts incurred by the minor during the period of emancipation."

NORTH CAROLINA: The age of majority in North Carolina is 18. A minor must be at least 16 years of age in order to seek an order of emancipation from the court. The court will consider several factors–including the parents' need for the minor's earnings as well as the minor's ability to accept adult responsibilities–in determining the best interests of the minor.

If the emancipation is granted, the minor will have the adult rights to sign contracts, take part in lawsuits, and conduct other adult-related business. The parents' duties of support to the minor are thereby ended.

OREGON: The age of majority in Oregon is 18. A minor must be 16 years of age to seek an order of emancipation from the court. The minor must show that they can support him or herself and otherwise assume adult responsibilities. If the court determines that an order of emancipation is in the best interests of the minor, then the minor "has all of the rights and is subject to all liabilities of a citizen of full age."

VERMONT: A minor must be at least 16 years old in order to seek an order of emancipation from the court. Minors are considered to be emancipated without a court order if they are married or have entered the armed forces. In order for the court to consider making an order of emancipation, the minors must have already lived separately from their parents, successfully taken care of their own finances, shown that they can take care of other personal business, either have received a high school diploma or are working toward one, and not be a ward of the social services or corrections department.

WASHINGTON: A child seeking a court order for emancipation must show the following by clear and convincing evidence: (1) the child is a resident of Washington; (2) the child has the ability to handle financial affairs; (3) the child can handle other affairs, including educational, personal, social, and other affairs; and (4) denying emancipation would harm the child.

WEST VIRGINIA: A minor must be at least 16 years old in order to seek an order of emancipation from the court. Minors must also show the court that they can provide for themselves and their "physical and financial well-being and have the ability to make decisions" for themselves. If an emancipation order is entered, minors have the rights and privileges of adults.

ADDITIONAL RESOURCES

De Witt, John Gregory, Peter N. Swisher, and Sheryl L. Wolf. *Understanding Family Law*. 3d ed. Newark, NJ: LexisNexis, 2005.

Katz, Sanford N. *Family Law in America*. New York: Oxford University Press, 2011.

Krause, Harry D. and David D. Meyer. *Family Law*. 4th ed. Eagan, MN: West, Thomson Reuters, 2009.

Oliphant, Robert E., and Nancy Ver Steegh. *Family Law: Examples and Explanations*. 3d ed. New York: Aspen Publishers, 2010.

ORGANIZATIONS

Focus Adolescent Services

PO Box 4514
Salisbury, MD 21803
Phone: (410) 341-4216
URL: http://www.focusas.com

Legal Information Institute

477 Myron Taylor Hall
Ithaca, NY 14853
URL: http://www.law.cornell.edu/wex/table_emancipation

Northwest Justice Project (NJP)

401 Second Avenue South, Ste. 407
Seattle, WA 98104
Toll Free: (888) 201-1012
URL: http://www.nwjustice.org/

FAMILY LAW

FAMILY PLANNING/ABORTION/ BIRTH CONTROL

Sections within this essay:

- Background
- History
- Birth Control
- Abortion
- *Roe v. Wade*
- After *Roe v. Wade*
- Additional Resources

BACKGROUND

Family planning involves decisions made by women and men concerning their reproductive lives and whether, when, and under what circumstances they have children. Family planning most often involves the decisions of whether to engage in sexual activity that could lead to pregnancy, whether to use birth control, and whether to terminate a pregnancy. Individuals faced with these decisions often rely on moral or religious beliefs. Because moral and religious beliefs vary widely in the United States, family planning laws are frequently controversial.

HISTORY

During the nineteenth century in the United States, birth rates began to decline, in part due to an increase in scientific information about conception and contraception, or birth control. The average white woman in 1800 gave birth seven times; by 1900, that number dropped to an average of three-and-a-half. At the beginning of the nineteenth century, early stage abortions generally were legal. The use of birth control and abortion, however, declined as growing public opinion considered information about birth control methods to be obscene and abortion to be unsafe.

BIRTH CONTROL

Birth control is any method used to protect a woman from getting pregnant. Beginning in the 1800s, laws in the United States prohibited birth control, when temperance and anti-vice groups advocated outlawing birth control devices and information about birth control devices. These groups considered birth control information to be obscene, a belief that was popular enough that in 1873, Congress passed the Comstock Act outlawing the dissemination of birth control devices or information through the mail. Most states followed suit by passing their own laws outlawing the advertising, sale, and distribution of contraception.

The turn of the century brought increasing attention to issues involving women's rights. Margaret Sanger, a strong advocate of birth control, opened the country's first birth control clinic in New York City in 1916 and was prosecuted for violating New York's version of the Comstock Act. She served a 30-day sentence in a workhouse but later established the National Committee for Federal Legislation for Birth Control. Sanger proposed a federal bill that outlined the health and death risks to women who underwent illegal abortions or who completed unwanted pregnancies. The bill sought to reverse the federal position prohibiting birth control, but under pressure from religious groups such as the Catholic Church, Congress did not pass Sanger's bill.

Sanger then sought to challenge the Comstock Act by sending contraception through the mail to a doctor. Her actions were prosecuted, but she achieved her goal when a federal district court deemed that the Comstock Act did not prohibit the mailing of contraceptives when such an act could save a life or promote the health of a doctor's patients. Sanger continued to lead a growing national movement advocating more information and access to birth control, and in 1921 she founded the American Birth Control League.

In 1942, the American Birth Control League became the Planned Parenthood Federation of America, still in existence today. Planned Parenthood advocates for a range of safe, legal, and accessible birth control options. In the 1950s, Sanger and Planned Parenthood supported the research efforts of Dr. Gregory Pincus that led to the development of the birth control pill. The birth control pill revolutionized family planning, and by the 1960s popular opinion was shifting in favor of making contraception and information about contraception readily available.

By the 1950s and 1960s, most states had legalized birth control, but many state laws still prohibited the dissemination of information about contraception, and some states still prohibited the possession of contraception. A 1965 landmark Supreme Court decision further eroded these laws sanctioning birth control. In *Griswold v. Connecticut,* the Court addressed the prosecution of a Planned Parenthood executive director charged with violating a Connecticut state law that prohibited the distribution of contraceptives and information about contraceptives, and prohibited the possession of contraceptives. The Court found that although the U.S. Constitution does not explicitly offer a right to **privacy**, that right can be inferred from the language in various sections of the **Bill of Rights**. The Constitution therefore does contain what the Court called a "zone of privacy." Connecticut's **statute** violated that zone of privacy in the realm of marriage because it permitted police officers to search the bedroom of a married couple for **evidence** of contraception. The Court deemed this action to be overly intrusive and an unconstitutional violation of the right to marital privacy, and it threw out the Connecticut law insofar as it applied to married couples.

In 1966, the federal government, with an endorsement by U.S. President Lyndon B. Johnson, began public funding of contraception services for low-income families. President Richard M. Nixon in 1970 signed into law an act promoting research of population and family planning issues. Finally, in 1971, Congress repealed the key elements of the Comstock Act.

Some states, however, kept birth control laws despite the **repeal** of the federal Comstock Act. In 1972, the Supreme Court found unconstitutional a Massachusetts law that only permitted married couples to receive contraception. The Court found this law to violate the **equal protection** rights of single persons. In 1977, the Court addressed a New York state law that permitted only physicians to distribute contraceptives to minors under the age of sixteen, and only physicians or pharmacists to distribute contraceptives to adults. The Court struck down this law as well. It became clear that the Supreme Court viewed as constitutionally protected the right of an individual, married or unmarried, to make personal decisions regarding whether to have children.

ABORTION

Abortion occurs when an embryo or fetus is expelled from a woman's body. Abortions can be spontaneous or induced. In the legal context, discussions about abortions usually involve induced, or intentional, abortions.

Before the United States became a country, the **common law** of England permitted abortions before the fetus "quickened." Quickening was the term used to describe the mother's first feeling of the fetus moving in her uterus. Typically, quickening occurs between the sixteenth and eighteenth weeks of pregnancy.

After the founding of the United States, laws regarding abortions did not exist until the 1800s. Women at that time were not allowed to vote and were not allowed to be doctors or members of the American Medical Association, which, along with religious leaders, advocated the passage of laws outlawing abortion. Abortions in the nineteenth century were generally unsafe, and women who survived abortions frequently were left sterile. By the 1880s, all states had laws criminalizing abortions. These laws stayed on the books until the 1960s and 1970s.

Beginning in the mid-twentieth century, women's groups, along with doctors and lawyers, organized a movement to reform abortion laws. Reformers cited inequalities between men and women that were exacerbated by women's inability to adequately control their reproductive lives. The post World War II population explosion also increased awareness about the environment and the need to limit family size. In other countries, abortions were legal and generally safe, but in the United States, women continued to undergo illegal abortions and risk permanent injury or death. In the 1960s, the anti-nausea drug thalidomide and an outbreak of German measles caused a rash of birth defects in babies born during that decade. The increase in birth defects brought further attention to the issue since women wishing to avoid the birth of a seriously deformed child could not seek legal abortions.

Women's rights organizations, including the National Organization for Women (NOW), lobbied for abortion law reform and filed lawsuits when **lobbying** efforts failed. States responded, reforming their laws about abortion, but women's rights groups continued to fight for unfettered access to abortion services for women. Anti-abortion groups fought back, arguing that a woman's right to reproductive freedom is no greater than the right of an unborn child to be born. The battle ultimately went before the U.S. Supreme Court, which in 1973 decided the landmark abortion case of *Roe v. Wade*.

ROE V. WADE

Jane **Roe** was a pseudonym for Norma McCorvey, an unmarried pregnant Texas woman who sought an abortion but was denied under Texas law. Roe, with the help of attorneys, filed a federal lawsuit seeking to have the Texas law thrown out as unconstitutional. She argued that a law prohibiting her from obtaining an abortion violated her constitutional right to privacy. The Supreme Court, voting 7-2, agreed with Roe that the law criminalizing abortion violated her right to privacy. But the Court held that states do have an interest in ensuring the safety and well-being of pregnant women as well as the potential of human life. Acknowledging that the rights of pregnant women may conflict with the rights of the state to protect potential human life, the Court defined the rights of each party by dividing the pregnancy into three 12-week trimesters. During a pregnant woman's first trimester, the Court held, a state cannot regulate abortion beyond requiring that the procedure be performed by a licensed doctor in medically safe conditions. During the second trimester, the Court held, a state may regulate abortion if the regulations are reasonably related to the health of the pregnant woman. During the third trimester of pregnancy, the state's interest in protecting the potential human life outweighs the woman's right to privacy, and the state may prohibit abortions unless abortion is necessary to save the life or health of the mother. The Court further held that a fetus is not a person protected by the constitution.

AFTER *ROE V. WADE*

Roe v. Wade established the limited right of a woman to have an abortion. Recognizing that fact, states liberalized their abortion laws following the Supreme Court's decision, but abortion soon became an even more divisive issue in the United States. Groups opposed to abortion, including the Catholic Church, became organized and politically powerful. The issue of abortion became a platform issue for all candidates for federal office, including the office of the U.S. president. During the 1980s, President Ronald Reagan, an opponent of abortion, used his presidency to argue for a reversal of *Roe v. Wade*. He appointed C. Everett Koop, another abortion opponent, to the position of surgeon general and

referred to abortion as a "silent holocaust." Reagan believed that abortion caused pain to the fetus and that the rights of the fetus were not outweighed by the rights of the pregnant woman.

Groups opposed to abortion, known as pro-life groups, have worked in various ways to reduce or eliminate entirely abortions in the United States. These groups have sponsored legislation limiting access to abortion and have attempted unsuccessfully to reverse *Roe v. Wade* by way of a **constitutional amendment**. Some groups opposed to abortion attempt to persuade patients not to undergo abortions by demonstrating outside of abortion clinics. In some extreme cases, individuals and groups opposed to abortion have bombed abortion clinics, injuring and killing patients and staff members, or have murdered doctors who provide abortions. Because of these extreme actions, many doctors are unwilling to perform abortions and many abortion clinics have shut down, making access to abortion difficult in some regions.

Other attempts to reduce the number of abortions have involved eliminating public funding of abortions and even prohibiting health care clinics that receive public funding from counseling women about the option of abortion. Soon after taking office in 1993, President Bill Clinton effectively reversed federal regulations that prohibited staff members at health care clinics that receive public funding from dispersing information about abortions or referring women to abortion providers. Once this so-called "gag rule" was lifted, these clinics once again were able to give women information about abortion.

Also complicating the issue of abortion rights are rules requiring a woman to get **informed consent** or parental consent. Informed consent involves a requirement that before undergoing an abortion, the abortion provider must give the woman information about the risks of abortion, alternatives to abortion, the age of the fetus, and the availability of government assistance for carrying the pregnancy to term. Parental consent involves a requirement that a minor wishing to undergo an abortion first obtain consent from her parent or **guardian**. The Supreme Court generally has upheld parental consent laws provided the laws allow a minor the ability to obtain permission to have an abortion from a judge rather than a parent and provided that the judge's decision take into account the minor's best interests, maturity, and ability to make decisions. As of 2012, 37 states required some level of parental involvement regarding a decision by a minor to have an abortion. In 22 of these states, one or both parents must consent to the abortion procedure. The Supreme Court generally has upheld laws requiring the notification, as opposed to consent, of parents of minors seeking to undergo an abortion. The Supreme Court generally has upheld informed consent laws so long as the laws do not create an undue burden on the woman seeking an abortion. The Supreme Court has not upheld laws requiring a woman to obtain her spouse's permission before undergoing an abortion.

Other state laws on abortion vary. The list below summarizes the laws as of 2012:

- In 39 states, a license physician must perform an abortion, and in many of these states, a second physician must participate at certain stages of the pregnancy, such as when the fetus is viable.

- In 21 states, abortions must be performed in a hospital if the fetus is viable or if the pregnancy has reached a certain period, such as 20 weeks.

- In 41 states, abortions are prohibited altogether after the pregnancy has reached a certain period, except in cases where the mother's life is endangered.

- In 18 states, "partial-birth" abortions are banned, though courts in several of these states have enjoined enforcement of these bans.

- Every state allows some funding for abortion, but in a majority of states, funds are limited to instances where the mother's life is at risk or the pregnancy was the result of rape or incest.

ADDITIONAL RESOURCES

Hendershott, Anne. *The Politics of Abortion*. New York: Encounter Books, 2006.

Johnson, John W. *Griswold v. Connecticut: Birth Control and the Constitutional Right to Privacy*. Lawrence, KS: University Press of Kansas, 2005.

Linton, Paul Benjamin. *Abortion Under State Constitutions: A State-by-State Analysis*. 2d ed. Durham, NC: Carolina Academic Press, 2012.

ORGANIZATIONS

Feminists for Life
PO Box 320667
Alexandria, VA 22320
Phone: (703) 836-3354
URL: http://www.feministsforlife.org

National Abortion and Reproductive Rights Action League (NARAL)
1156 15th Street Suite 700
Washington, DC 20005
Phone: (202) 973-3000
URL: http://www.naral.org

National Right to Life Committee
512 10th Street, NW
Washington, DC 20004
Phone: (202) 626-8800
URL: http://www.nrlc.org

Planned Parenthood Federation of America
434 West 33rd Street
New York, NY 10001
Phone: (212) 541-7800
URL: http://www.plannedparenthood.org

FAMILY LAW

FOSTER CARE

Sections within this essay:

BACKGROUND

Children in foster homes is a concept which goes as far back as the Old Testament, which refers to caring for dependent children as a duty under law. Early Christian church records indicate orphaned children lived with widows who were paid by the church. English Poor Laws in the 1500s allowed the placement of poor children into indentured service until they became adults. This practice was imported to the United States and was the beginning of placing children into foster homes. Even though indentured service permitted exploitation, it was an improvement over almshouses where children did not learn and were exposed to unsanitary conditions and abusive caretakers.

In 1853, Charles Loring Brace, a minister, founded the Children's Aid Society. Brace saw many immigrant children sleeping in the streets. He located families in the West willing to provide free homes for these children. These children were sent by train to these families and were often required to work long hours. Nevertheless, Brace's system became the foundation for today's **foster care** movement.

In the 1900s, social agencies began to pay and supervise foster parents. The government began state inspections of foster homes. Services were provided to natural families to enable the child to return home and foster parents were now seen as part of a team effort to provide for dependent children.

Legislative efforts during the 2000s to increase adoptions led to a decrease in the number of children in foster homes. In 2002, a total of 522,579 children were in foster homes. This number fell to 408,425 in 2010 according to the Administration for Children and Families of the U.S. Department of Health and Human Services.

FEDERAL CHILD WELFARE PROGRAMS

The Social Security Act contains the primary sources of Federal funds available to States for child welfare, foster care, and **adoption** activities. These funds include both non-entitlement authorizations (for which the amount of funding available is determined through the annual appropriations process) and authorized entitlements (under which the Federal Government has a binding

Children in foster care, FY 2007–FY 2011

Numbers at a glance

Fiscal year (FY)[1]	2007	2008	2009	2010	2011[2]
In foster care on September 30 of the FY	488,285	463,799	421,350	406,412	400,540
Entered foster care during FY	293,276	280,384	255,161	255,402	252,320
Exited foster care during FY	294,989	288,762	278,157	257,481	245,260
Waiting to be adopted on September 30 of the FY	133,682	125,741	114,450	109,456	104,236
Waiting to be adopted whose parental rights (for all living parents) were terminated during FY	82,020	79,376	71,093	65,611	61,361
Adopted with public child welfare agency involvement during FY	52,686	55,236	57,115	53,591	50,516

Note: Missing data are excluded and, therefore, the totals within each distribution may not equal the total provided for that subpopulation (e.g. number in care on September 30th may not match the sum across ages for that group).
[1]FY refers to the Federal Fiscal Year, October 1st through September 30th.
[2]Preliminary FY 2011 estimates as of July 2012.

SOURCE: U.S. Department of Health and Human Services, Administration for Children and Families, Administration on Children, Youth and Families, Children's Bureau, Adoption and Foster Care Analysis and Reporting System (AFCARS) FY 2011 Data. Available at http://www .acf.hhs.gov/sites/default/files/cb/afcarsreport19.pdf

TABLE BY PREMEDIAGLOBAL. ©2013 CENGAGE LEARNING.

obligation to make payments to any person or unit of government that meets the eligibility criteria established by law). Family preservation services are intended for children and families, including extended and adoptive families that are at risk or in crisis. Services include: programs to help reunite children with their biological families, if appropriate, or to place them for adoption or another permanent arrangement; programs to prevent placement of children in foster care, including intensive family preservation services; programs to provide follow-up services to families after a child has been returned from foster care; respite care to provide temporary relief for parents and other care givers (including foster parents); and services to improve parenting skills. The Foster Care Program is a permanently authorized entitlement that provides open-ended matching payments to States for the costs of maintaining certain children in foster care, and associated administrative, child placement, and training costs.

FOSTER CARE FUNDING

The Federal government provides funds to States to administer child welfare programs. State grant programs have their own matching requirements and allocations, and all require that funds go to and be administered by State child welfare agencies, or in some programs, Indian Tribes or Tribal organizations. In most states foster children are eligible for **Medicaid** cards which cover medical, dental, and counseling services. Foster parents receive reimbursement for the child's food and clothing. Some states provide a clothing **voucher** at the time of the child's first placement. Others provide clothing vouchers at the beginning of each school year. Foster children have

the same minimum health benefits as children in the Aid to Families with Dependent Children (AFDC) program. Most Federal funds for AFDC and foster children's health care come through Federal Medicaid (Title XIX of the Social Security Act).

MEDICAL ISSUES

As wards of the state, foster care children depend on government-funded health services. As a group, children in foster care suffer high rates of serious physical or psychological problems. Nearly half of these children suffer from chronic conditions such as asthma, cognitive abnormalities, visual and auditory problems, dental decay and malnutrition, as well as birth defects, developmental delays or emotional and behavioral problems. Over half require ongoing medical treatment. Studies indicate that well over half have moderate to severe mental health problems. These conditions stem from exposure to alcohol and drugs, lack of medical care, poor parenting, **domestic violence**, neglect, and unstable living conditions prior to family removal. The trauma of family separation, frequent moves, and the stress and disruptions brought about by impermanent placements in the foster care system aggravate the situation.

CHILDREN WITH DISABILITIES

Children with disabilities sometimes enter foster care because their parents have not received the type or level of support to meet their needs. In many cases, parents must work and responsible after-school childcare is not available. Sometimes the parents become overwhelmed with the needs of the disabled child and the demands of other children in the family. Children with disabilities are abused at a high rate. Their parents are often frustrated with their children's disabilities or with their own inability to help them. Disabled girls are more often sexually abused than other girls. Children with developmental disabilities have a hard time explaining what happened to the social worker or police. In foster homes, the foster parents are trained to care for these children and given support within the dependency system.

AGING OUT OF FOSTER CARE

Children age-out of foster care at age 18 or when they graduate from high school, whichever happens first. This event is referred to as **emancipation**. Some maintain a continuing relationship with their foster families while others do not. Many face a difficult future when state and federal funding ends, and housing, food, and medical care stops.

The John H. Chafee Foster Care Independence Program (CFCIP), Title I of the Foster Care Independence Act of 1999, provides funds to states to assist youth and young adults (up to age 21) in the foster care component of the child welfare system make a smoother, more successful transition to adulthood. This recent program replaces and expands the Social Security Act and allows states to use these funds for a broader array of services to youth "aging out" of the foster care system, including room and board. Most importantly, the Chafee program enables states to expand the scope and improve the quality of educational, vocational, practical, and emotional supports in their programs for adolescents in foster care and for young adults who have recently left foster care.

As of 2009, funding for CFCIP was $140 million as well as $45 million for the related Educational and Training Vouchers Program.

CHILD ABUSE

Many children become participants in the Foster Care system due to neglect or abuse by their primary caretakers. Investigations by child protective services (CPS) agencies in all States determine that close to a million children are victims of child maltreatment every year. More than half of all reports alleging maltreatment came from professionals, including educators, law enforcement and justice officials, medical and mental health professionals, social service professionals, and **child care** providers. Federal agencies have no authority to intervene in individual **child abuse** and neglect cases. Each State has **jurisdiction** over these matters and has specific laws and procedures for reporting and investigating. Individual States have a Child Protective Services agency set up to investigate complaints and allegations. In some States, all citizens are mandated reporters by State law and must report any suspicion of child abuse or neglect.

More children suffer neglect than any other form of maltreatment. Investigations determined that about half of children victimized suffered neglect, 22 percent physical abuse, 12 percent **sexual abuse**, 6 percent emotional maltreatment, 2 percent medical neglect, and 25 percent other forms of maltreatment. Some children suffer more than one type of abuse. Unfortunately, maltreatment is rarely the only issue of families who enter into the child welfare system. Substance abuse and other addictions, serious physical or mental illness, domestic violence, and HIV/AIDS are often critical factors. Poverty is pervasive, and inadequate or unsafe housing are significant problems. These serious difficulties can result in extremely complex family situations that need multiple and coordinated services.

FOSTER PARENT REQUIREMENTS

Generally, foster parents must be over 21, have a regular source of income, have no record of **felony** convictions, submit to a home assessment of all family members, and agree to attend parent training sessions. Foster parents can usually work outside the home, however, if the foster child requires day care, the foster parent is typically responsible for that expense. Foster parents need not make a certain minimum income, nor even own a large home. Foster children can usually share a bedroom with another child of the same sex. Both single persons and married couples are generally accepted as foster parents, however, some states do not certify homes in which unmarried adults are living together unless they are relatives.

The length of time a child may remain in foster care varies. The Adoption and Safe Families Act of 1997 requires states to seek a permanent placement for the child as quickly as possible, be it reunification with the birth parents, kinship care, or adoption.

GROUP HOMES

Group homes have a history of being problematic in the Foster Care system. Initially, there was a shortage of experienced operators and the industry was unregulated, and a few took advantage of it. Many were run by competent social workers or those in religious communities who, though without formal training, were instrumental in having a positive impact on these children. Unfortunately, in others, children were abused or forced to participate in the beliefs of their caretakers. Sometimes untrained workers tried behavior modification techniques that were cruel and inhumane. With little monitoring by the government, it was possible to cut back on food, clothing, education and programs to make a profit for the operators.

Group homes are now subject to a number of federal regulations. Any care facility that houses six or more children is considered a group home. Most group homes are small and try to integrate the children into the community. The residents attend local schools, are closely supervised, and have a structured life, with a counselor on duty around the clock in most cases and a schedule of counseling, tutoring, and other services.

KINSHIP CARE

Kinship care is the full time care of children by relatives, godparents, stepparents, or any adult who has a kinship bond with a child. The expansion of kinship foster care is, perhaps, the most dramatic shift to occur in child welfare practice over the past two decades. Informal kinship care is when a family decides that the child will live with relatives or other kin. In this informal kinship care arrangement, a social worker may be involved in helping family members plan for the child, but a child welfare agency does not assume legal **custody** of or responsibility for the child. Because the parents still have custody of the child, relatives need not be approved, licensed, or supervised by the state.

Formal kinship care involves the parenting of children by relatives as a result of a determination by the court and the child protective service agency. The courts rule that the child must be separated from his or her parents because of abuse, neglect, dependency, **abandonment** or special medical circumstances. The child is placed in the legal custody of the child welfare agency, and the relatives provide full time care. Formal kinship care is linked to state and federal child welfare laws. Federal legislation impacting kinship care includes The Adoption Assistance and Child Welfare Act of 1980, Title IV of the Social Security Act, and The Indian Child Welfare Act. Thus, kinship caregivers may be able to access Social Security Funds for the child, Temporary Assistance for Needy Families (TANF) funds for the child, and medical assistance for the child.

THE ADOPTION AND SAFE FAMILIES ACT

The Adoption and Safe Families Act of 1997 established time lines and conditions for filing termination of parental rights. The Act provides a new legislative framework that sets the direction and parameters for the operation of state and local child welfare agencies and courts. States must file a petition to terminate parental rights and concurrently identify, recruit, process and approve a qualified adoptive family on behalf of any child, regardless of age, if the child has been in foster care for 15 out of the most recent 22 months. Exceptions can be made to these requirements if a relative is caring for a child. The Act requires notice of court reviews and an opportunity to be heard is sent to relatives, foster parents, and pre-adoptive parents. A relative, foster parent or pre-adoptive parent caring for a child must be given notice of an opportunity to be

heard in any review or **hearing** involving the child. This provision does not require that any relative, foster, or pre-adoptive parent be made a party to such a review or hearing. The Act also mandates that the Federal Department of Health and Human Services (HHS) complete a study on kinship care.

THE INDIAN CHILD WELFARE ACT

The Indian Child Welfare Act (ICWA) of 1973 described the role that Native American families and tribal governments must play in decisions about the protection and placement of their children. It strengthened the role of tribal governments in determining the custody of Native American children and specified that preference should be given first to placements with extended family, then to Native American foster homes. The law mandated that state courts act to preserve the integrity and unity of Native American families.

ADOPTION OF FOSTER CHILDREN

If a child has been in placement with a foster care family for a significant period of time and the parental rights of the natural parents have been terminated, the foster parents may seek an adoption under the state law. In 2008, Congress enacted a law entitled Fostering Connection to Success and Increasing Adoptions Act, which reduced the number of children in foster homes by establishing funds for adoption assistance.

ADDITIONAL RESOURCES

Blatt, Susan McNair. *A Guidebook for Raising Foster Children.* Westport, CT: Bergin & Garvey, 2000.

De Witt, John Gregory, Peter N. Swisher, and Sheryl L. Wolf. *Understanding Family Law.* 3d ed. Newark, NJ: LexisNexis, 2005.

Katz, Sanford N. *Family Law in America.* New York: Oxford University Press, 2011.

Oliphant, Robert E., and Nancy Ver Steegh. *Family Law: Examples and Explanations.* 3d ed. New York: Aspen Publishers, 2010.

ORGANIZATIONS

Child Welfare League of America
1726 M St. NW, Suite 500
Washington, DC 20036
Phone: (202) 688-4200
URL: http://www.cwla.org

Court Appointed Special Advocates for Children (CASA)
100 West Harrison Street, North Tower, Suite 500
Seattle, WA 98119
URL: http://www.casaforchildren.org

FAMILY LAW

GAY COUPLES

Sections within this essay:

BACKGROUND

Within the already controversial realm of gay rights, no area is more controversial than gay marriage. For some, the idea that homosexual couples should have the same matrimonial benefits as heterosexual couples is purely a question of **civil rights**. According to this argument, the constitutional concepts of **equal protection** and due process require that same-sex couples be treated no differently than heterosexual married couples. Others see homosexual marriage as a moral question, and conclude that such unions violate traditional ethical values found in the Judeo-Christian moral tradition. Another argument is that it undermines family values: heterosexual marriage is founded upon the need to procreate, but that is something homosexual couples cannot do. To counter this argument, those in favor of same-sex marriages note that elderly, disabled, and infertile people are free to marry without thought to procreation, and that advances in fertility technology have opened many paths to parenthood.

The debate over gay marriage is not confined to the marriage ceremony itself, although being allowed to participate legally in that rite drives much of the emotionalism of the debate. It also has a more pragmatic side, including issues such as whether same-sex couples should receive the same tax and estate advantages, the same rights to surviving children, the same **community property** rights, and the same health care benefits as heterosexual couples.

Although same-sex marriages have occurred privately for years, only until relatively recent years has the issue been litigated. Only since 1993, with the Hawaii Supreme Court decision in *Baehr v. Lewin*, have gay rights supporters seen any measurable progress in state laws concerning homosexual marriage. Since that decision, both sides in the battle over same-sex marriage have experienced some victories and some setbacks.

PRE-1993

Unions between two members of the same sex in some sort of ceremony, religious or otherwise, existed for many years before anyone sought to gain legal recognition of them. Generally, these unions were kept private, with knowledge limited to immediate friends and family members. In 1971 the first lawsuit seeking to legalize a same-sex marriage was filed. *Baker v. Nelson* was inspired by the 1967 U.S. Supreme Court decision in *Loving v. Virginia*. In *Loving*, the Supreme Court invalidated a state **statute** that prohibited interracial marriage. The Court ruled that to deny marriage on the basis of race was a violation of the constitutional principles of equal protection and **due process of law**, because the law had "no legitimate purpose independent of invidious racial discrimination."

The Minnesota Supreme Court was not swayed by the reasoning in *Loving*. It struck down Jack Baker's attempt to gain legal status for his marriage to Mike McConnell. The court ruled that marriage was by definition between a man and a woman, and thus, unlike in *Loving*, there was no fundamental right to marry. Moreover, in a 1974 case, the Washington Supreme Court determined that the state's **Equal Rights Amendment** could not be held to allow homosexuals the right to marry. The law provided protection only on the basis of sex, not **sexual orientation**.

Following these cases, all attempts failed to get a state or federal court to recognize the right of homosexuals to marry. There were decisions allowing unmarried partners to sue for enforcement of promises of support or financial sharing (so-called "palimony" cases), beginning with the landmark *Marvin v. Marvin* case involving actor Lee Marvin in California in 1976. Gays also attempted to form legal relationships by having one partner "adopt" the other. Some municipalities, beginning with Berkeley in 1984, adopted domestic **partnership** laws that extended some recognition and benefits of marriage to registered same-sex couples. But gay activists considered that these gains fell far short of their ultimate goal: granting marriage recognition to gay unions.

BAEHR V. LEWIN

Activists scored their first major victory in 1993, in the Hawaii case of *Baehr v. Lewin*. Nina Baehr sued the state of Hawaii; she alleged that the state's refusal to issue her and her same-sex partner a marriage license amounted to illegal **discrimination**. In a **plurality** decision, the Hawaii Supreme Court said her case had merit. The court ruled the state's prohibition of same-sex marriages amounted to discrimination on the basis of sex. Under the state's Equal Rights Amendment, the state would have to establish a compelling state interest supporting such a ban, a fairly strict standard. Although the court did not directly rule that the state's prohibition of same-sex marriages was illegal, it left little doubt of its skepticism regarding the proposition. The court remanded the case to a lower court to determine whether the state could prove this compelling state interest in prohibiting same-sex marriage.

For the first time, a state supreme court had ruled that gay couples might have the right to marry. Although its immediate impact was only in Hawaii, the decision heartened gay rights supporters and discouraged opponents throughout the country. One reason for these responses was the Full Faith and Credit Clause, found in Article IV, Section 1, of the United States Constitution: "Full Faith and Credit shall be given in each state to the public Acts, Records and judicial Proceedings of every other state." The Clause requires states to grant full weight to legal actions in other states, including marriages, divorces, and other family-related situations. Both opponents and proponents of gay marriage realized that the Full Faith and Credit Clause of the Constitution might mean that if same-sex marriages were legal in Hawaii, the marriages would be entitled to legal recognition in other states as well.

The Reaction The *Baehr* decision mobilized opponents of same-sex marriages, who feared that gay marriage would soon be legal in Hawaii. Yet some disagreed over whether Hawaii's potential legalization of gay marriage would necessarily overrule other states' anti-gay marriage laws. Nevertheless, anti-gay marriage legislation was passed on both the state and federal level. Voters in Hawaii adopted a **constitutional amendment** allowing legislators to ban same-sex marriages, thus making the state's Equal Rights Amendment no longer applicable. In late 1999, the Hawaiian Supreme Court determined that this new ban was effective and refused to recognize same-sex marriages in the state.

The Defense of Marriage Act In 1996, in response to the *Baehr* decision, the U.S. Congress passed the Defense of Marriage Act (DOMA). President Clinton signed DOMA into law. The act was designed to prevent the Full Faith and Credit Clause from being applied to states' refusal to recognize same sex marriages. DOMA states in part that "No state, territory or possession of the United States . . . shall be required to give effect to any public act, record, or judicial proceeding of any other State, territory, possession or tribe respecting a relationship between persons of the same sex that is treated as a marriage under the laws of such other State, territory, possession, or tribe, or a right or claim arising from such a relationship."

DOMA does not ban same-sex marriages in itself. Neither does it require any state to ban them. DOMA defines marriage as a union between a man and a woman only. The act also specifically denies federal benefits to same-sex couples. The act states that any federal law that applies to married couples does not apply to same-sex couples: **statutory** and administrative use of terms such as "marriage" and "spouse" under federal law only apply to heterosexual couples. In addition to the federal law, many states passed their own defense of marriage laws.

RIGHTS EXPAND AS SUPPORT GROWS

The level of support for gay rights in general grew considerably throughout the 2000s. By 2012, some polls indicated that a slight majority of Americans supported the rights of same-sex couples to marry. In fact, President Barack Obama became the first sitting president in history to offer public support for gay marriage, which he announced in 2012.

As of 2012, a total of six states and the District of Columbia recognized gay marriage, either through legislation or from judicial opinions, while the issue is being debated heavily in other states. The U.S. Supreme Court may also issue an opinion on the issue at some point in the future.

MASSACHUSETTS: On November 18, 2003, the Supreme Judicial Court of Massachusetts ruled in *Goodridge v. Department of Public Health* that the state could not deny civil marriage to two members of the same sex who wished to marry. The court stayed its ruling for 180 days, so that the state legislature could address the issue. The legislature moved quickly to prohibit same-sex marriages, but voted to allow "civil unions," a category that was intended to be separate but legally equivalent to marriage. In February 2004, the Supreme Judicial Court issued an advisory opinion that concluded the proposed legislation was unconstitutional. This opinion paved the way for city and town clerks to issue marriage licenses to same-sex couples beginning in May 2004. As of 2012, Massachusetts was the only state in the United States where same-sex couples could legally marry.

CALIFORNIA: The State of California has had an even more complicated history with regard to same-sex marriage. At the same time the marriage debate raged in Massachusetts, the issue was heating up in San Francisco as well. In February 2004, the county clerk, acting on orders of San Francisco mayor Gavin Newsom, began to issue marriage licenses to same-sex couples. Couples from all around the U.S. flocked to the city to get married. Issuance of licenses was halted when the California Supreme Court issued a temporary stay on March 11, 2004. By that time, however, more than four thousand same-sex marriages had been performed.

The California legislature in 2005 and 2007 approved bills to permit gay marriages, but then-Governor Arnold Schwarzenegger vetoed both bills. As the debate continued, the California Supreme Court in a 4-3 vote ruled that California laws limiting marriage to one between a man and a woman were unconstitutional. By June 2008, several city offices began to issue marriage licenses.

However, in November 2008, voters approved Proposition 8, which limited the definition of marriage to one between a man and woman, effectively invalidating the California Supreme Court's decision. Marriages performed between June 2008 and November 2008 are still recognized, but as of 2012, the state did not recognize gay marriages.

Nevertheless, the fight has continued on several fronts. Parties have challenged Proposition 8 on federal constitutional grounds, and other parties in California have challenged the constitutionality of the Defense of Marriage Act.

CONNECTICUT: The State of Connecticut had approved a civil-union law, but parties continued to argue that the state should recognize full marriage rights. The state legislature approved a bill legalizing gay marriage, and the state began to perform same-sex marriages on November 12, 2008.

VERMONT: In 1999, the same year the Hawaiian Supreme Court refused to recognize same-sex marriages, the Vermont Supreme Court handed down its decision in *Baker v. State*. In that decision, the court said that same-sex couples must be granted the same benefits and protections that heterosexual couples received under state law. The court instructed the state legislature to determine how to grant homosexual couples those benefits and protections. It did not require the state to allow same-sex couples to be legally married but told the state legislature it had to find some way to treat those couples the same as if they were legally married.

The next year, the state passed a bill allowing same-sex couples to enter into civil unions. Town clerks were authorized to give licenses to same-sex couples for these unions in the same way they would give out marriage licenses. They could be married by anyone authorized to perform marriages under state law and would have to **divorce** under state law in the same way heterosexual couples would.

Similar to the circumstance in Connecticut, the Vermont legislature approved legislation that permitted same-sex marriage. The governor vetoed the bill, but the legislature overrode the veto, and gay marriage became legal on September 1, 2009.

IOWA: In a somewhat surprising move, the Iowa Supreme Court in 2009 ruled that denying marriage licenses to same-sex couples was unconstitutional. Iowa became the first state in the Midwest to recognize gay marriages, and despite strong opposition to the opinion, gay marriage has remained legal in the state.

DISTRICT OF COLUMBIA: The Council of the District of Columbia approved a bill allowing same sex marriage, effective on December 18, 2009.

NEW HAMPSHIRE: The New Hampshire legislature approved gay marriage, effective in 2010. The state had previously recognized civil unions, and those unions were automatically converted to marriages when the law became effective.

NEW YORK: After several proposals had previously failed, the New York legislature approved a bill legalizing gay marriage in 2011. The law became effective in July 2011.

OTHER STATE LAWS

Most of the remaining states limit the definition of marriage to the union of a man and a woman, and 31 states have approved amendments that explicitly prohibit same-sex marriages or unions. Nevertheless, several states provide some rights for same-sex couples that are available to married persons. The amount of protection provided varies greatly from just one or two rights in some states, to dozens of rights in other states. Following are some examples of rights that states have conferred to same-sex couples:

- hospital visitation
- the right to make health-care decisions
- eligibility for certain tort claims
- family leave
- workers' compensation
- inheritance under **intestacy** laws
- state tax deductions or exemptions
- eligibility for family health insurance for state employees

MUNICIPALITIES AND CORPORATIONS

In the past several years, municipalities have been generally more likely than states to grant same-sex couples the benefits of marriage than states. Since Berkeley passed the first domestic partnership law in 1984, dozens of cities and municipalities have enacted domestic partnership policies, including New York City and San Francisco. Although these policies do not legalize same-sex marriages (only the states can do that), they provide that same-sex couples will be treated the same as heterosexual couples under city ordinances and for such employment related purposes as health and **disability** benefits.

Many **corporations**, including companies such as Disney, Microsoft and IBM, also provide same-sex couples with the same benefits as married couples. This trend has grown. An estimated 52 percent of all employers offered domestic partner health benefits as of 2011. This represented a sharp increase from the previous year.

ADDITIONAL RESOURCES

Clifford, Denis, Emily Doskow, and Frederick Hertz. *A Legal Guide for Lesbian & Gay Couples.* 16th ed. Berkeley, CA: Nolo, 2012.

Mohr, Richard D. *The Long Arc of Justice: Lesbian and Gay Marriage, Equality, and Rights.* New York: Columbia University Press, 2005.

Myers, David G., and Letha Dawson Scanzoni. *What God Has Joined Together? A Christian Case for Gay Marriage.* New York: Harper, 2005.

Polikoff, Nancy D. *Beyond (Straight and Gay) Marriage: Valuing All Families Under the Law.* Boston, MA: Beacon Press, 2008.

ORGANIZATIONS

Human Rights Campaign
1640 Rhode Island Avenue NW
Washington, DC 20036-3278
Phone: (202) 628-4160
Toll Free: (800) 777-4723
Fax: (202) 347-5323
URL: http://www.hrc.org/

Lambda Legal Defense and Education Fund
120 Wall Street, Suite 1500
New York, NY 10005-3904
Phone: (212) 809-8585
Fax: (212) 809-0055
URL: http://www.lambdalegal.org/

FAMILY LAW

GRANDPARENTS' RIGHTS

Sections within this essay:

- Background
- Factors Considered for Custody or Visitation
  - Best Interests of the Child
  - Requirements for Awarding Custody to Grandparents
  - Requirements for Awarding Visitation to Grandparents
- Courts' Jurisdiction over Custody and Visitation Cases
  - Parties Residing in the Same State
  - Parties Residing in Different States
- State Provisions for Custody and Visitation
- Additional Resources

BACKGROUND

Grandparents in every state in the United States have rights, in some circumstances, to be awarded **custody** of their grandchildren or to be awarded court-mandated visitation with their grandchildren. Grandparents' rights are not constitutional in nature, nor did they exist at **common law**. Recognition of grandparents' rights by state legislatures is a fairly recent trend, and most of the statutes have been in effect for less than 50 years.

Federal legislation may affect grandparents' rights, though these rights are based primarily on state law. Congress passed the Parental **Kidnapping** Prevention Act in 1980, which requires that each state give full faith and credit to **child custody** decrees from other states.

Federal legislation passed in 1998 also requires that courts in each state recognize and enforce grandparental visitation orders from courts in other states. All states have adopted a version of the Uniform Child Custody **Jurisdiction** and Enforcement Act (UCCJEA, previously the Uniform Child Custody Jurisdiction Act), which requires courts in the state where a child resides to recognize and enforce valid child custody orders from another state. Though the UCCJEA is not a federal **statute**, the provisions of this uniform law as adopted in each state are similar.

Some courts have determined that state statutes providing visitation to grandparents are unconstitutional. The U.S. Supreme Court in the case of *Troxel v. Granville* (2000) determined that the Washington visitation statute violated the due process rights of parents to raise their children. This case and similar decisions by state courts caused several state legislatures to consider bills that would modify or completely revise the visitation rights in those states. Most state laws related to grandparent rights, however, have survived intact. Nevertheless, grandparents who seek to attain visitation rights should check the current status of state legislation in their respective states.

FACTORS CONSIDERED FOR CUSTODY OR VISITATION

Courts grant visitation or custody to grandparents only when certain conditions provided in state statutes are met. Conditions for a grandparent to attain custody differ from those conditions required for visitation rights. A grandparent should be familiar with the conditions for either custody or visitation before determining whether to file a petition to request either from a court of law.

Best Interests of the Child Courts in every jurisdiction must consider the "best interest of the child" when granting custody or visitation rights to a grandparent. In some states, the relevant statute provides a list of factors the court should consider when determining a child's best interests. Other states do not provide factors in the statute, but courts in those states typically identify factors in custody and visitation cases interpreting the state statutes.

The following factors in determining the best interest of the child are among those included in state statutes and **case law**:

- The needs of the child, including considerations of physical and emotional health of the child, the safety of the child, and the welfare of the child

- The capability of the parents and/or grandparents to meet the needs of the child

- The wishes of the parent(s) and the grandparent(s)

- The wishes of the child, if the child is capable of making decisions for himself or herself

- The strength of the relationship between the grandparent(s) and grandchild

- The length of the relationship between the grandparent(s) and grandchild

- **Evidence** of abuse or neglect by the parent(s) or grandparent(s)

- Evidence of substance abuse by the parent(s) or grandparent(s)

- The child's adjustment to the home, school, or community

- The ability of the parent(s) or grandparent(s) to provide love, affection, and contact with the child

- The distance between the child and the parent(s) or grandparent(s)

Requirements for Awarding Custody to Grandparents
Statutory Provisions for child custody (termed "conservatorship" in a few states) are usually less specific than the statutes regarding grandparent visitation. Courts must first consider the relationship of the parent or parents with the child before considering whether granting custody to grandparent(s) is appropriate. Several states specifically include consideration of grandparents as custodians if both parents are deceased. If either or both parents are alive, courts in most states will presume that the parent of the child should retain custody. Grandparents must generally prove the parent(s) unfit in order to overcome the judicial presumption in favor of the parent. Even if the relationship between the grandparent and grandchild is strong, it is very difficult for a grandparent to attain custody of a grandchild against the wishes of the parent or parents.

Requirements for Awarding Visitation to Grandparents
State statutes providing visitation to grandparents generally require that a number of conditions occur before visitation rights can be granted. The marital status of the parents must be considered in a majority of states before a court will evaluate the relevant factors to determine if visitation is appropriate. In some of these states, the parents' marital status is considered only if the grandparent or grandparents have been denied visitation by the parents. In other states, marital status is considered only if the grandchild resided with the grandparents for a certain length of time.

A minority of states require that at least one parent is deceased before a court can award visitation to the parent of the deceased parent of the child. For example, a maternal grandparent in one of these states may be awarded visitation only if the mother of the child is deceased.

State statutes vary in their treatment of cases in which a grandchild has been adopted. In several states, **adoption** by anyone, including a stepparent or another grandparent, terminates the visitation rights of the grandparent. In some states, adoption by a stepparent or another grandparent does not terminate visitation rights, but adoption by anyone else does terminate these rights. In other states, adoption has no effect on the visitation rights of grandparents, so long as other statutory requirements are met.

Once the statutory conditions for visitation are met, grandparents must establish the factors that courts may or must consider to grant visitation rights. In every state, grandparents must prove that granting visitation to the grandchild is in the best interest of the child. Several states also require that the court consider the prior relationship between the grandparent and the grandchild, the effect grandparental visitation will have on the relationship between the parent and child, and/or a showing of harm to the grandchild if visitation is not allowed.

COURTS' JURISDICTION OVER CUSTODY AND VISITATION CASES

Parties Residing in the Same State Each state provides the appropriate venue which can make custody and visitation determinations in a case where all of the parties reside in the same state. Where a **divorce** is pending, the appropriate venue for making a custody or visitation decision involving the grandparents and grandchildren is almost always the court **hearing** for the divorce proceedings. Some states require visitation petitions to be filed with another domestic relations suit. Some states also permit visitation requests after a domestic relations order has been rendered or as an original proceeding.

Parties Residing in Different States If a child's parents and/or grandparents live in different states, one of several laws will determine the appropriate court to hear a custody or visitation case. If a valid custody or visitation **decree** has been entered in one state, the Parental Kidnapping Prevention Act requires that another state must enforce and must not modify the decree. Another state may modify the decree only if the original state no longer has jurisdiction over the case or has declined jurisdiction to modify the custody or visitation decree. Congress amended this statute in 1998 to include a grandparent in the definition of "contestant."

If no state has made a valid custody determination, the provisions of the Uniform Child Custody Jurisdiction and Enforcement Act, as adopted by each state, will apply. A court in a particular state has power to hear a custody case if that state is the child's "home state" or has been the home state of the child within six months of the date the legal action was brought and at least one parent continues to reside in the state. Other situations include those in which a state with jurisdiction over a custody case declines jurisdiction or no other state may assert jurisdiction over the child.

STATE PROVISIONS FOR CUSTODY AND VISITATION

Grandparents should check a number of provisions in the statutes in their respective states to determine the conditions for visitation, the factors a court must consider to order visitation, and the proper venue to file a request for visitation. Though many state statutes are similar, state courts may apply statutory provisions differently. Every statute requires courts to consider the best interest of the child before awarding custody or visitation to grandparents.

As noted above, courts in a few states have ruled that statutes providing for grandparent visitation violate either the federal or the respective state constitutions. Several states have revised the statutory visitation provisions, but the constitutionality of these statutes may still be in question.

ALABAMA: Alabama courts struck down portions of the grandparent visitation statute as unconstitutional. The Alabama Legislature in 2003 amended the statute to comport with constitutional requirements, but in 2011, the Alabama Supreme Court ruled that the statute remained unconstitutional because it did not establish a presumption favoring parents. The Alabama Legislature

again amended the statute in 2011. Under the revised statute, a court may grant visitation to a grandparent if visitation is in the child's best interest and one of five events has occurred: (1) one or both parents of the child are deceased; (2) the marriage of the parents of the child has been dissolved; (3) a parent of the child has abandoned the child; (4) the child was born out of wedlock; or (5) the child lives with both biological parents, but one or both of the parents has prevented a grandparent from visiting the child. The state's custody statute requires courts to consider the moral character of the parents and the age and sex of the child to determine the best interests of the child.

ALASKA: Determination of grandparent visitation rights must be made in an action for divorce, legal separation, or child placement action, or when both parents have died. Adoption cuts off the visitation rights of grandparents unless the adoption decree provides for visitation between the child and the natural relatives.

ARIZONA: A court may award visitation rights if the child's parents' marriage has been dissolved for at least three months, or the child is born out of wedlock. Adoption cuts off the visitation rights of the grandparents unless the adoption is granted to a stepparent.

ARKANSAS: The custody statute requires that court grant custody "without regard to the sex of the parent but solely in accordance with the welfare and best interest of the children." Conditions for grandparent visitation rights include several circumstances where the grandchild has resided with the grandparent, the child's parents are divorced, the child is in the custody of someone other than a parent, or the child has been born out of wedlock. Adoption cuts off all visitation rights of the natural grandparents.

CALIFORNIA: Conditions for grandparent visitation rights include a determination of whether a parent is deceased, the child's parents are divorced or separated, the whereabouts of one parent is unknown, or the child is not residing with either parent. In addition to determining that visitation is in the child's best interests, the court must find that the grandparents had a preexisting relationship with the grandchild. The court must also balance visitation with the parents' rights. If both parents agree that the court should not grant visitation to the grandchild, the court will presume that visitation is not in the child's best interests. Adoption does not automatically cut off the visitation rights of grandparents. California law was amended in 2007 so that natural grandparents do not lose rights when a stepparent adopts a child.

COLORADO: A court may award visitation rights if the child's parents' marriage has been terminated, legal custody of the child has been given to a third party, the child has been placed outside the home of either of the child's parents, or the grandparent is the parent of a deceased parent of the child. Adoption cuts off the visitation rights of the grandparents unless the adoption is granted to a stepparent.

CONNECTICUT: A court may award visitation rights if visitation is in the child's best interest. Adoption does not automatically cut off the visitation rights of grandparents.

DELAWARE: A court may award visitation rights if visitation is in the child's best interest. Adoption cuts off all visitation rights of grandparents.

FLORIDA: The Florida Supreme Court has on more than one occasion ruled that the application of some provisions of the Florida statute providing grandparental visitation is unconstitutional. Under the current statute, Florida courts may award visitation to a grandparent when visitation is in the child's best interest and (1) the marriage of the child's parents has been dissolved; (2) a parent has deserted a child; or (3) the child was born out of wedlock.

GEORGIA: The custody statute does not list specific factors for the court to consider for determining the best interest of the child. A court may award visitation rights if an action is pending where there is an issue involving the custody of a minor child, divorce of the child's parents, termination of a parent's rights, or visitation rights. Adoption cuts off the visitation rights of the grandparents unless the adoption is granted to a stepparent or a natural relative of the child.

HAWAII: The custody statute requires courts to consider the child's wishes, if the child is old enough and has the capacity to reason, and evidence of any **domestic violence**, when determining the best interest of the child. A court may award visitation rights if Hawaii is the home state of the child at the time visitation is requested, and visitation is in the best interest of the child. Adoption cuts off all visitation rights of grandparents.

In 2007, the Hawaii Supreme Court ruled that lower courts must use a test under which the courts will uphold parents' wishes regarding visitation unless it would harm the child.

IDAHO: A court may award visitation rights if visitation is in the child's best interest. Adoption cuts off all visitation rights of grandparents.

ILLINOIS: In 2002, the Illinois Supreme Court determined that the Illinois Grandparent Visitation Act violated the Illinois Constitution. A new visitation statute became effective on January 1, 2005. Under the new statute, a court can grant visitation to a grandparent if visitation is in the best interest of the child and the grandparent has been unreasonably denied visitation to the child. A court may not grant visitation to a grandparent where both parents object to such visitation.

INDIANA: A court may award visitation rights if either of the child's parents is deceased, the child's parents' marriage has been terminated, or the child was born out of wedlock. In addition to considering whether visitation is in the child's best interest, a grandparent must show that he or she has had, or attempted to have, meaningful contact with the grandchild. Adoption cuts off the visitation rights of the grandparents unless the adoption is granted to a stepparent or a natural grandparent, sibling, aunt, uncle, niece, or nephew of the child.

IOWA: The custody statute requires courts to consider the best interest of the child that will provide the "maximum continuing physical and emotional contact with both parents." The Iowa Supreme Court has ruled on more than one occasion that the Iowa statute providing grandparental visitation is unconstitutional, but the Iowa Legislature adopted a new statute in 2007.

KANSAS: A court may award visitation rights in a custody order. Adoption cuts off the visitation rights of the grandparents unless the grandparent is the parent of a deceased parent and the surviving parent's spouse adopts the child.

KENTUCKY: A court may award visitation rights if visitation would be in the child's best interest. A court may award a grandparent the same visitation rights as a parent without custody if the grandparent's child is deceased and the grandparent has provided **child support** to the grandchild. Adoption cuts off the visitation rights of grandparents unless the adoption is granted to a stepparent, and the grandparent's child has not had his or her parental rights terminated.

LOUISIANA: A court may award visitation rights if the child's parent is deceased or declared legally incompetent, a grandparent is the parent of the deceased or incompetent parent to the grandchild, and visitation is in the child's best interest. Adoption cuts off the visitation rights of grandparents except in circumstances where the grandparents are the parents of a deceased party to the marriage or the parents of a party who has forfeited his or her rights to object to the child's adoption.

MAINE: A court may award visitation right if at least one of the child's parents is deceased, visitation is in the child's best interest, and visitation will not interfere significantly with the relationship between the parent and the child. Adoption cuts off all visitation rights of grandparents.

MARYLAND: The custody statute does not provide a list of factors for determining the best interest of the child. A court may award visitation rights if visitation is in the child's best interest. The factors for determining the child's best interest have been set forth in case law. Adoption cuts off all visitation rights of grandparents.

MASSACHUSETTS: The custody statute does not provide a list of factors for determining the best interest of the child. A court may award visitation rights if the child's parents' marriage is terminated, the parents are separated, one of the parents is deceased, or the child was born out of wedlock and **paternity** has been established. Adoption cuts off the visitation rights of grandparents unless the adoption is granted to a stepparent.

MICHIGAN: A court may award visitation rights if the child's parents' marriage is terminated, the parents separate, or custody of the child is given to a third party other than the child's parents. Adoption cuts off the visitation rights of grandparents unless the adoption is granted to a stepparent. The Michigan legislature in 2005 adopted a new statute after several cases struck down the prior law.

MINNESOTA: A court may award visitation rights if a child's parent is deceased and the grandparents are the parents of the deceased parent. Visitation may also be granted during or after divorce, custody, separation, **annulment**, or paternity proceedings. Adoption cuts off the visitation rights of grandparents unless the adoption is granted to a stepparent or another grandparent.

MISSISSIPPI: The custody statute does not provide a list of factors for determining the best interest of the child. If the child is at least 12 years old, he or she may choose who takes custody. Conditions for grandparent visitation rights include determination of whether one of the child's parents is deceased, or a parent has had his or her parental rights terminated. The court must also consider the relationship between the grandparent and grandchild. Adoption cuts off the visitation rights of grandparents unless the adoption is granted to a stepparent or a blood relative.

MISSOURI: A court may award visitation rights if the child's parents have filed for divorce, one parent is deceased and the other parent has unreasonably denied visitation to the grandparent, or when a parent or parents unreasonably deny visitation to a grandparent for more than 90 days. Adoption cuts off the visitation rights of grandparents unless adoption is granted to a stepparent, another grandparent, or a blood relative.

MONTANA: A court may award visitation rights if the court finds that visitation is in the child's best interest. Adoption cuts off the visitation rights of grandparents unless adoption is granted to a stepparent or another grandparent.

NEBRASKA: A court may award visitation rights if at least one parent is deceased, the parents' marriage has been dissolved or a petition for **dissolution** has been filed, or the child is born out of wedlock and paternity has been established. Grandparents must demonstrate that a beneficial relationship exists between themselves and the grandchild and that visitation is in the child's best interest. Visitation cannot interfere with the parent-child relationship. Adoption cuts off all visitation rights of grandparents.

NEVADA: A court may award visitation rights if the child's parents are deceased, the child's parents are divorced or separated, or one of the child's parents have had his or her parental rights terminated. The child's parent or parents must have unreasonably restricted visitation between the grandparent and grandchild before a court may award visitation to a grandparent. If a child's parent or parents has denied or unreasonably restricted access to a grandparent, a court will presume that visitation is not in the child's best interest. Adoption cuts off all rights of grandparents unless grandparents request visitation before the termination of the parental rights of the child's parent or parents.

NEW HAMPSHIRE: A court may award visitation rights if the child's parents are divorced or have filed for divorce, one of the parents is deceased, one of the parents has had his or her parental rights terminated, or the child has been born out of wedlock, if the child has been legitimated. Adoption cuts off all rights of grandparents.

NEW JERSEY: A court may grant visitation rights if visitation is in the child's best interest. Adoption cuts off the rights of grandparents, unless adoption is granted to a stepparent.

NEW MEXICO: A court may grant visitation rights if the child's parents are divorced, separated, or deceased. Visitation rights may also be granted if the child is over six years old, lived with the grandparent for more than six months, and was subsequently removed from the grandparent's home (if the child is under six, the residence requirement is reduced to three months). Adoption cuts off the rights of grandparents unless adoption is granted to a stepparent, a relative of the child, a caretaker designated in a deceased parent's will, or a person who sponsored the child at a baptism or confirmation.

NEW YORK: The custody statute does not provide statutory factors for determining the best interest of the child. A court may grant visitation rights if at least one of the child's parents is deceased or if the court finds that equity demands intervention based on the circumstances of the case. Adoption does not automatically cut off the visitation rights of grandparents.

NORTH CAROLINA: The custody statute does not provide statutory factors for determining the best interest of the child. A court may grant visitation rights as part of an order determining custody of the child. Adoption cuts off the visitation rights of grandparents unless adoption is granted to a stepparent or a relative of the child, where the grandparent proves that a substantial relationship exists between the grandparent and grandchild.

NORTH DAKOTA: A court must grant visitation rights unless the court determines that visitation would not be in the child's best interest. The amount of contact between the child, the grandparent, and the parent are factors to be considered when determining the child's best interest. Adoption cuts off the rights of grandparents, unless visitation was granted prior to the adoption.

OHIO: A court may grant visitation rights if the child's parents are deceased, divorced, separated, were parties to a suit for annulment or child support, or were never married to one another. Grandparents must show they have an interest in the child's welfare. Adoption cuts off the visitation rights of grandparents unless adoption is granted to a stepparent.

OKLAHOMA: A court may grant visitation rights if visitation is in the child's best interest. The statute provides special rules when the child is born out of wedlock. Adoption cuts off the visitation rights of grandparents unless the grandparents can show a previous relationship existed between them and the grandchild, and visitation is in the child's best interest.

OREGON: Determination of grandparent visitation rights include consideration of the relationship between the grandparent and grandchild, as well as the relationship between the parent and child. Adoption cuts off all visitation rights of grandparents.

PENNSYLVANIA: A court may grant visitation if at least one of the child's parents is deceased, the parents are divorced or separated for more than six months, or the child has lived with the grandparent for more than 12 months. Determination of grandparent visitation must include consideration of the best interest of the child, potential interference with the parent-child relationship, and the contact between the grandparent and grandchild. Adoption cuts off visitation rights of grandparents unless adoption is granted to a stepparent or grandparent.

RHODE ISLAND: The custody statute does not provide statutory factors for determining the best interest of the child. Determination of grandparent visitation must include consideration of the relationship of the grandparent and grandchild, including the best interest of the child. Courts may also grant visitation if the child's parents are divorced or the parent who is the child of the grandparent is deceased. Adoption cuts off all visitation rights.

SOUTH CAROLINA: A court may grant visitation if one parent is deceased, or the parents are divorced or separated. The court must consider the relationship between the grandparent and the child, as well as the parent and the child. Adoption cuts off all visitation rights of grandparents.

SOUTH DAKOTA: The custody statute does not provide statutory factors for a court to determine proper custody. A court may grant visitation if one parent is deceased, or the parents are divorced or separated. Adoption cuts off the visitation rights of grandparents unless adoption is granted to a stepparent or grandparent of the child.

TENNESSEE: Tennessee courts held that the previous version of the grandparent visitation statute was unconstitutional. The Tennessee Legislature amended the statute to comport with the state constitution. Under the revised statute, a court may grant visitation rights to a grandparent only in one of the following situations: (1) the mother or father of the child is deceased; (2) the child's parents are divorced or were never married to one another; (3) the child's mother or father has been missing for the preceding six months;

(4) a court in another state has ordered grandparent visitation; (5) the child previously lived with the grandparent for 12 months or more; (6) the child and grandparent(s) maintained a significant relationship for 12 months. If one of these events occurs, the court may award visitation rights if the child is in danger of substantial harm should the court deny visitation and visitation is in the best interests of the child.

TEXAS: The custody statute does not provide statutory factors for a court to determine proper custody. Conditions for grandparent visitation rights include a determination that one of the child's parents is deceased, incompetent, incarcerated, or has had his or her parental rights terminated. Visitation may also be awarded if the parents are divorced, the child has been abused or neglected, the child has been adjudicated a delinquent or in need of supervision, or the child has lived with the grandparent for at least six months within 24 months of the filing of the petition for visitation. Adoption cuts off the visitation rights of the grandparent unless the adoption is granted to a stepparent.

UTAH: Conditions for grandparent visitation rights include whether a parent is deceased, or whether the parents are divorced or separated. Adoption cuts off all visitation rights of grandparents.

VERMONT: Conditions for grandparent visitation rights include consideration of whether a parent is deceased or incompetent, or whether the child has been abandoned. Adoption cuts off all visitation rights of grandparents unless the adoption is granted to a stepparent or a relative of the child.

VIRGINIA: Determination of grandparent visitation is made during a suit for dissolution of the marriage of the child's parents. Adoption cuts off all visitation rights of grandparents.

WASHINGTON: The U.S. Supreme Court case of *Troxel v. Granville* ruled the Washington grandparent visitation statute unconstitutional. Although the Washington legislature subsequently amended the statute, the Washington Supreme Court in 2005 struck down the new law. Moreover, the Washington legislature has failed to enact a new law to replace the one struck down in 2005.

WEST VIRGINIA: The custody statute does not provide statutory factors for a court to determine proper custody. Conditions for grandparent visitation rights include

consideration of whether a parent is deceased, the child has resided with the grandparent and subsequently was removed by a parent, or the grandparent in several circumstances has been denied visitation by a parent. Adoption cuts off all visitation rights of grandparents.

WISCONSIN: Conditions for grandparent visitation rights include consideration of the relationship between the grandparent and grandchild. Visitation may also be permitted if one of the child's parents is deceased. Adoption cuts off the visitation rights of grandparents unless adoption is granted to a stepparent.

WYOMING: The custody statute does not provide statutory factors for a court to determine proper custody. Conditions for grandparent visitation rights include consideration of the child's best interest and the impairment of the rights of the parents.

ADDITIONAL RESOURCES

Katz, Sanford N. *Family Law in America*. New York: Oxford University Press, 2011.

Strauss, Carol Ann. *Grandparents: An Annotated Bibliography on Roles, Rights, and Relationships*. Lanham, MD: Scarecrow Press, 1996.

Truly, Tracy. *Grandparents' Right: Your Legal Guide to Protecting Your Relationship with Your Grandchildren*. 4th ed. Naperville, Ill.: SphinxLegal, 2005.

Warren, Kristine Taylor. *Grandparents' Visitation Rights: A Legal Research Guide*. Buffalo, NY: W.S. Hein & Co., Inc., 2001.

ORGANIZATIONS

AARP (American Association of Retired Persons)
601 E. St. NW
Washington, DC 20049
Toll Free: (888) 687-2277
URL: http://www.aarp.org

Association for Conflict Resolution (ACR)
12100 Sunset Hills Rd., Suite #130
Reston, VA 20190
Phone: (703) 234-4141
URL: http://www.acrnet.org/

Grandparent Rights Organization (GRO)
100 West Long Lake Rd., Ste. 250
Bloomfield Hills, MI 48304
Phone: (248) 646-7191
Fax: (248) 646-9722
URL: http://www.grandparentsrights.org

FAMILY LAW

GUARDIANSHIP

Sections within this essay:

BACKGROUND

A guardian is someone who is chosen, either by a court or by being named in a will, to make decisions for someone else when that person—generally referred to as the ward—cannot do the same for him or herself. These types of decisions include: giving consent to medical care or treatment; purchasing or arranging for purchase of such necessities as food, clothes, cars, household items, and other personal items; arranging for education; and managing finances and bank accounts.

A **guardianship** requires that someone act on behalf of and protect the ward during the period of time when the ward is incapable of doing so. When the court appoints a guardian in a particular situation, the court must be sure that the potential ward is

incapacitated and cannot make decisions for him or herself because of a mental or physical **disability**, disease, or addiction to alcohol or other drugs. The fact that potential wards are minors who lack someone to make certain decisions on their behalf until they reach the **age of majority** is also sufficient reason to ask the court to appoint a guardian.

The selection of a guardian is an extremely important task. Certain people with ties to the ward are preferred by courts as possible guardians. These include the person designated by the ward, before the period of incapacity occurred, by legal document or otherwise to handle his or her affairs; the spouse, parents, or another relative; or a state employee or private person familiar with the ward and the incapacity at issue. Whoever is chosen by the court must be willing and able to perform the duties at hand and to represent the best interests of the ward. In selecting the guardian, the court considers the prospective guardian's character, history, physical capacity, and other relevant attributes. A potential guardian's limited education or financial resources are not disqualifying conditions in and of themselves.

The guardianship statutes of each state detail the specific duties, responsibilities, and powers of the guardian. They should be examined in order to determine the regulations that apply to each situation.

GUARDIANSHIP OF MINORS

The guardianship of a minor can be over the actual minor (or what is commonly referred to as the minor's person), the property (or estate) of the minor, or both. Preferred guardians for a minor are parents and then other relatives. However, the primary consideration in selecting a guardian is the best interests of the minor. If the parents are still alive, before a nonparent is chosen as a guardian, the parents must be determined to be unable or unfit to look after the best interests of the minor. When minors are removed from the care and supervision of their parents, and **adoption** is either not forthcoming or not a viable option, guardianship is considered a reasonable alternative.

Even after a guardian is chosen for a minor, most state statutes allow that at age fourteen (or other reasonable age), the minor may select or at least voice a preference concerning who will be selected to serve a guardian.

The guardian of a minor looks after the direct physical well-being of the minor and the assets of the minor's estate. A guardian is also necessary to provide a **legal residence** in order for the ward to attend a public school; to apply for public assistance benefits for a minor if needed; to apply for public housing on behalf of a minor where necessary; and to bring a lawsuit on behalf of the minor. The guardian also receives and maintains any money due the minor for his or her care or support. The guardian is required to maintain, account for, and preserve any excess funds beyond what is necessary to support the minor. The guardian has a duty to look after the minor's **personal property** and assure the proper education of the ward. The guardian is also required to authorize any necessary medical or other care for the well-being and health of the ward. Generally, the guardian provides whatever care would be given to a child by its parents.

When a guardianship of a minor is instituted because of the age of the ward, the guardianship may be terminated when the minor reaches the age of majority. The guardianship may be reinstated by the court after the ward reaches the age of majority where it can be shown that the ward still requires supervision. Guardianship may be terminated if the ward marries. Guardianship is automatically terminated at the death of the ward. In addition, the guardianship may be terminated, and a new guardian appointed, when it can be shown that the guardian did not adequately perform his or her duties to the ward.

GUARDIANSHIP OF ADULTS

Every state allows courts to appoint a guardian or conservator (which essentially mean the same thing) for those who are no longer able to make decisions on their own. This is typical when the incapacitated person has not planned ahead by signing a durable **power of attorney** for finances and/or health care. Although the appointment of a guardian or conservator is generally common, the job of the guardian or conservator is time-consuming, and the process in general is expensive.

As of 2012, 34 states had adopted the Adult Guardianship and Protective Proceedings **Jurisdiction** Act, and more states had considered bills that would adopt the act. Additionally, the majority of states in the early 2010s considered reforms to their adult guardianship statutes.

TESTAMENTARY GUARDIANSHIP

Generally, parents may, in a properly drafted will, appoint or indicate their preference for a guardian for a minor child or an adult child with a disability who requires supervision over his or her person or estate. Courts will then make a determination as to the availability or appropriateness of the parents' selection.

TEMPORARY GUARDIANSHIP

Some state statutes provide for temporary or limited guardianships. These guardianships are generally granted by the courts to achieve a specific purpose for a certain amount of time. Once the purpose is accomplished, the guardianship is terminated.

Also, emergency guardianships have been granted. In these situations, an emergency situation exists and someone is needed to give approval in order for the person to receive emergency services. A temporary guardian is appointed by the court to serve during the existence of the emergency situation. Generally, the person being served by the temporary guardian is disabled or incapacitated in some way. The court must determine that the person being served by the guardian is unable to make the emergency decision because of mental disability, addiction, debilitating disease, or some other similar limitation. The court must also determine that if a guardian is not appointed, the person is at risk of serious harm or even death. Finally, the court must determine that there is no other person available who can make the emergency determination for the incapacitated person.

The order for emergency guardianship is generally granted for a short period of time which is sufficient to allow the situation to be handled properly. After the emergency situation has ended or subsided, the temporary guardian must file a report with the court detailing the nature of the services rendered by the guardian and describing the outcome of the situation.

GUARDIANSHIP OF PERSONS WHO ARE MENTALLY OR PHYSICALLY INCAPACITATED OR DISABLED

State statutes define mental and physical disability. However, generally, such disability or incapacity involves severe and long-term conditions that impose great limitations upon individuals' ability to take care of themselves, express themselves verbally, earn a living, and live independently of the care of others. Such a disability also reflects the necessity for a combination of treatments and services.

Guardianships for physically or mentally disabled or incapacitated persons have been understood to facilitate the independence and self-reliance of the ward. They are limited as much as is reasonable in order to allow wards to exercise as much control over their lives as possible while maintaining as much dignity and self-reliance as possible. The desires of the wards are given primary consideration. Also, wards are allowed to do as much of their own care giving as is physically and mentally possible.

The guardian will be granted only those powers necessary to accomplish for the ward what the ward cannot accomplish independently. These powers may include assuring the availability and maintenance of care for the ward, making sure that educational and medical services are maintained and adequate, and submitting updates to the court of the ward's condition. These court updates describe the ward's living situation and the status of mental and physical health based upon medical examinations and official records, provide a list of services being received by the ward, describe services rendered by the guardian, account for the ward's monetary assets, and provide any other information necessary to submit to the court in order for it to assess the status of the ward and the guardian's duties.

REMOVAL OF GUARDIAN

A guardian may be removed if a court determines that the ward no longer needs the services of the guardian. Also, a guardian may be removed when he or she has not provided adequate care for the ward or when it is determined that the guardian is guilty of neglect. Neglect can include using the ward's money or property for the guardian's own benefit and not obeying court orders. Upon court order, the guardian will be removed and a new guardian (or temporary guardian) will be substituted in place of the original guardian.

EXAMINATION OF CERTAIN STATE PROVISIONS ON GUARDIANSHIP

FLORIDA: The **statute** on guardianships for incapacitated persons requires that the court find the "least restrictive form of guardianship to assist persons who are only partially incapable of caring for their needs." The statute also confirms the legislative intent that incapacitated persons function and live as independently as possible, managing their finances and developing their potential for self-sufficiency. To that end, they will be encouraged to develop their living skills to the extent that they may, for

example, be able to marry, vote, travel, sign contracts, complete their educational objectives, and apply for a driver's license.

MASSACHUSETTS: Regarding the guardian of a minor, the statute states that the court will choose the guardian for any minor under the age of fourteen. A minor over the age of fourteen may suggest his or her own guardian and the court will try to honor that request. If the court does not find the guardian desired by the minor to be appropriate, then the court will appoint another guardian. Regarding the care of a mentally ill person by a guardian, the statute declares that a guardian will not have the authority to commit the ward to a mental institution or agree to the administering of "antipsychotic medication" unless the court first finds that such an action is in the "best interests" of the ward and then authorizes such a commitment or treatment. Regarding testamentary guardians, the statute allows parents to appoint such a guardian on behalf of a minor child, even if the child is not born at the time the testamentary instrument is drafted. Such a testamentary guardian will have the same powers and duties as one appointed by the court.

NEW HAMPSHIRE: Regarding the duties of a guardian for a minor, the guardian will "protect and preserve" the personal and real property assets of the minor and any income that comes from rents, income, or the sale of such property. The guardian is also given the authority, with the court's approval, to open a **trust** to which the minor's assets can be transferred. This trust would end no later than the ward's twenty-fifth birthday.

SOUTH CAROLINA: Regarding persons with disabilities, the spouse (if the incapacitated person is married) or parents of an incapacitated person may make a testamentary appointment of a guardian for the incapacitated person in their will. Such an appointment by a spouse or parent becomes effective after the incapacitated person and the person giving him or her care or the "nearest adult relative" has received twenty days written notice and "the guardian files acceptance of appointment in the court." When both a spouse and a parent appoint guardians in their **wills**, the appointment of the spouse has priority.

TEXAS: The Texas Legislature in 2011 approved several revisions related to adult guardianship. Many of these revisions provide procedural protections. When a person submits a petition to become another's guardian, the alleged incapacitated person and other interested parties are entitled to notice so that they can respond. The law also allows the alleged incapacitated person to retain his or her own attorney, without having to be represented by an attorney ad litem, who is typically appointed by the court.

ADDITIONAL RESOURCES

De Witt, John Gregory, Peter N. Swisher, and Sheryl L. Wolf. *Understanding Family Law.* 3d ed. Newark, NJ: LexisNexis, 2005.

Katz, Sanford N. *Family Law in America.* New York: Oxford University Press, 2011.

Oliphant, Robert E., and Nancy Ver Steegh. *Family Law: Examples and Explanations.* 3d ed. New York: Aspen Publishers, 2010.

ORGANIZATIONS

Administration for Children and Families, U.S. Department of Health and Human Services

370 L'Enfant Promenade SW
Washington, DC 20447

Phone: (202) 401-2337
URL: http://www.acf.gov

American Bar Association (ABA)

321 North Clark Street
Chicago, IL 60610
Phone: (312) 988-5000
Toll Free: (800) 285-2221
Fax: (312) 988-6800
URL: http://www.americanbar.org

National Guardianship Association (NGA)

174 Crestview Drive
Bellefonte, PA 16823-8516
Toll Free: (877) 326-5992
Fax: (814) 355-2452
URL: http://www.guardianship.org/

FAMILY LAW

MARRIAGE/MARRIAGE AGE

Sections within this essay:

- Background
- Consent
- Age
- Capacity
- Marriage Between Close Relatives
- Common Law Marriage
- Interracial Marriage
- Polygamy
- Same-Sex Marriage
- Change of Last Name
- State by State Summary (Age of Consent, Etc.)
- Additional Resources

BACKGROUND

Marriage requirements are defined by the laws of each state. Yet there are certain aspects of a valid marriage that are required of any couple. These additional considerations include the capacity of the parties to enter into the marriage, the consent of the parties, and the age of each person. Regarding age, if individuals are minors, they must obtain the consent of either one or both of their parents, depending upon the laws of the state.

The fact that the states can regulate marriage has given rise to laws that control other aspects of the ability of a couple to wed including the sex of each party and whether either party is already married. Although the states have the authority to regulate the institution of marriage and establish the laws that do so, some laws, such as those forbidding people of different races to marry, have been struck down by the Supreme Court of the United States as unconstitutional. The Congress of the United States has also enacted limitations to the marital union, the most recent being the enactment of DOMA, which not only defines marriage but also gives individual states the right not to recognize "a relationship between persons of the same sex that is treated as a marriage under the laws of such other State." In other words, such laws from one state do not have to be recognized by another state.

Marriage has traditionally been defined as a **contract** between a man and a woman who have consented to become husband and wife. In 1996, Congress passed the Defense of Marriage Act (DOMA), which defined marriage as "a legal union between one man and one woman as husband and wife." However, several lower federal courts as of 2012 had struck down parts of DOMA, and President Barack Obama instructed the Justice Department to cease defending the law in court. Six states recognize same-sex marriage, and a growing number of states have considered proposals that would allow it. However, 39 states continue to prohibit same-sex marriage either through **statute** or constitutional provision.

Because the laws regarding marriage vary considerably from state to state, couples desiring more specific information should contact their state government.

CONSENT

Before a marital union is recognized by a state, the parties of the union must, foremost, consent to be married. For consent to exist, both parties must agree to the marriage and there must be no mistake as to the nature of the union. In addition, no force must be used upon either party to enter into the union. Once consent is determined to exist, the laws of the individual states determine the status of the couple as husband and wife.

AGE

Age is an additional aspect of consent to marry. All states prescribe the age which must be reached by both parties to the marriage for the couple to be able to legally agree to become husband and wife without parental permission. For all but two states this "age of consent" is eighteen. In Mississippi, the age is 21, and in Nebraska, the age is 19.

The states vary in determining the minimum age at which a couple can marry with parental consent. For the majority of states, this age is sixteen, though in a very few states, this age is as low as fourteen.

CAPACITY

Capacity generally refers to the mental ability of one or both of the parties to the marriage to agree to become husband and wife. Both parties must be of "sound" mind and capable of agreeing to the marriage. Not all forms of mental illness and insanity serve to render someone incapable of entering into a marriage. A common test of capacity is the ability of individuals to understand the nature of marriage and what their responsibilities are to their partners once they enter into the union. Physical incapacity, and in particular the physical inability to have sexual intercourse, does not in and of itself render one incapable of marrying and does not on its face void a marriage that has already occurred.

MARRIAGE BETWEEN CLOSE RELATIVES

The laws of each state strictly regulate the marriage between relatives (also known as consanguinity). According to the "rules of consanguinity," no state allows marriage to a child, grandchild, parent, grandparent, uncle, aunt, niece, or nephew. However, for all other familial relationships, the states vary widely and the particular laws of the state of marriage must be consulted.

COMMON LAW MARRIAGE

Though laws regarding marriage are well regulated by the states, at one point, most state laws allowed for the institution of **common law** marriage. Common law marriages were based not just on the desire of the couple to live together or by their actually living or having lived together. For a common law marriage to achieve validity as a marriage, the couple must have lived together for a certain amount of time, had sexual relations, and represented themselves as husband and wife in all affairs

and to all people. Though no marriage ceremony had taken place, their children are viewed as legitimate and surviving families are entitled to state sanctioned **inheritance**.

Currently, the majority of states do not recognize common law marriage. Three states that do not recognize common law marriages (Georgia, Idaho, and Indiana) recognize unions that were entered into before certain dates (for Georgia and Idaho the year is 1997, for Indiana the year is 1958).

INTERRACIAL MARRIAGE

There are no prohibitions to interracial unions in the United States. At one time, many states had enacted statutes forbidding marriages between people of different races. Such a mixed-race union is also known as "miscegenation." These antimiscegenation statutes were found across the United States and particularly in Southern states. Though most states had repealed such laws by the time of the case of *Loving v. Virginia*, in 1967 the U.S. Supreme Court, in deciding that case, decreed all such laws to be unconstitutional because they violated the Equal Protection Clause of the U.S. Constitution.

POLYGAMY

Polygamy occurs when a spouse is married to more than one person at the same time. Polygamous marriages have been illegal in the United States since 1878 when the U.S. Supreme Court ruled that one of the basic tenets of Western civilization was the marriage of one man to one woman. Therefore, anyone who marries for the second time without ending a first marriage could be charged with polygamy.

SAME-SEX MARRIAGE

Traditionally in the United States, the marital union has been confined to a relationship between a man and a woman. That notion has been challenged in several states, culminating in Massachusetts becoming the first state to allow same-sex marriage. In response to these and other challenges, at least twenty-five states have passed marriage laws prohibiting same sex marriages. In almost as many states, bills prohibiting same sex/gay marriage have been defeated. In 1996, the Congress of the United States passed the Defense of Marriage Act (DOMA). This act defines the word marriage as a "legal union between one man and one woman as husband and wife." In addition, in response to the possibility that some states would recognize a same sex relationship as a marriage while others would not, DOMA determines that other states do not have to "give effect to" or recognize "a right or claim arising from" such unions which may be legal in other states.

On July 1, 2000, the state of Vermont enacted a law, the first in the country, permitting same sex couples to be parties to a "civil union." These unions, though not technically marriages, give same sex couples all the "benefits, protections, and responsibilities under Vermont law . . . as are granted to spouses in a marriage." This law also allows parties who reside outside Vermont to enter the state to achieve a civil union. However, in accordance with DOMA, other states are not required to recognize these unions.

President Obama stated that he believes DOMA is unconstitutional, and in 2012, he became the first sitting president to publicly support same-sex marriage.

Vermont spurred activists in other states to champion not just civil unions but same-sex marriage. As of 2012, the states of Connecticut, Iowa, Massachusetts, New Hampshire, Maine, Maryland, Washington, and New York, as well as the District of Columbia, joined Vermont in recognizing same-sex marriages. Other states have considered proposals that would allow same-sex marriage or have had the issue argued in the state courts. On the other hand, a large number of states have enacted bans on same-sex marriage through provisions in state constitutions or through statute. Many of these states also ban forms of same-sex unions.

CHANGE OF LAST NAME
A woman is not legally required to change her last name to that of her husband upon her marriage.

STATE BY STATE SUMMARY (AGE OF CONSENT, ETC.)
The following is a state by state summary of the "age of consent" for marriage and other pertinent marriage information for the fifty states, the District of Columbia, and Puerto Rico.

ALABAMA: The **age of consent** is eighteen. With parental consent, parties can marry at age fourteen. However, this parental consent is not required if the minor has already been married. (Other **statutory** laws apply.) Common law marriage is recognized.

ALASKA: The age of consent is eighteen. With parental consent, parties can marry at age sixteen. Parties can marry at a younger age, also with parental consent. Common law marriage is not recognized.

ARIZONA: The age of consent is eighteen. With parental consent, parties can marry at the age of sixteen. Parties can marry at a younger age, but with both parental and judicial consent.

ARKANSAS: The age of consent is eighteen. With parental consent, males can marry at the age of seventeen and under the age of seventeen can marry with parental consent and can receive a license by reason of pregnancy or the birth of a child. With parental consent, females can marry at age sixteen and under the age of sixteen can marry with parental consent and can receive a license by reason of pregnancy or the birth of a child.

CALIFORNIA: The age of consent is eighteen. With parental consent, there are no age limits regarding the minimum age for a couple to marry. (Other statutory laws apply.) California offers some spousal rights for registered same-sex domestic partners.

COLORADO: The age of consent is eighteen. Parties can marry at a younger age, also with parental consent. Common law marriage is recognized.

CONNECTICUT: The age of consent is eighteen. With parental consent, parties can marry at the age of sixteen. Parties can marry at a younger age, but with both parental and judicial consent. Like Vermont, Connecticut permits same sex couples to be parties to a "civil union."

DELAWARE: The age of consent is eighteen. Males can marry under the age of eighteen with parental consent and under the age of seventeen can receive a license by reason of pregnancy or the birth of a child. With parental consent, females can marry at age sixteen and under the age of sixteen can apply for and receive a license by reason of pregnancy or the birth of a child. Common law marriage is not recognized.

DISTRICT OF COLUMBIA: The age of consent is eighteen. With parental consent, parties can marry at age sixteen. However, this parental consent is not required if the minor has already been married. The District of Columbia offers some rights to registered same-sex domestic partners. Common law marriage is recognized.

FLORIDA: The age of consent is eighteen. With parental consent, parties can marry at age sixteen and parties under the age of sixteen can receive a license by reason of pregnancy or the birth of a child. However, this parental consent is not required if the minor has already been married. Common law marriage is not recognized.

GEORGIA: The age of consent is eighteen. With parental consent and/or the consent of a judge, parties can marry at age sixteen and under the age of sixteen can apply for and receive a license by reason of pregnancy or the birth of a child. Common law marriages are not recognized except for those that were entered into before 1997.

HAWAII: The age of consent is eighteen. With parental consent and/or the consent of a judge, parties can marry at age fifteen. Hawaii offers some spousal rights for registered same-sex domestic partners. Common law marriage is not recognized.

IDAHO: The age of consent is eighteen. With parental consent, parties can marry at age sixteen. Common law marriages are not recognized except for those that were entered into before 1997.

ILLINOIS: The age of consent is eighteen. With parental consent, parties can marry at age sixteen. If parents refuse to consent, judicial consent may be obtained on behalf of the parties. Common law marriage is not recognized.

INDIANA: The age of consent is eighteen. With parental consent, parties can marry at age seventeen and under the age of seventeen can receive a license by reason of pregnancy or the birth of a child. Common law marriages are not recognized except for those that were entered into before 1958.

IOWA: The age of consent is eighteen. With parental consent and/or the consent of a judge, parties can marry at age sixteen. Common law marriage is recognized.

KANSAS: The age of consent is eighteen. With parental consent and/or the consent of a judge, males can marry at age fourteen and females at age twelve. Common law marriage is recognized.

KENTUCKY: The age of consent is eighteen. With parental consent and/or the consent of a judge, parties can marry under eighteen years of age. Common law marriage is not recognized.

LOUISIANA: The age of consent is eighteen. Parties under eighteen years of age can marry with parental consent. Common law marriage is not recognized.

MAINE: The age of consent is eighteen. With parental consent, parties can marry at age sixteen. Maine offers some spousal rights to registered same-sex domestic partners. Common law marriage is not recognized.

MARYLAND: The age of consent is eighteen. With parental consent, parties can marry at age sixteen and younger parties may receive a license by reason of

pregnancy or the birth of a child. Parties giving consent must appear in person to give consent and provide proof of age if the parties seeking marriage are at least sixteen years old. Also, if one of the parents giving consent is ill, both an **affidavit** by the ill parent and from a physician are required to submit. Common law marriage is recognized.

MASSACHUSETTS: The age of consent is eighteen. With parental consent and/or the consent of a judge, males can marry at fourteen years of age and females can marry at the age of twelve. On May 17, 2004, Massachusetts became the first state to recognize same-sex marriage. Common law marriage is not recognized.

MICHIGAN: The age of consent is eighteen. With parental consent, parties can marry at age sixteen. Common law marriage is not recognized.

MINNESOTA: The age of consent is eighteen. With parental consent and/or the consent of the judge, parties can marry at age sixteen. Common law marriage is not recognized.

MISSISSIPPI: The age of consent is twenty-one. With parental consent and/or the consent of the judge, males can marry at age seventeen and females can marry at age fifteen. Common law marriage is not recognized.

MISSOURI: The age of consent is eighteen. With parental consent, parties can marry at age fifteen and younger parties may receive a license by reason of special circumstances. Common law marriage is not recognized.

MONTANA: The age of consent is eighteen. With parental consent and/or consent of a judge, parties can marry at age sixteen and younger parties may receive a license by reason of special circumstances. Common law marriage is recognized.

NEBRASKA: The age of consent is nineteen. With parental consent, parties can marry at age seventeen. Common law marriage is not recognized.

NEVADA: The age of consent is eighteen. With parental consent, parties can marry at age sixteen and younger. Common law marriage is not recognized.

NEW HAMPSHIRE: The age of consent is eighteen. With parental consent and the consent of the judge, males can marry at age fourteen and females can marry at age thirteen. Common law marriage is not recognized.

NEW JERSEY: The age of consent is eighteen. With parental consent, parties can marry at age sixteen or younger. Also, younger parties may receive a license by reason of pregnancy or the birth of a child or other special circumstances. New Jersey offers some spousal rights to registered same-sex domestic partners. Common law marriage is not recognized.

NEW MEXICO: The age of consent is eighteen. With parental consent, parties can marry at age sixteen and younger parties may receive a license by reason of pregnancy or the birth of a child or other special circumstances. Common law marriage is not recognized.

NEW YORK: The age of consent is eighteen. With parental and judicial consent, parties can marry at age sixteen. Common law marriage is not recognized.

NORTH CAROLINA: The age of consent is eighteen. With parental consent, parties can marry at age sixteen and younger parties may receive a license by reason of pregnancy or the birth of a child. Common law marriage is not recognized.

NORTH DAKOTA: The age of consent is eighteen. With parental consent, parties can marry at age sixteen. Common law marriage is not recognized.

OHIO: The age of consent is eighteen. With parental consent, males under the age of 18 can marry and females at age sixteen can marry and younger parties may receive a license by reason of pregnancy or the birth of a child. Common law marriage is not recognized.

OKLAHOMA: The age of consent is eighteen. With parental consent, parties can marry at age sixteen (and younger) and, in addition, younger parties may receive a license by reason of pregnancy or the birth of a child. Common law marriage is recognized.

OREGON: The age of consent is eighteen. With parental consent, parties can marry at age seventeen with the exception that if one party does not have a parent who resides in the state and one party has been a resident in Oregon for at least six months, then no permission is necessary. Common law marriage is not recognized.

PENNSYLVANIA: The age of consent is eighteen. With parental consent, parties can marry at age sixteen and younger parties may receive a license by reason of special circumstances. Common law marriage is recognized.

PUERTO RICO: The age of consent is twenty-one for males. The age of consent is also twenty-one for females who may apply for and receive a license at a younger age by reason of pregnancy or the birth of a child. Male applicants eighteen years of age and female applicants sixteen years of age may marry with parental consent. Younger males and females can marry with parental consent and receive a license by reason of pregnancy, the birth of a child, or other special circumstances. Common law marriage is not recognized.

RHODE ISLAND: The age of consent is eighteen. With parental consent, males can marry under age eighteen and females at sixteen and younger parties may receive a license under special circumstances. Common law marriage is recognized.

SOUTH CAROLINA: The age of consent is eighteen. With parental consent, males can marry at age sixteen and females at age fourteen and younger parties may receive a license by reason of pregnancy or the birth of a child. Common law marriage is recognized.

SOUTH DAKOTA: The age of consent is eighteen. With parental consent, parties can marry at age sixteen and younger parties may receive a license by reason of pregnancy or the birth of a child. Common law marriage is not recognized.

TENNESSEE: The age of consent is eighteen. With parental consent, parties can marry at age sixteen. Under special circumstances, younger minors can receive a license to marry. Common law marriage is not recognized.

TEXAS: The age of consent is eighteen. With parental and judicial consent, parties can marry but not below the age of fourteen for males and thirteen for females. Common law marriage is recognized.

UTAH: The age of consent is eighteen. With parental consent, parties can marry at age fourteen. However, this parental consent is not required if the minor has already been married. In addition, each county is authorized to provide premarital counseling before issuing a marriage license to applicants under the age of eighteen and those who are divorced. Common law marriage is recognized.

VERMONT: The age of consent is eighteen. With parental or judicial consent, parties can marry at age sixteen. Common law marriage is not recognized. In addition, a Vermont law, the first in the country, permits same-sex couples to be parties to a "civil union."

VIRGINIA: The age of consent is eighteen. With parental consent, parties can marry at age sixteen and under the age of sixteen may receive a license by reason of pregnancy or the birth of a child. Common law marriage is not recognized.

WASHINGTON: The age of consent is eighteen. With parental consent, parties can marry at age seventeen and at a younger age under special circumstances. Common law marriage is not recognized.

WEST VIRGINIA: The age of consent is eighteen. With parental consent, parties under the age of eighteen may receive a license at a younger age by reason of pregnancy or the birth of a child. Common law marriage is not recognized.

WISCONSIN: The age of consent is eighteen. With parental consent, parties can marry at age sixteen. Common law marriage is not recognized.

WYOMING: The age of consent is eighteen. With parental consent, parties can marry at age sixteen. They may obtain a license and marry at a younger age under special circumstances. Common law marriage is not recognized.

ADDITIONAL RESOURCES

De Witt, John Gregory, Peter N. Swisher, and Sheryl L. Wolf. *Understanding Family Law.* 3d ed. Newark, NJ: LexisNexis, 2005.

Katz, Sanford N. *Family Law in America.* New York: Oxford University Press, 2011.

Lind, Goran. *Common Law Marriage: A Legal Institution for Cohabitation.* New York: Oxford University Press, 2008.

Nichols, Joel A., ed. *Marriage and Divorce in a Multicultural Context: Multi-Tiered Marriage and the Boundaries of Civil Law and Religion.* New York: Cambridge University Press, 2012.

Oliphant, Robert E., and Nancy Ver Steegh. *Family Law: Examples and Explanations.* 3d ed. New York: Aspen Publishers, 2010.

ORGANIZATIONS

Family Life

PO Box 7111
Little Rock, AR 72223
Toll Free: (800) 358-6329
URL: http://www.familylife.com/

Human Rights Campaign

1640 Rhode Island Avenue NW
Washington, DC 20036-3278
Phone: (202) 628-4160
Toll Free: (800) 777-4723
Fax: (202) 347-5323
URL: http://www.hrc.org/

Marriage Missions International

12112 Rancho Vistoso Blvd.
Oro Valley, AZ 85755
URL: http://www.marriagemissions.com

Marriage Savers

9311 Harrington Drive
Potomac, MD 20854
Phone: (301) 469-5873
URL: http://www.marriagesavers.org

National Marriage Project

PO Box 400766
Charlottesville, VA 22904-4766
Phone: (434) 321-8601
Fax: (434) 924-7028
URL: http://nationalmarriageproject.org/

FAMILY LAW

PARENT LIABILITY CHILD'S ACT

Sections within this essay:

- Background
- Minors
- Civil Responsibility
  – Teenage Parents
  – Negligent Supervision
  – Family Car Doctrine
- Criminal Responsibility
  – Child Access Protection Laws
  – Computer Hacking and Internet Crimes
  – Juvenile Delinquents
- Insurance Coverage
- Selected State Laws
- Additional Resources

BACKGROUND

Parental liability is the term used to refer to a parent's obligation to pay for damage done by negligent, intentional, or criminal acts of that parent's child. In most states, parents are responsible for all malicious or willful property damage done by their children. Parental liability usually ends when the child reaches the **age of majority** and does not begin until the child reaches an age between eight and ten. Laws vary from state to state regarding the monetary thresholds on damages collected, the age limit of the child, and the inclusion of **personal injury** in the tort claim. Hawaii enacted such legislation in 1846, more than a century before statehood, and its law

remains one of the most broadly applied in that it does not limit the financial bounds of recovery and imposes liability for both negligent and intentional torts by underage persons. Laws making parents criminally responsible for the delinquent acts of their children followed civil liability statutes. In 1903, Colorado became the first state to establish the crime of contributing to the delinquency of a minor. Today, most states have laws relating to parental liability in various applications. Children's offenses can be civil and/or criminal in nature. Civil cases are lawsuits for money damages. The government brings criminal cases for violations of criminal law. Many acts can trigger both civil and criminal legal repercussions.

MINORS

A minor is a person under the age of majority. The age of majority is the age at which a minor, in the eyes of the law, becomes an adult. This age is 18 in most states. In a few other states, the age of majority is 19 or 21. A minor is considered to be a resident of the same state as the minor's custodial parent or **guardian**.

CIVIL RESPONSIBILITY

Each state has its own law regarding parents' financial responsibility for the acts of their children. Parents are responsible for their children's harmful actions much the same way that employers are responsible for the harmful actions of their employees. This legal concept is known a vicarious liability. The parent is vicariously liable, despite not being directly responsible for the injury. A number of states hold parents financially responsible for damages caused by their children. Some of these states, however, place limits on the amount of liability. The laws vary from state to state, but many cover such acts as **vandalism** to government or school property; defacement or destruction of the national and state flags, cemetery headstones, or public monuments/historical markers; and property destroyed in **hate crimes** based on race or religion, such as ransacking a synagogue. Personal injury in connection with any of these may also be included.

Teenage Parents Each year thousands of teenage girls, some as young as 12, enter into the Aid to Families with Dependent Children (AFDC) system because they become pregnant. These girls are eligible to receive welfare benefits for their children because the fathers are almost always noncustodial. Many of the fathers are also teenagers still attending high school and are frequently unable to pay **child support** because of their lack of income. These cases, commonly called "minor-mother" cases, are automatically referred to the state child support enforcement agency by the welfare department. When the agency receives a minor-mother referral, it begins **legal proceedings** against three parties: the father of the minor-mother, the mother of the minor-mother, and the father of the minor-mother's child. Because the parents of minor-mothers are legally responsible to support their daughters until **emancipation**, they must pay child support for their minor-mother daughters. The Welfare Reform Act has enacted important changes for teenage parents and minor-mothers. In order for a minor-mother to be eligible to receive AFDC benefits, she must enroll in high school or a state-approved GED program and live under adult supervision. The Welfare Reform Act has thus eliminated the enticement of physical and financial independence from one's parents. Another significant change implemented by the Welfare Reform Act is that parents of a noncustodial teenage father (the grandparents of the minor-mother's child) are liable to pay child support until their teenage son emancipates, if the minor-mother receives welfare. Prior to enactment of the Welfare Reform Act, grandparents were never liable to pay child support for their grandchildren, and the government could not collect child support from a minor-father until he became employed.

Additionally, the parents of a minor teenage noncustodial parent may face **paternity** action requests for child support from them, rather than the father of the newborn. When a minor child gives birth, that minor child is responsible for her baby, and the minor's parents remain responsible for her. However, if the young person under the age of 18 continues to live at home, the grandparents' income will be "deemed available" to the grandchild to determine eligibility for Temporary Assistance to Needy Families (TANF), and the mother may seek through the court to have the paternal grandparent's income "deemed available" for child support purposes.

As of 2012, a total of 37 states have enacted statutes that require at least one parent's approval before a minor can have an **abortion**. In some of these states, both parents must give permission. Typically, the parent or parents must be notified 24 to 48 hours before the abortion is performed.

The right of a parent to receive notification is not absolute, however. A total of 36 states have enacted procedures that allow a minor to request permission from a court to receive an abortion even without parental notification or permission. The majority of states that require parental involvement include an exception when the minor faces a medical emergency.

Negligent Supervision A parent is liable for a child's negligent acts if the parent knows or has reason to know that it is necessary to control the child and the parent fails to take reasonable actions to do so. This legal theory is known as negligent supervision. Liability for negligent supervision is not limited to parents. Grandparents, guardians, and others with **custody** and control of a child may also be liable under these circumstances. There is usually no dollar limit on this type of liability. An umbrella or homeowner's insurance policy may offer the adult some protection in a lawsuit.

Family Car Doctrine The family car doctrine holds the owner of a family car legally responsible for any damage caused by a family member when driving if the owner knew of and consented to the family member's use of the car. This doctrine is applied by about half of the states. Thus, even if a parent does not have a minor household member listed on the auto insurance policy, under the family car doctrine, the adult remains liable. Most insurance policies have special provisions for members of the household under eighteen. Typically, minor drivers must be included on the policy. The car owner would not be able to invoke the uninsured motorist provision for a minor child driver residing in the insured's household, driving the insured's vehicle.

CRIMINAL RESPONSIBILITY

Although some states impose criminal liability on parents of delinquent youth, many more have enacted less stringent types of parental responsibility laws. Kansas, Michigan, and Texas require parents to attend the hearings of children adjudicated delinquent or face **contempt** charges. Legislation in Alabama, Kansas, Kentucky, and West Virginia requires parents to pay the court costs associated with these proceedings. Other states impose financial responsibility on parents for the costs incurred by the state when youth are processed through the juvenile justice system. Florida, Idaho, Indiana, North Carolina, and Virginia require parents to reimburse the state for the costs associated with the care, support, detention, or treatment of their children while under the supervision of state agencies. Idaho, Maryland, Missouri, and Oklahoma require parents to undertake **restitution** payments.

Child Access Protection Laws Some states have laws which hold parents liable when children gain access to a firearms. At least nine states hold adults criminally responsible for storing a loaded firearm in such a way as to allow a minor to gain access. Some of these provisions include an enhanced **penalty** if the minor causes injury or death and create exceptions for parental liability when the minor gains access to a weapon by unlawful entry into the home or place of storage or if the firearm is used in **self-defense**. In addition, several states have provisions that create criminal liability when a custodial adult or parent is aware that his or her child possesses a firearm unlawfully and does not take it away. A number of jurisdictions have enacted laws making it a crime to leave a loaded firearm where it is accessible by children. Typically, these laws apply, and parents can be charged, only if the minor gains access to the gun. There are usually exceptions if the firearm is stored in a locked box, secured with a trigger lock, or obtained by a minor through unlawful entry. In most states, the penalty for unlawful access is a **misdemeanor** unless the minor injures someone else, in which case the parent can be charged with a **felony**.

Computer Hacking and Internet Crimes Another kind of illegal access by minors is that which involves computer and Internet activities. In 2003, the Recording Industry Association sued 261 persons for downloading protected music onto their personal computers and infringing copyrights. Among the defendants were several surprised parents who had no knowledge of their minor child's downloading activities. In *Thrifty-Tel v. Bezenek*, the California Court of Appeals upheld a verdict against the parents of juvenile computer hackers who accessed the phone company's network in order to make long-distance calls without cost. And with the appearance of camera cell-phones and computer video cameras in the early 2000s, the opportunity for minors to sell pornographic images of themselves or otherwise engage in illegal Internet activities increased dramatically. In such matters, federal law (e.g. Section 301 of the **Copyright** Act) may preempt state laws and provide a more uniform guidance for resolution. However, these examples point to the need for a more comprehensive approach to parental liability across state lines.

Juvenile Delinquents In addition to Access Protection Laws, some states hold parents responsible for paying restitution as well as criminal fines where crimes are committed by minors. Once a minor becomes involved in the juvenile justice system, parents may find themselves reimbursing the state for costs associated with their child's prosecution and rehabilitation. Minors who run away from home, exhibit chronic truancy, or refuse to obey their parents are classified by many states as incorrigible. Incorrigible minors are often referred to as status offenders because they would not be in court but for their status as minors. When a minor commits a criminal act that would still be a crime if committed by an adult, most states will classify the minor as a juvenile delinquent.

INSURANCE COVERAGE

Since homeowners insurance includes both property and liability coverage, wrongful acts of children or negligent supervision claims may be covered even if the act took place away from a policyholder's residence. Homeowner's policies typically cover legal liability in the event that anyone suffers an injury while on the insured property, even if the injury was committed by another household member or the result of **negligence** on the part of the policyholder.

SELECTED STATE LAWS

ARIZONA: Parents are liable for intentional acts of their children that injure others or damage their property. Parents can be held automatically liable for up to $10,000 in damage. Although not automatic, under some circumstances, this legal responsibility may extend to the full value of the victim's damages.

CALIFORNIA: Parents are responsible if the parent has knowledge of the child's potential for misconduct and fails to take reasonable steps to prevent such misconduct; if the parent has signed the child's driver's license application or the child drives the parent's car with the parent's knowledge and permission; if the child is guilty of willful misconduct; or if the child is given ready access to a firearm.

COLORADO: The governor signed Senate Bill 253 in 2003, which validates certain parental liability waivers, signed for their minor children who engage in various sports or recreational activities.

ILLINOIS: It is illegal for a person to store or leave any loaded firearm in a way that allows a minor to gain access to the firearm without permission from a parent or guardian and use it to injure or kill. A firearm is properly stored if it is secured by a trigger lock, placed in a securely locked box, or placed in some other location that a reasonable person would believe to be secured from a minor.

INDIANA: If the juvenile is adjudicated a delinquent, the parents or custodians of the juvenile may be required to participate in programs of care, treatment, or rehabilitation for the juvenile and will be held financially responsible for any services provided. These costs may include the costs incurred by the County on behalf of the juvenile for attorneys, institutional or **foster care** placement, detention, inpatient/outpatient treatment, or counseling. It may also include the costs of returning the child from another **jurisdiction** and court costs associated with the juvenile proceedings. If the parent or guardian defaults in reimbursing the county or fails to pay any fee required, the Juvenile Court may find him/her in contempt and may enter judgment for the amount due. A parent is liable to another person for up to $5,000 in actual damages arising from harm to person or property caused by a child in their custody and may be fully liable for all actual damages resulting from gang activity.

MASSACHUSETTS: It is unlawful to store or keep any firearm, rifle, or shotgun including, but not limited to, large capacity weapons or machine guns in any place unless such weapon is secured in a locked container or equipped with a tamper-resistant mechanical lock or other safety device, properly engaged so as to render such weapon inoperable by any person other than the owner or other lawfully authorized user. Dealers must conspicuously post at each purchase counter the following warning in bold type not less than one inch in height: "IT IS UNLAWFUL TO STORE OR KEEP A FIREARM, RIFLE, SHOTGUN OR MACHINE GUN IN ANY PLACE UNLESS THAT WEAPON IS EQUIPPED WITH A TAMPER-RESISTANT SAFETY DEVICE OR IS STORED OR KEPT IN A SECURELY LOCKED CONTAINER." Each dealer must provide the warning, in writing, to the purchaser or transferee of any firearm, rifle, shotgun, or machine gun in bold type not less than one-quarter inch in height.

MISSOURI: Parents may be liable in an amount up to $2,000 under the parental liability **statute**. Parents may be liable for greater amounts if the court determines that the child's actions were a result of parental negligence. The child must act purposely before the parent is liable.

NEW YORK: Parents are liable when their children "willfully, maliciously, or unlawfully" damage property. There is a cap of $5,000 per incident. Damages may be mitigated by a limiting financial status of the parents, or by showing diligent supervision.

TEXAS: It is a misdemeanor offense when a child gains access to a firearm because an adult fails to secure a readily dischargeable firearm or leaves the firearm in a place to which the person knew or should have known that a child could gain access. It also requires firearms dealers to post a sign with this warning: "It is unlawful to store, transport, or abandon an unsecured firearm in a place where children are likely to be and can obtain access to the firearm."

VIRGINIA: It is a misdemeanor to recklessly leave a loaded firearm so as to endanger the **life or limb** of any child under the age of fifteen.

WISCONSIN: The Grandparents Liability Law holds grandparents (parents of minor children) financially responsible for the support of any grandchildren born to their minor teen sons or daughters (under 18).

ADDITIONAL RESOURCES

Chambliss, William J. *Juvenile Crime and Justice.* Thousand Oaks, CA: Sage, 2011.

De Witt, John Gregory, Peter N. Swisher, and Sheryl L. Wolf. *Understanding Family Law.* 3d ed. Newark, NJ: LexisNexis, 2005.

Katz, Sanford N. *Family Law in America.* New York: Oxford University Press, 2011.

Oliphant, Robert E., and Nancy Ver Steegh. *Family Law: Examples and Explanations.* 3d ed. New York: Aspen Publishers, 2010.

ORGANIZATIONS

Administration for Children and Families, U.S. Department of Health and Human Services
370 L'Enfant Promenade SW
Washington, DC 20447
Phone: (202) 401-2337
URL: http://www.acf.gov

American Bar Association (ABA)
321 North Clark Street
Chicago, IL 60610
Phone: (312) 988-5000
Toll Free: (800) 285-2221
Fax: (312) 988-6800
URL: http://www.americanbar.org

Child Welfare League of America
1726 M St. NW, Suite 500
Washington, DC 20036
Phone: (202) 688-4200
Fax: (202) 833-1689

National Association Counsel for Children
13123 E. 16th Street, B390
Aurora, CO 80045
Toll Free: (888) 828-NACC
URL: http://www.naccchildlaw.org

FAMILY LAW

PATERNITY

BACKGROUND

Consider the early days of courtroom drama: a resistant father would be wrestled into court, and a **jury** would compare the physical features of the alleged father and the fatherless child in question to render their verdict. In later years, blood grouping tests were performed, but this only served to rule out a certain class of blood types (such as men with type A, B, or O blood types). Cases were often dismissed if witnesses could show that the mother had sexual relations with other men during the same time as the alleged father.

Today, the use of **DNA testing** for positive identification in paternity **litigation** has rendered most of the previous legal practice and procedure obsolete. The alleged father need only submit a painless DNA sample (usually in the form of a saliva swab) to prove or disprove his parentage. DNA matching has replaced the Human Leukocyte Antigen (HLA) Test, which was used to match not only blood type, but also tissue type and other genetic factoring. Experts had asserted that the HLA was at least 98 percent accurate. But presumptive fathers (based upon HLA results) could rebut those presumptions by proving they were out of the state, impotent (in pre-Viagra years), or sterile at the time the child was conceived. Conversely, DNA testing has a more conclusive accuracy (close to 100 percent) that becomes almost impossible to defeat.

SIGNIFICANCE

A child born to a married couple is considered legitimate in the eyes of the law. However, the fact that a person's name appears on a birth certificate is not conclusive proof of paternity. Since there is no requirement that a father sign a birth certificate, a mother may list anyone whom she believes is, or wants to be, the father.

The significance of a paternity determination is multifold. For a father who resists parentage, it means that he will now be held accountable for his share of support and responsibility. For a father who wishes to establish that he is the biological parent, he can do so with relative ease of procedure. Importantly, if the child is born out of wedlock, consent from the biological father is needed before the mother can give the child up for **adoption**.

For a mother, paternity determinations secure financial support as well as **custody** and visitation rights. For a child, at stake is the right to shelter and aid, as well as the emotional and psychological relief in knowing who his or her father is. Paternity also secures the right to **inherit**, the right to access personal information about the known health risks and profiles of the paternal family, and the right to sue for harm or death of the father, resulting in loss to the child. Likewise, a child for whom parentage has been established may also be eligible to receive **workers' compensation** benefits resulting from the father's death, or other dependent-based governmental assistance.

VOLUNTARY PATERNITY DETERMINATIONS

The establishment of paternity need not always conjure up images of court battles and adversity. A father may be very willing to support a child, but simply wants to ensure that he is indeed the biological parent. He may want a judicial determination before he commits to making **child support** payments or playing an emotionally-committed supportive role in the child's life.

Other fathers believe they have been unjustly denied knowledge of, or access to, children they may have fathered. This may occur following a contentious parting of ways between parents, when the mother wants no further involvement or contact with the father, and does not want the father involved in the child's life.

Finally, some men fear that they may not learn until years later (and perhaps at an inopportune time) that they have fathered a child. To ensure against this, men may wish to voluntarily submit to DNA testing and (in limited circumstances) compel women with whom they have had prior sexual contact to undergo a pregnancy test. (Generally, only a man alleging that he is the father of an expected child has legal standing to initiate a paternity action.) This brings closure to the relationship, and men know their future lives will not be unexpectedly jolted by news of having fathered children unknown to them.

Voluntary Petitions Most states will permit a father to execute an **affidavit** acknowledging paternity, which eliminates the need for a court action. The affidavit must be signed by both mother and father, notarized, and filed with the court. Once a paternity affidavit is filed and signed by a judge (if required by state law), the father cannot later attempt to **rescind** or void the affidavit. If the father's name does not already appear on the child's birth certificate, a corrected one will be reissued, showing the names of both parents.

Paternity affidavits are often encouraged to remove the stigma sometimes attached to children who may grow up believing they were unwanted because a parent denied or avoided parentage. Attendant to a voluntary petition for a paternity determination are other determinations that the court may rule on at the same time, mostly addressing the support, involvement, and active role in a child's life that the father will assume.

Voluntary Testing Likewise, voluntary submission of a DNA sample produces the same result as voluntary affidavits, without an adversarial court proceeding. Generally, testing involves a saliva sample, taken from the mouth with a cotton swab. Costs usually range from $200 to $600, and some health or medical insurance companies will cover the cost of the test. Laboratories that may perform such voluntary tests are generally listed in telephone directories under "Genetic Screening."

FORMAL PATERNITY PROCEEDINGS

In most states, a paternity action takes the form of a civil lawsuit, and is clearly not a criminal matter. Importantly, in most instances, paternity actions must be filed prior to the alleged father's death, to provide for a fair and just defense. In posthumous actions, the alleged father must have affirmatively done something to acknowledge the child prior to death (e.g., putting his name on the child's birth certificate or identifying himself as the father in some other legal or formal action).

Legal Standing Only certain persons or parties have legal standing to bring a paternity action:

- the mother of the child
- the mother of an expected child
- a man alleging that he is the biological father of a child
- a man alleging that he is the biological father of an expected child
- the child
- a personal representative of the child
- the mother and father of a child (a voluntary action filed together)
- the mother and father of an expected child (a voluntary action filed together)
- a state social service agency, interceding in cases of child neglect or need
- a prosecutor's office, interceding in cases of child neglect or need

Complaint for Paternity The complaining party has the legal burden of establishing requisite facts in a paternity action. A petition filed with the court should contain the following basic statements:

- a **citation** of the state paternity **statute** under which the action is being brought (the legal authority)
- a statement of residency for the complaining party (for establishing the court's **jurisdiction** over the parties)

- a statement of residency for the responding party (for establishing the court's jurisdiction over the parties)

- the child's full name and date of birth

- a statement of relationship between the complaining party and the child or unborn child

- a statement of relationship between the responding party and the child or unborn child

- a statement that the child was or was not born while the mother was married to someone else

- a statement addressing the status of any pending custody or visitation actions related to the child

- a statement of any facts tending to support a finding of paternity

Similar to other civil suits, the party who files the action will be responsible for providing supporting documents, paying the filing fee with the court, and serving the responding party with a **summons** and copy of the complaint. There is usually a requirement that other necessary parties be notified. For example, if the action is filed by a **guardian** of the child or a social services office, the mother or anyone having legal custody of the child must be served along with the alleged father.

A court will not automatically order paternity tests simply because a paternity action has been filed. It will review the petition to determine if there is sufficient information contained therein to **warrant** or justify the compelling of such a test. If the court orders a paternity test, the mother, child, and alleged father will all be tested at a court-designated facility. If the man did not initiate the paternity action, and test results determine that he is not the father, the cost of the testing will be charged to the party who filed the paternity action.

A court determination of paternity is final, and a copy of the court's order will be needed to establish the child's rights, both present and future. Parties should seek court-certified "true copies" of original orders.

CHALLENGING PATERNITY

Even with the proven accuracy of DNA testing, it is possible, though improbable, that the results are incorrect. Some of the grounds for challenging a paternity determination include:

- Tainted lab results (e.g., **evidence** of prior errors in lab results and routinely substandard work)

- Fraudulent lab results (e.g., evidence that the opposing party sent someone else to take the lab test on his behalf)

- Proof of infertility/sterility

- Proof that test results were tampered with

THE UNIFORM PARENTAGE ACT

The Uniform Parentage Act was first approved in 1973, and a total of 14 states adopted it. This uniform act was revised in 2000 and amended again in 2002, and nine states as of 2012 have adopted the current version. One of the most significant provisions in the current uniform act is an expansion of persons with standing to bring a paternity action before a court. Under the Act, any interested party may file a paternity suit on behalf of a child.

STATE LAWS

The following state provisions address proper designation of parties in an action for paternity, custody, child support, and termination of parental rights. All of these issues may be ruled upon in conjunction with a paternity action.

ALABAMA: (C.A. 30-2-1) Custody Factors: moral character, age and gender of child. Child Support: until age 19, either party may be ordered to pay, "as may seem right and proper," based on moral character and prudence, age and gender of child. Termination of Parental Rights: **abandonment**; emotional illness or mental illness or deficiency; excessive substance abuse; physical injury resulting from neglect; **felony conviction**.

ALASKA: (A.S. 25.24.010) Custody Factors: best interests of the child, various criteria. Child Support: until age 18. Termination of Parental Rights: non-custodial parent withholds consent to adoption, child conceived as a result of **sexual abuse** of a minor.

ARIZONA: (A.R.S. 25-311) Custody Factors: best interests of the child, various criteria. Child Support: until age 18, either party may be ordered to pay, "as may seem right and proper," based on moral character and prudence, age and gender of child. Termination of Parental Rights: abandonment; neglect or willful abuse; emotional illness or mental illness or deficiency; felony conviction; potential father failed to file paternity action within 30 days as prescribed by law; formal relinquishment of rights.

ARKANSAS: (A.C.A. 9-12-301) Custody Factors: best interest of child, without regard to gender of parent. Child Support: until age 18. Termination of Parental Rights: abandonment; neglect or abuse; non-custodial parent withholds consent to adoption.

CALIFORNIA: (Several Code provisions) Irrebuttable presumption of paternity for husband for all children born during marriage. Custody Factors: best interests of child;

nature and contact with each parent; any other relevant factor. Child Support: until age 18. Termination of Parental Rights: abandonment; neglect or abuse; emotional illness or mental illness or deficiency; substance abuse.

COLORADO: (C.R.S.A. 14-10-106) Custody Factors: best interests of child, including wishes of all parties. Child Support: until age 21. Termination of Parental Rights: physical or sexual abuse; emotional illness or mental illness or deficiency; substance abuse; violent conduct.

CONNECTICUT: (C.G.S.A. 46b-40) Custody Factors: best interests of the child; law favors joint custody. Child Support: until age 18, either party may be ordered to pay; various criteria. Termination of Parental Rights: abandonment or neglect.

DELAWARE: (D.C.A. 13-1502)) Custody Factors: best interests of child. Child Support: until age 18. Termination of Parental Rights: abandonment or neglect; emotional illness or mental illness or deficiency; felony conviction in which child was a victim.

DISTRICT OF COLUMBIA: (D.C.C. 16-901-916) Custody Factors: best interest of child. Child Support: until age 18. Termination of Parental Rights: physical, emotional or mental illness or deficiency; substance abuse.

FLORIDA: (F.S. 61.001) Custody Factors: Joint is preferred, but best interests of child to establish primary residence. Child Support: until age 18. Termination of Parental Rights: abandonment; egregious conduct which threatens life or wellbeing of child; **incarceration**.

GEORGIA: (C.G.A. 19-5-1) Custody Factors: non-specific, but children over 14 can choose which parent to live with. Moral character, age and gender of child. Child Support: until age 18. Termination of Parental Rights: abandonment; emotional illness or mental illness or deficiency; excessive substance abuse; physical or emotional neglect; felony conviction.

HAWAII: (H.R.S. 580-41) Custody Factors: best interests of child, child's wishes. Child Support: until age 18. Termination of Parental Rights: abandonment; emotional illness or mental illness or deficiency; neglect.

ILLINOIS: (750 ILCS 5/101) Custody Factors: wishes of the parties and child, and additional criteria. Child Support: until age 18 (750 ILCS 5/505). Termination of Parental Rights: abuse.

INDIANA: (A.I.C. 31-1-11.5) Custody Factors: wishes of the parties and child, and additional criteria. Child Support: until age 18. Termination of Parental Rights: abandonment; emotional illness or mental illness or deficiency; best interest of the child.

IOWA: (I.C.A. 598.1) Custody Factors: best interests of child, various factors. Child Support: until age 18. Termination of Parental Rights: abandonment; abuse or neglect; emotional illness or mental illness or deficiency; excessive substance abuse.

KANSAS: (K.S.A. 60-1601) Custody Factors: moral character, age and gender of child. Child Support: until age 19, either party may be ordered to pay, "as may seem right and proper," based on moral character and prudence, age and gender of child. Termination of Parental Rights: emotional illness or mental illness or deficiency; abuse or neglect; substance abuse; physical injury resulting from neglect; felony conviction.

KENTUCKY: (K.R.S. 403.010) Custody Factors: best interest of the child, considering various factors. Child Support: until age 18. Termination of Parental Rights: abandonment; abuse or neglect.

LOUISIANA: (LSA C.C. Art. 102) Custody Factors: Joint custody is preferred; best interest of child using various factors; moral character, age and gender of child. Child Support: until age 18 (LSA Rev. St. 9:315). Termination of Parental Rights: abandonment; extreme abuse, all forms; misconduct of parent toward child.

MAINE: (19 M.R.S.A. 661) Custody Factors: best interest of child, various factors. Child Support: until age 18. Termination of Parental Rights: abandonment; misconduct toward child; felony conviction where child was the victim.

MARYLAND: (A.C.M Family Law 7-101) Custody Factors: none. Child Support: until age 18. Termination of Parental Rights: child has been out of the custody of natural parents for over one year; abuse conviction; crime of violence conviction.

MASSACHUSETTS: (A.L.M. C208-1) Custody Factors: none in statute. Child Support: until age 18. Termination of Parental Rights: abandonment; all forms of neglect or abuse; felony conviction.

MICHIGAN: (M.C.L.A. 552.1/M.S.A. 25.96) Custody Factors: best interest of child, with various factors. Child Support: until age 18 or beyond if still completing high school. Termination of Parental Rights: abandonment; all forms of abuse; parental long-term **imprisonment**; chronic neglect.

MINNESOTA: (M.S.A. 518.002) Custody Factors: the parties' wishes and child's preference, if of sufficient age; various factors. Child Support: until age 18 (M.S.A. 518.551). Termination of Parental Rights: abandonment; unfit parent; chemical dependency of parent; abuse or neglect; child experienced severe harm while in parent's care.

MISSISSIPPI: (M.C. 93-5-1) Custody Factors: none by statute, but child of 12 may choose. Child Support: until age 21. Termination of Parental Rights: abandonment; emotional illness or mental illness or deficiency; abusive incidents; substance abuse.

MISSOURI: (A.M.S. 452.300) Custody Factors: best interest of child, various factors. Child Support: until age 18. Termination of Parental Rights: abandonment; abuse or neglect; child was conceived as a result of rape; substance abuse; felony conviction in which child was victim.

MONTANA: (M.C.A.40-4-101) Custody Factors: parties' wishes, various factors. Child Support: until age 18, various factors. Termination of Parental Rights: unfit parent; absence of child-parent relationship; irrevocable **waiver**.

NEBRASKA: (R.S.N. 42-301) Custody Factors: best interest of child, considering various factors. Termination of Parental Rights: abandonment; emotional illness or mental illness or deficiency; excessive substance abuse; physical injury resulting from neglect; felony conviction.

NEVADA: (N.R.S.A. 125.010) Custody Factors: best interest of child, various factors. Child Support: until age 18, several factors. Termination of Parental Rights: abandonment; neglect; parental unfitness; risk of physical, mental, or emotional harm to child.

NEW HAMPSHIRE: (N.H.R.S.A. 458:4) Custody Factors: joint custody presumed in the child's best interest. Child Support: until age 18, both parties responsible. Termination of Parental Rights: abandonment; emotional illness or mental illness or deficiency; all forms of abuse or neglect; felony conviction.

NEW JERSEY: (NJSA 2A:34-2) Custody Factors: best interest of child, various factors. Child Support: until age 18.

Termination of Parental Rights: abandonment; or potential for harm to child.

NEW MEXICO: (N.M.S.A. 40-4-1) Custody Factors: best interest of child, various factors. Child Support: until age 18. Termination of Parental Rights: abandonment; neglect or abuse; child placed in the permanent care of others.

NEW YORK: (C.L.N.Y, D.R.I 170) Custody Factors: best interest of child. Child Support: until age 18; needs are determined as a percentage of parents' combined income. Termination of Parental Rights: abandonment; emotional illness or mental illness or deficiency; surrender of child to authorities.

NORTH CAROLINA: (G.S.N.C. 50-1) Custody Factors: best interest of child. Child Support: until age 18, various factors. Termination of Parental Rights: neglect or abuse; leaving child in **foster care** for more than 12 months; abandonment.

NORTH DAKOTA: (N.D.C.C. 14-05-01) Custody Factors: several factors. Child Support: until age 18. Termination of Parental Rights: neglect or misconduct; faults or habits of parent; physical illness or mental illness or deficiency; child suffers from mental, moral, or emotional harm.

OHIO: (O.R.C. 3105.01) Custody Factors: best interest of child, with various factors. Child Support: until age 18; medical insurance payment must be made to enforcement agency. Termination of Parental Rights: abandonment; abuse or neglect.

OKLAHOMA: (43 O.S.A. 101) Custody Factors: best interest of child and child preference. Child Support: until age 18. Termination of Parental Rights: abandonment; conviction for **child abuse** or neglect; all forms of abuse; emotional illness or mental illness or deficiency.

OREGON: (O.R.S. 107.015) Custody Factors: joint custody only awarded if both parties agree. Child Support: until age 18. Termination of Parental Rights: physical or sexual abuse or neglect; emotional illness or mental illness or deficiency; substance abuse.

PENNSYLVANIA: (Pa.C.S.A. 3101) Custody Factors: best interest of child, various factors. Child Support: until age 21. Termination of Parental Rights: abandonment; abuse or neglect; child removed from parents by court; child conceived as a result of rape or **incest**.

RHODE ISLAND: (G.L.R.I. 15-5-1) Custody Factors: best interest of child. Child Support: until age 18. Termination of Parental Rights: abandonment; emotional illness or mental illness or deficiency; parental unfitness.

SOUTH CAROLINA: (C.L.S.C. 20-3-10) Custody Factors: various factors in interest of child. Child Support: until age 18. Termination of Parental Rights: best interest of child; abuse or neglect; abandonment; substance abuse; mental or physical deficiency of parent.

SOUTH DAKOTA: (S.D.C.L. 25-4-1) Custody Factors: "as may seem necessary and proper." Child Support: until age 18. Termination of Parental Rights: abandonment.

TENNESSEE: (T.C.A. 36-4-101) Custody Factors: Best interest of child, various factors. Child Support: until age 18. Termination of Parental Rights: abandonment; child removed by court order; severe child abuse; incarceration sentence of 10 years; **incompetency.**

TEXAS: (T.C.A., F.C. 3.01) Custody Factors: referred to as "managing conservatorship." Various factors; moral character, age and gender of child. Child Support: until age 19, either party may be ordered to pay, "as may seem right and proper," based on moral character and prudence, age and gender of child. Termination of Parental Rights: abandonment; abuse or neglect; sexual abuse of other child by parent.

UTAH: (U.C. 30-3-1) Custody Factors: best interest of child, various factors. Child Support: until age 18 (U.C. 78-45-7). Termination of Parental Rights: abandonment; neglect or abuse; parental unfitness.

VERMONT: (15 V.S.A. 551) Custody Factors: best interest of child, various factors. Child Support: until age 18. Termination of Parental Rights: failure to support child or exercise parental responsibility; conviction of crime of violence; risk of harm to child.

VIRGINIA: (C.V. 20-91) Custody Factors: best interest of child, various factors. Child Support: until age 18. Termination of Parental Rights: emotional illness or mental illness or deficiency; neglect or abuse; **habitual** substance abuse.

WASHINGTON: (R.C.W.A. 26.09.010) Custody Factors: each party's relative fitness and agreement between parties, other criteria. Child Support: until age 18. Termination of Parental Rights: habitual substance abuse; emotional illness or mental illness or deficiency.

WEST VIRGINIA: (W.V.C. 48-2-1) Custody Factors: none, but presumption in favor of primary caretaker. Child Support: until age 18. Termination of Parental Rights: abandonment; abuse or neglect.

WISCONSIN: (W.S.A. 767.001) Custody Factors: "legal custody and physical placement." Best interest of child. Child Support: until age 18. Termination of Parental Rights: abandonment; continuing need for protective services; abuse; failure to assume parental responsibility; incestuous parenthood; intentional killing of other parent.

WYOMING: (W.S.A. 20-2-104) Custody Factors: best interest of child. Child Support: until age 18. Termination of Parental Rights: abandonment; neglect or abuse; parental incarceration or unfitness.

ADDITIONAL RESOURCES

De Witt, John Gregory, Peter N. Swisher, and Sheryl L. Wolf. *Understanding Family Law.* 3d ed. Newark, NJ: LexisNexis, 2005.

Katz, Sanford N. *Family Law in America.* New York: Oxford University Press, 2011.

Oliphant, Robert E., and Nancy Ver Steegh. *Family Law: Examples and Explanations.* 3d ed. New York: Aspen Publishers, 2010.

Stanley, Jacqueline D. *Unmarried Parents' Rights.* 2nd ed. Naperville, IL: Sphinx Publishing, 2003.

ORGANIZATIONS

American Coalition for Fathers and Children

1718 Main Street NW, Suite 187
Washington, DC 20036
Toll Free: (800) 978-DADS
URL: http://www.acfc.org

Parents Anonymous

981 Corporate Center Drive, Suite 100
Pomona, CA 91768
Phone: (909) 236-5757
URL: http://www.parentsananymous.org

FAMILY LAW

PHYSICIAN-ASSISTED SUICIDE

Sections within this essay:

- Background
- Supreme Court Rulings
- Oregon's Death With Dignity Act
  - The DWDA and the Controlled Substances Act of 1970
- Other States
- Additional Resources

BACKGROUND

Physician-assisted suicide involves the hastening of death through the administration of lethal drugs, upon request of the patient. Physician-assisted suicide is sometimes known as active euthanasia. It differs from withholding or discontinuing medical treatment in circumstances that will result in death. Withholding or discontinuing medical treatment is sometimes called passive euthanasia. Passive euthanasia is generally accepted, although not without controversy, in the United States as an individual's right to refuse medical treatment. Examples of passive euthanasia include turning off respirators, stopping medication, discontinuing food and water, or failing to resuscitate.

The Hippocratic Oath has been used by physicians as a code of ethics for more than two thousand years. Attributed to Hippocrates (ca. 460-370 BCE), the oath provides in part: "I will follow that method of treatment, which, according to my ability and judgment, I consider for the benefit of my patients, and abstain from whatever is deleterious and mischievous. I will give no deadly medicine to anyone if asked, nor suggest any such **counsel**."

The American Medical Association takes this stance: "It is understandable, though tragic, that some patients in extreme duress—such as those suffering from a terminal, painful, debilitating illness—may come to decide that death is preferable to life. However, allowing physicians to participate in assisted suicide would cause more harm than good. Physician-assisted suicide is fundamentally incompatible with the physician's role as healer, would be difficult or impossible to control, and would pose serious societal risks."

Dr. Jack Kevorkian, self-styled "Dr. Death," garnered much publicity for his role in physician-assisted suicides. Kevorkian escaped **conviction** on murder charges several times during the 1990s as he assisted in numerous suicides. Kevorkian operated on his own set of rules to determine whom he would assist; he supposedly assisted more than 130 patients. When he began, Michigan did not have a law that specifically prohibited assisted suicide. As his notoriety grew, the Michigan legislature passed a law prohibiting assisted suicide. The Michigan Supreme Court upheld the **statute** in 1994, ruling that no constitutional right to suicide exists, including assisted suicide. Kevorkian's second-degree murder conviction was upheld. He was released from prison in 2007 and died in 2011.

The Supreme Court has determined that no right exists for physician-assisted suicide. However, states are free to enact laws to permit it. Oregon was the first state to permit physician-assisted suicide. Technically, however, a death under Oregon's Death with Dignity Act is not considered suicide, assisted suicide, or **homicide**. Oregon's law has survived numerous legal challenges since its enactment in 1994. In *Gonzales v. Oregon* (2006), the Supreme Court upheld the law, ruling that the Attorney General could not use the Controlled Substances Act to bring charges against doctors who prescribe drugs under the Death with Dignity Act. The State of Washington passed its own Death with Dignity Act in 2008.

In 1997, President William Jefferson Clinton signed the Assisted Suicide Funding Restriction Act of 1997. The law's intent was "to clarify Federal law with respect to restricting the use of Federal funds in support of assisted suicide," euthanasia, or mercy killing. The act banned the funding of assisted suicide through **Medicaid**, **Medicare**, military and federal employee health plans, veterans' health care systems and other federally funded programs. It also prohibited the use of taxpayer funds to subsidize legal assistance or other advocacy in support of legal protection for assisted suicide.

SUPREME COURT RULINGS

In two cases from 1997, the U.S. Supreme Court ruled that physician-assisted suicide is not a protected liberty interest under the Constitution. However, the rulings in *Vacco v. Quill* and *Washington v. Glucksberg* left the door open for states to permit physician-assisted suicide. *Washington v. Glucksberg* dealt with the constitutionality of a Washington statute that made it a **felony** for a person to assist in the suicide of another. According to the statute, "A person is guilty of promoting a suicide attempt when he knowingly causes or aids another person to attempt suicide." Maximum punishment for conviction was five years' **imprisonment** and a $10,000 fine. Another statute in Washington, the Natural Death Act, provided, "Withholding or withdrawal of life-sustaining treatment" at a patient's direction "shall not, for any purpose, constitute a suicide." A number of physicians and their terminally ill patients brought suit to challenge the constitutionality of the assisted suicide law. These plaintiffs claimed "the existence of a liberty interest protected by the Fourteenth Amendment which extends to a personal choice by a mentally competent, terminally ill adult to commit physician-assisted suicide."

The district court agreed with the doctors and patients. The court ruled that the law placed an undue burden on the exercise of a constitutionally protected liberty interest. The state appealed the case to the Ninth Circuit Court of Appeals. A three-judge panel reversed the district court ruling. According to that opinion, this country has never recognized a "constitutional right to aid in killing." However, a subsequent en banc **hearing** before all the judges of the Ninth Circuit resulted in victory for the doctors. According to the en banc decision,

"the Constitution encompasses a due process liberty interest in controlling the time and manner of one's death–that there is, in short, a constitutionally-recognized 'right to die.'" Furthermore, Washington's law was unconstitutional, "as applied to terminally ill competent adults who wish to hasten their deaths with medication prescribed by their physicians."

The state appealed, and the Supreme Court reversed. The opinion, written by Chief Justice William Rehnquist, traced the history of assisted suicide. The court noted that few exceptions to the rules against assisted suicide exist anywhere in Western democracies and states. Moreover, the punishment or disapproval of suicide or assisted suicide reaches back more than 700 years. The earliest statute to outlaw assisted suicide came in 1828, but long before that, **common law** recognized it as a crime. The court noted that advances in medicine and technology have caused many states to reexamine their stances on assisted suicide. For the most part, states have reaffirmed deeply-rooted bans on assisted suicide. To rule in favor of the doctors, the court noted, it would have to "reverse centuries of legal doctrine and practice, and strike down the considered policy choice of almost every State." Quoting another case, the court recognized that if something has been practiced for two hundred years by common consent, it will "need a strong case for the Fourteenth Amendment to affect it." The court also noted the danger of allowing policy preferences of the members of the court to subtly transform constitutional law.

Based on the history of assisted suicide laws in this country, the Supreme Court ruled that there is no fundamental liberty interest in a right to assisted suicide that is protected by the due process clause. Moreover, the ban on assisted suicide, as set forth in Washington's law, was rationally related to legitimate government interests. Those government interests include:

- To preserve life
- To prevent suicide
- To avoid the involvement of third parties and the use of arbitrary, unfair, or undue influence
- To protect the integrity of the medical profession
- To avoid future movement toward euthanasia and other abuses

The Supreme Court did not, however, ban assisted suicide. The opinion recognized the right of states to engage "in serious, thoughtful examinations of physician-assisted suicide."

OREGON'S DEATH WITH DIGNITY ACT

Only in Oregon is physician-assisted suicide legal. Voters in Oregon passed the Death With Dignity Act (DWDA) in 1994 by a narrow margin. The measure legalized physician-assisted suicide under certain circumstances. Physicians may not be forced to participate in the DWDA. A person who sought to employ the law needed to show:

- Patient must be at least 18 years of age
- Patient must be suffering from a terminal illness with a life expectancy of six months of less
- The patient must make two oral requests for assistance in dying
- The patient must make one written request for assistance
- Two physicians must be convinced that the patient is sincere, not acting on a whim, and that the decision is voluntary
- The patient must not be influenced by depression
- The patient must be informed of "feasible alternatives" such as hospice care and pain control
- The patient must wait 15 days between the verbal requests

Almost immediately after passage, court challenges succeeded in suspending the law. After the Supreme Court rulings in *Glucksberg* and *Vacco v. Quill* in 1997, the Ninth Circuit Court of Appeals lifted an injunction on DWDA. The law took effect on October 27, 1997. Voters in Oregon were asked to vote whether to retain the law in 1997. This time, 60 percent of voters approved of it.

In each year between 2006 and 2011, the number of patients who received prescriptions for assisted suicide has increased. In 2005, a total of 37 patients committed suicide, compared with a total of 71 who did so in 2011. As of 2012, a total of 935 people have received prescriptions, and 596 patients have died from ingesting medications prescribed under the law.

The median age of a patient receiving a prescription under DWDA in 2011 was 70; in 2004, the median age was 64. Just under half in 2011 had at least a baccalaureate degree. Although more males tended to use the drugs between 1998 and 2010, a total of 63.4 percent of those who died in 2011 were female. Malignant tumors accounted for 82.4 percent of the illnesses. According to the report, the three most frequently cited reasons for requesting assisted suicide were: a decreasing ability to participate in activities that made life enjoyable, loss of autonomy, and a loss of dignity. Death came anywhere from five minutes to 31 hours after ingestion of either pentobarbital or secobarbital.

The DWDA and the Controlled Substances Act of 1970

The stated purpose of the Controlled Substances Act is

"to provide increased research into, and prevention of, drug abuse and drug dependence ... and to strengthen existing law enforcement authority in the field of drug abuse." A regulation promulgated under the act provided, "A prescription for a controlled substance to be effective must be issued for a legitimate medical purpose by an individual practitioner acting in the usual course of his professional practice."

In 1984 the act was amended to give the U.S. Attorney General the authority to revoke a physician's prescription privileges upon a determination that the physician has "committed such acts as would render his registration ... inconsistent with the public interest."

On November 6, 2001, U.S. Attorney General John Ashcroft issued an interpretation of the Controlled Substances Act. Ashcroft's interpretation made it illegal for doctors to prescribe controlled substances under Oregon's Death With Dignity law. According to Ashcroft's determination, prescribing such drugs was a violation of the Controlled Substances Act because physician-assisted suicide was not a "legitimate medical purpose." A doctor who made such prescriptions could have his or her registration to distribute controlled substances under the act revoked or could be criminally prosecuted.

Ashcroft's determination reflected a reversal of administration policy from Clinton's presidency to that of George W. Bush. Janet Reno, attorney general under President Clinton, had determined that the pertinent section in the Controlled Substances Act would not apply in states where physician-assisted suicide was legal. Ashcroft's decision on the subject has come to be known as the "Ashcroft Directive."

The state, along with a doctor, a pharmacist, and a group of terminally ill patients, filed a lawsuit to challenge Ashcroft's interpretation of the Controlled Substances Act. On November 20, 2001, a federal judge issued a **restraining order** blocking implementation of the Ashcroft Directive. In April 2002 U.S. District Court Judge Robert Jones upheld the DWDA in light of the Controlled Substances Act. The U.S. appealed; the Ninth Circuit Court of Appeals upheld the federal district court decision. The **appellate** decision opined that the Ashcroft Directive violated the plain language of the Controlled Substances Act: "Contrary to the Attorney General's characterization, physician-assisted suicide is not a form of 'drug abuse' that Congress intended the CSA to cover." Moreover, the Ashcroft Directive undermined Congressional intent, and overstepped the bounds of the attorney general's authority.

Judge Richard Tallman's decision also noted that the federal government was interfering in an area delegated to the states. "The principle that state governments bear the primary responsibility for evaluating physician assisted suicide follows from our concept of federalism, which requires that state lawmakers, not the federal government are the 'primary regulators of professional [medical] conduct,'" Tallman wrote. He concluded, "The Attorney General's unilateral attempt to regulate general medical practices historically entrusted to state lawmakers interferes with the democratic debate about physician assisted suicide and far exceeds the scope of his authority under federal law." Moreover, "To be perfectly clear, we take no position on the merits or morality of physician assisted suicide. We express no opinion on whether the practice is inconsistent with the **public interest** or constitutes illegitimate medical care. This case is simply about who gets to decide."

On January 17, 2006, in a 6-3 decision, the Supreme Court upheld Oregon's statute. Writing for the majority, Justice Anthony Kennedy found that the "authority claimed by the attorney general is both beyond his expertise and incongruous with the **statutory** purposes and design." Although the Oregon law may stand under the decision, the case did not resolve the controversy surrounding physician-assisted suicide. Congress could amend the Controlled Substances Act to allow the Attorney General to determine whether Oregon's law is permissible under the statute, and this amendment would effectively negate the Court's decision.

OTHER STATES

MONTANA: In 2009, the Montana Supreme Court considered a case brought by a terminally ill patient and four doctors. The plaintiffs argued that the state's constitution guaranteed the right for the patient to receive drugs that would end the patient's life. The court ruled that although the constitution did not guarantee the right to physician-assisted suicide, nothing in the constitution prevented doctors from doing so. Accordingly, doctors in the state may prescribe lethal drugs to terminally ill patients.

WASHINGTON: In 2008, voters in Washington considered a proposal that would permit physician-assisted suicide. The language of the initiative was as follows: "This measure would permit terminally ill, competent, adult Washington residents medically predicted to die within six months to request and self-administer lethal medication prescribed by a physician. The measure requires two oral and one written request, two physicians to diagnose the patient and determine the patient is competent, a waiting period, and physician verification of an informed patient decision. Physicians, patients and others acting in **good faith** compliance would have criminal and civil immunity." Voters passed the law with 57.82 percent in favor.

The law applies to those who are 18 or older and who are mentally competent. Two physicians must verify that the patient is terminally ill with less than six months to live; that the patient makes the request voluntarily; and that the patient is informed of other options. The law also imposes a waiting period before a doctor can write a prescription.

ADDITIONAL RESOURCES

Alters, Sandra. *Death and Dying: Who Decides?* Detroit: Gale, Cengage Learning, 2004.

McDougall, Jennifer Fecio, and Martha Gorman. *Euthanasia: A Reference Handbook.* Santa Barbara, CA: ABC-CLIO, 2008.

Paterson, Craig. *Assisted Suicide and Euthanasia: A Natural Law Ethics Approach.* Burlington, VT: Ashgate, 2008.

State of Oregon. "Physician-Assisted Suicide Homepage." http://public.health.oregon.gov/ProviderPartnerResources/EvaluationResearch/DeathwithDignityAct/Pages/index.aspx (accessed August 19, 2012).

ORGANIZATIONS

American Medical Association (AMA)
515 North State Street
Chicago, IL 60610
Toll Free: (800) 621-8335
URL: http://www.ama-assn.org/

FAMILY LAW

PRENUPTIAL AGREEMENTS

Sections within this essay:

- Background
- Requirements for Prenuptial Agreements
- Provisions of a Prenuptial Agreement
  - Inventory
  - Character of Property
  - Spousal Support
  - Escalator Clause
- Contested Agreements
- Child Custody and Child Support
- Postmarital Agreements
- Living Together Agreements
- Engagement Rings
- Probate Concerns
- Additional Resources

BACKGROUND

A prenuptial agreement is a **contract** between two persons who are planning to marry. Prenuptial agreements are often called premarital agreements, and, if entered into subsequent to the marriage, postmarital or antenuptial agreements. These types of contracts typically set forth the rights that each party has to the other's property. Couples can enter into prenuptial agreements prior to a first marriage or prior to a subsequent marriage after death or **divorce** of a prior spouse. Premarital agreements become

operative in the event of divorce or the death of one spouse.

Prenuptial agreements can avoid uncertainty about how a judge would divide property and decide spousal support if the marriage ends in divorce. Either party may be seeking to avoid a major loss of assets, income, investments, or a business in the event of a divorce. People marrying for a second or third time often want to make their children the beneficiaries of all of their assets, rather than have the property pass to a second spouse and that spouse's offspring from a prior marriage. A valid prenuptial agreement will generally supersede whatever state law exists regarding **probate** or divorce issues.

REQUIREMENTS FOR PRENUPTIAL AGREEMENTS

In general, as with any contract, in order to be valid, a prenuptial agreement must be in writing and signed by the parties. In most states, the parties must fully disclose all income and assets to the other party. In a few states, it may be possible to waive a full disclosure of income and assets, but the spouse waiving that right must do so knowingly. If it is difficult to determine the exact validity of all of the assets, for example in a small family-owned business, the agreement should acknowledge some type of approximate value.

Additionally, the terms of the agreement must be reasonable. An agreement cannot be unusually harsh and unfair or the court will likely decline to uphold it. Blatantly unfair agreements are termed unconscionable agreements. Usually this means no reasonable person would enter into agreement with such terms. If a court finds an agreement to be unconscionable, the agreement will not be enforced.

Finally, both parties must have a fair opportunity to review the proposed agreement and to have independent legal **counsel**. While an agreement where both parties did not hire counsel is not necessarily invalid, hiring attorneys is another step that can demonstrate to the court that the agreement is fairly drafted and that both parties are making informed decisions. This is particularly true if two attorneys negotiate the agreement, drafting and redrafting various provisions to the satisfaction of the parties.

PROVISIONS OF A PRENUPTIAL AGREEMENT

Although each couple will have different circumstances, prenuptial agreements generally address a number of different aspects of the couple's agreement. These usually include the following:

Inventory The agreement should have an inventory, often attached as an exhibit to the agreement of each party's property, assets and debts which will be brought into the marriage.

Character of Property The agreement should specify the character of certain types of property, whether they will be owned as marital or separate property, or a combination thereof. This would include investment earnings from property previously owned, the earnings of each spouse, and any subsequent **inheritance**. The agreement should also set forth how property will be distributed in the event of death of either spouse or in the event of divorce.

Spousal Support The agreement should also specify the level (if any) of spousal support in the event of divorce. State laws do not set a specific amount of support that must be provided for premarital agreements. Many courts will apply broader notions of fairness and require support at a level higher than subsistence, so the level of support must be reasonable given the party's circumstances.

Escalator Clause An escalator clause increases the amount of assets or support given to one spouse based on the length of the marriage or sometimes on a significant increase in one spouse's assets or income. If one spouse is concerned that assets or income could devalue in the future, that spouse could include a provision that the amount of property given to the other spouse would never exceed a certain percentage of the entire value of all the assets.

CONTESTED AGREEMENTS

A prenuptial agreement can be contested, not simply during a divorce of the parties, but by the children or parents of a deceased spouse. The party contesting the agreement is usually seeking to have it declared void so that the existing probate or divorce laws will apply. Claims may be made that a spouse did not fully understand the agreement or that one spouse forced the other, physically or mentally, to sign the agreement. A challenge of this type is often termed **duress**. To avoid this sort of challenge, the couple should enter into the agreement well before the wedding. While most jurisdictions do not specify a particular time frame, the more time the couple has to review and consider the provisions of the agreement, the more chance a court would find it voluntary. While an agreement proposed and signed a day or two before the wedding is not **per se** invalid, it may be a factor which the court considers in deciding whether to uphold the agreement at a later date.

Other grounds for contesting an agreement may be that some misrepresentations took place which induced one spouse to sign the agreement. One spouse may have made misrepresentations about the agreement itself, perhaps that it was non-binding, only for tax purposes, or temporary. The agreement may also face a serious challenge if all assets were not fully disclosed. Although this is another form of misrepresentation, a challenge of this sort is typically termed **fraud**. An agreement may well be invalid on this basis if one spouse intentionally misrepresents certain aspects of income or assets.

Another theory used to contest prenuptial agreements is that one spouse lacked capacity. If a party was ill, taking medication which affected mental capacity, or was intoxicated by alcohol or influenced by other drugs, the agreement may not be valid under the rules of basic contract law.

CHILD CUSTODY AND CHILD SUPPORT

A prenuptial agreement may contain provisions regarding **child custody**, visitation, and **child support**; however, a divorce court would not be bound by such provisions. Courts have the power to decide on child custody, visitation rights, and child support. The court would look with particular disfavor on these provisions for children of both parties who were not even born at the time of the prenuptial agreement.

POSTMARITAL AGREEMENTS

Postmarital or antenuptial agreements are drafted after the marriage has taken place but before either party separates, divorces, leaves, or dies. These contracts contain provisions similar to those in premarital contracts. Courts look carefully at these types of agreements since once the marriage has taken place it is sometimes the case that one of the parties is unwilling to enter into the agreement. A postmarital agreement may alter the rules for the division of property between the spouses in the event of divorce or death. A married couple may seek to enter into a postmarital agreement after a significant financial change or after a reunification subsequent to a separation. A Marital Settlement Agreement is a particular form of postmarital agreement that specifies the distribution of property and responsibility for debt between the respective spouses as part of a divorce.

LIVING TOGETHER AGREEMENTS

The same concerns and considerations by couples who do plan to marry and who draw up a premarital contract apply to couples who plan never to marry. There is nothing illegal about an unmarried couple living together. Any governmental interference with a couple's right to live together would be considered a violation of the couple's right to free association under the First Amendment to the United States Constitution. An unmarried couple living together can enter into an agreement to share expenses or acquire property, including real estate. An unmarried couple can also enter into a **trust**, which would allow for a more specific distribution of certain assets and would protect the couple in the event of **disability** or incapacity of one of the partners.

ENGAGEMENT RINGS

There are two legal theories with respect to engagement rings. One theory is that an engagement ring is a gift and belongs to the person receiving it. The other theory is that an engagement ring is a conditional gift given in anticipation of marriage. Under this theory, if the marriage will not take place, the condition upon which the gift was given has been removed, and the ring belongs to the giver. A number of court cases have actually addressed this issue. In some states, if the person who gave the ring broke off the engagement, the person who received the ring is entitled to keep it. Since property which is a gift is generally considered separate property, once the marriage takes place, the ring then belongs to the wearer even if the marriage ends in divorce.

PROBATE CONCERNS

When a couple enters into a prenuptial agreement, the parties may also sign other documents relating to probate concerns and plans. The couple may contract to make a will or a trust with particular terms once they are married. (Signing new **wills** at the same time as a prenuptial agreement is an option; however, once the marriage takes place, the wills would need to be redrafted to reflect the marriage in order for the terms to remain valid.) The couple may choose to create a trust to manage certain aspects of estate planning. A trust created in connection with a premarital agreement might be used as a tool to manage and protect the assets of each spouse, as well as to establish a fund for the benefit of the less wealthy spouse. The prenuptial agreement might provide that in the event of divorce or death, the less wealthy spouse's entitlement to assets might be limited to the money or property in the trust.

In many estate plans, the Trust is the central tool that is used to control and manage property. A Trust continues despite the incapacity or death of the grantor. It determines how a **Trustee** is to act with respect to the Trust estate. It determines how property is to be distributed after the death of the grantor. A properly drawn Trust is a separate entity that does not die when the creator dies. The successor Trustee can take over management of the Trust estate and pay bills and taxes and promptly distribute the Trust assets to the beneficiaries, without court supervision, if the Trust agreement gives the Trustee that power. Trusts, unlike Wills, are generally private documents. The public would be able to see how much the descendent owned and who the beneficiaries were under a Will, but typically not with a Trust. Like a Will, however, a Trust can be used to provide for minor children, children from a prior marriage and a second spouse in the same trust, transfer a family-operated or closely-held business, provide for pets, provide for charities and can remove life insurance benefits from a taxable estate, while still controlling the designation of insurance beneficiaries.

ADDITIONAL RESOURCES

American Bar Association. "Five Myths About Premarital Agreements." *Law Trends & News* vol. 7, no. 3 (spring 2011).

Rickard, Jacqueline. *Complete Premarital Contracting: Loving Communication for Today's Couples.* New York: Evans, 1993.

Wallman, Lester, and Sharon McDonnell. *Cupid, Couples, & Contracts: A Guide to Living Together, Prenuptial Agreements, and Divorce.* Boring, OR: Master Media, 1994.

ORGANIZATIONS

American Academy of Matrimonial Lawyers
150 N. Michigan Ave, Suite 1420
Chicago, IL 60601
Phone: (312) 263-6477
URL: http://www.aaml.org

American Bar Association (ABA)
321 North Clark Street

Chicago, IL 60610
Phone: (312) 988-5603
Toll Free: (800) 285-2221
Fax: (312) 988-6800
URL: http://www.americanbar.org

Children's Rights Council
9470 Annapolis Road, Suite 310
Lanham, MD 20706
Phone: (301) 459-1220
URL: http://www.crckids.org

FAMILY LAW

TERMINATION OF PARENTAL RIGHTS

Sections within this essay:

- Introduction
- Grounds to Terminate Parental Rights
- Exceptions to Termination
- Federal Legislation
  – Adoption Assistance and Child Welfare Act
  – Adoption and Safe Families Act
- Constitutional Rights
- Consequences of Termination
- State Laws on Termination of Parental Rights
- Additional Resources

INTRODUCTION

Each state and territory in the United States has enacted a **statute** governing situations where a court can terminate a parent's rights to a child. In many situations, the parent and child often have no relationship, and by terminating this relationship, the court effectively allows the child to be placed for **adoption**. As a general matter, a court will only terminate the parent-child relationship if such a termination is in the child's best interests. Nevertheless, the process can be rather contentious.

State statutes establish the grounds on which the parent-child relationship can be terminated. Most states provide a list of criteria. In some states, the list is shorter, and the particular criteria is more general. In other states,

the list of factors is longer and more detailed. Several states have also approved exceptions to termination. For instance, a parent may not have the financial resources to care for a child, and several state laws prevent termination of the relationship if the lack of financial resources was the reason for the parent not caring for the child.

Federal legislation also applies to some termination cases, and courts must also protect the **constitutional rights** of both parents and children.

GROUNDS TO TERMINATE PARENTAL RIGHTS

In some situations, a child's birth parents may wish to terminate their rights to a child, especially if the parents are considering putting the child up for adoption. Even in voluntary termination cases, the court must make some decisions before terminating the relationship. As a general matter, the court must decide, by clear and convincing **evidence**, that a parent is unfit. Moreover, the court must also decide that terminating the relationship is in the child's best interests.

The specific grounds a court will consider before terminating a parent's rights vary by state law. In general, state laws allow a court to terminate the parent-child relationship when the child cannot be returned to the parent's home. This usually means there is a risk of harm to the child or the parent cannot provide for the child. Common factors under state law include the following:

- The parent severely or chronically abuses or neglects the child.
- The parent abuses or neglects other children in the household.

- The child is abandoned.
- The parent suffers from long-term mental illness or deficiency.
- The parent is incapacitated by long-term alcohol or drug use.
- The parent has failed to support or maintain contact with the child.
- The parent has had rights to another child terminated.
- The parent has been convicted of a violent crime against the child or another family member.
- The parent has been convicted of a **felony**, the parent's **incarceration** will have a negative impact on the child, and the child can only receive care through **foster care**.

EXCEPTIONS TO TERMINATION

More than half the states, as well as the District of Columbia, have statutes providing that the court will not terminate parental rights under certain circumstances. These include:

- The child has been placed in the care of another family member or relative.
- A state agency has found compelling reasons showing that terminating the parent's rights is not in the child's best interests.
- The parent has not received services required under state law to allow for the parent to be reunited with the child.
- The parent lacks financial resources to care for the child.

FEDERAL LEGISLATION

In addition to state law requirements, two federal statutes also apply to cases involving termination of parental rights. These statutes include:

Adoption Assistance and Child Welfare Act Congress enacted the Adoption Assistance and Child Welfare Act in 1980. This Act was designed to address the problem with children remaining in foster homes for too long. Under this Act, states are encouraged to employ reasonable efforts to prevent a child's removal and bring a child back into a home. The Act also requires states to engage in "permanency planning" and review a child's case periodically.

Although the Act does not provide for an independent cause of action, states receive certain funds for complying with the Act.

Adoption and Safe Families Act The second federal Act is the Adoption and Safe Families Act, which Congress approved in 1997. This Act was designed to limit the amount of time that children spend in foster care. The Act was also designed to speed up the adoption process. Under the Act, if a child is in foster care for 15 of the preceding 22 months, then the state should pursue termination proceedings. The Act generally requires the proceeding to occur within one year, but the proceeding may occur sooner if there are aggravating circumstances such as **sexual abuse**.

The Act also provides for exceptions. The Act's requirements do not apply if the child has been placed with a relative, if services for reunification have not been provided, or the court does not believe that termination is in the child's best interests.

Several states have incorporated the requirements and exceptions from the Adoption and Safe Families Act as part of their **statutory** schemes.

CONSTITUTIONAL RIGHTS

The U.S. Supreme Court has recognized that parents are entitled to rights under the Constitution. For instance, in the case of *Santosky v. Kramer* (1982), the Court concluded that for a state to terminate a parent's rights, the state must meet requirements by showing clear and convincing evidence. The Court considered this standard to strike an appropriate balance between the state's interests and the rights of parents.

Parents have successfully argued that other constitutional provisions protect their rights. For instance, a state statute establishing grounds for termination may be unconstitutionally vague, which would provide grounds for an **appellate court** to set aside a termination.

On the other hand, many arguments based on constitutional rights have failed. For example, several parents have argued that they should be entitled to a lawyer when faced with a termination proceeding. However, the courts have held that a parent does not generally have the **right to counsel** in these proceedings. Likewise, courts have rejected arguments based on free speech or freedom of religion.

CONSEQUENCES OF TERMINATION

A termination proceeding may sever the rights to one or both parents. If both parents lose their parental rights, the state must assume **custody** of the child as well as the responsibility of finding permanent placement for the child. This permanent placement must take the form of adoption or **guardianship**, and it must take place within a reasonable period of time.

In a minority of states, a state must achieve permanent placement within the period of time set forth in the statute. If the state fails to do so within this time period, a parent may request reinstatement of parental rights, which the court may grant if the parent is able to show that the parent can provide a safe home for the child.

STATE LAWS ON TERMINATION OF PARENTAL RIGHTS

Although state statutes on termination of parental rights vary from state to state, different states often have similar requirements. Every state establishes specific grounds on which a court may terminate a parent's rights, and several states also establish exceptions to such terminations. Examples of state statutes are:

ALABAMA: If the court finds from clear and convincing evidence that the parents of a child are unable or unwilling to discharge their responsibilities to their child, it may terminate the parental rights of the parents. In making this determination, the court shall consider, but not be limited to, the following:

- The parent has abandoned the child.
- Emotional illness, mental illness, or mental deficiency of the parent, or excessive use of alcohol or controlled substances has rendered the parent unable to care for the child.
- The parent has tortured, abused, cruelly beaten, or otherwise maltreated the child; or attempted to torture, abuse, cruelly beat, or otherwise maltreat the child; or the child is in clear and present danger of being thus tortured, abused, cruelly beaten, or otherwise maltreated as evidenced by the treatment of a sibling.
- The parent has been convicted of and imprisoned for a felony.
- The parent has committed any of the following: (1) Murder or **manslaughter** of another child of that parent; (2) Aiding, abetting, attempting, conspiring, or soliciting to commit murder or manslaughter of another child of that parent; (3) A felony **assault** or abuse that results in serious bodily injury to the surviving child or another child of that parent; (4) Unexplained serious physical injury to the child proved to be the result of the intentional conduct or willful neglect of the parent.
- Reasonable efforts to rehabilitate the parent have failed.
- Parental rights to a sibling of the child have been involuntarily terminated.

- The parent has failed to provide for the material needs of the child or to pay a reasonable portion of support of the child when the parent is able to do so.
- The parent has failed to maintain regular visits with the child in accordance with a visitation plan.
- The parent has failed to maintain consistent contact or communication with the child.

CALIFORNIA: Parental rights shall not be terminated if:

- The child is living with a relative who is unable or unwilling to adopt the child.
- The court finds a compelling reason for determining that termination would be detrimental to the child due to one or more of the following circumstances: (1) The parents have maintained regular visitation and contact with the child. (2) A child age 12 or older objects to the termination. (3) The child is placed in a residential treatment facility and adoption is unlikely or undesirable. (3) The child is living with a foster parent or Native American custodian who is unable or unwilling to adopt the child because of exceptional circumstances. (4) There would be substantial interference with a child's sibling relationship.

The statute also includes provisions that apply specifically to Native American children.

IDAHO: The court may grant an order terminating parental rights when it finds that such termination is in the best interests of the child and that one or more of the following conditions exist:

- The parent has abandoned the child.
- The parent has neglected or abused the child.
- The presumptive parent is not the biological parent of the child.
- The parent is unable to discharge parental responsibilities, and such inability will continue for a prolonged indeterminate period and will be injurious to the health, morals, or well-being of the child.
- The parent has been incarcerated and is likely to remain incarcerated for a substantial period of time during the child's minority.
- The parent caused the child to be conceived as a result of rape, **incest**, lewd conduct with a minor child under age 16, or sexual abuse of a child under age 16.
- The parent has subjected the child to torture, chronic abuse, or sexual abuse.
- The parent has committed murder or intentionally killed the other parent of the child; has committed murder or voluntary manslaughter of another child;

or has aided, abetted, conspired or solicited to commit such murder or voluntary manslaughter.

- The parent has committed battery that resulted in serious bodily injury to a child.

- The court determines the child to be an abandoned infant, except in a parental termination action brought by one parent against another parent.

KANSAS: The court may terminate parental rights when it finds by clear and convincing evidence that the parent is unfit by reason of conduct or condition that makes the parent unable to care properly for a child, and the conduct or condition is unlikely to change in the foreseeable future. In making a determination of unfitness, the court shall consider, but is not limited to, the following:

- Emotional illness, mental illness, mental deficiency, or physical **disability** of such duration or nature as to make the parent unable to care for the child

- Conduct toward a child of a physically, emotionally, or sexually cruel or abusive nature

- The use of intoxicating liquors or dangerous drugs that render the parent unable to care for a child

- Physical, mental, or emotional abuse, neglect, or sexual abuse of a child

- Conviction of a felony and imprisonment

- Unexplained injury or death of another child or stepchild of the parent

- Failure of reasonable efforts made by appropriate public or private agencies to rehabilitate the family

- Lack of effort on the part of the parent to adjust the parent's circumstances, conduct, or conditions to meet the needs of the child

- Whether the child has been in extended out-of-home placement as a result of actions or inactions attributable to the parent and any of the following factors

In addition, when a child is not in the physical custody of a parent, the court shall consider, but is not limited to, the following:

- Failure to assure care of the child when able to do so

- Failure to maintain regular visitation, contact, or communication with the child

- Failure to carry out a reasonable plan approved by the court directed toward the integration of the child into a parental home

- Failure to pay a reasonable portion of the cost of substitute physical care and maintenance based on ability to pay

OKLAHOMA: Under Oklahoma law: (1) The incarceration of a parent shall not in and of itself be sufficient to deprive a parent of parental rights; and (2) a finding that a parent has a diagnosed cognitive disorder, extreme physical incapacity, or a medical condition, including behavioral health or substance dependency, shall not in and of itself deprive the parent of parental rights.

ADDITIONAL RESOURCES

De Witt, John Gregory, Peter N. Swisher, and Sheryl L. Wolf. *Understanding Family Law.* 3d ed. Newark, NJ: LexisNexis, 2005.

Katz, Sanford N. *Family Law in America.* New York: Oxford University Press, 2011.

Krause, Harry D. and David D. Meyer. *Family Law.* 4th ed. Eagan, MN: West, Thomson Reuters, 2009.

Oliphant, Robert E., and Nancy Ver Steegh. *Family Law: Examples and Explanations.* 3d ed. New York: Aspen Publishers, 2010.

ORGANIZATIONS

Administration for Children and Families, U.S. Department of Health and Human Services

370 L'Enfant Promenade SW
Washington, DC 20447
Phone: (202) 401-2337
URL: http://www.acf.gov

American Bar Association (ABA)

321 North Clark Street
Chicago, IL 60610
Phone: (312) 988-5000
Toll Free: (800) 285-2221
Fax: (312) 988-6800
URL: http://www.americanbar.org

National Guardianship Association (NGA)

174 Crestview Drive
Bellefonte, PA 16823-8516
Toll Free: (877) 326-5992
Fax: (814) 355-2452
URL: http://www.guardianship.org/

FAMILY LAW

UNMARRIED PARENTS

Sections within this essay:

- Background
- Unmarried Parents Living Together
- Paternity Actions
- Paternity Tests
  - Blood Tests
  - DNA Tests

- Custody and Visitation
- Artificial Conception
  - Artificial Insemination
  - Invitro Fertilization
  - Surrogate Mothers

- Welfare
- Names
- Taxes
- Additional Resources

BACKGROUND

Children born out of wedlock are entitled to the same rights and protections as children born in wedlock. Unmarried fathers have rights and duties similar to those of married fathers. One of the most important legal responsibilities of parents is supporting their children. Parents are legally obligated to provide their children with all the necessities of life. The failure of parents to marry does not affect their responsibility to support their children. If parents are unmarried and cannot agree upon how much each should contribute toward the support of their children, the courts may decide. A court can order one parent to make specified payments to the other for **child support**.

State laws provide that biological parents make all the decisions involving their children, including education, health care, and religious upbringing. Parents are not required to secure the **legal right** to make these decisions if they are married and are listed on the child's birth certificate. However, if there is disagreement about who has the right to make these decisions courts can decide.

UNMARRIED PARENTS LIVING TOGETHER

Couples who are living together but are not married should take steps to ensure that both are recognized as the legal parents. Both parents can be listed on the birth certificate. A parent who is not listed can be added after the birth of a child if the parent contacts the state Bureau of Vital Statistics in which the birth took place. Most states require unmarried fathers to sign an **affidavit** or acknowledgment of **paternity**.

PATERNITY ACTIONS

A paternity action is a legal proceeding that allows unmarried parents to resolve issues about **child custody** and visitation similar to those dealt with in a **divorce** proceeding. Establishing paternity means establishing the identity of the child's father. A father can acknowledge paternity by signing a written admission or voluntary acknowledgment of paternity. All States have programs under which birthing hospitals give unmarried parents of a newborn the opportunity to acknowledge the father's paternity of the child. States must also help parents acknowledge paternity up to the child's eighteenth birthday through vital records offices or other entities designated by the State. Parents are not required to apply for child support enforcement services when acknowledging paternity.

Paternity cases do not have to involve a dispute between the parties about who the father is. Sometimes the parties will stipulate that they are the parents of the child. If, however, parentage is an issue in the case, then it must be handled prior to addressing other matters such as support and visitation. Paternity establishment can provide basic emotional, social, and economic ties between a father and his child. Once paternity is established, a child gains legal rights and privileges. Among these may be rights to **inheritance**, rights to the father's medical and life insurance benefits, and rights to social security and possibly veterans' benefits. The child also has a chance to develop a relationship with the father and to develop both a sense of identity and connection. It may be important for the health of the child for doctors to have knowledge of the father's medical history.

PATERNITY TESTS

Paternity can be determined by highly accurate tests conducted on blood or tissue samples of the father, or alleged father, mother and child. These tests have an accuracy range of between 90 and 99 percent. They can exclude a man who is not the biological father and can also show the likelihood of paternity if he is not excluded. Each party in a contested paternity case must submit to genetic tests at the request of either party. If the father could be one of several men, each may be required to take a genetic test. It is almost always possible to determine who fathered a baby and to rule out anyone who did not. There are several different ways to establish whether an alleged father is the natural and legal father of the minor child.

Blood Tests Paternity blood testing was first performed in the middle half of the twentieth century by comparing blood types of tested parties. This involved isolation of blood sera from antigen-challenged individuals that did not possess certain red blood cell antigens. These antigens are protein molecules that may be combined with sugar molecules and reside in the red blood cell membrane. These sera cause coagulation of red blood cells in individuals that possess that particular red blood cell antigen. In the ABO blood typing system, humans can possess the A antigen (A blood type), the B antigen (B blood type), both the A and B antigen (AB blood type), or neither of these antigens (O blood type). Red blood cell antigen systems of this sort can be used for paternity testing because there are genes that code for the antigens and these are inherited genes. A mother who has Type B

blood and a father who has Type O blood could not have a child who has type AB blood. The true father of the child must have the gene for the A antigen. Using RBC antigen systems for paternity testing did not provide for a very powerful test because the frequencies of the genes that coded for the antigens are not very low.

In the 1970s a more powerful test using white blood cell antigens or Human Leukocyte Antigens (HLA) was developed. This produced a test that was able to exclude about 95 percent of falsely **accused** fathers. Several milliliters of blood are required to perform the test. Blood types cannot be used to determine who the father is; however, blood types can be used to determine the biological possibility of fatherhood.

DNA Tests DNA (Deoxyribonucleic Acid) is the genetic material present in every cell of the human body. Except in the case of identical multiple births, each individual's DNA is unique. A child receives half of his or her genetic material (DNA) from the biological mother and half from the biological father. During **DNA testing**, the genetic characteristics of the child are compared to those of the mother. Characteristics that cannot be found in the mother must have been inherited from the father. DNA paternity testing is the most accurate form of paternity testing possible. If DNA patterns between the child and the alleged father do not match on two or more DNA probes, then the alleged father can be totally ruled out. If the DNA patterns between mother, child, and the alleged father match on every DNA probe, the likelihood of paternity is 99.9 percent. Either a blood test known as Restriction Fragment Length Polymorphism (RFLP) or a procedure called a Buccal scrap is used for DNA testing. A swab is rubbed vigorously against the inside of the subject's cheek. This provides a DNA sample for testing. Children can be tested at any age. Paternity testing can even be done on an umbilical cord blood specimen at birth. DNA testing is one of the easiest medical procedures for children. Since DNA is the same in every cell of the human body, the accuracy of testing performed on cheek cells utilizing the Buccal Swab is the same as an actual blood sample.

CUSTODY AND VISITATION

In most states, when a child is born to an unmarried mother, if there is no **adjudication** or registration of paternity, the mother has **custody**. Once paternity has been established, a father has the right to seek custody of or visitation with his child. Even after paternity has been adjudicated or registered, as long as there is no court order on custody, many states presume that the mother has custody of the child. A custody agreement between the parents or a court order can clarify custody and visitation issues. Unmarried parents without custody are entitled to the same visitation rights as divorced parents, absence extraordinary factors such as abuse or **domestic violence**.

ARTIFICIAL CONCEPTION

Modern medicine and science have allowed opportunities for conceiving children through **artificial insemination**, in vitro fertilization, and embryo transplantation. Combined with these techniques is the practice of **surrogate motherhood**. These new techniques have also created legal questions and disputes regarding the child's status and the rights and designation of the parents.

Artificial Insemination When a married woman, with the consent of her husband, conceives a child by artificial insemination from a **donor** other than her husband, the law generally recognizes the child as the husband's legitimate child. Most states have presumption laws which presume a child born to a married woman is the child of her husband, and the designation of the husband as father in a case involving artificial insemination derives from those laws.

Invitro Fertilization Invitro fertilization and egg transplantation involves the fertilization of the egg outside the womb. Where the egg is donated by another woman, the birth mother will be treated in law as the legitimate mother of the child.

Surrogate Mothers Undoubtedly a legally complex area is that of surrogate motherhood. In the most common arrangement, a married couple in which the husband is fertile but the wife is unable to carry a pregnancy enter into a privately arranged **contract** with a fertile woman. This fertile woman (the surrogate mother) agrees to be artificially inseminated with the sperm of the fertile husband. Alternatively, the surrogate mother may be impregnated with an embryo produced by the wife's ovum. In either case, the surrogate mother carries the pregnancy until delivery, and then, per the contract, assumes no parental rights or responsibilities and relinquishes the infant to the couple initiating the contract. These reproductive arrangements enable one woman to bear a child for another, thus separating genetic, gestational, and rearing parentage. Surrogate motherhood raises medical, psychological, ethical, and legal questions involving procreative **privacy** and the nature of parenting and family life.

The desire to have a child who is genetically related to at least one parent may make surrogacy a more attractive option than **adoption** for some couples. When women take on the role of surrogate mother to assist members of their own family, few legal complications arise. In some cases where women have agreed to the procedure for financial compensation, major legal issues have arisen. About half the states have laws which address surrogacy. In some states, surrogate mother contracts are illegal and entering into them can result in criminal charges. Other states rule that such contracts are invalid.

In an artificial insemination case, in which the husband is the donor to the surrogate, a court order can be obtained prior to the birth of the child that the husband is the father of the child. After the child is born, the surrogate mother signs consent forms which either terminate her parental rights, leaving the man with sole custody of the child, or which allow the wife of the couple to adopt. In a case involving egg fertilization outside the womb and an embryo transplant to the womb of the surrogate, a pre-birth court order can be obtained indicating that the couple is the child's biological parents. In this case, no adoption is necessary.

WELFARE

Federal welfare law requires minor custodial parents receiving cash assistance to attend school and live with their parents or in an adult-supervised setting. Congress established these requirements as part of the Personal Responsibility and Work Opportunity Reconciliation Act (PRWORA), which created the program for Temporary Assistance for Needy Families (TANF) and abolished the Aid to Families with Dependent Children (AFDC) program. A number of States have also established similar requirements.

Welfare policies that apply specifically to teenage parents pose a special challenge, because many young parents do not head their own cash assistance case. When an assistance case includes an older adult, an adolescent, and a very young child, it is often unclear whether the adolescent or the older adult is the parent of the young child, at least for assistance purposes. States are not supposed to use TANF block grant funds to provide financial assistance to unmarried minor custodial parents who do not have a high school diploma or its equivalent unless they are attending school. To meet this requirement, state welfare agencies must define school attendance requirements, obtain attendance information, and follow up with teenager parents who fail to attend school.

NAMES

The parents (as recognized by law) of a child are allowed to name the child whatever they choose. This is true for the first, middle and last names. A child is not required to have the last name of the father, or of either parent. Unmarried parents may give the child the last name of the father on the theory that a name is something inherited and passed down through paternal lineage. Unmarried parents may give the child the last name of the mother on the theory that if men were the ones spending numerous hours in labor, they would hardly be naming their children after women. The parents may select a hyphenated name or an entirely unrelated name.

TAXES

If a couple is unmarried, only one person can claim the child as a dependent for **income tax** return purposes in any given year. An unmarried couple can alternate years or decide that the person with the higher income takes the tax **deduction**. While both parents may be entitled to claim a child, only one person can legally take the exemption each year.

ADDITIONAL RESOURCES

Katz, Sanford N. *Family Law in America*. New York: Oxford University Press, 2011.

Ross, Julie. *Joint Custody with a Jerk: Raising a Child with an Uncooperative Ex*. New York: St. Martin's Press, 1996.

Wallman, Lester, and Sharon McDonnell. *Cupid, Couples, & Contracts: A Guide to Living Together, Prenuptial Agreements, and Divorce*. Boring, OR: Master Media, 1994.

ORGANIZATIONS

American Bar Association (ABA)

321 North Clark Street
Chicago, IL 60610
Phone: (312) 988-5603
Toll Free: (800) 285-2221
Fax: (312) 988-6800
URL: http://www.americanbar.org

Child Welfare League of America

50 F Street NW, 6th Floor
Washington, DC 20001-2085
Phone: (202) 638-2952
Fax: (202) 638-4004

National Association of Child Advocates

1522 K Street, NW, Suite 600
Washington, DC 20005-1202

FIRST AMENDMENT LAW

ASSEMBLY

Sections within this essay:

- Background
- Content-Based vs. Content-Neutral Restrictions on Free Speech
- Public vs. Private Speech
- Reasonable Time, Place, and Manner Restrictions
- Overbreadth and Vagueness
- Permissible and Impermissible Restrictions on Rights of Assembly
  - Speech and Assembly in Public Streets and Parks
  - Parade Permits and Other Restrictions
  - Speech and Assembly in Libraries and Theatres
  - Speech and Assembly in Airports and Other Public Transportation Centers
  - Picketing and Other Demonstrations
  - Loitering and Vagrancy Statutes
  - Speech and Assembly on Private Property
- State Laws Affecting Rights of Assembly
- Additional Resources

BACKGROUND

The First Amendment of the **Bill of Rights** provides that "Congress shall make no law . . . abridging . . . the right of the people peaceably to assemble." This provision applies to state government entities through the Due Process Clause of the Fourteenth Amendment. Though neither the federal Constitution nor any state constitution specifically protects rights of association, the U.S. Supreme Court and other courts have extended assembly rights to include rights of association.

Rights to free speech and assembly are not absolute under the relevant **jurisprudence**. Government entities may restrict many types of speech without violating First Amendment protections. Many of the Supreme Court's First Amendment cases focus on two main questions: first, whether the restriction on speech was based on the content of the speech; and second, whether the speech was given in a traditional public forum or elsewhere. Some questions focus exclusively on the actual speech, rather than on aspects of the right to assembly. Other questions contain aspects of both the right to free speech and the right to assemble peacefully. Cases addressing free speech plus some conduct in the exercise of assembly rights often pose complex questions, since either the speech rights or the assembly rights may not protect the parties in these types of cases.

Since the courts take into consideration such a variety of factors when determining whether a particular speech or a particular assemblage is protected by the First Amendment, it is difficult to provide a concise definition of rights of assembly. Even in areas where a government entity may restrict speech or assembly rights, courts are more likely to find a violation of the First Amendment if speech or assembly is banned completely. Some restrictions merely involve the application for a permit or license to assemble, such as obtaining a license to hold a parade in a public street. Other time, place, and/or manner restrictions may also apply.

CONTENT-BASED VS. CONTENT-NEUTRAL RESTRICTIONS ON FREE SPEECH

The outcome of a First Amendment case may very well hinge on whether the restriction of speech is based on the content of the speech. If the restriction is content-based, courts scrutinize the restriction under a heightened standard, compared with restrictions that are content-neutral. When courts apply this heightened scrutiny, they are more likely to find a First Amendment violation. Courts also recognize that content-neutral restrictions may cause as much or more harm than content-based restrictions. For example, a ban on all parades on public streets is much more intrusive than a ban on only some parades. If a restriction is content-neutral, a court will employ an intermediate standard of scrutiny.

Determining whether a restriction is content-neutral or content-based may be more difficult in the context of assembly rights than in the context of speech rights. For example, if a city requires that all groups obtain a permit to hold a parade, the restriction is more likely, at least on its face, to be content-neutral. However, if the city, through official or unofficial action, only issues permits to certain groups and restricts issuing permits to other groups, the restriction in its application is content-based, not content-neutral.

PUBLIC VS. PRIVATE SPEECH

In addition to determining whether a restriction is content-based or content-neutral, courts also consider whether the speech or assembly is given or held in a public or private forum. Government property that has traditionally been used by the public for the purpose of assembly and to disseminate ideas is considered a traditional public forum. Content-based regulations in a traditional public forum are the most likely forms of speech to be found in violation of the First Amendment. Some content-neutral restrictions on the time, place, and manner of the speech are permitted, however, even in the traditional public forum.

Public-owned facilities that have never been designated for the general use of the public to express ideas are considered nonforums. Government may reasonably restrict speech, including some content-based speech, in these nonforums. This does not mean that all speech may be restricted on such property, but it does mean that speech can be restricted to achieve a reasonable government purpose if is not intended to suppress the viewpoint of a particular speaker.

Some public property that is not a traditional public forum may become a designated or limited public forum if it is opened to the use of the general public to express ideas. Examples include a senior center that has been opened for the general public to express ideas or a state-operated television station used for political debates. Courts will strictly scrutinize content-based restrictions in a designated or limited public forum when the restriction on speech is related to the designated public use of the property.

REASONABLE TIME, PLACE, AND MANNER RESTRICTIONS

Government entities may make reasonable content-neutral restrictions on the time, place, and manner of a speech or assemblage, even in a traditional public forum. This action directly affects the rights of assembly, since a government entity may restrict the time and place where an assembly may take place, as well as the manner in which the assembly occurs. The restrictions must be reasonable and narrowly tailored to meet a significant government purpose. The government entity must also leave open ample channels for interested parties that wish to communicate.

OVERBREADTH AND VAGUENESS

Statutes and ordinances are often found to infringe on First Amendment rights because they are unconstitutionally vague or the breadth of the **statute** or **ordinance** extends so far that it infringes on protected speech. For example, some statutes and ordinances prohibiting loitering on public property have been found to be unconstitutional on the grounds of overbreadth since some people could be prosecuted for exercising their protected First Amendment rights. Similarly, statutes and ordinances restricting speech may be so vague that a person of ordinary intelligence could not determine what speech was restricted based on a reading of the law.

For example, in *Virginia v. Hicks* (2003), the City of Richmond, Virginia, was challenged for restricting access to a street by non-residents, in an attempt to stop suspected drug dealers from frequenting the area. Loitering notices were served on outsiders, including Hicks, who told the police that he was delivering diapers. As a non-resident, he had previously been served notice, and this time, was arrested. He challenged the law as overbroad, alleging interference with his First Amendment rights. However, the Supreme Court upheld the law, finding First Amendment restrictions too speculative or insignificant to outweigh the government's interest in controlling known crime in the area.

PERMISSIBLE AND IMPERMISSIBLE RESTRICTIONS ON RIGHTS OF ASSEMBLY

It is difficult to make general statements about when assembly rights are guaranteed and when they are not. Whether assembly is or is not guaranteed depends largely on where and when the assembly takes place, as well as the specific restrictions that were placed on this right by government entities.

Speech and Assembly in Public Streets and Parks Public streets, sidewalks, and parks are generally considered public forums, and content-based restrictions on these will be strictly scrutinized by the courts. However, reasonable time, place, and manner restrictions are permitted if they are neutral regarding the content of the speech.

The use of public streets, sidewalks, and parks may not always be considered use of public forums, which often causes confusion in this area. For example, in the 1990 case of *United States v. Kokinda*, the Supreme Court held that a regulation restricting use of a sidewalk in front of a post office was valid because, in part, that particular sidewalk was not a public forum. Similar results have been reached with respect to some public parks.

Parade Permits and Other Restrictions The right to assemble and hold parades on public streets is one of the more important rights of assembly. However, these rights must be balanced with the interests of government entities to maintain peace and order. The Supreme Court in the 1992 case of *Forsyth County v. Nationalist Movement* held that a government entity may require permits for those wishing to hold a parade, march, or rally on public streets or other public forums. Local officials may not be given overly broad discretion to issue such permits.

Speech and Assembly in Libraries and Theaters The Supreme Court has held that a publicly owned theatre is a public forum. Thus, government may not make content-based restrictions on speech or assembly in these theaters. However, government entities may make reasonable time, place, and manner restrictions in publicly owned theaters. Libraries, on the other hand, are not considered public forums and may be regulated "in a reasonable and nondiscriminatory manner, equally applicable to all and administered with equality to all."

Speech and Assembly in Airports and Other Public Transportation Centers The Supreme Court has held that airports are not traditional public forums, so government may make certain reasonable restrictions on assembly and speech rights in these areas. Courts have reached different conclusions with respect to other centers of public transportation, such as bus terminals, railway stations, and ports.

Picketing and Other Demonstrations The act of picketing is unquestionably intertwined with the First Amendment right to peaceful assembly. Courts have often recognized the right to picket and hold other peaceful demonstrations particularly in public forums. The right to picket, however, is limited and depends on the specific activities of the participants and the location of the demonstration. For example, if a demonstration breaches the peace or involves other criminal activity, law

enforcement may ordinarily end the demonstration in a reasonable manner. Similarly, a government entity may reasonably restrict demonstrations on public streets in residential areas.

Loitering and Vagrancy Statutes State and local governments have often sought to eliminate undesirable behavior by enacting statutes and ordinances that make loitering a crime. Many of these statutes have been held to be constitutional, even those that prohibit being in a public place and hindering or obstructing the free passage of people. Such rulings have a significant effect on the rights of assembly, since these crimes involve a person's presence in a certain place, in addition to suspicious behavior.

A number of courts have held that specific antiloitering statutes and ordinances have been unconstitutional. Some of these decisions are hinged on First Amendment rights, while others hinge on other rights, such as Fourth Amendment protections against unreasonable searches and seizures. Several of these statutes have been struck down on grounds of vagueness or overbreadth. Similarly, courts have struck down statutes and ordinances outlawing **vagrancy** on the grounds of vagueness or overbreadth.

Speech and Assembly on Private Property The general rule is that owners of private property can restrict speech in a manner that the owner deems appropriate. Some older cases have held that private property, such a privately owned shopping center, could be treated as the equivalent of public property. However, modern cases have held otherwise, finding that private property was not subject to the same analysis regarding First Amendment rights as public property.

STATE LAWS AFFECTING RIGHTS OF ASSEMBLY

Some municipalities in every state require interested individuals to file for a permit to hold a parade or other gathering on public property. These ordinances are often the subject of **litigation** regarding alleged **infringement** on First Amendment rights of peaceful assembly. Antiloitering statutes are also commonplace, though several of these have been challenged on First Amendment grounds as well. Whether a specific ordinance, statute, or official action constitutes a violation of the First Amendment depends largely on the specific facts of the case or the specific language of the statute or ordinance.

ALABAMA: Several municipalities require that interested parties file for a permit to hold a parade in public streets. A number of these ordinances have been attacked on First Amendment grounds, and some ordinances have been found to be in violation of First Amendment rights. The state's criminal laws prohibit loitering, including begging and criminal **solicitation**.

ARIZONA: Several municipalities require that interested parties file for a permit to hold a parade in public streets. The state's criminal laws prohibit loitering, including begging and criminal solicitation.

ARKANSAS: Several municipalities require that interested parties file for a permit to hold a parade in public streets. Some of these ordinances have been attacked on First Amendment grounds, and some ordinances have been found to be in violation of First Amendment rights. The state's criminal laws prohibit loitering.

CALIFORNIA: Several municipalities require that interested parties file for a permit to hold a parade in public streets. A number of these ordinances have been attacked on First Amendment grounds, and some ordinances have been found to be in violation of First Amendment rights. The state's criminal laws prohibit loitering, and these laws have generally been upheld in First Amendment challenges.

COLORADO: Several municipalities require that interested parties file for a permit to hold a parade in public streets. A number of these ordinances have been attacked on First Amendment grounds, and some ordinances have been found to be in violation of First Amendment rights. The state requires a permit for parties to use the state capitol building grounds. The state's criminal laws prohibit loitering, including begging and criminal solicitation. The Colorado Supreme Court held that the state's loitering statute was unconstitutional; this statute was subsequently modified.

DELAWARE: Several municipalities require that interested parties file for a permit to hold a parade in public streets. The state's criminal laws prohibit loitering, including begging, criminal solicitation, and loitering on public school grounds.

FLORIDA: Several municipalities require that interested parties file for a permit to hold a parade in public streets. The state's criminal laws regarding loitering have been the subject of several lawsuits. These laws make it a crime to loiter or prowl in a place, at a time or in a manner not usual for a law-abiding individual.

GEORGIA: Several municipalities require that interested parties file for a permit to hold a parade in public streets. A number of these ordinances have been attacked on First Amendment grounds, and some ordinances have been

found to be in violation of First Amendment rights. The state's criminal laws regarding loitering have been the subject of several lawsuits. These laws make it a crime to loiter or prowl in a place, at a time, or in a manner not usual for a law-abiding individual.

HAWAII: Several municipalities require that interested parties file for a permit to hold a parade in public streets. The state's criminal laws prohibit loitering for solicitation of prostitution.

IDAHO: Several municipalities require that interested parties file for a permit to hold a parade in public streets.

ILLINOIS: Several municipalities require that interested parties file for a permit to hold a parade in public streets or public assembly. A number of these ordinances have been attacked on First Amendment grounds, and some ordinances have been found to be in violation of First Amendment rights. The state statutes permit municipalities to prohibit vagrancy, and loitering is prohibited in the state by criminal statute.

INDIANA: Several municipalities require that interested parties file for a permit to hold a parade in public streets. Criminal gang activity is a separate offense under state criminal laws.

IOWA: Several municipalities require that interested parties file for a permit to hold a parade in public streets. The state provides specific laws prohibiting loitering and other congregation on election days near polling places.

KANSAS: Several municipalities require that interested parties file for a permit to hold a parade in public streets.

KENTUCKY: Several municipalities require that interested parties file for a permit to hold a parade in public streets. The state's criminal laws prohibit loitering for the purpose of engaging in criminal activity.

LOUISIANA: Several municipalities require that interested parties file for a permit to hold a parade in public streets. The state's criminal laws prohibit vagrancy and loitering, though these statutes have been attacked on First Amendment grounds several times.

MAINE: Several municipalities require that interested parties file for a permit to hold a parade in public streets.

MARYLAND: Several municipalities require that interested parties file for a permit to hold a parade or other public assembly in public streets or areas. The state's criminal laws prohibits loitering or loafing around a business establishment licensed to sell alcohol.

MASSACHUSETTS: Several municipalities require that interested parties file for a permit to hold a parade in public streets, though a number of these ordinances have been the subject to challenges on First Amendment grounds. The state's criminal laws prohibit loitering in some specific venues, such as railway centers.

MICHIGAN: Several municipalities require that interested parties file for a permit to hold a parade in public streets. A number of these ordinances have been attacked on First Amendment grounds, and some ordinances have been found to be in violation of First Amendment rights.

MINNESOTA: Several municipalities require that interested parties file for a permit to hold a parade, march, or other form of procession on public streets and other areas. The state's criminal laws prohibit vagrancy, including some instances of loitering.

MISSISSIPPI: Several municipalities require that interested parties file for a permit to hold a parade in public streets. A number of these ordinances have been attacked on First Amendment grounds, and some ordinances have been found to be in violation of First Amendment rights.

MISSOURI: Several municipalities require that interested parties file for a permit to hold a parade in public streets. The state's criminal laws prohibit vagrancy, including some instances of loitering.

MONTANA: Several municipalities require that interested parties file for a permit to hold a parade in public streets. The state's criminal laws prohibit vagrancy and loitering around public markets.

NEBRASKA: Several municipalities require that interested parties file for a permit to hold a parade in public streets. The state's criminal laws prohibit loitering in specified venues.

NEVADA: Several municipalities require that interested parties file for a permit to hold a parade in public streets. The state's criminal laws prohibit loitering around schools and other areas where children congregate. The state permits municipalities to enact ordinances to prohibit loitering.

NEW HAMPSHIRE: Several municipalities require that interested parties file for a permit to hold a parade in

public streets. The state's criminal laws prohibit loitering and prowling in specified circumstances.

NEW JERSEY: Several municipalities require that interested parties file for a permit to hold a parade in public streets. A number of these ordinances have been attacked on First Amendment grounds, and some ordinances have been found to be in violation of First Amendment rights. The state's criminal laws prohibit loitering for the purpose of soliciting criminal activity or in public transportation terminals.

NEW YORK: Several municipalities require that interested parties file for a permit to hold a parade in public streets. A number of these ordinances have been attacked on First Amendment grounds, and some ordinances have been found to be in violation of First Amendment rights. The state has enacted a number of laws prohibiting loitering, including loitering for the purpose of soliciting passengers for transportation, loitering for the purpose of criminal solicitation, and loitering in public transportation centers. The statute permits municipalities to enact ordinances prohibiting loitering. Several of the antiloitering laws have been the subject of litigation attacking the laws on First Amendment grounds.

NORTH DAKOTA: Several municipalities require that interested parties file for a permit to hold a parade or other processions in public streets.

OHIO: Several municipalities require that interested parties file for a permit to hold a parade or engage in the solicitation of business. The state's criminal laws prohibit loitering in public transportation centers and in polling centers during elections.

OKLAHOMA: Several municipalities require that interested parties file for a permit to hold a parade in public streets. The state's criminal laws prohibit loitering for the purpose of engaging in specified criminal acts.

OREGON: Several municipalities require that interested parties file for a permit to hold a parade in public streets. Some municipalities also require a noise permit when playing amplified noise in a public place.

PENNSYLVANIA: Several municipalities require that interested parties file for a permit to hold a parade in public streets. A number of these ordinances have been attacked on First Amendment grounds, and some ordinances have been found to be in violation of First Amendment rights. The state's criminal laws prohibit loitering for the purpose of engaging in specified criminal acts.

RHODE ISLAND: Several municipalities require that interested parties file for a permit to hold a parade in public streets. The state's criminal laws prohibit loitering for indecent purposes, loitering in public transportation centers, and loitering at or near schools.

SOUTH CAROLINA: Several municipalities require that interested parties file for a permit to hold a parade in public streets. The state's laws prohibit loitering in public transportation centers.

TENNESSEE: Several municipalities require that interested parties file for a permit to hold a parade on public streets. The state's criminal laws prohibit loitering for the purpose of engaging in specified criminal acts.

TEXAS: Several municipalities require that interested parties file for a permit to hold a parade on public streets. The state's laws prohibit loitering in polling centers during elections.

UTAH: Several municipalities require that interested parties file for a permit to hold a parade on public streets.

VERMONT: The state's laws prohibit loitering in public transportation centers and other public property.

WASHINGTON: Several municipalities require that interested parties file for a permit to hold a parade or march on public streets. The state's laws prohibit loitering in public transportation centers.

WEST VIRGINIA: Several municipalities require that interested parties file for a permit to hold a parade on public streets. The state's laws prohibit loitering at or near school property.

WISCONSIN: Several municipalities require that interested parties file for a permit to hold a parade on public streets. The state's laws prohibit loitering in public transportation centers.

ADDITIONAL RESOURCES

Abernathy, M. Glenn. *The Right of Assembly and Association*. 2nd rev. ed. Columbia: University of South Carolina Press, 1981.

Fellman, David. *The Constitutional Right of Association*. Chicago: University of Chicago Press, 1963.

Garvey, John H., and Frederick Schaver. *The First Amendment: A Reader*. 2nd ed. Eagan, MN: West, Thomson Reuters, 1996.

Gutman, Amy. *Freedom of Association*. Princeton, NJ: Princeton University Press, 1998.

Shiffrin, Steven, and Jesse H. Cooper. *The First Amendment: Cases, Comments, Questions*. 5th ed. Eagan, MN: West, Thomson Reuters, 2014.

Soifer, Aviam. *Law and the Company We Keep*. Cambridge, MA: Harvard University Press, 1995.

Weaver, Russell L. *Understanding the First Amendment*. 4th ed. New Providence, NJ.: LexisNexis, 2012.

ORGANIZATIONS

American Civil Liberties Union (ACLU)

125 Broad St., 18th Fl.
New York, NY 10004
Phone: (212) 549-2500
Email: info@aclu.org
URL: http://www.aclu.org/

National Coalition Against Censorship (NCAC)

275 Seventh Avenue
New York, NY 10001
Phone: (212) 807-6222
Fax: (212) 807-6245
Email: ncac@ncac.org
URL: http://www.ncac.org/

National Freedom of Information Coalition (NFOIC)

400 S. Record Street, Suite 240
Dallas, TX 75202
Phone: (214) 977-6658
Fax: (214) 977-6666
Email: nfoic@reporters.net
URL: http://www.nfoic.org/

Thomas Jefferson Center for the Protection of Free Expression

400 Peter Jefferson Place
Charlottesville, VA 22911-8691
Phone: (804) 295-4784
Fax: (804) 296-3621
Email: ch@tjcenter.org
URL: http://www.tjcenter.org

FIRST AMENDMENT LAW

CENSORSHIP

Sections within this essay:

- Background
- Early History
- Censorship in the United States
  - Book Censorship
  - Music Censorship
  - Press Censorship
- Electronic Censorship
- Additional Resources

BACKGROUND

"Congress shall make no law respecting an establishment of religion, or prohibiting the free exercise thereof; or abridging the **freedom of speech**, or of the press; or the right of the people peaceably to assemble, and to petition the Government for a **redress** of grievances." Despite the guarantee implicit in the words of the First Amendment to the U.S. Constitution, there have been many attempts in the ensuing two centuries to censor or ban speech, both in print and in other media.

Censorship is at best problematic and at worst dangerous when it tries to silence the voice of the powerless at the behest of the powerful. History has shown that power and influence are not reliable guides for judgment when it comes to information. The Nazi government in Germany in the 1930s and 1940s, and the governments of the Soviet Union and the People's Republic of China, have shown the world what happens when large, powerful nations choose to deprive their own citizens of knowledge and a voice. In the United States, Americans pride themselves on **freedom of speech** and freedom of the press—but many of them have experienced censorship. Boards of education frequently try to ban certain books from their school districts; television and radio stations ban certain programming; and newspapers may alter certain stories. The reasons for censorship are numerous, but they all share a common goal: protection. Perhaps children are the most frequently protected group. Books are banned when they depict violence or sexually suggestive material. Motion pictures are rated to protect young people from sex and violence on the screen. Internet resources are filtered to ensure that students will be unable to log into pornographic websites.

Society, and often the courts, have determined that some information does need to be censored, and that not all media deserve First Amendment protection. Deciding which materials fall into which categories is a subject of ongoing debate.

EARLY HISTORY

Censorship laws existed in ancient Rome and Greece more than 2,500 years ago; ancient societies in the Middle East and China also had censorship regulations. The role of censorship was to establish moral standards for the general population; civilizations that exercised it saw censorship as a means of helping the people by providing them with guidance.

The invention of movable type in the middle of the fifteenth century revolutionized the printing industry; it made more books available and helped literacy spread beyond just the most educated in society. A more literate public meant more need for censorship. The Roman

Catholic Church released a list of Prohibited Books, or *Index Librorum Prohibitorum*, in 1559, the first of 20 such lists (the last was issued in 1948). This list included books deemed by the Church to be heretical. Authors such as Galileo were denounced, and some authors (such as Sir Thomas More) were put to death. Prohibitions were not only religious; in 1563, Charles IX of France issued a **decree** that all printed material required his special permission.

Nonetheless, it became harder to suppress information, and by the end of the seventeenth century, there was a movement toward freedom of speech and the press. Sweden established a law guaranteeing **freedom of the press** in 1766, followed by Denmark in 1770. The newly formed United States put the First Amendment into its Constitution in 1787, and the French government moved in the same direction in 1789 at the dawn of its revolution.

CENSORSHIP IN THE UNITED STATES

The First Amendment has long been the standard by which the U.S. government has measured the freedom of individuals to speak or write their opinions without fear of reprisals. That freedom is not absolute; one of the most commonly cited examples warns that people do not have the right to walk into a crowded theater and shout, "Fire!" thus causing people to panic and trample over each other. Through the decades, the government has attempted to determine legitimate curbs to this freedom as opposed to arbitrary or discriminatory prohibitions.

Book Censorship Censorship existed in the United States from its beginnings, the existence of the First Amendment notwithstanding. But although there were federal anti-obscenity laws, censorship itself was not mandated by federal or state governments. What codified censorship was the 1873 Comstock Act, which called for the banning of literature deemed sexually arousing, even indirectly. The man for whom the act is named, Anthony Comstock, was the leader of the New York Society for the Suppression of Vice and a special agent for both the U.S. Post Office and the New York state prosecutor's office. The Comstock Act banned the mailing, importation, and transportation of any printed material (even private letters) that contained lewd or lascivious material. It also banned the transport of any sort of contraceptive drug or device, as well as literature describing contraceptive devices. What this meant was that a book that in any way made mention of any sort of **birth control** could be considered lewd and subject to confiscation. Violators of the Comstock Act (Comstock himself was deputized and arrested many violators himself) faced steep fines and even time in prison.

Other books that were affected by the Comstock Act included *The Decameron* (written by Giovanni Boccaccio in the fourteenth century), Tolstoy's *Kreutzer Sonata,* Hemingway's *For Whom the Bell Tolls,* and D.H. Lawrence's *Lady Chatterley's Lover.*

In Boston, the Watch and Ward Society, which had long championed against what it deemed indecent, organized book bans in the 1920s, which gave the language the phrase "Banned in Boston." Groups such as the American Civil Liberties Union (ACLU) fought to challenge the censorship laws. These groups were successful on several occasions, winning the right in 1933 for James Joyce's *Ulysses* to be imported into the United States and in 1960 when federal courts allowed the full version of *Lady Chatterley's Lover* to be published here.

Beginning in the 1950s, a series of U.S. Supreme Court cases helped change the scope of censorship laws in the United States.

Butler v. State of Michigan. The Butler case determined in 1957 that adult reading material did not need to be restricted to protect minors. It struck down a Michigan law that outlawed any printed material with obscene language (which could corrupt children), noting that the material's existence by itself was not a danger to young readers and the law was too sweeping. Justice Felix Frankfurter wrote that the Michigan law limited the entire adult population to "reading only what is fit for children."

Roth v. United States. Also decided in 1957, this case upheld a **conviction** for mailing materials that were deemed to be "in the prurient interest." Although *Roth* made clear that obscene material was not subject to First Amendment protection, the court did note that material that has *some* redeeming social value or importance. (**Obscenity**, wrote Justice William Brennan, was "utterly" without such value.)

Jacobellis v. Ohio. This case was decided in 1964. It held that "national" standards for obscenity determined "community" standards. A Cleveland Heights, Ohio theater had shown a foreign film with an explicit sex scene. The theater owner was arrested for violating the state obscenity **statute**, but the Supreme Court held that since the film in question had been screened across the country without incident, it was not obscene. "The Court has explicitly refused to tolerate a result whereby 'the constitutional limits of free expression in the Nation would vary within state lines,'" wrote Justice William Brennan. "We see even less justification for allowing such limits with town or county lines." *Jacobellis* was the case in which Justice Potter Stewart made his famous observation about obscenity: "I know it when I see it."

Memoirs v. Attorney General of Massachusetts. This case, decided in 1966, reversed a state court's ruling that the 1749 book *Memoirs of a Woman of Pleasure,* commonly known as *Fanny Hill,* was obscene. The reason, explained the court, was that the book, despite its content (much of which could be construed as offensive) geared toward prurient interest, the book was not "utterly" without redeeming social value. To be obscene, the book would have to have prurient **appeal**, offensiveness, *and* utter lack of redeeming social value.

Ginzburg v. United States. This case was decided in 1966, and the court upheld the conviction of a publisher who had marketed and mailed three sexually explicit publications. The reason the court reached this decision was that the material, though potentially not patently obscene, had been marketed solely as erotic material and thus could be reasonably construed on that basis to be obscene.

Ginsberg v. State of New York. In this 1968 case, the Supreme Court upheld a statute that a state can create more stringent obscenity standards for minors than for adults. The **defendant** had sold two adult magazines to a 16-year-old boy, and argued that the anti-obscenity statute violated that minor boy's right to read under the First Amendment. The court found that there was no violation of the child's rights because the material in question was obscene for children.

Miller v. California. This landmark 1973 case established a new definition for obscenity, replacing the standard set by *Roth.* The defendant had been convicted under California's obscenity law for mailing sexually explicit advertisements to sell adult books and films. An **appellate court** upheld the conviction, but the Supreme Court vacated the appellate court's decision and sent it back for reconsideration using the new definition. Chief Justice Warren Burger, writing for the majority, outlined the definition: "The basic guidelines ... must be: (a) whether the average person applying contemporary community standards would find that the work, taken as a whole, appeals to a prurient interest; (b) whether the work depicts or describes, in a patently offensive way, sexual conduct specifically defined by the applicable state law; and (c) whether the work, taken as a whole, lacks serious literary, artistic, political, or scientific value."

Board of Education v. Pico. Decided in 1982 by a 5-4 majority, this case ruled that school boards do not have the absolute right to remove books from school libraries. A school board in Island Trees, New York, removed several books from the school library shelves, including *The Fixer* by Bernard Malamud, *Slaughterhouse Five* by Kurt Vonnegut, *Best Short Stories of Negro Writers* (edited by Langston Hughes), *A Hero Ain't Nothin' But A Sandwich* by Alice Childress, and *A Reader for Writers* (edited by Jerome Archer). The school board, when challenged about its decision, called the books "anti-American, anti-Christian, anti-Semitic, and just plain filthy." Although

it was determined by a separate committee that several of the books should be replaced, but the board refused. A group of students sued the district.

Justice William Brennan wrote that "the special characteristics of the school library make that environment especially appropriate for the recognition of First Amendment rights of students." While the court noted that school boards do have discretion in what books to acquire for the school, and it could reject any works deemed to be "pervasively vulgar."

School boards continue to attempt to ban books, with classics such as *The Adventures of Huckleberry Finn* and *Of Mice and Men* among the most frequently challenged, according to the American Library Association. In the early 2000s, the Harry Potter series of books, which tell the story of a young aspiring wizard and his adventures in wizard school, became a focal point for many who oppose the focus on wizardry and magic.

Music Censorship Musical lyrics have been the subject of censorship through the years, particularly those that were deemed sexually suggestive or violent. Censorship has affected the works and performances of such disparate artists as Cole Porter, Frank Zappa, Bruce Springsteen, Rosemary Clooney, the Carpenters, Sheena Easton, Perry Como, and Bob Dylan.

In 1954, for example, Cole Porter's "I Get A Kick Out of You" was edited for radio broadcast to remove the line "I get no kick from cocaine" (it was replaced with "I get perfume from Spain"); the American Broadcasting Company bans Rosemary Clooney's performance of "Mambo Italiano," citing inadequate standards for "good taste"; and police in Long Beach, California, and Memphis, Tennessee, confiscated jukeboxes thought to contain songs with suggestive lyrics. (The owners were fined as well.)

Sometimes, the censors' rationale had nothing to do with the lyrics. In 1968, a radio station in El Paso, Texas, banned the playing of songs performed by Bob Dylan because his lyrics were hard to understand. (They did not ban performances of his lyrics when sung by other artists.) And in 1990, a radio station in Nebraska led a **boycott** against the music of k.d. lang—not because of what she sang, but because she was a vegetarian.

Although the music industry has frequently come under attack by opponents they deemed too reactionary or literal-minded, mainstream concerns about lyrics were being expressed more openly. In 1985, twenty wives of politicians and business leaders in Washington, D.C. (including Tipper Gore, wife of then-senator Al Gore) formed the Parents Music Resource Center (PMRC). The group's goal was to lobby the music industry for a ratings system for music similar to that used in the film industry, the printing of lyrics on album covers, and an overall reassessment of musicians and lyricists whose work could be deemed violent or explicitly sexual. In 1990, a parental warning sticker system was adopted by the recording industry that would place warning stickers on records deemed explicit. A year later, Wal-Mart, the nation's largest retailer, announced that it would refuse to stock any stickered albums in its stores. In 1995, former U.S. education secretary William Bennett and national Political Congress of Black Women chair C. Delores Tucker addressed a shareholders' meeting of Time-Warner, Inc., deploring rap music lyrics that promoted violence or that degraded women.

After the attacks in New York and Washington, D. C., on September 11, 2001, Clear Channel Communications (the largest broadcast station owner in the United States) released a list of 150 suggested songs it deemed "lyrically questionable" because they had metaphoric references to planes, crashing, and death. The list included Steve Miller's "Jet Airliner," the Dave Matthews Band's "Crash Into Me," Pat Benatar's "Hit Me with Your Best Shot," and the Jerry Lee Lewis song "Great Balls of Fire."

Press Censorship The concept of "freedom of the press" was established in New York when it was still a British colony. In 1734, John Peter Zenger, publisher of the *New York Weekly Journal,* was charged with libel against colonial governor William Cosby when he printed articles critical of Cosby's decision to remove the chief justice of New York from office. He was imprisoned for nine months before his case went to trial. Philadelphia attorney Andrew Hamilton argued that statements could not be **libelous** if they were true. Although English law did not accept truth as a defense to libel, Hamilton pressed the issue with the **jury**, which found Zenger not guilty on August 4, 1735. This case set a precedent that truth is an absolute defense to libel.

Over the years, freedom of the press has been an important element of American society. Newspapers have traditionally been given considerable leeway in what they publish, and there has never been a shortage of opinions expressed in print in the United States. Nonetheless, censorship is hardly unknown in the press or in broadcast news programs.

Often, the press censorship is voluntary. In times of war, for example, the press is careful about publishing material that could provide enemy forces with sensitive information about U.S. troops. On a more personal level, public figures were long afforded the courtesy of not having their private lives printed in newspapers or broadcast through other media. President Franklin D. Roosevelt could not stand unassisted after his 1921 bout with polio, but during his presidency the press voluntarily refrained from publishing photographs or releasing film footage of Roosevelt being assisted or using a wheelchair. (As the twentieth century progressed, this sort of courtesy eroded steadily, which sometimes may have given the public more information than it wanted about the private lives of public figures.)

Also, the press and broadcast media have often felt compelled to be sensitive to advertisers and sponsors. There are countless examples of brave publications running unsympathetic stories about advertisers, who would promptly cancel all future advertising with the offending publication. And there are examples of publications refusing to run stories that could offend a potential advertiser. But these are not examples of government-sanctioned censorship.

That said, there have been charges of government censorship over the years from the press, particularly during war time. One of the most noteworthy examples comes from the Iraq War, which began in March 2003. Not long after the war began, the Pentagon issued an order banning the release of photographs of flag-draped military coffins returning from the battle zone. (The ban had actually been in effect for several years before the war but not enforced.) Proponents of the ban argued that publishing the photos did a disservice to the **privacy** of the fallen soldiers and their families. Opponents of the ban countered that it was nothing more than a public relations ploy to minimize the true scope of American war casualties.

The **Freedom of Information Act** (FOIA), enacted in 1966, establishes the public's right to obtain information from any agency of the federal government. Any group or individual (foreign nationals as well as American citizens) can file a request. Each government agency is required by law to provide the public with information on how to file FOIA requests. There are exemptions to FOIA, including national security information, internal personnel information, confidential business information, inter- and intra-agency confidential communications, law enforcement records, financial institutions, and geological information. FOIA was amended in 1996 to allow increased access to electronic information.

ELECTRONIC CENSORSHIP

As a resource for information, the Internet has been both exciting and exasperating for precisely the same reason: the volume of unrestricted material that can be accessed instantly from virtually anywhere in the world. This means that inaccurate information can be distributed as quickly and easily as carefully researched material. It also means that offensive material, including **pornography**, can be posted and accessed. Balancing the First Amendment right to free speech with the need to protect against unprotected material has been a key focus of the U.S. government since the 1990s.

In 1996, Congress passed the Communications Decency Act (CDA), which prohibited the posting of materials deemed "indecent" or "patently offensive." There were already laws prohibiting child pornography and obscenity; CDA went further and ultimately prohibited what opponents claimed was protected speech under the First Amendment. The U.S. Supreme Court unanimously struck down CDA in 1997, claiming that its reach was too broad.

Congress passed the Child Online Protection Act (COPA) in 1998 and the Children's Internet Protection Act (CIPA) in 2000. COPA established criminal penalties for anyone who distributed indecent online material to minors, and CIPA required libraries and schools to place filters on their computers or face the loss of federal funding. COPA was challenged in the courts and in 2003 the Third Circuit Court of Appeals found that is was unconstitutional. The U.S. Supreme court upheld that decision in 2004 by a 5-4 margin.

More challenges to COPA awaited, however. In 2007, Judge Lowell A. Reed Jr. of the U.S. District Court for the Eastern District of Pennsylvania struck down the law again, ruling that it violated the First Amendment as well as the **Fifth Amendment**. The Third Circuit Court of Appeals upheld the ruling about year later, and the U.S. Supreme Court declined to review the case. Accordingly, COPA has never taken effect.

First Amendment arguments have also allowed unsolicited email (better known as spam) to clog the email boxes of millions of individuals, not to mention commercial, **corporate**, and even government email accounts. Proponents of spam claim that it is the electronic equivalent of bulk mail and is protected speech. Opponents claim that spam is far more insidious because many spammers use false email addresses and subject lines, making it impossible to contact the source to ask to be removed from the mailing list. (Experts on spam advise against sending a reply to "opt-out" links because this merely assures the spammer that the sender's address is active.) In December 2003, Congress passed the CAN-SPAM Act, which requires all commercial emailers to provide an opportunity to opt out, prohibits false headers and subject lines, and imposes civil penalties on offenders. Though well-intentioned, CAN-SPAM did little to make a real impact, in part because it is easy for spammers to find electronic loopholes that allow them to remain uncaught. The Coalition Against Unsolicited Commercial email (CAUCE) is a volunteer nonprofit organization that works to find ways to help reduce spam. Information on consumer guidelines, and on the group's progress, can be found at http://www.cauce.org.

ADDITIONAL RESOURCES

Barbour, Scott, ed. *Censorship*. Detroit: Greenhaven Press, 2010.

Nye, Valerie, and Kathy Barco, eds. *True Stories of Censorship Battles in America's Libraries*. Chicago: American Library Association, 2012.

Ramey, R. Chace. *Student First Amendment Speech and Expression Rights: Armbands to Bong Hits*. El Paso, TX: LFB Scholarly Pub., 2011.

Shiffrin, Steven, and Jesse H. Cooper. *The First Amendment: Cases, Comments, Questions*. 5th ed. Eagan, MN: West, Thomson Reuters, 2011

Weaver, Russell L. *Understanding the First Amendment*. 4th ed. New Providence, NJ.: LexisNexis, 2012.

ORGANIZATIONS

American Civil Liberties Union (ACLU)

125 Broad St., 18th Fl.
New York, NY 10004
Phone: (212) 549-2500
Email: info@aclu.org
URL: http://www.aclu.org/

American Library Association (ALA)

50 East Huron Street
Chicago, IL 60611
Toll Free: (800) 545-2433
URL: http://www.ala.org

Fairness and Accuracy in Reporting (FAIR)

104 W. 27th St., Suite 10B
New York, NY 10001
Phone: (212) 633-6700
Fax: (212) 727-7668
URL: http://www.fair.org

Federal Communications Commission (FCC)

445 12th Street, SW
Washington, DC 20554
Toll Free: (866) 225-5322
Fax: (866) 418-0232
Email: fccinfo@fcc.gov
URL: http://www.fcc.gov

FIRST AMENDMENT LAW

ESTABLISHMENT CLAUSE

Sections within this essay:

BACKGROUND

The First Amendment to the U.S. Constitution states, in part, that "Congress shall make no law respecting an establishment of religion, or prohibiting the exercise thereof." This two-part protection guarantees not only religious liberty, but also freedom from governmental action that purports to establish or support religious causes. The Establishment Clause, or "establishment of religion" Clause, is most often invoked in constitutional challenges regarding separation of church and state, whereas the "Free Exercise" Clause is invoked when challenging governmental interference with personal and fundamental religious freedom. The Fourteenth Amendment makes these protections applicable to the states and subdivisions thereof.

In its purest form, the Establishment Clause prohibits the state or federal government from establishing or setting up a church or religion as the official state or federal religion; it is said to provide "a wall of separation between church and state," in the words of Thomas Jefferson. Several U.S. Supreme Court justices, including prior long-term Chief Justice William Rehnquist, believed that the literal translation of the term meant that it only intended to prohibit the establishment of a single national church or the preference of one religion over another. This interpretation was premised on the historical context of the Constitution being drawn up by colonists fleeing oppression under the national Church of England. But other justices interpret a broader application of the term, to include prohibiting the government from promoting religion in general. This broader interpretation prohibits the government from passing laws that tend to favor or show preference for one or all religions, or tend to force belief or disbelief in any particular religion.

Accordingly, over the years, courts have eked out parameters of what government can or cannot do with respect to religion. For example, courts of law cannot adjudicate religious/ecclesiastical questions, nor can a religious test be used for election to public office. Likewise, providing **testimony** under oath need not be done by using a Bible and swearing before God; persons may substitute with an "affirmation," a solemn declaration that does not invoke or mention God.

However, in reality, constitutional challenges invoking the Establishment Clause tend to be more complicated and/or subtle. Judicial interpretation of the Establishment

Clause is an ever-evolving area of law, made more so in the 20th and 21st centuries because of the increasing cultural and ethnic diversity of the American population, as well as advancement in scientific technology that speaks to creationism and evolution.

TESTS USED TO DETERMINE CONSTITUTIONAL VIOLATIONS

To pass muster under the Establishment Clause, governmental actions are scrutinized by courts, using a few key tests. One of the most often used and quoted is that outlined in the U.S. Supreme Court case of *Lemon v. Kurtzman*, (1971). In that case, the Court struck down a Pennsylvania state program providing aid to religious elementary and secondary schools, in the form of reimbursement for salaries, textbooks, and instructional materials. However, payment was premised upon the condition, among others, that the courses taught be secular in nature, similar to those presented in the public schools. Notwithstanding, the high court was presented with the issue of whether payment of salary supplements was unconstitutional under the Establishment Clause.

The *Lemon* Court, under Chief Justice Warren Burger, outlined a three-prong test to be used in such challenges. To pass constitutional muster, a government action: (1) must have a secular legislative purpose; (2) its principal or primary effect must neither advance nor inhibit religion; and (3) it must not foster an excessive governmental entanglement with religion. The Court found the Pennsylvania school aid passed the first two prongs, but also found there was excessive entanglement with religion in its cumulative effect. While religion and government must co-exist in society and normally will interact at some points, they should not so overlap and intertwine as to cause persons to have difficulty differentiating between the two.

In 1997, the Supreme Court modified the *Lemon* test in its *Agostini v. Felton* decision. It combined the last two prongs (effect and entanglement), now using only the "purpose" and "effects" prongs. It still used the "excessive entanglement" criterion, but within the context of determining whether a governmental action had a primary effect of advancing religion.

In other Establishment Clause cases, courts also look to a test first advanced by Justice Anthony Kennedy, known as the "coercion" test. Under this test, government actions would be deemed constitutional unless they (1) provided direct aid to religion in a way that tended to establish a state church; or (2) coerced people to support or participate in religion against their will.

Still another, the "endorsement test" advanced by Justice Sandra Day O'Connor, asks whether the government action amounts to an endorsement of religion. Her primary focus was whether a government action conveyed "a message

to non-adherents [of religion] that they are outsiders, not full members of the political community, and an accompanying message to adherents that they are insiders, favored members of the political community," (from her dissenting opinion in the 1984 case of *Lynch v. Donnelly*). The endorsement test has been somewhat subsumed into the remaining *Lemon* prongs. The endorsement test is often used to consider cases in which the government is engaged in expressive activities, such as graduation prayers or, religious signs on government property.

RELIGIOUS EDUCATION IN PUBLIC SCHOOLS

Religious instruction in public schools is prohibited under the Establishment Clause. But seldom is the constitutional challenge so well defined. Instead, questions arise about the nature of the instruction (whether it is truly "religious") or what constitutes instruction or teaching.

In 1948, the U.S. Supreme Court struck down "released time" programs in public schools, which allowed early release from classes in order to receive religious instruction. However, the religious instruction was conducted elsewhere in the same public school buildings. The Court found that, in essence, the government was allowing publicly funded facilities to be used for the teaching of specific religious doctrine.

School Prayer For almost one hundred and fifty years, courts permitted schools to require student prayer. Finally, in 1963, the U.S. Supreme Court held that requiring prayer or Bible study in public schools, even if generalized and nondenominational, violated the Establishment Clause of the First Amendment (*Abington School District v. Schempp*). Since then, various school systems have attempted to comply with this holding, but still allow some freedom. In the latter part of the twentieth century and the early twenty-first century, the high court has increasingly been petitioned to refine and clarify the parameters of separation of church and state as it relates to prayer. While early cases prohibited praying out loud, later decisions also forbade compelled moments of silence or meditation. In *Wallace v. Jaffree* (1985), the Court banned a compelled "daily moment of silence" during which students were "encouraged" to use the time for silent prayer. In *Lee v. Weisman* (1992), the Court struck down invocations at public school graduation ceremonies, on the grounds that they had the effect of advancing religion and promoting excessive entanglement between church and state.

In the 1990s, the Supreme Court issued some decisions that seemed to suggest the need or desire to carve some exceptions out of the stricter separation of church and state decisions. In *Westside Community Board of Education v. Mergens* (1990), the Court held that if a school provided its facilities to some groups during off-hours, it must also make those facilities available to religious groups as well. In another case, the Court held that allowing a public employee to serve as a sign-language interpreter for a deaf child attending a religious school was permissible, even though the public employee would be spending at least part of his time interpreting religious beliefs and translating religious teachings.

Creationism, Evolution, and Intelligent Design Despite the 1925 Scopes "Monkey Trial," it was not until much later that a formal approach to teaching evolution was outlined. The general rule, set down in the 1987 U.S. Supreme Court case of *Edwards v. Aguillard* is that evolution must only be taught as scientific fact. Creationism may not be taught as a science. Moreover, the Court struck down a law requiring both theories to be taught side by side in public schools. In *Freiler v. Tangipahoa Parish Board of Education* (cert. denied 2000), the **appellate court** struck down a Louisiana school board rule mandating that teachers read a disclaimer to students stating that the teaching of evolution was "not intended to influence or dissuade the Biblical version of Creation or any other concept."

In the *Aguillard* case (above), the high court offered some guidance, by stating that "teaching a variety of scientific theories about the origins of humankind to school children might be validly done with the clear secular intent of enhancing the effectiveness of science instruction." In the 1990s, some teachers and school boards began telling students (by presenting only *scientific* **evidence** that supported it) about the scientific theory of "Intelligent Design." This theory, vouched for by many world-renowned scientists, does not displace Darwinism's focus on evolution, but rather adds to it the scientific theory of an organized, planned, and designed evolution far too complex for coincidence or happenstance. Critics have belittled Intelligent Design as merely a veiled teaching of creationism, but legal scholars believe its scientific basis and arguments actually fulfill the Supreme Court's mandate.

School Vouchers As mentioned, in matters of government expression, courts often look to the endorsement test, but when involving the use of government funds, courts are most interested in determining the *neutrality* of the financial aid. By determining whether the governmental action is neutral in treatment, the Supreme Court has allowed religious schools to participate in generally-available state **voucher** programs. It also has allowed states to provide computers to both public and religious schools, as well as provide remedial teachers to low-achieving students, whether attending religious or public schools. *Mitchell v. Helms* (2000), *Zelman v. Simmons-*

Harris (2002), Under this analysis, the faith-based initiatives of the Bush administration, when structured appropriately, appeared to conform to constitutional standards.

RELIGIOUS DISPLAYS ON GOVERNMENTAL PROPERTY

Happy Holidays Nativity scenes and other religious displays are generally permitted on public property if used in conjunction with the secular celebration of holidays. A publicly-sponsored Nativity scene standing alone is unconstitutional. The same holds true for publicly sponsored Christmas pageants with religious music, unless other secular holiday songs are included. Interestingly, *privately-sponsored* nativity scenes displayed on public property are constitutional, even in the absence of other secular symbols. However, equal access must be provided to competing interests/symbols, and to avoid confusion or challenge, public acknowledgment of the private sponsorship should be posted conspicuously.

The first big legal case resolving nativity scenes was *Lynch v. Donnely* (1984), a 5-4 decision allowing the display of a city-sponsored crèche scene in a public park, alongside other secular symbols of the holiday (Christmas tree, Santa Claus, and cut-out figures of a clown, teddy bear, and dancing elephant). In 1989, the Court ruled against a different nativity display (in another narrow 5-4 decision), striking the privately owned nativity scene displayed in a public county courthouse because the scene stood alone, without the display of other secular holiday symbols, making this one indisputably religious in nature. *Allegheny County v. ACLU* (1984).

Ten Commandments As early as 1980, the Supreme Court had banned the posting of the Ten Commandments on public school walls. *Stone v. Graham* But the Court continued to be pressed into making determinations about displays in other settings. Proponents for display argued that the Ten Commandments were non-denominational and were part of the historical under-pinnings of America: a moral reminder of right and wrong applicable to all citizens. Opponents argued that it was an impermissible endorsement of Judeo-Christian religion.

The issue was revisited in 2005, with two highly publicized cases before the Supreme Court. Both decisions evidenced a split court; both decisions were 5-4 rulings. In *Van Orden v. Perry,* the high court narrowly ruled in favor of allowing the Ten Commandments to be displayed at the Texas state capitol. But in *McCreary County, Kentucky v. ACLU,* the Court, again narrowly, ruled that they could not be displayed (in framed copies) at two Kentucky court houses. In the Texas case, the six-foot-high granite monument of the Ten Commandments was one among several national and historical markers spread across 22 acres of the state capitol grounds. The Court noted that 40 years had passed, without challenge, since the monument was first erected in the 1960s. The Court concluded that the Texas display represented a mixed but primarily non-religious purpose.

Conversely, the framed copies of the Ten Commandments displayed inside Kentucky courthouses stemmed from a governmental effort "substantially to promote religion," concluded the Court. (In an image that hangs above the courtroom in the Supreme Court, Moses is seen carrying the Ten Commandments. However, the tablets' text is not shown, and he is one of many historical figures depicted, including Mohammed and Confucius.)

GOVERNMENTAL ASSISTANCE OR BENEFITS

Financial aid given indiscriminately to all parents of school children (whether in public or religious schools) has tended to pass muster when challenged in court. If the aid is limited or directed to only parochial schools, it will generally fail for inability to show that the aid or assistance was limited to a non-religious purpose.

Paying bus fares and lending secular text books to parochial and private schools do not violate the Establishment Clause. However, direct grants, including the supplementing of salaries is prohibited.

NATIONAL SYMBOLS

Legal scholars have continued to dissect Supreme Court decisions to reach some palpable and instructive guidance in matters relating to the separation of church and state when it involves national symbols created by colonial Americans and steeped in historical symbolism. U.S. currency carries the motto "In God We Trust," and most school students (at least in the elementary grades) begin each day reciting the Pledge of Allegiance to "one nation, under God." Each meeting of the U.S. Congress begins with an invocation, which the Supreme Court found quite permissible, since the very first Congress paid a chaplain to provide an opening prayer.

Most legal authorities distinguish a general acknowledgement of God from the acknowledgement of a particular religious belief. They also make the distinction between invocations at the commencement of a congressional session, attended by adults, and school prayer, which may involve teachers and other students exerting influence over children more vulnerable to external suggestion or example.

In *West Virginia Board of Educ. v. Barnette* (1943), the parents of Jehovah's Witnesses school children brought suit after their children were expelled from West Virginia public

schools. A tenet of that faith is the commandment against bowing down to "graven images," which practitioners believe forbids them to recite the Pledge of Allegiance to one nation, under God. The West Virginia Board of Education defended that the children who refused to recite the Pledge disrupted the order and discipline of the classroom, which the board had a responsibility to maintain. The U.S. Supreme Court, reversing an earlier decision that resulted in gross harassment toward Witnesses, ruled that the expulsion of the children was an unjustified intrusion upon their religious freedom and was tantamount to a governmental censure of their religious beliefs.

The issue about the constitutionality of the Pledge of Allegiance again arose in federal courts in California. In 2005, U.S. District Judge Lawrence Karlton ruled that use the phrase "under God" violated the Establishment Clause, such that a teacher-led recitation of the Pledge was unconstitutional. In *Newdow v. Lefevre* (2010), a panel of the Ninth Circuit Court of Appeals reversed Karlton's judgment, deciding that the reading of the Pledge is "a predominantly patriotic exercise" and not in violation of the First Amendment.

BLUE LAWS AND SUNDAY CLOSINGS

Generally, Sunday closing laws (blue laws) have been upheld, because they were deemed to have been created to provide a day of rest and not a day of religious observation.

ADDITIONAL RESOURCES

Horwitz, Paul. *The Agnostic Age: Law, Religion, and the Constitution.* New York: Oxford University Press, 2011.

Shiffrin, Steven, and Jesse H. Cooper. *The First Amendment: Cases, Comments, Questions.* 5th ed. Eagan, MN: West, Thomson Reuters, 2011.

Weaver, Russell L. *Understanding the First Amendment.* 4th ed. New Providence, NJ.: LexisNexis, 2012.

ORGANIZATIONS

Americans United for Separation of Church and State
1301 K Street NW, Suite 850, East Tower
Washington, DC 20005
Phone: (202) 466-3234
Fax: (202) 466-2587
URL: http://www.au.org

First Amendment Center at Vanderbilt University
1207 18th Ave.S.
Nashville, TN 37212
Phone: (615) 727-1600
Fax: (615) 727-1319
URL: http://firstamendmentcenter.org

FIRST AMENDMENT LAW

FREE SPEECH/FREEDOM OF EXPRESSION

Sections within this essay:

- Background
- Protection of Core Political Speech
- Permissible Restrictions on Freedom of Expression
  - Speech that Incites Illegal or Subversive Activity
  - Fighting Words
  - Symbolic Expression
  - Commercial Speech
  - Freedom of Expression in Public Schools
  - Obscenity and Pornography
  - Regulation of the Internet
- State Law Protecting Free Expression
- Additional Resources

BACKGROUND

The First Amendment to the U.S. Constitution provides that "Congress shall make no law . . . abridging the freedom of speech." The rights protected under the First Amendment are among the freedoms most cherished by Americans. Democratic societies by definition are participatory and deliberative. They are designed to work best when their representative assemblies conduct informed deliberation after voters voice their opinions about particular issues or controversies. But neither elected representatives nor their constituents can fully discharge their democratic responsibilities if they are prevented from freely exchanging their thoughts, theories, suspicions, beliefs, and ideas, or are hindered from gaining access to relevant facts, data, or other kinds of useful information upon which to form their opinions.

Americans typically have strong opinions of the rights guaranteed by the First Amendment, especially with regard to free speech. In a survey conducted by Vanderbilt University's First Amendment Center in 2012, speech was the right most frequently recognized among the several rights recognized by the First Amendment. Of those who responded, only 13 percent agreed that the First Amendment "goes too far in the rights it guarantees," suggesting that the vast majority supports free-speech rights.

The theory underlying the Free Speech Clause of the First Amendment is that truthful and accurate information can only be revealed through robust and uninhibited discourse and that the best way to combat false, deceptive, misleading, inaccurate, or hateful speech is with countervailing speech that ultimately carries the day with a majority of the populace and its elected representatives. Of course, the majority is not always persuaded by countervailing truthful and accurate speech, especially in capitalistic democracies where factions that spend the most money tend to have the loudest and most prevalent voices through radio and television advertisements. Supreme Court Justice Oliver Wendell Holmes articulated an extreme view of the risks underlying freedom of speech when he wrote "that a law should be called good if it reflects the will of the dominant forces of the community, even if it will take us to hell." Similarly, in *United States v. Schwimmer* (1929), Holmes wrote that freedom of speech does not protect "free thought for those who agree with us, but freedom for the thought that we hate."

The Supreme Court has never literally interpreted the Free Speech Clause as an absolute prohibition against all restrictions on individual speech and expression. Instead, the Supreme Court has identified several kinds of expression that the government may regulate to varying degrees without running afoul of the Constitution, including the following: speech that incites illegal or subversive activity; fighting words; symbolic speech; commercial speech; student speech; and **obscenity** and **pornography**. The degree to which the government may regulate a particular kind of expression depends on the nature of the speech, the context in which the speech is made, and its likely impact upon any listeners. However, both state and federal courts will apply the same level of scrutiny to government regulation of free speech under the First Amendment, since the Free Speech Clause has been made applicable to the states via the Fourteenth Amendment's Equal Protection and Due Process Clauses.

PROTECTION OF CORE POLITICAL SPEECH

Core political speech consists of conduct and words that are intended to directly rally public support for a particular issue, position, or candidate. In one prominent case, *Meyer v. Grant* (1988), the U.S. Supreme Court suggested that core political speech involves any "interactive communication concerning political change." Discussion of public issues and debate on the qualifications of candidates, the Supreme Court concluded, are forms of political expression integral to the system of government established by the federal Constitution. Thus, circulating handbooks and petitions, posting signs and placards, and making speeches and orations are all forms of core political speech, so long as they in some way address social issues, political positions, political parties, political candidates, government officials, or governmental activities.

The First Amendment elevates core political speech above all other forms of individual expression by prohibiting laws that regulate it unless the laws are narrowly tailored to serve a compelling state interest. Known as "strict scrutiny" analysis, the application of this analysis by a court usually sounds the death knell for the law that is being challenged. This application is especially true when the core political speech is expressed in traditional public forums, such as streets, sidewalks, parks, and other venues that have been traditionally devoted to public assembly and social debate. Strict scrutiny is also applied to laws that regulate core political speech in "designated public forums," which are areas created by the government specifically for the purpose of fostering political discussion. For example, state fair grounds may be considered designated public forums under appropriate circumstances. In non-public forums, however, courts apply a lower level of scrutiny, allowing the government to limit core political speech if the limitation is reasonable and not aimed at silencing the speaker's viewpoint. Examples of nonpublic forums include household mail boxes, military bases, airport terminals, indoor shopping malls, and most private commercial and residential property.

Protection of political speech was the central point of the Supreme Court's controversial decision in *Citizens United v. Federal Election Commission* (2010). The case arose because of a challenge to the Bipartisan Campaign Reform Act, which was passed in 2002 to regulate financing during political campaigns. A provision of the Act restricted **corporations** and unions from making political expenditures within 30 days of a primary election or 60 days of a general election. A nonprofit group that wanted to fund advertisements during the 2008 election campaigns challenged the law. In a narrow decision, the Supreme Court ruled that the restriction on expenditures was a restriction on political speech protected by the First Amendment. Accordingly, the Court struck down provisions of the Act, which led to an outcry of criticism from members of Congress and President Barack Obama.

PERMISSIBLE RESTRICTIONS ON FREEDOM OF EXPRESSION

Speech that Incites Illegal or Subversive Activity Some speakers intend to arouse their listeners to take constructive steps to alter the political landscape. Everyday in the United States people hand out leaflets imploring neighbors to write Congress, vote on a referendum, or contribute financially to political campaigns or civic organizations. For other speakers, existing political channels provide insufficient means to effectuate the type of change desired. These speakers may encourage others to take illegal and subversive measures to change the status quo. Such measures have included draft resistance during wartime, threatening public officials, and joining political organizations aimed at overthrowing the U.S. government.

In *Brandenburg v. Ohio* (1969), the Supreme Court held that government may not prohibit speech that advocates illegal or subversive activity unless that "advocacy is directed to inciting or producing imminent lawless action and is likely to incite or produce such action." Applying the *Brandenburg* test, the Supreme Court has ruled that the government may not punish an antiwar protestor who yells "we'll take the f———— street later" because such speech "amounted to nothing more than advocacy of illegal action at some indefinite future time." (*Hess v. Indiana*, [1973]). Nor could the government punish someone who, in opposition to the draft during the Vietnam War, proclaimed "if they ever make me carry a rifle, the first man I want in my sights is [the President of the United States] L.B.J." (*Watts v. United States*, [1969]). Such politically charged rhetoric, the Supreme Court held, was more hyperbole and not a threat intended to be acted on at a definite point in time.

Fighting Words "Fighting words" are another form of speech receiving less First Amendment protection than core political speech. Fighting words are those words that "by their very utterance inflict injury or tend to incite an immediate breach of the peace" or have a "direct tendency to cause acts of violence by the person to whom, individually, the remark is addressed." (*Chaplinski v. New Hampshire*, (1942)). Where subversive advocacy exhorts large numbers of people to engage in lawless activity, fighting words are aimed at provoking a specific individual. For example, calling someone a derogatory epithet, such as "fascist," "kike," or "faggot" may result in a street brawl but cannot be accurately described as subversive speech.

Fighting words should also be distinguished from speech that is merely offensive. Unkind and insensitive language is heard everyday at work, on television, and sometimes even at home. But the Supreme Court has ruled that the First Amendment protects speech that merely hurts the feelings of another person. The Court has also underscored the responsibility of listeners to ignore offensive speech. Television channels can be changed, radios can be turned off, and movies can be left unattended. Other situations may require viewers of offensive expressions simply to avert their eyes. In *Cohen v. California* (1971), the Court ruled that a young man had the right to wear a jacket in a state courthouse with the aphorism "F—— the Draft" emblazoned across the back because persons in attendance could look away if they were offended. "One man's vulgarity," the Court said, "is another's lyric," and the words chosen in this case conveyed a stronger message than would a subdued variation such as "Resist the Draft."

Symbolic Expression Not all forms of self-expression involve words. The nod of a head, the wave of a hand, and the wink of an eye each communicate something without resort to language. Other forms of non-verbal expression communicate powerful symbolic messages. The television image of the defenseless Chinese student who faced down a line of tanks during the 1989 democracy protests near Tiananmen Square in China is one example of symbolic expression that will be forever seared into the memories of viewers. The picture of three New York City firefighters raising the American flag amid the rubble and ruins at the World Trade Center following the terrorist attacks of September 11, 2001, is another powerful example of symbolic expression.

The First Amendment does not protect all symbolic expression. If an individual intends to communicate a specific message by symbolic expression under circumstances in which the audience is likely to understand its meaning, the government may not regulate that expression unless the regulation serves a significant societal interest unrelated to suppressing the speaker's message. (*Spence v. Washington*, (1974)). Applying this standard, the U.S. Supreme Court reversed the **conviction** of a person who burned the American flag in protest over the policies of President Ronald Reagan (*Texas v. Johnson*, (1989)), and invalidated the suspension of a high school student who wore a black armband in protest of the Vietnam War (*Tinker v. Des Moines Independent Community School District*, (1969)). To the contrary, however, the Court has upheld federal legislation that prohibited the burning of draft cards. (*United States v. O'Brien*, (1968).) Of the governmental interests asserted in these three cases, maintaining the integrity of the selective service system was the only interest of sufficient weight to overcome the First Amendment right to engage in evocative symbolic expression.

Commercial Speech Commercial speech, such as advertising, receives more First Amendment protection than subversive advocacy, fighting words, and obscenity, but less protection than core political speech. Advertising is afforded more protection than these other categories of expression because of consumers' interest in the free flow of market information. (*Virginia State Board of Pharmacy v. Virginia Citizens Consumer Council, Inc.*, (1976)). In a free enterprise system, consumers depend on information regarding the quality, quantity, and price of various goods and services. Society is not similarly served, for instance, by the free exchange of obscenity.

At the same time, commercial speech deserves less protection than core political speech because society has a greater interest in receiving accurate commercial information and may be less savvy in flushing out false and deceptive ads. The average citizen is more conditioned, the Supreme Court has suggested, to discount the words of a politician than the words of a Fortune 500 company. The average citizen may also be more vulnerable to misleading commercial advertising. Even during an election year, most people view more commercial advertisements than political ones and rely on those advertisements when purchasing the clothes they wear, the food they eat, and the automobiles they drive. Thus, the First Amendment permits governmental regulation of commercial speech so long as the government's interest in doing so is substantial (e.g., the prohibition of false, deceptive, and misleading advertisements), the regulations directly advance the government's asserted interest, and the regulations are no more extensive than necessary to serve that interest.

Freedom of Expression in Public Schools In *Tinker v. Des Moines School District,* (1969), the Supreme Court articulated one of its most cited First Amendment pronouncements when it said that "[n]either students [n]or teachers shed their **constitutional rights** to freedom of speech or expression at the schoolhouse gate." Despite the frequency in which other courts have quoted this passage in addressing the free speech rights of public school students, as a principle of First Amendment law the passage represents somewhat of an overstatement. The First Amendment does not afford public school students the same liberty to express themselves as they would otherwise enjoy if they were adults speaking their minds off school grounds. In fact, the Supreme Court has since qualified this principle by stating that a public school student's right to free speech is "not automatically co-extensive with the rights of adults in other settings." (*Hazelwood School District v. Kuhlmeier,* (1988).) In *Hazelwood*, the Court held that educators may control the style and content of school-sponsored publications, theatrical productions, and other expressive conduct, so long as the educator's actions are reasonably related to legitimate pedagogical concerns. In short, student speech that is not consistent with a school's educational mission can be censored.

Applying the standard set forth in *Hazelwood*, the U.S. Court of Appeals for the Sixth Circuit upheld the disqualification of a candidate for student council president after he made discourteous remarks about an assistant principal during a campaign speech at a school-sponsored assembly. "Civility is a legitimate pedagogical concern," the court declared. Even state universities may adopt and enforce reasonable, nondiscriminatory regulations as to the time, place, and manner of student expressions. However, a state university's refusal to recognize a gay student services organization violated the First Amendment because it denied the students' right to freely associate with political organizations of their choosing. (*Gay Student Services v. Texas A&M University,* ([1984]).)

Obscenity and Pornography Artful depictions of human sexuality highlight the tensions between lust and love,

desire and commitment, fantasy and reality. Vulgar depictions can degrade sexuality and dehumanize the participants, replacing stories about love with stories about deviance, abuse, molestation, and pedophilia. State and federal laws attempt to enforce societal norms by encouraging acceptable depictions of human sexuality and discouraging unacceptable depictions. Libidinous books such as *Lady Chatterley's Lover* and pornographic movies such as *Deep Throat* have rankled communities struggling to determine whether such materials should be censored as immoral or protected as works of art.

The Supreme Court has always had difficulty distinguishing obscene material, which is not protected by the First Amendment, from material that is merely salacious or titillating, which is protected. Justice Potter Stewart stated in *Jacobellis v. Ohio* (1964) that he could not define obscenity, but he quipped, "I know it when I see it." Nonetheless, in *Miller v. California* (1973), the Supreme Court articulated a three-part test to determine when sexually oriented material is obscene. Material will not be declared obscene unless: (1) the average person, applying contemporary community standards, would find that the material's predominant theme appeals to a "prurient" interest; (2) the material depicts or describes sexual activity in a "patently offensive" manner; and (3) the material, when taken as a whole, lacks serious literary, artistic, political, or scientific value.

Although the Supreme Court has failed to clearly define words and phrases such as "prurient," "patently offensive," and "serious artistic value," literary works that deal with sexually related material are protected by the First Amendment, as are magazines like *Playboy* and *Penthouse*. More difficult questions are presented in the area of adult cinema. Courts generally distinguish hard-core pornography that graphically depicts copulation and oral sex from soft-core pornography that displays nudity and human sexuality short of these "ultimate sex acts." In close cases falling somewhere in the grey areas of pornography, outcomes may turn on the "community standards" applied by the **jury** in a particular locale. Thus, pornography that could be prohibited as obscene in a small rural community may receive First Amendment protection in Times Square.

Regulation of the Internet Although the Internet has increased the amount of information available to the average person by many times, it has also become the medium for the transmission of information that some deem harmful. This is particularly true in the case of child pornography. Congress and several state legislatures have attempted to enact legislation that would ban the transmission of this type of pornography. For instance, the Child Pornography Prevention Act of 1996, Pub. L. No. 104- 208, 110 Stat. 3009, banned the electronic transmission of depictions of pornographic images of children, including computer-generated images.

Groups have successfully opposed these laws on the grounds that they are overly broad and infringe upon First Amendment rights to free speech. In *Ashcroft v. Free Speech Coalition* (2002), the Supreme Court struck down the Child Pornography Prevention Act. Although the **statute** banned pictures of actual children engaged in sexual acts, it is also applied to images that appeared to be of a minor engaged in such an act. Because the statute prohibited protected speech (i.e., images that did not involve children) in addition to unprotected speech (i.e., pictures of actual children), the Court found that the statute was unconstitutional.

Other statutes related to the use of the Internet have withstood constitutional challenges. In *United States v. American Library Association, Inc.* (2003), the Court reviewed the Children's Internet Protection Act, Pub. L. No. 106-554, 114 Stat. 2763 (2000), which requires libraries that receive public funds to install filters on their computers so that neither adults nor children can access inappropriate materials. Despite arguments that the filtering software could effectively block access to constitutionally protected speech, the Court held that the statute was a valid exercise of Congress' spending power. The Court noted that the use of filtering software was no different in a library setting than was the selection of books and other physical items and that patrons could request that the filtering software be disabled.

STATE LAW PROTECTING FREE EXPRESSION

The federal Constitution establishes the minimum amount of freedom that must be afforded to individuals under the First Amendment. State constitutions may offer their residents more freedom of speech than is offered under the federal Constitution, but not less. Below is a sampling of state court cases decided at least in part based on their own state's constitutional provisions governing freedom of speech and expression.

ARKANSAS: A state statute penalizing night-riding did not abridge the freedom of speech guaranteed by the state or federal constitutions. *Johnson v. State*, 126 S.W.2d 289 (Ark. 1939).

ALABAMA: A city's **ordinance** forbidding a business from permitting consumption of alcoholic beverages and nude dancing at the same time regulated conduct and not individual expression; thus, the ordinance did not violate the state's constitutional right to freedom of speech. *Ranch*

House, Inc. v. City of Anniston, 678 So. 2d 745 (Ala. 1996).

ARIZONA: The state's **statutory** ban on targeted residential picketing was a valid accommodation for the right to freedom of speech explicitly protected by the state constitution. *State v. Baldwin*, 908 P.2d 483 (Ariz. App. 1995).

CALIFORNIA: The free speech clause in the state constitution contains a state action limitation and, thus, that clause only protects against government regulation of free speech and not private regulation thereof. *Golden Gateway Center v. Golden Gateway Tenants Ass'n*, 29 P.3d 797 (Cal. 2001).

COLORADO: Although smoking by an actor as part of a theatrical production was expressive conduct for First Amendment purposes, a Colorado court determined that a state smoking ban as applied to a theater did not violate the First Amendment right to freedom of expression. *Curious Theater Co. v. Colorado Dep't of Public Health & Environment*, 216 P.3d 71 (Colo. App. 2008).

ILLINOIS: The defendants' **arrest** for protesting on the premises of an **abortion** clinic did not violate the defendants' state constitutional right of free speech, since the clinic's policy required removal of all demonstrators from the clinic's premises regardless of their beliefs, and there was no indication that the clinic's policy of excluding demonstrators was ever applied in a discriminatory manner. *People v. Yutt*, 597 N.E.2d 208 (Ill. App. 1992).

INDIANA: The Indiana Supreme Court ruled that the state could prevent the provider of a prerecorded political message to send automated messages in violation of the state's "autodialer" law. The law was content-neutral, served a significant government interest, left open alternative forms of communication, and did not impose a substantial obstacle on the provider's right to engage in political speech. *State v. Economic Freedom Fund*, 959 N.E.2d 794 (Ind. 2011).

MAINE: The state's statute allowing the State Employees Association to pay 80% of the **collective bargaining** unit dues for association members, while contributing nothing toward the dues of non-members, violated neither the state nor federal guarantees to freedom of speech. *Opinion of the Justices*, 401 A.2d 135 (Me. 1979).

MARYLAND: A county **zoning** ordinance for adult entertainment businesses violated the federal and state constitutions because the ordinance failed to leave open adequate alternative channels of communication. The land in the county that was available for adult businesses was less than one-tenth of one percent of the land available for commercial enterprises in the county. *Pack Shack, Inc. v. Howard County*, 832 A.2d 170 (Md. 2003).

MASSACHUSETTS: A conviction for threatening to commit a crime does not violate a defendant's free speech rights under the federal or state constitution if the **evidence** is sufficient to satisfy each element of the crime, since those elements are defined in a way that prevents a conviction based on protected speech. *Commonwealth v. Sholley*, 739 N.E.2d 236 (Mass. 2000).

MICHIGAN: A state administrative rule prohibiting simulated sexual conduct in licensed liquor establishments did not violate the state's constitutional provision guaranteeing free speech. *Kotmar, Ltd. v. Liquor Control Comm'n*, 525 N.W.2d 921 (Mich. App. 1994).

MINNESOTA: Differences in terminology between the free speech protection in the federal Constitution and the free speech protection under the state constitution did not support a conclusion that the state constitutional protection should be more broadly applied than the federal. *State v. Wicklund*, 589 N.W.2d 793 (Minn. 1999).

NEW JERSEY: Although the right to free speech under the state constitution is broader than the corresponding right under the federal Constitution, nothing in the state constitution gives a person the right to videotape public proceedings. *Tarus v. Borough of Pine Hill*, 886 A.2d 1056 (N.J. Super. 2005).

NEW YORK: A state statute banning the televising of any court proceeding in which the **testimony** of a witness by **subpoena** is or may be taken denies free speech guarantee by the state and federal constitutions. *Coleman v. O'Shea*, 707 N.Y.S. 308 (N.Y. Sup. Ct. 2000).

OHIO: The state constitution's separate and independent guarantee of free speech applies to defamatory statements only if those statements are matters of opinion, and citizens who abuse their constitutional rights to freely express their sentiments by uttering defamatory statements of fact will remain liable for the abuse of that right. *Wampler v. Higgins*, 752 N.E.2d 962 (Ohio 2001).

OREGON: A statute prohibiting a "live public show" during which participants engage in "sexual conduct"

violated rights to freedom of expression under the state constitution. However, a statute prohibiting the promotion of prostitution was not unconstitutional. *State v. Ciancanelli*, 121 P.3d 613 (Ore. 2005).

PENNSYLVANIA: Regulations that barred nude dancing in public places violated both the federal and state constitutions. *Pap's A.M. v. City of Erie*, 812 A.2d 591 (Pa. 2002).

TEXAS: The state constitution offers greater free speech protection than the federal Constitution for political speech, but this greater protection does not extend to exotic dancing businesses. Society has a lesser interest in protecting material on the borderline between pornography and artistic expression than it does in protecting the free dissemination of ideas of social and political significance. *Kaczmarek v. State*, 986 S.W.2d 287 (Tex. App. 1999).

UTAH: The Utah Supreme Court partially struck down a tax imposed on sexually explicit businesses and escort services. The court upheld much of the law on First Amendment grounds but ruled that the law was unconstitutionally vague as it applied to escort services. *Bushco v. Utah State Tax Comm'n*, 225 P.3d 153 (Utah 2009).

WASHINGTON: Nude dancing receives constitutional protection under the free speech guarantees of the First Amendment and the state constitution, although nudity itself is subject to the police powers of the state. *DCR, Inc. v. Pierce County*, 964 P.2d 380 (Wash. App. 1998).

ADDITIONAL RESOURCES

Amar, David. *The First Amendment, Freedom of Speech: Its Constitutional History and the Contemporary Debate.* Amherst, NY: Prometheus Books, 2009.

Nye, Valerie, and Kathy Barco, eds. *True Stories of Censorship Battles in America's Libraries.* Chicago: American Library Association, 2012.

Ramey, R. Chace. *Student First Amendment Speech and Expression Rights: Armbands to Bong Hits.* El Paso, TX: LFB Scholarly Pub., 2011.

Shiffrin, Steven, and Jesse H. Cooper. *The First Amendment: Cases, Comments, Questions.* 5th ed. Eagan, MN: West, Thomson Reuters, 2011.

Weaver, Russell L. *Understanding the First Amendment.* 4th ed. New Providence, NJ.: LexisNexis, 2012.

ORGANIZATIONS

American Civil Liberties Union (ACLU)

125 Broad St., 18th Fl.
New York, NY 10004
Phone: (212) 549-2500
Email: info@aclu.org
URL: http://www.aclu.org/

American Library Association (ALA)

50 East Huron Street

Chicago, IL 60611
Toll Free: (800) 545-2433
URL: http://www.ala.org

Federal Communications Commission (FCC)

445 12th Street, SW
Washington, DC 20554
Toll Free: (866) 225-5322
Fax: (866) 418-0232
Email: fccinfo@fcc.gov
URL: http://www.fcc.gov

FIRST AMENDMENT LAW

FREEDOM OF ASSOCIATION

Sections within this essay:

- Introduction
- Evolution of Freedom of Association
  - *NAACP v. Alabama*
  - *Bates v. City of Little Rock*
  - *Scales v. United States*
- Right to Intimate Associations
  - *Griswold v. Connecticut*
  - *Roberts v. United States Jaycees*
- Right to Expressive Association
- Freedom Not to Associate
  - *Abood v. Detroit Board of Education*
  - *Boy Scouts of America v. Dale*
- Select State Court Decisions
- Additional Resources

INTRODUCTION

Nothing in the United States Constitution explicitly mentions freedom of association. However, courts during the twentieth century began to recognize this right as an outgrowth of the rights to free speech and freedom to assemble peaceably. In *United States v. Cruikshank* (1875), the Supreme Court recognized that "The very idea of a government, republican in form, implies a right on the part of its citizens to meet peaceably for consultation in respect to public affairs and to petition for a **redress** of grievances." More than 60 years later, the

Court in *De Jonge v. State of Oregon* expanded upon this principle, noting "The First Amendment of the Federal Constitution expressly guarantees that right against abridgment by Congress. But explicit mention there does not argue exclusion elsewhere. For the right is one that cannot be denied without violating those fundamental principles of liberty and justice which lie at the base of all civil and political institutions-principles which the Fourteenth Amendment embodies in the general terms of its due process clause."

The modern doctrine addressing freedom of association has expanded, and citizens are guaranteed specific rights related to this freedom. As a general matter, cases addressing association fall within three categories: (1) rights to intimate associations; (2) right to expressive association; and (3) freedom not to associate. Although early cases principally addressed concerns about communism and **civil rights**, more recent cases have addressed issues related to gender equality and rights related to **sexual orientation**.

EVOLUTION OF FREEDOM OF ASSOCIATION

Although the Supreme Court recognized the basis for freedom of association before the 1950s, the modern doctrine began to evolve with a series of cases addressing civil rights. The doctrine further evolved when the Court addressed issues arising from the so-called Red Scare involving efforts to prevent the spread of communism in the United States.

NAACP v. Alabama During the 1950s, the State of Alabama attempted to keep the National Association for the Advancement of Colored People (NAACP) from setting up a regional office in that state. The state's attorney general attempted to bar the NAACP from conducting activities in the state on the grounds that the association had not complied with a state **statute** that qualifies an organization to conduct activities. A state district court further required the association to produce names of its members. When the association failed to comply, the district court ruled that the NAACP was in **contempt**.

The NAACP challenged the action to the Supreme Court. In a unanimous decision, the Court reversed. Of particular concern was the district court's requirement that the association disclose the affiliation of its members. In an opinion by Justice John Marshall Harlan, the Court noted, "It is hardly a novel perception that compelled disclosure of affiliation with groups engaged in advocacy may constitute as effective a restraint on freedom of association as the forms of governmental action in the cases above were thought likely to produce upon the particular **constitutional rights** there involved. This Court has recognized the vital relationship between freedom to associate and **privacy** in one's associations." Moreover, Harlan added, "Compelled disclosure of membership in an organization engaged in advocacy of particular beliefs is of the same order. Inviolability of privacy in group association may in many circumstances be indispensable to preservation of freedom of association, particularly where a group espouses dissident beliefs."

Bates v. City of Little Rock Two years after the Court's decision in *NAACP v. State of Alabama*, the Court addressed another case involving the NAACP. In *Bates v. City of Little Rock*, the Court addressed another case involving a government's attempt to compel disclosure of a NAACP membership list. The controversy arose when two cities in Arkansas amended their occupation tax license ordinances to require organizations to disclose information, including membership rosters.

Relying on its 1958 decision, the Court concluded that the disclosure violated the organization's freedom of association. Justice Potter Stewart wrote, "On this record it sufficiently appears that compulsory disclosure of the membership lists of the local branches of the National Association for the Advancement of Colored People would work a significant interference with the freedom of association of their members. There was substantial uncontroverted **evidence** that public identification of persons in the community as members of the organizations had been followed by harassment and threats of bodily harm. There was also evidence that fear of community hostility and economic reprisals that would follow public disclosure of the membership lists had discouraged new members from joining the organizations

and induced former members to withdraw. This repressive effect, while in part the result of private attitudes and pressures, was brought to bear only after the exercise of governmental power had threatened to force disclosure of the members' names."

Scales v. United States Fears about the spread of communism into the United States prompted the U.S. government to adopt measures to effectively ban the Communist Party from the United States. On statute on which the government relied was the Alien Registration Act, also known as the Smith Act. This Act established criminal penalties for those advocating the overthrow of the government.

In *Scales v. United States* (1961), the Court reviewed the **conviction** of a man based on membership in the Communist Party. He argued that the Smith Act violated his rights to freedom of association. A divided Supreme Court disagreed, concluding that the Act applied to active members who were engaged in illegal advocacy. The Court also concluded, however, that the government could not punish someone simply for being a member of the Communist Party.

Although the government eventually abandoned attempts to **prosecute** individuals under the Smith Act, the *Scales* opinion has been cited several times in the 2000s and early 2010s in the context of cases involving terrorist suspects. Parties charged for their terrorist activities have argued that they are being prosecuted merely for membership in an organization. Most courts, though, have rejected these arguments.

RIGHT TO INTIMATE ASSOCIATIONS

Freedom of association evolved from the early cases to address more personal relationships. This right addresses those associations that exist between spouses, family members, and others to whom a person is close or intimate. The Supreme Court has specifically recognized the right of individuals to maintain intimate relationships without undue intrusion from the state.

Griswold v. Connecticut One of the first cases to address the right of association in the context of personal or intimate relationships was *Griswold v. Connecticut* (1965). The Court addressed a challenge of a state **birth control** law that banned the use of contraceptives. In considering whether this statute violated privacy rights, the Court considered the Constitution protects the association of people.

Relying on statements in *NAACP v. State of Alabama* and other cases, the Court concluded that the Constitution indeed protected a right of association. Justice William O. Douglas wrote, "The right of 'association,' like the right of belief . . . is more than the right to attend a meeting; it includes the right to express one's attitudes or philosophies by membership in a group or by affiliation with it or by other lawful means. Association in that context is a form of expression of opinion; and while it is not expressly included in the First Amendment its existence is necessary in making the express guarantees fully meaningful."

The decision in *Griswold* led to the Court's conclusion in *Roe v. Wade*, which recognized a woman's right to choose to have an **abortion**. The Court in *Roe* relied more heavily on due process rights, but commentators still often cite to the case in the context of rights of association.

Roberts v. United States Jaycees Although the Supreme Court based *Roe* and other cases in due process rights, the Court has continued to recognize the right of intimate association. In *Roberts v. United States Jaycees* (1984), the Court stated "that choices to enter into and maintain certain intimate human relationships must be secured against undue intrusion by the State because of the role of such relationships in safeguarding the individual freedom that is central to our constitutional scheme. In this respect, freedom of association receives protection as a fundamental element of personal liberty."

The decision in *Roberts* was significant not only because it addressed freedom of association but also because the Court's actual conclusion. The Court addressed a state statute that would effectively require the United States Jaycees to accept women as regular members. The Court concluded that the Act did not abridge the male members' rights to freedom of intimate association because the organization lacked some features of highly personal relationships that were protected by this freedom.

RIGHT TO EXPRESSIVE ASSOCIATION

The Court in *Roberts* identified another right of association focused on the right of expressive association. This right is based largely on the exercise of other First Amendment rights, including **freedom of speech**. Some cases addressed forced disclosure of membership groups as instances where the government has infringed upon an organization's right to expressive association. Interference with the internal affairs of an organization is another example. The Court in *Roberts* actually concluded that the Minnesota law requiring admission of women infringed upon the organization's right to expressive association because the law interfered with the Jaycees' internal affairs. However, the Court concluded that the state could articulate a compelling state interest protected by the requirement to admit women to the organization.

Later decisions have concluded that organizations have ruled in favor of groups arguing that government action violated rights of expressive association. In *Hurley v. Irish-American Gay, Lesbian, & Bisexual Group of Boston* (1995), the Court held that a group could prohibit a group of gay and lesbian activists from marching in a parade because the parade organizers had a right to determine the viewpoints represented in the parade.

FREEDOM NOT TO ASSOCIATE

Unlike the conclusion in *Roberts*, the Court has ruled in several cases that freedom of association includes a related freedom not to associate. In other words, the Courts has recognized that citizens have some rights to choose to resist association.

Abood v. Detroit Board of Education The right to choose not to associate arise in the case of *Abood v. Detroit Board of Education* (1977). In that case, a Michigan statute required non-union members to pay a service charge to unions equal to the amount of union dues. Thus, the employees were not members of the union yet paid the same amounts as union members. The Court agreed that the statute infringed upon the non-union employees' right to choose not to associate with the union.

Boy Scouts of America v. Dale In 2000, the Court reviewed a case involving a policy of the Boy Scouts of America. The organization refused to admit members who were gay or lesbian. When an assistant Scoutmaster admitted he was gay, he was fired. He sued the Boy Scouts, arguing that the Boy Scouts had violated a state non-discrimination law. The Court, however, concluded that the Boy Scouts could reject members based on sexual orientation because of the organization's right to expressive association.

SELECT STATE COURT DECISIONS

Like the U.S. Constitution, state constitutions do not expressly provide for freedom of association. However, state courts construe state constitutions to protect this freedom, much the way that the Supreme Court recognizes such rights under the First Amendment.

The summaries below are examples of state court decisions addressing freedom of association.

FLORIDA: Florida state law prohibits a lawyer from acting as an advocate at a trial when the lawyer is likely to be a necessary witness on the client's behalf. In *Eccles v. Nelson* (Fla. App. 2006), a Florida **appellate court** considered an argument that the law violated a client's right to freedom of association because she could not choose her own **counsel**. The court, however, rejected the argument. The court stated, "State courts, however, have a valid governmental interest in protecting the integrity of **litigation** taking place within it, and may certainly in the exercise of that interest enact rules governing when and how lawyers may act vis-à-vis that litigation."

INDIANA: A complaint brought by an assistant fire chief and a district fire chief alleged they were demoted because they were exercising their rights of **freedom of speech** and freedom of association. Specifically, they argued that they were punished for not supporting an incumbent's bid for reelection. The court, in *Morris v. City of Kokomo* (Ind. App. 1978), held that the plaintiffs had alleged a valid cause of action. The court stated: "The threat of demotion for failure to support an incumbent's bid for re-election has the same coercive effect. Thus, the prohibited result is the same whether the threat is demotion or discharge a significant impairment of First Amendment freedoms."

MINNESOTA: In *In re GlaxoSmithKline, P.L.C.* (Minn. 2007), the Minnesota Supreme Court concluded that it was within a state district court's discretion to issue a **protective order** to protect the associational rights of an organization. The court established a two-step analysis that a district court must apply to this type of circumstance: "First, the court should determine whether a party asserting the need for a protective order has sufficiently established a potential chilling effect on its association right. Second, if the party meets this burden, the court should balance the party's association right against the state's interest in releasing the information to the public. The state must demonstrate a compelling governmental interest in order to release documents protected by the First Amendment right to association."

NEW JERSEY: A state statute requires an applicant for a casino license to produce evidence showing the applicant's reputation for good character, honesty, and integrity. A group of casino employees challenged this requirement, arguing that the law infringed on their freedom of association because the law required the employees to divulge associational ties. The New Jersey Supreme Court in *Application of Martin* (N.J. 1982) disagreed, holding that the law was tailored to protect important state interests.

TEXAS: A nonprofit organization challenged a trial court's orders requiring disclosure of the names of the organization's contributors, arguing that the order violated the organization's right to freedom of association. The

Texas Supreme Court recognized that "[c]ompelled disclosure of the identities of an organization's members or contributors may have a chilling effect on the organization's contributors as well as on the organization's own activity." The court in *In re Bay City Citizens Against Lawsuit Abuse* (Tex. 1998) held that requiring disclosure of any **donor** lists would violate the First Amendment.

UTAH: In *State v. Holm* (Utah 2006), the Utah Supreme Court rejected a criminal defendant's argument that his conviction for **bigamy** violated his right to freedom of association. The court concluded, "Holm's right to intrinsic association has not been unduly infringed upon because . . . the right to engage in polygamous behavior is not encompassed within the ambit of the individual liberty protections contained in our federal constitution. Consequently, Holm cannot argue that his associational rights prevent the State from interfering with his ability to engage in properly criminalized behavior, as the right of intimate association protects only those associations that further or otherwise support fundamental liberty interests."

WASHINGTON: An American Legion post challenged a state law prohibiting smoking in a place of employment. Specifically, the post argued that the statute violated the organization's right to intimate association. In *American Legion Post #149 vs. Washington State Department of Health* (Wash. 2008), the Washington Supreme Court disagreed. The court concluded that the post had a large number of members, and the smoking ban did not directly interfere with relationships or a person's ability to join the chapter.

ADDITIONAL RESOURCES

Amar, David. *The First Amendment, Freedom of Speech: Its Constitutional History and the Contemporary Debate.* Amherst, NY: Prometheus Books, 2009.

Bresler, Robert J. *Freedom of Association: Rights and Liberties Under the Law.* Santa Barbara, CA: ABC-CLIO, 2004.

Karst, Kenneth. "Freedom of Association," in *Encyclopedia of the Supreme Court of the United States*, edited by David S. Tanenhaus. Detroit: Gale, Cengage Learning, 2008.

Nye, Valerie, and Kathy Barco, eds. *True Stories of Censorship Battles in America's Libraries.* Chicago: American Library Association, 2012.

Ramey, R. Chace. *Student First Amendment Speech and Expression Rights: Armbands to Bong Hits.* El Paso, TX: LFB Scholarly Pub., 2011.

Shiffrin, Steven, and Jesse H. Cooper. *The First Amendment: Cases, Comments, Questions.* 5th ed. Eagan, MN: West, Thomson Reuters, 2011.

Weaver, Russell L. *Understanding the First Amendment.* 4th ed. New Providence, NJ.: LexisNexis, 2012.

ORGANIZATIONS

American Civil Liberties Union (ACLU)

125 Broad St., 18th Fl.
New York, NY 10004
Phone: (212) 549-2500
Email: info@aclu.org
URL: http://www.aclu.org/

American Library Association (ALA)

50 East Huron Street

Chicago, IL 60611
Toll Free: (800) 545-2433
URL: http://www.ala.org

People for the American Way (PFAW)

2000 M Street NW, Suite 400
Washington, DC 20036
Phone: (202) 467-4999
URL: http://www.pfaw.org/

FIRST AMENDMENT LAW

REGULATING VIDEO GAMES

Sections within this essay:

- Introduction
- Efforts to Restrict Video-Game Sales to Minors
  - State Regulations
  - *Brown v. Entertainment Merchants Association*
  - Warning Labels
- Other First Amendment Issues
- Intellectual Property Issues
  - Copyright Protection
  - Trademark Protection
- Privacy Issues
- Additional Resources

INTRODUCTION

The video-game industry was born in the 1970s, and it grew quickly to become one of the largest industries in the world. Producers create games for all sorts of devices, including computers, stand-alone gaming systems, and a large variety of mobile devices. According to some estimates, retail sales of video games in the United States alone amounted to more than $9 billion, and the total revenue of the industry as a whole was estimated to be more than $16 billion.

As the video game industry has evolved and grown, a myriad of legal issues has arisen. Many lawsuits have arisen because of efforts to regulate and control the content of video games. These games have become so realistic that some parents and organizations have wanted to restrict which games minors can access. Other efforts have focused on placement of warning labels or other means to protect minors from the dangers the video games present. Several cases have applied First Amendment principles to resolve disputes that have arisen from controversies focusing on video games.

Video games have also given rise to other legal disputes. Some of these disputes address **intellectual property** concerns, while others focus more on **privacy** issues.

EFFORTS TO RESTRICT VIDEO-GAME SALES TO MINORS

Some of the most heated debates about video games have focused on making video games available to minors. When video-game arcades became popular in the 1970s and 1980s, some cities adopted ordinances restricting how many game machines a single establishment could have on its property or limiting the location of a video-game establishment to a certain distance from a school. Other ordinances attempted to limit use of video games by minors, especially for games that featured graphic violence or sexual themes.

Owners of video-game establishments challenged several of these ordinances by arguing that the laws violated First Amendment rights of either the owners or the users. However, courts frequently upheld these challenges. In several cases, courts ruled that laws applying to use of video games by minors were reasonable time, place, or manner restrictions and did not violate the Constitution.

State Regulations Video games continued to evolve during the 1990s and 2000s, and the graphics became increasingly more realistic. Some groups (often consisting of parents) intensified their efforts to prevent children from accessing violent and/or sexually explicit games. A number of these efforts occurred during the mid-2000s.

The Michigan legislature, for instance, adopted a law in 2005 that created a fine for someone who knowingly disseminated to a minor "an ultra-violent explicit video game" that was harmful to minors. The **statute** defined "ultra-violent" as something that continually and repetitively depicts extreme and loathsome violence. The statute further defined "extreme and loathsome violence" as real or simulated graphic depictions of physical injuries or physical violence against parties who realistically appear to be human beings, including actions causing death, inflicting cruelty, dismemberment, decapitation, maiming, disfigurement, or other mutilation of body parts, murder, criminal sexual conduct, or torture. Moreover, the statute defined an "ultra-violent explicit video game" as harmful to minors if the game had the following characteristics: (1) Considered as a whole, the game appealed to the morbid interest in asocial, aggressive behavior of minors as determined by contemporary local community standards; (2) The game was patently offensive to contemporary local community standards of adults as to what is suitable for minors; and (3) Considered as a whole, the game lacked serious literary, artistic, political, education, or scientific value for minors.

A group of companies that produced, distributed, and sold video games challenged the law in federal court, arguing that the Michigan law violated the First Amendment. In *Entertainment Software Association v. Granholm*, the U.S. District Court for the Eastern District of Michigan ruled that the content of video games was expression protected by the First Amendment. Moreover, the court concluded that the state could not show the law was narrowly tailored to serve a compelling government interest. Therefore, the court enjoined enforcement of the Michigan statute.

A similar issue arose in Illinois, where the Illinois legislature approved two state laws: the Violent Video Games Law and the Sexually Explicit Video Games Law. Both of these laws established criminal penalties for the sale or renting of a violent video game or a sexually explicit video game to an individual under the age of 18. The statute relied on the rating systems established by the Entertainment Software Rating Board (ESRB) (discussed below) and required video-game retailers to place signs within a certain number of feet advising customers about the rating system used by the ESRB.

The Entertainment Software Association and other groups challenged the law on grounds similar to those raised in the Michigan case. Like the Michigan court, the U.S. District Court for the Northern District of Illinois in

Entertainment Software Association v. Blagojevich struck down the laws on First Amendment grounds. The court reviewed extensive **evidence** about the effect that video games have on minors, but the court ruled that the state could not establish a compelling state interest in preventing violent or aggressive behavior by minors or in preventing developmental or other harm to minors. Moreover, the court concluded that the language in both laws was unconstitutionally vague. Therefore, the court permanently enjoined enforcement of both statutes.

Brown v. Entertainment Merchants Association First Amendment issues about laws regulating the sale of video games to minors reached the Supreme Court in 2011. The California legislature passed a law in 2005 that prohibited the sale or rental of violent video games to minors. The law also required these video games have a label indicating "18." Failure to adhere to this law would result in a civil **penalty** of $1,000.

As they did with the laws in Michigan and Illinois, organizations within the video game industry challenged the law by arguing that the law infringed upon First Amendment rights. Justice Antonin Scalia wrote the opinion for the Court, which struck down the law by a vote of 7 to 2 in *Brown v. Entertainment Merchants Association*. Scalia stressed that the First Amendment's most basic principle is that the government cannot restrict expression because of the expression's message, ideas, subject matter, or content. Although the Court has recognized some areas of speech that the government may regulate, including **obscenity** and fighting words, this list is rather limited. In nearly every instance, categories of speech that are subject to restrictions are reserved for areas where there is an American tradition of regulating the speech.

With regard to video games, Scalia wrote that California had attempted to construct the law in the manner that it appeared to regulate obscenity. However, Scalia noted that obscenity only included depiction of "sexual conduct" and not the types of speech regulated by the California law. Moreover, California could not create a class of content-based restrictions aimed specifically at children. Although states may protect children from harm, Scalia wrote, this power does not give the state complete freedom to restrict children from being exposed to ideas.

Warning Labels Part of Scalia's opinion in *Brown* noted that the video-game industry had developed its own system to inform customers about the contents of various games. This system is based on ratings produced by the Entertainment Software Rating Board, which assigns one of six ratings to each game reviewed. The ratings include: Early Childhood (ages 3 and over); Everyone (ages 6 and over); Everyone 10+ (ages 10 and over); Teen (ages 13 and over); Mature 17+ (ages 17 and over); and Adults Only 18+ (ages 18 and over). As of July 2012, the Board had rated more than 22,000 games.

Scalia noted a study produced by the Federal Trade Commission about the rating system. The study concluded that the system was more effective as applied to video games than the comparable system developed to rate movies and music. Nevertheless, a bill was introduced in Congress in 2012 that would require the Consumer Product Safety Commission to issue regulations requiring warning labels on any game rated above "E" for "Everyone." This warning would state: "WARNING: Exposure to violent video games has been linked to aggressive behavior." The video game industry criticized the bill immediately, and it received little support in Congress.

OTHER FIRST AMENDMENT ISSUES

Several federal courts have addressed First Amendment issues in other contexts. In some cases, parties have argued that video game producers were responsible when someone who played video games acted out and killed someone else. Plaintiffs in these types of cases have alleged such causes of action as **negligence**, intentional infliction of emotional distress, and products liability. Defendants have often raised the First Amendment as part of their defenses.

A minor was allegedly addicted to, and obsessed with, the video game "Mortal Kombat," which featured graphic violence. The teen was so addicted to the game that he acted out what a character of the game does to kill opponents and killed a friend. The mother of child who was killed sued the video-game manufacturer based on claims for negligence and intentional infliction of emotional distress. In *Wilson v. Midway Games* (2002), the U.S. District Court for the District of Connecticut held that the game was an expression that the First Amendment protected, thus precluding the plaintiff's recovery.

Similar issues arose in two other cases decided in 2002. In *Sanders v. Acclaim Entertainment, Inc.* (2002), two students shot and killed a teacher during a shooting spree. Survivors of the teacher brought an action in the U. S. District Court for the District of Colorado based on claims for **wrongful death**. The court dismissed the claims on several grounds, including First Amendment grounds. Likewise, in *James v. Meow Media, Inc.* (2002), the Sixth Circuit Court of Appeals heard an **appeal** brought by the parents of students who were killed when a classmate discharged firearms at a group of students. The court agreed with a lower court that "attaching tort liability to the effect that such ideas have on a criminal

actor would raise significant constitutional problems under the First Amendment that ought to be avoided." Based on this conclusion, the court held that the plaintiffs could not maintain their claims.

INTELLECTUAL PROPERTY ISSUES

Legal controversies about video games are not limited to First Amendment issues. In fact, most **litigation** arising from video games focuses on intellectual property issues. The majority of these intellectual property cases focus on copyrights.

Copyright Protection The **Copyright** Act of 1976 protects "original works of authorship fixed in any **tangible** medium of expression." Courts have generally concluded that this protection applies to the audiovisual effects featured in video games. In fact, in *Atari Games Corp. v. Oman* (1992), the U.S. Court of Appeals for the District of Columbia Circuit ruled that it was unreasonable for the Register of Copyrights to refuse to register a video game. In that particular case, the Register concluded that the game "Breakout" was not copyrightable because it only consisted of simple shapes and coloring. The court disagreed, holding that the interrelationship between the shapes, colors, and sounds was sufficiently creative to be considered copyrightable.

Courts have also considered arguments about the **fair use** of video games. For instance, some video-game manufacturers have sued those who have produced so-called emulators, which are software applications that allow users to play certain video games on computer systems. Several courts have held that the emulators fell under the category of fair use.

Trademark Protection Another line of cases has evolved that has focused on allegations of trademark **infringement**. In several cases, parties have sold video game cartridges that were nearly identical to the cartridges of the party (Nintendo) that owned the **trademarks** for those cartridges. Courts reviewing these cases generally concluded that the actions constituted trademark infringement.

On the other hand, some courts have held that no trademark infringement occurred when users uploaded and downloaded video games on an Internet bulletin board or when a party developed an emulator that allowed users to play video games on personal computers rather than systems for which the games were originally designed.

PRIVACY ISSUES

Some video-game disputes have also focused on so-called privacy torts. An example of such a claim would be one where a video-game producer allegedly appropriates the name or likeness of a celebrity for commercial gain.

ADDITIONAL RESOURCES

Buckman, Deborah F. "Intellectual Property Rights in Video, Electronic, and Computer Games." *American Law Reports Federal* Second Series 106 (2006), 269-327.

Dannenberg, Ross, ed. *The American Bar Association's Legal Guide to Video Game Development*. Chicago: American Bar Association, 2011.

Festinger, Jon. *Video Game Law*. 2d ed. Markham, ON, Canada: LexisNexis, 2012.

Kemper, Kurtis A. "First Amendment Protection Afforded to Commercial and Home Video Games." *American Law Reports*. 5th Series 106 (2003), 337-375.

Lipson, Ashley Saunders and Robert D. Brain. *Computer and Video Game Law: Cases, Statutes, Forms, Problems, and Materials*. Durham, NC: Carolina Academic Press, 2009.

ORGANIZATIONS

American Bar Association (ABA)

321 North Clark Street
Chicago, IL 60610

Phone: (202) 662-1000
Toll Free: (800) 285-2221
Fax: (312) 988-6800
URL: http://www.americanbar.org

Entertainment Software Association

575 7th Street NW, Suite 300
Washington, DC 20004
URL: http://www.theesa.com

First Amendment Center at Vanderbilt University

1207 18th Ave. S.
Nashville, TN 37212
Phone: (615) 727-1600
Fax: (615) 727-1319
URL: http://www.firstamendmentcenter.org

First Amendment Coalition

534 4th Street, Suite B
San Rafael, CA 94901
Phone: (415) 460-5060
Fax: (415) 460-5155
URL: http://www.firstamendmentcoalition.org

FIRST AMENDMENT LAW

RELIGIOUS FREEDOM

Sections within this essay:

- Background
- The Establishment Clause
  - History Behind the Establishment Clause
  - Case Law Interpreting the Establishment Clause
- The Free Exercise Clause
  - History Behind the Free Exercise Clause
  - Case Law Interpreting the Free Exercise Clause
- State Laws Protecting Religious Freedom
- Additional Resources

BACKGROUND

The First Amendment to the U.S. Constitution provides that "Congress shall make no law respecting an establishment of religion or prohibiting the free exercise thereof." The U.S. Supreme Court has interpreted this provision as guaranteeing two separate rights: (1) the right to live in a society where the government does not sponsor an official religion that dictates what God citizens must worship or what church they must attend; and (2) the right to exercise one's own religious faith in accordance with his or her conscience free from governmental intrusion. The first right is protected by the Establishment Clause of the First Amendment, while the second right is protected by the Free Exercise Clause of the First Amendment. Both clauses have their origins in American colonial history, and that history sheds light on the subsequent development of the First Amendment by state and federal courts.

THE ESTABLISHMENT CLAUSE

History Behind the Establishment Clause Prior to the American Revolution, the English parliament designated the Anglican Church as the official church of the England and the American colonies. The church was supported by **taxation**, and English citizens were required to attend services. No marriage or baptism was sanctioned outside the church. Religious minorities who failed to abide by the strictures of the church were forced to endure civil and criminal penalties, including banishment and death. Some American colonies were also ruled by theocrats, such as the Puritans in Massachusetts.

The English and colonial experiences influenced the Founding Fathers, including Thomas Jefferson and James Madison. Jefferson supported a high "wall of separation" between church and state and opposed religious interference with the affairs of government. Madison, conversely, opposed governmental interference with matters of religion. For Madison, the establishment of a national church differed from the Spanish Inquisition only in degree, and he vociferously attacked any legislation that would have led in this direction. For example, Madison fought against a Virginia bill that would have levied taxes to subsidize Christianity.

The Founding Fathers' concerns about the relationship between church and state found expression in the First Amendment. Despite the unequivocal nature of its language, the Supreme Court has never interpreted the First Amendment as an absolute prohibition against all laws concerning religious institutions, religious symbols, or the exercise of religious faith. Instead, the Court has turned for guidance to the thoughts and intentions of the Founding Fathers when interpreting the First Amendment, in particular the thoughts and intentions of its primary architect, James Madison.

But Madison's views have not produced a uniform understanding of religious freedom among the Supreme Court's justices. Some justices, for example, have cited Madison's opposition to the Virginia bill subsidizing Christianity as **evidence** that he opposed only discriminatory governmental assistance to particular religious denominations but favored non-preferential aid to cultivate a diversity in faiths. Thus, the Framers of the First Amendment left posterity with three considerations regarding religious establishments: (1) a wall of separation that protects government from religion and religion from government; (2) a separation of church and state that permits non-discriminatory governmental assistance to religious groups; and (3) governmental assistance that preserves and promotes a diversity of religious beliefs.

Case Law Interpreting the Establishment Clause The Supreme Court attempted to incorporate these three considerations under a single test in *Lemon v. Kurtzman* (1971). In *Lemon*, the Court held that state and federal governments may enact legislation that concerns religion or religious organizations so long as the legislation has a secular purpose, does not have the primary effect of advancing or inhibiting religion, and does not otherwise foster excessive entanglement between church and state. Under this test, the Supreme Court held in *Engel v. Vitale* (1962) that the First Amendment prohibited a school from beginning each day with a 22-word, non-denominational prayer. Such a prayer was tantamount to the government sanctioning religion at the expense of agnosticism or atheism, the Court said, something not permitted by the Establishment Clause.

Similarly, in *Lee v. Weisman* (1992), the Supreme Court struck down a clergy-led prayer at a public school graduation ceremony as a violation of the First Amendment. By contrast, lower federal courts are split over the issue of whether a student-led, non-denominational prayer at a graduation ceremony violates the Establishment Clause, with some cases finding the prayers unconstitutional because they are initiated on school grounds at a school-sponsored activities and other cases finding no constitutional violation because the prayers are initiated by students and not public employees. However, the Supreme Court ruled in *Marsh v. Chambers* (1983) that the First Amendment does permit state legislatures to open their sessions with a short prayer each day. The Supreme Court concluded that history and tradition have secularized this otherwise religious act.

The Court has produced seemingly inconsistent results in other areas of First Amendment law as well.

In one case, the Court permitted a municipality to include a nativity scene in its annual Christmas display, *Lynch v. Donnelly* (1984), while in another case it prohibited a county courthouse from placing a cross on its staircase during the holiday season. *County of Allegheny v. American Civil Liberties Union* (1989). In *Allegheny*, the Court said that there was nothing in the county courthouse to indicate that the cross was anything other than a religious display, while in Lynch the Court said that the nativity scene was part of a wider celebration of the winter holidays.

The desire to avoid excessive entanglement between church and state has also produced a body of law that often turns on subtle distinctions. On the one hand, in *McCollum v. Board of Education* (1948), the Supreme Court ruled that public school programs violate the Establishment Clause when they allow public school students to leave class early for religious training in classrooms located on taxpayer-supported school property. On the other hand, such programs pass constitutional muster if the students leave class early for religious training off school grounds, where all of the program's costs are paid by the religious organizations. *Zorach v. Clauson* (1952).

THE FREE EXERCISE CLAUSE

History Behind the Free Exercise Clause The Establishment Clause and the Free Exercise Clause represent opposite sides of the same issue. Where the Establishment Clause focuses on governmental action that would create, support, or endorse an official national religion, the Free Exercise Clause focuses on the pernicious effects that governmental action may have on an individual's religious beliefs or practices. Like the Establishment Clause, the Free Exercise Clause was drafted in response to the Founding Fathers' desire to protect religious minorities from persecution.

The Founding Fathers' understanding of the Free Exercise Clause is illustrated in part by the New York Constitution of 1777, which provided that "the free exercise and enjoyment of religious...worship, without **discrimination** or preference, shall forever...be allowed...to all mankind." However, the same constitution cautioned that "the liberty of conscience, hereby granted, shall not be so construed as to excuse acts of licentiousness, or justify practices inconsistent with the peace or safety of this State." The New Hampshire Constitution of 1784 similarly provided that "[e]very individual has a natural and unalienable right to worship God according to the dictates of his own conscience, and reason; and no subject shall be hurt...in his person, liberty or estate for worshipping God" in a manner "most agreeable" to those dictates, "provided he doth not disturb the public peace."

Case Law Interpreting the Free Exercise Clause These eighteenth-century state constitutional provisions not only provide insight into the Founding Fathers' original understanding of the Free Exercise Clause, they embody the fundamental tenants of modern First Amendment **jurisprudence**. The Supreme Court has identified three principles underlying the Free Exercise Clause. First, no individual may be compelled by law to accept a particular religion or form of worship. Second, all individuals are constitutionally permitted to freely choose a religion and worship in accordance with their conscience and spirituality without interference from the government. Third, the government may enforce its criminal laws by prosecuting persons whose religious practices would thwart a compelling societal interest.

Only in rare instances is a law that infringes upon someone's religious beliefs or practices supported by a compelling state interest. The Supreme Court has held that no compelling societal interest would be served in offending someone's deeply held religious beliefs with a law coercing members of the Jehovah's Witnesses to salute the American flag in public schools (*West Virginia State Board of Education v. Barnette*, (1943)), a law denying unemployment benefits to Seventh Day Adventists who refuse to work on Saturdays (*Sherbert v. Verner*, (1963)), or a law requiring Amish families to keep their children in state schools until the age of sixteen (*Wisconsin v. Yoder*, (1972)). However, a compelling governmental interest is served by the Internal Revenue System (IRS), such that no member of any religious sect can claim exemption from paying taxes. (*United States v. Lee* (1982)).

A different question is presented when the government disputes whether a particular belief or practice is actually religious in nature. In some instances, the Supreme Court is required to determine what constitutes a "religion" for the purposes of the First Amendment. For example, this determination occurs when conscientious objectors resist the government's attempt to conscript them into military service during wartime. Some draft resisters object to war on moral or ethical grounds unrelated to orthodox or doctrinal religions. If a conscientious objector admits that he or she is atheistic or agnostic, the government asks, how can he or she rely on the First Amendment to avoid conscription when it protects the free exercise of religion?

In effort to answer this question, the Supreme Court in *Torcaso v. Watkins* (1961) explained that the government cannot "aid all religions against non-believers" any more than it can aid one religion over another. So long as a non-believer holds a sincere and meaningful belief that occupies a place in that person's life parallel to the place

held by God in a believer's life, then it qualifies as a religious belief under the First Amendment. As to conscientious objectors, the Court stated in *Welch v. United States* (1970) that the First Amendment will insulate them from criminal prosecution if they resist the draft based on "deeply and sincerely" held beliefs that "are purely ethical or moral in source and content but that nevertheless impose…a duty of conscience to refrain from participating in any war at any time." However, a religious, moral, or ethical belief that manifests itself in a person's selective opposition to only certain wars or military conflicts is not protected by the Free Exercise Clause. The same holds true for a religious, moral, or ethical beliefs that are insincere.

In 1993, Congress attempted to add to the body of law protecting the free exercise of religion by enacting the Religious Freedom Restoration Act (RFRA), which provided that the "[g]overnment shall not substantially burden a person's exercise of religion," unless in doing so it furthers "a compelling governmental interest" and "is the least restrictive means of furthering that…interest." Congress enacted RFRA in response to *Employment Division v. Smith* (1990), a Supreme Court decision that upheld the denial of **unemployment compensation** claims made by two employees who had been fired for ingesting an illegal drug during a religious ceremony. In passing the law Congress made a specific finding that the Supreme Court in *Smith* "virtually eliminated" any requirement that the government provide a compelling justification for the burdens it places on the exercise of religion. Congress hoped that RFRA would restore that requirement.

The constitutionality of RFRA was immediately challenged in a flurry of cases, one of which eventually made its way to the Supreme Court in *City of Boerne v. Flores* (1997). Acknowledging that section 5 of the Fourteenth Amendment grants Congress the authority to enforce the First Amendment through measures that "remedy" or "deter" constitutional violations, the Supreme Court said that this authority did not include the power to define "what constitutes a constitutional violation." Yet this is exactly what Congress attempted to do by enacting RFRA, the Court said. Congress cannot effectively overrule Supreme Court precedent, the Court continued, without violating the separation of powers and other constitutional principles vital to maintaining the balance of power between the state and federal governments. The powers of the legislative branch are "defined and limited," the Court concluded, and only the judicial branch of government is constitutionally endowed with the authority to interpret and apply the First Amendment or any other provision of the federal Constitution. Thus, RFRA was declared unconstitutional, and the precedential value of *Smith* was restored.

STATE LAWS PROTECTING RELIGIOUS FREEDOM

The Free Exercise and Establishment Clauses of the First Amendment have been made applicable to the states through the Fourteenth Amendment. In a series of cases the Supreme Court has ruled that the rights guaranteed by the First Amendment establish the minimum amount of religious freedom that must be afforded to individuals in state or federal court. States may provide more religious freedom under their own constitutions, but not less. Below is a sampling of state court decisions decided at least in part based on their own state constitution's guarantee of religious freedom.

ALABAMA: The state's constitutional provision guaranteeing freedom of religion did not bar the court from resolving a dispute between congregational factions over the title to church property, even though spiritual issues arguably prompted the congregation's dispute, since the case involved civil conflicts of trusteeship and property ownership and required the court to review church records and incorporation documents without delving into spiritual matters. U.S.C.A. Const. Amend. 1; Const. Art. 1, § 3. *Murphy v. Green*, 794 So. 2d 325 (Ala. 2000).

ARIZONA: A residential picketing **statute** did not facially infringe upon the religious freedom guaranteed by the state and federal constitutions as they were applied to an **abortion** protestor who was convicted for protesting abortion in a residential neighborhood. Even though her protest was motivated by a deeply held religious belief, the statute did not single out religious picketing or religious demonstrations for prohibition. U.S.C.A. Const. Amend. 1; A.R.S. Const. Art. 20, par. 1; A.R.S. § 13-2909. *State v. Baldwin*, 908 P.2d 483 (Ariz. App. 1995).

CALIFORNIA: In guaranteeing the free exercise of religion "without discrimination or preference," the plain language of the state constitution ensures that the state neither favor nor discriminate against religion. West's Ann.Cal. Const. Art. 1, § 4. *East Bay Asian Local Development Corp. v. California*, 13 P.3d 1122 (Cal. 2000).

CONNECTICUT: An appellate court's consideration of various tort and **contract** claims brought against an organization of church congregations would constitute an interference in church practice that would violate the First Amendment. *Thibodeau v. American Baptist Churches of Conn.*, 994 A.2d 212 (Conn. App. 2010).

FLORIDA: Inherent in parents' authority over their unemancipated children living in their parents' household is the parents' right to require their children to attend church with them as part of the children's religious training, and neither the state nor federal constitutions entitle unemancipated minors to prevent such parent-mandated religious training on grounds that it violates the minors' religious freedom. U.S.C.A. Const.Amend. 1; West's F.S.A. Const. Art. 1, § 3. *L.M. v. State*, 610 So.2d 1314 (Fla. App. 1992).

ILLINOIS: A state statute permitting certain burials on Sundays and legal holidays did not abridge the union members' freedom to contract. Nor did it violate the federal and state constitutional prohibitions against impairment of contractual obligations, since the statute's provisions were narrowly drawn to permit free exercise of religious rights guaranteed by the state constitution while allowing labor to restrict its working schedules accordingly. S.H.A. ch. 21, 101 et seq. *Heckmann v. Cemeteries Ass'n of Greater Chicago*, 468 N.E.2d 1354, (Ill. App. 1984).

KENTUCKY: A state constitutional ban on **appropriation** of public funds to religious schools did not violate the Free Exercise Clause of the First Amendment. *University of Cumberlands v. Pennybacker*, 308 S.W.3d 668 (Ky. 2010).

MICHIGAN: The Michigan Civil Rights Act's prohibition on housing discrimination based on marital status did not violate the state constitution's guarantee of religious freedom, and thus the act was violated when two landlords refused to rent their apartments to unmarried couples, even though their refusal was based on religious grounds. M.C.L.A. Const. Art. 1, § 4; M.C.L.A. § 37.2502(1). *McCready v. Hoffius*, 586 N.W.2d 723 (Mich. 1998).

MISSOURI: State and federal constitutions' guarantee of religious freedom entitled a taxpayer to delete every reference to God on the state's tax form before taking the oath or affirmation required by the form. U.S.C.A. Const. Amend. 1; V.A.M.S. Const. Art. 1, §§ 5, 7; V.A.M.S. § 137.155. *Oliver v. State Tax Commissioner of Missouri*, 37 S.W.3d 243 (Mo. 2001).

MONTANA: The freedom of religion provisions set forth in the state constitution protect the freedom to accept or reject any religious doctrine, including religious doctrines relating to abortion, and the right to express one's faith in all lawful ways and forums. Const. Art. 2, §§ 5, 7. *Armstrong v. State*, 989 P.2d 364 (Mont. 1999).

NEBRASKA: Ex parte communications in which a trial judge during a capital murder case asked the jurors to join hands, bow their heads, and say words to the effect of "God be with us" did not infringe on the defendant's religious rights under the state or federal constitutions, since the defendant's rights to freedom of religion and to worship as he pleased did not suffer in any way. U.S.C.A. Const.Amend. 1; Const. Art. 1, § 4. *State v. Bjorklund*, 604 N.W.2d 169 (Neb. 2000).

NEW HAMPSHIRE: The state's constitutional provision guaranteeing freedom of religion prohibited the state from revoking a psychologist's license for his religious views but did not prohibit revocation for acts that otherwise constituted unprofessional conduct, regardless of their religious character. Thus, the court upheld the state's revocation of the psychologist's license on the grounds that he had provided incompetent therapy to a patient, even though part of the therapy involved reading the Bible. Const. Pt. 1, Art. 5. *Appeal of Trotzer*, 719 A.2d 584 (N.H. 1998).

NEW YORK: The state constitution's guarantee of religious freedom entitled a state correctional facility inmate to participate in all Jewish religious observances open and available to any other inmate, even though the inmate was not recognized as Jewish by the Jewish chaplain at the facility. McKinney's Const. Art. 1, § 3; McKinney's Correction Law § 610. *Thomas v. Lord*, 664 N.Y.S.2d 973, (N.Y. Sup., 1997).

OHIO: A court order requiring that a noncustodial parent pay 40 percent of his child's tuition at a private Catholic school did not violate the Establishment Clause of the First Amendment or the religious freedom provision of the state constitution. U.S.C.A. Const.Amend. 1; Const. Art. 1, § 7. *Smith v. Null*, 757 N.E.2d 1200 (Ohio App. 2001).

TEXAS: A state court could not hear a lawsuit alleging that a church minister and his wife negligently or intentionally misapplied the church's doctrine in attempting to drive out demons from plaintiff's minor daughter, since the lawsuit would involve a searching inquiry into the church's beliefs and the validity of those beliefs, an inquiry that would infringe up the defendants' religious freedom. *In re Pleasant Glade Assembly of God*, 991 S.W.2d 85 (Tex. App. 1998).

VERMONT: The state's constitution expresses two related, but different, concepts about the nature of religious liberty: no governmental power may interfere with or control an individual's free exercise of religious worship, and no person can be compelled to attend or support religious worship against that person's conscience. Const. C. 1, Art. 3. *Chittenden Town School Dist. v. Department of Educ.*, 738 A.2d 539 (Vt. 1999).

WASHINGTON: Requiring a church to apply for a conditional use permit in a rural estate **zoning** district, while requiring a county to reduce or waive the application fee following a showing of the church's inability to pay, was not an impermissible burden on the free exercise of religion guaranteed by the state and federal constitutions. *Open Door Baptist Church v. Clark County*, 995 P.2d 33 (Wash. 2000). U.S.C.A. Const.Amend. 1; West's RCWA Const. Art. 1, § 11.

ADDITIONAL RESOURCES

Horwitz, Paul. *The Agnostic Age: Law, Religion, and the Constitution.* New York: Oxford University Press, 2011.

Shiffrin, Steven, and Jesse H. Cooper. *The First Amendment: Cases, Comments, Questions.* 5th ed. Eagan, MN: West, Thomson Reuters, 2011.

Weaver, Russell L. *Understanding the First Amendment.* 4th ed. New Providence, NJ.: LexisNexis, 2012.

ORGANIZATIONS

American Bar Association (ABA)

321 North Clark Street
Chicago, IL 60610
Phone: (202) 662-1000
Toll Free: (800) 285-2221
Fax: (312) 988-6800
URL: http://www.americanbar.org

Americans United for Separation of Church and State

1301 K Street NW, Suite 850, East Tower
Washington, DC 20005
Phone: (202) 466-3234
Fax: (202) 466-2587
URL: http://www.au.org

First Amendment Center at Vanderbilt University

1207 18th Ave.S.
Nashville, TN 37212
Phone: (615) 727-1600
Fax: (615) 727-1319
URL: http://firstamendmentcenter.org